Sicut lilium inter spinas sic amica mea inter filias

On The Cover: We use the symbol of the "lily among the thorns" from Song of Solomon 2:2 to represent the Baptist History Series. The Latin, *Sicut lilium inter spinas sic amica mea inter filias*, translates, "As the lily among thorns, so is my love among the daughters."

THE

BAPTIST ENCYCLOPAEDIA.

Volume 2 of 3

WILLIAM CATHCART, D.D.
1826-1908

THE

BAPTIST ENCYCLOPAEDIA.

A DICTIONARY

OF

THE DOCTRINES, ORDINANCES, USAGES, CONFESSIONS OF FAITH,
SUFFERINGS, LABORS, AND SUCCESSES, AND OF THE
GENERAL HISTORY OF THE

BAPTIST DENOMINATION IN ALL LANDS.

WITH

NUMEROUS BIOGRAPHICAL SKETCHES OF DISTINGUISHED AMERICAN
AND FOREIGN BAPTISTS, AND A SUPPLEMENT.

EDITED BY

WILLIAM CATHCART, D.D.,

AUTHOR OF "THE PAPAL SYSTEM," "THE BAPTISTS AND THE AMERICAN REVOLUTION,"
AND "THE BAPTISM OF THE AGES."

———◆◆❀◆◆———

WITH MANY ILLUSTRATIONS

———◆◆❀◆◆———

PHILADELPHIA:
LOUIS H. EVERTS.
1881

he Baptist Standard Bearer, Inc.

NUMBER ONE IRON OAKS DRIVE • PARIS, ARKANSAS 72855

Thou hast given a *standard* to them that fear thee;
that it may be displayed because of the truth.
-- Psalm 60:4

Reprinted
by

THE BAPTIST STANDARD BEARER, INC.

No. 1 Iron Oaks Drive
Paris, Arkansas 72855
(501) 963-3831

THE WALDENSIAN EMBLEM
lux lucet in tenebris
"The Light Shineth in the Darkness"

ISBN #1-57978-403-8

THE BAPTIST ENCYCLOPAEDIA

sins. Under God, he was instrumental in the salvation of hundreds, while many Christians were strengthened and encouraged in the discharge of their duties.

It is not too much to say that Radford Gunn was a remarkable man. He possessed uncommon talents. In his community he was a leading man; and in his Association, the Georgia, he wielded a strong influence. He was a thorough Baptist, and all who knew him could bear witness to his many personal excellences. Rigidly honest and unflinchingly bold, he avowed his opinions on any subject and under any circumstances; still he was not obtrusive. He was generous to a fault, and he deemed nothing he had too good for his friends.

He spent a large part of the years 1862 and 1863 in the Virginia army, in evangelistic and charitable labors, breaking down his health and contracting the disease which ended his life. Unable to preach or do anything for his Master except exercise the grace of patience under suffering, he would frequently exclaim, "And now, Lord, what wait I for? My hope is in thee." "Lord, on thee do I wait all the day." "Now, lettest thou thy servant depart in peace, according to thy word, for mine eyes have seen thy salvation." When death did come he welcomed it with manifest joy; for his soul longed to escape from its crumbling tabernacle of clay. His work on earth was done, and he was anxious to depart and be with Christ. He died at his residence in Warren Co., Ga., June 15, 1866. His death was a very easy one, for he passed away as one falling into a sweet and peaceful sleep.

Gurney, William Brodie, was born in London in 1778. His father being a deacon of the Maze Pond church, he became acquainted in early life with the original members of the Baptist Missionary Society, and delighted them by the interest he manifested in the missionary enterprise. He followed his father's profession, stenography, and attained to such distinguished excellence in that art that at an early age he was appointed short-hand writer to the House of Lords, a lucrative office, which enabled him to give large sums for missionary and benevolent purposes. He took a leading part in the organization and direction of the Sunday-School Union, and liberally stimulated the production of a distinctive Sunday-school literature. This great and useful institution was in a large measure his creation. The Baptist Missionary Society was also greatly indebted to his enterprise and munificence for its present strength. As its treasurer for many years the duties of his office were no mere matters of finance. He took the liveliest interest in all the efforts of the society, and especially set himself to the development of a spirit of liberality towards evangelistic work at home and abroad. His

example and influence produced a happy effect, which he lived to see. He died in London, March 25, 1855, aged seventy-seven.

Guthrie, Hon. James, an eminent lawyer, statesman, and capitalist, was born in Nelson Co., Ky., Dec. 5, 1792. He was educated at Bardstown, and studied law under the distinguished Judge John Rowan. He established himself in practice in Louisville, Ky., in 1820. Though not a communicant in any church, he was a Baptist in sentiment, and attended Walnut Street Baptist church, with his family, all of whom became eminently useful members of this church. He quickly established an extensive reputation as a lawyer, and acquired property with great rapidity. Was elected to the lower house of the Kentucky Legislature in 1827; was in the Kentucky senate from 1831 to 1840, and in 1849 was president of the convention that formed the present State constitution; was Secretary of the U. S. Treasury from 1853 to 1857, and in 1865 was elected U. S. Senator, which position he resigned in 1868, on account of declining health. From 1860 to 1868 he was president of the Louisville and Nashville Railroad. Besides these, he held many other prominent positions of trust and honor. He was a man of superior business qualifications, and was said to have become the wealthiest man in his State. He died in Louisville, March 13, 1869.

Gwaltney, Luther Rice, D.D., the son of Rev. James L. Gwaltney, was born in Isle of Wight Co., Va., and is now about fifty years of age. In early life he received a thorough collegiate education, graduating with distinction from Columbian University, Washington, D. C., thence he went forth as an ambassador of the Cross. Where his first pastorate was is not known to the writer of this sketch. He was called from Murfreesborough, N. C., in 1857, to take charge of the church in Edgefield village, South Carolina, where he labored with great fidelity and success for eleven years, both in his pastorate and in the educational interests of the community. In 1868 he left Edgefield and took charge of the church in the city of Rome, Ga., where he remained for eight years. Here he worked with the most constant zeal in the ministry, in the temperance cause, and in the interests of education, bearing a prominent part in the founding of Shorter Female College. In 1876 he was called to the presidency of the Judson Female Institute, in Marion, Ala., where he now labors with great acceptance. With the highest culture, a dignified and graceful appearance, a pure life. and deep piety, the best kind of sense, and fine scholarly attainments, an earnest worker and an able preacher, Dr. Gwaltney has proven himself a success wherever he has been tried. He has the art of endearing himself in the lasting affections of his people. His *alma mater* in

Washington conferred the degree of D.D. upon him a few years since, as a fit tribute to his distinguished merit. He is one of our most valuable men, and would be a leading man in any community.

Gwaltney, Rev. W. R., was born in Alexander Co., N. C., in 1834; graduated at Wake Forest College; taught in Wilkes and Alexander Counties; has served the churches of Hillsborough, Chapel Hill, Weeksville, and Winston, and is now the laborious and beloved and very successful pastor of the Second Baptist church of Raleigh. Mr. Gwaltney is a trustee of Wake Forest College.

Gwin, D. W., D.D., pastor of the First Baptist church, of Atlanta, Ga., is a Virginian by birth, and at the present time is about forty years of age. He is a man of fine person and splendid natural abilities, heightened by study and training. To unusual mental powers he adds eloquence, grace of action, a fine command of language, and large intellectual acquirements. He graduated at Richmond College, Va., before he was twenty-one years of age. Soon after graduating he was elected Professor of Ancient Languages by the Brownwood Institute, La Grange, Ga., where he speedily manifested his proficiency and his skill as an instructor. To an intimate knowledge of Greek and Latin, which he has studied enthusiastically, he has added an acquaintance with Hebrew since graduating. To learn a language is with him a pastime, and he ranks now with the first linguists of the land; and yet philosophy and theology are his favorite studies. He was called by the Baptist church at Rome, Ga., and was there ordained in 1861. Compelled to leave Rome on account of the war, he moved to Griffin, Ga., and took charge of the church there, remaining four years, during which he founded and conducted the Griffin High School. In 1868 he accepted a call from the First Baptist church of Montgomery, Ala., where he preached with distinguished ability and eloquence for six years. He then moved to Atlanta and assumed his present charge. He is a member of the board of trustees for the Southern Baptist Theological Seminary, and though a man of great modesty and diffidence, his worth and abilities are highly appreciated by his brethren, who have placed him upon the State Mission Board, situated at Atlanta. His wife is a daughter of the distinguished Dr. R. B. C. Howell, of Nashville, Tenn.

Gwynn, Hon. W., is a native of Kentucky, but has been in Florida many years. During the administration of Gov. Broome, Mr. Gwynn was a State-house officer, and was appointed State treasurer on the election of Gov. Drew, which important position he now holds. He is a man of spotless character and incorruptible integrity, and hence is much respected by the masses of the people in his adopted and beloved State.

Mr. Gwynn was converted under the ministry of Dr. E. W. Warren, and was baptized by him at Tallahassee. He took an active interest in the Baptist cause there, and has recently labored hard and contributed liberally to relieve the church property of an embarrassing debt, and to repair the house of worship and sustain the gospel. Not easily excited, very cautious and conservative, sagacious and discerning, he is a very safe adviser.

H

Hackett, Prof. H. B., D.D., LL.D.—Horatio Balch Hackett was born in Salisbury, Mass., Dec. 27, 1808. The Hackett family is believed to be descended from the Scotch and the Danes. Few of the name emigrated to America. During the Revolution, John Hackett, grandfather of Horatio, superintended the building at Salisbury of the Continental frigate "Alliance." His maternal grandfather, the Rev. Benjamin Balch, was chaplain on the same ship. Richard Hackett, a son of John, was also a ship-builder, and married Martha Balch, a daughter of the clergyman first mentioned, who was settled in Barrington, N. H. Horatio was the second of four sons. His father died in 1814, at the early age of thirty. In 1821 he attended the academy at Amesbury, under the charge of Michael Walsh, a graduate of Trinity College, Dublin, and a celebrated teacher. In September, 1823, he became a pupil in Phillips Academy, Andover, Mass., under John Adams. Among his schoolmates were Oliver Wendell Holmes, Ray Palmer, D.D., Jonathan F. Stearn, D.D., Wm. Newell, D.D., and H. A. Homes, LL.D., State Librarian at Albany, N. Y. He graduated in August, 1826, with the valedictory address. A month later he was admitted to Amherst College. It was while a student that he became a Christian. He united with the College church Nov. 2, 1828. Having graduated at Amherst, with the valedictory, Mr. Hackett returned to Andover and entered the theological seminary. At the end of his first year in the seminary Mr. Hackett was honored with an

PROF. H. B. HACKETT, D.D., LL.D.

appointment to a tutorship in the college which he had so lately left, and held this position during the year 1831–32. He then returned to theological studies at Andover, pursuing the course to the end, and engaging in some occasional literary work. He graduated in 1834, in which year he for some time ministered to the Congregational church in Calais, Me.

Mr. Hackett was married to his cousin, Mary Wadsworth Balch, Sept. 22, 1834, and spent the academic year of 1834–35 as a member of the faculty of Mount Hope College, Baltimore, in charge of the classical department. In the summer of 1835 he was baptized, and united with the First Baptist church of Baltimore, a step resulting from investigations about the proper subjects of baptism. In September, 1835, he became a professor in Brown University, Providence, R. I., with the title at first of Adjunct Professor of the Latin and Greek Languages, and in 1838 he was elected Professor of Hebrew Literature. Among his associates in the faculty were Drs. Wayland, Elton, and Caswell. Aug. 5, 1839, he was chosen Professor of Biblical Literature and Interpretation in Newton Theological Institution, becoming the colleague of Drs. Chase, Ripley, and Sears. Sept. 1, 1841, he sailed for Europe, and was absent a year, studying at Halle and Berlin, attending the lectures of Tho-

luck, Gesenius, Neander, and Hengstenberg. He also fulfilled a commission from the Board of Managers of the Baptist General Convention for Foreign Missions in behalf of Christian brethren in Denmark.

About a year after his return he published, with annotations, the treatise of Plutarch, "De Sera Numinis Vindicta" (1844). A revised edition, with notes by Profs. H. B. Hackett and W. S. Tyler, was published in 1867. In 1845 appeared his translation of Winer's "Chaldee Grammar," and in 1847 his own "Exercises in Hebrew Grammar." In 1852 he traveled in the East, and has given a record of his observations in the book entitled "Illustrations of Scripture, suggested by a Tour through the Holy Land." In 1858–59 he was abroad again, and resided six months in Athens, Greece, under the auspices of the American Bible Union. Shortly before this he published the second edition of his "Commentary on the Acts," the first having appeared nearly seven years earlier. This has been styled by Dr. Peabody, in the *North American Review*, "one of the very few works of the kind in the English language which approaches in point of massive erudition the master-works of the great German critics, differing from them only in possessing a soundness and accuracy which they sometimes lack." A few months after his return from Europe, Prof. Hackett delivered an able and eloquent address on Bible revision before the American Bible Union in the city of New York, Oct. 6, 1859. The society published the address, and also Dr. Hackett's "Notes on the Greek Text of the Epistle of Paul to Philemon," etc., in 1860. He contributed thirty articles to Dr. Wm. Smith's "Dictionary of the Bible," published in England in 1860–63, and in 1861 wrote an introduction to the American edition of Westcott's "Introduction to the Study of the Gospels." He compiled a volume entitled "Christian Memorials of the War," published in 1864. In 1866 he began to edit an American edition of "Smith's Dictionary of the Bible." Its publication took place between 1867 and 1870, and in this task he had the special co-operation of Prof. Ezra Abbot, D.D., LL.D., and some of the most able scholars of America. In 1868 appeared his translation of Van Oosterzee's "Commentary on Philemon," with additions, for Dr. Schaff's edition of Lange's Commentaries.

In the same year he terminated his professorship of twenty-nine years at Newton, intending, however, still to dwell there, and to labor more exclusively for the Bible Union. But after a year of literary occupation he listened with favor to an invitation made to him through the Rev. E. G. Robinson, D.D., LL.D., then president of the Rochester Theological Seminary, to resume there his career as a teacher. A year later, in September,

1870, he entered upon his duties as Professor of Biblical Literature and New Testament Exegesis, having just returned, with his daughter, from his fourth European trip. In 1870 was published his translation of Braune's "Commentary on Philippians," with additions, for Dr. Schaff's work before mentioned. He wrote an introduction to an American edition of "The Metaphors of St. Paul and Companions of St. Paul," by John S. Howson, D.D., dean of Chester, published in 1872, and in 1873 made additions, notes, and appendices to Rawlinson's "Historical Illustrations of the Old Testament." His many and valuable contributions to the "Bibliotheca Sacra," *Christian Review*, and kindred works cover a period of forty years from 1834. "The Book of Ruth," the common version revised, was a posthumous publication, in 1876. His visits to the Old World were marked with attentions from eminent English and Continental scholars. A few weeks after this final one he died suddenly, Nov. 2, 1875, having just returned to his residence from an exercise with one of his classes.

Prof. Hackett was chosen to the membership of many learned societies in Europe and America, and only a few days before his death he attended a stated meeting of the New Testament Company of the American Bible Revision Committee. He received the degree of D.D. from the University of Vermont in 1845, and from Harvard University (where he was long an examiner) in 1861, and that of LL.D. from Amherst College in 1862. His memory was widely reverenced at the time of his death, and the tributes thus evoked were edited, some entire and others partially and in biographical connection,[*] by one who had been his pupil and colleague, and whom he had honored with his confidence and affection. In Newton's beautiful cemetery, not far from the spot and column consecrated by Prof. Hackett's patriotic discourse to the fame of her soldiers, a massive granite monument marks his own resting-place. Upon one side are the principal dates of his life and services. The reverse characterizes the writer and scholar who, fervent in spirit, serving the Lord, instructed a generation of Christian ministers.

Those who knew Dr. Hackett in later life will recognize the permanence of traits ascribed to him as a young man by the Rev. Ezekiel Russell, D.D. : "In character, H. B. Hackett was the beauty of our college Israel; modest, sincere, truthful, just, conceding to all their dues; claiming little for himself, and from his soul loathing everything in the form of affectation, intrigue, and selfish management."

He has a secure fame, and is held in the affec-

tionate remembrance which he was himself so ready to accord. "Having once loved Andover as the place of his intellectual nativity, he loved it unto the end," said Dr. Park at his burial. At the centenary celebration of Phillips Academy, in 1878, a poem was delivered by Dr. O. W. Holmes, whose prose portrait of his schoolmate, the future great Biblical scholar, was published in 1869, and is well known. In commemorating

"The large-brained scholars whom their toils release,
The bannered heralds of the Prince of Peace,"

he laid these fresh *immortelles* upon the grave of Hackett,—

"Such was the gentle friend whose youth unblamed
In years long past our student-benches claimed;
Whose name, illumined on the sacred page,
Lives in the labors of his riper age."

Hackett, Rev. J. A., the present able pastor of the First Baptist church, Shreveport, La., was born in Illinois in 1832. When he was quite young his father removed to Mississippi, where he was brought up. He was educated at Mississippi College, in which he recently preached the commencement sermon, which has added greatly to his reputation as a clear thinker and forcible speaker. He served as pastor at Jackson, Miss., and at Clinton and Hazelhurst in the same State. He was called to Shreveport in 1876. During his present pastorate the church has erected a beautiful house of worship. He has also successfully established a mission station in the suburbs of the city at a former Sunday resort for amusement.

Hadley, Rev. Moses, a pioneer preacher in Southwestern Mississippi, came to the State some time previous to 1806, and at that time labored in Wilkinson County. The estimation in which he was held in that day is seen in the fact that he was chosen moderator of the Association at its second session, when both David Cooper and Thomas Mercer were present. In 1810 he wrote the circular letter of the body on religious declension, an able document, in which he treats of the causes and cure in a forcible manner. In 1812 he wrote again on "Union of the Churches." The same year he was sent to Opelousas to ordain Mr. Willis and constitute the First church in Louisiana. He was, in 1817, one of a committee to write a summary of discipline for the churches. He died in 1818, much regretted by his brethren, who by resolution expressed their high appreciation of his labors.

Hadley, Judge T. B., was born June 30, 1801, in Beaufort District, S. C. In childhood his parents moved to Woodville, Wilkinson Co., Miss., where he was educated; was admitted to the bar, and was sent to the Legislature of Mississippi. In 1830 he was auditor of public accounts for the State of Mississippi; in 1838 was State senator from Hinds

[*] Memorials of Horatio Balch Hackett. Edited by George H. Whittemore. 1876.

County, and he was greatly applauded for his indefatigable exertions in procuring a law for the "Protection of the Marital Rights of Women," long and familiarly known as "Hadley's Law." He moved to Houston, Texas, in 1844, and served his county as chief justice, and the city of Houston as recorder. He joined the Baptist church at Jackson, Miss., in 1839 ; served as clerk and deacon of the Houston church, and always took a deep interest in its prosperity and in the progress of Christ's cause. The Baptist ministry of Texas will ever remember the generous hospitality which his family at all times dispensed. A good man and an honored citizen, he passed to the rest which remaineth for the people of God, Sept. 25, 1869.

Haetzer, Ludwig, a Hebraist, an able polemical writer, a hymnist, and an Anabaptist. In 1523 we find him earnestly supporting Zwingli in his reformatory efforts. His writing against images did much towards securing their removal from the Zürich churches. When the Anabaptists come forward, in 1524, we find him sympathizing with them in their efforts to secure pure churches, but still seeking to maintain the favor of Zwingli, Œcolampadius, etc. In 1525 he published the ablest plea for temperance to be found in the literature of the Reformation period, in which he condemned unsparingly the social gatherings of the clergy, where wine was drunk immoderately, and where worldly talk, even indecent conversation, was freely indulged in. Driven from Switzerland, he labored in Augsburg, Strasburg, and Constance. In 1526, in connection with Hans Denk (see article), he published a meritorious translation of some of the prophetical books of the Old Testament. He was beheaded at Constance in 1529, ostensibly for adultery, but probably on account of his Anabaptist views.

Hague, Rev. John B., was born in New Rochelle, N. Y., in 1813, and was a graduate of Hamilton College in the class of 1832. He pursued his theological studies at Newton, graduating in 1835. His ordination took place at Eastport, Me., where he continued as pastor for ten years. Mr. Hague has devoted the larger part of his life to teaching young ladies. He has had schools in Jamaica Plain, Newton Centre for six years, at Hudson, N. Y., for ten years, and at Hackensack, N. J., where he removed in 1870.

Hague, William, D.D., was born in Pelham, Westchester Co., N. Y., Jan. 4, 1808, and was a graduate of Hamilton College, N. Y., in the class of 1826. He took his theological course at the Newton Institution, graduating in 1829. He was ordained Oct. 20, 1829, as pastor of the Second Baptist church in Utica, N. Y., the sermon being preached by Rev. Dr. B. T. Welch, of Albany. Here he remained until called to the pastorate of

the First church in Boston, to fill the vacancy caused by the resignation of Rev. C. P. Grosvenor. His installation took place Feb. 3, 1831, Rev. Dr. Wayland preaching the sermon. His connection with this church continued until June, 1837, when he was dismissed to enter upon his duties as pastor of the First church in Providence, over which he was installed July 12, 1837, the sermon being preached by Rev. Dr. B. Sears. The church commemorated while he was pastor the second centenary of its foundation, Nov. 7, 1839, and he preached an historical discourse on the occasion, which was published. During nine months of the year 1838–39 he was abroad, the Hon. S. G. Arnold being his traveling companion. He resigned his office Aug. 20, 1840, and accepted a call to the Federal Street church, Boston, where he commenced his labors Sept. 20, 1840. His subsequent pastorates have been in Jamaica Plain, Mass., Newark, N. J., Albany, N. Y., New York City, and Boston. He is now pastor of a church at Wollaston Heights, one of the pleasant suburbs of Boston. Dr. Hague received the degree of Doctor of Divinity from Brown University in 1849, and from Harvard College in 1863. He was chosen a trustee of Brown University in 1837, and is now, with one exception, the oldest living member of the board. Among the productions of his pen are "The Baptist Church transplanted from the Old World to the New," "Guide to Conversation on the Gospel of John," "Review of Drs. Fuller and Wayland on Slavery," "Christianity and Statesmanship," "Home Life." He has also written much for the reviews and the periodical press, especially for the *Watchman*, of Boston, with which he was at one time connected editorially, and whose columns he has often enriched over his well-known signature "Herbert." Dr. Hague is justly regarded as one of the ablest and most scholarly ministers of his denomination.

Haigh, Deacon Daniel.—Mr. Haigh was born at Marsden, Yorkshire, England, in December, 1801. After his conversion he united with the Independent church at Huddersfield of which Dr. Boothroyd, the Bible commentator, was the pastor. He was afterwards baptized into the Baptist church at Wakefield, and served as deacon for some years. In 1847 he came to Illinois and settled near Long Grove. He was for many years an officer in the Pavilion and Bristol churches, and an active member of the Fox River Association, and helper in all denominational work. He still lives, retaining at advanced age his warm interest in the progress of Christ's kingdom.

Haigh, William Morehouse, D.D., was born at Halifax, Yorkshire, England, in April, 1829. Converted at the early age of thirteen, he was baptized at Wakefield by Rev. J. Harvey, in 1842. In

1852 the family removed to this country, settling at Pavilion, in the northern part of the State. He was licensed to preach by the Pavilion church in 1852, and began his pastorate over it in January, 1853, being ordained in November of that year. His subsequent pastorates were at Chillicothe, Bristol, Woodstock, Mendota, and Galesburg, in Illinois. In August, 1862, Mr. Haigh entered the army as chaplain of the 36th Regiment Ill. Infantry, continuing in that service until November, 1864. A year was then given to the service of the Baptist Union for Theological Education as agent for the seminary. In 1877, while pastor at Galesburg, having been tendered the appointment of district secretary of the Home Mission Society for Illinois, Iowa, Wisconsin, and Minnesota, he accepted the service, and is still prosecuting it with marked ability and success. His field has since been extended so as to include Nebraska, Dakota, and Kansas, a vast territory, which he nevertheless succeeds in reaching with measures promotive of missionary work.

Dr. Haigh has rendered important service in writings for the press. His "Letters to Young Converts," and his "Spiritual Life," first published in the Baptist paper at Chicago, have had a considerable additional circulation in more permanent forms.

Haile, Judge Levi, was born in Warren, R. I., and graduated at Brown University in the class of 1821. Having studied law, he practised his profession in his native town. From 1835 to the close of his life he was one of the judges of the Supreme Court of Rhode Island. For many years Judge Haile was a prominent member of the Baptist church in Warren. He died July 14, 1854.

Haldeman, Rev. Isaac Massey, was born at Concordville, Delaware Co., Pa., Feb. 13, 1845. He removed with his father in 1852 to West Chester, Pa., where he received a thorough academic education. From the age of nineteen to twenty-five he was engaged in business with his father. He was converted in 1866, and baptized by the Rev. J. A. Trickett into the fellowship of the West Chester church. From his conversion he was impressed with the conviction that it was his duty to preach, to which service his mother had from his infancy devoted him. His father designed him for business, but his own tastes were literary. He devoted his leisure hours to a course of study embracing the English classics and the ancient and modern languages, and he wrote for the magazines. Pursued by the "Woe is unto me if I preach not the gospel," he resolved to give himself to the ministry. He accepted the invitation of his pastor to preach during a revival, which lasted for thirty consecutive nights. He proclaimed also the gospel in other churches. He was called in April, 1871, to the pastorate of the Brandywine Baptist church,

Delaware Co., in which he was ordained. Having remained there four years, preached to crowded houses, and baptized over 200 persons, he became pastor of the Delaware Avenue Baptist church,

REV. ISAAC MASSEY HALDEMAN.

Wilmington, Del., in April, 1875. Here again the house was thronged. Meetings held in the fall and winter resulted in the quickening of the members and in the addition of 400 to the church. The baptisms have since reached 800, and the membership over 1000. "As a speaker," says an intimate friend, "he is exceeding rich in imagery, clothing his ideas as they flow from a fountain of clear and logical thought with choice words and fitting metaphors. He always speaks extempore."

Hale, Rev. William, an early minister in Mississippi, whose labors laid the foundation of many of the churches in the northern part of the State, was born in Tennessee in 1801, and began to preach in his nineteenth year; came to Mississippi in 1835. He was a man of strong native abilities, and with his co-laborer, Martin Bull, abounded in evangelistic labors. He assisted in the organization of the Chickasaw Association, which has since grown into four large Associations, viz., Aberdeen, Judson, Tippah, and Tishamingo. He died Sept. 21, 1855.

Hall, Jeremiah, D.D., was born at Swanzey, N. H., May 21, 1805. He was religiously educated by his parents, and in 1816 was baptized at Colerain, Mass., by Rev. George Witherell.

His education was obtained in part at the academy in Ashfield, Mass., and at Brattleborough, Vt. But having prosecuted the studies of the college course as opportunity permitted, he was admitted in 1847, by Madison University, to the degree of Master of Arts, and in 1854 the degree of Doctor of Divinity was conferred on him by Shurtleff College.

In 1827 he entered the Newton Theological Institution, and finished the course of study in 1830. He was ordained a minister of the gospel, Feb. 3, 1831, in Westford, Vt. In his joint pastorate of the Westford and Fairfax churches he was greatly blessed, and large accessions were made to their numbers.

In the spring of 1832 he accepted the charge of the First Baptist church in Bennington, Vt. During this pastorate the church was greatly strengthened, and a flourishing Baptist Academy, originated by him, was established at Bennington, which for some years exerted a wide influence in promoting the cause of Christian education in that vicinity.

In the spring of 1835 he removed to Michigan, and settled at Kalamazoo. Here, in the following winter, under his labors was organized the First Baptist church, which he served as pastor till the close of the year 1842.

Soon after his arrival at Kalamazoo he learned that the Michigan and Huron Institute, which had been brought into corporate existence chiefly through the efforts of Rev. T. W. Merrill, was seeking a home in the western part of the State, and that strong inducements were offered to locate it about six miles east of Kalamazoo. Believing that it should be established in the town of Kalamazoo, he assumed such pecuniary obligations in the purchase of land for its site as induced the trustees to locate what is now Kalamazoo College at that town. The unredeemed pledges of others, and the financial depression which soon came on, caused him great embarrassment and loss.

Early in 1843 he became pastor of the church in Akron, O., and in 1845 he took charge of the church in Norwalk, O., with special reference to the founding of the Norwalk Institute, a flourishing Baptist Seminary, over which he presided five years. Though greatly prospered in this work, he resigned it to become pastor of the church in Granville, O.

In 1853 he was elected president of Granville College. Soon after he entered upon his duties the name of the college was changed to Denison University, and a new site was selected in the immediate vicinity of the village of Granville, handsome buildings were erected, a valuable library was procured, and additions were made to the faculty. He was subsequently pastor of the Tabernacle church in Kalamazoo, and of the churches in Chillicothe, Mo., and Shell Rock, Iowa. For the last few years he has resided in Port Huron, Mich. He has two sons in the ministry.

Hall, Rev. John P., was a brother of Rev. Wm. S. Hall. Both these brothers left their impress upon the denomination in Pennsylvania. John labored extensively and for many years in the eastern portion of Pennsylvania, where his consistent life won him many friends. His latter years were spent in the pastoral care of the Mount Moriah church, Fayette Co., Pa., and the Nixon Street church, Alleghany City, Pa. After a very short illness he fell asleep in Christ, and his departure cast a deep gloom over the entire church.

Hall, Rev. Robert, of Arnsby, England, was born April 15, 1728, old style; his birthplace was Black-Heddon, about twelve miles from Newcastle. His father was an Episcopalian and his mother a Presbyterian. The death of his father when he was a child removed him from his mother's care to the guardianship of an uncle. With his family he attended the ministry of an Arminian, whose teachings filled him with great distress without pointing him to the blood of atonement. His convictions were deepened by other causes, until, at twelve years of age, the lad was filled with " black despair, accompanied by horrid temptations, and by blasphemies which ought not to be uttered." And this unhappy state continued for more than seven years. For some time he thought that God would have been unholy to have saved him. Then he imagined that if he could live without sin there might be some hope for him. To secure this object he made a covenant with God, which was written with his own blood, agreeing to be lost eternally if he ever sinned again. This compact of course was soon broken, and he supposed now that his destruction was irrevocable. After some calculations he concluded that as his sins in a little while would soon exceed the crime of self-murder, he would commit suicide. He appointed a time to execute this design, but concluded that he would first look at the Bible, and as he opened it his eyes fell on the words, " Come, now, and let us reason together, saith the Lord; though your sins be as scarlet, they shall be as white as snow; though they be red like crimson, they shall be as wool." These words destroyed his plan to kill himself, though they gave him no solid hope. At another time as he was reading in the New Testament the words arrested him, " God sent forth his Son, made of a woman, *made under the law to redeem them that were under the law.*" Immediately this thought impressed him, " Christ was *made under* the law ; then he was not under it originally ; for what *end* was he made under the law ? to redeem them that *were under the law ; were* under the law ! then they are not *under the law* now, but *redeemed.* There is, therefore, a way of redemption for sinners from the curse of the law by which it is possible even I may be saved ;" and in a little time he soon put his entire trust in the Saviour; and ever after became valiant for the truth, and especially for the truth as Paul revealed it, and as John Calvin expounded it.

Mr. Hall's brother Christopher joined the Baptists, much to his indignation, for he regarded them with aversion. He and some friends had a discussion with a Baptist minister, in which they were silenced but not convinced; but on further examination Mr. Hall fully received believer's baptism, and like an honest man, and like so many other intelligent Pedobaptists, he came out publicly, and was baptized Jan. 5, 1752. The next year Mr. Hall became pastor of the church at Arnsby on a salary which seldom amounted to £15 a year. His family increased fast, until he was the father of fourteen children; and by the force of self-denial and the plans and cares of a good wife, he kept out of debt.

For a time after his settlement he was greatly troubled about his call to the ministry. One Sunday morning he came to tell the church that he could not preach. An aged brother asked him to enter the pulpit and pray, and if he obtained help then he could preach, and if not they would unite in prayer for him. He took the advice and soon found a text and a sermon. That season of prayer gave the death-blow to doubts about his call to preach.

He was blessed in winning many souls to Jesus Christ, in setting forth the glorious gospel in becoming and in heaven-given thoughts and words; and he was successful in leading a life of untarnished loyalty to his divine Master. His ministering brethren loved him, his church with which he labored for thirty-eight years was devoted to him, and even the ungodly regarded Mr. Hall with reverence.

He had a penetrating and clear mind, and a heart often overflowing with the love of Jesus. These qualities are strikingly exhibited in his little work, "Help to Zion's Travellers," which has had a wide circulation in Europe and America, and which has rendered great service to the children of God. Mr. Hall was an able and honored servant of the king of Zion. He died suddenly, March 13, 1791. His son, the celebrated Robert Hall, differed widely from the doctrines of his father, and obtained a distinguished reputation for eloquence.

Hall, Rev. Robert, of Leicester, England, was born at Arnsby, near Leicester, May 2, 1764. He was the youngest of fourteen children, and when two years old he could neither speak nor walk. He learned to read through the efforts of an intelligent nurse, who took him for air and exercise to a small cemetery near his father's residence. From its grave-stones she taught him the alphabet, spelling, and reading. Before he was nine years old

he had become familiar with Jonathan Edwards on "The Freedom of the Will," and on "The Religious Affections," and with Butler's "Analogy." During his whole life Edwards was a favorite with him. Before he was ten years of age he had written many essays on religious subjects. When he was eleven his teacher, Mr. Simmons, dismissed him from his school because he was farther advanced in education than his instructor. Mr. Simmons, while young Hall was his pupil, had frequently to spend the night in preparation to keep up with him, and to relieve himself from this trouble Robert Hall was compelled to leave his school.

In his fifteenth year he entered Bristol College to study for the ministry. Here his progress was equally remarkable, and speedily inspired the brightest hopes for his future usefulness. During his first summer vacation he preached at Clipstone, in Northamptonshire, before his father and a number of ministers. His text was, "God is light, and in him is no darkness." The service was one of peculiar trial to him, and from which he earnestly begged to be relieved. Never till then had he assumed the responsibility of a preacher. But the effort was a success, and congratulations were showered upon him.

According to custom, while at Bristol he was required to give an address in the vestry of Broadmead church before his instructors and fellow-students. Its commencement was brilliant, but his nervousness overcame him, and "covering his face in an agony of shame, he exclaimed, 'Oh! I have lost all my ideas.'" He was appointed again to deliver the same address the next week, and a second time he made a worse failure than the first. Robert Hall was extremely sensitive, and these discouragements, while intensely mortifying, only summoned up or called down greater strength for the next trial, through which when it came he passed with flying colors.

After studying three years at Bristol he went, in 1781, to King's College, Aberdeen, where he remained four years. He pursued his studies in Greek and Latin, in philosophy and mathematics, with wonderful success. He was the first student in each of his classes, and the most distinguished young man in the college. While in Aberdeen Mr. Hall became acquainted with the celebrated Sir James Mackintosh, then a student in the same institution, and a young man of rare intellectual endowments. They discussed all important philosophical questions together on the sea-shore, or on the banks of the Don above the old town; they sat together in the class-room; they read Xenophon, Herodotus, and Plato together; and as their pursuits and friendships were well known, it was common for the students to say when Hall and

Mackintosh were seen together, "There go Plato and Herodotus." The regard that sprung up between them in Aberdeen lasted until death.

Immediately after leaving Aberdeen Mr. Hall became assistant to Dr. Caleb Evans, then pastor of Broadmead church, Bristol. The preaching of Mr. Hall speedily attracted very large congregations and an unusual amount of interest. Many of the leading men of Bristol, and quite a number of Episcopal clergymen, were occasionally among his hearers. His position, however, in the church, owing to misunderstandings between Dr. Evans and himself, and suspicions that the eloquent young preacher was not quite orthodox, became uncomfortable, and in 1791 he accepted a call to succeed the learned and erratic Robert Robinson as pastor of the church in Cambridge. In that city, famous for its Episcopal university, Mr. Hall soon acquired the reputation of being the most finished scholar and eloquent preacher in the British Islands. His "Apology for the Freedom of the Press," published in 1793, made him troops of friends and exhibited talents of the highest order. In 1801, Mr. Hall published a sermon on "Modern Infidelity," which carried his fame into every circle of society, and elicited the admiration and gratitude of the friends of Jesus throughout Great Britain. Dr. Gregory, his biographer, says, "The most distinguished members of the university were loud in his praises; numerous passages of the sermon that were profound in reasoning, or touching and beautiful in expression, were read and eulogized in every college (there are seventeen colleges in the University of Cambridge) and in almost every company;" and all over the land it was commended in reviews, periodicals, newspapers, and discourses. From this period Mr. Hall was at the head of the British pulpit; he was spoken of as "The prince of preachers," and his opinions and sayings were treasured up and quoted as if they had been the utterances of an inspired oracle. When his next sermon was printed, in 1803, which he named "Sentiments Proper to the Present Crisis," it was received all over the country with enthusiasm; and even England's great prime minister, perhaps her greatest, William Pitt, declared that "the last ten pages were fully equal in genuine eloquence to any passage of the same length that could be selected from either ancient or modern orators." His subsequent publications confirmed the splendor of his reputation. At Cambridge his intellect gave way twice for short periods from nervous prostration, but his recovery was perfect. He spent fifteen years at Cambridge and nearly twenty at Leicester, and then returned to Bristol in 1825, and entered the heavenly Canaan Feb. 21, 1831. His success in Leicester and Bristol was quite equal to his usefulness in Cambridge. He was the greatest

preacher that ever used the English tongue, and his works will be read while the language of Britain is spoken. They were first published in six volumes, in 1833, and they have passed through eleven editions up till 1853.

Mr. Hall never read his sermons, and very seldom wrote them entire. He studied them with the greatest care, though his use of paper was exceedingly limited.

He was the victim of a painful disease from boyhood till death. His brothers had frequently to carry him part of the way to and from school; he was often in mature years compelled to lie down on his back on the floor to gain relief from his anguish. For more than twenty years he was unable to pass a whole night in bed. He carried with him continually "an internal apparatus of torture," ready for work any moment, and certain not to be idle for any considerable time; and yet when free from pain he was one of the happiest of men.

At thirty-three years of age he was "a well-proportioned, athletic man, with a deportment of unassuming dignity, with winning frankness in all that he uttered, and with a speaking countenance animated by eyes radiating with the brilliancy imparted to them by benevolence, wit, and intellectual energy." "His mind was equally distinguished by power and symmetry, where each single faculty is of imposing dimensions and none out of proportion to the rest. His intellect was eminently acute and comprehensive; his imagination prompt, vivid, and affluent." He had the readiest command of the most appropriate language and beautiful imagery ever given to a mortal. His reading was enormous, from six to eight hours a day he often spent at it, and it ran over the Greek and Latin poets, orators, historians, and philosophers; the early Christian fathers, the Reformers, the Puritans, and Episcopalians of the seventeenth century, and more modern theologians, French and English. Nor was there any branch of literature with which he had not a remarkable acquaintance.

His piety was deep and abiding. Soon after his first attack of mental aberration he felt in himself the most extensive change in his relations to Jesus. His heart became the Saviour's more unreservedly than ever; his habits were more devotional than they had been previously, and his spiritual exercises more fervent and more elevated. The light of God's countenance followed him, and the peace of God was continually with him, and when he came to die, though his was a death of extreme physical pain, his faith was triumphant, and strong in the Lord he passed away joyfully to his eternal home.

He held Arminian views of the atonement, and in a measure of some of the other doctrines of grace, and he spoke scornfully of the works of Dr.

Gill, a writer who knew immensely more of the languages and teachings of the Bible than himself; he believed that unbaptized persons might come to the Lord's table. He had other peculiarities of doctrine as unscriptural as those just named. But while we discard his errors without hesitation, notwithstanding the authority of his great name, and in disregard of the sublimest eloquence by which false doctrine was ever commended to human consciences, we rejoice in the mighty preacher of Cambridge, Leicester, and Bristol as an illustrious servant of king Jesus.

Hall, Rev. Robert S., a leading Baptist preacher and educator in Northwestern Louisiana, was born in Ireland, in 1825, of Presbyterian parents, who devoted much time to his religious culture. Being designed for the ministry, he received a liberal education at Queen's College, Belfast. He emigrated to the United States, and engaged in teaching. He united with the Baptists, and in 1852 settled in Caddo Parish, La. He began to preach in 1867, and from his talents and learning at once became a man of mark. He died much regretted in 1873.

Hall, Rev. Wm. S., was born of Quaker parentage, in Blockley, Philadelphia, Pa., Nov. 27, 1809, and died in White Deer Valley, June 8, 1867, in his fifty-eighth year. Converted at the age of sixteen, he was baptized by Rev. J. H. Kennard, D.D., and ordained Oct. 4, 1829. His labors were spread over Berks, Schuylkill, Lancaster, Chester, and the Northumberland region as a mission-field, and as a pastor they were given to Frankford and Milestown in Philadelphia, Zanesville, O., Ridley, Pa., Phœnixville, Pa., Laight Street, N. Y., and the North church in Philadelphia.

The peculiarities characterizing Brother Hall were uncommon energy, surprising fluency in language, suavity of manners, and great firmness in advocating and in defending unpopular sentiments. This led him to strongly press the claims of free missions, and the revision of the Bible. To his praise let it be said that in the hour when his position was deemed the very height of folly, he never gave up his principles, even at the period of his ministry when to be a free mission or Bible Union advocate was to invite bitter opposition. His record shows that he baptized 2459 persons, founded 9 churches, and built 8 meeting-houses.

Hallett, Capt. Benjamin, was born in Barnstable, Mass., Jan. 18, 1760. He saw active service, both in the navy and the army, during the Revolutionary war. He was among the most enterprising merchants of his time, and was recognized as a man of rare qualities. For nearly seventy years Capt. Hallett was a consistent member of a Baptist church. We are told that "when he visited Boston he was hailed with a welcome wherever he went, whether he made his appear-

ance on the exchange, in marts of trade, or in Dr. Stillman's vestry, where his voice was often heard." He exerted his influence, and most successfully, in the Bethel, and stirred up the hearts of his Christian friends in Boston to labor and pray for the spiritual good of seamen. He died at his residence in Barnstable, Dec. 31, 1849, in the ninetieth year of his age.

Halliburton, Rev. Henry, an eloquent young Baptist minister of Northern Arkansas, was born in Tennessee in 1845. He began to preach in 1873, and developed rare abilities as an evangelist. At the time of his death, in 1877, he was a missionary in the White River region.

Halliburton, Col. W. H., is a distinguished lawyer at De Witt, Ark., who has taken an active part in the work of the Baptist denomination in the State for a number of years. He was born in Tennessee in 1815. He has never sought public position, but has filled several offices of trust with great credit to himself. During the war he was Confederate States marshal, and has always been efficient in church work.

Halteman, Rev. David Emory, pastor of the First Baptist church in Delavan, Wis., is a native of Montgomery Co., Pa., where he was born Aug. 28, 1834. His ancestors in the paternal line were

REV. DAVID EMORY HALTEMAN.

German Mennonites. The family came to America from Germany in 1698, and settled at Germantown, Pa. This old town was the birthplace of three successive generations of the family. His mother was Scotch by birth, although her parents emigrated to America when she was a child. When the subject of this sketch was four years old his father removed to Ohio and settled at Dayton, which became subsequently his home. Mr. Halteman's earliest religious instruction came from his godly Presbyterian mother. He attended the Sunday-school of the First Baptist church in Dayton, O. At twelve years of age he was converted and baptized into the fellowship of the First Baptist church in Dayton.

When seventeen years of age he was licensed by the church of which he was a member to preach the gospel. He was educated at Granville College (now Denison University) and Rochester University. He was formally set apart to the work of the Christian ministry by a council called by the Baptist church in Bloomfield, Ill., in December, 1857. This church he supplied six months. Having received an invitation to the pastorate of the Baptist church in Marengo, Ill., he entered upon his labors there in July, 1858, and continued in this relation eleven years. The church was small in numbers, and during his pastorate of eleven years it grew to be the largest in the Association, the membership being over 400 when he closed his labors there. The meeting-house and parsonage were built during his pastorate. Frequent revivals, in two instances of great power, blessed his ministry. In July, 1869, Mr. Halteman accepted a call to the pastorate of the First Baptist church in Delavan, Wis., one of the most important churches in the State. He began his ministry there in the autumn of the same year, and has continued it with fidelity and success up to the present time. Though it is of twenty-three years' duration it has been confined to two fields, and the results abundantly show the advantage of faithful labor in a prolonged term of pastoral service. He has frequently been tempted by calls to other important fields, but has uniformly declined to consider them, feeling that, as a rule, the more permanent the pastoral relation the better is the cause of Christ served. He has been an indefatigable worker in the study, in visits among his people, and in the State. During his ministry he has preached 4120 times, including sermons at Conventions, Associations, councils, dedications, and funerals. He has received 856 members into the two churches of which he has been pastor, 505 of whom were baptized by him; adding 180 persons baptized into other churches, he has immersed altogether 685 persons. His ministry builds up the churches strong doctrinally, develops generous habits of benevolence, and establishes the members in spiritual life and power. Just now his church is erecting a fine house of worship.

For eight successive years Mr. Halteman has been the president of the Wisconsin Baptist State Convention, and an active member of its board. As a presiding officer of a deliberative body he has few superiors, displaying rare tact, impartiality, and familiarity with parliamentary law. At the dedication of meeting-houses his services have been in frequent requisition.

During the war he served as chaplain of the 15th Regiment Ill. Volunteers one year, but his pastoral relation was not disturbed while he was absent.

Frank, open-hearted, generous to a fault, he has fulfilled in a high degree the promise with which he began his ministry. He has for many years taken a leading part in the denominational work of the State. If personal qualities, acquired knowledge, large experience, purity of aim and life, are of any value in the ministry, our brother is fitted to do the best work of his life in years yet to come.

Ham, Rev. Mordecai F., a prominent and useful minister in Southern Kentucky, was born in Allen County of that State, April 30, 1816. He united with Trammels Fork Baptist church, in his neighborhood, in April, 1838; was licensed to preach in 1842, and ordained in 1843, at which time he became pastor of Bethlehem, the oldest and largest church in his county, and has continued to serve in that capacity to the present time. He has preached statedly to four churches, and, on account of the scarcity of preachers in his region, has sometimes supplied as many as six. He has received into the churches he has served over 2000 members, by experience and baptism. Mr. Ham has performed considerable missionary labor, and has, with the assistance of his co-laborers, formed several new churches. For some years he has been collecting at his own expense a library for the use of young ministers in his locality. He has expended several hundred dollars in this enterprise, and has commenced the formation of a valuable library, especially rich in the subject of Baptist history. He has been eighteen years moderator of Bays Fork Association. His only son, Rev. Tobias Ham, is a young preacher of excellent promise.

Hamberlin, Rev. John B., pastor at Vicksburg, Miss., a descendant of Deacon Wm. Hamberlin, who accompanied Richard Curtis and company of Baptists to Mississippi in 1780; graduated at Mississippi College with the first honor of his class in 1856, and at Rochester Theologic. Seminary, N. Y., in 1858; pastor at Clinton and Raymond, Miss., from 1858 to 1862; two years chaplain in Confederate army, during the rest of the war was State superintendent of army missions. After the war he established Meridian Female College, and supplied Meridian and several surrounding churches, and edited *The Christian Watchman* and *College Mirror.* This excessive labor impaired his health, and he retired to the Gulf coast. Here he began a missionary work that resulted in the establishment of eight churches on the line of the New Orleans and Mobile Railroad, and the Gulf Coast Association. He became pastor at Vicksburg in 1880.

Hamilton, Rev. Alexander, was born in Ireland; his parents were Scotch-Irish; educated at the Royal College, Belfast, for the Presbyterian ministry, he embraced Baptist sentiments and united with that denomination in 1845; was employed by the Irish Missionary Society of the English Baptists, and labored at Conlig, Banbridge, and Belfast. He came to the United States through the influence of Spencer H. Cone, D.D., and Benjamin M. Hill, D.D., secretary of the American Baptist Home Mission Society. Soon after reaching this country he was ordained by the First Baptist church of New Haven, Conn., in 1851. He immediately went to Wisconsin as the missionary of the American Baptist Home Mission Society, where he has served in the Christian ministry until the present. He has been pastor at Barton, Appleton, Walworth, Eau Claire, and Waukau, spending twenty-eight years with these churches. He is living in retirement at Ripon, Wis. His ministry has been fruitful.

Hamilton, Rev. Hiram, was born Dec. 25, 1820, in Portage Co., O.; baptized in March, 1843, at Napoleon, Mich.; was soon after licensed. He studied at Madison University, and graduated at the University of Michigan in 1849. In 1850 he crossed the plains to California, and for eight years was at the head of the first Protestant female seminary in that State. In 1855 he was ordained, and served as pastor six months at San José. In 1864 he was appointed missionary to Idaho by the American Baptist Home Mission Society; organized a church and built a meeting-house at Idaho City. In 1866 he built a house at Boise City, at a cost of $3000, taught a school, and was chaplain of the first Legislature. He collected the Benneau and Shoshone Indians, and preached the gospel to them. In 1869 he returned to California, located in the San Joaquin Valley, began missionary work, established a church, into whose membership over fifty were soon baptized. His life-work is that of an educator. In this he is still active; is a member of the San Joaquin board of education, a zealous Christian, and ever ready to aid in advancing the interests of the denomination in California.

Hamilton Theological Seminary was founded at Hamilton, N. Y., May 1, 1820, by the Rev. Daniel Hascall as teacher in Ancient Languages, and Rev. Dr. Nathaniel Kendrick as teacher in Theology. It is certain, however, that as early as 1816 Daniel Hascall suggested the idea of a literary and theological institute to Nathaniel Kendrick. Out of this institution came Madison University, Hamilton Theological Seminary, and Colgate Academy. See these articles in this work, and also articles DANIEL HASCALL and NATHANIEL KENDRICK.

Hancock, B. F., Esq., was born in Philadelphia, Pa., Oct. 19, 1800, and he died Feb. 1, 1867. Two sons were born to him,—John Hilary, and Winfield Scott, now a major-general in the U. S. army, and lately a candidate for the Presidency of the United States. He served as deacon in the Norristown Baptist church, and also as superintendent of its Sunday-school for several years. He was a constituent member of the Bridgeport Baptist church, and served as deacon, church treasurer, and clerk, and he was Sunday-school superintendent until his death. He was regarded as a wise counselor, a conscientious, diligent, liberal, and faithful Christian. He loved the prayer-meeting, was invariably in his place, always prompt in taking part, and earnest and tender in urging his brethren to work for their blessed Lord and Saviour. Tears were often in his eyes while praying or speaking, or listening to the preaching of the gospel. At times, when pleading for his children, for the conversion of sinners, and for the prosperity of the church, his feelings would so completely overcome him as to compel an abrupt conclusion. He was not only uniformly present at all the services of the sanctuary and Sabbath-school, but was always in time. He was honored by the North Philadelphia Association with several successive elections as moderator.

No citizen of Norristown ever exerted a more decided Christian influence, or commanded more general respect. The Bridgeport Baptist church and Sunday-school are feeling the blessed influence of his counsels and prayers to-day, and will doubtless continue to be benefited thereby even to the end of time.

Hand, Rev. George, was born at Cape May, N. J., Sept. 2, 1821; graduated from the University of Pennsylvania with the first honor in 1849; was ordained pastor of the West Kensington church, Philadelphia, Pa., Nov. 7, 1849; was pastor of the Hatborough church, Pa., for ten years, from 1852. He has devoted much time to teaching, for which he has superior qualifications, but he has always maintained his calling as a preacher by proclaiming the Word of life on the Lord's day.

Mr. Hand is a scholar, a Christian, and a faithful laborer for Jesus in the seminary and in the pulpit.

Hand, Rev. Henry, was a native of New Jersey. He was converted Oct. 23, 1783, about which time he moved with his father to Georgia from South Carolina. He began to preach first as an itinerant minister, but afterwards had charge of a number of churches. He was a most laborious and zealous preacher, scattering the good seed of the gospel, on both sides of the Savannah River, from Savannah to Augusta, most faithfully and earnestly, during a period of not less than fifty years, from about 1785 to 1835. He died Jan. 9, 1837.

Hanks, Rev. Robert Taylor, was born April 23, 1850; a man of more than ordinary ability and of enviable reputation. His theological education was received in the Southern Baptist Theological Seminary at Greenville, S. C. After graduating he took charge of Barea church, near Greenville, having been ordained in 1871 at Dalton. In 1872 he went to Alabama, and entered Howard College, where he remained some time, but left that institution to enter Richmond College, Va., in 1873, where he spent three years. In the summer of 1875 he preached for the Petersburg church, in the interim between the resignation of Dr. Hatcher and the settlement of Dr. Eaton. On the 15th of October, 1876, he took charge of the Baptist church at Dalton, Ga., resigning in January, 1879, to assume the pastorate of the Albany church, where he is laboring most efficiently at present. As a preacher he is pleasant and graceful in manner, fluent in utterance, sound in his presentation of truth, and, at the same time, tender and pathetic. His social and genial disposition, combined with an earnest and sincere piety, has always won for him the affection, confidence, and esteem of those among whom he labors. He is an industrious worker, and fully abreast of the times in all the great benevolent schemes of the day.

Hanna, Judge William Brantly, was born Nov. 23, 1835, in the district of Southwark, now within the limits of the city of Philadelphia. His parents were, and still are, members of the First church, Philadelphia. He was educated at both private and public schools, and graduated from the Central High School of Philadelphia in July, 1853, when he determined upon a professional life; he began to study law in the office of his father, John Hanna, Esq. He graduated from the law department of the University of Pennsylvania, and was admitted to practise Nov. 14, 1857. He was subsequently appointed an assistant to the district attorney of the county, and remained in that position between two and three years. In 1867 he was elected to the common council of the city; was re-elected in 1870, and, before the expiration of the term, was chosen a member of the select council. In October, 1872, he was sent to represent the second senatorial district of the city in the convention that then assembled to revise and amend the constitution of the State of Pennsylvania. While serving as a member of the convention he was re-elected to the select council for the term of three years beginning Jan. 1, 1874. The new

constitution having been ratified by the vote of the people, and having provided for the establishment of an orphans' court in the city and county of Philadelphia, he was nominated as one of the

JUDGE WILLIAM BRANTLY HANNA.

three judges who should compose the court. In November, 1874, he was elected for the term of ten years beginning Jan. 1, 1875, and he has been commissioned president judge, which office he still holds.

Judge Hanna is a member of the First church, Philadelphia, having been baptized April 3, 1859. He has served as clerk and trustee, and is at present one of the deacons of the church. He is also the president of the "Baptist Orphanage of Philadelphia," and a member of the board of managers of the "American Sunday-School Union." These varied and repeated appointments in secular and religious affairs are a fitting testimony to his marked ability, his sterling uprightness, and his exemplary Christian character. He is one of the best judges in the State.

Hanna, Rev. Thomas Alexander Thomson, son of Thomas Thomson and Matilda (Carson) Hanna, was born in County Derry, Ireland, Aug. 6, 1842; his grandfather, Surgeon Thomas Hanna, R.N., served under Nelson; his mother is a daughter of Rev. Alexander Carson, LL.D.; spent his childhood in Glasgow, Scotland; came to America at the age of seven : converted in New York in 1858, and baptized by Rev. Ira R. Stuard ; studied eight years in Hamilton, N. Y.; ordained in 1866 as first pastor of Central Baptist church, Williamsburg,

N. Y., and served about three years; then first pastor of Fifth church in same place more than four years; in 1874–75 traveled in Europe and the East; settled in Plantsville, Conn., in 1875; secretary of

REV. THOMAS ALEXANDER THOMSON HANNA.

Connecticut Baptist State Convention for past three years; has written small commentary for Bible Union, and numerous articles for leading Baptist periodicals; married, in 1870, Emily Frances, daughter of Dr. Adoniram and Emily Judson; a very scholarly man; a student in several languages.

Hannan, Rev. Barton, was a pioneer preacher in the Mississippi Territory, who suffered persecution under the Spanish rule. He was imprisoned for preaching soon after the government passed into the hands of the Spaniards, and remained several years in jail, until near the time of the change of government. When his wife went to the commandant, Don Manuel Gayoso de Lemos, and demanded the release of her husband, he endeavored to evade her demand by caressing her babe and making it rich presents. The resolute woman said to him, "I don't want your presents; I want my husband." He replied, "I cannot grant your request, madam." She answered, "I will have him before to-morrow morning, or this place shall be deluged in blood; for there are men enough who have pledged themselves to release him before morning or die in the attempt." The governor deemed it prudent to yield to the demand of this resolute woman, and Hannan was released. He lived to preach the gospel unmolested under the flag of the United States.

Hansard Knollys Society, The, was instituted by our English brethren to republish some of the valuable writings of their fathers, and to issue important records never printed before. Ten volumes are the results of its judicious efforts. The first appeared in 1846, and contains "Tracts on Liberty of Conscience and Persecution," from 1614 to 1661; the second, "The Unpublished Records of the Broadmead Church, Bristol," from 1640 to 1686; the third, "The Pilgrim's Progress," printed from the first edition; the fourth, "The Bloudy Tenent of Persecution," by Roger Williams; the fifth, "A Necessity of Separation from the Church of England," by John Canne; the sixth and eighth contain Van Braght's "Martyrology of the Churches of Christ," translated from the Dutch; the seventh contains Du Veil's "Commentary on the Acts of the Apostles"; the ninth, "The Records of the Fenstanton, Warboys, and Hexham Churches," from 1644 to 1720; the tenth, "Confessions of Faith and other Public Documents of the Baptist Churches of England in the Seventeenth Century."

These works are of rare value, and they have numerous and important notes. No Baptist minister who can secure them should be without them. Unfortunately, the Hansard Knollys Society is dead.

Hanson, James Hobbs, LL.D., was born in China, Me., June 26, 1816. His ancestors on both sides were of English origin, and among the early settlers of New England. His youth was spent amid the scenes and toils of farm-life, in the enjoyment of such intellectual advantages as the common school and an occasional term at the village academy were capable of affording. His earliest and strongest wish was to obtain an education. When he was eighteen years of age he became a hopeful Christian. Soon after he commenced his regular preparation for college. Even at that early period he had decided to make teaching the business of his life. He was a graduate of Waterville College, now Colby University, taking a distinguished position as a scholar in the class of 1842. The year after graduation was spent in teaching in Hampden, Me. In September, 1843, he entered upon his duties as principal of Waterville Academy, where he remained till March, 1853. At that time he took charge of the high school in Eastport, Me. In January, 1857, an invitation to become principal of the boys' high school in Portland, Me., was accepted. Here he taught for a little more than eight years, at the end of which he was urged to return to Waterville to take charge of the academy with which he had formerly been connected. Here he commenced anew his labors, and has continued at his post up to the present time. In addition to the discharge of his duties as a teacher,

Mr. Hanson has annotated and published Cæsar's "Commentaries on the Gallic War," Sallust's "Catiline," a volume of Cicero's orations in connection with Mr. J. W. Rolfe, of Cambridge, Mass., a volume of extracts from Ovid, Virgil, and Horace, called "The Hand-Book of Latin Poetry." In 1872 he received from his *alma mater* the honorary degree of LL.D.

Haralson, Judge Jonathan, a fine jurist, judge of the city court of Selma, a most useful member of the Selma Baptist church, and president of the Baptist Convention of Alabama, was born Oct. 18, 1830, in Lowndes County. Mr. Haralson graduated in the State University, under Dr. Manly, in 1851, and in 1852 in New Orleans in the law-school of Louisiana. In 1853 he settled in Selma, where he maintained a first-class practice until 1875, when he was appointed by the governor of the State judge of the city court of Selma. He is a trustee of Howard College and of the Agricultural and Mechanical Colleges of the State.

He united with the Baptist Church when fourteen years of age,—and he became a deacon of the Selma church in 1855; was the efficient superintendent of the Sunday-school for seven years; has been sent to Europe on important professional business twice. Judge Haralson may be reckoned among the most distinguished laymen in the State, and his brother Hugh is not less so.

Hardin, Charles Henry, ex-governor of Missouri and founder of the female college that bears his name, was born in Kentucky in 1820. His ancestors from colonial times lived in Fairfax Co., Va. His father removed to Kentucky, and afterwards to Missouri, where he settled in Boone County. Charles H. had good literary opportunities, of which he availed himself, and, after graduating with honor, pursued the study of law, and in 1843 commenced practice at Fulton. Being elected a justice of the peace, he was early noted for his correct decisions. His business increased, until he was recognized as one of the most laborious, efficient, and sound lawyers within reach. In 1852 he was elected to the Legislature, and afterwards re-elected; and he was chosen while there, with two others, to revise and compile the State statutes, and then to superintend their publication. After serving in the house of representatives six years he was elected to the senate, in which he was honored as chairman of the judiciary committee.

In 1861 he removed to his present home in Mexico, Audrain Co. Here his professional services were extensively sought. After a period of ten years he was again sent to the senate, and honored as before with the chairmanship of the judiciary committee, and also with that of the asylum committee. In 1874 he was elected governor of the State by a majority of more than 40,000, and by his wise management he was instrumental in restoring the credit of the State bonds. After serving out his term, he retired to his home, where he is honored and beloved for his great abilities, unswerving honesty, and Christian generosity. The cause of

GOVERNOR CHARLES HENRY HARDIN.

education finds in him a devoted friend. The female college, one of the results of his benefactions, which he has endowed, and which he continues to aid, exerts an extensive influence over the State. He is a member of the Baptist Church.

Hardin College.—This young ladies' school was founded in 1873, by Gov. Charles H. Hardin. He gave $40,000 in lands and cash to establish it. The college buildings are complete, and of modern style. The grounds are extensive and finely arranged. Mrs. H. T. Baird is the experienced and accomplished president. The course of study is comprehensive and thorough. Upwards of 100 students were in attendance last year. It is located at Mexico, Audrain Co., Mo.

Harding, Rev. Harris, one of the fathers of the Baptist denomination in Nova Scotia, was born Oct. 10, 1761, in Horton, Nova Scotia; converted under Henry Alline's preaching, in Cornwallis, in 1783; evangelized in 1785 in Colchester and Cumberland Counties; in Chester in 1788; in Annapolis County in 1789; in Yarmouth, Onslow, and Amherst in 1790; in Liverpool, Argyle, and Barrington in 1791; ordained at Onslow, Sept. 16, 1794; was immersed as a Baptist in Yarmouth, Aug. 28, 1799, by Rev. James Manning; took part in forming the Baptist Association, June 23, 1800; was a pioneer of the gospel in 1817 to Cape Canso, to Westport in 1818. Mr. Harding had a passion for the conversion of sinners; and to his labors, under God, is largely to be attributed the growth of the Baptist denomination in Yarmouth. Died March 7, 1854, in the ninety-third year of his age.

Harding, Rev. John, a prominent and useful preacher of Green Co., Ky., was born, of Baptist parentage, in Washington Co., Ky., Jan. 16, 1785. His education was finished under Rev. N. H. Hall. He joined Pitman's Creek Baptist church, in Green County, at the age of twenty-five. Two years afterwards he was ordained to the ministry, and became pastor of Pitman's Creek and other churches. He was a man of extensive reading, and he was a strong logical preacher and writer. He was a

tered to the Baptist church, Fredericton, New Brunswick, three years from 1818; evangelized in Pictou and in Prince Edward Island in 1826. The church celebrated the jubilee of his pastorate Feb. 13, 1846; died June 8, 1855. Was a warm friend of Horton Academy and Acadia College. Strongly doctrinal, deeply emotional, quick and elastic, Theodore Seth Harding was pre-eminently the Baptist orator of the Maritime Provinces.

Hardwicke, J. B., D.D., was born in Buckingham Co., Va., Aug. 9, 1830. At the age of twelve he made a profession of religion, and united with the Enon Baptist church. In 1852 he was ordained at the Enon church, in order that he might accept calls to two churches in Campbell Co., Va. He at once became prominent among the young preachers

HARDIN COLLEGE.

brother of Hon. Aaron Harding, and uncle of Chief-Justice M. R. Harding. Died Nov. 11, 1854.

Harding, John H., was born in St. John, New Brunswick; converted and baptized in Wolfville, Nova Scotia, while attending Horton Academy, in 1834; is a deacon of the Baptist church, Germain Street, St. John; was treasurer of the New Brunswick Baptist Home Missionary Board, and is a firm friend of all denominational enterprises.

Harding, Rev. Theodore Seth, a founder of the Baptist denomination in Nova Scotia, was born in Barrington, Nova Scotia, March 14, 1773; converted in 1787; commenced preaching in 1793; withdrew from the Methodist denomination, and was baptized at Halifax, May 31, 1795; ordained pastor of the Horton church, July 31, 1796; evangelized and baptized in Cobiquid, 1799; took part in forming the Baptist Association, June 23, 1800; minis-

of the country. In 1853 he accepted a call to Greenfield, Va., where he remained for seven years. Here his special mission seems to have been to aid in rescuing the churches from the growing influence of anti-mission teachers. His next call was from Danville, which he declined, and after the call was repeated, he agreed to divide his time with them until they could secure a pastor. In 1860 he accepted a call to the Second church of Petersburg, and remained there until 1864. Now his time was divided between his church and the hospitals that were established in Petersburg during the war. His next field was Goldsborough, N. C., where he spent several years of successful labor. Afterwards he removed to Parkersburg, W. Va. Here he commenced the publication of the *Baptist Record*, which he edited for five years. His efforts here aided in uniting the Baptists of West Virginia in their support of one general organization, and in harmonizing churches that had been rent asunder by the civil war. In 1873 the College of West Virginia conferred upon him the degree of Doctor of Divinity. The year following he accepted a call to Atchison, Kansas. He served there for two years and nine months, was then called to Leavenworth, the largest city in the State. While in Kansas he was recording secretary, then president, and afterwards corresponding secretary of the State Convention. He was also a member of the board of directors, and a trustee of Ottawa University. He rendered valuable aid in freeing this school from financial embarrassments and difficulties that hindered its prosperity. At present Dr. Hardwicke lives at Bryan, Texas, and is pastor of a large and influential church. From early life he has been a regular contributor to various secular and religious periodicals, and he has published several sermons.

Hardy, Col. William H., a prominent lawyer at Meridian, Miss., was born in Alabama in 1837, and became a Baptist at the age of fourteen. He took a partial course at Cumberland University, Tenn. In 1856 he came to Mississippi and engaged in teaching. He began the practice of law in 1858, and at once became prominent at the bar, and he now occupies the front rank of his profession in Eastern Mississippi. He commanded a company in the Confederate army, and was afterwards on the staff of Gen. J. A. Smith as assistant adjutant-general. In 1872 he was elected grand master of the Masons; was tendered the nomination for governor of the State; was once elected vice-president of the Southern Baptist Convention; Presidential elector in 1876. Col. Hardy has always taken an active part in the denominational work in Mississippi.

Harkness, Prof. Albert, Ph.D., LL.D., was born in Mendon, Mass., and was a graduate of Brown University in the class of 1842. For nearly six years after his graduation he held an important position as an instructor in the Providence High School. In the fall of 1853 he went abroad to pursue his studies in the German universities, and was absent two years. He first attended lectures at the University of Bonn. From Bonn he went to Berlin, and from it to Göttingen. The degree of Doctor of Philosophy was conferred upon him by the University of Bonn. Returning home early in the fall of 1855, he entered upon his duties as Professor of the Greek Language and Literature in Brown University. In 1870 he went abroad the second time, and was absent a little over a year, studying at Bonn, Heidelberg, and Berlin, and making extensive tours through different parts of Europe. Prof. Harkness has published several works connected with his special department, and others designed to aid the student in Latin. Of these the best known and most popular is his Latin grammar, first published in 1864, which has had a very large circulation. He was one of the founders of

PROF. ALBERT HARKNESS, PH.D., LL.D.

the Philological Association, and its president in 1876–77. It is matter for just pride that we have in the Baptist denomination so accomplished and well known a scholar as Prof. Harkness.

Harmon, Rev. G. W., was born in Davidson Co., N. C., March 29, 1847; baptized by Rev. Wm. Turner in 1866; attended Abbott's Creek Academy and New Garden College; was ordained in August, 1871, Revs. Wm. Turner, W. M. Bostick, Enoch Crutchfield, J. H. Brook, and J. B. Richardson forming the Presbytery; graduated at Southern Baptist Theological Seminary in May, 1874; settled as pastor at Wadesborough in January, 1875, where he still remains.

Harper, Rev. Pleasant Howard, is a leading preacher and missionary in Washington Territory. Born in Claiborne Co., Tenn., Feb. 1, 1836; educated in the public schools; baptized in 1860; licensed and ordained in 1871, he began his ministry at once in the Territory as pastor at Elma two years; labored two years as missionary of the Home Mission Society on the line of the Northern Pacific Railroad; organized the Centerville church, and was its pastor two years; then labored with the White River church two years; gave important help to the Brush Prairie church, and is now at Goldendale, where he is aided by the Baptist Convention of the North Pacific coast. He is a good scholar, a steadfast Christian worker, and has held important civil and military positions which were thrust upon him by the people. Throughout the Territory he is recognized as one of the most important men in that new and growing field, where the harvest is great and the laborers are few.

Harris, Rev. Austin, a teacher and preacher of prominence in North Louisiana, was born in Georgia in 1835; was ordained in 1858, and the next year removed to Louisiana. He founded a school at Arizona, in Claiborne Parish, where he has successfully taught, and preached to surrounding churches.

Harris, Rev. Benjamin N., was born in Brookline, Mass., in 1783. For twelve years he was a Methodist minister. He changed his views on the subject of baptism, and connected himself with a Baptist church in Wrentham, Mass. His service for Christ in the ministry of the gospel extended over a period of fifty years. He preached in all the New England States, in New York, and Canada, and came at last to be known everywhere as "Father" Harris, and was greatly beloved and esteemed. He died in Bolton, Mass., March 3, 1859.

Harris, Rev. David, was born in Cornwallis, Nova Scotia, in 1785; converted at Bridgetown, Nova Scotia, in 1806, and subsequently baptized; ordained July 23, 1814, pastor of the Baptist church, Sackville, New Brunswick. His pastoral and missionary labors were very successful in the Maritime Provinces, especially in Nova Scotia. Died April 15, 1853.

Harris, Rev. E. L., was born in Ira, Cayuga Co., N. Y., Jan. 12, 1816. In 1833 he united with the Baptist church at Cato. In 1839 he entered Hamilton Literary and Theological Institution, from which he graduated in 1843. He was ordained August 31 of the same year by the church in Pike, Wyoming Co., N. Y., which he served two and a half years, the church at Rushford, Allegany Co., five years, and in the fall of 1850 he came to Wisconsin and settled with the Baptist church in Beloit as pastor. Here his ministry was blessed with an extensive revival. He subsequently served as pastor the Baptist church in Walworth three years, the Baptist church in Darien ten years (this church he gathered and organized, and built their meeting-house), the Baptist church in Sugar Creek two years, the Baptist church in East Delavan one year, the Baptist church in Greenwood, Ill., nearly one year. He was called a second time by the Baptist church in Walworth, serving eighteen months.

During the war he spent some months as chaplain in the army.

Mr. Harris has frequently been moderator of the well-known Walworth Baptist Association, and he was for one year president of the Wisconsin Baptist State Convention.

His ministerial labors have often been interrupted by ill health. He resides near Delavan, Wis., which has been his family home for many years. He has been a faithful and devoted minister of the gospel.

Harris, Rev. George W., was born in Nassau, Rensselaer Co., N. Y., Jan. 8, 1813, the son of Rev. John Harris. He studied at Hamilton, completing the collegiate course in 1840 and the theological course in 1842. He was ordained in Pittsfield, Mass., in January, 1843, and the next year became pastor in Jackson, Mich. In 1848 he became editor of the *Michigan Christian Herald,* and served in that office fifteen years. Since 1863 he has resided in Battle Creek, writing for various periodicals, and preaching as opportunity has offered. He is a ready and perspicuous writer.

Harris, Henry Herbert, D.D., was born in Louisa Co., Va., Dec. 17, 1837. Trained by parents

HENRY HERBERT HARRIS, D.D.

of piety and intelligence, in consequence of early afflictions his mind frequently turned to Jesus, and in November, 1852, at the age of fifteen, he was baptized, and united with the Lower Gold Mine church, Va. He entered at once on active work in the Sunday-school and prayer-meetings, and in 1857 was licensed to preach. His preparation for his college course had been so advanced and thorough, that in October, 1854, he entered the Junior class of Richmond College, graduating with the degree of A.B. in July, 1856. In 1857 he entered the University of Virginia with his younger brother, Prof. J. M. Harris, now of Furman University,

S. C. At the termination of three years he received the degree of A.M., having studied Hebrew and applied mathematics in addition to the regular course. He was at this time invited to the chair of Greek in Richmond College, but having a strong predilection for scientific studies, he accepted a proffered position in the Albemarle Female Institute. At the close of the first session, July, 1861, though exempt from military duty and frail in health, he volunteered as a private soldier, and made the campaign of that summer and fall in the Kanawha Valley as an infantry rifleman, engaged in scouts and skirmishes. In December his company was disbanded, and, thinking the war already over, he entered, in January, 1862, the Southern Baptist Theological Seminary at Greenville, S. C. After one month's stay at the seminary he learned that his old regiment was in peril at Roanoke Island, N. C.; left at once to join them, and was prevented from doing so by their capture. He went to Virginia; joined a battery of field artillery, afterwards attached to the corps of Gen. Stonewall Jackson, and took part in most of the great battles fought under that leader, including his last at Chancellorsville. In June, 1863, he was honored with an unsought commission as first lieutenant in a regiment of engineer troops, about to be organized for the army of Northern Virginia, in which capacity he was engaged in the manifold duties of reconnoitring, selecting routes of march and lines of battle, bridging streams, running countermines, and, upon occasion, taking active part in engagements up to the time of Gen. Lee's surrender at Appomattox Court-House, in April, 1865. In the following October he resumed his former position as instructor in the Albemarle Female Institute; and, on the reorganization of Richmond College, in July, 1866, he was again invited to the chair of Greek, which he accepted, and has continued to fill up to this time, with the exception of an interruption of six months in 1878, spent in a visit to Palestine and Greece.

Prof. Harris began his ministry in 1859 by preaching to a congregation of colored persons. In 1860–61 he filled an appointment once a month at an old free church near Charlottesville. In 1864 the colonel of an infantry regiment applied to the War Department for his appointment as chaplain, but the application was refused, on the ground " that so good an officer could not be spared, and that he was already doing much of a chaplain's work in his own command." From 1868 to 1870, Prof. Harris preached regularly at a small house in the suburbs of Richmond, where he had gathered a Sunday-school and congregation. When a church was organized at this place, he was ordained, July 4, 1869, and became the pastor. In less than a year, in consequence of ill health, he was compelled to resign, and since that time he has been able to preach but seldom. In the field of literature, Prof. Harris is known by several admirable reports and addresses before educational meetings in his own State, at Marion, Ala., at Philadelphia, and also by contributions to periodicals, chiefly to the *Religious Herald*, Richmond, Va. From 1873 to 1876 he was the editor of the *Educational Journal* of Virginia, and in 1877 of the *Foreign Mission Journal*, the organ of the boards of the Southern Baptist Convention. Upon the organization of the Virginia Baptist Historical Society, in June, 1876, he was elected its secretary and treasurer, which offices he still holds. In addition to his other duties, Prof. Harris is now the junior editor of the Richmond *Religious Herald*.

Harris, Judge Ira, was born May 31, 1802, at Charleston, Montgomery Co., N. Y., and died in Albany, N. Y., Dec. 2, 1875. In 1808 his parents

JUDGE IRA HARRIS.

moved into Cortland County and settled on a farm. In 1815 he entered the academy in Homer, where he was prepared to enter college. In 1822 he joined the Junior class in Union College, and graduated with the highest honors in 1824. He commenced the study of law under Augustus Donnelly, Esq., of Homer, and subsequently entered the office of Chief-Justice Ambrose Spencer, at Albany, and was admitted to the bar in 1827. He soon rose to prominence in his profession. In 1844 and 1845 he represented Albany County in the Assembly, and in 1846 he was chosen to a seat in the State convention to revise the constitution.

In the autumn of the same year he was elected to the State senate, and in 1847 he was chosen to a seat on the bench of the Supreme Court of the State. At the expiration of four years he was re-elected for the entire term of eight years.

On leaving the bench, Judge Harris spent a year in foreign travel, and in 1861 was elected by the New York Legislature to the Senate of the United States to succeed William H. Seward, who had been called to Mr. Lincoln's cabinet. As a lawyer, a legislator, a judge, a statesman, Ira Harris was above reproach. In the dark days of the war he stood firmly by the government.

After the expiration of his term he was again elected to the State constitutional convention of New York, when he delivered the celebrated speech on the "Government of Cities."

He was an ardent promoter of higher education. He was president of the board of trustees of Union College, president of Albany Medical College, and of the board of trustees of Vassar College; also one of the founders of Rochester University. He also filled the chair of Equity, Jurisprudence, and Practice in the Albany Law School.

Judge Harris was a devoted Christian, an officer of the Emmanuel Baptist church, Albany, and for years was president of the American Baptist Missionary Union. He traced his ancestors back to the colonists in Rhode Island led by Roger Williams, whose principles of religious liberty he seemed to inherit. His lecture on the life and character of the great founder of the Baptist denomination in America will long be remembered by the people of Albany.

Harris, Rev. John, was born in Rensselaer Co., N. Y., Sept. 19, 1790, and died in Battle Creek, Mich., Oct. 11, 1864. In the summer and fall of 1812 he served in the army of the United States. In 1815 he was baptized by Rev. Enoch Ferris, whom he succeeded as pastor at Nassau, N. Y., the next year. For ten years he was pastor here, and for ten years following at South Ballston. He then settled in Battle Creek, where he spent the remainder of his life preaching to various churches in that vicinity during twenty-eight years of hard labor and privation. He was recognized as a representative Baptist clergyman of Michigan, and an earnest advocate of all beneficent and wholesome reforms.

Harris, Prof. J. M., is one of Virginia's many valuable gifts to South Carolina. Although the soil of the two States does not touch, "they have always," as Dr. Jeter once said in the South Carolina State Convention, "sympathized and generally gone hand in hand, and this is especially true of the Baptists of the two States."

Prof. Harris is now a little over forty years of age. His parents were pious, and tried to bring up their children in the ways of the Lord, and their son's conversion in his thirteenth year was the fruit of their training.

He entered the University of Virginia Oct. 1, 1859, and received the degree of A.B. in July, 1860, and of A.M. July 1, 1861. He served in the artillery during the war. In February, 1869, he became Professor of Natural Sciences in Furman University, and is still doing excellent service in that position.

Harris, Rev. Tyre, was born in Boone Co., Mo., Aug. 9, 1824. He made a profession of religion when seventeen years of age, and joined the Bethlehem Baptist church. He was baptized by the beloved Fielding Willhite, pastor of the church. He commenced preaching when nineteen years of age. He was a young man of brilliant talents and deep piety, and he was eminently successful in winning souls to Christ.

He was a warm advocate of missionary and benevolent efforts. He was pastor at Fayette, Mount Pleasant, Booneville, Big Lick, and Mount Nebo. He was president for one year of Stephens College, Columbia, and he was also pastor of the church in that place.

He afterwards took the care of the Baptist church in Lexington, Mo., and died a few months after, in September, 1854.

He was highly esteemed by all. Happy in his associations with the people, earnest and eloquent in his preaching, he was a great blessing during his ministry. It was thought that his zeal and labors shortened his life.

Harrison, Rev. Edmund, Professor of the Latin Language and Literature in Richmond College, Va., was born at "The Oaks," Amelia Co., Va., Feb. 17, 1837. He prepared for college in the Amelia Academy, an institution established and conducted by his father, Wm. H. Harrison. During the year 1854 he was engaged in studying law, and afterwards attended lectures at the law-school of the University of Virginia. During 1855 he was engaged in teaching school in Cumberland Co., Va., after which he returned to the university, took the literary course, and graduated in most of the schools. After graduation, Mr. Harrison was engaged in teaching in the Southern Female Institute at Richmond, where his scholarship was held in high esteem. The war breaking out about this time, he entered the Confederate army, joining the "Powhatan Troop" as a private soldier, and continuing in active service until failing health sent him to stationary duty in the Nitre and Mining Bureau. In 1864 he received the appointment of assistant in the Nitre and Mining Corps, with the rank of captain of cavalry, and was promoted, in 1865, to the rank of major, in consequence of a valuable report prepared and presented by him to Gen. St. John.

He was with the army under Gen. Johnston when it surrendered at Greensborough, N. C. During 1865 he was engaged in teaching in the Richmond Female Institute, and in 1866 was elected Professor of Latin in Richmond College, a position which he still holds, with honor to himself and advantage to the institution. Prof. Harrison was converted at the age of sixteen, and united with the Mount Tabor Baptist church, Amelia County. For some years he was actively engaged in Christian labors, and, feeling it to be his duty to consecrate himself to the ministry, he, in 1874, received ordination, and is now engaged in preaching regularly to two country churches. Prof. Harrison writes occasionally for different periodicals, secular and religious.

Harrison, Gen. James E., was born in South Carolina; early joined the Baptist Church; was prominent in Baptist affairs in Mississippi many years; served in the State senate of Mississippi; was attached to the Confederate army during the

GEN. JAMES E. HARRISON.

whole civil war, attaining the rank of major-general. In civil life he was occupied from boyhood to old age as a farmer. He was an earnest worker in all the missionary and educational enterprises of Texas, and was first president of the General Association. He died at Waco, about the sixty-fifth year of his age, in 1874 or 1875.

Harrison, Richard, M.D., was born in South Carolina; educated in Mississippi; received the degree of M.D., and successfully practised medicine in Mississippi and Texas. At an early age he professed religion, and joined the Baptist Church;

zealously labored for benevolent enterprises, and served the Mississippi Baptist State Convention as its president. He represented Monroe Co., Miss., in the State senate. After moving to Texas he took an active part in Baptist affairs. He possessed high natural gifts as an orator. He was a younger brother of Gen. James E. Harrison, and twin-brother of Col. Isham Harrison, who fell at the head of his regiment during the civil war, in Mississippi. Dr. Harrison was married three times. His last wife was a daughter of Rev. Wm. C. Beech. Died at Waco, Texas, in 1877.

Harrison, Rev. T., was born in Sussex Co., Va., Dec. 9, 1839; graduated at Columbian College, Washington, D. C., in 1859; taught in Georgia two years; served through the late war in the cavalry; taught from 1865 to 1873 in Virginia and North Carolina; was ordained in Edenton, N. C., in 1872, and has been pastor at Hartford, Apex, Carthage, and Greensborough. Is now agent of Foreign Mission Board for North Carolina.

Harrison, Gen. Thomas, was born near Nantwich, Cheshire, England. His father, like the fathers of Henry Kirke White and Cardinal Wolsey, was a butcher, a circumstance that led such an excellent lady as Mrs. Lucy Hutchinson to say that " he was a mean man's son." He had a respectable education, and in early life he was a solicitor's clerk. His employer was on the side of Charles I.; but Harrison, from the beginning of the trouble, was with the friends of liberty. When the war commenced he became a cornet in the Parliamentary army. " He advanced," says Clarendon, " by diligence and sobriety to the grade of captain without any signal notice being taken of him, till the army was remodeled, when Cromwell, who possibly had knowledge of him before, found him of a spirit and disposition fit for his service, much given to prayer and to preaching, and otherwise of *an understanding capable of being trusted in any business;* and then he was preferred very fast, so that by the time the king was brought to the army he was a colonel of horse, and looked upon as inferior to few after Cromwell and Ireton in the councils of the officers and in the government of the agitators ; and there were few men with whom Cromwell more communicated, or upon whom he more depended for the conduct of anything committed to him."* Lord Clarendon was no friend of Gen. Harrison, and his testimony to his ability and prominence may be taken at its full worth. Harrison was speedily known all over the United Kingdom as a soldier of skill and daring, and he was raised to the rank of major-general, and for a considerable period was justly regarded as second only to Oliver Cromwell. When Charles I. was to

---

* Clarendon's History of the Rebellion, iii. 247. Oxford, 1706.

be tried for treason against his subjects, Harrison was deemed the safest man to bring him from Hurst Castle to Windsor and London; for he was regarded as proof against bribery or fears for the future. The soldiers relied upon him for his well-known piety; he prayed in their meetings for religious worship, and sometimes delivered gospel addresses burning with holy fervor; and his life was without a guilty stain. And then he was a decided republican; so that the hero of Naseby, as long as he fought against tyranny, could trust Harrison, in whom, after himself, the army confided. " Harrison," says Hume, " was raised to the highest dignity, and was possessed of Cromwell's confidence."* By the favor of Cromwell, and of the Parliament, of which he was a very influential member, he had acquired an estate worth $10,000 a year, in addition to his professional income; and he lived in a style corresponding with his ample means. He was selected as one of the judges to try the king, and his name stands boldly at his death-warrant. He reluctantly consented to aid Cromwell in dispersing the Long Parliament. When the fatal day arrived, Cromwell, during the session, told him " that the Parliament was ripe for a dissolution," and the general tried to persuade him to give the subject further consideration; and when some time after, Cromwell declared the members " no Parliament," and called in soldiers to remove them, Gen. Harrison intimated to the speaker that he should leave the chair; he refused to vacate his position without force; " I will lend you my hand," says Harrison. Then, according to Gen. Ludlow, of the Parliamentary army, " putting his hand within his, the speaker came down."† This was the greatest mistake of Gen. Harrison's life, but Cromwell was a dear friend; and from no other man could he obtain such necessary assistance to shield him from the anger of his countrymen, who reverenced the very name of a Parliament, and abhorred a military despotism. His fervent piety, his warm regard for Cromwell, and his intimacy with him are strikingly expressed in the following letter, written him as he assumed the command of the army which, on Sept. 3, 1650, vanquished the Scotch at Dunbar:

" To spare you trouble, I forbear to give you my excuse for not waiting on you to Ware. *I know you love me*, therefore are not apt to except, though in this particular I had not failed, but that orders from the Council superseded me. Considering under how many and great burdens you labor, I am afraid to say any more, that I may not add to them, but love and duty make me presume. The business you go upon is weighty as ever yet you undertook. The issue plainly and deeply concerns

the life or death of the Lord's people, His own name, and his Son's. Nevertheless may you rejoice in God, whose affair it is, who, having heretofore given you numberless signal testimonies to other parts of the work, will in mercy prosper this, that he may perfect what he hath begun; and to omit other arguments, that in Deut. xxxii. 27, hath much force on my heart, especially the last words, ' *And the Lord hath not done all this.*'

" I believe, if the present enemy should prevail, he would as certainly reproach God, and all that hitherto has been done aforesaid, even as I now write; but the jealousy of the Lord of hosts, for his great name, will not admit it. My Lord, be careful for nothing, but pray with thanksgiving, to wit, in faith. Phil. iv. 6, 7. I doubt not your success; but I think faith and prayer must be the chief engines; as heretofore, the ancient worthies, through faith, subdued kingdoms, out of weakness were made strong, waxed valiant in fight, and turned to flight the armies of the aliens. Oh that a spirit of supplication may be poured forth on you and your army! There is more to be had in this poor simple way than even most saints expect. My Lord, let waiting upon Jehovah be the greatest and most considerable business you have every day; reckon it so, more than to eat, sleep, or counsel together. Run aside sometimes from your company and get a word with the Lord. Why should you not have three or four precious souls always standing at your elbow, with whom you might now and then turn into a corner? I have found refreshment and mercy in such a way. Ah! the Lord of compassion own, pity your burdens, care for you, stand by and refresh your heart each moment. I would I could in any kind do you good. My heart is with you, and very poor prayers to my God for you. The Almighty Father carry you in his very bosom, and deliver you, if it be his will, from touching a very hair of any for whom Jesus hath bled. I expect a gracious return in this particular.

" But I am sorry to be thus tedious. Pardon me. . . . The Father of mercies visit and keep your soul close to him continually, protect, preserve, and prosper you, is the prayer of, my Lord,

" Your excellency's loving servant, whilst I breathe, T. HARRISON.

" WHITEHALL, 3d July, 1650.

" For his excellency the Lord-General Cromwell, humbly present these."‡

That Gen. Harrison was in the closest relations with Cromwell and with Cromwell's Saviour is clear from every line of this letter. He was the right-hand man of England's great uncrowned

---

* Hume, Smollett, and Farr, i. 730. London.
† Memoirs of Ludlow, ii. 457. Vevay, 1699.

‡ Confessions of Faith, etc., pp. 315-17. Hansard Knollys Society, London.

ruler, loving him tenderly, and beloved by him in return, until he proclaimed himself Protector, or, as Gen. Harrison viewed it, Despot. From that moment, as Hume states, Harrison and the other Baptists deserted him. Rapin says, "The Anabaptists* were all of the republican party," and, having fought to dethrone a king, they had no intention of waging war to support the government of one man under any other name. Cromwell, afraid of the military talents and great popularity of Gen. Harrison, cast him into prison, until the masses of his country acquiesced in his dictatorship, when his former trusted friend was set at liberty.

The general and his wife were baptized† in the winter of 1657, though they held Baptist principles for years before their immersion. At the time of their baptism the cold was intense and the ice very thick.

The Protector's displeasure removed from the general the pretended friends who sought the patronage of Cromwell through him, but he still enjoyed the love of the hosts who appreciated patriotic worth, Christian character, and military genius.

When the English people for a season became demented, like the French in their great revolution, and showed their aberration of intellect by giving their throne to Charles II., the basest and the most immoral of men, Gen. Harrison was quickly sent to the Tower of London, and in due time he was brought before unprincipled judges for trial as a regicide. The court sat in the Old Bailey in London, and when he was required to answer, as Gen. Ludlow states, "He not only plead *Not Guilty,*‡ *but he justified the sentence passed upon the king,* and the authority of those who commissioned him to act as one of his judges. He plainly told them, when witnesses were produced against him, that he came not thither to deny anything he had done, but rather to bring it to light; he owned his name subscribed to the warrant for the execution of the king, as written by himself; he charged divers of his judges with having formerly been as active for the cause in which he had engaged as he or any other person had been; he affirmed that he had not acted by any other motive than the principles of conscience and justice, in proof of which he said it was well known that he had chosen to be separated from his family, and to suffer a long imprisonment, rather than to comply with those who had abused the power they had assumed (Cromwell) to the oppression of the people. He insisted that having done nothing, otherwise than by the authority of Parliament, he was not

justly accountable either to this or any other inferior court, which, being a point of law, he desired counsel assigned upon that head ; but the court overruled (the question) ; and by interrupting him frequently, and not permitting him to go on in his defense, clearly manifested a resolution to gratify the resentments of the court (the king) on any terms. So that a hasty verdict was brought in against him ; and the question being asked, if he had anything to say why judgment should not pass, he only answered that, since the court had refused to hear what was fit for him to speak in his defense, he had no more to say. Upon which Bridgman pronounced the sentence. I must not omit (to state) that the executioner, in an ugly dress, with a halter in his hand, was placed near the general, and continued there during the whole time of his trial, but having learned to contemn such baseness, after the sentence had been pronounced against him, he said aloud, as he was withdrawing from the court, *that he had no reason to be ashamed of the cause in which he was engaged.*"

On Nov. 13, 1660, Harrison was executed at the place where Charing Cross formerly stood, that the king might have the pleasure of the spectacle, and inure himself to blood."§ In the "Trials of the Regicides"‖ the sickening scene is thus described : "He was drawn on a hurdle from Newgate to Charing Cross. Within certain rails lately there made a gibbet was erected, and he was hanged with his face looking toward the banqueting-house at Whitehall (the palace). Being *half dead,* he was cut down by the common executioner ; his bowels were burned, his head severed from his body, and his body divided into quarters. His head was placed upon a pole on the top of Westminster Hall, and the quarters were exposed on some of the city gates." Ludlow declares that "he was cut down *alive,*¶ and saw his bowels thrown into the fire." It was intended that he should be alive and conscious of his pain when the human butcher of his most gracious majesty should thrust his knife into his body. Samuel Pepys, "Clerk of the Acts of the Navy" in 1660, writes :** "I went out to Charing Cross to see Maj.-Gen. Harrison hanged, drawn, and quartered ; which was done there ; he looking as cheerful as any man could do in that condition. He was *presently* cut down, and his head and heart shown to the people."

From Ludlow†† we learn that when Chief-Justice Coke was executed, he was drawn to the scene of death on a sled, upon the front of which was the head of Gen. Harrison, with the face uncovered and

* Rapin's History of England, ii. 603. London, 1733.
† Evans's Early English Baptists, ii. 254. London, 1864.
‡ Memoirs of Ludlow, iii. 61–64.

§ Idem, iii. 69.
‖ Trials of the Regicides, p. 282.
¶ Memoirs of Ludlow, iii. 63.
** Pepys's Diary, i. 146.
†† Ludlow's Memoirs, iii. 75.

directed towards him, the object being to fill him with terror; but there was an expression in the face of the brave warrior that filled the chief justice with heroism, and frustrated the designs of his cruel murderers.

Harrison was fully informed of the purpose to arrest and execute him; but he refused to fly from the deadly danger, "regarding* such an action as a desertion of the cause in which he had engaged." Gen. Ludlow, who knew Harrison better than most men of his day, commenting on this remarkable fidelity to principle, says, "I shall not take upon me to censure the major-general, not knowing what extraordinary impulse a man of his virtue, piety, and courage may have had upon his mind in that conjunction. Sure I am, he was every way so qualified for the part he had in the following sufferings, that even his enemies were astonished and confounded."

As we think of the manly defense made by the general, with the executioner and his halter at hand all the time, and of his last words, which he uttered aloud as he left his judges, condemned to a frightful death by their wicked decree, "that he had no reason to be ashamed of the cause in which he was engaged," and of his choice of martyrdom instead of flight, we are filled with admiration for the faith and the courage of the praying and preaching general. And then when we think of him, in full view of Charles II., and, no doubt, of several of his fair and frail companions, butchered and dressed, a victim of royal vengeance, full of the most triumphant endurance that ever made the death of a martyr glorious, we bless God for his invincible grace, and we praise him for our Baptist ancestry.

The enemies of Gen. Harrison were ready to confess his extreme conscientiousness, his fearless daring, and his fervent piety, and his memory should be cherished as a sacred legacy by his Baptist brethren while the world lasts.

Harriss, Col. Samuel, was among the most effective preachers that ever proclaimed the glad tidings in this country. He was born Jan. 12, 1724, in Hanover Co., Va. He was at one time church-warden, sheriff, justice of the peace, colonel of the militia, and captain of the Mayo Fort. His position was respectable, and his genial disposition made him exceedingly popular. His education had been liberal. He first became anxious about his soul in his thirty-fourth year. On one of his journeys to visit the fort officially he called at a small house, where he learned there was to be Baptist preaching; the ministers were Joseph and William Murphy. He seated himself behind a loom to hide his uniform. The eye of God, however, was upon

* Ludlow's Memoirs, iii. 12.

him, and his heart was very deeply affected; but some time afterwards the Lord revealed his love to him in such fullness that, in an ecstasy of joy, he exclaimed, "Glory! glory! glory!" He was baptized by Rev. Daniel Marshall in 1758, it is believed. He forthwith, like converted Paul, began to preach Jesus. At first his labors were restricted to some neighboring counties of Virginia and North Carolina; but in process of time he preached throughout all Virginia and many parts of North Carolina. He was not ordained for years after he had been preaching. This event occurred in 1769; then he administered the ordinances. The first candidate he baptized was James Ireland, a much persecuted and very useful Baptist minister in Virginia. Mr. Harriss was the best-known man in his native colony, and it is doubtful if Patrick Henry could control a vast assemblage by a power superior to that of Samuel Harriss. His ministry was attended by conversions in very large numbers; churches sprang up on the line of his missionary travels; he was truly the apostle of Virginia. Not a few of his spiritual children became preachers after the order of Mr. Harris, and the aristocratic Episcopalian colony was agitated from one end to the other by these Baptist innovators.

Mr. Harriss feared nothing; legal prosecutions and private persecutions had no effect upon him. He was the owner of a respectable estate, and when he was converted he devoted the greater part of it to religious objects. He had been erecting a new and capacious residence before the Saviour called him, and when it was "covered in" he made it a meeting-house, and lived in his former confined abode. During the Revolutionary war, when salt was scarce, he kept two wagons running to Petersburg to bring it up for his neighbors.

When the Baptists in Virginia mistakenly supposed, in 1774, that the apostolic office still existed, Mr. Harriss was elected an apostle, but he held this honor for only a few months. At all meetings of delegates of the churches he was the presiding officer. Virginia Baptists loved to honor him, and, under God, he was chiefly instrumental in opening the prison-doors of the Old Dominion for the persecuted, and in sweeping away the foul ties uniting church and state.

He made a great mistake in the earlier part of his Christian life in denouncing the acceptance by ministers of any compensation for preaching the Word. This unscriptural and unjust doctrine nearly ruined some of God's faithful shepherds and their families; but Col. Harriss was led to see his error and renounce it. Take him "all together," he was a glorious man of God, a Virginia Whitefield, for which we gratefully bless our divine Redeemer. He died in the year 1795.

Hart, Rev. Jesse M., pastor at El Dorado, Ark.,

and president of the Arkansas Baptist Convention, was born in Alabama in 1838; began to preach in Louisiana in 1860, near the Arkansas line; has preached to a number of churches in both States, beside filling the important pastorates of Camden and El Dorado, Ark. By application Mr. Hart has made himself an effective minister.

Hart, John, a signer of the Declaration of Independence, was the son of Edward Hart, of Hopewell, a man of considerable importance, who raised a company of volunteers in the French war, and fought bravely in the campaign against Quebec. John was born early in the last century at Hopewell, N. J., grew up in high esteem among his neighbors, and became eminent for his honesty, kindness, modesty, and benevolence. He had no taste for political life, made few speeches, but was

driven away by the Hessians. Though the old man was a fugitive, pursued with unusual malice, sleeping in caves and in thickets, not permitted to visit his dying wife, his spirit was not broken, nor did he despair of the cause. After the battle of Princeton he came from his hiding-place, and convened the Legislature at Trenton. He died May 11, 1779, worn out by his labors and privations.

In 1865 a fine monumental shaft of Quincy granite was erected by the State of New Jersey near the old Baptist meeting-house in Hopewell to honor his memory. It was dedicated July 4, 1865, with imposing ceremonies, among which was an eloquent oration by Joel Parker, governor of the State, upon the life and services of John Hart. This monument prominently exhibits the words, "HONOR THE PATRIOT'S GRAVE."

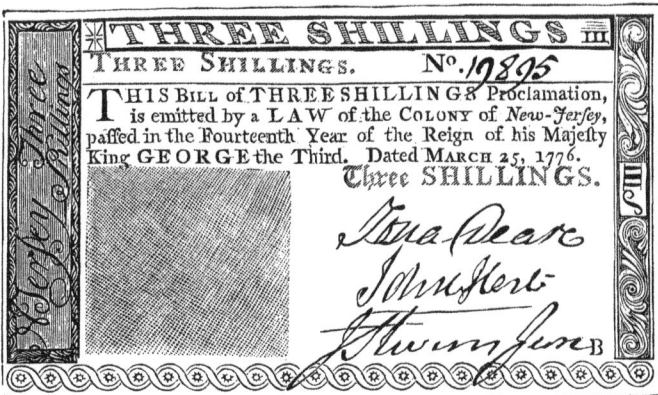

SPECIMEN OF NEW JERSEY MONEY IN 1776, BEARING THE SIGNATURE OF JOHN HART.

ready with brave sacrificing deeds. Such a man could not remain in the background during the period preceding the birth of his country's nationality. He was identified with the cause of the patriots from the beginning. When he entered the Continental Congress of 1774 he was about sixty years of age. He resigned the next year, and became vice-president of the Provincial Congress of New Jersey. He was again elected to Congress in 1775, and he was re-appointed to the same body by the convention of New Jersey in 1776, and took his place among the signers of the Declaration of Independence. In the same year he was chosen Speaker of the Assembly, and re-elected in 1777 and 1778. He was also an important member of the Committee of Safety, and particularly obnoxious to the British and Tories. When, in 1776, the Legislature fled from Princeton to Burlington, to Pittstown, in Salem Co., and to Haddonfield, where it dissolved, Mr. Hart returned to find that his wife and children had fled to the mountains, that his crops were consumed, and that his stock had been

The following is an extract from Gov. Parker's address:

"As his public career was without blemish so was his private life pure and exemplary. He was a consistent member of the old Hopewell Baptist church, and gave to the congregation the land on which the meeting-house was erected, and in which his remains are now deposited. He was a true patriot. I am of opinion, after a careful examination of the history of New Jersey during and immediately preceding the Revolutionary war, that John Hart had greater experience in the colonial and State legislation of that day than any of his cotemporaries, and that no man exercised greater influence in giving direction to the public opinion which culminated in independence."

Hart, Rev. Oliver, A.M., was born in Warminster, Pa., July 6, 1723; made a public profession of religion in the eighteenth year of his age; was ordained at Southampton, Pa., Oct. 18, 1749. The same year he was called to the Baptist church in Charleston, S. C., where he continued thirty

33

years. He was well acquainted with Whitefield and Tennent, and, as a patriot, traveled in South Carolina to enlighten the people in regard to their political interests. He was chiefly instrumental in establishing the Charleston Association. He became pastor at Hopewell, N. J., in 1780, and died there in triumph Dec. 31, 1795. Two funeral sermons were preached, one by Rev. Dr. Rogers, of Philadelphia, the other by Rev. Dr. Furman, of Charleston. The College of Rhode Island (now Brown University) constituted him M.A. at its first commencement. Among his publications are " Dancing Exploded," " A Discourse on the Death of Rev. Wm. Tennent, 1777," " The Christian Temple," " A Circular Letter on Christ's Mediatorial Character," and " The Christian Remembrancer."

Hartly, Rev. Wm., is a native of England ; ordained, in 1871, at Troy, Mich., where he began his work as a minister ; came to Wisconsin in 1873, and became the pastor of the Baptist church in Hudson, where he has labored seven years with growing usefulness as a pastor. Mr. Hartly is a man of fine natural powers, and by thorough and most industrious devotion to study he is proving himself a " workman that needeth not to be ashamed." He is a close student of the Bible, and he is familiar with the best works on theology. His genial disposition and Christian spirit have obtained for him the respect and friendship of many besides his own church and beyond his own denomination.

Hartman, Rev. Jno. H., pastor of the Fourth Avenue Baptist church, Pittsburgh, was born April 17, 1841, in Canaan, Wayne Co., O. Converted at the early age of nine, he soon after deemed it a personal obligation to devote his life to the work of the ministry. At the age of nineteen he entered upon his studies, and graduated at Vermillion College, O., in 1867, and from Newton Theological Seminary in 1870 ; ordained Nov. 17, 1870, in Canton, Mass. ; baptized, while pastor in Canton, 71 persons ; became pastor of Salisbury and Amesbury church in Massachusetts, June, 1874, where he baptized 99 on profession of faith ; resigned June, 1878, and traveled in England and on the Continent. His present pastorate commenced, after three months of supply service, Oct. 1, 1880. Previous to his acceptance of the doctrines distinguishing the Baptists he was connected with the " Church of God," of which body his father was a licensed preacher.

Hartsfield, Rev. Green W., a prominent minister of Grand Cane Baptist Association, La., who resides at Mansfield, was born in Georgia in 1833 ; came to Louisiana in 1849 ; educated at Mount Lebanon University ; ten years pastor at Mansfield ; has devoted much of his time to the colored popula-tion, preaching to them, holding ministers' institutes, and aiding in the organization of the Northwestern Louisiana (colored) Baptist Association, of which he is secretary. As president of Grand Cane Sunday-School Convention he has promoted such interest in the work that every church in the Association has its Sunday-school. He is at present laboring successfully as an evangelist in the employ of the State Convention.

Hartt, Prof. Charles Frederick, son of Jarvis W. Hartt, was born at Fredericton, New Brunswick, Aug. 23, 1840 ; was baptized at Wolfville, Nova Scotia ; studied at Horton Academy, of which his father was principal ; graduated from Acadia College in June, 1860 ; studied geology extensively in the Maritime Provinces and the United States, and became Professor of Geology in Cornell University, N. Y., and continued in this position until his death, March 18, 1878. He was leader and director of the Brazil Geological Survey, and finished a brilliant career in that great scientific undertaking.

Hartt, Jarvis W., was born in New Brunswick ; taught in the Baptist Seminary, Fredericton ; also in the high school at Wilmot, Nova Scotia, and was principal of the Horton Collegiate Academy from 1851 to 1860, when he removed to St. John, New Brunswick, and conducted a young ladies' school for several years. Died in 1873.

Hartwell, Jesse, D.D., was born in Massachusetts in 1795 ; graduated at Brown University in 1816 ; ordained in 1821 ; supplied Second church, Providence, one year. He then removed to South Carolina ; became pastor at High Hills and Sumterville, and a Professor in Furman Theological Institute. In 1836 he went to Alabama ; was pastor at Carlowville, president of the Alabama Baptist Convention, Professor of Theology in Howard College, president of the Domestic Mission Board of the Southern Baptist Convention. In 1847 he removed to Arkansas, and founded Camden Female Institute. In 1857 he removed to Louisiana, and became president and Professor of Theology in Mount Lebanon University. He passed away Sept. 16, 1859.

Hartwell, Jesse Boardman, D.D., son of Jesse Hartwell, D.D., and grandson of Rev. Jesse Hartwell, of Massachusetts, was born in Darlington, S. C., Oct. 17, 1835. His father was an ardent friend of missions, and gave him to that work from his birth. When Luther Rice returned from India he called upon the father. At the door he met his friend, saying, " Brother Rice, my missionary has come," and that day the babe was dedicated as a missionary to the heathen. He was baptized July 14, 1850 ; studied at Howard College, Ala. ; graduated at Furman University, S. C., in 1855 ; was Professor in Mount Lebanon University, La., until December, 1857. In 1858 he was appointed by the

Southern Baptist Foreign Mission Board a missionary to China, and sailed for his field in November, with his wife, Miss Eliza H. Jewett, of Macon, Ga., to whom he was married September 29. They labored two years at Shanghai ; then for many years at Tung Chau Foo, in the Shantung province of Northern China, where they opened the first mission, organized a church, and Mr. Hartwell's first convert was ordained as a minister. Here they were alone for many years, until two Presbyterian families came to labor on the same field. Mrs. Hartwell died in June, 1870. She was one of the best female missionaries ever sent to the foreign field ; she spoke the Chinese tongue fluently. On his return to the United States he married Miss Julia C. Jewett, his deceased wife's sister, in 1872, returned to China, but was compelled by his wife's health to come back to the United States. After four years he was appointed by the American Baptist Home Mission Society to mission work in California among the Chinese. His wife died Dec. 2, 1879, ten days after their arrival at San Francisco. Dr. Hartwell has a mission chapel in that city, and is an enthusiastic teacher and preacher to the Chinese of California in their own language.

Hartwell, John Bryant, was born in Alstead, N. H., Oct. 17, 1816. He became a member of the Freshman class in Brown University in September, 1838. It was his purpose to pursue a course of study in order to fit himself to enter the Christian ministry. Having changed his mind for reasons satisfactory to himself, he left college, and commenced business in Providence, and was a successful merchant, consecrating his talent and his property to the cause of his Master. He became a deacon in the Central Baptist church of Providence, and was an honor to the office. For six years he was a member of the board of trustees of Brown University. Death suddenly overtook him, and he passed away in the prime of a life of great usefulness, Dec. 9, 1872. "It is the testimony of those who knew him most intimately," says President Robinson, "that he was a man of deep religious convictions, gentle in spirit, persistent in purpose, active in life, and ready for death."

Harvey, Rev. Adiel, was born at Ashfield, Mass., July 29, 1805, and was baptized when twelve years of age. He graduated at Amherst College in the class of 1832. After teaching for a time, he entered Newton in 1835, and took the three years' course. On completing his studies at Newton, he settled over the church in Westborough, Mass., where he remained some eight years, and then went to Plymouth, Mass., where he was pastor for thirteen years. In the summer of 1858 he removed to Needham Plains, and took charge of a young ladies' school, and continued in his work until his death, which occurred June 23, 1864.

Harvey, Hezekiah, D.D., was born in Hulven, County of Suffolk, England, Nov. 27, 1821 ; came to America in 1830, and was graduated by Madison University and Hamilton Theological Seminary in 1847. It was his intention to become a foreign missionary, but poor health did not allow his cherished desire to have accomplishment. In 1847 he became tutor of Languages in Madison University, and pastor in Homer, N. Y., in 1849 ; pastor of the First church in Hamilton in 1857, and Professor of Ecclesiastical History in Madison University in 1858 ; Professor of Biblical Criticism and Interpretation and Pastoral Theology in 1861 ; pastor in Dayton, O., in 1864, when failing health compelled his resignation ; re-elected to a professorship in 1869 in Madison University, where he still retains the chair of Pastoral Theology and New Testament Exegesis ; received the degree of D.D. from Colby University in 1861.

Prof. Harvey has recently yielded to the desire of his students, and placed in the hands of the Baptist Publication Society his lectures on the Christian ministry and Baptist polity, and the society has given them to the public in two neat volumes bearing the titles of "The Pastor" and "The Church." The works have been most favorably received, and commended as invaluable alike to the minister and the layman.

Hascall, Rev. Daniel, A.M., was born in Bennington, Vt., Feb. 24, 1782, of Christian parents, originally from Connecticut. His father was a Baptist and his mother a Congregationalist. They were careful to give their children sound religious instruction, based upon their constant reading of Edward Hopkins and Bellamy, and paying particular attention to the Westminster Catechism. In 1785 his parents removed to Pawlet, Vt. Here the educational opportunities were very limited, being confined to school in the winter months, to a small public library, and to private instruction ; but of these Daniel Hascall took the largest advantage, and laid the foundations of his future great and abiding usefulness. After some very serious and protracted religious struggles he was converted in 1799, and united with the Baptist church in Pawlet. At the age of eighteen he began teaching during the winter, and employed his evenings and free moments in hard study, so that in 1803 he entered the Sophomore class of Middlebury College, from which he was regularly graduated in 1806. During these years he defrayed his expenses by his own personal effort. From 1806 to 1808 he taught in Pittsfield, Mass., and, so far as his duties would allow, used his time in reading theology. In 1808 he became pastor of the Baptist church in Elizabethtown, Essex Co., N. Y. In 1813 he settled as pastor of the First Baptist church, Hamilton, N. Y., a place at that time described as located in a "region new and unsettled." In addition to his duties as pastor he was engaged in teaching, and he also edited in part the *Christian Magazine.* Feeling very deeply the need of an educated ministry for

REV. DANIEL HASCALL, A.M.

the Baptist denomination, he began to receive pious young men into his family about 1815, and through his efforts, in 1817, the Baptist Education Society of the State of New York was formed, which resulted in the establishment of the Hamilton Literary and Theological Institution, now Madison University (see that article). Until 1828 he continued as pastor and teacher, when he resigned the pastorate, giving himself more largely to the work of the institution and Education Society. In 1835 his relations with the institution were terminated, but he now gave his attention to the interests of an academy at Florence, Oneida Co.; removed in 1837 to West Rutland, Vt., and interested himself in the Vermont Baptist Convention; in 1848 became pastor at Lebanon, N. Y., and in 1849 resided in Hamilton amid scenes so dear to himself. At the time when the removal of the institution was debated, as one of the original founders, and being the only person who could properly stand forth as the legal representative of this location,—one of those who proposed to the citizens of Hamilton the raising of a certain sum of money for its location at Hamilton,—he plunged into the controversy, and at times alone, and at times reproached, he stood firm to his position, "It shall not be moved," and through his efforts a perpetual injunction against removal followed. His prophecy that he should

live to see the institution saved and then die was fulfilled. He died June 28, 1852. His published works were a sermon, "Cautions against False Philosophy,"—Col. ii. 8 (1817); "Definition of the Greek Baptizo" (pamphlet, 1818); "Elements of Theology for Family Reading," pp. 260, and a smaller work for Sunday-schools. Daniel Hascall was a great man, deeply pious, versatile in his genius, heroic in his positions, sometimes risking his property to aid the enterprise in which he was engaged; industrious, and apparently possessing inexhaustible resources of physical strength and religious faith. To him more than to any other man does the denomination owe a debt of gratitude for the advance in the arts and sciences, and in Biblical scholarship of its ministry in the United States. (See Sprague's "Annals" and Dr. Eaton's "Historical Discourse in First Half-Century," Madison University.)

Haskell, Samuel, D.D., was born in Bridgeton, Me., March 20, 1818. While he was a child the family removed to Rockford, Ill., where he was baptized by Prof. S. S. Whitman, March 9, 1840. He fitted for college in Suffield, Conn., graduated from Brown University in 1845, and studied theology at Hamilton, finishing the course in 1847.

SAMUEL HASKELL, D.D.

He was ordained in Suffield, Aug. 4, 1847; was pastor of the First church in Detroit from 1847 to 1852, of the First church in Kalamazoo from 1852 to 1871, and in Ann Arbor from 1871 till now. Each of these churches grew in numbers and strength under his pastoral care. For thirty-three years he has been identified with every important enterprise conducted by the Baptists of the State. No man, living or dead, has had a larger share than he in the direction of our denominational work in Michigan. He was secretary of the State Convention in 1854, and president in 1866. Madison University conferred on him the degree of Doctor of Divinity in 1867.

Hastings, Rev. John, son of Rev. Joseph Hastings, was born in Suffield, Conn., in 1743; in early life he was worldly; became a true Christian; was settled as assistant pastor, with his father, by the First Baptist church of Suffield in 1775; became sole pastor after his father's death, in 1785, and so remained till his death; traveled extensively through the country, and aided in gathering a number of churches; his own became the most efficient church in Connecticut for the time; he baptized first and last about 1100 persons; a man of candor, kindness, strength, and fervor; died in Suffield, March 17, 1811, at the age of sixty-eight. His wife was Rachel Remmington, of Suffield.

Hastings, Rev. Joseph, of Suffield, Conn.; at first a member of the standing order; seceded in the Great Awakening; aided in forming a separate church in the west part of the town, of which he became pastor; immersed in 1752; in 1763 assisted in organizing the First Baptist church in Suffield, and became pastor; was at this time sixty-six years of age; remained pastor till 1775, when his son John was associated with him; traveled and preached in various places around; was a man of power; died in 1785, aged eighty-two years.

Haswell, James M., D.D., was born in Bennington, Vt., Feb. 4, 1810, and graduated at the Hamilton Literary and Theological Institution, now Madison University, in 1835. The question of his future service in the kingdom of his Lord having been settled by his decision to become a missionary to the heathen, he received his appointment from the Executive Board of the Missionary Union, Aug. 3, 1835, and sailed from Boston September 22, arriving at Maulmain in February, 1836. Having qualified himself for active service by mastering the language, he turned his attention to the evangelization of the Peguans, or, as they are more generally called, the Talaings. Into the language of this people he translated the New Testament, and wrote and published tracts for their religious benefit. For this people he always felt a deep interest even after he had learned the Burmese language, and performed missionary labor among the Burmese. He urged the appointment of a missionary to the people for whose spiritual welfare he had labored in some of the last letters he wrote home. "About the last work wrought by his trembling hand was the revision and preparation of tracts in their language." In 1849, Dr.

Haswell visited the United States, and remained here not far from three years, and in 1867 he also made a short visit of nine months. More than forty years of his life, with the exceptions just referred to, he spent in missionary labors. He died Sept. 13, 1876.

The Executive Board, in their sixty-third annual report, speak of Dr. Haswell in terms of deserved commendation. "He was a man of high character, an industrious scholar, an adept in the languages and literature of the races for whom he labored, an able minister of the new covenant, and a devoted servant of Christ. He had few superiors in point of personal character and missionary efficiency."

Haswell, Rev. James R., son of Dr. James M. Haswell, was born in Amherst, Burmah, Sept. 4, 1836. It was his father's hope and prayer that in due time his son would be his associate in missionary labor among the Burmese. Accordingly he took special pains in his early days to make him thoroughly familiar with the language. He received his collegiate education at the Madison University, where he graduated in 1857, and from the theological school two years later. In September, 1859, he sailed for Burmah. It was not long after his arrival at his destined station that he was stricken down by disease, and left in so shattered a condition that it was deemed best for him to return to this country with the hope that he might recruit his health. He had in a measure lost his voice and his hearing was impaired. He recovered his voice in a good degree, but not his hearing. A few years having been spent in the United States, he returned once more to Burmah, and gave himself to his work as a missionary with great zeal and success. Again he was attacked with a violent disease,—the cholera,—and in a few hours was no more. His death took place May 20, 1877.

Hatch, Rev. E. B., was born in East Hardwick, Vt., Feb. 8, 1831; baptized at the age of sixteen, and educated in Williston and Johnson, and in the theological seminary at Fairfax; was licensed by the Johnson church in October, 1852, and ordained in Lowell, Vt., Jan. 3, 1856; labored as an evangelist at St. Armand and Standbridge, province of Quebec. In 1857 became pastor for one year at Lancaster, Wis. In 1858 settled at Clinton Junction, and remained there six years. In 1865 moved to Thorn Hill, N. Y. In October, 1870, moved to California, where he has labored one year at San Rafael, four years at Vallejo, and three years at Yountville. In the last two places he built two houses of worship. He is a good pastor and preacher, has baptized many converts, and is an earnest and zealous minister of the gospel.

Hatcher, Rev. Harvey, was born in Bedford Co., Va., July 16, 1832, in the same house in which

Dr. Jeter was born, of whom he was a near relation. He was baptized by Rev. Wm. Harris in 1849; was graduated from Richmond College in 1858; served the churches of Portsmouth, Va., Keytesville, Mo., Sidney, and Richmond, Va., and is now associate editor of the *Biblical Recorder*. Mr. Hatcher is an older brother of Dr. W. E. Hatcher, of Virginia, and possesses much of the wit and humor of that distinguished pastor. He has attained distinction as a newspaper writer under the *nom de plume* of *G. Washington Jones*.

Hatcher, William E., D.D., of Virginia.— Among the first men of Virginia stands Rev. Dr. W. E. Hatcher, pastor of the Grace Street Baptist church, Richmond. Born July 25, 1835, in the county of Bedford, Va., he passed his youth among those blue mountains where were raised such preachers as Dr. Jeter, the late Dr. Daniel Witt ("the golden-mouthed orator"), and a large number of the most distinguished ministers which Virginia ever produced. He entered Richmond College, and his native talent and close application soon enabled him to take rank among the best students in his class, and to graduate in June, 1858, among the first.

In August, 1858, he took charge of a very weak church in Manchester (opposite Richmond), and, by faithful, judicious, and most untiring work, he added 400 to the church, and made it not only self-sustaining, but one of the most efficient in the State.

From Manchester Dr. Hatcher went, in March, 1867, to the pastorate of the Franklin Square Baptist church, Baltimore. He had a pleasant and successful year with this church, but in October, 1868, he returned to his native State, and took charge of the First Baptist church in Petersburg. During his seven years' pastorate there Dr. Hatcher refused a number of most tempting calls to other pastorates, and labored on in his chosen field, where he added to the church 360, and built up the cause to an extent rarely equaled.

Besides his labors in the pastorate, Dr. Hatcher has been a remarkably successful preacher in protracted meetings, and several thousand persons have professed conversion in connection with his labors. In 1875 he accepted the pastorate of the Grace Street church in Richmond. Dr. Hatcher is a man of rare and varied gifts. As a preacher he is a remarkable sermonizer, and an earnest and most effective proclaimer of the soul-saving truths of the gospel. Able, simple, earnest, pathetic, and always *practical*, large and delighted congregations wait on his ministry.

But Dr. Hatcher is even more efficient in his pastoral work than in the pulpit. His genial humor, keen wit, and winning manners make him the centre of attraction to the social circle, while his de-

vout piety, warm sympathies, and deep earnestness make him always a welcome visitor to the houses of his people and the "house of mourning." He is especially popular among the young, is a first-class Sunday-school man, and has had very large success in leading boys and girls to the Cross, and putting them to work for Jesus.

Dr. Hatcher has won a wide reputation as a writer of keen satire and a popular lecturer, and he is destined to still higher renown in this direction. He was one of the most untiring and successful workers in the great Virginia Memorial enterprise, and has won a place among the best collecting agents in the country. There opens up before few young ministers a brighter career of successful work for the Master whom he serves so faithfully.

Havelock, Maj.-Gen. Sir Henry, K.C.B., was born at Bishop Wearmouth, County of Durham, England, April 5, 1795. He had six brothers and sisters. It was the custom of his mother to assem-

MAJ.-GEN. SIR HENRY HAVELOCK, K.C.B.

ble her children in a room for the reading of the Scriptures and prayers, and as a result of this in early youth, Henry had serious religious impressions. When at the Charterhouse School, he and his companions met together regularly in one of the sleeping-rooms for religious reading and conversation. In 1814 he became a law pupil of Chitty, a distinguished "special pleader" of that day; the future Judge Talfourd was his fellow-student. Having a taste for the military profession, he obtained a commission in the English army about a month after the battle of Waterloo. To fit himself for his new calling he read every military work which he could procure, and made himself familiar with all the great battles in history and the tactics of all famous military commanders.

While sailing to India in the "General Kyd" in 1823 he first found peace with God through the blood of the Lamb. Until this time he had a great reverence for Jehovah and his religion, but he had never realized that his sins were blotted out by faith in the crucified Saviour. This rich revelation of divine love and grace in his soul was, as it is in every case, as lasting as life, and will be as continuous as eternity ; and it produced the greatest results in his future career. In the first British war with Burmah, while in Rangoon his attention was attracted by the "magnificent Shway-dagong" pagoda. It had a chamber, with images of Buddha all around it in a sitting posture. Havelock selected this room for the prayer-meeting of his pious soldiers. An officer once heard the sound of "psalm-singing" coming from the pagoda, and, following it, he was led into the place of worship. Havelock was expounding the Scriptures ; about a hundred soldiers were around him ; the only light which they had came from lamps placed in the laps of the surrounding idols. The scene was a strange one in every way, and yet it was as glorious as it was remarkable. But in this fashion the young officer trained his men, and the result was that they became the bravest and the most moral soldiers in the army, in which they were called "Havelock's saints" ; and they were often employed on occasions demanding special heroism. While on a mission to the king of Burmah, Havelock was "formally invested with a title of nobility and an official dress."

He was married Feb. 9, 1829, to Hannah, the third daughter of Dr. Marshman, one of the celebrated companions of Dr. Carey, the missionary. He was baptized April 4, 1830, at Serampore by the Rev. John Mack, and was ever after identified with the Baptists.

In Afghanistan, in 1842, after 13,000 English troops had been destroyed by a treacherous surprise, Havelock was with Sir Robert Sale at Jellalabad ; famine stared the soldiers in the face ; hosts of Afghan warriors surrounded them ; retreat was certain destruction. Havelock commanded one of three columns, each of them five hundred strong, in an attack upon the besieging Afghans. After a short but fierce struggle his division routed the wing opposed to it, and, being speedily joined by the other two, the enemy, many thousand strong, fled in terror, leaving great numbers of their dead and wounded upon the field. He fought bravely in the Sikh war, but secured the greatest distinction in the Indian mutiny. When that frightful calamity fell upon the Europeans of India Have-

lock rushed to the scene of danger. He gained several victories near Cawnpore, and rescued it from Nana Sahib, the butcher of hundreds of European women and children, whom, wounded and dead, he cast into a great well. Then Havelock, in a second attempt, reached Lucknow, fighting, it is supposed, nearly 50,000 drilled Sepoys with 2500 men, and carrying on a battle through three miles of the city, "where each house formed a separate fortress," until he reached the British Residency, and gave ample protection to the women and children and the slender garrison, who expected death every day. He continued here until Sir Colin Campbell brought a powerful reinforcement, and rescued the Europeans in Lucknow. Brave Havelock after this deliverance sank rapidly under a deadly disease, and passed away Nov. 22, 1859.

In his last moments he said to Sir James Outram, "For more than forty years I have so ruled my life that when death came I might face it without fear. I am not in the least afraid ; to die is gain. I die happy and contented." To his oldest son, who waited upon him with great tenderness, he said, "Come, my son, and see how a Christian can die."

Gen. Havelock believed that God was with him and that he ruled everything, and he was as cool in appalling dangers as if nothing could injure him. Wherever he was he found out the people of God and joined in their worship. He maintained his religious character among the most ungodly young officers of the English army in India, and he was always ready to confess his supreme attachment to the King of Kings. His death created the greatest gloom in the British Islands ; as a Christian and as a military hero he is revered throughout his own country, and known and esteemed over the world. Just before his death he was made a baronet, with a pension of £1000 a year. A statue by public subscription has been erected to his memory in Trafalgar Square, London. Had this eminent Baptist lived a few years longer no doubt he would have risen to the highest grade of the British peerage ; but the Lord elevated him to be a king and a priest with himself in the skies.

Hawthorne, J. B., D.D., pastor of the First Baptist church, Richmond, Va., was born May 16, 1837, in Wilcox Co., Ala. His father was a devoted Baptist minister of an old and honored family. Young Hawthorne was converted early in life, and after completing his literary studies at Howard College, in his native State, he spent about three years in the study and practice of law in Mobile. Under a conscientious sense of duty he decided to abandon his profession and engage in the ministry. He re-entered Howard College, and pursued a course of study in the theological department. On the 22d of September, 1859, at Friendship Baptist church, in his native county, he was ordained to the work of the ministry. Soon afterwards he became pastor of the Second Baptist

J. B. HAWTHORNE, D.D.

church in the city of Mobile. Here his reputation as a preacher and pastor was rapidly rising, when, in 1863, he entered the Confederate army as chaplain of an Alabama regiment, in which capacity his labors were very useful. At the close of the war he accepted the care of the Baptist church in Selma, Ala., where he remained two years, and was then called to the pastorate of the Franklin Square Baptist church, Baltimore. After a successful pastorate there of two years, he accepted a call to the First Baptist church of Albany, N. Y. From Albany he was called to the Broadway Baptist church, Louisville, Ky., where his labors were greatly blessed. While here a beautiful church edifice was erected, costing over $100,000, and dedicated entirely free of debt. From Louisville he was called to the pastorate of the Tabernacle Baptist church of New York City, which greatly prospered under his faithful labors. Failing health and the rigors of a Northern climate culminating in a sickness which was nigh unto death, compelled him reluctantly to leave this field of labor, and late in the year 1875 he accepted a call to the First Baptist church of Montgomery, Ala. Here in his native State his health greatly improved, and his ministry was largely blessed. The denomination increased in numbers and in influence, and the special tenets of the Baptist faith won their way to the favorable consideration of all sects. In the autumn of 1879, Dr. Hawthorne was invited to the pastorate of the First Baptist church, Richmond, Va., which he accepted. Succeeding such pastors as Manly, Burrows, and Warren, he has at once won the regard and admiration of the vast audiences which regularly crowd the church. Dr. Hawthorne is in the prime of life, tall, dignified, and of commanding presence. He has great power as an impressive speaker. His thoughts are fresh and stimulating, his language graceful, his utterance deliberate. He has considerable dramatic power, easily winning and holding the attention of his hearers. As a lecturer, also, he has secured a flattering reputation, and in evangelistic labors he has been greatly blessed by gracious revivals and numerous conversions.

Hawthorne, Rev. Kedor, was born in Robinson Co., N. C., in January, 1797, and moved to Alabama in 1817 and settled in Conecuh County; was baptized by the Rev. Alex. Travis in 1825, and began to preach two or three years afterwards; spent about fifty years in the ministry, planted many churches in South Alabama and West Florida, baptized about 4500 believers in Christ, and died in peace the latter part of August, 1877, at the age of eighty years. He was a pure man and an able minister of the New Testament. He reared a most interesting family, the gifted Rev. J. B. Hawthorne, D.D., now of Richmond, Va., and the Rev. Gen. Hawthorne, of Texas, being sons of his. The latter was a brigadier-general in the Confederate army, and the former has reached the highest celebrity as a preacher.

Haycraft, Rev. N. P., was born in Elizabethtown, Ky., April 9, 1797. He was converted in May, 1831; ordained in 1834 in Illinois. In 1835 he removed to Missouri and settled in Lewis County. He cultivated his farm, and was a missionary of the Bethel Association and of the General Association in North Missouri for six years from 1842. He baptized over 400 persons in the different churches in which he ministered. He endured heat and cold, toil and self-denial, for the Saviour's sake. In 1849 he went to California, and returning, began to preach Jesus. He has helped to organize thirteen churches and to ordain seventeen ministers. He is now eighty-four years old, and says, "My labors are well-nigh done."

Haycraft, Samuel, a distinguished citizen of Kentucky, was born in Elizabethtown, Aug. 14, 1795. He was clerk of the county and circuit courts, practised law, and represented his district in the State senate. Mr. Haycraft joined Severn's Valley Baptist church, the oldest congregation in the Mississippi Valley, in early manhood. He was one of the constituents of the Baptist Convention and General Association of Kentucky, and a generous contributor to its objects. He assisted liberally in the endowment of Georgetown College and the Southern Baptist Theological Seminary. He was connected with the Sabbath-school of his

SAMUEL HAYCRAFT.

church as superintendent and teacher forty years. He was a brilliant and humorous speaker and charming writer, a gentleman of superior culture, an almost unrivaled conversationalist, and during his long life made good use of his talents in devotion to Christianity and practical benevolence. He died Dec. 22, 1878.

Haycroft, Nathaniel, D.D., for several years one of the most eminent ministers of the English Baptists, was born near Exeter, Feb. 14, 1821. Having joined the church at Thorverton, Devonshire, in early youth, and manifesting a desire to enter the ministry, he was admitted to Stepney College, and subsequently studied at Edinburgh and Glasgow. His first settlement was at Saffron, Walden, in Essex, as co-pastor with the Rev. T. Wilkinson. Thence, after some years of successful labor, he was invited to the pastorate of the Broadmead church, Bristol. During this pastorate, which continued for eighteen years, he rose to the eminent place in the denomination which he held at his death. In 1866 he removed to Leicester to take charge of a new church, and in the midst of his work and the fullness of his powers, died Feb. 16, 1873, aged fifty-two. His indomitable energy and high culture secured him the respect of the community, whilst his services to the denomination endeared him to his brethren, and marked him as a

leader to whom the highest trusts might be confidently committed. Though a prolific writer and a brilliant orator, he published little. He received the degree of D.D. from Glasgow University, with appropriate congratulations upon his high attainments.

Hayden, Lucian, D.D., was born in Winsted, Conn., in 1808; baptized in Bethany, Wayne Co., Pa., in August, 1830; was graduated in Hamilton, N. Y., in 1836; ordained in Dover, N. H., in June, 1838. He was pastor there four years, at Saxton's River, Vt., fourteen years, and at New London, N. H., eleven years; had charge of Theological Institute for Freedmen at Augusta, Ga., for a few months, and for three years of Indianapolis (Indiana) Female Institute; pastor at Grafton, Vt., for three years, and now is settled at Dunbarton, N. H.; was two years president of Vermont Baptist State Convention, and one year of New Hampshire State Convention; elected a member of New Hampshire Legislature from New London in 1865; author of "Pure Christianity Characterized by Spirituality," published by American Baptist Publication Society; received D.D. from Madison University. Dr. Hayden is an excellent pastor and preacher, distinguished for piety and practical wisdom, and has long been esteemed one of our prominent men in Northern New England.

Haygood, Rev. Francis M., of Lithonia, was born in Clark Co., Ga., Aug. 18, 1817. He professed a hope and united with Mars Hill church in 1835; was licensed in 1840; attended the theological department of Mercer University in 1840 and 1841, at Penfield, and was ordained at Canton in 1847. For a few years he taught school, but for forty years has been an evangelistic preacher, and a laborious and faithful colporteur and Sunday-school worker. He has had charge of several churches in different parts of the State; was for some years the depository agent of the Georgia Baptist Bible and Colporteur Society at Macon, and for many years the successful agent of the American Tract Society of New York, a position he fills at present. All his life he has been a hard-working and faithful Christian laborer.

Hayman, Rev. J. M.—Henry Hayman, paternal grandfather of our subject, was born on the Eastern Shore of Maryland. He was a lieutenant in the Revolutionary war, and after its close he married Mollie Goodall, and settled in Burke Co., Ga. Here he reared his family. James, his son, was the father of the subject of this sketch. His maternal grandfather, Rev. James Martin, of Bryan Co., Ga., was a Dunkard Baptist minister. James Martin Hayman, of whom we write, is the oldest child of James and Delila (Martin) Hayman, and was born in Bryan Co., Ga., Dec. 28, 1822. He professed religion and was baptized by Elder John Tucker, in

Hernando Co., Fla., Aug. 7, 1844, and was licensed to preach by Alafia church, of Hillsborough County, June 17, 1851, and at the request of the same church was ordained to the ministry Nov. 10, 1851, Elders John Tucker, Daniel Edwards, and M. N. Strickland constituting the Presbytery.

He informs the writer that his diary shows that he has traveled 25,000 miles in the discharge of ministerial labors, preached 500 sermons, besides lectures and other labor, and baptized 319 persons.

Elder Hayman moved to South Florida when it was almost a wilderness, and so sparsely inhabited that he would often ride forty miles from one community to another. He has lived to see the fruit of his labors to a considerable degree. Mr. Hayman is a prudent man, whose ministry has been a blessing.

Haymore, Rev. C. C., was born in Yadkin Co., N. C., in 1848 ; baptized in 1869 by Rev. J. H. Lewellyn ; ordained in 1870 ; was a student for a while at Wake Forest College, and is now the efficient pastor of Mount Airy church.

Haynes, Albert G., was born in Greene Co., Ga., Aug. 1, 1805 ; was educated at Monticello, Jasper Co., Ga. ; resided for two years in the forks of the Tallapoosa River, Ala. ; resided seven years in Noxubee Co., Miss. ; removed to Texas in the fall of 1842. He was a prominent participator in the efforts to establish the Baptist church at Independence. He served as moderator of the Union Association at one or two important sessions. He acted as deacon for nearly thirty years, and, besides contributing liberally of his means to the cause of Christ, dispensed a princely hospitality at his residence during his lifetime. He held the offices of notary and magistrate, and represented the county of Washington in the State Legislature, and was a trustee and treasurer of Baylor University for many years, aiding by all means in his power in promoting the cause of religion and education. He died May 22, 1870. He was a leading man in all religious and political assemblies in Texas from 1842 to 1870.

Haynes, Rev. Dudley C., was born in Portland, Me., Sept. 15, 1809. He was converted in the winter of 1831, and united with the First Baptist church of Portland, by which he was licensed to preach. He entered the preparatory department of Newton Theological Institution in 1832, and graduated from the seminary in 1837. He became pastor of the Baptist church at Marblehead, Mass., by which he was ordained immediately on leaving the seminary. He has also been pastor at Middletown, Conn., Utica, N. Y., Brunswick, Me., Hyannis, Mass., Philadelphia, Pa., Bainbridge and Union, N. Y., where now, in the seventy-second year of his age, he is actively engaged in pastoral work. During these forty-four years of uninterrupted labor, he has at different times served the Amer-

ican Baptist Missionary Union and American Tract Society. On resigning his pastorate at Philadelphia he became the district secretary of the American Baptist Publication Society for New England, in which work he was very successful. He was afterwards corresponding secretary of the American and Foreign Bible Society for four years. During the war he was engaged as the general agent of the American Freedmen's Relief Association and the American Freedmen's Union Commission, visiting California twice for these societies, and Europe once, and raising large sums of money.

He has also had charge at different times of the affairs of the American Colonization Society and of the American Peace Society in specially designated fields. During Mr. Haynes' secretaryship for the Publication Society he wrote "The Baptist Denomination," a book published by Sheldon & Co., which had a large sale previous to the war.

This is a brief sketch of a life of unceasing activity and usefulness. Few men have done so much hard work and enjoyed such remarkable health.

Haynes, Rev. Emory J, was born at Cabot, Vt., Feb. 6, 1846. His father and grandfather were Methodist Episcopal ministers of considerable note in that denomination. In 1863 he made a public profession of religion, and united with the Methodist Episcopal Church. In 1868 he was graduated from the Wesleyan University, of Middletown, and was immediately settled as pastor of a Methodist Episcopal church in Norwich, Conn. In 1870 he was put in charge of St. Paul's church, Fall River, and two years later he was transferred to Hanson Place Methodist Episcopal church, Brooklyn, N. Y. Here he drew great throngs of people, and the church found it necessary to increase the capacity of their house. In 1875 he took charge of the Seventh Avenue church in the same city. Two years later his convictions led him reluctantly to sever his connection with the Methodists and unite with the Baptists. He was baptized in the Fifth Avenue Baptist church by Thomas Armitage, D.D., and on that occasion made public his reasons for the change. He was very soon called to the pastorate of the Washington Avenue Baptist church, Brooklyn. During the three years of his labor a large number have been added to the church. He is a fluent and eloquent preacher, his discourses abounding in illustrations, showing a warm heart and an earnest desire for the spiritual welfare of the people. He is the author of a work entitled " Are These Things So ?" gems of thought selected from his sermons.

Haynes, J. A., M.D., D.D., was born in King and Queen Co., Va., Dec. 13, 1822. He was educated by his father in part, and at the Virginia Baptist Seminary (Richmond College). He subsequently entered the Columbian College, where he graduated in 1843. After having served for a year as principal of the Bruington Academy, he attended lectures at the National Medical College (the Columbian College) during the session of 1844–45, and completed his medical course at the Jefferson Medical College, Philadelphia, where he graduated in 1846. After practising his profession in King and Queen and Clarke Counties, Va., for some time, he felt it to be his duty to preach the gospel, and was licensed by the Berryville church, Clarke County, in 1853, and ordained in 1857. After laboring for a while in behalf of the State Mission Board, he became principal of the Clarke Female Seminary, at Berryville. In the fall of 1860, Dr. Haynes removed to Loudon County, having accepted the pastorate of the Ebenezer and of Middleburg churches, the former in 1858, and the latter in 1859. In 1867 he left Ebenezer and took charge of Long Branch. While residing at Middleburg, he also had charge of a young ladies' seminary until 1876. Dr. Haynes has preached frequently in the adjoining counties, assisting in protracted meetings, and rendering efficient services in Associational and kindred meetings, by means of his good judgment and independence. Richmond College conferred the honorary degree of D.D. upon him in 1877. Dr. Haynes died very suddenly in the early part of 1880.

Haynes, Lucius M. S., D.D., is the son of Rev. D. C. Haynes, and was born at Marblehead, Mass., in February, 1838. He was graduated at the High School, Philadelphia, and studied at Newton Theological Seminary. He was ordained as pastor at Augusta, Me.

Early in the war he enlisted in the army, and was commissioned first lieutenant of the 4th Maine Light Artillery. After serving one year he resigned, and accepted the pastorate of the Baptist church of Oswego, N. Y. He was afterwards induced to accept a call from Watertown, then from Norwich, and, after the death of the lamented Dr. Lyman Wright, he was called to the pastorate of the Binghamton Baptist church, N. Y. His earnest and faithful labor in all these leading churches in Central New York, his fidelity to his denomination, and his ability in the pulpit, have given him a high position in the estimation of his brethren. The honorary degree of Doctor of Divinity was conferred upon him by Madison University.

Haynes, Rev. Sylvanus, was born in Princeton, Mass., Feb. 22, 1768; commenced to preach in March, 1789; was ordained pastor of the Baptist church in Middletown, Vt., where he remained twenty-six years, his ministry being accompanied with abundant fruits. He removed to Elbridge, Vt., in 1817, and there preached with great success for several years. He died Dec. 30, 1826.

Hazen, Rev. J. H., for many years a pastor in

Illinois, now laid aside in consequence of injuries received while a chaplain in the army, is a native of Pennsylvania, and was born Sept. 10, 1824, of Massachusetts Puritan stock on the father's side, and on the mother's of Scottish descent, his grandmother having come from the Highlands of Scotland. He was converted at twelve, and licensed to preach at seventeen, by the First church of Providence, into whose fellowship he had been baptized. He studied at Providence Academy and at the Northwestern Institute, Sharon, Pa., taking, subsequently, a two years' course in theology in a private class under Dr. John Winter. During the twenty-eight years of his pastoral service he has labored with churches at Salem, where he was ordained in 1844, Georgetown, and Meadville, Pa., and in Illinois at Brimfield, Peoria, and Amboy. During the war he served in the army both as chaplain and as surgeon, and by injuries and overwork was completely disabled. His present home is in Amboy, where, though released from active service, he shares the sympathy and esteem of his brethren as a true man and " a good minister of Jesus Christ."

Heard, Rev. George Felix, son of Col. Abram and Nancy Heard, was born in Greensborough, Ga., Feb. 29, 1812; prepared for college at Athens, Ga.; entered University of Georgia in same place, and graduated with honor in 1829; joined the Presbyterian church at Athens in 1827; shortly after his graduation he entered Princeton Theological Seminary; remained a year; then went to Andover for a year; then returned to Princeton, and continued till May, 1833, when, convinced that the views of the Baptists could be sustained by the Scriptures, he was constrained to change his ecclesiastical relations and cast in his lot with the Baptists. Accordingly he left the Princeton Seminary, joined the First Baptist church in Philadelphia, and completed his studies under Rev. Wm. T. Brantly, Sr., D.D. He returned to Georgia, and in February, 1834, was called to Black Swamp church, S. C. But the next year he removed to Mobile, Ala., became pastor of the church, laboring with great zeal and fidelity five years, during the latter three of which he edited a Baptist paper called *The Monitor*. In 1841 he removed to Harrison Co., Texas, where his course was one of constantly increasing usefulness, until it was terminated by death in 1844. He was an admirable public speaker. Had he lived longer he would have produced a much deeper impression in reference to his powers as a scholar, a theologian, and a preacher.

Heath, Rev. Moses, A.M., was born in Kingwood, N. J., May 13, 1827, and graduated at Madison University, N. Y., in 1854. Having taught for two years, he was ordained in September, 1856, by the Baptist church at Flemington, N. J., where he had been baptized, licensed to preach, and married.

Immediately after ordination he became pastor at McKeesport, Pa. Sixty were added to the church during his pastorate there. In 1859 a long-cherished desire for missionary work induced him to remove to Minnesota. Commissioned by the American Baptist Home Mission Society, he settled at Belle Plaine, remaining six years as pastor of the church and missionary for the surrounding region. In this field he baptized about seventy. Compelled by ill health to leave it, he accepted the charge of the church at Anoka, Minn. There, amidst his pastoral duties, he served as county superintendent of public schools. After two years of happy labor he left a loved and loving people in order to take charge of the Minnesota Baptist school, then at Hastings, where he also became pastor of the Baptist church. In a few months, however, bronchial disease laid him aside from all labor and necessitated a change of residence. Benefited by climate and rest, he took charge of the Loller Academy, Hatborough, Pa., where he remained four years. Since 1872 he has been principal of Wyoming Institute of Delaware, preaching occasionally as health permits, and assisted in his educational work by members of his family.

Heath, Rev. William, was born in Newport, N. H., March 9, 1798. He graduated at Dartmouth College in the class of 1826. Among his classmates was the late Chief-Justice Chase. For a year after his graduation he was a tutor in the preparatory department of the Columbian College at Washington. He graduated at the Newton Theological Institution in 1832, and soon after became principal of the South Reading Academy. He was ordained as an evangelist July 1, 1835. His pastorates were with the churches in Shelburne Falls and North Reading, Mass. He was in the book trade for several years, having charge of the Baptist Sabbath-School Depository in Boston. His death took place Jan. 19, 1869, at Wakefield, Mass.

Hedden, Rev. Benjamin Franklin, son of Bartholomew, was born in Stonington, Conn., in 1803; was an excellent school-teacher; licensed and ordained by the First Baptist church in Groton, and succeeded Rev. John G. Wightman in its pulpit; labored in various fields with marked success,—Martha's Vineyard, Mass.; East Greenwich, R. I.; Manchester, N. H.; Mansfield, Conn.; Camden, N. J.; the Twelfth Baptist church in Philadelphia; an able and devout man. From ill health and a fall he resigned his pastorate in Philadelphia in 1871, and died Feb. 27, 1872, aged sixty-eight years. His brother, Rev. Harlem Hedden, was a useful preacher in different parts of New London Co., Conn.

Hedden, Rev. William D., the son of Presbyterian parents, was born at East Orange, N. J., Nov. 6, 1829. He was converted at seventeen, and being convinced that the immersion of believers only is New Testament baptism, he united with the church at East Orange. After pursuing studies at Hamilton he was ordained at Meridian, N. Y., in 1853. May 13, 1855, he became pastor of the church with which he first united, where, with the exception of a few months, he has continued to labor till the present time. Mr. Hedden has corresponded considerably for the religious press, and cultivates the poetic talent.

Helwys, Thomas, was a native of England, who went to Amsterdam, in Holland, and united with a church of English Separatists, founded in the early part of the reign of Queen Elizabeth. In this church a controversy arose about the validity of infant baptism, which led to the exclusion of those who rejected that unscriptural custom, and of Thomas Helwys with his Baptist brethren. While a member of the Brownist Church they looked upon him as a man of eminent faith, charity, and spiritual gifts.

In the Baptist church formed by the expelled Separatists, Mr. Helwys enjoyed the warmest regards of the entire people; and when, in 1611, their pastor, the Rev. John Smyth, died, Mr. Helwys was elected his successor.

Very soon after entering upon his office, probably early in 1612, Mr. Helwys became uneasy about staying out of England; it appeared to him to savor of cowardice, and he was convinced that it was his duty and that of his church to return home at once and bear testimony to the truth, since persecution threatened its extinction, and encourage and comfort their brethren who were suffering for Christ's sake. The church and pastor decided speedily, and soon commenced worship in London. The community flourished greatly in its new home, and its members were often the victims of royal and episcopal hatred. Mr. Helwys was a man of power, and his influence lived long after he slept with his fathers. His doctrines were said to be Arminian. His views of civil government in relation to religion were thoroughly Scriptural, and in that day were held by none but Baptists. In a Confession of Faith received by his people, and probably written by him, published about 1611, it is said, "The magistrate is not to meddle with religion or matters of conscience, nor to compel men to this or that form of religion; because Christ is the king and lawgiver of the church and conscience." (Crosby, i., Appendix, p. 71.) Nothing more emphatic was ever written on the question of soul liberty in any age or country. But in the days of Helwys this doctrine was denounced by Robinson, the father of the Puritans who founded New Plymouth in 1620. Mr. Helwys and his Baptist brethren were detested as much for the liberty of conscience for which they pleaded as for the believer's baptism which they practised.

Henderson, Rev. Samuel, D.D., a native of Jefferson Co., Tenn., was born March 4, 1817; united with the church in September, 1832. Reared to the business of a practical printer, when quite a youth he removed to Alabama, and established one of the first political news-papers of Talladega, which he published and edited for several years. He was ordained to the gospel ministry in the church in Talladega in 1840, this being his first pastorate. Moved to Tuskegee in 1846, where he was pastor for twenty-one years. To the Baptists Tuskegee was, during that period, one of the most important centres of influence in the State. In addition to its refined and wealthy church membership, it was the site of the East Alabama Female College, a property whose erection cost our brethren not less than $40,000. It was also the seat of publication of the *Southwestern Baptist*, the denominational organ of the State, which was conducted with marked ability by Dr. Henderson, it being then one of the most influential religious journals in the whole South. (See ALABAMA BAPTIST NEWSPAPERS.) In 1868, Dr. Henderson returned to Talladega County to the charge of several country and village churches, among the best country churches in the State, where he is pleasantly located on a handsome and fertile farm, and passes his time in visiting the churches, writing for the papers, being one of the editors of the *Christian Index*, of Atlanta, Ga., and in making further search into the contents of his splendid library. For the last thirty years Dr. Henderson has been among the most prominent and useful of Alabama ministers. Liberally educated at the start, he has become one of our erudite men, an able and distinguished preacher, an adviser of first-class judgment, a graceful, cultivated, and powerful writer, and withal a sound theologian, thoroughly *read-up*. Dr. Henderson has published a number of able sermons, review articles, and other strong and well-prepared documents. It was in his discussion with the Rev. Mr. Hamill of the Alabama Conference on "Methodist Episcopacy," more than twenty years ago, that he gained a distinguished reputation as a ready and cogent ecclesiastical controversialist. It was first published in his paper in Tuskegee, and subsequently in a book of 380 pages, by the Southern Baptist Publication Society at Charleston. Nothing can be found more satisfactory on that subject. His father, Deacon John F. Henderson, was for many years one of the most useful members of the church in Talladega. Of this church his younger brother, Hon. John Henderson, an able and upright judge of the Circuit Court, is now a member and a deacon.

Hendricks, Rev. John, who had been a Methodist minister, lived in Greensborough, Ga., where he was very useful as a preacher in the Baptist churches of that section. Becoming troubled on the subject of baptism, because of doubt as to its proper administration, and unwilling to remain in a state of uncertainty, he investigated the subject, and became convinced of the propriety of immersion. He was baptized by Dr. Adiel Sherwood about 1827. He afterwards removed to Cherokee, Ga., where he resided until his death.

Hendrickson, Charles R., D.D., was born Feb. 18, 1820, in Gloucester Co., N. J. His parents belonged to the Methodist Church, and, upon making a public profession of religion in the fifteenth year of his age, he identified himself with it.

He had early impressions that it was his duty to preach, and in the nineteenth year of his age he entered the Methodist ministry, and traveled one year in connection with the New Jersey Conference. He afterwards was transferred to the Kentucky Conference, and served two years in that connection. During his residence in Kentucky he was called upon to defend infant baptism and other doctrines of the Methodists; but the result of his investigations, instead of furnishing him arguments in favor of the tenets of his own church, caused him to see the error of his position and to adopt the sentiments of the Baptist denomination.

He immediately severed his connection with the Kentucky Conference, returned to Philadelphia, and was baptized by Rev. Dr. J. Lansing Burrows in 1842. Up to the time of his uniting with the Baptists he had never heard a sermon upon the subject of Scriptural baptism and the ordinances of the church, but at his baptism he preached upon this subject, setting forth the arguments that had led him to change his views.

He entered at once upon the work of an evangelist, and traveled extensively in Pennsylvania and Maryland. In 1846 he was called to the pastorate of the First Baptist church, Norfolk, Va. In 1852 he became pastor of the First Baptist church, Memphis, Tenn., where he was instrumental in building up a large and influential community. Owing to rheumatism, from which he has been a great sufferer, he left Memphis for California in 1859, and became pastor of the Baptist church at Stockton, and afterwards of the First Baptist church of San Francisco. He remained in California eleven years, and then returned to Philadelphia, and became pastor of the North church. He served it two years, during which time he baptized more than one hundred persons. In 1873 he accepted a call to the church at Jackson, Tenn., where he is now laboring with success.

Dr. Hendrickson is distinguished for his piety and the possession of those Christian graces that so beautifully adorn his life. While he is a sound Baptist, his gentleness and Christian charity secure for him the esteem and high regard of other denominations. His studies and varied reading have made Dr. Hendrickson a highly-cultured minister.

As a writer, his style is easy and natural, and his thoughts are forcibly and logically expressed. Few men are more completely at home in the pulpit. As a preacher, he is distinguished for his attractive delivery, his elegant English, his clear arguments, his honest sincerity, and his thorough comprehension of the subject.

The Southwestern Baptist University, located at Jackson, Tenn., owes much to Dr. Hendrickson. He has been chairman of the executive board of trustees from the date of its organization to the present.

Henricians, The.—Henry, a monk in the first half of the twelfth century, became a great preacher. He was endowed with extraordinary powers of persuasion, and with a glowing earnestness that swept away the greatest obstacles that mere human power could banish, and he had the grace of God in his heart. He denounced prayers for the dead, the invocation of saints, the vices of the clergy, the superstitions of the church, and the licentiousness of the age, and he set an example of the sternest morality. He was a master-spirit in talents, and a heaven-aided hero, a John Knox, born in another clime, but nourished upon the same all-powerful grace.

When he visited the city of Mans the inferior clergy became his followers, and the people gave him and his doctrine their hearts, and they refused to attend the consecrated mummeries of the popish churches, and mocked the higher clergy who clung to them. In fact, their lives were endangered by the triumph of Henry's doctrines. The rich and the poor gave him their confidence and their money, and when Hildebert, their bishop, returned, after an absence covering the entire period of Henry's visit, he was received with contempt and his blessing with ridicule. Henry's great arsenal was the Bible, and all opposition melted away before it.

He retired from Mans and went to Provence, and the same remarkable results attended his ministry; persons of all ranks received his blessed doctrines and forsook the foolish superstitions of Rome and the churches in which they occupied the most important positions. At and around Thoulouse his labors seem to have created the greatest indignation and alarm among the few faithful friends of Romanism, and Catholics in the most distant parts of France heard of his overwhelming influence and his triumphant heresy with great fear. In every direction for many miles around he preached Christ, and at last Pope Eugene III. sent a cardinal to overthrow the heretic and his errors. He wisely took with him, in 1147, the celebrated St. Bernard. This abbot had the earnestness and the temper of Richard Baxter, whom he resembled in some respects. He was a more eloquent man, and he was probably the most noted and popular ecclesiastic in Europe. He speaks significantly of the state of things which he found in Henry's field: "The churches (Catholic) are without people, the people without priests, the priests without due reverence, and, in short, Christians are without Christ; the churches were regarded as synagogues, the sanctuary of God was not held to be sacred, and the sacraments were not reckoned to be holy, festive days lost their solemnity, men died in their sins, souls were snatched away everywhere to the dread tribunal, alas! neither reconciled by repentance nor fortified by the holy communion. The life of Christ was closed to the little children of Christians, whilst the grace of baptism was refused, nor were they permitted to approach salvation, although the Saviour lovingly proclaims before them, and says, 'Suffer the little children to come to me.'"[*]

Elsewhere, St. Bernard, speaking of Henry and other heretics, says, "They mock us because we baptize infants, because we pray for the dead, because we seek the aid of (glorified) saints."[†] That Henry had a great multitude of adherents is beyond a doubt, and that he was a Bible Christian is absolutely certain, and that he and his followers rejected infant baptism is the testimony of St. Bernard and of all other writers who have taken notice of the Henricians and their founders. We incline to the opinion of Neander that Henry was not a Petrobrusian. We are satisfied that he and his disciples were independent witnesses for Jesus raised up by the Spirit and Word of God. The Henricians were Baptists, and their founder perished in prison.

Henricks, Rev. William, was born in 1800. His father was an Austrian, who emigrated to America to escape Romish persecution because of his conversion to Protestantism, and settled first in North Carolina and then in Greene Co., Ga., in 1808. Wm. Henricks was converted in 1826, under the preaching of Lovick Pierce, and was baptized in 1828 by Dr. A. Sherwood, after a thorough investigation of the subject of baptism. He was ordained in 1832. He became an able and zealous minister of the gospel, with few superiors as a revivalist. For eighteen years he preached among the churches of Greene, Morgan, Clarke, Monroe, and Walton Counties, with great power and usefulness. For fifteen years he was moderator of the

---

[*] Parvulis Christianorum Christi intercluditur vita, dum baptismi negatur gratia; nec saluti propenquare sinuntur; Salvatore licet pie clamante pro eis; *Sinite*, inquit, *parvulos venire ad me.* (Sancti Bernardi Genuina Opera, i. Ep. 241, p. 237. Parisiis, 1690.)

[†] Irrident nos, quod baptizamus infantes. Idem, i. p. 1497.

Appalachee Association; indeed, remaining so until his removal to Floyd County in 1850. He assisted in the organization of the Oostanaula Association in 1852, and was elected moderator. He died at Rome, Ga., June 18, 1856. He was a man of mark and of great usefulness in his day, and stood side by side with the first Baptist ministers of his time in promoting the interests of the denomination in Georgia.

Henry, Rev. Foster, was born in Perkinsville, Windsor Co., Vt., in 1817. He took the full courses of study at Brown University and at the Newton Theological Institution, graduating at the former in the class of 1845, and at the latter in the class of 1848. He was ordained to the ministry in November, 1852, and was pastor of the church in Tyringham, Mass., five years, when he removed to Pawtuxet, R. I., remaining there four years, then at Danversport, Mass., for three years, then at Newport, N. H., for six years. From Newport he went to North Bennington, Vt., and is at this time pastor of the church in that place.

Henson, Poindexter S., D.D., was born in Fluvanna Co., Va., Dec. 7, 1831; entered Richmond College in 1844, and graduated with the first

POINDEXTER S. HENSON, D.D.

class, in 1848, being then sixteen years of age. After teaching for one year in his native county, he entered the University of Virginia, and spent two years in that institution, graduating in various "schools." In the fall of 1851 he became principal of the Milton Classical Institute in North Carolina, and retained the position two years, in the mean

while studying law with the Hon. M. McGee, and editing the *North Carolina Democrat,*—a weekly paper published in the town of Milton. When about entering upon the practice of law he was elected Professor of Natural Science in the Chowan Female College at Murfreesborough, N. C. This position he retained for two years, at the expiration of which he married Miss A. C. Ruse, of Hicksford, Va., and returned to Fluvanna County.

Was converted in 1846, while a student at Richmond College, and was baptized by Rev. J. B. Jeter, D.D., into the fellowship of the First church at Richmond. At the close of the year 1855 he abandoned the law and devoted himself to the ministry of the gospel; was ordained in February, 1856, and settled as pastor of the Fluvanna church. In connection with his pastorate he established the Fluvanna Female Institute, and remained there preaching and teaching until the summer of 1860, when he accepted a call to the Broad Street church, Philadelphia, and entered upon his labors Dec. 27, 1860. With this church he remained until September, 1867, when under pressure of demand for a new interest in a rapidly-growing section of the city, he, with others, went out to organize the Memorial church, where he still continues a faithful and efficient ministry. He received the degree of D.D. in 1867 from the university at Lewisburg. In 1878 he declined an urgent call to the presidency of that institution.

Dr. Henson possesses a keenly logical mind, and is thoroughly skilled in his methods of attacking error and defending the truth. As a preacher, he stands in the front rank of loyal and brilliant pulpit orators, and his sermons abound in the rich results of Bible study and devout piety. As a lecturer his services are in frequent requisition, and large audiences are ever ready to show their appreciation of his native wit and cultured scholarship. He is prominently and actively engaged in the management of local and general denominational societies, and as editor of the *Baptist Teacher* he continues to exert helpful and healthful influence upon Sunday-school work and workers. He has the largest Protestant congregation in Philadelphia.

Herndon, Rev. Thaddeus, was born in Fauquier Co., Va., May 9, 1807. He was the eldest of four brothers, all of whom were ministers of the gospel, and all of whom preceded him to their final reward. He was baptized by Dr. W. F. Broaddus in 1828, and united with the Long Branch church, being licensed to preach by it in 1833. For some years he was employed by the Salem Union Association as missionary, traveling over large districts of country in Loudon, Fauquier, Prince William, and Fairfax Counties. In 1837 he was called to the pastorate of Antioch church, Prince William Co., and about the same time to North Fork church,

Loudon Co., both of which he faithfully served for about forty years. He was the pastor also of two other churches. Although Mr. Herndon had the care of a farm and a large family, he very rarely failed in regularly meeting his church appointments, riding on horseback through the storms of winter and the heats of summer. He was an earnest gospel preacher and a welcome guest at many a fireside. He died June 2, 1878.

Herndon, Rev. Traverse D., the brother of the Revs. Thaddeus and Richard Herndon, was born March 11, 1810. His father was the Rev. John C. Herndon, a resident of Fauquier County. About the age of eighteen, being hopefully converted, he was baptized by Dr. W. F. Broaddus, and united with the Long Branch church. Being a young man of ardent piety, and longing to honor his Master by a life wholly consecrated to his service, he was persuaded to prepare himself for the work of the ministry. Having been for a short time engaged in mercantile business in Alexandria, Va., he relinquished his position in that place and entered the Columbian College, where he remained during five years, graduating in 1838, the year of his ordination. His first pastoral charge was the Falmouth church, which he held in connection with an engagement as missionary under the Salem Union Association. Owing to his precarious health, however, he was soon obliged to relinquish both these positions, and for nearly two years he was unable to preach. When he had recovered a good measure of health he took charge of four churches, Liberty, Mount Holly, Fiery Run, and Front Royal. These churches being too remote from his residence, he took charge of the Middleburg, Long Branch, and Ketocton churches, with which he labored up to the time of his death, which occurred Sept. 10, 1854. Mr. Herndon stood high among his brethren as a preacher. His sermons were plain, practical, and saturated with earnest descriptions of the love of Christ for sinners. Human guilt and divine redemption were the great themes upon which he loved to dwell, and his teachings were blessed to the conversion of many souls and the encouragement of God's people. More than three hundred were baptized by him during his ministry, while thousands of others who listened to him during his journeyings from home at protracted meetings were greatly quickened in their spiritual energies. As a Christian man in all the various relations of life he was a model. "His natural qualities, controlled as they were by a constant sense of the obligations on him as a Christian, made him, in the estimation of all who knew him well enough to appreciate his personal worth, most emphatically a Christian gentleman." Dr. Wm. F. Broaddus, who knew Mr. Herndon well, says, "But this I can say in all honesty, that after an acquaintance with him

of nearly thirty years, and for many years an intimate acquaintance, such was his entire deportment both as a man and a Christian, that if he had faults, my admiration of the characteristics uniformly exhibited in his life and conversation so occupied me, that those faults entirely escaped my observation."

Herr, Joseph Daniel, D.D., was born in Sharpsburg, Pa., Feb. 23, 1837. At the age of seventeen he was converted and immersed as a member of the Methodist Protestant Church. In 1858, having completed a collegiate course at Madison College, Pa., he was ordained to the ministry. His reputation for ability in the pulpit led to his serving prominent churches in Pittsburgh and Cincinnati. He was also made secretary of the board of trustees of Adrian College, and of the Missionary Society of the Methodist Protestant Church. In August, 1870, in accordance with his early convictions, and impressed with the great truth that faith should precede baptism, he resigned the charge of the Second Methodist Protestant church of Pittsburgh, and immediately thereafter accepted the pastorate of the Union Baptist church of the same city. A few months later he assisted in the formation of the Penn Avenue Baptist church, and became its first pastor. Nov. 1, 1875, he resigned to take charge of the Central Baptist church of New York. Dr. Herr as a preacher is eloquent, and is noted for his fervor and earnestness. His pastorates have been marked by progress and spiritual prosperity. In 1876 he was made D.D. by Otterbein University, Ohio.

Hewes, Rev. and Prof., was born in Lynnfield, Mass., in 1818; converted and baptized at the age of fourteen; graduated at Brown University and the Newton Theological Seminary. In 1844 he was ordained as pastor at Lonsdale, R. I. In 1849 he began an eight years' pastorate at Lansingburgh, N. Y. In 1857–58 he was professor in the Troy University. From Troy he was called to the presidency of the Indianapolis Institute, holding his position there seven years. Removing to California, he was two years a professor in the Female College of the Pacific, two years pastor and lecturer on Natural Sciences in the Mills Seminary, five years pastor at St. Helena, and two years pastor of the Fifth church, San Francisco. Though much of his life has been spent in educating the young, he has baptized over three hundred converts. Since his arrival in California he has spent three years in extensive travels in Europe, Egypt, and the Holy Land.

Hewitt, C. E., D.D., was born Oct. 16, 1836, in Galway, Saratoga Co., N. Y., being a son of Deacon Edmund Hewitt, well known for more than half a century as a prominent member and officer of the Galway Baptist church, of which the son became a member at sixteen years of age. He graduated at the University of Rochester in 1860, and at the seminary in 1863. His pastorates have been at Ypsilanti, Mich., 1863–68; Bloomington, Ill., 1868–76; Centennial church, Chicago, 1877–79; and now (1880) he has charge of the First Baptist church, Peoria, Ill. During his service at Ypsilanti the membership of the church increased from 200 to 300, and at Bloomington from 300 to 500. His work in Chicago was in a time of great financial and spiritual depression, and though equally faithful, showed less of immediate result. Dr. Hewitt has always been active and interested in the general work of the denomination. In Michigan he was an influential member of the Board of State Missions, and one of the trustees of Kalamazoo College. In Illinois he has held like positions, especially as connected with the State missions and with the theological seminary; an ardent Sunday-school man; also for several years president and secretary of the State Sunday-School Association.

Hick, Col. J. M., was born in 1831, in West Virginia; was bred to the law; a member of the secession convention of Virginia in 1861; commanded a regiment at Cheat Mountain, and was captured there; was baptized in Raleigh, N. C., by Dr. T. H. Pritchard, in March, 1864; was president of the Baptist State Convention in 1875; was for several years chairman of the Sunday-School Board; is a trustee and a liberal benefactor of Wake Forest College, he and J. G. Williams, of Raleigh, having presented a building, known as the Library Building, to the college, which cost $10,000.

Hickman, David H., was born in Bourbon Co., Ky., Nov. 11, 1821. He died June 25, 1869. His father was a pioneer, having moved to Missouri in 1822. David was educated at Bonne Femme Academy. He was of studious habits, and for a time he was a teacher. He was delicate, but very energetic and successful. He was converted at seventeen, and united with the Bonne Femme church, and died in its membership. Mr. Hickman had no taste for public life, yet he served in the State Legislature of Missouri, and was moderator of the General Association when young. He framed the law for the common-school system of the State, which was adopted by the Legislature. He loved his home, and he was devoted to the church, in which he was a wise counselor and useful member. He was eminently successful in business, and gave $10,000 to Stephen College, of Columbia. He remembered in his will the poor of Bonne Femme and Columbia churches. Over the departing couch of David Hickman a voice from heaven said, "Blessed are the dead who die in the Lord."

Hickman, Col. H. H., for many years a deacon of the First Baptist church at Augusta, Ga., was born in Elbert Co., Ga., in 1818. He removed to Augusta when nineteen years of age. He was baptized in 1841, after a profession of faith, by Dr. William T. Brantly, Jr., then pastor of the church. Developing business talent early, he was admitted to membership in the firm, which was for many years known as that of Cress & Hickman. On the retirement of his partner, Mr. Hickman continued the business with uniform success until the close of the war between the States, although, like a host of others, he was injured financially to a serious extent. But after the return of peace his sagacity, his integrity, and his energy soon restored all that was lost. He became president of the Graniteville Manufacturing Company and of the Bank of Augusta, and was eminently successful in both of these positions.

Mr. Hickman was elected deacon of the Augusta (Greene Street) church more than twenty years ago, in which capacity he has served with great fidelity, always manifesting a deep interest in the welfare of the church, aiding it by his prayers, his counsels, and his substance. In the city with which he has been identified for more than forty years he has the highest standing as a business man of intelligent views and trustworthy character.

Hickman, Rev. William, one of the most famous of the pioneer Baptist ministers in Kentucky, was born in King and Queen Co., Va., Feb. 4, 1747. He was by early training an Episcopalian, and entertained great contempt for the Baptists. During a sermon by the renowned John Waller, in 1770, was deeply impressed. After struggling with his sins and his prejudices about three years, he obtained peace in Christ and was baptized by Reuben Ford, in April, 1773. At this time he lived in Cumberland County. There being few preachers in that region, he, with others, established prayer-meetings. In February, 1776, he started to Kentucky, and arriving at Harrodsburg, he remained several weeks, and during the time, though not licensed, he attempted on one occasion to preach. Upon his return home to Virginia he was soon set apart for the ministry, and spent several years as a preacher in his native State. In 1784 he removed to Fayette Co., Ky., where he preached with great zeal and activity in the surrounding settlements. In 1788 he changed his residence to what is now Franklin County. Here, in the same year, he formed the Forks of Elkhorn church, and was chosen the pastor. From this place he made preaching tours among the settlers, often attended by a guard of soldiers to protect him from the Indians. The new churches he formed were watched over and nurtured until they grew strong and the savages were driven from the country. He was greatly blessed in his ministry. A contemporary supposes that in his day he "baptized more people than any other minister in Kentucky." He probably formed more churches than even the famous Lewis Craig. He " baptized over 500 during one winter." He died suddenly in 1830. His son William was long pastor of South Benson church, and Hickman Co., Ky., was named after his son, Col. Paschal Hickman, who fell in the battle of the river Raisin.

Hickson, Rev. Edward, A.M., was born Oct. 13, 1824, at New Bandon, County Gloucester, New Brunswick, and was converted when quite young. He was baptized at Wolfville, Nova Scotia, in 1855. He graduated from Aca'dia College in June, 1860. He was ordained as pastor of the North Esk church, New Brunswick, July 27, 1862, where he labored successfully for ten years. He was pastor at St. George, New Brunswick, and is now in charge of a church at Carleton, St. John.

Hiden, J. C., D.D., is a young man of uncommon native powers. To enjoy his conversation is a treat, and to hear him lecture, a feast. Born at Orange Court-House, Va., Nov. 5, 1837, he spent three years in the Virginia Military Institute as a cadet, graduating in July, 1857. Elected as Professor of Ancient Languages in the Chesapeake Female College of Virginia when nineteen, he occupied that chair one year, and then entered the University of Virginia, where he spent two years, pursuing a wider range of study. He was ordained at Orange Court-House, Va., in 1859, and served the Hillsborough Baptist church, Albermarle Co., as pastor during the last year he spent at the university. During 1860 and 1861 he taught a private school at Orange Court-House, then entered the Confederate army as chaplain, and served throughout the war. Afterwards he taught school at Orange Court-House, and at Staunton; in 1866 he was elected pastor of the Fourth Street Baptist church, Portsmouth, serving two years, when he was called to the care of the Wilmington, N. C., First Baptist church, which he served for more than six years. In March, 1875, he was called by the Greenville church, of South Carolina, which call he accepted. He is well read, a superior preacher, and a fine scholar. He possesses great physical strength and powers of endurance, and yet those who know him best would rather meet him in the field than on the platform or forum. His mother is a niece of Jas. Barbour, who was governor of Virginia, U. S. Senator, Secretary of War, and minister to England, and she is a sister of Philip P. Barbour, who was a member of Congress and justice of the U. S. Supreme Court. She is still living. Dr. Hiden has a fine fund of anecdotes, and tells them remarkably well. As a speaker, he is clear, vigorous, original, unique. He is a true and noble man, and those who know him best love him most. Still young, of good constitution, an ardent student and full of energy, he may naturally expect to attain a high degree of distinction.

Higgins, Rev. George, was born at Marcus Hook, Pa., Dec. 16, 1798 ; baptized in Spruce Street church, Philadelphia, in 1817 ; ordained in Reading, February, 1829. He was among the first missionaries in the service of the State Convention, now called the General Association, and had for his field the Schuylkill Valley, but soon after labored chiefly on the West Branch of the Susquehanna. The writer bears pleasant witness to his untiring zeal and fidelity during the ten years of service in this region. In this space of time he baptized nearly 500 converts, mostly gathered from regions where Baptist sentiments were unknown and opposition was strong. Several churches, now enjoying comparative strength, were planted by his labors, while other existing churches were much enlarged. In 1859 he returned to Philadelphia, and aided materially in founding the Calvary church in 1841. Here also his memory is fragrant. In 1850 he settled as pastor of the Montgomery church, Montgomery Co., Pa., and closed a useful and honored life March 9, 1869, in his seventy-sixth year. During his ministry he baptized nearly 1500 persons.

No discouragements dampened his ardor ; he met all opposition with calmness. His blameless life disarmed adverse criticism of much of its force, and, though necessarily involved in frequent discussions during his missionary career, he never lost control of his temper. In argument he was clear and scholarly ; in preaching, plain and simple. Even opponents were compelled to respect him, while friends loved him with great warmth.

Higgins, Rev. John S., was born in New Jersey, Dec. 29, 1789. His early life was spent in Ohio, and in Woodford Co., Ky. In 1813 he was converted and joined a Baptist church. In 1815 he removed to Lincoln Co., Ky., where he was ordained to the ministry, and became the stated preacher of McCormack's, Hanging Fork, and Forks of Dix River churches. He assisted in forming the Baptist church in Danville, Ky., and was for a time its pastor. He was active in the benevolent enterprises of his denomination, and eminently successful as a minister. He died in 1872.

Hill, Benjamin H., D.D., was born in Newport, R. I., April 5, 1793 ; studied in Newport Academy and at the University of Pennsylvania ; took two courses of medical lectures ; converted and baptized in Thompson, Conn., in 1812 ; licensed Feb. 5, 1815 ; preached two years in Leicester, Mass. ; in 1818 was ordained pastor of Baptist church in Stafford, Conn. ; was engaged for Connecticut Baptist Missionary Society ; in 1821 settled with the First Baptist church in New Haven and was prospered ; in 1830 took charge of the First Baptist church in Troy, N. Y. ; in 1840 was chosen secretary of the American Baptist Home Mission Society, and served with remarkable success till 1862; in 1865 removed to New Haven, Conn., from which he was recently translated to the skies; received the degree of D.D. from Madison University in 1852; wise in judgment and in speech; a true man in the faith.

Hill, President David J., son of the Rev. Daniel T. Hill, was born at Plainfield, N. J., June 10,

PRESIDENT DAVID J. HILL.

1850. Received his early education in the public schools of Glen's Falls, N. Y., and Plainfield, N. J., and at the academy at Deckertown, N. J. Prepared for college at Suffield, Conn., and Cooperstown, N. Y. While at Cooperstown, in 1867–68, began writing for the press, the contributions consisting of short sketches and poems and a biography of Gen. U. S. Grant, in six numbers of five columns each. In April, 1870, was baptized by his father at Pauling, N. Y., and united with the church. In August of the same year entered the university at Lewisburg as a Freshman. Took the first "Lung Prize for Oratory" in 1873, and on graduating, in 1874, delivered the valedictory addresses, the first honor of the class. Was at once called to the pastorate of the Baptist church of Madison, Wis., but declined, accepting a call as tutor in Ancient Languages in the university at Lewisburg. At the close of the collegiate year 1874–75, Mr. Hill was appointed instructor in Rhetoric in the university, and in 1877, Crozer Professor of Rhetoric. At the same time he published, through Sheldon & Co., of New York, "The Science of Rhetoric," an advanced text-book

for colleges, which was at once adopted in the University of Michigan, Vassar College, and other first-class institutions. At the request of Sheldon & Co., Prof. Hill prepared "The Elements of Rhetoric," for schools of lower grade, which is now used in every State of the Union. In 1879, Prof. Hill began a series of brief biographies of American authors, similar to Morley's "English Men of Letters." Two volumes, on Irving and Bryant, respectively, were issued by Sheldon & Co., and were widely accepted and highly praised. The preparation of this series was interrupted by his election to the presidency of the university at Lewisburg, in March, 1879, to succeed the Rev. Justin R. Loomis, LL.D., the position which he now occupies. Since his election to the presidency President Hill has confined his pen, to lectures, sermons, and review articles. He has an engagement with Sheldon & Co. to prepare an elementary work on Logic as soon as his duties permit. President Hill, though quite young, is one of the ablest men in the Baptist denomination, with unusual prospects before him.

Hill, Rev. Noah, was born in Virginia, June 11, 1811; educated at Mercer University, Penfield, Ga.; commenced preaching in 1838; came to Texas in 1846, and prosecuted faithfully the work of the ministry at Brazoria, Matagorda, Wharton, and Brenham until 1869, when he was called away to his eternal home. He was a preacher of imposing personal appearance, and ably presented and enforced the great doctrines of the gospel. Few men in Texas labored under more difficulties and with more success.

Hill, Rev. Reuben Coleman, M.D., is one of the most distinguished and successful Baptists in Oregon. Born in Kentucky, March 27, 1808, of Baptist parents; baptized in 1833; ordained as deacon and licensed to preach by the Clear Creek church in 1835; ordained in 1845. He removed to Keetsville, Mo., in 1846; organized the church there, and increased its membership to 100. In 1851 he removed to Oregon; located at Albany, where he still resides; organized the Cowallis and Albany churches; was pastor of one church eighteen years, of the Albany church eleven years, and has served other churches shorter periods. He has baptized 1014 converts, among them six whole households. He is a physician as well as preacher; is liberal in his gifts; a member of all Baptist missionary, educational, and Bible organizations in the State, and has served two terms as a member of the Oregon Legislature.

Hill, R. J., M.D., was born in Ashland Co., O., June 15, 1836. He was educated at Vermilion Institute and Granville College. He was teacher and pupil till he closed his course. In 1859 he began a course of medical study with Drs. Rupert and

Thompson, of Mount Vernon, and graduated at the Starling Medical College, Columbus, O. In 1862 he became surgeon of the 45th Ohio Regiment of Volunteers; was captured in Tennessee by Gen. Longstreet in 1863; spent a month in Libby Prison; was exchanged November 20, and, after a brief visit home, re-entered the army, and remained till the end of the war. Came to St. Louis in 1866, where he has acquired an extensive practice and a flattering reputation. He is now president of the Public School Board of St. Louis. He was for years a deacon in the Baptist church in Green Town, O., and he is now a consistent and useful member of the Second Baptist church of St. Louis, Mo.

Hill, Stephen P., D.D., was born in Salem, Mass., April 17, 1806, and received his early edu-

STEPHEN P. HILL, D.D.

cation at the Salem High School. His parents and all his family connections were Unitarians. About the age of fourteen, casually entering a Baptist church, he heard a sermon from the venerable Father Grafton, of Newton, on the unbelief of the Apostle Thomas, which was instrumental in his conversion. He was baptized by the Rev. Lucius Bolles in June, 1821, being then about fifteen. At the age of twelve young Hill had entered the law-office of the Hon. David Cummins, but desiring a more active life, he was occupied for a while in mercantile pursuits. But his heart was in the work of the ministry. He began preaching at the early age of seventeen, and, in connection with the Rev. G. D. Boardman, then a student at Andover,

he frequently preached for the colored people. Wishing to prepare himself more thoroughly for his life-work, he entered Waterville College in 1825, and in 1827 removed to Brown University, graduating in 1829. During his winter vacations he was engaged in teaching. He entered the theological seminary at Newton, and finished his course in 1832, at which time he was ordained as pastor of the First Baptist church in Haverhill, Mass. His connection with it, though pleasant, was short; he removed to a warmer climate in consequence of a threatened pulmonary complaint. He passed the winter of 1833–34 near Charleston, S. C., and, at the urgent request of Dr. Basil Manly, supplied the pulpit of the church in Georgetown in that State. On his return to the North, he was taken sick in Baltimore, and on his recovery he was invited to become pastor of the First Baptist church in that city, which position he accepted. His ministry here was long-continued and successful, the membership having increased during the first eight years of his pastorate from 80 to nearly 600. A Sunday-school numbering upwards of 500 was gathered, and several auxiliary schools organized in various parts of the city. After seventeen years of fruitful labor in this field, Dr. Hill removed to Washington, D. C., and took charge of the First Baptist church, in which relation he continued, greatly prospered, until 1861, when he resigned. Since that time he has had no regular charge, but has frequently preached to feeble congregations unable to support pastors. He has also taken a deep interest in the welfare and progress of the colored Baptist churches, often preaching for them, and always ready to give them encouragement and counsel. Dr. Hill has also added to the literature of the denomination. He is the author of several prize monographs,—one on "The Theatre," one on "The Church," etc., and has also published, among other works, an essay on "The Best Plan of an International Tribunal for Peace." He has also written some poetry,—"The Unlimited Progression of Mind," which was delivered before the literary societies of Brown University at the commencement in 1839; on "The Problem of Truth," delivered before the societies of Madison University in 1859; and on "The Triumphs of the Gospel," delivered before the Knowles Society of the Newton Theological Seminary in 1839. He has also written a number of shorter poems, published in various papers and periodicals. But few men are more familiar with the history of hymnology, and his refined taste in this department of literature led to his selection as one of the committee which had charge of the preparation of the hymn-book so extensively used at one time,—"The Psalmist." Dr. Hill is also the author of a collection of hymns under the title of "Christian Melodies," as well as of several small works for the young,—"Time, the Price of Wisdom," "The Youth's Monitor," and a "Comprehensive Catechism." He is an active member of the board of trustees of the Columbian University, and deeply interested in its welfare. Mrs. Hill is a sister of W. W. Corcoran, LL.D., the well-known and generous benefactor of so many good causes.

Hill, Rev. Thomas, was born Sept. 12, 1797. He was converted in 1822, and was ordained in 1825. He was the first missionary for Southern Indiana appointed by the American Baptist Home Mission Society. He served it and the Indiana State Convention thirteen years. He was pastor of the Coffee Creek church thirty years, and he was moderator of the Coffee Creek Association thirty-nine years. He was a strong thinker and an eloquent preacher. Hundreds have been led to Christ by his ministry. He died March 27, 1876.

Hillman, Walter, LL.D., a distinguished educator in Mississippi, was born on Martha's Vineyard, Mass., in 1829. After a preparatory course at the Connecticut Literary Institution and Worcester Academy, he entered Brown University in 1849. While in it he spent one year in teaching as sub-principal of Worcester Academy and as classical instructor in Pierce Academy. He graduated in 1854 with the degree of A.M., and was immediately elected Professor of Mathematics and Natural Philosophy in Mississippi College, at Clinton. In 1856 he became principal of Central Female Institute in the same town,—a connection he has retained until the present. During this time he also held the presidency of Mississippi College for six years. Under his administration these institutions greatly prospered. Ordained to the ministry in 1858, he has since occasionally preached.

Hillman, William, was born in the city of New York, Nov. 21, 1794, and died April 14, 1864. In his nineteenth year he was converted and baptized into the fellowship of the First Baptist church by the pastor, Rev. William Parkinson. For more than fifty years he was a member of that church. While a young man he was elected one of its deacons, and its honored pastors, Wm. Parkinson, Spencer H. Cone, A. Kingman Nott, and Thomas D. Anderson found him a safe adviser, an efficient helper, and a liberal supporter of the church and all the great evangelizing enterprises of the Baptist denomination. With Dr. Cone he entered heartily into the work of the American Bible Union. He was one of the eighteen men who on a stormy day met in Deacon Wm. Colgate's parlor and took preliminary measures for its organization. He paid the first hundred dollars into its treasury to make his pastor a life-director. He possessed a strong faith in God, was a man of ardent piety, and left this world by a death remarkable for its peaceful, joyful, triumphant demonstration of Christian victory.

Hillsman, Matthew, D.D., was born in Tennessee, near the town of Knoxville, Aug. 7, 1814.

MATTHEW HILLSMAN, D.D.

With the exception of two years in Talladega, Ala., he has spent all his life in his native State. Mr. Hillsman was converted at the age of nineteen, and was ordained in 1835. For many years he supplied Baptist pulpits in a number of cities and towns in Tennessee. Among his successful pastorates was the one with the church at Murfreesborough, from which there were sent out as foreign missionaries Dr. Burton, T. P. Crawford, and Rev. Mr. Gilliard. For one year he was president of Mossy Creek College, and subsequently for years corresponding secretary of the Bible Board of the Southern Baptist Convention. In 1862 he became pastor of the church at Trenton, Tenn., where he still resides, ministering to it and preaching with great acceptance in the surrounding country. As president of the board of the West Tennessee Baptist Convention, and sometimes president of the Convention itself, he has done much to promote its efficiency. A trustee of the Southern Baptist Theological Seminary, he was one of the committee who selected Louisville as its location; and he was also on the committee which presented a plan for the organization of the Southwestern Baptist University. For more than forty years he has been intimately connected with the educational, missionary, and benevolent enterprises of Tennessee, and he has always been zealous in aiding the

Domestic and Foreign Boards of the Southern Baptist Convention. Dr. Hillsman presides well over deliberative bodies, and is frequently called upon to act in that capacity, and is now the moderator of the Central Association. As a preacher he is widely known, and has great influence in all parts of Tennessee. As a teacher, editor, or pastor, he has been identified with all the great Baptist movements with credit to himself and honor to the denomination. No man has the confidence of his brethren more completely or stands higher in their estimation. In his sermons he is sound in doctrine, clear in exposition, and powerful in appeal, and entirely free from sensationalism. His style is plain, practical, and direct, his best efforts being those of his regular service. The degree of Doctor of Divinity was conferred on him by the Union University. He is at present one of the editors of the Nashville *Reflector*.

Hillyer, Rev. John F., LL.D., was born May 25, 1805, in Wilkes Co., Ga.; educated at University of Georgia and Georgia Medical College; practised medicine two years; professed religion in 1825, and soon thereafter commenced preaching; was connected as a professor with Mercer University, Penfield, Ga., from 1835 to 1839; preached and taught at Eatonton until 1847, when he became pastor of the Galveston Baptist church, Texas; was successful in establishing Gonzales College, of which he was first president. From 1860 to 1865 was Professor of Mathematics and Natural Philosophy in Baylor University. From the last-named institution he received the degree of LL.D.; was at the organization of the Georgia Baptist State Convention, the Southern Baptist Convention, and the Texas Baptist State Convention; has preached fifty-three years; is a brother of Rev. S. G. Hillyer, D.D., and Hon. Junius Hillyer, late member of Congress from Georgia; was chaplain of Texas house of representatives two sessions, and ministers now to two or three churches regularly. He has been a successful preacher and teacher, and always a hard worker.

Hillyer, Shaler G., D.D., president of Monroe Female College, Forsyth, Ga., stands among the first Baptist preachers and scholars of the State. For nearly fifty years he has been thoroughly identified with both the secular and religious affairs of the Baptists of Georgia, and is universally recognized as a man of great ability, high culture, and deep piety, and of eloquence far above ordinary. He was born June 20, 1809, in Wilkes County, and was educated at the State University, graduating with the class of 1829. He united with the Baptist church at Athens in 1831, and was ordained in 1835. During his long life he has been the pastor of Baptist churches in all parts of the State,—at Athens, Milledgeville, Macon, Madison, Forsyth,

White Plains, Rome, Penfield, Crawfordville, Cass Spring, Albany, and various other places; and his piety, zeal, amiability, scholarship, pulpit ability, and theological learning have united in making him both useful and successful. As a sermonizer and orator he has very few, if any, superiors in the State, for to a noble and dignified style, amounting often to striking eloquence, he unites a strong current of manly thought, arranged in a systematic train most attractive to cultivated minds. He was tutor in the State University during the year 1834, and Professor of Rhetoric and Belles-Lettres in Mercer University from January, 1847, to May, 1856. From September, 1859, to May, 1862, he was Professor of Theology in the same institution, and in both these positions he sustained himself with marked ability. When the war broke up Mercer University temporarily, his professorship ceased, and as it has never been re-established, his connection with Mercer University has not been resumed. He and Prof. Asbury, after the war, took charge of the Monroe Female College, at Forsyth, Ga., where he now resides. He is president of the college and pastor of the Forsyth church.

Dr. Hillyer is a devoted Christian, pure in heart, unselfish, confiding, and faithful. As a preacher, his sermons move the heart and excite the sensibilities. He is a guileless man, and stands high in the Christian confidence of his brethren.

Himes, Rev. Palmer C., was born in Clarendon, Vt., April 3, 1804. He was hopefully converted at the age of fifteen, and was baptized Dec. 19, 1824, by Rev. John Spaulding, and united with the Berkshire, Vt., Baptist church. He commenced preaching in Sheldon, and the seal of the divine blessing at once rested upon his labors. After preaching for a time, he went to the Madison Theological Institution, pursuing his studies a little less than two years. He was ordained at Enosburg in March, 1833. He labored as a minister of the gospel for forty-two years, in Vermont, New Hampshire, and Maine. It has been estimated that not far from one thousand persons were converted under his ministry. He died at Enosburg, Vt., March 5, 1871.

Hinckley, Rev. Abel R., was born in Livermore, Me., Dec. 24, 1809. He was converted in 1831, and joined the Baptist church in Augusta. He was licensed to preach by that church in 1832. Soon afterwards he began a course of study, spending some time in Waterville College, Newton, and New Hampton. Sept. 14, 1834, he was ordained by the Swanzey church, N. H., during the session of the Dublin Association, and shortly afterwards moved to Lawrenceburg, Ind. He was called to the pastorate of the Sparta church in 1836. After a few months he received a call from the church at Franklin, and his great interest in the "Manual

Labor Institute," then lately started, led him to accept it. He removed to Franklin in November, 1837. The church had no house of worship. Under his leadership it built a large, commodious edifice, and the membership rapidly increased. In July, 1842, he had a second attack of hemorrhage of the lungs, which obliged him to cease public labor. He died in the following September. He was for five consecutive years secretary of the State Convention. His efforts for the promotion of the institute were untiring. One of the present deacons of the Franklin church says that he was the best and purest man he ever knew.

He published in pamphlet form a series of letters on "Baptism," in reply to a sermon preached by Dr. Monfort, of the Franklin Presbyterian church. This pamphlet was extensively circulated and well received, and produced a good result in the State. He was Indiana editor of the *Banner and Pioneer*, published at Louisville, Ky. He spent much of his time in planning for the enlargement of the Redeemer's kingdom among Indiana Baptists.

Hinton, Rev. Isaac Taylor, was born in Oxford, England, July 4, 1799. In 1821 he was baptized by his father. He sailed from London for Philadelphia, April 9, 1832. In June, 1833, he took the oversight of the First Baptist church of Richmond, Va. In 1835 he took charge of the First Baptist church of Chicago, then in its infancy. In 1841 he accepted a call to the Second church in St. Louis, Mo. In December, 1844, he received an invitation from the Baptists of New Orleans to labor in that city, and immediately removed to this new field. He was instrumental in building a church edifice for them, which was opened in February, 1846, and in greatly increasing their numbers, so much so that it was planned by the pastor and his people to erect a larger structure in the autumn of 1847. He died of yellow fever on the 28th of August, 1847.

Mr. Hinton was the author of a "History of Baptism," and of "Prophecies of Daniel and John, illustrated by the Events of History."

The churches over which Mr. Hinton presided, without exception, prospered, and he was instrumental in forming other churches in localities near these seats (cathedræ) of his ministry.

In fourteen years of his life in America he made a name as widely known as our country, and his memory is fragrant still in the land of his adoption. Like the saintly Wilson, a recent martyr, in the same city, by the same plague, Mr. Hinton left a numerous family. He possessed a remarkable amount of historical information and of Biblical knowledge, and he had a deep experience of the love of Christ.

He was invited to the presidency of Alton College, Ill., and he was justly regarded as one of the purest and most learned and talented ministers in the denomination.

Hinton, Rev. John Howard, M.A., was the son of the Rev. James Hinton, pastor of the Baptist church at Oxford, England, and was born in that city March 24, 1791. His father conducted a private school for many years with much credit and success, and was well known as an able and scholarly minister. Not a few men of brilliant reputation were educated by him. His mother was of the famous family of the Taylors, being the daughter of the eminent engraver, Isaac Taylor, the first of five in lineal descent of that name. Among Mr. Isaac Taylor's friends was John Howard, the philanthropist, and when he was about to take his last journey abroad, he said to his friend's daughter, "I have now no son of my own : if ever you have one, pray call him after me." Mrs. Hinton possessed much of the family ability, and her influence upon her eldest son, whom she named John Howard, determined him to devote himself to the ministry. At first he studied medicine, but when he was in his twentieth year, having been called by the church to exercise his gifts in the ministry, he was entered at Bristol College, then under the presidency of Dr. Ryland. Here he studied for two years, and proceeded to Edinburgh University in 1813. He had received an excellent scholastic training with his father's pupils at home, and the curriculum of the celebrated Scottish university, together with the theological studies of Bristol College, gave him a very complete furnishing for the work of his life. He took the M.A. degree at Edinburgh at the close of the third year of the academical course, and after preaching for some time in various places, he accepted a call to the Baptist church in Haverford-West, Pembrokeshire, and preached his first sermon there on May 19, 1816. After five years' ministry at Haverford-West, he removed to Reading, and in this more advantageous position he found scope for his great talents, and became prominent in the denomination. His native ability and very superior culture gave him a leading place among the foremost Non-conformist ministers in all public movements. In 1837 he entered upon the pastorate of the ancient church in Devonshire Square, Bishopsgate Street, in the very heart of London. In denominational work he was ever foremost. The Baptist Union, of which for many years he was the indefatigable secretary, would have miserably perished but for his persistence and faith in its utility as a means of securing denominational unity. In the operations of the Baptist Missionary Society he had taken the liveliest interest in his youthful days, when Andrew Fuller and other founders of the mission used to come to Oxford to confer with his father and pray together for divine direction. After coming to London he bore an influential part in the counsels of the Missionary Committee, and threw himself heart and soul into the enterprise of William Knibb to render the Jamaica Baptist churches self-supporting. His life of Knibb gives a lively and stirring presentation of the work and its claims upon Christian benevolence. For a quarter of a century, without any abatement of energy, he pursued these manifold labors, and all the while he was busy with his pen on theological and kindred topics suggested in the course of events. He entered warmly into controversies in which the fundamental truths of religion were assailed, and he enjoyed the remarkable experience of being suspected of heterodoxy in his youth for the maintenance of opinions which in his old age procured him the highest reputation for orthodoxy. He could boast that it was not he who had changed his sentiments. His collected works, published by himself, on his retirement from his London pastorate in 1863, form seven volumes. His intimate friend, the Rev. C. M. Birrell, says of his works, that " thousands could tell the tale of recovery from infidelity ; of increased reverence for the authority of the Word of God ; of the dispersion of sluggish formalism, and the creation of a vivid and vital realization of admitted truths, which had come to them through his penetrating and awakening pen." His figure was of commanding height, and his countenance was singularly calm and thoughtful. An admirable portrait of him hangs in the board room of the Baptist Missionary Society. He was "instant in prayer," steadfastly preserving the habits of devotion in the midst of exciting and absorbing public labors. During the last four or five years of his life his bodily powers gently and steadily diminished, until at last he fell asleep in Jesus in perfect peace, and with unclouded mind, on Dec. 22, 1873, aged eighty-two. As a preacher he excelled in analysis and exposition. His sermons were pre-eminently instructive, rich in argument, wrought in the fire of a fervid evangelical zeal for the salvation of men. Besides his collected works, in seven volumes, he edited the English edition of Dr. Wayland's " Principles and Practices of Baptists," Rev. Isaac Taylor Hinton's work on the "History of Baptism." He contributed several works to general literature, the most popular being the biography of William Knibb. In early life he published a work on the "History and Topography of the United States, from their First Discovery and Colonization to 1826," which was completed in 1832, and favorably received on both sides of the Atlantic. Later editions have been published in England and in America. His pamphlets on the voluntary principle and other stirring public questions were characterized by incisive force, with peculiar accuracy and lucidity of statement.

Hinton, James, M.D., eldest son of the Rev. John Howard Hinton, was for many years a distinguished London physician, and published several valuable works, some of which were widely known,—" The Mystery of Pain," "Man and his Dwelling-Place," " Life in Nature," etc. Dr. Hinton was baptized by his father in early life, and his writings are marked by a devout, reverent spirit, as well as high intelligence. His death, in London, was recently announced.

Hires, Rev. Allen J., was born in Bridgeton, N. J., Sept. 26, 1822. At the age of sixteen years he was baptized into the fellowship of the Baptist church in that town. After a course of study preparatory to the work of the gospel ministry he was ordained when twenty-five years old, and became pastor of the Vincent church, Chester Co., Pa. From his ordination up to the present time his life has been devoted to labor for the salvation of men and for the upbuilding of the cause of Christ. His pastoral relations have been, in addition to the above-named place, at Glen Run, Chester Co., Pa. ; Jersey Shore, Lycoming Co., Pa. ; Woodstown, N. J. ; Cape May Court-House, N. J. ; and with the Second church, Baltimore, Md. For four years he was also district secretary of the American Baptist Home Mission Society in Pennsylvania and New Jersey. Mr. Hires has been greatly honored of God in his ministry.

Hiscox, Edward T., D.D., was born in Westerly, R. I., Aug. 24, 1814. His mother was a member of the Society of Friends, and his father was a Seventh-Day Baptist. One of his ancestors, Rev. William Hiscox, was the first pastor of the first Seventh-Day church in America. In September, 1834, he was baptized by Rev. Flood Shurtleff, and became a member of the First Baptist church of Wakefield, R. I. He was graduated from Madison University in 1843, and in 1844 he accepted the pastorate of the First Baptist church of Westerly, R. I. During his three years of labor there the church had a rapid growth, built a spacious house of worship, and became one of the ablest churches in the State. In 1847 he took charge of the Central church, in Norwich, Conn., where, during five years, his labors were greatly blessed. In 1852 he accepted a call to Stanton Street church, New York. He remained there several years, during which about four hundred were added to the church, chiefly by baptism. At the present time he is pastor at Mount Vernon, N. Y., laboring with his usual vigor and success. He is an able preacher and a prolific writer. He is the author of " The Baptist Church Directory," a manual of Baptist Church order and polity, 30,000 copies of which have been sold. It has been translated into six foreign languages, and is generally used by our foreign missionaries ; also, " The Baptist Short

Method," an examination of the characteristic features of the Baptists as distinguished from other denominations of Christians ; " The Star Book for Ministers," a manual for ministers of all denominations ; " The Star Book of Christian Baptism," a manual in reference to this ordinance. He is about to bring out " The Star Book on the Lord's Supper," " The Star Book on Baptist Councils," and a large volume on the mutual relations and responsibilities of pastors and churches, entitled " Pastor and People."

Historical Society, The American Baptist. —At the annual meeting of the American Baptist Publication Society, held May 4, 1853, in the Spruce Street Baptist church, Philadelphia, a special meeting was called for the next evening to organize a " Historical Department" in connection with the Publication Society. The motion to convene the meeting was made by John M. Peck, D.D., and the mover, together with Hon. H. G. Jones and Henry E. Lincoln, were appointed a committee to report a plan of organization. At the meeting of the Publication Society, on Thursday evening, the committee reported a constitution, which was unanimously adopted, establishing a national society, to be called " The American Baptist Historical Society," and they gave it " a separate and permanent form," and required " its officers to be elected by the Publication Society." William R. Williams, D.D., was its first president. " The objects of the society were to collect and preserve all manuscripts, documents, and books relating to Baptist history," etc.

The society made progress in various directions, but rather slowly until 1860, when the late Dr. Malcom became its president. Ardently attached to its objects, and free from public duties, he gave his entire time to the increase of its treasures, and in a few years its library was enriched by thousands of volumes, many of them of priceless value to our denominational history.

In 1861 the society was incorporated under a new constitution, which gives it as the constituency to elect its officers and board, not the Baptist Publication Society, " but all persons who pay ten dollars or more towards its objects." The secretary of the Publication Society and the president and secretary of its board of managers are ex officio members of the board of the Historical Society.

Constant accessions are made to the library, to the increase of which all the funds donated to the society are devoted.

The Historical Society has at least six thousand volumes, among which there are many rare works by the Baptist writers of other days,—books which it would be difficult, if not impossible, to replace ; and it also has the writings of many Pedobaptists assailing our peculiarities. It needs financial support to secure the literary treasures which are fre-

quently within its reach, and it should receive it liberally.

It is believed that the society should have a warm place in the hearts of our entire denomination, and that it should speedily be furnished with a fire-proof building to protect its invaluable collection of books and other treasures.

Rev. William Cathcart, D.D., is the president of the society, Rev. Job H. Chambers, secretary, and H. E. Lincoln, Esq., librarian and treasurer.

Hobart, I. N., D.D., for over ten years connected with the direction of State missions in Illinois, was born in Lyme, N. H., Feb. 20, 1812. His conversion took place July 4, 1831, and his baptism in August of the same year. In 1834 he was licensed, and on Aug. 12, 1841, he was ordained as pastor of the church at Radnor, Pa., Rev. Elon Galusha preaching the sermon. He remained pastor at Radnor nearly six years, returning to New England with impaired health in 1847, and for about two years remaining without pastoral charge. Jan. 1, 1849, he became pastor of the church at North Oxford, Mass., where he labored between three and four years, when he accepted the pastorate of the church at Bristol, R. I. Here his health failed again, and in 1855 he removed to St. Lawrence Co., N. Y. From Jan. 1, 1856, to Oct. 1, 1868, he labored in that State. At the last date he was appointed by the Home Mission Society to take charge of its work in Illinois. In the year following the society and the Illinois Baptist General Association adopted the co-operative plan in State missions, and Dr. Hobart was chosen superintendent of missions for that State. When the co-operative plan was discontinued he was appointed district secretary for the States of Illinois, Iowa, and Wisconsin. At the earnest solicitation of the Board of the General Association he decided to remain in the superintendence of its missions, and to this post has been elected from year to year to the present time (1880), conducting the Baptist missions of the State with marked self-devotion and administrative ability.

Hobbs, Smith M., M.D., an eminent physician of Mount Washington, Ky., was born in Nelson County in 1823. His early education was under the superintendence of Noble Butler, A.M., a well-known author, and was completed at St. Joseph's College, at Bardstown. He graduated at the Kentucky School of Medicine in 1852, and immediately commenced practice at Mount Washington. He is a gentleman of fine culture and a close student, a man of tireless energy, and has performed an incredible amount of professional labor. He was a member of the Kentucky Legislature in 1868, and was the author of a bill which largely increased the common-school fund of the State, and of a report in favor of " prohibiting the marriage of first cousins." In 1876 he was one of the two commissioners appointed to superintend the interest of Kentucky in the Centennial Exposition at Philadelphia. He

SMITH M. HOBBS, M.D.

became a Baptist early in life, and is a liberal contributor to Baptist enterprises.

Hobgood, Prof. F. P., was born in Granville Co., N. C., in 1846; was prepared by James H. Horner for college; graduated from Wake Forest College in 1869; taught an academy at Reidsville, N. C.; came to Raleigh and took the position of his father-in-law, Dr. Royall, as principal of a female college, which he conducted successfully until 1880, when he removed his school to Oxford, N. C.

Hodge, James L., D.D., son of Rev. William and Elizabeth Hodge, was born in Aberdeen, Scotland, in 1812, and at the age of twelve accompanied his parents to America. In 1831 he became a member of the First Baptist church of Hartford. In 1835, after graduating at the Literary Institution, Suffield, he was ordained pastor of the First Baptist church of that town. He was subsequently called to the First Baptist church in Brooklyn, which proved to be one of the longest and most successful settlements of his life. In the midst of his prosperity he was impressed with the importance of founding a church in the upper part of the city, on Washington Avenue. After a pastorate of some years with the new interest, which was crowned with success, Dr. Hodge was induced to settle in Newark, N. J. In 1864, after an absence of eight years, he was called to his present highly successful pastorate with the Mariners' church, New York. During his long experience as a min-

ister, Dr. Hodge has been regarded as an eloquent champion of Scriptural truth, and has been especially fitted for the performance of his duties by his tender sympathies, magnetic nature, and analytical powers. In 1848 he was made D.D. by Madison University.

Hodge, Marvin Grow, D.D., was born in Hardwick, Vt., in 1822; educated at Derby Academy; ordained at Charleston in 1843, where he began his ministry. Subsequently he was settled at Colchester and Hinesburg, Stillwater and Brooklyn, N. Y., Kalamazoo, Mich., Beaver Dam, Janesville, and Milwaukee, Wis. At the last place he now resides, and is the pastor of the First Baptist church in that city. His pastorates at Hanson Place, Brooklyn, N. Y., Janesville, Wis., and Kalamazoo, Mich., were nearly seven years each. At Janesville he was very successful. He added not only large numbers to the church, but led the church to erect the finest Baptist meeting-house in the State. He left it a large, intelligent, and influential body. The church in Milwaukee is strengthening itself under his ministrations and entering upon a new era of usefulness. Dr. Hodge was one year district secretary of the New York Baptist Convention, and district secretary of the American Baptist Home Mission Society for New England two years. He received the honorary degree of A.M. from the University of Vermont in 1849, the like honor from

MARVIN GROW HODGE, D.D.

the University of Rochester in 1864, and the title of D.D. from the University of Chicago in 1867. He excels as an expository preacher. His sermons are nearly all clear expositions of the divine Word. Theologically exact and Scriptural, always thoroughly prepared with the riches of a ripe Christian experience, he brings to his people in his pulpit ministrations a gospel feast. His people love to see him in the pulpit. They are sure to be instructed. As the result, he indoctrinates his congregations and builds them up. Few congregations are better instructed in the doctrines of the Word of God than the churches at Janesville and Kalamazoo during his ministry over them. As a pastor, Dr. Hodge is wise, sympathetic, knows his people thoroughly, is their recognized leader and guide, and feeds his flock like a shepherd, gathering the lambs in his arms and carrying them in his bosom. With his fine abilities as a preacher, his decided executive talents, and excellent gifts for pastoral labor, he has for many years been regarded as one of the ablest of Christian ministers. In the State where he now resides, and where ten years of his life have been spent, he is known as a good man and a faithful herald of Jesus Christ, " watching for souls."

Hodgen, Rev. Isaac, " in some respects one of the most brilliant preachers of Kentucky," was the son of Robert Hodgen, a distinguished citizen and a leading Baptist among the first settlers of Kentucky. He was born in La Rue County about 1780, became a member of Severn's Valley church in 1802, and was licensed to preach at Nolin church in 1804. In 1805 he removed to Green County and united with Mount Gilead church, where he received ordination the same year. He devoted most of the energies of his life to the work of an evangelist, though he was stated preacher for several churches at different periods. He traveled and preached almost unceasingly, and multitudes were turned to the Lord wherever he labored. In 1817, accompanied by William Warder, he made a tour as far as Philadelphia, returning through Virginia. They traveled the entire distance on horseback, and preached almost every night. It was estimated that " over 600 were baptized who were awakened under their preaching in Virginia." Mr. Hodgen continued in this course of tireless zeal and energy till the Lord called him home in the maturity of his manhood, in 1826.

Hodges, Rev. Cyrus Whitman, was born in Leicester, Vt., July 9, 1802; became a Christian, and united with the Congregational church in Salisbury, Vt., in July, 1821. Within a few months, finding his views more in harmony with those of the Baptists, he joined the Baptist church in Brandon, and was licensed by them to preach in 1822. He was ordained at Chester, N. Y., in 1824, and remained there three years. His other pastorates were Arlington, Shaftsbury, and Springfield, Vt., Westport, N. Y., Bennington, and finally Bristol,

Vt. In each of these places he rendered good service to the cause of his Master. He died April 4, 1851.

Holcombe, Henry, D.D.—Among those who took an active and beneficial part in shaping the destinies of the Baptist denomination in the State of Georgia was Henry Holcombe. Born in Prince Edward Co., Va., he moved to South Carolina, with his father, Grimes Holcombe, in early life. He was a captain of cavalry in the Revolutionary war, and, at the age of twenty-two, while in command of his company, was hopefully converted to God. He began at once to proclaim the unsearchable riches of Christ, making his first address on horseback, at the head of his command. He soon became distinguished as a preacher, and met with extraordinary success in his work. He was pastor of the Baptist church in Beaufort and other places in South Carolina until 1799, when he was invited to Savannah as " supply" to what is now known as the Independent Presbyterian church of that city, which then occupied the Baptist house of worship, having leased it for a number of years. In November of 1800 he, with his wife and ten others, united in organizing and constituting the First Baptist church of Savannah, which still exists. He became the pastor, soon gathered a large congregation, to which he ministered until 1811, when he accepted a call to Philadelphia. As pastor of the First Baptist church he preached in Philadelphia until his death, in 1824.

The degree of A.M. was conferred on him in early life by Columbia College, S. C., and the degree of Doctor of Divinity, which meant far more then than it does now, was conferred on him in 1810 by Brown University, R. I.

Dr. Holcombe never took any part in politics, but when quite a young man he was a member of the convention in South Carolina which ratified and adopted the Constitution of the United States. Several points in his life are worthy of mention:

1. He baptized the first white person ever immersed in the city of Savannah.

2. He was the originator of the penitentiary system of Georgia, *in lieu* of death, for ordinary crimes.

3. He was the founder of the Savannah Female Orphan Asylum, and wrote its constitution.

4. He published the first religious periodical in the Southern States, and one among the first in the United States,—a magazine called the *Analytical Repository*,—it was begun in May, 1802.

5. He was one of the Baptist ministers who met by appointment at Powelton, Ga., in May, 1802, and originated the "General Committee," which was the germ of the Georgia Baptist Convention.

6. He was the main instrument in the foundation of Mount Enon Academy, near the line of

Burke County,—a Baptist institution of learning, unfortunately located, but which prospered as long as Dr. Holcombe resided in Georgia. This was the first institution of the kind in the South established under the influence of Baptists, and it was the precursor of Mercer University.

Dr. Holcombe was a man of wide information and elegant culture. He was a great reasoner, mighty in the Scriptures, and a born orator. His bearing was dignified, his manners graceful, his presence commanding, and he had great personal magnetism. In its softer tones his voice was gentle and persuasive; at other times it was full of power and majesty. A man of very tender feelings and sympathetic nature, he was, indeed, a "son of consolation" to the poor, the widows, and the orphans, many of whom have been heard to speak with tears of his gentle ministrations a whole generation after his death. He condescended to men of low estate, was a friend to the friendless and the outcast, and would take to his home and to his bosom those who were spurned by society. On the very day when a man was put to death on the gallows in Savannah, his children were gathered together at Dr. Holcombe's house,—the abode of sympathy and love,—where they were cared for, comforted, counseled, and cherished with more than fatherly tenderness.

With these almost womanly qualities Dr. Holcombe's character possessed another side. He was a bold, brave man, immovably stern when occasion required, and at times imperial if not imperious in his bearing, and these qualities, in a man of herculean physique and of immense intellectual and moral momentum, inspired awe and even fear in the minds of many. He was a man of warm impulses, and, it is said, "liberal to a fault," lavishing his means with an almost reckless generosity. Add to all this wonderful preaching ability, intense zeal, and enthusiasm in the cause of Christ, and it need excite no wonder that he made a deep impress upon the State, and that his presence was felt as that of a great power. He died calmly, in possession of all his mental faculties, and fully aware of his approaching end; and the concourse of people attending his funeral was such, it is said, as was never before seen in Philadelphia. Dr. Holcombe was six feet and two inches in height.

Holcombe, Rev. Hosea, a native of North Carolina, was born about the year 1780. For some years a minister in upper South Carolina, he settled in Jefferson Co., Ala., early in the history of the State. Was unquestionably a leader in projecting the plans of the early Baptists of the State, taking a bold and aggressive part in everything that looked to the elevation of the Baptist cause, or to the progress of Baptist principles. Organized nearly all the churches for many miles around where he lived,

and established them on a sound basis; and traveled and preached over a large part of the State; went to Associations far and near, and was universally regarded as able to guide them; was six years president of the State Convention; more than any other man in the State he withstood the anti-missionaries; was in the strength of his ministerial influence when the anti-missionaries were doing their work of mischief among Alabama Baptists. He was the man for the times, and performed his work well. One of the founders of our State Convention, and a most earnest advocate for the establishment of good schools by the denomination, and for ministerial education. He was an able minister of the New Testament, doctrinal and argumentative in preaching, clear and forcible in delivery, mighty in the Scriptures, a noble and impressive person, commanding respect and veneration everywhere; though not so great a man, he holds a position in the history of Alabama Baptists not unlike that of Dr. Mercer among the brethren of Georgia. He wrote a number of controversial pamphlets, compiled a hymn-book, and a history of the Baptists in Alabama,—a work of 375 pages, which brings its history down to the year 1840. He passed his ministry as pastor of a number of churches, and as a missionary evangelist. He died in 1841 at his home, and was buried on his farm, near Jonesborough. Two of his sons became Baptist ministers.

Holcombe, Rev. William H., a minister in Northeast Mississippi, distinguished for eloquence and piety, was born in Alabama in 1812. He began to preach very young; came to Mississippi at an early day; successfully filled the pastorate at Columbus, Aberdeen, Okalona, and at Pontoloc and Ripley. He died in 1867.

Holden, Rev. Charles Horace, of Modesto, Cal., is a young and most prominent Baptist pastor. He was born in West Milford, Va., Aug. 23, 1853; educated, converted, and baptized in Webster, W. Va.; removed to California; ordained in July, 1879, and became pastor at Modesto, where the baptism of converts, the awakened interest in the gospel, and other tokens of divine favor give great promise of increasing usefulness and power in connection with his ministry.

Holden, Charles N., was born at Fort Covington, N. Y., May 13, 1816, of parents who had emigrated to that place from New Hampshire, and were among the earlier settlers of Northern New York. His father, W. C. Holden, an energetic and patriotic man, was present and participated in the battle of Plattsburg, so important among the battles of the war of 1812-15. At twenty years of age, Charles N. Holden, the eldest son, having received such education as the opportunities of a new country afford,—though these were well improved,—engaged in teaching. Deciding at length to try his fortunes in the new West, Mr. Holden, in 1837, removed to Chicago. After a little time spent upon the farm of his uncle, P. H. Holden, in Will County, he returned to Chicago in the fall of the year just named, and in the spring of the following year began business as a lumber-dealer, afterwards as a grocer. In 1852, retiring from the business in which he had been so long engaged, he entered that of insurance and real estate; was one of those who organized the Firemen's Insurance Company, holding in that company the office of secretary; subsequently being elected treasurer of the Firemen's Benevolent Association, in which service he still remains. Mr. Holden has been called to repeated offices of trust,—as alderman, as commissioner of taxes for the city of Chicago, as city treasurer, and in other posts of important public service. Converted in early life, Mr. Holden has been during many years a valued and useful member of the Baptist denomination. In Chicago his church connection has been with what is now the Second church, always one of its most trusted and efficient members. He was also during many years a trustee of the university, and was one of those who laid the foundations of the theological seminary at Chicago. To no one man is it more due that the financial affairs of that institution have been always so judiciously guided, while his own donations to its funds have been ready and liberal. Held in high esteem by his fellow-citizens during his whole career, he has especially been remarkable for his firm, consistent, and useful course as a Christian, a friend of reform, and a worker in every good cause.

Holden, Gov. W. W., was born in Orange Co., N. C., in November, 1818; learned the printer's trade; settled in Raleigh in 1836; was foreman of the *Raleigh Star* office four years, during which time he read law, and was licensed to practise 1st January, 1841. Became proprietor and editor of the *Standard* in 1843, which he conducted with distinguished ability for twenty-five years. He was a member of the House of Commons from Wake County in 1846; was several times State printer; was for seven years a member of the State Literary Board; elected a trustee of the State University in 1856; served several years as one of the board of directors of the insane asylum and the institution for the deaf and dumb; was a member from Wake County in the secession convention of 1861; was provisional governor of North Carolina for seven months in 1865, having been appointed by President Johnson; was elected governor of North Carolina in 1868 by a large majority, and served two years and six months, when he was impeached by the State Legislature; was offered the mission to San Salvador by President Johnson, and that to Peru by President Grant, both of which he declined.

Gov. Holden professed faith in Christ in December, 1870, at a meeting held by Rev. A. B. Earle, in Raleigh, and was baptized by Dr. T. H. Pritchard, pastor of the First Baptist church of that city. He has been an active and useful church member, and has a Bible-class of young men in the Sabbath-school, which numbers 40 members. He has been the postmaster of Raleigh for six years.

Hollins Institute, Botetourt Springs, Va.— About the year 1841, the Rev. Joshua Bradly, of New York, went to Virginia. He was a Baptist minister, and enthusiastic on the subject of education. At this time Botetourt Springs, now the seat of Hollins Institute, was for sale, and Mr. Bradly at once conceived the plan of purchasing it for school purposes. Without a dollar in his possession he contracted for the purchase of the property, relying upon his own tact and energy to secure the necessary funds. He opened a school for boys and girls with the purpose of supplying the neighboring districts with good teachers. There was a large attendance of pupils, but financial and other troubles soon arising, he resigned at the end of a year and left the State. Before his departure he had formed an organization under the title of "The Valley Union Education Society of Virginia," which afterwards procured a charter as a joint-stock company, and continued the school. The Rev. George Pearcy, late missionary to China, and now deceased, was elected principal, and continued such for several years with varying success. Mr. Pearcy, about to leave for China, urged Mr. Cocke to take charge of the school, which, relinquishing his position in Richmond College, he consented to do on the following terms: that he would advance a sum sufficient to save the property from immediate sale; he should be both principal and steward of the school, becoming responsible for all salaries of teachers whom he might employ; and the society should furnish premises and buildings, but should be subjected to no liabilities whatever beyond the cost and repair of the premises. Mr. Cocke found the grounds and everything on them in a most unattractive condition, but by his untiring energy they were soon made to present a beautiful appearance. He opened the school, and the first year the number of pupils was small, but soon there was not room enough for all the applicants. Finding that the education of young men and young women together, and their living in the same building, was not desirable, Mr. Cocke advised the discontinuance of one class; and as there was no chartered school in Virginia for young ladies, he counseled the continuance of the school as an institute of high grade for that sex, and in 1852 the change took place. The session of 1852–53 of the newly organized school for girls alone opened with cheering prospects. Soon the rooms of the institution were filled, and so great was the success, and so marked the interest in female education throughout the South, that there speedily rose into being Hampton Female College, Richmond Female Institute, Albemarle Female Institute, Warrenton Female Institute, and Danville Female College, all under the patronage of the Baptists, and a like number started by other denominations. In the year 1855, Mr. John Hollins, of Lynchburg, Va., at the suggestion of his wife, a pious Baptist lady, proposed to the company that if they would relinquish their stock he would give as much as all their shares aggregated, and place the institution in the hands of a self-perpetuating board of trustees. The proposition was accepted, and the amount given by Mr. Hollins was $5000, which in a few years was supplemented by a public subscription amounting to $10,000, Mr. Cocke acting as agent during vacation, and giving his services gratuitously. After Mr. Hollins's death his widow continued her donations, the whole amount from the Hollins family being about $19,000. With this assistance, Prof. Cocke managed to remove all the old buildings of the institute, which at this time, under the new charter, assumed the name of "Hollins Institute," and as such had perpetual succession. Handsome buildings were erected adapted to the wants of a school for young ladies, and the institution placed upon a new and higher career of usefulness. The exercises were continued throughout the long and weary years of the war, with an overflowing patronage, being the only institution in the State that preserved its organization during that terrible period of conflict and blood. Subsequent to the war the Virginia patronage diminished in consequence of the universal financial distress, but this loss was more than repaired by patronage from other States. Prof. Cocke's accomplished wife and daughters have been most efficient co-laborers with him in giving success to all departments of the institute, and they are highly appreciated by the public. The course of instruction is thorough and complete, and its certificates and diplomas are eagerly sought for. There are in the institute seven schools,—1. The English Language and Literature; 2. Ancient Languages and Literature; 3. Modern Languages and Literature; 4. Mathematics; 5. Natural Science; 6. Mental and Moral Science; 7. History. These schools constitute the collegiate department, besides which there is a normal department and an ornamental department. The faculty embraces fourteen experienced instructors.

Hollis Family, The.—Vice is often hereditary, and benevolence frequently descends from father to son; it remained in the Hollis family for generations, and we trust that it flourishes among the descendants of such worthy forefathers to-day.

Thomas Hollis was for more than sixty years a member of the church in Pinner's Hall, London. He was a man of unbounded liberality to benevolent and religious enterprises. Like many other persons who give away great sums, he systematically subjected his personal expenditures to the most rigid economy, that he might make larger donations to cherished objects. He died in September, 1718.

His son Thomas was baptized in 1680, when he was twenty years of age, and in gifts to sustain and extend education and religion he was the most prominent man of his day. He was a sagacious and successful merchant of London, who traded and toiled to make money that his resources might assist every noble cause.

He sent over a library of valuable theological books to the Philadelphia Baptist Association, which for many years was exceedingly useful to our fathers in the ministry. "The Assembly's Annotations on the Scriptures," a commentary in two folio volumes, now in possession of the American Baptist Historical Society, is supposed to have been one of the works given to the first Baptist Association in America. It bears his name, evidently in his own handwriting, and the date 1721.

Thomas and his brother John gave the Baptist church of Boston, Mass., £135 for repairing their meeting-house. Thomas Hollis founded a professorship of Theology in Harvard University, with a salary of £80 per annum, and an "exhibition" of £10 each per annum to ten scholars of good character, four of whom should be Baptists, if there were such persons there, and £10 a year to the college treasurer for his trouble, and £10 more to supply accidental losses or to increase the number of students. According to the charter, at the time Mr. Hollis made these gifts to Harvard the ministers of Boston (Congregational) were part of the overseers of the college, and when Mr. Hollis proposed the Rev. Elisha Callender, pastor of the Baptist church of Boston, as a fit person to have a seat in the board of overseers, Mr. Callender was refused the position, evidently because he was a Baptist. Isaac Backus gives this statement without expressing any doubt of its correctness, and he names his authority.

Six years after his first donation he founded a professorship of Mathematics and Experimental Philosophy in Harvard, with a salary of £80 a year, and he gave an apparatus for the professor which cost about £150, and he sent books for the library. Until that time, no man, according to Isaac Backus, who examined the records, had been so liberal to Harvard as this eminent Baptist. Mr. Hollis died in 1731. Prof. Wigglesworth, in a discourse which he published on the death of Mr. Hollis, says, "By his frequent and ample benefactions, for the encouragement of theological as well as human knowledge among us, who are Christians of a *different denomination from himself*, he hath set such an example of generous, catholic, and Christian spirit as hath never before fallen within my observation, nor, as far as I now remember, within my reading." We had no college in America at this period, and like a true Baptist, Mr. Hollis showed himself the friend of light.

The donations of this family of Baptists continued to enrich Harvard for nearly a century, and exceeded £6000. If the money was properly invested, it must to-day be worth many times more than $30,000.

We know nothing of the way by which these funds for Baptist students have been appropriated; for the honor of old Harvard we trust that the requisite number of Baptist students have regularly received the £10 per annum which Mr. Hollis left them. But we fear if the godly Calvinist, Thomas Hollis, heard the divinity taught in Harvard now he would bitterly regret his well-meant generosity. In a letter to Elder Wheaton, of Swanzey, Thomas Hollis writes: "God, that hath shined into our hearts by his gospel, can lead your sleeping Sabbatarians from the Sinai covenant and the law of ceremonies into the light of the new covenant and the grace thereof. I pity to see professors drawing back to the law, and desire to remember that our standing is by grace."

Hollis, Rev. J. A., was a native of South Carolina, but of English parentage. He was born in 1824. He graduated at Georgetown College, and subsequently entered the ministry in Mississippi. He removed to Missouri in 1844, and resided in that State till the time of his death, in 1870. He was pastor of several churches, and became president of Stephen Female College, at Columbia, in 1865, and held the office till his decease. He was a man of learning and ability, of eminent piety and noble characteristics, possessing a rare talent for the instruction of the young. He ended a laborious and useful life without a stain upon his memory. The institution, the church, and the community felt his loss deeply. His name will long live in the hearts of thousands.

Holman, Deacon James Sanders, a prominent and influential Baptist, died in Polk Co., Oregon, Jan. 14, 1880. He was born in Tennessee, Nov. 28, 1813; he moved to Oregon in 1847. He was baptized at Turnedge, Mo., at sixteen, and was for many years a deacon of that church. He was the first president of the Oregon Baptist Education Society, and a charter-member of McMinnville College. He was sheriff of Polk County several terms, and served two years in the Oregon Legislature. He carried his religion into public life, was honored by all, and spoken of by men as "the peace-maker." He was one of the first to plant the Baptist banner on the Pacific coast, and was faithful to God and his country until death called him to his rest.

Holman, Judge Jesse L., was born in Mercer Co., Ky., Oct. 22, 1783. He learned his letters while very young, and in his childhood was a daily reader of the Bible. He recollected a sermon that he heard when he was only four years old. He joined the Clear Creek Baptist church in his seventeenth year. After completing his studies he was admitted to the bar in New Castle, and afterwards practised in Frankfort. He, like his father, was an emancipationist, and he decided to remove north across the Ohio, and accordingly, in 1811, he passed over the river, and settled on a romantic bluff that he called Verdestan, and this was his home for the remainder of his life. When he removed to Verdestan the whole country was a wilderness, and Indians were roaming everywhere. At the time of his removal to Indiana he received from Gov. Harrison commissions for district attorney of the State for the counties of Dearborn and Jefferson. In 1814 he was elected a member of the house of representatives of the Territorial Legislature, and was chosen president by a unanimous vote. Near the close of the same year he was appointed the presiding judge of the district in which he lived, and in 1816, under the State government, he was appointed presiding judge in the second and third districts, and in the same year was chosen one of the electors of the President and Vice-President of the United States. In December, 1816, he was appointed judge of the Supreme Court of the State, which office he filled with great acceptance for fourteen years. In 1831 he was a candidate for the United States Senate, and was defeated by one vote. In 1835 he received the appointment of judge of the United States district for Indiana, which office he filled with singular ability till his death. He was a constituent member of the Laughery church. He also aided in gathering the Aurora church, and was a liberal giver to all worthy causes. In 1834 he was ordained, and thus entered upon a work that his soul longed to engage in. So unsullied was his public as well as his private life that men were always glad to hear him preach. While traveling the judicial circuit it was no unusual thing for him to address his fellow-citizens on Bible operations, missions, Sabbath-schools, general education, and temperance. So consistent and earnest was his life that there seemed no incongruity, but rather a singular harmony in his two offices of judge and minister. He was a leader in the organization of a Sabbath-school association in his own county. He took particular interest in the distribution of religious books and tracts. He was for many years vice-president of the American Sunday-School Union, and was president of the Western Baptist Publication and Sunday-School Society.

Mr. Holman was a warm and consistent friend of missions. Indeed, it may be said that in that time, when the gifts to missions were small in Indiana, a circuit of churches, of which Aurora may be said to be the centre, was the headquarters for missions. During the agency both of Dr. Bennett and Dr. Stevens, this portion of the State was always represented in donations. The Holmans, the Ferrises, the Hinckleys, the Dows, and others never refused or neglected to give. Judge Holman was for five years president of the Indiana State Convention. He was also from the first a member of the Indiana Baptist Education Society, and during several years was president of the board of trustees. His constitution was naturally feeble, and an attack of pleurisy caused his death, March 28, 1842. He knew that he must die, and expressed perfect confidence in the pardon and love and power of the Master.

Holman, Rev. John W., M.D., was born in Canaan, Me., in 1805; converted in 1818; studied at Waterville; ordained in 1824 in the Christian denomination; preached in Eastern Maine, New Brunswick, Philadelphia, and Boston; in latter city joined the Free-Will Baptists, and preached fifteen years; united with the regular Baptists at Mystic River, Conn.; settled with First Baptist church in Norwich, Conn., and with various churches in New York and Maine, with Franklin church, Mass., and finally with Third Baptist church in North Stonington, Conn.; in forty-nine years preached over 5000 sermons and organized 11 churches; was withal a poet, a painter, and a physician; a man of rare talents and great labor; left some interesting poetical and exegetical papers; while pastor in North Stonington was prostrated by sickness, and died May 16, 1873, aged sixty-eight years. All his four sons are Baptist ministers.

Holman, Russell, D.D., was born in Warwick, Mass., Aug. 14, 1812. The instruction and integrity of his parents gave him those virtues which made him a pure, conscientious man in after-life. He graduated at Brown University. He removed to Kentucky in 1839, and became pastor of two churches in Green County. Weak in body, he served there till 1842. He was ordained July 29, 1840. He performed missionary work in addition to his pastoral labor in these two churches.

In 1842 he went to New Orleans, and finding no Baptist church there, with great zeal, and against much opposition, he established what is now called the Coliseum Baptist church of New Orleans. In 1845 he was elected secretary of the Home Mission department of the Southern Baptist Convention. His skill and energy made the board efficient in home mission work. In 1851 he retired from this office from ill health, and left the work in the height of its prosperity. He became pastor till 1856, and was re-elected to the secretaryship, and held the office till 1862. Ill health caused him again to resign. During the war he tenderly ministered to the sick and wounded, and preached the gospel to them. Afterwards he was sent to collect the scattered flock of the Coliseum church in New Orleans. He succeeded in re-establishing the church six months after beginning his efforts. In 1867 he went to Illinois, and labored there and in Kentucky and Missouri till 1876, when a severe stroke of paralysis put an end to his active toils. His zeal and heart kept warm for the cause, and he patiently submitted to his lot. Says Dr. Wm. H. McIntosh, " As a preacher Dr. Holman was instructive, sometimes eloquent. He accepted the doctrines of grace, and enforced them upon the consciences of his hearers. His life was in constant conformity to the rule and spirit of the gospel. His heart was tender to all. In his family he was loving and true." His last days were spent in Miami and Marshall, Mo. On Dec. 2, 1879, he went to his eternal rest after a few hours of illness.

Holman, Judge William S., son of Hon. J. L. Holman, was born in Verdestan (now Aurora), Ind., Sept. 6, 1822. He had the advantages of the common schools and a partial course at Franklin College. Soon after he left college he was elected to the State Legislature. He was a member of the constitutional convention in 1850. He was elected judge of the Common Pleas, and served from 1852 to 1856. He was elected to the Thirty-sixth Congress, and made chairman of Revolutionary Claims. He was re-elected to the Thirty-seventh and Thirty-eighth, and served with marked ability. His untiring care for the expenses of the government has given him among the people the *sobriquet* " watch-dog of the treasury." He was elected again to the Fortieth Congress. He is a member of the Aurora Baptist church. He occupies the home of his father,—a beautiful spot on one of the hills on the Ohio River. No man has been so uniformly popular in his district as Mr. Holman.

Holme, Deacon George W., was a constituent member of the Baptist church at Holmesburg, and for thirty years one of its deacons. After a life of great usefulness, he died July 9, 1864, in his seventy-sixth year, in the house in which he was born.

Holme, Judge John, was one of the early settlers in Pennsylvania. He is supposed to have been the first Baptist, of any prominence at least, in the colony. Mr. Holme appears in the affairs of the colony in 1685–86. Whether he arrived in the country at this time, or earlier, is uncertain.

Mr. Holme is said to have been a native of Somersetshire, England, on what authority it is not known. He does not seem to have been a relative of Thomas Holme, the surveyor-general, as

Thomas Holme, in one of his letters, addresses him as "namesake" merely. John Holme brought with him to this country four sons,—John, Samuel, Ebenezer, and Benjamin. He came hither by way of the Barbadoes, where he resided some time, and was engaged in sugar-planting. That Mr. Holme was a man of wealth and social standing appears from many circumstances. It was he who gave one-half of the lot on which the First Baptist meeting-house was erected, on Second Street near Arch Street. His name appears with that of Gov. Markham, and two or three men of prominence in the colony, to a petition to the council to put the colony in a state of defense against the hostile Indians, who, at the instigation of the French, were threatening it during the French and English war. His name is also found next to that of the mayor of the city as signer of a petition relative to "the cove at Blue Anchor,—that it should be laid out for a convenient harbor, to secure shipping against ice or other danger of the winter, and that no person for private gains or interests may incommode the public utility of a whole city."

John Holme was appointed justice in the County Court in 1690; and he represented the city of Philadelphia in the Assembly of 1692.

He married as his second wife, Mary, the widow of Nicholas More, the first chief justice of the colony, and president of the "Free Society of Traders of Pennsylvania." Chief-Justice More was a man of great legal acquirements and general learning. The closest friendship existed between him and John Holme. At the death of Judge More, Mr. Holme was made the executor of his estate and the guardian of his children. There is reason to believe that they had been acquainted before they came to this country, and if so, it would seem that they both came from Bristol.

That John Holme was himself a man of more than ordinary culture appears from his library, which for an emigrant at that time was certainly remarkably large and well selected. It must have contained several hundred volumes. In his will John Holme bequeaths to his eldest son, John, several large folios,—Wilson's "Christian Dictionary," Haak's "Dutch Annotations," and Newman's "Concordance." Besides these, there are still in possession of his descendants many books of great value that he owned, among which are Baxter's "Theology," Bunyan's works, a Baptist Confession of Faith (London, 1652), and the writings of many stalwart old Baptist worthies, such as "The Pulpit Guard Routed, by Thomas Collier, London, 1652;" "The Foundations of the Font Discovered, by Henry Haggar, London, 1653;" "The Storming of Antichrist in his Strongest Garrisons, Compulsion of Conscience and Infant Baptism, by Ch. Blackwood. Printed Anno 1644. *Being one* of those years wherein Antichrist threatened the storming of the churches;" "An Appeal for the Use of the Gospel Ordinances, by Henry Lawrence, Esq.," and the more generally known works of Hanserd Knollys and Benjamin Keath. Together with these are some controversial works of a more general character, such as "The Three Conformities, or the Harmony and Agreement of the Romish Church with Gentileism, Judaism, and the Ancient Heresies, by Francis De Croy G. Arth, London, 1620;" "A Large Examination taken at Lambeth, according to His Maiesties direction, taken point by point of M. George Blakwell, made Archbishop of England by Pope Clement 8, &c. Imprinted at London by Robert Barker, Printer to the Kings Most Excellent Maiestie, 1607;" "Triplicinodo, triplix cuneus, or an Apologie for the Oath of Allegiance, &c. Imprinted at London by Robert Barker, Printer to the Kings Most Excellent Maiestie, 1609." This book is supposed to have been written by King James himself. Among the general philosophical works in Mr. Holme's library are Bacon's "Essays," and among the devotional are works of Thomas Brooks, Thomas Vincent, and Thos. Dookitol, and others. But what is still more remarkable is that a copy of Milton's "Paradise Lost" is found among the books that belonged to him. Unfortunately the title-page of this book is gone, but it is undoubtedly among the earliest editions of the poems.

If the character of John Holme may be judged of from his books, he was a man of very much more than ordinary culture, for in the library of very few emigrants, in the seventeenth century certainly, were found the works of Lord Bacon, Baxter, Bunyan, and Milton. The writings of the last two mentioned were at that time scarcely known over half of England. No Macaulay had yet appeared to set forth their merits. We have from the pen of John Holme himself, in verse, a manuscript of some 20 pages (published in 1848, in the Bulletin of the Historical Society of Pennsylvania, vol. i. No. 13), entitled "True Relation of the Flourishing State of Pennsylvania."* This is probably the first metrical composition written in the State, and though worth little as poetry, it is valuable historically, as one of the earliest and most extended and accurate accounts of the condition of the colony; and as in it he avows himself a Baptist, it is a creditable testimony of an impartial witness to the general good government of the Quakers, and shows great foresight of the natural resources and coming greatness of the State of Pennsylvania.

But the incident which has given most interest

---

* The original manuscript of this work is lost. It was loaned by the family at Holmesburg to a gentleman for exhibition to the Pennsylvania Historical Society, and has never been returned.

and historic importance to John Holme is that he was one of the judges that presided at the trials of George Keith, William Bradford, and others, which may be considered the *causes cèlebre* of the administration of William Penn, and so serious in their consequences to Penn in England and here, as to occasion for a time the loss of the governorship to the proprietary. Of the eight judges that sat upon the bench at these trials, six were Quakers, Lacey Cock, a Lutheran, and John Holme, a Baptist. George Keith, who was a man of great ability, and previous standing and influence among the Quakers, was charged with defaming the character of Thomas Lloyd, the president of the council, in phrases, such as calling him an "impudent rascal," and saying "that his memory would stink," etc., of tending to encourage sedition and breach of the peace by his comments on the arrest of Babbit, a pirate, and also of aiming a blow at the proprietary's government. Judge Holme dissented from the majority of the bench on these charges, and boldly expressed his views, and was tacitly sustained in them by Judge Cock. Mr. Holme maintained that the whole affair was essentially a religious dispute, pertaining to matters of doctrine and practice among the Quakers, and was not fit to be adjudicated by a civil tribunal; that the arraignment was in effect a religious persecution, and without justification in a colony that proclaimed religious liberty. He especially maintained that the exceptions of Keith to the jury, as prejudiced and not impartial, ought to be admitted. But in this also he was overruled by the majority of the bench. In the trial of William Bradford he was again a dissentient. Mr. Bradford was the first printer in the colony, and was arraigned for unlawfully printing the appeals and attacks of George Keith upon the Quakers. And a tailor was also put on trial for posting one of Mr. Keith's protests in his shop. In all these matters Judge Holme persistently dissented from the majority of the bench, and it is said actually resigned his office rather than seem to be made a party in any degree to what he regarded a case of religious persecution, and of the infringement of the liberty of the press.

It is flattering to our denominational pride, that if you meet a Baptist you will find a friend both of religious liberty and the freedom of the press. It is not too much to say that in the person of Judge Holme, who stands as both the pioneer and the representative of the Baptists in this country, south of Rhode Island, is found a man of the broadest views, of a far-sighted state policy, of courage and patriotism and piety, a champion of religious liberty, even against the encroachments of the Quakers themselves, and the first fearless advocate of the freedom of the press, in his defense of William Bradford, the first printer of the colony.

Judge Holme removed in the latter part of his life to Salem, N. J., where he was again made a judge, which office he retained to the time of his death, in 1703. He was one of the constituent members of the Baptist church in Salem, and often exercised his gifts in religious meetings, but was at no time a minister. Many of the descendants of Benjamin Holme, his youngest son, still reside at Salem and in the vicinity.

His eldest son, John Holme, settled at Pennypack Mill, and his lineal descendants live in the very same town to this day. Every one, in line, having adhered strictly to the religious faith practised by their great Baptist progenitor.

Holme, John Stanford, D.D., was born in Holmesburg, now a part of the city of Philadelphia, March 4, 1822. His ancestors came to America from England in 1683, and purchased lands from William Penn. John Holme was a magistrate under Penn, but resigned by reason of what he deemed the intolerance of his Quaker associates. An ancestor named Rev. Abel Morgan was one of the earlier writers in defense of Baptist doctrines in the colonies, as appears by a volume which was published by Benjamin Franklin in 1747.

He prepared for college at New Hampton, N. H. He studied law in Philadelphia, but desiring to enter the ministry he graduated at Madison University in 1850, and was first settled over the Baptist church in Watertown, N. Y. Four years afterwards he accepted a call to the Pierpont Street Baptist church, Brooklyn, one of the most important churches in the denomination. He labored there ten years with marked success. He then devoted two years to literary pursuits. Afterwards he organized the Trinity Baptist church, corner of Third Avenue and Fifty-second Street.

Of his ancestors above mentioned, John Holme was the first Baptist of Philadelphia. Abel Morgan was from Wales, a talented minister, highly educated. He was the author of the first Welsh concordance ever printed.

Dr. Holme has a large library of choice and rare books, and is an enthusiastic student of history and of sacred learning.

While pastor of Pierpont Street, he adapted the Plymouth collection of hymns for the use of Baptist churches, which had a wide circulation. He also compiled a work entitled "Light at Evening Time," published by the Harpers. It is a collection of rare spiritual gems for the comfort of aged Christians. So great is the demand for it that already eight editions of it have been printed. He has recently organized the River-Side Baptist church, on the corner of Eighty-sixth Street and the Boulevard, in New York, of which he is pastor, and it gives promise of being a strong church.

Holmes, Rev. Obadiah, was born at Preston,

Lancashire, England, about 1606, and came to this country, as is supposed, about 1639. His religious connections were with the Congregationalists. At first, in Salem, Mass., from which he removed to Rehoboth, where for eleven years more he continued in the church of his early choice. He there became a Baptist, and united with the Baptist church in Newport, R. I. In the month of July, 1651, in company with Dr. John Clarke and Mr. Crandall, he made a visit to William Witter, a Baptist, who resided at Lynn, Mass., about twelve miles from Boston. The day after their arrival being the Sabbath, they arranged to have a religious service at the house of their host. In the midst of the discourse which Dr. Clarke was preaching two constables presented to him the following warrant: "By virtue hereof, you are required to go to the house of William Witter, and to search from house to house for certain erroneous persons, being strangers, and them to apprehend, and in safe custody to keep, and to-morrow morning at eight o'clock to bring before me. Robert Bridges." The three "erroneous persons, being strangers," were at once arrested and carried, first to "the ale-house or ordinary," and then forced to attend the meeting of the day. At the close of the meeting they were carried back to the "ordinary." The next morning they were taken before Mr. Bridges, who made out their *mittimus*, and sent them to prison at Boston. Having remained a fortnight there, they were brought before the Court of Assistants for trial, which sentenced Dr. Clarke to pay a fine of twenty pounds, Mr. Holmes thirty pounds, and Mr. Crandall five pounds, and in default of payment they were to be publicly whipped. Unknown to Mr. Clarke some one paid his fine, and Mr. Crandall was released on promise that he would appear at the next court. Mr. Holmes was kept in prison until September, when, his fine not having been paid, he was brought out and publicly whipped. Mr. Holmes says, "As the strokes fell upon me I had such a spiritual manifestation of God's presence as the like thereof I never had nor felt, nor can with fleshly tongue express; and the outward pain was so removed from me that indeed I am not able to declare it to you; it was so easy to me that I could well bear it, yea, and in a manner felt it not, although it was grievous, as the spectators said, the man striking with all his strength (yea, spitting in his hand three times, as many affirmed) with a three-corded whip, giving me therewith thirty strokes."—(Backus, i. 94. Newton.) Such was the charity of New England Congregationalists of that day. Gov. Joseph Jenks has left on record the following: "Mr. Holmes was whipped thirty stripes, and in such an unmerciful manner that in many days, if not some weeks, he could take no rest, but as he lay upon his knees and

elbows, not being able to suffer any part of his body to touch the bed whereon he lay."

Mr. Holmes soon after removed to Newport. In 1652 he was ordained to preach the gospel, and took Dr. Clarke's place as pastor of the Baptist church in Newport. He died in 1682. He left eight children, one of whom, Obadiah, was a judge in New Jersey.

Holmes, Rev. O. A., was born in New Woodstock, Madison Co., N. Y., in 1825; joined the Baptist church in his native town when sixteen years of age. He was ordained pastor in La Fayette, O., when twenty-three. Five years after his ordination he came to Iowa, and has labored in the State as pastor for twenty-seven years,—at Maquoketa, Webster City, Marshalltown, and Tama City. While at Webster City, which was entirely a new field, he also organized a church at Boonsborough and one at Iowa Falls, supplying them until they became strong enough to secure pastors. His labors were extended through a wide range of country, and the results were marked and lasting. Mr. Holmes has given to the Baptist cause and to every good work in Iowa many years of efficient service. While faithful in his own field as pastor and preacher, he has contributed largely, by earnest labor, hearty co-operation, and wise counsel, to all the good results which have been accomplished by the Iowa Baptists in their general work.

Holmes, Willet, was born May 14, 1807, in

WILLET HOLMES.

Shelby Co., Ky.; was converted in 1847, baptized by H. L. Graves, and has been a deacon ever since;

was one of the three hundred colonists who, under Moses Austin's grant from Mexico, settled the province of Texas; was twice a member of the Congress of the republic of Texas, twice a magistrate, once a county commissioner, postmaster under the republic, and postmaster under Abraham Lincoln. His time, his talents, and his money have always been freely given to the church, the cause of missions, and as a trustee to Baylor University.

Home Mission Society, The American Baptist, and other Home Missions.

—In the early history of the Baptists in this country most of our pastors were home missionaries. It was a common custom for the settled shepherd of one flock to make a tour through several counties in his own colony or State, or through other colonies or States, preaching the gospel almost every night in barns, private houses, school-rooms, or public halls. Months were spent frequently in this apostolic occupation. And many churches were founded and hosts of souls converted by these gratuitous labors of our saintly fathers in the faith. All the original colonies were frequently traversed by this almost extinct order of heaven-blessed home missionaries. Churches and Associations often rendered assistance in this form of home mission service. And nowhere on earth in any period of Christian history has Jesus had nobler missionaries among their countrymen, or grander results, than those furnished by the Baptist pioneers of the maritime provinces of Canada and of the country now called the United States.

In the year 1800 the *Boston Female Society for Missionary Purposes* was formed. It had at first only fourteen members, and of these some were Baptists and some Congregationalists. In its first year it raised $150 for home missions. This is said to have been the first society established in this country of a purely missionary character. It should not be forgotten when we award honors to the benefactors of their race, that *women* formed the first distinctively missionary organization in America.

Two years later the *Massachusetts Domestic Missionary Society* was founded. Among its first officers were Dr. Thomas Baldwin, Dr. Daniel Sharp, and Heman Lincoln. Its field included Massachusetts, Maine, Western and Southern New York, Pennsylvania, Virginia, Missouri, Ohio, and Lower Canada. Among the numerous missionaries of this society were John M. Peck, James E. Welch, and Nathaniel Kendrick.

In 1807 the *Lake Missionary Society* was organized in Pompey, Onondaga Co., N. Y. Its proposed field was the region of country adjacent to the lakes. Ashbel Hosmer was its first president and Elisha Payne its secretary. Among its early missionaries were John Peck and Alfred Bennett,—men whose

names are still held in reverence for the divine power that attended their ministrations.

In 1822 the *Baptist Missionary Convention of the State of New York* was formed, and in 1825 the two New York organizations united, and in a few years the society had an income of $17,000, and missionaries in the Middle States, in some of the Western States, and in Canada.

The *American Baptist Home Mission Society* was formed in New York, April 27, 1832. Heman Lincoln was its first president, Jonathan Going its corresponding secretary, William R. Williams its recording secretary, and William Colgate its treasurer. Men mighty with God established one of the greatest agencies to spread the gospel that ever blessed any land. The Home Mission Society in 1880 had 285 missionaries and teachers, and, according to Dr. Morehouse, its secretary, an income of $213,821; and deducting $48,369.70 for loans repaid to the church edifice and trust funds, its remaining receipts from other sources were $165,452.11. Its missionaries during that year baptized 1160 persons, founded 67 churches, and organized 32 Sunday-schools. From its report in 1880 we learn that since its formation the society has commissioned 8301 missionaries and teachers, formed 2704 churches, and through its agents baptized 84,077 disciples. Many of the largest churches in the great cities of the West are the fruits of its wise efforts.

The church edifice fund, now amounting to $255,679, in 1880 was aiding by loans 213 churches in 34 States and Territories. The Home Mission Society in 1880 had eight institutions for the education of colored teachers and ministers. The Richmond Institute, located at Richmond, Va., has 5 instructors, 92 students, 61 of whom are candidates for the ministry, and a property valued in 1871 at $30,000 at least. Wayland Seminary, located at Washington, D. C., has 7 instructors, 92 students, 36 young men preparing for the ministry, and a property worth $40,000. The Benedict Institute, located at Columbia, S. C., has 6 instructors, 150 students, 50 of whom intend to preach the gospel, and a property valued at $43,700, with an endowment of $18,700. The Nashville Institute, of Nashville, Tenn., has 8 instructors, 231 students, 55 of whom are preparing for the ministry, and a property worth $80,000. Shaw University, of Raleigh, N. C., has 15 instructors, 277 students, 59 of whom intend to preach, and a property worth $125,000, with an endowment of $1000. The Atlanta Baptist Seminary, at Atlanta, Ga., has 4 instructors, 100 students, 60 of whom are candidates for the pulpit, and a property worth $12,000. Leland University, at New Orleans, has 5 instructors, 148 students, 41 of whom expect to enter the ministry, and a property worth $85,000, with an endowment of $10,000. The Natchez Seminary, of Natchez, Miss., has a property worth $15,000; 4 instructors and 120 students, 31 of whom are studying for the ministry. The Home Mission Society in these eight institutions has property worth $430,700, and endowments amounting to $38,700; 54 teachers labor in them, 1572 young men and women pursue their studies in them, of whom 393 are qualifying themselves to preach Jesus. In these colored colleges the society is working gloriously for the salvation and education of our African millions. In the records of organized missionary effort few societies can show such a blessed series of successes and so grand a list of instrumentalities.

But we have other home missionary organizations. The *American Baptist Publication Society* in 1880 had 35 colporteur and 28 Sunday-school missionaries, with an income for all benevolent purposes of $68,321. The *Home Mission Board of the Southern Baptist Convention* had 34 missionaries and an income of $20,624. The *Women's* and the *Women's American Baptist Home Mission Societies* had 21 missionaries. From the " Year-Book," and from direct communications with brethren in various States, after making allowance for the union between the Home Mission Society and State organizations in the West, and for a similar connection between the Home Mission Board of the Southern Baptist Convention and kindred institutions in the South, we learn that the number of men receiving aid from State organizations to assist them in preaching the gospel in the United States is at least 766, and that the income of these State societies is $150,190. Many Baptist Associations and individual churches support additional missionaries.

This would give us a grand total of 1169 missionaries and teachers (missionary teachers in colored seminaries in the South), sustained by national and State organizations at an annual expense of $413,619.

Dr. G. W. Anderson, of Philadelphia, in a carefully prepared pamphlet, states that during the last fifty years (down to 1876), " nearly six millions of dollars had been raised by the Baptists of the United States for home mission work." The five years that have elapsed since would add more than two millions to that amount. For this liberality, and for the thousands of churches that have sprung from it, and from God's blessing upon it, millions of souls will praise Christ throughout all eternity. See articles on SOUTHERN BAPTIST CONVENTION, AMERICAN BAPTIST PUBLICATION SOCIETY, and the various State Conventions and General Associations.

Home Mission Societies, The Women's.— The organization and success of the Women's Baptist Missionary Societies for heathen lands drew the attention of Baptist ladies to the advantages to be secured by a similar agency for the necessities of the home field. The appeals of the devoted Miss J. P. Moore, in New Orleans, for help in prosecuting her mission among the colored people, and similar calls from other sections, together with the very able advocacy of the evangelization of the heathen Indians by Major G. W. Ingalls, led to the formation of the " Women's Baptist Home Mission Society," which took place Feb. 1, 1877. Subsequently the Women's American Baptist Home Mission Society was organized in Boston.

At first the Chicago Society adopted a constitution which placed it in close relations with the great Home Mission Society of the Northern Baptists, but six months later the constitution was changed and the institution became independent, with the avowed purpose of being a vigorous ally to the old society in its vast field, and of carrying on, according to its ability, the general home mission work.

The distinctive aim of the society is to perform women's work, through its missionaries, for women and children in the degraded homes of our country, especially among the colored people, the Indians, and the teeming foreign population of the West. " The (missionary) women visit from house to house, reading the Bible and familiarly teaching its truths to all who will listen." " They organize Sunday-schools, training the teachers for their work in teachers' meetings and Bible readings." They give lessons in cleanliness, industry, temperance, and purity.

At a meeting held in New York, Jan. 14, 1880, to secure union in labors between the Chicago and the Boston societies, it was

" *Resolved*, That the two societies should retain their separate existence; that the society located at Boston shall have New England for its territory, and that each society shall prosecute the work embraced in its constitution; that the missionaries appointed by the society located at Boston shall be commissioned by the society at Chicago and their salaries paid through its treasury; and that all missionary supplies shall be reported to the society at Chicago."

It was also resolved among other things that " Each society shall hold its own annual meeting, and that a yearly anniversary of the two societies shall be held at such time and place as may be agreed upon by their respective boards." These arrangements have been fully carried out, and harmony and success have marked the combined efforts of the two societies.

The Woman's Baptist Home Mission Society of Michigan and the Woman's State Board of Minnesota are earnestly toiling in the same glorious service.

The first home missionary society in the United

States was formed in Boston in 1800 by ladies, and it is a proper cause for thanksgiving that they have resumed the work once more, determined not to relinquish it while there is an unconverted woman or child within the broad limits of our mighty republic.

The receipts of the societies at Boston and Chicago in 1880 were $9098.66 in cash, and $2601.81 in goods and donations to missionaries and pastors on the frontier.

Twenty-one missionaries have labored under the auspices of the two societies during 1880.

Hooper, Wm., D.D., LL.D., was the ripest scholar North Carolina has yet produced. He was

WM. HOOPER, D.D., LL.D.

a grandson of Wm. Hooper who signed the Declaration of Independence for North Carolina, and was born near Wilmington in 1792; graduated at Chapel Hill about 1812, read theology at Princeton, N. J., and was elected Professor of Ancient Languages at the University of North Carolina at Chapel Hill in 1816. In 1818 he entered the ministry of the Episcopal Church, and was for two years rector of St. John's church in Fayetteville, when, because of a change of views on baptism, he resigned his position as pastor, and again became connected with the university as Professor of Rhetoric. In 1829 he was transferred to his old chair of Ancient Languages. He was baptized in 1831 by Rev. P. W. Dowd into the fellowship of Mount Carmel church, Orange Co. In 1838 he removed to South Carolina, and taught theology for two years in Furman Institute, when he became for six years Pro-

fessor of Ancient Languages in South Carolina College, at Columbia, but was recalled to North Carolina to become the president of Wake Forest College in 1846. The financial embarrassments of the college discouraged him, and he did not remain in this position long. In 1852 he settled as pastor in Newbern; in 1855 became president of Chowan Female Institute; retired from this position in 1862; he taught school in Fayetteville for several years, and in 1867 became co-principal with his son-in-law, Prof. De B. Hooper, at Wilson, N. C.

A very important event in the history of Dr. Hooper was the killing of a young lady, his cousin, by the accidental discharge of a neglected gun, while playing with the children in his uncle's family. His whole life seemed from this circumstance to have been tinged with melancholy. The year before he died he addressed a letter to Prof. Hooper, while living in the same house with him, expressing the sadness that still weighed down his spirits as he looked into the years that were passed. He died at Chapel Hill, where so much of his life had been spent, Aug. 19, 1876, and if he had lived eleven days more would have been eighty-four. His remains were fittingly laid by the side of Dr. Joseph Caldwell, the founder of the college, in the campus of the State University at Chapel Hill.

It may well be questioned whether any man has lived in the South, or for that matter in America, who wrote better English than Dr. Hooper, and it is greatly to be regretted he died without issuing from the press a few volumes of his sermons or some other work by which future generations might have been certified of the lowly piety, exquisite taste, sparkling wit, and rich stores of learning of this great and good man.

Hooten, Rev. Enoch M., was born in Henry Co., Ga., June 30, 1837. At the age of fourteen he joined the Presbyterians, but in 1865 changed his religious views and united with the Baptists. On the 7th of November, 1866, he was ordained, and since then has served various Baptist churches in Middle Georgia, baptizing about 40 persons each year. For some years he taught school, and for several sessions was clerk of the Flint River Association. Mr. Hooten is a good pastor, a very clear and forcible preacher, and a graceful speaker. He enjoys the full confidence and 'esteem of all who know him.

Hopkins, Rev. Charles J., was the child of Quaker parents. He was born in Philadelphia, Pa., April 2, 1800. Converted in early life, he was baptized by Rev. Dr. Holcombe, and received into the First church, Philadelphia, in October, 1818. He was ordained at the First church, Camden. N. J., in 1824. From May, 1829, to April, 1835, he was pastor of the church at Salem, N. J. Then for five years he served the church at Bridgeton.

In the fall of 1843 he took the pastorate of Bethesda church, New York City. In October, 1859, he became pastor of the Salem church, which was his last charge. He died in Salem, July 14, 1863. Mr. Hopkins was a good, faithful, earnest minister of the gospel. His beaming countenance, ready wit, musical voice, and enthusiastic manner attracted attention. He was an ardent temperance man, and was in great demand as a speaker upon that subject.

Hopper, A. M., D.D., was born at Long Branch, N. J., Jan. 12, 1822; received his university education at Madison; ordained pastor of Academy Street church, New Haven, Conn., in the autumn of 1850; took charge of the First church of Charlestown, Mass., in 1855. He was also pastor in Auburn, N. Y., in Bridgeport, Conn., and in Scranton, Pa. In 1870 Madison University conferred upon him the degree of Doctor of Divinity. In 1872, Dr. Hopper had baptized more than 500 candidates. He is a genial, godly, and able minister of the Saviour.

Hopps, Herman K., one of the most interesting and promising of the early graduates from the University of Chicago, was drowned at Newport Beach, R. I., Aug. 1, 1873, while bathing. He was converted while a boy, and during his student course was remarkable not only for scholarly diligence and success, but also for his genial Christian spirit. He graduated in the class of 1870, and immediately entered the Rochester Theological Seminary. Spending a little time, however, with the church in Batavia, Ill., his preaching awakened so much interest that he found it his duty to remain for a year, in which time 70 were added to the church. He then entered the middle class at Newton. At the time of his death he was preaching for the church at Lynn, Mass., where a promising work was already in progress. His remains were taken to Lamoille, Ill., where his home had been, and where his parents still reside.

Hornady, Rev. Henry Carr, of Atlanta, Ga., is one of the most distinguished and influential ministers of the State. Born Feb. 22, 1822, in Jones County, he has spent all his life and exerted all his energies within his native State. He enjoyed excellent academical advantages and availed himself of them fully, until his twentieth year. Converted in 1843 and ordained in 1848, he became pastor of the Americus church, where he remained eight years. Since that time he has occupied various responsible positions in the denomination, as agent for Mercer University, editor of the *Cherokee Baptist*, and the pastor of various churches. He is now pastor of the Third Baptist church, in Atlanta. He is a Baptist in the strictest sense of the term, and consequently is a devoted Christian; he is a good pastor, and an earnest, tender, pathetic, and faithful preacher.

Hornberger, Rev. Lewis P., was born in the city of Philadelphia, Pa., Oct. 25, 1841. He was converted at the age of fifteen, and baptized one year after into the fellowship of the Olivet Baptist

REV. LEWIS P. HORNBERGER.

church, Philadelphia, by Rev. N. B. Baldwin, Oct. 4, 1857. On the 14th of October, 1858, he entered Madison University as a student for the gospel ministry, and graduated Aug. 2, 1865. On the 1st of July preceding he accepted the unanimous call of the Spring Garden Baptist church, Philadelphia. He entered upon the duties of his first charge Aug. 20, 1865.

The church had been for some time without a pastor. It had a membership of 279 and a debt of $7000. The young pastor entered with ardent zeal and vigorous faith upon his work. The church rallied nobly under the new leadership, and soon gave evidence of rapid and vigorous growth.

Mr. Hornberger remained with the Spring Garden church six years and nine months. During this period it was blessed with uninterrupted harmony and prosperity. The house was thoroughly repaired, the debt was paid, and 629 persons added to the membership, 415 of whom were baptized, 190 came by letter, 16 by experience, and 8 by restoration. Mr. Hornberger had a very pleasant trip to Europe during the summer of 1870. The membership and congregation having increased beyond the capacity of the house of worship, and the dimensions of the lot rendering an enlargement of it impossible, the project of a removal was seriously considered, but was afterwards dismissed as impracticable. Mr. Hornberger was finally induced, at the solicitation of many members of his church, as well as of a number of influential members of other churches, to undertake the establishment of a new church in the northwestern part of the city. Accordingly, in the early part of the year 1872, he retired from the pastorate of the Spring Garden church, and, with a constituency of 257 persons, 186 of whom were dismissed from the Spring Garden church for the purpose, he organized, March 28, 1872, the Gethsemane Baptist church. A lot was immediately secured at the northwest corner of Eighteenth and Columbia Avenue, and the work of building begun. It progressed rapidly, and the house was completed and dedicated April 30, 1874. The entire cost of the house and lot, with the furniture, was $100,000. The edifice is of brown-stone, substantially built, and handsomely furnished. It has a lecture-room which will comfortably seat 400 persons, and an audience-room seating about 1000. At the present date, 1880, the membership is 652, and the usual congregations are among the largest in the city. The Bible-school numbers 988, with an average attendance of 700.

As a preacher, Mr. Hornberger is eminently earnest and practical, sound in doctrine, clear in his statements of gospel truths, and uncompromising in their advocacy. He is a fluent, ready, and graceful speaker, equally good in extemporizing or reading.

As a pastor, he has unusual influence and power. Easily accessible and courteous, he is loved and respected by his people. He possesses a warm and sympathizing heart, and is ever a most welcome visitor in the homes of the sick and the sorrowing. His guiding hand is manifest in all the important movements of the church, and the almost unexampled success that has marked his career as a pastor is perhaps owing to a happy combination of qualities, shared in part by all, but not often so symmetrically united in one.

His church edifice is out of debt. Mr. Hornberger is one of the most useful ministers that ever labored in Philadelphia, and his talents and piety deserve the rich harvests he has garnered.

Horner, Rev. T. J., was born in Orange Co., N. C., Nov. 23, 1823 ; was baptized by Rev. Joseph King in 1855 ; was educated at the famous Bingham Academy, of Hillsborough ; ordained at Mount Zion church, Granville Co., Rev. Joseph King and his son, Rev. Thomas King, forming the Presbytery, and has been pastor of this church for eighteen years. Mr. Horner has served other churches in Granville and Person Counties, and has taught for thirty-five years. He is now the senior principal of a flourishing academy at Henderson, N. C.

Horton, Hon. Albert C., was born about 1800, in Georgia ; removed to Green Co., Ala. ; engaged in farming and became wealthy ; served in the Senate of Alabama ; removing to Texas in 1835 ; commanded a company of cavalry, the advance-guard of Col. Fannin, whose force was savagely massacred at Goliad ; narrowly escaping the same fate, his command being cut off from the main force. He was a member of the first Congress of the republic, with Houston, Rusk, Grimes, and Lester. He was a member of the convention which formed the constitution of Texas as a State, and was elected the first lieutenant-governor, and during the absence of Gov. J. Pinckney Henderson, who commanded the Texas troops during the war between the United States and Mexico, in 1846, he filled the chair of governor for several months with signal honor. The latter part of his life was spent in managing his large estate in Wharton and Matagorda Counties, dispensing a liberal hospitality to all classes, taking a deep interest in the religious welfare of his numerous slaves. Joining the Baptist church in his early days, he was to the end of his life a consistent, zealous, liberal, and active Christian. As a member of the body that formed the Texas Baptist State Convention, and as a trustee of Baylor University, his counsels and services will live as a heritage of blessings to education, and to the denomination of which he was so honored a member. He died in 1865.

Hoskinson, Thomas J., was born at Waynesburg, Greene Co., Pa., May 14, 1821 ; was bap-

THOMAS J. HOSKINSON.

tized in 1855, by Rev. Thomas R. Taylor, into the fellowship of the Sandusky Street church, Alleghany City, Pa. In 1871 he removed to Philadelphia, where he still remains an esteemed member of the Memorial church.

In early life he engaged in mercantile pursuits, and subsequently associated himself with others in the manufacture of iron. His enterprise and integrity enabled him to prosper abundantly, and others reaped the advantage of his benefactions. He has been long and prominently identified with the educational and missionary work of the denomination, and is widely known as a wise counselor and careful manager. As a trustee of the university at Lewisburg, and president of the Pennsylvania Baptist Education Society, he has especially aimed to advance and exalt the education of young men for the gospel ministry. Mr. Hoskinson is one of the leading Baptists of Pennsylvania; and he is known and honored by his brethren throughout the State.

Hotchkiss, V. R., D.D., was born June 5, 1815, in Spafford, Onondaga Co., N. Y.; was educated in Madison University; has been pastor in Poultney, Vt., in Rochester, N. Y., in Fall River, Mass., in Buffalo, N. Y., from 1849 to 1854, and from 1865 to the present time, 1880. He was a professor in Rochester Theological Seminary from 1854 to 1865. Dr. Hotchkiss is one of the strongest men in our denomination in the Empire State. Madison gave him his doctorate of divinity.

Hough, Rev. Silas, M.D., was born in Bucks Co., Pa., Feb. 8, 1766. He was thirty years of age before he exercised saving faith in the blessed Redeemer. He was baptized into the fellowship of the Montgomery church, in his native county, May 8, 1796. Dr. Hough was possessed of more than ordinary gifts for the ministry, and in June, 1804, he was ordained as pastor of the Montgomery church, which he served till December, 1821; eighteen months after his resignation, his spirit entered the heavenly rest.

Dr. Hough left $1000 to the Philadelphia Association, the interest of which is to be appropriated forever to the support of the widows of Baptist ministers. He was the first man to start this fund. Dr. Hough had a strong faith, an undying zeal, and a blameless life.

Hougham, John S., LL.D., a native of Indiana, graduated in Wabash College in 1846. In July, 1848, he was elected Professor of Mathematics and Natural Philosophy in Franklin College. He was after a short time transferred to the chair of Chemistry and Related Sciences. He built up an excellent laboratory, and, in addition to his teaching, established and superintended the manufacture of chemical and philosophical apparatus. He was also of great service to the institution by the aid he gave in its financial management. He is acknowledged to be a man of great practical ability.

He made some original investigations in respect to the influence of mercury upon the body. He resigned in 1862, and several months later accepted a professorship in the Kansas Agricultural College. He accepted a professorship in the Indiana Agricultural College, and was appointed to superintend the laying out of the grounds and the structure of the buildings. He served the institution several years, and finally resigned to care for his real estate in the West. His home is in La Fayette.

House, Rev. Horace Lee, one of the youngest pastors in the State, a native of Otselic, N. Y., where he was born in 1850, was graduated from Cornell University, New York, in 1874, and from the Theological Seminary in 1877; ordained June 27, 1877. Mr. House's first pastorate was with the Fifth Avenue Baptist church in Minneapolis, Minn., from June 1, 1877, to Feb. 1, 1880, at which time he was called to the pastorate of the Baptist church in Racine, where he now resides. He has a fine field of labor and one of the best churches in Wisconsin.

Houston, Mrs. Margaret Moffette, daughter of Temple and Nancy Lea, was born in Perry Co., Ala., April 11, 1819. She belonged to a family of marked individuality. Her brother, Hon. H. C. Lea, was a distinguished member of the Alabama State senate. Her education was mainly received from Prof. J. A. McLain, a well-educated Scotch Baptist. She possessed poetical talent, which she occasionally exhibited by contributing articles for the journals of the day, and her conversational powers rendered her society attractive. Her views of Christian truth and duty were in full accord with the gospel. She was married to Gen. Sam Houston, in April, 1840. During the ministry of Rev. Peter Crawford at Marion she was converted and baptized. She was always ready to contribute of her means to the promotion of the cause of Christ. Eight children survive her,—Sam Houston, Jr., Mrs. Nannie Morrow, Mrs. Mary Morrow, Mrs. Maggie Williams, Mrs. Antoinette P. Bringhurst, Andrew Jackson Houston, William Rogers Houston, and Temple Houston. She died at Independence, Texas, Dec. 3, 1869. The following lines indicate both her Christian spirit and poetical gift:

A MOTHER'S PRAYER.

WRITTEN WHILE UNCERTAIN AS TO THE FATE OF HER SON, LIEUT. SAM HOUSTON.

O Thou! 'neath whose omniscient eye
    The footsteps of the wanderer roam
Far from his own loved native sky,
    Far from the sacred ties of home.
A captive on some hostile shore,
    Perchance his young heart pineth now
To join the household band once more,
    That 'round the evening altar bow;
Or, 'mid the cannon's roar again
    And gleam of clashing steel, perchance

Upon the bloody battle-plain
Hath met the deadly foeman's lance.
I cannot tell: my dim eye now
His wanderings may not trace;
But, oh! 'tis sweet to feel and know,
Through every scene, in every place,
Thy glorious eye doth follow him.
On toilsome march, 'mid prison gloom,
On Southern soil, through Northern clime,
Or 'mid the cannon's dismal boom,
His life is safe beneath thy sight,
As though a mother's love could soothe
And for the weary head each night
With tender hand his pillow smooth.

Houston, Gov. Sam, was born near Lexington, Rockbridge Co., Va. ; with his mother, six broth-

GOVERNOR SAM HOUSTON.

ers, and three sisters he removed to Blount Co., Tenn., when about twelve years old; spent some time before his sixteenth year among the Cherokee Indians; entered the United States army in his nineteenth year; was under Gen. Andrew Jackson at the battle of Tohopeka, against the Creek Indians, serving as ensign, fighting heroically, and receiving two wounds from rifle-balls and one from a barbed arrow, from whose effects he never wholly recovered; was appointed a lieutenant, and stationed a while at Nashville and New Orleans; resigned when about twenty years of age; studied law at Nashville, Tenn., for about six months, under Hon. James Trimble; was licensed to practise, and in less than twelve months afterwards was elected district attorney of the Davidson circuit; settled first at Lebanon, and served as district attorney one year at Nashville; resigned, and devoted himself to the practice of law, until 1823,

when hardly thirty years of age, he was elected to Congress without opposition, and also, in 1825, almost by acclamation, and in 1827 was chosen governor by 12,000 majority resigned Jan. 1, 1829, three months after his first marriage, leaving his wife, because she declared that neither at that time nor at their marriage did he have her heart; went among the Cherokees, and remained three years, with varying incidents of great political moment, then removed to Texas; aided in forming its first constitution, April, 1833; engaged in vigorous efforts for the liberation of Texas, until as commander of the Texan army, at the battle of San Jacinto, April 21, 1836, he succeeded in securing the freedom of the republic. At the battle of San Jacinto he received another wound. President of the republic from 1836–38; member of the Texan Congress from 1839–41; President of the republic from January, 1841, to January, 1845; Senator from Texas, in the United States Senate, from 1845–57; governor of Texas from January, 1859, to March, 1861; died July, 1863, at Huntsville, Walker Co. Married to Miss Maggie Lea, April, 1840; lived scrupulously devoted to morality, and his wife's views of religious truth, until he was converted. The influence of his wife over his later life was ever cheerfully and gratefully acknowledged by him. Was baptized at Independence, Texas, November, 1855, by Rev. Rufus C. Burleson, D.D.; regularly attended upon Dr. Geo. W. Samson's ministrations during the whole of his senatorial career at Washington. He took an active share in prayer-meetings, at Associations and Conventions when present, and delivered numerous lectures during the latter part of his life in aid of temperance. As a soldier, lawyer, general, President, Senator, governor, orator, Christian, he was one of the remarkable men of the nineteenth century.

Hovey, Alvah, D.D., LL.D., was born in Greene, Chenango Co., N. Y., March 5, 1820. In the autumn of that year his parents returned to their native place, Thetford, Vt., where his childhood and youth were passed, the summers mostly on a farm and the winters in a district school. He prepared for college in Brandon, Vt., and was graduated from Dartmouth College in 1844. He had been already principal of an academy in Derby, Vt., two years, and was principal of the academy at New London, N. H., one year. He studied at the Newton Theological Institution three years, and after graduating preached one year in New Gloucester, Me. Returning to Newton in the autumn of 1849, he has been engaged as a teacher in the institution from that time to the present (with the exception of ten months spent in Europe). From 1849 to 1855 he was tutor in Hebrew; from 1853 to 1855, Professor of Church History; from 1855 to the present time, Professor of Theology and Christian Ethics; and for the last twelve years president of the institution. Dr. Hovey has contributed a large amount of matter to the *Christian Review*, the *Baptist Quarterly*, the *Bibliotheca Sacra*, the

ALVAH HOVEY, D.D., LL.D.

Examiner and Chronicle, the *Watchman*, the *Standard*, and other papers. He is the author of the following books: "A Memoir of the Life and Times of Rev. Isaac Backus, A.M.," 1859; "The State of the Impenitent Dead," 1859; "The Miracles of Christ as attested by the Evangelists," 1864; "The Scriptural Law of Divorce," 1866; "God with us; or the Person and State of Christ," 1872; "Religion and the State," 1876; "The Doctrine of the Higher Christian Life, compared with the Scriptures," 1877; "Manual of Theology," 1878. Dr. Hovey has published several unbound discussions, as "Close Communion," "State of Men after Death," "Semi-centennial Discourse at Newton," etc. Brown University conferred on him the degree of D.D., and Richmond College and Denison University that of LL.D. He has been a member of the Executive Committee of the American Baptist Missionary Union for many years.

Howard, Rev. Amasa, son of Amasa Howard, was born in Woodstock, Conn., Sept. 9, 1832; converted in his twelfth year, at Slatersville, R. I.: baptized in North Uxbridge, Mass., in May, 1845: began to study with his brother, Rev. Johnson Howard, pastor of Baptist church in Dover, N. Y.; was at the academy at New Ipswich, N. H., and at Worcester Academy, Mass.; colporteur of American and Foreign Bible Society; connected with

academy at Shelburne Falls for two years; entered Madison University; spent two years with a mission church in South Boston, Mass.; became city missionary in Hartford, Conn., in 1857, and labored eight years; ordained in 1861; in 1865 settled with Wethersfield church; in 1867 with Third Baptist church, Providence, R. I.; in 1870 returned to Hartford, Conn., and became pastor of the newly formed Washington Avenue church; resigned in 1877; supplied Bloomfield and other churches till health failed; in June, 1879, was chosen chaplain of Connecticut State Prison, where he is now laboring.

Howard College, located at Marion, is the Baptist male college of Alabama. It was founded in 1843. Prof. S. S. Sherman, Rev. H. Talbird, D.D., Rev. J. L. M. Curry, LL.D., Rev. S. R. Freeman, D.D., and Prof. J. T. Murfee, LL.D., have been presidents of this institution. Its buildings and grounds are estimated to be worth $150,000. And before the war its endowment was valued at as much more, which, however, was lost in that unhappy struggle. It belongs to the State Convention of Alabama, and that body appoints its trustees and devotes a great deal of attention to its welfare. It has a deep hold on the confidence and affection of the denomination in the State, as is seen in the fact that after its buildings had been twice destroyed by fire they were promptly rebuilt, with improvements, by the Baptists of the State; and in the further fact that although without an endowment, it is successfully competing with richly-endowed colleges in and out of the State. Dr. Murfee, the present president, who has occupied that position for eight years, has, with his able corps of professors, established for Howard College the reputation of imparting a thoroughness of scholarship and of manly deportment unsurpassed in the whole country. Besides, the moral tone and religious surroundings of the institution are of the first order. Every effort is made to develop the nobler traits of human character, and to bestow the best education that can be had. The graduates of Howard College are taking some of the highest stations in all the learned callings.

Howard, Hon. James L., son of Rev. Leland Howard, was born in Windsor, Vt., Jan. 18, 1818; settled in Hartford, Conn., in October, 1838; an extensive and successful merchant and manufacturer; well and widely known for ability, integrity, good judgment, and courtesy; largely trusted with public interests; to his fine taste Bushnell Park, Hartford, owes much of its attractiveness; baptized into the fellowship of the First Baptist church, Jan. 7, 1841; chosen deacon Sept. 4, 1857; active in this church and prominent in the denomination; president of Connecticut Baptist State Convention from 1871 to 1877; president of Connecticut Baptist Social Union from its origin in 1872, as he was its chief originator; president of American Baptist Publication Society from 1873 to 1878; for many years an efficient trustee of Connecticut Literary Institution; generous contributor to benevolent operations.

Howard, John, the Philanthropist, was born at Enfield, England, Sept. 2, 1726. His education

JOHN HOWARD.

was respectable. In his early manhood he traveled extensively in France and Italy, purchasing works of art, and inspecting the ruins of the glorious past and the creations of modern genius. In his travels he learned to speak the French language with great accuracy, which was of signal service to him in future life. Some time after his return from the Continent he became so ill that he was convinced that the attentions of his nurse alone saved his life, and as the only adequate expression of his gratitude he married her when she was fifty-five and he was twenty-five. She lived but a short time to enjoy her new position and the wealth of love in her husband's noble heart. On the 2d of May, 1758, he married Henrietta Leeds, with whom he spent nine happy years at Cardington. During this period his active mind found constant occupation in building school-houses and model cottages for the poor of the town, and in many other labors for the education and improvement of the neglected villagers. He was appointed sheriff in 1773. To accept this required him to produce a certificate stating that he had taken the Lord's Supper in an Episcopal church within a reasonable time. How-

ard was a Dissenter, and he abhorred such contemptible methods of sustaining the interests of a church; neither would he decline the office and pay a fine as his father had done. He accepted the position, determined to contest to the uttermost any suit brought against him for breaking the law. No one prosecuted the good man. After the assizes were over he descended into the prison to see the condition of its inmates. It was the home of John Bunyan for twelve years, in which he wrote his immortal "Pilgrim's Progress." Everything in it was shocking, and appealed to his whole humanity to remove the horrid evils that reigned all over the place. From that moment he seems to have consecrated himself to fight prison abuses and the powers of the plague throughout the world. How he traveled, how he suffered, how he labored with kings, emperors, empresses, parliaments, and governors of jails; how he gave his money to relieve oppressed prisoners and victims of the plague; and how he risked his life times without number, it is not possible to tell in an article like this. It is sufficient to say that the name of Howard stands high above every other philanthropist to which our race has given birth. The Howard Associations of our country and of other lands show the extent and duration of his fame. He died at Kherson, in the Crimea, of camp fever, contracted in his warfare against that scourge, on the 20th of January, 1790. Mr. Howard's efforts have been followed by marvelous improvements in prison-life, and by a multitude of benevolent societies to aid the victims of the pestilence.

He was a member of the Baptist community of which Dr. Samuel Stennett was pastor, in London. On the 1st of March, 1790, Dr. Stennett preached a funeral sermon for his lamented friend. In that discourse, in describing Mr. Howard's faith, says, "Nor was he ashamed of those truths he heard stated, explained, and enforced in this place. He had made up his mind, as he said, upon his religious sentiments, and was not to be moved from his steadfastness by novel opinions intruded upon the world. Nor did he content himself with a bare profession of these divine truths. He entered into the spirit of the gospel, felt its power and tasted its sweetness. You know, my friends, with what seriousness and devotion he attended, for a long course of years, on the worship of God among us. It would be scarcely decent for me to repeat the affectionate things he says, in a letter written me from a remote part of the world, respecting the satisfaction and pleasure he had felt in the religious exercises of this place."* The historian Ivimey gives the letter entire. It was written from Smyrna, on the 11th of August, 1786. In it he says, "The

---

* Works of Samuel Stennett, D.D., iii. 295. London, 1824.

principal* reason of my writing is most sincerely to thank you for the many pleasant hours I have had in reviewing the notes I have taken of the sermons I had the happiness to hear under your ministry ; these, sir, with many of your petitions in prayer, have been, and are, my songs in the house of my pilgrimage. With undoubted pleasure I have attended your ministry ; no man ever entered more into my religious sentiments, or more happily expressed them. It was some little disappointment when any one occupied your pulpit. Oh, sir, how many Sabbaths have I ardently longed to spend in Little Wild Street (Dr. Stennett's) : on those days I generally rest, or, if at sea, keep retired in my little cabin. It is you that preach, and I bless God I attend with renewed pleasure. I bless God for your ministry ; I pray God to reward you a thousandfold."

Mr. Howard had been a Congregationalist, but from "the many years" during which he had worshiped with Dr. Stennett, and the declaration that " no man ever entered more into his religious sentiments, or more happily expressed them," it is certain that John Howard was a Baptist.

Howard, Rev. Leland, was born in Jamaica, Vt., Oct. 13, 1793. During a revival in Shaftsbury he was hopefully converted, and baptized when about seventeen years of age, by Rev. Isaiah Madison. At an early age he commenced to preach. In 1814, having been invited by Gen. Abner Forbes, a wealthy citizen of Windsor, Vt., to come to that place to pursue his studies, he accepted the invitation. He was placed under the instruction of Rev. Joseph Bradley, pastor of the Baptist church, his board and tuition bills being paid by his kind friend. He completed his theological studies with Rev. J. M. Winchell, of Boston, and was ordained pastor of the church in Windsor, Vt., in November, 1817. In 1823 he became pastor of the First Baptist church in Troy, N. Y., where he remained five years. For a time he was again with his old church in Windsor, and then in Brooklyn, N. Y. He preached in Meriden, Conn., in the year 1837–38. Subsequently he was pastor in Newport, R. I., Norwich, N. Y., North church in Troy, then at Hartford, N. Y., and finally in Rutland, Vt., where his pastorate closed in 1852. He died May 6, 1870. Few men have left a better record in the places where he labored as a minister of the gospel than " Father" Howard. One of his sons is Hon. James L. Howard, of Hartford, Conn., president of the American Baptist Publication Society.

Howard, Rev. Mark William, was ordained at Ukiah, Cal., in 1859, and has been pastor of the Ukiah and other churches in that part of the

State ever since. He was born in 1818, converted at nine, and joined his mother's church, the Methodist. In 1838 he removed to Fort Smith, Ark., three years after to Southwest Missouri. In 1844, having previously become a Baptist by studying the Bible, he was immersed and joined a Baptist church. In 1856 he removed to California, spent one year in San Joaquin County, one year in Sonoma County, and joined the Healdsburg church. In 1858 he settled near Ukiah, where he was soon after ordained. God has blessed him both in his business and in his labors in the pulpit, and given him great influence as a citizen and as a Christian pastor.

Howard, Wm., D.D., was born in Manchester, England, Dec. 17, 1828. In early life he ran away from home. For several years he was occupied as a cabin-boy in a sailing-vessel. While thus engaged he made the acquaintance of Rev. A. P. Repiton, D.D., at Wilmington, N. C. This good brother took him to his home and adopted him as a son. Through his instrumentality he was converted, and baptized in 1847. He early indicated strong powers of native intellect. Cherishing high desires for thorough education, he entered Howard College, Ala., in 1849, and graduated in 1852, receiving the degree of A.M. in 1854. In January, 1855, he became pastor of the Gainesville church, Ala., in the charge of which he continued until the close of 1866, when he assumed the pastorate of the First Baptist church in Galveston, Texas. At different times, while living in Alabama, he served as pastor at Providence and Sumterville churches, Ala., and Macon and Enterprise churches, Miss., preaching to them once a month. During the war he acted as a chaplain and general missionary in the Confederate army. For several years he was moderator of the Bigby River Association, Ala., and was for some months general agent in Texas of the Home Mission Board of the Southern Baptist Convention. He has represented Alabama and Texas in the Southern Convention, and in May, 1876, at Buffalo, N. Y., represented the same Convention in the general Baptist anniversaries. For several years he has been president of the Texas Baptist Sunday-School Convention. Baylor University conferred on him the degree of D.D. in 1870. He is a student, possessing a library rich in the variety, rarity, and number of its volumes. He is ranked by no minister of the " Island City." His commencement sermons at Baylor University and other educational centres have given him a prominent place among Southern ministers. He holds a warm place among the Galveston people.

Howe, Rev. Phineas, was born in Fitzwilliam, N. H., in 1792; was converted at the age of twenty-eight; licensed by the church in Fitzwilliam; studied with Rev. J. M. Graves, and was ordained in 1824 to the pastorate of the Marlborough and Newfane, Vt., church, where he remained for seven years. After brief pastorates in one or two other places, he returned, in 1834, to the church which he had first served, where he continued his labors for another term of seven years. Broken down in his health, he suspended his ministerial labors for a season. His last settlements were in Hinsdale and Troy, N. H. He returned to spend the close of his life among his old friends, and died at Newfane, Vt., Jan. 17, 1869. During the nearly twenty-five years of his active ministry he baptized 308 persons, and was otherwise very useful.

Howe, Rev. Samuel, was pastor of the church meeting in Deadman's Place, London, for about seven years. Neal says that "he was a man of learning, and printed a small treatise called 'The Sufficiency of the Spirit's Teaching'" (vol. ii. 316, Dublin, 1755). Others speak of him as a cobbler, and, consequently, an illiterate person. He might have carried on the shoe business, because he could not support himself by preaching to a small persecuted Baptist church, and yet not be an ignorant man. Neither does the fact that his book seems to disparage learning prove that he was destitute of it. Many in his day represented learning as the CHIEF qualification for the ministry. Baptists never have entertained this opinion, though they regard learning in their pastors as of immense importance, and have given more money, perhaps, than any other denomination, with their numbers and resources, in this country to erect and endow institutions for the education of their ministry.

Mr. Howe attracted the attention of the persecuting clergy and their instruments, by whom he was imprisoned and excommunicated. Dying in jail, he was refused burial in consecrated ground ; a constable's guard protected the parish cemetery at Shoreditch from profanation by the reception of his body. He was buried at Agnes-la-Clair ; and several members of his church, at their own request, were buried afterwards with him.

Mr. Howe's people, after his death, according to Dr. Thomas Fuller, on Jan. 18, 1641, to the number of 80 meeting at St. Saviour's, Southwark, "preached," among other things, "*that the king was only to be obeyed in civil matters.*" Crosby states that they were arrested while at their place of worship and committed to the Clink prison, and that the next morning six or seven of the men were taken to the House of Lords and strictly examined about their principles. They freely admitted that "they owned no other head of the church but Jesus Christ, *that no prince had power to make laws to bind the consciences* of men, and that laws made contrary to the law of God were of no force." Crosby states that this church was of the independent order. Fuller says they were Anabap-

tists ; Crosby's and Mr. Howe's contemporaries represent him as a Baptist. The principles his people avow are emphatically the doctrines of the Baptists. They may have been Independents, who added believer's immersion to their Congregationalism. Mr. Howe was bitterly persecuted and deeply lamented. His reputation as a manly, talented, and learned Non-conformist was so favorably and widely known, that Crosby tells us "he was very famous for his vindication of the doctrines of separation."

Roger Williams, in "The Hireling Ministry," etc., says, "Among so many instances, dead and living, to the everlasting praise of Christ Jesus and of His Holy Spirit, breathing and blessing where He listeth, I cannot but with honorable testimony remember that eminently Christian witness and prophet of Christ, even that despised and yet beloved Samuel Howe, who, being by calling a cobbler and without human learning (probably he meant a university education, which Dr. Carey never had), which yet in its sphere and place he honored, who yet, I say, by searching the Holy Scriptures, grew so excellent a textuary, or Scripture-learned man, that few of those high rabbies that scorn to mend or make a shoe, could aptly or readily from the Holy Scriptures outgo him. And, however, through the oppressions upon some men's consciences, even in life and death, and after death, in respect of burying, as yet unthought and unremedied, I say, however, he was forced to seek a grave or bed in the highway, yet was his life and death and burial (being attended by many hundreds of God's people) honorable and (how much more on his rising again !) glorious."

It is probable that Roger Williams learned "soul liberty" from Samuel Howe, whose church believed that "the king was only to be obeyed in civil matters ;" that "no prince had power to make laws to bind the consciences of men."

Howell, Judge David, was born in New Jersey in 1747, and graduated at Princeton in 1766. By the advice of President Manning he came to Rhode Island, and was his associate in the new Rhode Island College, just commencing operations in Warren. He was appointed Professor of Mathematics and Natural Philosophy in 1769, and continued to give instruction in his department until college exercises were suspended in consequence of the breaking up of the college in the Revolutionary war. He was Professor of Law in the university for over thirty years, and a Fellow for fifty-two years. For many years he ranked among the first lawyers of Providence, was a member of the Congress of Confederation, and in 1812 was appointed U. S. judge for the district of Rhode Island, holding the office until the time of his death, in 1824.

Prof. Goddard, in a sketch of Judge Howell, remarks, "He was endowed with extraordinary talents, and he superadded to his endowments extensive and accurate learning. Upon all occasions which made any demands upon him, he gave the most convincing evidence of the vigor of his powers, and of the variety and extent of his erudition."

Howell, R. B. C., D.D., was born in Wayne Co., N. C., on the 10th of March, 1801, and died in Nashville, Tenn., on Sunday, April 5, 1868. He commenced preaching about 1825, and was ordained, in 1827, in Cumberland Street church, Norfolk, Va., where he labored until 1834, after which he came to Nashville. Here he built for the First Baptist church of Nashville a fine house of worship, and gathered a membership of over 500. He resigned April, 1850, to take charge of the Second Baptist church of Richmond, Va., in which he labored until the 19th of July, 1857, when he returned to the scene of his early successes, where he had acquired the reputation of one of the most learned and eloquent divines in the country. Here his labors were again attended with the same blessings that crowned his efforts in past years, until paralysis obliged him to relinquish the pulpit he had filled so acceptably for more than a quarter of a century. In the earlier days of his ministry he had to contend with the anti-missionaries of his own denomination and with the followers of Alexander Campbell. He was often found in debate with them by voice and pen, and he always acquitted himself as a loyal disciple of our Lord Jesus Christ. At the request of the Tennessee Baptist Convention, in 1854, he wrote a work on the "Terms of Christian Communion," of 456 pages, which ran through several editions in this country and three or four in England. In 1846 he published a work entitled "The Deaconship: its Nature, Qualifications, Relations, and Duties," which was issued by the American Baptist Publication Society, and ran rapidly through six editions. "The Way of Salvation" was his next literary effort, which passed through several editions. A small work entitled "The Evils of Infant Baptism," followed, which caused a good deal of newspaper comment from Pedobaptist denominations. In 1854 he was the author of a work entitled "The Cross," which was published by the Southern Baptist Publication Society, at Charleston, S. C., and the Virginia Baptist Sunday-School and Publication Society, at Richmond. "The Covenants," published by the same societies, was written in 1856. These works evince a high order of learning, and some of them are authorities in the Baptist denomination. His scholarship was universally conceded. He was educated in Columbian College, Washington, D. C. The degree of Doctor of Divinity was conferred upon him by Georgetown College, Ky., about the year 1844. Besides the works of Dr. Howell just named, he died leaving four others in manuscript, upon which a great amount of thought and labor were bestowed. "The Early Baptists of Virginia," written in 1857, was printed by the American Baptist Publication Society, Philadelphia, for his children, and is the only one of the four that has been published. As a minister, he was regarded as one of the ablest and most learned men in the South, and no one exercised a greater or more beneficial influence within or outside of the church. His life was unspotted, his Christian course was marked by the highest virtues. His courtesy and kindness of heart made him a universal favorite, notwithstanding the fierce theological debates in which he was often engaged. He was a thorough Baptist, and always jealous of the fair fame of his denomination. Dr. Howell was for many years president of the Southern Baptist Convention, and one of its vice-presidents at the time of his death. He had filled also the post of vice-president of the American Baptist Historical Society. He was a member of the Historical Society of Tennessee, and was president of the board of trustees of the asylum for the blind, an institution endowed and sustained by the State of Tennessee. He administered the ordinance of baptism to an immense number of people, first and last, during the long course of his ministry. His death occurred on Sunday, about noon, at the very hour in which, for more than forty years, he had stood up for Jesus in the pulpit. For a week before his death he was speechless but conscious. He knew all that was said around him; and when the pastor of the First church of Nashville spoke of the infinite pity and compassion of the Saviour for his suffering servant, he burst into tears. On being asked if he saw Jesus, he answered by pointing first to his heart and then to heaven.

In addition to the positions held by Dr. Howell already mentioned, he was frequently the moderator of the Concord Association and other bodies. His capacity as a presiding officer of deliberative bodies was rare.

Howes, Prof. Oscar, A.M., was born near Carmel, N. Y., April 20, 1830; was converted while in college; graduated from Madison University in 1850; spent a year at Rochester University; went to Europe in 1852, and was abroad two years, devoting his time, with the exception of a few months spent in traveling, to the study of the German and French languages; in 1855 became Professor of the Greek and Latin Languages in Shurtleff College; in 1863 made a second visit to Europe, spending six months at Athens in the study of the Greek language, ancient and modern, attending daily lectures on the latter at the University of Athens.

After a tour through Greece, Egypt, and Palestine he returned to his duties at Shurtleff. In 1874 he accepted the chair of Latin and Modern Languages at Madison University, where he still labors. He went abroad for the third time in 1878, accompanied by his family.

Howlett, Rev. Thomas R., was born in Cambridgeshire, England, March 19, 1827. He was converted in Richfield, O., when fifteen. He graduated from Madison University in 1856, and from the seminary in 1858. He has been pastor in New Brunswick, N. J.; of the Pearl Street church, Albany, N. Y.; the Central, Trenton, N. J.; the Calvary, Washington, D. C.; in Hudson City, N.Y.; and of the Second church of Plainfield, N. J. During his seven years' pastorate in Washington, the Calvary church erected and paid for an edifice costing $120,000. Mr. Howlett is an able preacher, a sound theologian, a successful pastor, and a genial and loving Christian. In every way fitted to hold the conspicuous positions to which he has been called, and with many years apparently still before him, the denomination may yet expect much valuable services from him.

Hoyt, Col. James A.—Modestly declines to furnish any material for a biography. This notice will, consequently, be "short." Nearly fifty years ago the first Baptist newspaper was published in South Carolina. The numerous changes of name and place, proprietors and editors, tell the sad tale that not one of them was self-sustaining.

In 1878, Col. Hoyt became proprietor of the *Working Christian*, published in Columbia. He soon after removed it to Greenville, and called it the *Baptist Courier*. It has gradually improved until he has a paper sustained on business principles; and the brethren owe very much to him and his cultured coadjutor, Rev. J. A. Chambliss, D.D., for giving them an organ amply worthy of the liberal support it is receiving.

Col. Hoyt is a large-hearted Christian man, who enjoys the warm regards of all South Carolina Baptists, and of many outside our denominational fold.

Hoyt, James M., LL.D., was born in Utica, N. Y., Jan. 16, 1815; graduated from Hamilton College in 1834; read law in Utica and Cleveland, O.; engaged in the practice of law until 1853, when he turned his attention to the development and sale of real estate. In 1835 he united with the Baptist church at Utica, and on removing to Cleveland became connected with the First church of that city. For twenty-six years was superintendent of the Sunday-school, and subsequently teacher of a large Bible-class. In 1854 he was licensed to preach, but has never received ordination.

In State and national affairs Dr. Hoyt has been very prominent. In 1854 he was chosen president of the Ohio Baptist State Convention, and for twenty-five years was annually elected to that position. He was also chosen president of the American Baptist Home Mission Society, and was annually re-elected until his voluntary retirement

JAMES M. HOYT, LL.D.

in 1870. He was for thirteen years president of the Cleveland Bible Society. In 1870 he was made a member of the Ohio State Board of Equalization, —a body requiring great ability and worth. In 1873 he was appointed to represent the city on the Cleveland Board of Public Improvements.

Dr. Hoyt, while an active and successful lawyer and business man, has given himself largely to literary studies. His addresses before various bodies have always evinced wide study and the best taste. He published in the *Christian Review*, October, 1863, an analytical and exhaustive article on "Miracles." In September, 1879, he also published in the *Baptist Review* a defense of the intuitional philosophy, entitled "Theism Grounded in Mind," which has been very favorably received. Dr. Hoyt was married in 1836 to Miss Mary Ella Beebee, in the city of New York. Of six children born of this union five are still living. Their eldest son, Wayland Hoyt, D.D., is pastor of the Strong Place church, Brooklyn, N. Y. Their second son, Colgate Hoyt, is in business with his father. James H. Hoyt, their third son, and Elton Hoyt, their fourth son, are practising law. In 1870 Denison University, in consideration of Dr. Hoyt's varied talents, services, and learning, conferred upon him the honorary degree of LL.D.

Hoyt, Wayland, D.D., was born in Cleveland,

O., Feb. 18, 1838. In 1860 he was graduated from Brown University, and in 1863 from Rochester Theological Seminary. He was ordained over the Baptist church of Pittsfield, Mass. After one year

WAYLAND HOYT, D.D.

there he removed to Cincinnati, O., and took charge of the Ninth Street Baptist church. Three years later he took charge of the Strong Place Baptist church, Brooklyn. It was a large and influential church, and in this relation began the development of his powers as a profound thinker, a scholarly writer, and an able preacher. In the hope of establishing a great Baptist tabernacle in New York, he accepted a call from the Tabernacle Baptist church, New York, and commenced services in Steinway Hall. It promised well in the beginning, but there were insurmountable difficulties, and the enterprise was abandoned. He then accepted a call to Shawmut Avenue Baptist church, Boston, Mass. The Strong Place church, Brooklyn, recalled him to that important field, where he now labors. He is a prolific writer. His contributions are eagerly sought by the great leading journals of the Baptist denomination. He is the author of "Hints and Helps of the Christian Life," and he is about to bring out a new work, the subject of which is not announced.

As a preacher, he is earnest, logical, and persuasive. He shows that he has thoroughly investigated the subject of his discourse. As a platform speaker, he is ready, clear, and forcible, and as a pastor he is faithful and successful.

Hubbard, Gov. Richard Bennett, was born

36

Nov. 1, 1832, in Walton Co., Ga.; graduated with the degree of A.B. at Mercer University, Penfield, Ga., in 1851; pursued the law course at the University of Virginia, and graduated with the degree of LL.B. in the Law Department of Harvard University, Massachusetts; commenced practising law at Tyler, Texas, in 1854; was appointed United States attorney for the western district of Texas by President Franklin Pierce in 1856; resigned this office to accept a seat in the State Legislature of Texas in 1858–59; was a delegate to the convention which nominated President James Buchanan; during the war between the States he was colonel of the 22d Regiment of Texas Infantry; in 1872 was a Presidential elector; in 1874 was president of the Democratic State convention at Austin; during the same year was elected lieutenant-governor of Texas, and was re-elected to the same office in 1876; delivered by appointment Centennial oration for Texas at Philadelphia in 1876; became governor of Texas Dec. 1, 1876. All his ancestry and his immediate family belong to the Baptist Church. "The Baptists are the people of his fathers." At fourteen years of age he joined the church at Liberty, Jasper Co., Ga.

Gov. Hubbard is one of nature's noblemen. He is a thoroughly learned lawyer, an able statesman, and an orator of the highest order, whose utterances arouse intense enthusiasm among the people.

GOV. RICHARD BENNETT HUBBARD.

His administration of the executive office was remarkably popular with the people, and had he been a candidate for re-election he would have received fully two-thirds of the votes of the people at the polls. His earnestness in behalf of education, virtue, philanthropy, and religion make him a popular favorite; and as he is only yet in the prime of his powers, a brilliant and useful future may be anticipated for him.

Hubbard, Rev. William, was born in Boston, Mass., Jan. 28, 1778. His early associations were not with Baptists, his parents and friends being Episcopalians. When he became interested in the matter of his personal salvation, he was brought under the ministry of Rev. Dr. Stillman, and he united with his church. Encouraged by his pastor, he prepared for his life-work, and entered upon itinerant labors in Maine and Connecticut. The churches which he served as pastor were in the western part of Massachusetts, at Martha's Vineyard, the Third Baptist church in Middleborough, and fourteen years were spent at Goshen. He died at Lakeville, Mass., Jan. 3, 1858.

Hübmaier, Balthazar (Friedberger, Pacimontanus), is the most honorable name among the Anabaptists. He had not the impulsiveness of Grebel, nor the brilliancy of Hätzer and Denk; but for calmness, soberness, logical clearness and consistency, absolute devotion to truth, and freedom from important errors, he stands unrivaled by any man of the Reformation time. Born in 1480, educated at the University of Freiberg, where his principal teacher was John Eck, he spent some years in school-teaching, then became tutor at Freiberg, and in 1512 followed Eck to Ingoldstadt, where he became preacher and Professor of Theology. Here he was created Doctor of Theology. In 1516 he was called to be preacher in the cathedral church in Regensburg. His great eloquence led to this appointment. Here he preached so powerfully against the Jews as to cause their expulsion from the city. In 1519 he declared himself for Luther, and was driven from Regensburg. In 1522 he became pastor at Waldshut, near Zürich. Here he was among the most zealous of the supporters of the Zwinglian doctrine; but soon came to deny the Scripturalness of infant baptism. In 1524 he published eighteen axioms concerning the Christian life, in which he set forth his reformatory views, and he soon secured from the town council recognition and protection for the preachers. His writing on "Heretics and their Burners" soon followed. In this he shows that only those are heretics who contradict the Scriptures, especially the devil and the papists. This is the earliest and clearest plea for liberty of conscience of the Reformation time. He shows that heretics can be overcome by instruction only, and that to try to overcome them by violence is contrary to the teachings and spirit of Christ. In 1525 he wrote against infant baptism, and was elaborately answered by Zwingle and

Œcolampadius. Hübmaier's tract against infant baptism is an admirable production alike in matter and in spirit. The straightforward earnestness and Christian courtesy of Hübmaier's tract are in striking contrast with the sophistry and reviling of Zwingle's reply. He was one of the chief participants in the disputations with Zwingle during this year. Assured of the support of the civil power, Zwingle, on these occasions, acted the part, not of a brother in Christ, but of a lord, and by his air of superior wisdom and authority, by his fluent sophistry, easily persuaded the members of the council that his adversaries had been fairly vanquished. Hübmaier was imprisoned at Zürich, where he suffered great hardship. Having been released from prison, he went to Moravia (1526), where Anabaptists already existed in considerable numbers. At Nicolsburg he established a strong church, and published in quick succession a large number of tracts on ordinances, worship, and doctrine. Most of these have been preserved, and are among the choicest products of the Anabaptist movement. In 1527 he was taken to Vienna and thrown into prison. In 1528 he died heroically at the stake, a martyr to his Baptist principles.

Huckins, Rev. James, was one of the best men the writer has ever known. He was born in New Hampshire in April, 1807. He was left an orphan at four or five years of age, and was baptized at fourteen. He graduated at Brown University at an early age. He went among the first Baptist ministers to Texas, under the patronage of the Home Mission Society. His singular insight into human character, his high courage tempered finely with gentleness, and, what is no less important, his tact, fitted him peculiarly for usefulness among the frontiersmen.

After many years of incessant and successful labor as a missionary, he became pastor of the church in Galveston, where his influence over all classes was both wide and deep. The esteem in which he was held was manifested by the presentation of a heavy pitcher and pair of goblets of solid silver, on his departure, from the citizens at large.

In 1859 he accepted the pastorate of the Wentworth Street Baptist church, in Charleston, S. C. Here he was ready for every good word and work, especially among the poor. From the commencement of the war his labors in the hospitals in and around Charleston were incessant, and in the double toils of pastor and chaplain he fell on the 14th of August, 1863.

Hudson, Hon. Nathaniel C., was born in St. Johnsbury, Vt., Oct. 9, 1828. After receiving a common school education, he entered Leland Seminary, Vt., and prepared for the Sophomore class in college, but went south for his health. In 1852 he took charge of Twiggs Academy, in Georgia, where he proved a popular teacher. He studied law, came north, entered the National Law School at Poughkeepsie, and graduated in 1855. He then removed to Iowa, and entered upon his profession at Sioux City. He removed to St. Louis in 1866. Mr. Hudson was elected to the State Legislature in 1874 from St. Louis, and served on important committees. In 1876 he was elected a senator to the General Assembly of Missouri, and served on the committees of Ways and Means, Penitentiary, Bank and Corporations, Insurance, and Constitutional Amendments. He is courteous, frank, outspoken, cordial, and popular. His business relations are marked by integrity, and his church duties by fidelity. He is a member of the Second Baptist church of St. Louis.

Huff, Rev. Jonathan, a useful minister of the Hephzibah Association, was born in Warren Co., Ga., in August, 1789. Licensed by Little Brier Creek church, he was ordained in 1823. In 1829 he was elected moderator of the Hephzibah Association, in which capacity he served for thirteen years consecutively. His practical good sense and sterling integrity and unaffected piety gained him the confidence and esteem of his brethren. For thirty-one years he was pastor of Ways church, and of Reedy Creek church he was pastor thirty-seven years consecutively. In addition he labored with other churches to an extent which always occupied his whole time. A faithful student of the Bible, he was a safe expounder of its teachings; conscientious and tender of spirit, he was touching in his addresses to the unconverted; and hence he was very successful in winning souls to Jesus and in building up churches that were sound in the faith. He was indomitably persevering, and possessed an equanimity that nothing could disturb. He was usually slow of speech, yet few men have accomplished more good or exerted a wider influence. He was an ardent and intelligent supporter of the missionary and temperance causes, and heartily co-operated with the denomination in its benevolent enterprises. He died in the vicinity of his birthplace on the 25th of November, 1872, at the age of eighty-three.

Hufham, Rev. Geo. W.—Among the older living ministers of North Carolina is the Rev. Geo. W. Hufham, who was born in 1804; baptized in 1830 by Rev. Geo. Fennell, began to preach soon after, and has served many of the churches of Sampson and Duplin Counties. Mr. Hufham is a gentleman of respectable learning, and in his youth was a popular preacher. Ill health has prevented him from preaching as much as his heart desired. Honored and loved, this good man is resting in the Beulah Land, waiting for the call to pass over the river.

Hufham, J. D., D.D. The son of an esteemed

minister, Dr. Hufham is one of the most noted of the living ministers of North Carolina. He was born in Duplin Co., N. C., May 26, 1834; was fitted

J. D. HUFHAM, D.D.

for college by the Rev. Dr. Sprunt, of Keenansville; graduated at Wake Forest College in 1856; was baptized at the college by Dr. Wingate in February, 1855, and ordained in 1857, Revs. A. Guy, B. F. Marable, and L. F. Williams comprising the Presbytery. In 1861 he purchased the *Biblical Recorder*, which he conducted with distinguished success till the close of 1867. For three years he was pastor of the Lanyino Creek church, Camden Co. He then became corresponding secretary of the Baptist State Convention, and, after four years' service in this position, became pastor of the Second church of Raleigh and associate editor of the *Biblical Recorder*. For the past three years Dr. Hufham has labored in Scotland Neck, and the adjacent country for a hundred miles up and down the Roanoke River, and so remarkable have been the results of his efforts, that it may be truly said that, though always active and useful, he never did such effective service in the cause of Christ as now. Dr. Hufham is a ripe scholar, refined and critical in his tastes, a born editor, and the prince of agents. He never seems so happy as when managing an Association or taking up a collection. He is the author of an admirable memoir of Rev. J. L. Prichard, is a trustee of Wake Forest College, and was for many years recording secretary of the State Convention. He received his D.D. from his *alma mater* in 1877.

Hughes, Rev. Joseph, was born in London, Jan. 1, 1769. He was baptized by Dr. Samuel Stennett into the fellowship of the church in Little Wild Street in his native city. He studied for the ministry at Bristol College, and at Aberdeen and Edinburgh, in Scotland. He was ordained in Battersea in 1797. He was appointed secretary of the Religious Tract Society of London in 1799, and continued to discharge the duties of that office during the remainder of his life.

In 1802 the Rev. Thomas Charles, of Bala, in Wales, came to London to secure, through private friends, a supply of Welsh Bibles. He appeared before the committee of the Religious Tract Society, and his appeal was the subject of deliberation at several of their meetings. At one of these meetings Mr. Hughes suggested that Wales was not the only part of the empire destitute of the written Word of God and requiring assistance; that Great Britain itself was not the only part of Christendom which needed to be supplied; and that it might be desirable to form a society which, while it met the demands of Wales and the necessities of all parts of the British Islands, might be comprehensive enough *to embrace within its scope the entire world.* Mr. Hughes was recommended to embody his thoughts in writing. In compliance with the request he prepared his celebrated paper entitled "The Excellency of the Holy Scriptures." In this document Mr. Hughes earnestly advocated the importance of forming an association of Christians of all denominations with the sole object of giving the Word of Life to the nations. The paper was widely circulated, and the plan was approved immediately by large numbers. After various preliminary arrangements, a meeting was held at the "London Tavern," March 7, 1804, consisting of about three hundred persons belonging to various denominations, at which the British and Foreign Bible Society was formally organized, and Mr. Hughes appointed one of its secretaries. This was the first Bible Society in the world, and the parent of all similar institutions everywhere. This noble organization received its origin and its very name from a Baptist. (History of the British and Foreign Bible Society, vol. i. pp. 4–9. London, 1859.) The thought that started this society on its career of usefulness and power was placed in the mind of our Baptist brother by the Comforter, the Guardian Spirit of revelation, and of the redeemed race.

In 1833 Mr. Hughes entered the eternal rest. The British and Foreign Bible Society passed resolutions expressing in the most touching and eloquent terms their appreciation of his exalted worth, and of the great loss their institution had suffered in his death. Evangelical Christians in throngs lamented the demise of one of the most useful men that had toiled for centuries for the spread of pure truth. The well-known Jay, of Bath, said of him, "I am thankful for my intimacy with him. My esteem for him always grew with my intercourse. I never knew a more consistent, correct, and unblemished character. He was not only sincere, but without offense, and he adorned the doctrine of God our Saviour in all things." His long pastorate at Battersea was a great blessing to the church which he loved, and by which to the last he was tenderly cherished, and it was only terminated by his death.

Hughes, Rowland.—This excellent brother had considerable property, which he used largely for benevolent purposes. Mr. Hughes was gentle in spirit and conservative in his views; he was ready for every good work, and he had the confidence of all his brethren and their highest esteem. After a protracted and painful illness he died of typhoid fever, Feb. 7, 1855. The Baptists of Missouri, where he so long lived, cherish his memory with great love.

Hulbert, E. B., D.D., was born at Chicago, Ill., July 16, 1841, and was baptized at Burlington Flats, N. J., in 1854. Entering Madison University, he continued in study there through his Junior year, taking his Senior year at Union College, where he graduated in 1863, and at the theological seminary in Hamilton in 1865. His first service was in connection with the Christian Commission, in Grant's army, while before Richmond, continuing in this until the close of the war. For three years from September, 1865, he was pastor at Manchester, N. H. In November, 1868, he began labor with the Rolling Mills Mission at Chicago, and continued there until its organization as a church, in March, 1870. In that year he accepted a call to the First Baptist church, St. Paul, Minn.; in 1874 was invited to the First Baptist church, San Francisco, Cal.; and in 1878 became pastor of the Fourth Baptist church, Chicago. Dr. Hulbert as a thoughtful, earnest, inspiring preacher, has great power with intelligent congregations, while as a lecturer before the theological seminary at Chicago, as well as before ministers' institutes, he has developed rare facility in handling profound and weighty subjects.

Hull, Rev. John, was born in Manchester, Nova Scotia. He was converted there in 1819; engaged in missionary labor in Cape Breton in 1821, where spirituality in religion was very little known or recognized. He was baptized by Rev. Joseph Dimock in 1825, and ordained at Wilmot, Nova Scotia, June 28, 1826. He died Aug. 13, 1829, at Sydney, Cape Breton.

Hull, Rev. Robert Bruce, pastor of the Tabernacle church of New York City, was born Jan. 12, 1841, in Kirkcudbrightshire, Scotland. His parents shortly after his birth removed to Liverpool, England, and after remaining there a few years came to America and settled at Buffalo, N. Y., where they now reside. His father, Robert Hull, while in Liverpool, was one of the preachers to a Scotch Baptist church in that city. In June, 1860, Robert B. was baptized into the fellowship of the Cedar Street Baptist church of Buffalo. He went to Tennessee in 1864, and there, with a relative, entered into business. Soon the conviction grew upon him that he must preach the gospel, and closing up a prosperous establishment, he returned to Buffalo to prepare for college. This was done, under a private tutor, in one year. In September, 1867, he entered the University of Rochester. While in his Freshman year he took charge of a mission Sunday-school, near the city, where, on Sunday evening, Feb. 16, 1868, he preached his first sermon. God set his seal on the work, and about twenty persons were converted. Finding that the preparation of sermons interfered with college studies, he ceased to preach, except in his vacations. His course in college was successful. He took the second prize for declamation in his Sophomore year; was honorably mentioned in connection with the Greek prize, and also for extra studies in French in his Junior year; and received a first prize for the Senior prize essay at his graduation. He then entered the Rochester Theological Seminary, and preached through the entire course, chiefly at Royalton and Dansville, N. Y. He supplied the Lockport, N. Y., Baptist church during his Senior year in the seminary, and accepted a unanimous call to become its pastor on his graduation. During this year a revival took place, and, at the request of the church, he was ordained Feb. 17, 1874. Over 100 were baptized as the result of the revival. He continued his studies, and graduated in May, 1874. During his pastorate at Lockport, the accessions to the church by baptism were more than doubled. Its membership was more than doubled. In March, 1877, the Tabernacle church of New York, hearing of his success, unanimously invited him to become its pastor. He accepted the call, and is now the honored successor of Everts, Lathrop, Kendrick, Hoyt, and Hawthorne.

Humble, Rev. Henry, a pioneer preacher in Louisiana, was born in South Carolina in 1765; settled in Catahoula Parish, La., 1822, and in 1826 gathered the First church on the Ouachita; was moderator on the Louisiana Association in 1828, and the following year died while attending the Association.

Humble, Rev. Thos. J., the leading minister of the Ouachita Baptist Association in Louisiana, was born in Caldwell Parish, La., in 1829; has long been the efficient clerk of his Association, and frequently its moderator.

Hume, Rev. Thomas, was the son of the Rev.

Thomas Hume, of Edinburgh, Scotland, who, soon after his graduation from the university of that city, and his ordination as a minister of the Established (Presbyterian) Church, removed to the United States. Having settled in Virginia, he married there, and united to the duties of his sacred calling the office of classical teacher. His only child, Thomas, was born in Smithfield, Isle of Wight Co., Va., March 15, 1812. The sudden death of the father, while in the act of preaching the opening sermon as moderator of the Baltimore Presbytery, occurred when the son was scarcely six years of age. His education was interrupted in his sixteenth year by his acceptance of an assistant's place in a store in Petersburg, Va. At the age of eighteen he made a profession of religion, and joined the First Baptist church of Petersburg. His marked decision of character, his intellectual sprightliness, and his earnest piety attracted the attention of the devoted church, and he was soon licensed to preach. After a brief but fruitful training at the Virginia Baptist Seminary (now Richmond College), he made his first attempt at preaching in Chesterfield Co., Va. Just before his twenty-first year, he was called to the pastorate of the Court Street Baptist church, Portsmouth, Va., which was then small in numbers and influence, as well as burdened with temporal and spiritual troubles. His modest and scrupulous reluctance was overcome by the kind importunities of the community, and the rapid growth of the church, as indicated by the erection of a spacious and elegant house of worship within four years after his installation, and by the increase of the membership from a mere handful to 650, proved the wisdom of his choice. During this pastorate of nearly twenty-five years, his enlightened public spirit, his financial knowledge and administrative talent, gave him great influence in the commercial and charitable enterprises of the city. He was a director of the Seaboard and Roanoke Railroad Company, president of the Providence Society, general superintendent of education in Portsmouth and Norfolk Counties, president of the Portsmouth Insurance Company, and prominently connected, also, with other institutions. His reputation and usefulness in the denomination are attested by the number of important positions to which he was called. As president of the Virginia Baptist Bible Board, clerk and president of the Portsmouth Baptist Association, president of the Baptist General Association of Virginia, trustee of the Columbian College (from which he received the honorary degree of A.M.), and of Richmond College, owner (in part) and treasurer of the Chesapeake Female College, organizer and pastor of the Fourth Street Baptist church, Norfolk, Va., he was constantly active in the service of God and man. His self-sacrificing interest in the community to which he gave his consecrated life is specially remembered in connection with the yellow-fever epidemic, which, in 1855, desolated the twin cities of Norfolk and Portsmouth. He was the fearless, faithful pastor throughout all those sad and weary months, and the special guardian and friend of the many orphans, while his complete exemption in his own person from the pestilence enabled him to multiply his usefulness in every direction. As a preacher, Mr. Hume was marked for Scriptural soundness of doctrine, spiritual unction and pathos, and by practical wisdom. Great revivals of religion in his earlier ministry accompanied the orderly and successful administration of the work of the church and Sunday-school; while his financial skill was such as to distinguish him not only in his profession, but also in business circles, yet the sincere fervor of his piety restrained his undue absorption in worldly affairs, and kept his character and his reputation alike unsullied. In the vigorous maturity of his powers, he became suddenly enfeebled after exposure in the Virginia Baptist Memorial Campaign of 1872, and after two years died, lamented and beloved by all who knew him.

Hume, Rev. Thomas, Jr., son of the Rev. Thomas Hume and Mary Ann Gregory Hume, was born in Portsmouth, Va., Oct. 21, 1836. He enjoyed excellent opportunities both at home and at the collegiate institute of the city. At the age of fifteen he entered Richmond College, where he obtained the degree of A.B., followed by that of A.M. His studies were continued at the University of Virginia, where, after graduation in several schools, his course was interrupted by a serious illness. While at the university he was one of the editors of *The Literary Magazine*, and president of the Young Men's Christian Association. As he purposed devoting himself to the business of teaching, he accepted the professorship of Latin, French, and English Literature in Chesapeake Female College, near Old Point Comfort, but had not fairly commenced work when the war broke up that prosperous institution. During his residence there the church in Portsmouth, of which he was a member, corresponded with him with regard to his duty to enter the ministry, and learning that his informal services with the Christian Association had been blessed, urged upon him the propriety of accepting a license to preach. Having entered the Confederate service at the opening of the war, he was soon called by the 3d Va. (Infantry) Regiment to officiate for them, and he received an appointment as their chaplain. The authorities, however, soon transferred him to the post-chaplaincy at Petersburg, Va., a very important hospital station, around which the lines of a protracted siege were fast closing.

Since the war Mr. Hume has been at various times principal of the Petersburg Classical Institute (at the same time supplying country pulpits in Sussex and Chesterfield Counties, Va.), Professor of Languages and Literature in Roanoke Female College, Danville, Va., pastor of the Danville Baptist church, and of the Cumberland Baptist church, Norfolk, Va., and Professor of the English Language and Literature in the Norfolk (Female) Collegiate Institute. His interest in literary pursuits, especially in English studies, has accompanied but not interfered with his regular devotion to the higher work of the ministry. Mr. Hume is an earnest and forcible preacher and a successful pastor. As a writer he is vigorous, classical, and chaste, and among the younger of the Virginia ministers is marked for his genial social qualities, his intellectual acuteness, and his accurate and varied attainments.

Humphrey, Hon. Friend, was born in Simsbury, Conn., March 8, 1787; at nineteen he was

HON. FRIEND HUMPHREY.

converted and baptized; in 1810 he removed to Albany, N. Y., and commenced business for himself; in 1811 he was one of the constituent members of the First Baptist church of his adopted city; in 1834 he was one of the constituent members of the Pearl Street church. He was several terms mayor of Albany. He was also a member of the State senate. He was a man of great courage in times of pestilence, and as unselfish as he was brave. His liberality was universal; "no improvement, no enterprise, no mission, no charity that commended itself to the wise and liberal," was without his aid. It is supposed that his contributions to benevolent objects reached $100,000. "He was a noble specimen of a man, a universal philanthropist. The name of Friend Humphrey will never be forgotten in Albany." He died March 14, 1854. The stores of the city were closed during the services at his funeral; a profound stillness showed the love and sorrow of Albany; the city government and a large concourse of people followed the remains to their last resting-place, and tears fell from many eyes.

Humphrey, Rev. Luther, was born in Glover, Vt., Aug. 19, 1808; died at Augusta, Wis., Aug. 17, 1876; educated at Potsdam Academy and at Amherst College. After teaching as the principal of Southport Academy, N. Y., he prosecuted a course of theological study at Hamilton, N. Y. He was settled as pastor at Lorraine, Covington, and Massena, in New York, and at Mazomanie and Augusta, Wis. For a number of years he was not in the active work of the ministry owing to enfeebled health.

Humpstone, Rev. John, was born in Manchester, England, May 4, 1850. He is the son of Rev. William Humpstone, and came to America with his father when a lad. At twelve years of age he assisted his father in public worship in Music Hall, Worcester, England, by reading from the pulpit the Scriptures and the hymns, thus forecasting the work of his life. On the 25th of December, 1864, he was baptized by Rev. J. E. Cheshire, and became a member of the Baptist church of Falls of Schuylkill, Philadelphia. A few months later he gave promise of usefulness by the delivery of an address of remarkable ability for one of his age. In 1871 he was graduated from Lewisburg University, and in 1874 from Crozer Theological Seminary. Before his studies were completed he was compelled to leave school for a year, during which time he supplied the church in Galway, N. Y. A revival was the result, and 43 converts desired to be baptized by him, and for this reason a council was called and he was ordained at Galway in 1873. His first pastorate was at Manayunk, Philadelphia, where he was settled in 1874. In 1877 he accepted a call to the Calvary Baptist church, Albany, N. Y., where at the present writing his labors are greatly blessed.

Hunt, Rev. Abraham S., A.M., was born near Digby, Nova Scotia; converted and baptized in St. John, New Brunswick; graduated from Acadia College, June, 1844; ordained at Dartmouth the following November; became co-pastor, in 1847, with the venerable Edward Manning, of the Cornwallis church, and his successor in 1851; returned to Dartmouth in 1869; appointed superintendent of education in Nova Scotia in 1870, and conscientiously performed his duties till he died, in 1877.

Hunt, Rev. George, was born in Fayette Co., Ky., June 9, 1831. He united with East Hickman Baptist church in 1844; was educated at Georgetown College, and graduated in 1849. He was ordained to the pastorate of Maysville Baptist church in 1856. In 1858 he was elected Professor of Theology in Georgetown College, where he remained until 1861. In 1862 he was elected president of Bethel College, and occupied the position two years. He has since been pastor of Main Street Baptist church, in Bowling Green, the First Baptist church in Lexington, the church at Versailles, and is now pastor of the church at Hillsborough, Woodford Co., all in Kentucky. He has baptized about 400 persons into the churches of which he has been pastor. He is now conducting a school at Versailles in connection with his pastoral work.

Hunt, Judge Joseph D., was born in Fayette Co., Ky., in 1838. He is a brother of Rev. George Hunt, who, on the death of their father, became his guardian and superintended his education. He graduated with the honors of a class of forty-nine at Center College, Ky., in 1857. He graduated in the law department of the University of Louisville. In 1862 he entered the Confederate army as a volunteer, and remained until the close of the war. On the return of peace he resumed his profession. In 1873 he was appointed by Gov. Leslie judge of the tenth judicial district of Kentucky to fill a vacancy caused by the death of Judge Thomas. In 1874 he was elected by the people to the same position and served six years, but declined re-election and resumed the practice of law. He is an honored member of East Hickman Baptist church.

Huntington, Adoniram Judson, D.D., the youngest son of the Rev. Elijah Huntington, was born in Braintree, Vt., July 6, 1818. Though he lost his father before he was ten years of age, yet he was blessed, during his boyhood and youth, with the careful guidance of a mother eminent for prudence and tenderness, and for consistent and earnest piety. At the age of thirteen he united with the Baptist church in Braintree, of which his father was for a long period the pastor. He entered, in September, 1837, the Freshman class in Brown University. Here he remained less than a month, on account of that ill health which had before, as it has often since, been a serious obstacle to his intellectual pursuits, and from this cause he was compelled to suspend his studies for an entire year, the latter part of which he spent with a very kind relative and benefactor, the late Dr. Eleazer Parmly, in the city of New York. In the pleasant home of this gentleman he passed also the following year, at the same time pursuing his studies as a member of the Freshman class of the Columbia College. In this class he attained the second place in scholarship, the Hon. A. S. Hewitt having occupied the first. In September, 1839, he returned to Brown University, where he spent the Sophomore and a part of the Junior year, when failing health made it necessary for him again to leave college. Soon

ADONIRAM JUDSON HUNTINGTON, D.D.

afterwards he engaged as a teacher, as in those days so many Northern students were accustomed to do, in the more genial climate of the South, and in this occupation passed a year and a half in Middlesex Co., Va. Fearing the rigors of a Northern climate, he completed his collegiate course at the Columbian College, D. C., where he graduated in October, 1843. Immediately after he became tutor in the same institution in the Greek and Latin languages. In June, 1844, he married Miss Bettie G. Christian, the daughter of Dr. R. A. Christian, of Middlesex Co., Va. Having filled the office of tutor for three years, he was elected professor of the same departments, and after filling this position with great success for three years, he resigned it for the purpose of entering upon what he regarded as the chosen vocation of his life,—the ministry of the gospel,—and was ordained in June, 1849. His first pastoral charge was in Lexington, Va., which he relinquished (and to which he was afterwards again invited) for a wider field of labor in Chelsea, Mass. After a year of successful service in the First Baptist church of this place (having been called also at a later period to the Carey Avenue Baptist church of Chelsea), he received an unsolicited invitation to resume his former professorship in the Columbian College, which, from considerations of health, he accepted. After occupying this

chair for seven years he again retired from it, in 1859, in hopes of being able to resume the duties of the ministry. After spending between one and two years in Farmville, Va., where his labors were signally blessed, he accepted, in September, 1860, a call from the First Baptist church of Augusta, Ga., and in this field, which was regarded as one of the most important in the denomination in the South, and in those troublous war times he so discharged the duties of his office for some five years that, with the divine blessing, the peace and prosperity of the church were promoted. Within this period he was selected to deliver, at the Georgia Baptist State Convention, an annual address before the Bible and Colportage Society, and again to preach the annual sermon on ministerial education. Soon after the resignation of the charge of this church, in August, 1865, he was again invited to the Columbian College to fill the Greek professorship, on which he entered in September, 1866. This position he has ever since occupied, excepting some fifteen months spent in Europe in 1867–68, partly in travel in pursuit of health as well as knowledge, and partly in study at Athens and Heidelberg. During the periods of his professorship he has given a considerable part of his Sabbaths to the preaching of the gospel. He published while in Augusta a tract of some thirty pages on the "Moral and Religious Training of Children," and in April, 1877, in the *Baptist Quarterly*, an article on "Ancient Attica and Athens;" besides which he has made occasional contributions to religious journals. He received the degree of D.D. from Brown University in 1868. Dr. Huntington as an educator is clear, thorough, and exact; as a preacher impressive and instructive ; and as a man genial, affable, and of "good report of them which are without."

Huntington, Rev. Elijah, was born in Mansfield, Conn., Aug. 21, 1763. His ancestors settled in that State at an early period, and from them has sprung the numerous family of Huntingtons in Connecticut and other States. He was a soldier of the Revolutionary army, and soon after its close he removed to Vermont, where he was employed for a time as a teacher. When about twenty-seven years of age he was converted, and united with the Baptist church at Royalton. In June, 1800, he was ordained in Braintree, Vt., as an evangelist. Immediately he became pastor of the Baptist church in that town, and he held this office till his death, June 24, 1828.

Mr. Huntington had a strong, discriminating, and well-balanced mind. He was a successful teacher of youth, a forcible and acceptable speaker, and an instructive preacher of the gospel. In every relation of life he may be said to have been an example worthy of imitation.

In regard to his piety, it may probably be safely

asserted that no man in the region in which he lived was more distinguished for a holy and blameless life. It seemed to be his constant aim to know and to do the will of that Master to whom he had devoted himself without reserve. " The law of God seemed to be engraven on his heart." From the very thought of violating the divine commands he apparently shrunk with horror. And yet he placed a very low estimate upon his own piety ; his humility was one of his most striking characteristics.

As a preacher he thoroughly and prayerfully studied the Bible, clearly expounded its doctrines, and faithfully enforced its precepts. His sermons were thoughtful, able, evangelical, earnest, and faithful. " Occasionally he rose above himself, and, as though endued with extraordinary power, presented truth in a manner the most clear and impressive."

His influence was extensive, permanent, and in every respect salutary. Nor were his efforts to do good limited to his own neighborhood. " He was an ardent friend of foreign missions, and prayed and labored, as well as gave of his substance, for the spread of the gospel. His end was peace. In view of it he said, " I wish not to choose for myself ; I think it is my greatest desire that God may be glorified by me in life and in death."

A biographical notice of Mr. Huntington appeared in the *American Baptist Magazine* of February, 1829, written by Rev. A. Nichols, of blessed memory, then pastor of the Congregational church in Braintree, who, for twenty years, lived only three or four miles from Mr. Huntington. Appended to that obituary the following note appears : Mr. Huntington was at the house of a friend, when conversation was casually introduced respecting Mr. Nichols. Mr. Huntington remarked, " I do not know of a man I should be willing to exchange for Mr. Nichols." Not long after Mr. Nichols was at the same place, and conversation was in a similar manner introduced concerning Mr. Huntington. Mr. Nichols observed, " I do not know of a man I should be willing to exchange for Mr. Huntington." The references to each other mentioned in this note show both the high character of the two men and their mutual friendship.

Huntington, Rev. Joseph, son of Rev. Elijah Huntington, was born in Braintree, Vt., July 27, 1811. In the ordinary frivolities of childhood and youth he had little disposition to engage. He was habitually serious and contemplative, and often exhibited deep convictions of sin and anxiety for his salvation. It was not, however, till the revival of 1831 that he found peace in believing, and united with the Baptist church in Braintree. As he had felt a deep and most painful sense of his need of Christ as a Saviour, so his love to him was ardent and his consecration unreserved. Having deter-

mined to devote himself to the ministry of the gospel, he commenced the study of the Greek and Latin languages, in which he made great progress. He entered Middlebury College, in his native State, from which, at the expiration of four years (in 1837), he graduated, having maintained during his whole course a standing second to no one in his class. As a proof of the estimation in which he was held by his fellow-students they assigned to him the most honorable part in the anniversary exercises of their literary society on the day before commencement, while the offer of a tutorship in the college, soon after his graduation, showed the respect entertained for him by the faculty of the institution. This, however, he did not accept. In 1838 he entered the theological institution at Newton, Mass. ; but, in hope of finding the duties of a country pastor more favorable to his declining health, and in consideration of the pressing need of ministers in his native State, he reluctantly returned to Vermont in less than a year, and was ordained as pastor of the Baptist church in East Williamstown. After a few months of very acceptable and useful service he was compelled to relinquish all ministerial duties. Soon afterwards, to recruit his health, he went to South Carolina and Georgia, where he passed a winter, but in the following spring he returned to Vermont without improvement. Here, at the home of his mother, he lingered for a year, and died of consumption April 26, 1843. Thus prematurely passed away this devoted servant of Christ, who nevertheless had lived long enough to secure the high esteem, the warm friendship, and the strong confidence of all who knew him well. His mind was strong and logical. He had great power of acquiring knowledge as well as untiring industry. He was a speaker of uncommon readiness, conciseness, earnestness, and force. His sermons were methodical, lucid, and pungent. His piety was ardent and consistent, characterized by deep feeling, and still more by inflexible principle. Nothing could make him swerve from what he deemed to be right. His conduct was not only above reproach, but also above suspicion. He seemed to have brought his passions and appetites, his heart, his intellect, and his will into subjection to Christ. The delineation, indeed, of his character would be an enumeration of the virtues that most adorn the man and of the graces that most closely liken the Christian to his Master.

As his grand aim in life was to do the divine will, so he cheerfully submitted to that will when he saw his earthly career coming to so early a close, and at last, knowing in whom he believed, he calmly and even joyfully committed his soul to his keeping.

Hurd, Rev. James Christie, M.D., was born in Nova Scotia, April 17, 1829. He early prepared himself for the practice of medicine, but soon felt that it was his duty to preach. In 1873 he became pastor of the Cedar Street Baptist church, Buffalo, N. Y. While residing in Buffalo he practised medicine for a time, and afterwards occupied an editorial position on the Buffalo *Express*. From Buffalo he went to St. Thomas, Ontario, as pastor of the Baptist church. He came to Iowa in 1876 and took charge of the Baptist church at Marshalltown, and soon became identified with his brethren of the State in all the general interests of the denomination. In October, 1878, he was elected president of the Iowa Baptist State Convention, and was re-elected in 1879, always meeting the duties of this position with signal ability. In 1878 he became pastor of the First Baptist church, Burlington. He died in the harness on Sunday, Dec. 21, 1879.

Hurley, Rev. William, was born in Warwickshire, England, Feb. 5, 1795. At eighteen he was converted and soon commenced preaching. He was ordained in 1822. Preached for ten years in England with marked success. In 1828 he came to America; preached a year in Providence, R. I., and afterwards came to St. Louis, Mo. In 1831 he took charge of the Fee Fee Baptist church. He was at the organization of the General Association of Missouri in 1835, and that year he became pastor of the Palmyra church, and afterwards of Bethel Baptist church. Subsequently for years he labored as an evangelist. He was earnest, self-denying, and very successful in leading souls to Jesus.

Dr. Fisk wrote his memoir, which shows that he was a man of unusual talent, culture, and eloquence. His last address was at the laying of the corner-stone of an institution of learning. He was a Mason of high standing and lectured eloquently to the "craft." He loved standard literature, and advocated its study. He was a man of deep piety; his memory will long be lovingly cherished in Missouri, and his influence for good be perpetuated. He died Aug. 3, 1856, in Troy, Lincoln Co., Mo., in the sixty-first year of his life.

Hutchens, Prof. Allen Sabin, a native of Spafford, Onondaga Co., N. Y., was born Dec. 8, 1817. He spent his early youth in Medina, N. Y. When but a boy his father removed to Adrian, Mich., where he grew up to manhood. He was educated at Denison University, Granville, O., from which he graduated in 1843. He subsequently studied theology at Newton, Mass. He taught at Denison University and at the Baptist Academy at Norwalk, O. But the chief work of his life has been done in connection with Wayland University, at Beaver Dam, Wis. He was called to the presidency of this institution in 1857, and has been connected with it, with the exception of a few years, throughout its entire history. Prof. Hutchens is a Chris-

tian teacher of fine culture and attainments. He stands high as a Greek scholar. He has been a hard worker, and in the very prime of his life, with health so impaired as to prevent his further labor in the class-room, at present he is living in retirement at Beaver Dam.

Hutchins, Rev. Hiram, was educated at Madison University; ordained in Richfield, N. Y., in August, 1840; served the church of Charlestown, Mass., as pastor, and the church of Roxbury, and in 1860 took charge of a church in Brooklyn, of which he is still the beloved pastor. For several years he was president of the American Baptist Free Mission Society. His long ministry of forty years has been blessed with many tokens of divine approbation.

Hutchinson, Rev. Elijah, was born in Marion, N. Y., June 7, 1810, and removed with his parents to Newport, N. H., when he was a child. He was baptized by Rev. Ira Pearson. Impressed that it was his duty to preach the gospel, he studied at New Hampton, and at Portsmouth, under the tuition of Dr. Baron Stow, and took the full course at Newton. In the autumn of 1834 he was ordained pastor of the church at Windsor, Vt., and continued in office for twenty years. After suspending his work for two years, he resumed his pastorate with the church at Windsor, where he labored for five years longer. This ministry of twenty-five years with one church, his only charge, was full of blessing to his people. His labors also, at times, extended beyond his more immediate field, and the feeble churches in his neighborhood enjoyed the benefit of his instructions. He came to be regarded as a leader in all good enterprises, and his counsels were sought and followed by those who asked his advice. He enjoyed a very large measure of the respect and esteem of his brethren in Vermont, and left the impress of his Christian influence upon the Baptist cause in that State. Mr. Hutchinson died at Windsor, April 5, 1872.

Hutchinson, Rev. Elisha, was born in Sharon, Conn., Dec. 22, 1749. After his conversion, at twenty, there seemed to be an awakening of his intellectual powers. He longed to preach the gospel, which had done so much for him. He commenced a course of preparatory study under the tuition of Rev. Dr. Wheelock, at Lebanon, Conn., and joined the Congregational church of which his instructor was the pastor. He was a member of the first class that graduated at Dartmouth College in 1775. Shortly after leaving college he was licensed as an evangelist, and preached some years, when he was ordained in the year 1778 as pastor of the Congregational church in Westford, Conn., where he remained five years. In 1785 he accepted a call to the Congregational church in Pomfret, Vt., where he remained for about ten years. For the next few years he supplied churches in Vermont and Massachusetts. In 1800 he changed his views on the mode and subjects of Christian baptism, and became a decided Baptist. . After various charges he was invited to become the pastor of the Baptist church in Newport, N. H., in 1814. Four years after, he was blessed with a powerful revival of religion, and in about ten months 110 united with the church, adding very greatly to its efficiency. After this revival, feeling the infirmities of age, Mr. Hutchinson resigned his pastorate, but remained a resident in the place where his labors had been so signally blessed until his death, which occurred April 19, 1833.

Hutchinson, Rev. Enoch, was born in Marion, N. Y., in June, 1810, and was a graduate of Waterville College in the class of 1834, and of the Newton Theological Institution in the class of 1837. He was ordained in Boston, Nov. 26, 1837. He was pastor of the church in Framingham, Mass., one year, and Professor of Theology in the Maine Baptist Theological Institute at Thomaston, Me., for one year. For some time he was editor of the *Baptist Memorial,*—1846–51. The results of his Oriental studies are embodied in his "Syriac Grammar." He is the author of "Music of the Bible." Mr. Hutchinson has resided for several years in Brooklyn, N. Y.

Hutchinson, Gov. John, was born at Nottingham, England, in September, 1616. He was the son of Sir Thomas Hutchinson, and of the Lady Margaret, daughter of Sir John Biron, of Newstead. When he reached a proper age he spent five years in the University of Cambridge, where he greatly improved his opportunities for acquiring a superior education. After his marriage, which occurred July 3, 1638, he retired with his wife to Owthorpe, near Nottingham. There his mind became deeply exercised about religion, and he spent two entire years in the study of divinity. During this period he was enabled to put his whole trust in the Saviour, and he was led to see that salvation never entered a human heart through free will or creature merits, but through sovereign grace and the blood of Christ. From that period his faith warmly embraced the doctrine of God's election and of his minute overruling providence. He cherished a fervent love for the Saviour and his people, and a tender compassion for the impenitent and for personal enemies. The cavaliers and high-churchmen of his day, the men who caught the spirit of Archbishop Laud and his fellow-conspirators against Christ's truth and British liberty, were all Arminians, and Mr. Hutchinson was necessarily placed in the ranks of the defenders of the Commonwealth.

In the struggle which resulted in the overthrow and death of Charles I., he was made governor of the castle and town of Nottingham, and he became colonel of a regiment which he raised. The castle was a ruin and the town was full of traitors, some of whom were fitted by talents and malice to give

GOV. JOHN HUTCHINSON.

much trouble. Nottingham was a place of great importance to Charles and the Parliament. Under the care of the new governor the castle was greatly strengthened, and forts were erected to guard the town, malcontents were kept in check, the love of liberty was fostered, and the best interests of the people were secured. Repeated attacks of the foe were ignominiously defeated, and difficulties that overwhelmed others, and that would have crushed any ordinary leader, were surmounted with ease and honor. And when the sword of the king could not conquer the valiant governor and his men, immense sums of money were offered to corrupt Gov. Hutchinson and secure the stronghold. But it was held for the Parliament until Charles lost his head and the civil war was ended.

The fame of the governor spread all over his country. His skill, heroism, patience, and success made him dear to the hearts of all the friends of liberty in his native country. He was elected to the House of Commons, and he occupied a conspicuous and influential place in its debates. Cromwell early saw his extraordinary ability, and tried to enlist him on his side, but the governor quickly penetrated the selfish schemes of the "uncrowned king" of England, and though Ireton, the son-in-law of Cromwell, was his cousin and trusted friend, he speedily informed the hero of

Marston Moor that he had not fought against one tyrant to assist in building the throne of another. And from that moment the coming Protector used every art to keep him from military promotion. Had it not been for Cromwell, Gov. Hutchinson would have been in a position, in all human probability, to have perpetuated a republic in the British Islands. He was one of the judges that tried Charles I., and signed his death-warrant.

After the return of Charles II. the English people for a time acted as if a wave of insanity had swept over the nation; the son of a deceitful and bloodthirsty despot, himself a treacherous libertine, was hailed with rapturous joy wherever he went; the enthusiasm was so general that hosts of the followers of Cromwell were carried away either through terror or a change of mind, and they made the air ring with their shouts for the king. The governor during this period of national madness kept his mind calm, and his heart courageous in his God, and while he took proper measures to protect himself he recanted no principle, he denied no act, he betrayed no friend. In a time when life could be purchased and large estates protected by information treacherously imparted, any amount of which was at his disposal, repeated opportunities to communicate which were given him by the attorney-general and others, he despised the meanness so common and so frequently commended of protecting himself by the sacrifice of others.

For a season he was unmolested at Owthorpe. He carefully attended to home duties, avoiding all connection with politics, expounding the Scriptures on the Lord's day to his family instead of attending the ministry of some semi-Catholic in the parish church. But at last he was arrested, and soon after he was removed to the Tower of London, and from it he was taken to Sandown Castle, in Kent, where he died Sept. 10, 1664, in the forty-ninth year of his age. During the eleven months of his imprisonment he enjoyed a large measure of the sustaining grace of God, and a foretaste of heavenly blessedness made his death-bed a scene of special joy.

Gov. Hutchinson believed that in religious affairs secular legislation had no place. He abhorred all persecution for conscience' sake. When George Fox, the founder of the "Society of Friends," was imprisoned in Nottingham, he extended to the persecuted Quaker his powerful protection.

He was a man of fearless courage, and when he saw his friends of the Commonwealth butchered by the bloody mandates of King Charles II., he was only restrained by his wife from giving himself up to die with them.

He and Mrs. Hutchinson became Baptists in this way: "When formerly the Presbyterian ministers had forced him, for quietness' sake, to go and break up a private (religious) meeting in the cannonier's chamber (of Nottingham Castle), there were found some notes concerning Pedobaptism, which were brought into the governor's lodgings, and his wife then having more leisure to read than he, having perused them and compared them with the Scriptures, found not what to say against the truths they asserted concerning the misapplication of that ordinance to infants; but being then young and modest, she thought it a kind of virtue to submit to the judgment and practice of most churches, rather than to defend a singular opinion of her own, she not being then enlightened in that great mistake of the national churches. But in this year, expecting to become a mother, she communicated her doubts to her husband, and desired him to endeavour her satisfaction; which while he did, he himself became as unsatisfied, or rather satisfied against it. First, therefore, he diligently searched the Scriptures alone, and could find in them no ground at all for that practice: then he bought and read all the eminent treatises on both sides, which at that time came thick from the presses, and was still more satisfied of the error of the Pedobaptists. After the confinement of his wife, that he might if possible give the religious party no offense, he invited all the ministers to dinner, and propounded his doubt and the ground thereof to them. None of them could defend their practice with any satisfactory reason but the tradition of the church from the primitive times, and their main buckler of federal holiness, which Tombs and Denne had so excellently overthrown. He and his wife then professing themselves unsatisfied in the practice, desired their opinions what they ought to do. Most answered, to conform to the general practice of other Christians, how dark soever it were to themselves; but Mr. Foxcraft, one of the Assembly (which framed the Westminster Confession of Faith), said that except they were convinced of the warrant of that practice from the Word they sinned in doing it: whereupon the infant was not baptized. And now the governor and his wife, notwithstanding that they forsook not their assemblies, nor retracted their benevolences and civilities from them, yet were they reviled by them, called fanatics and anabaptists, and often glanced at in their public sermons. And not only the ministers but all their zealous sectaries conceived implacable malice against them upon this account; which was carried on with a spirit of envy and persecution to the last; though he, on his side, might well have said to them, as his Master said to the old Pharisees, 'Many good works have I done among you; for which of those do you hate me?' Yet the generality even of them had a secret conviction upon them that he had been faithful to them and deserved their love; and in spite of their own bitter zeal, could not but have a reverent esteem for him whom they often railed at for not thinking and speaking according to their opinions." (Life of Colonel Hutchinson, by his Widow Lucy, pp. 299, 300, 301. London, 1846.)

This Christian hero, a graduate of Cambridge, like Judson, Noel, Carson, Dunster, and a host of others, sacrificed his feelings, his friendships, his interests, and his social comfort for no earthly gain, but for heaven-born truth. Gov. Hutchinson is an illustration of the resistless force of God's pure Word.

Hutchinson, Rev. John Blanchard, was born in Long Sutton, Lincolnshire, England, Dec. 16, 1825. His father was a respected minister of the Wesleyan body, and under his faithful labors his son was awakened. He also united with the Wesleyans, by whom he was licensed when but eighteen years of age. He came to America in May, 1856, and was minister in charge of the Methodist Episcopal church, South Orange and Jefferson Village, nearly three years.

His views of Bible truth becoming more matured he was baptized by Rev. William Hind, and entered into the membership of Northfield Baptist church, by which he was licensed to preach. On Oct. 1, 1860, he was ordained, and assumed charge of the Livingston church, in Essex Co., N. Y. Mr. Hutchinson has won for himself a strong place in the hearts of his brethren, and has rendered good service in the Olivet church, Philadelphia, the Centennial in Wilkesbarre, and in the Hatboro' church, Montgomery Co., Pa., where he now labors.

Hutchinson, Mrs. Lucy, was born the 29th of January, 1620, in the Tower of London. Her father was Sir Allen Apsley, governor of the Tower; her mother was Lucy, daughter of Sir John St. John, of Lidiard Treegooze, Wiltshire, England. Her parents were both the children of God, and by precept and example from her earliest years showed her the blessedness of a holy life.

When about seven years old she had eight teachers in as many different branches: languages, music, dancing, needlework, and writing. She hated needlework, and cared nothing for music and dancing. When children came to see her she wearied them with grave instructions, and treated their dolls so roughly that they were glad when she forsook their company for the society of older persons. Books were everything to her even in childhood; during hours intended for amusement she was reading, and at all other times when she had an opportunity. And when she reached womanhood her information was equal to that of any young lady in England, if she was not the best-informed woman in her country. Soon after she ceased to be a mere child she was called by Jesus into the kingdom of his grace; and she entered

upon his service with a heart wholly his, and without a doubt of his love for her. This blessed condition fitted her to despise her own fancies, and every form of danger, and made Christ the Lord of

MRS. LUCY HUTCHINSON.

all her doctrines, and of her entire conduct. After her marriage with Mr. Hutchinson, when he was appointed governor of the castle and town of Nottingham, she went with him; and when the horrors of war visited Nottingham there was not a braver heart in the place than Mrs. Hutchinson's.

When five of her husband's soldiers were wounded and carried to the castle, and there was no surgeon to dress their wounds, with some assistance from a soldier, this young lady fearlessly bound up the bleeding limbs and bodies of the sufferers; and seeing some of the enemy carried in as prisoners in the same unfortunate situation, and consigned to a miserable dungeon, crowded with other prisoners, she sent for them and cleansed and bound up their wounds, while Capt. Palmer, an officer on her husband's side in the civil war, was helping her by declaring that " his soul abhorred to see this favor to the enemies of God."

Throughout life she ever showed a strong faith, a generous benevolence, and a lofty courage. She adopted Baptist sentiments from reading the notes found in the cannonier's room, in Nottingham Castle, where the Baptist soldiers had held a prayer-meeting; and from comparing them with the Scriptures; her husband, after careful and protracted examination, followed her example. But not all her quickness to perceive affronts; nor the exquisite pain inflicted by them upon her refined feeling; nor the certainty that insults, if not severe wrongs, would be heaped upon her for becoming a Baptist, could keep her from honoring and obeying her Lord. She confessed her principles in the most public way, in an age when Baptists alone understood Christ's law of religious liberty.

She helped her husband with more than the power of half a dozen ordinary men; and then she wrote his "Memoirs" in a style so charming and eloquent that it chains the reader from beginning to end. I doubt very much if in the seventeenth century, except the "Pilgrim's Progress," there was another book written in prose by such a masterly pen as that of Lucy Hutchinson. It is the best biography in the English language, and one of the most popular that ever was written in any tongue.

Hutchinson, Rev. William, was born in Drumlamph, Ireland, in August, 1795, of Scotch-Irish parents; came to the United States in 1818; entered Hamilton in 1821; ordained on leaving the institution, and labored as a missionary for three years in his native land; returned to this country in 1827, and has been pastor of seven churches in New York, and of Lower Dublin, Pa. Mr. Hutchinson has been blessed in delivering his glorious message, and he has walked with God in his own heart.

Hyatt, Rev. B. C., pastor at Monticello, Ark., was born in South Carolina in 1815; removed to Arkansas in 1846; ordained in 1857. His labors have been chiefly confined to the counties of Bradley, Drew, Ashley, and Lincoln; has gathered seven churches in his field, and baptized about one thousand persons.

Hyde, Rev. G. W., son of Richard and Eliza D. Hyde, was born near Chancellorsville, in Spottsylvania Co., Va., March 25, 1838. When a little more than one year old his parents removed to Missouri and settled near Keytesville, Chariton Co., where he was reared. He professed conversion and united with the Keytesville Baptist church in May, 1853. He entered the State University at Columbia, Mo., in September, 1855, and graduated with honors in July, 1859. In September, 1859, he entered the Southern Baptist Theological Seminary, then located at Greenville, S. C., and graduated in full in 1862. He was licensed to preach while a student at the university by the church in Columbia, and was ordained at Peterville church, Powhatan Co., Va., in August, 1863. He has twice been made financial agent of William Jewell College, and has been pastor at Keytesville and Brunswick, in Chariton Co., and also at Mount Nebo, Beulah, Concord, Mount Herman, and Boonville, in Cooper County. For ten years he has been an active member of the board of trustees of William Jewell College, and also a visitor of the Vardeman

School of Theology. He has also been honored with the position of curator of Stephens College for a number of years.

Hyman, Rev. John J., was born Sept. 21, 1832. He is principal of the Mount Vernon Institute, at Riddleville, Ga. He was ordained April 12, 1863, and served all through the war as a chaplain of the 49th Ga. Regiment in Gen. Lee's army, and was considered one of the best chaplains in the army. During the war he baptized 260 soldiers, and since the war he has been a great worker both as pastor and teacher. He is an earnest, faithful pastor, a good preacher, and has served as moderator of Mount Vernon Association.

Hymns, and their Authors.—It is undeniable that in the infancy of the church, as Cave says, "It was usual for any person to compose divine songs in honor of Christ, and to sing them in the public assemblies." (Primitive Christianity, page 134, Oxford, 1840.) In the beginning of the second century, Pliny, in giving the emperor Trajan an account of the Christians, says, "They were accustomed to meet on a certain day before it was light and sing a hymn alternately to Christ as God." (Pliny, lib. x., Ep. 97.) This was evidently an uninspired composition. Eusebius, speaking of early hymns, says, "Whatever psalms and hymns were written by the brethren *from the beginning* celebrate Christ, the Word of God, by asserting His divinity." (Eccles. Hist., lib. v. cap. 28.) That there were many hymns written in the first and second centuries we have no doubt. These were all composed by Baptists. The oldest hymn now known among Christians in its most *ancient* form is, "Glory be to the Father, and to the Son, and to the Holy Ghost, world without end, Amen." In this form a Baptist was its author. And it was first given to the churches in the second century, or earlier. The additional words, "As it was in the beginning, is now, and ever shall be," were placed in this sacred song at an early period.

In modern times some of the most popular hymns in our language were written by Baptists. "My country, 'tis of thee," was written by Dr. S. F. Smith. This is the most popular patriotic hymn sung in the United States. "He leadeth me: oh, blessed thought," was written by Prof. J. H. Gilmore, of Rochester University. This is one of the finest hymns that ever was published. "Come, thou fount of every blessing," is from the pen of Robert Robinson. Rev. Dr. Fawcett wrote "Blest be the tie that binds." Dr. Samuel Stennett is the author of "On Jordan's stormy banks I stand," and the Rev. Edward Mote composed "My hope is built on nothing less." The following table gives the names of some Baptist authors of hymns, with their nationality, the date of their birth, and the first line of one of their hymns:

Name.	Born.	Country.	Hymns.
Adams, John	1751	England	" Sons we are through God's election."
Anderson, G. W.	1816	United States	" Onward, herald of the gospel."
Anderson, Mrs. G. W.	18:9	France	" Our country's voice is pleading."
Balfern, W. P.	.....	England	Author of a volume containing 139 hymns.
Baldwin, Thomas	1753	United States	" Come, happy souls, adore the Lamb."
Baxter, Mrs. Lydia	1809	"	" The Master is coming ; he calleth for thee."
Beddome, Benjamin	1717	England	" Come, Holy Spirit, come."
Brown, J. Newton	1803	United States	" Go, spirit of the sainted dead."
Burnham, Richard	1749	England	" Jesus, thou art the sinner's friend."
Burton, John	1773	"	" Time is winging us away."
Cleveland, Benjamin	.....	United States	" Oh, could I find from day to day."
Colver, Nathaniel	1794	"	" Weep for the lost; thy Saviour wept."
Cocks, Mrs. Sarah	.....	England	Author of a volume of 216 original hymns.
Cole, Charles	1733	"	" Hark how the gospel trumpet sounds."
Cutting, S. S.	1816	United States	" Oh, Saviour, I am blind : lead thou the way."
Davis, Eliel	1803	England	" From every earthly pleasure."
Deacon, Samuel	1746	"	" To Jordan's stream the Saviour goes."
Denham, David	1791	"	" 'Mid scenes of confusion and creature complaints."
Doane, W. H	.....	United States	" Safe in the arms of Jesus."
Draper, B. H.	.....	England	" Ye Christian heralds, go proclaim."
Dracup, John	17—	"	" Thanks to thy name, O Lord, that we "
Dyer, Sidney	1814	United States	" Go preach the blest salvation."
Elvin, Cornelius	1797	England	" With broken heart and contrite sigh."
Evans, James H	1785	"	" Faint not, Christian, though the road."
Evans, John M	1825	United States	" Amid the joyous scenes of earth."
Fanch, James	1704	England	" Beyond the glittering, starry sky."
Fawcett, John	1739	"	" Blest be the tie that binds."
Fellows, John	.....	"	" Jesus, mighty king in Zion."
Flowerdew, Alice	1759	"	" Fountain of mercy, God of love."
Fountain, John	1767	"	" Sinners, you are now addressed."
Francis, Benjamin	1734	Wales	" My gracious Redeemer I love."
Franklin, Jonathan	1760	England	" Thy church, O Lord, that's planted here."
Gadsby, William	1773	"	" Holy Ghost, we look to thee."
Giles, John E.	1805	"	" Thou hast said, exalted Jesus."
Gilmore, J. H.	1834	United States	" He leadeth me: oh, blessed thought."
Grace, Robert	.....	England	Author of 240 hymns.
Groser, William	1791	"	" Praise the Redeemer, all mighty to save."
Groser, William House	18—	"	" Spirit of truth, celestial fire."
Harbottle, Joseph	1798	"	" See how the fruitless fig-tree stands."
Hinton, John H.	1791	"	" Once I was estranged from God."
Hill, Stephen P.	1806	United States	" The Lord is my shepherd and guide."
Horne, W. W.	1773	England	" Death is no more the frightful foe."
Hupton, Job	1762	"	" Jesus, omnipotent to save."
Ide, George B.	1805	United States	" Son of God, our glorious head."
James, R. S.	1824	"	" Hast'ning on to death's dark river."
Jessey, Henry	1606	England	" Unclean, unclean and full of sin."
Jones, Edmund	1722	"	" Come, humble sinner, in whose breast."
Judson, Adoniram	1788	United States	" Our Father God, who art in heaven."
Judson, Sarah B.	1803	"	" Proclaim the lofty praise."
Keach, Benjamin	1640	England	" My soul, mount up with eagle wings."
Keith, George	.....	"	" How firm a foundation, ye saints of the Lord."
Knowles, J. D.	1798	United States	" O Lord, where'er thy saints apart."
Leland, John	1754	"	" The day is past and gone."
Lowry, Robert	1826	"	" Shall we gather at the river."
Lewis, W. G.	.....	England	" Awake, my soul, thy God to praise."
Lawson, John	.....	"	" Father of mercies, condescend."
Manly, Basil	1825	United States	" Holy, holy, holy Lord."
Medley, Samuel	1738	England	" Awake, my soul, in joyful lays."
Mote, Edward	1797	"	" My hope is built on nothing less."
Milton, John	1608	"	" Let us with a gladsome mind."
Needham, John	1710	"	" Holy and reverend is the name."
Newton, James	1733	"	" Let plenteous grace descend on those."
Norman, ——	.....	"	" 'Tis not as led by custom's voice."
Noel, B. W.	1799	"	" There's not a bird with lonely nest."
Pal, Krishna	1764	India	" O thou, my soul, forget no more."
Pearce, Samuel	1766	England	" In floods of tribulation."
Phelps, S. D.	1816	United States	" This rite our blest Redeemer gave."
Pledge, Ebenezer	1813	England	" I went alone: 'twas summer-time."
Poindexter, ——	.....	United States	" Head of the Church, we bow to thee."
Rawson, George	.....	England	" Cast thy burden on the Lord."
Rippon, John	1751	"	" There's joy in heaven and joy on earth."
Robbins, Gurdon	.....	United States	" There is a land mine eye hath seen."
Robinson, Robert	1735	England	" Come, thou fount of every blessing."
Rowland, A. J.	1840	United States	" There is rest in the shadow."
Ryland, John	1753	England	" In all my Lord's appointed ways."
Saffery, Mrs. M. G.	1773	"	" 'Tis the great Father we adore."
Scott, Jacob R.	1815	United States	" To thee this temple we devote."
Sherwin, W. F.	.....	"	" Sound the battle-cry."
Smith, Samuel F.	1808	"	" My country, 'tis of thee."
Spurgeon, C. H.	1834	England	" The Holy Ghost is here."
Steele, Anne	1716	"	" The Saviour! Oh, what endless charms."
Stennett, Joseph	1663	"	" Another six days' work is done."
Stennett, Samuel	1727	"	" On Jordan's stormy banks I stand."
Swain, Joseph	1761	"	" Who can forbear to sing."
Sutton, Amos	1804	"	" Hail, sweetest, dearest tie that binds."
Thurber, Charles	.....	United States	" From yonder Rocky Mountains."
Tritton, Joseph	.....	England	" Spirit of glory and of grace."
Tucker, William	1731	"	" Amidst ten thousand anxious cares."
Turner, Daniel	1710	"	" Jesus, full of all compassion."
Turney, Edmund	1817	United States	" Oh, love divine! oh, matchless grace."
Upton, James	1760	England	" Come ye who bow to sovereign grace."
Wallin, Benjamin	1711	"	" Hail, mighty Jesus! How divine."
Washburn, H. S.	1811	United States	" Father, gathered round the bier."
Winkler, Edwin T.	.....	"	Author of 140 hymns.
Wyard, George	1803	England	" Oh, charge the waves to bear our friends."
Ward, William	1769	"	" Oh, charge the waves to bear our friends."
Willmarth, J. W.	1835	France	" O Father! Lord of earth and heaven."
Yeager, George	1821	United States	" On the cross behold the Saviour."

I.

Ide, George B., D.D., was born in Coventry, Vt., in 1804, and was the son of Rev. John Ide, a Baptist minister of considerable reputation in the section in which he lived. Young Ide received an

GEORGE B. IDE, D.D.

academic and collegiate education, and he graduated at Middlebury College. It was his purpose to practise law, and he and his fellow-townsman Redfield, afterwards Judge Redfield, of Vermont, commenced a course of legal study in Brandon, Vt. Like Adoniram Judson, whose father also was a minister, Mr. Ide was inclined to be a skeptic, and did not hesitate sometimes to avow his infidel sentiments. But he was reached by the power of divine grace, and finally became settled in his belief of those doctrines which he so eloquently preached in after-life. At once he threw himself into the work of preaching the gospel, and as a revivalist preached with great power in different sections in Northern Vermont. For a short time in each place he was pastor of the churches in Derby, Passumpsic village, and Brandon, Vt., from which place he was called to the pastoral care of the First Baptist church in Albany, N. Y. Here he remained until, having completed a four years' pastorate, he was called to

the Federal Street, now Clarendon Street, church, in Boston, where he continued for two years. He then went to Philadelphia to take charge of the First Baptist church in that city, where he remained for fourteen years, taking rank with the ablest and most eloquent preachers of any denomination in that city. From Philadelphia, Dr. Ide was called to the First Baptist church in Springfield, Mass., and was its pastor from 1852 to the time of his death, a period of nearly twenty years. Twice during this time he was called to important positions in New York, with double the salary he was receiving in Springfield, but he declined, not wishing to take upon himself the burdens of a large city church.

Without doubt Dr. Ide was one of the most vigorous and effective preachers that the Baptist denomination has had in this country. He has given to the public some of his more elaborate discourses in two volumes, bearing the titles "Bible Pictures" and "Battle Echoes," the latter a series of sermons preached during the late civil war. He was also the author of a Sunday-school book, which reached a considerable popularity, entitled "Green Hollow." He published also a missionary sermon, and several works of a denominational character.

Ide, Rev. John, was born in Vermont in 1785. For more than half a century he was a devoted minister of Christ. He was converted when he was about thirty years of age, and commenced his ministerial labors in Coventry, Vt. He was greatly prospered in his work. In one of the revivals which occurred under his ministry, six of his own children were converted and baptized together. In the different pastorates which he held, he was successful in the vocation upon which in early manhood he had entered. When he commenced his ministry the Baptists in Vermont were comparatively few in number, and were "everywhere spoken against." They were taxed to support the "standing order" by the laws of the State. In case of refusal to pay their taxes they were subject to the "pains and penalties" of the law, obedience to which they could not conscientiously render. In the meridian of his days Mr. Ide was associated with Gov. Butler, and men who sympathized with him, in fighting the battles of religious freedom in the Vermont Legislature. They were at last successful, and the Baptists were no longer compelled to support a ministry which did not preach what they regarded as the whole truth. Mr. Ide died at Potsdam, N. Y., July 27, 1860.

Illinois, Missionary Organizations.—What seems to have been the beginning of organized missionary work in Illinois was the appointment, by a meeting of Baptists held at Edwardsville in 1831, of a committee, instructed to arrange and superintend "a system of traveling preaching to promote the interests of religion within the limits of Illinois." The members of this committee were James Lemen, Paris Mason, George Stacey, James Pulliam, B. F. Edwards, J. M. Peck, and Hubbell Loomis. Rev. J. M. Peck was the missionary placed under appointment by this committee, receiving his support from the East, through an arrangement with the Massachusetts Baptist Missionary Society. The committee named above do not seem to have attempted independent work of any kind, but simply served as an agency for correspondence with the Massachusetts board, through Dr. Going.

Of the missionaries put into the field under this joint arrangement may be named, besides Mr. Peck, Alvin Bailey, Moses Lemen, Gardner Bartlett, Jacob Bower, and Elijah Dodson,—all names of note in the Baptist pioneer history of Illinois. The committee continued under appointment from year to year by what was called the General Union Meeting of Illinois Baptists, until October, 1834. At that time the Illinois Baptist State Convention was organized at Whitehall, Green Co. Three Associations and two churches were represented in its formation. The scope of the society was soon enlarged, so that at the third anniversary, which was held at Peoria, Oct. 12, 1837, eight Associations and ten churches were represented. The support of missions in the State was made a chief feature of the Convention's yearly plans, and at the anniversary just alluded to it was resolved to raise, in the ensuing year, $2000 for this purpose. Attention was also given to ministerial education, the institution at Upper Alton being one of the objects reported upon regularly at the yearly meetings.

At the anniversary of the Convention, held at Bellville, Oct. 3, 1844, a committee was appointed to confer with a committee of the Northwestern Baptist Convention upon the subject of a union of the two bodies. These committees met at Canton, November 21 following, and a new organization was made, called the Illinois Baptist General Association, covering the whole State. The Northwestern Convention had been formed in 1841, in consequence of dissatisfaction with the proceedings of the State Convention, "and to accommodate and bring into concerted action the brethren residing in Wisconsin, Iowa, and Northern Indiana," along with the Baptists in Northern Illinois. By the recent action, this body was now merged in the Illinois

Baptist General Association, which has remained until the present date the missionary organization for the State. A "Baptist Convention for Southern Illinois," composed of churches and Associations declining to enter into the new organization, continued for some years to exist, but the strength of the Baptist body in the State has been concentrated in the General Association from the time of its organization at Canton, in 1844. Since that date, as nearly as can be ascertained, the number of missionaries bearing its commission has been about 600, the number of baptisms by these missionaries not far from 4000, and the amount of money raised and expended in salaries to missionaries nearly $125,000.

Illinois Woman's Baptist Missionary Society.—The Woman's Baptist Missionary Society of the West was organized at Chicago, May 9, 1871. Its first officers were Mrs. Robert Harris, President; Mrs. A. M. Bacon, Recording Secretary; Mrs. C. F. Tolman, Corresponding Secretary; Mrs. S. M. Osgood, Treasurer. The society is auxiliary to the American Baptist Missionary Union, having been formally accepted as such at the anniversary meeting in May, 1871. At the first annual meeting Mrs. A. L. Stevens was present, the first applicant for appointment to the foreign field. Since that time 24 missionaries have been sent out, of whom one has returned in feeble health, two have died, seven have, by marriage, been transferred to the service of the Missionary Union; leaving as missionaries of this society (1880), six in Burmah, three in India, and five in China. Miss Daniels, of Swatow, China, is the only medical missionary connected with the society of the West. During the year 1879–80 the society supported 13 missionaries, 17 schools, and 31 Bible-women. It sent within the year contributions to 18 missionaries of the Union, and to 2 supported by the Society of the East.

The contributions during the first year of the society were $4244.69. Those reported for the year 1879–80 amounted to $18,483.91. The present officers of the society are Mrs. A. J. Howe, President; Mrs. C. F. Tolman, Vice-President; Mrs. J. O. Brayman, Recording Secretary; Mrs. A. M. Bacon, Corresponding Secretary; Mrs. F. A. Smith, Treasurer.

Immersion.—We have a profound regard for the theology of John Calvin, and for many of his utterances. We view his declaration, "The word *baptize*, however, signifies *to immerse*, and it is certain that immersion was observed by the ancient church,"[*] as displaying sound learning, an accurate knowledge of church history, and fidelity

---

[*] Ipsum baptizandi verbum mergere significat, et mergendi, ritum veteri ecclesiæ observatum fuisse constat. Inst. Christ. Relig., lib. iv. cap. 15, sect. 19. London, 1576.

to truth. No man fully acquainted with the facts upon which the opinion of the great Genevan was based, could speak otherwise and maintain fidelity to the truth. Luther says, "Baptism is a Greek word; in Latin it can be translated immersion, as when we plunge something into water that it may be completely covered with water."[*] Luther and Calvin translate the Greek word baptism as it was understood by those who used the language of which it was a part, before Christ's days, and ever afterwards. In the sense of immersion it is employed in the New Testament. The whole church of Christ practised immersion for at least twelve centuries of our era, and several nations baptize in that manner still.

Tertullian, in the end of the second century, writes, "The act of baptism itself belongs to the flesh, because we are immersed in water."[†] Jerome, in his notes on Ephesians iv. 5, says, "We are immersed three times[‡] to receive the one baptism of Christ." Ambrose, expounding the baptismal death in Romans vi. 3, says, "The death, therefore, is a figurative, not a real bodily death, for when you are immersing you present a likeness of death and burial."[§] Pope Leo the Great, speaking of baptism in the fifth century, says, "Trine IMMERSION is an imitation of the three days' burial (of Christ), and the EMERSION out of the waters is a figure (of the Saviour) rising from the grave."[||]

According to Bede, who died in 735, Paulinus, the apostle of the north of England, "washed" some of his converts "in the river Glen," baptized others "in the river Swale" of Yorkshire," and a "great multitude in the river Trent."[¶] Laufranc, archbishop of Canterbury in the eleventh century, commenting on Phil. iii. 10, says, "Being made conformable unto his death in baptism, for as Christ lay for three days in the sepulchre, so let there be a trine immersion in baptism."[**] St. Bernard, the most prominent ecclesiastic in France in the twelfth century, in his sermon on the Lord's Supper, says, "Baptism is the first of all the sacraments, in which we are planted together in the likeness of his (Christ's) death. Hence trine immersion represents the three days we are about to celebrate."[††]

There are many baptisteries in Italy that were used for centuries for the immersion of candidates for baptism. The most remarkable of these is in the catacomb of San Ponziano, Rome. It is on the right side of the Via Ostiensis, and at a short distance beyond the Porta Portese. Through this cemetery a stream of water runs, the channel of which is diverted into a reservoir, which was used for administering baptism by immersion from the first to the fourth centuries;[‡‡] and within a few years candidates for primitive baptism have been buried under its waters once more. Dr. Cote[§§] gives a list of sixty-seven of these baptisteries that exist in Italy now, some of them ready for service and others greatly changed. Not a few of the edifices reared to cover the baptismal pools are spacious and magnificent. The baptisteries above ground were erected from the fourth to the fourteenth century. The sacristan who shows the sacred structure has no hesitation in telling the visitor that the church formerly practised immersion. Until the beginning of the thirteenth century immersion was the mode of baptism of all Western Christendom, except in cases of sickness, and it was a common practice long afterwards in many parts of the papal dominions; it was the general usage in England until after the Reformation, and it was frequently observed down to the middle of the seventeenth century. There is a record of the immersion of Arthur and Margaret, the brother and sister of Henry VIII.,[||||] and there is no doubt that immersion was the mode of baptism that prevailed all over his kingdom in Henry's day.

William Wall, the learned Episcopalian writer, says, that "in 1536 the lower house of Convocation sent to the upper house a protestation, containing a catalogue of some errors and some profane sayings that began to be handed about among some people, craving the concurrence of the upper house in condemning them. Some of them are these:

"'That it is as lawful to christen a child in a tub of water at home, or in a ditch by the way, as in a font-stone in the church.'

"I think," says Wall, "it may probably be concluded from their expressions, that the ordinary way of baptizing at this time in England, whether in the church or out of it, was by putting the child into the water."[¶¶] He then proceeds to give the others.

In Tyndale's "Obedience of a Christian Man," published in 1528, he writes, "Ask the people what they understand by their baptism or washing, and

* Latine potest verti mersio, cum immergimus aliquid in aquam ut totum tegatur aqua. De Sacram. Bapt. Opera Lutheri, i. p. 319. 1564.

† In aqua mergimur. De Baptismo, cap. 7, pars ii. p. 37. Lipsiæ, 1839.

‡ Ter mergimur, tome ix. p. 109. Basle, 1516.

§ Cum enim mergis, mortis suscepis et sepultaræ similitudinem. De Sacramentis, lib. ii. cap. 7.

|| Trina demersio, ep. 16, vol. liv. p. 699, Patrl. Lat.

¶ In fluvio Gleni . . . in Sualo fluvio. In fluvio Treenta. Hist. Eccles., ii. 14, p. 104; ii. 16, p. 107. Oxonii, 1846.

** Sic in baptismate trina sit immersio.

†† Trina mersio.

‡‡ Baptism and Baptisteries, p. 102. Amer. Bapt. Publication Society.

§§ Idem, 110–112.

|||| Cathcart's Baptism of the Ages, pp. 41–43. Amer. Bapt. Publication Society.

¶¶ History of Infant Baptism, p. 648. Nashville.

thou shalt see that they believe how that the very plunging into the water saveth them." . . . "Behold how narrowly the people look on the ceremony. If ought be left out, or if the child be not altogether dipt in the water, or if, because the child is sick, the priest dare not plunge him into the water, but pour water on his head, how tremble they! how quake they! 'How say ye, Sir John' (the priest), say they, 'is this child christened enough? Hath it his full christendom?' They verily believe that the child is not christened."*
At this time plunging into water was the mode of baptism in England, and the exception of sick children was evidently unpopular; and the substitute for immersion, according to good William Tyndale, the translator of the English Bible, was regarded with grave suspicions.

The Book of Common Prayer, issued by the authority of Edward VI., in 1549, says, "Then the priest shall take the child in his hands, and ask the name. And naming the child, shall dip it in the water thrice. First, dipping the right side; second, the left side; the third time dipping the face toward the font; so it be discreetly and warily done. And if the child be weak it shall suffice to pour water upon it."† Immersion was still the custom as well as the law in England, with the exception for which the Prayer Book made provision.

On May 18, 1556, a complaint was made against a considerable number of persons who favored the gospel in Ipswich, before Queen Mary's council, sitting in commission at Beccles, in Suffolk. Among the charges preferred was a refusal to have children dipped in the fonts:

"Mother Fenkel, and Joan Ward, alias Bentley's wife, refused to have children dipped in the fonts. Mother Beriff, midwife, refused to have children dipped in the fonts."‡

There is no hint given by Fox, who records the names and accusations of these servants of God, that they preferred sprinkling or pouring for the children. They were Baptists undoubtedly, and dipping in the font was still the common mode of baptism.

Mr. Blake, vicar of Tamworth, in Staffordshire, the author of a pamphlet published in 1645, entitled "Infant's Baptism Freed from Antichristianism," writes on the first page, "I have been an eye-witness of many infants dipped, and know it to have been the constant practice of many ministers in their places for many years together." Mr. Blake is supposed to have been forty-three years of age when he wrote his pamphlet.

In the Westminster Assembly of Divines, on Aug. 7, 1644, according to Dr. John Lightfoot, when a vote was taken on the question, "The minister shall take water and sprinkle or pour it with his hand upon the face or forehead of the child," "it was voted so indifferently that we were glad to count names twice, for *so many were unwilling to have dipping excluded* that the vote came to an equality within one; for the one side was twenty-five, the other twenty-four, the twenty-four for the reserving of dipping and the twenty-five against it."§ The question was finally decided against immersion the next day, and "it is said entirely by the influence of Dr. Lightfoot," as Ivimey states.‖ It seems surprising that an assembly of Presbyterians should be nearly equally divided about retaining immersion as a mode of baptism, and that "so many (in it), though none of them were Baptists, were unwilling to have dipping excluded." Learned Roman Catholics and Episcopalians have no prejudices against immersion; but, in 1876, Rev. J. H. Clark, of the Lackawanna Presbytery, Pa., immersed an applicant for membership in his church, for which he was censured by his Presbytery. His appeal to the Synod of Philadelphia resulted in the following decision: "In view of the teachings and principles entering into the doctrine of baptism, we judge that the administration of baptism by Rev. J. H. Clark, in the case excepted to came within the *possible limits of a permissible* administration of the rite, and although without *any sanction of command or fact in the Sacred Scriptures*, yet did not involve a moral wrong. The mode of administration, however, not being accordant with the distinctive mode of baptism accepted and appointed by the Presbyterian Church, we do approve of the spirit of the exception of the Presbytery of Lackawanna, as,"¶ etc. The ministers composing the Synod of Philadelphia are men of broad culture and Christian integrity, but they differ widely from Mr. Coleman and Mr. Marshall and "many" others in the Westminster Assembly, who were "*unwilling to have dipping excluded;*" but the men of English birth who took part in framing the Confession of Faith of the Presbyterian Church in the United States, in 1644, had seen immersions all around them in the state church, the older men in large numbers, the younger men less frequently; and many of them loved the baptism of their fathers and of the Founder of Christianity.

Mr. Crosby mentions that "many sober and pious people belonging to the congregations of the Dissenters about London were convinced that

* Doctrinal Treatises, i. 276–77. Parker Society.
† Liturgies of King Edward VI., pp. 111, 112. Parker Society.
‡ Acts and Monuments, viii. 599. London, 1839.

§ The Whole Works of Lightfoot, vol. xiii. 301. London, 1824.
‖ History of the English Baptists, i. 183. London, 1811.
¶ Burrage's Act of Baptism, p. 210. Amer. Bapt. Pub. Soc.

believers were the only proper subjects of baptism, and that it ought to be administered by immersion," and not being satisfied with the qualifications of any administrator in England, they sent Richard Blount to Holland, who received immersion there; and on his return he baptized according to the primitive mode Samuel Blacklock, a minister, and these baptized the rest of the company.* This event *may* have occurred, and if it did, it was probably about the beginning of the reign of Charles I.; no regular *Calvinistical* Baptist minister may have been permitted to live in England by the oppressions of the king and Laud, and though large numbers of persons then living in that country had been immersed, in the majority of cases it was not after believing. Mr. Hutchinson, from whom Crosby quotes, says about these persons, " The great objection was the want of an administrator, which, *as I have heard*, was removed by sending certain messengers to Holland." Crosby himself says, " This agrees with an account given of the matter in an ancient manuscript, *said to have been written* by Mr. William Kiffin." We would not bear *heavily* on the testimony adduced by these good men.

The Rev. John Mason Neale, a learned Episcopalian, whose " History of the Holy Eastern Church" is an authority on most of the topics on which it treats, writes, " The Constantinopolitan (Greek Church) ritual says, ' The priest baptizes him, holding him upright, and facing the East, and saying, " The servant of God is baptized in the name of the Father, and of the Son, and of the Holy Spirit," etc. At each sentence plunging and raising him up from the water.'

" The Coptic ritual says, ' He thrice immerses him, and after each immersion raises him up and breathes in his face.'

" The Armenian ritual says, ' Then the priest takes the child in his arms, and immerses him thrice in water, as an emblem of the three days' burial of Christ.' "†

In a celebrated Syriac liturgy it is written, " The priest stands by the font, and invokes the Spirit, who descendeth from on high, and rests on the waters, and sanctifies them, and makes new sons to God.

" When the child *is plunged into the water* the priest saith, ' N. is baptized for sanctity and salvation and a blameless life, and a blessed resurrection from the dead, in the name of the Father. Amen. And of the Son. Amen. And of the living and Holy Ghost for life everlasting. Amen.' "‡ " All the Syrian forms prescribe or assume trine immersion."§

Badger gives the baptismal ritual of the Nestorians, which says, " Then they shall take him (the child) to the priest, standing by the font, who shall place him therein, with his face to the East, and he shall dip him therein three times. . . . In dipping him he shall dip him up to the neck, and then put his hand upon him, so that his head may be submerged ; then the priest shall take him out of the font and give him to the deacon." ‖

In Picart's description of Abyssinian baptism, we learn that " As soon as the benediction of the font is over the priest plunges the infant into it three times successively. At the first he dips one-third part of the infant's body into the water, saying, ' I baptize thee in the name of the Father;' he then dips him lower, about two-thirds, adding, ' I baptize thee in the name of the Son;' the third time he plunges him all over, saying, ' I baptize thee in the name of the Holy Ghost.' "¶

The same author, as quoted by Burrage, describing the baptism of " the Rhynsburgers, or Collegiants, a branch of the Mennonites, originating in Holland," says,—

" The candidate for baptism makes publicly his profession of faith on a Saturday, in the morning, before an assembly of Rhynsburgers held for that purpose. A discourse is pronounced on the excellency and nature of baptism. The minister and candidate go together to a pond behind a house belonging to his sect (we might call it a hospital, since they received for nothing those who had not wherewithal to pay their hotel bills). In that pond the neophyte, catechumen, or candidate is baptized by immersion. If a man, he has a waistcoat and drawers ; if a woman, a bodice and petticoat, with leads in the hem."** Picart's work was published in Amsterdam in 1736.

The Russian Church, the Greek Church in Turkey and in the little kingdom of Greece, the Armenian, Nestorian, Coptic, Abyssinian, and the other Christian communities of the East, have always practised immersion, and that is their usage at this hour. About a fourth of the whole Christian people on earth still immerse in baptism ; and counting the centuries when immersion was the mode of baptism used by all Christendom, and the millions that employ it still, we are safe in affirming that a majority of all Christians, living and dead, were immersed in baptism. (See articles on SCRIPTURAL MODE OF BAPTISM, BAPTISM OF CLOVIS, BAPTISM OF TEN THOUSAND ENGLISH.)

Immersions, Great European.—There are several remarkable baptisms which took place when Christianity was triumphantly introduced into some

---

* History of the English Baptists, i. 161–63.

† History of the Holy Eastern Church, p. 949. London, 1850.

‡ Neale's History of the Holy Eastern Church, pp. 992–93. London, 1850.   § Idem, 950.

‖ The Nestorians and their Rituals, pp. 207, 208. London, 1852.

¶ Burrage's Act of Baptism, p. 182.

** Idem, p. 180.

of the European nations in which the mode was positively immersion. Saint Patrick baptized more than 12,000 men at one time in a spring in Ireland. (See article on PATRICK, THE APOSTLE OF IRELAND.) Clovis, king of the Franks, with 3000 warriors, his two sisters, and other women and their children, was baptized by "trine immersion" in 496. (See article on THE BAPTISM OF CLOVIS.) Ten thousand English were immersed in the river Swale, near Canterbury, in 597. (See article on BAPTISM OF TEN THOUSAND ENGLISH.) Three thousand English were baptized by Paulinus in 627, in a fountain in Northumberland, England. (See article on BAPTISTERY OF PAULINUS IN ENGLAND.) The whole population of the city of Kieff were immersed in the Dneiper at one time, about 988. (See article on BAPTISM OF THE POPULATION OF KIEFF.) These great baptisms must have conformed to the recognized mode of administering the ordinance.

Imposition of Hands after Baptism was a common custom among Baptists in the seventeenth century, in Europe and America, though it never was a general practice. Its observance often occasioned bitter controversies, which sometimes rent churches. The First church of Providence, R. I., continued the laying on of hands till the end of Dr. Manning's ministry; and the supposition that he held the observance of it rather to satisfy the consciences of others than to meet the demands of his own, subjected him to much opposition. When the Philadelphia Association adopted the English Baptist Confession of Faith of 1689, they added two articles to that document, one " On Singing of Psalms," and another on " Laying on of Hands." In the latter article the Confession of Faith says, " We believe that laying on of hands, with prayer, upon baptized believers, as such, is an ordinance of Christ, and ought to be submitted unto by all such persons as are admitted to partake of the Lord's Supper; and that the end of this ordinance is not for the extraordinary gifts of the Spirit, but for a further reception of the Holy Spirit of promise, or for the addition of the graces of the Spirit, and the influences thereof; to confirm, strengthen, and comfort them in Christ Jesus; it being ratified and established by the extraordinary gifts of the Spirit in the primitive times, to abide in the church, as meeting together on the first day of the week was, Acts ii. 1, that being the day of worship or Christian Sabbath, under the gospel; and as preaching the Word was, Acts x. 44, and as baptism was, Matt. iii. 16, and prayer was, Acts iv. 31, and singing psalms, etc., was, Acts xvi. 25, 26, so this of laying on of hands was, Acts viii. and xix.; for as the whole gospel was confirmed by signs and wonders, and divers miracles and gifts of the Holy Ghost in general, so was every ordinance in like

manner confirmed in particular." This article was adopted with the Confession, Sept. 25, 1742. The Roxborough and Second Baptist churches of Philadelphia still practise this observance. Before the hand of fellowship is given to the newly baptized the pastor places his hands upon the head of each one and prays for the person.

By most modern Baptist churches the article quoted from the Philadelphia Confession of Faith is regarded as one of the unwise things received by our American religious ancestors. The few churches that still retain this usage see something in it to admire.

Imputed Righteousness. See article on JUSTIFICATION.

Index, The Christian, a weekly Baptist paper, has been published in the State of Georgia since the year 1833. It was first issued in Washington, D. C., under the auspices of the Baptist Board of Foreign Missions, under the name of *The Columbian Star*, and was removed to Philadelphia, where it was edited by Dr. Wm. T. Brantly, the elder, with the approval of the board. In 1833 it was transferred to Jesse Mercer, who began its publication in Washington, Wilkes Co., Ga., for his own convenience, securing the services of Rev. Wm. H. Stokes as assistant editor. In 1840, Mr. Mercer transferred the paper to the Georgia Baptist Convention, by which body it was published in Penfield until 1856, when it was removed to Macon. In 1861 it was sold to S. Boykin, at that time its editor. By him it was published until the close of the civil war, when he sold it to J. J. Toon, of Atlanta, who transferred it to that city. A few years ago Mr. Toon sold his entire publishing establishment, including the *Index*, to Jas. P. Harrison & Co., who now issue the *Index*. It is doubtful if there is any other one instrumentality by which the denomination in Georgia has been more benefited and united than *The Christian Index*. Its present editor is Dr. H. H. Tucker, a writer of great clearness and power, of extensive erudition, of mature judgment, full of love for the truth, one of nature's noblemen, whose journal is an honor to the Baptist denomination.

Indian Missions.—The attention of the Baptist Triennial Convention was early turned to the spiritual condition of the Indian tribes of North America. At the first meeting of the Convention after its formation in 1814, steps were taken to commence evangelical work among these "wards of the nation." In the directions given to Messrs. John M. Peck and James E. Welch, they were specially enjoined in the performance of their duties as domestic missionaries, stationed at St. Louis, to carry the gospel to the Indians with whom they might be brought in contact. The first person appointed to devote his whole time to this work was

Rev. Isaac McCoy, who was stationed at what was at that time—1818—the far West,—Fort Wayne, Ind. The several tribes of Miamies, Kickapoos, Ottawas, and Pottawatomies, all speaking dialects which had among them much that was common, came within the sphere of Mr. McCoy's labors. He was so far successful in his attempts to reach the people in the field of his missionary operations that he succeeded in gathering a school of 48 pupils, and in various ways had brought the truths of the gospel to the knowledge of these heathen of North America.

In 1822 a new station was established on the banks of the St. Joseph's River. This new station, which was named Carey in honor of the distinguished missionary, was a hundred miles from the nearest settlement of white men. To this place those who had been gathered under the fostering care of the missionary at Fort Wayne were removed, so that it was not long before there was a church at Carey of 30 or 40 members, many of whom were Indians, and it is said that "its exercises of public worship on the Sabbath often attracted large companies of natives from the adjacent settlements."

A third station was formed on the Grand River among the Ottawas, which was called Thomas, in honor of the English missionary of that name. When, in 1829, the station at Carey was partially abandoned, the missionaries withdrew to the new settlement, where the prospects of success were more hopeful. In 1832 several of the Indians gave such evidence of genuine conversion that they were baptized and received into the church. One of the principal chiefs of the Ottawas, Noonday, was among the number, and his after-life furnished proof that he was a sincere disciple of the Lord Jesus. While there were there things to encourage, there were others to depress. The Indians retire before the approach of civilization, and their territories fall into the hands of white men. The settlement at Thomas was broken up, and the mission, with the Indians connected with it, removed to Richland, fifty miles farther south. The most of the Ottawas have long ago disappeared from Michigan, and there is but little left to indicate what was done for their spiritual benefit by the self-denying missionaries who labored so earnestly to do them good.

The history of the mission among the Ojibwas deserves a passing notice. The board of the Triennial Convention, in 1828, accepted the funds appropriated by Congress to be expended for the benefit of this tribe, and established a mission at Saut Ste. Marie, one of the trading-places of the tribe, not far from fifteen miles southeast of Lake Superior. Rev. Abel Bingham was appointed missionary. His efforts were directed to both the whites and the Indians, and so successful was he that during a time of awakened religious interest, in 1832, forty persons were baptized and added to the church. Eleven of this number were Indians. A translation of the New Testament into Ojibwa was made and printed in 1833 in Albany, N. Y., and circulated among the people. The mission passed through various fortunes, adverse and prosperous, until 1857, when it was discontinued.

The mission among the Cherokees has yielded as much substantial fruit as any that has been attempted by the Baptists among the Indians. In the list of the early missionaries sent to this tribe, we find the honored name of Evan Jones. Through his labors, and those of his associates, we find that up to the time of the removal of the Cherokees by order of the United States government, in 1838, hundreds of them had been converted and formed into Christian churches. Mr. Jones followed the Cherokees to their new home, and continued to labor for their spiritual good until his removal to Kansas in 1862. In 1842 all the churches were reported as having meeting-houses, and a printing-office had been furnished at the expense of the Cherokees. In 1846 the translation of the New Testament was completed. The progress of the mission was steadily maintained year after year, and the influence of the gospel in elevating and blessing the people was of the most marked character. In 1863 the estimate of the number of church members was 1500.

Other Indian tribes among whom Baptist missionaries have labored are the Choctaws, the Creeks, the Otoes, the Omahas, the Delawares, and the Shawanees. Among the honored servants of Christ who have labored among these different tribes may be mentioned Rev. Moses Merrill, Rev. Jotham Meeker, Rev. Leonard Slater, Rev. Thomas Frye, Rev. Jesse Busyhead, a native preacher, Rev. John B. Jones, Rev. Ira D. Blanchard, Rev. J. G. Pratt, Misses E. S. and H. H. Morse, Rev. J. Lykins, and Rev. Francis Barker.

The Home Mission Society has spent nearly $28,000 since 1865 in supporting missionaries among the Indians. It has at present three white missionaries, one colored, and six Indian, laboring among the Indians in the Indian Territory. It also supports the principal of a normal and theological school. In the Indian Territory there are 100 Baptist churches, with a membership of 6000.

See article on SOUTHERN BAPTIST CONVENTION.

Indiana Baptist Papers.—The *American Messenger* was first begun in Madison in 1843, with Rev. E. D. Owen as editor. It was then a biweekly, afterwards a weekly. In 1846 he removed it to Indianapolis, and after about one year sold it to the *Cross and Journal*, of Ohio, and it became a part of what is now the *Journal and Messenger*.

At a meeting of brethren attending commencement exercises at Franklin College, in June, 1856, it was unanimously resolved " that we make an effort to start a paper at Indianapolis," and " that the matter be put into the hands of a publishing committee, until such time as a suitable editor can be found." The paper was called *The Witness.* Very soon Rev. M. G. Clarke became editor. He was succeeded by Rev. E. W. Clark, who conducted it till 1867, when it was sold to the *Christian Times,* of Chicago, and became a part of what is now *The Standard.* Three different papers have been started by the presidents of Franklin College, as aids in their work. Dr. Chandler published a few numbers of *The Baptist Inquirer* in 1843. President Wayland issued twelve or fifteen numbers of the *Camp-Fire* in 1870, and President Stott has for three years conducted *The Link* in the immediate interests of the college.

Rev. A. R. Hinckley was for several years associate editor of the *Baptist Banner and Pioneer,* published in Louisville, Ky. Hon. J. L. Holman was likewise, for several years, associate editor of the *Baptist Advocate,* published in Cincinnati, O.

Rev. W. N. Wyeth, D.D., Indianapolis, is at present one of the editors of the *Journal and Messenger.*

Indiana Baptist State Convention, The, was organized at a church called Brandywine, in Shelby County, in April, 1833. Rev. Samuel Harding was elected President; Rev. J. L. Holman, Recording Secretary; Rev. Ezra Fisher, Corresponding Secretary, and Henry Bradley, Esq., Treasurer. The annual sermon was preached by Rev. Ezra Fisher. There were present 37 delegates, and the treasurer's receipts were $17.00.

The receipts in 1840 were $1265.05; 1850, $1139.73; 1860, $2464.23; 1870, $410.05; 1879, $3495.30.

The first policy adopted for the evangelization of the State was that each minister should spend several weeks in traveling, holding a series of meetings in destitute places.

These brethren received very little compensation, in some cases none. The next plan was to collect money in the several Associations, and employ a few men to travel and preach all the time. But little money was expended at any one point, and so the fruits of the labor were not apparent for any length of time. Next the " village fund" policy, introduced from Ohio by Rev. T. R. Cressy, who came into the State as pastor, was tried. In this plan men pledged themselves to give $5 or $10 per year for five years, to aid in planting Baptist churches in the villages. It did not contemplate the permanent settlement of a pastor over the church, and so it failed of any great fruit. Finally it was agreed that the money gathered should be expended only at such places as gave promise of success. For several years there was much discussion as to what points gave such promise. At the present time the settled policy of the State board is that no place shall be aided that does not give hopes of *becoming self-supporting* within a reasonable time, and the success of State missions was never so fully assured as now. The Convention at this time employs ten missionaries, and through the efficient labors of the general agent, Rev. A. J. Essex, the salaries are paid quarterly. The board is especially seizing opportunities to plant churches in country towns. Within five years a new departure has been taken as to the relation the State Convention sustains to foreign missions, home missions, education, etc.

It was formerly thought that the body having State missions in charge was the State Convention, and that the other organizations met with it for convenience, and by courtesy. The present conviction is that each of these organizations is a part of the State Convention. The Convention, through appropriate standing committees or boards, attends to State missions, home missions, foreign missions, publication society, education, etc. The organization under its present management seems to be in a high state of efficiency.

The past year 260 churches contributed to State missions; that was the largest number ever giving money for this purpose. This year the number will be 300.

Indiana Baptists, their Origin and Growth. —The first church organized in what is now the State of Indiana was originally called Owens, next Fourteen-Mile, and then Silver Creek. While bearing the name Silver Creek, the church was divided by the doctrines of A. Campbell; the portion holding fast the doctrines of the Philadelphia Confession of Faith retaining their organization, and finally becoming the Charlestown church. The original church was constituted in 1798, under the leadership of Rev. Isaac Edwards, a native of New Jersey. The church is best known in history by the name Silver Creek. Around it was gathered at length the Silver Creek Association, which in turn become three or four Associations. The first settlements were along the rivers, and so the centres of Baptist strength were at first along the Wabash on the west, the Ohio on the south, and White Water on the east, the main rivers of the State. The first Association in the State was White Water, formed in 1809, the next was Silver Creek, formed in 1812. As an indication of the unstable condition of affairs during the earlier history of Indiana Baptists, it may be stated that there have been formed in all, up to this time, sixty Associations.

There are now but thirty. Exact statistics as to membership can only be approximated. In

1812, 1376; 1832, 11,334; 1840, 16,234; 1845, 15,795; 1850, 18,311; 1857, 25,282; 1860, 28,038; 1866, 29,103; 1876, 40,015; 1880 (estimated), 42,159,—in 568 churches. The apparent decrease from 1840 to 1845 is to be accounted for by the fact that several *anti-mission* Associations withdrew from all correspondence with the State Convention. Indeed, it may be said that most of the thirty Associations dropped from the list have died because of their anti-mission policy and spirit. A few yet survive as working bodies, and some were merged into other missionary Associations. A brother, who is constantly traveling over the State, estimates the anti-mission membership at 5000. Their strength is now a mere fragment of what it once was. No account is made of them in the general statistics of the State.

Indiana, Educational Institutions of.—The first meeting having for its object the founding of an institution of learning for Baptists was held in Indianapolis, June 5, 1834. The final result was the establishment of Franklin College, which with a variety of experiences " continues to this day," and is now in a more prosperous condition than ever before. In 1848, Rev. J. G. Craven and his father founded a school at College Hill, Jefferson Co., for the education of all colors and both sexes. In 1849, Rev. J. C. Thompson, of Ohio, came to their assistance. The name given the institution was Eleutherean College. The Cravens put great energy at the service of the school, and for some time it prospered notwithstanding its persecutions. One of the most distinguished of its colored pupils is Rev. Moses Broyles, of Indianapolis. There have been several attempts to revive the school, but without permanent success. It had no endowment, and hence it could not live. About the year 1854, Revs. Anson Tucker and D. Taylor were appointed by the Education Society of Indiana to proceed in the work of founding a school for young women at La Fayette. They reported $12,000 pledged. Prof. W. Brand resigned his place in the faculty of Franklin College to enter upon his duties as agent of the school,—The Western Female Seminary. The effort finally failed, and the interest aroused in behalf of the enterprise was in a measure transferred to Ladoga in the Freedom Association. Ladoga Female Seminary, established in 1855, was intended at first to supply the wants of its own Association, but it was found that Northwestern Indiana was its appropriate field. It has done successful work under Principals Rev. G. Williams, M. Bailey, Rev. A. J. Vawter, and Rev. W. Hill. For lack of endowment it finally suspended.

The same may be said in general of Crown Point Academy, under the principalship of Rev. T. H. Ball, and Huntington Academy, founded by Deacon John Kenower. The lack of endowment, and

the fact of the establishment of public high schools in the State within a few years, led to the suspension of all schools except the college at Franklin. The last to succumb was the Indianapolis Female Institute. This was founded in 1858. Rev. G. Williams was its first principal. The total expended for site and buildings was $53,000. Rev. L. Hayden, D.D., was the last principal. It suspended in 1872.

Indiana Baptists have also taken considerable interest in the Baptist Theological Seminary in Chicago, and contributed several thousand dollars to that institution. The largest sum given is $5000, by M. L. Pierce, Esq., of La Fayette.

Ministerial training is receiving new attention in the State. During the year there were 42 young men receiving education for the ministry, 23 of whom were at Franklin College.

Indiana, Publication Society in.—The American Baptist Publication Society began work in the State about the year that it took its present name. Revs. G. C. Chandler and T. C. Townsend took special interest in the circulation of its tracts, the one from Franklin as a centre, the other from Anderson. The State has made contributions to the society, giving in 1857, $85; 1865, $438; 1870, $663; 1875, $1081; 1880, $1873. Some legacies have been given, among the largest is one of $5000 from J. L. Allen. Rev. E. A. Russell was the Sunday-school missionary of the society for Indiana.

Indiana, The Sunday-Schools of, were not general before 1850. Many churches, however, had schools as early as 1833. Most of the schools at first, especially in the country, were *union schools*, and were what are now called "summer" schools. In 1848, the missionaries of the Indiana Baptist State Convention were instructed "to make it a prominent part of their business to establish Sabbath-schools, and labor to promote their interests." There was no persistent effort made to gather Sunday-school statistics till 1868, when Rev. E. A. Russell was appointed Sunday-school missionary for Indiana by the American Baptist Publication Society. His report for 1870 is as follows : schools, 285; officers and teachers, 1628 ; scholars, 22,369 ; converted during one year, 770 ; volumes in libraries, 17,111. Of the 285 schools, 51 were *union*. There is a marvelous increase since 1870. In 1878 there were: schools, 542 ; officers and teachers, 5000; scholars, 58,000 ; volumes in library, 30,000 ; benevolent contributions, $71,615. Indiana now comes to the front in the number of scholars.

Indianapolis, Ind., Baptists of.—The *First Baptist church* was constituted Sept. 28, 1822, with 17 members. The pastors have been Revs. B. Barnes, A. Smoch, J. L. Richmond, M.D., G. C. Chandler, D.D., T. R. Cressy, S. Dyer, Ph.D., J.

B. Simmons, D.D., H. Day, D.D. (who was pastor for fifteen years and built the present house of worship), W. Randolph, D.D., H. C. Mabie (present pastor). The church at present numbers 515. The superintendent of the Sabbath-school is W. C. Smoch. The church has planted three other churches in the city.

South Street was organized in 1869 with 73 members. Its pastors have been Revs. W. Elgin, H. Smith, G. W. Riley, J. S. Gillespie, and J. N. Clark (present pastor). Present membership, 217.

North Street was organized in 1871 with 27 members. Its pastors have been Revs. E. K. Chandler, J. B. Schaff, I. N. Carman, and G. H. Elgin (present pastor). Present membership, 120.

Garden church was organized in 1872 with 16 members. Its pastors have been Revs. S. Cornelius, D.D., P. Shedd, and C. B. Allen, Jr. Present membership, 112. Sabbath-school superintendent, H. Knippenberg.

Infant Baptism in all Ages has required Faith before its Administration.—This is one of the most remarkable features of that unscriptural practice. Neander alludes to this demand when he says, "Infant baptism also furnished probably the first occasion for the appointment of sponsors or godfathers; for as this was a case in which the persons baptized could not themselves declare their confession of faith, it became necessary for others to do it in their name." (Church History, i. 315. Boston.) From the first intimations of the existence of infant baptism the sponsor is spoken of, who professed faith for the child. Though it should be remembered that sponsors were required for others as well as infants, and that Neander was mistaken in saying that "infant baptism also furnished *probably* the first occasion for the appointment of sponsors." He only gives his opinion as a probability. As Bingham says, "There were sponsors for such adult persons as could not answer for themselves," who were speechless from some cause, and there were sponsors for persons of full intelligence, "whose duty was not to answer in their names" (the candidates for baptism), "but only to admonish and instruct them." (Antiquities of the Christian Church, pp. 526, 527. London, 1870.) Tertullian mentions the existence of sponsors in his day, when *child*, not *infant*, baptism was first proposed. (De Baptismo, cap. 18.) It is probable, since sponsors were in the church in the end of the second century, before infant baptism existed, that they were first used in times of persecution to guard the Christian communities against spies who sought membership in them to betray them, and that afterwards they were employed to instruct and guard those for whose character they had become responsible. There is no lack of evidence among early writers to sustain

Bingham's three classes of sponsors, so that when the word sponsor is found in the fathers it may have no reference to infant baptism; but when infant baptism was introduced sponsors were always required to profess faith for the unconscious subjects of the rite.

When Augustine baptized an infant he asked, "Does this child believe in God? Does he turn to God?" And he declares expressly in another place that sponsors answered for the children. (Patrologia Latina, xxxiii. 363. Parisiis.) The great bishop of Hippo, the man who gave its chief impetus to infant baptism, insisted on faith before its administration. Martin Luther's "Smaller Catechism" has these questions and answers:

"When did the Holy Ghost begin this santification in you?" "In the holy ordinance of baptism the Holy Ghost began this sanctification in me."

"What did God promise you in holy baptism?" "God promised, and also bestowed upon me, the forgiveness of sins, life, and salvation."

"But what did you promise God?" "I promised that I would renounce the devil and all his works and ways, and *believe in God the Father, Son, and Holy Ghost.*"

"Through whom did you make this promise in holy baptism?" "I made this promise in holy baptism through my sponsors." (Catechism, p. 58. New York, 1867.)

"The Garden of the Soul" (pp. 184, 185. London), a popular English Catholic prayer-book, has these questions and answers about baptism:

"Dost thou renounce Satan?" "I do renounce him."

"And all his works?" "I do renounce them."

"And all his pomps?" "I do renounce them."

"Dost thou believe in God, the Father Almighty, creator of heaven and earth?" "I do believe."

"Dost thou believe in Jesus Christ, his only Son, our Lord, who was born into this world and suffered for us?" "*I do believe.*"

"Dost thou believe in the Holy Ghost, the holy Catholic Church, the communion of saints, the forgiveness of sins, the resurrection of the body, and life everlasting?" "I do believe."

It is stated at the commencement of these questions that "the priest interrogates the person to be baptized, or the sponsors, if an infant, as follows;" so that the sponsors not only make solemn renunciations for the infant, but profess a comprehensive faith for it before it can be baptized.

In the Greek Church the priest, as a prerequisite to baptism, asks, "Hast thou renounced Satan?" And the catechumen or *sponsor* replies, "I have renounced him."

"Hast thou joined thyself unto Christ?" And he answers, "I have joined myself."

"And dost thou believe on him?" The catechumen replies, "I *believe* on him as king and God." (Neale's History of the Holy Eastern Church, Part I. 956. London, 1850.) Of course, in the case of an infant the faith is professed by the sponsor, and it must be confessed before baptism.

In the Episcopal Church, when a child is brought for baptism, the minister asks each godfather and godmother the following questions, and receives the answers given to them :

"Dost thou, in the name of this child, renounce the devil and all his works, the vain pomp and glory of the world, with all covetous desires of the same, and the carnal desires of the flesh, so that thou wilt not follow nor be led by them?" "I renounce them all."

"Dost thou believe in God, the Father Almighty, maker of heaven and earth? And in Jesus Christ, his only begotten Son, our Lord? And that he was conceived by the Holy Ghost, born of the Virgin Mary; that he suffered under Pontius Pilate, was crucified, dead, and buried; that he went into hell, and also did rise again the third day; that he ascended into heaven and sitteth at the right hand of God, the Father Almighty, and from thence shall come again at the end of the world to judge the quick and the dead?" etc. "All *this I steadfastly believe*." (Book of Common Prayer: Public Baptism of Infants.) Such is the profession of faith made by sponsors for an unconscious infant in the Episcopal Church. The "Westminster Confession of Faith," chap. xxviii. sec. 4, says, "Not only those that do actually profess faith in and obedience unto Christ, but also the infants of one or both *believing* parents, are to be baptized." Here there is no provision made for the baptism of any infant unless one of its parents had faith in Christ; and upon that faith the baptism of any infant depends among the Scotch, Scotch-Irish, English, and American Presbyterians.

The British Congregationalists, though having the "Savoy Confession," prepared by their own brethren, according to Neale (History of the Puritans, iv. 164. Dublin, 1755), "have in a manner laid aside the use of it in their families, and agreed with the Presbyterians in the use of the Assembly's (Westminster) Catechism." Robinson gives an account of a Congregational baptism at which the minister stated that "not only those that do actually profess faith in and obedience unto Christ, but also the infants of one or both believing parents, were to be baptized." (History of Baptism, p. 681. Nashville.) These are the exact words of the "Westminster Confession of Faith," and they require faith in one parent for the baptism of an infant.

Throughout the Christian ages all the great churches that baptized infants before the Reformation, and all the large communities that were formed during or soon after it that followed that practice, insisted on faith as essential to baptism as strongly as the Baptists have ever done. When the "Episcopal Catechism," in answer to the question, "What is required of persons to be baptized?" says, "Repentance, whereby they forsake sin, and faith, whereby they steadfastly believe the promises of God made to them in that sacrament," it gives the doctrine held by all the great historic communities of the Christian world since infant baptism arose about the absolute need of faith before baptism. This has always been the teaching of Baptists during the Christian centuries when only believers were immersed, and throughout all the dark and enlightened ages since. The difference between us and Pedobaptists is that they are satisfied with healing faith in a sponsor, or in a parent, while the infant has the disease of sin and is without faith in Christ. If it reaches years of responsibility it will surely be without God and without hope in the world; and we want the healing faith in the heart of the candidate, according to the Master's saying, "He that believeth and is baptized shall be saved."—Mark xvi. 16.

We furnish candidates for immersion with suitable robes in which to receive Christian baptism; but we can only loan the garments, the needed faith is the gift of God. The five wise virgins in the parable, as they beheld their five foolish companions in the throes of despair because they had not the oil of saving faith in their lamps, full of compassion for them as they were, and enjoying the faith that gave everlasting life, had no faith to loan them or to profess for them. And no Christian ever had a faith which he could place to the credit of any one, infant or adult. A man might as well attempt to loan an unconscious child the vigor of his mature mind, or the power of his strong right arm, or a dozen of the heavenly worlds.

Infant Baptism in the first Four Christian Centuries.

—There is not a single recorded case in the first two ages of Christian history of the baptism of an unconscious babe. Men have searched this period with a scrutiny and a measure of learning never surpassed to find one undeniable instance of the kind, but the literature of Christianity has been examined in vain, and it ever will be. Justin Martyr gives a full account of the manner of conferring baptism in the latter half of the second century. "As many," says he, "as are *persuaded and believe that the things which we teach and declare are true, and promise that they are determined to live accordingly, are taught to pray to God, and to beseech him with fasting to grant them the remission for their sins*, while we also pray and fast with them. We then *lead them* to a place where there is water, and there they are regenerated in the same manner as we also were; for they are there washed in that water in the name of God the Father and Lord of the universe, and of our Saviour Jesus Christ, and of the Holy Spirit." (Patrologia Græca, vol. vi. p. 240. Migne. Parisiis, 1857.)

In Justin's time candidates for baptism believed that the statements of Christian teachers were true; they promised to live according to gospel requirements, and they prayed for pardon. These were believers, and he names no other class of persons who were baptized. Tertullian, just at the close of the second century, while yet orthodox, says, " It behooves those who are going to be baptized to pray with frequent supplications, fasts, kneelings, and vigils, and with the confession of all past faults, that they may show forth even John's baptism; they were immersed," he says, " confessing their sins." (De Baptismo, cap. xx.) No unconscious babe could make these preparations, or at this period enjoyed Christian baptism. There was in Tertullian's time an effort made to introduce, not the baptism of new-born infants, but of little children, which he denounced. The learned Salmasius and Suicerus have been criticised by Bingham for the statement, " For the first two ages no one received baptism who was not first instructed in the faith and doctrine of Christ, so as to be able to answer for himself that he believed, because of those words, ' He that believeth and is baptized.' " (Antiquities of the Christian Church, Book xi. chap. iv, sec. 5.) But Bingham, profoundly versed as he was in the doctrines and practices of the early church, brings forward no case of the baptism of an unconscious infant during this period, or a positive account of the existence of the rite. *He could not.*

There is but one case of unconscious infant baptism in the entire third century. The facts about it are found—in the letter of Cyprian and sixty-six bishops addressed to Fidus—in the works of Cyprian bishop of Carthage. Fidus, an African bishop, living in scenes of rustic ignorance, wrote to Cyprian to learn the earliest time when an infant might be baptized. Cyprian could not answer the question; but a council of sixty-six bishops, of which he was a member, decided that it might be baptized as soon as it was born. They also gave their reasons for their conclusion. One was because the sins of a babe were not as grave as those of a man, and as baptism took away the greater sins it could remove the smaller; and another was that Elisha placed his body upon the lifeless body of the child which he restored, his mouth to its mouth, his eyes to its eyes, and his hands to its hands, *the spiritual sense of which was that infants are equal to men, and therefore should have their baptism.* This is the first record of unconscious infant baptism on the page of Christian history, and there is no other instance in the third century. The council was supposed to have been held about

A.D. 256. This letter in Cyprian is supposed by many to be spurious; and we are inclined to that opinion, chiefly because the progress of the infant error was so very slow; the great theologian, Augustine, a North African by birth, who was born in 354, whose mother was the saintly Monica, was not baptized till he was thirty-three years of age,—an occurrence nearly impossible if the infant rite had been sanctioned by Cyprian and the other authorities of the North African Church a century before. The Christian writers of the East in the third century treat of *child*, not infant, baptism,—children of six years or more.

In the fourth century the greatest church leaders, and some of them the most eminent Christian authors of all the ages since Jesus, though the children of believers, were not baptized in infancy. Ambrose, whose family were all Christians, was governor of Milan, and elected to be its archbishop before he was baptized. In 381, Nectarius was elected archbishop of Constantinople, when, according to Sozomen, "he was of advanced age," and unbaptized. Gregory Nazianzen, who was born while his father was bishop of Nazianzum, was baptized in his thirtieth year, and he was archbishop of Constantinople. The eloquent John Chrysostom, both of whose parents were Christians, was baptized when he was twenty-eight, and he, too, presided over the See of Constantinople. Basil the Great, whose fathers were Christians for generations, who died in 379, was baptized in his twenty-eighth year. Jerome, the first Hebrew and Greek scholar among Christians in the fourth century, who was born of believing parents in 331, was not baptized till about 366. Theodosius the Great, after proving himself a valiant warrior, was baptized, though he had Christian parents, as Sozomen relates.

The baptism of the fourth century required candidates to profess faith in Jesus, as we learn from Ambrose in his " De Sacramentis." " Thou wast asked," says he, addressing candidates, " ' Dost thou believe in God, the omnipotent Father?' and thou saidst, ' I believe,' and thou was immersed, that is, thou wast buried. Again thou was asked, ' Dost thou believe in our Lord Jesus Christ, and in his cross?' And thou saidst, ' I believe'; and thou was immersed, and therefore thou wast buried with Christ. . . . A third time thou wast asked, ' Dost thou believe in the Holy Spirit?' And thou saidst, ' I believe'; and a third time thou wast immersed." (Patrol. Lat., vol. xvi. p. 448. Migne. Parisiis.) This faith was the general demand at the baptisms of the fourth century throughout Christendom. Masses of men whose parents were Christians, and who attended churches and loved Christ, had never been baptized either in childhood or in later years. They were waiting for baptism till the approach of death, that its waters might give full cleansing from sin and a perfect fitness for heaven.

The clergy of the fourth century were continually appealing to the regular members of their congregations to be baptized, throngs of whom had never received the rite; and in times of threatened war or pestilence multitudes hastened to baptism and the ministers could with difficulty immerse them. "Infant baptism," says Neander, "though acknowledged to be necessary, entered *so rarely and with so much difficulty* into the church life, during the first part of this period." (Church History, ii. 319. Boston.) The cases of infant baptism in the fourth century, outside of North Africa, are scarcely worthy of being named. And in that Roman colony the earnest appeals and arguments of Augustine show that its strength was not great. Dean Stanley only claims that "*after the fifth century* the whole Christian world . . . have baptized children." (*Nineteenth Century*, p. 39, October, 1879.) It is perhaps true that in all parts of Christendom *some* persons immersed children after the fifth century had entirely passed, but if the dean intends to state that the unconscious infants of Christians everywhere were baptized, his declaration is incapable of proof though the piercing eye of an archangel sought the evidence.

Infant Baptism, Unfit Supports of.—As Baptists view the bases upon which its friends place infant baptism, they seem wholly inadequate to sustain it.

Among the oldest of these is the assumption that baptism has come in the place of circumcision. Augustine of Hippo uses this argument as if it were infallible; and it is employed to-day with the same childlike confidence which marked the great African bishop when he framed it. But what Scripture confirms the statement? By implication or declaration the assertion has no more support in the New Testament than the claims of Leo XIII. to be the successor of Peter as the supposed prince of the apostles. If baptism took the place of circumcision, no man should have both rites. But Christ received both; so did the thousands of Pentecostal converts; so did Paul, the greatest of all the apostles. There is then no connection between the two ordinances. Dr. Halley, a distinguished English Congregationalist, in his celebrated work in defense of infant baptism, says, "The general opinion that baptism is substituted for circumcision, as a kind of hereditary seal of the covenant of grace, appears to be ill-sustained by Scriptural evidence, and to be exposed to some very serious, if not absolutely fatal, objections." (The Sacraments, p. 34. London, 1855.)

Another argument to sustain the infant rite is taken from Matthew's gospel, xix. 13, 14, 15: "Then were there brought unto him little chil-

dren, that he should put his hands on them and pray; and the disciples rebuked them. But Jesus said, 'Suffer little children, and forbid them not, to come unto me: for of such is the kingdom of heaven.'" This passage is regarded by many as absolutely proving that infant baptism is invested with the sanction of Jesus. From it we learn that the apostles knew nothing of the baptism of children, for they would not let them approach Jesus till he commanded them to permit them to come; and, as baptism had been in existence for some time, it is quite clear infants had no part in the baptismal ordinance. Besides, they were only brought to him that he might "put his hands on them and pray," and it is said that "he laid his hands on them;" but he did not baptize them. The words "of such is the kingdom of heaven" do not mean that *of children is* the kingdom of heaven. If the Saviour had said of the little children, "of *them* is the kingdom of heaven," then no adult could have entered Christ's gospel kingdom of love. Jerome, in the fourth century, commenting on these words, in his Latin vulgate, observes, "Jesus said *of such*, not *of them*, to show that not *age* but *morals* should rule, and that to those who had *similar* innocence and *simplicity* a reward was promised." This is the Saviour's meaning, given by the famous monk of Palestine. This transaction has nothing in favor of infant baptism, and something against it.

In 1 Cor. vii. 12, 13, 14, Paul recommends a Christian not to put away an unbelieving husband or wife if the unbeliever will stay. Now the unbeliever might be a Pharisee or an idolater, and he adds, "For the unbelieving husband is sanctified by the wife, and the unbelieving wife is sanctified by the husband, else were children unclean; but now are they holy." The holiness spoken of here is not sanctification of the heart, but the legality of the wedded relations. The idolatrous companion or the unbelieving partner can be sanctified in no other way. Peter says, "Ye know that it is an unlawful thing for a man that is a Jew to keep company, or come unto one of another nation."— Acts x. 28. Paul tells these converted Israelites that they shall not forsake their Christ-rejecting partners, that their relations are proper, and their children legitimate. Because the children are said to be holy, it is argued that they should be baptized. For the same reason the ungodly idolatress or Jewess, the idolater or scornful Pharisee, should be baptized, for the adjective that describes the *children as holy is from the verb that sanctifies the unbelieving husband and wife*. The apostle is not treating of baptism, but of the sacredness of wedded relations and the legitimacy of children; and infant or unbelieving adult baptism can obtain no aid here.

The household baptisms furnish another argument for infant baptism. "There must have been infants in them," it is said, "and they must have been baptized, and therefore the children of all believers should be baptized." There is not a tittle of evidence that there was an infant in one of the households. Dr. J. H. Borum, of Dyersburg, Tenn., has baptized forty-six households in his ministry, and there was not an infant in one of them. And until it is proved that there were infants in these households, and that they were immersed, *infant baptism rests upon a supposition,*—a mere conceit, not worth the one-hundredth part of the chaffy covering of a corn of wheat. (See article on THE SCRIPTURAL SUBJECTS OF BAPTISM.)

Infant Salvation.—The following is from a tract entitled "Infant Salvation, Dedication, and Baptism," issued by the American Baptist Publication Society : " Are not infants, dying in infancy, saved? Certainly. Of a child which was the fruit of sin, David says, ' I shall go to him, but he shall not return to me.' 2 Sam. xii. 23. We have no reason to suppose that God will consign to hell infants who have never known good from evil. There is no controversy between Baptists and evangelical Pedobaptists on this point." If any statement could be regarded as authoritative for the whole Baptist denomination, this declaration might be received in that character. It comes from our great Baptist tract and book society, which is governed by the Baptists of America.

The doctrine of the quotation is held by all Baptists everywhere. Every child that dies before it knows " right from wrong," in any country under heaven, enters the regions of the blessed.

Ingalls, Mrs. M. B., the second wife of Rev. L. Ingalls, of the Arracan Mission, was born in Greenville, N. Y., Nov. 25, 1828. She was married in December, 1850, and sailed for the field of her labor July 10, 1851. Mr. Ingalls was transferred in 1854 to the Burmese department of the Rangoon Mission, where Mrs. Ingalls was his co-laborer until he died, March 14, 1856, after a faithful service of twenty-one years. Mrs. Ingalls superintended his schools for the education of Burmese girls, in 1857, and on one occasion, early in the year, made a tour of twenty-three days into the jungle in company with some of the native disciples, and found everywhere eager listeners. In April of this year she returned to America, remaining here until re-embarking for the scene of her former labors, Nov. 26, 1858, where she met a cordial welcome on her arrival in Rangoon from the missionaries and native converts. She took up her abode in the midst of a Burmese population, two miles north of the Kemendine Karen Mission, in a place called Zay-Ghee. In this place and at Thongzai her labors were greatly blessed. She removed to Thongzai in the latter part of 1860, from which

place she wrote home a letter, soon after her settlement, full of hope and good cheer. The most remarkable success followed her labors,—a success in some respects unprecedented in the history of the Burmese Missions. One cannot but admire the good common-sense sort of way in which Mrs. Ingalls did, and always has done, her work. She wrote of herself, in 1864: " It is not a day of romance with me, but a day when my strength and trust in God must be tested." The trial came in one of the severest forms, in July, 1864, when the new and beautiful chapel was destroyed by fire. Mrs. Ingalls lost nearly all her personal effects, and among them various manuscripts which probably could never be replaced. The effect of this loss, in addition to the weight of the burdens she had so long carried, so prostrated her health that she returned to this country in 1865, remaining here until the fall of 1868, awakening a deep interest in the churches she visited in the cause of missions. On her return she found a new chapel nearly completed, and the church ready to give her a cordial welcome, and for several years the work went on hopefully and successfully, until the night of the 12th of March, 1876, when the torch of the incendiary was applied to the mission compound, and again nearly everything was destroyed except the chapel. But amid all these sorrows there were joys ; so that of the year 1876 it could be said, "it was a year of troubles and a year of blessings." The last published report of the Executive Committee says that, " so far as outward circumstances are concerned, the mission under the charge of Mrs. Ingalls is in better condition than ever, and that the prospects of usefulness are as great as ever."

Ingels, Deacon George, was born in White Marsh Township, Montgomery Co., Pa., Feb. 26, 1746. When sixteen years of age he came to Philadelphia, and soon after the Holy Spirit made him the subject of serious religious impressions. In October, 1767, he was baptized into the fellowship of the First Baptist church of his adopted city. Five years after his baptism he was chosen a deacon by the church, and for fifty-five years he served the church in that honorable office.

He was a patriot full of self-sacrifice in Revolutionary times, and by his courage in the battlefield, and in the camp in the coldest of winters, he earned the character of a brave soldier and an unmurmuring sufferer. In civil life he was elected to various responsible offices by his fellow-citizens, and both the State and general government enlisted his services.

He was perhaps the most active man in Philadelphia in ministering to the victims of yellow fever in 1797. His efforts were unwearied, and brought comfort to the homes of suffering thousands in that visitation of terror and death.

Mr. Ingels had a strong faith in the Lord Jesus Christ, and a heart full of generous affections; and among the laymen connected with the "mother-church" of Philadelphia, in her long and honored history, no one rendered more efficient service to the Redeemer's cause than Deacon Ingels. He died in his eighty-first year, enjoying the confidence and love of the people of Philadelphia.

Ingersoll, Hon. George, of Marshall, Mich., was born in Victor, Ontario Co., N. Y., Feb. 5, 1819. He became a member of the Baptist Church in 1842, and has been a chief pillar of the church ever since. He has been superintendent of the Sunday-school fifteen years. He has also been president of the board of education of the city for fifteen years, and is now judge of probate for Calhoun County.

Ingham, Richard, D.D., author of the "Hand-book on Christian Baptism," and "Christian Baptism, its Subjects and Mode," was born at Halifax, Yorkshire, England, in 1810. He was baptized Nov. 20, 1829, and received authority to preach from the General Baptist church at Slack, Yorkshire, in 1833. Relinquishing his business some time after, he studied for the ministry under the Rev. J. Jarrow, of Wisbeach, and was ordained pastor at Bradford in 1839. He spent the years of his ministry in Louth, Halifax, Vale, and Bradford, and died June 1, 1873. As a preacher he was highly esteemed, and his labors as a student were untiring and successful. His "Hand-book" is allowed to be a work of great value, carefully and thoroughly executed.

Inman, Rev. G., a native of Sumner Co., Tenn., was born in 1836; educated at Union University, Murfreesborough, Tenn.; ordained by the Hillsborough Baptist church in Washington Co., Ky., where he began his ministry in 1858; labored as pastor of the Baptist churches of Clarksville and Spring Creek, Montgomery Co., Ky., five years, of the Central Baptist church, Nashville, Tenn., five years, of the Baptist church in Decatur, Ill., three years, of the Baptist church of Fox Lake, his present field of labor, two years. His ministry has been fruitful in results. He has baptized about 500 persons into the fellowship of the churches of which he has been pastor. He is a very active and able worker in the temperance cause. In his native State he held a leading position in the ranks of temperance reformers, and no great temperance assembly was considered complete without his presence. By his pen and voice he has furnished to this important reform some of its most effective weapons. His own pulpit is always a stronghold of total abstinence, and from it are struck heavy blows against the sin of drunkenness and drunkard-making.

Installation in recent years has become general in large cities when an ordained minister enters upon a new field. The pastor and his people on such occasions commonly hear a sermon from some brother in the ministry, the hand of fellowship is given to the stranger, and a charge; a charge is also delivered to the church. The object of the service is to give a welcome to the pastor, and to stir up him and his people to appreciate the weighty responsibilities that rest upon them.

Intercessor, The.—A belief in intercessors is universal among the adherents of every false religion. Heathenism abounds in such mediators. Mohammed is supposed to intercede for all true Moslems. Tertullian expresses the conviction that Satan has something to imitate every institution of God. This observation is eminently true of intercession. Romanism has an intercessor in every canonized saint.

The Jewish high priest, by divine appointment interceded in the holy of holies for his nation. And God cannot be approached acceptably now, except through Christ the great intercessor, of whom the chief of the Jewish priesthood was an humble type. "For there is one God, and one Mediator between God and men, the man Christ Jesus."—1 Tim. ii. 5. "My little children, these things write I unto you, that you sin not; and if any man sin, we have an advocate with the Father, Jesus Christ the righteous."—1 John ii. 1. "Jesus saith unto him, I am the way, the truth, and the life; no man cometh unto the Father but by me."—John xiv. 6. God has appointed but one intercessor; every other claimant to that office is a sacrilegious impostor; and the fact that Jehovah ordained Christ as an advocate for all who ventured to approach him is infallible evidence that the purest and the foulest of our race, in their approaches to the eternal throne, need the all-prevailing Mediator.

Our intercessor bases his pleadings for us upon his expiatory sacrifice. When the high priest of Israel entered the holy of holies to plead for the Jews, he first sprinkled the mercy-seat with blood and then presented his supplications. Paul says, "Which hope we have as an anchor of the soul, both sure and steadfast, and which entereth into that within the veil (the holy of holies); whither the forerunner is for us entered, even Jesus, made a high priest forever after the order of Melchisedec."—Heb. vi. 19, 20. Christ enters into the holy of holies in paradise with his own blood, and, as the high priest of the whole elect family, he pleads its merits for them all.

He observes every supplicant who seeks his intercessions. His honored mother has no more power to see or hear than any other glorified believer, and, consequently, is totally unfitted to be an intercessor. But, "being in the form of God, and thinking it no robbery to be equal with God," he sees every petitioner at his throne, and he observes the prayerful desires of his heart before he clothes them in words.

He is unwearied in his intercessions. " He ever liveth to make intercession for us." Men die, and empires perish, and night hides the glory of the day, but the pleadings of our advocate are continually poured out in the ear of Deity ; nor will they cease till the last gift needed by the last believer on earth has given him perfect preparation for heaven.

He is a tender-hearted intercessor. " Wherefore in all things it behooved him to be made like unto his brethren, that he might be a merciful and faithful high priest."—Heb. ii. 17. The fountain of compassionate love, from which all the affection of angels and men has streamed forth, is in his heart ; and it exercises a boundless influence over his movements.

He will plead for *any penitent* who trusts his name, and he will seek *every needful gift* for each supplicating child ; and his eloquent advocacy has such a power on high that the Father *always hears him*, and the trusting one who commits his case to him is invariably successful.

Iowa Baptists, History of.—There were some Baptists among the earliest settlers of Iowa. In succeeding years, as the tide of emigration flowed into the territory, Baptists were fairly represented. The fullest and most reliable account of Iowa Baptists in their earlier history is found in a paper carefully prepared by Rev. J. F. Childs some years ago, entitled " The History of the Rise and Progress of Iowa Baptists." This history is still unpublished, but, through the kindness of the author, it contributes largely to the facts of this sketch. The Danville, or, as originally called, the Long Creek, church, was the first Baptist church in Iowa. Brother and Sister Manly came from Kentucky, bringing with them the Articles of Faith adopted by the Bush Creek Baptist church, Green Co., Ky. They settled within six miles of Danville, where they continued to reside. Together with a few Baptists from Illinois, they organized a church, and invited Elders John Logan and Gardner Bartlett, of Illinois, to preach for them. Elder Logan preached in a log cabin the evening of Oct. 19, 1834, probably the first sermon by an evangelical minister in this part of the Territory. The next day the church was constituted and named " The Regular Baptist Church at Long Creek."

In 1838 another church was organized, about six miles southwest of Burlington, through the labors of Elders James and Moses Lemon and Clark, from Illinois. It was called " The Baptist Church of Christ, Friend to Humanity, at Rock Spring, Iowa." The Union and Pisgah churches were organized in 1839. In 1839 three churches, Long Creek, Union, and Pisgah, were organized into an Association, the first Baptist Association in the Territory. The meeting was held in a grove, west of what is now Danville Centre. The membership of the three churches was less than 90, and the number of delegates in attendance was 10. The organization was effected and the entire business of the meeting transacted while 9 of the delegates were seated in a row on a log and the moderator standing before them, supported by the back of a chair. The body was called " The Iowa Baptist Association." In 1843, after the organization of the Davenport Association, its name was changed to the " Des Moines Association."

The Baptists of Iowa went on gaining from year to year. Their strength and efficiency were increased by accessions to the ministry of able and earnest men, many of whom came under the appointment of the American Baptist Home Mission Society, by the constant tide of emigration from the older States bringing in many faithful Baptists, and by the conversion of souls. New fields of Christian labor were occupied, churches were multiplied, a general organization for missionary work was formed, additional Associations were established, the Sunday-school enterprise was pressed forward, means were proposed and devised for the advantages of higher education, and institutions of learning were founded.

Baptist churches are found in most of the principal cities and towns of the State. There are now in Iowa 24 Baptist Associations, 410 churches, having a membership of 24,700 ; over 1000 were added to these churches by baptism during the year 1879-80. They have about 250 Sunday-schools, with 20,000 pupils, and are well represented numerically in their institutions of learning now at work. The Baptist ministry of Iowa has many men of sterling worth. Not a few of them have supported their families in part or altogether by the labor of their own hands while preaching the gospel to others. Iowa Baptists have been, and they still are, represented in the civil and educational interests of the State and nation, holding places of prominence and trust in halls of legislation, in executive and judicial positions, and among professional men. Iowa Baptists have contributed some noble men and women for the work of foreign missions, and for missionary toils in the dark places of our own land. Among the biographical sketches of this work will be found the names of a few men who are now living in the State or are sleeping in its soil. These by no means exhaust the list of men worthy of special notice, but may be accepted as representatives of the different classes whose lives and labors occupy an important place in Iowa Baptist history.

Iowa Baptists have a future which has the promise of marked advancement and blessed results to those interests of Christ's kingdom committed to their trust.

Iowa, Baptist Centennial Academy of, is located in Malvern, Mills Co., Southwestern Iowa. The enterprise was begun mainly by Rev. J. W. Roe, pastor at Malvern, in 1876. The expense of building was borne almost wholly by the church. The subscriptions taken by Mr. Roe amounted to $8000, but he died before the edifice was begun. It was erected in 1877-78, during the pastorate of his successor, the Rev. O. T. Conger, the name of Mr. Roe being chiseled in the corner-stone. The building is a beautiful structure, and cost, as it now stands, about $12,000. The first and only principal the school has had thus far is R. M. Bridges, A.M., a man of scholarly attainments.

Iowa Baptist State Convention.—"In response to a call of the Des Moines Association, a Convention of brethren from the Baptist churches in Iowa Territory was held in Iowa City, June 3-4, 1842, to consider the expediency of forming a Territorial Association for missionary purposes." Twenty-five delegates were present. Some had walked seventy-five miles. Three of these delegates, C. E. Brown, William Elliott, and M. W. Rudd, are still living and in Iowa. B. Carpenter was made president, and W. B. Morey secretary, of "The Iowa Baptist General Association." In 1851 the name was changed to "Iowa Baptist State Convention." The constitution then adopted said, "The object of this Association shall be to promote the preaching of the gospel, ministerial education, and all the general objects of benevolence throughout this Territory." Though the name of the organization has been changed, the declared object has remained the same.

At the time of this organization there were about 380 Baptists in the Territory, and not more than 15 Baptist churches, while Iowa then had a population of about 52,000. For the first fourteen years of its history this Association was little more than an agent for the American Baptist Home Mission Society, to advise and assist that society in its work. In 1854 and 1855 the Convention attempted some direct labors in behalf of the German population. In 1856 the Rev. I. M. Seay received the first commission ever issued by this body. During the same year two other missionaries were sent forth, and the Convention entered heartily upon its declared work. During 1857 twenty-five missionaries were appointed, and Rev. J. Y. Aitchison was chosen agent. From 1858 to 1861, Rev. D. P. Smith labored in the interest of the Convention as financial agent, and a band of earnest-working missionaries were kept on the field. "In 1863, Rev. S. H. Mitchell became missionary agent, and labored till the fall of 1869. Other men have toiled in the general agency and missionary work of the

Convention for shorter periods and rendered good service, while during all these years a number of noble, earnest-hearted men have been laboring as missionaries in the destitute and remote parts of the State. Among the secretaries have been Rev. T. S. Griffith, Rev. J. F. Childs, and Rev. T. F. Thickstun. Rev. J. Sunderland, the present missionary secretary and general missionary, in a recent circular says, "The Home Mission Society has aided missionaries in Iowa for forty-one years, issuing about 600 commissions. Besides all the churches organized, houses of worship built, Sunday-schools established, and souls saved, more than 5000 persons have been baptized into our churches in this State by its missionaries. Its work has equaled the labor of one man for four hundred and forty-two years, or an average of eleven missionaries constantly at work for the forty-one years. It has expended in this State $115,000. The State Convention has aided missionaries for the last twenty-five years, issuing 386 commissions. Its missionaries have baptized 3029 persons, organized 69 churches, and aided in building 66 meeting-houses. Their work equals the labor of one man for two hundred and sixty-one years, or an average of eleven men for the twenty-five years. There has been raised and expended in this work $65,300. In the whole work of Baptist missions in Iowa there has been expended $180,000.

The Convention is now prosecuting its missions in co-operation with the Home Mission Society,— holding the control of the work in its own hands with such guarantees of assistance from the Home Mission Society as enabled the Convention to extend it and increase its efficiency. There are at present thirty missionaries under appointment, including one Scandinavian and one German. There is a growing interest in this work, and a very deep conviction of the responsibility and promise of the present and future.

The Convention has its Sunday-school department and Sunday-school secretary. Formerly there was an organization called "The Iowa Baptist Sunday-School Union," formed in 1867, and having for its object "To promote the interests of Baptist Sunday-Schools in Iowa." This continued till 1878, and did good service. Now the Sunday-school work is a department of the Convention. It is put in the hands of a committee of five, known as "the Sunday-School Committee co-operating with the American Baptist Publication Society." The plan includes the employment of a Sunday-school missionary, "to do a general pioneer missionary work in destitute fields, by establishing Sunday-schools, organizing churches, holding meetings with feeble churches, holding Sunday-school institutes," etc. In the Baptist churches of Iowa there are about 250 Sunday-schools, having a membership of officers, teachers, and pupils of over 20,000. A number of the smaller churches join union schools, and some of the weaker, scattered churches have no schools. For two years the American Baptist Publication Society and the Iowa Baptist State Convention have sustained a Sunday-school missionary. Through the efforts of these missionaries new churches and schools have been organized, and twelve Associations have formed Sunday-school Conventions. Other Associations devote a part of their time to Sunday-school interests. Institutes have been held, awakening greater enthusiasm in the work. These Sunday-school missionaries have sold several hundred volumes of denominational works, besides giving away books, Testaments, and tracts.

In connection with their State Convention Iowa Baptists have "The Iowa Union for Ministerial Education," and "The Iowa Baptist Pastors' Conference." These assemble annually with the Convention, and also at the quarterly meetings of the board. The Union for Ministerial Education was organized in 1867. Its object is "the assistance of young men of Baptist churches in their educational preparation for the gospel ministry." The union has assisted over fifty brethren, several of whom are ordained pastors.

The Pastors' Conference was organized in 1867. Its object is "the mutual improvement of its members in Biblical knowledge and in the duties connected with the ministry." Ministers' institutes are occasionally held under the guidance of this Conference.

Ireland, Rev. James, was born in Edinburgh, Scotland, in 1748. He was brought up in the Presbyterian Church of his fathers. His education and talents were respectable. He came to America after reaching manhood, with pleasing manners, and without Christ in his heart. He was something of a poet, and in revising one of his religious pieces he was deeply convicted of guilt, from which faith in a suffering Saviour delivered him. He became eminent as a preacher soon after his baptism; his learning and the tenderness of his manner produced a powerful impression upon his hearers, and the Spirit's blessing upon the truth he proclaimed made him a great enemy of Satan's empire. He formed several Baptist churches during his ministry, which extended over forty years, and his influence in favor of truth was very great.

This led the Episcopal clergy of Virginia to stir up social and legal persecutions against him. He was thrust into jail in Culpeper for preaching without the authority of law; abuse was heaped upon him on his way to prison; within its walls an attempt was made to blow him up with gunpowder, and on its failure an effort was put forth to suffocate him by burning brimstone at the door and window of his jail. It was also planned to poison him. His persecutions permanently injured his health; two accidents completed the work begun by State church tyranny, and Mr. Ireland entered upon his rest May 5, 1806.

Ireland, Joseph Alexander, M.D., a distinguished physician and surgeon, was born in Jefferson Co., Ky., Sept. 15, 1824. At the age of seventeen he commenced studying, and graduated in the Kentucky School of Medicine in 1851, and immediately began the practice of his profession in the

JOSEPH ALEXANDER IRELAND, M.D.

city of Louisville. In 1854 he removed to Jefferson County, where he practised as a physician about ten years. In 1848 he was set apart for the ministry by a Baptist church, of which he had been a member from his youth, and preached statedly to several churches in his neighborhood. In 1864 he was elected Professor of Obstetrics and Diseases of Women and Children in the Kentucky School of Medicine, and afterwards was made a professor in the university at Louisville. Since 1875 he has filled the chair of Diseases of Women and Children in both the Kentucky School of Medicine and the Louisville Medical College.

Irish Baptists. See ENGLISH BAPTISTS.

Irwin, Rev. Charles Mercer, eldest son of Maj. Isaiah T. and Isabella Irwin, was born in Wilkes Co., Ga., Nov. 11, 1813. He was converted in early life, and was baptized into the fellowship of Sardis church by Rev. Enoch Callaway. His father, being wealthy, gave him the best educational advantages of the day. Prepared for college by Rev. Otis Smith at Powelton, he went through most of the regular course in the State University at Athens, and then studied law in the University of Virginia. On his return to Georgia he was admitted to the bar in 1834, married a most amiable lady, Miss Harriet E. Battle, settled in Washington, Wilkes Co., and for two years practised law successfully. He then settled on a plantation in Hancock County. There the Spirit of God met him and moulded him to his own sacred purposes. The feelings which made him say at sixteen, "If, when grown, I feel as I do now, I shall preach," constrained him to consecrate himself to the Lord for life. He entered the ministry and was ordained at Powelton. After devoting several years to missionary labor in the southern part of the State, he settled as pastor of the Baptist church in Madison, where he remained eight years, developing preaching talents of a high order, and manifesting remarkable executive ability. So successful were his labors that his church increased largely, and soon was regarded as a model. His next two pastorates were at Atlanta and in Albany, Ga., in which latter place he labored with wonderful success for three or four years. Broken down in health, he took a northern trip for recuperation in 1860. Then came sad years of war. Residing on his plantation in Lee County, he preached gratuitously to country churches until peace spread her balmy wings over the land once more. Although he has been a pastor twice since the war, his health has not been equal to the demands of the position, and he has devoted most of his time for the last ten years to agency work in the State of Georgia in behalf of foreign missions, for the Southern Baptist Convention. In this he has been faithful and efficient. Mr. Irwin is a man of fine and varied talents, he is modest as to his own merits, but a fluent speaker. By nature he is strictly honest, affectionate, and very devoted to his family, two children having blessed this union. In disposition, he is pleasant and genial; in manners, courteous and obliging. His piety is undoubted, and he has been a successful pastor and preacher, and a good business man. For several years he was clerk of the State Convention; has, for a long time, been a member of the board of trustees for the Mercer University. Few men are more generally beloved among the Georgia Baptists for their usefulness in the past, their excellence of character and qualities of sterling worth.

Irwin, Isaiah Tucker, a pious and wealthy deacon of the Sardis church, in Wilkes Co., Ga., who was born in Amherst, Va., Aug. 15, 1783, and died in April, 1856. His parents moved to Georgia when he was quite young, and, settling in Wilkes County, engaged in farming, which occupation he himself pursued, gradually accumulating a large landed property. At nineteen he married Miss Isabella Bankston, a woman in whom all the virtues of mind, heart, and person were blended, and who reached the age of ninety-one. Mr. Irwin was a very popular and useful man. He represented his county in the Legislature for many years, and served in the Creek war, rising to the rank of major. In 1827 the prayers of his pious wife were answered, and he was converted and united with the church of which he was afterwards an active, liberal, and useful member. He was ordained a deacon soon after uniting with the Sardis church, and filled the office well. His house was the seat of a princely hospitality; nor did he ever permit a minister who was his guest to leave without bestowing on him a pecuniary gift. To his children he gave the very best educational facilities that the country afforded, and he lived to see them all happily married and followers of Jesus. A daughter became the wife of the distinguished Baptist minister, Rev. J. L. Brookes; his second son was Speaker of the Georgia House of Representatives; and his eldest son, Rev. C. M. Irwin, a useful Baptist minister, is still living. To his servants Mr. Irwin was remarkably kind and considerate, providing liberally for their religious instruction. In return they almost idolized him. Affectionate and warm-hearted by nature, he was the tender husband, the kind and loving father, the sympathizing and generous neighbor, and faithful Christian. With full barns, he never forgot the poor, whether in the church or out of it, and at his mills the widows' sacks were always filled, and their wants were supplied in many other ways. When he died gloom pervaded the community, and at his funeral the poor exclaimed, "We have lost our best friend." In person he was tall and commanding, being in that, as in every other respect, one of nature's noblemen.

Ives, Dwight, D.D., son of Abraham and Eunice (Day) Ives, was born in West Springfield (now part of Holyoke), Mass., Sept. 20, 1805; pursued academical studies in New Ipswich, N. H., under Robert A. Coffin; graduated at Brown University in class of 1835, at the age of thirty; preached for the First Baptist church in Springfield, Mass., where he was ordained; settled with the Baptist church in Alton, Ill., where he won a high reputation, but was compelled from ill health to return to the East; settled with the Second Baptist church in Suffield, Conn., by the side of the Connecticut Literary Institution; guided in the erection of a beautiful church edifice, and drew a large congregation and built up a strong church; labored in this important field from 1839 to 1874 with most remarkable success, baptizing more than 1200 persons, and greatly aiding the Connecticut Literary Institution and benefiting the whole State; was a leading man in all ministerial circles and all educational and missionary affairs; received the honorary degree of Doctor of Divinity from Brown University in 1857; left two sons, the elder of which, William C., graduated at Brown University

DWIGHT IVES, D.D.

in 1865; resigning in Suffield in 1874, from age and ill health, he removed to Conway, Mass., and preached as he was able to the church in that place; died in Conway, Dec. 22, 1875, aged seventy years; one of New England's noblest men and most effective preachers.

Ives, Rev. Jeremiah, was pastor of a General Baptist church in London, England, for more than thirty years. He had a peculiar talent for discussion, which enabled him to use with much readiness his great intellect and his stores of learning. He had controversies with the Quakers and the Presbyterians, in which he obtained considerable reputation. Crosby says that his fame reached Charles II., who sent for him to dispute with a Romish priest. Mr. Ives entered upon the discussion in the habit of an Episcopal clergyman, and pressed the priest very closely. He showed that the "pretended antiquity of their doctrines and practices fell short of the days of the apostles; for they were not to be found in any writings which remain of the apostolic age." The priest, after much wrangling, in the end replied "that this argument was of as much force against infant baptism as against the doctrines and ceremonies of the Church of Rome." To which Mr. Ives replied that he readily granted what he said to be true. The priest upon this broke up the controversy, saying

"he had been cheated, and that hé would proceed no farther, for he came to dispute with a clergyman of the Established Church, and it was now evident that this was an Anabaptist preacher." There is no community of Christians who are entirely invulnerable to the assaults of Rome except the Baptist denomination, a church ages older than the apostasy of the popes.

Ives, Moses Brown, was born in Providence, R. I., July 21, 1794, and was the son of Thomas Poynton and Hope Brown Ives. His father was the senior partner of the old and everywhere respected firm of Brown & Ives, and his mother the sister of the Hon. Nicholas Brown, the generous patron of the university which bears his name.

It was the intention of his father in due time to introduce him into the firm of which he was a member. Believing, however, that mental discipline and culture are not inconsistent with the calling of the merchant, he decided to give him a full collegiate education. He graduated at Brown University in 1812, and wishing to pursue his studies still farther, he entered the law-school at Litchfield, Conn., which then ranked among the best professional schools of its character in the country. On completing his course of study here he was still comparatively a youth, and it was deemed wise that he should reap the benefits of foreign travel, especially in so far as they had a bearing on his future calling in life. "While abroad," says Dr. Wayland, " his object seems to have been, not so much to see sights and walk through galleries, as to observe men and acquaint himself with the habits and manners of merchants of distinction. I have heard him frequently refer to this period of his life, but I think never for any other purpose than to illustrate the modes of doing business in the several capitals which he had occasion to visit."

Having passed through the preparatory training, he entered the counting-room of Brown & Ives, and at once applied himself to the work to which he proposed to devote his life, and he became, in the best sense of the word, " a model merchant." His opinion on all matters connected with his profession was received with the highest respect. He believed that there were great principles which were as certain and undeviating in business as the laws of nature, and he rigidly adhered to them. But it is not as a successful merchant that we wish to call attention to Mr. Ives, but to the deep interest he took both in popular and liberal education. The city of Providence owes to him a debt of gratitude for what he did in elevating the standard of common-school education which it can never pay. His relations to Brown University were of the most intimate character. He was elected a member of its board of trustees in 1822, and in 1825 he was chosen its treasurer, and without compensation, and as a labor of love to his *alma mater*, discharged its onerous and sometimes complicated duties for the long period of thirty-two years. " During the twenty-nine years of my connection with the university," says Dr. Wayland, " I do not remember an examination at some of the exercises of which he was not present unless detained by sickness, and in which he did not take a lively interest. His interest never flagged when anything could be suggested to improve the condition of the institution which he loved so well. If in any respect Brown University has gained in favor with the public; if it has taken a more honorable rank among the colleges of New England ; if its means of education have been rendered, in any respect, ample, and its board of instruction such as would adorn any similar institution in our country ; to no one are we more indebted for all this than to the late treasurer of the university."

Mr. Ives, although like his uncle, the Hon. Nicholas Brown, not a member of the church, was an habitual worshiper in the venerable meeting-house of the First Baptist church. He was not wont to give expression to his religious views, but as the shadows of time passed away, and the solemn realities of eternity rose to his view, he did not hesitate to make known the ground of his hopes. " I am now on my death-bed," said he, in a note dictated to a friend, " but my mind is perfectly clear. I am firm and unwavering in my belief in Jesus Christ and him crucified." To another he sent this message, "Give him this short message from me,—' Look unto Jesus.' " Such testimony to his firm and unshaken trust in his Redeemer, coming from the lips of such a man, meant all it expressed.

Ivey, Rev. F. H., was born in Fayetteville, N. C., in 1834; bred in the *Observer* office under the training of E. J. Hale, baptized by Dr. James McDaniel, and graduated at Wake Forest College, it is not strange that Mr. Ivey is a capital writer and an excellent preacher. He was for eleven years pastor of the Baptist church of Athens, Ga. ; returned to North Carolina in 1873 ; did good work as agent for Wake Forest College for more than a year, and has been for the last four years pastor in Goldsborough.

Ivimey, Rev. Joseph, was born at Ringwood, Hampshire, England, May 22, 1773. When a youth he was convicted of sin, and a gospel hope first entered his heart through the stanza,—

> " In the world of endless ruin
> It shall never once be said,
> There's a soul that perished suing
> For the Saviour's promised aid."

This hope was soon after confirmed, so that he could regard the Saviour as his. He was baptized Sept. 16, 1790. He was ordained pastor of the Eagle Street church, Red Lion Square, London, Jan. 16, 1805. His labors were attended with great success. He was gifted with much energy, with

REV. JOSEPH IVIMEY.

an unusual power of gaining and keeping information, and with fearless faithfulness in proclaiming the whole truth of God. He had the happiness of baptizing his own father and mother. His father was seventy years of age at the time of his immersion, and only partook of the Lord's Supper once after he was received into the church.

Mr. Ivimey wrote a life of John Bunyan, which enjoyed considerable popularity, and " A History of the English Baptists," in four octavo volumes, the last two of which were published in 1830. This history is invaluable. It is only seldom for sale, and when it can be purchased it is held at a high price. He was also the author of other works.

Mr. Ivimey closed his useful life Feb. 8, 1834. A little before his departure he said,—

> " Not a wave of trouble rolls
> Across my peaceful breast."

J.

Jackson, Gov. Charles, son of Hon. Richard Jackson, and brother of Rev. Dr. Henry Jackson, was born in Providence, R. I., March 3, 1797, and was a graduate of Brown University in the class of 1817. He pursued his law studies in the office of Hon. James Burrill, of Providence, and was admitted to the bar in 1820. After practising his profession for three years, he retired from it, and devoted himself to the manufacture of cotton, and resided for several years in a village which took its name from him,—Jacksonville. He returned to Providence in 1839, and devoted himself during the remainder of his life to the manufacturing interests of the State and of the country at large. For several years he was a member of the General Assembly of Rhode Island, and Speaker of the House in 1841–42. He was chosen governor of the State in 1845, and held the office one year. His death occurred at Providence, Jan. 21, 1876. Although not a professor of religion, he had a pew in the First Baptist meeting-house in Providence, and regarded that place as his religious home.

Jackson, Henry, D.D., was born in Providence, R. I., June 16, 1798. By family connection he was related to some of the first people in the city of his birth and in Rhode Island. Having completed his preparatory studies in the university grammar school, he entered Brown University in 1813. During his second year in college he was baptized, and became a member of the First Baptist church in Providence, then under the pastoral charge of Rev. Dr. Gano. At once he took a decided stand as a Christian worker, and, obeying what he recognized as the call of God, he resolved to devote himself to the work of the Christian ministry. To fit himself for it he repaired to the Andover Theological Institution, and pursued the full course of study there. The First Baptist church in Providence, with which he was connected, gave him a license to preach the gospel in 1820. He was ordained as pastor of the Baptist church in Charlestown, Mass., Nov. 27, 1822. For fourteen years he labored with great zeal, and was rewarded by seeing the growth of his church, both in numbers and spiritual efficiency. It was largely owing to his influence and practical aid that the Charlestown Female Seminary was founded, an institution which did an incalculable amount of good in the intellectual training of young ladies, and fitting very many of them for positions of great useful-

ness in after-life. His ministry in Charlestown closed Oct. 19, 1836.

Dr. Jackson had received an invitation to take charge of the First Baptist church in Hartford,

HENRY JACKSON, D.D.

Conn., before his resignation of his pastorate in Charlestown. After a few weeks of cessation from his ministerial work, he was installed at Hartford. Serious illness interrupted his labors after he had been in his new field a little more than a year. After a season of rest, he was anxious once more to be engaged in the work of the ministry, and accepted a call to the First Baptist church in New Bedford, where he was installed Jan. 1, 1839. Seven years were spent in New Bedford. Once more he found himself overworked, and compelled, in comparative retirement, to recruit his wasted energies. He resumed his work in January, 1847, and was settled as the pastor of the Central Baptist church in Newport, R. I. The church had recently been formed, and he was its first pastor. This was his longest pastorate, extending from January, 1847, to the close of life, a period of a little more than twenty-three years. When the end of his long ministerial career came, he had been in the vocation which, in his young days, he had accepted with such a hearty consecration of himself to his Lord, nearly forty-one years. During this time he had welcomed into the different churches of which he had been pastor nearly 1400 persons, having administered the ordinance of baptism to 870 of this number.

Dr. Jackson was greatly interested in all forms of educational institutions. In 1828 he was elected a member of the corporation of Brown University. He was one of the founders of the Newton Theological Institution, and a trustee from 1825 through the remainder of his life. By his will he left generous bequests to both these seminaries of learning. He published a history of the Baptist churches in Rhode Island, and by his industry and diligent search gathered up materials which, but for his labors, might have been irrecoverably lost.

The death of Dr. Jackson was almost a translation. He was on his way to East Greenwich, R. I., going there on some errand of Christian love. While engaged in pleasant conversation with a friend who sat by his side, without a moment's warning, life was extinct, and he was transferred from the scene of his labors to that of his reward. It was without doubt a stroke of apoplexy. The event occurred March 2, 1863, at the age of sixty-four years and eight months and four days. He had filled so prominent a place in the denomination in which for so long a time he had exercised his ministry, that his sudden departure was a great shock to his friends. It is difficult to realize the sum total of the good which sprang from all those years of service for the Master. That he owned and blessed the service was the servant's exceeding great reward.

Jackson, Col. Moses, a member of the Mississippi senate from Wilkinson and Amite Counties, was born in Amite Co., Miss., in 1822; became a Baptist in 1852, and has since lived a consistent Christian life in the midst of public duties; twenty-two years a trustee, and twenty-four years a deacon, and twenty-five years clerk of his church. When the General Association of South Mississippi and Eastern Louisiana was formed, in 1866, he was elected moderator. He entered the Confederate army as a private, and was promoted through several grades to that of lieutenant-colonel of the 33d Miss. Regiment. Besides several minor offices which he has held, in 1861 he was elected to the State Legislature, and re-elected in 1863. In 1865 he was elected to the State senate, and re-elected in 1877.

Jackson, Hon. Richard, was born in Providence, R. I., July 3, 1764. His early boyhood brought him within the period of the Revolutionary war. When there were grave fears that Providence would be attacked by the British, the father of young Jackson removed his family to Pomfret,

Conn., where they remained for some time away from the dangers and excitements of the war. Mr. Jackson early showed a taste for business pursuits, and embarked in mercantile and manufacturing enterprises, in the prosecution of which he was eminently successful. He also developed a taste for political life, and was honored several times with the votes of his fellow-citizens to fill places of important civil trusts. In 1815 he was elected a member of the Tenth Congress of the United States, and so acceptable were his services to a majority of the people of his native State that he was re-elected to the Eleventh, Twelfth, and Thirteenth Congresses. The whole period of his service as one of the representatives from Rhode Island was nearly seven years, covering the period between November 11, 1808, and March 4, 1815. In all matters affecting the welfare of his native town he took a great interest. Of one of the leading insurance companies of Providence—the Washington—he was the president for thirty-eight years. He took also an abiding interest in the affairs of the First Baptist church, in whose meeting-house he worshiped for so many years. Brown University chose him as a member of its corporation in 1809, and he held this office until his death, which took place at Providence, April 18, 1838. Mr. Jackson was the father of Rev. Henry Jackson, D.D., and of Hon. Charles Jackson, who was governor of Rhode Island during the gubernatorial year 1845–46.

Jackson, Rev. R. S., a gifted young minister, a native of Louisiana, was born near the mouth of Red River, Sept. 12, 1844; was educated at Mount Lebanon University and the State Seminary at Alexandria. He left school to enlist in the Confederate army, and rose to the rank of captain. After the war he engaged in teaching; began to preach in 1869 to the creoles in their vernacular; was subsequently tutor in Mississippi College; secretary of the Ministerial Educational Board of the Louisiana Convention, and missionary of Bayou Macon Association, La. After a successful pastorate at Bastrop, La., he entered the Southern Baptist Theological Seminary. As a contributor to the religious press he attained distinction. He died at the seminary from an old army wound in 1874.

Jackson, Thomas, a prominent Baptist layman in Eastern Louisiana, was one of "Marion's men" during the Revolution, and accompanied the old "Swamp Fox" throughout the war. It was he who prepared the dinner of roasted sweet potatoes for the British officers who visited Marion's camp under a flag of truce, and who reported that it was impossible to conquer men who fought for liberty and lived upon roots. He came to East Feliciana Parish, La., in 1806, and either united in the organization of the Hepzibah church in 1813, or became a member soon after. He died in 1844. Several of his descendants have been prominent Baptists in the State.

Jackson, Wade M., a pioneer among the Baptists of Missouri, was born in Fleming Co., Ky., Dec. 3, 1797, and died in Howard Co., Mo., March 22, 1879. He removed to Missouri in 1824, and settled on the farm where he died. He was the father of Mrs. Judge James Harris, of Boone Co., Mo., and brother of Claiborne F. Jackson, late governor of Missouri. As an honored citizen of Central Missouri he stood in the front rank. He became a Baptist forty-one years before his death, and consecrated his life to Christ, and served his denomination faithfully. He was a member of the Executive Missionary Board of the General Association for years, and a trustee of William Jewell College. He rendered valuable aid in drawing up the charter of that institution, and helped to organize it. Many old friends followed him to his resting-place in the family burying-ground near his home.

Jackson, Rev. Wingate, was born in 1776 in Virginia, and removed in early life to Kentucky, where he reached eminence as a preacher. He came to Missouri about 1809, and labored in and around Cape Girardeau and Jackson. He belonged to Bethel Association, and great success attended his ministry. He was clear in doctrine, eloquent in speech, wise in counsel, and untiring in labor. He died in 1835. His opinions for years after his death were quoted to settle controversies.

Jacobs, B. F., Esq.—This name is one well known among active and enterprising Christian workers throughout the land. Mr. Jacobs was born at Paterson, N. J., in September, 1834. He was baptized in Chicago in 1854, by Rev. J. C. Burroughs, then pastor of the First Baptist church, uniting with that church, of which he has remained a member until now. Previous to his removal to Chicago he had lived for some years in Detroit, where he was a member of the Bible-class of Mr. S. N. Kendrick. His conversion occurred while there. Immediately upon uniting with the church in Chicago he began active Christian work, at first as a teacher in the Taylor Street Mission School, the first of such schools established in Chicago, being engaged also in a similar way in the home school. In 1856 the first of the mission schools of our own denomination in Chicago was opened in what was then called New Street, now Seventeenth, and named the New Street Mission ; subsequently, in recognition of the generous aid given it by Miss Shields, of Philadelphia, called the Shields Mission. Of this mission Mr. Jacobs remained the superintendent for eight years, and under his guidance it grew to be one of the most efficient agencies of the kind in the city. In 1865, when Deacon S. Hoard, by reason of his connection with the Sec-

ond church, upon the west side of the river, left the superintendency of the school at the First church, Mr. Jacobs was elected superintendent in his place. The church was at that time building a new house of worship on Wabash Avenue, and was meeting meantime in Bryan Hall. On the first Sunday in January, 1866, it removed to the lecture-room of the new house, a room made for the accommodation of 800. The school numbered only 90, and seemed at first almost lost in the new quarters, but began at once to grow, and so continued until it had reached nearly 1200. During this time Mr. Jacobs remained the superintendent, and continued such until the house on Wabash Avenue had been destroyed by fire, in 1874. Upon the erection of a new house in the south part of the city, Mr. Jacobs, with others, organized a school and evening congregation upon Wabash Avenue near the site of the house that was burned. This, under the name of the Tabernacle, has been continued until the present time. The school at present numbers 400. There are 126 members of the organization holding their formal membership with the First church, but having otherwise a distinct identity. The weekly evening prayer-meeting numbers from 75 to 100, fully three-fifths of whom are men. Of those who have connected themselves with the organization most have come in by baptism, many of them rescued from the lowest depths of dissipation. At the evening service, which is always well attended, Mr. Jacobs preaches.

The large place which Mr. Jacobs has filled in general church work would deserve detailed record if space would allow. He was one of the founders, and has always been one of the most active members of the Young Men's Christian Association of Chicago, an organization which grew out of the revival of 1857–58. In 1861, Mr. Jacobs, Mr. Moody, and Mr. Tuthill King inaugurated the religious work at Camp Douglas, in Chicago, which was continued during the war with the happiest results. As one of the first who visited on a like errand the troops in service in the South, he may be said to have had a share in creating the Christian Commission, with which he remained connected to the end of the struggle, serving as its secretary for the West, and raising for its uses the sum of more than $100,000. In the general Sunday-school work, State and national, he has labored during many years ; was the originator of the International Sunday-School Committee, and remains a member of that committee to this day. This is but the meagre outline of a career of remarkable Christian activity, carried on amidst the exacting demands of an engrossing business, and which, we rejoice to say, has still the promise of many years' continuance.

Jacobs, Capt. William S., commanded at sea

for many years, and on retiring, resided at Liverpool, Nova Scotia. He became a member of the Baptist church in that town ; was liberal in support of all denominational objects, and at his death, in 1863, left handsome bequests to Acadia College, to home missions, and infirm ministers.

James, Prof. Charles Sexton, Ph.D., was born in Philadelphia, Pa., Feb. 6, 1820. He was prepared for college at the Haddington Institution, under the care of Rev. J. L. Dagg, D.D. He entered Brown University at sixteen, and was a member of the famous class of 1840, in which he was associated with James R. Boise, Wm. T. Brantly, Ebenezer Dodge, ex-Gov. Gaston, of Massachusetts, J. R. Kendrick, Heman Lincoln, and Henry G. Weston. His course was, however, interrupted by a three years' absence, and his graduation deferred until 1843. He distinguished himself as a student, and particularly in Greek. He was chosen to membership in the Phi Beta Kappa Society in his Junior year. He was converted during a revival at Brown University in 1835, and was baptized into the fellowship of the Tenth Baptist church, Philadelphia, by Rev. J. H. Kennard, D.D. After his graduation he became an instructor with his uncle, T. D. James, in the academy at Eleventh and Market Streets, Philadelphia, until 1851, when he was called to the Professorship of Mathematics and Natural Philosophy in the university at Lewisburg, Pa. As a scholar, Prof. James was exact and thorough. As a teacher, for more than a third of a century, he was enthusiastic and eminently successful. The dry problems of pure mathematics were poetry to him, and in his hands were clothed with unknown charms to his classes. Many of Lewisburg's best and most useful graduates refer to his class-room as the place of their first and lasting inspiration to exact reasoning and earnest scholarship.

As a student of the Bible and a member of the church, Prof. James was reverent and diligent. He was always an active worker in the Sunday-school. His knowledge of the New Testament was founded upon a thorough study of the original Greek. For years he has conducted a Sunday morning Bible-class of college students in his parlor, the New Testament being studied in Greek.

In 1859, the degree of Ph.D. was conferred upon him by Columbian College. Prof. James was singularly modest. In his class-room, and within the circle of his appointed labors, he was devotedly loved by those who knew him best, as a man of self-sacrificing generosity and earnest devotion to the cause of Christian education.

James, Rev. John, was pastor of the Baptist church meeting in Bulstake Alley, Whitechapel, London. In the latter end of 1661, Mr. James was rudely interrupted twice by officers of the law while preaching to his own people, and commanded to come down. Then he was dragged out of the pulpit. A perjured wretch named Tipler, a journeyman pipe-maker, charged him with uttering treasonable words against the king; and so disreputable a person was Tipler that the justice refused to commit Mr. James on his testimony, unless it was corroborated ; but this was done, and the good pastor was sent to the Tower.

On the 14th of November he was brought before Chief-Justice Forster, and three other judges, at Westminster Hall, where he was charged with " endeavoring to levy war against the king; with seeking a change in the government; with saying that the king was a bloody tyrant, a blood-sucker, and a bloodthirsty man, and that his nobles were the same; and that the king and his nobles had shed the blood of the saints at Charing Cross, and in Scotland." To this indictment he pled " not guilty, neither in matter nor form." And there was not a tittle of evidence to substantiate one of the charges in any just court on earth. Mr. James was remanded to Newgate for four days, when the trial was to proceed. In the mean time he received a letter from a friend of distinction, who informed him that for many years there had not been such efforts to pack a jury, and that his only hope of safety lay in challenging them, or " most of the chief men of them." When Mr. James was brought before the court, the chief justice exclaimed, " Oh, oh, are you come ?" " and this was a specimen of the way in which his trial was conducted." He was condemned according to the plot of those who planned his murder ; and the next day, after the court had sentenced him, his wife presented a petition to King Charles II. proving his innocence, and appealing for mercy; but the only reply of his majesty was, " Oh ! Mr. James, he is a sweet gentleman," " and the door was shut against her." The next morning she made another appeal to him ; and his cruel response was, " He is a rogue, and shall be hanged."

When he was asked if he had anything to say why sentence of death should not be pronounced upon him, his answer was: " As for me, behold, I am in your hand : do with me as it seemeth good and meet unto you. But know ye for certain that if ye put me to death, ye shall surely bring innocent blood upon yourselves, and upon this city, and upon the inhabitants thereof. Precious in the sight of the Lord is the death of his saints. He that toucheth you toucheth the apple of mine eye." And when Mr. James heard his sentence, he immediately added, " Blessed be God, whom man hath condemned God hath justified."

At Tyburn, where he was *hung, drawn and quartered*, his remarks were gentle and loving, and his soul brave and full of hope. " His quarters were taken back to Newgate prison on the sledge which brought him to the gallows, and they were afterwards placed on the city gates, and his head was set upon a pole opposite his meeting-house.''

John James was an inoffensive and benevolent man, free from any blemish in his character, and guiltless of every charge in the indictment. He was savagely murdered by Charles II., his courtiers, and his tools, the judges, to terrify the Dissenters, and especially the Baptists, into loyalty. Undoubtedly the vengeance of God, invoked by the innocent blood of John James, had something to do with driving the Stuarts from the throne of England. Mr. James was a Seventh-Day Baptist.

James, Rev. John Angell (colored), was born Nov. 5, 1826, in De Kalb Co., Ga. He was raised on a farm, but became a mechanic. He professed religion, and was baptized by Rev. S. Landrum in 1849, and joined the Cotton Avenue Baptist church in Macon, Ga., Feb. 10, 1850. He was licensed in 1856 by the Cotton Avenue church. In September, 1865, the Second Street (colored) church was formed by members who took letters from the Cotton Avenue church. They called Mr. James to ordination, and he was set apart to the gospel ministry by a Presbytery consisting of Rev. E. W. Warren (white), Rev. F. M. Haygood (white), and Rev. Frank Quarles (colored), on the 14th of October, 1866. He assumed the pastorate of the Second Street church in October, 1867, and served nine years with much success, and baptized over 300 persons. He then went to Houston County, where he organized the Springfield (colored) church, which he served sixteen months. Returning to Macon, he organized the Fulton church, which he served two years as pastor. He then went to Forsyth, Ga., and organized the St. James (colored) Baptist church in 1867, where he still labors industriously and usefully. He has baptized into the fellowship of that church 374 persons. The total number baptized by him during his ministry to the present time, 1880, is 738. Mr. James is one of the most intelligent, useful, and laborious ministers among the colored Baptists of Georgia, and one who stands high in the denomination. For years he was clerk of the Middle Georgia Association (colored), a large and working body. For eight years he has been assistant secretary of the Colored State Baptist Convention, and is a vice-president of that body and secretary of its executive board. He is liberal, earnest, and devout, and he is a faithful pastor, enjoying the confidence of all, and a man of marked ability as a preacher and writer among his race.

James, J. H., a banker of Atlanta, Ga., was born in Henry County, July 14, 1830. His father removed to Georgia from North Carolina, of which State he was a native. Until manhood Mr. James resided on his father's farm. There was, however, in him a genius for business that could not brook such a life, so, at twenty, he went to Atlanta and accepted a situation at $10 per month, which, before

J. H. JAMES.

a great while, was increased to $100 per month. In 1860 he opened a banking-house in Atlanta, and when the war began was wealthy; but the end of the war found him worth about $12,000 only. He opened his bank again, and prosecuted his business with such success that he is now one of the wealthiest men in Georgia. His business capacity and integrity are such that he enjoys the confidence of all who know him, and has now established for himself the reputation of a financier of the first order. In manner Mr. James is pleasant and friendly; free from affectation, and full of geniality. As a citizen, he is charitable and public-spirited; as a Christian, generous and sincere, taking part in all denominational affairs, and in the family circle he is kind, affectionate, and considerate. He has occupied the position of mayor of Atlanta, is a trustee of Mercer University, and a trustee and superintendent of the Baptist Orphans' Home of Georgia, located at Atlanta.

In 1876 his name was suggested in connection with the gubernatorial election, and many, desiring to secure for the State the benefit of his financial ability, entreated him to allow his name to be placed before the nominating convention, but this he declined.

Mr. James is a man of great liberality. At his individual expense he erected two Baptist houses of worship in Atlanta, at a cost of $2500 each; and to the completion of another he contributed the sum of $3500, besides generously aiding in the support of ministers for these churches. Thousands of his minor charities have relieved the necessities of the poor, and if the worth of men should be measured by their gifts to the needy, that of Mr. James would appear pre-eminent. His donations to churches since the war sum up more than $15,000, an amount considerably in excess of the entire capital with which he resumed business.

He is one of those noble men who win their way in life by capacity, integrity, and sound judgment, and who rise, not on the ruin of others, but through the legitimate exercise of their own abilities and good sense in the ordinary business affairs of life. During the panic of 1873, when many of the wealthiest bankers were compelled to suspend, some going into bankruptcy, a heavy pressure was brought to bear upon the establishment of Mr. James, by the unexpected demands of depositors. At this juncture he closed his bank until he could collect assets, when a number of the wealthy men of Atlanta, voluntarily and through the press, proposed to assume, in his behalf, liabilities varying from five to fifty thousand dollars each. Such a manifestation of faith is seldom met in the history of bankers or banking institutions, and this was an expression of confidence unmistakably sincere, since it was based upon the advance of large sums of actual capital for immediate use.

Mr. James frequently attends the denominational gatherings of his brethren, and his speeches are always plain, practical, and full of good sense.

James, Rev. J. J., was born in Halifax Co., Va., Nov. 30, 1814; was for three sessions a student at Wake Forest Institute, and, after teaching for two years in Virginia, graduated at Columbian University, Washington, D. C., in 1841. Mr. James was baptized at the age of eighteen by the Rev. John G. Mills, and was ordained in 1842, Rev. J. G. Mills and Rev. A. M. Poindexter constituting the Presbytery. After laboring for many years with much success as pastor in Caswell Co., N. C., aiding in the organization of Oxford Female College, and being a useful member of the various boards of the Convention, he became editor of the *Biblical Recorder* in 1854, which position he held till 1861. He now resides on his farm in Caswell County, and preaches only occasionally.

James, Rev. Owen, was born Oct. 30, 1848, in the County of Carmarthen, Wales. Until his sixteenth year his time was spent partly at school and partly in agricultural pursuits. He was converted in the summer of 1864, was baptized, and became an active and useful church member. His marked ability at so early an age prompted the church to advise him to prepare for the ministry,

to which his own inclinations strongly urged him; but circumstances for the time made it impracticable. Soon after this he united with another Baptist church, and here, again, after a most useful membership of nearly four years, the church urged him to devote himself to preparation for the ministry. Through the advice of Dr. Thomas Price, of Aberdare, Mr. James made his arrangements to come to the United States. He entered the preparatory department of Lewisburg University in September, 1870, and the college in 1872, from which he was graduated in 1876 with the highest honors of his class. In the fall of the same year he entered Crozer Theological Seminary, and was graduated from it in 1879. He was immediately called to the pastorate of the North Baptist church, Washington, D. C., which he accepted, where he was ordained, and where he still labors. Mr. James is an interesting and instructive preacher; is gifted with unusual logical and analytical power, and presents his themes in so fresh and original a manner that the most thoughtful minds listen to his expositions of Scriptural truth with both pleasure and profit. His congregation, though not very large, contains some of the most cultured of the denomination among its members.

James, Rev. Richard S., M.D., president of Judson University (Judsonia, Ark.), was born in Philadelphia, Pa., in 1824; educated at Brown University and Columbian College, Washington, D. C.; ordained in 1859; pastor nine years at Camden and Marlton, N. J.; was pastor at West Newton, Mass., and Market Street church, Zanesville, O.; and professor in Hillsdale College, Mich.; was pastor at Medina, Mich., where he was also principal of Oak-Grove Academy. At the beginning of the present year (1880) he was called to Judsonia, Ark., and soon after his arrival was elected president of the Judson University, located at Judsonia. Dr. James is an enthusiastic teacher, an eloquent preacher, and a sprightly writer.

Jameson, Ephraim H. E., D.D., was born at St. George, Me., May 19, 1835. His father, Rev. Thomas Jameson, was for many years a Baptist pastor in Maine, but removed to Illinois, where he died in 1870, at the age of eighty years. Mr. Jameson was educated at the Lebanon and South Berwick Academies, in Maine, and the Kingston Academy, N. H. He then entered upon the profession of teaching. In 1854 he was born into the kingdom of Christ. With a change of heart came convictions of duty in another direction, and he entered the New Hampton Collegiate and Theological Institution, at Fairfax, Vt., to prepare for the ministry. After completing his classical course, difficulties arrested his efforts, and he resolved to engage in secular pursuits till the way should open for him to preach the gospel. He went West, spent some time in teaching, and afterwards several years in the editorial profession in St. Louis, Mo. He bore an honorable part in the war as colonel of a U. S. regiment. He was elected to a seat in the Mis-

EPHRAIM H. E. JAMESON, D.D.

souri Legislature, and being re-elected, filled the Speaker's chair one year.

During all this time the voice of conscience was calling him to his real life-work. He endeavored to compromise by engaging in Sunday-school and mission efforts, but this only led him to follow Christ more fully. He was licensed to preach in 1874, by the Park Avenue Baptist church of St. Louis, and on May 9, 1876, he was publicly ordained to the ministry.

Dr. Jameson was chosen pastor of the First Baptist church of Omaha, Neb., Aug. 1, 1876. He still continues in that office. The completion of their large church edifice will remain for years a monument to his indefatigable energy. Shortly after his settlement in Nebraska he was chosen corresponding secretary of the Baptist State Convention, a position which he still holds, and in which he has rendered the State valuable service. In June, 1880, he received from Central University, Iowa, the degree of D.D.

Jameson, Rev. J. D., late pastor at Camden, Ark., was born in Georgia in 1850; began to preach in Columbia Co., Ark., in 1870; after a course of study at Mississippi College, interrupted by bad health, he spent one year in the Southern Baptist Theological Seminary; was successful as agent of the Southern Baptist Publication Society; as pastor

at Mineral Springs and at Camden, Ark.; at present he is State evangelist.

Janes, Col. Absalom, a prominent, consistent, and efficient member of the Baptist denomination in Georgia, was born in Wilkes County, June 8, 1796. In 1839 he took up his residence in Penfield, where he dwelt until his death, Sept. 25, 1847.

He was for eleven years treasurer of the Georgia Baptist Convention, and managed the finances of the body during years of extreme monetary depression with remarkable success. He was a trustee of Mercer Institute until it became Mercer University, and until his death, in 1847, he continued to be one of its trustees. In sustaining and in firmly establishing these two institutions, and all the other benevolent Baptist enterprises of Georgia, he was an active and most efficient co-laborer with Mercer, Mallary, Stocks, Sherwood, Dawson, Thornton, Battle, Davis, Campbell, and Walker. Col. Janes had talents of a high order, with a strong, active, discriminating intellect. He possessed great quickness of perception, excellence of judgment, and energy of character. He was liberal, public-spirited, and philanthropic, claiming and receiving nothing for his services while treasurer of the Convention. In practical financial affairs his judgment was inferior to that of no one. For several years he represented Taliaferro County in the State senate, and in 1844 he ran against Hon. A. H. Stephens for Congress, and, though defeated, he received a larger vote than any candidate who ever opposed A. H. Stephens. Col. Janes was distinguished for unvarying courtesy and kindness in all the relations of life, and he is justly considered one of the chief builders of the Baptist denomination in Georgia.

Japan, Mission to.—At the annual meeting of the Missionary Union in 1872, it was resolved to accept Rev. N. Brown, D.D., and Rev. Mr. Goble as their missionaries to Japan, they having been in the employ of the American Baptist Free Mission Society. These brethren returned to the field of labor to which they had been designated, arriving at Yokohama in February, 1873, and immediately entered upon their work. Mr. Goble's connection with the Union continued only for a short time. Rev. J. H. Arthur and wife were appointed as missionaries to Japan in 1873, and in December of the same year Rev. J. T. Doyen, formerly connected with the Episcopal Church, and a resident of Yokohama, was also appointed as a missionary of the Union. Dr. Brown entered, very soon after reaching the field of his labors, upon the work of translating the Scriptures into Japanese, and in 1876 was able to report good progress in this direction. From January, 1875, to April, 1876, there had been published 614,600 pages of various translations, including the gospels of Matthew and Mark, the

Epistle of James, and several distinct portions of the New Testament, as the parables, the sermon on the mount, etc., and other religious reading. A new missionary station was commenced in Tokio (Yeddo) by Mr. and Mrs. Arthur in 1876. Rev. F. S. Dobbins and wife were sent out by the Union in October, 1876, to be connected with Dr. Brown. Mr. Dobbins was obliged to return to this country in a few months, on account of the sickness of his wife. Mr. Arthur, one of the most promising of all the missionaries that have been sent to the foreign field, also, was compelled to retire from his labors, and sailed for California, hoping that a short respite from his work would restore his health. He died at Oakland, Cal., Dec. 9, 1877. The church which was formed by him in Tokio had, on the 1st of January, 1878, 23 members. The outlook for the mission in Japan is favorable. Dr. Brown says in his report to the Executive Committee, " here are 33,000,000 of people, all speaking the same language, and using the same written characters." Having referred to the fact that previous translations of the Bible had been made by those who were not favorable to Baptist views, he says, " We marvel that Baptists should for a moment hesitate as to the duty of giving this people a faithful translation of the New Testament. We have printed, within the last three years, over 1,000,000 pages of Scripture, including the first three gospels, and portions of the Old Testament."

In Yokohama in 1880 there were 7 male and female missionaries, and one church with 39 members. In Tokio there were 5 missionaries, one man and four women, and one church with 37 members.

Jarman, Prof. G. W., A.M., was born May 14, 1826, in Lawrence Co., Ala. He joined the Baptist church in 1843 ; graduated at La Grange College, Ala., in 1847. Before graduating he had employed his vacation and leisure hours in studying medicine with a view of becoming a physician. November, 1847, he was elected tutor in Union University, Murfreesborough, Tenn., and commenced teaching January, 1848. In 1850 was elected Professor of Latin in Union University, and in 1855 the professorship of Greek was added to that of Latin. He succeeded Rev. Dr. Jos. H. Eaton as president of Union University in 1860; resigned his position in Union University in 1873, and in 1874 was elected principal of the Southwestern Baptist University, Jackson, Tenn. In 1875 was elected Professor of Latin and Greek in the same institution, and in 1876 was elected chairman of the faculty, which position he now holds. He has had students from every quarter of the globe, and those who have attended his instruction number many thousands. With slight intermissions, has been engaged in teaching for thirty-three

years. Prof. Jarman is still in his prime, and looks as though he might have another thirty years before him. Thorough in scholarship, skillful in discipline, dignified in bearing, he commands the respect and esteem of his students. He has left his impress upon great numbers who now occupy the higher walks of life as ministers, lawyers, physicians, teachers, and statesmen.

The Baptist churches of Tennessee and the Southwest are greatly indebted to this veteran teacher for his very efficient labors in their behalf. His name will be forever associated with the educational work of the denomination in Tennessee, and will grow brighter and brighter as his labors and sacrifices become better known in their far-reaching influence.

Jeffery, Rev. William, was born at Penhurst, England, about the year 1616. At Seven-Oaks he was one of the chief supporters, if he was not the founder, of the Baptist church. Of this church, then called Bradburn, he became the pastor, and under his zealous labors it enjoyed remarkable prosperity. Mr. Jeffery preached in various places in the county of Kent, and with some help from others was instrumental in founding more than twenty churches. He was the author of a valuable work called " The Whole Faith of Man," the second edition of which was issued in 1659. He was a gentle but steadfast Christian, and a very decided Baptist, never inviting controversy, and never permitting his heaven-born principles to lack a defender while he could wield a spiritual weapon to protect them.

Mr. Jeffery suffered much for his principles. On one occasion the magistrates of Seven-Oaks arrested all the men in his congregation while they were at worship, and kept them in prison an entire night. The next day the justices, after an examination, dismissed them. They returned to the church to thank God for their deliverance. To their astonishment, as they entered the house of God, they saw the women there, who, from the time of their arrest, had continued in fasting and prayer for their release until their supplications were visibly and joyfully answered. Mr. Jeffery was imprisoned after the restoration of Charles II., and subjected to many hardships.

After a life of great usefulness, of universal benevolence, and of abundant labors and sufferings, Mr. Jeffery rested from his toils in a good old age, and he was succeeded in his pastoral office by his son, the Rev. John Jeffery.

Jeffrey, Reuben, D.D., was born in Leicester. England, Feb. 15, 1827, and came to America when ten years of age with his parents, who settled in Geneva, N. Y. He was graduated from Madison University and the theological seminary connected with it. His first settlement was at Nantucket, where, in 1847, he was ordained and entered on a very successful ministry.

He has filled the pastoral office in the First church of Albany, N. Y.; the Fourth church in

REUBEN JEFFREY, D.D.

Philadelphia, Pa.; the North church in Chicago, Ill.; and the Ninth Street church, in Cincinnati, O. On the 14th of December, 1873, he accepted a call to the Marcy Avenue church, in Brooklyn, N. Y. It was a new and feeble organization, with about 40 members, meeting in a chapel. The house very soon became too small for his audiences. A new one was built, and that also in a few months was overflowing. It was enlarged, and more than a thousand people filled it at every service. The membership has increased to more than 600, the largest portion by baptism. Many of them are among the most substantial people in that section of the city. His friends regard this as the most successful work of his life.

Dr. Jeffrey's sermons are never sensational. He speaks without a manuscript or notes, yet his discourses are delivered with ease, force, and clearness. His rhetoric is good and his logic conclusive. He often thrills his hearers by impassioned bursts of eloquence, especially when presenting the great truths of the gospel.

Several of his sermons have been published. Recently he has removed to Denver, Col., where his new charge are building a spacious house of worship.

Jenckes, Gov. Joseph, was born in Pawtucket, R. I., in 1656. His grandfather, of the same name,

was, without doubt, in the company of emigrants who came from England in 1630, under the leadership of Gov. Winthrop. The father of Gov. Jenckes is supposed to have taken up his residence in Pawtucket about the year 1655. He was a blacksmith by trade, and the articles of his manufacture were in ready demand in the section of the country where he lived. He was honored and respected in the colony, and filled several important offices of civil trust. Like his father, the subject of this sketch also took a prominent part in civil affairs. As early as 1705 he was a commissioner to aid in the settlement of the perplexing questions which arose about the boundary-line between Rhode Island and Massachusetts. He was elected, in 1715, deputy governor of Rhode Island, and was in office until May, 1721. Before he had completed his term of service he was sent, in 1720, to England to bring the boundary disputes between Rhode Island as the one party, and Connecticut and Massachusetts as the other, to the direct notice of the king. He was again re-elected deputy governor in 1722, and continued in this office for five years, making eleven years in all that he occupied this honorable position. In 1727, upon the death of Gov. Cranston, who had been in office for the long period of twenty-nine years, Mr. Jenckes was chosen as his successor, and occupied this post of honor for five years. During a large part of this time Gov. Jenckes resided, by the special request of the General Assembly, in Newport. When Gov. Jenckes completed his term of gubernatorial service he was well advanced in years. He is said to have been the tallest man of his time in Rhode Island, standing seven feet and two inches. His death took place June 15, 1740. Gov. Jenckes was a decided Baptist. Among other things we read from the inscription that was placed on his tombstone, that "he was a bright example of virtue in every stage of life. He was a zealous Christian, a wise and prudent governor, grave, sober, beautiful in person, with a soul truly great, heroic, and sweetly tempered."

Jenkens, Rev. C. A., was born in Benton, Miss., Jan. 20, 1850; educated at the University of Virginia; taught school in Virginia. He was a layman and vestryman of the Episcopal Church in 1875, when he was baptized by Dr. C. Manly in Staunton, Va. He came immediately to North Carolina, and took charge of Warsaw High School, and began to preach. He was at one time pastor of Louisburg church, then of Franklinton, and now of Oxford. Mr. Jenkens edited "Baptist Doctrines," published in St. Louis in 1880, a large and valuable work, several thousand copies of which have already been sold.

Jenkins, Charles J., was a prominent layman, for many years, among the Baptists of Georgia.

He was the father of ex-Gov. Chas. J. Jenkins of that State, who is still living. He was born in 1780, but moved from Georgia to Beaufort District, S. C., in 1804, on his marriage to Miss Susan Emily Kenny of that State. He resided in Beaufort District until the spring of 1815. Mr. and Mrs. Jenkins became deeply interested in the subject of religion, and both united with the Baptist church at Beaufort.

During several years of his residence in South Carolina Mr. Jenkins was ordinary of Beaufort District, an office then in the gift of the State Legislature, and always most carefully bestowed because of its great importance.

About the beginning of 1816 Mr. Jenkins removed to Jefferson Co., Ga., and united with the Providence Baptist church, on Rocky Comfort Creek, twelve miles above Louisville. He afterwards resided a short time in Washington County, near Fenn's Bridge; but, about the beginning of 1819, he removed to Madison County, where he built a Baptist house of worship and organized a Baptist church near his residence. In October of the following year, during the annual meeting of the Sarepta Association, at Ruckersville, Elbert Co., he, as clerk, presented the following resolution, drawn up by Rev. Adiel Sherwood, D.D.:

"*Resolved*, That we suggest for our consideration, and that of sister Associations in this State, the propriety of organizing a general meeting of correspondence."

The resolution was adopted, and resulted in the formation of the General Association on the 27th of June, 1822, at Powelton, which name was changed to the Baptist Convention of the State of Georgia in 1828.

In 1822, Mr. Jenkins was appointed surveyor and collector of the port of Apalachicola, in West Florida, where he remained three years, resigning and returning to Georgia on account of his deprivation of church privileges in Apalachicola. He settled in Jefferson County, where he had formerly resided, on his return to his native State, and there he died, in July, 1828, in his forty-ninth year. Mr. Jenkins was a quiet, unassuming man, very useful, kind and benevolent in disposition, and of the strictest integrity. He was exceedingly energetic and liberal, but seldom let his right hand know what his left was doing. He was a man of culture and refinement. He never sought office; and it was only because he positively declined that he was not elected State senator for both Jefferson and Madison Counties. His heart was in his religious denomination, and, outside of his domestic circle and private business affairs, all his efforts and energies were devoted to extending its borders, and widening its influence and power. In every community in which he dwelt he was a leading and an influential man, and enjoyed the respect and confidence of all who knew him. For years he was clerk of the Sarepta Association, and took hold of religious and educational measures with a strong hand, and he was able to accomplish much that was useful.

Jenkins, Rev. Nathaniel, was born in Wales in 1678; was converted, and began to preach in his native country. He settled at Cape May, N. J., in 1712, and became the founder and first pastor of the church at Cape May Court-House. He continued to preside over this church until 1730, when he took charge of Cohansey, where he died in 1754. His talents shone both in the church and state. He exemplified his belief in liberty of conscience on an important occasion. When he was a member of the Colonial Legislature of New Jersey, in 1721, a bill was introduced to punish all who denied the doctrine of the Trinity, Christ's divinity, and the inspiration of the Scriptures. He could not be persuaded to vote for it, but, rising in his place, said, among other things, with Welsh warmth and eloquence, "I believe the doctrines in question as firmly as the promoters of that ill-designed bill; but will never consent to oppose the opposers with law, or any other weapon save that of argument." The bill was defeated.

Jenkins, Samuel, was born in Wales, Feb. 12, 1789. At the age of six he was able to read in Welsh, and he loved to read the Bible. In 1801 his parents came to Philadelphia, and in 1804 he joined the Welsh Calvinistical church in that city, of which his father was pastor. Having settled in the Great Valley, Chester County, he was baptized, and united with the church in that place in 1816, and from that time to the day of his death he was a thorough Baptist.

Mr. Jenkins possessed a wonderful memory, and his knowledge of Welsh history was remarkable. He wrote much for the press. In 1852 he published a work entitled "Letters on Welsh History," which exhibited a thorough acquaintance with the records of that ancient people. He died Sept. 12, 1871.

Mr. Jenkins was a good man, a sincere Christian, and a friend to every worthy cause.

Jenkins, Rev. S. G., a native of Georgia, was ordained in that State by Elders Sanders, Lumpkin, Thornton, and Hillyer. In 1832 he removed to Mississippi, where he successfully served churches for some years. In 1840 he came to Alabama and settled on the picturesque spot where he now resides, in Talladega County. Soon he planted a number of churches. Has been pastor of Antioch and Cold Water churches, respectively, thirty-nine years, and has baptized 1006 members at these two churches, many of them from other denominations. He has been abundant in labors and success. He has baptized 13 households and 22 men who entered the ministry. He has always been a farmer, and before the late war was in good worldly circumstances. Has constantly been a fearless gospel preacher. Has reared an interesting family; is about seventy years old, and now often rides forty miles in a day, and preaches three sermons.

Jenks, Prof. John W. P., was born in West Boylston, Mass., May 1, 1819. He graduated at Brown University in the class of 1838. On leaving college he went to Georgia, where he taught four years, for a part of the time acting as colleague of Rev. Jesse Mercer, D.D., in the last year of his life in Washington, Wilkes Co., Ga. In 1842 he became the principal of the Peirce Academy, in Middleborough, and continued in that relation twenty-nine years. During his administration the academy rose to a high rank among the best institutions of its kind in New England. In 1872 he was elected Professor of Agricultural Zoology and curator of the Museum of Natural History in Brown University, which position he now holds. By his untiring efforts Prof. Jenks has brought his special department into a condition far in advance of what it was when he entered upon the duties of his professorship. Brown University has a museum of natural history of which it may justly be proud.

Jennings, Rev. John, was born in Danbury, Conn., Dec. 8, 1809; was hopefully converted at the age of fourteen, and baptized into the fellowship of the church in the place where he had passed his youthful days. He was licensed to preach when he was but seventeen years of age, June 17, 1826. He entered upon a course of preparatory study, and without going through college, he graduated at the Newton Theological Institution in the class of 1834. He was ordained pastor of the church in Beverly, Mass., Sept. 15, 1834, remaining here for two years, and then settling at Grafton, where he continued for six years, at the end of which period he was called to the pastorate of the newly organized Second Baptist church in Worcester, Mass. He commenced his labors here in March, 1842, and continued in this pastorate for eight years. For some time he was in the service of the American Tract Society. In 1852 he became the pastor of the Baptist church in Fitchburg, Mass., where he remained until 1859, when he was invited to Woonsocket, R. I., and labored there three and a half years. His last settlement was in Westfield, Mass., where he continued seven and a half years, when his failing health obliged him to resign, and he moved to Auburndale, Mass., where he died, June 26, 1871. An appreciative notice of this worthy minister of Christ, written by his friend, Rev. W. C. Richards, says of him, "Few men have lived more respected and beloved as a Christian man and a Christian minister by all who knew his vir-

tues and piety. He leaves a clean record; his life was a success.''

Jerome, Rev. Edward Miles, son of Chauncey and Salome (Smith) Jerome, was born in Bristol, Conn., June 15, 1826; removed to New Haven in 1843; graduated from Yale College in 1850; converted when a Sophomore, and united with Third Congregational church in New Haven; studied in Yale Law-School and in Baltimore, Md.; received LL.B. in 1852, and was admitted to the bar; manager of his father's business in New York; became a Baptist; baptized by Rev. R. Turnbull, D.D., and united with First Baptist church in Hartford, Conn., in 1856; licensed by that church and studied theology; ordained, in 1859, as an evangelist in Holyoke, Mass.; supplied First Baptist church in New Haven, Conn.; in 1861 settled as pastor in Northampton, Mass.; in 1862 settled with church in West Meriden, Conn., and remained four years, till disabled by throat affection; preached in New Haven occasionally; in 1869 settled in Westfield, Mass., but health again failed; in 1871 established the *Naugatuck Valley Sentinel* in Ansonia, Conn.; aided in gathering there a Baptist church, of which he became pastor; served as Sunday-school missionary of the Baptist State Convention; in 1879 returned as associate editor of the *Sentinel* in Ansonia; in April of present year (1880) became proprietor and editor of *The Shore Line Times*, in New Haven; good preacher and ready writer.

Jesse, Rev. John Samuel, one of the most influential young pastors in the Sacramento River Association, is located at Biggs Station, Cal. He was born in Missouri, Nov. 4, 1852. His father, W. M. Jesse, of Virginia, and five relatives were ministers. He was immersed in 1870; received a good education at Mount Pleasant College and the schools in Missouri; entered the ministry by license in 1873; was ordained in October, 1874. His preaching for three years in Missouri was greatly blessed. In 1877 he went to California, preached for a time for the Sutter and Calaveras churches, and in 1878 became pastor at Biggs Station, and he is also giving pastoral aid to the Virginia and Wheatland churches. He is a fine writer and liberal contributor to the religious press.

Jessey, Rev. Henry, A.M., was born at West Routon, Yorkshire, England, Sept. 3, 1601. When he was seventeen years of age he entered St. John's College, Cambridge, in which he continued six years. In his twenty-first year, while still at the University of Cambridge, the Spirit of God gave him a new heart, and a blessed hope through the Saviour's blood.

After leaving Cambridge he became a chaplain in the family of Mr. Brampton Gordon, of Assington, Suffolk, for nine years, during which he advanced rapidly in such knowledge as would qualify him for his holy calling. In 1627 he received episcopal ordination, and in 1633 he was appointed rector of Aughton, Yorkshire. In 1637 he became pastor of a Congregational church in London, in

REV. HENRY JESSEY, A.M.

which his labors were greatly blessed. But his church was repeatedly invaded and robbed by Baptist principles. In 1638 "six persons of note" were carried off; in 1641 a greater number still; and in 1643 the departing members were more numerous than ever. Many of those who joined the Baptists were persons of superior intelligence and piety. Mr. Jessey was forced to examine the Scriptures about the mode of baptism, and the result of his investigations was that immersion was the inspired mode of baptism, and that sprinkling was a modern innovation. From that time forward for two or three years he always dipped children when he administered baptism. In 1645, after an anxious examination of the subjects of baptism, and after earnest appeals to heaven for divine light, he became decided in the conviction that only believers should be baptized, and in the June of that year he was immersed by Hanserd Knollys. He was pastor for many years of the church meeting in Swan Alley, Coleman Street, London. He was one of the Triers appointed by Cromwell to examine candidates for the ministry in the national church, and to investigate the character and claims of "ignorant and scandalous ministers" with a view to their expulsion from the pulpits of the state church. He was rector of St. George's church, Southwark, London, and pastor of a Baptist church

in the same city. In the morning of the Lord's day he preached at St. George's church, and in the afternoon he was among his own people. He was a man of great learning; he had an extensive knowledge of Greek, Hebrew, Syriac, and Chaldee. It was the ambition and labor of his life to produce a new translation of the Scriptures, which was about completed when the restoration of Charles II. poured a deluge of evils over the Non-Conformists of that country, and made worthless the labors of Mr. Jessey in revising the Scriptures. He was a man of boundless charity; he even employed efforts to send money to the poor Jews of Jerusalem to preserve them from threatened slavery.

His labors were unremitting, and they were attended with great success. He was the author of eight published works, and with some help from Mr. Row, Professor of Hebrew in Aberdeen, he was the author of a revised and unpublished version of the Scriptures. His literary labors were highly appreciated and widely known. His character was marked by unselfishness and an intense love for the truth and its Divine Author.

By the cruel Act of Uniformity he was ejected from St. George's church, Southwark, and soon after, through his zeal for the Saviour, he was cast into prison, where he died Sept. 4, 1663, full of peace, humility, and hope.

At his funeral, three days after his death, several thousand pious persons of various denominations attended, whose manifest grief showed the great esteem in which Mr. Jessey was held.

Jeter, Jeremiah Bell, D.D., was born in Bedford Co., Va., July 18, 1802. He was baptized on the first Sunday in December, 1821, by the Rev. Wm. Harris, in the North Fork of the Otter River. His first public address was made on the banks of this stream, in coming out of it, on the occasion of his baptism. On the evening of the 15th of January of the same year he preached his first sermon to a small congregation of mountaineers in the gorge between the Flat Top and Luck Mountains, in Bedford County. He was present at the organization of the Baptist General Association of Virginia in 1823, was the first missionary appointed by that body, and the last survivor of the men who formed it. On the 4th of May, 1824, he was ordained to the work of the ministry at High Hills church, Sussex Co., by the Revs. N. Chambliss and J. D. Williams, for the former of whom he acted as assistant. Leaving Sussex in the spring of 1826, his first pastorate was with Hills Creek and Union Hill churches, Campbell Co. In the autumn of 1827 he removed to the Northern Neck of Virginia, where he was installed pastor of Moratico church in Lancaster Co., and subsequently of Wicomico church in Northumberland Co. His ministry was eminently successful in this field of labor, he having baptized over one thousand persons in about nine years.

In the latter part of 1835 he became pastor of the First Baptist church, Richmond, Va., and was

JEREMIAH BELL JETER, D.D.

for nearly fourteen years its faithful and successful leader, baptizing into its fellowship nearly 1000 converts, among whom were the Rev. Dr. Garlick, of Richmond, and the Rev. Dr. Henson, of Philadelphia. During his pastorate the First church built the house of worship which it now occupies, and organized its colored membership of 2000 into the First African church of Richmond, since so well known for its large congregations, its efficient church regulations, and its excellent singing. The latter church was put into possession of the old house of worship at the corner of Broad and College streets.

In October of 1849, Dr. Jeter was invited to the pastorate of the Second Baptist church, St. Louis. He remained here three years, baptized 150 persons, and was instrumental in organizing two other churches in that city. In September of 1852 he returned to Richmond, and became pastor of the Grace Street Baptist church, whose membership was nearly doubled during his ministry, having increased from 322 to 600. About the close of the war he became the senior editor of the *Religious Herald*, and continued until his death, Feb. 18, 1880, to furnish for its columns the mature gleanings of his long, rich, and varied experience.

As preacher and pastor, Dr. Jeter was remarkably successful. His form was commanding, his
39

face intellectual, and his eye expressive, all which secured for him marked advantages as a speaker. The interest of his preaching consisted in the earnest simplicity with which he presented and enforced the great truths of the gospel. He constantly aimed to establish from the Word of God some great doctrine, or to enforce some practical duty in gospel ethics. As a pastor, he was kind, genial, and gentle, welcomed alike by old and young, rich and poor, learned and ignorant. In the large deliberative assemblies of the denomination, Dr. Jeter always occupied a prominent place. As a debater, he was ready, self-possessed, courteous, wisely conservative, added to which qualities were a force and ability that won universal attention.

Dr. Jeter was quite successful as an author. In 1837 he published the "Life of the Rev. A. W. Clopton"; in 1845, "A Memoir of Mrs. Schuck, Missionary to China"; in 1850, the "Life of the Rev. Andrew Broaddus"; in 1854, "Campbellism Examined," which work won for him a wide reputation as a skillful polemic, and subsequently "Campbellism Re-examined"; in 1858, "The Christian Mirror"; in 1871, "The Seal of Heaven" and "The Life of the Rev. Daniel Witt," besides numerous tracts, sermons, addresses, and other works of minor importance. His writings were all characterized by that clearness and vigor, as well as that chivalrous courtesy, which won the regard of the most persistent opponents, and gained for him as a writer so wide a reputation.

Dr. Jeter was equally successful as an editor. For fourteen years the *Religious Herald* has been the medium of conveying his sage counsels, evangelical opinions, and earnest Christian appeals in behalf of everything noble, just, and good into thousands of Christian families. He displayed an excellent judgment and discrimination in selecting topics at once of genuine importance and yet of general interest.

Dr. Jeter also preserved an abiding and growing interest in all the great denominational movements of the day. Missions, education, a more thoroughly equipped ministry, higher schools for young women, reformatory movements, with kindred plans for the well-being of men and women, and the conversion of the world, always received his most cordial support. A long life was devoted to the cause of Christ and the good of the world, and it was as spotless to its protracted close as the perfect azure of a sunset flecked by no single cloud. "No one who knew Dr. Jeter would hesitate to put him among the aristocracy of the world. As a preacher, a pastor, an editor, a citizen, a Christian, he lived up to the measure of developed faculties, and was an Israelite in whom there was no guile."

Jewell, William, M.D., was born near Alexandria, Va., Jan. 1, 1779; removed with his father to Kentucky in 1800; graduated from Transylvania University with the degree of M.D. In 1820 he came to Missouri, and settled permanently in Columbia. He united with the Bonne Femme Baptist church. He had a capacious and acquisitive mind, and a fixed purpose to excel in his profession. His library was large and choice, and his practice was extensive. He was familiar with learned medical authors of all lands. He took a deep interest in his patients, and when his medical skill failed, he pointed them to the heavenly physician. He attained great eminence as a medical practitioner, citizen, and Christian. His gifts of more than $17,000 to the Baptist college at Liberty gave it the name of William Jewell. He superintended the erection of the college buildings, and at his death bequeathed his library and $3000 to the institution. He gave nearly half his property to benevolent objects. He died in Liberty, Clay Co., Aug. 7, 1852. He gave $1800 to the State University, at Columbia. He often represented Boone County in the State Legislature. He was a zealous student of the Bible. His religion was manifest at home, and in his professional experience, as well as in public worship. His death was deeply mourned, and deserved eulogies were pronounced over his Christian life.

Jewett, Lyman, D.D., was born in Waterford, Me., March 9, 1813. He was a graduate of Brown University and of the Newton Theological Institution. He served for some time as a supply of the Baptist church in Webster, Mass. His appointment as a missionary to the foreign field was made in 1847, and he was ordained to the work of the ministry in Boston, Oct. 6, 1848. Sailing a few days after for the East, he reached Nellore, April 16, 1849. For somewhat more than three years the mission had been without American helpers. Mr. Jewett found, at first, many things that were discouraging, but he addressed himself to his work with zeal, preaching his first regular Teloogoo sermon in the chapel Dec. 3, 1849. As he became more familiar with the language his ability to be useful increased, and his contact with the heathen was closer. Weeks and months passed in the usual routine of missionary labor. We learn from the report of 1852 that there was preaching in the chapel twice every Sabbath, the attendance varying from 40 to 150 persons. Considerable audiences were collected to listen to street preaching. Visitors calling at the mission house for instruction often received spiritual benefit. Excursions were made by Mr. Jewett to the neighboring villages and hamlets, and sometimes great crowds thronged to hear the Word, and receive Bibles and religious tracts. But while Mr. Jewett and his co-laborers were encouraged by these signs of outward success, and felt that could the mission be well reinforced and evangelical agencies plied with zeal, the best results would be secured, it was evident that many of the friends of missions at home were beginning to think that the Teloogoo Mission was not a successful one. The whole matter was submitted to the Missionary Union in 1853, and it was decided to continue to carry on the mission. The departure of Mr. Day from Nellore early in 1853 left Mr. Jewett the only American male missionary on the field. With what courage and hope he prosecuted his work appears from his own words, written Nov. 5, 1854: "The last month has been one of constant labor in preaching the gospel. I am earnestly looking for fruit. I feel in my soul that our labors will not be in vain." Again he writes with almost prophetic vision of the glorious ingathering of the harvests of souls which has been lately witnessed: "For the last few months I have felt more than ever not only the importance of the mission, but the certainty of accomplishing, in the Lord's good time, a great and glorious work for this people." Before this vision became a reality the faith of Mr. Jewett was often and most severely tried. Rev. F. A. Douglass joined Mr. Jewett, April 14, 1855, and the mission, thus reinforced, continued to enjoy a good degree of prosperity. In 1859 an increased interest in religion was reported. Mr. Jewett visited Ongole to see for himself what prospect of success there was in that place. In March, 1861, such was the state of his health that it was thought best that he should return to the United States and obtain needed rest and recuperation. He remained here until November, 1864, when he sailed the second time, and arrived at Nellore, April 22, 1865. He at once resumed his labors. Mr. Timpany became associated with him in missionary work in April, 1868. A part of the time of Dr. Jewett was occupied in the work of translating the Bible into the Teloogoo language. In 1875 he was again in his native country for the restoration of his wasted strength. He has returned to the scene of his labors, where he is now actively engaged in the service of him whose cause lies so near his heart.

Jewett, Prof. Milo P., LL.D., was born in Johnsbury, Vt., April 27, 1808. His father, Calvin Jewett, was an eminent physician of Johnsbury, and his mother was a highly cultivated lady. Milo was prepared for college at the Bradford Academy, Vt., and graduated from Dartmouth College in the class of 1828. Upon his graduation he became principal of Holmes Academy at Plymouth, N. H. Having the law in view as a profession, he spent a part of that year and of the following year in the office of Hon. Josiah Quincy, of Rumney, N. H. Abandoning the law in 1830, he entered the theological seminary at Andover, completing the course of study. Mr. Jewett, upon the invitation of Josiah Holbrook, of Boston, founder of the American lyceum system, spent his vacations during his theological course in lecturing in New Hampshire, Massachusetts, and Connecticut on "Common Schools." He had had much success in teaching, and his soul was full of his subject,—a higher grade of common-school education for the masses. His addresses on this subject are believed to have been the first of a popular character delivered in the country. They created extensive interest in the subject among our best educators. Through J. Orville Taylor, a fellow-student of Mr. Jewett, who became interested in the matter, a movement was started in New York City, which resulted in the establishment of the present common-school system of the Empire State.

Having decided that teaching and not preaching was the work for which God had fitted him, and in which he had already given him marked success, Mr. Jewett devoted himself to that profession, and in 1834 accepted a professorship in Marietta College, Marietta, O., just then founded. Before entering upon the active duties of his chair he spent some time among the Congregational churches of New England in soliciting funds for the college. He based his plea on "the perils which threaten our civil and religious liberties from the progress of Roman Catholicism in the Mississippi Valley." His addresses awakened a deep interest, and made the raising of funds an easy task. In 1836, Mr. Jewett was associated with Prof. Calvin E. Stowe and William E. Lewis by the State Educational Convention of Ohio to urge upon the Legislature the establishment of a new common-school system. He not only accomplished his object, but much more. Prof. Calvin Stowe went to Europe, under the direction of the State, to investigate the best school systems there, and Wm. E. Lewis became the first State superintendent of public schools in Ohio. But this was not all. His report on the subject created the deepest interest over the country, and resulted in the special educational mission and work of Horace Mann in New England.

In January, 1839, having changed his views on baptism, and united with the Baptist Church, Prof. Jewett resigned his professorship in Marietta College, and, going South, he established the Judson Female Institute in Marion, Ala. It soon became the most flourishing educational institution for ladies in the South. In connection with this school he established the *Alabama Baptist*, which became the Baptist organ of the State. In the autumn of 1855 he returned North, and purchased the Cottage Hill Seminary at Poughkeepsie, N. Y. Here he first met with Mr. Matthew Vassar. Their acquaintance ripened into friendship. Prof. Jewett found that Mr. Vassar proposed to leave his large fortune for benevolent purposes. He suggested to him the founding of a thoroughly furnished and endowed college for young women during his own life. It met with Mr. Vassar's approval. He changed his will, in which he had left his property for another object, and turned his attention to this new purpose. Thus originated Vassar College. It was incorporated in 1861. Prof. Jewett was the adviser of Mr. Vassar in everything relating to the establishment of the college, and was its first president. In 1862, at the request of the trustees, he visited Europe to inspect the universities, libraries, art-galleries, etc., in Great Britain and on the Continent to obtain information about the best educational systems in the old world, that Vassar might have the benefit of his observations and experience.

In 1864, having almost entirely lost the sight of his eyes, he resigned the presidency of the college, to the great regret of Mr. Vassar and the board, and in 1867 he removed to his present home in Milwaukee. Prof. Jewett devotes himself to the interests of education, philanthropy, and religion. He is held in high esteem in the First Baptist church, of which he is a member. He is the president of Milwaukee Female College, though not required to teach, chairman of the board of visitors of the University of Wisconsin, president of Milwaukee board of health, president of the Wisconsin State Temperance Society, president of the Milwaukee County Bible Society, and chairman of the State Baptist Educational Commission.

Prof. Jewett is a man of extensive literary attainments, and in addition to occasional articles in newspapers and magazines, has written several publications of marked character. In 1840 he published "Jewett on Baptism"; in 1863, "Report of the President's Visit to Europe" and "Report on the Organization of Vassar College"; in 1874, "Relation of Boards of Health to Intemperance"; in 1875, "A Plea for Academies"; and the same year, "The Model Academy."

Prof. Jewett, although never engaged in the active work of the ministry, received ordination at the hands of a council called by the Siloam Baptist church of Marion, Ala., in 1839. He received the degree of LL.D. from Rochester University in 1861.

He takes a very deep interest in everything pertaining to the growth of the Baptist denomination, especially in the State of Wisconsin. His efforts for the more thorough establishment of Wayland Academy have been of the highest value. He is an active member of its board, and contributes most generously both time and means to its increased usefulness.

Johnson, Rev. Cæsar.—A useful man among the colored Baptists of North Carolina is Cæsar Johnson, who was born in Warren Co., N. C., in 1833, and until the war was a slave of Mr. John

V. Canthorn. He was baptized by Rev. N. A. Purefoy in 1862; attended Shaw University in Raleigh for nine years; served as missionary of the Home Mission Board, New York, for eight years, and is now employed as colporteur by the American and Foreign Bible Society. Mr. Johnson has been moderator of the Convention of colored Baptists for four years, and is much interested in collecting historical and statistical data concerning his people.

Johnson, Col. Daniel D., a younger brother of Okey, was born in Tyler Co., Va., April 28, 1836. He was partly educated at Marietta College, and graduated a Bachelor of Philosophy from Columbian College, Washington, D. C., in 1860. He enjoyed the warm friendship, which yet continues, of Dr. Samson, then president of the college. In 1861, when the civil war broke out, as a firm friend of the Union he helped to raise the 14th Va. Regiment, of which he was elected major. He was soon promoted to the colonelcy, which post he filled until the close of the war. He participated in a number of hard-fought battles, among them Cloyd Mountain, Carter's Farm, Opequan, and Winchester. At the battle of Opequan he was severely wounded, and was granted leave of absence. At the battle of Winchester, on the 24th July, 1864, he commanded a brigade. When the Union forces were defeated and compelled to fall back, he covered the retreat in a masterly manner, for which the credit was unjustly given to another. Although a colonel, he commanded a brigade frequently. In 1865, after the close of the war, he received an honorable discharge, and at once set about the work of reconciliation with those against whom he had fought. He was an enemy in war, but in peace a friend. He received them cordially when they returned, and treated them as his equals in the government, being actuated by the same Christian spirit which had ruled his boyhood and manhood. He went to the Legislature in 1865, and served for several terms in the lower house. He was elected a member of the constitutional convention of 1872, where he distinguished himself as much perhaps as any member of that body, being an earnest, eloquent, and lucid speaker, and being by far the best parliamentarian in the State. In 1872 he was elected a member of the State senate, which position he yet holds, and for the whole time, except for two years, he has been president of the senate. He is one of the most active men in the State in the cause of education, and is now president of the board of regents of the West Virginia University. He is a thorough Baptist, and has been one for over twenty years. He has a number of times been moderator of his Association, and also president of the West Virginia Baptist Convention, and he is superintendent now of a Sabbath-school. In all these various relations he has shown himself a Christian gentleman.

Johnson, George J., D.D., was born in Vernon, N. Y., Oct. 9, 1824; was baptized before he was fifteen; studied at Madison University and Hamilton Theological Seminary, graduating from the latter institution in 1848; was soon after ordained at Trenton Falls, N. Y., and settled as missionary pastor in Burlington, Iowa. Here he organized a church of 12 members, which numbered 318 at the close of his pastorate in 1858. Among the converts was Rev. John E. Clough, present missionary to the Teloogoos at Ongole, Burmah. He also performed arduous and efficient labors in connection with the Burlington Collegiate Institute. He subsequently organized a church at Fort Madison, Iowa, and remained pastor five years. Returned to Burlington as district secretary of the American Baptist Publication Society for the Northwest, and afterwards became district secretary for the Southwest, with headquarters at St. Louis, Mo. In 1876–77 he engaged in celebrating the semicentennial of Shurtleff College at Upper Alton, Ill., by raising an additional endowment fund of $100,000. In this enterprise his incessant and self-sacrificing labors were crowned with magnificent success. In 1878 he was appointed missionary secretary of the American Baptist Publication Society, with headquarters at Philadelphia. This position he still holds, and the society is prospered by the large results of his faithful and unceasing toil. He received the degree of D.D. from Madison University in 1871.

Dr. Johnson has given the best years of his life to pioneer missionary work, and few men have accomplished such wide-reaching and abiding results. With varied and consecrated talents, and robust physical powers, and with an energy born of intense love for the truth, and an invincible determination to succeed, he has broken the soil and planted the seeds of the kingdom far and wide. The blessed and increasing fruitage of his past toil is a perpetual inspiration to his present unwearied and useful endeavors.

Johnson, Rev. Hezekiah, son of Rev. Eleazar Johnson and Martha Rounds, was born March 6, 1799, in Maryland; converted and ordained in Highland Co., O., in 1824. He was pastor at Frankfort and Greenfield, O., and labored in Iowa under the Baptist Home Mission Society from 1839 to 1844, and organized some of the first churches and Associations in that State. In 1845 he went, with Rev. E. Fisher, as missionary of the Home Mission Society, to Oregon, and settled at Oregon City, where he formed a church. This was his home until his death, in August, 1866. He traveled, preached, helped to organize churches and Associations, and lay the foundations of religious and educational institutions in the new State. He wrote and published many sermons and pamphlets, in furtherance of the cause of religion and reform, completing the last on his death-bed. He was one of the strong Baptist leaders in the early days of Oregon. His faithful wife accompanied and upheld him in all his labors. They are buried near Oregon City. Over their graves a memorial stone bears this inscription,—" Pioneer Baptist Missionaries."

Johnson, Hon. James, a son of Col. Robert Johnson, and a brother of Col. R. M. Johnson, was born in Orange Co., Va., from which he removed with his parents to Kentucky. He united with Great Crossing Baptist church about 1801, of which he remained a faithful member until his death. He was a lieutenant-colonel in the war of 1812–15, and distinguished himself in the battle of the Thames. In 1808 he was elected to the State senate from Scott County. He was Presidential elector in 1821, and was elected to a seat in the U. S. Congress in 1825. He died at Washington while a member of Congress, in December, 1826.

Johnson, John L., LL.D., Professor of English Literature in the University of Mississippi, was born in Virginia in 1835. After receiving a liberal education at the University of Virginia, he was ordained in 1860. During the war he served as chaplain of the 17th Va. Infantry, and subsequently as pastor of the colored Baptist church at Lynchburg. After the war he was two years pastor at Portsmouth, Va., and about as long at Free Mason Street, Norfolk. He then retired to the country, engaging in literary pursuits, supplying some churches, and teaching in the Albemarle Female Institute. For some months he supplied Dr. Fuller's church in Baltimore. He also taught for a time in Roanoke Female College. He accepted his present position in 1873. While discharging the duties of his professorship he has also engaged in preaching at Oxford, Miss., and in the surrounding country. Dr. Johnson is the author of " The University Memorial" and a number of published sermons.

Johnson, Gov. Joseph, was born Dec. 19, 1785, in Orange Co., N. Y. His father having died when he was but five years old, his widowed mother soon after removed to Sussex Co., N. J., and from it, in 1801, to Harrison Co., Va. Here, at the age of fifteen, he was employed on the large farm of a Mr. Smith, whose chief manager he soon became, and at the age of twenty-one he married one of that gentleman's daughters. Four years after his marriage he purchased the estate on which he had been living, and continued to occupy the same until his death, a period of more than seventy years. Early in life Mr. Johnson became one of the most popular and influential men in the county. During

the war of 1812 with Great Britain he organized a rifle company, was made its captain, marched to Norfolk, and continued in service until peace was secured, in 1815. His talents, decision of character,

GOV. JOSEPH JOHNSON.

and strict integrity forced him at this time into political life, and on his return from military service he was elected a member of the State Legislature, defeating his opponent, the distinguished Mr. Prunty, who had been in the Legislature during twenty-five consecutive years. Having served for four years in this body with great usefulness, he declined a re-election, and returned to the farm-life which he loved so well. In 1823 he was elected to Congress after one of the most exciting and thoroughly contested canvassings that Harrison County had ever witnessed, defeating his able and distinguished opponent, Mr. P. Doddridge. He was re-elected to Congress in 1825, returned to his home in 1827, and in 1832 was elected to fill the vacancy caused by the death of Mr. Doddridge. He was also elected to Congress in 1835, serving six years, and in 1845, serving two years. He had thus been elected to Congress seven times, and during his whole career in that body maintained the reputation of being one of the most punctual and laborious members of the body. In consequence of the urgent solicitations of his friends he served in the State Legislature during the session of 1847; was a member, in 1850, of the State convention which remodeled the constitution, and while a member of that body was elected governor of the State under the conditions of the old constitution, entering on his official duties in December, 1851. In the fall of 1851 he was elected governor by the popular vote for the term of four years. He was the first and only man ever elected governor of Virginia from that part of the State now comprised in West Virginia. As governor he took an active part in originating or carrying out greatly needed internal improvements, which, unfortunately, were sadly retarded by the breaking out of the war. At the close of 1855 he retired to his country home, having served his generation most faithfully in the State and national halls for more than forty years. Gov. Johnson followed Virginia during her terrible war experiences, and threw all the weight of his great influence and experience into the cause of the Confederacy. At the termination of that fearful contest, with the burdens of eighty years upon him, he withdrew, as much as such a man could, from public life. For more than ten years he enjoyed the coveted quiet of a lovely home, the attentions of kindred and loved ones, and the warm regards of troops of friends. He died Feb. 27, 1877, in the ninety-second year of his age, in the home which he had entered more than seventy years before, in the assured hope of a blissful immortality.

In private life, Gov. Johnson was modest, affable, genial, and kindly considerate of the interests of all. In appearance he was below the medium height, of a dark complexion, with a bright black eye that flashed as if on fire when in debate. During the last few years of his life his thoughts were almost constantly occupied with Biblical themes. He was punctual in the performance of religious duties, and would let nothing interfere with them. The last two years of his life were spent in superintending and liberally contributing to the rebuilding and furnishing of the Baptist meeting-house near his residence, where he was a member, and where his mother and wife had worshiped, frequently testifying himself in the meetings to the comfort, truth, and power of the gospel of Christ. As a man, he was beyond reproach, as a statesman, he was one of the strictest of the "Jacksonian" school, and as a follower of Christ, he adorned the doctrine of the Saviour by a "well-ordered life."

Johnson, Rev. J. E., was a native of Tolland, Conn., where he was born, Oct. 27, 1827. His early youth was spent in Willington, Conn., to which place his parents removed soon after his birth. He was baptized and united with the Baptist church in that place when but a mere lad. He was educated at Suffield Institute, Conn., and at Brown University, R. I., from which he graduated with honor in the class of 1853. He spent one year at Newton Theological Seminary. He was ordained by the Baptist church in Jackson, Mich., in 1855, and remained its pastor seven years. He was subsequently pastor of the Baptist church in

Madison, Wis., four years, of the Baptist church in Delavan two and a half years, of the Grand Avenue Baptist church, Milwaukee, one year, and of the Baptist church at Beaver Dam three years, where he died Oct. 20, 1872. His ministry of seventeen years was highly successful. He was an excellent preacher, of clear, analytical mind, and of most earnest spirit. But he was pre-eminent in his simple, unostentatious piety, and devotion to the work of the ministry, to which he had consecrated his life.

Johnson, Rev. N. B., a distinguished missionary in the mountains of Kentucky, was born in Fayette County of that State, March 28, 1820. In early life he joined the Campbellites, but in 1842 he experienced a change of heart, was baptized, and united with the Baptist church at Georgetown. He was ordained to the ministry in 1862, and was pastor of several country churches along the border of the mountains. In 1866 he entered the mountain field as a missionary. During the thirteen years that followed he traveled, on horseback and on foot, 13,000 miles, preached 2800 times, besides delivering numerous addresses, visited a large number of families, organized 60 Sabbath-schools, baptized 1200 persons, and, with the assistance of proper helps, constituted 24 churches. He is, in 1880, pastor of four churches.

Johnson, Judge Okey, was born in Tyler Co., Va., March 24, 1834. His parents were both immersed into the fellowship of the Baptist Church over fifty years ago, by Rev. Jeremiah Dale, whose biography appears in "The Lives of the Virginia Baptist Ministers." Okey united with the Long Reach Baptist church on the 7th of July, 1849. He graduated at the Marietta High School in 1856. The same year he entered the law-school of Harvard University, where for two years he had the benefit of the lectures of those distinguished men Profs. Parsons, Washburne, and Parker, and graduated with the degree of LL.B. in July, 1858. He engaged in agriculture for nearly two years, and made two successful trading expeditions to Memphis and New Orleans, on flat-boats, in the fall and winter of 1859 and 1860, and left New Orleans on the 21st day of March, 1861. In May, 1862, he located in Parkersburg, Va., and commenced the practice of law in good earnest. On the 4th of July, 1862, at Parkersburg, while the United States troops were thundering at the gates of Richmond, he made an oration in favor of his candidate for the Presidency to a great multitude; and his effort was so full of lofty patriotism that it called forth the loudest plaudits, and on request of the vast throng it was published. Although a Union man, he was a decided Democrat, and very conservative on all questions involving the conduct of the war, and when that unhappy strife ended he was for general amnesty and peace, and did much in the State of West Virginia, which was the " Child of the storm," to arrest and repeal the legislation against the returned Confederate soldiers. In 1870 he was

JUDGE OKEY JOHNSON.

elected a member of the West Virginia senate. He was elected to the constitutional convention called by the Legislature of 1870, largely through his influence, by a triumphant majority. He was a very active and distinguished member of this convention, and when the new constitution was submitted to the people he was an eloquent advocate for its ratification, and it was adopted by a handsome majority.

In 1874 Marietta College conferred upon him the honorary degree of Master of Arts. From 1860 to 1870 he was annually elected moderator of the Parkersburg Association. And he was repeatedly elected president of the West Virginia Baptist Convention. Notwithstanding his political relations, he uniformly enjoyed the highest esteem of his brethren. His law practice was large and successful, rarely ever losing a case in the Supreme Court of Appeals. In 1876 he was nominated for the office of judge of the Supreme Court of Appeals, and elected for twelve years to that office, by a majority of 17,000 votes. He now holds that position, and fills it with fidelity and ability, and to the entire satisfaction of the people of West Virginia, by whom he is regarded as one of the purest men in the United States.

Johnson, Col. Richard Mentor, son of Robert Johnson, was born at Bryant's Station, Fayette Co.,

Ky., Oct. 17, 1780. He studied law after finishing his literary education at Transylvania, and was admitted to the bar at the age of nineteen. He was elected to the Kentucky Legislature in his twenty-first year, and was a member of the U. S. Congress, 1807–19. He accepted a colonel's commission, and was in active service in the war of 1812–15. In the battle of the Thames, Oct. 5, 1813, he rendered brilliant service, and was desperately wounded. He was, however, able to resume his seat in the House in February following. After serving several terms in the lower house of Congress, he was elected to the U. S. Senate in 1819, and remained a member of that body until 1829. After this he was again a member of the House in 1829–37. In 1837 he was elected Vice-President of the United States by the Senate, the choice having devolved upon them under the Constitution. In March, 1841, he retired to his farm in Scott County, where he spent the remainder of his life, except during two terms through which he served in the Kentucky Legislature. He died at Frankfort, Nov. 19, 1850, while a member of the Legislature. Col. Johnson appears to have been a member of Great Crossing church as early as 1801.

Johnson, Col. Robert, the head of one of the most distinguished families in Kentucky, was a native of Virginia. He removed to Kentucky during the Revolution and settled at Bryant's Station, but shortly afterwards he settled near the present site of Georgetown, in Scott County, where he was the principal instrument in organizing Great Crossing Baptist church, of which he was a member. He was prominent in the councils of the Baptists in the early settlement of the country, conspicuous as a leader in the Indian wars of the period, and a member of most of the councils of state. He was a member of the convention which formed the first constitution of Kentucky in 1792, and of that which formed the second constitution, in 1799. He was eight times elected to the Kentucky Legislature. Three of his sons were members of Congress from Kentucky, and several of his descendants have been members of Congress from other States. He died at a ripe old age at his residence in Scott Co., Ky.

Johnson, Rev. Thomas, was born in Georgia. He visited Missouri in 1799, and preached near Cape Girardeau ; one person at his first service made a profession of faith and was baptized, a Mrs. Blair. This is said to have been the first believer immersed west of the Mississippi River, in Missouri. The baptism was administered in Randal's Creek, where, in 1797, a number of Baptists settled near the village of Jackson. Here they built the first Baptist house of worship in Missouri. It was of logs, and was erected in 1806. Around this old church are graves with rough tombstones, which mark the resting-place of the first Baptists, and the first Protestants in Missouri.

Johnson, Rev. Thomas C., one of the best qualified and most successful ministers in the State, was born at Long Reach, Tyler Co., W. Va., Sept. 18, 1848. He is next to the youngest of nineteen children of Wm. Johnson, of Mineral County. In 1867 he entered college; was baptized the following April by Rev. J. D. Griebel, and graduated in 1872. He preached his first sermon in October, 1871, and was licensed to preach by the Long Reach church in the summer of 1872. He entered Crozer Theological Seminary in the fall of 1872, and graduated in 1875. He then took charge of the Willow Island church, in West Virginia, and the Valley church, in Ohio. He was ordained at Willow Island in 1875.

In December, 1877, he became pastor of the Baptist church in Charleston, W. Va., at which place he is now located. The church was in a low and scattered condition and deeply in debt, but he has, in less than three years, been instrumental in greatly promoting its efficiency and in enlarging its membership.

Johnson, Rev. Thomas Thornton, was born July 20, 1803, in Fauquier Co., Va. He was converted at the age of thirteen years, and baptized by Elder James Lugget, of Kentucky. He removed to Missouri in 1828. He contended for missionary principles against bitter opposition. Helped to form a missionary society in 1838, and labored much as a pastor, and was at home in protracted meetings. He was remarkably effective in exhortations. He aided in the formation of many churches in Ralls, Pike, Lincoln, and Montgomery Counties. He died at Truxton, Mo., Feb. 25, 1877.

Johnson, Rev. William, is a very remarkable man in some respects. He was born in Barnwell District, S. C., Jan. 9, 1803, and is related doubtless to Col. Richard M. Johnson, who killed Tecumseh in Kentucky. His father died before he was born, and his mother died when he was seventeen years old, at which time he was "bound" to a man in Augusta, Ga.

Here he remained till nearly twenty-one years of age, when he disagreed with his master for the first time, and leaving him, returned to South Carolina, and went to school a few months. He often quotes,—

"No mother to nurse and to guide,
No father to protect and provide,
No fortune to shield from hunger and cold,
A poor little orphan, cast on the world,"

as being almost literally true in his case.

Elder Johnson was converted and baptized about 1829, his baptism occurring at a branch of Darien church, and was performed by Prescott Bush, a Revolutionary soldier. He was ordained, while a

member of Philippi church, by W. B. Johnson, D.D., Peter Galloway, John Landrum, and Joseph Morris. He was a constituent member in the organization of the Edisto Association, and was its moderator several times. He removed to Florida in 1854, and joined Pleasant Grove church, in Alachua County, and at different times has served that church, and Wacahoota, Eliam, and Ockwilla, in the same county; Paran, in Putnam County, and Providence, in Bradford County, besides aiding in building up some new churches. He aided in the formation of the Alachua Association, and has been perhaps its only moderator, and was for a few sessions moderator of Santa Fé River Association.

Mr. Johnson is strong in body and mind. His ancestors were Irish, and from them he inherited a robust constitution and a fondness for humor. In his preaching his favorite themes are divine sovereignty, election, grace, etc. He is a decided Baptist, and contends earnestly for the faith. He had a struggle before consenting to enter the ministry, and would never after take any civil office.

Mr. Johnson has been a tower of strength in Florida, and is yet popular and exerting a good influence, but he is not able to preach much.

Johnson, W. B., D.D., was one of the most active and useful ministers that ever labored in South Carolina. "Soon after 1820" he was a member of the Saluda Association, and presided over its deliberations for a number of years. Subsequently he was the acting pastor at Edgefield Court-House, and a member of the Association bearing the name of his church, and of this Association he was chosen moderator.

The State Convention founded in 1821 had a very warm friend in Dr. Johnson. He was one of a committee of three who drafted its constitution. In 1822 he preached the introductory sermon, and prepared the address of the Convention to the churches, which was printed in the minutes of that year, a document of great ability, and penetrated by a thoroughly missionary and evangelical spirit. In 1823 he was elected vice-president of the Convention. In 1824 he preached the annual charity sermon, and in 1825 he was chosen president on the death of the honored Dr. Richard Furman, whose name is justly venerated in South Carolina, and by hosts of Baptists all over our country. Dr. Johnson held this position for a great many years, an office the duties of which were discharged not only by Dr. Richard Furman, but by Dr. Basil Manly, Chief-Justice O'Neall, and other distinguished men. The reputation of Dr. Johnson spread over our whole country, and for three years he was president of our great national missionary society, "The Triennial Convention of the United States," and after the division in that body he was chosen the first president of the Southern Baptist

Convention. In no section of our country was any Baptist minister more highly honored by his brethren.

He was a solid and impressive preacher, deeply

W. B. JOHNSON, D.D.

versed in the sacred writings, and full of his Master's spirit. He was very hospitable, and his life was blameless. To the Saviour he rendered noble service, which was fruitful in an unusual measure.

Under Dr. Wayland's presidency Brown University gave him the degree of Doctor of Divinity. He died at Greenville, S. C., in 1862, when he was about eighty years of age.

The State Convention, in 1863, appointed its president, Dr. J. C. Furman, to preach a sermon "in honor of the memory of their venerable brother, the late Rev. W. B. Johnson, D.D.," and after the delivery of the discourse the Convention requested a copy for publication, and a committee was also appointed "to raise funds to erect a monument over his remains."

Johnson, Hon. William Carey, son of Rev. Hezekiah Johnson, was born in Ohio, Oct. 27, 1833. In 1845 he removed to Oregon with his parents, and has since then lived at Oregon City. He received a good academic education ; was converted in 1854, and baptized by Rev. E. Fisher. He entered and attained a high position in the legal profession, and in 1866 became State senator. In 1868 he was married to Miss Josephine De Vore, the first woman to win the degree of A.B. on the Pacific coast, graduating with honor from the full course of Willamette University, at Salem, Oregon, in

1868. Mr. Johnson has continued one of the most active laymen in the work of the Baptists in his State, clerk of the Willamette Association, and for many years its moderator. In his church at Oregon City he has a leading influence, and in its Sunday-school is a devoted Bible-class teacher and superintendent.

Johnston, Judge James William, was born in 1791 ; studied law in Annapolis, Nova Scotia, and became distinguished in his profession ; was converted and baptized in Halifax, Nova Scotia; strongly supported the educational movement which commenced among the Baptists of Nova Scotia in 1828, which resulted in the establishment of Horton Academy in 1829, and Acadia College in January, 1839 ; represented Annapolis County in the Provincial Parliament for twenty years ; was leader of the government and attorney-general for several years ; became, in 1865, judge of the Supreme Court, Nova Scotia, and judge in equity. James W. Johnston possessed a gigantic mind, unsullied integrity, indomitable energy, commanding eloquence, and Christian humility. On the death of Gov. Howe, Judge Johnston was appointed to succeed him as governor of Nova Scotia, but death interposed his veto Nov. 21, 1873.

Johnston, Judge James W., a son of Judge James W. Johnston, graduated from Acadia College in 1843 ; studied law with his father, and practised his profession in Halifax for many years; was appointed judge of the Halifax County Court in 1877, and performs his duties with ability. Judge Johnston is a member of the Dartmouth Baptist church.

Johnston, Col. John W., was born at Paltonsburg, Botetourt Co., Va., July 6, 1839. Having received his early intellectual training in the neighboring schools, he entered upon and finished his studies in law in Lexington, Va., and afterwards prosecuted his profession with great success. At the beginning of the war he entered the Confederate service, first as second lieutenant of riflemen of the 48th Regiment Va. Militia, and a few weeks after became second lieutenant of the 28th Va. Infantry, Provisional army of the C. S. A. Near the close of 1861 he became first lieutenant of Anderson's Battery, Light Artillery, and in the early part of 1863, captain of the Botetourt Artillery. During this year he served also as captain and inspector-general of artillery on Maj.-Gen. C. L. Stevenson's staff. During 1864 he held the position of major of artillery in the P. A. C. S., and until April, 1865, was in command of a battalion of light artillery, in all these positions he displayed the highest ability. During the sessions of 1875–77 Col. Johnston was a member of the house of delegates of Virginia from Botetourt County, and served with marked efficiency. April 24, 1877, he was elected president of the James River and Kanawha Company, and also president of the Buchanan and Clifton Forge Railway Company. Col. Johnston is a member of the Buchanan Baptist church, and actively engaged in all movements designed for the advancement and strengthening of the denomination.

Johnston, Rev. Jonas, was born in Beaufort Co., S. C., March 11, 1821; received a sound academic education; was converted and baptized in August, 1846. After ordination ministered to the following churches: Lawtonville, S. C.; Anderson, Bedias, Danville, Waverly, Bethel, Montgomery, Huntsville, Ebenezer, Planterville, and Navisota, Texas. He has been prospered in his worldly business beyond most ministers of the gospel, but at the same time he has been a laborious and very successful preacher, exerting extended influence and commanding general esteem. He is now the business manager of the Texas *Baptist Herald*, and is efficiently promoting the great educational and missionary operations of Texas. He is a sound theologian and an able counselor.

Jones, Rev. C. B.—For nearly twenty years the Baptist denomination in Florida had the valuable labors, influence, and advice of Rev. Charles B. Jones, who was born on Wilmington Island, near Savannah, Ga., in the year 1798, and died at Palatka, Fla., March 5, 1879. " In early life he was of a generous and jovial disposition, having plenty of money, and withal possessing a commanding personal appearance, he was not only a favorite, but an acknowledged leader among his associates."

He was deeply convicted by the killing of an uncle in a duel, he being present at the scene. He was soon after converted, and he united with the First Baptist church in Savannah. In a short time he began to preach, and was popular. He frequently filled the pulpit of the First Baptist church of Savannah during the annual vacations of the pastor, and at one time was its pastor. He was greatly beloved by all the churches he served.

" Few men could present the doctrines of the gospel with greater power. His favorite theme was the love of Christ, and when speaking upon this his countenance would become radiant, and he would seem to be almost inspired."

Upon going to Florida he settled in Marion County, and was for a time pastor of the church at Ocala. Soon after the close of the late war he moved to Palatka, where he labored as a missionary of the Northern Home Mission Society, preaching in Palatka and the surrounding country. Mr. Jones was a man of general intelligence and a ready use of language. He was tall, with a fine head, and a countenance that was a true index of his generous heart and noble impulses.

Perhaps his crowning gift was his power of conversation, in which he was ready, easy, and expressed himself in language well chosen, beautiful, and chaste. He was always welcome in every circle, and exerted a powerful social influence.

Jones, Rev. David, A.M., chaplain in the Continental army, was born in White Clay Creek Hundred, Newcastle Co., Del., May 12, 1736. His parents were Morgan and Eleanor (Evans) Jones, and his grandparents were David and Esther (Morgan) Jones. Esther Jones was a sister of Enoch and Abel Morgan, well known Baptist ministers, who were children of Morgan ap Rhyddarch, a famous Baptist minister, who resided in Llanwenog, South Wales. Mr. Jones was baptized May 6, 1758, joined the Welsh Tract Baptist church, and was one of the pupils of Isaac Eaton, at Hopewell Academy, N. J., but studied divinity with his cousin, Abel Morgan, at Middletown, N. J. He was ordained Dec. 12, 1766, as pastor of the Freehold Baptist church, Monmouth Co., N. J. While there he was impressed with a desire to preach the gospel to the Indians, and was the first Baptist missionary among that people.

REV. DAVID JONES, A.M.

No doubt the example of David Brainard influenced his heart, and the wretched condition of the poor red men for this and for the future life prompted his course. They then occupied what is now the State of Ohio, and he made them two visits. His first began May 4, 1772, and ended in August; his second began Oct. 26, 1772, and ended in April, 1773. He kept a journal of his missionary labors, which was published in 1773, and was reprinted in New York by J. Sabin, in 1865. Mr. Jones continued his pastorate at the village of Freehold until his outspoken views in favor of the rights of Americans rendered him unpopular, and in April, 1775, he became pastor of the Great Valley church, Chester Co., Pa. In that year the Continental Congress recommended a day of fasting and prayer, and he preached a sermon before Col. Dewees's regiment, entitled " Defensive War in a Just Cause Sinless," which was printed and extensively circulated. He took high ground even at that early day in favor of independence. In 1776 he was appointed a chaplain in Col. St. Clair's regiment, and was at Ticonderoga, where, just before battle, he delivered a patriotic address, which roused the courage of the soldiers to a high degree. Subsequently he served under Gen. Horatio Gates and Gen. Wayne, and was in many battles, and always proved himself to be a wise counselor and a devoted patriot. He was at the Paoli massacre, and narrowly escaped death. While the army was at Valley Forge he frequently showed his devotion to the cause, and was highly trusted by Washington. When news arrived that France had recognized our independence, he preached an appropriate sermon to the troops at the Forge. He continued in the army until the capitulation at Yorktown, and then retired to his farm in East Town, Chester Co., adjoining the farm of his old commander, Gen. Wayne. In 1786 he became pastor of the Southampton church, Bucks Co., where he remained until 1792, when he returned to the Valley church, with which he remained, part of the time as senior pastor, until his death. When Gen. Wayne was appointed to the command of the army, and undertook to put down the Indians in the Northwestern Territory, he induced Mr. Jones to accompany him as chaplain, and he acted in that capacity during 1794–95–96, and was present at the treaty of Greenville. When the war of 1812 broke out, although seventy-six years of age, he again volunteered his services, and was appointed chaplain by his old companion in arms, Gen. John Armstrong, then Secretary of War, and he served under Gens. Brown and Wilkinson until peace was declared. He then retired to his farm and devoted himself to its cultivation, and also to arboriculture, of which he was very fond. He thus passed the evening of a busy life, varying it with visits to his relatives, both near and far, preaching wherever he went, and often writing for the press on public affairs, in which he never ceased to take a deep interest.

Mr. Jones was a prominent member of the Philadelphia Baptist Association, of which he was moderator in the year 1798, and was often appointed on committees to answer queries or to settle difficulties among the churches. When the great Winchester defection occurred in the church of Philadelphia, and a majority of the members followed Elhanan Winchester, who had become a Universalist, or as he was then called a Restorationist, Mr.

Jones was one of the ministers appointed by the church to advise them in their troubles.

Mr. Jones died at his farm, Feb. 5, 1820, in the eighty-fourth year of his age, and was buried at the Valley church-yard. The funeral services were conducted by Rev. Thomas Roberts, Rev. Wm. E. Ashton, and Rev. William Latta. The Rev. Dr. William Rogers delivered a funeral sermon on the next Sunday. The following notice of Mr. Jones appeared in Poulson's *Daily Advertiser :*

" In sketching the character of this venerable servant of the Cross, truth requires us to say that he was an eminent man. Throughout the whole of his protracted and eventful life Mr. Jones was peculiarly distinguished for the warmth of his friendship, the firmness of his patriotism, the sincerity and ardor of his piety, and the faithfulness of his ministry. In the army of the Revolution he was a distinguished chaplain, and was engaged in the same arduous duties during the last war. As a scholar he was accurate; possessing a mind of superior texture, he embellished it with the beauties of classical literature and the riches of general science. The Fellowship of Brown University, in the year 1774, as a testimony of respect for his learning and talents, conferred upon him the degree of Master of Arts."

In early life he studied medicine, and his services during the wars were often called for, and, although not a physician, yet he frequently prescribed when applied to.

Mr. Jones was the author of several works: 1st. A journal of two visits made to some nations of Indians on the west side of the River Ohio, in the years 1772 and 1773. 2d. A treatise on the work of the Holy Spirit. 3d. A treatise on laying on of hands. 4th. Another on the same subject, in reply to a broadside of Rev. Samuel Jones, D.D. 5th. " Peter Edwards' Candid Reasons examined."

Mr. Jones was married Feb. 22, 1762, to Anne, daughter of Joseph and Sarah Stilwell, of Middletown, N. J., and had issue: 1st. Morgan, who died near Wheeling, Va. 2d. Eleanor, who married John Garrett, and died at Garrettsville, O. 3d. Mary, who married Archibald McClean. 4th. Horatio Gates Jones, who died at Philadelphia. All his children left issue.

In danger he knew no fear, in fervent patriotism he had no superiors and few equals, in the Revolutionary struggle he was a tower of strength, especially in the section now known as the Middle States, and in piety he was a Christian without reproach.

Jones, Rev. David, was born in Wales, in April, 1785. Though bearing the same name, this is not the heroic David Jones, the Pennsylvania chaplain in the Revolutionary war. He landed in Philadelphia in 1803, when the yellow fever was raging;

he went to Ohio, and more than two years afterwards he was baptized into the fellowship of the Columbia church, near Cincinnati. He studied under Dr. Samuel Jones, of Lower Dublin, Pa., for some time. In January, 1814, he took pastoral charge of the church of Newark, N. J., where the Lord revived the church and converted many souls through his ministry. In 1821 he succeeded Dr. Samuel Jones as pastor of the Lower Dublin church, and he continued to serve it until the Lord took him home; in this church the Great Shepherd gave him several revivals, in one of which, in 1831, he baptized 65 persons, though the population around was small. He died April 9, 1833, in the enjoyment of a blessed hope through his Saviour's blood.

Jones, Rev. Evan, was born at Brecknockshire, Wales, in May, 1789. Previous to his coming to this country he was for thirteen years a merchant in London. He was appointed by the board of the Baptist Triennial Convention, July 24, 1821, a missionary among the Cherokee Indians. For several years before the removal of the Cherokees from North Carolina Mr. Jones labored with great success among them, establishing churches and schools, and proving that some of the Indian tribes of this country can be civilized and Christianized. In 1838, in carrying out the treaty of New Echota, the Cherokees were removed to what was known as the Western Territory, and Mr. Jones followed his flock to their new home, and in two years after their removal 130 persons were baptized and a new church formed. Mr. Jones's connection with the Cherokees covered a period of fifty years. It is said that "the confidence in which he was held by them was never impaired." He died at Tahlequah, Aug. 18, 1873, having reached the age of eighty-three years and three months. "He was a man of quiet home virtues, of unostentatious life, and of such purity of character that even suspicion presumed not to tarnish it."

Jones, Rev. F. H., was born in Surry Co., N. C., Sept. 4, 1836; educated at Union Academy, Davie Co., Beulah Institute, and Yadkin Institute; baptized by Rev. C. W. Bessant; has done much missionary work; is now pastor of the Yanceyville church, moderator of the Beulah Association, and the leading man in that body.

Jones, Rev. G. S., was born in Pasquotank Co., N. C., Dec. 23, 1837; graduated at Wake Forest College in 1860; ordained in 1861, Revs. T. B. Justice, Thomas Stradley, and Dr. J. D. Hufham forming the Presbytery; served the Hendersonville church as pastor from 1861 to 1868, since which time he has been in the employ of the American Sunday-School Union, and has organized and aided about 900 schools.

Jones, Rev. Henry V., was born in North Wales, Feb. 24, 1808. Left an orphan when four years old, he went to live with an uncle in London. After attending an academy, he entered mercantile life at seventeen. He was converted and baptized in August, 1826, into the fellowship of the Dean Street church, London, and was disowned by his uncle (an Episcopalian) the next day. He came to America in 1831, and was ordained in New York State, April 8, 1835. His first pastorate was in Palmyra. He held important positions in New York, New England, and New Jersey. In the latter State he accomplished a great work. When he took charge of the First church in Newark the cause was very low. Differences of doctrine and diverse views as to measures among the members had long prevented growth. Under his genial and loving preaching and administration union was secured, the congregation more than filled the house, a building for the South church was begun, and a colony was designated to occupy the new house. This was the beginning of church extension in Newark, and Mr. Jones was a moving spirit in the work. His health requiring a change, he accepted a call to the old church at Piscataway, N. J., where he spent six years of loving, successful labor. After good work was done at Rondout and West Troy, N. Y., and Noank, Conn., he served the church at Princeton, N. J. His brethren felt that his qualifications to incite the churches to benevolent work ought to be more extensively used, and he was persuaded to accept the position of district secretary of the Home Mission Society. He also acted at other times as financial secretary of Peddie Institute and South Jersey Institute, collecting large sums for these schools. He was a clear, sound, solid preacher, having the Welsh power of illustration blended with the sober judgment of a master in Scripture doctrine. He was a valuable helper in the First church, New Brunswick, of which he was a member the last seven years of his life. His last sermon was at the old church at Piscataway, on Sunday, June 16, 1878. He preached with great power, and seemed to be in usual health. The next evening, after two hours' sickness, he went to his heavenly home. A prominent periodical well spoke of him as "a man of strong common sense, singular magnanimity and devotedness, and great purity of character."

Jones, Hon. Horatio Gates, A.M., the youngest son of Horatio Gates Jones, D.D., was born Jan. 19, 1822, in Roxborough, Philadelphia. He graduated at the University of Pennsylvania in 1841; was admitted to the Philadelphia bar in May, 1847; formed an acquaintance early in life with the annalist of Philadelphia, John F. Watson, which in a great measure gave tone to the future studies of his life; in 1848 became a member of the Historical Society of Pennsylvania, and in 1849 its secretary, a position which he held for eighteen years, and in 1867 he was chosen one of its vice-presidents, and still holds that office; in 1856 he became connected with the Welsh Society of Philadelphia, of which he is now president; in 1858 he was elected clerk of the Philadelphia Baptist Association, and filled the office for fifteen years, when he was chosen moderator. He has been president of the board of trustees of the Philadelphia Association for thirteen years. He was elected in 1865 by the councils of Philadelphia a director of Girard College. He has been secretary of the board of trustees of Crozer Theological Seminary for thirteen years. In 1874 he was elected to the State senate from Philadelphia, and re-elected in 1876 and in 1878. Mr. Jones is a member of the historical societies of Rhode Island, New York, Delaware, Wisconsin, Minnesota, and Florida; and also of the Moravian Historical Society, the New England Historic Genealogical Society, and the American Antiquarian Society; and in 1877 he was elected an Honorary Fellow of the Royal Historical Society of Great Britain.

Mr. Jones was largely interested in the organization of the Baptist Home of Philadelphia, and he has been secretary of its board of trustees from its establishment.

Mr. Jones united with the Lower Merion church in 1840, of which his father was pastor, and he still remains a member of it.

He is the author of a number of valuable works, which show great research and literary ability.

In the senate of Pennsylvania, while not neglecting other interests of the State, he has devoted much time to religious liberty; his aim has been to secure freedom from the penalties of the Sunday law of April 22, 1794, for all persons who observed the seventh day as the Sabbath. In 1876–77–78–79, and in 1880, he introduced bills for this purpose into the senate, and though on each occasion he was defeated, yet the vote in favor of his motion was always larger. Mr. Jones cherishes an enthusiastic love for Baptist soul liberty; he understands the subject thoroughly, his efforts on its behalf have been well planned and valiant; and ultimate victory is certain under his generous leadership. He might justly be called the American champion of religious liberty.

Mr. Jones has an enviable reputation, an extensive influence, an unselfish disposition, and a heart full of love for his Master, his truth, and his servants.

Jones, Horatio Gates, D.D., of Roxborough, Philadelphia, Pa., youngest son of Rev. David Jones, of the Great Valley church, was born Feb. 11, 1777, at East Town, Chester Co., Pa., and passed his early youth there and at Southampton, Bucks Co. After acquiring such education as the schools there could give, when nineteen he was placed under the care of Rev. Burgiss Allison, D.D.,

who was principal of an academy at Bordentown, N. J. The celebrated Dr. Stoughton was one of the teachers, and the acquaintance then formed ripened into a friendship which lasted through life. The system of instruction was quite varied, and the attendance of many French refugees was of great advantage to the students, who could thereby acquire a knowledge of French. On his return from school, Mr. Jones devoted himself to farming. He also mingled in politics, and, being a fluent speaker, he soon acquired a prominent position, even before he had attained his majority. But about this time his mind was directed to religious concerns, and he made a public profession of his faith June 24, 1798, and became a member of the Valley church. He soon began to exercise his gifts as a speaker, and the church being satisfied with his efforts, licensed him to preach Sept. 26, 1801. The young man had before him the prospect of political preferment if he remained in civil life, but convictions of duty made him sacrifice all such aspirations, and he entered on his new work with an energy which proved the earnestness of his purpose. He preached in Chester and Delaware Counties, and also in the State of Delaware, where his Welsh ancestors had settled nearly a century before. Having been invited to preach at Salem, N. J., he visited that church, of which Rev. Isaac Skillman, D.D., had been pastor. His labors were appreciated, and on Feb. 13, 1802, he was ordained, and labored in Salem until April, 1805, when he was obliged to leave on account of enfeebled health; the climate not suiting him. He removed to a farm in Roxborough, Philadelphia, and preached every Lord's day, where an opening was had. Among other places he preached in "Thomson's Meeting-House," in Lower Merion, Montgomery Co., which belonged to Hon. Charles Thomson, first secretary of the Continental Congress. Mr. Thomson was a highly-educated man, had once been a tutor in the College of Philadelphia, was a thorough Greek scholar, and is well known as a translator of the Bible. He gave Mr. Jones a warm welcome, and in many ways exhibited an interest in the preaching of the gospel in that neighborhood. Although residing six miles from the meeting-house, yet he was generally the first person there, and for a period of three years he continued his labors without any signs of success. But in May, 1808, he was privileged to baptize the first convert in a small dam on Mill Creek, which he erected the previous day with his own hands. Other hopeful conversions and baptisms followed, until on Sept. 11, 1808, the Lower Merion Baptist church was organized with 19 members, with Mr. Jones as pastor. Rev. William Rogers, D.D., and Rev. William Stoughton, D.D., officiated on the occasion. In two years' time a meeting-house was built on a lot of ground the gift of Mr. Thomson, who, although a Presbyterian, ever continued to attend the Merion church, until over ninety years of age, and proved himself a warm friend of Mr. Jones. Notwithstanding Mr. Jones was a laborious minister, and was constant in visitations among his people, yet he took a deep interest in civil affairs, and to the close of his life filled many important posts of honor, but none of profit. For more than twenty years he was a director of the Bank of Germantown, and director and controller of the public schools.

In 1814, when the Baptist Board of Foreign Missions was organized in Philadelphia, he was present, aided 'in its formation, was one of the Board of Managers, and for many years acted as secretary of the board. He was warmly interested in the cause of education, and especially the education of young men for the ministry. It was chiefly through his influence that the Philadelphia Association was induced to organize a manual labor school at Haddington, Philadelphia Co., which afterwards became Haddington College. As long as the college existed he was president of its board of trustees, and spared neither time nor money in promoting its interests. In 1812, Brown University conferred on him the degree of Master of Arts, and in 1852 the university at Lewisburg bestowed on him their first degree of Doctor of Divinity, he being at the time the chancellor of the institution. In 1829 Mr. Jones was chosen president of the trustees of the Philadelphia Baptist Association, and he held that honorable position until 1853, a period of twenty-four years. He was chosen moderator of the Association in 1816 and 1822, and was clerk in 1808, 1810, 1813, 1815, and 1835.

The Lower Merion church, of which he was the first pastor, continued under his care for a period of forty-five years. It assisted all the benevolent and missionary organizations as they arose, and it was owing to a query from this church to the Association, that the Baptist State Convention, now known as the Pennsylvania Baptist General Association, for missionary purposes, was organized. Dr. Jones continued his active duties until 1845, when his health began to fail; but still he would not consent to give up his pastorate. And so he continued to preach and pray for his beloved Merion until called home to his reward on high, on the 12th of December, 1853, in his seventy-seventh year.

Mr. Jones was twice married, first to Miss Esther Righter, by whom he had three children,—Hon. John Richter Jones, Ellen Maria, married to Rev. George Higgins, Hetty Ann Jones, all of whom are deceased. His second wife was Miss Deborah Levering, and by her he had issue,—Sarah, married to Hon. Anthony D. Levering, Col. Charles Thomson Jones, Nathan Levering Jones, died April 19, 1879, leaving issue, Horatio Gates Jones.

Jones, Rev. Howard Malcom, son of the missionary, Rev. John Taylor Jones, D.D., was born in Bangkok, Siam. He was a graduate of Brown University in the class of 1853, and of Newton Theological Institution in the class of 1857. He was ordained pastor of the church in Schoolcraft, Mich., in 1858, where he remained one year, and then went to Racine, Wis., where he was a pastor four years. On leaving the Racine church, he settled in Fredonia, N. Y., where he was pastor six years, and then accepted a call to Bristol, R. I. Since 1869, Mr. Jones has been preaching in Bristol with much acceptance.

Jones, Hugh, D.D., president of Llangollen College, Wales, was born in Bodedern, Anglesea, July 10, 1831. He became the subject of religious convictions while yet a boy. When about twelve years of age he connected himself with the Welsh Calvinistic Methodist Church. In his sixteenth year he removed to the neighborhood of Llanfachreth, where the Baptists had a stronghold. His associations with them led him for the first time to examine the New Testament on the subject of baptism, and the result was his conversion to the Baptist faith. He was baptized in the river Alaw by the Rev. Robert D. Roberts in his seventeenth year. His abilities were soon discovered by the brotherhood at Llanfachreth, and he was urged to exercise his gifts as a preacher. Having spent some time in the grammar-school of the neighborhood, he entered Haverford West College in June, 1853. His progress in this institution was such as to command particular mention. In Hebrew, mathematics, and the classics he was the distinguished student of his class. In May, 1857, he settled as pastor over the Baptist church at Llandudno, Caernarvonshire. In a little over two years he was enabled greatly to strengthen the cause, leaving them on account of ill health in October, 1859.

In the same month he became co-pastor with the Rev. John Prichard, D.D., at Llangollen. This fellowship of service was most fruitful of good. The elder and the younger were true yoke-fellows in Christ. They had joint charge of the Welsh and English churches of Llangollen, as well as of a branch church at Glyndyfedwy, Merionethshire. In 1862 the North Wales Baptist College was instituted at Llangollen, with Dr. Prichard as president, and Mr. Jones as classical and mathematical tutor. In 1866, Dr. Prichard resigned, and Mr. Jones became president, a position which he still holds with acknowledged efficiency.

Dr. Jones has not confined himself to his collegiate and ministerial duties. Some of the most valuable productions in the Welsh language are from his able pen. In 1862 he issued a small book on "The Mode and Subjects of Baptism, with the History of the Rise of Infant Baptism and Sprinkling," which has been widely read. In 1863 there appeared a volume on "The Act of Baptism, or an Enquiry into the Mode of Baptism." An abbreviated edition of this book has appeared in English, and has been very well received. It is in the Welsh language what Carson is in the English. Its excellence and value are universally recognized. Another volume which has been a rich boon to the Welsh people is a masterly production on "The Bible and its Interpretation, or an Introduction to the Holy Scriptures." Dr. Jones has done himself great credit both in the conception and execution of this work. It will do for the Bible-loving Welsh people what no other book could. There was nothing more needed in the vernacular of the principality than a scholarly treatise on Bible exegesis, and Dr. Jones has supplied the need in a manner that cannot fail to command the gratitude of every lover of the Book of books in the land. Several other minor productions have been issued from Dr. Jones's pen that have taken a high place in his country's literature: "The Church of Christ," being the inaugural address from the chair of the Welsh Baptist Union, 1876; "The History of the Protestant Reformation in Great Britain, with Special Reference to Wales;" "Popery: its History and Characteristics, with the Remedy Against It," being the inaugural address from the chair of the Welsh Baptist Union for 1877. He has also written many essays and sermons for the Welsh periodicals, together with a Commentary on Ecclesiastes for Mr. Gee, of Denbigh's family Bible.

Few men of this generation have done more to enlighten and elevate their countrymen than Dr. Hugh Jones, of Llangollen. His writings have all been of a sterling character.

Jones, Rev. Jenkin, was born about 1690, in Wales, and he came to this country in 1710. He took charge of the First church of Philadelphia, May 15, 1746, at the time the church was "reconstituted." Previous to that time the Philadelphia body was only a branch of the Lower Dublin church, and of it Mr. Jones had been pastor for twenty-one years. He died July 16, 1761. Mr. Jones was "a good man," and performed valuable service to his church and denomination; he was the cause of changing the marriage laws of the colony, so that "dissenting" ministers might celebrate marriages; he built a parsonage largely at his own expense; he left "a legacy towards purchasing a silver cup for the Lord's table which is worth £60. His name is engraven upon it."

Jones, Rev. John, an eloquent colored Baptist minister, long pastor of the First African Baptist church in Shreveport, La., was a native of North Carolina, and came to Shreveport under the protection of Deacon John N. Howell about 1840. He was ordained in 1856 by a Presbytery consisting of Dr. W. H. Stokes, George Tucker, Jesse Lee, and A. J. Rutherford. In the early part of the civil war a law was passed requiring all free persons of color, not natives, to leave the State. Under the operation of this law he went to Ohio, but his loss was soon felt, and it was known that he could do more than all the police in keeping the Africans in order; consequently a special act of the Legislature was passed inviting his return, the terms of which he accepted, to the great joy of the people of both races. He was often invited to preach to the whites, and always drew large and interested audiences. He died in 1877, much regretted.

Jones, John Emlyn, LL.D., was born in the town of Newcastle, Emlyn, Caermarthenshire, Wales, on the 8th of January, 1820, and died at Ebbeo Vale on the 18th. of January, 1873. He was a man of commanding presence and oratorical ability. He was editor at different times of the two leading organs of the Baptists of Wales. He was a voluminous contributor to various Welsh periodicals. He translated into the Welsh language Gill's Commentary and Hamilton's Grammar, and he wrote "The History of Great Britain for the Past Half-Century." During the last years of his life he was engaged in a work in the Welsh language called "The History of the World," one volume of which was published, and he had written about half of the other. He was likewise a poet of no mean order. He won during his lifetime a large number of prizes for poetical compositions. At the Abergavenny Eisteddfod, in 1838, he was invested with the degree of B.B.D. (Bard by Privilege and Usage). At the Denbigh National Eisteddfod, in 1860, he won the chair, with the accompanying prize, for the best ode on the "Pentecost," also at Llanerchymedd for the best ode on "Time." Among his poetical productions, "The Poor Man's Grave" is regarded for its pathos, simplicity, and heart-touching effect as equal to anything of its kind in the literature of the country.

Jones, Judge John Richter, the eldest son of Rev. Horatio Gates Jones, was born in Salem, N. J., Oct. 2, 1803, and was educated at the Germantown Academy, and was graduated from the University of Pennsylvania in the year 1821. He was admitted to the Philadelphia bar Nov. 17, 1827. For many years he was one of the judges of the Court of Common Pleas of Philadelphia County, during which time he lived at Roxborough. On retiring from the bench he settled in Sullivan Co., Pa. When the late war began he felt it to be his duty to devote himself to the service of his country, and with all the patriotic ardor of his renowned grandfather, Rev. David Jones, of the Continental army, Judge Jones immediately raised a regiment, the 58th Penna. Vols., of which he was commissioned colonel. He sought as soon as possible for active service, and was ordered to Norfolk, Va., and finally was sent to Newbern, N. C., where he soon achieved much renown for the boldness of his attacks. He did not know what fear was, and hence sought for the place of greatest danger. One of his last and most successful marches was made in May, 1863, against a force which had encamped at a place called Gum Swamp. He had placed at his command a number of regiments, over which he exercised the power of acting brigadier-general. After a long and arduous march he succeeded in capturing the whole of the force without losing a single man. But the song of victory was soon changed into a wail of sorrow, for shortly after his return to camp at Newbern his troops were attacked, and placing himself at the head of a force to reconnoitre, he was suddenly shot through the heart, and died without a groan. Most truly can it be said of him, *Dulce et decorum est pro patria mori.* Judge Jones was a devout Christian, and was a member of the Lower Merion church. He was a classical scholar, and carried with him to the camp his Septuagint version of the Old Testament, which he was accustomed to read daily. His death occurred May 23, 1863.

Jones, John Taylor, D.D., was born at New Ipswich, N. H., July 16, 1802. He joined the Congregational church in Ashby, Mass., when he was but fifteen years of age. He graduated at Amherst in 1825, and studied theology at Andover, where his views underwent a change on the mode and subjects of baptism, in consequence of which he thought it would be more expedient for him to complete his course of study at Newton. He was baptized by Rev. Dr. Malcom in 1828, and became a member of the Federal Street church, in Boston. He was appointed a missionary to Burmah, and reached Maulmain in February, 1861. He immediately addressed himself with great zeal to his missionary work. He was able to preach both in the Burman and the Taling languages before many months had elapsed. Believing that there was a favorable opportunity to preach to the Talings in the kingdom of Siam, it was decided by the board that Dr. Jones was the most suitable person to make the effort. To carry out this purpose he went to Bangkok. Providence soon pointed out to him what was to be his special mission to Siam. It was to translate the New Testament into the tongue of that country. He engaged in this congenial occupation with the greatest interest, and completed the work upon which he had set his heart in October, 1843. Meanwhile, circumstances brought him to his native land, where he remained for a short time, and then returned to the scene of his labors. Again, in 1846, the state of his wife's health led to another visit. He spent a year in this country, presenting everywhere, as opportunity offered, the claims of foreign missions to the churches, and in 1847 he returned to his post of labor. In Bangkok he was regarded with the highest respect. We are told that "the magistrates, and even the king, did not hesitate to consult him in cases of difficulty." He continued at his favorite work as a translator, and in the preparation of many books which he hoped would be useful to the natives. In the summer of 1851 he had an attack of dysentery, which so prostrated him that he died September 13, being a few weeks over forty-nine years of age.

His associates in missionary labor place Dr. Jones very high on the list of those who have devoted themselves to the services of Christ in the foreign field. His great work, the translation of the New Testament into the Siamese language, says Dr. Dean, "compares favorably with the translation of the New Testament made in any of the Asiatic languages, including the life-work of such men as Carey, Marshman, Judson, and Morrison, and their worthy successors." He adds, " I have met men on the missionary field who exhibited some stronger points of character, and some particular qualifications, or greater fitness for missionary usefulness, but, take him altogether, I have never seen his equal, and among more than a hundred men I have met among the heathen, I would select Dr. Jones as the model missionary."

Jones, Jonathan, A.M., principal of the University Female Institute at Lewisburg, Pa., was born in Chester County in that State, June, 1845. His early education was received in the schools of his native county, and in those of Reading, whither his family removed in 1860. Here he was fitted for college, but he did not enter the University of Lewisburg until 1864, having previously to this time served in the late war. He graduated from college in 1868 with high honors. The two succeeding years were spent in Minnesota in teaching and preaching. In the summer of 1870 he returned to Lewisburg, having been elected to take charge of the academy connected with the university. He remained here until 1873, when he accepted the principalship of the Classical and Scientific Institute at Mount Pleasant, Westmoreland Co., Pa. Here he remained five years. Although the school sustained great financial losses during that time, yet there was a steady increase in the attendance, largely due to his excellent management. In 1878 he accepted the principalship of the institute at Lewisburg,—the ladies' department of the university. Since his election to this position, the board of curators have introduced into the school, at his suggestion, a full classical course of instruction. The institute now confers on young women the advantages of a college, and it is the determination of the principal to keep the standard of scholarship equal to that of the most advanced institutions for women. His work as an instructor is in the line of psychology, ethics, and Greek.

Jones, Judge J. H. C., was born at Rockville, Md., July 31, 1823. He was educated at the Rockville Academy, and graduated at the Columbian College in 1841. He removed to King and Queen Co., Va., in 1842, where he taught school two years; he afterwards studied law, and was admitted to the bar in 1845. He was baptized into the fellowship of the Bruington church in October, 1842, of which church he has been clerk since 1861. He was elected clerk of the Rappahannock Association in 1863, which office he held continuously until 1869, when he was elected moderator of the body, to which office he has been annually re-elected ever since. He also filled the office of president of the Baptist General Association of Virginia at its annual sessions in 1875–76–77. In March, 1865, he was elected to represent the counties of King and Queen and Essex in the house of delegates of Virginia, but the failure of the Confederate cause shortly afterwards prevented the assembling of the body to which he was elected. He represented the counties of King and Queen and King William in the house of delegates under what was then called "the restored government of Virginia," during the sessions of the Legislature of 1865–66 and 1866–67. In April, 1870, he was elected by the Legislature of Virginia, under the new constitution, just then adopted, judge of the County Courts of King and Queen and Middlesex, and upon the expiration of his term of office, Jan. 1, 1874, he was re-elected by the same body judge of the County Courts of King and Queen and King William for six years, which office he holds at present. Judge Jones is warmly interested in everything pertaining to the progress of the denomination.

Jones, J. Wm., D.D., was born at Louisa Court-House, Va., Sept. 25, 1836, and was baptized Aug. 26, 1854, into the fellowship of the Mechanicsville church, Louisa Co. He received his literary and scientific education at the University of Virginia during the years 1855–59, and his theological education at the Southern Baptist Theological Seminary. He was ordained at Charlottesville, Va., June 10, 1860, with three well-known and beloved brethren, C. H. Toy, J. L. Johnson, and J. B. Taylor, Jr., all college-mates and intimate friends. On July 3, 1860, he offered himself to the Foreign Mission Board of the Southern Baptist Convention for appointment as missionary to Canton, China, was accepted, and had made arrangements to sail in the autumn with his friend (now Rev. C. H. Toy, D.D.), who was under appointment for Japan. The political troubles of that year caused the board to postpone their sailing, and the war finally prevented it. Dr. Jones's interest in foreign missions led him, in 1860, to visit many of the Associations and

J. WM. JONES, D.D.

churches to stimulate them to greater zeal in behalf of the cause, and he accomplished much good. During the winter of 1860–61 he became pastor of Little River church, Louisa Co., preaching once a month. In May, 1861, he enlisted as a private in the Confederate army, and followed its varying fortunes from Harper's Ferry to Appomattox Court-House. In 1862 he was made chaplain of his regiment, and in 1863 missionary chaplain to Gen. A. P. Hill's corps; and he was present and an active participant in all the great movements and battles from Manassas to the surrender. Dr. Jones knew intimately all the prominent officers in the Confederate service. He was an active worker in those great revivals in the army in Virginia in which over 15,000 of the soldiers under Gen. Lee professed conversion, baptizing himself 520 soldiers, and laboring in meetings which resulted in the conversion of at least 2000. In 1865 he took charge of Goshen and Lexington churches, Rockbridge Co., Va., and in 1866 devoted himself exclusively to the latter, remaining until July, 1871. His services here were greatly blessed. During his six years' pastorate in the valley he baptized 200 persons, and labored in meetings in which 250 others professed conversion. Dr. Jones's residence in Lexington opened up to him special opportunities for doing good, for he was one of the chaplains of Washington College, of which Gen. R. E. Lee was

40

president, and also gave much time to the students of the Virginia Military Institute, where, during one session, there were over 100 professions of conversion in connection with a series of prayer-meetings which he conducted. Of those whom he baptized while at Lexington, eight have become useful Baptist ministers, and fifteen clergymen in other denominations. During 1871 he acted as agent for the Southern Baptist Theological Seminary, laboring mainly in Georgia and Alabama. In 1872 he became general superintendent of the Virginia Baptist Sunday-School and Baptist Board, and held the position until June, 1874. In 1875 he took charge of the Ashland Baptist church, of which he is still the pastor. Dr. Jones has performed some admirable literary work. In 1874 he published, through the Appletons, of New York, "Reminiscences, Anecdotes, and Letters of Gen. R. E. Lee," which received the warmest commendations of critics in all parts of the country, and which an accomplished scholar designates as "one of the most charming semi-biographies in the language." Of this work 20,000 copies have already been sold. He is diligently at work now on several historical works, among which are a "Life of Gen. Stonewall Jackson," and a "History of the Revivals in the Confederate Army," the latter of which, from the fact that he was actively engaged in them, will be looked for with eager interest by the Christian public. He is also at the present time secretary of the Southern Historical Society, and editor of their monthly paper. Dr. Jones also had the reputation of being one of the best "special correspondents" that prepared for the newspapers accounts of the terrible battle-scenes of the war. One who knows the subject of our sketch intimately describes him as "a noble man every way,—large in body and heart, liberal to a fault, the truest of friends, and a man of such strong will that he would die for his convictions on any point."

The honorary degree of D.D. was conferred upon him in 1874 by the Washington and Lee University, Virginia.

Jones, Rev. Miller, A.M., was born July 3, 1830, in Hilltown Township, Bucks Co., Pa. His father, John M. Jones, died Nov. 30, 1839; his mother, Mary Hines Jones, is still living, in her seventy-sixth year. Both parents were baptized at an early age by Rev. Joseph Matthias. The subject of this sketch was baptized by Rev. Joseph H. Kennard, D.D., in April, 1846. He was subsequently licensed by the Tenth Baptist church, Philadelphia, to preach the gospel; graduated from the university at Lewisburg in 1856, and from the theological department in 1858; ordained as a Baptist minister a few weeks afterwards by a council convened by the Marcus Hook Baptist church, Pa.

He continued pastor of this church for three years and three months, and was greatly prospered. His second pastorate was over the Bridgeport Baptist church, Montgomery Co., Pa., and continued with most encouraging results for more than two years. The third settlement was with the Moorestown, N. J., Baptist church, which continued for four years. Here a most delightful and extensive revival was enjoyed. His fourth pastorate was with the Marlton, N. J., Baptist church, which continued, with many tokens of divine favor, for three years. His fifth charge was the Second Baptist church of Reading, Pa. Here a large number of conversions occurred, and much prosperity was enjoyed, but a call coming from the Bridgeport Baptist church to assume a second time the pastoral charge, his sixth settlement was with this beloved church. Here a steady and solid growth of the church was enjoyed during the eight years of a very happy pastorate. Jan. 1, 1880, he entered upon the pastorate at Village Green, Pa. A Baptist church has since been organized and recognized. A baptistery, with additional rooms for the convenience of the candidates, is now being constructed, and the whole property is being put in the best repair through the liberality of Mrs. J. P. Crozer. The prospects for growth are encouraging. About 300 persons have been baptized during his ministry.

Jones, Nathan Levering, A.M., of Roxborough, Philadelphia, Pa., was born Aug. 3, 1816, and was a son of Rev. Horatio Gates Jones, D.D. He received his early education at the Roxborough Academy, and also at Haddington College, and was one of its first students. Before graduating he entered into business, and located at Roxborough, in the lumber trade, which he continued to pursue during the remainder of his life. When quite young he joined the Lower Merion Baptist church, of which his father was pastor, and he was a constituent member of the Balligomingo church. His membership was finally removed to Merion, of which church he was a deacon at the time of his death. Mr. Jones was highly esteemed, and was elected to many offices of trust and honor. He was a director and also controller of the public schools of Philadelphia, a director of the Bank of Germantown, and of the Germantown Mutual Insurance Company. For over twenty years he was president of the Roxborough Lyceum. His death, which was sudden, occurred on Saturday evening, April 19, 1879. As a husband and father he was loving and affectionate, as a neighbor he was most highly esteemed, as a citizen he was honored, and as a Christian he was devoted. His memory is highly cherished in the community where he had so long lived. Mr. Jones for several years was active in the temperance work, and as a public man exerted a great influence in that direction among his associates. He was also largely interested in the cause of education, especially of ministerial, and was a manager of the Pennsylvania Baptist Education Society. In their obituary report for 1879, the committee, speaking of Mr. Jones, say, " He was a man of considerable prominence in the community where he was born and lived. He filled many positions of public trust with a fidelity which commanded confidence and inspired respect. His memory is blessed both in the church and in society, for he was a staunch Christian and a true and noble man." The honorary degree of Master of Arts was conferred upon him by the University at Lewisburg.

Jones, Rev. Philip L., was born in England in 1838; was baptized at East Clarence, N. Y., in 1854; was educated at the University of Rochester and at Rochester Theological Seminary, graduating from the latter institution in 1868; ordained the same year at Dunkirk, N. Y. In 1870 he was called to the pastorate of the South Broad Street church, Philadelphia, then a mission of the First church. He still continues to labor in this field, which has quietly and steadily grown under his efficient and faithful ministry. He is a member of the board of managers of the Pennsylvania Baptist Education Society, and was for several years the secretary of the Philadelphia Conference of Baptist ministers. He is a man of gentle and winning manners; and his sermons and writings are clear, forceful, and poetic.

Jones, Rev. Robert B.—The Baptists of North Carolina have produced no more remarkable man than Robert B. Jones. He was born in Person Co., N. C.; baptized into the fellowship of the Mill Creek church; went as a soldier to Mexico, to get rid of the duty of preaching; fought bravely till the army reached the city of Mexico, when he was pronounced an incurable consumptive, and told by the surgeons that he would never again see North Carolina. On his way to Vera Cruz, expecting to die, he promised the Lord that if he would allow him to reach North Carolina again he would preach as much as he wished. From this time he began to improve; he entered Wake Forest College in 1854, but after studying a year or two was obliged to leave on account of ill health. He went up on the Catawba River and did good service for the Master, and in 1858 returned to college, and graduated in 1861. He was pastor of Hartford church for several years, became agent of his *alma mater* in 1866–67, and died at the college in December, 1867.

Jones, Samuel, D.D., was born Jan. 14, 1735, in Glamorganshire, Wales, and was brought to this country two years afterwards by his parents. He received his education at the College of Philadelphia, and graduated in 1762; and in the begin-

ning of the next year he was ordained to the ministry of the gospel. In 1763 he became pastor of the Lower Dublin Baptist church, and he held that office until his death, which occurred Feb. 7, 1814.

SAMUEL JONES, D.D.

Dr. Jones, if not superior in scholarly attainments to every other American Baptist of his day, was equaled by few, and surpassed by none. His wisdom in managing difficult matters was as striking as his learning was remarkable. At an early period of his life he became the most influential Baptist minister in the middle colonies, and probably in the whole country. Dr. Jones, when a young man, was sent by the Philadelphia Association to Rhode Island, to assist in founding Rhode Island College. At Newport he remodeled the rough draft of the college charter, which soon after obtained the sanction of the Legislature of Rhode Island. He prepared a new treatise of discipline for the Philadelphia Confession of Faith by request of the Association in 1798. Dr. Jones, Rev. David Jones, and Dr. Burgiss Allison compiled a selection of hymns for the use of the churches. In 1807 he preached the centenary sermon of the Philadelphia Association, which was published with the volume of " Minutes for One Hundred Years," by the Baptist Publication Society. His name occurs continually in the minutes of the Association for half a century, as moderator, preacher, committeeman, or writer of the circular letter. " Dr. Jones was a ready writer and a fluent speaker; he was a large and firmly-built man, six feet or more in height, and in every way well-proportioned. His face was the very image of intelligence and good nature, which, with the air of dignity that pervaded his movements, rendered his appearance uncommonly attractive."

He educated many young men for the Christian ministry, some of whom attained distinction for their talents, learning, and usefulness.

On the death of Dr. Manning, Dr. Jones received a letter from Judge David Howell informally offering him the presidency of Rhode Island College. Secretary Howell informed him that "the eyes of the corporation (of the college) seemed to be fixed on him for a successor to Dr. Manning."

This great and good man was largely blessed in his ministry; and he exerted a vast and useful influence over the rising Baptist churches of our country.

Jones, Rev. Thomas Z. R., was born in the parsonage of the Great Valley church, Pa., July 23, 1803, and died in Kalamazoo, Mich., July 2, 1876. His father was Rev. Richard Jones, a native of Wales. In 1835, Brother Jones came to Michigan Territory to take up his work. Years before he had selected that as his field of labor. He took the right wing of the little army of invasion that was strung along the rivers St. Clair, Detroit, Raisin, and Maumee. Up and down the St. Clair and back into the woods wherever a settler had pushed, he preached in the wilderness and sought the sheep. There he nursed his sick, and buried the members of his young family, and saw the salvation of God. The China church, as then called, was a visible result, and much seed for other harvests was sown. The missionary spirit thrusting him on, he reached the spiritual solitude between Jackson and Kalamazoo, and struck in on its eastern edge. Spring Arbor, Concord, Albion, Marengo, and Marshall in turn responded to his work, and he saw the churches in them planted and acquiring growth, and watered by gracious revivals. Then he struck through to Grand Rapids, and was one of the first and best master-builders on the Baptist foundation there. He went to Kalamazoo, from which he has gone to and fro in his agency services, with occasional short pastorates so mixed in as not to break up his home, where so many youth of the schools have been succored, and where he still lives. All older Michigan is a road where his wheels have made and worn marks as he sought supplies for domestic mission and educational works; also for our societies for evangelization, foreign as well as home.

His sympathies were broad as human want, his contributions from the smallest of incomes—with which he always seemed contented—were constant and liberal, his business habits painstaking and just, and his heart sincere. He gave forty-one years of good and faithful work to Michigan.

Jones, T. G., D.D., is a native of Virginia, and like many other Virginians, not a little proud of his State. His father, Wood Jones, of Nottoway, was a relative of U. S. Senator Jones, and of John

T. G. JONES, D.D.

Winston Jones, Speaker of the House of Representatives; and his mother, Elizabeth Trent Archer, of Powhatan, of U. S. Senator Wm. S. Archer, and of Branch T. Archer, who figured conspicuously in the earlier councils of Texas. He was early doubly orphaned, his mother dying when he was about three years old, and his father a few months later. In his boyhood he was with one of his brothers, who afterwards graduated at the University of Virginia and became a lawyer of distinction. When about eighteen years of age he entered the Virginia Baptist Seminary, now Richmond College. After being there some time he decided to devote himself to the ministry, and was licensed by the Second Baptist church of Richmond, whose pastor, the late revered James B. Taylor, had a few years before baptized him. Leaving that institution, he entered the University of Virginia, from which, after a two years' course, he went to William and Mary College, where he graduated. Immediately after taking his degree he went to Alabama, and for a year or two taught a few hours daily in a private family, devoting the rest of his time to theological study and occasional preaching. Returning to Virginia, he preached for a few months in Clarksville, on the North Carolina border; when, although not yet ordained to the full work of the ministry, he was elected the first pastor of the Freemason Street church of Norfolk, with which, though often invited to more prominent positions in the larger cities, he continued until the late war, when he was compelled to leave. He found an asylum in Baltimore as pastor of the Franklin Square church. When the war closed he was recalled to Norfolk, where he remained until he was elected to the presidency of Richmond College. Continuing at the head of that institution for several years, he was again recalled to his old charge at Norfolk. About ten years ago, having been elected pastor of the First Baptist church of Nashville, he removed to that city, where he still resides. Dr. Jones has been honored by the colleges. At the University of Virginia he was the valedictory orator of his society, and received the same honor upon his graduation at William and Mary College. While pastor of the church at Norfolk he was elected president of Wake Forest College, North Carolina, and a few years later, president of Mercer University, Ga. Both these appointments, however, he felt constrained to refuse from his reluctance to leave his first beloved and loving charge. Richmond College conferred upon him the degree of D.D., and, as already stated, called him a few years later to its presidency. Closely engaged in preaching and other pastoral work, he has not written much. Still, his pen has not been idle altogether. Besides a number of published addresses before literary and other bodies, unpublished lectures, and papers in various periodicals, he has written three small books, the first a prize essay, on "The Duties of Pastors to Churches," which was published in Charleston by the Southern Baptist Publication Society ; the second on the "Origin and Continuity of the Baptist Churches," published by the American Baptist Publication Society ; and the third entitled "The Great Misnomer, or the Lord's Supper, miscalled the Communion." These have met with a ready sale, and are highly commended. Dr. Jones is regarded as one of the finest pulpit orators of the nation, and highly esteemed by his charge in Nashville.

He has been for several sessions one of the vice-presidents of the Southern Baptist Convention, and is now first vice-president of the board of trustees of the Southern Baptist Seminary. He is possessed of rare dignity of manners, fine scholarship, and a blessed record.

Jones, Washington (son of William G. Jones), was born in Wilmington, Del., Jan. 5, 1818 ; commenced business for himself in his native place in November, 1839 ; was a director of what is now the National Bank of Wilmington and Brandywine for thirty years, of which he was elected president in 1868, which position he still holds. He is a manager of the Saving Fund, a prosperous institution, whose object is to help the poor to save their earnings ; was prime mover in the introduction of gas into the city in 1850, and has been a director of the gas company since its formation.

WASHINGTON JONES.

The emperor Dom Pedro, of Brazil, when in this country in 1876, visited the factory of Mr. Jones, by whom he was shown through the establishment and the various processes explained to him. He seemed much pleased with the operations and took extensive notes.

Mr. Jones was converted in 1841, and baptized into the fellowship of the Second Baptist church on the 2d of January in that year ; was elected a trustee of the church July 9 of the same year, and president of the board April 26, 1860, which office he held until 1876, when he resigned ; was elected a deacon in June, 1853, which office he still holds ; was treasurer of the church for seventeen years, and superintendent of the Sabbath-school fifteen years.

In 1852 the church resolved to rebuild in a new location, and Mr. Jones was made chairman of the building committee, and took an active part in erecting their present handsome and commodious house of worship, both by his own large contributions and zealous efforts in collecting funds from others. Besides, he gave much time and personal attention to the erection of the edifice, and when it was completed gave his individual note for part of the debt remaining upon it.

Mr. Jones is the largest contributor to the funds of the church of which he is a member, besides giving for missions and other benevolent objects at home and abroad. He has the respect of the whole community and the love of his brethren. A man of piety, he is active in church work, prompt and faithful in the discharge of his Christian duties, and speaks and prays with great acceptance in the public meetings of the church and of the denomination.

Jones, Rev. William, was born in the county of Denbigh, in Wales, June 17, 1762. When young he removed to Poulton, in Cheshire, where he received a classical education. In October, 1786, he was baptized by the Rev. Archibald McLean, of Edinburgh, then on a visit to Chester, in the river Dee.

In 1793 he established himself in Liverpool as a wholesale bookseller and publisher. In that city he began to hold meetings in his own spacious drawing-room, at first for his own family, for prayer, praise, reading the Scriptures, exhortation, and exposition. These assemblies were speedily frequented by neighbors and others, and soon they were transferred to a chapel, when a church was formed, and Mr. D. S. Wylie and Mr. Jones were appointed pastors.

Mr. Jones left Liverpool for London, and in 1812, soon after he went to the metropolis, he began his "History of the Waldenses and Albigenses."

In 1815 he started the *New Evangelical Magazine,* in London; this periodical, subsequently called the *New Baptist Magazine,* was conducted by Mr. Jones with great success for eleven years.

He spent three years in preparing a " Dictionary of the Sacred Writings," the first edition of which, consisting of 2000 copies, was quickly sold. His Church History, of which his " History of the Waldenses and Albigenses" is not quite a half, is a work highly creditable to the research and candor of its author and worthy of a conspicuous place in every Baptist library.

Mr. Jones was the author of biographies of Rowland Hill, Edward Irving, Adam Clark, and of several other works.

He was a writer of great industry and conscientiousness; and in the latter part of his life his works were very popular among Baptists.

In 1843, when his means were very limited, the queen offered him a place in the Charterhouse, where all his wants would be cared for during the rest of his life; but, as the acceptance of it required him to become an Episcopalian, he declined the royal offer. The queen on learning the fact ordered £60 to be paid Mr. Jones in three annual installments. He died in January, 1846.

Jones, Rev. William, was born in Wake Co., N. C., about 1800; was graduated at Wake Forest in 1839, and for many years was the agent of the

State Convention. He was a good and useful man.

Jones, William G., was born in Wilmington, Del., Sept. 3, 1784; was baptized April 3, 1803, upon profession of his faith, in the Brandywine, by Rev. Daniel Dodge, pastor of the First Baptist church. He was the first person baptized in Wilmington by Mr. Dodge, who afterwards became pastor of the Second Baptist church, Philadelphia.

About 1812 he, with others, united in the organization of another church, which disbanded after an existence of two years. He then united with the Marcus Hook church, and was at once elected deacon. For years he walked to and from "the Hook," a distance of twenty miles, to attend the services on the Sabbath.

In 1843, when Rev. Morgan J. Rhees became pastor of the Second church, Wilmington, Mr. Jones united with that body, by which he was chosen a deacon. He retained his membership and office until his death, Jan. 26, 1873. He died in the house in which he was born, and in which he lived nearly all his life.

Mr. Jones was to a large extent identified with the Baptist history of Delaware and Southeastern Pennsylvania. His house was a home for ministers, and among the many eminent men who enjoyed its hospitalities were John Leland, Dr. Staughton, Luther Rice, and Dr. J. L. Dagg.

His fidelity to truth was unswerving, and his business integrity unquestionable. He was urbane even in old age, and his conversation highly entertaining and instructive to the young. His Christian character was of the positive type, and the conversion of most of his children, and of many of his grandchildren, bears testimony to his domestic piety. By industry and economy he acquired the pecuniary means which he used to support and advance the cause of Christ, to which he also devoted his time, energies, and prayers.

Jones, Wm. P., M.D., of Nashville, Tenn., was born in Adair Co., Ky., Oct. 17, 1819. At the age of twenty he entered the Louisville Medical Institute, and subsequently received a diploma from the Medical College of Ohio and the Memphis Medical College. He first established himself in the practice of his profession at Edmonton, Ky., afterwards removing to Bowling Green, and finally to Nashville, Tenn.

Dr. Jones is a member of the American Medical Association, Association of American Superintendents of Hospitals for the Insane, American Association for the Advancement of Science, Tennessee State Medical Society, and the Medical Society of Davidson County. He was one of the editors of the *Southern Journal of the Medical and Physical Sciences* in 1853, and for several years thereafter; he established and edited the *Parlor*

Visitor in 1852, and in 1874 became associate editor of the *Tennessee School Journal.*

In 1858 he, with others, founded the Shelby Medical College, in which he was Professor of Materia Medica.

Academy Hospital, the first established in Nashville after the arrival of the Union forces, was

WILLIAM P. JONES, M.D.

under his charge. In 1862 he was elected superintendent of the Tennessee Hospital for the Insane. Through his persistent and earnest appeals to the State Legislature the funds were provided for, and Dr. Jones had the pleasure of erecting a separate and suitable building for the insane colored people, the first institution of the kind in America.

The affairs of the State institution were administered fairly and impartially, and Dr. Jones was unanimously re-elected for a period of eight years.

In 1876 he was elected president of Nashville Medical College.

The people have frequently demanded his public services, and he has rendered them with great distinction as president of Nashville city council and as State senator from Nashville. While acting in the last capacity he was made chairman of the school committee, and introduced the present public school law of Tennessee, which provides equal educational advantages for all the children of the State without regard to race, color, or previous condition.

Dr. Jones has been a member of the Baptist church since 1836, and he is now president of the Tennessee Baptist State Convention, and an honor to the Baptists in Tennessee.

Jordan, Rev. F. M., was born in Montgomery Co., N. C., June 4, 1830; was baptized by Rev. Eli Phillips in 1843; went to Wake Forest College in 1850, and was ordained in 1853. He has labored as pastor in Orange, Caswell, Person, and Davidson Counties.

For the last six years Mr. Jordan has given himself to the work of an evangelist; 1900 persons have professed faith in Christ under his preaching. He has been a laborious and useful minister of the gospel. He has one son in the ministry, W. T. Jordan, pastor at Lumberton.

Jordan, Hon. O'Bryan, was an active member of the Concord Association formed in 1823 at Mount Nebo church, in Cooper Co., Mo. He was appointed clerk of the Association at its organization. He was a member of the Mount Nebo church, and in 1824 he read a circular letter before it which he had prepared upon the Scriptural argument for the support of the ministry. The reasons were clear and convincing. He was a layman of remarkable devotion and purity of life. He was for years a member of the Legislature from Cooper County, and he came out unstained by the corruptions of politics.

Jordan, The.—From יָרַד, "yarad," to descend; "the river of God;" probably referred to in Ps. lxv. 9; the "Descender," now known among the Arabs as "esh Sheriâh," the watering-place. Three main sources of the river have been indicated: one at Tell-el-Kâdi, the site of the ancient Dan of the Israelites, where from the base of an oblong mound about eighty feet above the plain the water gushes out in rivulets numerous enough to form a considerable stream; another, a little northeast of this point, at Banias, the ancient Cæsarea Philippi, where the stream can be traced to a cave,—itself the outlet of a more remote *fons*,—whence it flows by a subterranean course, and reappears a considerable stream a short distance from the grotto. The third leading source of the river may be found, according to Lieut. Lynch, U.S.N., a short distance above the town of Hâsbeiyêh, where two copious streams burst from the base of a precipitous wall of rock, the immediate source of the river Hâsbeiyêh, which Lieut. Lynch regards, however, as the *true* Jordan, rather than as a tributary only.

From Tell-el-Kâdi the river flows for a few miles down the fertile valley, till it expands into Lake Hûlêh, "the waters of Merom" of Scripture, and about nine miles below this pours itself into the "Sea of Galilee." It emerges from the lake at its southern end, and finally buries itself in the Dead Sea. Lieut. Lynch, who gives us the natural history of the river and the region through which it passes, speaks of it at one stage of its course as describing "a series of frantic curvilinears, and returning in a contrary direction to its main course." Between the Lake of Tiberias and the Dead Sea, distant in latitude only about 60 miles, the river describes a course of fully 200 miles, through a valley averaging but 4 or 5 miles in width. The same authority represents it, in this part of its course, as ranging from 3 to 12 feet in depth, and in width from 25 to 180 yards, where it pours into the Dead Sea.

As "the Jordan" or "Descender," the river is most appropriately named. From the Lake of Tiberias to its final outlet in the Dead Sea its descent is over 1000 feet in the short distance of 60 miles. As a consequence, the American explorers encountered during the passage of the river between these points no less than twenty-seven threatening rapids, many others of lesser note, and numerous cascades and waterfalls. By its annual inundations the river appears to have burrowed out a channel above the one it ordinarily pursues, so that for a considerable part of its course there are plain indications of terraced or double banks. For some distance below the Lake of Tiberias, Lieut. Lynch found a luxuriant vegetation along its borders, while in patches here and there the valley bore traces of careful cultivation. But the lower Ghor, until the stream was lost in the Salt Sea, presented a picture of dreary sterility, and almost savage desolation. Tracks of the tiger and boar were clearly discerned, where the banks of the river were low enough to furnish a thicket for their lair. Numerous small islands, a number of tributaries, and the remains of several bridges of Roman and Saracenic architecture were passed in the descent of the river. But little need be said of the fords. There does not appear to have been at any time more than three or four places where the river could be safely forded when swollen after the winter rains. But two fords of any importance are indicated by explorers,—one at a point now known as Sûkwâ, in line with the road from Nâblûs to Es-Sâlt; the other, about five miles from the mouth of the river, and over against Jericho, now designated "El-Meshra," the Pilgrim's Bathing-Place. Boats may have been anciently used in crossing the river, but as an appliance now in going from bank to bank they are unknown. The course of the stream at times is between high banks of rock or alluvium; at other points, on one or both sides, they recede from the river, and in such cases are covered with thicket or jungle.

It is not necessary to dwell at length on the circumstances and incidents that lend such a peculiar and sacred interest to this river, or even to enumerate all of them. The Jordan was the eastern boundary of the Promised Land. Josh. i. 11. Abraham sojourned at a point where the fertile valley through which the river coursed could be seen. Gen. xiii. 3. Jacob, when he went into his long

exile, crossed it with his staff alone, and recrossed it when he returned as two bands. Gen. xxxii. 10. His descendants, as they terminated their long wilderness pilgrimage, passed dry-shod through its waters. Josh. iv. 10. Elijah and Elisha successively smote it with their mantles, and it divided for their passage. 2 Kings ii. 8 and 14. Naaman dipped in it and was cleansed of his leprosy. 2 Kings v. 14. And last of all it was the stream where not only "all Judea and Jerusalem" were baptized by John (Matt. iii. 5, 6), but the Lord himself. v. 16. Here the interest of the sacred river fitly culminates. Enon, near to Salem (John iii. 23), where the Baptist in his later ministry baptized, cannot now with absolute certainty be identified. It appears, however, most probably to have been situated at a point a few miles below the ancient Bethshean, now Beisân, near or at one of the fords of the river, and where, either from the depth or quantity of water, or the nature of its banks, there were the desired facilities for the administration of baptism. Whatever the uncertainty, however, attending the site of Enon, manifold and unbroken tradition points to the ford nearly opposite Jericho, and about five miles from the Dead Sea, as the place hallowed by the baptism of the Messiah. Above and below this locality, now known, as intimated, as "the Pilgrim's Bathing-Place," the river flows through alluvial banks of considerable height, but at this point the western line of the stream forms a cove, where the strand and a convenient depth for immersion or bathing is at once reached by a gradual and easy descent. In the narrative of his expedition, Lieut. Lynch, who was an eye-witness, describes the annual ceremony of the baptism of the pilgrims. On this occasion, from 5000 to 8000 of them having come down from Jerusalem, plunged tumultuously into the stream, immersing themselves and each other three times, in the name of the Trinity. At this point he describes the river as 120 feet wide and 12 feet deep, the current dangerously swift, as the writer of this article himself discovered when bathing in the river but a few feet from the banks. Tradition locates the ancient Bethabara, "the House of the Ford or Passage," at a point near the eastern bank of the river, and opposite the Pilgrim's Bathing-Place.

Jordan, Rev. William Hull, was born in Bertie Co., N. C., Aug. 15, 1803. His mother afterwards married the Rev. Mr. Poindexter, and by him became the mother of Dr. A. M. Poindexter, and to the piety and force of character of this good woman, who consecrated her sons to God's service at their birth, is our Southern Zion indebted for two of the ablest and most eloquent ministers who have distinguished her annals. Mr. Jordan was educated at Chapel Hill, professed a hope in Christ on the 9th of December, 1823, preached his first sermon on the 25th of December of the same year, and was baptized by Rev. Reuben Lawrence, Jan. 25, 1824. It will thus be seen that Mr. Jordan was induced by the pressure of his brethren to preach before he was baptized. This has always been a source of sincere sorrow to him, but it may be doubted whether it should be, since it is said a great revival began from his preaching, spreading over several counties, and resulting in the conversion of 2000 souls. Besides serving a number of churches in the country, Mr. Jordan has been pastor of churches in Raleigh, Wilmington, Lilesville, and Wadesborough, N. C., Clarksville and Petersburg, Va., Norristown, Pa., and Sumter, S. C. He was for a long time the corresponding secretary of the Baptist State Convention; was twice agent for Wake Forest College, giving his time and money for its release from financial distress, and has worked faithfully for its prosperity as a trustee. Mr. Jordan calls himself a high-church Baptist, and has spent no small part of his life in vindicating by voice and pen Baptist and Calvinistic principles. He is a very devout man and a singularly eloquent preacher.

Joslyn, Rev. Adoniram Judson, during many years a denominational leader in Illinois, and one of the most effective preachers in the State, was born Oct. 5, 1819. He was baptized at the age of fourteen years, uniting with the Baptist church in Nunda, N. Y., where his early life had been spent. He removed to Illinois in 1838, settling at Crystal Lake, in the northern part of the State, where his first occupation was that of a farmer. Drawn to the ministry by his ardent love for the cause of Christ, he had a partial course of study with a neighboring pastor. His first pastorate was at Warrensville, where he was ordained in 1842. After two years he removed to Elgin, where he remained eleven years. In 1855 he accepted an agency for Shurtleff College, and in that form of labor, as well as in efforts of a like kind in behalf of the University of Chicago, he rendered important service in the cause of education. In November, 1856, he organized the Union Park church in Chicago, and became its first pastor, remaining in that relation three years. His health having become impaired, he returned to his old home in Elgin, and purchasing the *Gazette* in that city, entered upon journalism, holding at the same time the office of postmaster of the town; in the mean time preaching for destitute churches as his state of health would allow. The disease which had begun its inroads continued to make progress in spite of all efforts to check it. He lingered, however, until Oct. 9, 1868, when his labors and sufferings ended in rest. Mr. Joslyn was an ardent friend of reform, an outspoken temperance man, always bold, direct, and effective in his advocacy of whatever cause enlisted his zeal.

In his relations with his brethren he was an acknowledged leader, with marked executive ability and rare powers of public speech.

Journal and Messenger.—The first number of a paper called the *Baptist Weekly Journal of the Mississippi Valley* was issued at Cincinnati, O., July 22, 1831. John Stevens, D.D., was the editor, and Noble S. Johnson publisher. It was a folio, 20 by 13 inches to the page, and the subscription price was $2.00 in advance or $3.00 at the end of the year. It had in three years a subscription list of 1300. In 1834 the *Cross*, the Baptist paper of Kentucky, was united with it, and it became *The Cross and Baptist Journal of the Mississippi Valley.* At the end of seven years it was removed to Columbus, and Rev. George Cole, D. A. Randall, D.D., and James Batchelder became the editors and publishers, the name being changed to *The Cross and Journal.* This name was subsequently still further changed to the *Western Christian Journal.* In 1850 *The Christian Messenger,* of Indiana, having been united with it, it was removed again to Cincinnati, and called the *Journal and Messenger,* Rev. E. D. Owen and J. L. Batchelder being the editors and publishers. In December, 1856, a stock company was formed called the Central Baptist Press Company, which bought out the interest of the former publishers, and Rev. George Cole again became editor, continuing in that capacity until 1865, when Rev. T. J. Melish succeeded him. In 1867 the form was changed from folio to quarto. In 1872, Rev. J. R. Baumes, D.D., became the editor, with Rev. W. N. Wyeth as associate editor. In 1876, having purchased all the stock and the entire interest of the paper, Rev. G. W. Lasher, D.D., became editor and proprietor, and so continues until the present time. The present form of the paper is a large quarto, 47 by 35 inches. In its circulation it ranks fourth among the Baptist papers of this country. It is devoted to the advocacy of Baptist principles, and is very enterprising in gathering denominational news.

Judd, Rev. J. T., a native of Canada, was born in Toronto Nov. 29, 1851, and became a graduate of Columbian University, D. C., in 1872, and of Crozer Theological Seminary in its full course in 1875. He was ordained at the call of the Harrisburg church Sept. 2, 1875. In this church he has remained ever since, and has succeeded where many others have failed. The church has become, after many years of painful struggling, a self-supporting body. Better still, it has developed the Christian grace of benevolence to a remarkable degree.

Judson, Adoniram, D.D., the eldest son of Adoniram and Abigail Judson, was born in Malden, Mass., Aug. 9, 1788. In the sixteenth year of his age, being sufficiently advanced in his studies, he entered the Sophomore class in Brown University, becoming a member of the institution on the 17th of August, 1804. He graduated in 1807 with the highest honors of his class. At the time of leaving college he was inclined to be skeptical in his religious opinions. The sudden death of a classmate, under circumstances of peculiar interest, was the means of arresting his thoughts and putting him upon a course of serious examination of the claims of religion to his personal attention. For the purpose of pursuing his inquiries, he was admitted as a "special student" into the Andover Theological Institution. He soon became a hopeful Christian, and was received into the fellowship of the Third Congregational church in Plymouth, Mass., of which his father was the pastor, on the

ADONIRAM JUDSON, D.D.

28th of May, 1809. Regarding himself now as not his own but the Lord's, he began to seek for light upon the pathway of his future career. The result of his prayerful deliberation was the determination reached, in February, 1810, to consecrate himself to the work of foreign missions. In the seminary he found other young men of kindred spirit, who joined with him in urging upon the Christian churches the claims of the heathen. The zeal and earnestness of these students gave power to the spirit of missions, which had already been aroused in the hearts of Christians. That honored society, the American Board of Commissioners for Foreign Missions, was formed June 28, 1810. Mr. Judson had been licensed on the 17th of May previous by the Orange Association of Congregationalist ministers, in Vermont. September 24 of this year he

graduated at Andover. Soon after his graduation he was sent to England by the American Board to confer with the London Missionary Society on the matter of combining the efforts of the two societies in the work of carrying the gospel to the heathen. He embarked Jan. 1, 1811, in the ship "Packet." The vessel had not been long at sea when she was captured by the French privateer "L'Invincible Napoleon," and carried to Bayonne in France, where he was immured in a dismal dungeon. From his short confinement he was soon released, and, after various adventures, he reached England, presented his credentials, and was cordially received by the Christian friends to whom he had been commended. He and his fellow-students, Newell, Nott, and Hall, were appointed by the London Missionary Society as missionaries in India, with the expectation that their pecuniary support would be provided for by the friends of missions in America. The object for which he was sent to England having been accomplished, Mr. Judson returned to this country. The board, after mature deliberation, came to the conclusion that the wiser course to pursue was to enter upon the work of missions independently of any other organization, and they accepted as their missionaries the four young men, and pledged themselves to see that they were supported in the undertaking upon which they had embarked. Mr. Judson, with his wife, Ann Hasseltine Judson, and Messrs. Nott, Newell, Hall, and Rice, sailed Feb. 19, 1812, from Salem, Mass., and reached Calcutta the 17th of the following June. During the voyage Mr. Judson's views on the mode and subjects of baptism underwent a change, and, on reaching Serampore, he was baptized by Rev. William Ward, Sept. 6, 1812. This event severed his connection from the American Board of Commissioners for Foreign Missions, and led to the formation of the Baptist Triennial Convention, on the 18th of May, 1814, under whose patronage Mr. Judson and his Baptist associates were taken. After experiencing months of hardship, on account of the hostility of the East India Company, who opposed the establishment of his mission in India, Mr. Judson decided to commence his work among the Burmese. On the 14th of July, 1813, he reached Rangoon, and began at once the study of the language. It was a formidable task, and taxed all his powers to accomplish it. At nearly the end of his five years' residence in Rangoon a zayat was built, and opened with appropriate religious services, and Mr. Judson made this place his religious headquarters. Inquirers began to visit him, and he had the satisfaction of baptizing the first convert to the Christian faith, Moung Nau, on the 27th of June, 1819. No sooner, however, did there appear some signs of success than a spirit of opposition began to be awakened, and Mr. Judson had reason to fear that his work would be stopped by the arm of the civil power. With the hope of securing toleration, he went to Ava with Mr. Colman, and sought permission to preach the new faith in Burmah. But the king would not grant the request, and they returned to Rangoon, and continued the prosecution of their mission work regardless of the opposition which had been awakened. Mr. Judson devoted himself especially to the translation of the Scriptures and the preparation of religious tracts, to be circulated among the people.

We have now reached one of the most interesting periods of the life of Dr. Judson. Dr. Price, who had arrived at Rangoon in December, 1821, was summoned to the court of the king, in his capacity as a physician, and it was necessary that Mr. Judson should accompany him. His reception was favorable, and he had more than one opportunity to proclaim the gospel to the members of the royal family. The prospect for usefulness seemed so bright that he returned to Rangoon for Mrs. Judson, bringing her back to Ava, and began his missionary work, encouraged by the hope of greater success in his labors. But this hope was destined soon to meet with utter disappointment. War broke out between England and Burmah. Rangoon fell into the hands of the British on the 23d of May, 1824, and the tidings of its capture reached the capital two weeks after. The jealous Burman officers, regarding Dr. Price and Mr. Judson as spies, caused them to be arrested and thrown into a loathsome jail. where, for nine months, they were kept in the closest and most barbarous confinement. They were then sent to a wretched place called Oung-pen-la, where they were ordered to be put to death. The sentence, however, was not carried into execution. With the continued success of the English arms, the fears of the king and his court became so aroused that negotiations were entered into, in which Mr. Judson took a prominent part, and, as one of the results, he obtained his freedom. As soon as practicable he left Ava, and once more returned to Rangoon, and soon removed with his family to Amherst, designed henceforth to be the capital of British Burmah. For several months his was occupied with the English commissioner, Mr. Crawford, at Ava, in negotiating with the Burman government a commercial treaty. During his absence Mrs. Judson died at Amherst, Oct. 24, 1826. Dr. Judson removed to Maulmain Nov. 14, 1827, and entered once more upon his missionary work, which he carried on in Maulmain, Prome, Rangoon, and other localities, and he became especially interested in the conversion of the Karens. On April 10, 1834, he married Mrs. Sarah Boardman.

For many years Dr. Judson devoted a part of his time to the translation of the Scriptures into the Burmese language, and the compilation of a Burmese dictionary. On the last day of January, 1834, the closing page of the now wholly translated Bible was written by Dr. Judson. Many years were given to the careful revision of this work. In its completed state it is pronounced by competent judges to be nearly perfect. For several years Dr. Judson kept up his missionary labors, the blessing of God accompanying him in his toil. The failing health of Mrs. Judson forced him, in 1845, to leave Burmah for America. She died at St. Helena, where she was buried. Dr. Judson continued his voyage, and reached Boston in the month of October. During his stay in this country he was everywhere the recipient of the kindest attentions, and when, after a few months of residence in this country, he returned to his Oriental home, with the third wife, who was to share his fortunes, the prayers of thousands of Christian hearts followed him. " It was no sectarian adulation offered to a distinguished name, but rather the natural homage which Christian civilization pays to the cause of Christian philanthropy,—the instinctive admiration of an intelligent and religious people for the character of one who has proved himself a great benefactor of mankind." After this visit of Dr. Judson to his native land a few more years were allotted to him to render service to the cause to which he had given so large a part of his life. He hoped to live long enough to complete the Burmese dictionary, and was busily engaged in its preparation when he was attacked by the fever of the country, which completely prostrated him. A sea-voyage was recommended. The vessel sailed April 8, and four days after he died, and his body was committed to the deep.

Judson, Mrs. Ann Hasseltine, the first wife of Dr. Judson, was born in Bradford, Mass., Dec. 22, 1789. She received her early education at the academy in her native place. Her conversion took place when she was not far from seventeen years of age. The interest which she exhibited for religious reading of the most elevated character was remarkable in a person comparatively so young. She became a member of the Congregational church in Bradford Sept. 14, 1806. With a desire to be useful and to secure the means of an independent support, she engaged for several years, at intervals, in teaching. At the meeting of the Massachusetts Congregational Association at Bradford in June, 1810, Mr. Judson met his future wife. His persuasive words induced her to consent to share the fortunes of his missionary life, as well as to be the first American woman who " resolved to leave her friends and country to bear the gospel to the heathen in foreign climes." She was married to Mr. Judson Feb. 5, 1812. On the outward voyage to Calcutta she changed—as did her husband—her views on the mode and subjects of baptism, and was baptized with her husband by Rev. Mr. Ward. The missionary life of Mrs. Judson is so intertwined with that of Dr. Judson that the record of the latter contains all that needs to be said in that of the former. With the same fidelity and patience which characterized her husband, she applied herself to learning the language, and at the close of 1815 she states that she can both read and write it with a good degree of ease. She was the efficient helper of Dr. Judson for several years, when she was compelled by her failing health to return to her native land. On the 21st of August, 1821, she embarked for Bengal, and on reaching Calcutta took passage for England. The kindest attention was shown to

MRS. ANN HASSELTINE JUDSON.

her both in England and Scotland. She embarked on board the ship "Amity" at Liverpool, Aug. 16, 1822, and arrived at New York the 25th of the September following, and after a brief visit in Philadelphia she hastened to her old home in Bradford. The severity of a Northern climate to one who had lived so many years in the East was more than her enfeebled constitution could endure, and she was forced to make her winter home in Baltimore with her brother-in-law, Dr. Elnathan Judson. Here she rapidly improved in health, and was able to write an interesting account of the Burman mission. A few weeks of the following spring she spent among Christian friends in Washington, and then returned to Massachusetts. On the 21st of June, 1823, she embarked on her return voyage to Calcutta, having as her companions Rev. Jonathan

Wade and his wife, and arrived at Rangoon on the 5th of the following December.

The narrative of the fortunes of Dr. and Mrs. Judson in Ava, to which city they proceeded soon after the arrival of the latter in Rangoon, is told in the sketch of the life of the former. The pitiful story of the dreadful sufferings of Oung-pen-la reads almost like a romance. The noble, heroic character of this most gifted woman has touched the sensibilities of thousands of Christian hearts, and the memorial of all that she did and endured for her husband will not soon be forgotten. When the anxiety and the intense and prolonged excitement connected with eighteen months of bitter trial had passed away, there came the natural reaction, and when the disease which forced her to return to her native land assumed a more violent type her weakened physical system was unable to endure the attack, and she yielded to its force. Early in the month of October, 1826, she was stricken with the fever which finally proved fatal, and died the 24th. The sad event was followed in a few months by the death of " little Maria," and together they were buried under the " Hopia" tree at Amherst. She was one of the noblest women that ever bore the Christian name. Her hallowed fame will be handed down with reverence to the last generation of Christ's followers on earth.

Judson, Prof. C. H., was born in Monroe township, Conn., in 1820. His early opportunities were limited to the common school. At eighteen his attention was powerfully turned to the subject of religion under the preaching of Rev. J. Robards. He became thoroughly convinced that the aim of man's life should be something higher than a mere subsistence. He resolved to seek the salvation of his soul, and soon he found peace in believing.

Some remarks of Mr. Robards called his attention to Locke's " Essay on the Human Understanding," which he read with eager interest, which opened up before him a new field of thought. He then resolved to secure an education. He spent two years at Hamilton Literary and Theological Institution. Afterwards he taught about three years, then he spent two years in the University of Virginia, graduating in five schools.

After leaving the university he taught in Virginia and North Carolina until 1851, when he was elected Professor of Mathematics and Natural Philosophy in Furman University, which position he held until 1861, when the war closed the university. In 1862 he was elected president of the Greenville Female College. He was recalled to his former position in the university in 1869, which he still holds.

He is singularly modest and retiring in his manners. His methodical habits fit him well for the post of treasurer of the university and of the Baptist State Convention. As a mathematician he probably has no superior in the South.

Judson, Rev. Edward, the son of Dr. Adoniram Judson, the missionary, was born at Maulmain, Burmah, Dec. 27, 1844. He graduated at Brown University in 1865. After teaching as principal of a seminary in Vermont he became tutor in Madison University, and in 1868 was appointed Professor of the Latin and Modern Languages. In 1875 he listened to the call of the church at North Orange, N. J., and was ordained pastor. He ministers to a large and intelligent audience in one of the finest meeting-houses in the State; and has seen a wonderful blessing upon his work. Between three and four hundred have been baptized by him within five years, and the denomination holds great prominence in the city of Orange. He has been often called to preach and speak before Associations, colleges, and denominational societies, and in 1880 he was elected a trustee of Brown University.

Judson, Mrs. Emily Chubbuck, was born in Eaton, N. Y., Aug. 22, 1817. Under the name of "Fanny Forrester" she wrote a number of articles in prose and poetry for the magazines of the day, which were afterwards collected together and published under the title of "Alderbrook," Boston, 1846, 2 vols. She became the third wife of Dr. Judson, being married to him June 2, 1846, and left the country the 11th of the month, reaching Calcutta the 30th of November following. Dr. Judson re-established himself in Maulmain, his wife submitting with courage to all the hardships and self-denials of a missionary's life. Dr. Judson found in her a sympathizing companion and friend, helping him to the utmost of her power in his missionary and literary work. She was not destined, however, to be long associated with him. In less than four years after their marriage he left her to enter upon that "long voyage" from which he never returned. After the death of her husband Mrs. Judson returned to this country, and died at Hamilton, N. Y., June 1, 1854. Besides "Alderbrook," she wrote an interesting biography of the second wife of Dr. Judson, Mrs. Sarah B. Judson.

Judson Female Institute, located at Marion, Ala., was first opened for students Jan. 7, 1839, with the Rev. Milo P. Jewett as president,—a position which he held for sixteen years with great distinction and a constantly increasing fame. Indeed, it is not too much to say that to Prof. Jewett, more than to any other man, the Judson is indebted for its existence and for the solid foundation on which its celebrity is laid. It is worthy of remark that the same distinguished gentleman was the first president of Vassar Female College.

After Dr. Jewett, Prof. S. S. Sherman, A.M., was president from 1855 to 1859. Prof. Noah K. Davis was president from 1859 to 1864. Prof. J. G. Nash was president in 1864–65. Prof. A. J. Battle, D.D., was president from 1865 to 1872. Prof. R. H. Rawlings was president from 1872 to 1875. Rev. M. T. Sumner, D.D., was president in 1875–76. Rev. L. R. Gwaltney, D.D., was elected president in 1876,—a position which he still holds to the universal satisfaction of the friends of that famous institution of learning. There have been but three presidents of the board of trustees of the Judson Institute,—Gen. E. D. King, for twenty-three years; Deacon W. W. Wyatt, for four years; and Hon. Porter King, from 1868 to this time. The Judson, one of the oldest, is confessedly one of the best, female colleges in the United States. While it does not neglect solid and thorough education, it has always given special attention to the esthetic branches, and as a consequence has gained great reputation for the accomplishments which it bestows upon and weaves into the character of young ladies who are educated under its management. Its buildings and property are worth at least $75,000. It reports annually to the Baptist Convention of Alabama.

Judson, Mrs. Sarah Boardman, the second wife of Dr. Judson, was born in Alstead, N. H., Nov. 4, 1803, and was the daughter of Ralph and Abiah Hall. At an early age she became a member of the First Baptist church in Salem, Mass., then under the pastoral charge of Rev. Dr. Bolles. Her thoughts began, soon after her conversion, to be turned towards the condition of the perishing heathen, and she longed to go forth and tell the story of a Saviour's love to those who were "sitting in darkness." While cherishing such desires as these she was introduced to George Dana Boardman, and found in him one whose tastes and wishes were like her own. Shortly before their departure from this country they were united in marriage, and took passage in the ship "Asia" for Calcutta, reaching the place of their destination Dec. 13, 1825, where they remained until March, 1827, and then proceeded to Amherst, at which they stayed for a few weeks, and then went to Maulmain to enter upon their missionary work in that place. Here, among some things to try their faith and others to encourage them, she continued a faithful helper to her devoted husband. Under date of Jan. 1, 1828, he writes, "Mrs. Boardman is now surrounded by a group of Burman girls, and is delighted with her employment." When it was decided to commence a station at Tavoy, in order that Mr. Boardman might be brought into closer contact with the Karens, she entered into the plan with all her heart. Again her husband writes under date of Aug. 17, 1828, describing the manner in which the Sabbath was observed, "After family worship and breakfast Mrs. Boardman and myself, with the Chinese

Christians, have worship, and a printed sermon is read. Mrs. Boardman is engaged in the afternoon in giving religious instruction to the scholars and domestics." A year from this date came the revolt of Tavoy, and Mrs. Boardman, with George, hastened away, amid many perils, to a place of safety at Maulmain, her husband joining her in a few days. They returned early the next October to the scene of their labors in Tavoy. An alarming illness of Mrs. Boardman, early in 1830, awakened the fears of her friends that she might soon be taken away. She rallied at length, and was able to resume her work for a time, but the state of her health was such that it was thought best that she should make a temporary home in Maulmain. After some months she returned again to Tavoy, and accompanied her husband on his last journey to the villages of the Karens, and was with him to close his eyes in death on the 11th of February, 1831.

Mrs. Boardman, after the death of her husband, continued to prosecute her missionary work as her health and strength permittted. On the 10th of June, 1834, she became the wife of Dr. Judson, and proved a most worthy successor of her who had so deservedly won his respect and love. For a little more than eleven years they shared each other's confidence and affection. After the birth of her last child, in December, 1844, she became the victim of a chronic disease, and the physicians decided that nothing would save her life but a long voyage. She embarked with her husband and three children April 26, 1845. Some encouraging symptoms were apparent in the early part of the voyage, but they proved deceptive, and she died on shipboard, in the port of St. Helena, Sept. 1, 1845. Mrs. Judson's knowledge of the Burmese language was singularly accurate. She translated the New Testament into the Peguan language, and the " Pilgrim's Progress" into Burmese. Dr. Judson, in the warmest terms, gave his testimony to her great worth. No one can read those charming lines of his commencing

"We part on this green islet, love,"

without feeling that hers was a character of singular grace and beauty. She was the mother of Dr. Boardman, the honored pastor of the First Baptist church of Philadelphia.

Judson University, located at Judsonia, White Co., Ark., was founded by some self-sacrificing Baptists, under the leadership of Prof. M. R. Forey, formerly of Chicago University, who became its first president. It was chartered in 1871, suitable buildings were erected, and an able Faculty organized. In 1874, Prof. Forey resigned, and Rev. Benjamin Thomas, D.D., late of Ohio, was elected in his place. Dr. Thomas continued to discharge the duties of the position until 1880. He was succeeded by Rev. R. S. James, M.D., a distinguished

educator, whose enthusiasm has infused new life into the enterprise. The institution is yet young, but under its present able management bids fair to become permanently successful. The location is healthy, and it is surrounded by a thrifty population and superior lands.

Justice, Rev. T. B.—A great friend to missions is this venerable man, who was born in Henderson Co., N. C., July 27, 1813; was baptized by Rev. Benjamin King in August, 1835; ordained in 1842; has frequently been moderator of the Green River and other Associations. A man of faith and fervor, and greatly beloved.

Justification is not regeneration. A new heart lifts the affections from sinful objects, keeps them, by the aid of divine grace, from an immoderate love for proper earthly things, and fixes them supremely upon Jesus. It is not sanctification. It is a state in which holy principles, planted in the soul at the new birth, are cultivated and strengthened by the Spirit of God, until the disciple of Christ is fitted for the church in glory. It is not pardon. Barabbas, guilty of sedition and murder, was forgiven and set at liberty by Pilate. But no intelligent man would have said that he was justified by the governor of Judea when he was released from prison. Pardon and justification are great but widely differing privileges.

In justification the law underlies everything. It has been broken. and it must be satisfied. It was inscribed upon the human conscience by the Creator. The Saviour's version is no doubt the one received by Adam and revealed by Moses: "Thou shalt love the Lord thy God with all thy heart, and with all thy soul, and with all thy mind; . . . thou shalt love thy neighbor as thyself."—Matt. xxii. 37, 39. This law can never be abrogated or modified: "Till heaven and earth pass, one jot or one tittle shall in no wise pass from the law till all be fulfilled." Its requirements must be met to the very letter before a man can be justified, and without justification no one can enter heaven.

The judge who pronounces the sentence of justification is God the Father. "It is God that justifieth, who is he that condemneth? It is Christ that died, yea, rather, that is risen again, who is even at the right hand of God, who also maketh intercession for us."—Rom. viii. 33, 34. From this we learn that the Saviour, as advocate, moves the Chief Justice of the universe to give his decision of justification, and that the First Person of the Trinity, on hearing his appeals, pronounces the justification of all believers.

Forgiveness seems to be the special work of Christ, as the bestowment of the new birth is the peculiar office of the Holy Spirit. He gave the price of the soul, in obedience and sufferings, to the eternal Judge, the Vindicator of the holy law, and, after receiving this consideration of submission and dying throes, as a holy Jehovah he justifies all who receive Christ. The Saviour, who presented the redemption price, turns to those who have believed, and says, " I forgive you." Hence it is written, " Him hath God exalted with his right hand to be a Prince and a Saviour, for to give repentance to Israel, and forgiveness of sins."—Acts v. 31. The Father, who receives the payment of the debt, justifies the soul; the Son, who made it for men without a claim upon him, forgives them.

Christ is the occasion and the sole cause of our justification. The word צדק in the Old Testament, translated righteousness, and δικαιοσύνη, its representative in the New, describe Christ's grandest gift to his redeemed children. He imputes or reckons his righteousness to every one of them, and it becomes their own just as really as if they had " wrought it out" for themselves.

By the righteousness of Christ we are to understand his complete submission to the precepts and penalties of the law of God, his perfect earthly obedience, and his unparalleled anguish; these he places to the credit of each member of his elect family.

The law we have already described was only kept by Adam and Eve before their fall. The purest unregenerate man on earth would not claim to have observed it, and if he did the pretense would be baseless. The holiest saint of the entire Christian family, though stained with the blood of his own martyrdom, never fully kept the law, one breach of which, though no greater than a jot or a tittle, is death : " For whosoever shall keep the whole law, and yet offend in one point, he is guilty of all."—James ii. 10. Like a vessel anchored near the shore in a hurricane with one weak link in her anchor-chain, which breaks in the moment of greatest need, and destroys the ship, so one guilty act is an offense against the majesty of God and against his whole law, and it ruins the righteousness of its perpetrator. If one man had all the excellences of the whole American people from the landing of the Pilgrims or the first settlement of the Cavaliers, and, in addition, the good qualities of all the rest of Adam's children, past and present, there would be thousands of broken links in the chain of his righteousness, and the ship of his hopes would surely be dashed to pieces. " Therefore by the deeds of the law (human performances) there shall no flesh be justified in his sight."—Rom. iii. 20. Jesus became our substitute to obey the law and suffer its penalty. When God arrested the descending hand of Abraham, about to kill Isaac, he seized a ram caught by Providence in a thicket near by, and offered it up instead of his son ; its blood was spilled instead of his, its life was sacrificed for his, its body was given

to the flames which would have reduced Isaac's to ashes. And so " Christ also hath once suffered for sins, the just for the unjust, that he might bring us to God."—1 Peter iii. 18. He took our place before the violated law, and with it our guilt and pains, and he ended both, and gives the righteousness he acquired to every saint.

Paul says, " For he (the Father) hath made him (the Son) to be sin for us, who knew no sin, that we might be made the righteousness of God in him."—2 Cor. v. 21. The word ἁμαρτιαν, translated sin, means, in its New Testament use, sin, vice, wickedness. And it is without doubt properly translated in 2 Cor. v. 21. He was made sin, not by any guilty act of his own, but because the Lord laid on him the iniquities of us all. It was this that made the Father abandon him in death, and it was this that overwhelmed the glorious sufferer with horror as he realized the desertion. And just as he was made sin for us we are " made the righteousness of God in him." He creates a mutual exchange between himself and his redeemed ones ; he takes their guilt, and they become the righteousness of God (δικαιοσύνη Θεοῦ), " For Christ is the end (τέλος) of the law for righteousness (justification) to every one that believeth,"—Rom. x. 4,—that is to say, he has obeyed all its precepts, and suffered all its pains, for every trusting disciple, and he gives him this divine righteousness; this is " the righteousness of God, which is by faith of Jesus Christ, unto all and upon all them that believe."—Rom. iii. 22; of which the Psalmist speaks when it is said, " David also describeth the blessedness of the man to whom God imputeth righteousness without works."—Rom. iv. 6. The great apostle declares that this righteousness justifies without any of our own works : " Therefore we conclude that a man is justified by faith without the deeds of the law." —Rom. iii. 28.

In the New Testament, Christ and his people are represented as being one. Various figures are used to describe this union, but the most remarkable is that of a human body. " Now," says Paul, " ye are the body of Christ and members in particular." 1 Cor. xii. 27. Jesus is the head of this heaven-favored body, and, as a consequence, the acts of the head belong to the whole body, and its privileges, powers, and sacred attributes. According to this teaching Christ's obedience and death are as much ours as they are his. Hence Paul says, "For the love of Christ constraineth us, because we thus judge, that if one died for all, then were all dead."—2 Cor. v. 14. It follows from this undoubted and blessed union that we all died with Christ upon the cross, that the same spotless robe that belongs to the head flows down in unstained beauty and purity over the whole body of Christ, of all names, ages, and worlds.

It is no wonder then that Paul says, "There is, therefore, now no condemnation to them who are in Christ Jesus." "It is God that justifieth, who is he that condemneth?" "Who shall lay anything to the charge of God's elect?"—Rom. viii. 1, 33, 34. The righteousness of the holiest archangel is but the obedience and purity of a creature. The righteousness of a true believer is the immaculate robe of Immanuel, the righteousness of God, which shall for ever hide each moral defect, mortal weakness, and guilty stain. This robe envelops the soul and justifies it through the instrumentality of faith. As the hawser coming from a great steamship, when fastened to a dismasted and helpless vessel, gives her all the force of her powerful engines, and saves her, so faith binds the soul to Jesus, and gives it his justifying righteousness; and for this reason it is written, "Being justified by faith, we have peace with God, through our Lord Jesus Christ."—Rom. v. 1. Faith is one of the fruits of the Holy Spirit in the soul (Gal. v. 22), and whatever merit there is in it belongs to the Comforter, as the whole merit of our righteousness is Christ's. So that every ransomed man, as he enters the eternal world and examines his entire religious exercises, will feel and affirm, "By the grace of God I am what I am;" and his chief glory will be, "Jehovah *is* our righteousness."—Jer. xxiii. 6.

"Jehovah Tsidkenu (our righteousness)! my treasure and boast;
Jehovah Tsidkenu! I ne'er can be lost;
In thee I shall conquer by flood and by field,
My cable, my anchor, my breastplate and shield."

Jutten, David B., D.D., present pastor of the Sixteenth Street Baptist church of New York, was born in that city Jan. 7, 1844. His parents, Benjamin and Emma Jutten, were Baptists. His early education was received in the public schools. In 1859, at the age of fifteen, he united with the Berean Baptist church, having been baptized by the late Dr. Dowling. Soon after his membership was changed to the Bloomingdale Baptist church, now merged into the Central. From this church he received a license to preach in 1862. He entered Madison University in May of the same year, from which he graduated in 1867, and from the theological seminary in 1870. During this time he supplied for short periods, with acceptance, three churches, one in Connecticut, one in New Jersey, and one in New York State. After graduation, and in the same year, he was called to the E Street Baptist church, Washington, D. C. Here he passed three years in successful work.

In 1873 he received a unanimous call from the Sixteenth Street church of New York City, after having preached one Sabbath with great acceptance. The morning sermon on "The Office of the Spirit" indicated a man who realized the source of power in the church. In June, 1873, the new pastor was installed. Dr. Jutten preaches generally without notes. He is a man of large sympathy, and exhibits toward all a truly charitable spirit. He gives special attention to pastoral work. It is his endeavor to call upon every member of the church once a year, holding with all religious conversation and offering prayer with the family in accordance with the good old custom. He has been greatly blessed in his labors during the past five years, and is still prospering. During this time there have been added to the church about 300 members, of whom more than 200 have been received by baptism.

K.

Kalamazoo College.—For the beginning of the enterprise which resulted in the establishment of Kalamazoo College we must go back to the year 1829. In November of that year Thomas Ward Merrill, a graduate of Waterville College in the class of 1825, having finished the course of theological study at Newton in 1828, reached Michigan, seeking, as he then wrote, "to promote the intellectual as well as moral advancement of the people of the Territory of Michigan." He was the son of that Rev. Daniel Merrill who, in Sedgwick, Me., in 1805, became a Baptist, and was accompanied in his adoption of Baptist views by a large part of the Congregational church of which he had been many years pastor. The son was like his father in very hearty devotion to Baptist principles.

In the prosecution of his plans he opened a classical school in Ann Arbor. It, being the only one of the kind, as is supposed, in the Territory, was patronized by Detroit and the other early settlements, and enjoyed prosperity.

From it the next season, July, 1830, Mr. Merrill issued, and traversed the Territory with a petition, of which he was the author, asking the Territorial Legislature to charter an institution under the name of the Michigan and Huron Institute, and secure its control to the Baptist denomination by prescribing that three-fifths of its trustees should be of that faith. The object of the petition was favorably considered in the Legislature, but finally, meeting with objections from those opposed to its denominational features, the bill was laid over to the next session.

Meanwhile, under the influence of those who had opposed it, an academy was incorporated and started at Ann Arbor, of which Mr. Merrill was urged to take charge. But feeling that his Christian and denominational aims and hopes would thus be compromised, he declined.

And the same season, concluding that the eastern shore of the peninsula was to prove uncongenial to the growth of his cherished enterprise, he resolved

untrodden grasses and the unbent bushes of the Western prairies and openings, and encamping with enthusiastic admiration beneath the majestic forests and beside the miniature lakes of Western Michigan. And among the waymarks which he was setting up, some of the first were those which, in his own mind, designated the places where his children should be baptized, his neighbors have their house of prayer and praise, and his denomination their Hamilton of Christian learning, for he had come from where the long shadow of the Hamilton of Hascall and of Kendrick had swept over him.

In the autumn of 1831 there were to be seen traces of these two pioneers coming together and planning methods by which to raise money to purchase land

KALAMAZOO COLLEGE.

to transfer it to the western shore. And as Kalamazoo was a forest through which but the smoke of one log cabin rose, he sought the older settlement of Prairie Ronde, among whose first settlers he assisted in building a house for schools and meetings, and occupied it for those uses as early as the winter of 1830–31.

The question now was where to drive the stake for the permanent institution, and how to purchase lands for its use, for it was then the design that it should incorporate the manual-labor system. And another question was how to reappear before the Legislature and secure the act of incorporation.

Fortunately the practical wisdom, the generous liberality, and the intelligent Christian citizenship of Caleb Eldred stood now waiting to ally themselves with the high aims and the unconquerable tenacity of Thomas W. Merrill. Judge Eldred was then just dragging his surveyor's chain through the

for the occupancy of the contemplated institution. And an appeal to the benevolent Baptists of the East was agreed upon. Accordingly, Mr. Merrill visited the meeting of the Michigan Association at Pontiac in September of that year, and secured the recommendation of that body for him to visit the East on such an agency. A month later he was at the Baptist Convention of the State of New York, and received a hearty commendation of his object signed by Elon Galusha, John Peck, C. M. Fuller, Archibald Maclay, Charles G. Somers, Jonathan Going, B. T. Welch, B. M. Hill, Philander D. Gillette, and others.

So far as appears, the first subscriptions paid in this work, except what Mr. Merrill paid in defraying his own expenses, were seven ten-dollar ones from these seven honored and ever to be remembered names: Jonathan Going, Nathan Caswell, James Wilson, John H. Harris, Byron & Green,

41

William Colgate, and E. Withington. This money went to purchase the property first bought for the institute in Bronson (now Kalamazoo).

Returning from this agency in 1832, Mr. Merrill, Judge Eldred, and others renewed the petition to the Legislature for the incorporation of the institution, under the name of the Michigan and Huron Institute, and without any provisions for denominational control, suggesting, however, the names of the petitioners and others as trustees. These names embraced the early ministers and active brethren of the Baptist denomination then resident in the Territory.

The bill, introduced in answer to the petition, had to work its way through some objections, but receiving the helping hand of Judge Manning, in addition to the watchful efforts of the petitioners, it passed, and, after lodging some time in the hands of the governor, was helped over his scruples by a committee, consisting of John Booth, F. P. Browning, and T. W. Merrill, and was finally approved April 22, 1833.

The first president of the board of trustees was Caleb Eldred, who for twenty-five years worthily filled the office, and was relieved of it only after his repeated and earnest solicitations.

As the charter did not locate the institute, a tedious work awaited the trustees in determining that important matter. There were long journeys over primitive roads to meetings in Clinton, Troy, Ann Arbor, Comstock, Whitmansville, and elsewhere, often resulting in a failure of the necessary quorum, and sometimes issuing in nearly a deadlock of rival contestants for the prize. But at length, in the autumn of 1835, Providence gave the weary fledgling a nest in Kalamazoo, through the subscription of $2500 by residents there, and the purchase of 115 acres of land in what is now the south part of the village, which property was afterwards converted into the site and building accommodations now occupied on the west side of the village, where, through favoring providences, no complaint of ineligibility has ever arisen, or can ever arise, to be among the embarrassments of the enterprise. Twenty years later the adjoining site was secured through the liberal and timely supply of $1500 by Mrs. H. E. Thompson; and the beautiful and commodious building which now graces it was entered and dedicated in the autumn of 1859.

No effort was made to endow the institution, nor was any debt suffered to accrue from its operation during the first twenty years of its history. Its expense for instruction was not large, as its course of study was chiefly preparatory. Moreover, the inferior condition of the public schools, and their lack of all high school facilities, left the people quite ready to extend to a good select school a remunerative patronage. And much of the time

other corporations assumed the current expenses of the institute; for a while the State University supported it as one of its branches, and afterwards the Baptist Convention adopted it as the literary helpmate for its theological education. Yet the property of the institute always remained distinct, and its board of trustees allowed no intermission of their meetings and controlling care.

The privileges of the institute were free alike to both sexes from the first, except during, and for a little after, the time that the Baptist Convention paid the teachers; and, indeed, throughout this period, rooms were supplied free of rent, in which a school for young women was maintained.

In February, 1855, the charter was amended so as to confer full college powers, the name changed to Kalamazoo College, and the corps of instructors enlarged so as to meet the demands of the college course, which was required by the charter to be of as high grade as that of the State University.

The successive principal teachers from the establishment of the school till it became a college were Mr. Marsh, Walter Clark, Nathaniel A. Balch, David Alden, William Dutton, and James A. B. Stone. The last named of these had charge of the school from 1843, and, with the entrance of the institution on its career as a college, he was appointed its president, and remained until 1864. Mrs. Stone was associated with him during all these years.

From 1864 to 1867, Rev. John M. Gregory, LL.D., was president, and, after an interval of more than a year, was followed, in 1868, by the present president, Rev. Kendall Brooks, D.D.

In 1870 the "ladies' course," which prescribed a somewhat lower range of studies than the regular college course, was discontinued, and since that time both sexes have had equal admission to all the courses of study.

In 1853 the sum of $20,000 was secured by subscription towards the endowment of the college and, in 1858, $10,000 for the new building. A few years later the sum of $30,000 was subscribed, and, immediately after the election of President Brooks, $50,000.

The ground and buildings occupied by the college are not wholly its property. The Baptist Convention of the State of Michigan owns the older edifice, used for students' dormitories, containing also the library and two halls for the literary societies of the young men. The new building, designated at its dedication as Kalamazoo Hall, in recognition of the fact that the expense of its erection was mostly paid by citizens of Kalamazoo, contains chapel, recitation-rooms, apparatus-room, and music-room. The whole real estate is estimated to be worth $100,000. The present endowment is about $80,000, of which a part is not now productive. There is nominally one endowed professorship of $10,000, established by Mr. Merrill, who also offered $15,000 as scholarships, the income to be given to students preparing for the ministry in Baptist churches. Of the whole sum, however ($25,000), only one thousand dollars was paid in cash, and the paper in which the rest was paid is not at present yielding any income. It is hoped that both endowments will become productive ere long.

Among those who have held professorships in the college the following may properly be named: William L. Eaton, Samuel Graves, D.D., Edward Olney, LL.D., Daniel Putnam, Edward Anderson, H. L. Wayland, D.D., Silas Bailey, D.D., LL.D., James A. Clark, Samuel Brooks, D.D., William C. Morey, Nathan S. Burton, D.D.

Honorary degrees have been very sparingly given. Only four men have received the degree of Doctor of Divinity, and three that of Doctor of Laws, from the college, during the first twenty-five years of its history.

We rejoice, in looking through the history of the college, that we are brought into something of the presence of an indwelling God. Revivals of religion have not been strange things in its history. For a long time nearly every year witnessed the cloud of God's saving and consecrating presence standing at the door of the institution. Some years the companies that have joined themselves to the Lord in covenant have been large. Fifty in a year have entered our Baptist family through the appointed door, while many more confessed Christ otherwise or elsewhere; and not a few have owed their call to the Christian ministry to these seasons of quickening from spiritual death.

Kalloch, Rev. Amariah, was born in 1808 at Warren, Me. He was one of the foremost ministers in his native State from 1830 to 1849, when he sailed for California. There having contracted a fever, and unwilling to remain quiet until fully restored, he set out upon a mission from Sacramento to Placerville, where he died in 1850. He belonged to a family of preachers well known in New England. He had great natural talents, and was distinguished for his piety, enthusiasm, and marked success in revival preaching and pastoral work. In 1832 he was ordained at Thomaston, where he organized a church at a small hamlet four miles distant, at Rockland. The church increased to 400 members under his oversight. In 1847 he was settled at Augusta, from which he removed to California. He was universally beloved. Many hundreds were baptized as the fruit of his labors.

Kane, Chaplain James J., U. S. Navy, was born in the city of Ottawa, Canada, Oct. 18, 1837; was sent to Europe at an early age; spent two years at a French, and four years at a leading English, college; in consequence of ill health was com-

pelled to give up his studies, and went on a voyage to the Arctic regions. He followed the sea for several years, rising to the command of a vessel. In 1857 joined the Methodist Episcopal church. In 1861 was baptized in the Delaware River by Rev. Jos. Perry, pastor of the Mariners' Baptist Bethel of Philadelphia. Feeling called to preach the gospel, Mr. Kane made preparation to enter upon a theological course at Lewisburg, Pa. The civil war breaking out, he entered the naval service as an officer, and during the four years of the conflict performed the additional duties of a chaplain.

At the close of the war he entered the theological department of Lewisburg, Pa., and graduated in regular course in the class of 1867. He was ordained to the ministry the year previous in the Mariners' Baptist Bethel, in order to file his application for a chaplaincy in the navy.

By the special request of Admiral D. G. Farragut, Mr. Kane was commissioned as chaplain in June, 1868; has served in various ships and stations since that time. In 1870 he spent one year at Harvard Law-School. Chaplain Kane is the author of the work, "Adrift on the Black Wild Tide."

Kansas Baptist State Convention was organized in 1860, before Kansas became a State, and when there were only about 40 churches in the Territory. Its first officers were Rev. I. S. Kalloch, president; Rev. L. A. Alderson, vice-president; and Rev. E. Alward, secretary.

In 1861, Rev. A. Perkins, D.D., was present as pastor of Atchison church, and 26 Baptist ministers were reported as residing in the Territory, and about 1200 members.

In 1864 the churches were reported as numbering 54, and the additions during the previous year 191 persons.

In 1866 Leavenworth was represented by Rev. Winfield Scott, Ottawa by Rev. Isaac Sawyer, and Lawrence by Rev. E. D. Bentley. Rev. J. G. Pratt and C. Journeycake were delegates from the Delaware Reserve.

In 1868, Rev. C. A. Bateman was general missionary, and the names of Deacon S. J. Nugent, Prof. J. R. Downer, Hon. J. S. Emery, Rev. Robert Atkinson, and Rev. H. K. Stimson are reported among the active delegates at the Convention.

In 1869, Prof. Downer made an interesting report concerning church building along the line of the Kansas Pacific Railroad.

In 1870, Rev. Winfield Scott resigned his charge at Leavenworth to do general missionary work throughout the State. Judge Emery stated in his report on statistics that there were in the State 146 Baptist churches, of which 22, with a membership of 350 persons, had been organized during the year, and that of 84 ordained Baptist ministers in the State, and 9 licentiates, all but 2 or 3 were proclaiming the gospel. The aggregate membership at this time was about 6087, and great progress was made in erecting houses of worship.

In 1871 it was reported that nearly $60,000 had been expended in beginning or completing church edifices during the preceding year, and that the State contained 179 churches, with an aggregate of 7000 members. M. A. Clark was present this year as Sunday-school missionary for the State.

In 1872, Rev. Robert Atkinson was general missionary of the Home Mission Society, and Rev. F. M. Ellis, of Lawrence, was secretary of the Convention, and Deacon E. J. Nugent, of Ottawa, its treasurer. Mr. Atkinson reported that 3 general missionaries and 19 missionary pastors had been employed in the State during the year, at an expense of $6750, which was appropriated by the Home Mission Society for the purpose, the amount raised in Kansas for State purposes being included in this amount.

The decade from 1870 to 1880 began with a desire for church edifices far beyond the ability of the people to erect, and it had a very demoralizing effect on the churches, which were crippled greatly on account of it. Rev. E. Gunn labored faithfully as the district secretary of the Home Mission Society during a portion of this time, but under very great disadvantages. In 1879 and 1880, Rev. James French, who had been stationed at Denver, Colorado, as district secretary of the Home Mission Society over a large territory, including the mountain regions, was directed to include with his other work the attempt to liquidate the debts on Kansas church edifices. This, with the aid of pastors and others, was accomplished, and a new method of co-operation with the Home Mission Society was successfully inaugurated; so that with the beginning of a new decade, in 1880, and with a general missionary highly esteemed by the churches (Rev. Granville Gates), and Prof. Ward, of the State Agricultural College, as corresponding secretary, the Baptists of Kansas occupy a more favorable position than ever before. According to the "Year-Book" of 1881, the Baptists of Kansas had

Associations	21
Churches	441
Ordained ministers	309
Members	17,648

Karens.—See article on BURMAH.

Karen Theological Seminary.—Early in the history of our missions the conclusion was reached that the mission churches must be taught, as soon as possible, to be self-sustaining, and that a native ministry must be trained to take the pastoral oversight of them. The ministry thus raised up must be educated, and the necessary facilities furnished to secure the needed instruction. At the annual meeting of the board of the Missionary Union, in Albany, in 1843, Dr. Wayland, as chairman of a committee on

the education of native teachers and preachers, reported in favor of the establishment of a theological school for the Karens. Immediate steps were taken to carry into effect this recommendation, and Rev. Dr. Binney and his wife sailed from this country in November, 1843, to take charge of the new institution. The location first selected for it was in the neighborhood of Maulmain, and it was named Newton. The first term was opened May 28, 1845, and thirty-six students were in attendance at the close of the first year. For the next few years the school was successful under the supervision of Dr. Binney. In September, 1850, Dr. Binney was obliged to leave, with Mrs. Binney, who was ill, for the United States, and the institution was left in charge of Rev. N. Harris, and in 1853 it was placed under the care of Rev. J. H. Vinton. In consequence of the ravages of the cholera, it was suspended at the close of the first term. When it was reorganized, in 1854, Dr. Wade was selected to take charge of it until the return of Dr. Binney, who resumed his old position May 25, 1860, the institution having been removed from Maulmain to Rangoon. In 1863, Rev. C. H. Carpenter was added to the corps of teachers, and Rev. D. W. Smith in 1865. After six years of faithful service, Dr. Binney was obliged again to return to this country on account of the impaired health of Mrs. Binney. For some two years Messrs. Carpenter and Smith had the oversight of the institution, and then Dr. Binney once more returned to his post, Mr. Smith retiring to Henthada, to fill the place made vacant by the removal of Mr. Thomas to Bassein. From the opening of the institution, in 1843, to Sept. 30, 1867, the sum of $12,330.16 had been expended in meeting its wants. The late Prof. Ruggles, of Washington, has been a liberal donor to the funds of the seminary, and to him more than to any other person is to be attributed, under God, its present prosperity. Mr. Smith returned to the seminary in 1869 and remained for a short time, and then resumed his duties at Henthada. For the past few years the institution has done its work with success. Dr. Binney's health failing, he left Rangoon Nov. 14, 1876. The seminary for more than a year was under the care of native teachers. Mr. Smith, who had again been placed on the corps of instructors, reached Rangoon in the latter part of 1876, soon after the departure of Dr. Binney, and at once entered upon the duties of his office as the presiding officer of the seminary. Its affairs are in a hopeful and prosperous condition, and the happiest results may be predicted for it in the future.

Kay, Robert G., was born in Culpeper Co., Va., Sept. 10, 1804. About the year 1825 he was converted, and united with a Baptist church in Christian County of which the lady whom he married, Miss Cynthia A. Burruss, and who survives him, was already a member. In October, 1833, he removed with his family to Illinois and settled at Payson, where he resided for more than forty years upon the same homestead. From this farm his family of eleven children, as they successively reached manhood and womanhood, went forth to do their life-work. Among these children was Mrs. E. P. Scott, well known as formerly a missionary, with her husband, Rev. E. P. Scott, in Assam. Mr. Kay always took an active interest in all public questions, but it was in the name of Christ that his energies were chiefly enlisted. Here he loved to bestow his prayers, his labors, and gifts. In donations he sometimes seemed almost prodigal, yet what he gave was always returned to him in larger measure. He was one of the constituent members of the Payson Baptist church at its organization, in 1834 ; was chosen to the deaconship in 1836, and continued in that office until his death. The Sabbath-school of the church was organized in 1840 ; he was its first superintendent, and while he lived continued to labor in the school either in this or in some other capacity. He also had an active share in the organization of the Quincy Baptist Association. His death occurred at Payson, Adams Co., Ill., May 12, 1877.

Keach, Rev. Benjamin, was born in Stokehaman, England, Feb. 29, 1640. He found peace through Christ in his fifteenth year ; and being unable to discover infant baptism or baptism by sprinkling in the Bible, and being fully satisfied that every believer should be immersed, he was baptized after the Saviour's example by John Russel, and united with a neighboring Baptist church. This community, perceiving his remarkable talents, encouraged him, when he was eighteen years old, to exercise his gifts as a minister.

At first he was an Arminian about the extent of the atonement and free-will, but the reading of the Scriptures and the conversation of those who knew the will of God more perfectly relieved him from both errors. In 1668, in the twenty-eighth year of his age, he was ordained pastor of the church of Horsleydown, Southwark, London. The congregation increased so rapidly after Mr. Keach became pastor, that they had repeatedly to enlarge their house of worship.

Mr. Keach soon became a famous disputant on the Baptist side ; he had taken Richard Baxter in hand, to the serious injury of the bishop of Kidderminster, and others had felt his heavy blows.

The Rev. John Tredwell, of Lavingham, a friend of Mr. Keach, was blessed in his ministry by the conversion of several vicious persons, who united with his church ; this stirred up the indignation of the Rev. Wm. Burkitt, the commentator, a neighbor of Mr. Tredwell, who cast many unjust reflections upon the Baptists and their doctrines. Mr.

Tredwell wrote Mr. Burkitt giving some reasons why he should abandon the unchristian course he was pursuing. Mr. Burkitt, at a time when Mr. Tredwell and his people were gathered in the sanctuary for public worship, with a number of his parishioners, entered the meeting-house, and demanded that Mr. Tredwell and his church should hear his view of the points in dispute. Mr. Tredwell, taken aback somewhat by "such a riotous and tumultuous challenge," agreed to let him speak against Baptist beliefs and usages, provided that he should have an opportunity to reply. For nearly two hours Mr. Burkitt sustained infant baptism, and then he and his "riotous company departed without giving Mr. Tredwell an opportunity of making any return, except to a few of his own

REV. BENJAMIN KEACH.

persuasion that were left behind." Mr. Burkitt speedily published the substance of the address so rudely intruded upon the Baptist minister and his people. Mr. Keach, as a valiant defender of the faith, was invited to reply to Mr. Burkitt's arguments, which he did effectively in "The Rector Rectified and Corrected." Mr. Burkitt was rector of Dedham.

He was challenged by some Episcopal ministers to discuss baptism at Gravesend, near London. As he went to that place in a boat with some friends, he incidentally alluded to the proposed meeting in a way that permitted a stranger, an Episcopal minister, to know that he was Mr. Keach. This person attacked him about infant baptism, and received such a complete drubbing that as soon as the boat touched land he started for his Episcopal brethren and informed them of the arguments which Mr. Keach would use and of his method of putting them. The result of the interview between Mr. Keach's fellow-traveler in the Gravesend boat and his brethren was that they went away as quickly as possible, leaving Mr. Keach without an antagonist.

Mr. Keach was often in prison for preaching, and his life was frequently in danger. Some cavalry sent down to Buckinghamshire to suppress the religious meetings of Dissenters found Mr. Keach preaching, and swore that they would kill him. He was seized and bound and laid on the earth, and four of the troopers were ready to trample him to death with their horses; but just as they were going to put spurs to their horses an officer who perceived their object rode up and stopped them. He was taken to prison, from which he obtained a release after suffering great hardships.

In 1664 he wrote "The Child's Instructor." For the heresies against the Episcopal Church in the little work he was arrested, and bound over under heavy penalties to appear at court. The assizes began at Aylesbury Oct. 8, 1664. The judge was Lord Chief Justice Hyde, afterwards Lord Clarendon, who acted like Jeffreys at the "Bloody Assizes." He abused Mr. Keach outrageously, he threatened the jury, and he evidently wanted to have Mr. Keach executed if he could terrify him into making some unwise statements. The jury brought in a verdict that Mr. Keach was guilty in part. And when asked to explain their verdict the foreman said, "In the indictment he is charged with these words, 'When the thousand years shall be expired, then shall all the rest of the devils be raised'; but in the book it is, 'Then shall the rest of the dead be raised.'" The judge informed the jury that they could bring him in guilty of all the indictments but that sentence. They brought in the prompted verdict. And immediately the judge said: "Benjamin Keach, you are here convicted for writing, printing, and publishing a seditious and schismatical book, for which the court's judgment is that you go to jail for a fortnight without bail, and the next Saturday stand upon the pillory at Aylesbury in the open market for the space of two hours, with a paper upon your head with this inscription, 'For writing, printing, and publishing a schismatical book entitled "The Child's Instructor, or a New and Easy Primer,"'" and the next Thursday to stand in the same manner and for the same time in the market of Winslow; and then your book shall be openly burnt before your face by the common hangman in disgrace of you and your doctrine. And you shall forfeit to the king's majesty the sum of twenty pounds; and shall remain in jail until you find

sureties for your good behavior and appearance at the next assizes, there to renounce your doctrines and make such public submission as shall be enjoined upon you." The sheriff was as rigorous in executing this infamous sentence as the judge was insolent in pronouncing it.

On the pillory at Aylesbury Mr. Keach defended himself and the truth with great boldness. The jailer frequently interrupted him, and finally the sheriff himself threatened to have him gagged. The people, contrary to custom, had no words of mockery for the good, persecuted minister, and no offensive missile was hurled at him. An Episcopal minister who ventured to assail Mr. Keach in the pillory was immediately reproached by the people with the ungodliness of his own life, and his voice was drowned in laughter. At Winslow, where he lived, he suffered the same shameful penalty, and a copy of his little book was burned.

Mr. Keach was a zealous Baptist; he aided ministers who came to him from all parts of his country, he had many meeting-houses built, and his works in defense of Baptist principles were read all over the kingdom. Before his death men spoke of him as the "famous" Mr. Keach, and he is still described by writers as a man of great celebrity. His two most popular works are "Tropologia, or a Key to open Scripture Metaphors," and "Gospel Mysteries Unveiled, or an Exposition of all the Parables." The latter work is more frequently offered for sale in the catalogues of the great London second-hand bookstores than any production of Richard Baxter, John Howe, or Jeremy Taylor. Mr. Keach was the author of forty-three works. He died July 18, 1704, in his sixty-fourth year. He was a devout Christian who led a blameless life and died in the triumphs of faith.

Keach, Rev. Elias, was born in 1667. He was the only son of the Rev. Benjamin Keach, a distinguished Baptist minister of London, England. He came to Philadelphia in 1686, when he was nineteen years of age. At the time of his arrival in this country he was a very ungodly young man. To make himself appear to be a clergyman he wore black clothing and bands, and he was at once taken for a minister. He speedily had an opportunity of showing his clerical talents by conducting a public service. He succeeded with his imposition until he had preached a considerable portion of his sermon. Then he stopped abruptly and "looked like a man astonished." The people supposed that he had been taken by some serious and unexpected complaint. But as they gathered around him they learned from him that he was neither a minister nor a Christian, and he made the communication with tears and "much trembling." Great was his anguish, and to obtain relief he went to Elder Dungan, of Cold Spring, near Bristol, Pa., who encouraged him to take his guilty soul to the sin-cleansing Redeemer. Soon the young man was a happy believer, full of ardent love to the Lord Jesus, and anxious to be a true preacher of his glad tidings. Elder Dungan baptized him; and from the Cold Spring church and pastor he went forth ordained to preach Jesus.

Mr. Keach constituted the Lower Dublin church in January, 1688. This church immediately elected him its pastor; and from it has sprung the wealthy and influential sisterhood of churches that now makes Philadelphia the home of the greatest number of Baptists in any large city in America. Mr. Keach labored in Pennsylvania and New Jersey with burning zeal, journeying far, preaching often, and succeeding marvelously. The Lower Dublin church at one time embraced in its membership all the Baptists in Pennsylvania and New Jersey; and to accommodate its widely scattered communicants the Lord's Supper was administered at Burlington and Cohansey, N. J., and at Chester, Philadelphia, and Lower Dublin, Pa. Lower Dublin at that time was the seat and centre of the Baptist denomination in several colonies, and from the community founded and extended so widely by Mr. Keach the Philadelphia Baptist Association arose, the first Association of our brethren on this side of the Atlantic.

Mr. Keach married Miss Moore, a daughter of Chief Justice Nicholas Moore, of Pennsylvania. Owing to some difficulties in the Lower Dublin church, Mr. Keach returned to England in 1792. After his return to London he organized a church, of which he became pastor, into the membership of which he baptized about 130 souls in nine months after reaching London. He died in 1701 in the thirty-fourth year of his age.

He was a preacher of popular talents and of undoubted piety. He often had a congregation at the morning lecture, supported by the Baptists in Pinner's Hall, London, of 1500 persons. Mr. Keach published "Four Sermons on Justification," "A Treatise on Discipline," and "Two Sermons on the Nature and Excellency of the Grace of Patience."

Keachi Female College, located at Keachi, De Soto Parish, La., was chartered in 1857, with a capital stock of $18,000, and with buildings donated by Thomas M. Gattin, which cost $4500. The school opened in 1858 under Dr. J. S. Bacon, of South Carolina, who resigned in a short time, and Rev. J. H. Tucker succeeded him. At the beginning of the war 125 young ladies were in attendance. During the war the school was suspended, and the buildings used for a Confederate hospital. After the war it was reorganized, under Peter Crawford, who held the position until 1871, when he resigned, and Rev. J. H. Tucker was

again called to the presidency, and has continued in office until the present time. The college has gradually regained its former prosperity.

Keely, Rev. George, was born at Walsham, County of Suffolk, England, July 26, 1772. Early in life he lost his father, and was thrown upon the care of an affectionate mother, whose instructions and wise counsels exerted an influence upon his youthful mind which was most salutary. When he was eighteen years of age he went to London, friendless and alone. By diligence and application to business he soon made for himself a position in which he bade fair to secure prosperity in his worldly affairs. The providence of God directed him to the place of worship where Dr. Rippon was the pastor, the same church of which Mr. Spurgeon is now the minister. Here he was converted and baptized. Soon after, he abandoned business, and prepared for the ministry at Bristol College under the charge of Dr. Ryland. He became the pastor of the Baptist church in Northampton in 1799, remaining there ten years, at the end of which period he became pastor of a church in Ridgemount, in the County of Bedford, and continued there until he resigned in 1818 to come to this country. Soon after reaching the United States he became the pastor of the First Baptist church in Haverhill, Mass., and was recognized as such Oct. 7, 1818. For nearly fourteen years he continued his labors in this important church, and established a reputation for being one of the ablest ministers in the denomination in Massachusetts. Upon his resignation he declined all overtures again to settle as a pastor. He passed the remainder of his life in such employments as were congenial with his tastes, and died, at the great age of ninety-four years, at Hampton Falls, N. H.

Keely, Prof. George Washington, LL.D., was born in Northampton, England, Dec. 25, 1803. His father, Rev. George Keely, came to this country in 1818, and for several years was pastor of the First Baptist church in Haverhill. George entered Brown University in 1820, and graduated with the highest honors of his class in 1824. He was appointed tutor of the Latin and Greek Languages in Brown University in 1825, and continued in the office for three years, and gained for himself a high reputation as an accomplished instructor. Having taught a private school for a year, he was appointed in 1829 Professor of Mathematics and Natural Philosophy in Waterville College. A new direction was soon given to his studies, which hitherto had been in the department of languages. He had so vigorous a mind that it was not difficult to turn his intellectual energies into new channels, and he soon mastered the more abstruse studies to which he now directed his attention, and proved himself to be one of the ablest scholars in the land in the special direction to which he applied himself. For twenty-three years he held the office of Professor of Mathematics and Natural Philosophy, securing for himself the sincere respect and the warm admiration of the students who came under his supervision. He resigned his professorship in 1852, and returned to more private life. He was employed for several years in the United States Coast Survey, and was also a correspondent of the Royal Observatory of England. Prof. Keely combined in himself what might be regarded as opposite traits of character. He was modest almost to timidity and lived the life of a scholastic recluse, and yet no man in the community kept himself better informed as to what was going on in the world, or was more entertaining and instructive in his conversation with those who were the sharers of his hospitality or casually met him in the ordinary walks of life.

Prof. Keely was an habitual worshiper at the First Baptist church in Waterville, in whose prosperity he always felt interested. The writer of this sketch, once his pastor, cherishes for him a regard and an affection which he has felt for but few men. Brown University conferred upon him in 1849 the honorary degree of Doctor of Laws. His death took place almost without a moment's warning, at Waterville, June 13, 1878.

Keely, Rev. Josiah, son of Rev. George Keely, was born in England May 26, 1806. He was baptized by his father June 18, 1826, ordained Dec. 21, 1843, as pastor of the church in Wenham, Mass., where he remained until called to the church in Saco, Me. He continued to act as pastor of this church for eleven years, when he resigned, having received an appointment as chaplain of the 13th Maine Regiment, Jan. 1, 1864. The hard service of military life undermined his health, and suffering from disease, he was taken to St. James Hospital, New Orleans, where he died June 24, 1864.

Keen, Joseph.—Jöran Kyn (Keen), the ancestor of Joseph Keen, came to this country from Sweden at about the age of twenty-three with Gov. John Printz in 1643. He was the founder of Upland, now Chester, Delaware Co., Pa.; and the Crozer Theological Seminary (in which Dr. W. W. Keen, the grandson of Joseph Keen, is one of the constituent trustees) stands on a portion of what was once his land. (See "The Descendants of Jöran Kyn," in the *Penna. Mag. Hist. and Biog.*, 1878–81.) Like not a few of his descendants, Jöran Keen was of such eminent piety that he is referred to in early colonial documents as "the pious." The family were originally Swedish Lutherans, and the grave-stone of Matthias Keen, the great-grandfather of Joseph, is (with the exception of that of two children) the oldest in the old Swedes' (Gloria Dei) church-yard, Philadelphia.

The father of Joseph Keen, Matthias, of Tacony, Oxford township, near Philadelphia, was a member of the Church of England (as most of the Swedish Lutherans became), and was a vestryman for many years of Trinity church, Oxford. His mother, through whose influence Joseph became a Baptist, was Margaret Thomas, whose father, John Thomas, came to America from Wales, settled near Philadelphia, and died in 1747. Joseph was born July 14, 1762. At the age of eighteen he left Tacony, and was apprenticed to George Oakley, a tanner and currier, for £150, which sum, with characteristic integrity, he worked out. He continued in this business to the end of his life in co-partnership with John Sellers, an eminent and devoted Quaker. He was married by Dr. Rogers, Jan. 24, 1788, to

JOSEPH KEEN.

Margaret Williams, a woman of superior character and eminent worth, who died Oct. 16, 1815. He related his personal Christian experience before the First Baptist church, Philadelphia, April 5, 1790, was unanimously elected a deacon Nov. 25, 1799, and served as such for nearly twenty-two years until his death, May 12, 1821, at the age of fifty-nine.

"No one can peruse the minutes during his long connection with the church without being impressed with the variety and intensity of his Christian activities, the kindliness of his heart, the loyalty of his faith, and the high esteem in which he was held by the entire church." When the Baptist Sunday-school enterprise was first started in Philadelphia it was approved by some, mildly countenanced by Dr. Holcombe, the pastor, but heartily encouraged by Deacon Keen, and when, in October, 1815, the first session was held, he "opened the school with the first public prayer connected with the Baptist Sunday-school enterprise in this city" (see Spencer's "Early Baptists of Philadelphia," pp. 186–8),—a service he repeatedly rendered to the cause in its early days.

Keen, William Williams, son of Joseph and Margaret (Williams) Keen, was born Sept. 4, 1797, in Tacony, near Philadelphia. His mother had taken refuge there during the epidemic of yellow fever, and he was born in a house built by his great-grandfather, John Keen, on a tract of 300 acres of land originally obtained from Sir Edmund Andros in 1676. He was associated with his father

WILLIAM WILLIAMS KEEN.

in business at the age of nineteen. At his death he succeeded him, with his brothers Joseph and Samuel W., and was for many years one of the most prominent men in his branch of trade. He retired from active business in 1851. He was married Feb. 20, 1823, by Dr. Holcombe, to Susan Budd, a descendant of William Budd, who came over from England and settled in Burlington Co., N. J., in 1678. She came of a robust religious stock. Rev. Thomas Budd, the father of William, while rector of Martock, Somersetshire, England, in 1660, under Charles the Second, became a Quaker. In 1662, on account of his religious opinions, he was thrown into jail at Ilchester, and remained there, resolutely adhering to his conscientious convictions, till liberated by death June 22, 1670, after

eight years of imprisonment. After an honored and most useful life, she died Oct. 27, 1877, in the seventy-fourth year of her age. He became a member of the First Baptist church, Philadelphia, Oct. 24, 1831, he and his wife being baptized with a large number of candidates, including seven married couples, by Dr. Brantly. As was then the custom, the whole company, in baptismal robes, attended by the members of the church, marched to Arch Street wharf, crossed to Cooper's Point, Camden, and were there baptized in the Delaware. Both his personal and his family ties have ever bound him closely to this ancient church. His father was a deacon in it for nearly twenty-two years; his brother Joseph was a deacon for twenty years; his brother Samuel a trustee and church clerk; and he in his turn became a trustee Jan. 20, 1834, and a deacon Nov. 22, 1838.

In May, 1843, he removed to West Philadelphia. Here he quickly gathered a few scattered brethren into a determined and hopeful band, and in October, 1843, less than five months after their first meeting, they laid the corner-stone of a neat building for the First Baptist church, West Philadelphia, on a lot given to the church by him, and afterwards repurchased on their removal to the present site at the corner of Thirty-sixth and Chestnut Streets. In 1860 the present handsome brown-stone church and chapel were erected. Few who have never gone through the trials of building two churches know what zeal and determination, and often what real sacrifices, are necessary to carry them through. His brethren deserve all praise for their heroic endeavors to carry the load, but the main burden, financially at least, fell upon him, and when failure threatened he sold his horses and his carriages, curtailed family expenses in every direction, often at personal discomfort, and made even his garden and his grapery aid in the work of building the Lord's house. Most men settle on a scale of expenses, family and personal, suitable to their means and social position, and give away what they can afford out of the remnant of their income, but with him the sum devoted to the Lord was the standard by which all expenses, family and personal, were regulated, and many a debate was held with his conscience before a grapery, a green-house, a coachman, or a pair of horses was decided upon, lest the unusual expense should curtail his beneficence. When he retired from business he resolved on his knees never to lay up another dollar, a resolution he has fulfilled for more than twenty-seven years. He has frequently given away more than half his income, and an aggregate sum amounting to more than all he is worth at present. Next to his church, the American Baptist Publication Society was his cherished field of denominational work. In 1837, while it was a feeble institution, occupying a small building belonging to his father's estate on Fourth Street above Chestnut, he became its treasurer, and faithfully administered its finances for eighteen years. He was one of the most earnest advocates of its removal to 530 Arch Street, and headed the subscription list with $5000. After serving the society as treasurer, vice-president, and manager from 1837 to 1872, his joy has been great in its removal to such a splendid home as the exceptional liberality of its friends has now provided for it. More than usually trusted by his brethren, he has been called to many offices of usefulness and responsibility in the denomination. Besides his service in the Publication Society, he was a constituent trustee of the university at Lewisburg, and served for three years (1846–49); a member of the first and most carefully chosen board of managers of the Missionary Union, organized in 1845 after the dissolution of the Triennial Convention, a position he filled for two years; manager of the Philadelphia Baptist Association since 1856; trustee of the Ministers' and Widows' Fund since 1858; manager of the Pennsylvania Education Society for twenty-five years (1842–67), to which society he gave, in 1856, its first scholarship; manager of the Pennsylvania Baptist General Association for twenty-two years (1832–54); and in the two churches of which he has been a member a deacon for nearly forty-three years.

Not only in the church, but also in the commercial community, he has been confided in, having been a manager in the Woodlands cemetery for nineteen years, a director in the Bank of North America, the oldest bank in the country, for nearly twenty years, and as a constituent manager of the Western Saving-Fund since 1847, has served nearly thirty-four years.

Now, in a ripe though feeble and blind old age, honored by all who know or know of him, he is awaiting with expectation and delight the summons of his Lord, "Well done, good and faithful servant; enter thou into the joy of thy Lord."

Keen, William Williams, M.D., son of William W. and Susan (Budd) Keen, was born in Philadelphia, Jan. 19, 1837. Graduated from the Central High School, January, 1853. Entered Brown University in 1855, and graduated in 1859. After pursuing scientific studies as a resident graduate for one year in Providence, entered Jefferson Medical College in 1860, and graduated M.D. in March, 1862.

During several years of the war, as Assistant-Surgeon, U.S.A., Dr. Keen discharged duties belonging to his office both on the battle-fields and in the general hospitals with great success. Resigning from the service in 1864, he went abroad and pursued his studies in Paris, Berlin, and Vienna. In 1866 he settled in private practice in Philadelphia,

where he has remained, chiefly devoting himself to anatomy and surgery, and has attained an enviable reputation for skill and ability in his profession. Dec. 11, 1867, he married E. Corinna, daughter of Jefferson Borden, of Fall River, Mass.

As a medical teacher, especially of anatomy, and as an author, Dr. Keen is widely known throughout this and other countries. He was appointed Lecturer on Pathological Anatomy in the Jefferson College from 1866 to 1875. During the same period he occupied the chair of Anatomy and Operative Surgery in the Philadelphia School of Anatomy, in which institution he gathered the largest private anatomical class ever assembled in this country. In 1876 he was appointed Professor of Artistic Anatomy in the Pennsylvania Academy of Fine Arts, and in 1878 was made Lecturer on the Anatomy of Animal Forms as applied to Decorative and Industrial Art in the schools of the Pennsylvania Museum. He has also for five years been special Lecturer on Clinical Anatomy in the Woman's Medical College of Pennsylvania.

Dr. Keen has made extensive contributions to medical literature. Among his principal works are "Gunshot Wounds, and other Injuries of Nerves," 1864; "Reflex Paralysis," 1864 (both with colleagues); "Clinical Charts of the Human Body," 1872; editor of the "American Health Primers, vols. i.–xii.," by various authors; Heath's "Practical Anatomy," 1870; Flower's "Diagrams of the Nerves," 1872. In 1876 he delivered the fifth Toner Lecture before the Smithsonian Institution on the "Surgical Complications and Sequels of the Continued Fevers." He has published also interesting lectures on the "History of Practical Anatomy," 1870; the "History of the Philadelphia School of Anatomy," 1875; and on "Medical Missionary Work in Japan," 1878. In addition to these he has contributed a large number of articles to journals and reviews.

His activities are by no means confined to his professional sphere. As a manager of the American Baptist Publication Society, a trustee of Crozer Theological Seminary and of Brown University, and as a deacon and trustee of the First Baptist church of Philadelphia, Dr. Keen gives a practical illustration of the vast influence that may be exerted by men who, while serving suffering humanity, are led by the teachings of Jesus.

Keith, Hon. George H., was born in Randolph, Orange Co., Vt., May 4, 1825. He is of Scotch descent. His ancestors came to this country early in the seventeenth century. He received his elementary education at the public school in his native town. At the age of sixteen he entered the Kimball Union Academy at Meriden, N. H. Here he devoted four years to study and teaching. He then received the appointment of superintendent of the primary department of Franklin College, Ind. After holding this position one year he commenced the study of medicine, and graduated from the medical college at Woodstock, Vt., in 1852. In 1855 he came to Minneapolis, Minn., where he now resides. He was elected to the first Legislature of Minnesota in 1858 and 1859. In 1862 he was appointed surgeon of the expedition sent to relieve Fort Abercrombie. In 1863 he was appointed provost marshal for the second district of Minnesota, which position he filled until the close of the war. In May, 1871, he was commissioned by President Grant postmaster of Minneapolis, which office he yet honorably fills.

HON. GEORGE H. KEITH.

He was converted in October, 1838, and applied for membership in the Free-Will Baptist church, of which his parents were members. His experience was satisfactory, but the pastor and church thought him too young to make a profession of religion, and advised him to wait six months. At the end of that time he was baptized and received into the fellowship of the church. In 1846 he united with the First Baptist church in Indianapolis, Ind., Rev. T. R. Cressey pastor. He has ever been an earnest worker in all departments of Christian labor. He was the first president of the Minnesota Baptist State Convention, and has been a continuous member of its board of trustees, except when absent during the war. He was active in the establishment of the Minnesota Academy at Owatouna.

Keithian Quaker Baptists.—In the early his-

tory of William Penn's colony a serious controversy broke out among the Quakers about "the sufficiency of what every man naturally has within himself for the purpose of his own salvation." Some denied this sufficiency, and, as a consequence, exalted Christ and the Scriptures more than Barclay had done. George Keith, an impetuous and talented Scotchman, was the leader in resisting Quaker orthodoxy. The dispute was carried on with much bitterness, and in 1691 it led to a division and the establishment of separate meetings in Pennsylvania and New Jersey. Keith and his friends published a confession of their faith, and other works in favor of their views, and in denunciation of " the slanders, fines, imprisonments, and other persecutions which they endured from their brethren." Keith soon turned Episcopalian ; others were reconciled to their brethren ; and many became Baptists, Seventh-Day and Regular. According to Morgan Edwards, the Keithian Quakers started the Seventh-Day Baptist denomination in Pennsylvania. The Regular Baptists obtained valuable accessions from the Keithians in Philadelphia, Lower Dublin, Southampton, and Upper Providence. They were called Quaker Baptists because they retained the language, dress, and manners of the Quakers.

Kellar, Rev. William, an eminent pioneer Baptist minister, of German extraction, was born in Shenandoah Co., Va., in 1768. His early life was spent in East Tennessee, and afterwards in what is now Oldham Co., Ky. He was instrumental in forming Harrod's Creek church in 1797, Eighteen-Mile church in 1800, and Lick Branch (now Lagrange) church in 1802. In 1803, Long Run Association was constituted, of which he was chosen moderator, and filled that office four years. In 1812 he raised a company of volunteers, of which He was commissioned captain. At the close of the war he resumed his pastorates, and labored diligently in his profession. He was greatly beloved by the people, and led many souls to Christ. He died Oct. 6, 1817.

Kelley, Rev. Edwin D., was born in North Clarendon, Vt., June 18, 1846, pursued his preparatory studies at Rutland, Vt., and graduated at the University of Michigan in 1866. After teaching a while in Granville, O., he entered Newton Theological Institution, and graduated in June, 1871. He was appointed a missionary to the Shans, and reached Toungoo Feb. 20, 1872. He had so far made himself familiar with the language, that he was able to teach and to preach in it in less than one year, which was all the time that he had to devote to his missionary work. He was drowned in Shanland, Jan. 1, 1873. The editor of the *Missionary Magazine* says of him : " Mr. Kelley was a good scholar, and possessed a remarkable aptness for the acquisition of languages. He was also a well educated theologian, and a devout and earnest Christian. He was modest and firm in following his convictions, a man of sound and discriminating views of truth, and of much promise as a missionary."

Kellis, Rev. Lewis C., an active and efficient minister, who resides at Monroe, La., but supplies the churches at Bastrop, Oak Ridge, Delhi, and Wynn Island, situated between the Ouachita and Bayou Macon Rivers; was born in Mississippi; educated at Summerville Institute and Mississippi College. He removed to Louisiana in 1874, and became pastor at Alto. In the fall of the same year he became pastor at Trenton and Delhi. Mr. Kellis has been successful in his work. He is a ready writer, and has contributed largely to the Baptist papers of Mississippi and Louisiana. He is about thirty years of age.

Kelly, Robert, son of Robert Kelly, an Irish patriot, who in 1796 emigrated to New York, was born in the city of New York, Dec. 15, 1808. From early youth Robert Kelly was inclined to study. He was diligent, pure-minded, and honorable. He entered Columbia College the first of his class, and maintained that position to his graduation in 1826. In mercantile life he was distinguished by industry and energy. His integrity and sense of honor were utterly beyond the reach of temptation. He learned the French, Spanish, Italian, German, and Hebrew languages. On retiring from business he followed this bent of his mind, and remained to the end of life a student. Naturally, he became a leader in all matters pertaining to higher education. He was conspicuous in the organization of the institution now known as the College of the City of New York.

For many years he was a trustee of the University of New York, and also of Madison and Rochester Universities, which institutions are largely indebted to his generosity, his judgment and labors. He was chairman of the committee which organized the course of study in the University at Rochester. His services in education were recognized by his election as one of the regents of the University of the State of New York. In the House of Refuge and in the Institution for the Benefit of Merchants' Clerks he took a leading part. At the time of his death he was chairman of the board of trustees of the New York Society Library. There was scarcely a form of public activity in the city, whether financial, fiduciary, charitable, commercial, or literary, in which, in some way, he did not bear a prominent part.

Without political office, except that of city chamberlain, he was fitted to adorn any civic station, and, at the time of his death, at the height of his powers, he was without question one of the very foremost citizens of New York. He never made a

public profession of religion, but was a Christian man, a Baptist by conviction, and a devoted attendant on the ministry of Wm. R. Williams, D.D., his lifelong friend. He died in New York City, April 27, 1856.

Kelly, Hon. William, son of Robert Kelly, an Irish patriot who fled from his native land in 1796 to find liberty in the New World, was born in the city of New York, Feb. 4, 1807. His father became a very prosperous merchant, and died in 1825, leaving three sons, John, William, and Robert. They continued his business for several years with great success. In 1836 John died, and in 1837 William and Robert retired, each with an ample competence. In all their arduous business days the brothers maintained a love for literature, refinement, and the high moral and religious tone for which their early home had been so long conspicuous. In 1842, William purchased a property on the Hudson, near Rhinebeck, which he made his permanent residence, and which his energy and taste invested with every attraction. For two years he was a member of the senate of the State of New York, and he was a candidate for governor against Edward D. Morgan, his successful competitor. Mr. Kelly was a man of large heart, and constantly, though silently, dispensed his gifts and charities. He was trustee at the beginning, and for some years after, of Cornell University, the mathematical portion of which bears his name in acknowledgment of a generous donation. He was also a trustee of Vassar College and of Rochester University at the time of his death, of the first from its inception, and of the last from the death of his brother Robert, whose vacant seat he was called to fill. He was a liberal contributor to Rochester, a final subscription of $20,000 being made not long before his decease. He was a member of the Baptist church at Rhinebeck, where his widow still resides. He died in Torquay, England, whither he had gone in hope of restoration to health, Jan. 14, 1872.

Kelton, Rev. William H., was born in 1835; entered the New Hampton Institution in 1855, having previously spent some time in the Bangor Theological Seminary, and graduated in 1858. He was ordained, soon after his graduation, as pastor of the church at Bluehill, Me., and subsequently was pastor for a time at West Waterville, Me. His health was broken down in consequence of his hard experience in the army as a worker, sent to the seat of war by the Christian Commission, and he did not attempt ministerial labor until 1865, when he took charge of the church in North Scituate, Mass. Here he did excellent service for the cause of Christ until the Master called him to his reward. He died April 4, 1871. He was very greatly beloved by a large circle of friends, who sincerely mourned over what to them seemed his untimely end.

Kemper, Rev. Burdette, a popular and useful minister of Garrard Co., Ky., where he was born Feb. 24, 1788, was of German extraction. He was converted, and became a member of Forks of Dix River church in 1830, and at the age of forty-five was ordained to the ministry. He was immediately associated with John S. Higgins in ministering to the church of which he was a member. On the resignation of Mr. Higgins, in 1839, Mr. Kemper became the pastor, and under his ministry the church greatly prospered and increased in numbers, until it embraced a membership of more than 500. Besides performing his pastoral labors, Mr. Kemper preached to several of the churches of South District Association, of which he was moderator twenty-five years. He died March 18, 1876.

Kempton, George, D.D., was born in South Carolina in 1810. He graduated from Hamilton Literary and Theological Institution in 1839. After preaching a few years in the South he became pastor of Spruce Street church, Philadelphia, and remained for eight years. He also had charge of the Lower Dublin church, in Philadelphia, for five years. He presided over the First church in New Brunswick, N. J., for five years. From a partial failure of health, in 1863 he located in Hammonton, N. J., and has preached for the church there with great acceptance. In 1859 Madison University gave him the degree of D.D. He is a sound theologian and a logical preacher.

Kempton, Rev. S. Bradford, A.M., was born in November, 1834, at Milton, Queens County, Nova Scotia; converted and baptized there in 1853; graduated from Acadia College in 1862; ordained pastor at New Minas, Sept. 16, 1863; took charge of the First Cornwallis church in 1868, being the third minister that has held that position since 1808; sound theologian, good preacher, and pastor.

Kendall, Hon. Amos, was born near Woburn, Mass., Aug. 16, 1789. By great self-denial and perseverance he prepared for college, and entered Dartmouth in the spring of 1808, from which he graduated with distinction. After leaving college he entered the law-office of W. M. Richardson, at Groton, Mass., but, encountering numerous perplexing difficulties, he made preparations for leaving New England. Accordingly he removed to Kentucky, and engaged as tutor in the family of Henry Clay, then residing near Lexington. After continuing in this position for a few months, he became editor of a newspaper in Georgetown, and at the same time opened a law-office there. In 1816 he became co-editor and proprietor of the *Argus*, a journal published at Frankfort. He held this position for several years, and became one of the most influ-

ential writers on local and State politics in Kentucky. In 1826 he was appointed fourth auditor of the treasury by President Jackson, and in consequence removed to Washington. This position he filled with great advantage to the government and honor to himself for five years, when, through his great executive ability, and the vigorous aid which he gave to the administration, he was appointed, in 1835, postmaster-general. The energy with which he carried on this important department of the government was soon evident, but the fidelity with which he managed its affairs subjected him to some vexatious and damaging prosecutions at the hands of his enemies. In 1840, in consequence of impaired health, he sent to the President his resignation from the office, and was thus relieved of the

HON. AMOS KENDALL.

great burden. Mr. Kendall while residing in Washington was connected with several different daily journals, in which many of the absorbing questions of the day were discussed with much pungency and power. He became interested at a very early day in Prof. Morse's telegraph operations, and by his business energy and tact gave a great impetus to the movement. In 1857 he gave a house and two acres of land, near the boundary-line of the city of Washington, for an institution for the deaf and dumb, which, under the judicious guidance of its superintendent, Edward M. Gallaudet, LL.D., and the generous appropriations of the United States government, has become the only college in the world with a regular and full curriculum for deaf mutes.

Mr. Kendall, although indulging the thought that he had been converted early in life, was not baptized until April, 1865, the ceremony taking place in the E Street church; he became a member, however, of the Calvary Baptist church, whose pastor at the time was the Rev. J. S. Kennard. He took a deep interest in securing a church edifice for the society with which he became thus connected, and contributed for the purpose nearly $100,000. On the 3d of June, 1866, the new house was dedicated, and the church entered at once on a most prosperous career. In June of 1866, feeling the need of rest and recreation, Mr. Kendall visited Europe, being absent about fifteen months. On Sunday morning, Oct. 15, 1867, the beautiful edifice of the Calvary church was destroyed by fire, nothing being left but the blackened walls. Encouraged by Mr. Kendall, a new structure was soon reared, towards the cost of which (the insurance money received being $80,000) he gave upwards of $15,000. This new building was dedicated July 11, 1869. He gave to the Columbian College, of which he was always a stanch friend and counselor, $6000, to purchase a classical scholarship, which should be enjoyed during six years by the best-prepared pupil in any one of the public schools of Washington. He also endowed two mission Sunday-schools, his contributions to them amounting in all to about $25,000. He died in Washington, Nov. 12, 1869.

Kendrick, Adin A., D.D., the present president of Shurtleff College, was born at Ticonderoga, N. Y., Jan. 7, 1836. He was the son of Dr. Albert Kendrick. Dr. Kendrick is of the family to which have belonged several eminent men of that name, including Adin Kendrick, M.D., of Poultney, Vt., his grandfather; Rev. Ariel Kendrick, of New Hampshire; Rev. Nathaniel Kendrick, D.D., the first president of what is now Madison University, and one of its founders; and Rev. Clark Kendrick, of Vermont; with whom may be included, as still living, Prof. A. C. Kendrick, D.D., of the University of Rochester, and the Rev. J. R. Kendrick, D.D., of Poughkeepsie.

President Kendrick received his education at Granville Academy, in Washington Co., N. Y., at Middlebury College, Vt., and at the Rochester Theological Seminary. Upon leaving college, and before commencing his theological course, he studied law, and was admitted to the bar, practising that profession at Janesville, Wis., and afterward for a short time at St. Louis. Deciding to study for the ministry, he went to Rochester for his theological course, graduating there in 1861. His first pastorate was in Chicago, where he served in that capacity the North Baptist church until 1865, when he returned to St. Louis as assistant pastor of the Second Baptist church, Rev. Galusha Anderson being the senior pastor. After a year and a

half he became pastor of the Beaumont Street church. In 1872 he was chosen president of Shurtleff College.

Although comparatively a young man, Dr. Kendrick discharges the duties of his present responsible post with marked efficiency and success. With unusual gifts of attractive public address he combines studious habits, a special taste for the high themes which belong to his chair as instructor, and qualities as a teacher and disci-

ADIN A. KENDRICK, D.D.

plinarian which give him every year a stronger hold upon his work and upon those under his care. The college has never prospered more than under his administration; year by year it is taking higher rank upon the roll of American colleges. Dr. Kendrick is always cordially received on the various public occasions, in his own State and elsewhere, when service is required of him, and invariably acquits himself in a way which commands the respect of all.

Kendrick, Albert, M.D., of Waukesha, Wis., is a native of Vermont, and a son of Adin Kendrick, a prominent physician of Poultney, where the subject of this sketch was born Aug. 1, 1813. At the age of seven years Albert had his right hand nearly severed from the arm, disabling him ever afterward for all kinds of manual labor. He was therefore kept at school through the early years of his life. He studied at Hamilton Literary Institution (now Madison University). He graduated from the medical school in Woodstock, Vt., when twenty years of age. He commenced the practice of his profession in Poultney, Vt., where he resided three years. Subsequently he removed to Ticonderoga, N. Y., and remained three years. He then settled in Granville, N. Y., and practised medicine for sixteen years, and in June, 1855, he located in Waukesha, Wis., which has since been his home.

Dr. Kendrick is a man of fine standing in his profession, and thoroughly conscientious. He has been a member of the Baptist Church since he was sixteen years of age. He is a nephew of Nathaniel Kendrick, D.D., once president of Madison University, a cousin of A. C. Kendrick, D.D., the eminent Professor of Greek in the University of Rochester, and the father of A. A. Kendrick, D.D., the president of Shurtleff College, at Upper Alton, Ill.

In the Baptist church at Waukesha he is a trusted pillar. In the denomination of the State he is highly esteemed for his wise counsels and intelligent views. He is a liberal contributor to the religious and benevolent work of his denomination.

Kendrick, Asahel C., D.D., LL.D., was born in Poultney, Vt., Dec. 7, 1809. When thirteen years of age he went to Hamilton, N. Y., where his uncle, Nathaniel Kendrick, D.D., held the presidency of Hamilton Literary and Theological Institution. He pursued a course of study to prepare himself for college. He entered the junior class of Hamilton College, at Clinton, N. Y. At the end of one year he returned to Hamilton, and was employed as teacher in the village academy. He then re-entered Hamilton College, and was graduated in 1831. He was appointed tutor in the literary and theological seminary at Hamilton (now Madison) University, and the next year he was elected Professor of Greek and Latin. Relieved after a few years of the Latin department, he held the Greek chair until 1850, when, on the establishment of the University of Rochester, he accepted the Greek professorship in that institution, which he still continues to fill. In 1852 he went to Europe, perfecting his knowledge of Greek in the University of Athens. He also visited several Italian and German universities, studying the educational methods of those celebrated centres of learning. After two years he returned to his duties at Rochester. While he is an admitted authority in Greek, he is not lacking in other languages, ancient and modern. For many years he has been employed in the revision of the New Testament. He is the author of several Greek text-books. He brought out a revised edition of Olshausen's "Commentary on the New Testament." He is also the author of a memoir of Mrs. Emily C. Judson, wife of Dr. Judson, the missionary. His poetic talent was shown when a mere lad by anonymous contributions to the village papers of Hamilton, which created consider-

able discussion among the students and people as to their authorship. In later years he has brought out a volume of poems entitled "Echoes," some of which were greatly admired in literary circles. As a teacher of the Greek language he has no superior in America. He has made that a specialty. He has never been a pastor, but he has often, to the great satisfaction of the churches, supplied the pulpits of pastors. His profound learning, especially in the field of New Testament exegesis, gives his discourses a value and a public interest rarely found in sermons.

Kendrick, Rev. Clark, was born in Hanover, N. H., Oct. 6, 1775. The death of his father was the occasion which led to his removal to Vermont, in which State most of his life was spent in constant efforts to advance the Redeemer's kingdom. His conversion took place in 1797. He seems at once to have been impressed with the conviction that it was his duty to prepare himself for the Christian ministry. Although at first shrinking from assuming the responsibilities of the sacred office, he concluded, after much struggle, to obey what he regarded as a divine call, and, with such preparation for the work as he could obtain, he entered upon his ministerial labors, and was ordained April 20, 1802, at Poultney, Vt. Revivals of religion followed his preaching, one of which, that in 1816, resulted in an addition of more than 100 persons to his church.

Mr. Kendrick possessed in an eminent degree the missionary spirit. The religious destitution of his adopted State deeply touched his sympathies. He made tours to different sections of Vermont, the northern parts of New York and Canada, and labored most zealously to give the gospel to multitudes who were deprived almost wholly of the means of grace. His interest in missions extended to heathen lands, and he was among the most efficient agents in giving momentum to the efforts of the Baptist churches—aroused to new life by the stirring appeals of Luther Rice—to carry the news of salvation to the dark corners of the earth. Ministerial education also was another cause which enlisted his zeal and called forth his earnest efforts. The Vermont Baptist Education Society was formed mainly through his instrumentality, and he was chosen its president, and became its agent to visit the churches. To provide an educational home for these young men, the Baptists in Vermont proposed to start an institution of learning having special reference to the training of indigent students to become preachers of the gospel. The Baptists of the central and western districts of the State of New York had a similar plan in their minds. It was decided at length to unite efforts and establish the desired institution in some locality that would be convenient to all the parties concerned.

This locality was Hamilton, N. Y., the seat of the now flourishing Madison University. Mr. Kendrick was selected as an agent to solicit funds for the new institution, and for the remainder of his life devoted himself with great singleness of purpose to this work, and to him the infant seminary owed a debt of gratitude larger than it could ever repay.

Thus it was that the life of Mr. Kendrick was filled with deeds of Christian benevolence and unwearied activity in the cause of his Master. He was a recognized power .in his State, greatly honored and respected wherever he was known. Middlebury College conferred on him the honorary degree' of Master of Arts in 1819. His death occurred Feb. 29, 1824. The loss of the denomination by this premature cutting down of one of its strongest pillars was very great. It was not easy to supply the vacancy thus made. It is pleasant to know that the mantle of the father fell on sons who have risen up to render honor to their beloved parent. The influence which he so widely exerted has been extended in many directions by those who bear his venerated name and inherit the virtues which shone so brightly in his character.

Kendrick, James Ryland, D.D., youngest child of Rev. Clark and Esther Thomson Kendrick, was born in Poultney, Vt., April 21, 1821. He pursued his early studies at Hamilton Seminary, N. Y., where he made a profession of religion and joined the church, February, 1837. He entered the Junior class of Brown University in September, 1838, and graduated with the "classical oration" in 1840. In the latter part of the same year he removed to the State of Georgia, where he taught school for two years, having been licensed and ordained at Forsyth in the autumn of 1842. In the spring of 1843 he entered on his first pastorate in Macon, Ga. After a ministry of nearly five years in Macon, Dr. Kendrick was called, in 1847, to the First Baptist church in Charleston, S. C., where he remained for nearly seven years. He left this position to accompany a little colony of Baptists who established what is now known as the "Citadel Square church," of Charleston, and who built what is probably the best Baptist house of worship south of the Potomac. The civil war having straitened his flock, he retired from this field in May, 1862, after a pastorate of nearly eight years. During the further continuance of the war he preached for the Baptist church in Madison, Ga. At the close of the great struggle his Union sentiments led him North, and he settled with the Tabernacle Baptist church, New York City, in November, 1865, where he remained nearly seven years. In September, 1873, he became pastor of the church in Poughkeepsie, where he still labors, having secured the building of a fine and commo-

dious house of worship. He has no living children. The degree of Doctor of Divinity was conferred on him by Rochester University in 1866. He was for some time associate editor of the *Southern Baptist* newspaper, published in Charleston, S. C. Several tracts from his pen have been published, among them the following: "Responsibility for our Belief," "Human Depravity," "Address to Christians on the Subject of Temperance." He has also published several sermons on a variety of subjects. Of late years he has been a frequent contributor to the *Examiner and Chronicle,* New York. He is a brother of Prof. A. C. Kendrick, D.D., LL.D., of Rochester University. He is noble-minded, generous, cordial in his manners, of commanding presence, devout in spirit, and a good preacher.

Kendrick, Nathaniel, D.D., was born in Hanover, N. H., April 22, 1777. His parents, among the first settlers of the town, were both members of the Congregational Church. He labored on the

NATHANIEL KENDRICK, D.D.

farm until he was twenty, and then, with his father's consent, divided his time between teaching a school and attending the academy. About this period he was converted, through a revival that occurred in a small Baptist church; but, not being ready to give up the faith of his childhood, he sought from both a Baptist and a Congregational minister a statement of their views, and their reasons for holding them. Not satisfied by this method, he resolved to examine the New Testament, and after prosecuting his studies for nine months he became satisfied that the peculiarities of the

Baptists were derived from and supported by the New Testament, and he was immersed in April, 1798.

During the succeeding four years he engaged in farm labors and academic studies, uncertain as to his permanent life-work, feeling a strong disposition to enter the ministry, but shrinking from its responsibilities. Satisfied at length that it was his duty to preach, he spent some time in studying with Rev. Mr. Burroughs, of Hanover; with Rev. Dr. Asa Burton, of Thetford; with Dr. Emmons, of Franklin; and with Drs. Stillman and Baldwin, of Boston. By the church of the latter he was licensed to preach in the spring of 1803, at the age of twenty-six.

He began preaching as a supply at Bellingham, Mass., where he remained one year. Declining their call, he was ordained at Lansingburg, N. Y., in August, 1805. In 1810 he settled at Middlebury, Vt., dividing his time between this and three other feeble churches.

In 1817 he settled with the churches at Eaton and Morrisville, N. Y., resigning the latter in 1820 to lecture in the Hamilton Literary and Theological Institution. In 1821 he was elected Professor of Systematic and Pastoral Theology. In 1823 received D.D. from Brown University. In 1824 he located in Hamilton Village. In 1825–37 was one of the overseers of Hamilton College, at Clinton, N. Y. In 1836 was chosen president of the Hamilton Literary and Theological Institution, but, while acting as such, did not formally accept the office; corresponding secretary of New York Baptist Educational Society from 1834 to 1848; died Feb. 11, 1848, after a lingering and painful illness caused by a fall in 1845.

Dr. Kendrick's great work was in the Hamilton Institution. In his manners he was a dignified Christian gentleman. His theology belonged to the Edwards form of Calvinism. As a counselor he was wise and safe. See also article MADISON UNIVERSITY, and for a complete sketch see "Nathaniel Kendrick" (American Baptist Publication Society); consult also "Sprague's Annals," jubilee volume Madison University.

Kennard, Joseph Hugg, D.D., was born in Haddonfield, N. J., April 24, 1798; baptized by Rev. Daniel Dodge, at Wilmington, Del., July 3, 1814; began to preach when but seventeen years of age, and attracted at once great attention on account of his youth and fervor; was licensed in September, 1818, and in 1819 undertook an agency to present the claims of missions, under the direction of Luther Rice. Became pastor at Burlington, N. J., Nov. 14, 1819; at Hopewell, N. J., January, 1822; and at Blockley, Pa., in October, 1823. In 1832 took charge of the New Market Street church, Philadelphia, Pa., where he remained six years. In

1838 went with a colony from the New Market Street church to form the Tenth church, and remained pastor of it until his death, June 24, 1866,— a period of twenty-eight years. A natural, graceful and vigorous style in presenting doctrinal as well as practical truths, united with tenderest sympathies, made Dr. Kennard one of the most successful preachers of his day.

During his ministry of nearly fifty years he was the means of the conversion of over 3000 people, 2500 of whom he himself baptized. No man in Philadelphia was more sincerely loved, or is more affectionately remembered. Nor was he merely a pastor. All agencies for the redemption of men had his sympathy and support. In his early life he traveled much in destitute regions to preach

JOSEPH HUGG KENNARD, D.D.

Christ and establish Baptist churches. He was one of the founders of the Pennsylvania General Association, and a life-long member of the Board of the Publication Society. He was among the first to advocate the temperance cause. In the great noonday prayer-meetings of 1857 he was a most conspicuous leader. A number of the Baptist churches of Philadelphia owe their origin to him. No man was more earnest in his advocacy of foreign and home missions. He sought in every way to secure a first-class education for the rising ministry.

Dr. Kennard was married June 27, 1822, to Miss Beulah E. Cox, of Burlington, N. J., who died June 26, 1862. He left six children, five daughters and a son, Rev. J. Spencer Kennard,

D.D., who in 1867 edited a memoir of his father, which was issued by the American Baptist Publication Society.

Kennard, J. Spencer, D.D., was born in Philadelphia, Sept. 24, 1833. He was converted when twelve years old; baptized by his father, Rev. Dr. Jos. H. Kennard, in April, 1846, and united with the Tenth Baptist church, Philadelphia.

After graduating from the Philadelphia High School, he entered the senior class of Lewisburg University. Here he consecrated himself to the ministry New Year's Eve, 1852. Graduating with honor, he entered Princeton Theological Seminary, and, completing a two years' course, accepted the pastorate of the First Baptist church of Bridgeton, N. J., October, 1856. After three years of successful work he became pastor of the E Street church, Washington, D. C., in 1859, succeeding Dr. George W. Samson. The church suffered distraction during the civil war, the flock being scattered North and South. The shepherd remained with his charge, working in a government clerkship during the week, preaching on the Sabbath, laboring for the sick and wounded on the battle-field; but health failed, and the Woburn church, Mass., called him in 1862 to that field.

He removed from Woburn to Albany, N. Y., after gathering a rich harvest of souls. In 1865, Dr. Kennard accepted the pastorate of the Calvary Baptist church, Washington, D. C. The new interest became a vigorous church. On the death of his father he was called to the Tenth church, Philadelphia, in April, 1867. After four prosperous years, 196 converts having been added to that church by baptism, and various mission enterprises successfully started, he removed to New York, and became pastor of the Pilgrim church. Here 300 persons were baptized by him. In 1879 a call from the Central Square church, East Boston, was accepted, and he is now the pastor. The doctorate was conferred on him by Madison University, N. Y., in 1879.

Dr. Kennard's literary labors have been the memoir of his father, many contributions to the press, especially a series of articles on "Pulpit Eloquence," and a work, in preparation, on the "Relation of Oriental Religions to Christianity."

During his ministry Dr. Kennard has baptized 1100 converts.

Kennedy, Rev. W. M., was born in Duplin Co., N. C., Aug. 26, 1825; baptized by Rev. Jesse Howell, Feb. 14, 1847; ordained by Revs. G. W. Hufham, G. W. Wallace, L. F. Williams, and Jesse Howell, in November, 1849; has been a pastor for thirty-one years; was moderator of Easton Association two years; was for many years president of the board of trustees of Warsaw High School; has baptized 1800 persons, traveled over 90,000 miles

in preaching the gospel, and he is as full of zeal and efficiency as ever.

Kentucky Baptists.—"The Baptists were the pioneers of Kentucky." The first explorers of its territory were the brothers Daniel and Squire Boone. The latter was a Baptist preacher. The first settlement was made at Boonsborough, in what is now Madison County, in the summer of 1775, by Col. Daniel Boone, his wife and daughters being the only women in the small colony. Col. Richard Calloway and his family joined the settlers the first day of September. They also were Baptists. The same fall a small settlement was made at Harrodsburg, some thirty miles southwest of Boonsborough. Early in the spring of 1776, Thomas Tinsley and William Hickman, Baptist ministers, came to Harrodsburg. "Mr. Tinsley," says Mr. Hickman, "preached almost every Sunday." Hickman also preached. Nothing more is known of Mr. Tinsley except that "he was," says Hickman, "a good old preacher." Mr. Hickman returned to Virginia the following summer. Emigrants, principally from Virginia, now began to pour into the new country rapidly. Among these were Gen. Henry Crist, Gen. Aquilla Whitaker, Gen. Joseph Lewis, Col. Robert Johnson, Col. William Bush, Hon. James Garrard, Gabriel Slaughter, the Clays, and many others, who became prominent in the camps and councils of the State. These were all Baptists.

During the years 1779 and 1780, William Marshall, John Whitaker, Benjamin Lynn, John Garrard, and Joseph Barnett, Baptist ministers, settled in the new country. John Taylor and Joseph Reding visited it and preached during this period.

The first Baptist church formed in Kentucky, or in the great Mississippi Valley, was constituted of 18 members by Joseph Barnett and John Garrard, on the present site of Elizabethtown, forty miles south of Louisville, June 18, 1781. It still bears its ancient name, Severn's Valley. The second church was constituted by the same ministers, July 4, 1781. It is called Cedar Creek, and is located forty miles southeast from Louisville. The third church in Kentucky was Gilbert's Creek, in Garrard County. It was constituted in Spottsylvania Co., Va., and removed to Kentucky, under the pastoral care of Lewis Craig, in the fall of 1781. Here it held its first meeting the second Sunday in December of that year.

Then followed Forks of Dix River, in 1782; Providence, in 1783; South Elkhorn, in 1783; Gilbert's Creek (Separate Baptists), in 1783; Beargrass, in 1784; Cox's Creek, Clear Creek, Great Crossings, Tate's Creek, Limestone, Brashear's Creek, Rush Branch, Pottinger's Creek, and Head of Boone's Creek, in 1785.

In 1785 three Associations were formed, Elkhorn and Salem of Regular Baptists, and South Kentucky of Separate Baptists. In 1793 an effort to form a union between the Regular and Separate Baptists failed in its object, and resulted in the formation of Tate's Creek Association of United Baptists. From this period till 1799 religion was at a low ebb, and open infidelity much abounded. In 1800 the religious awakening known as "The Great Revival in Kentucky" began, and continued three years. In this period the number of Baptists in the State was more than doubled. It was at this time that the jerks and the barking and dancing exercises prevailed in some degree among the Baptists, but much more extensively among the Presbyterians and Methodists.

In 1801 the Regular and Separate Baptists formed a union, and all assumed the name of United Baptists. From that time until 1818 the Baptists of Kentucky continued to prosper, with little to interrupt their harmony. About this period Daniel Parker introduced his two-seed doctrine, and with it the anti-mission spirit. This caused much trouble, dividing many churches and Associations. These factions still exist, but have become weak and insignificant. In 1823, Campbellism began to disturb the denomination, and continued to distress the churches until the Campbellites were cut off. The formal separation began in 1829, but was not completed till 1835, when the Campbellites became a distinct sect, known by various names in different localities.

In 1832 the Baptist State Convention was organized. Its operations were unsatisfactory, and, after a trial of four years, it was dissolved. In 1837 the General Association of Kentucky Baptists was constituted. Its special object was to promote the spread of the gospel in the State. Its success was encouraging from the beginning. It is estimated that 50,000 persons have been baptized under its auspices. Meanwhile, the anti-missionary spirit, which had first manifested itself in the churches about the year 1818, was fully aroused by the organization of the General Association. Divisions were produced in many churches and Associations. In not a few of these a majority was on the anti-missionary side. The formal division began in 1840. Since that time the Baptists of Kentucky have been divided into missionary and anti-missionary churches. The latter have now an aggregate membership of about 7000.

Since the division last referred to the denomination has enjoyed a good degree of harmony and prosperity. Until the close of the late civil war, the white and colored people worshiped together in the same churches. Since that period the colored people have formed churches and Associations of their own. The separation was harmonious, and

the feeling between the brethren of the two races is kind, and their correspondence is fraternal.

The subjoined table will show the growth of the Baptist denomination in Kentucky from 1790 to 1880:

Date.	Population of the State.	Number of Baptists.	Date.	Population of the State.	Number of Baptists.
1790.........	73,677	3,105	1850.........	982,405	69,894
1810.........	406,511	....	1860.........	1,155,684	81,262
1812.........	....	21,666	1870.........	1,321,011	....
1830.........	687,917	....	1875.........	....	144,269
1831.........	....	34,827	1878.........	....	159,743
1840.........	779,828	47,325	1879.........	....	161,190
1846.........	....	60,991	1880.........	....	163,696

Kentucky, General Association of.—The first general organization of the Baptists in Kentucky was effected in 1832 at Bardstown. It was styled "The Kentucky Baptist Convention." There was much opposition to it among the churches. It continued to meet for about four years, and then dissolved. In 1837 "The General Association of Baptists in Kentucky" was organized in Louisville. Its leading objects were to promote preaching among the destitute within its bounds, to encourage literary and theological education, and to foster foreign missions. The churches watched its movements with doubt and suspicion, and some of them openly opposed it. But immediately after its organization an extensive revival swept over the whole State, and the General Association grew rapidly in favor. It employed a large corps of missionaries, and built up many churches that were weak, and constituted a large number of new ones. It is estimated that its missionaries, and those of its auxiliary societies, have averaged at least a thousand baptisms a year, from its organization until the present time. It has stimulated the churches to support their pastors, kindled the spirit of home and foreign missions, encouraged the building up of schools and colleges, and checked the ravages of intemperance, and has been in every way of incalculable advantage to the denomination in Kentucky.

Kenyon, Rev. Archibald, as the pastor during three years and a half of the Tabernacle church in Chicago, and afterwards for several years of the Berean Baptist church, is to be remembered with those who have contributed to build up the Baptist denomination at important points. He was born in Athol, Warren Co., N. Y., July 31, 1813. Until eighteen years of age his home was at Hague, on the west side of Lake George. His conversion occurred in the fall of 1831, and he was baptized by Elder Daniel Tinkham July 6, 1832. Feeling himself called to the work of the ministry, he was licensed by the church at Hague. He studied at the Sandy Hill Academy, also at East Bennington, then conducted by Messrs. A. Macomber and A. N.

Arnold. He was ordained in 1836. His first pastorate was at Lakeville and Shushan, in Washington County. Subsequently he was engaged at White Creek, Shaftesbury, and Hoosac. During the years 1840–41 he had the care of a Baptist church in Providence, R. I., but in 1842 the relation was dissolved. After a year at Vernon, Oneida Co., N. Y., and three and a half years at Clinton, eight miles away, he came West, and accepted pastorates in Chicago as above mentioned. From 1852 to 1856 he served the Tabernacle church, and later the Berean. His subsequent pastorates have been at Iowa City, at Peoria, and other places in Illinois. Though his pastorates have for the most part been brief, they have been fruitful, in nearly every instance considerable accessions being made to the church. He has been an active champion of every kind of reform, in that department of effort being a valued associate and co-laborer of Dr. Nathaniel Colver. He now suffers a great affliction in nearly a total loss of sight, but continues in service as pastor of two small churches near the central part of the State.

Kerfoot, Franklin H., D.D., was born in Clarke Co., Va., Aug. 29, 1847. Until the age of fourteen he was educated at schools in Berryville. He was engaged in the Confederate service during the war. In 1866 he entered the Columbian University, graduating in the college with the degree of Bachelor of Philosophy, and in the law school with the degree of Bachelor of Law, in 1869. He spent a year and a half at the Southern Baptist Theological Seminary, but, his health failing, he was obliged to suspend all study for nearly a year. Subsequently he entered the Crozer Theological Seminary, and after one year's study graduated in 1872. Afterwards he traveled over Europe, Egypt, and Palestine, and spent a year at the University of Leipsic. On his return to this country he became pastor of the Midway and Forks of Elkhorn churches, Ky., entering on his labors in those fields Feb. 1, 1875. On the death of the lamented Dr. Richard Fuller, of the Eutaw Place Baptist church, Baltimore, Mr. Kerfoot was elected his successor, and he entered on the pastoral charge of that church in November, 1877. While in Kentucky, Mr. Kerfoot held for one session the professorship of German in Georgetown College, Ky.,—a position for which he was admirably fitted by his studies in Germany. During his absence in the East he published in the *Religious Herald* some interesting letters descriptive of classical and Biblical scenes. The Columbian College conferred upon Mr. Kerfoot, in 1872, the honorary degree of A.M.

Kermott, Rev. Wm. Judson, was born in Carrolton Co., New Brunswick, in 1833. In his infancy his parents removed to Canada West, where he remained until twelve years of age, when he became a member of the family of his brother-in-law, Rev. E. J. Scott, a Baptist minister. He made a profession of religion at fifteen years of age, and united with the Baptist church at New Market, Canada West. He very early in life felt that God called him to preach the gospel, and made preparation for it as opportunity afforded up to manhood. He was ordained by the Baptist church in Almond, Allegany Co., N. Y., in 1857, and at once became the pastor of the church. This pastorate he resigned after two years' labor to accept an appointment from the American Baptist Home Mission Society as general missionary for Kansas. This position he held for eleven years, accomplishing during the time a very successful and important work. In 1866 he became the pastor of the First Baptist church in Omaha, Neb. The church there was largely gathered through his labors, and its fine meeting-house built and completed so as to enable the church to meet for worship in the basement. In 1870 he removed to Chicago, Ill., where he was pastor of the Coventry Street Baptist church six years, and of the Halsted Street Baptist church two years. This last pastorate Mr. Kermott resigned for the purpose of again entering the service of the American Baptist Home Mission Society as district missionary for Southwestern Wisconsin, which is his present field of labor.

During his ministry of twenty-three years, devoted largely to the new States and Territories, Mr. Kermott has been an indefatigable worker and a highly successful minister. He has organized a number of churches, built several meeting-houses, aided in the formation of the Kansas and Nebraska Baptist State Conventions, assisted struggling churches encumbered with heavy debts to provide the means for their payment, and all his work is of a substantial character. He has fine acquisitions in literary and theological learning, and is a highly esteemed minister of Christ.

Kerr, Judge John, LL.D., distinguished as a jurist, orator, statesman, and above all as a devout Christian, was born in Pittsylvania Co., Va., Feb. 10, 1811, and was the son of the Rev. John Kerr, the most eloquent preacher of the gospel who has yet appeared in North Carolina or Virginia. Mr. Kerr was educated in Richmond, Va.; was the first law student of the late Chief-Justice Pearson, and settled in Caswell, N. C., his father's native county, at the age of twenty-one, and was baptized in 1832 into the fellowship of the Yanceyville Baptist church by the Rev. J. J. James. Mr. Kerr was a decided Baptist, and was called on by his brethren to fill many important positions. He was a trustee of Wake Forest College, vice-president of the Southern Baptist Convention, president of the Baptist State Conventions for many sessions, and frequently moderator of the Beulah Association. He represented his county in the State Legislature; was in the Congress of the United States in 1852-53, and again in 1858–59; was judge of the Superior Court during the war, and was again elected judge by the people in 1874 for eight years. He was the orator of the Mecklenburg Centennial, celebrated May 25, 1875.

He was also a trustee of the State University, president of the North Carolina Historical Society at the time of his death, and received the title of LL.D. from both Trinity College and the State University.

When a young Christian his faith and zeal were so great that many predicted that he would follow his father into the pulpit, but worldly ambition tempted him into politics. God, however, was gra-

JUDGE JOHN KERR, LL.D.

cious to him and restored his first love, and for many years before his death he became eminent for godliness. He loved the society of Christ's children, and while he was attending to his judicial duties it was a common thing for this magnificently endowed man to forsake the fashionable circles which eagerly courted his society and find his chief delight in some humble prayer-meeting. He was never ordained as a preacher, but no Sabbath was permitted to pass, no matter where he was, without his bearing witness to the love of Jesus, and his exhortations were all the more forcible because of his position on the bench. He died Sept. 5, 1879, at his home in Reidsville, N. C., after a protracted illness.

Kerr, Rev. John, was born in Caswell Co., N. C.,

Aug. 4, 1782. His father was of Scotch descent, and was eminently pious. His early education was superior to that of most of those by whom he was surrounded. He was converted under the preaching of Rev. Wm. Paisley, a Presbyterian clergyman, and was baptized Aug. 12, 1801. Shortly afterwards he was licensed to preach, and was everywhere listened to with the most earnest attention. Having been engaged in teaching previous to his conversion, he now abandoned it and gave himself wholly to the ministry. He made extensive tours in all directions, visiting South Carolina and Georgia, and preaching to large assemblies of people. Lower Virginia, also, was the scene of his labors. About the year 1811, Mr. Kerr, at the earnest solicitation of friends, allowed himself to become a candidate for Congress. At first he was defeated, but he was subsequently elected, and continued to serve his constituents in that body during the war of 1812. Mr. Kerr always regarded this step as a grievous error, inasmuch as it diminished his own spirituality and injured his influence as a minister of the gospel; and his belief was that he was brought back from political life only by a painful special providence. In March of 1825 he removed to Richmond, Va., and took charge of the First Baptist church in that city. During the six years he spent as pastor of this church, nearly a thousand persons were baptized by him, so powerfully did the Word of God prevail. Mr. Kerr was deeply interested in all the benevolent movements of the day, and for many years presided over the General Association of Virginia, as well as over the Dover Association. He took an active part also in protesting against the dangerous errors of Alexander Campbell. In 1832 he resigned the care of the church in Richmond in order to devote himself more especially to evangelistic labors. His time was thenceforth given to protracted meetings and visiting destitute churches. In the year 1836 he removed to a farm near Danville, Va., still prosecuting his labors among the feeble churches, and accomplishing much good. He died Sept. 29, 1842. As a preacher Mr. Kerr was greatly gifted. With a fine person, a well-modulated voice, and a graceful manner, he won and held the attention of the largest assemblies for hours. His sermons were exceedingly interesting and impressive, and one who knew him has said, "Under his stirring and almost seraphic appeals I have frequently, I judge, seen thousands at one time bathed in tears." "Thousands have acknowledged him," says the same writer, "as their spiritual father; and in Virginia and North Carolina multitudes were turned to righteousness through his labors."

Keyser, Charles, D.D., was born at Albany, N. Y., May 13, 1827; received his literary and theological education at Madison University and

Rochester Theological Seminary; ordained at Wallingford, Conn., in 1851; was pastor at Mount Norris, Niagara Falls, and Binghamton, N. Y., in Providence, R. I., in Philadelphia, Pa., in Trenton, N. J., and in Wakefield, Mass., where he died. In 1865 he received the prize offered by the American Baptist Publication Society for the "Baptist Catechism." Lewisburg University conferred upon him the degree of Doctor of Divinity.

Dr. Keyser was the owner of a clear, powerful intellect; he was logical, orthodox, fearless, and faithful. The writer lamented his early and unexpected death, and thousands shared in his sorrow.

Kidder, Rev. Wm. S., of Igo, Shasta Co., Cal.; born in Charing, County of Kent, England, Nov. 15, 1834; came to New York in 1842; was converted at fifteen, and baptized into the fellowship of the Morris church, N. Y.; removed to California in 1858, and was ordained at Sacramento in 1860. He is a devoted pioneer preacher in Northern California,—almost the only Baptist minister in that wide and destitute field. He has acted as pastor at Red Bluff, Weaverville, Mount Shasta, and Eagle Creek, laboring with his own hands for his bread, and riding forty or fifty miles at his own expense to serve some poor church or minister to the afflicted, looking for his reward on high. He has been greatly blessed in his work and has secured much influence among the people, who have honored him with some of their most important offices.

Kieff, Baptism of the Population of.—Vladimir the Great, Prince of Russia, was a heathen until he married the Princess Anna, of Constantinople, when he repudiated his god Perune, and about A.D. 988 ordered the entire inhabitants of Kieff to be baptized. The proclamation stated that "Whoever, on the morrow, should not repair to the river (Dnieper), whether rich or poor, he should hold for his enemy." . . . "Some stood in the water up to their necks, others up to their breasts, holding their young children in their arms. The priests read the prayers from the shore, naming at once whole companies by the same name."—Mouravieff's "History of the Church of Russia," pp. 13, 15. Oxford, 1842. In this baptism thousands were immersed, and Christianity of a certain kind was triumphantly introduced into Russia.

Kiffin, Rev. William, was born in London in 1616. In 1625 the plague, which swept over his native city, deprived him of both his parents and left him with six plague sores, the cure of which was regarded as impossible. Through two sermons preached by Mr. Davenport and Mr. Coleman, in London, Mr. Kiffin obtained from Christ a divine life which defied the evils of seventy stormy years. He united with a Congregational church, by which he was first called to the ministry. In 1638 he

joined the Baptist church of which the Rev. John Spilsbury was pastor. From this community a colony went forth in 1640 which formed another church. The new organization met in Devonshire Square. It elected Mr. Kiffin pastor,—an office which he retained for sixty-one years, the duties of which three assistant pastors at different times aided him to discharge.

Mr. Kiffin was a merchant, carrying on business with foreign countries, and especially with Holland. He conducted his mercantile affairs with so much skill that in a few years he was among the wealthiest men in London, and known by all classes of society throughout the kingdom as one of the greatest of English merchant-princes. This made him a conspicuous object for persecuting spite, and

REV. WILLIAM KIFFIN.

it stirred up the cupidity of a base horde of informers, whom the Stuarts employed to ruin Dissenters. Lord Arlington, one of the secretaries of Charles II., told Mr. Kiffin that he was on every list of disaffected persons whose freedom was regarded as dangerous to the government.

He was arrested many times. Once he was committed to the White Lion jail in London, where some prisoners formed a conspiracy to murder him, but he was unexpectedly set at liberty. Gen. Monk arrested him for an alleged conspiracy against the king, but the charge was shown to be false, and he was released. About midnight, on another occasion, he was taken into custody, accused of having hired two men to kill the king, but soon after this wicked fabrication was exposed, and he was permitted to depart. His position among Dissenters exposed him to extreme peril for many years. Kiffin's influence was very great. Macaulay says, "Great as was the authority of Bunyan with the Baptists, William Kiffin's was greater still." He had talents of the highest order; his education was respectable; his sagacity was uncommon; his manners were polished; his piety was known everywhere; and for half a century he was the first man in the Baptist denomination. With the business community of London, or with the great trades of other cities, the credit of Kiffin stood higher than the financial promises of kings. Even the haughty nobles of Britain were not too proud to be his friends, and among these Clarendon, the Lord High Chancellor, stood the first. Thurloe, the chief secretary of Cromwell, in his "State Papers," frequently mentions Mr. Kiffin's name with respect, and the "Whitlocke's Memorials" are equally just to the great and good Baptist. Even King Charles himself, as far as his heartlessness would permit him to show affection, was the friend of Mr. Kiffin. There were ten Baptist men and two women arrested at a Dissenting religious meeting at Aylesbury, for which offense against the Church of England they were sentenced to three months' imprisonment. At the expiration of that time they were brought before the court and commanded to conform to the Episcopal Church or to leave the country immediately. These sturdy Baptists refused to do either, and they were sentenced to death *according to law*. A man forthwith started off to Mr. Kiffin, in London, who interceded with the king, and saved their lives. And on several other occasions the king gave substantial proofs of his regard to the great city merchant. He was so friendly to Mr. Kiffin that he sent to borrow £40,000 from him, no doubt as a return for favors he had granted his brethren, which Mr. Kiffin compromised by a gift of £10,000, and felt that he had saved £30,000 by the arrangement. When King James II. abolished the charter of the city of London he wanted to make Mr. Kiffin an alderman to secure the influence of his great name to help him in his illegal suspension of many charters, and of all penal laws against Dissenters and Catholics. But he disliked the king's illegal measures, and lent him no willing aid, direct or indirect, to assist him in their execution.

Mr. Kiffin's ample means were chiefly used in works of benevolence. He gave large sums to the poor; he contributed with great liberality to the feeble churches and their persecuted ministers; he assisted in the education of young men for the ministry, and he was ever ready for any labor or gift of love.

The only work he ever published was a treatise in favor of "close communion," the arguments in

which are as sound as the principles that governed his pure and noble life.

One of the sons of Mr. Kiffin was poisoned by a Catholic priest in Venice because he had been too free in denouncing his religion. Two of his grandsons, the Hewlings, were murdered by Jeffreys, the basest of judges, and James II., the meanest of kings. Macaulay speaks of them as "the gallant youths, who, of all the victims of the Bloody Assizes, had been most lamented." Their sister Hannah married Major Henry Cromwell, the grandson of the great Protector.

Mr. Kiffin was evidently raised up by the providence of God and invested with his talents, influence, and wealth to shield his persecuted brethren in times specially calamitous; and in a spirit of supreme love to Jesus, for half a century, he was the father of the English Baptists. He died Sept. 29, 1701, when the sword of William III. of blessed and of "Boyne Water" memory had terrified the last Stuart from the English throne.

Kilborne, Rowley, was born in the town of Bristol, Addison Co., Vt., Sept. 28, 1780. He removed to Canada in 1820. Converted with his wife in the winter of 1827–28, he joined the Baptist church in the township of Lobo. In 1832 he removed to Beamsville, and two years after was chosen deacon of the church there, in which office he continued to the day of his death, Oct. 17, 1880. He was the first president of the Baptist Missionary Convention of the Province of Ontario. For forty years he was a magistrate, and in several other official positions he served the public with rare skill and fidelity.

Killingsworth, Judge Thomas, was probably a native of Norwich, England, and came to this country very soon after his ordination. We find him at Middletown and Piscataway exercising his ministry in 1688 and 1689. His name was prominently associated with Baptist movements in New Jersey, and especially in Piscataway. He was the first pastor at Cohansey, continuing for nineteen years, until his death. The destruction of the old church records for the first century of its existence deprives us of facilities for securing information about him. Mr. Killingsworth was appointed judge in Salem County, and discharged the duties of the bench as well as those of the pulpit satisfactorily. He died in 1709. He was a firm Baptist, but avoided any rash illegal act; so we find that in 1706 at a court held in Salem he took out a license under the Toleration Act for a preaching-place at the house of one Jeremiah Nickson.

Kilpatrick, Rev. J. H. T., was one of those who aided greatly in elevating our denomination in Georgia to its present high standard in a missionary point of view. He was born in Iredell Co., N. C., June 24, 1793. In his younger years he had excellent educational facilities, received an exceptionally classical education, and prior to his permanent settlement in Georgia he taught school in several places in Louisiana. While in that State he married his first wife, and also took an active part in the campaign of 1814 and 1815, participating in the battle of New Orleans, Jan. 8, 1815. He was converted in 1817, and joined the Baptist church at Cheneyville, La., June 22. In 1820, after the death of his wife, he returned to the East, was prevailed upon to remain and preach at Robertvill, S. C., from whence he removed to Burke Co., Ga., where he married Miss Harriet Eliza Jones, June 23, 1822. Afterwards he removed to Richmond County, and at once identified himself with the most prominent Baptists in the State, taking a high

REV. J. H. T. KILPATRICK.

position among them. His field of labor lay within the Hephzibah Association, which, when he first became connected with it, was violently anti-missionary. With great zeal and prudence he promulgated missionary sentiments, and after the lapse of thirteen years had the pleasure of seeing it entirely revolutionized on the subject of missions. A tract written by him in 1827 or 1828, entitled "A Plain Dialogue on Missions," which was afterwards published in the "Baptist Manual" in connection with denominational articles by Pengilly, Booth, and Andrew Fuller, was prepared specially for the Hephzibah Association, and had a most salutary influence. Mr. Kilpatrick was, through the force of circumstances, a great champion of baptism and temperance in his Association, and to him those

two causes owe much able and eloquent support by both pen and voice. He aided, too, greatly in promoting the Baptist educational interests of Georgia. The land upon which Hephzibah High School is situated was donated by him, and at the State Convention of 1829, at Milledgeville, he, Sherwood, Sanders, and Mercur promptly raised the $2500 necessary to secure the Penfield legacy,—an action which proved to be the inception of Mercer University. His life was prolonged until Jan. 9, 1869, and was one of remarkable usefulness.

The following is part of a sketch of Mr. Kilpatrick, written by Gen. G. W. Evans, of Augusta, which appeared in the minutes of the Hephzibah Association for 1869:

"As a citizen, he was quiet, retiring, and unobtrusive; as a man, open, honest, and unsuspecting; as a friend, true but undemonstrative; as a pastor, laborious and constant, always punctual to his appointments; as a preacher, he was logical and profound, and when aroused oftentimes sublimely eloquent; as a writer and controversialist, he was true, accurate, and resistless; as a Christian, uniform and faithful; and in his expiring moments, as if to seal the holy record of his life with his dying testimony, his last words were 'Precious Jesus!'

"Such, brethren, is the brief and imperfect record of the man now gone to his reward, who, before many of us were born, became, by the power of his intellect, we might almost say the father of this Association, and who, by pen and voice, aided by the late Rev. Joshua Key, was the main instrument of building up the missionary interest among us, and who for years was the triumphant defender of our peculiar views and the eloquent vindicator of our denominational honor. Gifted with a massive intellect and an iron constitution, he literally wore out in the service of his Master. We deem it no injustice to the living or the dead to express our honest conviction that in his death is extinguished the brightest intellectual light which it has ever been our pride to honor."

Kilpatrick, Rev. James Hines, youngest son of Rev. J. H. T. Kilpatrick and Miss Harriet E. Jones, was born in Burke Co., Ga., Oct. 18, 1833. He entered Mercer University in 1849 and graduated in 1853, sharing the highest honors of his class. While at Mercer he made a public profession of religion and united with the church, and was called to ordination by the White Plains church, Greene County, in 1854. He began his labors as pastor of that church in 1855, succeeding Rev. V. R. Thornton. Since that time his energies have been concentrated upon the White Plains church, of which he has been the pastor ever since, though he has had charge of other churches, and he has succeeded in so developing its capabilities that it has become one of the most spiritual, efficient, liberal, and enlightened churches in the State. For years it has been regarded as a model church, and Mr. Kilpatrick as the model pastor of the State. In his preaching he makes no effort at display, his aim being to present gospel truth in such a manner that all may understand and few fail to appreciate it; and perhaps no minister in the State is uniformly heard with more interest and profit.

In public life he is very quiet and unobtrusive, but is ever ready to maintain his opinions with ability. He has always taken a prominent part in the affairs of the Georgia Association, and since his majority has invariably occupied a seat in the Georgia Baptist and Southern Baptist Conventions.

In private life he is simple in his habits, affable in manners, and pleasant in social intercourse. He is fond of books and study. He has published several valuable sermons and a series of articles in the *Christian Index* on the subject of " Baptism," which were masterly in character and exhaustive in execution. He exerts a strong influence in the denomination within his own State, and might deservedly occupy a much more prominent position were it not for his modesty. He is a strong, terse, sensible writer, a forcible speaker, and a man of great power every way.

Kilpatrick, Rev. Washington L., eldest son of Rev. J. H. T. Kilpatrick, was born in Burke Co., Ga., Oct. 18, 1829. He was graduated from Mercer University, with the first honors of his class, in 1850; was ordained in 1852, entered upon the duties of a country pastor, and to the present time, with persistent and untiring energy and faithfulness, has labored in the ministry, serving different churches within the bounds of the Hephzibah Association. So eminent have been his abilities, so exalted his character, so uniform his courtesy and kindness, and so efficient have been his labors and so Christian his deportment, that he wields an influence possessed by no other in his Association. He is commanding in person, with a fine open countenance, great benignity of expression, and a pleasing address that secures the confidence of strangers. Having a tender heart and liberal impulses, the suffering have ever found him a ready friend and the poor a generous almoner. As a preacher, he speaks extemporaneously, is always practical, pointed, and clear. Too deeply concerned in presenting sound and wholesome instruction, which he does in a solemn and impressive manner, to seek for mere ornamentation in speech, he makes no special effort to embellish his sermons. By his preaching he has attained the most gratifying results, and has secured for himself an enviable reputation; for, while an unflinching Baptist, and ardently devoted to the spread of Baptist sentiments, he seeks for success more by the firm maintenance of truth than by directly combating error.

But other labors pertaining to the welfare of our Baptist Zion, besides those of a pastor, have engaged his attention. For twenty-two consecutive years he managed the mission and colporteur work of the Hephzibah Association. Chiefly through his instrumentality the Hephzibah High School was established in 1861, and that school he taught, as president, with eminent success, from 1866 to 1876. In 1868 he organized the Walker Colored Association, and since its formation he has been the chief and trusted counselor of its ministers and churches. Prior to emancipation the members of those churches belonged to the Hephzibah Association. Since 1869 he has faithfully discharged the duties of a trustee of Mercer University; and in 1878 he succeeded in securing the organization of the Georgia Baptist Historical Society, of which he is the efficient corresponding secretary.

Mr. Kilpatrick has sought to make his attainments more and more available for wide-spread usefulness; and, whatever his influence may be as a public man,—and unquestionably it is very great, —it is but the natural and logical sequence of an unblemished private record and consecrated talents.

Kimbro, Rev. W. C., M.D., a prominent minister and physician in Drew Co., Ark., was born in North Carolina in 1835; came to Arkansas in 1860 and settled near his present residence, and engaged successfully in the practice of medicine. He united with the church in 1868, and was soon after licensed to preach, and ordained in 1870. While pursuing his profession he has done much to relieve the destitute around him. Hopewell and Centre Point churches have enjoyed his labors, and have been much blessed under his efficient ministry.

Kimbrough, Rev. Bradley, son of Rev. Duke Kimbrough, was born in Jefferson Co., Tenn., Nov. 3, 1799. He studied and practised law for a time, and was regarded as one of the first lawyers of the State.

In 1834 he was a leading member of the convention which revised the constitution of the State of Tennessee. He afterwards refused political preferment and became a minister of the gospel, and was ordained by the Madisonville Baptist church in the year 1835. His efforts as a pastor were very successful; he assisted in the organization of a number of churches, and labored in protracted meetings, which were abundantly blessed of the Lord.

His ministerial gifts were of a high order. In 1845 he was chosen agent to endow Union University, located at Murfreesborough, Tenn. He accepted, and completed the work in 1847. At one time he was agent of the Bible Board. He was successful in whatever he undertook. For many years he was moderator of the Liberty Association, and he was also president of the General Association. He closed his earthly labors June 30, 1874. While living he was one of the brightest lights in our beloved Zion.

Kincaid, Eugenio, D.D., was born in the State of Connecticut, and brought up in Southern New York; was one of five students who formed the first class in Madison University, Hamilton, N. Y. Under the influence of sermons preached by Dr. Carey, during his second year at Hamilton, he determined to become a missionary. At the time of his leaving college there was war between the English and Burman governments, which led to the breaking up of the Burmese mission and delayed his departure for heathen lands. He then became pastor of the church at Galway, N. Y., where, however, he became dissatisfied, and resolved that if no door was yet open for labor among the heathen, he would find some destitute region in his own country where he could do missionary work. His attention being directed to the mountainous districts of Central Pennsylvania, he commenced work at Milton, where at that time there was but one Baptist, and she a poor widow with six children. He preached in court-rooms, school-houses, and occasionally in groves, for four years, with manifold tokens of the Divine favor.

While thus engaged he received a letter from the executive committee of the Missionary Union asking him to go to Burmah. He replied at once that he would. In the spring of 1830 he sailed from Boston, and towards the close of the year he reached Maulmain, where he found Drs. Judson and Wade and Mr. Bennett.

Dr. Kincaid commenced the study of the language under a native preacher, giving twelve hours every six days of 'the week to the work. Meanwhile, he preached for the English soldiers then stationed in those parts. After a year of preparation he went to Rangoon and gave his entire time to work among the Burmans. In a little more than a year he left the Burman church at Rangoon under the care of a native pastor, and proceeded to Ava, the capital, and subsequently spent three months in visiting every town and village along the banks of the Irrawaddy. For nearly two months he lived in his boat, subjected to severe hardships; but he heroically continued his work among the natives, and at the end of fifteen months had baptized eleven converts and organized them into a church.

He continued his labors for many years in foreign lands, and subsequently returned to America broken in health by his incessant toil. At his quiet home in Girard, Kan., the enfeebled body detains a little longer "the hero missionary" from his home beyond the skies.

Kincaid, Rev. J. P., was born in Garrard Co., Ky., March 4, 1848. In 1852 his parents removed to Danville, where, at the age of thirteen, he united with the Baptist church. In 1868 he transferred his membership from the church at Danville to New Providence church, in the same county, where, July 14, 1872, he was ordained to the gospel ministry in the Baptist church by the following Presbytery: T. M. Vaughn, R. L. Thurman, W. P. Harvey, I. M. Sallee, and A. D. Rash. About this time he was called to the pastoral care of the Drake's Creek church, in Lincoln Co., Ky. After this he took charge of the Logan's Creek church also. About forty persons were added to the Drake's Creek church during his first year's labors there. In the latter part of 1873 he resigned the care of these churches, and removed to Covington, Tenn. During the summer and fall of the year he labored in protracted meetings in Topton, Lauderdale, and Dyer Counties, and in October, 1874, was called to the care of the Elam Baptist church, Durhamsville, Tenn.

He is a decided Baptist. He is now pastor of the church in Gallatin, Tenn. Mr. Kincaid, though a young man, stands among the first preachers of our State; he is a reasoner, and knows how "rightly to divide the word of truth."

"Kind Words" and "The Child's Gem."— *Kind Words* is the Sunday-school paper of the Southern Baptist Convention. It is published at Macon, Ga., and edited by Rev. S. Boykin. This useful paper wields a strong, extended, and healthy influence. Its lesson expositions of the "International Series" are studied to advantage by perhaps 200,000 persons each week in all the editions, counting the Lesson Leaflets. Its tone is highly evangelical, and at the same time it is strikingly denominational and a decided advocate of the mission cause. It first appeared in January, 1864, in the very midst of the throes of war, and was originated by Mr. C. J. Elford, of Greenville, S. C., assisted by Rev. Basil Manly, D.D., president, and Rev. John A. Broadus, corresponding secretary, of the Sunday-School Board of the Southern Baptist Convention, and soon reached a circulation of 25,000. For years it was a small monthly sheet, and its price was ten cents. It was then published at Greenville, S. C. In 1868 the Sunday-School Board was removed to Memphis, Tenn., and *Kind Words* was transferred to that city, where, in 1870, it was consolidated with the *Child's Delight*, a Sunday-school paper published by Rev. S. Boykin, at Macon, Ga., who was employed as editor. The *Child's Delight* was a semi-monthly paper, and thus *Kind Words* became a semi-monthly. Two years later a weekly edition was also issued, and its circulation became very extensive throughout the South and Southwest. In 1873 the Sunday-School Board was merged into the Home Board of the Southern Baptist Convention at Marion, Ala., and *Kind Words* was transferred to the care of that board, by which it has been issued ever since. Its publication office was changed to Macon, Ga., where satisfactory printing arrangements were made with the firm of J. W. Burke & Co. by the secretary of the Home Board. It is beautifully illustrated and elegantly printed, and yields the Home Board of the Southern Baptist Convention an income of $1000 per annum above expenses. The different editions of the paper are a weekly, semi-monthly, and monthly. The monthly issue contains no lessons; the weekly and semi-monthly issues contain them. Four-page Lesson Leaflets are also published.

The Child's Gem, a beautiful little four-page weekly illustrated Sunday-school paper for infant classes, is published by Rev. S. Boykin, Macon, Ga. It contains appropriate matter for the very young, with the lesson-story and questions adapted to the capacity of children unable to read. It has now been in existence two years, and has quite a wide circulation. It was first published under the title of *The Baptist Gem*.

King, Rev. Alonzo, was born in Wilbraham, Mass., April 1, 1796. When he was three or four years of age his family removed to Newport, N. H. He pursued his studies preparatory to college at the Newport Academy, and under the tuition of Rev. Leland Howard, of Windsor, Vt., and was a graduate of Waterville College, now Colby University, in the class of 1825. He was invited, immediately on his graduation, to become pastor of the church in what is now Yarmouth, Me., then North Yarmouth, which had become vacant by the removal of its pastor, Rev. Stephen Chapin, D.D., afterwards president of Columbian College, Washington, D. C. He was ordained Jan. 24, 1826, and was eminently successful in his ministry till failing health forced him to resign, in the spring of 1831. A year afterwards he was so far recovered that he was able to accept a call to the pastorate of the Baptist church in Northborough, Mass. While residing at Northborough he was for a time agent of the Massachusetts Baptist Convention, and also soliciting agent to raise funds for the endowment of the Newton Theological Institution. He was several times urged to take charge of important churches in cities and large towns, but his modest estimate of his abilities led him to decline all these overtures. In the spring of 1835 he removed to Westborough, Mass., where he died November 29 of the same year. As an author he is known by his "Memoir of George Dana Boardman." "In my own memory," says Baron Stow, "and in that of every one who knew him, his name is fragrant."

King, Rev. Daniel, was born July 1, 1803, on what was then the disputed border line of Kentucky and Tennessee. He was converted and baptized in 1831, and soon began missionary work in Mississippi. For twenty-five years he was a most faithful and successful evangelist and pastor, conducting many revivals, building up new churches, and baptizing large numbers. He was robust and had great natural force, swaying large audiences with the powers of a splendid eloquence. In 1853 he went to California and located on the Solano plains, where he built up one of the strongest and wealthiest churches, now known as the Dixon church. He died at Dixon, Oct. 3, 1877. He was honored and loved by all, and his influence on the Baptist cause, in its missionary and educational departments, will be felt for many generations on the Pacific coast.

King, Gen. E. D., was born in Greene Co., Ga., April 12, 1792; was a captain in the command of Gen. Floyd in the principal Indian war, fought in several battles, and was twice wounded. He removed to Alabama while it was yet a Territory, commenced life there in a log cabin, and became princely wealthy. For many years he was a trustee of the University of Alabama, one of the projectors of Howard College and of the Judson Female Institute, and president of the board of trustees of the last-named institution from its beginning to his death; contributed liberally of his time and means to the cause of education and religion; deacon in the Baptist church at Marion, and one of its most useful members; ardent and sincere in his attachments and convictions; of a strong and determined will; noted for his eminently practical judgment and good sense. He was the father of the Hon. Porter King.

King, Rev. Eustace E., pastor at Senatobia, Miss., was born in Mississippi in 1850; graduated at Mississippi College in 1873; began to preach at the age of eighteen; spent two years at the Southern Baptist Theological Seminary, then located at Greenville, S. C.; after which he was called to his present pastorate, where his labors have been eminently successful.

King, Rev. G. M. P., principal of the Wayland Seminary, Washington, D. C., was born at Oxford, Me., in 1833. He was fitted for college at Hebron Academy, and graduated from Colby University in 1857. He spent one year at Newton Theological Seminary. For the school year of 1858–59 he had charge of the rhetorical department of the Maryland Agricultural College. In 1860 he became pastor of the Baptist church in East Providence, R. I., and remained there five years. In April, 1865, while spending a few weeks with the army, in the service of the Christian Commission, he became interested in the education of the colored people of the South. He wrote and urged the granting of the first request to be allowed to open a school in Richmond, Va., for the teaching of the freedmen. In 1867 he took charge of the National Theological Institute, Washington, D. C.,—a school for their education. After two years it was united with Wayland Seminary, and Prof. King became the principal,—a position which he still holds. In the beginning they had no building and but few students; now they have a property free from debt, worth nearly $50,000, a handsome building in a beautiful location. It has numbered nearly 100 students annually for the last ten years, about half of whom have been connected with the theological department, and already more than 50 of the students are doing effective work as pastors, while a much larger number have engaged in teaching. The last class numbered 17, the largest ever graduated at this excellent institution.

King, Rev. H. M., was born in Ralls Co., Mo., April 8, 1839. He attended for some time the Shelbyville Seminary, at Shelbyville, Mo., and afterwards continued his studies under a graduate of Berlin, and finally with a Presbyterian minister of Kentucky. He was converted at Shelbyville, Mo., in 1859, in February, and baptized the same month. In August of that year he commenced to preach, and in the December following was ordained.

Mr. King labored for some years acceptably in Missouri, when, on account of being frail, he removed to Texas, hoping that its milder climate would suit him better. He was quite successful at Chapel Hill, Texas. Here his health gave way again, and he concluded to go to Florida. He arrived there a few years ago, and settled at Gainesville. His first pastorate was at Fernandina. He has been constantly engaged in the ministry, and his health is restored.

Mr. King is a man of fine intelligence, and as a preacher he has few equals. He thinks closely and clearly, and expresses himself perspicuously. He is remarkably prudent, conservative, and firm. He is able to adapt himself to the various classes of society, and he is beloved alike by all, which, in a country with such a complex population, adds very materially to his usefulness. He is one of the most valuable men in the denomination in Florida.

King, Rev. I. D., was born in Baltimore, Md., Feb. 4, 1824; was baptized into the fellowship of the Spruce Street church, Philadelphia, by Rev. T. O. Lincoln, May 8, 1842; was ordained in May, 1854, and settled as pastor of the church at Smithfield, Pa., where he remained two years; was subsequently pastor of the churches at Uniontown, Pa., Portsmouth, O., Granville, O., Phœnixville, Pa., and Chestnut Hill, Philadelphia. In 1876 he took charge of a new mission interest in Philadelphia,

which, under his efficient labors, soon became the Centennial church. With this church he still continues as pastor, and God is still blessing his ministry.

King, Hon. Judge Porter, was born in Perry Co., Ala., April 30, 1824; educated at the University of Alabama and at Brown University, R. I., whilst under the presidency of Dr. Wayland; studied law under Thos. Chilton, Esq.; was judge of the circuit court of one of the judicial circuits of the State before the late war, and held the office until deprived of it by Federal authority in 1865; for many years a trustee of the State University and of the Hospital for the Insane, taking a deep interest in these institutions; deacon in the Baptist church at Marion, trustee of Howard College, and president of the board of trustees of the Judson Female Institute. Judge King is a wealthy, cultivated gentleman, a lawyer of distinction, and a Baptist of sterling worth. He is a son of the late Gen. E. D. King.

Kinnear, Judge William Boyd, was born in St. John, New Brunswick, Oct. 12, 1796; converted in that city, and baptized in Halifax, Nova Scotia, in 1827; was one of the founders of the Baptist seminary at Fredericton; elected member of the Provincial Parliament in 1832; appointed to the Legislative Council in 1838; was judge of probate in St. John for many years, and was deacon of Brussels Baptist church. Judge Kinnear possesses a keen, well-cultured mind, accurate knowledge of law, deep Christian experience, zeal for education and other denominational enterprises, and the strictest integrity.

Kinnersley, Rev. Ebenzer, was born in Gloucester, England, Nov. 30, 1707. He arrived in America Sept. 12, 1714, was ordained in 1743, and ministered in Philadelphia and elsewhere until 1754. He had serious doubts about the character of Whitefield's preaching, and involved himself in grave trouble with the Baptist community in Philadelphia by proclaiming in the pulpit his convictions.

"In 1746," says Senator Jones, of Pennsylvania, "his attention was first directed to the wonderful and unknown properties of the electric fire, as it was then termed, and he was brought into close companionship with Benjamin Franklin. He was intimately associated with Franklin in some of his most splendid discoveries, and he more than once gratefully acknowledged his aid. He attracted the attention of many of the most eminent philosophers on both sides of the Atlantic, and he was chosen a member of the American Philosophical Society, which was then composed of the most learned and scientific men in the city." He was elected Professor of the English Tongue and of Oratory in the University of Pennsylvania in 1755. He held this position with advantage to the institution for eighteen years, and resigned it to the great regret of the students and their teachers. He died July 4, 1778. In the splendid building recently reared for the University of Pennsylvania a beautiful memorial window commemorates the worth of Ebenezer Kinnersley.

Kinney, Deacon Albert William, eldest son of Hon. R. C. Kinney, is deacon of the Baptist church of Salem, Oregon. He is successor to his father in an immense business at Salem, is noted for his devotion to Christ and for his lovely spirit. He is a large contributor to Baptist benevolent objects and other charities on the Pacific Coast. He was born at Muscatine, Ia., Oct. 3, 1843, became a Christian in early life, and is a zealous and steadfast member of the Baptist church.

Kinney, Hon. Robert Crouch, one of the most distinguished of Baptist benefactors in Oregon, was born July 4, 1813, in St. Clair Co., Ill.; removed to Muscatine, Ia., in 1838, and to Oregon in 1847; successful in large business enterprises, kind to the poor, just in his dealings, liberal to all, especially

HON. ROBERT CROUCH KINNEY.

to churches and colleges. He died at Salem, Oregon, March 2, 1875; all business was suspended, the Capitol was in mourning, and State officials wept as for a brother at the funeral. When death was near, his son, Dr. Kinney, was summoned at midnight to a distant town. The night was stormy, and the son, being reluctant to leave his father, was urged to go. "It may be some poor man that cannot pay you, Alfred; but go; don't let him suffer."

His marriage in early life was a happy one. He and his wife were Baptists; their children illustrated their parents' piety in the consecration of their wealth to the upbuilding of McMinnville College, the support of missions, and all other objects of benevolence. Mr. Kinney was a member of the Iowa Constitutional Convention; also a member of the Territorial Legislature, and of the Constitutional Convention of Oregon.

Kirk, Rev. A. G., is of Scotch origin on his father's side, and of English on his mother's. He was born in Lancaster Co., Pa., Nov. 14, 1809, of Quaker parentage. His great-grandfather, Benjamin Gilbert, and his family, were taken prisoners by the Indians in April, 1780, and suffered a miserable captivity, passing their days in constant terror of being killed, but, in the language of the chief, Rowland Mintour, "The Great Spirit would not let us kill you."

The son remained with his father's family until his marriage, in 1833, and in the subsequent year removed into Ohio, and engaged in teaching until 1845. On Jan. 15, 1843, he was baptized, and made his first public speech to a large assembly, partly composed of his scholars and of skeptical friends attracted to the solemn scene. He was ordained Jan. 12, 1845, at Salem, Columbiana Co., O. He was the first resident pastor of the church in New Castle, Lawrence Co., Pa., and the first pastor of the Nixon Street church, Alleghany City, Pa. At New Castle he enjoyed a prosperous ministry of eleven years. In Alleghany City and other churches he was highly favored. His entire ministry has been richly blessed. In labors he has been abundant, having preached during thirty-three years about 5000 sermons, and during the entire period losing only eight Sabbaths by any indisposition of the body. He is still in service.

Kirtley, Rev. E. N., a prominent minister in Louisiana, is a native of Virginia, and nearly fifty-five years of age. He came to Louisiana about 1850 as a licensed preacher in the Methodist church. He was convinced of the truth of Baptist sentiments from reading "Pendleton's Three Reasons." He was ordained as a Baptist minister in 1854, and became a missionary of the Grand Cane Association. He labored here until the war. About 1863 he removed to Springville, in Red River Parish, and engaged in teaching and preaching. He then removed to Ringgold, in Bienville Parish, where he taught and preached until he was called to Minden, in 1873. He then took a school at Red Land, in Bossier Parish, where he still lives, supplying the church at Bellevue, the capital of Bossier Parish.

Kirtley, Rev. Robert, was born in Culpeper Co., Va., May 30, 1786. In 1796 he with his parents emigrated to Boone Co., Ky., where he spent the remainder of a long and eminently useful life.

He professed religion and united with the Baptist church at Bullittsburg in 1811. In 1812 he entered the army as a lieutenant, and at the close of the campaign returned home and engaged in the active duties of religion. He was licensed to preach in 1819, ordained in 1822, and in 1826 he succeeded the beloved Absalom Graves in the pastoral care of Bullittsburg church. He was the leading preacher for years in North Bend Association, of which he was moderator thirty-one years. He died April 9, 1872.

Kitchen, Hon. W. H., who represents the Second District of North Carolina in the U. S. Congress, was born in 1837 ; received a collegiate education in Virginia ; read law ; entered the army in 1861, and attained the rank of captain of infantry, 12th Regiment N. C. troops ; was baptized by Rev. C. Durham in 1876. Mr. Kitchen is a man of great worth.

Kitts, Rev. Thomas J., was born in 1789, and was licensed to preach by the First Baptist church of Wilmington, Del. He was ordained to the pastorate of the church of Canton, N. J. In 1823 he took charge of the Second Baptist church of Philadelphia. This office he held for nearly sixteen years, till death summoned him to the skies.

His preaching was able and his ministry successful. He was a man of prayer ; he was thoroughly conversant with the Word of God ; he lived near the Eternal, whose love lifted his heart above the world and gave him the warm regards of all the friends of Jesus with whom he came in contact. He died Jan. 26, 1838, in the forty-ninth year of his age.

Knapp, Halsey Wing, D.D., was born in the city of New York in October, 1824. His father, Rev. Henry R. Knapp, was a successful Baptist minister, and his mother a woman of piety and force of character. In his youth and early manhood he was impulsive, energetic, and jovial, leading a restless life, some years of which were spent at sea. In 1846 he settled in business in New York. He was converted in 1857, and in 1858 was ordained to the ministry by a Council of the Baptist churches of New York. From this time his career has been especially eventful. His pastorates have been at West Farms and Hudson City, and in New York City with the South, Pilgrim, and Light Street churches. These important positions he has filled and at the same time conducted an extensive business. During nineteen years of pulpit service he has given away his entire salary to religious and benevolent objects. He daily transacts business, preaches every night in the week, during revival seasons traveling at night to keep his appointments, without any expense to the churches, and he often gives largely of his own means to assist new churches. His donations are without ostentation, and aggregate many thousands of dollars. As a preacher Dr. Knapp is eloquent and impressive, and he is greatly beloved by his denomination. A Western college conferred upon him the degree of D.D. in 1876.

Knapp, Rev. Henry Reynolds, was born in the city of New York Dec. 6, 1800; converted at the age of twenty-four; with his half-brother, William, organized a Sunday-school and preaching service in the basement of his father's house, out of which grew the Sixteenth Street Baptist church; licensed by McDougal Street Baptist church in 1832; ordained pastor of Greenport church, L. I., Oct. 8, 1834; having evangelistic gifts, afterwards settled with Baptist church, Essex, Conn.; First Baptist church, New London; Baptist church, Preston City; Second Baptist church, Groton; church in Rockville; church at Rondout, on the Hudson; returned to Greenport, L. I.; with church at Noank, Conn.; with the church at Hastings, on the Hudson; clear and forcible preacher; sound in doctrine and devoted in labors; his ministry crowned with many and happy revivals; occupying different fields in order to do the most good; in every place honored and held in sweet remembrance; has three sons now living, Rev. Halsey W. Knapp, D.D., Rev. Samuel J. Knapp, and Prof. Knapp of Yale College; had in his wife an eminent helpmeet; died May 13, 1862, in his sixty-second year, and the thirty-first of his ministry.

Knapp, Rev. Jacob, was born Dec. 7, 1799, in Otsego Co., N. Y., and died at Rockford, Ill., March 3, 1874. He studied at Hamilton in 1821–25, and was ordained August 23 in the year last named. Entering the pastorate at Springfield, Otsego Co., N. Y., he remained there five years; then removed to Watertown, N. Y., where he remained three years. Entering there upon the work of an "evangelist," he continued in that service during the remaining forty-two years of his public ministry. Fifteen years he resided at Hamilton, N. Y., twenty-five upon his farm near Rockford, Ill. In his revivalist work he ranged widely over New York, New England, and the Western States, including California. "He preached about 16,000 sermons," says Prof. Spear, of Madison University, "led about 200 young men to preach the gospel, and baptized 4000." Mr. Knapp's physique was in some sense a type of his mental and spiritual habit. He was of moderate height, strongly built, with broad shoulders and a muscular frame capable of great endurance. His conspicuous physical, like his mental, quality was that of robustness, while the business-like air with which he moved about in his ordinary avocations was typical of the serious, earnest, unflinching way in which he preached and toiled in the face of severe personal exposure and reproach. His preaching was doctrinal, direct, unsparing, even sometimes to the verge of coarseness; but his power over audiences was remarkable, and the fruits of his long toil in his chosen sphere, while not always genuine, were believed in many cases to be so, and always abundant. Among his last words were, "Oh, I have come to the everlasting hills!"

> "On Christ the solid rock I stand,
> All other ground is sinking sand."

He was buried at Rockford, Ill., Drs. Cole and Osgood and Hon. Messrs. Fulton, of Belvidere, and Holman, of Rockford, participating in the service.

Knapp, William J., Ph.D., was born at Greenpoint, Long Island, March 10, 1835; received his collegiate education in Madison and New York Universities. At graduation, in Madison, he was elected Professor of Modern Languages, for which he possesses remarkable qualifications. For a time he was Professor of Ancient and Modern Languages in Vassar College. In 1867 New York University conferred upon him the honorary degree of Doctor of Philosophy. For some years he was engaged in successful missionary labors in Spain. He is now a professor in Yale College.

Kneeland, Rev. Levi, was born in Masonville, N. Y., in 1803; converted at the age of fifteen, and united with the Baptist church in Masonville; at twenty licensed to preach; in 1824 entered Hamilton Literary and Theological Institution, and remained four years; ordained at Packerville, Conn., Oct. 8, 1828, with church just formed; held meetings in remote neighborhoods; established branch church at Voluntown; preached at Jewett City, Sterling, and Plainfield; assisted in protracted meetings at Norwich and elsewhere; held protracted meetings at Packerville every year; bold, aggressive, mighty in prayer, powerful in exhortation, full of illustrations, affable, sociable; intent on saving souls and greatly beloved by his brethren; in the six years of his ministry baptized more than 300; died at Packerville, Aug. 23, 1834, aged thirty-one.

Knight, Rev. Aaron Brightwell, A.M., was born in Todd Co., Ky., Feb. 24, 1824. He united with the Baptist church at Russellville in 1842, was licensed to preach in 1846, and was ordained in 1850. He was educated at Centre College, Ky., and graduated in 1845, after which he pursued a three years' course at Princeton Theological Seminary, in New Jersey. He received several flattering calls to city and village churches, but preferring the quiet of a country home, after preaching a short time for Salem church in Christian County, in his native State, he settled on a farm in Shelby Co., Ky., in 1858, where he still resides. He has been pastor of Burk's Branch church since 1858, and for a short time of Clay Village church. Since 1871

he has been pastor at Simpsonville church. In 1863 he was moderator of the General Association, and has been thirteen years moderator of Long Run Association, which includes the churches of Louisville. He was active in establishing the Kentucky Female College at Shelbyville; was its first president, and chairman of its board of trustees until it was destroyed by fire. He is a good preacher, and is much beloved and honored by his people.

Knight, Rev. Richard, author of the "History of the General and Six-Principle Baptists in England and America," in two parts; and the son of Deacon Stephen Knight, was born in Cranston, R. I., Oct. 5, 1771; a descendant of Richard Knight, one of the first settlers of Cranston; united with the Six-Principle Baptists in 1804; ordained pastor of the church in Scituate, R. I., Oct. 19, 1809, by Revs. Westcott, Manchester, and Sprague; served this church till his death; favored with powerful revivals; his church finally numbered over 400 members: published his history (8vo, 370 pages) in 1827; occupied his pulpit for fifty-three years; a man of great worth, industry, and strength; died in Cranston, R. I., April 10, 1863, in his ninety-second year.

Knollys, Rev. Hanserd, A.M., was born at Chalkwell, in Lincolnshire, in 1598. His parents gave their son religious instruction and a superior education. He was sent to the University of Cambridge, where he remained until he graduated. He had some religious exercises before he came to Cambridge, but sermons which he heard during his residence there were blessed to his conversion.

In June, 1629, he was ordained by the Bishop of Peterborough, and soon after he received the living of Humberstone from the Bishop of Lincoln. While at Humberstone he preached in many parishes beside his own, and at several hours in the day. He frequently proclaimed Christ at Holton at seven in the morning, at Humberstone at nine, at Scartha at eleven, and at Humberstone again at three in the afternoon, besides preaching on every holiday. After he became a Non-conformist he was in the pulpit just as frequently. For above forty years he delivered three or four sermons a week, and when he was in prison he preached every day. While he was a clergyman of the National Church and a Conformist he knew of no case of conversion resulting from his labors, but when he set out without state support he had throngs of converts.

He was convinced that many things in the Episcopal Church were destitute of Scripture warrant, and he first resigned his parish, and then two or three years afterwards his ministry and membership in the Anglican Church. This event occurred in 1636. That year he was arrested by order of "The High Commission Court," a tribunal second only to the Inquisition in wickedness, but by the connivance of the man who had him in charge he escaped. He started for New England by way of London. There he had to wait so long for a vessel that his entire money was spent except six brass farthings. His wife, however, was able to give him five pounds. They were twelve weeks on their passage, and their provisions became nearly unfit for use.

When he arrived at Boston, which was in 1638, he was speedily and falsely denounced as an Antinomian, and though he met with some kindness he had to work with a hoe to secure his daily bread. He was there but a brief time when he had an opportunity to go to Dover, then called Piscataway, in New Hampshire, and preach the gospel to the

REV. HANSERD KNOLLYS, A.M.

people of that place. That he was a Baptist at this time we see no reason to doubt. Mr. Mather says in his "Ecclesiastical History of New England," "I confess there were some of those persons (more than a score of emigrant ministers that had arrived in Massachusetts) whose names deserve to live in our book for their piety, although their particular opinions were such as to be disserviceable unto the declared and supposed interests of our churches. Of these there were some godly Anabaptists; as namely Mr. Hanserd Knollys, of Dover, who, afterwards removing back to London, lately died there, a good man, in a good old age." That Mr. Mather was acquainted with the religious opinions held by Hanserd Knollys when he was in Dover is evident to us. There was a bitter contro-

versy between two sections of Mr. Knollys' church during his residence there, and his doctrines unquestionably were well known, and Mather speaks of him as an Anabaptist when he came. We wish no better testimony to the good character of Hanserd Knollys whilst in Dover, and to his Baptist principles, than Mather furnishes. Knollys probably had a sort of union church there for a time, such as Backus had for a short period at Middleborough. Mr. Lechford, an Episcopalian, visited Dover in April, 1641, and he describes a controversy existing between Mr. Knollys and a ministerial opponent there as being about baptism and church membership. "They two," says he, "fell out about baptizing children, receiving of members," etc. And Mr. Knollys' section of the Dover church evidently held Baptist sentiments. The Baptists taught by Knollys, to escape persecution from Massachusetts, to which Dover was recently united, removed, in 1641, to Long Island. After Long Island fell under the power of the English and of Episcopalianism they removed again, and located permanently in New Jersey, near New Brunswick, and they called their third American home Piscataway, after their first on this continent. The Piscataway church is to-day as vigorous a community as bears the Baptist name in any part of our broad country.

Mr. Knollys was summoned to England by his aged father, and on his return immediately commenced to preach in the churches. For this he was drawn into frequent troubles. At last he set up a separate meeting in Great St. Helen's, London, where the people thronged his house, and his congregations commonly numbered a thousand. For this innovation he was summoned before a committee of "The Westminster Assembly of Divines," by whose chairman he was commanded to preach no more. But his ready reply was that "he would preach the gospel publicly, and from house to house."

In 1645 he was formally ordained pastor of the Baptist church which he had gathered in London. This position he retained till his death. His popularity as a preacher was very great, and it continued till a late period of life.

He was imprisoned frequently for breaking the laws against the worship of Dissenters. Even in his eighty-fourth year he was in jail six months, and just before his incarceration he refused to employ his immense influence with the Baptists to secure their approval of the suspension of the penal laws by James II.

He was a strong Calvinist, a devoted servant of God, a decided Baptist, a firm friend of every true Christian, and a man of great learning in the ancient languages and in general literature. He was the author of eleven works, among which was a grammar of the Latin, Greek, and Hebrew languages. He was regarded, and he is still revered, as a shining light by the denomination whose name he honored and whose bounds he extended. He died in London, Sept. 19, 1691, in the ninety-third year of his age.

Knowles, Prof. James Davis, was born in Providence, R. I., in July, 1798. His father having died when he was but twelve years old, he was left to the care of an affectionate mother, who lived to see the successful career of her son. He was placed when quite young in a printing-office in Providence, which became to him an excellent school for the acquisition of knowledge. At the age of twenty-one he became the co-editor of one of the leading journals of Rhode Island.

It was about this time that he made a public profession of his faith under Rev. Dr. Gano's ministry, and he became a member of the First Baptist church in Providence, and soon after was licensed to preach the gospel. All the previous plans which he had formed with reference to his future life were abandoned, and he resolved to give himself to the work of the ministry. To prepare for it he pursued a course of theological study with Dr. Stoughton, first in Philadelphia, and then in Washington when his teacher removed to that city to take charge of Columbian College.

Along with his theological studies he was able to pursue a collegiate course with such success that at the end of two years he graduated with the highest honors of his class. He was at once appointed tutor in the college, which office he held until the summer of 1825, when he returned to New England, having received a call to become the pastor of the Second Baptist church in Boston, as the successor of the venerated Dr. Baldwin. He was ordained Dec. 28, 1825. After a pastorate of seven years he felt compelled to resign his charge, and by a change of occupation relieve his overtaxed energies. Having been appointed Professor of Pastoral Duties and Sacred Rhetoric in the Newton Theological Institution, he retired from the church, between which and himself there was the warmest affection. He found renewed health in the position to which the providence of God had called him, and made his experience as a minister of Christ of the highest importance to him in his new field of labor. It was during his connection with the seminary that he conducted the *Christian Review* with an ability that placed it among the best quarterlies in the country. Prof. Knowles was the author of the biography of Mrs. Ann Hasseltine Judson, one of the most finished memoirs ever published in America. He was also author of a memoir of Roger Williams.

The connection of Prof. Knowles with the Newton Theological Institution terminated very sud-

48

denly. While on a visit to New York he contracted the smallpox, and shortly after his return sunk under the attack and died May 9, 1838, being within a few weeks of forty years of age. His apparently premature decease was lamented by all who knew him. Prof. Knowles was a man of great energy and indomitable will. His life was one of diligence, and of quiet but persistent work. He was not to be led aside from the performance of his duties by the temptations of ease or by difficulties besetting his path. The denomination has cause for rejoicing in his devotedness to the service of Christ.

Knowles, J. Sheridan, author of "Virginius" and other dramas of great literary excellence and celebrity, joined the Baptist church at Torquay, Devon, England, in 1847, when he was about sixty years of age. He had maintained a high moral character throughout his literary career, but received no serious religious impressions until late in life. The semi-popery prevalent in the Established Church at Torquay, where he resided, disgusted him, and he resorted to the Baptist meeting-house, where, under the ministry of the late Rev. J. King, he found the joy of salvation. Soon after his conversion he went forth as an evangelist, and crowds came together to hear him. Always a graceful elocutionist, his reading of the Scriptures was very impressive. Until his death, which took place Nov. 30, 1862, he manifested the deepest interest in evangelical Christianity and a firm attachment to Baptist principles. His eminent literary services were recognized by the government, and a pension was awarded him, which, after his death, was continued to his widow.

Knowles, Deacon Levi, a merchant of Philadelphia, was born in New Jersey in 1813. He early commenced business, and determined to pursue it with energy and industry. He began life without the advantage of capital, but resolved to use all the talent he possessed to succeed. He joined the church in his youth, adopting the Baptist faith, that had been handed down through two generations in his family. He gave some of his best efforts to the Sunday-school cause and other objects of benevolence. He was unanimously elected a deacon in three different churches while he was in their membership. His services were sought for to take charge of the funds of various organizations, for twelve of which he is now treasurer, and in none of which is any compensation given. His firm has maintained its credit through all the vicissitudes and panics of years. Mr. Knowles is familiar with the great writers of the past and present. He married wisely and was blessed with children, in whose society he spends many of his happiest hours. He is strong in his friendships, liberal in his gifts, and one of the pillars of the Baptist denomination in Philadelphia. Mrs. Knowles, with rare wisdom and generous giving, has made the Baptist Home of Philadelphia, of which she is president, one of the most successful institutions of its class on either side of the Atlantic.

Knowles, William B., son of Deacon Levi and Mrs. E. A. Knowles, was born in Philadelphia, Feb. 20, 1848, and died Sept. 22, 1875, at the early age of twenty-seven years. Mr. Knowles was possessed of fine natural abilities, and, in addition to a liberal education, he received a thorough training for mercantile pursuits, enabling him in early manhood to occupy a prominent position in the business community of his native city. As a member of the firm of L. Knowles & Co., so widely and honorably known, he was brought into relations with merchants in all parts of the country, and gained by his deportment and honorable bearing a wide circle of friends.

The Christian character of William B. Knowles was an exemplification of the great beauty and usefulness that the Lord often causes to be manifested in a life devoted from tender years to his service. Very early he gave clear evidence of a change of heart, and at the age of twelve he spoke of his love for Jesus to the Tabernacle church of Philadelphia, and on the last Lord's Day in February, 1860, he was "buried with Christ in baptism."

From this date until his triumphant death his life was one of faith manifested by works. Clerk of Beth-Eden church from its organization, active in the Sunday-school, young people's association, and in the prayer-meetings of the church, he was always solicitous for the spiritual interests of Zion. In his daily life he commended to others the religion of the Lord Jesus by maintaining a high Christian reputation. In his early bloom, just as the promise of his youth began to be fulfilled, he passed away, and, to use his last faint words, he was " Safe, safe in the arms of Jesus."

His loss was severely felt, and the most tender sympathy was expressed for his parents and loving wife by the Commercial Exchange of Philadelphia, merchants in this and other cities, and by ministers and hosts of brethren in the Christian faith.

Knowlton, Miles Justin, D.D., was born in West Wardsborough, Vt., Feb. 8, 1825. Both his parents were persons of more than ordinary excellence of character, and took the deepest interest in the early development of their son. He prepared for college at West Townsend, and completed both his collegiate and his theological course at Hamilton. Near the close of his college course he seems to have had a fresh baptism of the Holy Ghost, which was followed by a new and thorough conse-cration of himself to any work which his Lord had for him to do. A missionary life, either at home or abroad, appeared to him to be that to which he regarded it both as a privilege and a duty to devote himself. At length his mind settled upon the foreign field, and he offered himself to the Missionary Union and was accepted, and China was designated as the field of his labor. He was ordained in his native town Oct. 8, 1853, and soon after sailed for China, arriving at Ningpo in June, 1854, which henceforth was to be his home, and where he was to labor as a servant of the Lord Jesus Christ. There he continued for a little more than twenty years, deducting two years for his temporary sojourn in this country, whither he had come to recover his shattered health. With singleness of aim and the utmost persistency he gave himself to the one great business of preaching "the glorious gospel of the blessed God" to the Chinese. In season and out of season he determined to know only one thing among the heathen, and that was the gospel of Christ. He was full of energy and moral heroism, and he knew how to kindle the enthusiasm in the souls of others which he felt in his own.

Dr. Knowlton, in Ningpo, did not spare himself if he might but win souls to Christ. At the post of labor he was found when death came to him, on the 10th of September, 1874. It is thus that the executive board speak of him in their sixty-first annual report: "With what earnestness, what zeal, what love for Christ and the souls of men, what devotion to the special evangelization of the great empire of China, and with what success in his personal work as a missionary of the cross, our lamented Brother Knowlton gave himself to his life-work for twenty years, is partially and imperfectly recorded in the history of your work in China, but it is all registered in completeness in the book above. He died in the city of Ningpo, on the 10th of September last, in the very midst of his usefulness. China mourns."

Knox, Rev. George, was born in Saco, Me., Oct. 24, 1816, and fitted for college at the academy in Yarmouth, Me. He graduated at Waterville College, in the class of 1840. Having spent a year at the Newton Theological Institution, he was ordained as pastor of the Baptist church in Topsham, Me., where he remained for four years, when he removed to Cornish, where he was pastor two years, and then to Lewiston, where his relation with the Baptist church in that city continued for thirteen years. He had two brief pastorates after leaving Lewiston, one at Brunswick, and the other at Lawrence, Mass. While acting as chaplain of the 3d Me. Regiment in the late war he died, in Virginia, Oct. 31, 1864.

Krishna Pal was the first Hindoo led into the

baptismal waters by Dr. Carey ; he had courage and faith to stand alone in renouncing the abominations of his countrymen in the presence of his kindred. He was born about 1764, at Chandernagore, Bengal.

Krishna was by trade a carpenter ; and in listening to a discourse on the folly of idolatry and the great truths of Christianity, he became deeply affected and shed tears. He visited the missionaries soon after for religious instruction, and received with great eagerness the truths which they communicated. Soon he felt that he had put his trust in Jesus, and that he was a Christian. He then requested baptism, and laid aside openly his allegiance to idolatry. He sat down at the table of the missionaries in presence of their Hindoo servants, and by this act renounced caste. The news spread rapidly, and soon Krishna was besieged by a mob of 2000 persons, who poured out torrents of maledictions upon him, and then dragged him to the magistrate, who immediately released him and commended him for the piety of his course, and commanded the mob to disperse. The magistrate placed a Sepoy at Krishna's house to guard him, and offered armed protection to the missionaries during the celebration of the rite of baptism. The immersion occurred in the Ganges, on the 28th of December, 1800. Mr. Carey walked to the river from the chapel with his eldest son, Felix, on one side, and Krishna on the other. At the landing there were gathered the governor and a number of Europeans, and a great throng of Hindoos and Mohammedans. Mr. Ward preached a sermon in English from John v. 39, " Search the Scriptures." Dr. Carey delivered an address in Bengali after a Bengali translation of the hymn was sung,—

> " Jesus, and shall it ever be,
> A mortal man ashamed of thee ?"

Then he baptized Felix Carey and Krishna amid profound silence and deep solemnity. Krishna was the first baptized convert after seven years of labor. Krishna the same day partook of the Lord's Supper, and he enjoyed an unusual measure of the love of God as he waited upon Him in both ordinances. For more than twenty years Krishna Pal preached the blessed gospel to his countrymen with great success and ability. He led a holy life and he possessed a strong faith, and when he came to the end of his earthly journey his heart was full of peace, and of the light of a bright hope of immediate entrance into heaven. A European who was present at his dying couch says, " I myself witnessed the last moments of Krishna, and heard his aged and quivering lips speak of the preciousness of Christ." Krishna composed the beautiful hymn from which the following stanzas are taken :

> " O thou my soul, forget no more
> The Friend who all thy misery bore ;
> Let every idol be forgot,
> But, O my soul, forget Him not.

> " Jesus for thee a body takes ;
> Thy guilt assumes, thy fetters breaks,
> Discharging all thy dreadful debt ;
> And canst thou e'er such love forget ?"

Kutchin, Rev. T. T., was born in Philadelphia, Pa., Nov. 5, 1815, died at Dartmouth, Wis., Aug. 7, 1877. He entered the ministry at New Britain, Pa., at the age of twenty-one, and at once became popular as a preacher. He came to Wisconsin in 1855. For many years he was the editor of the *Milwaukee Sentinel*, and subsequently of the *Fon du Lac Commonwealth*. He was distinguished for remarkable intellectual power united with great kindness of heart. His two sons are esteemed ministers of the gospel, occupying important pulpits in the State.

L.

La Grange College was chartered in 1859, and a commodious brick building was erected, 90 by 70 feet, which was finished in 1866. It had superior chemical and philosophical apparatus when J. F. Cook, LL.D., became president. Both sexes are admitted to this institution. In the fourteen years of his presidency there have been more than two thousand matriculations, and among the number about sixty students for the ministry. Nearly $15,000 have been raised for improvements and for the removal of debts during the administration of Dr. Cook. One hundred and fifty children of ministers have been gratuitously educated in La Grange. Dr. Sawyer is now vice-president of the institution. It has eleven able instructors, who render excellent service, as the character of their graduates testifies. This college is beautifully located on the bluffs of the Mississippi, one hundred and thirty-seven miles north of St. Louis. (See page 668.)

Lailey, Thomas, was born Aug. 29, 1820, in the parish of Poplar, London, England. When quite young he came with his parents to Canada. He owns the largest wholesale house in his business in the province of Ontario. He united, by baptism, with the Bond Street church, Toronto, in 1849. In 1867 he, with several others, left this old mother-church to form a new interest on Alexander Street. The cost of the neat and comfortable edifice which they at once proceeded to erect was chiefly borne by him; and he has been from the first by far the largest contributor toward the current expenses of the church. The erection of the College Street and Lewis Street church edifices was also mainly due to his enterprise and liberality, and he is now (1881) promoting a scheme of church extension in the western part of the city. He has purchased an eligible site, on which a mission chapel is to be commenced immediately. He was president of the Home Mission Convention of Ontario in 1868–69.

tions, which he has filled with great ability and fidelity.

For forty years Mr. Lain has been a member of the Baptist church in Waukesha. He is known as a man of great purity of character, and of blameless Christian life. Until the failure of his health, which occurred a few years ago, he was very efficient and active in promoting the Baptist cause in his city, and in strengthening the denomination in the State.

Lake, Rev. J. B., was born in Fauquier Co., Va., May 4, 1837; attended school in Alexandria, Va., where he received a thorough training at the hands of the well-known Benjamin Hallowell, and afterwards studied at the University of Virginia, where he was graduated from several of its schools. While still at the university he was elected to a professorship in Edgeworth Female College, Greens-

LA GRANGE COLLEGE.

Lain, Hon. Isaac, of Waukesha, was born in Orange Co., N. Y., Dec. 18, 1820. His ancestors were from England, and settled at an early day on Long Island, N. Y. Isaac Lain's father was a farmer, and to this calling the son devoted himself until 1833. He then learned the business of architect and builder. In June, 1842, he settled in Waukesha, Wis., where he still resides. Here he engaged extensively for many years in his new business. In 1852 he established a real estate and insurance agency, and in 1860 he took an active part in founding the Waukesha County Manufacturing Company, of which he is now a heavy stockholder and secretary. In 1861, at the outbreak of the civil war, Mr. Lain was a member of the State Legislature, and took an active part in the measures which placed Wisconsin in the front rank of States for the promptness and efficiency with which her regiments were raised and sent to the front. Mr. Lain has held many local and county posi-

borough, N. C. Subsequently, Mr. Lake held a professorship in Chesapeake Female College, Va., four years, and then had charge of the Roanoke Female College, at Danville, Va., nine years. In 1872 he left Danville to become pastor of the church in Upperville, Va., where he still remains as a most successful preacher and pastor. His mind is vigorous and logical, and his sermons are filled with cardinal doctrinal truths and enriched by apt and numerous historical illustrations.

Lake, Rev. P. W., came to Wisconsin in 1839, and settled in Walworth County, and performed much foundation work in the early history of the State. He was an interesting preacher. Earnestness and spirituality were distinguished characteristics in his ministry. He died many years ago, but his name and labors are held in remembrance in many of the churches of Walworth County.

Lamar, Rev. A. W., editor of the *Baptist Courier*, was born at Leavenworth Mills, S. C.,

March 30, 1847. His father was Col. Thomas G. Lamar, who distinguished himself in the late war as commander at the battle of Secessionville, near Charleston, in June, 1862, and who died soon after. In honor of his memory the State Legislature sent the subject of this sketch to the State Military School to be educated. Being strongly impressed that it was his duty to preach, he sold a tract of land—obtained from his father's estate—to procure means for educating himself. Entering first Furman University, and then the theological seminary at Greenville, he afterwards accepted a call of the Mount Zion church in Newberry County, where he was ordained Jan. 15, 1871, at the age of twenty-four. At the meeting of the State Convention in November, 1871, he was elected its general agent. In November, 1873, the State Convention manifested its appreciation of his ability and success by electing him both corresponding secretary and general agent, charging him with all the work of the body during its recess. He was converted when at the military school, and began at once to work for Jesus among the cadets, praying with and for them, holding prayer-meetings, and reading Spurgeon's sermons to them. At first he met with much opposition, was treated with every indignity, but in the end those who led in these things asked him to pray for them. He has met with extraordinary success in the work assigned him, being imbued with zeal, perseverance, and earnestness, and blessed with great tact and good judgment. He is a young man, self-reliant and with good judgment, who takes hold of his work and does it like a veteran, having the confidence and esteem of all. His present field of labor is Camden.

Lamb, Rev. Amherst, was born in Phillipston, Mass., July 28, 1796, and spent his childhood and youth in Guilford, Vt. Soon after making a public profession of faith he commenced to preach, but, feeling the necessity of a better preparation for his work, he placed himself under the tuition of Rev. Dr. Young, then of Worcester, Mass. He was ordained in December, 1821, as pastor of the church at Guilford, Vt., and remained there for six years, when he became pastor of the church in Whitingham, September, 1827, and continued there until 1836. He then went to Charlemont, Mass., and preached there for nine years, having charge of the church in Buckland during a part of this period,—for half the time. Recalled to the church in Whitingham in 1845, he gave it twelve years of additional service, after which he supplied churches in his neighborhood, where his labors were much blessed. He died at Whitingham, May 29, 1870. His record was one of a high character wherever he was known.

Lamson, William, D.D., was born in Danvers, Mass., Feb. 22, 1812. He prepared for college at the academy in South Reading (now Wakefield), Mass., and graduated at Waterville College in the class of 1835. After his graduation he served as tutor for one year. In the autumn of 1837 he was ordained as pastor of the church in Gloucester, Mass. Wishing to pursue a more extended course of theological study, he entered the Newton Theological Institution in 1839, and remained until 1841, when he was settled as pastor of the church at Thomaston, Me. He returned to Gloucester, where he continued until called to Portsmouth, N. H., in 1848. He was pastor of the church in Portsmouth for eleven years. The church in Brookline, Mass., called him in 1859, and he was their pastor until 1875, when failing health obliged him to give up his ministerial work. Since his resignation he has lived chiefly in Salem and Gloucester, Mass.

Dr. Lamson has been one of the most useful and acceptable ministers in the denomination. By his pen, as well as his voice, he has made his talents subservient to promote the interests of truth.

Lancaster, Rev. William, was born in Warren Co., N. C., in 1753; was baptized by Rev. Wm. Walker; was the founder of the churches at Maple Spring and Poplar Spring, Franklin Co., about 1793; was a member of the State Convention, of the convention to ratify the Federal Constitution, and for many years chairman of the Court of Pleas and Quarter Sessions of Franklin County. He closed his long and useful life Sept. 16, 1826.

Landrum, Rev. John G., was born in Tennessee in 1810. At eighteen he removed to Union Co., S. C., and the next year began to preach. His slender form made him look much younger than he was, and for some years he was called the boy preacher. He became pastor of the Mount Zion and Bethlehem churches, in Spartanburg County, in 1830, and still serves them. He has had charge of the New Prospect church since 1835. The Baptist church at Spartanburg Court-house was organized under his ministry, where he preached for twenty-five years.

He has baptized about 5000 persons in fifty years. He exercises a very extensive influence in Spartanburg and the surrounding counties. Perhaps he could not say that his "natural force is not abated," but his labors are as abundant as ever.

Landrum, Sylvanus, D.D., pastor of the Baptist church at Savannah, Ga., has exerted a strong influence among the Baptists of Georgia. For many years he has been on the board of trustees of Mercer University, and for a long time acted as secretary of the board, and, besides, he has served the denomination in various positions with much success. He is a courteous gentleman, with a sound judgment, sincere piety, and intellectual ability.

He is an eloquent speaker. His congregations love and respect him. He was born in Oglethorpe Co., Ga., Oct. 3, 1820; his parents came from Virginia. He was educated at Mason Academy, Lexington, Ga., and at Mercer University. Ordained Oct. 23, 1846, he became, in January, 1847, pastor of the Baptist churches at Lexington and Athens, Ga.

SYLVANUS LANDRUM, D.D.

In December, 1849, he became pastor of the Macon (Ga.) Baptist church, where he served ten years, being instrumental there in the erection of a handsome and costly Gothic church edifice. In December, 1859, he accepted a call to Savannah, Ga., and there he remained twelve years, building up and uniting the Baptist cause in the city. He was there during the war, and never lost a single service on account of hostilities,—his was the only white Baptist church on the coast line from Baltimore to Texas which did not close at all during the conflict. He preached on one Sabbath to Confederate and the next Sabbath to Federal soldiers, at the time of the city's capture.

In 1871 he removed to Memphis, and became pastor of the Central Baptist church, remaining until after the severe yellow-fever scourge of 1878, during which he lost two sons, both prominent and talented young men. In 1879 he returned to Georgia, and again took charge of the Savannah church, where he is doing an admirable work.

Two colleges in one year conferred on him the Doctorate in Divinity,—Georgetown, Ky., Dr. Crawford president, and Columbian College, Washington, Dr. Samson president.

He is a man of national views, whose heart is in the pastorate, and whose chief aim is the advancement of Christ's kingdom on earth. His sermons are always good and never disappointing. To great administrative ability he unites remarkable excellence of judgment and a good knowledge of men and human nature. He is a wise and safe counselor, and makes his influence for good felt in the assemblies of his denominational brethren.

Landrum, Rev. William Warren, son of Dr. Sylvanus and Eliza Jane (Warren) Landrum, was born in Macon, Ga., Jan. 18, 1853. He was converted at the age of ten, and baptized in his fourteenth year. His early education was received at Chatham Academy, Savannah. He entered Mercer University, but subsequently went to Brown University, where he was graduated with distinction in 1872. He then became a student in the Southern Baptist Theological Seminary, at Greenville, S. C., from which he graduated in 1874, in nine of the thirteen schools in the institution.

At the call of the Central church of Memphis, he was ordained in May, 1874. His first pastorate was at Shreveport, La., where he labored with success for two years. He then accepted a call from the First Baptist church in Augusta, Ga., and removed to his native State in February, 1876. Of that church he is still the pastor. He was married Sept. 21, 1875, to Miss Ida Louise Dunster, a descendant of Henry Dunster, first president of Harvard University.

Mr. Landrum is a good preacher and pastor, and a man of more than ordinary abilities. He hates controversy, has great faith in the power of gospel preaching and the efficacy of a cheerful, loving piety, and his highest ambition is to be a consecrated and successful minister of Jesus Christ.

Lane, Rev. Dutton, was born Nov. 12, 1732, near Baltimore, Md. He was baptized by Shubael Sterns in 1758, and ordained to the ministry in October, 1764. He had a vigorous constitution, a powerful voice, and a heart on fire with the love of Jesus, and he was greatly blessed by his Master. In the Dare River church, Va., of which he was pastor, and for many miles around, the fruits of his ministry were visible to the whole community. His father, impelled by hatred to his religious fervor, tried to kill him, but "he himself was slain by the sword of the Spirit, from which he soon after revived with the hope of eternal life," and was baptized by his son.

Mr. Lane continued in the ministry till death, but the latter part of his life was marred by certain strange opinions which he adopted.

Lane, Rev. Thomas Jefferson, one of Tennessee's veteran Baptist ministers, was born in Jefferson (now Hamilton) Co., East Tenn., Oct. 9, 1804; son of Aquila and Agnes Lane, and grandson of

Elder Lane, one of the first Baptist ministers that settled in East Tennessee, in 1785.

Mr. Lane professed religion in 1834, and was baptized by Andrew Coffman, and regularly set apart to the ministry on the second Saturday in October, 1839, by the Bent Creek Baptist church, Elders Joseph Manning and Hugh Woodson acting as the Presbytery. From that time Mr. Lane has been doing effective service for the Master in the same section of country. Eternity alone will reveal the good he has accomplished for the cause of Christ and the salvation of sinners.

Lankershim, Deacon Isaac, is the Baptist benefactor of California. He is of Jewish birth; was converted to Christianity, baptized in Missouri, and removed with his wife, a converted Jewess, to California at an early day; joined the First Baptist church; was one of its deacons; became a constituent member of the Tabernacle church in 1865, and is still a member, the church having changed its name to Metropolitan in 1875. He is a large benefactor of Baptist institutions; purchased lots for the Second, Fifth, and Tabernacle churches; was a chief contributor to the building of the Tabernacle, and in 1875 provided the money, nearly $200,000, for the Metropolitan church lots and building. In 1874 he gave the second large subscription for California College, nearly $13,000. Always successful in business operations, careful, prudent, and conscientious, quiet and unassuming in manner, he is everywhere loved and honored. He has large city properties and immense farms in the country. His home is at Los Angeles. Though a converted Jew,—"an Israelite in whom there is no guile,"—giving quietly from principle, and not from impulse, he has never lost the respect of his Jewish kindred, with whom he is associated in many business enterprises. Deacon Lankershim is for California what the Crozers, Colgates, and Colbys are for the Atlantic States.

La Rue, Rev. Alexander Warren, whose ancestors were French and Irish, and firm Presbyterians, was born in La Rue Co., Ky., Jan. 23, 1819. He united with Severn's Valley church while attending an academy at Elizabethtown in 1837; was licensed to preach in November, 1838. In 1839 he entered Georgetown College, graduating in 1842. During the latter year he was ordained for the pastorate of Flemingsburg church. This church was in the Bracken Association, among the churches of which Mr. La Rue held many protracted meetings with encouraging success. In 1849 he removed to Louisville and became associate editor of the *Baptist Banner*, a weekly religious paper, since called the *Western Recorder*. While in this position he preached a short time to Bank Street Baptist church in New Albany, and afterwards to East Baptist church in Louisville. Having resigned his edi-

torial office, he accepted the pastorate of the church at Harrodsburg in 1853, where he remained three years, and then accepted a call to the church at Georgetown. Subsequently he was pastor of the church at Stanford, and finally at Salem, in Christian County. At the latter place he died, Sept. 11, 1864, after a life of singular consecration, devotion, and fruitfulness. His biography was written and published under the appropriate title of "La Rue's Ministry of Faith," by Rev. A. C. Graves, D.D.

Lasher, George William, D.D., was born in Schenectady Co., N. Y., June 24, 1831. His father

GEORGE WILLIAM LASHER, D.D.

was a farmer of Holland ancestry, and his mother traced her descent from a member of the "Boston Tea Party." He was converted at Hamilton, in 1853, while attending the academy, and in the same year entered Madison University, graduating in 1857. In 1859 he graduated from Hamilton Theological Seminary, and at once entered upon the pastorate of the Baptist church of Norwalk, Conn., where, on September 30, he was ordained. In 1860 he married Miss Lizzie C., daughter of Dr. G. W. Eaton, president of Madison University. In July, 1861, he became chaplain of the 5th Conn. Regiment, and served for six months on the upper Potomac, when he became pastor of the Baptist church at Newburg, N. Y. From 1864 to 1868 he was pastor of the Portland Street church, Haverhill, Mass., from 1868 to 1872 of the First church of Trenton, N. J., and from 1872 to 1875 was corresponding secretary of the New York Baptist Education Society. In 1875 he made a tour of Europe,

Egypt, and Palestine, and in August, 1876, became editor and proprietor of the *Journal and Messenger*, at Cincinnati, O. In 1874 he received the degree of D.D. from Madison University. Dr. Lasher has a commanding presence, and is a vigorous and successful preacher and editor. The *Journal and Messenger* under his management has a wide influence in the Central West.

Lathrop, Edward, D.D., son of Burel Lathrop, who early removed from Norwich, Conn., to Georgia,

EDWARD LATHROP, D.D.

was born in Savannah, Ga., March 14, 1814; baptized by Rev. H. O. Myer into the Savannah Baptist church in June, 1827; commenced study for the ministry at Furman Institution, S. C., in 1832; on the closing of that institution went to Hamilton, N. Y., and graduated in what is now Madison University in 1840; pursued a course of theological study at Hamilton; was called as assistant of Rev. Richard Fuller, D.D., at Beaufort, S. C.; in 1844 settled as pastor of the Tabernacle Baptist church in New York City, and labored with distinguished success for twenty-two years, until health failed; granted a long furlough by the church, but finally resigned; in 1866 became pastor of the Baptist church in Stamford, Conn., where he still labors with great honor; received the honorary degree of Doctor of Divinity from Rochester University; has been a trustee from the beginning of Vassar College, N. Y., and is now president of the board of trustees; is also president of the board of trustees of Connecticut Literary Institution; is one of the trustees of Madison University; engaged in all benevolent

objects; a strong preacher and able counselor; he has published several sermons by request.

Lattimore, Rev. Samuel S., was born in Rutherford Co., N. C., March 9, 1811; removed with his father while yet a child to Jennings, Ind. At fourteen years of age became a member of the literary institution at South Hanover, Ind. Supporting himself by his own exertions, he remained at this institution for nine years, until he completed his course, in July, 1833. During this period he became a member of the Presbyterian church, and remained in this connection for six or seven years. Leaving college soon thereafter, he went to Vicksburg, Miss., thence to Clinton, and shortly afterwards taught in the school at Society Ridge. In 1834 he joined the Baptist church. In 1835 he was ordained to the gospel ministry, and became general agent for the Mississippi Baptist State Convention. In December, 1837, he settled at Middleton, Carroll Co., Miss., where he engaged in preaching, and in teaching a school under Baptist auspices until 1840, when he removed to Sumter Co., Ala., where he preached to Providence and other churches. In 1845 he was again general agent of the Mississippi Baptist State Convention. In 1847 he was called to the pastorate of Macon church, Noxubee Co., Miss. Remaining there one year, he accepted a very urgent call from the Aberdeen church, with an understanding that he should return to Macon after the lapse of a year. Accordingly he returned to Macon, and remained till he again accepted an invitation to take charge of the Aberdeen church. In this relation he continued until his death. From 1849 to 1854 he was president of the Mississippi Baptist State Convention. He had various controversies on the principles and practices of the Baptists, and endured no little persecution. He was a man of marked ability, of warm and generous affections, eloquent as a preacher, able as a controversial writer, and eminently successful as a minister of the gospel.

Law, Rev. Francis Marion, was born in Sumter District, S. C., May 15, 1828; was educated for a physician, and received his diploma from the Medical College of Georgia, at Augusta; practised medicine at Wetumpka and Selma, Ala.; ordained in 1855; for five years financial secretary of Alabama Baptist Bible and Colportage Society; one year missionary and surgeon on the Bethel ship "Mobile Bay," under auspices of American Seamen's Friend Society; removed to Texas in November, 1859; pastor of Chapel Hill, Bellville, Brenham, Plantersville, and Bryan churches from 1860 to 1876; is a man of vigorous intellect and indomitable energy; now engaged in raising $250,000 for Texas Educational Commission.

Law, Rev. Josiah S., son of Samuel S. Law, was born in Saulsbury, Ga., Feb. 5, 1808. He received a classical education, and succeeded Rev. James Shannon as a teacher in Liberty County, when Mr. Shannon was called to Augusta, in 1827. It was while teaching at Sunbury that he was converted and joined the Baptist church there. He then took a three years' theological course at Newton Theological Seminary. In 1831 he entered upon his ministerial duties at Sunbury, and for twenty years served that church and neighborhood with great usefulness, except during two short intervals when he accepted calls to Macon and Savannah.

The colored people received great benefit from his preaching, among whom he was very successful. He died on the 5th of October, 1853. At that time sixty colored candidates were awaiting baptism at his hands.

Law, Rev. Samuel Spry, was born in Liberty County in 1774. He moved in the best society all his life, his family and connections being cultivated and wealthy. For forty years he lived a worldly-minded man and a moralist, but was converted in his forty-first year, and joined the Sunbury Baptist church on the 30th of April, 1815. He was ordained to the ministry Dec. 27, 1827, at the age of fifty-three. After laboring on the coast for some time, he was called to succeed Dr. C. O. Screven, at Sunbury. This connection continued for a year or so only, and he devoted his whole time to the colored people, and to the poor white churches of Liberty County. This work he continued with great usefulness for six or seven years, when his health began to fail gradually, and he expired on the 4th of February, 1837.

He was a man of great fervor and spirituality; prepared his sermons carefully, and became a good preacher. He was well acquainted with the Scriptures, and was much gifted in prayer. Few ever made more progress in piety and in the knowledge of our Lord Jesus Christ than he.

Lawler, Rev. B. F., was born in West Tennessee, Jan. 1, 1834; baptized in 1858; ordained in 1860; labored a number of years at Windsor, Mo. He is at the present time pastor of the Salem and Prairie Union Baptist churches, Neb. In connection with his ministerial labors, Mr. Lawler, while in Missouri, devoted a part of his time to teaching. In 1880 he published a volume of sermons, addresses, and letters.

Lawler, Judge Jacob, was born in North Carolina in 1796; while a youth his father removed to Tennessee, and the son subsequently located in North Alabama, and about the year 1820 settled in Shelby County. He held various offices of trust: judge of the county court, member of the House of Representatives of the State Legislature from 1826 to 1831, and was then elected to the State Senate; resigned that position to accept that of receiver of

public moneys for one of the land districts of the State, tendered him by President Andrew Jackson; held that office at Mardisville, in Talladega County, where it was located, until he was elected to Congress in 1835; was re-elected to Congress in 1837, and died on the 8th of May, 1838, in the city of Washington, while Congress was in session, and his remains now rest in that city. He was in office continuously from 1822 to 1838, never having suffered defeat or reproach.

In 1826, Jacob Lawler united with the Baptist church, and in a short time was ordained to the ministry. From the time of his ordination to his election to Congress he filled the office of pastor. The Talladega (now Alpine) and the Talladega town churches were originated by his ministry, and he was their pastor. It was characteristic of Mr. Lawler not to allow his secular duties to interfere with his religious obligations when it could be avoided.

Lawler, Gen. Levi W., was born in Madison Co., Ala., in 1816; with his parents, settled in

GEN. LEVI W. LAWLER.

Talladega County in early life; united with the Talladega church, of which his father was pastor, in 1835. After Judge Lawler resigned the office of receiver of public moneys at Mardisville he was succeeded by his son Levi, under appointment of President Jackson, and, though only nineteen years of age, he easily obtained the required bond of $100,000. After four years he was suspended on account of his opposition to the administration of President Van Buren, but was restored to the position by President Tyler in 1841, and held it for another term of four years. In 1848 he located in Mobile, and engaged in the commission business, which he has not yet relinquished. In 1861 his friends elected him to the Legislature without consulting him; was returned in 1863; was a member of that body during the whole period of the civil war, and he was three years chairman of the committee on ways and means. In 1874, Gen. Lawler was appointed by Gov. Houston one of the State commissioners to adjust and liquidate its burdensome debt. He drafted the plan of settlement, and performed the principal labor in its execution among creditors of the State,—a work which brought great relief to the people of Alabama. For many years he has been one of the trustees of Howard College, and of the Agricultural and Mechanical College of the State. He has been and is still a man of handsome fortune, of great energy, industry, and financial skill; liberal to objects of benevolence and to public enterprises. It is conceded that the gubernatorial honors of Alabama have been within his reach for years, but he has declined them. His vast influence affects for good all the higher relations of life, political and civil, social and educational, financial and denominational, in the State. He maintains the constant confidence of all grades of society. When a master he was famous for his tenderness to his slaves, and now that they are free he has their uniform confidence and highest regard. He has no superior in Alabama.

Lawrence, William Mangam, D.D., was born in Washington, D. C., May 11, 1848; was converted in early youth, and entered college at Amherst, Mass.; graduated from Madison University and Hamilton Theological Seminary; settled with the church at Amsterdam, N. Y., where he was ordained in August, 1871. The following year he received an urgent call from the Spring Garden church in Philadelphia, which he accepted, and entered upon his labors in October, 1872. It was an important period in the history of the church. A large colony had just gone out to form the Gethsemane church in a new and rapidly-growing neighborhood. A pastor was needed with power to hold and strengthen "the things which remained," and in this work he has, under God, been eminently successful.

Mr. Lawrence throws the vigor of his early manhood into all that he says and does. His sermons and occasional contributions to religious journals give evidence of an observing and thoughtful mind. His systematic methods enable him to accomplish a vast amount of pastoral work, and to render valuable service to other denominational interests with which he has become connected. His powerful intellect, scholarly attainments, and Christian spirit make him a power in the commu-

nity. In 1880 he became pastor of the Second Baptist church of Chicago.

WILLIAM MANGAM LAWRENCE, D.D.

Laws, Rev. M. L., was born in Virginia, Aug. 21, 1842. He made a profession of religion when eighteen years of age, and was baptized by Rev. J. S. Kennard in the E Street Baptist church, Washington, D. C., in November, 1859. He was ordained in 1871 at the Rehoboth Baptist church in Saline Co., Mo. Brother Laws has been pastor at Glasgow and Booneville, and of the Park Avenue church in St. Louis. He is now secretary of the Missouri Baptist Sunday-School Convention, and he is rendering efficient service in this position. He is a man of ability, industry, and usefulness.

Lawson, Rev. Albert G., was born in Poughkeepsie, N. Y., Jan. 5, 1842. In 1858 he made a public profession of religion, and was baptized by Rev. John Q. Adams, and became a member of the North Baptist church, New York. He studied in the College of the City of New York and in Madison University, and was ordained as pastor of Perth Amboy Baptist church, N. J., in June, 1862. In 1867 he took charge of the Greenwood Baptist church, where he still labors with marked success.

He is one of the most able laborers in the temperance cause. He is the author of "Methods of Church Work," "Duty of the Christian Church in Relation to Temperance," and the "Peace and Power of Temperance Literature," also an address on "Self-Culture." His discourses are clear, logical, and earnestly delivered.

Lawson, Admiral Sir John, was born near

Scarborough, Yorkshire, England. From very early life he was on the ocean. When the Parliament resolved to fight for the liberties of England, Lawson entered its naval service. His intelligence, faithfulness in executing orders, and religious behavior soon attracted attention and secured promotion. Having obtained the command of a small vessel, he made himself so useful that he was soon the captain of the finest ship in the British navy; and in process of time he became an admiral, and occasionally had the whole fleet placed under his authority. He fought under Blake in all the battles which gave him and his country so much naval glory. Cromwell looked upon him with special favor, and was always ready to promote his interests, until he became a king in everything but the name.

On the 2d of June, 1653, the British fleet attacked the Dutch off the coast of Flanders. Deane and Monk were admirals, Sir William Penn was vice-admiral, and Sir John Lawson was rear-admiral. Lawson charged through the Dutch fleet with forty ships, pouring destruction into the enemy, and so disabling De Ruyter's squadron that Van Tromp had to come to his relief; and after a hot engagement, in which Lawson was the foremost fighting man, the Dutch withdrew. The next day the battle was renewed and the enemy was routed. Six great ships of the Dutch were sunk, two blown up, and eleven of the largest and two smaller vessels were captured, with thirteen hundred prisoners, and nothing but flight saved the other Dutch vessels.

As soon as the power of Richard Cromwell ended, and the Parliament of the country had reassembled, the officers of the fleet, being largely Baptists, and consequently strong republicans, acknowledged the authority of Parliament in terms of loyal satisfaction. Immediately after, the Committee of Safety appointed by the Parliament ordered the equipment of six frigates to be ready for any emergency, and, to show their appreciation of our gallant brother, Sir John Lawson, they gave him the command of this squadron and created him vice-admiral of the fleet. For a considerable period after this Sir John had control of the whole British navy, and he was known throughout his country as a supporter of a free Parliament whom no bribes or persuasions could turn from his patriotic convictions.

The Parliament in power at this period was the Long Parliament dispersed by Oliver Cromwell, and recalled once more to the exercise of legislative and executive powers. Against this body the army determined to wage war, and they hindered the speaker and the members from reaching the house. Lambert and the principal officers of the army were bent on ruling the nation by the sword. Lawson brought his fleet into the Thames and declared for the Parliament by a voice which the Dutch had respected on the ocean, and which his countrymen reverenced everywhere. And his timely assistance, with the aid of Monk, overcame the friends of the sword, and the Parliament resumed its meetings and its authority. On the 3d of June, 1665, in a great naval battle between the English and the Dutch, in which the Duke of York was the nominal and Lawson the real commander of the British fleet, and in which the Dutch lost thirty-two ships and six thousand men, Sir John Lawson received a shot in the knee in the middle of the battle; the wound gangrened, and he died a few days after on shore, rejoicing in the blessed Saviour whom he was going to meet.

Lord Clarendon, a bitter enemy of Baptists and republicans, says of the admiral: "He was, indeed, of all the men of that time, and of that extraction and education, incomparably the modestest and the wisest man, and most worthy man to be confided in. He was in all the actions performed by Blake, some of which were very stupendous, and in all the battles which Cromwell had fought with the Dutch. He was commander-in-chief of the fleet when Richard (Cromwell) was thrown out; and when the contest grew between the Rump (the Long Parliament) and Lambert, he brought the whole fleet into the river and declared for that which is called the Parliament (Clarendon did not recognize this body as a Parliament), which broke the neck of all other designs, though *he intended only the better settlement of the Commonwealth.*" He had no wish to aid the Stuarts to mount the throne forfeited by Charles I. Elsewhere he says: "The present fleet, prepared for the summer service, was under the command of Vice-Admiral Sir John Lawson, an excellent seaman, but then *a notorious Anabaptist;* and they well remembered how he had lately besieged the city (London), and by the power of his fleet given that turn which helped to revive the 'Committee of Safety' (the government set up by the army) and restore the Rump Parliament to the exercise of their jurisdiction." Granville Penn, in his "Memorials of Admiral Sir William Penn," speaks of "the renowned Sir John Lawson," and he states that Oliver "Cromwell set aside Major Bourne and appointed Lawson rear-admiral of the fleet in his place." The great Protector held Sir John Lawson in the highest esteem. Except Cromwell himself, in his day no soldier stood higher than Gen. Harrison. And during the latter part of Lawson's life he was regarded as one of the greatest heroes in the naval history of Britain, and his death was felt to be a national calamity. These brave men were both decided Baptists. See "Memoirs of Ludlow," ii. 466, 666, 726, 736, 855, Vevay, 1699; Southey's "Lives of the British Admirals," v. 269, note,

London, 1837; Clarendon's "History of the Rebellion," iii. 728, Oxford, 1706; Rapin's "History of England," ii. 639, 640, London, 1733; "Memorials of Sir William Penn, Knt.," i. 312, 469, 470, London, 1833.

Lawton, Col. Alex. J., who died some three years ago, spent his life, which, "by reason of strength was fourscore and four years," in Beaufort, S. C. He was long a deacon of the Black Swamp church, and repeatedly a member of the State Legislature. He was dignified but extremely pleasant, especially among the young, with whom he was a great favorite. The writer met him about a year before his death, and found him the same genial Christian that he had always been. Few masters were so considerate of their slaves, and few had their affection in an equal degree. He used much of his large property for benevolent objects. Few have spent a life so long and so well regulated.

Lawton, Rev. Joseph A., may be called the Baptist patriarch of Barnwell, S. C., and of the surrounding counties. He held and used his large fortune, before the war, as a steward who must give an account. He now lives, in advanced years, in the midst of his spiritual children, white and colored, who revere him. Prudence and moderation have marked his whole life. His numerous servants, at the close of the war, cherished him in their hearts, and quite a number of them still live with him, and manifest the same respect as they did in the time of slavery. Baptist ministers in his section owe him much, because he refused to preach for wealthy churches unless they paid a salary in proportion to their ability, saying that if he preached for nothing it should be to churches not able to compensate him. They complied, and many brethren have been less stinted than they would have been had Mr. Lawton not insisted that "the laborer is worthy of his hire." He always gave his salary, and much more, to some worthy object. He has long been pastor of the Allendale church, one of the most active and liberal in the Savannah River Association.

Lawton, Rev. W. A., was born in Beaufort Co., S. C., in 1793. He was in the ministry fifty-five years, and at the time of his death, in 1878, he had been pastor of the Pipe Creek church for twenty-seven years. His remarkably strong constitution bore him up in good health almost to the close of life, which "by reason of strength was fourscore and five years." Next to Thomas Dawson, he was probably the oldest Baptist minister in the State.

Lea Female Seminary, located at Summit, Miss., on the line of the New Orleans and Jackson Railroad, Rev. Charles H. Otken, principal, is an admirable institution.

Lea, Hon. Fryer, was born in Tennessee, and is now nearly eighty years of age; joined the Baptist Church in Tennessee, where he practised law with success and distinction. Represented Tennessee in the Congress of the United States. He afterwards removed to Mississippi, and practised law at Jackson. Has served as State superintendent of public instruction in Texas, and now lives at Goliad. He has been a consistent Baptist under all circumstances.

Lea, Rev. Wm. M., a prominent minister in Arkansas, was born in North Carolina in 1817, but reared and educated in Tennessee. He came to Arkansas in 1851 as missionary of the Marion Board Southern Baptist Convention, and began his labors at Helena. The following year he severed his relations with the board, and boldly entered the State as an independent missionary, relying upon his field for support, and, with the exception of a few years, has ever since continued there to labor. Helena, Pine Bluff, Little Rock, Forest City, and other places have received the benefit of his labors. Just before the late conflict he raised a subscription of $75,000 towards endowing a State college, which was unfortunately lost by the war. Mr. Lea has distinguished himself as a polemic, having engaged in many debates, and considers himself specially set for the defense of the truth.

Leach, Beriah N., D.D., was born in Middletown, Vt., April 28, 1801; converted at fourteen; ordained pastor at Cornwell, Vt., in October, 1826; pastor at Middlebury, Fredonia, Wyoming, Hamilton, and Brooklyn, N. Y., and in Middletown, Conn. He received the degree of Doctor of Divinity from Madison University in 1859. He died Jan. 23, 1869, strong in his Redeemer's supporting grace. Dr. Leach was full of labors and of love for the Redeemer, and the favor of heaven rested upon his toils for Jesus as well as upon his own soul.

Leach, Rev. William, was born in Shutesbury, Mass., in 1804, and baptized by Rev. David Goddard, of Wendall. Relinquishing the business in which he was engaged, he pursued a select course of study at the Shelburne Falls Academy, and took a partial course at Newton. In 1840 he was ordained in Paterson, N. J. Subsequently he removed to Newark, N. J., and then to Wendall and South Hanson, Mass., and Omaha, Neb. To this latter place he had gone on business, but, seeing the destitution of the gospel in that rising city, he preached for some time there without compensation, and for two years as a missionary of the American Baptist Home Missionary Society. The Baptist church of Omaha is the child of his prayers and labors. Returning East, he had charge of the churches in East Stoughton, Holmes' Hole, South

Yarmouth, Harned, and Still River, all in the State of Massachusetts. He died at Still River, Mass., March 30, 1871.

Learning, Baptist Institutions of.

—Preceding and during the Commonwealth in England, large numbers of our ministers in that country were graduates of Oxford and Cambridge. After 1660, when Charles II. ascended the throne, the necessity for seeking education for Baptist pastors in some new quarter forced itself upon the attention of our brethren. Various plans were discussed in London and elsewhere to secure an object so dear to the churches. Edward Terrill, of Bristol, in 1679, set apart a portion of his property for the instruction of students for the ministry, which did not become available until the death of his wife. Though some aid was received from it for five years preceding 1720, it was in that year, under Rev. Bernard Foskett, that Bristol Baptist College was formally established.

In 1756, Rev. Isaac Eaton, of Hopewell, N. J., opened the first Baptist Seminary in this country "for the education of youth for the ministry." In the progress of this institution the Philadelphia and Charleston Baptist Associations took the deepest interest. They appointed trustees to watch over its affairs; and the Philadelphia Association raised about £400 to aid it in its work. The principal was a scholarly man, and he had the art of imparting knowledge to others. His school was in existence only eleven years, and in that time the following were among its pupils: Dr. James Manning, Dr. Samuel Jones, Dr. Hezekiah Smith, Dr. Isaac Skillman, and Revs. David Thomas, David Jones, the celebrated Revolutionary chaplain, and Charles Thompson. The distinguished Judge David Howell was also a student at Hopewell. The frame house in which Mr. Eaton presided over his seminary is still standing, and in excellent condition.

ISAAC EATON'S ACADEMY.

THE FIRST BAPTIST SEMINARY FOR THE EDUCATION OF MINISTERS IN AMERICA.

On the 12th of October, 1762, the Philadelphia Baptist Association, with twenty-nine churches in its fellowship, met in the Lutheran church on Fifth Street above Race Street, Philadelphia. Rev. Morgan Edwards was chosen moderator, and Rev.

Abel Morgan clerk. At this session of the mother Association of American Baptists it was decided that it was "expedient to erect a college in the colony of Rhode Island, under the chief direction of the Baptists." Morgan Edwards was "the principal mover in this matter," and to him and Dr. Samuel Jones the grand educational project was referred.

In 1763 an effort was made to secure the confirmation of a charter for the new college in the Rhode Island Assembly. The charter had been prepared by Dr. Ezra Stiles, of Newport, a Congregational minister, and it "was so artfully constructed as to throw the power into the Fellows' hands, whereof eight out of twelve were Presbyterians, usually called Congregationalists." "The trustees were presumed to be the principal branch of authority, and as nineteen out of thirty-five were to be Baptists, the Baptists were satisfied, without sufficient examination into the authority vested in the fellowship, which afterward appeared to be the soul of the institution, while the trusteeship was only the body" (Manning and Brown University, pp. 48–49). This unworthy effort of Dr. Stiles was frustrated by Daniel Jenckes and others in the Assembly. The amended charter was confirmed by the Legislature of Rhode Island in 1764. In that year the Philadelphia Association recommended the churches to be liberal in placing the new college upon an efficient basis; and in 1766 the Association "agreed to recommend warmly to the churches the interests of the college, for which a subscription is opened all over the continent." Dr. James Manning was the first president of Rhode Island College, now Brown University. This institution to-day has nineteen instructors, property valued at $1,750,000, an endowment of $650,000, a library of 53,000 volumes, 247 students, and a history of usefulness of which Americans, and especially American Baptists, may justly be proud. The Baptist colleges, theological seminaries, and academies of the United States, according to the report of the "Baptist Year-Book" for 1881, have property worth $11,988,883, and endowments of $4,960,730,—that is to say, these institutions own assets amounting to $16,959,613, nearly seventeen million dollars. Their reported income last year was $679,178, to which may be added $160,000 from 36 of them from which we have no report of receipts. They had, during 1880, 667 teachers, 8749 students, of whom 1532 were preparing for the Christian ministry.

In the United States most Pedobaptist communities receive large accessions from European emigration; the Baptists gain comparatively few members from this source. Besides, they have had to contend against powerful prejudices from the earliest period in the history of this country, prejudices which for a long time in several colonies clothed themselves in persecuting legal enactments, and which exist to-day, without the force of law, in unfounded charges of bigotry and saving sacramentalism. Nevertheless, by the favor of God, they have been able not only to rear a multitude of church edifices, but to invest seventeen million dollars in institutions of learning. Indeed, we have reason to believe that if all our educational enterprises were *reported*, and an exact examination of their property and endowments made, that the result would show an investment in these fountains of light of a sum little less than twenty million dollars.

BAPTIST INSTITUTIONS OF LEARNING.

UNITED STATES. IN 1881.

COLLEGES AND UNIVERSITIES.

Name.	When Founded.	President.	Location.	Instruct-ors.	Students.	Property.	Endow-ment.
Brown University	1764	E. G. Robinson, D.D., LL.D.	Providence, R. I.	19	247	$1,750,000	$650,000
Madison University	1819	E. Dodge, D.D., LL.D.	Hamilton, N. Y.	10	90	640,000	480,000
Colby University	1820	Henry E. Robins, D.D.	Waterville, Me	8	148	300,000	200,000
The Columbian University	1821	J. C. Welling, LL.D.	Washington, D. C.	25	343	370,000	110,000
Shurtleff College	1827	A. A. Kendrick, D.D.	Upper Alton, Ill	7	128	175,000	150,000
Georgetown College	1829	R. M. Dudley, D.D.	Georgetown, Ky	6	119	125,000	75,000
Denison University	1831	Alfred Owen, D.D.	Granville, O.	9	173	300,000	190,000
Franklin College	1834	W. T. Stott, D.D.	Franklin, Ind.	8	85	120,000	80,000
Wake Forest College	1834	T. H. Pritchard, D.D.	Wake Forest, N. C.	8	171	86,000	46,000
Mercer University	1838	A. J. Battle, D.D.	Macon, Ga.	9	108	300,000	100,000
Richmond College	1832	B. Puryear, A.M.	Richmond, Va.	8	125	300,000	95,000
Howard College	1843	Col. J. T. Murfee	Marion, Ala.	8	125	50,000	....
Baylor University	1845	W. C. Crane, D.D., LL.D.	Independence, Texas	6	119	70,000	26,000
University at Lewisburg	1846	J. F. Harris, A.M.	Lewisburg, Pa.	7	66	250,000	121,769
William Jewell College	1849	W. R. Rothwell, D.D.	Liberty, Mo.	7	145	175,000	100,000
University of Rochester	1850	M. B. Anderson, LL.D.	Rochester, N. Y.	9	146	846,443	255,540
Mississippi College	1850	W. S. Webb, D.D.	Clinton, Miss.	7	200	50,000	20,000
Carson College	1850	N. B. Goforth, D.D.	Mossy Creek, Tenn.	4	185	50,000	....
Furman University	1851	J. C. Furman, D.D.	Greenville, S. C.	5	86	100,000	....
Central University	1852	L. A. Dunn, D.D.	Pella, Iowa.	7	121	....	....
Kalamazoo College	1855	Kendall Brooks, D.D.	Kalamazoo, Mich.	9	169	175,000	75,000
Bethel College*	1856	Leslie Waggener, LL.D.	Russellville, Ky.	5	105	175,000	75,000
University of Chicago	1859	Galusha Anderson, D.D.	Chicago, Ill	16	250	150,600	600
McMinnville College	1858	Rev. G. J. Burchett, A.M.	McMinnville, Oregon.	4	100	30,000	20,000
Waco University	1861	R. C. Burleson, D.D.	Waco, Texas.	10	190	50,000	13,000
Vassar College	1861	S. L. Caldwell, D.D.	Poughkeepsie, N. Y.	31	303	992,154	281,250
University of Des Moines	1865	J. A. Nash, D.D.	Des Moines, Iowa.	4	78	70,000	20,000
La Grange College*	1859	J. F. Cook, LL.D.	La Grange, Mo.	8	131	36,000	....
Monongahela College	1867	H. K. Craig, D.D.	Jefferson, Greene Co., Pa.	6	108	40,000	20,000
California College	1871	U. Gregory, D.D.	Vacaville, Cal.	4	60	30,000	20,000
Southwestern Baptist Univ.	1874	Prof. G. W. Jarman, A.M.	Jackson, Tenn.	6	185	105,000	55,000
Total number 31	....			280	4609	$7,910,597	$3,279,159

* From previous reports.

THEOLOGICAL INSTITUTIONS.

Name.	When Founded.	President.	Location.	Instruct-ors.	Students.	Property.	Endow-ment.
Hamilton Theological Sem.	1819	E. Dodge, D.D., LL.D.	Hamilton, N. Y.	5	36	$70,000	$32,750
Newton Theol. Institution.	1825	Alvah Hovey, D.D.	Newton Centre, Mass.	6	67	426,878	314,801
Rochester Theological Sem.	1851	A. H. Strong, D.D.	Rochester, N. Y.	8	70	450,000	300,000
Southern Baptist Theol. Sem.	1858	Jas. P. Boyce, D.D., LL.D.	Louisville, Ky.	4	89	300,000	300,000
Shurtleff Theological Dept.	1862	A. A. Kendrick, D.D.	Upper Alton, Ill	...	...	....	....
Baptist Union Theol. Sem.	1867	G. W. Northrup, D.D.	Morgan Park, Ill.	7	78	....	....
Crozer Theological Seminary.	1868	H. G. Weston, D.D.	Upland, Pa.	4	42	403,000	244,130
Vardeman Sch. of Theology.	1868	W. R. Rothwell, D.D.	Liberty, Mo.	3	48	40,000	....
Total number 8	....			37	430	$1,689,878	$1,191,681

BAPTIST INSTITUTIONS OF LEARNING—*Continued.*

ACADEMIES, SEMINARIES, AND FEMALE COLLEGES.

Name.	When Founded.	President.	Location.	Instructors.	Students.	Property.	Endowment.
Alabama Central Female Col.	1857	Prof. A. K. Yancey, Jr..........	Tuscaloosa, Ala.............	12	110	$100,000	....
Atlanta Baptist Seminary† ...	1870	Rev. J. T. Robert, LL.D............	Atlanta, Ga..................	4	100	12,000	....
Baptist Female College.........	1855	John F. Lanneau, A.M............	Lexington, Mo..............	12	133	....	....
Bardstown M. and F. College.	1842	H. J. Greenwell, A.M............	Bardstown, Ky..............	7	85	10,000	....
Baylor Female College.........	1846	J. H. Luther, D.D................	Independence, Texas......	10	100	20,000	....
Benedict Institute†......	1870	E. J. Goodspeed, D.D............	Columbia, S. C.............	6	150	43,700	$18,700
Bethel Female College........	1852	J. W. Rust, A.M..................	Hopkinsville, Ky..........	8	100	30,000	....
Broaddus Female College.....	1871	Rev. E. J. Willis, LL.D............	Clarksburg, W. Va........	7	75	10,000	....
Burlington Colored Institute.	1852	Prof. E. F. Stearns...............	Burlington, Iowa..........	6	60	50,000	20,000
Cedar Valley Seminary*......	1863	Rev. A. Bush, A.M................	Osage, Iowa.................	6	172	22,000	9,000
Central Female Institute.....	1853	Walter Hillman, LL.D.........	Clinton, Miss..............	7	104	20,000	....
Chowan Baptist Female Inst.	1848	Dr. A. McDowell.................	Murfreesborough, N. C..	8	60	50,000	....
Colby Academy...................	1836	James P. Dixon, A.M............	New London, N. H......	6	76	181,000	81,000
Colgate Academy................	1872	Rev. F. W. Towle, A.M.........	Hamilton, N. Y............	5	111	125,000	55,000
Connecticut Lit. Institution..	1833	Martin H. Smith, A.M.........	Suffield, Conn..............	7	110	100,000	28,000
Cook Academy....................	1872	Prof. A. C. Hill....................	Havana, N. Y..............	10	120	168,708	....
Georgetown Female Sem......	1846	Prof. J. J. Rucker...............	Georgetown, Ky..........	10	115	25,000	....
Georgia Female College........	1850	Mr. P. F. Asbury.................	Madison, Ga...............	5	70	....	....
Grand River College............	1859	Prof. T. H. Storts...............	Edinburg, Mo.............	4	131	10,000	....
Greenville Baptist Fem. Col.,	1854	Prof. A. S. Townes..............	Greenville, S. C..........	10	153	20,000	....
Hardin Female College*......	1873	Prof. A. W. Terrill............	Mexico, Mo................	8	160	68,000	40,000
Hollin's Institute...............	1841	Prof. Chas. L. Cocke............	Botetourt Springs, Va....	12	114	75,000	....
Howe Literary Institute......	1874	Prof. S. F. Holt..................	East St. Louis, Ill........	4	84	25,000	....
Judson Female Institute......	1839	L. R. Gwaltney, D.D...........	Marion, Ala................	10	115	50,000	....
Keystone Academy.............	1868	Rev. J. H. Harris, A.M.........	Factoryville, Pa...........	7	145	30,000	....
Leland University†.............	1870	Rev. Seth J. Axtell, Jr..........	New Orleans, La..........	5	148	85,000	10,000
Lea Female College............	1877	Rev. C. H. Otken, A.M.........	Summit, Miss..............	6	75	10,000	....
Mary Sharp College............	1850	Z. C. Graves, LL.D.............	Winchester, Tenn........	8	110	16,000	....
Minnesota Academy*..........	1877	S. H. Baker, A.M................	Owatonna, Minn..........	6	173	12,000	5,190
Mount Pleasant Institute.....	1873	Rev. Leroy Stevens, A.M......	Mount Pleasant, Pa......	6	60	25,000	....
Nashville Institute†...........	1865	D. W. Phillips, D.D.............	Nashville, Tenn...........	8	231	80,000	....
Natchez Seminary†.............	1877	Rev. Charles Ayer..............	Natchez, Miss.............	4	120	15,000	....
Normal and Theol. School....	1878	Rev. H. Woodsmall.............	Selma, Ala.................	4	250	8,000	....
Peddie Institute.................	1865	Rev. E. J. Avery, A.M..........	Hightstown, N. J........	10	125	125,000	1,000
Reid Institute....................	1862	C. A. Gilbert, A.M..............	Reidsburg, Pa..............	3	68	10,000	....
Richmond Institute†............	1867	Rev. C. H. Corey, A.M.........	Richmond, Va.............	5	92	....	....
Shaw University†...............	1865	Rev. H. M. Tupper, A.M.......	Raleigh, N. C..............	15	277	125,000	....
South Jersey Institute.........	1870	Prof. H. K. Trask...............	Bridgeton, N. J...........	10	150	75,000	....
Stephen's Female College.....	1856	Prof. R. P. Rider...............	Columbia, Mo.............	14	170	50,000	20,000
University Academy...........	1846	W. E. Martin, A.M.............	Lewisburg, Pa.............	4	65	....	....
University Female Institute.	1846	Jonathan Jones, A.M...........	Lewisburg, Pa.............	10	72	75,000	....
Vermont Academy.............	1872	H. M. Willard, A.M.............	Saxton's River, Vt........	8	125	142,000	100,000
Wayland Seminary†...........	1865	Rev. G. M. P. King.............	Washington, D C...........	7	92	40,000	....
Wayland University............	1855	N. E. Wood, A.M................	Beaver Dam, Wis..........	6	120	50,000	19,000
Worcester Academy............	1834	Nath. Leavenworth, A.M......	Worcester, Mass..........	4	58	200,000	83,000
Wyoming Seminary............	1867	Rev. M. Heath, A.M.............	Wyoming, Del..............	5	88	....	....
Young Ladies' Institute......	1832	D. Shepardson, D.D.............	Granville, O................	9	100	....	....
Total number........48				350	5522	$2,388,408	$489,890

* From previous reports.   † Under the auspices of the American Baptist Home Mission Society.

ENGLAND, WALES, AND SCOTLAND.*

Name.	When Founded.	President.	Location.	Instructors.	Students.	Property.	Endowment.
Bristol College.....................	1720	F. W. Gotch, LL.D................	Bristol......................				
Chilwell College (Gen. Bap.).	1797	Rev. F. Goadby, B.A.............	Nottingham................				
Rawdon College..................	1804	Rev. T. G. Rooke, B.A...........	Rawdon, Yorkshire........				
Pontypool College	1807	Rev. W. M. Lewis, A.M.........	Pontypool, Wales..........				
Regent's Park College.........	1810	Joseph Angus, D.D., M.R.A.S...	London......................				
Haverfordwest College.........	1839	Thomas Davies, D.D.............	Haverfordwest, Wales....				
Theol. Institution of Scotland.	1856	James Culross, D.D..............	Glasgow.....................				
Pastor's College (Spurgeon's).	1856	Rev. C. H. Spurgeon.............	London......................				
Llangollen..........................	1862	Hugh Jones, D.D.................	Llangollen, North Wales.				
Manchester Bap. Theol. Inst.	1866	Rev. Edward Parker.............	Brighton Grove, M'ch't'r.				
Total number........10							

* These institutions had an income of $80,000 in 1880.

BAPTIST INSTITUTIONS OF LEARNING—*Continued.*

CANADA.—ONTARIO.

NAME.	WHEN FOUNDED.	PRESIDENT.	LOCATION.	INSTRUCT-ORS.	STUDENTS.	PROPERTY.	ENDOW-MENT.
Canadian Literary Institute..	....	Rev. John Torrance, M.A.........	Woodstock, Ontario......	10			
Toronto Theol. Institution....	1881	J. H. Castle, D.D....................	Toronto, Ontario	3			
Total.................................	....	....	....	13			

NOVA SCOTIA.

NAME.	WHEN FOUNDED.	PRESIDENT.	LOCATION.	INSTRUCT-ORS.	STUDENTS.	PROPERTY.	ENDOW-MENT.
Acadia College.......................	....	A. W. Sawyer, D.D................ ..	....	8	75		

In addition to these, we have missionary colleges and theological institutions in Jamaica, Burmah, India, France, Germany, and Sweden.

The Hollis family of London, earnest Baptists, were such generous friends of education, that down to 1735 they gave more than "£6000 currency of Massachusetts" to Harvard College, then a Congregational institution, that New England might have literary advantages. We had no American Baptist colleges in that day to receive such benefactions.

In establishing and sustaining institutions of learning, and in extending general education throughout our entire country, no denomination occupies a more honored place than the Baptists.

Leavitt, Rev. Samuel K., was born at Levant, Me., June 23, 1830; graduated at Colby University in 1855; after graduation taught in the literary and scientific institution at New London, N. H., in the high school at Holyoke, Mass., and at Halliwell, Me. In 1857 removed to Evansville, Ind., where he studied law and remained in the legal profession until the spring of 1870, with an interruption of three years' service in the army as captain in the 65th Regiment of Ind. Inf. Vols. Was converted in college in 1852, and baptized at Holyoke in 1855 by Rev. James French. In the spring of 1872 was ordained to the work of the ministry at Evansville, Ind. Has had only two pastorates, the first at Keokuk, Iowa, and the second at First church, Cincinnati, O., from December, 1872, to the present time. He is an earnest, thorough-going man, and he is profoundly interested in the reformatory as well as the religious movements of the day.

Lecompte, Rev. Edwin Augustus, was born in Boston, Sept. 14, 1835. He was religiously trained at home, and in the Sunday-school of the Charles Street Baptist church, under the ministrations of the Rev. Dr. Sharp. Having gone through the course of study pursued in the excellent schools of his native city, he decided to devote himself to business. When but fifteen years of age he was hopefully converted, and was baptized by Rev. A. H. Burlingham, then pastor of the Harvard Street church, Boston. His attention was now turned to the Christian ministry, and in order to fit himself for his chosen work he pursued his preparatory studies in part at the Middleborough Academy, under the tuition of Prof. J. W. P. Jenks, and graduated with honor at Harvard University in the class of 1862. "His subsequent work proved that his intellectual as well as moral culture was broad and thorough." He was ordained as pastor of the Fourth Street church, in South Boston, July 30, 1862. For seven years he labored successfully with this church, and then accepted a call to the pastorate of the First Baptist church, in Syracuse, N. Y., where he remained until 1864, when he was called back to his native State and became pastor of the Worthen Street church, Lowell, Mass. Here for fifteen years he "made full proof of his ministry," and his work was respected in the community in which he lived, inasmuch as he brought to the discharge of his duties a well-cultivated intellect and a warm, gentle, and guileless heart. "He was one of those men for whom we are never called on to explain or apologize." He died March 2, 1880, not having quite reached the forty-fifth year of his age.

Lee, Rev. David, was born in Johnston Co., N. C., Feb. 4, 1805. With his father, Joel Lee, and family, he removed to Alabama and settled in Conecuh County in 1817. David Lee was happily converted, and in November, 1827, was baptized by Rev. Alex. Travis, and the next year began to exhort sinners to repentance. Was ordained in 1833 by Revs. David Peebles and Alexander Watson. Has been pastor of Hopewell church, at Mount Willing, ever since he entered the ministry, and from time to time of other churches. Has attended every meeting, save one, of the Alabama Association since 1833, and has been moderator of that body for about thirty-five years, and is one of the best presiding officers in the State. All his life as a man and a minister he has exerted a commanding influence in that large and powerful Association. Has written extensively and ably for our religious papers; has ever been in good worldly circumstances.

Lee, Franklin, Esq., was born in New Jersey in 1787; was a member of the Second Baptist church, Philadelphia, Pa., for more than fifty years,

FRANKLIN LEE, ESQ.

and for about thirty years an honored deacon. He was treasurer of the Philadelphia Baptist Association for many years. He was a representative from Philadelphia in the Pennsylvania Legislature, and he held other public positions of importance in times when such offices sought the men to fill them. In his own church he was familiarly known as "Father Lee," and every member of it felt a special interest in him. He was known and venerated by

the whole denomination in Eastern Pennsylvania; he held a high place in the regards of all the leading citizens of Philadelphia among whom he mingled in business pursuits and in patriotic efforts.

His doctrinal sentiments accorded with those proclaimed by Dr. Gill and taught by inspired Paul; he was deeply devotional in his religious exercises, a generous friend of missions at home and abroad, and a liberal contributor to the necessities of the poor. While broad in his charities, Mr. Lee was a strong Baptist, and no struggling community of his denomination ever vainly appealed to him. For years before his death his ordinary gifts to the poor and the cause of Christ were about two thousand dollars annually.

Intimately conversant with God's Word, of which he was a diligent and intelligent student, he was strengthened by its doctrines and its promises, and led a life marked by unspotted purity. His hope was unusually bright; he often quoted the words of the poet to express his experience,—

> "More happy, but not more secure,
> The glorified spirits in heaven."

He entered the eternal inheritance Dec. 13, 1861, mourned by throngs in whose hearts he will ever live, and from whose memories the records of his worth can never be obliterated.

Lee, Rev. Hanson, distinguished as an educator, preacher, and editor, was born in North Carolina, but reared in Alabama, where he received a fine classical education, and afterward graduated at the Southwestern Theological Seminary, Marysville, Tenn. After several successful pastorates in Alabama, he became president of Mossy Creek College, Eastern Tennessee. In 1854 he came to Mount Lebanon, La., where he founded the *Louisiana Baptist*, which took rank among the best Southern religious journals. In connection with his intelligent wife he also founded Mount Lebanon Female College. He died May 7, 1862.

Lee, Rev. Jason, son of Rev. Joseph Lee, of Long Island, N. Y., was ordained pastor of the First Baptist church in East Lyme, Conn., in 1774, and with great honor sustained this relation till his death, which occurred in 1810, in the seventieth year of his age, and the thirty-sixth of his pastorate.

Lee, Rev. Jesse, was born in Alabama in 1803; became a preacher in 1837. He removed to Caddo Parish, La., in 1847. Through his labors the Shreveport church was greatly strengthened, and a large church built up at Summer Grove, of which he was pastor more than twenty years. He died Oct. 9, 1872.

Lee, Rev. S. C., pastor at Farmersville, La., and editor of the *Baptist Messenger*, was born in Alabama in 1826; has served several churches in

44

Concord Association, La., and has been often elected moderator of that body. He conceived the idea of establishing the Concord Institute, and as agent secured in a few months an endowment of $14,000.

Leigh, Hon. John T., is descended from Revolutionary stock. He was born in New Jersey in 1821. At twelve years of age he went into a store at New Brunswick as clerk. In 1844 he began business at Clinton, N. J., and has risen to a prominent place among business men in the community. He was one of the founders of the Clinton National Bank, has been twice mayor, and he has been a member of the Legislature. He is a deacon of the Baptist church in Clinton.

Leland, Rev. Aaron, lieutenant-governor of Vermont, was born in Holliston, Mass., May 28, 1761. He became a member of the Baptist church in Bellingham, Mass., in 1785, and soon after was licensed by that church to preach. He removed to Chester, Vt., where, in 1789, a small church of only ten members was formed, of which he took the pastoral charge. In ten years the church had grown so large, in consequence of a great revival which spread through that section, that it became necessary to divide it, and four churches were set off from the parent stock.

Mr. Leland did not confine his ministerial labors to his own vicinity, but went out, as our fathers in the ministry were wont to do, into the surrounding districts, making disciples and then gathering them into Christian churches. "It was not uncommon for him during the early years of his ministry to go from fourteen to twenty miles through the wilderness to attend a funeral."

Mr. Leland, from his known intelligence, and because in his political sentiments he harmonized with the people of the district in which he lived, was often called upon to act in civil affairs. For nine years he was representative in the General Assembly. He was speaker of the House for three years, and one of the governor's council for four years. For five years he was lieutenant-governor of the State, a part of the time being associated with Rev. Ezra Butler, who was governor. Probably this is the only instance in the history of the country where two Baptist ministers occupied together the two highest posts of honor within the gift of their fellow-citizens, as officers of a State government. For eighteen years he was one of the assistant justices of the County Court. He was proposed as a candidate for governor in 1828, but feeling that he must separate himself too much from the work of the ministry if he accepted the position, he declined to run for the office. We are told that "he had high qualifications for a popular and effective preacher. He had a noble form ; a mind of a powerful cast, that perceived quickly and composed easily ; a voice of vast compass, but

smooth and mellow ; great facility of utterance, and great fervor of spirit ; clear, but impassioned, he would carry with him the multitude irresistibly." With such traits of character, and ready to enlist heartily in any and every good cause, it is no wonder that he wielded an extensive influence throughout the State of Vermont. "He had great influence among his brethren, and commanded their high respect, as was evident from their almost uniformly making him the moderator of their meetings. He was a wise and safe counselor, always bringing to his aid the best light he was able to command, and forming his judgment with a discreet reference to all the circumstances of the case." He was one of the Fellows of Middlebury College, and received from that institution in 1814, and from Brown University in 1815, the honorary degree of Master of Arts. He died Aug. 25, 1833.

Leland, Rev. John, was born in Grafton, Mass., May 14, 1754. At the age of eighteen he passed through an experience not unlike that of John

REV. JOHN LELAND.

Bunyan, coming out gradually into the liberty of the gospel. Within a month after his conversion, in June, 1774, he made his first attempt at public speaking. Having connected himself with the church in Mount Poney, Culpeper Co., Va., he was ordained by the choice of the church. He preached from place to place, everywhere proclaiming "the unsearchable riches of Christ." Wonderful revivals everywhere followed the labors of Mr. Leland in Virginia. Hundreds came under the power of converting grace, and professed their faith in

Christ. The summary of his labors during the fifteen years of his ministry in Virginia is thus recorded,—3009 sermons preached, 700 persons baptized, and two large churches formed, one of 300 members, and another of 200.

Having finished the work which he thought his Master had given him to do in Virginia, Mr. Leland returned to his native State, and made his home for the most of the remainder of his life in Cheshire, Mass. Here, and in the region about, the same power and the same success followed his ministry. He reports the whole number of persons whom he had baptized down to 1821 as 1352. "Some of them," he says, "have been men of wealth and rank, and ladies of quality, but the chief part have been in the middle and lower grades of life. Ten or twelve of them have engaged to preach." Missionary tours were made in almost every direction, and multitudes crowded to hear him. The story of the "mammoth cheese" sent by the people of Cheshire to President Jefferson belongs to this period. He was the bearer of the gift to Washington. "Mr. Jefferson," remarks Rev. J. T. Smith, "treated him with much deference, among other things taking him into the Senate chamber." Year after year he went on doing that special work to which he believed the Lord had called him. "From seventy to beyond eighty years of age he probably averaged more sermons a week than most settled pastors." And it is interesting to have the following recorded of him by one who could speak intelligently about him, "The large attendance on his preaching was as creditable to the hearers as to the preacher. A sensational preacher he was not, nor a mere bundle of eccentricities. The discriminating and thoughtful listened to him with the most interest and attention." He was evidently "a born preacher." The life of a settled pastor would have been irksome to him. He wanted freedom from all restraint, and to do his own work at his own time and in his own way. In politics he was a Democrat of the Jeffersonian school, a hater of all oppression, whether civil or ecclesiastical. His warmest sympathies went out to his Baptist brethren in their efforts to secure a complete divorce of the Church from the State. Everywhere he pleaded with all the energy of his soul for civil and religious liberty, and he had the satisfaction of seeing it at last come out of the conflict victorious over all foes. Among the class of ministers whom God raised up during the last century to do the special work which it was given the Baptist denomination to perform, John Leland occupies a conspicuous place. We doubt if his equal will ever be seen again. Mr. Leland died Jan. 14, 1841.

Leland University, located at New Orleans,

La., was founded by the munificence of Holbrook Chamberlain, under the direction of the Home Mission Society. It is devoted to the education

LELAND UNIVERSITY, NEW ORLEANS, LA.

of freedmen. Mr. Chamberlain first gave $12,500 to found it, and the amount was duplicated by contributors to the society. He then gave $5000 more towards the buildings. He and his wife not only donated money to this noble object, but lent also their hearty personal efforts. This school has now been in successful operation several years, and has the warm sympathy of the Baptists of the city, and indeed of the Southwest. It is an important factor in the evangelization of the freedmen of the South.

Lemen, Rev. James, was born in Berkeley Co., Va., in 1760. In early life he was one of those who went North from Virginia with Gen. Washington, and was in some of the noted actions of the war of the Revolution. Returning to Virginia he settled near Wheeling, but in 1786 removed to Illinois, being one of the earliest settlers in that region of then almost unbroken wilderness. He went down the Ohio River in a flat-boat, with his family, and after much exposure and disaster arrived at length, though with a loss of all his household goods, which the river in the wrecking of his boat had swallowed up. His first home in Illinois was near Kaskaskia, at New Design, on the road from Kaskaskia to St. Louis. For many years his house was a stopping-place for travelers between the two places, and they were always entertained with Western hospitality. Under the preaching of Rev. James Smith, the first evangelical minister to visit Illinois, Mr. Lemen experienced conversion in 1787, but did not make a profession of his faith in baptism until 1794, when with his wife and two others he was baptized by Rev. Josiah Dodge. This was the first instance of the administration of baptism in what is now the State of Illinois. Two years later Mr. Lemen and his wife united with a few others in forming the first Christian church in Illinois, their minister being Rev. David Badgley. The Baptists thus led the way in the work of establishing churches in the great Prairie State. Even before Mr. Lemen had experienced conversion he had been one of a small company who met together on the Lord's day to read the Scriptures, with a sermon whenever one could be procured. After his conversion he was able to accompany these exercises with prayer. Finally, in 1808, he was licensed to preach, being now nearly fifty years of age. From that time until his death he was an active, zealous, and useful minister of the gospel, associating this with other public duties, such as, for some years, justice of the peace, and also as one of the judges of the County Court. He died Jan. 8, 1823, aged sixty-two. His son, James Lemen, Jr., who was in the ministry before him and assisted at his ordination, also preached his funeral sermon.

Lemen, Rev. James, Jr., third son of the foregoing, was born at New Design, Ill., Oct. 8, 1787. Converted at the age of twenty, he immediately began preaching, even before he had united with any church. Joining the church at New Design, he was by that church ordained, and he continued in the duties of an active ministry in various parts of Southern Illinois for more than sixty years. He took an active part also in public affairs ; was during sixteen years a member of the Legislature, both as representative and as senator. An election to the U. S. Senatorship was offered him but declined. He died Feb. 8, 1870, aged eighty-two.

Lemen, James H., was one of the family of Lemens who came into Illinois among its earliest settlers. He died in O'Fallon, Madison Co., Sept. 12, 1872, at the age of sixty-five. He had been a member of Bethel church since the age of twelve, was for many years clerk of the church, and for twenty years clerk of the South District Association.

Lemen, Rev. Joseph, was the second son of James Lemen, Sr., and was born near Harper's Ferry, Va., Sept. 8, 1785. He was only nine months old when his parents removed to Illinois. He was converted at a camp-meeting near Edwardsville, Ill., conducted by the Methodist bishop, McKendree, and by two Baptist ministers,— "Father Clark" and James Lemen, Sr. He was ordained Feb. 4, 1810, and was an active and useful minister for fifty-one years. He died June 28, 1861, at the age of seventy-five.

Lemen, Rev. Josiah, was born Aug. 15, 1794, at New Design, Ill. He was the sixth child of James Lemen, Sr. He also, like his brothers

Joseph, Moses, and James, became a minister of the gospel. He was baptized May 2, 1819, by Rev. John Clark, known in the former history of Illinois as "Father Clark," and united with the Canton, now Bethel church, near the place of his birth. He died July 11, 1862, aged seventy-two.

Lemen, Rev. Moses, was the youngest son of James Lemen, Sr., and he was born at the Illinois home of that remarkable family, Sept. 3, 1797. Though converted at ten years of age, he did not unite with the church until his twenty-second year. He was then baptized by "Father Clark." He and his brother Josiah were both baptized and ordained at the same time, their ordination occurring March 24, 1822. Moses Lemen, during thirty-six years, was one of the most laborious and useful ministers in Illinois. He died March 5, 1859, aged sixty-one.

Lemen, Rev. Sylvester, was also of the famous Lemen family, of Illinois, and he was for many years a member of the Bethel church. He died at Belleville, Ill., Sept. 28, 1872, at the age of fifty-six. He was, during some thirty-five years, one of the active and useful members of the South District Association.

Lennon, Rev. Haynes, was born Dec. 15, 1816 ; was deeply impressed with a desire to seek the Saviour at four years of age, but did not join a church till twenty-three ; was baptized by Rev. Wm. Ayers, in June, 1839 ; began to preach in May, 1841, and was ordained in March, 1842, Rev. Wm. Ayers and Rev. Dwight Hayes forming the Presbytery. He has been the pastor of the Antioch church, in Robinson County, N. C., for thirty-eight years, and of several others nearly as long. He was moderator of the Cape Fear Association, the second largest in the State, from 1850 to 1878, with the exception of the sessions of 1864 and 1865, when he was absent on account of sickness. In 1870 he became general superintendent of missions in his Association, and has been eminently useful in developing a missionary spirit among the churches. He is still an active and effective minister.

Lenox, Judge David T., whose parents were Scotch Methodists, was born at Catskill, N. Y., in 1801. He was baptized at Rushville, Ill., in 1832, with his wife (Miss Louisa Swan, of Lexington, Ky.). He organized and superintended two Sunday-schools ; he removed to Missouri in 1840 ; joined the Todd's Creek church ; was clerk of the church and Association until 1843, when he removed to Oregon, and located on the Tualatin Plains ; found five other Baptists in the wilderness, invited them to his house and there organized the West Union church, the first Baptist church west of the Rocky Mountains. In 1852 he spent $1500 of his own money, and raised $1200, to build a church edifice. He was deacon of the church. He was district judge and judge of Probate Court many years. In 1856 he removed to Weston, Eastern Oregon, where he closed a useful and consecrated life, Nov. 4, 1873.

Leonard, Rev. George, was born in Raynham, Mass., Aug. 17, 1802. He entered Brown University and graduated in 1824. He studied subsequently at the Newton Theological Institution, and was one of the first students who graduated from that seat of sacred learning. He was ordained pastor of the Second Baptist church in Salem, Mass., in August, 1826, where he labored until compelled to resign on account of ill health. On the 4th of July, 1830, he began his ministry as pastor of the First Baptist church in Portland, Me. Again his health failed. He gave up all ministerial work, and died at last, Aug. 11, 1831, in Worcester, Mass. If Mr. Leonard had been blessed with good health, and had lived longer, it may be safely predicted that he would have taken a high place among the ablest ministers of his denomination. Both the churches he served revere his memory.

Leonard, Judge John, was born in Knox Co., O., Aug. 20, 1825. He attended Denison University, at Granville, O. On leaving college he located in Morrow County, and at the age of twenty-three was elected county surveyor. While holding this office he devoted his spare time entirely to the study of law, and in 1852 was admitted to the bar in Wooster, Wayne Co., O. In the summer of 1853 he came to Iowa, and settled at Winterset, where he opened a law-office, and gradually built up an extensive practice. In 1862 he was elected district attorney, but resigned in 1864. In January, 1874, he entered upon his duties as judge of the Fifth Judicial District, to which he had been recently elected, and in which he continued to serve till the expiration of his term of office. He is an earnest and studious reader, especially in the line of his profession, and has one of the best libraries of any lawyer in Southwestern Iowa. He has long been a member of the Baptist church, and he is exemplary and faithful in his life and church relations. He still resides in Winterset, where his home has been for more than twenty-seven years. His eldest son, Byram Leonard, an attorney of much promise, a man of sterling Christian worth, and an earnest worker in the Baptist church of which he was a valued member, died in 1879, in his early manhood, and in the midst of a useful life.

Leonard, L. G., D.D., was born in Monson, Mass., Jan. 6, 1810; graduated at Newton in 1836; the same year became pastor of the church in Webster, Mass., where he remained nearly seven years. After two short pastorates in Thompson and New London, Conn., he took charge, in 1848, of the Market Street church, Zanesville, O. From 1855 to 1863 was pastor at Marietta, O., where he

was the means not only of greatly strengthening the home church, but was instrumental in forming several new churches in the surrounding country. In 1863 he took charge of the church at Lebanon, O., remaining until 1872, when he became pastor of the church at Bucyros, a position which he still holds.

Dr. Leonard has been closely identified with Baptist interests in Ohio. For thirty years he has been a member of the board of trustees of Denison University. His pastorates have been long and fruitful. A wise counselor and a faithful toiler for Christ, he has received during his many years of service the highest esteem and affection.

Leslie, Gov. Preston H., was born in Clinton Co., Ky., March 8, 1819, and was educated in the schools of his vicinity until the age of sixteen. Upon leaving school he spent a portion of his time

GOV. PRESTON H. LESLIE.

upon a farm near Louisville. At the age of eighteen he accepted a position in a store in Clinton County, and shortly afterwards entered the county clerk's office as a deputy. After this he attended a school of higher grade, and applied himself to study with great diligence, committing to memory the whole of a text-book on logic within a few weeks. When he left this school he entered the law-office of Gen. Rice Maxey, since Judge Maxey, of Texas, and father of United States Senator S. B. Maxey, of that State. In 1841 he was admitted to the bar. While a law-student, or just before he began the study of law, he professed religion and joined a Baptist church, and from that time made the Bible his study and his guide. When he commenced the practice of law he formed a resolution not to advocate knowingly an unjust cause for any consideration, and he determined never to neglect his duty to God for any worldly advantage however great. On these principles he began the business of life, and it is believed that he has adhered to them with unyielding tenacity. His success was assured from the beginning. From 1842 until 1853 his residence was upon a farm on Cumberland River, in Jackson Co., Tenn. Here he divided his time between farming and his profession. A few years later he removed to Glasgow, Ky., where he now resides. He was first elected to the Legislature from Monroe County in 1844, and was re-elected in 1850. He represented Barren and Monroe Counties in the State Senate from 1851 to 1855, and again in 1867, occupying the speaker's chair in the Senate in 1869. On the resignation of Gov. Stevenson he became governor *ex-officio* until the expiration of the term, in 1871. During that year he was elected governor by the extraordinary majority of 37,156. In the discharge of his duties as chief magistrate he attained a national reputation for diligence, wisdom, and integrity. At the close of his term, in 1875, he returned to his home in Glasgow and resumed his legal practice. Gov. Leslie is as faithful to his church as to the State, and he allows nothing but Providential circumstances to detain him from public worship or to prevent him from taking an active part in the business of his church. He superintended the Sunday-school at the Baptist church in Frankfort while he was governor, and was frequently moderator of the General Association of the Baptists. The State and the Church alike are justly proud of this pure statesman and devoted Christian.

Leslie, Rev. Robert, was born in Edinburgh, Scotland, in 1838, and came with his parents to the United States in 1851, stopping at Chicago, Ill., but subsequently locating at Schenectady, N. Y. In 1856 the family again removed to the West, establishing their home this time at Clinton, Iowa. According to the old established rule among the Scotch Presbyterians, the parents of Mr. Leslie designed him for the ministry, and while yet quite young he attended for some time the Rev. Dr. Andrew Thompson's school in Edinburgh. The conversion of his parents to Baptist views, and their removal to the United States, somewhat modified and changed these early purposes and also interrupted his education. Converted at the age of sixteen, he made a profession of religion in 1854, and united with the Baptist church in Clinton, Iowa. After his union with the church he prosecuted, in connection with his father, the business of architect and builder. During a number of years he had a painful conflict with his convictions

with reference to the Christian ministry, which finally culminated in his happy and entire consecration to that work. He was educated at the University of Chicago, graduating in the class of 1869, and at the Chicago Theological Seminary, graduating in 1870. He was ordained Oct. 12, 1870, as pastor of the Baptist church at Anamosa, Iowa. He was subsequently settled at Joliet, Ill., and in Waverly, Iowa. He took charge of the Baptist church in Waukesha, Wis., Aug. 1, 1879, where he is now the highly esteemed and useful pastor of the church of which Dr. Robert Boyd was pastor emeritus until his death. Thoroughly educated, fully consecrated to the work of the ministry, sound in his views of truth, and the pastor of one of the best churches in Wisconsin, Mr. Leslie has before him a bright and most promising future.

Lester, James S., was born in Virginia; is now over eighty years old; was a soldier against the Indians and Mexicans in Texas in 1842; was a member of the convention and signed the declaration of independence of Texas, March 2, 1836; has been a consistent Baptist all his life; a trustee of and liberal contributor to the endowment of Baylor University; joined the Baptist church in Texas at an early age, and lives now among his old friends in the enjoyment of their warm regard. He is one of the remarkable men of Texas.

Letters of Dismission are granted to members to unite with other churches of the same faith and gospel order. A letter of dismission is only a recommendation to the brother in whose favor it is granted. No church is obliged to receive it or him. It is found by experience that a letter should always be addressed to a particular church. General letters are unfavorable to permanent church relations. The letter is wisely limited in time, expiring in three, six, or twelve months. Until the accceptance of the letter by another church the person in whose favor it has been issued retains his membership in the church granting it unless a by-law provides otherwise. Authority to unite with another church ceases when the date of limitation in the letter is passed. According to Baptist usage the applicant for a letter should pay his church dues, if he is able, before he receives it. After receiving his letter of dismission, if he changes his mind about uniting with another community, he should return the letter to the church or its clerk. While retaining the letter, and before its date of limitation is reached, though still a member of the church, he should not vote at church meetings or take any part in the regular business of the church.

Every Baptist has a right to obtain a letter to unite with a regular Baptist church unless there is a charge against him. And this privilege, it is believed, would be sustained by the civil courts. And for the same reason, if a member is excluded from a church contrary to its by-laws, or, if it has none, against the usages of the denomination, the courts would order his restoration. An English authority recently makes the following statement on this question: " The courts say to a church, chapel, company, club, or partnership, Make what contract you please, but *when the agreement is made we will see that it is kept.*" There is no reason to doubt but that this is the law in every State of the Union for every association, secular and religious, legally holding real estate. When a member asks for a letter, and there is no accusation against him before the disciplinary committee or the church, unless some grave breach of duty has been committed no charge should be brought then. Baptist usage requires the clerk of a church receiving a letter to notify the church granting it that the brother commended by it has been received into fellowship. Regular Baptist churches do not grant letters of dismission to Pedobaptist religious communities. Neither do they receive letters from these bodies except as testimonials.

Form of a Letter of Dismission.

The Baptist church of ———— to the Baptist church of ————

DEAR BRETHREN:

This is to certify that ———— is a member with us in good standing and full fellowship; and at his own request he is hereby dismissed from us to unite with you. When received by you his connection with us will cease.

By order of the church.

———— ————, *Church Clerk.*

This letter will be valid for six months.

Leverett, Prof. Warren, was born Dec. 19, 1805; he and his twin-brother, Prof. Washington Leverett, are sons of William and Lydia (Fuller) Leverett, of Brookline, Mass. At the age of fourteen the two brothers went to live with Samuel Griggs, Esq., a brother of Mrs. Leverett's second husband, a farmer residing in Rutland, Vt. Here they remained until they reached their majority. In the mean time they had experienced conversion, and leaving the home in Vermont that they might pursue study under the direction of their eldest brother, Rev. William Leverett, of Roxbury, they united with the Baptist church in Cambridgeport. September, 1828, they entered Brown University, graduating in 1832. For a time the brothers were separated, Washington becoming one of the faculty of Columbian College, Washington, D. C., and Warren being compelled by broken health to travel, though engaged occasionally in teaching. He removed to the West and opened a school in Greenville, Ill, and successfully carried it on for a year and a half, when he removed to Upper Alton, becoming connected with Shurtleff College, and re-maining in that service until 1868. He died at Upper Alton in November, 1872. Prof. Leverett's department in Shurtleff College was that of ancient languages, in which studies he was a thorough, proficient, and an admirable instructor. While a member of the church in Cambridgeport he was licensed as a preacher, and frequently during his life officiated as such with much acceptance.

Leverett, Washington, LL.D.—Some account of the early life of Washington Leverett, professor in Shurtleff College during so many years, is given in connection with the notice of his twin-brother, Prof. Warren Leverett. Washington Leverett, after two years spent as teacher in Brown University, and in Columbian College, Washington, D. C., entered at Newton, where he graduated in 1836. Receiving at that time a call to the chair of Mathematics and Natural Philosophy in Shurtleff College, he accepted it, and removing to Illinois entered at once upon his duties. This post of service he continued to fill with marked acceptance for thirty-two years, resigning it in 1868. Since that date he has continued his connection with the college as a member of the board of trustees, and as librarian and treasurer. It is justly written of him that " as a teacher he was eminently successful, and possessed a thoroughness of scholarship and real worth that never failed to command the respect of his pupils, and which has endeared him to a large circle of warm friends."

Levering, Judge Charles, associate judge of the Circuit Court of Allen Co., O., was a lineal descendant of Wigard Levering, one of the pioneer settlers of Roxborough, in Philadelphia County, who emigrated to this country from Germany in 1685.

He was born in Roxborough township, Dec. 8, 1782.

Mr. Levering received the common rudiments of an English education at the district school of his native place.

In 1805 he indulged a hope in Christ, and was baptized into the fellowship of the Roxborough Baptist church, of which he was elected deacon March 24, 1821.

On Sept. 24, 1812, he was married to Esther Levering, eldest daughter of Deacon Anthony Levering, of Roxborough, a most estimable Christian wife and mother.

Mr. Levering was a patriot, and during the war of 1812–14, although he was major of a regiment, yet when he found his command was not to be ordered into active service until after six months, he enlisted as a private in the Roxborough Volunteers, of which company he subsequently became captain.

In 1822 he removed into the district of Southwark, and united with the Third church; subsequently he joined the Second church, during the pastorate of the Rev. Thomas J. Kitts.

In 1835, Mr. Levering removed to Allen, now Auglaize Co., O., soon after which he was appointed

JUDGE CHARLES LEVERING.

associate judge of the Circuit Court for that county, which position he held for several years.

He was active in everything pertaining to the success of our denomination. He was a constituent member and deacon of the Amanda and Wapaukoneta churches, and held the office of deacon in the latter until his death, which occurred March 14, 1860. His remains lie in a country church-yard, on the State road, about five miles north of Wapaukoneta, the county seat of Auglaize Co., O.

Levering, Eugene, Sr., was born in Baltimore, Md., April 24, 1819. He traced his family for seven generations to Rosier Levering, born probably in France about 1600, who fled to Holland or Germany on account of religious persecutions, and married Elizabeth Van De Walle, of Wesel, Westphalia. They had two sons,—Wigard and Gehard. The former, Eugene's ancestor, was born at Gamen, Westphalia, about 1648, and married, in 1671, Magdalene Böker. In 1685, accompanied by his wife and their four children, he came to America and settled at Germantown, Pa. In 1692 he removed to Roxborough, where he bought 500 acres of land. Wigard and his wife had ten children. Their son William, of the third generation, was born at Mulheim, in Germany, May 4, 1677, and came to America with his parents. He died a 1746, leaving five children. The eldest, Wil-

liam, of the fourth generation, was born at Roxborough, August, 1705. He married, May 2, 1732, Hannah Clement. He built the first hotel at Roxborough, now known as the " Leverington," which he carried on together with blacksmithing and farming, his farm embracing 250 acres. He died March 30, 1774. The first school-house in Roxborough was built through his exertions, and he gave the ground for it in 1748. It is now called "The Levering Primary School." William and Hannah had nine children, one of whom, Enoch, of the fifth generation, was born in Roxborough, Feb. 21, 1742. After conducting his large tannery there for many years, he removed to Baltimore, Md., between the years 1773 and 1775. Here he entered extensively into the grocery business. He married Mary Righter, and died aged fifty-four. They had nine sons. Peter was the first-born. Enoch's brother, Nathan, born in Roxborough, May 19, 1745, gave the lot on which the Roxborough Baptist church is built, and superintended its erection. This church, of which he was a constituent member, met at his residence prior to the erection of their house of worship. He also gave the ground for their cemetery. He was father-in-law to H. G. Jones, D.D., son of Rev. David Jones, A.M., a famous Revolutionary chaplain. Hon. H. G. Jones, the son of Dr. Jones, is the author of " A Genea-

EUGENE LEVERING, SR.

logical Account" of the Levering family, from which many of the facts of this article are taken. Peter, of the sixth generation, was born in Roxborough, Feb. 14, 1766, and removed to Baltimore with his parents, where he became engaged in the shipping and commission business. He married, May 22, 1798, Hannah, only daughter of William Wilson, of the firm of William Wilson & Sons, one of the most extensive shipping-houses of Baltimore. They both were members of the First Baptist church. Mr. Levering united with it late in life, but was a prominent member of the congregation, and his house was headquarters for the denomination. He died Dec. 7, 1843. They had fourteen children, Eugene being the twelfth, and the 455th descendant of Rosier Levering. He was born in Baltimore, April 24, 1819. After spending some years in preparation in private schools in Baltimore, he went to college, but his health compelled him to relinquish his intention. At an early age he was converted, and united with the First Baptist church, of which he became a most useful member. Subsequently he became a valued member of the Seventh Baptist church, Richard Fuller, D.D., pastor, of whom he was an intimate friend. He was for many years the treasurer of the Maryland Baptist Union Association. He married, Oct. 4, 1842, Ann, daughter of Joshua and Mary E. Walker, of Baltimore, and a descendant of Henry Sater, who came from England in 1709, and through whose liberality and efforts the first Baptist church in Maryland was formed. They had twelve children, nine of whom are now living. In 1842 he commenced business, in partnership with his brother, Frederick A., who married Martha E. Johnson, grandniece of the first governor of Maryland. Levering & Co. soon became a leading house in their business, and not only established for themselves an enviable reputation, but also added much to the prosperity of Baltimore. In 1861, when the war began, owing to their extensive trade with the Southern States, where they were unable to collect their debts, they were compelled to suspend and to compromise with all their creditors for fifty cents on the dollar. But near the close of the war, so successful and conscientious were they, that they paid the entire obligation, from which they had been legally released, with interest, amounting to nearly $100,000. In 1866, upon the death of his brother, Eugene took into partnership with him his sons William T., Eugene, and Joshua. The house took a position at the head of their special trade, and has been greatly instrumental in making Baltimore second in importance in their branch of business in the United States. Mr. Levering died, after an illness of four months, in June, 1870. He left $30,000 to charitable and religious objects. He made his three sons his executors, and left them in charge of the business. The present firm, composed of his sons William T., Eugene, Joshua, and Leonidas, succeeded the old firm in January, 1875, upon the settlement of their father's estate. It is the largest house in their business in Baltimore, and the third or fourth in the United States. Eugene is president of the National Bank of Commerce. Following in the footsteps of their fathers, the sons are living for Christ, being active in church and denominational matters, and being also among the largest contributors to the cause of Christ in the Baptist denomination North or South. Mr. Levering's widow survives him. She and her children—eight sons, one daughter, and four daughters-in-law—are all members of the Eutaw Place Baptist church. These children are left to testify by their worth of character and their noble deeds to the true principles and exalted reputation of their parents.

Levering, Franklin, was born in Baltimore, March 9, 1811. He united in early life with the First Baptist church in Baltimore. He removed to Clark Co., Mo., and united with Fox River church, and organized the first Sabbath-school in the county. In 1843 he located at Hannibal, and entered upon mercantile pursuits. He was a successful business man, and a zealous Christian, given to hospitality. His house was the home of visiting ministers. He united with the church in Hannibal, and was clerk, deacon, and Sabbath-school superintendent. The last office he held twenty-six years. He left his children the heritage of an unblemished character, and was held in the highest esteem as a citizen. He died July 26, 1870, and was deeply mourned in the church and in the community. His daily life exemplified the beauty of holiness. When dying he was asked if he wanted anything, he shook his head and replied, "Jesus is coming." When asked if he had any message to leave, he said, "Live holy lives."

Levy, Edgar Mortimer, D.D., was born in St. Mary's, Ga., Nov. 23, 1822; was converted when thirteen years of age, and united with the Presbyterian Church. After pursuing studies for two years in a private classical school, he spent three years in the University of Pennsylvania, and studied theology under the late Rev. Albert Barnes; was licensed to preach in 1843; became deeply interested in the subject of baptism, and after a year of prayerful study, was baptized April 14, 1844, by Dr. G. B. Ide, of Philadelphia. In the autumn of 1844 he was invited to supply the First West Philadelphia church, and soon after became pastor. After fourteen years of abundant labor he accepted a call to the South church, Newark, N. J., where he remained ten years. In 1868 he returned to Philadelphia, and became pastor of the Berean church, where he still remains, and where many have been gathered into the church under his ministrations. He received the degree of D.D., in 1865, from the university at Lewisburg. Dr. Levy has had much to do with the prosperity of the Baptist church in West Philadelphia.

Levy, Capt. John P., was born in St. Mary's, Ga., July 25, 1809; learned the trade of ship-carpenter, and on completing his apprenticeship shipped as a sailor on a Liverpool packet; was soon made commander of the vessel, and spent a number of years in seafaring life. At length he returned to Philadelphia, and established the well-known ship-building firm of Reaney, Neafie & Levy, which undertaking was attended with rapidly increasing success. In the spring of 1855 he was baptized by his brother, Rev. E. M. Levy, D.D., and united with the First church, West Philadelphia, of which his brother was at that time pastor. He subsequently became impressed with the necessity of establishing another interest in this rapidly growing section of the city, and united with others in organ-

CAPT. JOHN P. LEVY.

izing the Berean church. The beautiful meeting-house of this church was secured mainly through his munificent benefactions, and was dedicated free of incumbrance June 22, 1860. As a thank-offering for continued prosperity, he built an attractive parsonage adjoining the sanctuary, and conveyed it to the church, together with an annuity of $600. Nor were his benefactions confined to the church of which he was a member. He was a man full of generous impulses, and his wealth was largely distributed. He died at Aiken, S. C., whither he had gone to recruit his feeble health, Dec. 26, 1867.

Lewis, Rev. Cadwallader, LL.D., an eminent scholar, and one of the most eloquent pulpit orators of the South, was born in Spottsylvania Co., Va., Nov. 5, 1811. He was educated by his father, who conducted a classical school many years at Llangollen, Va., but finished his course of study, which was a very full one, at the University of Virginia. In 1831 he went to Kentucky, and taught school in Covington. The following year he took charge of the preparatory department of Georgetown College. In 1844 he commenced the study of medicine, but his health failed, and he located on a farm in Franklin County, where he has lived until the present time. During the same year he made a profession of religion, and united with Buck Run Baptist church, near his home. He was very soon after licensed to preach, and was ordained in 1846. He was invited to take pastoral charge of the Baptist church at Frankfort, but his health would not admit of his leaving his farm. He took charge of country and village churches convenient to his residence, preaching one Sunday in the month to each, and has thus employed himself to the present time, except when, in consequence of a crushed limb, he was unable to travel. He occupied the chair of Theology in Georgetown College four years. He is a strong, logical writer, and exercises a leading influence in the councils of the denomination in his State.

Lewis, Rev. Charles Casson, son of Horatio and Betsey Lewis, was born in Stonington, Conn., June 8, 1807; became a sea-captain; converted in 1842 under the preaching of Rev. J. S. Swan; joined Third Baptist church in Groton, Conn.; began preaching at Key West, Fla., where he planted a church and was ordained; afterwards settled with the following churches: First Groton, Conn.; Lisbury, Mass.; Second Hopkinton, Exeter, North Kingstown, Block Island, and Lattery Village, R. I.; and Second North Stonington, Conn.; from Block Island he was elected to the senate of Rhode Island; was a man of fervor and power; died in the pastoral office with the Second Baptist church of North Stonington, Conn., March 10, 1864, in his fifty-seventh year.

Lewis, Rev. Daniel D., was born in Barnstable, Mass., July 21, 1777. He was converted in early life, and joined the First church in Portland, Me., then composed of nine members. These persons were full of the grace of Christ, and the church soon became numerous and widely influential.

Mr. Lewis took charge of the church at Ipswich, Mass., on first entering the ministry. He was subsequently pastor of the Second church of Providence, R. I., of the church in Fishkill, N. Y., in Frankford, Pa., in Wilmington, Del., and in Paterson and Piscataway, N. J. In Piscataway he spent years rich in divine blessings, and from it he entered the "general assembly and church of the first-born," Sept. 25, 1849. He delivered his last sermon on Sunday evening, and died on the following Tuesday.

Mr. Lewis was an able preacher, full of the Spirit and Word of God, and a successful pastor of the churches for whose welfare he labored. He healed church wounds, built up disciples in the glorious doctrines of grace, led throngs of converts to Jesus, and enjoyed the warm affection of large numbers. His memory is precious still in the churches for whose eternal interests he employed his time and talents, and his fervent prayers.

Lewis, Rev. Geo. W., was born in Ellisburgh, Jefferson Co., N. Y., April 14, 1822, where he was baptized in March, 1833; ordained in Lowell, Ind., Jan. 18, 1866; labored in Indiana, Illinois, and Iowa; and became pastor of the Aurora Baptist church, Neb., in 1878. Mr. Lewis has enjoyed the divine blessing in his pastorates.

Lewis, Hon. Henry Clay, of Coldwater, Mich., was born in Orleans Co., N. Y., May 5, 1820. He has resided in Coldwater since 1844, where he has been engaged in business, first as a merchant and afterwards as a banker. He is president of the Coldwater National Bank, and has been mayor of the city. He has been a member of the Baptist Church nearly twenty years. He is chiefly known as the owner of an art-gallery, which he founded in 1868, which is open to the public without charge. It is larger than any other art-gallery on this continent. Mr. Lewis takes great pleasure in affording

HON. HENRY CLAY LEWIS.

enjoyment to others, and has made his gallery, in its surroundings as well as in itself, beautiful and attractive, and a most important element in the educational influences of the city of Coldwater.

Lewis, Prof. John J., A.M., was born in Utica, N. Y., Dec. 25, 1843, of Welsh Congregational parentage; entered the grammar school of Madison University in 1859; entered Madison University, and afterwards Hamilton College (Clinton), and was there graduated in 1864; Professor of Belles-Lettres and Elocution in Brooklyn Collegiate and Polytechnic Institute from 1864 to 1866. In the fall of 1866 he removed to Syracuse, and began preaching in a small mission chapel; was settled March, 1867, as pastor of First Baptist church, Syracuse; was very successful, the increase in sixteen months being over 140. In 1868 he became Professor of Belles-Lettres in Madison University, which position he still retains, to the great satisfaction of students, alumni, and friends of the institution; has contributed largely to the press, many of his articles being founded on his travels in Japan, Burmah, India, and the Orient.

Lewis, Rev. John W., one of the most distinguished Baptist ministers of North Georgia, was born near Spartanburg, S. C., Feb. 1, 1801. Educated at a classical academy near Spartanburg, he studied and practised medicine at Greenville, S. C., becoming a skillful and popular physician. He united with the Baptist church of that town. During the years 1830 and 1831 he was a member of the South Carolina Legislature. About that time he began to preach, and was ordained in 1832. He removed to Canton, Ga., in 1839 or 1840, becoming pastor of that and other churches in Cherokee, Ga., and acquiring a great influence. He was a preacher of much force and energy; a strong and bold defender of the faith; an able expounder of the Word, and an eloquent advocate of the truth. A man of fine practical sense, he had a strong mind, and was a deep, original thinker. He had a benevolent heart, and was steadfast in his friendships. He had extraordinary forecast, and managed business matters with great ability and success. In 1857 he was appointed superintendent of the State road by Gov. Brown, and his management was eminently successful. During the war he served in the Congress of the Confederate States, as Senator, with great ability, and previous to the war he served in the State senate, and was instrumental in the establishment of the Supreme Court of Georgia. His character stood extraordinarily high in Georgia. A man of firm faith, deep piety, and unabated zeal, he won many souls to Jesus. After a life of great usefulness, he died in Cherokee County, in June, 1865.

Lewis, Rev. Lester, was born in Suffield, Conn., Oct. 15, 1817; baptized by Rev. Henry Jackson, D.D., and united with First Baptist church in Hartford, Feb. 11, 1838; studied in Connecticut Literary Institution; ordained pastor of the church in Agawam, Mass., Oct. 7, 1840; in 1846 began to labor for Connecticut Baptist State Convention, but soon settled with the church in Bristol; in 1853 became pastor of the church in Middletown, where, after great success, he died, Feb. 7, 1858; large-hearted, sound in the faith, a clear and forcible preacher, fervent in prayer, and beloved by all who knew him.

Lewisburg, Pa., the University at.—In the year 1845, some intelligent Baptists of the North-umberland Association saw the need of higher edu-cation for their sons and daughters, under the religious auspices of their own denomination. Their perception of this need at first took form in a plan for a first-class academy. The natural beauty, healthfulness, and economic advantages of the borough of Lewisburg, in Union Co., Pa., on the West Branch of the Susquehanna, and in the geographical centre of the State, determined the location of the school in that village. Through the Rev. Eugenio Kincaid and the Rev. J. E. Bradley, Stephen W. Taylor, who had recently resigned his professorship in Madison University, became en-listed in the new enterprise. Under the principal-ship of Prof. Taylor, assisted by his son, Alfred Taylor, A.M., and I. N. Loomis, A.M., a school was opened in the fall of 1846 in the basement of the Baptist church, since destroyed.

Prof. Taylor combined prophetic insight with the powers of a rare teacher, and saw in the new school the germ of a university. Others approved the project of founding at Lewisburg such an in-stitution as would meet the higher educational de-mands of the whole State. A charter incorporating "The University at Lewisburg, Pa.," was approved on the 5th day of February, 1846, with the follow-ing trustees: James Moore, James Moore, Jr., Joseph Meireell, William H. Ludwig, Samuel Wolfe, Levi B. Christ, Henry Funk, Joel E. Brad-ley, Eugenio Kincaid, Benjamin Bear, William W. Keen, William Bucknell, Thomas Wattson, James M. Linnard, Lewis Vastine, Oliver Black-burn, Caleb Lee, Daniel L. Moore.

It was provided in the charter that ground should be purchased and buildings erected when $100,000 had been raised, that a fourth part should be per-manently invested in a productive form, that the property should not be mortgaged or debt incurred under any pretext whatever, that no misnomer should defeat or annul a grant or bequest, and that ten acres of ground with improvements should be exempt from taxation. The management was committed to two boards: 1st, a board of trustees, not to exceed twenty members, all of whom must be Baptists; and, 2d, a board of curators, not to exceed forty members; the majority of whom must be Baptists. Both boards are self-perpetuating.

The subscription of $100,000 was declared to be se-cured on the 17th day of July, 1849, through the ef-forts of Drs. Eugenio Kincaid and William Shadrach, who traversed the State soliciting funds. Previous to this a tract of land to the south of the borough of Lewisburg, including a fine hill of nearly a hundred feet elevation, covered with a beautiful natural grove, and commanding extended views over river and valley, had been secured for the university. In 1848 an academy building was begun and nearly completed. In January, 1849, the trustees felt justi-fied in electing professors for the college, and in commencing a college building. Two graduates of Madison University, the Rev. G. W. Anderson, A.M., editor of the *Christian Chronicle*, of Phila-delphia, and the Rev. G. R. Bliss, of New Bruns-wick, N. J., were appointed, respectively, to the chairs of Latin and Greek. Both soon afterwards began their labors, the students of the academy and the college, consisting of both sexes, reciting together in the academy building, Prof. Taylor still acting as principal.

In 1851 the west wing of the college building was completed, and the college students moved into dormitories and studies regarded at the time as "unsurpassed in pleasantness by those of any in-stitution." In the spring of this year Prof. Taylor resigned his position to accept the presidency of Madison University, but remained to preside at the first Commencement, August 20, 1851, when a class of seven was graduated in the chapel of the acad-emy. It is but just to the memory of this good man and great teacher to quote the words of a co-worker who knew him well: "Without him it is almost certain that our university would never have existed, and existing in an essential measure by his agency, it is well for us that that agency was not only earnest, benevolent, laborious, and pious, but also in the main judicious and beneficial."

The Rev. Howard Malcom, D.D., of Philadelphia, an alumnus of Princeton, and ex-president of Georgetown College, had been chosen president of the university, and Charles S. James, A.M., a graduate of Brown, and Alfred Taylor, A.M., a graduate of Madison, were added to the faculty of the college, the former as Professor of Mathematics and Natural Philosophy, and the latter as Professor of Belles-Lettres. With these additions began the collegiate year 1851–52. The college now became a distinct department of the university, the academy became gradually a preparatory school for boys only, while, in 1852, the "University Female In-stitute" became a separate department. A theo-logical department was added in 1855. From this point, therefore, we may consider the departments separately.

THE COLLEGE.

The presidency of Dr. Malcom continued from 1851 to 1857, during which the college building was completed, consisting of a main building 80 feet

THE UNIVERSITY AT LEWISBURG, PA.

square, of three stories, for recitation-rooms, chapel, society halls, library, cabinet, and Commencement Hall, and two wings, each 120 feet long and 35 feet wide, of four stories, for students' study-rooms and dormitories. In 1852 the sum of $45,000 was added to the funds by a few friends without a general canvass. About $20,000 were received from lands sold from the original campus, leaving finally about twenty-six acres as university grounds.

Thus established, the college began a work of incalculable value to the intellectual and spiritual progress of the denomination in Pennsylvania. On the resignation of President Malcom, in 1857, the Rev. Justin R. Loomis, Ph.D., who had been called from Waterville, Me., in 1854, to fill the chair of Natural Sciences, succeeded him as president. During twenty-five years President Loomis devoted his best energies to the work of building up the college, and establishing the youth who came under his moulding hand in the principles of a deep Christian philosophy. The invasion of Pennsylvania by Lee's army, in 1863, caused the closing of the college during a campaign of six weeks, officers and students uniting to form Company A of the 28th Regiment of Pa. Vols. A memorial tablet in Commencement Hall commemorates the names of those who fell in the war for the Union. In 1864, President Loomis increased the funds of the university by collecting subscriptions amounting to $100,000. In 1876 an attempt was made to secure additional endowment, but owing to other interests in the field the effort was abandoned after about $20,000 had been promised, mostly in private subscriptions offered by a few liberal friends.

In 1879, President Loomis resigned the presidency, and Prof. David J. Hill, A.M., a graduate of the college, and at the time of his appointment Crozer Professor of Rhetoric, was chosen president of the university, a position which he still occupies.

The following were presidents and acting presidents from the foundation of the college to the year 1880:

PRESIDENTS.

Elected.		Resigned.
1851.	Rev. Howard Malcom, D.D., LL.D.	1857
1857.	Rev. Justin R. Loomis, Ph.D., LL.D.	1879
1879.	Rev. David J. Hill, A.M.	

ACTING PRESIDENTS.

Stephen W. Taylor, LL.D., prior to 1851.
Rev. Geo. R. Bliss, D.D., LL.D., during 1871-72.
Rev. Francis W. Tustin, Ph.D., for six months in 1879.

The university has an endowment of $121,000, and property worth $117,000, and an effort is now started by which its endowment is certain to be greatly increased. The institution has no debts.

The college is now in possession of a fine library of nearly 10,000 volumes, a museum of about 10,000 specimens for the illustration of the sciences, a chemical laboratory and apparatus. There are two flourishing literary societies with libraries of their own. They publish a monthly journal called *The College Herald*. There is also a "Society for Moral and Religious Inquiry." There are two prizes for preparation for college and one for excellence in oratory in the Junior year. Tuition is free to the sons of ministers. The expenses range from $125 to $250 per annum.

The courses of study have expanded greatly since the opening of the college, as shown in comparative tables published in "A Historical Sketch of the University at Lewisburg," edited by O. W. Spratt, LL.B., in 1876, and printed by the Society of Alumni. There are now two courses leading to a degree : (1) The classical course, of four years, leading to the degree of A.B., and (2) the Latin scientific course, leading to the degree of S.B. Both courses have been brought up to the standard of the best Eastern colleges, and have recently given some scope to the optional element. Anglo-Saxon, American literature, comparative zoölogy, analytical chemistry, and constitutional law have been added to both courses. A good collection of engravings, heliotypes, and casts has stimulated the study of the fine arts, and illustrated lectures are given to the Senior class. Lectures on Grecian history, life, and literature ; Roman history, life, and literature ; mediæval history ; English history and literature ; the history of philosophy ; natural theology ; and the evidences of Christianity are regularly delivered. The introduction of a short course of lectures on practical ethics and hygiene for the Freshman class is believed to be distinctively peculiar to this college. The government is thus based on ethical ideas, and so far has proved that an appeal to manhood develops it and secures self-government.

The graduates of the college number 322. Honorary degrees have been bestowed as follows : LL.D., 12; D.D., 36 ; Ph.D., 10; A.M., 52.

Since 1851, when the first class was graduated, important changes bearing upon the prosperity of the college have gradually taken place. The Philadelphia and Erie Railroad runs within one mile of Lewisburg, and the Lewisburg and Tyrone Railroad passes through it. The town is lighted with gas, and contains several miles of well-paved sidewalks. A new church edifice, costing nearly $60,000, has been built by the Baptists. The natural beauty of the place has been enhanced by these improvements, yet it remains a quiet, moral, and rural retreat admirably adapted to the seclusion which thorough study demands for the young.

THE INSTITUTE.

This department of the university began its separate organization as a school in 1852, under the principalship of Miss Hadassah E. Scribner, of

Maine, who retained her position for two years. In 1854 two young ladies, the first class of the institute, were graduated. At this time all the teachers resigned, and Miss Amanda Taylor, of Easton, Pa., with a new corps of assistants, undertook the work. Strong prejudices existed in the community against the liberal education of women, but this was gradually overcome by persistent effort, and in 1858 fifteen young ladies were graduated in the presence of an audience of 1500 people. Since then classes ranging from ten to twenty have been graduated every year. In 1857 six acres of a beautiful grove were appropriated for a suitable building on the university grounds. The building is pleasantly and healthfully located, warmed with furnaces, and lighted with gas, and it will accommodate ninety boarders. In 1869 a wing was added, at the cost of $10,000, containing rooms for students and a large gymnasium, which has been suitably fitted up.

In 1863, Miss Taylor resigned, and was succeeded by Miss Lucy W. Rundell, of Alden, N. Y. She continued her work ably until 1869, when she was succeeded by Miss Harriet E. Spratt, daughter of the Rev. Geo. M. Spratt, D.D., and a graduate of the institute. This rare Christian woman had already spent fourteen years in the school as a teacher. She continued as principal until the Commencement of 1878. A few months later she ended a career of extraordinary usefulness by death, having been made Emeritus lady principal after her resignation. For twenty-four years her life was devoted to the successive classes of young women that passed through the institute, and hundreds mourned for her as for a sister.

In 1878, Jonathan Jones, A.M., was elected principal, a position which he now holds. The institute is provided with an able corps of instructors, who live in the institute building and make it a school home. There are five courses of study, ranging from a preparatory English course to a full classical collegiate course. The young ladies recite in their own building, apart from the young gentlemen, but attend the lectures of the college, enjoy the use of the library and museum, and witness the experiments of the professor of natural sciences. There are excellent advantages for instruction in music, drawing, crayoning, and painting. The graduates number 293.

THE ACADEMY.

When, in 1849, the college emerged into a distinct department of the university, the academy was intrusted to the principalship of Isaac N. Loomis, A.M., sharing the new academy building with the college. This arrangement continued until the college building was completed, H. D. Walker, A.M., succeeding Principal Loomis in 1853, and George Yeager, A.M., following in 1857.

Isaac C. Wynn, A.M., became principal in 1859, and in January, 1860, the academy building being used then solely for that department, it was fitted up for a boarding-school for boys and young men. Until 1868 the academy embraced the classical preparatory classes of the university, but in that year "The Classical Preparatory Department" was organized, with Freeman Loomis, A.M., as principal, the academy being confined to English branches only. This arrangement continued, the English academy having in the mean time a succession of separate principals, until 1878, when the departments were reunited under the principalship of William E. Martin, A.M. "The Classical Preparatory Department," from 1868 to 1878, was established in the west wing of the college building.

The academy, as reorganized in 1878, is a thorough English and classical school, designed to prepare young men for college, for business, or for teaching in the common schools. The students have access to the college library and reading-room. When prepared they are admitted to the college upon the certificate of the principal, without examination. Special attention is given to English and commercial branches. Many improvements have been made in the building, rendering it a pleasant home for boys. Students of small means are allowed to board in clubs, which reduces their expenses considerably.

THE THEOLOGICAL DEPARTMENT.

The charter of the university permits the establishment of any professional school by the corporation. A school of theology, however, is the only department of this kind so far attempted. This was opened in 1855 under the charge of Thomas F. Curtis, D.D., and continued during thirteen years. On the resignation of Prof. Curtis, in 1865, the school was reorganized, with Lemuel Moss, D.D., as Professor of Theology, and Lucius E. Smith, D.D., as Professor of Sacred Rhetoric and Pastoral Theology, Geo. R. Bliss, D.D., being continued as Professor of Biblical Interpretation. In 1868 the department was removed to Upland, Pa., and reorganized by the family of the late John P. Crozer as "The Crozer Theological Seminary," under a new corporation, but still retaining a close connection with the university at Lewisburg, whose graduates supply its classes in a large measure. While at Lewisburg the department enrolled 38 graduates. These have been received and enrolled among the alumni of the Crozer Seminary.

Liberia.—The people of Liberia are of the African race, by the way of the United States. They are very enterprising, and there is reason to believe that the providence of God designs to accomplish great spiritual good for the country of their fathers through their instrumentality. There are 26 Baptist churches in the republic with a membership of about 2000. At the last meeting of "The Liberia Baptist Association," in December, 1879, a considerable amount of prosperity among the churches was reported. The Providence church in Monrovia had received 56 by baptism, the Arthington church 24, and the First church in Edina 39; 275 baptisms were reported for the year.

At the annual meeting of the Liberia Baptist Association the members agreed to form another Association and a national organization.

Liberty, American Religious.—Much has been said and written about the originator of our religious freedom. Some have zealously claimed Lord Baltimore as its author. This nobleman was a Roman Catholic, and on that account a large amount of very clear evidence is necessary to establish his right to this honor. He was a talented man, with many of the qualities of a statesman. He knew that the English people in 1633, when his first settlers left their country for the New World, would never tolerate a colony in the British dominions where the Protestant religion was excluded, and, as a matter of absolute necessity, he had to permit its existence in Maryland. He deserved no credit for showing common sense. His first settlers were Catholics, and to them his colony appealed for recruits; and nothing in the history of Maryland shows him to be an unselfish friend of religious liberty. He simply appears as a yielding statesman bending to the necessities of the times.

John Leeds Bozman's "History of Maryland" was published by the General Assembly of that State in 1837. It is derived largely from "the written memorials which then existed in the public archives of the State," to which the author had free access, and it bears the authority of the government of Maryland. In 1639, Bozman says, "A very short bill was introduced into the house (the Legislature), entitled 'An act for church liberties,' and was expressed nearly in the following words: '*Holy Church* within this province shall have all her rights, liberties, and immunities safe, whole, and inviolable in all things.' When we reflect on the original causes of their emigration (the colonists of Maryland), we cannot but suppose that it was the intention of those in whose hands the government of the province was, a majority of whom were without doubt Catholics, as well as much the greater number of the colonists, to erect a hierarchy, with an ecclesiastical jurisdiction similar to the ancient Church of England *before the Reformation.*"* "Holy Church" is the Catholic Church, and this was but the entering wedge of a Romish persecuting religious establishment.

Another bill of the same session provided, that "eating flesh in time of Lent, or on other days, Wednesdays excepted, wherein it is prohibited by the law of England, without case of infirmity, to be allowed by the judge; and the offender shall forfeit to the lord proprietary five pounds of tobacco, or one shilling sterling, for every such offence."† This is liberty of conscience at the expense of a shilling, or five pounds of tobacco, for each indulgence in such freedom. In 1640, Bozman says, "The *first of the acts* passed at this session, entitled 'An act for church liberty,' is nearly *verbatim* the same as the first section of the second act of the preceding session;"‡ that is, that "Holy Church within this province shall have all her rights, liberties, and immunities safe, whole, and inviolable in all things;" and the Catholics of Maryland would probably have given force to their law, and erected a persecuting popish established church in their colony, if they had not heard the commencing thunder that roared with such fury a little later at Marston Moor and Naseby. Their church act was the second of the preceding Legislature, and the first of this, showing their great earnestness on the subject.

Cromwell wrought wonders in England; the Church was completely overthrown, Satan was as popular in Great Britain as a Catholic, and Lord Baltimore, certain to lose his province unless he suited his sails to the fierce hurricane then raging, at once appointed a Protestant governor (Stone) instead of Gov. Greene, a Catholic; he also appointed a Protestant secretary of the province and a Protestant majority in the council. Bozman, speaking of the change, says, "In this measure of his lordship we discern *the commencement* of that general toleration of all sects of religion which prevailed under the early provincial government of Maryland."§ No principle of toleration required Baltimore to place Protestants at the head of his government. He certainly did not love Protestantism at this very time, for he required Gov. Stone to take the following as a part of his official oath: "And I do further swear that I will not, by myself nor any person directly or indirectly, trouble, molest, or discountenance any person whatsoever in the said province professing to believe in Jesus Christ, *and in particular no Roman Catholic for or in respect of his or her religion, nor in his or her free exercise thereof within the said province.*"|| A councillor had to take the same oath. It certainly was not love for the men or their religion that led Baltimore to make his new appointments. It was "an enlightened measure of state policy" to save his province from Cromwell.

With this change in the rulers of Maryland his

---

* History of Maryland, ii. 107–9.

† Idem, 137.
§ Idem, 336.
‡ Idem, 174.
|| Idem, 648, note lxi.

lordship proposed, and his Legislature enacted, a law with the following clauses in it: "Whatsoever* person or persons within this province and the islands thereunto belonging shall from henceforth blaspheme God, that is, curse him, or shall *deny our Saviour Jesus Christ to be the Son of God, or shall deny the Holy Trinity, the Father, Son, and Holy Ghost,* or the Godhead of any of the said three persons of the Trinity, or the unity of the Godhead, or shall use or utter any reproachful speeches, words, or language concerning the Holy Trinity, or any of the said three persons thereof, shall be punished with death and confiscation or forfeiture of all his or her land and goods to the lord proprietary and his heirs." "Whatsoever person or persons shall from henceforth use or utter *any reproachful words or speeches concerning the blessed Virgin Mary,* the mother of our Saviour, or the holy apostles or evangelists, or any of them, shall in such case for the first offence forfeit to the said lord proprietary, and his heirs lords proprietaries of this province, the sum of £5 sterling, or the value thereof, to be levied on the goods and chattels of every such person so offending; but in case such offender or offenders shall not then have goods and chattels sufficient for the satisfying of such forfeiture, or that the same be not otherwise speedily satisfied, then such offender or offenders *shall be publicly whipped, and be imprisoned during the pleasure of the lord proprietary,* or the lieutenant or chief governor of this province." For the second offense the fine is £10, *or a public and severe whipping,* and imprisonment as for the first. For the third offense, *the forfeiture of all lands and goods, and expulsion from the province.* A subsequent part of the *same law* says, "*Except as in the act is before declared and set forth,* no person or persons whatsoever within this province, or the islands, ports, harbors, creeks, or havens thereunto belonging, professing to believe in Jesus Christ, shall from henceforth be anyways troubled, molested, or discountenanced for or in respect of his or her religion, nor in the free exercise thereof within this province, or the islands thereunto belonging, nor any way compelled to the belief or exercise of any other religion against his or her consent." The penalty for breaking this enactment is "treble damages to the party wronged," and a fine of 20s.; and in case of failure to pay the fine, a severe public whipping, and imprisonment at the pleasure of the proprietary or his governor. This is the celebrated toleration law of Lord Baltimore for which his liberality has been lauded extravagantly, and for which Catholics have been represented as the first founders of religious liberty on this continent. The act was passed in the end of April, 1649, and Charles I. was executed three months before. This

event, and the motives that prompted it, and the men whom they governed, account wholly for Lord Baltimore's liberality. The toleration was partial and poor. Those who denied the Trinity—all Jews, Unitarians, and Arians—were condemned to death. The gallows was the liberty it gave them. Respect for the Virgin Mary was encouraged by fines and whippings, and, in obstinate cases, by the loss of all property, and by exile. There was, indeed, some liberty in this law, accompanied by cruel and wicked limitations; and for this liberty no thanks are due to Lord Baltimore or his Maryland Catholics.

Bozman, in another work† published in 1811, truly says, "In most of the States the penalties of the common law in matters of religion still subsist. The *bloody statutes* also of some of them only *sleep.* Not being repealed, they are liable to be called up into action at any moment when either superstition or fanaticism shall perceive a convenient time for it. *What Jew, Socinian, or Deist, possessing a sound mind, would venture, in the State of Maryland for instance, to open his lips in defence of his own religion?*" Even in 1811 the statute book of Maryland contained cruel, persecuting enactments; and only by asserting what is flagrantly untrue can the Baptist State be robbed of her just glory to bestow it upon the founder of Maryland, or upon his colony.

The "Colonial Records of Rhode Island" were published by order of the Legislature in 1856, and in them we learn that Roger Williams landed on the site of Providence in the month of May or early in June, 1636, and that he and his friends on their "first coming thither did make an order that *no man should be molested for his conscience,*" even though he was an Israelite, a Unitarian, or an infidel. And a woman had her religious freedom protected by the same law. In August, 1636, the celebrated compact was entered into and signed at Providence, by which its people "subjected themselves in active and passive obedience to all such orders or agreements as shall be made for public good of the body in an orderly way, by the major consent of the present inhabitants, masters of families, incorporated together in a Town fellowship, and others whom they shall admit unto them, *in civil things only.*" No laws for favoring or prohibiting any form of religion were to be enacted. On the 21st of May, 1637, Joshua Verin was sentenced to lose the right of voting "for restraining the liberty of conscience" of his wife.‡ On the 27th of May, 1640, among certain proposals agreed upon at Providence to form a government, these words are found: "We agree, as formerly

---

* History of Maryland, 662, 663, note.

† A Sketch of the History of Maryland, during the Three First Years after its Settlement, p. 374. Baltimore, 1811.
‡ Colonial Records of Rhode Island, printed by order of the Legislature, i. 13, 14, 16. 1856.

have been the liberties of the town, so still, to hold forth liberty of conscience."*

The first charter of Rhode Island was signed March 14, 1643, and adopted in the colony in May, 1647. Arnold, in his "History of Rhode Island," truly says, "The use of the word *civil* is everywhere prefixed (in the charter) to the terms 'government' or 'laws' wherever they occur . . . to restrict the operation of the charter to purely political concerns. In this apparent restriction there lay concealed a boon of freedom such as man had never known before. They (Rhode Islanders) held themselves accountable to God alone for their religious creed, and no earthly power could bestow on them a right which they held from heaven. . . . At their own request their powers were limited to *civil matters*."† The first instrument of government in the world's history disavowing all right to make laws for or against religion, and thereby giving the widest religious liberty, was adopted in Rhode Island two years before Lord Baltimore's bigoted toleration act was passed in Maryland. After making a code of laws for the *civil affairs* of the colony occur these striking words: "These are the laws that concern all men, and these are the penalties for the transgression thereof, which by common consent are ratified throughout the whole colony; and otherwise than thus what is herein forbidden (*non-religious crimes only*), all men may walk as their consciences persuade them, every one in the name of his God. And let the saints of the Most High walk in this colony, without molestation, in the name of Jehovah their God, for ever and ever,"‡ etc.

Roger Williams gives a striking view of liberty of conscience in his letter to the town of Providence in 1654. "It hath fallen out," says he, "sometimes that both Papists and Protestants, Jews and Turks, may be embarked in one ship, upon which supposal I affirm that all the liberty of conscience that I ever pleaded for turns upon these two hinges: that none of the Papists, Protestants, Jews or Turks, be forced to come to the ship's prayers or worship, nor compelled from their own particular prayers, if they practise any."§ In the charter of 1663, inspired by their convictions and their Baptist agent in London, it is written, "*No person* within the said colony, at any time hereafter, shall be anywise molested, punished, disquieted, or called in question for any difference of opinion in matters of religion."‖ Even the Quakers, as may be seen in "Laws agreed upon in England by the Governor of Pennsylvania (William Penn) and Divers Freemen thereof," restrict their legal toleration to "all persons who confess and acknowledge the one

almighty and eternal God to be the creator, upholder, and ruler of the world."** The Baptists of Rhode Island had no laws upon religion, the greatest infidel of the human race carried no *legal* stigma in that colony for his opinions from its first settlement by our Baptist fathers; it had the only government in the world where religion was entirely free. Maryland's mean toleration was *not* freedom of conscience, except for certain classes, and poor as it was, Rhode Island gave full liberty thirteen years sooner. In 1789, Washington, at the request of the Virginia Baptists, recommended to Congress that amendment to our national Constitution which says, "Congress shall make no law respecting an establishment of religion, or prohibiting the free exercise thereof." It was through their influence that grand article was added to our great instrument of government.†† The religious liberties of our country were first established in Rhode Island by our Baptist fathers, and only through Baptist channels have the nations of the earth learned soul freedom.

Liberty of Conscience among the English Baptists before the Publication of "The Bloudy Tenent" of Roger Williams.

—In 1589, as Crosby states, Dr. Some, a man of great reputation in England, wrote a work against certain prominent Puritans, whom he compares in some things to the Anabaptists. In his book he represents the Anabaptists as holding, among their doctrines, that ministers of the gospel ought to be maintained by the voluntary contributions of the people, and that the civil power has no right to make and impose ecclesiastical laws. This is the great Baptist doctrine of soul liberty, the proclamation of which about fifty years later has given undying fame to the illustrious founder of Rhode Island. These men in demanding that religion should be completely delivered from state patronage and persecution were the successors of a line of Baptists who claimed the same privileges in every Christian age up to the Teacher of Galilee. Leonard Busher, a citizen of London and a Baptist, presented to James I. and to Parliament his "Religious Peace, or a Plea for Liberty of Conscience," and published in pamphlet form in 1614. The work of Mr. Busher is both able and eloquent, and, considering his times, one of the most remarkable productions ever printed. He says,—

"Kings and magistrates are to rule temporal affairs by the swords of their temporal kingdoms, and bishops and ministers are to rule spiritual affairs by the Word and Spirit of God, the sword of Christ's spiritual kingdom, and not to intermeddle

---

* Colonial Records of Rhode Island, i. 28.
† History of Rhode Island, i. 200.   ‡ Idem, 201.
§ Idem, 255.   ‖ Idem, 292.

** Minutes of Provincial Council of Pennsylvania, p. 41. Published by the State. Philadelphia, 1852.
†† Cathcart's Baptists and the American Revolution, pp. 97–111. Philadelphia, 1876.

one with another's authority, office, and function." Again, "All those bishops that force princes and people to receive their faith and discipline by persecution do, with Judas, go against Christ in his members, with swords, staves, and halberds, who, seeing God's Word will not help them, betake themselves with all haste and hazard unto the authority of the king and magistrate." Again, "It is not only unmerciful, but unnatural and abominable, yea, monstrous, for one Christian to vex and destroy another for difference and questions of religion." Again, "Neither suffer the bishops with persecution to defend their faith and church against their adversaries. If they have not anything from God's Word against us, let them yield and submit themselves. If they think they have anything against us, let them betake themselves only to God's Word, both in word and writing." Again, "By persecution are the Jews, Turks, and Pagans occasioned and encouraged to persecute likewise all such as preach and teach Christ in their dominions; for if Christian kings and magistrates will not suffer Christians to preach, and preach the gospel of Christ freely and peaceably in their dominions, how could you expect it of the infidels? . . . And the king and Parliament may please to permit (liberty to) ALL SORTS OF CHRISTIANS; YEA, (to) JEWS, TURKS, AND PAGANS, so long as they are peaceable and no malefactors, as is above mentioned." This is the true liberty for which our denomination has always contended,—liberty of conscience for all mankind. Busher says, "Persecution for difference in religion is a monstrous and cruel beast, that destroyeth both prince and people, hindereth the gospel of Christ, and scattereth his disciples that witness and profess his name. But permission (liberty) of conscience in difference of religion saveth both prince and people; for it is a meek and gentle lamb, which not only furthereth and advanceth the gospel, but also fostereth and cherisheth those that profess it."* Leonard Busher delivered a noble testimony for liberty and truth.

His work was speedily followed by another treatise on the same subject, entitled "Persecution for Religion Judged and Condemned." It was published in 1615 "by Christ's unworthy witnesses, his majesty's faithful subjects, commonly, but falsely, called Anabaptists." No writer in the nineteenth century, in Europe or America, has a clearer conception of religious liberty than the author of this book. He says, "The power and authority of the king are earthly, and God hath commanded me to submit to all ordinances of man, and therefore I have faith to submit to what ordinance of man soever the king commands; if it be a human ordinance, and not against the manifest Word of God, let him require what he will, I must of conscience obey him with my body, goods, and all that I have. But my soul, wherewith I am to worship God, belongeth to another King, whose kingdom is not of this world, whose people must come willingly, whose weapons are not carnal but spiritual." Again, "The whole New Testament throughout, in all the doctrines and practices of Christ and his disciples, teaches no such thing as compelling men by persecutions to obey the gospel, but the direct contrary." Again, "I unfeignedly acknowledge that God hath given to magistrates a sword to cut off wicked men, and to reward welldoers. But this ministry is a worldly ministry, their sword is a worldly sword, their punishments can extend no further than the outward man; they can but kill the body. And therefore this ministry and sword are appointed only to punish the breach of worldly ordinances, which is all that God hath given to any mortal man to punish." Again, "Christ's kingdom is spiritual, his laws are spiritual, the transgressions are spiritual, the punishment is spiritual, everlasting death of soul, his sword is spiritual; no carnal or worldly weapon is given to the supportation of his kingdom. The Lawgiver himself hath commanded that the transgressors of these laws should be let alone until the harvest, because he knows that they that are now tares may hereafter come to repentance and become wheat." Again, "Magistracy is a power of this world; the kingdom, power, subjects, and means of publishing the gospel are not of this world." Again, "But if I defend the authority of Christ Jesus over men's souls, which appertaineth to no mortal man, then know you that whosoever would rob him of that honor, which is not of this world, he will tread them underfoot. Earthly authority belongeth to earthly kings, but spiritual authority belongeth to that one spiritual King, who is King of kings. . . . I have showed you *by the law of Christ that your course is most wicked, to compel any by persecution to perform any service to God*, as you pretend."†

The Anabaptists presented James I. a petition in 1620 pleading for liberty of conscience and deliverance from persecution. The soul freedom, so dear to Baptists in all ages, is conspicuous in this "Supplication." The writer of this document says, "The vileness of persecuting the body of any man, only for cause of conscience, is against the Word of God and law of Christ." Again, "Oh, be pleased to consider, why you should persecute us for humbly beseeching you, in the words of the King of kings, to give unto God the things which are God's, which is to be Lord and Lawgiver to the soul in that spiritual worship and service which he re-

* "Religious Peace," in Tracts on Liberty of Conscience, Hanserd Knollys Society, pp. 23, 24, 25, 33, 41. London, 1846.

† Persecution for Religion Judged and Condemned. Idem, pp. 107, 108, 120, 121, 122, 133, 135.

quireth. If you will take away this from God, what is it that is God's? Far be it from you to desire to sit in the consciences of men, to be lawgiver and judge therein. This is antichrist's practice, persuading the kings of the earth to give him their power to compel all hereunto. You may make and mend your own laws, and be judge and punisher of the transgressors thereof, but you cannot make or mend God's laws, they are perfect already. You may not add nor diminish, nor be judge nor monarch of his church; that is Christ's right. He left neither you nor any mortal man his deputy, but only the Holy Ghost, as your highness acknowledgeth; and whosoever erreth from the truth, his judgment is set down and the time thereof."[*] The author of the "Humble Supplication," according to the famous Roger Williams,[†] was committed "a close prisoner to Newgate, London, for the witness of some truths of Jesus, and having not the use of pen and ink, wrote these arguments in milk, in sheets of paper brought to him by the woman, his keeper, from a friend in London as the stopples of his milk-bottle. In such paper written with milk nothing will appear; but the way of reading it by fire being known to this friend who received the papers, he transcribed and kept together the papers, although the author could not correct nor view what himself had written." From the "Humble Supplication" were taken the arguments, which, being replied to by Mr. Cotton, gave rise to the work of Mr. Williams, and which he has so significantly called "The Bloudy Tenent of Persecution Discussed." This theory, so nobly advocated by English Baptists, so ably defended by the illustrious founder of Rhode Island in his celebrated work, was carried out in practice by the Baptists in England. In 1655, John Biddle, a Socinian, was arrested on the charge of heresy in London; his danger was very great; with his opinions Baptists had no sympathy; but for his liberty of conscience they cherished a profound regard, and many Baptist congregations petitioned Cromwell for his release. They made common cause with the man whose life was endangered by an attack upon his rights of conscience. How the theory of Roger Williams has been carried out first in Rhode Island, and now in every State in the Union, all the world knows.

In 1644, when "The Bloudy Tenent" was published in London, the Baptists were the only advocates of full liberty of conscience on earth, that year Mr. John Goodwin, a Congregationalist, came to their help. The Congregationalists as a body, in England and America, were willing to grant liberty only to those "sound in fundamentals."

Daniel Neal, an Independent (Congregationalist), says, "The Independents pleaded for a toleration so far as to include themselves and the *sober* Anabaptists, but did not put the controversy on a general foot (ing). They were for tolerating all that agreed in the fundamentals of Christianity; but when they came to enumerate fundamentals they were sadly entangled, as all those must be who do not keep the religious and civil rights of mankind on a separate basis." Neal writes of his brethren in 1645, and from the last sentence we quote, he would have given them a better character as friends of true liberty if the facts would have permitted him. The Parliament of Scotland appealed to the legislature of England, and declared their conviction "that the piety and wisdom of the honorable houses (of Parliament) will never admit toleration of any sects or schisms contrary to our Solemn League and Covenant." This covenant was taken in England in the end of 1643 and in the beginning of 1644. Neal says that "at the same time they appealed to the people, and published a declaration against toleration of sectaries and liberty of conscience, in which, after having taken notice of their great services, they observe that there is a party in England who are endeavoring to supplant the true religion by pleading for liberty of conscience, which, say they, is the nourisher of all heresies and schisms. They then declare against all such notions as are inconsistent with the truth of religion, and opening a door to licentiousness, which, to the utmost of their power, they will endeavor to oppose; and as they have *all entered into one covenant*, so to the last man in the kingdom they will go on in the preservation of it. And however the Parliament of England may determine in point of toleration and liberty of conscience, they are resolved *not to make the least start*, but to live and die for the glory of God in the entire preservation of the truth;"[‡] that is, in suppressing liberty of conscience. This was the spirit of Presbyterian Scotland in 1645.

Richard Baxter, the most influential Presbyterian minister in England, as quoted by Crosby, writes, "My judgment in that much debated point of liberty of religion I have always freely made known; I abhor unlimited liberty, or toleration of all." The Westminster Assembly of Divines, which framed the creed of all British Presbyterians, Dec. 15, 1645, in response to an application of the Congregationalists for a very moderate toleration for themselves, declared that "this opened a perpetual gap for all sects to challenge such a liberty as their due; that this liberty was denied by the churches of New England, and that they have as just ground to deny it as they; that this

---

[*] An Humble Supplication to the King's Majesty. Idem, pp. 192, 230.

[†] Bloudy Tenent, page 36, Pref. 30, 35. London, 1848.

[‡] Neal's History of the Puritans, iii. 244, 240. Dublin, 1755. See also Collier's Ecclesiastical History, viii. 300, 301. London, 1841.

desired forbearance is a perpetual division in the church, and a perpetual drawing away from the churches under the rule ; for upon the same pretense those who scruple infant baptism may withdraw from their churches, and so separate into another congregation. Are these divisions, say they, as lawful as they are infinite? or must we give that respect to the errors of men's consciences as to satisfy their scruples by allowance of this liberty to them? That *scruple of conscience is no cause of separation ;* nor doth it take off causeless separation from being schism, which may arise from errors of conscience as well as carnal and corrupt reason." The Assembly flatly denied the toleration solicited by the Congregationalists ; and for the moment the English government was ready to enforce their decision. These godly men in the Assembly and the leading ministers and laymen of their denomination in London, and in the country at that time, were fierce enemies of liberty of conscience. To-day our Presbyterian brethren are friends of true liberty, secular and sacred. But down to 1644 the Baptists were the only advocates of liberty of conscience for all Christians, and *all other men on earth.* They have the honor of being the first preachers of this doctrine, and of converting the masses of other denominations to this part of their creed ; and they have the glory of founding Rhode Island, the first State on earth where this doctrine received legal recognition ; and through Rhode Island the Baptists have given this doctrine a place in the Constitution of the United States, and in the legal enactments of every State in the American Union.

License, A Form of.—As a Baptist church is the highest ecclesiastical authority in the denomination, or in the Sacred Book, upon whose teachings our churches are built, the church, after hearing a brother exercise his gifts as a preacher, gives him a license, not to administer baptism and the Lord's Supper, but to proclaim the blessed gospel. This license gives him no ministerial standing, and no position beyond that of a layman, except that it expresses the opinion of the church of which he is a member that he has qualifications for preaching the gospel. The following form of license has been used :

" *To all whom it may concern.* The Baptist church of Blanktown sends greeting: Our beloved brother, Joshua Smith, a man of good repute, undoubted piety, and sound knowledge of divine things, after exercising his ministerial gifts in private and in public to our entire satisfaction, is hereby licensed to preach the gospel, wherever the Lord may open a door for him. We recommend him to the favor of our brethren ; and we pray that the Lord may greatly bless him.

" Done at our regular meeting for business, etc."

Ligon, William Claiborne, was born in Prince Edward Co., Va., Dec. 18, 1796. He studied at Golgotha Academy ; was converted at eighteen years, and ordained in 1825 by Elders P. P. Smith and Clapton. He came to Missouri in 1841, and settled near Carrollton. For thirty years he labored in that part of the State ; was pastor at Lexington, Dover, Liberty, Richmond, and Carrollton. He gave much time and effort to the establishment of William Jewell College. He was successful as an evangelist, in Clay, Ray, Lafayette, and Saline Counties. He died in Dover, April 13, 1877.

Lilburn, Maj.-Gen. Robert, was a soldier of great daring. When the Earl of Derby placed himself at the head of 1500 horse and foot in Lancashire, Lilburn met him near Wigan, and with 800 men routed his forces, though they fought bravely for about an hour. Lilburn killed many of the enemy, captured between 300 and 400 prisoners, and lost only 11 men.

In Scotland his military administration was marked by a spirit of devout piety, and of great kindness. The Baptist church of Hexham, Northumberland, England, has several allusions to the general in old letters belonging to its records ; and one of its letters written to the general is still preserved. In this epistle the church writes :

" HONORED SIR,—It hath been matter of great joy and consolation to our spirits, ever since we heard of the glorious appearances of the divine nature in you, which manifests itself through your love, which you have towards all saints, and particularly towards us. We desire to admire the good hand of our God in it, that we, who are less than the least of saints, should have favor given us in your eyes, whom God has so highly honored to set in a place of so great eminency."* They then proceed to thank him for his great kindness to three of their brethren,—Edward Hickhorngill, Charles Bond, and Thomas Stackhouse,—and for his great love to their entire church. Ten of the brethren sign the letter on behalf of the church. It is dated the 22d day of the Fourth month, 1653. Gen. Lilburn had Baptist chaplains, and maintained loving relations with the churches of that denomination wherever he was stationed. In 1647 he was governor of Newcastle ; next year he was one of the judges that tried Charles I. and condemned him to death ; and the name of Robert Lilburn is appended to the warrant for his execution.

Cromwell for a time imprisoned him because of his inflexible republicanism, as he served Harrison and others. But this only showed the immense influence wielded by Gen. Lilburn ; for it was not to punish him that Cromwell subjected him to arrest, but to protect himself from the attacks of a powerful military leader, who was opposed to all govern-

---

* Fenstanton Records, etc., 328. London, 1854.

ments administered* by "one man." Cromwell knew his great worth, and it was he who made him a major-general.

Lilburn† was very active in securing the recall of the remnant of the Long Parliament, when the system of government instituted by Oliver perished in the hands of Richard Cromwell. Largely through his great influence in the army was this course pursued. He felt that no military chieftain should exercise dominion in his country, nor any committee of generals ; and that government was the creation of the people themselves ; and as the Long Parliament was the only fragment of legal government in England capable of being invested with life, he lent effectual aid in giving it the sceptre of power once more.

When Charles II. was placed upon the throne Lilburn was tried as a regicide ; he offered no defense, and of course was condemned ; he was exiled to the Isle of St. Nicholas, off Plymouth, where he died in 1665. Why he was not executed we cannot conceive ; it was not because of any mercy possessed by Charles II., nor on account of any bribe given to the frail but all-powerful companions of the king's dearest pleasures. Probably, legal murder, accompanied by the horrible custom in treason cases of "drawing and quartering," had begun to arouse the indignation of the nation against the Stuarts; and Lilburn's life was spared because its sacrifice might cost too much. We love the memory of Maj.-Gen. Robert Lilburn, the "fanatic Anabaptist," as Guizot, in his Memoirs of Monk, is pleased to call him.

Lillard, Rev. Jas. M., was born in Mercer Co., Ky., Sept. 27, 1806, and has been a Baptist minister for forty-seven years. He removed from Kentucky to Lewis Co., Mo., in 1832, being the first Baptist preacher north of Palmyra, Mo. He traveled far and near, traversing large prairies in the severest weather, preaching the gospel and receiving little or no compensation. He was truly a missionary. He often went down the Mississippi River, and occasionally returned to Kentucky, where he held, and assisted his father in conducting, a number of great revival meetings, in which hundreds professed faith in Christ. He has exerted a wonderful influence for good throughout all Northeast Missouri, and though now old and much afflicted, often preaching while sitting, he travels almost continually, laboring for Christ. He has organized a great many Baptist churches ; assisted in ordaining at least twenty-five Baptist ministers, and has baptized more than 3000 persons.

Lillard, Rev. Robert Rodes, A.M., a man of remarkable gifts and attainments, was born in Anderson Co., Ky., Jan. 10, 1826. After a pre-

paratory course he entered Georgetown College as a Sophomore in 1842, and graduated in 1845. Having professed religion and united with the Baptist church at Lawrenceburg, in his native county, in 1841, he was licensed to preach the following year, and was ordained to the ministry in 1846. He now placed himself under the instruction of the distinguished Dr. J. L. Waller, and the following year became associated with his preceptor in the editorship of the *Western Baptist Review*, at that time the ablest periodical in the West. His career was a most brilliant one, and within a few months he was placed among the ablest periodical writers of his time, but shortly after, death closed his too brief career, on June 7, 1849.

Lincoln, Ensign, was born in Hingham, Mass., Jan. 8, 1779. He enjoyed good educational opportunities in his youthful days, and the inestimable blessing of an early religious training. When he reached the age of fourteen he was placed as an apprentice at the business of printing. Having become a Christian he was baptized by Rev. Dr. Baldwin in 1799, of whose church he was a member until he transferred his relation to the Third Baptist church, for so many years under the pastoral charge of Rev. Dr. Sharp. As he had evidently gifts which fitted him to preach the gospel, he was induced to exercise them. The churches at Lynn, East Cambridge, Cambridgeport, Roxbury, South Boston, and Federal Street, Boston, owe to him a great debt of gratitude for what he did among them in the days of their early weakness. While engaged in promoting the Redeemer's kingdom by the use of the talents which God had given him as a preacher of righteousness, he was also in another way accomplishing a vast amount of good. As the leading partner in the publishing house of Lincoln & Edmunds, he was instrumental in sending out from the press a healthful religious literature, which proved a blessing of great value to multitudes of people. He spent a life of purity and blamelessness among his fellow-men, until God took him home to receive the reward of a faithful servant. His death occurred Dec. 2, 1832. Dr. Wayland says of him, "Since his death was mentioned to me, I have been striving to think of one who was of more value to the church as a layman. I could not think of one. I have thought of clergymen, and the result was the same. You may look over a dozen cities before you find a man in a private station who has cleared away around himself so large and so fertile a field of usefulness. I know of no man to fill up his place."

Lincoln, Hon. Heman, was born in Hingham, Mass., Jan. 7, 1779. He was one of a family of eleven children, whose parents were honored and loved in the community in which they lived for their consistent piety. When Heman was fourteen

---

* Hume, Smollett, and Farr, i. 730. London.
† Rapin's History of England, ii. 605. London, 1733.

years of age he was apprenticed to a carpenter in Boston. He was baptized by Dr. Baldwin, May 19, 1799, and in 1809 he was chosen a deacon of the church.

A man of his sterling worth could not remain long in private life. His fellow-citizens, recognizing his abilities, were not backward in soliciting him to occupy public positions. At different times, as representative and senator, he served in the Legislature of Massachusetts. He was chosen a member of the convention for the revision of the State constitution, and, as an intelligent Baptist, he made an earnest plea in behalf of religious liberty and the rights of conscience. Ten years, however, passed before the cause which he so earnestly advocated triumphed over the prejudices with which it had been called to contend.

Deacon Lincoln was among the earliest and most steadfast friends of home and foreign missions. For several years he was the president of the American Baptist Home Mission Society, and when the conversion of Mr. and Mrs. Judson to Baptist sentiments called forth an appeal to the churches in this country for help in the establishment of the missions in Burmah, he was among the first to respond. In 1824 he was chosen treasurer of the Baptist General Convention, and he held the office twenty-two years. So deep was his interest in the cause that he gave up his regular business, and spent his time at the mission rooms in Boston, and proved himself a most valuable assistant to Rev. Dr. Bolles, at the time the corresponding secretary of the Convention.

But it was not merely the two great denominational organizations for the prosecution of home and foreign missions that awakened the regards of Deacon Lincoln. He was ready to unite with all good men for the advancement of any cause which aimed at the improvement of mankind and the glory of God. He was a steadfast friend of the American Bible Society, the American Tract Society at New York, the American Temperance Society, and kindred organizations. For twenty-seven years he was a trustee of Brown University. He was one of the founders of the Newton Theological Institution, and for several years one of its trustees. For twenty-two years he was chairman of the executive committee of the American Baptist Missionary Union. The missionaries under appointment found in his hospitable dwelling a happy home while waiting the time of their departure to the distant fields of their labor, and when, worn down with protracted toil, they returned to recruit their wasted strength in their native country, Deacon Lincoln was among the first to give them a hearty welcome under his own roof. A life of more than ninety years was consecrated to the service of his Master, and when he died, Aug. 11, 1869,

it was felt that a good man had gone home to heaven. Most truthfully was it said of him, "The cause of Christ was dearer to him than personal reputation or any earthly good. His record was remarkably unsullied, and all the churches with which he was connected may count that record as among their choicest ornaments."

Lincoln, Heman, D.D., was born in Boston, Mass., April 14, 1821. He graduated at Brown

HEMAN LINCOLN, D.D.

University in the class of 1840. Among his classmates were Prof. J. B. Boise, LL.D., Rev. Dr. W. T. Brantly, President E. Dodge, LL.D., Rev. Dr. J. R. Kendrick, and President H. G. Weston, D.D. He graduated at the Newton Institution in the class of 1845, and was ordained immediately after his graduation, in Boston, September, 1845. He was pastor of the church in New Britain, Pa., for five years, when he removed to Philadelphia to take charge of the Franklin Square church. After three years of service he was called to Jamaica Plain, Mass., where he continued six years. He accepted a call to the Central Baptist church in Providence, of which he was pastor for eight years, the connection being terminated by his appointment to the professorship of Ecclesiastical History in the Newton Theological Institution, the duties of which he performed for five years, when he was transferred to the chair of Homiletics and Pastoral Duties, which position he now holds. Dr. Lincoln has had much experience in writing for the press during all his professional life. For five years he was editorially connected with the *Christian Chronicle*, and for thirteen years with the *Watchman and Reflector*. Rochester University conferred upon Dr. Lincoln the degree of Doctor of Divinity in 1865.

Lincoln, Prof. John, LL.D., son of Ensign Lincoln, was born in Boston, Mass., Feb. 23, 1817, and was graduated at Brown University in the class of 1836. Immediately after which he was chosen a tutor in Columbian College, Washington, D. C., where he remained during the academic year 1836–37. In the fall of 1837 he entered the Newton Theological Seminary, where he remained until the fall of 1839, when, having been elected a tutor in Brown University, he removed to Providence. He held this office two years, at the end of which he went abroad, in company with Prof. H. B. Hackett, in order to pursue his studies at the German universities. He spent the academic year 1841–42 in Halle, studying theology with Tholuck and Julius Müller, and philology with Gesenius, in Hebrew, and with Barnhardy in the classics. The vacation of July and August was spent in an excursion through Switzerland and Northern Italy, with Tholuck as a companion. The second academic year, 1842–43, was spent in Berlin, under Neander, in church history, Old Testament history with Hengstenberg, and the classics with Boectch. The fall of 1843 he spent in Geneva, where he devoted himself to the study of French, and then went to Rome, where he remained until May, 1844. In the fall of 1844 he entered upon his duties as Assistant Professor of the Latin Language and Literature in Brown University, and was appointed full professor in 1845. In 1857 he went abroad a second time, and was absent six months, a part of which was passed in Athens. Again in the summer of 1878 he took a third trip to the Old World. Prof. Lincoln has prepared editions of Livy and Horace, which have been well received. He has also contributed able articles for reviews, magazines, and the religious papers.

Lincoln, Mrs. Nancy Hanks, the mother of Abraham Lincoln, was born in Virginia, and when quite young removed to Kentucky with some members of her family. In 1806 she married Thomas Lincoln, of Hodgenville, Hardin Co., Ky.

In 1843 La Rue County was created, which included the home of Thomas and Nancy Lincoln. This county was named after John La Rue, and Hodgenville after Thomas Hodgen. A biographer of Abraham Lincoln says, "Both these pioneers were men of sterling integrity and high moral worth ; they were consistent and zealous members of the Baptist church, and one of their associates, Benjamin Lynn, was a minister of the same persuasion. Such were the influences under which, more than twenty years before Thomas Lincoln settled there, this little colony had been founded, and which went far to give the community its permanent character." In this Baptist settlement Abraham Lincoln, afterwards President of the United States, was born, Feb. 12, 1809.

Nancy Hanks Lincoln was a woman of rare qualities of mind and heart, and though she died in 1818, when her son was only nine years old, she left impressions upon him which could never be effaced, and which directed his whole future movements. "All that I am on earth," said President Lincoln to Rev. Dr. A. D. Gillette, then of Washington City, "I owe to my Baptist mother. I am glad to see you, doctor ; you remind me of my Baptist mother."

Mrs. Lincoln lived and died unknown beyond a very limited circle, but her light has been carried over this land and over all the world by the fame of Abraham Lincoln, her distinguished son.

Lindsay, Edmond J., a well-known Christian business man of Milwaukee, was born in Dundee, Scotland, in 1838. His father, in 1841, emigrated with his family to New York, and in 1843 came to Dodge Co., Wis., where he engaged in farming. He was a prominent member and officer in a Scotch Baptist church in Dundee, a man of decided Christian influence. When he came to Wisconsin and found himself in a newly-settled country, where the institutions of religion were not yet established, he had a church in his home, teaching his children the way of God, expounding the Scriptures, and holding regular worship until churches were established.

It was in this Christian atmosphere young Lindsay's childhood and youth were passed. He obtained his education in the log school-house of the newly-settled neighborhood, and an occasional term of study in the classical schools at Waupun and Fox Lake. But Mr. Lindsay has been a student all his life, having a fine library and other facilities for the acquisition of knowledge.

When eleven years of age his father died, and the care of the farm devolved upon him.

Mr. Lindsay is the senior member of the firm of E. J. and W. Lindsay. The business was established by Mr. Lindsay in 1869, and is now one of the most extensive establishments of its class west of the Lakes, having relations with every State and Territory in the Northwest. As its manager Mr. Lindsay displays qualifications of a high order.

But it is chiefly as a Christian that he has become widely known. He made a profession of religion when fourteen years of age, and united a few years later with the Baptist church at Fox Lake. He is one of the best-known members of the First Baptist church in Milwaukee, a member of its board of trustees, has been its Sabbath-school superintendent, and in all the work of the church a chief actor. In the city, outside of his church, he is a leader in all benevolent enterprises. In the denominational work of the State he takes a prominent part. He is a member of the board of the Wisconsin Baptist State Convention, and of its Executive Committee, and he is its efficient treasurer.

Lindsay, Rev. W. C., was born in Virginia in 1840. He spent four years at a literary and two at a medical college, and afterwards three in the study and practice of law. At the close of the war he resumed the study of medicine, but having "tasted and seen that the Lord is good," "immediately he conferred not with flesh and blood," but came to the Southern Baptist Theological Seminary, and spent four years and graduated.

His first pastorate was at Wilson, N. C., where he had the society and warm friendship of the celebrated Dr. Hooper. In five months his health failed, pneumonia contracted in camp having left his lungs in a diseased condition. Having rested a few months, he took charge of the church at Barnwell Court-House, when, as an evidence of their appreciation, they almost doubled the compensation they were accustomed to give. The young men who avoided the church not only went, but contributed liberally to his salary. Five years in the pine belt, as frequently happens, restored his health. He next spent a year, 1876, as agent for the Southern Baptist Theological Seminary and Furman University, and then settled in Columbia, S. C., where he is now pastor.

He probably has not an enemy in the world.

Lindsey, Rev. E. H., a prominent minister of Dallas County, Ark., was born in Alabama in 1831. He embraced Christ and united with the Methodist Church in 1848, and was a preacher in that denomination for seven years. A careful examination of the subject of baptism led to a change of views, and he united with the Baptists in 1859, and in the following year was ordained to the ministry. He came to Arkansas and settled in Dallas County, where he has remained ever since, having served the following churches in Dallas and the adjoining counties: Cold Water, ten years; Hampton, nine years; Millville, seven years; Holly Springs, three years; Edinburg, two years; Chambersville nearly twenty years. During the time he has baptized about 400.

Lineberry, Rev. William, a useful minister in the Sandy Creek Association, N. C. He had been a minister of the Protestant Methodist Church, but became a Baptist, and was baptized by Rev. Enoch Crutchfield in 1843. He was agent for the State Convention in 1845 and 1846. He died in 1875.

Link, Rev. J. B., was born in Rockbridge Co., Va., May 7, 1828; converted in October, 1840; baptized at the Natural Bridge, Va., in October, 1841; ordained at Mount Pleasant, Jessamine Co., Ky., in 1852, Drs. D. R. Campbell and Wm. M. Pratt acting as the Presbytery; prosecuted the

four years' course of study at Georgetown College, Ky., graduating in 1853; studied theology at, and graduated from, Rochester Theological Seminary, after a two years' course, in 1855; pastor of the churches at Paris, Ky., and Liberty, Mo.; acted as agent for William Jewell College for nearly two years, and raised $20,000 for that institution; entered the Confederate army, spent most of the time as a chaplain; went to Texas as agent of the Home Mission Board of the Southern Baptist Convention, especially for army missions. At the close of the year was occupied in efforts to establish the *Texas Baptist Herald*. Since 1866 has published and edited that journal with indefatigable energy, placing it upon a solid foundation. He is a man of indomitable will and courage, clear-headed,

REV. J. B. LINK.

patient, wise, and logical. He has been a vice-president of the Southern Baptist Convention, and is now laboring for the "Texas Educational Commission," in connection with his editorial management of the *Texas Baptist Herald*.

Linnard, James M., was born in September, 1784; was baptized about the year 1830, by Rev. Gideon B. Perry, into the fellowship of the Spruce Street church, Philadelphia, Pa. He continued in membership with this church until his death, which occurred Oct. 16, 1863. Few men have left behind them the record of a Christian life more abundant in the blessed results of intense consecration and large-hearted benevolence. Nor do these results pertain to his own life alone; for it appears to be well and widely known that his example and influence were agencies divinely employed to inspire similar consecration and benevolence among others possessed of greater wealth, whose princely benefactions still continue to aid the advancement of the Redeemer's kingdom. He was for many years, and up to the time of his death, the president of the Pennsylvania Baptist General Association. The growth and usefulness of this organization were largely due to his love for Christ and zeal for his cause. He had a clear, sound mind, and was a warm friend and wise counselor in every department of benevolent and religious effort. He was one of three laymen who have been moderators of the Philadelphia Baptist Association.

Linsley, Rev. James Harvey, son of James and Sarah (Maltby) Linsley, was born in North Branford, Conn., May 5, 1787; in 1809 went South; converted in 1810; taught school in Cheshire, Conn.; baptized in 1811 in North Haven; studied in Wallingford Academy; graduated from Yale College in 1817; taught in an academy at New Haven, also at New Canaan, also in a select school at Stratford; began to preach in 1828; ordained, in 1831, as an evangelist, at Meriden; preached in Milford and Stratfield; in 1835 was delegate to Triennial Convention in Richmond, Va.; health failed in 1836; went to Florida; was a member of Yale Natural Historical Society, of Connecticut Academy of Arts and Sciences, of Hartford Natural Historical Society, of Boston Society of Natural History; published valuable scientific papers. He died Dec. 29, 1843, leaving a precious record as a scholar and as a Christian.

Lisk, Rev. James, was born near Coshocton, O., Oct. 16, 1839; was baptized April 27, 1855, by Rev. A. W. Odor; graduated from Denison University in 1862, and from Rochester Theological Seminary in 1865; was ordained in June, 1865, and settled with the Second church, Cincinnati, O.; removed to Rockford, Ill., in 1867, and remained for two years; accepted a call to his present field of labor, the Second church, Germantown, Philadelphia, and entered upon his duties June 1, 1870. He is an able and impressive preacher and a faithful pastor, diligent in personal efforts for the salvation of souls, and strong in defense of "the faith once delivered to the saints." He is actively identified with the educational and missionary work of the denomination, and is conscientious in the performance of duties assigned to him in the management of important trusts. In 1879 he was made moderator of the Philadelphia Baptist Association. His people, after worshiping for years in a neat chapel, are now building a handsome church edifice.

Literature, Baptist.—The list of authors in this article contains the names of only a portion of the great body of Baptist writers ; and often but one book is mentioned where several came from the

same hand ; or three, as in the case of Benjamin Keach, where forty-three were the fruits of his active mind.

THE SACRED TEXT AND WORKS UPON IT.

Our Lord was immersed in the river Jordan when he reached adult years, and founded the Baptist denomination. The writers of the New Testament, like the Saviour, were Baptists, whose "one (material) baptism" is believer's immersion. In translating the New Testament into the language of a heathen people, Baptists have always insisted upon *translating* Βαπτίζω, instead of transferring it. The first versions of the Scriptures followed this plan. The Peshito, a Syriac version, made early in the second century for the Jews in Palestine, renders the act of baptizing by the verb ܥܡܕ, to immerse.

About the same time a Latin translation was prepared for the people who used that tongue. Probably from this first version Tertullian quotes the Saviour's commission, "Go, teach the nations, immersing them in the name of the Father, and of the Son, and of the Holy Spirit."—Matt. xxviii. 19. (Ite, docete nationes, tinguentes eas in nomen Patris, etc. De Baptismo, cap. 13.) In the next chapter Tertullian quotes Paul's statement, that he was "not sent to baptize, but to preach," and he uses the words *ad tinguendum*, to immerse, to describe the baptismal act. The men who made these earliest translations, like the inspired writers of the New Testament, were Baptists. Jerome, in his Vulgate, uses *baptizo*, instead of *tinguo* or *immergo*, not because immersion was abandoned, but on account of a mass of ceremonies that in his day burdened the baptismal rite, authority for which could readily be claimed under a foreign word, the meaning of which was only known to scholars. What was true of the Syriac and Latin versions is true of other primitive translations of the New Testament; and from these and other considerations we claim the versions of the first three centuries as substantially Baptist productions. Like modern Baptists, the early Christians multiplied versions of the Scriptures, and distributed the Word as widely as possible. Augustine says, "Those who have translated the Bible into Greek can be numbered, but not so the Latin versions, for in the first ages of the church whoever got hold of a Greek codex ventured to translate it into Latin, however slight his knowledge of either language."

In 1229, at a Catholic council held in Thoulouse, in France, a canon was passed prohibiting "laics from having the books of the Old or New Testament, unless it be a Psalter, or a Breviary, and the Rosary, and it does not permit them so much as to *translate them into the vulgar tongue.*" Du Pin after recording the above adds, "This restraint was doubtless founded on that frequent abuse which was made of them in that country." (Eccles. Hist., ii. 456. Dublin, 1724.) This canon was enacted to rob our Baptist Albigensian fathers of the Scriptures, parts of which they had for a time in French, and subsequently the whole of them. Their version was a Baptist work. In 1526, Denk and Haetzer, two Anabaptists, commenced the translation of the Hebrew Bible in Strasburg, and succeeded well with the prophets, which were published early in the following year, nearly five years before Luther's Bible. The Rev. Henry Jessey had a translation of the Scriptures prepared in 1660, when the persecutions that followed the accession of Charles II. to the throne of England rendered its publication impossible, and resulted in its destruction.

Dr. William Carey translated the Scriptures into Sanscrit, Hindu, Brijbbhassa, Mahratta, Bengali, Oriya, Telinga, Karnata, Maldivian, Gurajattee Bulooshe, Pushtoo, Punjabi, Kashmeer, Assam, Burman, Pali, or Magudha, Tamul, Cingalese, Armenian, Malay, Hindostani, and Persian. Before the death of Dr. Carey the mission press at Serampore had sent forth the Scriptures in forty different languages and dialects, the tongues of 330,000,000 of human beings.

Dr. Judson translated the Scriptures into Burmese, Dr. Marshman into Chinese, Dr. Mason into Sgau Karen, Dr. Nathan Brown into Japanese. Dr. H. F. Buckner translated the gospel of John into the language of the Creek Indians. The New Testament, " with several hundred emendations," was edited by Spencer H. Cone and William H. Wyckoff. The American Bible Union, controlled by Baptists, though not exclusively composed of them, revised the entire English New Testament, and a large part of the Old; and they also revised the Spanish and Italian New Testaments, and made a new translation into the Ningpo colloquial dialect of China. It may be added that the Bible Union did much to create the public opinion that has resulted in the movement in England to make a revision of the Bible of 1611. The Rev. Joseph S. C. F. Frey edited an edition of Van Der Hooght's Hebrew Bible.

Dr. John Gill was the author of a commentary on the Old and New Testaments, in nine quarto volumes. This great work was republished in Philadelphia by a Presbyterian in 1819, and in Ireland many years later by an Episcopal clergyman. It is the richest treasury of Biblical and Oriental learning and of gospel truth which exists in the form of a commentary. Dr. John Fawcett was the author of a commentary in two folio volumes. The Baptist Publication Society is preparing a commentary under such auspices as will secure the fruits of the ripest scholarship and of the most recent discoveries in Bible lands. Robert Haldane

was the author of " Notes on the Epistle of the Romans," and a work upon " The Verbal Inspiration of the Scriptures." Dr. C. M. Du Veil, a converted Israelite, led to embrace Baptist sentiments when an Episcopal clergyman, by reading our books in the library of the bishop of London, to which he had access, in 1685, published " A Literal Explanation of the Acts of the Apostles." James A. Haldane wrote an " Exposition of the Epistle to the Galatians." Prof. H. J. Ripley prepared "Notes on the Gospels and Acts," and on the " Epistle to the Hebrews." Prof. Hackett wrote a commentary on the " Acts of the Apostles ;" Spurgeon has a commentary upon the Psalms, called " The Treasury of David," in six volumes. Dr. Adiel Sherwood was the author of " Notes on the New Testament." Dr. George W. Clark has prepared " Notes on the Gospels."

Rev. William Jones was the author of " A Dictionary of the Sacred Writings." Dr. Hacket edited an American issue of Smith's " Dictionary of the Bible," to the English edition of which he contributed thirty articles. John Canne spent "more than thrice seven years" in preparing marginal references for the English Bible. A marginal Bible, printed in 1747, now before the writer, after the dedication to King James, presents Mr. Canne's " Letter to the Reader." Dr. Malcom's " Dictionary of Names, Objects, and Terms Found in the Holy Scriptures" has had a circulation of nearly 200,000.

Dr. Samuel G. Green's " Handbook to the Grammar of the New Testament, Together with a Complete Vocabulary (Lexicon) and an Examination of the Chief New Testament Synonyms," is a work of great learning and value.

RELIGIOUS WORKS.

In this list we might include a large number of the books written by primitive Christians, whose authors, like Justin Martyr, speak only of the " washing in water," of " persuaded believers" (Just. Philos. Mart. Apol. I. Pro Christ. Patrol. Græca VI. p. 240, Migne), or of trained catechumeni. Tertullian in his orthodox days wrote on the mode and subjects of baptism like a very zealous Baptist, and a part of his works might be legitimately reckoned to the credit of Baptists. The Confession of St. Patrick, and his Letter to Caroticus, are Baptist productions ; he immersed throngs of believers in wells in various parts of Ireland. The Swiss Anabaptist Confession of 1527, as far as it goes, is almost entirely in harmony with modern Baptist opinions. The religious literature of this period, of the sober Anabaptists of the Continent of Europe, may be largely claimed by our denomination to-day. The writings of Leonard Busher and others " On Liberty of Conscience," from 1614 to 1661, published by the Hanserd Knollys Society, are vigorous Baptist productions. The Confessions, issued by the same society, beginning with 1611 and ending with 1689, belong to us. "Tropologia, or a Key to Open Scripture Metaphors," and "Gospel Mysteries Unveiled, or an Exposition of all the Parables," are the two most popular works of the celebrated Benjamin Keach. The "Exposition of all the Parables" is more frequently offered for sale now in London catalogues of second-hand books, than any of the works of John Howe, Dr. John Owen, or Bishop Jeremy Taylor. John Bunyan's works, in 761 royal octavo double-column pages, of which the "Pilgrim's Progress" occupies but 120, are not as well known as they should be, except "Grace Abounding," "The Holy War," and "The Pilgrim's Progress." Of the last, we may truly say that it is the most popular book ever written. Until 1847 it had been translated into French, Flemish, Dutch, Welsh, Gaelic, Irish, Hebrew, Spanish, Portuguese, Italian, Danish, German, Armenian, Burmese, Cingalese, Orissa, Hindostani, Bengali, Tamul, Mahratta, Canarese, Gujaratti, Malay, Arabic, Samoan, Tahitian, Pehuana, Behuana, Malagasy, New Zealand, and Latin; and undoubtedly it has been translated into several languages since that time. The prose writings of John Milton were numerous and popular. Some of these were political, like his first and second "Defence of the People of England;" but a number of them treated of ecclesiastical questions, like his "Reformation in England," his "Prelatical Episcopacy," his "National Establishments of Religion," his "True Religion, Heresy, Schism, and Toleration;" others were devoted to "Education," "The History of Britain," and to miscellaneous subjects. His Treatise "On Christian Doctrine," edited by Charles R. Sumner, librarian and historiographer to his majesty, and prebendary of Canterbury, and published in 1825, is a very remarkable work. In it there are some opinions from which we decidedly dissent, but upon many questions, and conspicuously about the mode and subjects of baptism, Milton was a strong Baptist. "Anti-Christ Unmasked," by Henry Denne; "The Necessity for Separation from the Church of England," by John Canne; Delaune's "Plea for Nonconformists," according to Daniel De Foe, "perfect in itself; never author left behind him a more finished piece;" in 1739 it had passed through seventeen editions; "Ill News from New England, &c.," by John Clarke, a celebrated work in defense of liberty of conscience.

"Gill's Body of Divinity" and his other theological works are invaluable. The works of Andrew Fuller, in 1012 double-column imperial octavo pages, are necessary to the completeness of any Protestant theological library. The works of Robert Hall, in six 12mo volumes, breathe the eloquence which made their author the greatest preacher of his day, and the equal of any orator of the Anglo-Saxon race. The following works are favorably known: Buck's "Philosophy of Religion," Pendleton's "Christian Doctrines," "Baptist Doctrines," edited by C. A. Jenkens; Dagg's "Moral Science," "Evidences of Christianity," and "Manual of Theology," Stock's "Handbook of Revealed Theology," Carson on "The Knowledge of Jesus, the Most Excellent of the Sciences," and "The Providence of God Unfolded in the Book of Esther." The works of Archibald McLean, in six volumes, 12mo; "Help to Zion's Travelers," by Robert Hall, Sr.; "Exhortations Relating to Prayer and the Lord's Supper," by Benjamin Wallin; "First Fruits," and "Primitive Theology," by Henry Holcombe; Edmund Botsford's "Spiritual Voyages;" "Writings of John Leland," by L. F. Green; complete works of Abraham Booth; "Church Order," "The Election of Grace," "Internal Call to the Ministry," and "Sermons," by Isaac Backus; "Treatise on Various Subjects," and "Vindication of Natural Religion," by John Brine; Magowan's "Dialogues of Devils," "The Deity and Atonement of Christ," by John Marshman; the works of John H. Hinton, in seven volumes 12mo; the writings of Dr. Francis Wayland, educational, philosophical, and religious; the "Miscellanies," and "Lectures on Baptist History," of William R. Williams; Angus's "Handbook of the Bible," "The Power of the Cross," by Richard Fuller; "Apostolic Church Polity," by William Williams; "Preaching: its Ideal and Inner Life," by Thomas Armitage; "Preparation and Delivery of Sermons," by John A. Broadus; "Wheat from the Fields of Boaz," by A. G. Thomas; "Christian Experience," by D. W. Faunce; "The Atonement," by Octavius Winslow; "The Atonement," by J. A. Haldane; "Soul Prosperity," by C. D. Mallary; "Maxcy's Literary Remains," by Romeo Elton; "Lectures on Biblical Antiquities," by F. A. Cox; "Christ in History," by Robert Turnbull; "The Apostolical Constitutions, including the Canons," by Irah Chase; "Internal Evidences of Christianity," by John Aldis; "Book of Worship for Private Families," "The Sanctuary, Its Claims and Power," by W. W. Everts; "Pulpit Eloquence," by Henry C. Fish; "The Spirit, Policy, and Influence of Baptists," by T. G. Jones; "Black Diamonds," "Great Wonders in Little Things," and "Ocean Gardens," by Sidney Dyer; "A Pedobaptist Church no Home for a Baptist," by R. T. Middleditch; "Baptist History, Faith, and Polity," by D. B. Cheney; "Encyclopedia of Religious Knowledge," by J. Newton Brown; "Campbellism Examined," by J. B. Jeter; "Morning by Morning," and "Evening by Evening," by C. H. Spurgeon; "The

Church, its Polity and Ordinances," by H. Harvey; " Baptist Short Method," by Edward Hiscox ; " The Papal System from its Origin to the Present Time," " A Historical Sketch of Every Doctrine, Claim, and Practice of the Church of Rome," by William Cathcart ; " History of Romanism," by John Dowling ; " The Pernicious Effects of Infant Baptism," by Norman Fox ; " The Philosophy of Atheism Examined and Compared with Christianity," by B. Godwin ; " Duties of a Pastor to his Church," by Franklin Wilson ; Dr. Malcom's " Travels in South-Eastern Asia," " A Year's Tour in the Holy Land," by S. D. Phelps ; " Plea for Baptist Principles," by G. W. Anderson ; " Text-Book of Campbellism," by D. B. Ray ; " Text-Book of Popery," by J. M. Cramp ; Dr. J. R. Graves is among the first of living Baptist writers, his last work is " Old Landmarkism, What is it ?" " Religious Denominations in the United States and Great Britain," by Joseph Belcher ; " The Creative Week," and " The Mountain Instruction," by George Dana Boardman ; " Priscilla," by Joseph Banvard ; " Western Empire, or the Drama of Human Progress," by E. L. Magoon ; " Corrective Church Discipline," and " Parliamentary Practice," by Chancellor P. H. Mell.

Sermons in volumes have been published very extensively by Baptists. In 1876, Spurgeon had issued twenty-one volumes. Some of his sermons have been translated into German, Danish, Swedish, French, Italian, and Welsh. Maclaren has published sermons which have been very popular. We shall only add the following as authors of volumes of sermons : Dr. Samuel Stennett, Dr. William T. Brantly, Sr., Dr. Samuel Stillman, Rev. Oliver Hart, and Rev. William Parkinson.

The following are among a large number of works on baptism and the Lord's Supper : " Anti-Pedobaptism," by John Tombes (Mr. Tombes wrote fourteen distinct works on baptism) ; " A Treatise of Baptism, wherein that of Believers and that of Infants is Examined by the Scriptures," by Henry D'Anvers ; " Anti-Pædo-Rantism, or Mr. Samuel Finley's Charitable Plea for the Speechless Examined and Refuted, the Baptism of Believers Maintained, and the Mode of it by Immersion Vindicated," by Abel Morgan, Philadelphia, printed by B. Franklin, in Market Street, 1747 ; Mr. Finley was subsequently president of New Jersey, now Princeton, College ; " The Baptism of John" and " Letters on Baptism," by Thomas Baldwin ; " Pedobaptism Examined," by Abraham Booth ; " Infant Baptism a Part and Pillar of Popery," by John Gill ; " History of Baptism," by Robert Robinson ; " Scripture Guide to Baptism," by Richard Pengilly ; Gale's " Reflections on Wall's History of Infant Baptism ;" " Baptism, a Term of Communion at the Lord's Supper," by Joseph King-

horn ; " Baptism in its Mode and Subjects," by Alexander Carson ; " Infant Baptism an Invention of Men," by Irah Chase ; " Essay on Christian Baptism," by B. W. Noel ; " Baptism and Terms of Communion," by Richard Fuller ; " Doctrine of Baptism on the Principles of Biblical Interpretation," by J. J. Woolsey ; " Baptism," by F. W. Broaddus ; " Handbook on the Mode of Baptism," and " Handbook on the Subjects of Baptism," by Robert Ingham ; " Theodosia Ernest," by A. C. Dayton ; " Grace Truman," by Mrs. S. R. Ford ; " Baptism and Baptisteries," by W. Cote ; " The Meaning and Use of Baptizein Philologically and Historically Investigated," by T. J. Conant ; Howell on Communion ; " Immersion Essential to Christian Baptism," by John A. Broadus ; " Church Communion as Practised by the Baptists," by W. W. Gardner ; " Studies on the Baptismal Question," by D. B. Ford ; " Baptism in Harmony in the East and in the West," by J. C. Long ; " The Position of Baptism in the Christian System," by Henry H. Tucker ; " History of Baptism," by Isaac T. Hinton ; " The Act of Baptism," by Henry S. Burrage ; " The Baptism of the Ages and of the Nations," by Wm. Cathcart.

The following histories were written by Baptists : Kench's " History of the English Baptists," Crosby's " History of the English Baptists," Ivimey's " History of the English Baptists," Orchard's " History of the English Baptists," Taylor's " History of the General Baptists," Robinson's " Historical Researches," Backus's " History of the Baptists," Cramp's " Baptist History," Benedict's " History of the Baptists," " Materials for a History of the Baptists in Delaware and in other States," by Morgan Edwards ; Semple's " History of the Rise and Progress of the Baptists in Virginia," Cook's " Delaware Baptists," Orchard's " History of Foreign Baptists," " Historical Vindications," by S. S. Cutting ; Duncan's " History of the Baptists," " The Early English Baptists," by Benjamin Evans ; Asplund's " Baptist Register," Hague's " Historical Discourse," Callender's " Historical Discourse on the Civil and Religious Affairs of Rhode Island and Providence Plantations ;" the materials gathered by John Comer for a history of American Baptist churches are of great value to all who have engaged in the undertaking, from which death removed the talented collector ; Curry's " Struggles and Triumphs of Virginia Baptists," Hayne's " Baptist Denomination, its History and Doctrines," Ford's " Origin of the Baptists," Wm. Jones's " Church History," " Sketch of the Lower Dublin, or Pennepek Church," by H. G. Jones ; " History of the First Baptist Church of Newport," by C. E. Barrows ; " Religious Liberty and the Baptists," by C. C. Bitting ; Anderson's " Annals of the English

Bible," Ray's "Baptist Succession," Mrs. T. J. Conant's "History of the English Bible," Curtis's "Progress of Baptist Principles," Cox's "History of English Baptist Missions," Gammel's "History of American Baptist Missions," McCoy's "History of Baptist Missions among American Indians," "Baptists and the American Revolution," by Wm. Cathcart; "Annals of the Christian Commission," by Lemuel Moss; "History of Missions," by John O. Choules; "Bunhill Memorials," by J. A. Jones; Bunhill is the London cemetery for Dissenters, where the ashes of Bunyan repose; "Manning and Brown University," by Reuben A. Guild; "The Baptist Encyclopædia," edited by William Cathcart.

BIOGRAPHIES.

"Life of Colonel Hutchinson, 'written by his widow Lucy;'" Ivimey's "Life of John Milton;" "Life of Henry Dunster," first president of Harvard College, by Jeremiah Chaplin; "Life of William Kiffin," by Joseph Ivimey; "Virginia Baptist Ministers," by J. B. Taylor; Hovey's "Life and Times of Isaac Backus;" Lives of Roger Williams, by J. D. Knowles, Romeo Elton, William Gammel, and Benjamin Evans; Wallin's "Life of Dr. John Gill," Wilkin's "Life of Joseph Kinghorn," Gregory's "Life of Robert Hall," Fuller's "Life of Samuel Pearce," "Memoirs of Mrs. Ann Hasseltine Judson," by J. D. Knowles; "Memoir of Dr. Judson," by Francis Wayland; "Memoir of Dr. Wayland," by F. and H. L. Wayland; a "Biographical Sketch of Sir Henry Havelock," by William Brock; "Life of Mrs. Lydia Malcom," by H. Malcom; "Life of Jesse Mercer," by C. D. Mallary; "Life of Luther Rice," by James B. Taylor; "Life and Times of James B. Taylor," by George B. Taylor; "Life and Writings of Robert Robinson," by George Dyer; "Life of Joseph Stennett," by D. Turner; "Memoirs of Mrs. Theodosia Dean," by Pharcellus Church; "Life of Rev. Duncan Dunbar," by Jeremiah Chaplin; "Life of William Knibb," by J. Howard Hinton; "Life of Rev. Thomas Burchell," by W. F. Burchell; "Life of Dr. Eugenio Kincaid," by Alfred Patton; "Life of Joseph Ivimey," by George Pritchard; "Life of Dr. Richard Fuller," by J. H. Cuthbert; "Life of Mrs. Shuck," "Life of Andrew Broaddus," and "Life of Daniel Witt," by J. B. Jeter; "Life of John Thomas," by C. B. Lewis, the first Baptist who preached the gospel in India; "The Life of John Bates," by Justin A. Smith; "Memoir of Andrew Fuller," by A. G. Fuller; "Memoir of Dr. William Stoughton," by S. W. Lynd; "Life and Correspondence of John Foster," by J. E. Ryland; Lives of Carey, Marshman, and Ward, by J. C. Marshman; "Life of John P. Crozer," by J. Wheaton Smith; "Life of Dr. Joseph H. Ken-

nard," by J. Spencer Kennard; "Life of Spencer H. Cone, D.D.," by Edward and S. W. Cone; "Autobiography of John Gano," "Memoir of Dr. Baron Stow," by J. C. Stockbridge; "Life of Mrs. E. C. Judson," by A. C. Kendrick; "Memoir of Governor George N. Briggs," by W. C. Richards; "Life of John M. Peck, D.D.," by Rufus Babcock; "Life of William Colgate," by W. W. Everts; "Life of Joseph G. Binney, D.D.," by Mrs. J. G. Binney.

GENERAL LITERARY WORKS.

Hanserd Knollys wrote a Hebrew, Latin, and English grammar; Dr. Carey a Mahratta grammar, a Sanscrit grammar extending over a thousand quarto pages, a Punjabi grammar, a Telinga grammar, and a Mahratta dictionary, a Bengali dictionary, and a Bhotanta and a Sanscrit dictionary. Dr. Judson made a Burmese dictionary, and Dr. Mason a Pali grammar. Dr. J. Wade was the author of a Karen dictionary, and Dr. H. F. Buckner prepared a grammar of the language of the Creek Indians. The "Essays" of John Foster are among the finest productions in the literature of our tongue. Sir James Mackintosh justly describes their author as "one of the most profound and eloquent writers that England has produced." Dr. Gill's "Antiquity of the Hebrew Language, Letters, Vowel Points, and Accents" has been properly represented "as a masterly effort of profound research, which would have shown Dr. Gill to be a prodigy of learning, of reading, and of literature had he never published a syllable on any other subject." "Orators and Oratory" is one of several able works from the pen of William Matthews, LL.D. John M. Gregory, LL.D., wrote "A Handbook of History." Dr. Mason wrote "Burmah, its People and Natural Productions, or Notes on the Natives, Fauna, Flora, and Minerals, &c.;" F. S. Dobbins, "False Gods;" James De Mille, "The Dodge Club;" John Ash, LL.D., "A Grammar and Dictionary of the English Language;" Rev. F. Denison, the "History of the First Rhode Island Cavalry," and the "History of the Third Rhode Island Heavy Artillery;" Col. C. H. Banes, the "History of the Philadelphia Brigade;" Dr. James T. Champlin, a "Text-Book of Intellectual Philosophy." Prof. Cleveland Abbe for ten years has been meteorologist of the bureau of the army signal office, in which he compiles the published weather probabilities, the storm signals, monthly reviews, and international bulletin. He has made numerous contributions to the *American Journal of Science, Monthly Notices*, Royal Astronomical Society, the Smithsonian Annual Reports, and to Appleton's and Johnson's Encyclopædias. Rev. John Howard Hinton wrote a "History of the United States;" Lieut.-Gov. Arnold, a "History of Rhode Island ;" Dr. Joseph Angus, " The Handbook of the English Tongue," " The Handbook of English Literature," and " Specimens of English Literature ;" Dr. Hackett translated Winer's Chaldee Grammar and published his own exercises in Hebrew grammar ; Dr. Benjamin Davies prepared a "Student's Grammar" and a " Student's Lexicon" of the Hebrew language ; Dr. T. J. Conant translated Gesenius's Hebrew grammar, which he enlarged and improved ; this work is now the standard of the schools in America and Europe. Joseph S. C. F. Frey was the author of a Hebrew grammar, the ninth American edition of which appeared in 1835 ; he also compiled a Hebrew lexicon. Dr. Leechman wrote a work on logic. Prof. Noah K. Davis has published " The Theory of Thought, a Treatise on Deductive Logic ;" and President D. J. Hill has issued " The Elements of Rhetoric" and " The Science of Rhetoric." Dr. K. Brooks, in " Baptists and the National Centenary," says, " Dr. William Stoughton prepared an edition of Virgil, which had extensive use in his day. Adoniram Judson published an English grammar before he turned his attention to the Christian ministry. Dr. Francis Wayland was the author of very popular treatises on moral science, intellectual philosophy, and political economy. Dr. A. C. Kendrick has published introductory text-books in Greek and an edition of ' Xenophon's Anabasis ;' Dr. Hackett, ' Plutarch on the Delay of the Deity in Punishing the Guilty ;' Dr. John L. Lincoln edited Livy and Horace. Dr. J. R. Boise has given to the public seven volumes of Greek text-books, and Dr. Albert Harkness eight volumes of Latin text-books and one of Greek. Dr. J. T. Champlain has published a large number of school-books, including treatises on ethics and intellectual philosophy, and editions of Demosthenes and Æschines. Dr. J. R. Loomis is the author of treatises on geology, anatomy, and physiology. Dr. S. S. Greene has published a series of English grammars ; Prof. S. P. Sanford, a series of arithmetics ; Prof. J. F. Stoddard, a series of arithmetics and algebras ; and Dr. Edward Olney, a series of mathematical text-books, covering the whole ground of school and college study. Dr. J. H. Hanson has edited two volumes of the Latin authors usually read in preparation for college. Dr. G. W. Sansom is the author of a volume on art criticism ; Dr. S. H. Carpenter, of an Anglo-Saxon grammar ; and Prof. James G. Clark, of a treatise on the ' Differential and Integral Calculus ;' Dr. A. A. Gould was associated with Agassiz in preparing a treatise on geology ;" and Prof. S. M. Shute, D.D., " A Manual of Anglo-Saxon, comprising a Grammar, Reader, and Glossary."

The amount of secular literature coming from the intellect and the learning of Baptists is immense. They have written a multitude of books, and control many influential secular newspapers.

POETICAL WORKS.

" Paradise Lost," by John Milton ; Miss Ann Steele's " Hymns and Poems" were published in three volumes in 1780. Dr. John Fawcett was the author of 156 hymns which were printed in 1782. Benjamin Beddome wrote many precious hymns ; Benjamin Wallen, a book of hymns, published in 1750 ; Samuel Medley, a work with 232 hymns ; John Fellows, a book with 55 hymns. Turner's " Divine Songs, Hymns, and Other Poems" were published in 1748. Joseph Swain wrote 129 hymns, which were issued in 1792. Samuel Stennett furnished 40 hymns to Dr. Rippon in 1787 for his " Selection." Edward Mote published a " Selection" of hymns in 1797, 108 of which were written by himself; and Dr. Edmund Turney wrote " Baptismal Harmonies," containing 36 hymns and chants ; Richard Furman was the author of " Pleasures of Piety, and Other Poems ;" but no considerable part of our poetical treasures can be recorded in this article; with Dr. S. F. Smith, Hon. Charles Thurber, Prof. J. H. Gilmore, Dr. Robert Lowry, Dr. Sidney Dyer, and others among the living, and Milton and a large number among the dead, we have great reason to bless God for our gifts. (See article on HYMNS AND THEIR AUTHORS.)

SUNDAY-SCHOOL LITERATURE.

The American Baptist Publication Society has 1326 works on its list, of which 444 are for Sunday-school libraries. These were written with great care and ability. Many others have been issued by private publishers in different sections of our country. In foreign lands Baptists are equally interested in providing religious books for the young, and the efforts which they have used for this object have been attended with great success.

In periodicals for the religious instruction of the young the Baptists have shown great enterprise. The *Young Reaper* is probably the most popular paper in existence ; its pages are eagerly read by hundreds of thousands. *Our Young People*, intended for the period between childhood and adult years, is edited with great ability, and has a large circulation. The Baptist Publication Society has a list of periodicals, only two of which we have named, whose pages show remarkable adaptation to the various stages of childhood and youth for which they are intended. *The Teacher*, designed to benefit the young through their instructors, is one of the best Sunday-school papers in existence. *Kind Words*, issued by the Southern Baptist Convention, is a great blessing to throngs of the young. Baptists of all nationalities have numbers of religious papers for the enlightenment of the rising generation.

AMERICAN PERIODICALS.

Name.	Editor.	Issued.	Where Published.
Advanced Bible Lesson Quarterly	Dr. C. R. Blackall	Quarterly	Philadelphia, Pa.
Alabama Baptist, The	E. T. Winkler, D.D	Weekly	Marion, Ala.
American Baptist Flag	D. B. Ray, D.D	"	St. Louis, Mo.
American Baptist, The	A. C. Caperton, D.D	Monthly	Louisville, Ky.
American Baptist Year-Book	Rev. J. G. Walker	Yearly	Philadelphia, Pa.
Baptist, The	J. R. Graves, LL.D	Weekly	Memphis, Tenn.
Baptist Banner	James I. Morris	"	Cumming, Ga.
Baptist Banner	Rev. W. P. Throgmorton	"	Benton, Ill.
Baptist Beacon, The	Rev. W. J. Crawford	Monthly	Albany, Oregon.
Baptist Courier, The	Rev. A. W. Lamar	Weekly	Greenville, S. C.
Baptist Family Magazine	J. Eugene Reed	Monthly	Philadelphia, Pa.
Baptist Journal, The	Rev. A. R. Griggs	"	Dallas, Texas.
Baptist Missionary Magazine	S. F. Smith, D.D	"	Boston, Mass.
Baptist Pioneer, The	W. H. McAlpine	"	Marion, Ala.
Baptist Record, The	Rev. J. B. Gambrell	Weekly	Clinton, Miss.
Baptist Reflector, The	J. B. Chevis	"	Nashville, Tenn.
Baptist Review, The	J. R. Baumes, D.D	Quarterly	Cincinnati, O.
Baptist Signal	J. J. Spelman	Monthly	Jackson, Miss.
Baptist Teacher	P. S. Henson, D.D	"	Philadelphia, Pa.
Baptist Weekly, The	A. S. Patton, D.D	Weekly	New York, N. Y.
Biblical Recorder	Rev. C. T. Bailey	"	Raleigh, N. C.
Bible Lesson Monthly	Rev. J. W. Willmarth	Monthly	Philadelphia, Pa.
Canadian Baptist, The	Wm. Muir	Weekly	Toronto, Ontario.
Canadian Missionary Link	Mrs. H. J. Rose	Monthly	"
Central Baptist, The	Wm. Ferguson	Weekly	St. Louis, Mo.
Children's Picture Lesson	Mrs. M. G. Kennedy	Monthly	Philadelphia, Pa.
Christian Helper	H. E. Buchan, M.D	"	Toronto, Ontario.
Christian Index, The	H. H. Tucker, D.D., LL.D	Weekly	Atlanta, Ga.
Christian Messenger, The	S. Seldon	"	Halifax, Nova Scotia.
Christian Monitor, The	Dr. D. M. Breaker	"	Gainesville, Ga.
Christian Repository	S. H. Ford, LL.D	Monthly	St. Louis, Mo.
Christian Secretary	S. D. Phelps, D.D	Weekly	Hartford, Conn.
Christian Visitor	Rev. J. E. Hopper	"	St. John, New Brunswick.
Der Muntere Säeman (German)	Rev. J. C. Haselhuhn	"	Cleveland, O.
Der Sendbote (German)	Rev. J. C. Haselhuhn	"	" "
Die Sonntags Freude	Rev. J. C. Haselhuhn	Monthly	" "
Der Wegweiser	Rev. J. C. Haselhuhn	"	" "
Evangel, The	Rev. J. T. Prior	Weekly	San Francisco, Cal.
Evangel, The Arkansas {	B. R. Womask	"	Little Rock and Dardanelle.
	J. B. Searcy		
Evangelisk Tidskrift	Prof. J. A. Edgren	Monthly	Chicago, Ill.
Examiner and Chronicle, The	E. Bright, D.D	Weekly	New York, N. Y.
Foreign Journal	H. A. Tupper, D.D	Monthly	Richmond, Va.
Georgia Baptist, The	Rev. Wm. J. White	Weekly	Augusta, Ga.
Helping Hand		Monthly	Boston, Mass.
Herald of Truth	G. S. Abbott, D.D	Semi-monthly	Oakland, Cal.
Intermediate Lesson Quarterly	Mrs. M. G. Kennedy	Quarterly	Philadelphia, Pa.
Journal and Messenger	G. W. Lasher, D.D	Semi-monthly	Cincinnati, O.
Kind Words	Rev. S. Boykin	Weekly	Macon, Ga.
Le Moniteur	T. Amyrauld	"	Grunby, Quebec.
Michigan Christian Herald	Rev. L. H. Trowbridge	"	Detroit, Mich.
Missionary Baptist	C. C. Dickinson	Semi-monthly	Memphis, Tenn.
National Baptist, The	H. L. Wayland, D.D	Weekly	Philadelphia, Pa.
National Monitor, The	Rev. R. L. Perry	Semi-monthly	Brooklyn, N. Y.
National Watchman	Howard Bunts, Jr	Monthly	Albany, Ga.
New Jersey Baptist, The	John W. Moody	"	Trenton, N. J.
Our Little Ones	Dr. C. R. Blackall	Weekly	Philadelphia, Pa.
Our Young People	A. J. Rowland, D.D	Monthly	"
Picture Lesson Cards	Mrs. M. G. Kennedy	Weekly	" "
Religious Herald {	A. E. Dickinson, D.D	"	Richmond, Va.
	Prof. H. H. Harris, D.D		
Standard, The	J. A. Smith, D.D	"	Chicago, Ill.
Texas Baptist, The	Rev. R. C. Buckner	"	Dallas, Texas.
Texas Baptist Herald	J. B. Link, D.D	"	Houston, Texas.
Vermont Baptist, The	Rev. J. K. Richardson	Monthly	Rutland, Vt.
Watchman, The	Lucius E. Smith, D.D	Weekly	Boston, Mass.
Watch Tower, The	J. W. Olmstead, D.D	"	New York, N. Y.
Western Recorder	A. C. Caperton, D.D	"	Louisville, Ky.
Young Reaper	B Griffith, D.D	Semi-monthly	Philadelphia, Pa.
Y Wawr (Welsh)	O. Griffith	Monthly	Utica, N. Y.
Zion's Advocate	Rev. H. S. Burrage	Weekly	Portland, Me.

BRITISH PERIODICALS.

The Baptist Handbook, yearly ; *The Baptist Almanac*, yearly ; *The Baptist Year-Book and Almanac*, yearly ; *The General Baptist Almanac*, yearly ; *Spurgeon's Illustrated Almanac*, yearly ; *The Quarterly Reporter of the German Baptist Mission*, quarterly ; *Baptist Magazine*, monthly ; *Baptist Messenger*, monthly ; *The Church*, monthly ; *General Baptist Magazine*, monthly ; *Earthen Vessel*, monthly ; *Gospel Herald and Voice of Truth*, monthly ; *Missionary Herald*, monthly ; *Juvenile Missionary Herald*, monthly ; *Sword and Trowel*, monthly ; *The Irish Baptist Magazine*, monthly ; *The Freeman*, weekly ; *The Baptist*, weekly.

WELSH.

The Welsh Baptist Handbook, yearly ; *Y Greal* (*The Magazine*), monthly ; *Yr Athraw* (*The Teacher*), monthly ; *Cydymaith Y Plentyn* (*Child's Companion*), monthly ; *Seren Cymru* (*Star of Wales*) weekly.

SCOTLAND.

The Scottish Baptist Magazine, **monthly.**

Littlefield, Gov. Alfred Henry, was born in Scituate, R. I., April 2, 1829. Several of his ancestors occupied prominent positions in the administration of the civil affairs of Rhode Island. He was one of a family of eleven children. In the spring of 1851 he entered into partnership with his brother. The business of the firm was so successful that it has become one of the most prominent in the State. Gov. Littlefield had an appointment in the civil war as brigade quartermaster on the staff of Brig.-Gen. O. Arnold, and in various ways rendered efficient aid to the government, and extended his sympathy and pecuniary help to the families of the soldiers. He has filled, and continues to fill, important positions in different corporations in Pawtucket, R. I. He has represented the town of Lincoln in both branches of the General Assembly. He was chosen governor in 1880. Gov. Littlefield is an habitual attendant on the ministry of Rev. George Bullen, pastor of the First Baptist church in Pawtucket, of which his wife is a member.

Lloyd, Rev. W. B., the oldest Baptist minister in Mississippi, was born in Georgia in 1809; became a Baptist in 1825, and at once began to preach; was ordained the following year. He settled in Noxube Co., Miss., in 1830, where he engaged actively in the ministry. He was an able preacher and a successful revivalist, having baptized about 3000 persons during the fifty-five years of his ministry.

Lloyd, Rev. W. S., was born in Hyde Co., N. C., Feb. 27, 1811; ordained in South Carolina in 1835; educated in Furman University, in both the literary and theological courses. After a useful ministry of ten years in that State, he settled in Macon Co., Ala., in 1845, where he remained until his death. Soon attracting general attention, he became one of the most popular and useful, as he was one of the most gifted ministers in the State. A striking form, excellent social qualities, with the spirit of a Christian, he made friends of all with whom he came in contact. His churches were among a wealthy and highly-cultivated people. He fell dead in the pulpit in the midst of one of his eloquent sermons, at Mount Meigs, Ala., at eleven o'clock on Sabbath, March 12, 1854. Rev. W. E. Lloyd, of Auburn, one of the best preachers in Alabama, is his son, possessing many of the striking and noble traits of his brilliant father.

Locke, Rev. Jacob, an able and useful preacher of the Old Green River Association in Kentucky, was born in Berkeley Co., Va., about 1768. He removed to Mercer Co., Ky., in 1789, and subsequently to Barren County of that State about 1799. Here he was ordained to the ministry in 1801, and became pastor of the Mount Tabor Baptist church in 1803, besides supplying several other churches.

Mr. Locke was a man of wisdom, piety, and zeal. He was the leading man in planting and establishing the young churches and guiding their associational councils. He was moderator of Green River Association for more than twenty years, and then of Liberty Association from its constitution until his death, which occurred Jan. 18, 1845.

Lofton, George Augustus, D.D., pastor of the Third Baptist church, St. Louis, Mo., was born Dec. 25, 1839, in Penola Co., Miss. He finished his education in 1859–60 at Mercer University. It was his purpose to enter the Methodist ministry, but in 1859, from the study of the Greek New Testament, he was convinced of the Scripturalness of Baptist views, and was immersed into

GEORGE AUGUSTUS LOFTON, D.D.

the fellowship of the Second Baptist church, Atlanta, Ga. In 1861 he entered the service of the Confederacy, and continued through the war as an officer of artillery. He entered the Baptist ministry at Americus, Ga., in 1868; and since that time Dr. Lofton has served as pastor, principally, the Baptist church at Dalton, Ga., the First Baptist church at Memphis, Tenn., and the Third Baptist church at St. Louis, Mo. These churches have all flourished under his care, numerically, spiritually, financially, and socially. He has baptized some 600 converts in his churches; and he is regarded as a devoted, able, and successful pastor, a sound and practical preacher, an indefatigable worker, a friend to the poor, a popular speaker. Besides many articles and sermons for the periodical press, he has written and published some bound volumes, which have received favorable criticism, and which indicate culture and originality. He is in the prime of life, and has the promise of many years of usefulness. He and his present charge are in close bonds of sympathy, and are co-operating most successfully in religious work of all kinds in St. Louis, in the State, and in the regions beyond. Thoroughly evangelical, Dr. Lofton leads any church he serves as pastor in the most efficient methods of work, and into the widest fields of usefulness. He served faithfully and suffered greatly through the yellow fever scourge of 1873 in Memphis; and in 1875 he led his brethren in the centennial effort to endow the Southwestern Baptist University at Jackson, Tenn. He was also president for two years of the Southern Baptist Publication Society, located at Memphis. Dr. Lofton is especially prominent and well known in the South, and he is rapidly acquiring a national reputation.

Long, Rev. F. M., traces his ancestry to the "Mayflower" and Plymouth Rock. He was born Sept. 30, 1839, in East Tennessee, where he was converted. He was baptized in Macoupin Co., Ill., licensed in 1864, ordained in 1865 by the Honey Creek church, and preached with great success for ten years in Madison, Bond, and Montgomery Counties, Ill. In 1874 he removed to Oregon, and has since then been connected with the Oak Creek church, giving occasional aid to the Providence, North Palestine, and Lacreole churches. He is an earnest, doctrinal extempore preacher, and is one of the most logical reasoners in the Oregon pulpit. He does not put himself forward, but when called out carries all hearts with him. A diligent student and active pastor, he deserves the love of the brethren and the churches, which he possesses to an unusual degree.

Long, Prof. J. C., D.D., LL.D., was born in Campbell Co., Va., Nov. 28, 1833; graduated at Richmond College in June, 1856. The month following his graduation he was appointed tutor in the college, but resigned at the close of the first session; was ordained in Grace Street church, Richmond, Va., July 5, 1857. In the summer of 1857 he was elected teacher in the Florida State Seminary, and held the position for one year in connection with the pastorate of the Tallahassee church. He then became pastor of the Cumberland Street church, Norfolk, Va., and remained until 1861, when the relationship was broken up by the war. From 1861–65 he resided in Goochland Co., Va., and during part of the year 1863 was teacher of a school in Danville, Va. He subsequently became pastor of the Fine Creek and Mount Tabor churches. From 1866–68 he was pastor of the Scottsville and Hardware churches in Albemarle County. In 1868 he became pastor of

the church at Charlottesville, Va., where he remained until April, 1875, when he was elected Professor of Ecclesiastical History in the Crozer Theological Seminary. In this position he continues to render valuable service to the cause of ministerial education. He received the degree of D.D. from Richmond College in 1872, and that of LL.D. from Baylor University in 1880.

Dr. Long is a man of ripe scholarship, unassuming manners, and most genial social accomplishments. His writings evince the results of long-continued and patient research, and display his marked ability to interpret the facts of history in their relation to the church of Christ. His sermons are rich in the clear, simple, and devout exposition of the Word of God.

Long, Nimrod, a banker, merchant, and manufacturer, was born in Logan Co., Ky., July 31, 1814. At the age of fourteen he went to Russellville, the seat of justice of his native county, and entered a store as clerk. Three years afterwards he became a partner in the house. In a short time the senior partner died, and Mr. Long took his brother into the partnership. They were very successful. After some years Mr. N. Long withdrew from the business, and became a commission merchant, and afterwards established the banking-house of N. Long & Co., and in 1870 built the largest flouring-mill in the State. This, like all his enterprises, proved a success, and Mr. Long is now a wealthy capitalist. He became a member of the Baptist church in Russellville in early life, and has used his business talent and growing capital for the cause of Christ with rare liberality. He was ordained a deacon of his church in 1832, was made its treasurer in 1838, and has for many years been superintendent of the Sunday-school. He has been the leading spirit in founding and endowing Bethel College, one of the best and most flourishing institutions of the West. After contributing largely to the erection of its buildings, he endowed the chair of English, known as the N. Long professorship. In 1870 he conceived the idea of boarding students at actual cost, and, to carry it out, caused the erection of the N. Long Boarding Hall, capable of accommodating 100 students. He has also been a liberal patron of Georgetown College and other institutions of learning in his denomination.

Longley, Avard, M.P., was born in Wilmot, Annapolis County, Nova Scotia; is a member of the Wilmot Baptist church; represents the county of Annapolis in the Parliament of Canada. Mr. Longley has been much in political life; is a governor of Acadia College, a strong advocate for prohibition of all intoxicating liquors, and a friend of all denominational enterprises.

Loomis, Rev. Ebenezer, was born in 1794; baptized in 1809; preached first in Tolland Court-

House, Conn., in 1821; ordained in New London, Conn.; labored as pastor, exploring agent, and evangelist in Richfield, Otsego Co., N. Y.; First Newark, N. J.; Hudson, N. Y.; Springville, Boston, and Evans, Western New York; Detroit, China, and Coldwater, Mich.; Cincinnati, O.; North Lyme; First Colchester, Brooklyn; First North Stonington, Preston, and Killingly, Conn.; Fredonia, N. Y.; finally Bradford Co., Pa.; gifted, scholarly, amiable, devoted; gave thousands of dollars to churches, to Connecticut Literary Institution, and to the missionary press in Burmah; always traveled on foot; died in Bradford Co., Pa., in 1872, in his seventy-ninth year.

Loomis, Prof. Freeman, was born in Waterville, Me., May 21, 1844. His studies preparatory to admission to college were pursued mostly at the academy connected with the university at Lewisburg, and he was admitted to Freshman standing in June, 1862. He graduated in 1866, taking the second honors of his class. He passed at once to theological studies, the course in that department then occupying two years. Having finished his theological course, he was temporarily appointed to the principalship of the academy in the spring of 1867. At the commencement in June the board of trustees elected him principal, which position he held for two years. In 1869 the preparatory department became distinct from the academy, and he was placed at the head of it. In 1879 the preparatory department again became a part of the academy, and Prof. Loomis resigned his connection with it. In 1870 he obtained leave of absence, and occupied himself for two years in the study of French and German in Berlin and Paris. During his absence, in 1871, the trustees appointed him to the chair of Modern Languages in the university. This position he held in connection with that of head of the preparatory course till his resignation of the latter in 1879. Since that time he has held only the professorship of Modern Languages. In this department his instruction is faithfully given, and he is deservedly popular with his classes.

Loomis, Rev. Hubbell, died Dec. 15, 1872, in his ninety-eighth year, at Upper Alton, Ill. He was an example alike of the physical vigor and of the intellectual and spiritual robustness of the New England stock. He was born at Colchester, Conn., May 31, 1775. As his father, a descendant of Joseph Loomis, who emigrated from England to this country in 1638, was in moderate circumstances, he was thrown chiefly upon his own resources in procuring his education, graduating at Union College, Schenectady, N. Y., in 1799. Having studied theology under Rev. Joel Benedict, of Plainfield, Conn., he was licensed as a Congregationalist minister in 1801. His first pastorate was at Willing-

ton, Conn., where he continued twenty-four years, uniting with his pastoral duties the work of a teacher, one of his pupils being Jared Sparks, afterwards so eminent as president of Harvard College and author of "The Life of Washington," and other valuable works. In the later years of this pastorate, as a result of earnest study of the Scriptures with reference to questions of denominational difference, he became a Baptist, and united with the Baptist church of Willington; this event, of course, dissolving his connection with the church he had served so long, and necessitating great self-denial in other respects.

In 1829, Mr. Loomis removed to Illinois. After some months spent in Kaskaskia and Edwardsville, he settled in Upper Alton, and then founded the seminary which in 1835 became incorporated as Shurtleff College. His name stands first on the list in the college charter of incorporation. He was a liberal donor to the college, and to the end of his life its earnest friend, while in the various exigencies of its history his counsel was often sought. He was remarkable for conscientiousness; an ardent advocate of human rights, and a warm friend of moral reforms. One of his sons, Prof. Elias Loomis, of Yale College, ranks with the eminent men of science in this country, while others of his children have filled stations of great usefulness, one daughter, Sophia, having been the wife of Hon. Cyrus Edwards, another, Caroline, was married to Prof. Newman, of Shurtleff College, who died in 1844; a son, David B., residing in Minnesota, has filled several terms as a member of the Legislature of that State; while another, John Calvin, was at one time Professor of Languages in the Alabama University.

Loomis, Justin R., D.D., LL.D., was born in Bennington, Vt., Aug. 21, 1810. At the age of seventeen he went to Hamilton Literary Institution, and at a subsequent date he entered Brown University, and graduated with marked honor in 1835. Shortly after his graduation he was elected professor in Waterville College, now Colby University.

Determined to thoroughly inform himself in the field of his chosen studies, he visited South America, where he spent a profitable year in scientific explorations through Bolivia, Peru, and Chili. Thus prepared for more efficient service, he was elected Professor of Natural Science in the university at Lewisburg, Pa., and in 1858 succeeded to the presidency. This office he held with singular ability for twenty years, retiring from it in January, 1879.

His consistent and blameless life, his many acts of benevolence, his indomitable will, combined with practical good sense, his warm interest in the welfare of the university, and especially in the students, his influence in shaping the character of the town, and in making the Baptist church edifice, which was mainly erected by his own exertions, among the best in the State, have left a stamp of permanent value upon the history of the university.

As an author, he has prepared various standard

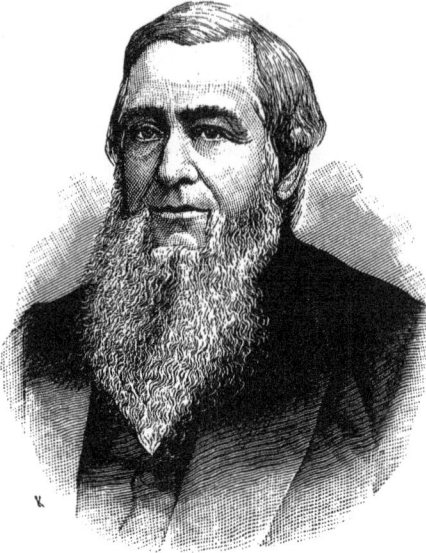

JUSTIN R. LOOMIS, LL.D.

works: "Principles of Geology," "Physiology," and "Anatomy," are works of great value, while various essays, lectures, pamphlets, and sermons attest the possession of talents of a high order. While he could lay no high claim to oratorial power as a public speaker, yet his presence and counsel at the meetings of the Associations and other bodies were always welcome, and were much desired.

His son, Freeman Loomis, is a professor in the university at Lewisburg.

Lord, Edward C., D.D., was born at Carlisle, N. Y., Jan. 22, 1817, and was a graduate of Madison University. He was ordained at Preston Hollow, N. Y., Aug. 27, 1846, having previously received an appointment as a missionary to China. He reached Ningpo June 20, 1847, and was connected with Dr. Macgowan in the care of that station. Having acquired the language, he was able to preach to the natives and hold conversation with them on religious subjects. The health of Mrs. Lord made it necessary for him to return to the United States, which he reached at the close of 1851. Remaining here a little less than two years, he returned to Ningpo. Arriving there June 1,

1854, he commenced again his missionary labors, taking, as far as possible, the place of the lamented Goddard, and having Mr. Knowlton as a co-worker with him. While occupied with these evangelical labors, Mr. Lord performed some work in his study. Writing to the Executive Committee, in 1860, he says, "My notes on the Epistles to the Hebrews and Romans have been completed, and considerable other labor of a similar kind has been performed." And the next year he writes, "My notes on the First Epistle to the Corinthians have been completed and put to press. My notes on Ephesians have been carefully revised, and those on Second Corinthians are in course of preparation." In 1863 he writes, "At Ningpo, in my own neighborhood, I have plenty of work, and I am thankful to say there is much encouragement. At the communion season, about three months ago, I baptized five persons, three men and two women, and I have at present several applicants." The connection of Mr. Lord with the Missionary Union closed in July, 1864. He was in the diplomatic service of the United States in China, and performing more or less of missionary service for several years. His formal connection with the Missionary Union has been resumed. He has had charge of two chapels in Ningpo, being aided in his work by three native preachers.

Lord's Supper, The.—The Lord's Supper, in its *form*, must be bread and wine; for Matthew says that Jesus took bread and blessed it, and brake it and gave it to the disciples and said, "Take, eat; this is my body. And he took the cup, and gave thanks, and gave it to them, saying, Drink ye all of it."—Matt. xxvi. 28. The retention of the cup from the laity in the Church of Rome, deprives her Eucharist of every divine sanction, and reduces it to a mere human invention.

The Supper is a *memorial* or *remembrancer* of a *slain* and *absent* Saviour. His wounds and death are shown by the broken bread and the flowing cup. His *bodily* absence is proved by the object of the Sacrament. Speaking of the bread Jesus says, "This is my body which is given for you; this do in *remembrance* of me."—Luke xxiv. 19. We can only *remember* absent persons. So that the purpose of the Eucharist as a remembrancer makes it certain that Christ's body is not in it. And Paul teaches the same truth when he writes, —"For as often as ye eat this bread and drink this cup, ye do show the Lord's death till *He come*."—1 Cor. xi. 26. In body, he is not in the Supper, for it is intended to be observed till Jesus, whom "the heaven must receive until the times of restitution of all things" (Acts iii. 21) shall come in the glories of his final advent. His humanity is now at the right hand of God. His Deity is everywhere, but peculiarly near the devout worshiper. The transubstantiation* of Rome, and the consubstantiation† of Luther are, therefore, without foundation either in Scripture or in fact.

The sole direct teaching of the Supper is: *The agony of Jesus the sustenance of redeemed men.* Strange that *bread* should be the figure to represent the body of Christ. Why not his image in gold or silver? His statue in marble or wood? His picture on canvas? Then each wound might have been seen, and every writhe of anguish. But no, bread, the *food of the world*, and wine, the beverage of many nations, are chosen to exhibit the wounded body of Jesus. Food and drink, the support of all human life, constitute the *monument* erected by Jesus for himself,—the food, *broken* bread, to remind us of his torn body—the cup, wine, to represent the purple current drawn from his veins. And these emblems are not *to be viewed, simply*, in solemn sadness, nor even in joyful faith,—we are *to partake* of them. Thus teaching that as food and drink sustain men, without which their bodies must perish, so the sufferings of Jesus *are the bread and the beverage* of the soul. And as it would be madness to try to support flesh and blood on anything but food and drink, so it is insanity to look anywhere but to Christ's woes for the nourishment of the undying spirit. And the true disciple, by a hungering faith, ought to make these sorrows bread for his soul; while by a thirsting frame of spirit he ought to drink at these crimson streams of divine torture. And as we need bread and drink *all the time*, the choice of these emblems by the Saviour proclaims to us that his wounds and death are a constant supply for the necessities of a soul perpetually in want. What other doctrines could be designed by such emblems? Beyond all doubt God speaks to us through them, and says, Like the body needing bread several times *every* day, so your souls require atoning blood each instant, and like the food of mankind there is an everlasting supply for all the weaknesses and criminal experiences that mark each footprint of your earthly journey, to which you are as welcome every moment as to the food that covers your own tables, or the fruits that wave in golden beauty on your own abundant harvest-fields. "He that spared not his own Son but delivered him up for us all, how shall he not with him also *freely give us all things?*"—Rom. viii. 33. "By one offering he hath *perfected forever* all them that are sanctified."—Heb. x. 14. "I give

---

* The Council of Trent decrees, "If any man shall deny, that in the sacrament of the most holy Eucharist, there is contained really, truly, and substantially, *the body and blood, together with the soul and divinity* of our Lord Jesus Christ, and so *whole Christ*, but shall say he is only in it in sign, or figure, or power, *let him be accursed*." De Eucharis, Can. i. Less. xiii. p. 63. Canones et Decreta Concilii Trid. Lipsiæ, 1863.

† The body and blood of Christ truly present in the Supper. Augsburg Confession, Article x.

---

unto them *eternal life;* and they shall *never perish,* neither shall any pluck them out of my hand."— John x. 28. Thank God for the Lord's Supper!

The Supper has no commission to teach us charity for each other. Examine the descriptions given of it in Matt. xxvi. 26–28, in Mark xiv. 22–23, in Luke xxii. 19, 20, in 1 Cor. xi. 20–29, and allusions made to it elsewhere, and in *every instance* it is a memorial of the Saviour's *wounds and blood*,—a picture of Christ's only *food* for perishing souls, and in each case *destitute* of any other allusion. Many Christians turn it into a feast of charity for members of their own and of other sects, and speak *with unloving harshness* of those who observe it solely as a remembrancer of a Saviour in the throes of death. Charity in its own place is a truly blessed grace; he is not Christ's who has not a goodly measure of it; it is the chain whose golden links bind together the whole heavenly throng, from the Mighty One wielding the sword of Omnipotence to the lowliest shining spirit. From the depths of our hearts, *enthusiasm* surges up in a mighty current around charity, the darling of heaven,—the element of which God himself is composed. But we have a fervent love for the truth of God,—for that whole body of revelation, one fragment of which exceeds in worth the riches of time, and all the material splendors of the universe. And as the Lord's Supper, according to Jesus, has nothing to do with charity, as it is a MONUMENT upon which is sculptured the ANGUISH OF JESUS, THE FOOD AND DRINK OF THE SOUL, and a monument from which the most dazzling glories in the universe shine forth, and around which the most thrilling melodies of heavenly harmony shall ever float, why obliterate its *divinely* appointed inscription to trace upon it any other writing, even though you inscribe upon it man's love to his fellow,—where Christ's love *in lines of blood* was once read? Surely this is an impious act in any one, and peculiarly so in the adherents of that Protestantism which boasts that the "Bible and the *Bible alone* is its religion." You might with as much propriety assemble the pious business people of several localities together on New Year's day, who manifested the grace of Christian integrity by paying their debts, and induce them to celebrate the Supper as an exhibition of their uprightness and probity. And if it might be said, the cross shows Christ's love for us in the Supper, the example of which commands us to love one another, it might with equal justice be affirmed, the sufferings of Jesus seen in the Supper *as our surety*, show him as wonderfully honest in paying our debts to the violated law, and following in his footsteps, we should refuse all gains not righteously secured.

Lorimer, George C., D.D., was born near Edinburgh, Scotland, in 1838, and in that city he spent the early part of his life. For a short time he followed the sea, then for a brief period he had some business connection with a theatre, and occasionally performed some parts, but God had something higher

GEORGE C. LORIMER, D.D.

and better for him than the stage. He came to the United States when he was about eighteen years of age, and having been providentially led to the city of Louisville, Ky., he was brought under the influence of the preaching of the pastor of the Walnut Street Baptist church. That preaching was blessed to him, and he became a hopeful Christian. The whole purpose of his life was at once changed. He entered upon a course of study in Georgetown College, Ky., preparatory to the Christian ministry, and in 1859 was ordained pastor of the church at Harrodsburg, Ky. He remained there until called to Paducah, Ky., and from there to Louisville, where he was a pastor for eight years. The degree of Doctor of Divinity was conferred upon him by Bethel College while he was in Louisville. From Louisville he was called to Albany, N. Y., where he remained two years, and then accepted an invitation to the Shawmut Avenue church, Boston. While in the midst of a successful ministry with this church, the attention of the Tremont Temple church was directed to him, and he was urged to occupy that central and important position, in which, for several years, his labors have been so much blessed. About eighteen months ago he took charge of the First church, Chicago. Dr. Lorimer is in the prime of his life, and, it is to be hoped, of his usefulness. His ministry is a

popular one, in the best sense of the word. He believes in a genial religion, and seeks to draw men to Christ by the sweet words of a Saviour's love. His preaching has been blessed to the building up of a large church and congregation in Boston; and it has been equally effective in his present charge.

He has just sundered his happy relations with the First church to minister to a new community occupying the field vacated by the Michigan Avenue Baptist church.

Lothrop, Rev. J. Grafton, was a brilliant young minister in Eastern Louisiana, who died, very much regretted, at Greensburg, La., June 16, 1868. He began to preach in 1861.

Louisiana, one of the Gulf States, was long a part of the territory of France, but was purchased by the United States in 1803. It has about 20,000 white Baptists and about 30,000 colored.

The sentiments of the Baptists were first propagated in this State by preachers from the contiguous parts of Mississippi. Rev. Bailey E. Chaney removed with his family into Eastern Louisiana, then called West Florida, in 1798, and settled with a number of other South Carolinians not far from Baton Rouge. He began to preach to his American neighbors, but he was not long without molestation. He was arrested and imprisoned at Baton Rouge by the Spanish authorities. But he purchased his liberty by promising to abstain from preaching in the future, and subsequently returned to Mississippi.

Soon after the cession of the French portion of the Territory, Joseph Willis, a mulatto, who was a licensed Baptist preacher, and who had been a co-laborer with Richard Curtis in Mississippi, boldly crossed the Mississippi River, and in 1804 preached at Vermillion and Plaquemine Brulé. The following year he returned and settled on Bayou Chicot in St. Landry Parish, where he began to preach, and in 1812, with assistance from Mississippi, organized a church, of which he became pastor.

About the beginning of the present century a number of young ministers crossed into West Florida, at the peril of their liberty. By the labors of these, two churches were gathered on Pearl River, called Mount Nebo and Peniel, which were constituted in 1813.

Previous to 1806, Ezra Courtney, who had settled in Mississippi in 1802, made frequent visits into the Felicianas and East Baton Rouge, and about that time removed and settled near the present town of Clinton, and in 1814 Hepzibah church was constituted. In 1819 West Florida was ceded to the United States. Other ministers came into this part of the State. Elisha Anders settled in West Feliciana, Howell Wall and W. B. Wall in St. Helena. As early as 1818 a small church was gathered in New Orleans, and enjoyed the labors of Benjamin Davis.

West of the Mississippi Joseph Willis continued for several years to labor alone, and organized churches at Cheneyville, Vermillion, Plaquemine Brulé, and Hickory Flat. In 1816 he was joined in this field by Ezekiel O'Quinn and Isham Nettles. On the 31st day of October, 1818, six churches met by delegates at Cheneyville, and organized the Louisiana Baptist Association, of which Joseph Willis was elected moderator. Other ministers were ordained, and churches increased, mainly through the zealous labors of Mr. Willis.

In 1822, Rev. Henry Humble settled on the Ouachita River, in the parish of Catahoula, and in 1826 the First church in Catahoula was established. Here, at a somewhat later day, labored Asa S. Mercer, John Hill, the Meridiths, Thomas and James, and many churches were gathered in the Ouachita region.

In 1820, Rev. James Brinson, with a number of other Baptists, settled at Pine Hills, not far from the present town of Vienna, and organized a church in 1821. Here they were joined by John Impson. They extended their labors westward, and gathered a church about four miles east of Mount Lebanon, called Providence. It was afterwards removed to Athens. Not far from the present town of Minden they found a few Baptists, whom they gathered into a church called Black Lake.

In 1837 a colony, most of whom were Baptists, removed from South Carolina and settled at Mount Lebanon, in Bienville Parish. In the company was Henry Adams, a colored man, who was an ordained Baptist preacher. A church was organized, and Mr. Adams became pastor. He was a man of some education, and was very much respected by the community. This church became one of the most active and influential in the State.

About the same time Elias George, Samuel J. Larkin, and William B. Larkin began to preach in Union Parish, and many churches were gathered in a few years.

In 1843, Rev. John Bryce, an eminent Baptist minister, was sent to Shreveport as collector of customs on imports from the republic of Texas. While discharging the duties of his office he preached in Shreveport and the surrounding country. In 1845 a church was gathered in Shreveport, and Mr. Bryce became pastor. His office of collector of customs having expired by the annexation of Texas, he continued to labor in this region until 1850. He was joined in 1847 by A. W. Jackson and Jesse Lee, two able ministers from Alabama, and on Dec. 21, 1849, the Grand Cane Association was organized.

In the Sabine region the churches were principally planted and consolidated by the labors of Nathan H. Bray after 1847. There were a few churches before this planted by Willis and his co-laborers, but they were feeble and scattered. In 1848, Mr. Bray formed them into an Association called Sabine.

The Bayou Macon region, between the Ouachita and Mississippi Rivers, had but few Baptists previous to 1850. Shortly after this J. P. Blake and D. D. Swindall began their labors there, and in 1855 organized the Bayou Macon Association.

Louisiana Baptist, a weekly newspaper, was started at Mount Lebanon, La., in 1855, by Rev. Hanson Lee, and conducted with such ability that it ranked with the ablest religious journals of the South. In 1862, Mr. Lee died, and the paper was continued by W. F. Wells, with Dr. Courtney as editor, and subsequently as part owner. At the close of the war Rev. A. S. Worrell bought it, but after a short connection, resold to W. F. Wells, and Dr. Courtney became editor, with W. E. Paxton associate. At the end of the year 1869 Mr. Wells sold his subscription to Rev. J. R. Graves of the *Memphis Baptist,* and the *Louisiana Baptist* was discontinued.

Louisiana Baptist Convention was organized in 1848. Its leading objects were educational and missionary. Under its fostering care Mount Lebanon University came into existence and other schools were encouraged. Its missionaries have penetrated into many destitute parts of the State, and laid the foundation for numerous churches now flourishing. With an active mission board, inspired by Rev. W. C. Friley, the State evangelist, the work of the Convention has greatly prospered for the last two years. Its operations during the past year secured about $6000.

President, Rev. J. P. Everett, Shiloh, La.; Recording Secretary, Rev. G. W. Hartsfield, Mansfield, La.

Louisiana, Baptist Messenger of, is a weekly paper published at Farmerville, La., Rev. S. C. Lee editor. It started in 1879 as a semi-weekly. It began its second year as a weekly. It is well conducted, and it is rapidly growing in public favor.

Louisville, Baptist Orphans' Home of, was established through the efforts of the ladies of Walnut Street church, in Louisville, in 1866. The building first occupied was a rented one. Soon after the house was opened, however, Mrs. J. Lawrence Smith, a member of the Walnut Street church, donated to the Orphans' Home Society $5000 in money and a lot of ground valued at $15,000, provided a sufficient amount should be raised to erect suitable buildings thereon. The sum of $22,000 was speedily secured, and in March, 1867, the ground was broken for the foundation. The new home was dedicated Dec. 19, 1870. During its existence 280 children have been received; 171

of these have been placed in good homes, 62 have been legally adopted in Christian families, and 41 remain in the home. The object of the home is to receive such orphans as cannot be well provided for otherwise, and to educate and train them for useful employments until such time as suitable homes can be procured for them in private families, or until they are able to take care of themselves. Under the management of Miss Mary Hollingsworth, who has been matron since its organization, the home has been very popular, and has been well sustained by voluntary contributions.

Louisville, Walnut Street Baptist Church of.—The First Baptist church in Louisville was organized by Rev. Henson Hobbs in 1815, and consisted of 14 members. In 1839 the church numbered 539. Eighteen withdrew and formed the Second Baptist church. In 1849, when both churches were without pastors, they invited Rev. Thomas Smith, who accepted both calls on condition that the churches would unite and build a good house in an eligible locality. On Oct. 29, 1849, both churches dissolved and formed the Walnut Street Baptist church, and the present magnificent house was erected the following year on the corner of Fourth and Walnut Streets. The first public meeting held in the finished house was the funeral of the pastor. The edifice cost $105,000. Since its erection it has been altered at considerable expense several times. At one time $20,000 was expended upon it. Its seating capacity is 1300. It is the mother of the other Baptist churches of Louisville,—a goodly family.

Lovelace, Rev. Colmore, was born in Maryland, Nov. 26, 1795. At five years of age his parents removed to Kentucky. At the age of fourteen he united with Mount Moriah Baptist church, in Nelson County. He was licensed to preach at Severn's Valley church, in Hardin County, in 1822, and ordained in 1823. He was pastor of several churches in Salem Association, and devoted much time to the work of a missionary. He was distinguished for his piety, zeal, and philanthropy. Few men were more devotedly loved or more extensively blessed. He baptized more than 1200 persons. He died in Hardin Co., Ky., March 16, 1864.

Lovell, Rev. Andrew Sprague, son of Stephen and Rhoda (French) Lovell, was born in Braintree, Mass., in September, 1807; converted in 1825; studied at Maine Wesleyan Seminary, Kent's Hill, Readfield, Me., at Connecticut Literary Institution, Suffield, Conn., and at Newton Theological Seminary, Mass.; chosen associate principal of the Connecticut Literary Institution in 1837; principal of the city high school in Middletown, Conn., for two years; for a time the editor of *The Ægis*, published in Worcester, Mass.; in 1847 became pastor of the Baptist church in Mansfield, Conn.; ordained

in 1848; in 1853 accepted a call to Bloomfield, Conn.; in 1857 settled with the Baptist church in East Longmeadow, Mass.; during the war was an agent for the Christian Commission at Newbern, N. C.; in 1868 settled with the Baptist church in Tariffville, Conn.; now living in Andover, Conn.; very scholarly, calm, penetrating, thorough in thought, elegant in style, eminently sound in the faith; mightier with his pen than with his voice: a poet of unusually delicate taste; a man of great purity and integrity.

Lovell, Rev. N. G., was born in Rowley, now Georgetown, Mass., in 1806. He graduated at Brown University in 1833, and in the following October entered Newton Theological Institution. He was ordained pastor of the Baptist church in Princeton, Mass., in July, 1834. His subsequent settlements were at Amherst, Bellingham, and North Attleborough. Seventeen years of his life were thus devoted to the ministry. His labors were blessed in all his pastorates, especially in that of Bellingham, where there was an interesting revival of religion, followed by large additions to his church. He died at Valley Falls, R. I., Nov. 15, 1851.

Lowry, Gen. M. P., president of Blue Mountain College, Miss., ten years president of Missis-

GEN. M. P. LOWRY.

sippi Baptist Convention, distinguished as an educator, preacher, editor, and as a brigadier-general in the Confederate army, was born in Tennessee in 1828. He began to preach in Mississippi in 1852; supplied the churches at Farmington, Corinth,

WALNUT STREET BAPTIST CHURCH, LOUISVILLE, KY.

Rienzi, Ripley, and other places; in 1861 entered the Confederate service as a captain, was elected colonel, and for gallant conduct was made brigadier-general, and although he refused further promotion, he was often assigned to the command of a division, and served with distinguished ability at Corinth, Perryville, where he was wounded, and in that terrible succession of battles that followed Sherman's advance into Georgia. During the war he preached regularly to the soldiers, and at its close resumed his old field; founded Blue Mountain Female College; contributed two years to *Georgia Index*, and was six years associate editor of the *Memphis Baptist*. He is also a Doctor of Divinity.

Lowry, Rev. Jennings O'Bannon, pastor of Coliseum Place Baptist church, New Orleans, was born in Georgia in 1851, but reared in South Carolina. He took a literary course at Erskine College, S. C. After a course in theology at the Southern Baptist Theological Seminary, he spent some time at Leipsic, Germany; was pastor of St. Francis Street church, Mobile, Ala., five years; called to New Orleans, in December, 1879.

Lowry, Robert, D.D., was born in Philadelphia, Pa., March 12, 1826. His parents were members of the Associate Presbyterian Church. At the age of seventeen he became a subject of divine grace. After reading the New Testament, he was convinced that it was his duty to follow Christ in baptism. He was immersed April 23, 1843, by Dr. George B. Ide, pastor of the First Baptist church, Philadelphia. He began his religious life with Christian work in helping to organize a Sunday-school in a destitute part of the city. For several years he felt an irrepressible drawing towards the ministry, but did not venture to disclose it until his pastor probed his feelings and encouraged him to begin a course of study. In 1848 he entered the university at Lewisburg, Pa., and was graduated in 1854, receiving valedictory honors. In the same year he was ordained, and called to the pastorate of the First Baptist church, West Chester, Pa. Here he remained four years, during which time a new church edifice was built. In 1858 he was called to the Bloomingdale Baptist church, New York City. A movement for a new church edifice was interrupted by the breaking out of the civil war. In 1861 he accepted a call to the Hanson Place Baptist church, Brooklyn, N. Y., where he labored over eight years. During this pastorate about 400 members were added to the church. In 1869 he was induced to accept the professorship of Belles-Lettres in Lewisburg, and the pastorate of the Baptist church. While here the new church edifice was dedicated. After performing this double work for six years, he retired, with the honorary title of D.D., to Plainfield, N. J. He was subsequently elected chancellor of the university.

Shortly after reaching Plainfield a new church was organized, which called him to its pastorship. This movement led to the erection of the Park Avenue church at a cost of $40,000. He has always been an active worker in the Sunday-school. He preaches extemporaneously, and holds tenaciously to the distinctive views of Baptists. Multitudes know him as a composer of sacred song rather than as a preacher. His melodies are sung in every English-speaking land. Some of his hymns have been translated into foreign tongues. Music and hymnology are favorite studies with him. Of five sons, three of whom are living, the oldest has given himself to the work of the ministry.

Loxley, Col. Benjamin, was born in Yorkshire, England, Dec. 20, 1720; came to Philadelphia at the age of sixteen, and served five years at the carpenter's trade. Married first Jane Watkins, sister of his master, and on her death, Catherine Cox, of Upper Freehold, N. J. He had fifteen children. About 1755 he helped to form the 1st Artillery Company of Philadelphia, and went as lieutenant into the service under Gen. Braddock, sharing his defeat at Great Meadows. In 1758, Gen. Forbes appointed him to take charge of the king's stores in the province, which he did for seven years. In 1764 he had command of the artillery which awaited the invasion of the " Paxton boys," of which Mr. Graydon gives an amusing account in his " Reminiscences." He describes Capt. Loxley as a very honest little man, " who was always put foremost when great guns were in question." In 1775, Col. Loxley was on the Committee of Safety for Dock Ward, and served in the Provincial Conference and Convention of the times. Commanded the artillery at Amboy, at Germantown, and was constantly engaged in casting and in supplying various munitions of war. While driven out of Philadelphia by the British, they burned five of his buildings and destroyed other property. Some of his family also served in the army. Col. Loxley was early a member of the First Baptist church, and liberal and conspicuous in erecting its meeting-house at La Grange Place. Among other Baptist houses, public or private, where Whitefield preached in Philadelphia, was Loxley's residence, near 177 South Second Street, then said to be in the country. The front of the house was arched, and there the great preacher addressed thousands on the gentle hill, whose slope afforded a resting-place. The neighborhood was where Cadwallader drilled his " silk-stocking company," some of whom proved doughty warriors in times that tested men's souls. About opposite was the house of William Darrah, whose wife (Lydia) overheard a plot laid by certain British officers, quartered upon them, to surprise Washington at Whitemarsh. She "went to mill" early next morning, and contrived to convey information whereby the danger was averted, the British not knowing why their plans failed. Col. Loxley died in the fall of 1801, aged about eighty-one years, leaving many of his name and blood in Pennsylvania and New Jersey. One, Benjamin R. Loxley, was long a useful home missionary in Philadelphia. Another is wife of Robert Lowry. D.D.

Lucas, Rev. Elijah, was born in Plymouth, England, in December, 1828. When quite a lad he accepted Christ, and united with the Wesleyan Methodists. In the spring of 1850 he came to

REV. ELIJAH LUCAS.

America, and having been for a long time troubled on the subject of baptism, and being convinced that the law of Christ required immersion, he offered himself to the First Baptist church of Troy, N. Y., as a candidate for baptism, and was baptized by Rev. Geo. C. Baldwin, D.D., and some time afterwards that church licensed him to preach. Mr. Lucas always shrank from the work of the ministry, and was at last almost thrust into it by the providence of God.

His first settlement was at Waterford and Half-Moon, in Saratoga Co., N. Y. He served both those churches, preaching three times each Lord's day. After laboring for about two and a half years, he removed in 1855 to Stanford, in Dutchess Co., N. Y. In 1859 he accepted a call from Greenport, and continued there three years. He served the First Baptist church in Harlem, New York City, nine years, after having labored about two and a

half years in Hastings, on the Hudson. On returning from Harlem he went to Europe, and on his return he accepted the unanimous call of the First Baptist church of Trenton, N. J., and began his labors there in 1873, and he is still with that church.

Mr. Lucas has baptized a large number at Trenton. His church has over 1000 members, being the largest Baptist church, except the First of Newark, in the State. Mr. Lucas is an able preacher and a devoted servant of the Redeemer.

Luck, Rev. William Francis, was born Nov. 7, 1801, in Campbell Co., Va., in 1827. He removed to Tennessee, and lived there thirty years. In 1857 he located in Lincoln Co., Mo. He professed religion in 1830, and joined the Pleasant Valley church, Tenn. At one time he was missionary of the General Association of Middle Tennessee and North Alabama. He preached until within a few days of his death, and chiefly to four churches. As a preacher, he was bold and impressive. As an evangelist, he was efficient. In Missouri he labored much in revivals. He died Dec. 26, 1878. Rigid in discipline, prompt in reproof, and full of the spirit of Jesus, he commanded the confidence and love of his brethren.

Ludlow, Gen. Edmund, was born at Maiden-Bradley, in Wiltshire, England, in 1620, and educated at Trinity College, Oxford. He was one of the judges that condemned Charles I.; he was a distinguished general in the Parliamentary forces, and for a time at the head of the large English army necessarily kept in Ireland. He was endowed with a penetrating and independent mind; and he could not be moved by fear for the mighty power of Cromwell, or by a desire for the great favors he had to bestow, to change the course he had selected for himself. Ludlow was a decided republican, and when Cromwell assumed the Protectorate, he made a vigorous protest against the step, and gave up his command in Ireland. After the return of Charles II. to England, he went to Vevay, in Switzerland, where he died in 1693. His "Memoirs" are necessary to complete the history of the Parliamentary war in England.

Richard Baxter, speaking of Cromwell, says, "He sent his son Henry into Ireland, who mightily supprest the Anabaptists, . . . so that Maj.-Gen. Ludlow, who headed them in Ireland, was forced to submit."* Ludlow was a Baptist, and worthily he walked in days of danger and temptation.

Ludlow, Rev. James Peter, grandson of Rev. Dr. Stephen Gano, of Rhode Island, was born at Charleston, S. C., Jan. 5, 1833. He was converted at sea, on the whale-ship "Helen Augusta"; baptized at Honolulu, Sandwich Islands, in February,

---

* Baxter's Life, pp. 69, 70.

1853, by the seamen's chaplain, S. C. Damon; the first immersion ever witnessed at Honolulu. He graduated at Rochester, in 1861 from the university, and in 1864 from the theological seminary, and was ordained in 1864 by the Central church, Newport, R. I.

The American Baptist Home Mission Society sent him to San Francisco, Cal., in 1864, at which place he organized, in 1865, the Tabernacle church, and was for six years its successful pastor. In 1872 he was pastor of Calvary church, Sacramento. Failing health induced him to take a sea-voyage around the world. With health restored, he became pastor at Olympia, Washington Territory, where he served with great success. In 1879 he became missionary for Puget Sound, with residence at Seattle. He is deputy clerk of the U. S. District Court of Washington Territory, over which the Hon. Judge Roger S. Greene, his friend, and also a Baptist preacher, presides with marked ability.

Lumpkin, Rev. John, the third of eight brothers, all of whom attained prominent positions, was the son of John and Lucy Lumpkin, who removed from Virginia and settled in Oglethorpe Co., Ga. He was born in Pittsylvania Co., Va., Nov. 4, 1785, but was brought to Georgia in his infancy, and in Oglethorpe County he was reared and educated, and in it he labored and died. He was a Baptist minister of prominence, usefulness, sterling worth, ability, and conscientious rectitude. Gov. Wilson Lumpkin, of Georgia, was his elder brother, and Judge Joseph Henry Lumpkin, chief justice of the Supreme bench, was his younger brother. He united with County-Line church, Morgan Co., in 1808, and was ordained the same year, and immediately was called to the care of churches. During his ministry he constituted the churches at Antioch and Salem, in Oglethorpe County, and Sardis, in Wilkes County; and at the time of his death, Aug. 1, 1839, the buildings of these three churches were draped in mourning.

His life was a shining example of true Christianity. As a preacher, his sermons were more remarkable for their practical bearing than for brilliancy. In his ministerial career he labored diligently and persistently to win souls for Christ; and God blessed his labors wonderfully. By conforming his example to his precepts he made a deep impression upon the community where he lived, and left to his children a spotless name. During his last moments an aged minister stepped in to bid him a final adieu, and said, "Brother Lumpkin, you are now entering Jordan, how do you find it?" "The deeper I wade the firmer the bottom," was the reply.

Lumpkin, Ex-Gov. Wilson, of Georgia, was born in Pittsylvania Co., Va., Jan. 14, 1783, and died at Athens, Ga., on the 28th December, 1870, at the age of eighty-seven.

In 1786 his parents moved to Georgia, bringing with them the infant destined to fill so many conspicuous positions in the State of his adoption. At eighteen years of age his mind became awakened to the great importance of salvation, and he experienced peace through faith. Personal investigation of the Scriptures led to his adoption of Baptist views, although his parents were Methodists, and his predilections were towards the Presbyterians. In the course of time his parents, affected by his baptism, became Baptists themselves, after searching the Scriptures. Subsequently, others of the

EX-GOV. WILSON LUMPKIN.

family followed the parents into the waters of baptism, and in a short period all the adult members of the family united with a Baptist church. "God made me a Baptist," said Gov. Lumpkin to a friend, in after-life, "and I can never be anything else. I must be of this faith, if I am the only person in the world professing it," and to the end of his long life he remained steadfast to his convictions.

Hardly had he attained his twenty-first year before he was elected a member of the Legislature of Georgia, which met in 1804, and he discharged his responsible duties so satisfactorily that he was elected for several consecutive sessions. In 1814 he was chosen to represent his district in the national councils, and took his seat at Washington the same year,—a year memorable for the destruction of the national capital by the British troops.

For several sessions Mr. Lumpkin was returned to Congress, bearing off the prize from all competitors. In 1831 he was so prominent with his party—the old Union party, as it was then termed—that he received the nomination for governor, and his election followed. Having served the State for two years, he was triumphantly re-elected in 1833. On retiring from the gubernatorial chair he received, from Gen. Jackson, an important commission in connection with Indian affairs, after the discharge of which duty he became, in 1838, a United States Senator.

He had now enjoyed all the political honors the State could bestow, and being nearly threescore years of age, he sought retirement; and, purchasing a comfortable home in the vicinity of Athens, Ga., he spent in that locality the remainder of his days. The only public service he afterwards rendered was as a member of the board of trustees of the State University, of which he was the senior member and honored president for many years.

Few men have lived in Georgia more universally popular than Gov. Lumpkin. He never failed to secure any office for which he was a candidate before the people. For forty consecutive years he was retained in positions of high trust and honor, and for a much longer period, if we include his service as trustee of the State University. His popularity was due, in a good degree, to his unswerving fidelity to the trusts he had received. If not a bold and dashing leader, he was a prudent officer, and the people felt that the public interests were safe in his hands. He was always ready to serve his friends at any reasonable sacrifice, whilst towards his political opponents he deported himself with so much courtesy that he was constantly disarming their opposition and winning them to his support.

He was endowed by nature with an active and inquiring mind. He early learned to think for himself, and by this process his fine intellectual gifts were drawn out or educated. There were few subjects of importance connected with the science of government which had not been carefully examined by him, and his opinions were promptly forthcoming whenever required. His official papers while governor, and his speeches while a member of Congress, are able and statesmanlike, evincing a thorough knowledge of the subjects discussed; and they are written with the perspicuity and good sense characteristic of a man who has something to say and is intent only in lodging his meaning in the minds of those whom he addresses.

But it was the elevated moral and religious character dignifying and adorning the life of Gov. Lumpkin which constituted his highest excellence. He was a Christian statesman, not indifferent to the approbation of his fellow-men, but far more anxious for the honor which comes from above. With some honorable exceptions, politicians make poor church members; but Gov. Lumpkin never furled his religious colors for fear it might lose him the votes of those who were of a different religious faith. Whether at his country home, where he first professed faith in Christ, or at Milledgeville, or in Washington City, or Athens, he always took his stand for Christ, identifying himself with his Baptist brethren, however obscure they might be. Assuming nothing on account of the high honors he had received from the State, he took his place among the humblest members of the church, ever counting it a privilege to be even a door-keeper in the house of God. When the work of the Lord was revived, no one rejoiced more than he; and it was a touching sight to see him exhorting the youthful converts to be faithful to their vows, when they presented themselves for church-membership. His silvery locks and tearful eye and tremulous voice emphasized his pious advice with a power and pathos which subdued every heart.

He courted the confidence of his brethren more than the praises of politicians. Late in life he attended a meeting of the Sarepta Association, and, quite unexpectedly to himself, was elected moderator. His heart was touched by the respect thus expressed, and he subsequently remarked that no office which worldly men had conferred ever gave him such pleasure as the confidence thus exhibited by his brethren in calling him to preside over their deliberations. He was a man of great faith and large heart, and with a nature as tender and sensitive as a woman's. Afflictions severe and frequent kept his heart soft. "He had," said one who knew him most intimately, "as much real, heart-breaking, continued trouble as any one I have ever known, yet such was his faith in God that he could rejoice at all times." He was accustomed to say, "I would rather walk in the dark with God than go alone in the light. My dear Lord appoints all my troubles, and I brush away the coming tears when I think that it is his will."

At the time of his death he was probably the oldest Baptist, as he was certainly among the oldest citizens, of the State. He served his generation faithfully, by the will of God, and then fell asleep,—that

" blessed sleep,
From which none ever wakes to weep."

Lung, Rev. A. H., was born in Rush, Susquehanna Co., Pa., Nov. 1, 1826. He received his first lessons at school from Benj. F. Bently, now Judge Bently, of Williamsport, Pa.

At the age of eleven years he found Christ, and was baptized at thirteen by Rev. Davis Dimock, and became a member of the Rush Baptist church.

For two years he taught school. He then became a student in Hartford Academy, in Northeastern Pennsylvania, and after two and a half years was admitted into Lewisburg University, and graduated in 1853. He entered the theological seminary at Rochester, N. Y., and completed his course in the class of 1855.

Acting as a supply, he preached as opportunity offered until May, 1857, when he became pastor of the Baptist church at Canandaigua, N. Y., and was ordained the following August.

Here he labored with marked success until the breaking out of the war. In January, 1862, he was commissioned as chaplain of the 33d Regiment N. Y. Vols. While on the Peninsula, Va., he was attacked with severe illness, and for several days lay in the hospital at Fortress Monroe at the point of death. Recovering, he remained with his regiment until it was mustered out of service, a little before the battle of Gettysburg, after which he resumed his pastorate at Canandaigua. In September, 1864, he was called to the pastorate of the First Baptist church of Germantown, Philadelphia. Here his ministry was signally blessed in the conversion of many souls. In 1866 he laid the cornerstone of the chapel now known as the Second Baptist church of Germantown, and his church dismissed a colony to aid in forming the organization.

In 1867 he was permitted to enjoy the most gracious revival of his whole ministry. In a single year he gave the hand of fellowship to 202 new members, 179 of whom were received by baptism.

In 1868 he planted a mission in Lower Germantown, erected a chapel, and organized a church, which became the Third Baptist church of Germantown.

He became its pastor, and remained with it with much success until June, 1872. In that year he was called to take the pastorate of the Trinity church of Camden, N. J. He is now in his ninth year with this church, which has grown from 90 to about 400 members. Mr. Lung has baptized 712 persons during his ministry.

He is a member of the board of trustees of Lewisburg University and of South Jersey Institute. He is also a member of the board of managers of the New Jersey Baptist Education Society and of the American Baptist Historical Society. He is a diligent worker, a conscientious Christian, and a successful pastor.

Lunsford, Rev. Lewis, was born in the county of Stafford, Va., about the year 1753. He was baptized by the Rev. Wm. Fristoe, and, uniting with the Potomac church, now Hortwood, he began at once to preach. His labors in the Northern Neck of Virginia were greatly blessed, and many were added to the churches which he himself had organized. In the year 1778 he was chosen pastor of the Moratico church, just then constituted, and he continued in that relation until his death, which occurred Oct. 26, 1793. Mr. Lunsford, in many respects, was a remarkable man. His zeal in the work of his Master is seen in the fact that he would sometimes rise from his sickbed and preach a thrilling sermon to the waiting crowds; also in the fact that he would start on long and wearisome journeys in the most stormy weather to meet either regular or special appointments. His journeyings took him three different times as far as Kentucky, preaching the gospel everywhere, and he was listened to by thronging crowds of anxious and delighted hearers. In his spare hours he was a diligent student, and among his acquirements was quite an accurate knowledge of medicine, which made him specially useful among families to whom he might, otherwise, not have had access. As a man, Lunsford stood among the foremost in his State for consistency of character, amiability of deportment, and an example of all the nobler traits of human nature; while his powers of reasoning, the keenness of his sarcasm, and his undaunted spirit, made him a terror to the wicked. As a preacher, he had but few equals in his day. His presence was commanding; his voice strong and well modulated; his conceptions quick and elevated; and his whole manner attractive in the highest degree. Lunsford, with other Baptists of those days, met with considerable persecution at the hands of the ignorant and the bigoted. He was frequently threatened, sometimes assaulted, and more than once in great danger; but his prudence and perseverance overcame, in a measure, this hostility. Dr. Jeter has said of him, " He was eminently useful, and the churches which he founded have enjoyed a large measure of prosperity. . . . He would have been distinguished in any age and country; . . . and, though taken from the field of labor in the vigor of his days, but few have accomplished more than he for the extension of the Redeemer's kingdom.''

Lush, The Right Honorable Sir Robert, a lord justice of the English High Court of Appeals, has been for many years a prominent member of the Baptist denomination in England. He was born at Shaftesbury, Wiltshire, Oct. 25, 1807, and was educated in his native town. He was called to the bar in 1840, and practised with success in the Chancery courts, his professional services being held in high esteem by the leading commercial men of the metropolis. In 1857 he obtained the dignity of Queen's counsel, and in 1865 he was elevated to the bench and received the honor of knighthood, to which has since been added the dignity of a Privy Counsellor. Sir Robert Lush married the daughter of the Rev. Christopher Woollacot, many years pastor of the venerable church in Little Wild Street, London, and with that church he was associated until the organiza-

THE RIGHT HONORABLE SIR ROBERT LUSH.

tion of the Regent's Park church, under Dr. Landels, in 1857. Since that time he has served the church in the office of deacon with zeal and devotion, and has been a ready helper of the pastor in every good work. He has also taken a lively interest in the Missionary Society, and has been for several years one of the treasurers of the Particular Baptist Fund. Several treatises on points of law attest his professional eminence, and he was gazetted in 1878 as one of the members of the Royal Commission appointed to inquire into the provisions of the Draft Code relating to Indictable Offenses.

Luther, John Hill, D.D., was born in Warren, R. I., June 21, 1824. On his mother's side he is of Huguenot origin, while his ancestors on the father's side were among the Welsh emigrants who founded one of the earliest Baptist churches on the American continent, the Rev. Samuel Luther being the second pastor of the Swansea Baptist church. He graduated at Brown University in 1847. Among his classmates were Prof. G. P. Fisher, of Yale College ; Dr. J. P. Boyce, of the Southern Baptist Theological Seminary ; R. A. Guild, LL.D., of Providence ; and Benjamin Thomas, a missionary to Burmah. He graduated at Newton Theological Seminary in 1850 ; taught three years in Georgia before ordination ; was pastor of Blackswamp and Old Pendleton churches, S. C., 1854–58 ; president of Young Ladies' Seminary in Kansas City, Mo., 1858–61 ; pastor of Miami church during the war, 1861–65 ; of Palmyra

church, 1865–68 ; established *The Central Baptist* in St. Louis, Mo., in 1866, and edited it for nine and a half years ; pastor of Fee Fee church in ·St. Louis Co., Mo., the oldest Protestant church west of the Mississippi ; pastor of Second Baptist church, Galveston, Texas, one year, ending August, 1878 ; now president of Baylor Female College, Independence, Texas. His training under Wayland. Sears, and Hackett, his association with Sherwood and Campbell, of Georgia, Johnson and the elder Manly, of South Carolina, have fitted him for extended usefulness. The journals of Louisville and Boston speak of him as a fine rhetorical scholar, a thorough theologian, and an accomplished editor. William Jewell College conferred on him the de-

JOHN HILL LUTHER, D.D.

gree of D.D. He is also a member of the Phi Beta Kappa Society. He is in the prime of his powers.

Luther, Rev. Robert M., was born in Philadelphia, Pa., in 1842. At the age of fifteen he united with the Chambers Presbyterian church, in Philadelphia. For more than two years he continued his connection with this body, and pursued preparatory studies with a view to entering the Christian ministry. In August, 1859, through witnessing a baptism in the Tabernacle church, Philadelphia, administered by Rev. W. T. Brantly, D.D., he was led to be baptized according to the requirements of the Scriptures.

This course involved a temporary separation from his relatives, and gave him a practical experience of the blessedness of putting his whole trust in the Lord, which determined to some extent his after-course.

He was licensed to preach by the Nicetown church of Philadelphia in 1860, and after completing his studies at Princeton, N. J., was ordained April 4, 1864, by a council called by the Nicetown church. About a year previous to this time he had decided to enter the foreign mission field. In May, 1864, having recently married Calista, only daughter of Rev. Dr. J. H. Vinton, our sainted missionary to the Karens, Mr. Luther and his wife sailed for Burmah, and having joined the Rangoon mission to the Karens, they began there the work of educating the future preachers and teachers of the mission. Mr. Luther was chosen president of the Pegu High and Normal School. The mathematical department was committed to Mrs. Luther. The theological class numbered usually about 25 members, and was conducted entirely by Mr. Luther. The vacation of four months was spent in jungle work and in conducting a series of evangelistic labors among the heathen. Having studied medicine, much of the influence attained over the heathen communities was due to Mr. Luther's medical skill, and thus by a combination of labors he and his faithful wife were enabled to do good service for Christ and the church. They were not appointed by any society, preferring to labor independently, and upon the work of the Rangoon mission they expended their entire property. Excessive labor and exposure ruined Mr. Luther's health, and he was carried on board ship in January, 1870, and supposed to be at the point of death. The voyage, however, and the unwearied care of his devoted companion, saved his life, and he landed, after more than six years absence, in July, 1870, upon his native shores.

He has since been actively engaged in the work of the ministry in this country. He served the Fifth Baptist church of Philadelphia for seven months as stated supply, during which period about 100 were led to Christ, principally from the Sabbath-school. Needing a colder climate in order to control the frequent attacks of the malarial disease contracted in the Burmese jungles, he accepted a call to Bennington, Vt., where he remained for more than nine years, having a very successful pastorate. He resigned his charge at the request of the Executive Committee of the American Baptist Missionary Union, at the same time declining a call from the church at Waltham, Mass., to accept the position of district secretary of the Missionary Union for the Southern District. He entered upon his labors Oct. 1, 1880.

Lyndon, Gov. Jonas, was born in Newport, R. I., March 10, 1704. His relatives were among the honored and respected citizens of his birthplace, and he received in early life a good education. At the age of twenty-six he was chosen clerk of the lower house of the General Assembly, and of the Superior Court of the county of Newport, which offices he held for many years, discharging his duties with great fidelity. The year 1758 is memorable in Rhode Island history, it being the year in which commenced an exciting struggle for the governorship between the friends of Samuel Ward and Stephen Hopkins. Strife raged with great violence until, as we are told, " such was the heart-burning hostility of the belligerent parties as very greatly to impair the enjoyment of domestic tranquillity and interrupt the hospitalities of social life." Success and defeat at different times fell to the lot of the rival candidates, and for ten years the State was the scene of bitter animosity. At last the parties interested seem to have been aware that the time had come to put an end to the quarrel, and amicable arrangements were made for the election of a governor, both Mr. Ward and Mr. Hopkins stepping aside to give place for the introduction of a new name. It is an indication of the esteem in which Jonas Lyndon was held by his fellow-citizens that he was at once selected as a candidate to fill the most important position in the State, and chosen by them to occupy the gubernatorial chair, his term of service commencing May 1, 1768. Gov. Lyndon came into office at a time of great interest in the colonies. Signs of growing hostility to the arbitrary measures of the British government were exhibiting themselves on all hands. In Rhode Island, where there was the declaration of sincere loyalty to the crown, there was no hesitancy in giving utterance to an earnest protest against the infringement of the rights of the citizens. In Bartlett's " Records of the Colony of Rhode Island" we find a lengthy correspondence between Gov. Lyndon and the Earl of Hillsborough touching matters in which the citizens of Rhode Island felt the deepest interest, and a letter also which the governor wrote to the king. In the letter, after giving expression to the most loyal affection for " His Most Excellent Majesty," Gov. Lyndon and the " Company of the English Colony of Rhode Island and Providence Plantations in New England in General Assembly convened, beg leave with great humility to lay before your majesty a representation of our grievances, and to offer our humble supplications for redress." After alluding to the close ties which unite them to the mother-country, and briefly rehearsing the history of the events which led to the establishment of the New England colonies, and dwelling with emphasis on the rights and immunities guaranteed to Rhode Island by the charter of King Charles II., especially the " exclusive right of giving and granting their own money by themselves or by their representatives," the letter of Gov. Lyndon goes on to say, " It is with the greatest concern and grief that your majesty's loyal subjects in this colony find their property given and granted by your majesty's Parliament without their consent. Although we have the highest veneration for that most august body, to whom we cheerfully and readily submit, as to the supreme legislature of the whole empire, in all things consistent with the first and most fundamental rights of nature, yet we humbly conceive that the late acts of Parliament imposing duties and taxes upon your majesty's subjects in America, not for the regulation of commerce merely, but for the express purpose of raising a revenue, thereby giving and granting the property of the Americans, without their consent, to be an infringement of those rights and privileges derived to us from nature, and from the British constitution, and conformed by our charter, and the uninterrupted enjoyment of them for more than a century past." This letter, expressive of the sentiments of the General Assembly of Rhode Island, and signed by its patriotic governor, was accompanied with two others to the Earl of Hillsborough, in which the same views were presented. The three communications were sent to Joseph Sherwood, Esq., the agent of the colony in London, to whom the governor wrote, "By these you will know the sentiments of the General Assembly upon the late acts of Parliament for raising a revenue upon the free inhabitants of the colonies without their consent. They look upon them as incompatible with their rights, and with their existence as a free people; and they have no doubt but that you will exert your utmost endeavors to obtain a repeal of these acts." Those letters to the king and the Earl of Hillsborough produced no change in the policy of the British Parliament. Mr. Sherwood in communicating the circumstances that he had delivered the documents forwarded to his care, writes, "We learned yesterday from one of his majesty's ministers that the legislature is determined not to repeal those acts for the present, but to enforce the execution of them; yet such enforcement is intended to be executed with lenity and mildness if it can; but at all events the execution of those acts will at present be enforced, according to the best information we can get."

The administration of Gov. Lyndon continued but for one year, from May 1, 1768, to May 1, 1769. His declination for another term seems to have been a voluntary act on his part. It may be that he saw that difficulties and dangers were gathering around the colony, and he shrank from the grave responsibilities which might fall upon him as the chief magistrate of the State. His habits of life rather fitted him for the quiet clerical pursuits in which he had so long been engaged. The Hon. J. R. Bartlett speaks of him as "of an amiable and something of a literary character; he 47

had been many years clerk of the Court of Common Pleas for the county of Newport, which place he held undisturbed by either party. He was of mild and inoffensive manners; moderate in politics, as well as in his general deportment. He held the place of governor only one year, when, by his own consent, he left the gubernatorial chair to resume his former office of clerk of the Common Pleas, which place he held until his death."

Although not a communicant, Gov. Lyndon was a warm friend and supporter of the First Baptist church of Newport, and a constant attendant on its worship. In conjunction with another person, Hezekiah Carpenter, he gave the lot on which the church edifice stands, and also a parsonage, which stood on the lot on which the "Perry House" was subsequently built. Upon the occupancy of Newport by the British he removed to Warren, R. I., where he died of smallpox, March 30, 1778.

Lynn, Rev. Benjamin, "the Daniel Boone of the Kentucky pulpit," is known only as the hunter-preacher of Southern Kentucky. The earliest account we have of him is that he was a wandering hunter in the Green River Valley before its settlement. As soon as a few people had settled in stockade forts along the river to which he had given his name, he formed No-Lynn (now called South Fork) church of Separate Baptists, in 1782, according to tradition, in what is now La Rue County. Three years after he gathered Pottingess Creek church, in Nelson County, and a little later Levelwoods church, in La Rue County. His name is connected with the traditions and, in some cases, with the earliest records of the oldest churches located in Southern Kentucky, near the Tennessee line. His name is preserved in No-Lynn (now written Nolin) River, *Lynn* Camp Creek, *Nolin* church, *Lynn* Association, and other localities and religious bodies.

Lyon, Rev. Albert Jonathan, was born in Sturbridge, Mass., July 11, 1848. When he was ten years of age his family removed to Newport, Minn. He was prepared for college by Rev. Dr. Drury. While pursuing his studies he became a Christian, and was baptized by his father, Rev. A. S. Lyon, in June, 1863. One year of his university course was spent in Shurtleff, and the last three in Rochester University, where he graduated in 1871. He entered the Rochester Theological Seminary to prepare for the ministry, and decided to offer himself as a missionary. He sailed from New York Oct. 24, 1877, and arrived at Rangoon December 27. He reached Bhamo Feb. 13, 1878. He was soon attacked by a fever, and died March 15. Thus, on the threshold of life a promising young missionary was cut off. His loss was deeply felt by his companions in Christian labor.

M.

MacArthur, Robert Stuart, D.D., was born at Dalesville, Quebec, Canada, July 31, 1841. His parents came from the Highlands of Scotland to Canada. His father is a Presbyterian, but his

ROBERT STUART MACARTHUR, D.D.

mother and other members of the family are Baptists. He was converted at the age of thirteen, and baptized at Dalesville. He was zealous as a church member, and at eighteen began to hold religious meetings and address the people. He prepared for college at the Canadian Literary Institute at Woodstock, Canada; was graduated at the University of Rochester in 1867, taking in the course the Sophomore prize for declamation, and the gold medal for the best written and delivered oration at graduation. He was licensed to preach Sept. 25, 1868; was graduated in the theological seminary at Rochester in 1870. While in the seminary he preached on Sunday evenings at Lake Avenue chapel, which resulted in many conversions and the organization of a church now flourishing.

In June, 1870, he accepted the call of the Calvary Baptist church, on Twenty-third Street, New York, where he has since labored with marked ability and success. He is now one of the leading ministers in that city.

Macgowan, Rev. John, was born in Edinburgh, Scotland, about 1726. He was converted among the Wesleyan Methodists, and by them ordained to the ministry. Discovering the unscriptural character of Arminianism, he left the Methodists and united with the Congregationalists; light continuing to increase upon him, he followed the Saviour in immersion. In July, 1767, he was ordained pastor of the Devonshire Square church, London. He continued in this office till his death, which occurred Nov. 25, 1780.

Mr. Macgowan had a powerful imagination, a clear intellect, and a heart full of love to Jesus.

As an author, he became well known beyond the limits of his own denomination. His "Dialogues of Devils" has passed through a number of editions, and its pages are well known on both sides of the Atlantic; this book deserves a place in the library of every Christian. His other books are "The Shaver, or Priestcraft Defended; a sermon, occasioned by the expulsion of six young gentlemen from the University of Oxford for praying, reading, and expounding the Scriptures; humbly dedicated to Mr. Vice-Chancellor and the Heads of Houses;" "Sermons on the Book of Ruth;" "The Arian and Socinian Monitor."

Mackenzie, Hon. Alexander, ex-prime minister of the Dominion of Canada, was born Jan. 28, 1822, in Logierait, Perthshire, Scotland. In his boyhood he attended the public schools of Moulin, Dunkeld, and Perth; but at the age of fourteen the death of his father made it necessary for him to engage in industrial pursuits. He learned the business of an architect and builder, which he followed for a time in the neighborhood of Irvine, on the coast of Ayrshire. During his stay there he became the subject of saving grace, and united with the Baptist church in Irvine, then under the pastoral care of the late Dr. Leechman. In 1842 he emigrated to Canada, and settled in Sarnia, on the St. Clair River, where he commenced business as a contractor, meeting with well-merited success. This was a period of great political excitement in the Canadian colony, on the subject of Responsible Government. The masses of the people, in opposition to the ruling faction, demanded that public affairs should no longer be managed under the irresponsible control of Downing Street nominees, but that Cabinet ministers should have seats in the Canadian Legislature, and be responsible to the Parliament of Canada for every executive act.

The contest was long and bitter; but at a general election, in 1848, the Reformers were completely victorious, and popular government became firmly established. It was not possible for a man

HON. ALEXANDER MACKENZIE.

of Mr. Mackenzie's strong political convictions and sympathies to stand idly by when such a struggle was in progress. Very shortly after his arrival in the country he espoused the cause of the people, and was soon recognized as one of its most earnest and fearless advocates. In process of time he became the acknowledged editor of the *Lambton Shield*, a Liberal paper, which he conducted for several years in Sarnia with distinguished ability. He was first elected to Parliament in June, 1861, as member for the county of Lambton, of which Sarnia is the county town, and at every succeeding election he has been returned for the same constituency. From the beginning of his parliamentary career he has taken a prominent part in the councils of the nation. He contributed very largely to the success of the scheme of British American confederation, which was accomplished in 1865. In the fall of that year he was offered a seat in the Federal Cabinet, which he declined because he could not approve the commercial policy of the government. In 1871 he was elected to the local Legislature of Ontario, as representative of West Middlesex, and soon after became a member of the Provincial Administration. But finding it inexpedient for a member of the Federal Parliament to busy himself with local legislation, he resigned both seat and office in 1872, and has since given

his undivided attention to the politics of the Dominion. Soon after this he became the recognized leader of the Liberal party, and in 1873 he was made prime minister of Canada. For five years he discharged the duties of this exalted position with rare wisdom and fidelity, laying the country of his adoption under a debt of gratitude, which history will not fail to record. In 1875–76 he visited Great Britain, where he was warmly welcomed by Queen Victoria and the leading statesmen of the empire. In Scotland his visit was a series of ovations, men of all ranks and parties uniting to do him honor. He received the "freedom" of several Scotch burghs, and many other marks of popular appreciation; but the order of knighthood, tendered him by her majesty in recognition of his distinguished public services, he felt himself obliged to decline.

Mr. Mackenzie is a man of superior mental culture and of great intellectual power. In private life he manifests the most kindly disposition, without the slightest ostentation or assumption. He is (1881) a member of the Jarvis Street Baptist church, Toronto, Ontario, a trustee of the Toronto Baptist College, and a warm friend to the work of the denomination generally.

Maclaren, Alexander, D.D., was born in Glasgow, Scotland, in 1825. His father was for many years a pastor of the Scotch Baptist church in that city, and was held in high reputation by his brethren as an expositor of the divine Word. On his father's removal to Australia, he attended the ministry of Dr. James Paterson, for forty-six years pastor of the Hope Street Baptist church in Glasgow, and was baptized on May 7, 1840. When not much more than sixteen years of age he was entered at Stepney College, London, as a student for the ministry. He made thorough and honorable progress in all the studies of that seminary, and at the close of the course took the B.A. degree at the London University, with the prize for proficiency in the Hebrew and Greek Scriptures. His first settlement was at Portland chapel, Southampton, where a notable minister, Rev. John Pulsford, had preached for a few years, and a very mixed congregation had been gathered. At the time of Mr. Maclaren's settlement the attendance was small, and for some years few, if any, signs of progress appeared. The young minister was for a time uncertain whether his ministry should be continued, but he persevered in his course, making for himself the reputation of an original and reverent thinker. His peculiar treatment of sacred themes in the pulpit, and his unclerical attire, led some of his neighbors to think he was heterodox. But Mr. Maclaren lived down all suspicion of heterodoxy, and it became evident to all that the town possessed in the young Baptist pastor a public teacher of great gifts. The church was filled, and ultimately crowded. In 1858 he was induced to remove to Manchester, to become pastor of a church founded on similar principles of organization to that at Southampton. Since that time his fame as a preacher and writer has steadily risen. The great mercantile city cherishes his name as one of her choice possessions, while the literary and theological world esteems Dr. Maclaren one of the foremost preachers of the age. By the denomination he is regarded as a tower of strength; his attachment to the distinctive tenets of the body being known to all. He filled the chair of the Baptist Union in 1875, and is a zealous promoter of the missions and other denominational enterprises. He is in great request as a lecturer, but for the most part he gives himself to pulpit and pastoral work. A very large edifice recently built is already too small to accommodate the congregation, and the church is the centre of evangelistic activity. Several editions of his sermons have been published on both sides of the Atlantic. He has also written a little book on Italy, which attracted favorable notice. The Edinburgh University gracefully tendered him the degree of D.D. in 1878, in recognition of his distinguished ability as a theologian and a preacher.

Maclay, Archibald, D.D., was born in Killearn, Scotland, May 14, 1778, and died in New

ARCHIBALD MACLAY, D.D.

York, May 2, 1860. The family removed to Glasgow, where he formed the acquaintance of the learned Christian philanthropist, Robert Haldane. To him he made known his wish to prepare for the min-

istry, and Mr. Haldane gave him the means to procure an education. In 1802 he commenced preaching as a Congregationalist at Kirkcaldy, in Fifeshire. In 1804 he was appointed a missionary to the East Indies, but the British government interfered and the project was abandoned. Then, through the advice of Mr. Haldane, he sailed for New York; commenced preaching in Rose Street, and soon organized a Congregational church. Three years later his investigations and convictions led him to unite with the Baptists, and the majority of his church in Rose Street followed him.

A Baptist church, now known as the Tabernacle church, was organized, of which he remained pastor until 1837, when he resigned, to become the general agent of the American and Foreign Bible Society. He labored with great success in this work for thirteen years, traveling over all parts of the United States and the British provinces. The Bible Translation Society of England was one of the results of his labors. In 1850 he assisted in organizing, and became the general agent of the American Bible Union, whose main object was the revision of the English Bible. Becoming dissatisfied with its management, he withdrew from it in 1856, and published his reasons for so doing.

One of his addresses in favor of faithful translations was issued in several languages, and more than a hundred thousand copies of it circulated. He was a superior preacher, an able writer, and a successful minister.

Maclay, Hon. William B., son of Archibald Maclay, D.D., was born in New York in 1812. After four years at the University of New York he was graduated with the highest honors of his class in 1836, the valedictory being awarded to him by the faculty. He was immediately elected a member of the council of the university, which position he still holds. He was elected to the Legislature of New York in 1840, 1841, and 1842. He is known as the author of bills which passed the Legislature which greatly improved the facilities of the higher courts in their work, and lessened the expenses of litigation. In 1842 he drafted a bill, which became a law, establishing the present system of public schools of New York, of which he has the honor of being the founder. Mr. Maclay has been five times elected a representative in Congress from his city. With great credit he served on the Committee of Ways and Means, on the Committee on Naval Affairs, and on other important committees. He was prominent in securing a reduction of letter postage, and published his views in *Hunt's Merchants' Magazine*. He had the faculty of stating his opinions on all public questions with clearness and force, and therefore carried his points in State and national legislation. It is admitted by statesmen that he has given the clearest account of our title to Oregon of any man, and put that matter beyond dispute. Since his retirement from Congress he has held no office except that of commissioner of the New York and Brooklyn Bridge Company. He is a member and supporter of the Madison Avenue Baptist congregation.

Maclay, William W., a grandson of Rev. Dr. Archibald Maclay, was born in the city of New York, March 27, 1845. He was graduated from the U. S. Naval Academy in 1863, and was immediately commissioned ensign in the navy. For gallant conduct he was promoted to the grade of master in 1865. He served with Admiral Porter in both bombardments of Fort Fisher, in 1864 and 1865. In 1867 he was commissioned lieutenant, and in 1868 was again promoted, to lieutenant-commander. In the same year he was made fleet-lieutenant and acting fleet-captain in the U. S. Asiatic Squadron. Again, in 1868, he was appointed instructor of mathematics in the Naval Academy at Annapolis. In 1870 he was elected corresponding member of the U. S. Geographical Society, and was awarded the gold medal by the society on practical engineering, and was then appointed an engineer of the dock commission of the city of New York, which position he still holds. His rapid promotion was the result of his peculiar fitness and ability for the service assigned him. His essay was published in a pamphlet of over fifty pages in the " Transactions of the American Society of Civil Engineers," and shows great industry and remarkable talent in that field of labor.

Macon, Hon. Nathaniel, was born in Warren Co., N. C. He was a soldier of the Revolution, and a member of the U. S. Congress for thirty-six years; whom John Randolph, his life-long friend, remembered in his will, describing him as " the wisest man I ever knew;" and whom Jefferson characterized as " the last of the Romans." He was a great reader of the Bible and a staunch Baptist, because the New Testament made him one. While in college at Princeton, N. J., nigh the then seat of war, in 1777, he enlisted in the Continental army for a short term. When the emergency passed he studied law, but when the seat of war was transferred south he again enlisted. Refusing a commission, he served as a private; was at the fall of Charleston and the defeat at Camden, S. C.; retreated with Greene before Cornwallis in Virginia, but saw his surrender at Yorktown; retired from the army only when the preliminary treaty of peace was signed in 1782, and refused all pay during his service and a pension after the war. His ability and integrity led to his choice, while a youth and in the army, in 1780, as a State senator, where he served till 1785. He opposed the payment of the depreciated State currency except at its market value, on the ground that speculators from covetousness had robbed the soldiers in their need. From 1787 to 1789 he opposed the adoption of the U. S. Constitution as giving a power liable to be abused to the oppression of the people. In 1791 he entered the U. S. Congress; was a member of the lower house till 1815, and Speaker from 1801 to 1806, and was then in the U. S. Senate from 1816 to 1828, serving as president *pro tem.* from 1825 to 1827. He steadily declined cabinet positions, twice refusing Jefferson's efforts to secure his services as postmaster-general, and remonstrating when, in 1824, Virginia cast her twenty-four electoral votes for him as Vice-President. In Congress, as in his State, he opposed speculators in the Continental currency. He supported the second war with Great Britain only on the ground that defensive, not offensive, war was justifiable. He voted for the embargo, but against privateering, the increase of the navy, and the building of forts, except for home defense. From the conviction that true philanthropy, as well as patriotism, could not be mercenary, he voted in 1795 against a grant of lands to the Count de Grasse, and in 1824 to the Marquis de La Fayette. When his principles triumphed in the election of Gen. Jackson, he felt that he could withdraw from national affairs. During his long public life, the sagacity as well as integrity of Mr. Macon won the esteem of all parties. Called in 1835 to preside in the convention that revised the constitution of North Carolina, his marked consistency again appeared. He opposed the " freehold" qualification of voters because it fostered a landed aristocracy. An avowed and devout Christian believer, he opposed all religious tests from official candidates, since the conscientious doubter was more reliable than an unscrupulous taker of an oath. The last public position held by Mr. Macon was that of Presidential elector in 1836, when Mr. Van Buren was chosen. To a friend who blamed his independent course, he explained in these memorable words, under date Warren Co., N. C., Oct. 6, 1836, " I think better of the people than most men. I have tried them in every way, and never found them wanting." He was taken sick only a few hours before his death. He had ordered a plain wooden coffin, and had directed that he should be buried on a rocky knoll, where the plow could never find soil to tear, and that a heap of loose stones only should mark his grave. The only memoir of his life, that of Edward R. Cotton, Baltimore, 1840, is out of print. He died June 29, 1837. The *Democratic Review* for October, 1837, Washington, D. C., thus opens its notice: " There is no man in the history of this country who is destined to a higher or a more perpetual fame than Nathaniel Macon of North Carolina." The pupils of Dr. Wayland will imagine his ethical views echoed as by telephone from

Rhode Island to North Carolina. The line of Christian heroes is not broken in this New World.

Madison University, Hamilton, N. Y., overlooks a village of rare beauty and healthfulness. It is near the geographical centre of the State, and near the centre of a new net-work of railways, which give easy communication with every part of the State. In all of its forms it is sixty years old; was opened as a school in 1820; organized as a seminary, college, and academy in 1834; chartered as a university in 1846. As a university, it at once appropriated the patronage, organism, faculty, classes, alumni, and what of property and other resources there then were in the Hamilton Literary and Theological Institution, and thus were united the vigor of a young life with the strength and prestige of the old.

Early patronage was wide-spread,—drawn not from New York only, but from Vermont, Massachusetts, Connecticut, New Jersey, Pennsylvania, Ohio, and Michigan. The body that founded it was at the time energetic and diffusive. It looked to this school with great hope, and on it concentrated its best offerings and fervent prayers. The school was strictly indigenous, springing up from the smallest of beginnings, brought from no foreign land, borrowing its plan from no existing institution. It grew under the pressure of an outward need and the workings of an inward zeal, and became the expression of a denominational sentiment. Free in its blessings to all, it yet acknowledged its chief allegiance to those representative Baptists who founded it.

The times that gave birth to this enterprise were eventful. The second war with England had closed with the Treaty of Ghent, Dec. 24, 1814, and English domination in the colonies had ceased. The country was stimulated by a new sense of freedom, and the American idea of independence and undisputed sovereignty in the Western World was for the first time having full scope. Emigration, with a fuller tide, was flowing west of the Hudson, and carrying New England arts, manners, education, religion, and thrift over this State, and through it into the Western States.

One of these tides moved down the beautiful valley of the Chenango, and towns, villages, schools, and churches sprung up in the valley and on the hill. Baptists had no college in the State of New York, nor had they any schools for common education or for the education of the ministry. But no Convention was called, no general concert of action, no resolutions passed determining when, where, or how. Almost unconsciously a seed was dropped, a prayer was offered,—

> "Sink, little seed, in the earth's black mould,
> Sink in your grave so wet and so cold;
> Earth I throw over you, darkness must cover you,"—

and the seed germinated and grew, almost unobserved, but vigorously.

In 1817 thirteen men met. They gave one dollar each, and these thirteen dollars were the beginning of the endowment. Soon Dr. Baldwin, of Boston, and thirty others gave 238 volumes, and this was the beginning of the library. A room was given in the chamber, and this was the beginning of the college buildings. Two students came in poverty,—Wade and Kincaid,—and these were the beginning of generations of students. True, such beginnings did not seem auspicious. But faith gave them superhuman energy. This energy had push, and this again, vitalized by the idea that Baptists must have an institution that furnished a complete education, gave unexpected development and growth.

The alumni, most of whom have graduated from some one of the courses,—academical, scientific, collegiate, or theological,—number about 2700. The first two students, Rev. Jonathan Wade, D.D., and Rev. Eugenio Kincaid, D.D., and 80 others, went out as foreign missionaries; 21 are counted as presidents of colleges; 88, professors and principals; 63, authors, legislators, and Congressmen. The alumni are found in all the professions, but the largest number are ministers of the gospel; 130 have been honored with the Doctorate from different colleges and universities, and these alumni are found in every quarter of the globe as true representative men. The three schools have graduated about as follows: from the theological seminary, 700; from the college or university, 830; from the academy or grammar school, 1200.

The annual average of students in attendance is about as follows: in the theological seminary, 35; in the college or university, 102; in Colgate Academy, 100. Ladies not counted in. The first class that took the full college course of four years, and graduated in 1836, numbered 26, 9 of whom are still alive, and 8 of these now living have been honored with the Doctorate. This class entered about fifty years ago.

If you inquire after the faculty that has taught this large body of students, you will find that many are gone,—Rev. Nathaniel Kendrick, D.D., Prof. Daniel Hascall, Prof. Seth S. Whitman, Prof. Joel S. Bacon, D.D., Rev. George W. Eaton, D.D., LL.D., Stephen W. Taylor, LL.D., Rev. John S. Maginnis, D.D., John H. Raymond, LL.D., Rev. Edmund Turney, D.D., Prof. John F. Richardson, Ph.D., Rev. David Weston, D.D., Rev. Barnas Sears, D.D.

The following have resigned: Rev. Thomas J. Conant, D.D., Rev. Asahel C. Kendrick, D.D., William Mather, M.D., Rev. George R. Bliss, D.D., Rev. Albert N. Arnold, D.D., Rev. Prof. Ezra S. Gallup, Prof. Wm. I. Knapp, Prof. Edward Judson, Prof. A. S. Bickmore, Ph.D.

EAST COLLEGE.

WEST COLLEGE.

ALUMNI HALL.

MADISON UNIVERSITY, HAMILTON, N. Y.

The following are the present faculty: Rev. E. Dodge, D.D., LL.D., Professor of Metaphysics and Theology and Præses; Rev. P. B. Spear, D.D., Professor of Hebrew and Latin Emeritus; Rev. A. M. Beebee, D.D., Professor of Logic and Homiletics; Rev. H. Harvey, D.D., Professor of New Testament Exegesis and Pastoral Theology; L. M. Osborn, LL.D., Professor of Natural Sciences; N. L. Andrews, Ph.D., Professor of Greek Language and Literature; J. J. Lewis, A.M., Professor of History, Literature, and Oratory; J. M. Taylor, A.M., Professor of Mathematics; O. Howes, A.M., Professor of Latin and Modern Languages; Rev. W. H. Maynard, D.D., Professor of Moral Philosophy and Ecclesiastical History; Rev. W. R. Brooks, D.D., Lecturer on Natural History; Rev. S. Burnham, A.M., Professor of Hebrew and Old Testament Exegesis; Rev. F. W. Towle, A.M., Professor of Greek Language and Principal of the Colgate Academy; E. P. Sisson, B.P., Professor of Mathematics; J. W. Ford, A.M., Professor of Latin Language; Geo. H. Coffin, Professor of English and Natural Sciences.

The four Presidents.—There have been four presidents. Dr. Nathaniel Kendrick, the first, died Sept. 11, 1848, from a fall and lesion of the spine, being seventy-two years old. He was elected in 1836, but was virtually president during the twenty-eight years of his connection with the institution. He was tall, six feet four, well proportioned, of large brain, lofty forehead, and benevolent expression. He was easily *primus inter pares*, and, of natural right, presided everywhere. His influence was as far-reaching as his name. He had a clear voice, an earnest look, and was truly eloquent. He is well described by B. F. Taylor, the "Jubilee" poet,—

"I see Kendrick's grand form towering up like a king's,
I hear accents at first like the waving of wings;
Now he warms with his theme into true welding weather,
And the word and the blow are delivered together.
The thought and the thinker are all in a glow,
The glasses he whirls from his dome of a brow.
His words that were halting grow freer and bolder,
And he strikes for the truth straight out from the shoulder.
It is Gabriel's trumpet and Gideon's sword,
'Tis the pillar of fire and the breath of the Lord;
It is crash after crash with the tables of stone,
'Tis the thrill of the thunder, the dread of the throne.
Then softer and sweeter his cadences grow;
It was Sinai before, it is Calvary now."

Standing by Dr. Kendrick is Rev. Prof. Daniel Hascall, who came to Hamilton in 1812, and settled as the pastor of the Baptist church. To him is accredited the original idea of a seminary in Hamilton. Dr. Kendrick, in 1816, became pastor of the church at Eaton. These two men supplemented each other, and harmonized in every good work. In 1820, when the "school" was opened, Hascall became Professor of Languages, and Kendrick of Theology. Hascall continued eighteen years and resigned. Kendrick remained till his death.

Around these men rallied other stalwart men, pioneers in the forest, in the churches, and in great enterprises,—Hon. Jonathan Olmsted, Judge Samuel Payne, Deacon William Colgate, Hon. Seneca B. Burchard, Judge James Edmunds, and others, —men ready at all times for great sacrifices and great achievements.

In 1851, Prof. Stephen W. Taylor, LL.D., was elected second president. He was graduated at Hamilton College; had made teaching his lifework; had been from 1834 to 1836 professor or principal of the academy at this institution; had in the mean time founded the university at Lewisburg, Pa., and, after the settlement of the question of removal, returned to Hamilton. He was of the English type, square, strong built, methodical, firm of purpose, a good organizer, and strong executive officer. He was connected with the university in different departments of instruction for eighteen years, and left his mark on its history. He died of disease of the spine, Jan. 7, 1856, at the age of sixty-five.

In 1856, Rev. George W. Eaton, D.D., LL.D., was elected the third president. In mind and body he was cast in a large mould. His features symmetrical, movements graceful, sympathies large, of good nature, in satire powerful, his language felicitous. He was a natural orator. In memory, imagination, and description he was masterly. A scene once before him, he could reproduce with all the freshness and vividness of the reality. His religious emotions and convictions were strong, and constituted the underlying current of his life. He was connected with the university in different capacities—as Professor of Mathematics, of History, of Philosophy, of Theology, and as president—for forty years, and died Aug. 3, 1872, at sixty-eight years of age.

The fourth president is Rev. Ebenezer Dodge, D.D., LL.D., elected in 1868. He has been connected with the university twenty-seven years as Professor of the Evidences of Christianity, of Metaphysics, of Biblical Interpretation, of Theology, and as president. He was graduated from Brown University and Newton Theological Seminary, and has earned a reputation as scholar, teacher, and author that places him among the best thinkers of the age.

The present faculty are well known among the educators of our country. Some who have left us deserve mention. Dr. Barnas Sears, the secretary of the Peabody Fund and former president of Brown; Dr. Thomas J. Conant, a well-known exegete and translator; Dr. A. C. Kendrick, a Greek scholar and author, have helped to make this university. Then the writer's room-mate and class-mate and colleagues in the faculty, Dr. John H. Raymond and Prof. J. F. Richardson, the one president of Vassar and the other Professor of Latin in Rochester, now both departed, have been free to acknowledge their indebtedness chiefly to this university for their success in life's work, and to accept the credit in turn given for their hand in this enterprise. What the university has done for them it can do for all the loyal.

Financial Condition.—The finances of them-selves would make a history, for these are the rock-bottom on which human endeavor builds. It should be noticed that since 1846 two corporations have a hand in this enterprise. The Baptist Edu-cation Society for twenty-seven years had the sole responsibility and management. For the last thirty-three years the Madison University has had the same in all except the nomination of theological professors and the support of needy young men for the ministry. All the salaries and running ex-penses of these three schools fall upon the Madison University. The annual income needed for this corporation is now about $40,000, the salaries alone being $30,000.

It were vain to attempt a history of the night and day struggles, of men who have had to dig a channel and create a depth of current sufficient to float this great enterprise. It were as easy to tell of the hidden forces of nature which underlie all her operations. Only results are known or seen.

When the university was chartered it had no property. It had none in 1850 on the adjustment of the removal controversy. It had only about $52,000 in 1864 when the war closed. Without a hired agency, the most quiet and energetic meas-ures were prosecuted to fill the treasury. The old policy of borrowing and paying was set aside, and the university put upon the most rigid cash sys-tem. For seventeen years, without debt or outside assistance, except from liberal donors, the uni-versity has each year balanced its accounts, draw-ing nothing from endowment funds. No pledges were counted or even reported till they were turned into cash or its equivalent. The progress has not been rapid, but of steady growth. In round num-bers: in 1864, $62,000: in 1865, $121,000; in 1868, $177,000; in 1870, $255,000; in 1874, $304,000; in 1876, $405,000; in 1880, $430,000, for endowment without debt.

Then the unproductive property, buildings, grounds, library, museum, apparatus, president's house, which have come of gifts within the last sixteen years, amount to $120,000 more, making the whole sum raised since the war $550,000. These figures are independent of the Education Society's accounts of scholarships, beneficiaries, and agencies. Deacon Alva Pierce has been treas-urer of the Baptist Educational Society of New York for the last forty-three years, and P. B. Spear treasurer of Madison University for the last seven-teen years.

This university has acted directly and indirectly on the schools and systems of instruction in our country to stimulate the standard for higher at-tainments. It has acted on its own denomination to lift it to a higher plane of moral power. It has given origin to three other universities of similar type, and has co-operated with like institutions to mould the national mind and to give Americans an enviable name among the nations of the earth.

To the above account of the financial prosperity must be added a gift of $50,000, one-half to go to Colgate Academy, given at Commencement in 1880 by Mr. James B. Colgate, of New York, as a thank-offering for his rescue at sea in the winter of 1879–80. See also articles HAMILTON THEOLOGICAL SEMINARY, COLGATE ACADEMY, and the biographical articles of persons alluded to in this sketch. For a full history, see also the historical discourse of President Eaton in Jubilee volume, or "First Half-Century of Madison University."

Magazine, Massachusetts Baptist Mission-ary, has the honor of being the first periodical publication by the Baptists of this country. It was established by the Massachusetts Baptist Mis-sionary Society in September, 1803. The society was organized somewhat more than a year before its executive officers announced a periodical which was felt to be necessary as a medium of communi-cation with the churches, to awaken interest in the cause of missions, and to give publicity to the re-ports and letters of the missionaries in their employ in different sections of the country. Only two numbers, of thirty-two pages each, were issued the first year, and two the second year. The twelfth number of the volume was published Jan. 1, 1808. The second volume was completed in the next two years. The issues were somewhat irregular until a new series was commenced in 1817, the numbers being issued in alternate months till the close of 1824. Since that time it has been published each month down to the present time. The area of its operations was enlarged in 1826, after the removal of the Foreign Mission Board to Boston, and it became the organ of the Triennial Convention, and when the Missionary Union was formed it held the same relation to the new society. Until the close of 1835 the contents of the magazine were of quite a miscellaneous character, being largely biographies of distinguished ministers and laymen, not always Baptists, but persons of note in the other denomi-nations, essays on literary subjects, reviews, letters, journals, etc. From the commencement of 1836 down to this date it is devoted to the publication of articles bearing directly or indirectly on the cause of foreign missions. As the organ of communication between the missionaries and the churches it has rendered invaluable service to the noble cause which it advocates. It is not easy for us to appreciate the eagerness with which in thousands of Baptist families the letters and journals of Boardman and Judson, in the earlier history of foreign missions, and those of Wade and Kincaid, and Dean and Bixby, and very many others in later times, have been read, and what an impulse has been given by their perusal to the great work of evangelizing the nations of the earth. Steady improvement in the magazine has been the aim of its editors. It may safely be said to take a high rank among the class of publications of which it is so good a representative, comparing favorably with the organ of the American Board of Commissioners for Foreign Missions, the *Missionary Herald.*

Magazine, The Baptist.—Our English brethren were occasionally troubled by their relations with *The Evangelical Magazine.* The profits of that publication were to be divided among the widows of Congregational and Baptist ministers. And it was sometimes unkindly hinted that Baptist widows needing its aid were more numerous than those of Independent ministers. Besides, our English brethren felt a crying need for a magazine to spread the tidings of their missions fully before their churches, and to discuss many denominational questions. *The Baptist Magazine* was established in 1809, and it has rendered immense service to our British brethren and to the cause of truth.

Magazine, The Baptist Family.—This pictorial monthly is published in Philadelphia, Pa. J. Eugene Reed, Esq., is editor and proprietor. Its contents include tales, biographical sketches. notes of travel, essays, poems, and editorials. It devotes special attention to the following departments: the young folks, literature, popular science, health in the home, music and art notes, farm and kitchen, and church and ministerial record. The pictures are numerous and well chosen. The editor is one of the most talented young men in the denomination, he is an earnest Baptist, and his magazine is full of interest and instruction. The young and the old read it with delight and profit.

Magee, Rev. John, son of Rev. Thomas Magee, was born in Cork, Ireland, but converted and baptized in St. Stephen, New Brunswick ; studied at the Baptist Seminary, Fredericton ; was ordained pastor of the Baptist church, Mangerville, New Brunswick, in 1840 ; was pastor at Macknaquack and Nashwaak, and performed much missionary work. Died Dec. 23, 1861, after a useful ministry of twenty years.

Magee, Rev. Thomas, was born in Ireland ; converted and baptized in the city of Cork ; ordained in New Brunswick, March, 1831 ; labored

as an evangelist extensively, not only in New Brunswick, but also in the State of Maine. He served the Baptist denomination in a faithful ministry of over twenty years.

Maginnis, John Sharp, D.D., was born of Scotch-Irish parents, in Butler Co., Pa., June 13, 1805. He was brought up a Presbyterian. He was converted young, in Vernon, O., and united with the Baptist church in that place. He received his literary and theological training in Waterville College, Brown University, and Newton Theological Seminary. In October, 1832, he was ordained pastor of the Baptist church of Portland, Me., and soon the community had such an increase that a second church was established. In 1838 he accepted the professorship of Biblical Theology in the institution at Hamilton. In this position he continued with great usefulness until he accepted the chair of Biblical and Pastoral Theology in the new seminary connected with the University of Rochester, and the professorship of Intellectual and Moral Philosophy in the university at the same time. He died Oct. 15, 1852.

In 1844 he received the degree of Doctor of Divinity from Brown University.

Dr. Maginnis was a vigorous Calvinist, and his students went forth with Paul's doctrines enshrined in their hearts or living in their minds to confound the Arminianism which they brought to the seminary, and which prejudice would not permit them to renounce.

He was a man of very extensive and varied learning, often reaching into the distant Christian past, so largely given up to Romanists and Anglicans. He had a powerful and penetrating, as well as a highly-cultured mind. He had not many equals in his day, and very few superiors, as an acute reasoner. While not offensive in his independence, he was unbending when truth required it, or wisdom seemed to demand it.

He was a devout Christian in the minute as well as in the grandest relations of the soul. The churches lost a noble leader and heaven gained a mighty soul when John Sharp Maginnis left his frail body for the skies.

Magoon, Elias Lyman, D.D., was born in Lebanon, N. H., Oct. 20, 1810. His grandfather was a Baptist minister, and a participator in the scenes of the Revolution ; his father an architect, who enjoyed considerable success in his profession and endured protracted sickness.

At sixteen years of age young Magoon was apprenticed to the bricklayer's trade, which he followed to his twentieth year, and by the use of his trowel during his vacations, and in the intervals of study, supported himself through ten years of preparatory studies at New Hampton Academy, Waterville College, and Newton Theological Institution.

He was ordained the night after graduating, in 1839, and he immediately settled at Richmond, Va., as pastor of the Second Baptist church, where he remained six years. A beautiful new edifice was

ELIAS LYMAN MAGOON, D.D.

erected, and all was prosperous until the division arose in the denomination on the question of slavery, which took place while the young pastor was in Europe.

Returning speedily, he quietly resigned, and was at once called to the Ninth Street Baptist church, Cincinnati, but remained in Richmond until a successor was procured. He served in Cincinnati four years, and in 1849 removed to New York, as pastor of the Oliver Street Baptist church. In 1857 he took charge of the First Baptist church in Albany, where he remained ten years, and from it removed to the Broad Street Baptist church, Philadelphia, where he still labors.

Rarely sick, this busy preacher has not been out of employment a single Sunday for forty years. His large and liberal congregation have just celebrated his seventieth birthday with unanimous congratulations, and both leader and people seem never to have been under more favorable auspices than now.

The usual honors of A.B. and A.M. were conferred at Waterville, now Colby University; and, in 1853, Rochester University added the D.D.

Dr. Magoon's published works are "Orators of the American Revolution" (New York, 1848); "Living Orators in America" (New York, 1849); "Proverbs for the People" (Boston, 1848); "Re-

publican Christianity" (Boston, 1849); and "Westward Empire" (New York, 1856). In their day many of these books were sold, but now are out of print.

Dr. Magoon possesses extensive culture, manly independence, a large heart, an unsullied record, and the warm love of throngs in and out of Philadelphia. His ministry has been greatly blessed. and his name is favorably known all over the land.

Main, A. H., is a native of Plainfield, Otsego Co., N. Y., where he was born June 22, 1824. His parents were Alfred and Semantha Main. His father removed from Connecticut to New York in his youth, and thence, in 1846, to Dane Co.. Wis., which has since been the family home. Mr. Main was educated in the common schools of New York. He engaged in mercantile business, and continued it after his removal to Madison, Wis., in 1856, until 1860. That year he became cashier of the Sun Prairie Bank, which position he held until he closed the business, in 1863. For many years Mr. Main has been at the head of one of the largest insurance offices in Madison, and in fact in the Northwest.

When quite young he united with the Baptist church. He is well known by the denomination in the State, and in his own Association, as well as in the State work, he has borne a generous and active part. In his own church at Madison he is a trusted leader; and in the Christian and philanthropic enterprises of the city he is one of the most able and earnest workers.

Maine Baptists.—The oldest incorporated town in what is now the State of Maine was Kittery. The presence of Baptist sentiments was recognized not far from the year 1681. A few Baptists were among the earlier settlers of this place. Among the more prominent of these was William Screven, who suffered no small amount of persecution from the "standing order" on account of his persistent adherence to Baptist principles. A church was formed in 1682, but in less than a year it was broken up and its members scattered. From the dissolution of the church in Kittery, a period of eighty-five years elapsed before the appearance of any other organized body of Baptists. In 1768 a church was formed in Berwick from persons converted under the preaching of Rev. Dr. Hezekiah Smith. That church lived through all the fiery trials of persecution, and is to-day the flourishing church of South Berwick. In a few years other churches were formed. As the district of Maine was settled, Baptist principles everywhere spread and new churches were organized. In the State there are now 13 Associations, embracing 261 churches, with a membership of nearly 21,000 persons.

The Maine Baptist Convention was formed in 1824. Its officers are: President, Rev. H. E.

Robins, D.D.; Vice-President, Rev. S. L. B. Chase; Recording Secretary, Rev. H. S. Burrage; Corresponding Secretary, J. Ricker, D.D. Its permanent invested funds are $9700, and its income from all sources as reported at its last meeting $8400.91.

The Maine Baptist Charitable Society has for its object to contribute to the wants of indigent ministers and to the needy families of deceased ministers. The president is P. Bonney, Esq.

The Maine Baptist Education Society furnishes aid to young men in a course of preparation for the Christian ministry. Its funds amount to nearly $3000. The president of the society is Rev. J. McWhinnie.

The Baptists of Maine constitute one of the strongest and most efficient denominational bodies in the country. Their college, Colby University, with the three academic institutions having a vital connection with it, the Waterville Classical Institute, Hebron Academy, and Hootton Academy, furnish the best facilities for the higher education of the young. An able ministry is guiding and moulding the churches. The spirit of benevolence pervades these churches, and they will compare favorably with other churches in their contributions to all good causes. Every year marks progress and religious enterprise. The Baptists of Maine have no reason to be ashamed of their past record, or of the position which they now hold among the other religious communities of the State.

Major, Samuel C., a deacon of the Fayette church, was born in Franklin Co., Aug. 26, 1805. In 1826 he removed to Fayette Co., Mo. Seven of eleven children survive him. One of them is Hon. Samuel C. Major, Jr. In 1832, Mr. Major was elected a justice of the peace, and held the office for thirteen years. In 1840 he was appointed public administrator. At different times he was mayor of the city of Fayette. He was alive to the public good and to religious interests.

In 1843 he made a profession of faith in Christ, and united with the Fayette Baptist church. He was for years the efficient president of the executive board of the General Association of Missouri. He left for his family the rich legacy of a well-spent life, whose characteristics were unfeigned modesty, strict integrity, genuine friendship, and devoted piety. He died March 13, 1880, aged seventy-five years.

Malcom, Howard, D.D., LL.D., was born in Philadelphia, Pa., Jan. 19, 1799. His father was of Scotch descent, and his mother a lineal descendant of Hugh Roberts, a distinguished Welsh Friend preacher, who was on terms of intimacy with Wm. Penn. Howard's father died at the age of twenty-three, in 1801, leaving his wife and child to the care of her father, John Howard, a retired merchant. This grandfather died when Howard was

nine years of age, and Mrs. Malcom devoted herself to the education of her only child. In 1813 he was placed at school in Burlington, N. J., to be prepared for college, and in September, 1814, he

HOWARD MALCOM, D.D., LL.D.

entered Dickinson College, at the age of fifteen. Most of the students here were insubordinate, and a serious difficulty between students and professors terminated, in April, 1815, in the closing of the institution. In 1815, Howard entered a counting-house to prepare for the life of a merchant, which had long been his ambition. While here, he says in his diary, August, 1815, "I have for some time past been tormented with the fear of dying," the first indication of an awakened conscience. In December an accident to his knee confined him to his room for three weeks, and he says, " This was one of the most merciful providences of God to me. The pain was not so great as to prevent my reading. . . . I learnt more about the Bible than I knew before altogether." On January 1, 1816, he related his experience before the Sansom Street Baptist church, and on the 16th of January this entry appears in his diary, " Have been much disturbed lately with an idea that intrudes itself upon all occasions, viz., that I must shortly quit the counting-house and prepare to go out and proclaim the glad tidings." . . . He was licensed to preach in 1818; entered Princeton Seminary soon after, where he remained until 1820. During these formative years, from 1816 to 1820, young Malcom's experiences, as given copiously in his diary, were most deep and interesting, and characterized by a singular maturity of thought and independence of action. But space here only permits a very brief sketch. He was ordained in April, 1820, was married to Miss Lydia Sheilds May 1, 1820, and in the same month became pastor of the Baptist church at Hudson, N. Y. Here he remained until 1826, when he became first general agent of the American Sunday-School Union. In this capacity he spent nearly two years, and visited all the principal cities of the country in establishing auxiliary societies and local depositories, in raising funds, and in the performance of the varied duties of this responsible mission. In November, 1827, Mr. Malcom became pastor of Federal Street church in Boston. His success with this church was very great. He was also a member of various boards and societies, and he delivered a great many lectures. He was the author, in 1828, of his "Bible Dictionary," which was immensely popular, reaching a circulation of over 200,000 copies, and it is still sold. He also prepared for the press a work on the "Extent of the Atonement," and one on "The Christian Rule of Marriage," both of which had a large sale. He edited "Law's Call," Henry's "Communicant's Companion," and Thomas à Kempis's "Imitation of Christ." Under these labors his health gave way, and in 1831 he spent eight months with his wife in visiting the countries of Europe. In December, 1833, his beloved wife died. In 1835, Mr. Malcom was obliged to resign his pastorate because his voice failed him, and in September, having been chosen to visit foreign missionary stations by the Triennial Convention in Boston, he sailed for Burmah, remaining two and a half years. The issue of this important journey was in the missionary field a cementing and unifying of the labors of our missionaries, and in this country, upon his return, the result was a general increase of interest and contributions for missionary purposes. These were accomplished by his numerous lectures in different parts of the country, and the publication of "Malcom's Travels," a work of 600 pages, which at once became a standard both in this country and Great Britain. Upon his return he could not resume his pastorate, as his voice had not been restored. In 1838 he married Miss Anne R. Dyer, of Boston, and in 1840 he was simultaneously elected to the presidency of Shurtleff College, Ill., and Georgetown College, Ky. He accepted the latter early in 1840. Under his fostering care and indomitable industry the institution received a great impulse. In 1842 he received from Dickinson College the degree of A.M., and the degree of D.D. at the same time from the University of Vermont and Union College, New York. In 1849 he resigned the presidency of Georgetown College, and within a few weeks was called to the pastorate of the Sansom Street church, Philadelphia, and again to the pres-

idency of Shurtleff College. He accepted the former. This church of his youth was not long permitted to have the benefit of his labors, for in 1851 he became the president of the university at Lewisburg, Pa. About this time he edited "Butler's Analogy," with a very full conspectus, which is now used largely as a text-book. After six years of successful labor for the university, Dr. Malcom resigned to complete his "Index to Religious Literature," which was published in 1869. During these years he became deeply interested in building up the American Baptist Historical Society, and to this noble work he was devoted to the end of his life. He was for many years the president of this society, as well as of the American Peace Society, senior vice-president of the Pennsylvania Colonization Society, and was one of the founders of the American Tract Society. In 1878 he sustained a severe trial in the loss of his esteemed and beloved wife, and from this time all his powers rapidly failed, and he died in Philadelphia in March, 1879, in the eighty-first year of his age, a member of the church in which he was converted, baptized, licensed, and ordained. A noble eulogy was pronounced by one in the expressive words, "It would be difficult to name any good cause to which his heart had not been given."

Mallary, Charles Dutton, D.D., was born in West Poultney, Vt., Jan. 23, 1801, and died July 31, 1864. He graduated with the first honor at Middlebury College, Vt., in August, 1817; was baptized and joined the church in 1822; and the same year moved to South Carolina, where he was ordained in 1824, at Columbia. There he married Miss Susan Mary Evans, granddaughter of Rev. Edmund Botsford. In 1830 he removed to Augusta, Ga., and took charge of the Augusta Baptist church. Four years afterwards he became pastor of the church at Milledgeville, but resigned to become the agent for Mercer University, in 1837, laboring as such for three years, when he began a life of evangelistic and pastoral labors for various churches in Middle and Western Georgia, which continued until 1852, when he retired to his farm, near Albany, where he resided, in feeble health, until his death, in 1864. In 1840 he married his second wife, Mrs. Mary E. Welch, a lady of superior worth and talents, who preceded him to the skies by two years.

Dr. Mallary was a man of most uncommon piety, and exerted a more wholesome influence than any other man of the denomination in the State. No other stood higher in the esteem of the brethren; nor did any other of his day, in the truest sense, do more for the cause of God and the denomination in the State. Dawson was a more brilliant orator, and Crawford was more learned and scholarly, but neither surpassed him in the highest and best characteristics, as a preacher. He had clear views of divine truth, and a deep experience of its sanctifying power in the heart. His voice was commanding; his elocution distinct and forcible; his

CHARLES DUTTON MALLARY, D.D.

imagination splendid; his language chaste, and his address affectionate and persuasive. While eminently pure and clear, his style was often ornate, and sometimes arose to sublimity. He loved to preach Christ crucified as the only foundation of a sinner's hope, and to exhibit a sovereign God, working all things after the counsel of his own will. These high themes he discussed with a clear head and a warm heart, and rendered them eminently practical by the manner in which he pressed them on the consciences of his hearers. Thoroughly instructed in the Scriptures, profoundly conversant with the workings of experimental religion, and knowing well " the windings and doublings" of man's deceitful heart, he was exactly fitted to take it captive with the sweet influences of revealed truth.

He had the happy talent of introducing religious subjects in his conversation with others, and of directing their attention to the great interests of eternity. To those who knew him intimately his conversation was simply delightful, for a spirit of piety pervaded almost every sentence of his discourse; and the power of a well-cultivated mind added interest and instruction to the other charms of his conversation. In all that he did and said his profound spirituality shone conspicuously as the distinguishing feature of his character. If any man ever had the full assurance of hope it was he, for

his faith in God seemed to know no misgiving. His chief joy was in the worship of God, and scarcely any possible contingency was permitted to interrupt his family and private devotions. At the domestic altar and in the closet he held sweet communion with the Father of spirits, and came forth to his public ministrations and religious efforts richly imbued with the spirit of his divine Master. Everywhere he exhibited a beautiful consistency of Christian character. He maintained always a close walk with God. His aim in life was to promote the glory of God and the good of mankind. Every personal interest was subordinated to this sublime purpose. No narrow-mindedness checked his expansive charity, for his benevolence embraced the whole human race,—the needy at his own door, and the heathen at the ends of the earth.

His private life was as pure as his sentiments were exalted, and in all his relations with his brethren he was a model of gentleness and unselfish Christian courtesy. He was distinguished for his controlling and peaceful influence in our denominational councils. He was most skillful and prompt to adopt measures in promotion of harmony and efficiency, and, by word and deed, led his brethren onward in the way of truth and righteousness, and in extending the Redeemer's kingdom throughout the world. When money was needed for the interests of the churches and for the spread of the gospel, he was a liberal contributor and a most successful agent in procuring the gifts of others. His example and influence survive in the memory of thousands; the seeds of truth which he has sown are still growing and bringing forth fruit in the lives and hearts of many who heard his voice. Besides these he has left written memorials which will be read with interest and profit for many years to come, among which are his memoirs of Mercer and Botsford, and that most excellent book entitled " Soul Prosperity." While a man of strong convictions and determined purposes, he was as meek and gentle as a lamb. With a will as determined as ever moved a despot, it was so tempered and subdued by grace that it would bear all things, believe all things, hope all things, endure all things. His self-control seemed to be complete; no unkind word or hasty speech, or anything to stain a most consistent and holy life, ever escaped his lips or characterized his actions. He never entered the arena of strife, but would pour oil on the troubled waters, and turn away anger by soft words, and with melting tenderness reprove the erring. So profound was his piety that nothing ever seemed to disturb it. The expression of his countenance when in the pulpit was tender and heavenly. While replete with doctrinal truth, his sermons were full of tenderness and pathos, his greatest strength consisting in what rhetoricians have denominated *unction;* for, as he stood in the pulpit, his audience *felt* that they were in the presence of a man of God. It was this, united to his native good sense, which gave him such influence in religious deliberative assemblies, and secured for him the most profound attention, and rendered his suggestions most likely to meet the approval of his brethren; and it was this, imbuing all his words and actions, which gave him such spiritual power among his brethren, and made him a pillar in the denomination, and which yet gives his memory a fragrance among Georgia Baptists.

Dr. Mallary was a warm advocate of temperance, missionary societies and Sunday-schools, and to the very end of life continued to preach whenever physically able. Though so energetic and laborious during his whole ministry, his services to God and his generation were performed with a feeble body, especially in the last years of his life, when he was subject to frequent attacks of nervous disease, attended with violent pain in the head. His death was peaceful and happy, and his last expression, uttered while gently clapping his hands, was, " Sweet, sweet home !''

Mallary, Hon. Rollin C., was born in Cheshire, Conn., May 27, 1784. Ten years after his birth his parents removed to Poultney, Vt. He was a graduate of Middlebury College, in the class of 1805. He studied law with Horatio Seymour at Middlebury, and Robert Temple at Rutland, and was admitted to the Rutland County bar in March, 1807. He soon became a leading lawyer in the county, and for five years was State attorney. He was elected a member of Congress in 1819, and took his seat in the House of Representatives Jan. 13, 1820. He had several re-elections, and remained a member continuously until his death. He gained a prominent position in Congress, second, perhaps, to no other member from New England in his time, and particularly distinguished himself as a friend and advocate of the " protective system.'' At the commencement of the Twentieth Congress he was made chairman of the Committee on Manufactures, and reported the tariff of 1828, and his efficient efforts doubtless contributed largely to secure its passage.

Mr. Mallary died at Baltimore, Md., in 1831, while on his return home from Washington.

Maltby, Rev. Clark O., was born in Rutland, N. Y., July 19, 1836; educated at the Normal College at Albany, from which he graduated in 1858. Mr. Maltby devoted a number of years to teaching and mercantile pursuits, in both of which he was very successful. Hearing the call of God to preach the gospel, he entered Rochester Theological Seminary in 1874, and graduated in 1877. Before he completed his course he received the unanimous call of the Baptist church in Madison, Wis., to its pastorate. He entered upon his labors

here in the autumn of 1877. The church had been in a very dispirited condition for a number of years. Through Mr. Maltby's pastorate a great change has been effected. The house of worship has been thoroughly repaired, a new organ purchased, a fine congregation gathered, and the future of the church is full of promise. He occupies one of the most important fields in the State,—the capital of the Commonwealth. He is bringing to his work the practical wisdom gained by large experience with men in business relations, mature and finely cultured intellectual powers, and a heart aglow with love for the highest and holiest calling. He has won in his brief ministry the place of a trusted shepherd in his flock, that of a Christian gentleman in the city, and that of a useful and respected minister of Christ throughout the State.

Mangam, William D., was born in Croton, Westchester Co., N. Y.; an uncommon man, with acute, strong, comprehensive mind, and noble, generous impulses; started in the city of New York without capital, and became one of the largest and most successful commission merchants; but lived not for himself; was an unswerving Baptist in his principles; bequeathed to the Clinton Avenue Baptist church of New York City, of which he was a member, a property worth $60,000; was habitually benevolent, and always active and noble.

Manly, Basil, D.D., was born in Chatham Co., N. C., Jan. 25, 1798; baptized Aug. 26, 1816, and licensed to preach in 1818. He graduated at the College of South Carolina, Dec. 3, 1821, with the first honor, when honors were given to such men as Preston, Pettigrew, and O'Neal. He was ordained in 1822. His first settled pastorate was at Edgefield Court-House, S. C., where the savor of his influence is yet felt. In March, 1826, he became pastor of the First Baptist church in Charleston. Seldom has a pastor been so loved by all, saint and sinner, old and young.

After about ten years of most successful labor in Charleston he became president of the State University of Alabama. He was the controlling spirit of the university, and it enjoyed unwonted prosperity for eighteen years under his administration.

In 1855 he returned to Charleston as pastor of the Wentmouth Street church. After four years of fruitful toil, he was again recalled to Alabama as State evangelist, a position for which he was peculiarly fitted, and his labors were abundantly blessed.

He spent the close of his life with his son, Rev. B. Manly, Jr., professor in the Southern Baptist Theological Seminary, at Greenville, S. C. It was a great pleasure to him to see the institution in successful operation for which he had so long labored and prayed. Doubtless he could have adopted the language of Simeon : " Lord, now let-test thou thy servant depart in peace, for mine eyes have seen thy salvation."

BASIL MANLY, D.D.

Dr. Manly was one of the most distinguished ministers with which the Spirit of God ever blessed the Baptist denomination.

Manly, Basil, Jr., D.D., LL.D., son of the distinguished Dr. Basil Manly, of South Carolina, was born in Edgefield District, S. C., Dec. 19, 1825. After attending a preparatory school in Charleston, he became a student at the State University of Alabama, where he graduated in 1843. He then entered Newton Theological Seminary, where he remained for a time, and subsequently graduated at Princeton. He was licensed to preach at Tuscaloosa, Ala., in 1844, where he was ordained in 1848. He preached two years to several country churches in Alabama. In 1850 he accepted a call to the First Baptist church in Richmond, Va. His health failing, in 1854 he superintended the erection of a building, costing $70,000, for the Richmond Female Institute, of which he became principal. In 1859, when the So .thern Baptist Theological Seminary was established at Greenville, S. C., he was elected one of its original professors. While the seminary was suspended during the war he preached to several churches in the neighborhood. Upon the re-opening of the seminary he resumed his professorship, in addition to which he collected money for the support of students, by means of which nearly a hundred young men were enabled to attend the institution. In 1871 he ac-

cepted the presidency of Georgetown College, which position he occupied until 1879, when he again accepted a professorship in the Southern Baptist Theological Seminary, now located at Louisville, Ky. He is regarded as a man of extensive learning and critical scholarship, and is still more highly esteemed for his " meek and quiet spirit" and his constant devotion to the cause of Christ.

Manly, Rev. C. G., was born in Hamden, Geauga Co., O., Jan. 14, 1834 ; converted and baptized in 1851. He attended the district school and Burton Academy, and studied at Kalamazoo and Franklin Colleges. He was ordained at Rolling Prairie, Ind., in February, 1865, and was pastor of the church there one year ; was missionary colporteur of the Baptist Publication Society for Northern Indiana to Southern Michigan one year ; organized the church at Three Oaks, Mich., during this year and became their pastor, and continued with them four years. He came to Kansas in November, 1869, and organized the second Baptist church west of Emporia ; assisted in constituting what is now known as the Southwestern Kansas Baptist Association, in October, 1871. He has been pastor of the Augusta church four years. During the fifteen years that he has been in the ministry he has supervised the building of three meeting-houses and the repairing of two. He is a modest, but faithful and efficient pastor.

Manly, Charles, D.D., was the son of Dr. Basil and Sarah M. Manly, May 28, 1837, in Charleston, S. C. He was prepared for college at Tuscaloosa, Ala., in the school of R. Furman, and was graduated from the University of Alabama July 11, 1855 ; was baptized April 24, 1853 ; licensed to preach by the Tuscaloosa Baptist church Oct. 2, 1855 ; was graduated from the Princeton Theological Seminary, N. J., April 29, 1859, and was ordained pastor of the church in Tuscaloosa, Ala., June 19, 1859. Dr. Manly continued in this field of labor until called to the pastorate of the church in Murfreesborough, Tenn., Sept. 24, 1871, whence he removed to Staunton, Va., as pastor of the church there, Oct. 12, 1873. Dr. Manly was connected, either as professor or president, from 1860 to 1873, with the Alabama Female College ; and, as president, with Union University, Murfreesborough, Tenn., from September, 1871, to September, 1873. The degree of A.M. was conferred upon him by the University of Alabama in 1859, and the degree of D.D. by William Jewell College in 1872. Dr. Manly has contributed frequently to the *Religious Herald*. In his pastoral labors he has been very successful, and is a polished and vigorous preacher. He is now pastor of the church at Greenville, S. C., where he labors with great acceptance and usefulness.

Manning, Rev. Edward, pre-eminent among

the founders of the Baptist denomination in the Maritime Provinces, was born in 1766, in Ireland; brought up in Falmouth, Nova Scotia; awakened by hearing Henry Alline pray, in 1784; converted April 29, 1789, under the ministry of Rev. John Payzant, and soon began to evangelize; had a revival at Kingsclear, New Brunswick, 1793; ordained Oct. 19, 1795; renouncing Pedobaptism, was immersed, in 1797, in Lower Granville, by Rev. Thomas Handley Chipman; became pastor of the Regular Baptist church, Cornwallis, Nova Scotia, Jan. 27, 1808, and continued in it till his death, Jan. 12, 1851; united in forming the Baptist Association, June 23, 1800; was a firm friend of Horton Academy and Acadia College. Edward Manning possessed a massive and powerful intellect, much firmness, keen penetration, great administrative ability, deep Christian experience; was a profound theologian and a very useful minister of Christ.

Manning, James, D.D.—So identified was the life of James Manning with Brown University that the history of the earlier years of that institution is also the history of his life. He was its first president, we might almost say its founder, and he ceased not from laboring for it till the hand of death interposed. The twenty-six years of his connection with the college were years calling forth the highest administrative and financial ability, the utmost prudence and indomitable perseverance; years always crucial to a young and financially feeble institution, but doubly so by the poverty consequent on the war of the Revolution. How ably he accomplished the arduous task that befell him the high position that Brown University occupies among the colleges of our country sufficiently attests.

James Manning was the son of Isaac and Catherine Manning, and was born at Elizabethtown, N. J., Oct. 22, 1738. About the age of eighteen he went to Hopewell, N. J., to prepare for college, under the instruction of the Rev. Isaac Eaton. In 1758 he entered the College of New Jersey, where he graduated four years later with the highest honors of his class. It was at the beginning of his college course that he made a public profession of his faith, and shortly after his graduation he entered the ministry. His marriage to Margaret Stites occurred in 1763, and a year was spent by him in traveling extensively through the country.

There was a strong feeling among the Baptists of their need of an educated ministry, and the Philadelphia Association, which met in 1762, resolved to attempt the establishment of a denominational college in Rhode Island, and to Mr. Manning was intrusted the carrying out of this object. A charter was obtained from the General Assembly in 1764 authorizing the establishment of the College of Rhode Island.

48

Mr. Manning then removed to the town of Warren, about ten miles from Providence, where he established a grammar-school, which soon became a flourishing institution. It was removed to Provi-

JAMES MANNING, D.D.

dence in 1770, and is now in existence as the University Grammar-School. A church was organized in Warren the same year,—1764,—and Mr. Manning was called to the pastorate. In 1765 he was formally appointed " President of the College of Rhode Island, and Professor of Languages, and other branches of learning, with full power to act in these capacities at Warren and elsewhere." The college opened at Warren in 1766 with one student. Three others, however, joined within a few days, and at the first commencement—1769—a class of seven was graduated.

In 1767 was formed the Warren Association, comprising at first but four churches, but it soon extended over New England. Mr. Manning was a prominent and useful member of this body, several times being chosen moderator. The Association was of much benefit to the college, giving it material aid and strength.

It was decided in 1770 that the time had come for the erection of a college building, and Providence was selected for the site, the town and county subscribing £4200 as an inducement thereto. The officers and under-graduates accordingly removed from Warren to Providence, and during the course of the year University Hall was erected. Mr. Manning having resigned the pastorate of the Warren church, and the pastor of the First Baptist church of Providence being desirous of retiring from the duties of his office, that church invited President Manning to preach for them, and in 1771 called him to be their pastor. His power in the pulpit was great, and during his pastorate the church was much blessed. Many additions were made to its membership, and several revivals were experienced, that of 1774 resulting in 104 conversions. The increased prosperity and membership of the church under Mr. Manning's charge made necessary the erection of a new house of worship. With the view also of holding there the commencement exercises of the college, the church was designed and made to be the largest and finest church edifice of the denomination in the colonies.

President Manning continued his arduous and multifarious duties as president, professor, and pastor till the breaking out of the war of the Revolution. The college had been growing in reputation and usefulness, and was fast attaining that high position and influence it now occupies. But the capture of the town by the British forces necessitated the closing of the college, the building being occupied by them as barracks. After their departure it was used as a hospital by the American and French forces, and not till 1782 was the course of instruction permanently resumed. Meanwhile, President Manning occupied himself with his pastoral labors, and efforts for the amelioration of the distress so prevalent during that period.

In 1786, President Manning was chosen by the General Assembly to represent Rhode Island in the Confederation of the States. He was induced to accept the position in the hope of gaining from Congress an appropriation for the use made of the college by the allied forces during the struggle for independence. He was granted leave of absence by the college and church from March until September, when he returned and resumed his duties.

The articles of the Confederation of the States proving inadequate for the purpose designed, a union upon a new basis was proposed. Our national Constitution, framed at Philadelphia in 1787, was adopted by a few of the States with serious opposition, but in some of them, and especially in New England, there was great danger of its final rejection. Dr. Manning, though holding no political office, was deeply interested in the result, believing that upon the adoption of the Constitution the future prosperity of the country depended. He attended the debates on the measure in Boston, and the favorable action of Rhode Island was in a large degree due to his counsels and influence.

Dr. Manning had long felt that his collegiate duties were too great to allow him to give the care his church required, and in 1791 he requested the appointment of a successor. In April of this year he preached his farewell sermon. He had the year

previous expressed a desire to be relieved from his collegiate duties, but before the request had been complied with he was stricken with apoplexy, and his useful life was ended July 29, 1791, in the fifty-third year of his age.

Manning, Rev. James, another founder of the Baptist denomination in Nova Scotia, was born in Ireland in 1764; brought up in Falmouth, Nova Scotia, and awakened under Henry Alline's ministry; converted in 1789, and joined the Congregational church, Rev. John Payzant, pastor; commenced to preach in 1792; evangelized with his brother Edward in New Brunswick, in 1793; in 1796, James, renouncing Pedobaptism, was immersed by Rev. Thomas Handley Chipman. After returning from a second tour with Edward in New Brunswick and Maine, he was ordained pastor of the church in Lower Granville, Sept. 10, 1798, and continued in this position to his death, May 27, 1818. James Manning was an earnest Christian and a faithful minister, a wise counselor and peacemaker in the church of God. His grandson, Rev. J. W. Manning, is now the useful pastor of the North church, Halifax, Nova Scotia.

Manning, Rev. Reuben Elias, late one of the principals of Wayland Academy, a native of Penfield, Monroe Co., N. Y., was born March 31, 1840. His parents removed while he was quite young to Salem, Mich., where he spent his childhood and youth, receiving in the common schools of the neighborhood the rudiments of an education. He devoted himself for a number of years to agricultural pursuits with marked success. As the result of his excellent management he became the owner of a fine farm, and was one of the most successful men in that calling in his neighborhood. He obtained a hope in Christ in 1858, and united with the Baptist church. He had frequent convictions that he was called to preach the gospel, and finally, in 1869, he abandoned farming and began to prepare for the work of the ministry. He graduated from Kalamazoo College, Mich., in 1873, and from the Baptist Theological Seminary at Chicago in 1874. Before graduating he received a call to the pastorate of the Baptist church in Beaver Dam, Wis., and was ordained by this church Feb. 28, 1874. His pastorate here was one of marked success, the church growing in numbers and efficiency, and obtaining through his influence a prominent position in the community.

In September, 1877, having become associated with Prof. N. E. Wood in the principalship of Wayland Academy, he resigned his pastorate to engage in the work of teaching in that institution. He was associate principal with Prof. Wood, and Professor of Mathematics until June, 1880, when he retired from the school with a view of again entering the pastorate.

He is a man of splendid executive abilities, with superior qualities as a pastor.

Mansfield, Rev. David Logan, a distinguished minister in Gasper River Association, was born in Logan Co., Ky., June 8, 1797. In early manhood he became a member of Stony Point church, in his native county. His education was completed at Glasgow, Ky., under the direction of that famous instructor, Rev. R. T. Anderson. He was ordained to the ministry in November, 1823 ; soon after which he became pastor of Providence church, in Warren County, to which he removed in 1825, and there he settled for life. He was pastor of several other churches, and was very successful in leading sinners·to Christ. In the winter of 1832–33 he baptized over 300 persons. He died about 1850.

Mansfield, Rev. James W., the most prominent minister of his day in Little River Association, in Kentucky, was born in Albemarle Co., Va., March 18, 1794. In 1815 he settled in Kentucky, stopping for a few months in Mercer County, where he was baptized, and then locating in Christian County. In 1819 he removed to Caldwell County, where he made his home. In May, 1820, he was licensed to preach, and was ordained pastor of Donaldson church in 1827, in which office he served twenty-five years. At the same time he had charge of three other churches, and from the scarcity of ministers, for a considerable period he preached to several other churches on "week-days." Among the churches he formed is that at Princeton, the county seat of Caldwell. He was fourteen years moderator of Little River Association. He died Oct. 15, 1853.

Manton, Rev. Joseph Randall, A.M., son of Dr. Shadrach and Amey Randall Manton, was born in Providence, R. I., Sept. 28, 1821 ; graduated at Brown University in 1842 ; united with the Fourth Baptist church in Providence ; taught in Worcester Academy ; studied theology at Hamilton, N. Y. ; ordained to the Baptist ministry at Gloucester, Mass., in 1848 ; from delicate health left the New England coast and settled with the church in Clarksville, Tenn., from 1850 to 1857, also preaching widely as an evangelist ; settled with the Vermont Street Baptist church in Quincy, Ill., from 1857 to 1860 ; from impaired health removed and settled with the Baptist church at Minneapolis, Minn., in 1860, and remained till 1865 ; removed to St. Joseph, Mo., and remained four years ; in 1869 settled with the church at Richfield, Minn., where he now labors ; a man of marked talents, true devotion, uncommon culture, and great eloquence, of delicate health, successful in his labors, and greatly esteemed.

Manz, Felix.—See article ANABAPTISTS.

March, John, was born in England ; removed to St. John, New Brunswick, in 1854 ; is a prominent Baptist of that city ; was connected for several years with the press ; is now the efficient secretary of the board of school trustees for St. John ; is earnest and liberal in support of all denominational objects.

March, Rev. Stephen, brother of John March, was born March 28, 1832, in England ; came to New Brunswick in 1854 ; was ordained at St. Francis, New Brunswick, July 5, 1856 ; became, in 1858, pastor of the Baptist church in St. George, New Brunswick ; took charge of the church in Bridgewater, Nova Scotia, in 1862 ; Onslow in 1874 ; Canning in 1877 ; returned to Bridgewater in 1879. He is a good preacher and pastor.

Marchant, Judge Henry, was born at Martha's Vineyard, Mass., in April, 1741. His early education was the best that could be obtained in the schools of Newport, R. I. He completed his studies at Philadelphia, in the institution which subsequently became the University of Pennsylvania. He spent five years in the study of law, and having been admitted to the bar, commenced the practice of his profession at Newport, R. I. Early in his career he advocated the rights of his country against the oppressions of Great Britain. At the October session of the General Assembly, in 1770, he was elected attorney-general of the State, and held this office until May, 1777. In 1771 he went to England in his official character to look after some matters affecting the interests of Rhode Island. While abroad he was brought into intimate relations with gentlemen of the Whig party, upon whom he exerted no little influence in favor of his country. Returning to his home in 1772, and anticipating the troubles which his sagacity told him would soon befall a town so exposed as was Newport, he purchased an estate in Narragansett, whither he moved his family. He was a delegate to the Continental Congress for three years, and was one of the signers of the Articles of Confederation. After the war he returned to Newport, which place he represented for a time in the General Assembly. President Washington appointed him judge of the District Court for Rhode Island, which position he held until his death, Aug. 30, 1796. In his religious sympathies Judge Marchant was a Baptist, and shared, with Roger Williams, an intense love of civil and religious liberty, which was transmitted to his posterity.

Marcom, Rev. J. C., was born in Orange Co., N. C., in 1814 ; baptized in June, 1835, by Thomas Freeman ; ordained in 1847, Revs. J. S. Purefoy, W. T. Brooks, W. A. Atkinson, and T. B. Horton forming the Presbytery ; has served many churches in Wake, Chatham, and Harnett Counties ; was reading clerk of Raleigh Association for thirty years, and moderator for two sessions ; has taught school, and is still active and useful.

Marcy, Gov. William Learned, was born in Southbridge, Mass., Dec. 12, 1786, and died at Ballston Spa, N. Y., July 4, 1857. He was graduated at Brown University, removed to Troy,

GOV. WILLIAM LEARNED MARCY.

N. Y.. studied law, and was admitted to the bar. He served as lieutenant in the war with England, in 1812. In 1816 he was appointed recorder of Troy, and in 1818 he became editor of the *Troy Budget*, a leading daily newspaper. In 1821 he was appointed adjutant-general of the State militia, and in 1823 was elected by the Legislature comptroller of the State, and removed to Albany. In 1829 he was appointed one of the associate justices of the Supreme Court of the State, which office he held till 1831, when he was elected United-States Senator. He served as Senator two years, when he resigned to accept the office of governor of New York. He was re-elected in 1834, and again in 1836. In 1845 he was made Secretary of War by President Polk, a post made peculiarly difficult by hostilities with Mexico. As a member of President Polk's cabinet he distinguished himself in the settlement of the Oregon boundary question, and other matters which engaged the attention of the government. In 1853 he was called into the cabinet of President Pierce to fill the high office of Secretary of State. In his correspondence with Austria, his state papers on Central American affairs, and the Danish Sound dues, his great ability as a writer, a statesman, and diplomatist was demonstrated to the world.

He was a constant attendant and liberal supporter of the Pearl Street Baptist church of Albany, and an ardent admirer of Dr. Bartholomew T. Welch. In all the varied relations of life, public and private, there is no stain on his memory. His wisdom, his faithfulness, and his integrity stand unchallenged, and his memory is justly revered by all who knew him.

Margrave, Rev. William G., was born in Lexington, Va., Nov. 23, 1793. The death of his father when he was an infant left his education entirely to his faithful mother, who was a member of the Presbyterian Church. When seventeen years of age he located in the town of Lewisburg, W. Va., where he spent the remainder of his life.

He was for a long time one of the most ungodly men in Lewisburg, a common drunkard, and a reproach to his neighbors. While engaged in his dissolute pleasures he was powerfully convicted of sin and was converted. It was with difficulty that he found a Baptist preacher to receive him. At length Rev. James O. Alderson heard of him, and came to his home and baptized him, and at once he began to preach. Whatever he did he performed with all his might. And such was the strength of his faith that he never doubted the reality of his conversion, and to the day of his death his zeal knew no abatement. His ministry was greatly blessed. An attack of pneumonia ended his work on the 24th of February, 1867. He died exhorting sinners to repent.

Marsh, Ebenezer, is one of the men long identified with Baptist progress in Southern Illinois. He has been for many years president of the Alton Bank, and a pillar in the Alton Baptist church. He was born in Sturbridge, Mass., Sept. 16, 1806. He was educated at Dudley Academy in that State, but in early life removed to Illinois, being one of the first settlers in Madison County in that State. His first occupation was that of teacher in the Rock Spring Seminary, St. Clair County, an institution founded by Dr. John M. Peck. In 1832 he removed to Alton, engaging first in the insurance business, subsequently as a banker. As a member of the church in Alton, of the Shurtleff College board of trustees, and in other positions of service, he has done much to promote denominational growth in his own section of the State.

Marsh, Rev. J. B., was born in Collisville, N. Y., May 26, 1830; converted at nine; baptized by A. B. Earle in May, 1848; was licensed by the Collisville church, but fearing that he was not called he returned the license; came to Virginia as a missionary of the Sunday-School Union in 1854; to North Carolina in April, 1855; was ordained in Ashville in September, 1858; preached for several years in Western North Carolina, but since 1868 has served churches in Catawba, Iredell, and Davie Counties.

Marsh, Rev. R. H., was born in Chatham Co., N. C., Nov. 8, 1837; graduated at Chapel Hill in 1858; was baptized by Dr. T. C. Teasdale at Chapel Hill, in October, 1856; spent two years at the Southern Baptist Theological Seminary in Greenville, S. C.; was tutor at Wake Forest College in 1859; professor in Oxford Female College in 1862–63: preached in Granville County until 1864, when the death of his father recalled him to Chatham; returned to Oxford in 1868, where he still resides, the blessed pastor of several excellent country churches. Mr. Marsh was for several years the pastor of the Oxford and Henderson churches; was for two sessions moderator of the Flat River Association, and has been for ten years a trustee of Wake Forest College.

Marshall, Rev. Abraham, to whom belongs the highest place among the Baptist pioneer preachers of Georgia, was born April 23, 1748, in the town of Windsor, Conn. He was the son, and probably the oldest, of Daniel Marshall, by his second wife, Martha Stearns. Although he was the subject of deep religious impressions from early childhood, yet it was not until he was about twenty-two years of age that he entertained well-grounded hopes of salvation. At that time his parents were living on Horse Creek, S. C., a few miles north of Augusta, and there, about 1770, he united with the church, and was baptized in the Savannah River. He was immediately seized with a desire to lead others to the Saviour, and soon began to call sinners to repentance. In January, 1771, in company with his parents, he removed to Columbia Co., Ga., and settled on Big Kiokee Creek, about which time he was regularly licensed to preach. He was not ordained, however, until May 20, 1775.

Just as he had chosen his life-work the Revolutionary war broke out, and Georgia became a scene of violence and blood. During almost the entire struggle the people were subject to the combined outrages of Britons, Tories, and Indians. Many sought safety in flight, among whom were those noble and useful men, Edmund Botsford and Silas Mercer, the former never to return as a permanent laborer, and the latter not until after an absence of six years. Abraham Marshall and his venerable father, however, remained at their posts, faithfully preaching the gospel. Sometimes they were taken prisoners, and subjected to great indignities, but through all God mercifully preserved them.

On the 2d of November, 1784, soon after the war closed, Daniel Marshall was called to his reward on high, and his son Abraham succeeded him as pastor of Kiokee church. In May, 1786, some business affairs, in connection with his father's estate, rendered it necessary for Abraham Marshall to visit his native town in Connecticut. He made the trip on horseback, and was absent several months, preaching almost every day during his journey. In New England his sermons drew together vast crowds, some comparing him to Whitefield in the fervor and power of his eloquence.

On his return, in November, 1786, he entered upon his ministerial labors with greater zeal than ever, and, being free from the care of a family, he engaged much in itinerant work, visiting various parts of the State, and preaching the Word with great power. In the spring of 1787 a wonderful revival began, and spread far and wide: thousands attended the ministrations of the gospel, and multitudes were converted. During the year more than 100 were baptized at Kiokee church alone, and the church membership soon increased to more than 300.

Now in the zenith of his powers, Abraham Marshall went everywhere throughout the State, preaching, baptizing, organizing churches, and ordaining ministers. So much assistance did he render in the work of constituting churches, and setting men apart to the ministry, that it was said to be " his business, his trade." This language will not appear extravagant when it is remembered that in three years the number of churches in the Association increased from 7 to 31, and in seven years to 56, while during the same period the ministers had increased from 6 to 36.

Mr. Marshall married Miss Ann Waller, of Virginia, in 1792, being then forty-four years old, and for twenty-three years they lived happily together, she preceding him to their heavenly home by four years only. Four sons were the issue of this marriage, only two of whom attained to manhood.

He retained the pastorship of the Kiokee church until his death,—a period of thirty-five years,—during which it kept its high position as the mother of churches and ministers. He from time to time had the oversight of other churches. In addition, during the whole course of his ministry, he continued his itinerant labors, his praise being emphatically in all the churches.

In the old family mansion, near the Kiokee meeting-house, Mr. Marshall, full of years and honors, ended his earthly life on Sunday, Aug. 15, 1819.

It is not too much to say, in conclusion, that for abundance of labors and general usefulness the first place among the pioneer Baptists of Georgia belongs to Abraham Marshall.

Marshall, Rev. Andrew, was for many years pastor of the First African church of Savannah, Ga. He was born in South Carolina about 1755. He was owned by different masters, and he acted as " body-servant" to President Washington when he visited Savannah. Andrew was a witness of many of the exciting events of the American Revolution and of the war of 1812, and in the latter war he showed a patriotism which proved him to be above the love of money.

Andrew purchased his liberty about the time he was converted, and he joined the church in 1785, and not long after he was licensed to preach. In 1806 he became pastor of the Second Baptist church of Savannah. This was a colored church ; the First church was a white community, of which Dr. Henry Holcombe was pastor. Mr. Marshall's church increased from 1000 to 3000 members, when he led off a colony and formed the First African church. Here his popularity was extraordinary, and his influence and usefulness unbounded. His congregations were overflowing ; his reputation was carried over the whole country, and it was known even in Europe. Andrew Marshall became one of the noted ministers of America. Every visitor who came to Savannah was likely to hear him, and when he was going to officiate in Augusta, Macon, or Charleston, throngs greeted his ministrations, many of whom were respectable white persons. It is said that " the Legislature of Georgia at one time gave him a hearing in an entire body." Sir Charles Lyell and Miss Frederika Bremer attended his church, and published sketches of him. But his wide-spread fame did not injure him. He was an intelligent man, and he was deeply pious ; he had wonderful executive ability in managing his immense church and his secular business ; he had great good sense and untiring perseverance ; he was endowed with a keen perception and with ready arguments, and he would have been a leader in any age or country.

He read and owned many books, among which was Gill's " Commentary," which shaped his theology and gave perseverance and stability to his converts.

" His voice was so deep, sonorous, and tender that its capacity for the expression of pathos was unsurpassed."

He baptized nearly four thousand converts.

He died in Richmond, Va., Dec. 8, 1856, and he was buried in Savannah on the 14th of the same month.

" An immense procession about a mile long, with fifty-eight carriages, either loaned by families in the city to their servants or other colored friends, or occupied, as in many instances, by respectable white people themselves, followed him from his church to his grave." So Andrew Marshall, a colored friend of law and order, a man of genius, a grand Calvinistical Baptist, a man upon whose ministry the broad seal of divine approval conspicuously rested, was honored in life and in death in his native South.

Marshall, Rev. Asa M., for many years one of the most beloved ministers of Georgia, was born in Jones County, Dec. 20, 1832, of parents who were pious and consistent Baptists. A. M. Marshall was left an orphan at seven ; at twenty he professed religion and united with the church ; entered the Freshman class of Mercer in 1856, and graduated in 1860, studying with a view to the ministry. He was ordained in the fall of 1860, and in the following year became chaplain of the 12th Ga. Regiment, and served through the entire war, preaching to the soldiers, nursing the sick, and taking part in those grand revival movements that occurred among the troops which resulted in the salvation of so many. After the war he returned home and entered upon pastoral duty, which he has continued to the present time, serving various churches in Putnam and Greene Counties. As a preacher, he is plain and unaffected, earnest, and forcible. His whole aim seemed to be to edify his churches, hold up the Cross, and win souls to Christ. He is a man of genuine piety, and during his entire ministry has maintained a consistent and godly character. He is a strong friend of missions and Sunday-schools.

Marshall, Rev. Jabez P., eldest son of Rev. Abraham Marshall, was converted after leading a wild life in youth, and became an able and useful minister. He succeeded his father in charge of the Kiokee church, which he served usefully until his death, which occurred in 1832, closing a period of sixty years, during which father, son, and grandson presided over the same church. He wrote a life of his father, and served as clerk of the Georgia Association for a number of years.

Marshall, Rev. William, belonged to one of the most distinguished families of Virginia, and one that has been equally famous in Kentucky. He was a brother of Col. Thomas Marshall, so noted among the pioneers of Kentucky, and an uncle of Chief-Justice John Marshall of the Supreme Court of the United States. He was born in Fauquier Co., Va., in 1735. He grew up to be a brilliant young man, and gave himself much to fashionable amusements. Upon his marriage with the daughter of Rev. John Pickett, a pioneer Baptist minister of that region, he was brought under the influence of the gospel. In 1768 he was converted and baptized. In a short time he began to preach with mighty power, and multitudes were converted. He was a singularly gifted orator, and continued to labor here about twelve years. Meanwhile he was ordained, and became pastor of South River church. As early as 1780 he removed to Kentucky, and settled in Lincoln County. He was active and diligent in the ministry, and in a short time aided in building up a number of churches. After a few years he settled in Shelby County, where he raised up Fox Run church, and became its pastor. He died in 1813.

Marshman, John C., son of the distinguished

missionary, Dr. Marshman, of Serampore, accompanied his parents to India in early childhood, and spent many years in that country in various secular employments, especially identifying himself with Christian journalism. While a mere boy he devoted himself with remarkable zeal and fidelity to the work in which the Serampore missionaries were engaged. In conjunction with his father he labored in producing the Chinese version of the Scriptures. He established the first paper-making works in India, issued the first newspaper published in the Bengali language, and founded the English weekly newspaper, the *Friend of India*, which in his hands became one of the most influential journals in the world, and a potent factor for good in the Indian dependencies of the British crown. In its early days this newspaper escaped suppression from the British authorities by the protection of the Danish government, under whose flag it was published at Serampore. It was outspoken in its denunciation of official misdoings, and fearlessly advocated the civil rights of the native population. But whilst Mr. Marshman continued to be a layman he did efficient work in connection with the Baptist missions, especially devoting himself to the interests of Christian education. He gave a very large proportion of his increasing income year by year to the maintenance of Serampore College and other educational institutions. He became in later life the friend and trusted adviser of the government in important affairs, and few men exercised a greater influence upon the rulers and the ruled. His literary labors also procured him high standing. The lives of Carey, Marshman, and Ward, together with his history of India, will long perpetuate his name. His eminent services were recognized by the English government by the bestowment of the honor of C.S.I. (Companion of the Order of the Star of India). He spent the closing years of life in his native land, enjoying the esteem of a large circle of friends, and serving the cause of Christian missions and philanthropy. He died July 8, 1877, in his eighty-third year, and was followed to his grave by many distinguished men, including Lord Lawrence, formerly governor-general of India, and other famous Anglo-Indian statesmen, who had personally known his character and worth. Mr. Marshman's views concerning missionary methods of operation occasioned much discussion. He held with tenacity the opinion that India and the other Eastern nations could not be converted to Christianity by Europeans, and that the business of missionaries was to raise up "native apostles." When he died he was engaged upon a series of biographies of the viceroys of India, a work for which he was universally regarded as better qualified than any man living.

Marshman, Joshua, D.D., was born at Westbury Leigh, Wiltshire, England, April 20, 1768. He received such education as the village school afforded, and eagerly perused all the books that came within his reach. His love of reading was so notorious, that when he proposed to join the Baptist church, the members were afraid he had too much head knowledge of the gospel to have much heart experience of it, but their apprehensions in time passed away. In 1794 he removed to Bristol to take charge of a school supported by the Broadmead Baptist church, and was soon afterwards baptized and received into church fellowship. He joined the classes of the theological seminary, and for upwards of five years studied the classics, and also Hebrew and Syriac. The periodical accounts which recorded the labors of Carey awakened in him a missionary spirit, and in 1799 he and his wife offered themselves for service in India. Three other missionaries embarked with him in an American ship, the "Criterion," on the 29th of May, 1799, and landed at Serampore on October 13, seeking protection under the Danish flag from their anti-missionary countrymen in Calcutta. When the authorities found that the missionaries had arrived without a permit from the India House, they threatened Capt. Wickes, of the "Criterion," that his vessel should be refused entry unless the four missionaries appeared at the police-office, and entered into engagements to return forthwith to England. Representations were, however, made to the governor-general, Lord Wellesley, which resulted in the abandonment of all hostile proceedings against the vessel, but the missionaries were compelled to remain at Serampore. After the establishment of the mission in Serampore, Mr. and Mrs. Marshman opened boarding-schools, which soon attracted large numbers of scholars, and were a source of permanent income to the mission. In association with Mr. Marshman, Carey labored on translations of the Scriptures, preaching, and other missionary work. In 1806, Mr. Marshman commenced the study of Chinese, with the view of translating the Scriptures into that language, and, after fifteen years of arduous toil, he carried through the press the first Chinese Bible. He received the diploma of D.D. from Brown University in June, 1811. In 1814 he published "Key to the Chinese Language," towards the expense of which the government of India voted £1000. On the 31st of May, 1818, the first newspaper ever printed in any Eastern language was issued from the Serampore press, and was very popular among the natives. After the death of Dr. Carey, his already enfeebled constitution gave way, and although he rallied for a time, the capacity for work was exhausted. He died on Dec. 4, 1837, and his remains were laid in the cemetery with his departed colleagues.

Marston, Rev. Charles C., pastor of the Baptist church in Clinton, Wis., a native of West Medway, Mass., was born in 1849. When he was but a child his parents removed to Washington Co., Iowa. At the age of twelve he made a public profession of faith in Christ. His parents were Baptists, and he had been from early youth instructed in this faith. But no Baptist church had yet been organized in the vicinity where he resided, and he united with the Winebrennarians,—a denomination holding views of faith and practice in some respects similar to those of Baptists. By them Mr. Marston was licensed in 1865, and ordained to the work of the ministry in 1866. He held pastorates at Boiling Springs, Spring Grove, and Lanark, Ill. In 1876 he united with the Michigan Avenue Baptist church of Chicago, Ill. He has since been fully identified with the Baptist denomination. He completed the usual course of study in the University of Chicago, preaching for the Norwood Park Baptist church while prosecuting his studies in the university. In 1878, having been called to the pastorate of the Baptist church in Clinton, Wis., he removed to that place, which continues to be his field of labor. His ministry has been more than usually successful, having been attended with revivals of considerable power. He is doctrinal in his preaching, a close student of the Bible, and one of the promising young ministers of the State.

Marston, S. W., D.D., was born in York Co., Me., July 23, 1826. He studied in academies in Maine and New Hampshire, and for four years in New Hampton Institute, and graduated with honor in 1852. He was baptized by Rev. Abner Mason in 1847, in Medway, Mass.; was pastor at Brookfield in 1852, and in 1853 went South for his health, and in a short time returned to Middleborough, Mass., and taught two years, and preached during this time at New Bedford. Subsequently he taught in Greenville, Ill., and in Burlington, Iowa. In 1860 he became pastor at Plainfield, Ill. In 1865 he took charge of the Boonville Institute in Missouri. In 1868 he began his Sunday-school labors in Missouri, and in five years he increased the number of Baptist schools from 74 to 603, and organized a Sunday-school Convention in each of the 59 Associations of the State, auxiliary to the State Sunday-school Convention, of which he was the secretary. In October, 1873, he became superintendent of State missions for Missouri, which position he held for three years, and then was appointed by President Grant United States agent for 57,000 civilized Indians in the Indian Territory, whose affairs he managed with great satisfaction to the government. In 1879 he was appointed by the American Baptist Home Mission Society superintendent of freedmen's missions in the South, which position he now holds. Dr. Marston is a thorough

Baptist, a logical thinker, an able preacher, and a successful minister of Jesus.

Martin, Rev. A. F., was born in 1812 in Missouri, and converted in 1830; has been preaching forty-seven years in Linn Co., Mo.; has served as missionary of the General Association of Missouri, and performed evangelistic work, through which many have been converted. He was ordained in 1833. His parents were constituent members of the Fee Fee church, St. Louis County, and his brother, Dr. Martin, was a constituent member of the Fourth Baptist church of St. Louis.

Martin, Hon. Isaac L., was born in New Brunswick, N. J., Jan. 11, 1829. He early entered into business with his father, a merchant in his native city. After years of success his father transferred the business to his sons. Mr. Isaac Martin has long been a director of the National Bank of New Jersey and of the New Brunswick Fire Insurance Company. After serving in the Legislature two terms he was, in 1879, elected senator from Middlesex County for three years. Mr. Martin while yet a youth united with the First Baptist church in New Brunswick; has been in the board of trustees, the Sunday-school, and other departments of church work.

Martin, Rev. James, B.A. (of London University), late president of the Baptist Association, Victoria, Australia, and distinguished among scholars and theologians for his translations from the German, was born in London, England, in September, 1821, and at an early age joined the church at Hackney. He studied at Stepney College, and then proceeded to Bonn, in Germany. Having completed his course with success, he settled first at Lymington, and subsequently at Stockport, Edinburgh, and Nottingham. During his nine years' pastorate at Nottingham he rose rapidly to distinction as a preacher and theologian. He translated upwards of twenty volumes of Clark's Foreign Theological Library, including several of the best works of Keil, Delitzsch, Kurtz, Ebrard, and Hengstenberg. In 1869 he received a pressing call from Melbourne, Australia, which at length he accepted. The position involved the honor and responsibility of denominational leadership in that rapidly growing city and colony, and high expectations were cherished by all who knew him, which, in his brief Australian career, were in no scanty measure fulfilled. But in the full tide of success and honor he was stricken down, and died Feb. 13, 1877, in his fifty-sixth year. Both in England and Australia his death was keenly felt as a severe bereavement to the denomination and the Christian church at large. Mr. Martin published little except an able treatise on "The Origin and History of the New Testament."

Martin, Rev. M. T., proprietor of *Baptist Record*,

Jackson, Miss., was born in 1842; was nine years Professor of Mathematics in Mississippi College; acted as agent of the college after the war; redeemed the property from mortgage; added $50,000 to the endowment, and extinguished an incumbrance in the form of scholarships, amounting to $42,000; began to preach in 1877, and is one of the most efficient evangelists in the State.

Martin, Rev. Robert, a prominent minister in North Louisiana Association, La., was born in South Carolina in 1814; began to preach in Georgia in 1841; removed to Bossier Parish, La., in 1852, and became the successful missionary of the Baptist State Convention, and was instrumental in planting most of the churches in Bossier Parish. After three years in this relation he became supply for a number of the churches which were planted by his instrumentality, and he has since labored in that capacity, supplying Salem, New Hope, Sarepta, and Spring Branch, in the parish of Bossier.

Martin, Rev. Samuel Sanford, was born April 15, 1820, in Colisville, Broome Co., N. Y., and was baptized at the age of sixteen. After a three years course at Hamilton, he was ordained at Colisville, Sept. 27, 1843. Removing to Illinois, he became pastor of the Knoxville, now Galesburg, Baptist church. His pastorates since have been at Lamoille, where he helped to build the first Baptist house of worship, at Dixon, Tremont, Delavan, —where also under his labors the first meeting-house was built, and Rev. D. H. Drake, missionary to Kurnool, India, was baptized,—Washington, Forest City,—a church being here gathered,—and San José. Mr. Martin is numbered with those in Illinois whose chief work has been the laying of foundations.

Martin, William E., A.M., principal of the University Academy, Lewisburg, Pa., was born in May, 1845, in Saltsburg, Indiana Co., Pa. Here he received his academic training. In 1868 he was baptized by Rev. Azariah Shadrach, and united with the Saltsburg Baptist church. In the following year he entered the Junior class in the university at Lewisburg, from which he was graduated in the class of 1871.

After a year spent in teaching in the preparatory department of the university, he entered the Crozer Theological Seminary, in fulfillment of his original purpose to prepare himself for the ministry. After a single session, however, he was recalled to the work of instruction at Lewisburg. He was principal of the English Academy until 1878, when the classical and English departments of the preparatory work of the university were consolidated into the University Academy, with Principal Martin at its head. He has been very earnest in his purpose to elevate the standard of scholarship. Under his excellent management,

and with his constant and self-denying labors, the academy is a success.

Maryland, The Baptists of.—The first Baptist church in Maryland was formed in 1742, at Chestnut Ridge, about ten miles north of Baltimore City. Its founder was Henry Sator, or Sater, a General Baptist, who came from England in 1709. It has ever since been known as "Sater's" church. It has a small brick meeting-house in a beautiful grove of about four acres, containing numerous graves of the Baptist fathers and their descendants. This church at first increased rapidly. In four years it numbered 181 members, and extended into Opeckon and Ketockton, in Virginia. In 1754 a church, principally originating from Sater's, was founded at Winter Run, in Harford County, which has since borne the name of the Harford church. For forty years it was under the pastoral care of the Rev. John Davis, who died in 1809, in the eighty-eighth year of his age, venerated and beloved. "Sater's" became nearly extinct under Antinomian influence, and is now a very feeble body.

The First Baptist church of Baltimore was organized Jan. 15, 1785, with 11 members, all of whom, except its pastor, the Rev. Lewis Richards, were dismissed from the Harford church. From the Harford church also arose the churches at Taneytown and Gunpowder. The First church worshiped until 1817 in a small house on the corner of Front and Fayette Streets. In that year they completed the edifice in Sharp Street, so long known as the "Old Round-top," at a cost of $50,000; but the debt thereby incurred was not entirely removed for thirty-five years, and seriously hindered the prosperity of the church. During ninety-five years it has had only five pastors, viz.: Lewis Richards, thirty-three years; E. J. Reis, three years; John Finlay, thirteen years; Stephen P. Hill, sixteen years; and J. W. M. Williams, the present pastor, nearly thirty years. From it originated several churches, principally the Waverly church, and the Seventh church in 1845, and the Lee Street church in 1854. In the year 1878, the vicinity of the meeting-house having become almost entirely occupied by warehouses, the church removed to Lafayette Avenue, near Tremont Street, where, in a new and beautiful house of white marble, renewed prosperity has been enjoyed.

The Second church of Baltimore was founded in 1797, by Elder John Healey, from Leicester, England, who with five others came to Baltimore in 1795. Elder Healey remained as pastor for *more than fifty years*, and died June 19, 1848. To this church belongs the honor of having established the first Sunday-school in the State of Maryland, in the year 1804.

The High Street Baptist church was constituted

Feb. 14, 1835, of 10 members, six of whom were Wm. Crane and his family, and two, the Rev. J. G. Binney, its first pastor, and his wife. It was at first called the "Calvert Street church." Mr. Binney remained but a few months, and in January, 1836, the Rev. George F. Adams became the pastor, and continued as such for about seven years, during which time the church increased to nearly 300 members. In 1843, the Rev. Jonathan Aldrich succeeded Mr. Adams, and in 1844 the church left the Calvert Street house and built a new one on High Street, first occupied in November of 1845. A crushing debt had been incurred in its erection, and in July, 1846, the pastor resigned and the house was offered for sale. After months of anxious solicitude relief was obtained by the concessions of creditors, the extra efforts of the church, the liberality of friends, and the election of a pastor, the Rev. Frankin Wilson, who served without salary, thus permitting the entire income to aid in reducing the debt. In November. 1850, a disease of the throat compelled Dr. Wilson to suspend his labors; but, in a large measure owing to his liberality, the house was saved, and the church has continued to prosper under his successors, the Revs. H. J. Chandler, John Berg, L. W. Seeley, E. R. Hera, Geo. P. Nice, R. B. Kelsay, M. R. Watkinson, and J. T. Craig. The above named may rightly be called the "mother-churches," as most of the others (except the Nanjemoy and Good Hope churches in Charles County) sprang from them either directly or indirectly.

ASSOCIATIONS.

The Salisbury Association, on the eastern shore of the Chesapeake Bay, was formed in 1782, under Elijah Baker and Philip Hughes. It probably never had over 600 members, and, having adopted anti-mission views, has almost dwindled into non-entity.

The first meeting of the *Baltimore Baptist Association* was held at Fredericktown, in August, 1793. Six churches, with 226 members, were represented there. It increased slowly, until, in 1820, it had 18 churches, with 1362 members. It was decidedly in favor of domestic and foreign missionary operations for more than forty years, with a few dissentients on the part of some pastors and churches. The anti-missionary spirit culminated at the meeting held in May, 1836, at Black Rock, in the adoption, by a vote of sixteen to nine, of resolutions against "uniting with worldly societies," and in a declaration of non-fellowship with those who had done so. By "worldly societies" were meant missionary, Sabbath-school, Bible, tract, and temperance societies. The Association was at once divided, and the two sections have since had only a nominal existence.

The Maryland Baptist Union Association was or-

ganized Oct. 27, 1836, with only 6 churches, 4 ministers, and 345 members. The ministers were Stephen P. Hill, Geo. F. Adams, Thos. Leahman, and Joseph Mettam. From the beginning it was a missionary body, and in favor of all the objects denounced by the "Black Rock" resolutions. For many years it included several churches in the District of Columbia; but in 1877 six white churches there withdrew to form a separate Association, and in 1879 the few colored churches of the District also withdrew, so that the Association is now confined to Maryland alone. Its present statistics will be found below. The largest number ever reported was in 1877, before the withdrawal of the District churches, viz., 51 ministers, 60 churches, 10,716 members. Nearly all the churches outside of Baltimore have been aided more or less by its contributions, and several of those within the city. During the forty-four years of its existence it has disbursed, in sustaining missionaries and aiding feeble churches, $130,518, besides assisting indirectly in the erection of a large number of meeting-houses, the education of young men for the ministry, the support and endowment of the Columbian University, and the distribution of Bibles and religious publications. A weekly paper, the *True Union,* was originated under its auspices in 1850, and continued until suspended by the war in 1861. Afterwards, in 1865, the *Maryland Baptist,* a monthly, was issued for one year. Subsequently, the Rev. O. F. Flippo for several years published a monthly,—the *Baptist Visitor.* The Association has an invested fund of $11,205 derived from special legacies, a "Superannuated Ministers' and Widows' Fund" of $3061.22, and a "Church Building Loan Fund" of $606.81.

The Baltimore Baptist Church-Extension Society, organized in 1854, has been of much value in planting churches in the city. The Lee Street and Franklin Square meeting-houses were built under its auspices, and more recently the Leadenhall Street house; and a new and handsome edifice for the First Colored church has been partly erected by this society aiding the members of the church. The recent progress of the colored Baptists in Baltimore has been wonderful. The First church, founded in 1836, had only 80 members in 1868, after an existence of thirty-two years; it now has 350. In 1848, the Rev. Noah Davis, then a slave in Virginia, was aided by Baltimore Baptists in purchasing his freedom. He became a missionary of the Association, and a small church was organized under his ministry in 1852. That church, united with fragments of others, has now grown to be the largest one in the Association; and the colored Baptists, who, twelve years ago, were comprised in 2 churches, with 273 members, have now 5 churches, with 2726 members.

REVIVALS.

Many revivals have occurred at intervals in separate churches, but some have had a general and marked influence on the denomination. The first was in 1839, when the additions by baptism (606) were more numerous than the whole previous aggregate of members (565). In 1857 the baptisms reported were 559. From 1870 to the present time (except in 1871-72) the annual additions have ranged from 531 to 1085.

EMINENT MINISTERS.

This sketch would be very incomplete without further reference to at least two brethren whose labors, under God, have been greatly blessed in building up the cause of truth in Maryland,—the Rev. George F. Adams and Richard Fuller. To Brother Adams was largely due the origin of the Maryland Baptist Union Association. As pastor of two churches in the city, and two or three in the country, as general State missionary for several years, as editor, historian, as a faithful, zealous, wise, consistent, devoted man of God, his labors and his character contributed much to the extension of our principles and the establishment of the churches in the faith. He died April 16, 1877, universally lamented, leaving behind him a precious memory, and a rich treasure in the "History of the Maryland Churches," carefully prepared by him.

The Rev. Richard Fuller, D.D., entered upon the pastorate of the Seventh church, Baltimore, June 1, 1847. After twenty-four years' labor there, during which the church increased from 104 to 1170 members, he went out, in 1871, with 134 members, to establish the Eutaw Place church. At the time of his death, October, 1876, that church had increased to 468 members. But his usefulness must not be measured by the hundreds converted and baptized under his ministry. The influence of his noble character, his splendid talents, his impassioned eloquence, his fame as one of the greatest pulpit orators of the age, his powerful advocacy of every philanthropic and Christian enterprise, did much to give his beloved denomination and the truth it maintains a higher estimate in the public mind, and to win for it a wider sway. Such transcendent abilities so thoroughly consecrated to Jesus, and permitted for nearly thirty years to shed their sacred lustre upon Baltimore and the surrounding country, formed indeed one of the richest gifts of God to the Baptists of Maryland.

Quite a large number of ministers have gone forth from the Maryland Baptist churches, many of them to do good in other States. Among them are the honored names of Spencer H. Cone, Bartholomew T. Welsh, Wm. Carey Crane, Elijah S. Dulin, Noah Davis, the founder of the American Baptist Publication Society, and Benjamin Griffith, for so many years its efficient corresponding secretary; the missionaries Rosewell H. Graves, Brethren Bond and Rohrer, whose mysterious loss at sea occasioned such profound sorrow; J. L. Holmes, murdered by the rebels in China; Jno. A. McKean, J. H. Phillips, J. B. T. Patterson, Levi Thorne, Isaac Cole, S. C. Borton, J. W. T. Boothe, J. L. Lodge, J. T. Beckley, C. J. Thompson, Richard B. Cook, J. H. Brittain, George McCullough, H. W. Wyer, W. S. Crowley, and many others.

CONDITION IN 1880.

Nearly all the Baptist churches in Maryland are connected with the Maryland Union Baptist Association. At its session in November, 1879, reports were received from 47 churches, 14 of them being in Baltimore City, and 33 in the country or in the smaller towns. The strength of the denomination is in the city of Baltimore. Ten of the city churches are white, numbering 3641 members; four colored, numbering 2686 members. Twenty-three of the other churches are white, numbering 1386 members; ten colored, numbering 605. In other words, there are in Maryland 8318 Baptists, of whom 5027 are white, 3291 colored. Of these, 6327 are in 14 churches in Baltimore, averaging over 452 members to each church, while only 1991 are in the 33 churches of the State at large, averaging about 60 members to each church. The largest church is the Union Colored church of Baltimore, with 1497 members. The largest white church is the Seventh, with 590 members, though several others nearly equal it; for instance, the First church, 528; the Eutaw Place, 519; the Franklin Square, 494; the High Street, 438; the Lee Street, 407; the Second, Broadway, 328.

All the city churches have good substantial houses of worship, none very large, but several of considerable architectural beauty. They are well located, at proper distances from each other, so as to reach all parts of the city. All except four, one German and one colored, are self-supporting and liberal in benevolent contributions. With each is connected a flourishing Sunday-school.

Many of the churches in the State are not well located. Of the 23 white churches only 7 are in towns or cities of over 2000 population, the remainder being in small villages or country places. All of them have suitable meeting-houses, generally paid for. Partly for want of material, their growth has been slow, and their struggles for existence severe. Several have become extinct.

Mason, Alanson P., D.D., was born in Cheshire, Mass., Jan. 19, 1813. He was graduated from Madison University in the class of 1836, and from the Hamilton Theological Seminary in 1838. He was pastor of four churches in the State of New

York,—Clockville, Groton, Binghamton, and Williamsburg, and of the First Baptist churches in Fall River and Chelsea, Mass. After serving the latter church for thirteen years, he resigned his pastorate to enter upon the duties of district secretary for New England of the American Baptist Home Mission Society. In this position he is now serving his thirteenth year. While pastor in Chelsea he was for seven years a member of the board of overseers of Harvard University by appointment of the Massachusetts Legislature. He received the degree of Doctor of Divinity from Madison University in 1859.

Mason, Rev. Auguste Francke, pastor of the Baptist church in Milwaukee, Mich., was born in Clockville, N. Y., Nov. 17, 1839. He is a descendant of sturdy old Samson Mason, a dragoon of the republican army of Oliver Cromwell, who came to America in 1650, and concerning whom the records of Rehoboth, Mass., contain the following curious mention: "Dec. 9, 1657.—It was voted that Samson Mason should have free liberty to sojourn with us, and to buy house, lands, or meadow, if he see cause for his settlement, provided that he lives peaceably and quietly." Anabaptist as he was, this permission was regarded a peculiar act of grace on the part of the New England Puritans. For generation after generation the descendants of Samson Mason were pastors of the Baptist church in Swanzey, Mass. The Rev. Alanson P. Mason, D.D., the sixth generation from the old Cromwellian, and Sarah Robinson Mason, were the parents of Auguste Francke Mason. Mr. Mason's father, an able and prominent minister of the Baptist church, after a pastorate at Clockville, N. Y., was settled for six years at Brooklyn, N. Y., and thirteen years at Chelsea, Mass. Mr. Mason's mother was the daughter of a New England farmer, and a woman of superior intelligence and great force of character. She was educated at Mrs. Willard's well-known seminary, Troy, N. Y., in which institution she afterwards became a teacher. Mr. Mason was educated at Chelsea, Mass. After leaving the high school he became a clerk in the counting-room of a mercantile house in Boston, where his energy and business aptitude pointed to a successful career. In 1857, during the great religious awakening, he was the subject of deep religious convictions, which caused him to withdraw from mercantile life and to turn his attention to the gospel ministry. After a course of study at Madison University, from which he afterwards received the degree of A.M., he was ordained at Barnstable, Mass., in June, 1859. Although comparatively a young man, his ministerial labors extend over a period of nearly twenty years, and have been attended with marked success. He has been settled as pastor at Meriden, New York City,

Leominster, and Washington, D. C. Mr. Mason is an earnest and forcible speaker, and his sermons exhibit much originality of thought and scholarly research.

Mason, Rev. Darwin N., was born in Indiana, and reared in New York, on the shore of Lake Erie, on a farm. He graduated at the State Normal School in Albany in 1856. He was ordained, and settled as pastor at Rochester, Minn., in 1861; removed to Iowa in 1868; served as pastor in Cedar Falls, as principal in Des Moines University, as pastor in Indianola, Boone, Marshalltown, and Marion. He was secretary of the Iowa Baptist State Convention 1874–77. He has been in his present pastorate at Marion since 1876.

Mason, Francis, D.D., was born in York, England, April 2, 1799. In early life there was developed in him a remarkable taste for mathematical studies. A love for the English classics was also awakened, and he made himself familiar with the works of the best authors in his native tongue. He came to this country in 1818. After his conversion he could not rest satisfied with the routine of his daily life. He wanted to do noble things for his Master. He was licensed to preach Oct. 1, 1827, and became a member of the Newton Theological Seminary in November following. Two years afterwards he received an appointment from the executive board of the Missionary Union, and sailed May 26, 1830, in company with Rev. E. Kincaid and wife, for Calcutta, and arrived in Maulmain in November. He joined Mr. Boardman in Tavoy in 1831, and was with him during the last weeks of his life, administering the ordinance of baptism to the Karen converts on the memorable occasion when, as a dying man, the worn-out missionary reclined on the banks of the stream in whose waters the new disciples were "buried with Christ by baptism." Dr. Mason's connection with the Tavoy mission continued for about twenty-two and a half years, or one-half of his whole missionary life. While at Tavoy Dr. Mason's life was an exceedingly active one, and the visible results of his labors were manifest in many directions. For some time the superintendence of the station rested on him. A seminary for the education of teachers and preachers was also under his charge. He translated the Scriptures into the Sgau Karen and Pwo Karen languages. He also made his collections for his "Notes on the Fauna and Flora of Burmah," published in 1852, and for a similar work which was published some time later.

Dr. Mason having obtained permission of the board, proceeded to Toungoo to commence a mission in that place, where he arrived Oct. 22, 1833. In a few weeks he was joined by San Quala, "the Karen apostle," and two assistants. The most remarkable success followed the labors of these devoted missionaries. Although Dr. Mason was obliged to leave Burmah for this country in the early part of 1854, the work went on with marvelous strides, so that when, three years later, he returned to Toungoo, there were 2600 baptized Christians and 35 churches connected with the mission. In ten years from the establishment of the station more than 6000 converts had been baptized and 126 churches had been formed.

In the midst of this wonderful prosperity occurred those singular circumstances which those who have made themselves familiar with the history of this mission will recall. Mrs. Mason, the wife of Dr. Mason, came under the influence of certain strange delusions, and through her teachings of the new converts the most lamentable defections from the simple gospel were the result. The peculiar hallucination which seemed to have taken possession of her mind was this: "She pretended to have found the language in which God spoke to Adam, the 'God language' as she called it, in the embroideries of the Karen women's dresses, in the pagodas, and other appendages of Buddhist worship, and claimed that all nations have this language, and that what is needed only is to read it according to the key which she stated she had received." It was in vain that the executive board protested against the inculcation of these wild vagaries, and set forth the great injury which the Karen churches must suffer from the propagation of such sentiments. Dr. Mason did not see fit to interfere in the matter, and there was no alternative but that his connection with the Missionary Union must cease. For a little more than seven years this separation continued, but at last the extravagant conduct of his wife forced him to believe that she must be laboring under a form of insanity, and he could no longer sanction the course which she was pursuing. His relation to the Missionary Union was restored July 11, 1871, and continued harmonious and pleasant until his death, which occurred March 3, 1874.

From the foregoing sketch it is evident that Dr. Mason was no common man. Placed in any position he could not fail to secure respect for his ability. He created a new literature for the Karens, giving to them the Word of God and other devout and instructive books in their own tongue. He was a careful observer of the natural history of the country in which he passed so many years of his life. Sir J. D. Hooker, an eminent English naturalist, says of his "Fauna and Flora, etc., of British Burmah and Pegu," "F. Mason, D.D., has made the most valuable addition to the history of the fauna and flora of British Burmah of any man of modern times." In many respects Dr. Mason will be regarded as holding a first place in the ranks of American missionaries.

Mason, Rev. J. O., D.D., was born in Fort Ann, Washington Co., N.·Y., Dec. 25, 1813. His parents were active members of the Baptist Church, and lived until a ripe old age. Their influence and training during his early years very largely moulded his subsequent life and character. When about to enter college, in his eighteenth year, he was converted, and began to prepare for the gospel ministry. In 1833 he became a student in the Literary and Theological Institution at Hamilton, N. Y., graduating in 1836. Shortly after appointed by the Foreign Mission Board as a missionary to the Creek Indians beyond the Mississippi. He was ordained Aug. 30, 1838, and, accompanied by his wife, started for his field. The unsettled state of the Indian tribes rendered mission work almost impossible, and, after many attempts to gain a foothold, he was compelled to abandon it. In May, 1840, he settled as pastor at Fort Ann, and remained with much success nearly four years. Sept. 1, 1844, he entered upon the great work of his life, as pastor of the Bottskill Baptist church, in Greenwich, N. Y. With an occasional brief intermission on account of ill health, he has labored with this honored church until the present time. During all these years he has been blessed in leading souls to Christ and in breaking the bread of life to a people in whose hearts he is held with affectionate regard.

Mason, Deacon John R., son of Deacon Mason, of Warren, R. I., is a member of the Central church, Oakland, and treasurer of the California Baptist State Convention. He was born at Warren, R. I., in 1826; spent some years at St. Louis, Mo.; crossed the plains for California in 1849; and has been a successful merchant. He was converted in 1868, and baptized by Rev. J. P. Ludlow, and has ever been active in church and denominational interests on the Pacific coast.

Mason, Rev. J. P., was born in Chatham Co., N. C., March 13, 1827; baptized by Rev. Johnson Olive, November, 1848; ordained in January, 1856, Revs. G. W. Purefoy, B. J. Hackney, and Thomas Yarboro forming the Presbytery. Mr. Mason has served Lystia church for twenty-two years, and served other country churches nearly as long. He is a good pastor.

Mason, Prof. Otis Tufton, was born in Eastport, Me., April 10, 1838; was baptized in 1856, and united with the First Baptist church, Washington, D. C., and was licensed to preach by the First Baptist church in Alexandria, Va., in 1859. Prof. Mason was educated at the Columbian College, where he graduated in 1861 with the degree of A.M. From that time to the present he has been the successful principal of the preparatory school of the university. He is superintendent of the Sunday-school of the First Baptist church,

Washington, D. C., and a deacon in the same. He is a collaborator of the Smithsonian Institution in anthropology, joint editor of the scientific department of Harpers' serials, and anthropological editor of the *American Naturalist.* He is the author of several papers on anthropology, published in the " Smithsonian Reports," and in the " Proceedings of the American Association." Prof. Mason is, at present, engaged in collating materials for an encyclopædia of the North American Indians, an atlas of the archæology of the United States, and a grammar and dictionary of the Southern Indian languages, a department of research in which he is deeply interested, and for which he has special aptitude.

Mason, Sumner R., D.D., was born in Cheshire, in the western part of Massachusetts, June 14,

SUMNER R. MASON, D.D.

1819. He was a lineal descendant of Samson Mason, who was at one time an officer in Cromwell's army, a radical in politics and a Baptist in religion. He came to America about 1650. For assisting in the building of the Baptist meeting-house in Swansey he was summoned before the authorities of Plymouth colony, fined fifteen shillings, and warned to leave the jurisdiction. When the subject of this sketch was about seven years of age his parents removed to Penfield, in the western part of New York. His father died in 1828, leaving a widow and a large family. Dr. Mason pursued his preparatory studies in Cincinnati, and entered Yale College in 1838, where he remained two years. He was baptized and united with the First Baptist

church in New Haven, March 1, 1840. For the next seven years he was engaged in teaching in Cincinnati and in Nashville, Tenn. He was licensed to preach by the First Baptist church of Nashville when Dr. Howell was pastor, Sept. 7, 1844. He pursued his theological studies under the direction of Dr. Howell, and was ordained pastor of the First Baptist church in Lockport, N. Y., Aug. 22, 1849, where he remained until called to the First Baptist church in Cambridge, Mass., where he commenced his ministerial labors March 4, 1855. Here he proved himself to be " a workman that needed not to be ashamed, rightly dividing the word of truth." The church under his ministry of sixteen years grew not only in its membership, but in sound doctrine and active benevolence, and every year added to its pastor's reputation and the weight of his influence in every direction in which that influence was exerted. It might have reasonably been predicted that many years of active service and great usefulness were before this devoted minister of Christ, but in the very prime of life he was suddenly cut down. What at the time was known as the " Revere disaster" sent a great shock through the minds of people residing in the neighborhood where the frightful event occurred. Dr. Mason was on his way to Beverly, Mass., to exchange pulpits with Rev. J. C. Foster. It was on Saturday evening, Aug. 26, 1871. At the Revere station, a few miles out of Boston, an express train from Portland met the outgoing train, and Dr. Mason, with a score of others, was instantly killed.

In an appreciative sketch of the life of Dr. Mason, his friend, Dr. O. S. Stearns, says of him, " He was a sincere friend, an earnest, sympathetic Christian, a truth-searching theologian, an effective preacher, a wise and judicious pastor. To his family he has bequeathed a life full of sunny memories. By his people his name will always be honored. In his denomination he will long be considered one of its choicest ornaments. By all who knew him he will be esteemed as a *prince in Israel.*"

Massachusetts Baptists.—We can trace the history of the denomination in the State of Massachusetts nearly to the settlement of Boston in 1630. Among the earlier inhabitants of the district taken possession of by Gov. Winthrop, and the nearly fifteen hundred people who accompanied him, there were found some who had grave doubts about the divine authority of the rite of infant baptism, and refused to have it performed in the case of their own children. The first president of Harvard College, Rev. Henry Dunster, took a decided stand on the subject, and openly avowed his sentiments against infant baptism. Then came the persecution of Thomas Gould, and the troubles through which the First Baptist church in Boston passed, beginning with the formation of the church in 1665 and extending through several years. Two years previous, in 1663, the church in Swanzey was formed, it being really a transfer of the Swansea church in Wales, organized in 1649, to this country. From the Boston church there were formed, from time to time, churches in different sections of the State, made up chiefly of members who, having been connected with that church because it was the only church of their faith which they could conveniently join, desired to enjoy church privileges in the locality where they lived. In this way commenced the church in Kittery, formed in Maine in 1682, and about the same time the church in Newbury. Thomas Hollis, an eminent merchant of London, proved himself the warm friend of his denomination by making generous provision for Baptist young men to be educated for the ministry in Harvard. As early as 1727 we find that there were Baptists in Springfield, the pastor of the First church in Boston, by special request, visiting that place to administer the rite of baptism to several persons. Before the close of the century there were about 50 churches in different sections of the State. Among the oldest of these we mention the church in Wales, 1736; Bellingham, 1737; the Second church, now Warren Avenue church, Boston, 1743; First Middleborough, 1756; West Harwich, 1757; Third Middleborough, 1761; and the First church in Haverhill, 1765. With rare exceptions very few of these 50 churches were churches of much pecuniary ability. But they were earnest followers of Christ, and contended for what they believed to be "the faith once delivered to the saints." They encountered persecution, they suffered many civil disabilities, and yet they continued to grow and multiply until they have reached a high rank among the other denominations of Christians in the State.

The latest statistics give us the following figures: There are 14 Associations, embracing 289 churches, with 232 pastors. The number of ordained ministers in the State is 328. The total membership of the churches is 48,764, and the amount of money raised for various purposes, so far as reported, for the year covered by the statistical tables to which we refer, was $713,125. The church having the largest membership is the Union Temple, Boston, the number being 1501.

Of the State denominational societies the Convention may be first mentioned. It was formed May 26, 1802, and was incorporated Feb. 28, 1808. It is authorized to hold real estate to the amount of $200,000. The receipts for 1880 were $13,800. The officers of the Convention at the present time are Eustace C. Fitz, president, and four vice-presidents, all laymen, Rev. G. W. Bosworth, D.D., secretary, and Rev. Andrew Pollard, D.D., treasurer.

directors is made up of 50 ministers and laymen, who represent the different sections of the State. Another organization is "The Baptist Charitable Society for the Relief of Widows and Orphans of Deceased Baptist Ministers." Rev. G. G. Fairbanks is its president. Its receipts in 1880 were over $2550. This society was formed in 1821. "The Massachusetts Baptist Pastoral Conference" was formed in 1829, its object being the relief of aged and indigent ministers. It is authorized to hold property to the amount of $75,000. The president is Rev. C. M. Bowers, D.D. "The Northern Baptist Education Society" was formed in 1814. It has a permanent fund of $32,400. The president is Rev. Henry M. King, D.D., and the secretary Rev. J. C. Foster. The society has aided during the year 52 young men studying for the ministry. Its income in 1880 was $6774.91. (See articles on FIRST BAPTIST CHURCH OF BOSTON, FIRST BAPTIST CHURCH OF SWANZEY, NEWTON THEOLOGICAL SEMINARY, PIERCE ACADEMY, WORCESTER ACADEMY, and THE WATCHMAN AND REFLECTOR.)

Mather, Rev. Asher E., was born in Canada in 1823; son of Deacon Alonzo T. Mather. The

REV. ASHER E. MATHER.

family removed to St. Lawrence Co., N. Y., in 1828, and to Michigan in 1836. He devoted some time to teaching, and then engaged in business in the city of Detroit. His attention was early turned to the gospel ministry, and many of his brethren thought he was called of God to this work before he could overcome his fear lest he was not qualified for it. At length, in 1851, turning away from pursuits that promised large pecuniary returns, he became pastor in Mount Clemens, where he was ordained in August, 1851. This pastorate continued only for a year, but was specially attended with the blessing of God. The Tabernacle church, in Detroit, of which he had been a deacon, called him to be its pastor, and he accepted the call. But the plans of the church could not be carried out with the means at its command, and after a brief period he removed to Romeo, where a small church was in a depressed condition. During the next four years his work was greatly blessed, a good house of worship and a parsonage were built, and the church, which had been aided by the American Baptist Home Mission Society, became self-supporting. His next pastorate was in Pontiac, and continued nine years. These were years of prosperity. At the opening of the war he rendered valuable service in raising a regiment of volunteers, and became its chaplain. He was absent from the church a year in this service.

In 1866 he became district secretary of the American Baptist Home Mission Society, and for ten years engaged in work for that society with great earnestness, and with constant tokens of divine approval. Having led in the organization of the church in Caro, in 1876, and the erection of its house of worship, he became, soon after, pastor in Portland, where he is now engaged in earnest work.

No Baptist in Michigan is more fully acquainted with the churches throughout the State, and none have rendered a service more widely felt. He has assisted at the dedication of more than fifty houses of worship. It was at his suggestion that the Woman's Baptist Home Mission Society of Michigan was formed,—the first society of its kind in the country. He served the State Convention as its secretary for seven years, and in 1879 was made its president.

Mathews, William, LL.D., is by far the best and most successful writer the West has yet produced. Having enjoyed in early life the culture of New England, and, later, having breathed for many years the stimulating atmosphere of the West, he combines with the finished scholarship of the one, the vigorous vitality of the other. He was born at Waterville, Me., July 28, 1818. His taste for study, and his proficiency in whatever in that way was undertaken, were shown very early in life. At the age of thirteen he entered Waterville College, now Colby University, and in 1835, at the age of seventeen, graduated. Two years were then spent in the Harvard Law School, and two years more in the office of Hon. Timothy Boutelle, of Waterville. Having been admitted to the bar, he first taught for a year in Virginia, but returning to Waterville in 1841, he began the practice of law, associating with that, however, the editorship of a literary paper,—*The Yankee Blade*. This latter proved to be for him the more congenial sphere. After two

years the paper was removed to Gardiner, Me., where for some four or five years its publication was continued with marked success; subsequently to Boston, in which city it achieved a circulation and popularity in all parts of the United States scarcely equaled by any other literary paper. As editor of the *Blade*, Mr. Mathews formed many interesting and valuable literary acquaintances, including several of the best known and most eminent of American writers.

In 1856, Mr. Mathews sold his paper and removed to Chicago. His work here was at first in the form of contributions to various journals; but in 1859 he was appointed librarian of the Young Men's Association, holding that office some three years. He was then elected Professor of Rhetoric and English Literature in the University of Chicago. This place he filled with eminent success until 1875, when he resigned it, with a view to devote himself entirely to authorship. In this new line of work he has been remarkably successful. His writings for the most part have the form of essays, upon subjects literary, biographical, and practical, covering a wide range, but so grouped as to give each of his volumes admirable unity of direction and general topic. His style is a model of elegance and vivacity, while his method, being largely illustrative, enables him to utilize the results of an almost ubiquitous reading and study. The titles of his principal books, and nearly in the order of their appearance, are "Getting On in the World," "Words, their Use and Abuse," "Orations and Orators," and "Monday Chats," the last named being a translation of Sainte-Beuve's "Causeries du Lundi," introduced by an appreciative biography of the great French *littérateur* and critic. Dr. Mathews's home is still in Chicago, where he enjoys the warmest esteem of a wide circle of cultured friends.

Mathias, Rev. Joseph, of Hilltown, Bucks Co., Pa., was born May 8, 1778. He was baptized on a profession of his faith in his twenty-second year. He was ordained to preach the gospel July 22, 1806, and he continued in the work of the ministry for more than forty-six years as pastor of the same church. He possessed a vigorous intellect, a spirit of stern loyalty to Jesus, and a heart overflowing with love to the Redeemer.

He was a strong Calvinist, fully persuaded that each believer owed his salvation to a gospel springing from the everlasting and personal love of God, a gospel bearing the whole treasures of grace to every heart that received it, and a gospel surely carrying each recipient to the world of glory.

He was untiring in the use of means to bring men to the Saviour. His prayers for the salvation of his people were marked by a fervor and a faith that nothing could surpass. His public appeals to saints and sinners to follow Jesus were unusually tender and earnest.

He preached three times on the Lord's day, and several times during the week. And it was his regular custom to make a tour annually, at a convenient season of the year, extending over several weeks, and to preach every night at the place where he stopped. To gather a congregation he sent word beforehand, and the people thronged to hear the gospel. In a brief account of one of these apostolic trips before me, it is stated that he preached in ten different places, and baptized ten persons at three of his meetings. Only one of these services was held in a church, the others were conducted in barns and school-houses. The labor performed for the Saviour in this way was effective and very extensive. Many were born again, and united with other denominations, and many others formed Baptist churches, several of which are in a flourishing condition at this time.

In one of his preaching journeys he tells of two persons "who requested baptism, but the relation they gave was not satisfactory, and their request was not granted." Mr. Mathias built up Christian churches in the truth, and with soundly converted members, whose future experience would encourage their brethren and commend the gospel.

He was an earnest advocate of missions all over our own country, and away to the ends of the earth. He was ever ready to speak for missions in his own church and in the region around. And it was his custom to commend Christian love for the perishing at home and abroad by a liberal contribution of his own, which gave him freedom of utterance in appealing to others, and which imparted a peculiar power to his missionary arguments.

He had five sons and three daughters, every one of whom was converted under his ministry, and buried in the waters of baptism by his hands.

No man was loved more in the old Philadelphia Association than Father Mathias. His fame had traveled over the entire State and a large section of New Jersey. Wherever he was known he had a warm place in the hearts of the friends of Christ.

He was a firm Baptist, and while he loved all Christians, he knew nothing of that charity that would sacrifice the smallest part of God's truth. Not for empires, nor for mines of gold, nor for worlds, would he slight his Lord that he might bribe the servants of that Master for their good will.

Mr. Mathias preached three times the Sunday before his death; on the following Tuesday evening his spirit suddenly entered the heavens. On Friday an immense concourse of people gathered at his funeral services, every one of whom felt that a father and a friend had been borne to the skies when Father Mathias fell asleep. And though this event occurred thirty years ago the memory of our venerable friend is as fragrant as ever, not in Hilltown only, but for hundreds of miles around it.

Mattoon, Rev. C. H., of Albany, Oregon, is an earnest and influential preacher, and known as the Baptist historian in that State. There is hardly any pastor or prominent Baptist in Oregon whose history is unknown to Mr. Mattoon. He has preached in nearly every part of the State. Born at Canastota, N. Y., of Old-School Presbyterian parents, he became a Baptist, and was immersed at Genoa, O., in 1844. He obtained a good education at Central College, O. He went to Oregon in 1851; was licensed in 1853; published The Religious Expositor six months; was Professor of Mathematics in McMinnville two years; and in agency work became familiar with Baptists in the State and adjacent Territories. In 1871 he was ordained by the Pleasant Butte church; is a strong Baptist writer of the Landmark school; in 1874 held a written discussion on that subject; is more logical than rhetorical in preaching; is positive, and so full of the facts in Baptist history that he is sometimes called "the Baptist Encyclopædia of Oregon." He is historical secretary of the Baptist Convention of the North Pacific coast.

Maxcy, Jonathan, D.D., was born in Attleborough, Mass., Sept. 2, 1768. In his case the moulding influence of a highly gifted mother was felt in the formative period of his life. Such was the intellectual development of young Maxcy that his parents determined to secure for him all the advantages of a liberal course of study. Having been prepared for college in the academy of Rev. William Williams, of Wrentham, not far from his native place, he became a member of the Freshman class in Brown University in 1783, when he was but fifteen years of age. All the hopes which had been cherished with reference to him were abundantly realized. He made rapid progress in the acquisition of knowledge and in mental discipline, and graduated with the highest honors of his class in 1787. His talents were brought into immediate service in the college where he had gained his laurels. He was appointed a tutor, and for four years devoted himself with great success to the duties of his office. But his Master had a higher service for him. Having become a subject of the converting grace of God, he was baptized by Rev. Dr. Manning, and connected himself with the First Baptist church in Providence. The church at once gave him a license to preach, and he was invited to supply the pulpit which President Manning had recently vacated. From the outset of his public efforts as a preacher of the gospel his rank as a pulpit orator was established. So pleased was the church with these efforts that he was solicited to resign his office as tutor in Brown University and accept a call to the pastorate of the flock to which he had ministered with so much satisfaction. The call was accepted, and Mr. Maxcy was ordained Sept. 8, 1791, when he was but twenty-three years of age, the Rev. Dr. Stillman preaching the ordination sermon. He was also appointed a professor in Brown University on the same day, as well as a trustee of the college.

In the midst of most congenial employments, and when he was constantly developing his powers as a preacher and a pastor, Dr. Manning was suddenly smitten down by a fatal disease and died. All eyes were at once turned to Maxcy as the most suitable person to fill the vacancy created by the decease of the lamented Manning, and he was unanimously elected president. He resigned his pastorship just one year from the day he was ordained, and entered upon his duties in the university. He was only twenty-four years of age, the youngest man, if we mistake not, that was ever called to fill so responsible a position in this country. His youth probably brought him in closer and more intimate relations with the students of the college than if he had been older. At any rate, he was from the first very popular, and the young men were proud of their youthful president. Several discourses which he published within a few years after he took charge of the university added greatly to his reputation as an able divine. In 1801 Harvard University conferred on him the honorary degree of Doctor of Divinity. He was at the time only thirty-three years of age. His official connection with Brown University continued for ten years, when he was called to the presidential chair in Union College, where he remained two years. Finding our Northern climate too severe for his delicate constitution, he accepted an invitation to take the presidency of the South Carolina College, where he remained for sixteen years, and was the means of raising the institution to a high rank among the colleges of the country.

From all the traditions that have come down to us there is reason to believe that Dr. Maxcy was one of the most eloquent preachers, not merely of his own denomination, but of any, in the country. It is said that " a profound and breathless silence, an intense feeling, and a delight amounting to rapture were the almost invariable attendants of his preaching. His manner was emphatically his own. There was no labored display, nothing turgid or affected, but everything was easy, graceful, dignified, and natural. His general manner of delivery was rather mild than vehement, and rather solemn than impetuous ; commencing in a moderate tone of voice, but becoming more animated and impassioned as he proceeded, he gradually influenced the hearts and feelings of his audience." Says Hon. Jas. L. Petigru, of South Carolina, " Never will the charm of his eloquence be erased from the memory on which its impression has once been made." Hon. Senator Evans, of South Carolina, " He was the greatest orator I have ever heard in the pulpit." Judge O'Neall, of South Carolina, " His were the finest specimens of eloquence and truth to which it has been my privilege to listen." Dr. Maxcy died June 4, 1820.

Maxey, Gen. Rice, was born in Barren, Ky., July 23, 1800. In 1829 he became a member of Mill Creek Baptist church, Monroe Co., Ky. Practised law from his twenty-first to his fiftieth year ; removed to Paris, Texas, Nov. 20, 1857 ; elected to the State senate to succeed his son, Gen. S. B. Maxey, in 1862. He lived to see his son, Samuel Bell Maxey, a U. S. Senator from Texas. He was a leader in Kentucky and Texas, both in religion and politics, and exerted great influence both by his lofty character and fine abilities. He was twice married. After a painful illness, borne with Christian fortitude, he died Jan. 11, 1878.

Maxey, U. S. Senator Samuel Bell.—The Maxey family are of Huguenot descent, having settled on James River soon after the revocation of the edict of Nantes. His great-grandfather, Rad-

ford Maxey, became a planter in Halifax Co., Va., and his grandfather, William Maxey, removed to Kentucky in the last century. His father, Rice Maxey, was born in Barren Co., Ky., in the year

1800, and was a lawyer by profession. His mother was the daughter of Samuel Bell, a native of Albemarle Co., Va.

Samuel Bell Maxey was born at Tompkinsville, Monroe Co., Ky., March 30, 1825. His father removed, in 1834, to Clinton County, where he was clerk of the Circuit and County courts. In 1857 he removed to Texas and settled at Paris. Samuel was educated at the best schools, studying Latin, Greek, and mathematics until he was seventeen years old, when he was appointed a cadet in the Military Academy at West Point. He was graduated there in 1846, and assigned to the 7th Infantry as a brevet second lieutenant. That fall he went to Mexico. He first joined Taylor at Monterey, and when Scott organized a new offensive line from Vera Cruz, Maxey went in Twiggs' column to Tampico. He shared in the siege of Vera Cruz, and was with Harvey's brigade at the battle of Cerro Gordo. He was brevetted a first lieutenant for gallant conduct at the battles of Contreras and Churubusco, and was also engaged at Molino del Rey and in the engagement which resulted in the capture of the city of Mexico. After the city fell into his hands Gen. Scott organized a battalion of five companies of picked men under Col. Charles F. Smith as a city guard. Maxey was assigned to the command of one of these companies, and he was thus provost of one of the five districts of the city. Maxey had learned French at West Point. While in Mexico he became familiar with the Spanish tongue, which subsequently proved useful to him in the practice of the law in Texas. He returned to the United States from Mexico in the summer of 1848, and was stationed at Jefferson Barracks, but finally resigned Sept. 17, 1849. He returned to his father's home, studied law, and in 1850 began the practice at Albany, Clinton County.

In 1857 he settled at his present home in Paris, a promising town in Northeastern Texas, and practised law until 1861. About the opening of the war he was elected to the State senate, but never took his seat, as he thought he ought to be in the army. He raised the 9th Texas Infantry for the army under Gen. Albert Sidney Johnston. In December, 1861, it marched by land and reached Memphis in time to join the army at Corinth. In the mean time he had been made a brigadier-general. He joined Gen. Johnston at Decatur, and was sent by him to Chattanooga to collect and reorganize troops there.

Gen. Maxey's services in the Confederate army were many and important. On the direct application of Gen. E. Kirby Smith, then in command of the Trans-Mississippi Department, in the fall of 1863 he was ordered to take command of the Indian Territory. Everything there was in terrible confusion. Maxey, with very little aid from head-quarters, put eight or ten thousand troops under arms. In the spring of 1864 he advised Gen. Smith of Steele's advance, and moved into Arkansas, where he joined Price and shared in his fight at Prairie Danne to check the enemy. He fought Steele at Poison Springs, April 18, 1864, and captured his entire train of 227 wagons. The loss of his transportation compelled Steele to retire. For his conduct on this occasion Maxey was made a major-general.

Gen. Maxey went to his home and devoted himself to the practice of the law, which soon proved both laborious and lucrative to him. He was appointed judge, but declined. In 1874 he was elected to the United States Senate, and took his seat March 5, 1875. Gen. Maxey undoubtedly owes his election to the popular conviction that he is stanch, diligent, and a representative man.

At first Gen. Maxey was placed on the Committee on Territories, but was transferred the same year, 1875, to that on Military Affairs. He has served continuously on the Committee on Labor and Education, and on Post-Offices, of which latter he is now chairman. He has had more than ordinary success in practical legislation. He has never made a report from any committee which was not sustained. The post-office committee is a very important one to a frontier State. Gen. Maxey has aided greatly in increasing the postal facilities of Texas. Among others, he has had established the stage route from Fort Worth to Fort Yuma, the longest stage line in the world.

Gen. Maxey is a member of the Baptist Church, to which his family has belonged for four or five generations. He is a gallant, genial gentleman, and a hard-working, useful Senator. Very few Senators enjoy so generally the affection and esteem of their colleagues.

Maxson, Rev. John, the first white child born on the island of Rhode Island, was born in 1638, shortly after his father had been killed by the Pequots. He was one of the purchasers of Westerly, R. I., in 1661, and one of the freemen there in 1669; ordained, when seventy years of age, "to the place and office of an elder" in the First Westerly (now Hopkinton) Seventh-Day Baptist church; had as assistants, in 1710, John Maxson (2d), William Davis, Joseph Clarke, Sr., George Stillman, Joseph Clarke, Jr., and Joseph Crandall, and in 1712 the church numbered about 130 members; died Dec. 17, 1720, aged eighty-two.

Mayfield, W. D., D.D., pastor of Central Baptist church, Little Rock, Ark., was born in South Carolina in 1837; began to preach in 1856; chaplain of the 3d S. C. Regiment in the Confederate army; after filling several important pastorates in his native State he became pastor at Helena, Ark., in 1868; from 1874 to 1877, corresponding secretary of the Southern Baptist Publication Society ; then removed to Nashville, Tenn., and began the publication of the *Baptist Reflector ;* he also published a literary magazine called *Happy Home ;* at the close of the year 1879 he removed to Little Rock. Dr. Mayfield is a fine writer, and as he is yet in the prime of life, much may be expected from his vigorous pen.

Mays, Rev. John L., a pioneer preacher in North Louisiana, by whose zealous labors many churches in Union, Claiborne, and Jackson Parishes were founded, was born in 1814, and died in the pulpit, Nov. 16, 1866.

Mays, R. G., M.D., was born in Edgefield Co., S. C., Oct. 5, 1800. "After finishing his regular course of study," writes his sister, Mrs. Judge Brevard, "he decided on medicine as his calling, and graduated at the medical college in Baltimore in 1822." Not caring for his profession, he devoted himself to farming and became a very successful planter.

In the extensive revival of 1831, Dr. and Mrs. Mays were converted, and baptized into Edgefield church by the Rev. Mr. Hodges. From his conversion to his death he was an earnest, zealous Christian. He was a natural orator, readily using beautiful expressions with a voice full of melody, and he was almost irresistible in exhortation. His prayers were from a heart imbued with the Spirit of God, and could scarcely be heard without emotion. His manners were genial and kind, and his hospitality overflowing and refined.

He was ready to aid every good work, and being blessed with a competency, and coming to Florida when the denomination was young and weak, he did much to build it up. He was specially interested in the spiritual welfare of his slaves, and employed ministers to preach to them.

He was called to pass through deep waters. Seven of nine children were taken from him, and in April, 1878, the wife of his youth died at their home at Orange Mills. Since that time Dr. Mays himself has gone to his eternal home.

McAlister, Rev. I. N., an active minister of Sabine Association, La., was born in Mississippi in 1813 ; came to Louisiana in 1853 ; was employed as a missionary of the State Convention, and did good service. He died Jan. 27, 1874.

McAlpine, Rev. Wm. H., is about thirty-six years old ; reared as a slave in a cultivated family ; received instruction and good breeding ; entered school at Talladega soon after he became free. Took a liberal course in the Congregational College at that place ; at the same time received instruction in theology from Dr. J. J. D. Renfroe, by whom he was baptized, ordained, and installed pastor of the colored church in the city. He has been State evangelist for his race ; now pastor of the large colored church at Marion. No man has done more for the elevation of the colored people in Alabama. He is an excellent preacher, and a rising man.

McArthur, Joseph Benjamin, was born Nov. 25, 1849, in the township of Lobo, County of Middlesex, Ontario, Canada. He attended the public school until fifteen years of age, and, after an interval of two years spent upon a farm, went to the Middlesex Seminary. In 1868 he matriculated into the Law Society of Upper Canada, and was entered as a student at Osgoode Hall, in the city of Toronto. He was called to the bar of Ontario in November, 1873, and was invited to join the eminent legal firm to whom he had been articled. The retirement of a member of the firm on Jan. 1, 1881, led to the formation of the present firm of Mulock, Tilt, McArthur & Crowther. Mr. McArthur was baptized in 1873, and united with the Alexander Street church, Toronto, of which he has been for several years a deacon. He is superintendent of the Sunday-school, one of the trustees of the Toronto Baptist College, and a vice-president of the Home Mission Board. For personal consecration and liberal giving he is conspicuous among the laymen of Canada.

McCall, Rev. G. R., of Hawkinsville, Ga., is one of the ablest, most prominent, and influential of the younger generation of Georgia Baptist ministers,—a man whose modesty equals his merit, and whose ability as a preacher is second to few of his age. He was born Feb. 7, 1829, in Screven Co., Ga., and was educated at Mercer University, graduating with the third honor, in a talented class, in the year 1853. He then spent one year in the same university studying theology. He joined the church at fifteen, was licensed at eighteen, and ordained Sept. 24, 1854, when nearly twenty-five. In January of 1855 he was called to preach once a month to the Richland church, Twiggs County, and has continued its pastor ever since. After the war he settled in Hawkinsville, and took charge of the Baptist church there in October, 1866, to which church he is still preaching. He has been a diligent and successful pastor. For years Mr. McCall has acted as the moderator of the Ebenezer Association, and his influence in all the region where he lives is very great, especially in the Baptist churches. For ten years in succession he has been the clerk of the Georgia Baptist Convention, and for two years was clerk of the Southern Baptist Convention. He has been a member of the board of trustees for Mercer University, acting as secretary of the board. He is a strong friend of missions, Sunday-schools, and of education. He is an excellent preacher and a wise counselor. He ranks very high in the estimation of his brethren.

McCallum, Rev. H. B., was born in Knox Co.,

Tenn., Jan. 9, 1837, and spent his childhood at Gravesville, in the northeastern part of that county. In his thirteenth year his father removed to Knoxville. Here Hugh spent his time from 1849 to 1853.

In 1852 he entered East Tennessee University, and remained several terms. During the fall of 1852 he was converted, and was baptized by Dr. Matthew Hillsman in December of that year. He was soon impressed with the duty of preaching the gospel, and resolved to devote his life to that work. In 1854 he entered Union University, Murfreesborough, Tenn., intending to take a full course, but his health declined so rapidly that he remained but ten months.

By advice of his physicians he visited Florida in December, 1856, and remained till spring. By doing this for two or three years he was restored to comparatively good health.

In 1859 he settled in Camden, S. C., and continued meanwhile to study theology. The following year he enlisted as a private, and was mustered into service in the Confederate army. In 1861 he was called to the chaplaincy of his regiment, and was ordained at the call of his church, and served as chaplain during the war.

At the close of the war he settled in Sumter District, S. C., and preached to country churches. In 1867 he removed to Florida, and in 1869 he located at Lake City, and was soon chosen to the pastorate of the church there. The little organization, with no house, was soon built up to an effective church, and one of the best houses of worship in the State erected. In 1873 he was induced to commence the *Florida Baptist*, and published it two years, and then transferred it to the *Christian Index*, of Georgia.

Mr. McCallum is a man of ability and energy. He is a ready, forcible writer and speaker, and by his pen and his preaching has done much to strengthen the Baptist denomination in the State.

McCloud, Rev. Constant S., a native of Vermont, was born in 1818; graduated at Georgetown College in 1846; removed to Mississippi, and became successively pastor at Starkville, Vicksburg, and Raymond. After the war he became pastor at Jefferson, Texas, where by his indefatigable labors he increased the membership from a mere handful to about two hundred, and erected one of the handsomest church edifices in the State, and a comfortable parsonage. In 1872 he became missionary of the Grand Cane Baptist Association, La. He fell a victim to yellow fever at Shreveport, Oct. 17, 1873.

McCoid, Hon. M. M., member of Congress from Iowa, was born in Logan Co., O., Nov. 5, 1840. His father, Robert McCoid, was of Irish, and his mother, Jane Bain, of Scotch, descent. Her father came from Ayrshire, Scotland, and was a Revolutionary soldier in the Virginia troops. McCoid removed with his parents to Iowa when he was eleven years old. He received a common-school education, and then attended Fairfield University, and Washington College, Washington, Pa., until the Junior year, leaving because of ill health. He soon after entered upon the study of law. He was admitted to the bar in 1861, but immediately enlisted as a private in Co. E, 2d Regiment Iowa Vols., in which he served for the full time of enlistment, being discharged May 28, 1864. He was promoted to be second lieutenant, and was for a considerable time acting adjutant of the regiment. He was in seven battles, including Fort Donelson, Shiloh, Corinth, and Stone River. In 1864 he returned to civil life, and began the practice of law. In 1866 he was elected district attorney of the sixth Iowa judicial district, and served for four years. In 1870 he was elected State senator, and re-elected in 1875; in 1878 he was elected from the first district as a member of the Forty-sixth Congress, and he was re-elected to the present Congress. He was brought up a Presbyterian, and learned the Shorter Catechism before he was able to read, but on his conversion, in 1865, he embraced the Baptist faith, and has been a member of the Fairfield Baptist church ever since. He is a man of great ability, integrity, and piety.

McConnico, Rev. Garner, was a native of Lunenburg Co., Va., where his family occupied a high social position. He became hopefully pious, under the instructions of an excellent mother, at a very early age, and united with the church; and such were the spirit and the ability which he manifested in the part he occasionally took in the social religious exercises that the church in due time licensed him to preach, and ordained him as a minister of the gospel before he had reached his twenty-eighth year. As the beautiful valley of the Cumberland presented extraordinary attractions as a place for settlement, Mr. McConnico sold his property in Lunenburg County near the close of the last century, and selected as his future home a spot in Williamson County than which it would be difficult to find another more beautiful. Here he secured a large tract of land, and spent thirty-five years rearing a large and estimable family, some of whom have since reached positions of usefulness and honor. His mansion was ever the scene of a profuse hospitality. In it was found the best society then in the West; and especially was it the home of ministers of the gospel. Mr. McConnico immediately commenced among the settlers his appropriate work. He was a diligent student of the Bible, and of standard theological writings, with which his library was furnished. He clung with unyielding tenacity to the great doctrines of the

Cross, and had an intelligent and definite view of the whole evangelical system. He prepared his discourses with much care, and they were characterized by remarkable perspicuity and directness, and they were delivered with graceful elocution and impressive fervor. For years he preached often in all parts of the middle district, and sometimes beyond it. Many professed religion, and a large number of churches were raised up mainly through his instrumentality. Of the Harpeth church, which was in his immediate neighborhood, and which was large, intelligent, and wealthy, he became the regular pastor, and continued in the office until the end of his life. Of seven other churches around him he was the stated supply, according to the practice of the times. His popularity was almost unbounded. He died suddenly, full of faith and hope, in the year 1833.

His piety was deep, and his presence neutralized every tendency to levity. Listening to him beneath the shade of the gigantic forest-trees, where he so often preached, you would have felt coming over you a strange reverence for his mighty mind. His memory and influence can never die.

McCoy, Rev. Isaac, the great apostle to the American Indians, was born in Fayette Co., Pa., June 13, 1784. He came with his father to Kentucky in 1790. In 1801 he was converted and joined the Buck Creek Baptist church. In 1803 he was married to Christiana Polk, daughter of Capt. Polk, whose wife and several children were captured by the Ottowas. Mr. McCoy and his wife were afterwards missionaries to that tribe.

In 1804 he came to Vincennes, Ind., and in 1805 removed to Clarke County, same State. He had a marked influence upon the churches and Associations of that part of the State. No one of the great benevolent enterprises of the denomination was allowed to pass unnoticed. Living in a part of the country where Antinomianism was industriously taught, he exerted himself to counteract its baneful influence. He was licensed to preach by the mother of all Indiana Baptist churches,—Silver Creek. In 1810 he was ordained by the Maria Creek church. In 1817 he received an appointment as missionary to the Indians of Indiana and Illinois. After his departure for his work the influence of Daniel Parker grew rapidly in the southwestern part of Indiana, and the missionary spirit waned. Mr. McCoy was appointed for one year, but had no thought that he should cease to labor for the red man at the expiration of that time; his plans embraced many years. After spending some time in Western Indiana, it occurred to him that he should move to Fort Wayne and establish a mission. He labored there till 1822, when he established a mission about one mile west of where Niles (Michigan) now is. He named it Carey, after the English missionary. Mr. McCoy and his wife entered upon this missionary work with all the zeal and strength of faith that characterized the life and labors of Mr. and Mrs. Judson. And their faith did not fail. Deprivations, sicknesses, and sorrows such as but few mortals know were not strangers to them. Mr. McCoy rode hundreds of miles through the wilderness, and swam the swollen streams, lying on the wet ground at night, for the sake of carrying forward his missions. He went on horseback to Washington several times to interest Congress in measures beneficial to the Indian. Many months would be occupied in these journeys. One of the severest trials that Mr. McCoy was called to bear was that during his absence from home sickness and sometimes death would visit his family. Five of his children were called by death at different times while he was absent from home. Persons of narrow selfish views would readily call him cruel and indifferent, but men who could rise to his plane of devotion to the work that he believed God had given him can see that his loyalty to the Master was superior even to parental affection. No man loved his wife and children more than he.

Many conversions occurred at the Carey mission. The hymns composed by him on the occasion of the first baptism at Fort Wayne and at Carey are expressive at once of his great joy and his great hope of what would yet be done for the Indian.

He records that the greatest obstacle by far that he was obliged to meet in his labors for the conversion of the Indians was the introduction of whisky among them by white men. So great were his annoyances at one time that he decided to send several of his Indian pupils East to be educated, so that they might become teachers for their own people. They found a ready welcome at Hamilton, N. Y.

His labors at Washington were to secure a territory for the Indians into which the white man might not intrude his wicked commerce. This he regarded as the only sure hope for the Christianization or civilization of the red men. He lived to see some of the tribes settled on their own territory, industrious and happy. In his labors for the passage of such acts as he recommended to Congress he speaks of the sympathy and co-operation afforded him by Spencer H. Cone, William Colgate, and others of his brethren.

Oct. 9, 1825, Mr. McCoy preached the first sermon in English ever delivered in Chicago or near its site. In 1826 he gave up the personal superintendence of the Carey mission for the purpose of selecting lands for the Indians farther West. He made surveys west of the Mississippi River, and several times went to Washington to communicate facts to Congress and to lay his plans before that body. In 1840 he published his "History of Indian Affairs," a volume of 600 octavo pages, and full of interest. In 1842 the American Indian Mission Association was formed, and he was made secretary, with headquarters at Louisville, Ky.

In June, 1846, as he was returning from Jeffersonville, where he had preached, he was caught in a rain-storm, from the effects of which he died in a few days at his home in Louisville.

"His life and labors were truly the connecting link between barbarism and civilization in this region of the country and over a large portion of the West. His perseverance and devotion were morally and heroically sublime. For nearly thirty years he was the apostle to the Indians of the West." His last words were, "Tell the brethren, never to let the Indian mission decline."

McCoy, Milton, M.D., was born in Kanawha Co., West Va., in January, 1824. He professed conversion, and joined the Hansford Baptist church in 1847, being baptized into the fellowship of that church by Rev. M. M. Rock. He commenced the practice of medicine in 1849; removed to Moniteau Co., Mo., in 1853, and to Boonville in 1863. He was a constituent member of the First Baptist church in Tipton, Mo., which was formed in 1858, and of which he was made a deacon. Upon his removal to Boonville he was made a deacon there, and has held the office ever since. For years he has been one of the main pillars in the church.

McCraw, Rev. A. G., a native of Newberry District, S. C., was born June 4, 1803. He is of Scotch descent. In 1818, with his father, he removed to Alabama, and located in Perry County. An industrious student, he pursued an extensive range of historic reading; was baptized at Ocmulgee church in May, 1828, and began at once to preach the gospel; was ordained in 1831, Rev. George Everett receiving ordination at the same time; these two labored much together, mainly as evangelists. They planted a number of churches, had many revivals, and baptized large numbers of converts; in one of their revivals 200 were baptized in Shelby County in 1832. In 1835 he became pastor of the large and influential church at Ocmulgee,—a position which he held for many years. In 1851 he became pastor in the growing city of Selma, where he led a career of success until his death, which occurred Jan. 14, 1861. Always in easy circumstances, Mr. McCraw labored constantly in the ministry, and with but small remuneration. He was prominently connected with the leading interests of Alabama Baptists, earnestly pleading every cause fostered by our State Convention. He was several years president of that body. He reared a highly accomplished family.

McCraw, Rev. N. F., an active and efficient minister of the Bayou Macon Association, La., was born in Tennessee in 1828; did much to strengthen the Baptist churches between the Mississippi and Ouachita Rivers. Died in 1874.

McCulloch, Rev. Jno. V., a pioneer preacher in Arkansas, was born in Tennessee in 1820. He settled in Dallas County, Ark., in 1839, and shortly afterwards began to preach, though not ordained until 1851. Abounding in labors in the gospel, he preached in all the surrounding country; was instrumental in forming most of the early churches in the region between the Ouachita and Saline Rivers. He even extended his labors into the region between the Bayou Bartholomew and the Mississippi River, where he died from malarial fever in 1874. This useful minister is affectionately remembered by the people.

McCully, Judge Jonathan, son of Rev. Samuel McCully, was born in Nappan, Nova Scotia, July 25, 1809. He was converted and baptized in 1849. He removed to Halifax soon after, and became deacon of the North Baptist church in that city, which office he held until his death, Jan. 2, 1877. He was a member of the Nova Scotia Legislative Council and of the Senate of Canada, and judge of the Supreme Court of Nova Scotia. He was an able lawyer, statesman, and judge. He left bequests to Acadia College and foreign missions.

McCully, Rev. Samuel, was born in Nova Scotia. He was converted under the ministry of Rev. Joseph Crandall, and embracing Baptist principles, was immersed by him in 1813. He was ordained at Sackville, New Brunswick, in 1820. From 1827 he was associated in labor with Rev. Charles Tupper at Amherst, Nova Scotia, but preached frequently in Cumberland and Westmoreland Counties. Faithful and earnest, firm yet pacific, his labors were highly prized.

McCune, Hon. Henry E., deacon of the Baptist church at Dixon, Cal., a man of great social, political, and religious influence, an intelligent Christian and generous Baptist. Through his liberality the large college property at Vacaville, worth $20,000, was secured for California (Baptist) College. He is president of its board, and a large contributor to its funds. The Dixon house of worship, an elegant edifice, was erected by his aid as a chief contributor. He was born June 10, 1825, in Pike Co., Mo.; baptized in March, 1840, and joined the Peno church; removed to California, and settled near Vacaville, Solano Co., in 1854; went into the organization of the Vacaville Baptist church in 1856; was ordained as deacon in 1863. In 1873 he was elected to the State senate of California, and served two terms. By occupation he is a farmer, and holds several thousand acres of fine land. Deacon McCune has been greatly prospered; but he holds his wealth as a trust for the Lord, and, though he gives wisely and largely for church and denominational enterprises, and is loved and honored by all who know him, he is one of the most modest and unassuming of men. His home and heart and purse are all for Christ.

HON. HENRY E. M'CUNE.

McDaniel, James, D.D., was one of the men whom the Baptists of North Carolina delighted

JAMES M'DANIEL, D.D.

to honor. He was born near Fayetteville, N. C., in 1803; was baptized in 1827, and began to

preach the same year. He was chiefly instrumental in the organization of the Fayetteville Baptist church, of which he was pastor for thirty-two years. For six years he was pastor of the First Baptist church of Wilmington, N. C., during a part of which time he was also editor of a religious journal.

Dr. McDaniel was one of the founders of the Baptist State Convention, being present at its organization in Greenville, Pitt Co., in 1830, and he had the honor of presiding over its deliberations for nineteen years. He was a trustee of Wake Forest College for many years, and his zeal in the cause of missions was ardent and unremitting. He was clerk of Cape Fear Association for fourteen years. Dr. McDaniel possessed in a rare degree the gifts and graces of the orator, and many are the traditions of the pathos and power of his preaching in his younger days. At a good old age, and with his natural force unabated, this eminent divine was gathered to his fathers in 1870. Wake Forest College conferred the degree of Doctor of Divinity upon him in 1868.

McDonald, Rev. Alexander, was born in 1814, in Scotland. He was converted at Margaree, Cape Breton, and baptized by Rev. Wm. Burton. He studied at Acadia College from 1838 to 1841. He was ordained pastor in Prince Edward Island. He was pastor of Carleton Baptist church, St. John, New Brunswick, from 1846 to 1849. He died Jan. 27, 1851. He was an earnest, faithful, and useful minister.

McDonald, Gov. Charles J., was born in Charleston, S. C., in July, 1793. His parents removed to Georgia during his infancy. In his youth he was sent to a classical school in Hancock Co., Ga., and was graduated at the University of South Carolina during the presidency of Jonathan Maxey, who at twenty-four years of age was president of Brown University. Returning to Georgia, young McDonald studied law, and even in his early manhood took rank with the best lawyers in the State. In a short time he was elected by the Legislature to a judgeship of the Superior Court. Though his duties were confined to a district, he acquitted himself in this office so handsomely that he became known throughout the State as one of its ablest jurists. Having previously been a member of the Legislature, he had acquired some standing among politicians, and in 1839 was elected governor of the State by a handsome majority. In 1841 he was re-elected to the same office, although the State, at an election held for President of the United States only a short time previously, had given a large majority to his political opponents. The fact shows that he was a far more popular man with the people than the party with which he was identified. Retiring from the gubernatorial chair, and being still in the vigor of his days, he resumed the practice of law. But in a short time the people called him to be a judge of the Supreme Court of the State, and he continued in the office until disabled by the illness which

GOV. CHARLES J. M'DONALD.

terminated in his death. He died at his beautiful home in Marietta, Ga., in December, 1860.

Perhaps no man was more popular in his day than Gov. McDonald. Besides commanding all the votes of his party when a candidate for office before the people, he was sustained, from personal considerations, by many who dissented from his political views. This was not because he descended to the low expedients of the partisan in seeking supporters. He utterly despised all unworthy means. It was his fine character which commanded universal respect. His integrity was above reproach, whilst as a politician he always aimed at the general good. On one occasion during a heated canvass, a friend suggested a method by which he might gain a great advantage over his opponent. "It is not honorable," said the governor. "What of that? It will never be known." "I shall know it myself; and a man cannot afford to know anything mean of himself."

The confidence which the people reposed in his judgment was another source of the support he enjoyed at their hands. His mind was remarkably well-balanced. He was singularly sagacious and discriminating; and had he been connected as intimately with the national as with State politics, would have left the impress of his wisdom on the legislation of the country. Throughout life he was

a man of the strictest probity and morality. It is believed by those who knew him best that he had experienced converting grace, and, though not baptized, he was a decided Baptist, and like Nicholas Brown, was closely identified with the Baptists.

McDonald, Rev. D. G., was born Feb. 15, 1843, at Uigg, Prince Edward Island, where his conversion and baptism took place in 1863. He studied at Acadia College, and was ordained at Newport, Nova Scotia, Jan. 16, 1873. He labored as a missionary for some time on Prince Edward Island. Subsequently he became pastor of the Baptist church at Charlottetown, the capital of that province, where his ministry proved highly beneficial.

McDonald, Henry, D.D., was born in the county of Antrim, in the north of Ireland, Jan. 3, 1832. He was nurtured in the Roman Catholic Church, to which his parents and ancestors all belonged. He was educated in the national schools of Ireland, and afterwards passed through the regular course of the Normal School, Dublin. In 1848 he left his native country in consequence of the failure of the patriots to throw from them the yoke of British oppression, and reached New Orleans, which city he left, after a few weeks, to visit Kentucky. He taught school for some time in Greensburg Co., Ky., and afterwards studied law and was admitted to the bar. During his residence in Greensburg County he made a thorough examination of the doctrines of Roman Catholicism, the result of which, after a severe mental struggle, was the rejection of the whole system as unscriptural. Abandoning his faith in the church's dogmas, he was led to a complete trust in Christ alone for salvation. In consequence of this radical change in his religious views and feelings, he publicly professed his faith in Christ, and united with the Baptist church in Greensburg, having been baptized by the pastor, the Rev. George Peck. He soon felt it to be his duty to devote himself to the ministry, and was accordingly licensed by the church and subsequently ordained, in May, 1854. He was invited to the pastorate of the church in Greensburg, and served it with great success for nearly ten years. During this period he was also pastor, at different times, of the Friendship and Campbellsville churches, in Taylor County, and the Mount Gilead church, in Greene County. For one year he was pastor of the Tate's Creek and Waco churches in Madison County, and for six years of the Danville church. He was afterwards pastor of the church in Georgetown, Ky., and at the same time elected to a professorship of Theology in the Western Baptist Theological Institute, from which position he subsequently retired to fill the chair of Moral Philosophy in the Georgetown College, Ky. The honorary degree of A.M. was conferred upon him by the Georgetown College, and the degree of

D.D. by both the Georgetown and Bethel Colleges, Ky. Several years ago, Dr. McDonald was invited to the pastorate of the Second Baptist church, Richmond, Va., which he accepted, and where he still labors with eminent success. In 1856 he married, in Greensburg, Miss Mattie Harding, daughter of the Hon. Aaron Harding, for several successive terms a representative in Congress from Kentucky. Dr. McDonald is greatly gifted as a preacher, impassioned, eloquent, and a master of men's emotional nature. Those who know him intimately honor him greatly.

McDougal, Rev. Alexander, was born in Dublin, Ireland, about 1738. In his twenty-first year he came to America and settled in Wilmington, N. C., from which he soon afterwards removed to Union District, S. C. He and his wife were Presbyterians, but about 1770 he became convinced that he was without Christ. He was deeply convicted of sin. When he found peace in Jesus he united with a Baptist church, and soon began to exhort. He was ordained to the ministry about 1775. This was at the commencement of the Revolution. Warmly espousing the cause of the colonies, "he divided his time, during the war, between cultivating his farm, preaching the gospel, and fighting the Tories." He continued preaching in his adopted State until about the year 1800, when he removed to Kentucky, and settled in Hardin County. Here, in 1803, he became pastor of Nolin church, and he was also pastor of Severns Valley church. He continued to serve these communities until his ninety-fifth year, when he resigned. He died March 3, 1841, aged one hundred and three years.

McDowell, Archibald, D.D., was born in Kershaw Co., S. C., in 1818; became a Christian early; graduated at Wake Forest College in 1849; was for a time tutor in that institution, then took charge of the new enterprise since known as the Chowan Female Institute, at Murfreesborough, and afterwards removed to Milton, where he preached and taught. In 1853–54 he taught in Raleigh, but returned in 1855 to the Chowan Institute, where he has been ever since, having become president in 1862. He received his degree of D.D. from Wake Forest College, of which he has long been a trustee.

McFarland, Rev. Arthur, a pioneer preacher in North Louisiana, was born in Tennessee in 1793; removed to Louisiana in 1821, and with his father-in-law, Elder James Brinson, united with the Pine Hills Baptist church, the first gathered between the Ouachita and Red Rivers. Shortly after he began to preach, and continued to labor in the region where he resided until disabled by age. He died at Athens, La., Aug. 21, 1878. He is mentioned by Benedict as one of his correspondents in Louisiana.

McGee, Rev. W. H., pastor at Minden, La., and secretary of Louisiana Baptist Convention, was born in Mississippi in 1846; graduated at Mississippi College in 1876; in 1877 called to his present field, where his labors have been greatly blessed.

McGuire, Rev. John A., a veteran Baptist minister, residing at Monroe, La., was born in Kentucky in 1799; began to preach at the age of seventeen. He labored successfully in his native State until 1850, when he settled permanently at Monroe, La., where he gathered a few Baptists into a church and became their pastor. The circumstances were most unfavorable, but he labored with such success that a comfortable house was built, and another church gathered at Trenton, on the opposite side of the river. He has lived to witness a commodious brick edifice take the place of the first humble house of worship, and two strong churches grown up from the seed he sowed.

McIntosh, W. H., D.D., a descendant of Gen. McIntosh of American Revolutionary fame, was

W. H. MCINTOSH, D.D.

born in McIntosh Co., Ga., April 4, 1811. After thorough preparation for college, he finished his education in Furman Institution, S. C., under the Rev. Samuel Furman and Dr. Jesse Hartwell. Preached for some years as voluntary missionary, under a license from the Sunberry Baptist church, and was ordained by the South Newport church in 1836. Became pastor at Darien in 1838, where he remained for eleven years. In 1849 he was called to the pastorate in Eufaula, Ala., and remaining there six years, in 1855 he accepted the call of the Siloam church in Marion; and, after a pastorate there of seventeen years, he was, in 1872, called to Macon, Ga., from which he returned to Marion, Ala., in the fall of 1875, to assume the corresponding secretaryship of the Home Mission Board of the Southern Baptist Convention, of which he was president during his long pastorate in that place. The degree of Doctor of Divinity was conferred on him by two institutions in 1868,—Columbian College, Washington, D. C., and Baylor University, Texas. Dr. McIntosh is a man of dignified presence, engaging manners, and high character. There is no minister in our acquaintance more widely honored and beloved. His letters and discourses are traced by a remarkably graceful and vigorous pen; and rare tact, energy, and executive power are displayed in the discharge of the duties of his responsible office.

McIver, Hon. Alex. M., a native of Darlington District, S. C., was born on the 21st of February, 1799. He graduated at the South Carolina College in 1817. He was admitted to practice in the law court in 1820, and in that of equity in 1828. He was a member of the Legislature from 1830 to 1833, and in 1841 was elected solicitor of the northern circuit. He was twice re-elected, and died in his third term, on the 10th of July, 1850. His descendants are among the most honorable in the State. As a Christian and a Baptist he adorned his profession, " walking in all the statutes and ordinances of the Lord blameless."

McIver, Rev. D. R. W., was born in Charleston, S. C., in 1794; was educated at the University of South Carolina. Being a man of large property his early labors were devoted to the poor, preaching on the plantations to the slaves. He filled a successful pastorate at Prattville and Wetumpka, Ala. In 1856 he removed to De Soto Parish, La. Here he labored with great success until 1862. He died Feb. 10, 1863.

McKay, Rev. Uriah, was born in the State of Indiana in 1821. At the age of eighteen he was baptized. He went to Franklin College to obtain a better education, to prepare for usefulness in the world without having the ministry in view; spent some time preaching and teaching in Indiana. He went to Illinois in 1854, and was ordained the next year. He spent fourteen years in Effingham Co., Ill., preaching most of the time for but little compensation. He came to Iowa in 1868, and is now living on a farm at Elm Grove, near Des Moines. He has been employed chiefly since coming to Iowa in preaching to feeble churches in destitute fields, doing good service for the cause of Christ by his earnest labors, his consistent and cheerful Christian life, and hearty co-operation in all denominational works. He represents a class of men in the ministry found in Iowa who, while supporting themselves by the labors of their own hands, have contributed largely to the growth and prosperity of the denomination.

McKenzie, Rev. David Banks, was born in Liverpool, England, June 26, 1836, and came to America, arriving at Boston April 15, 1848. In 1853 he became the subject of religious impressions, and was immersed by Rev. Mr. Pierce, at Gloucester, Mass. He had a natural love for the ocean, followed the sea in early youth, and during the civil war in the United States entered the navy, and was three times promoted for meritorious service. For many years, though he had professed Christianity, he lived in sin, gave himself to the world, was very intemperate, and apparently a moral wreck, until, in December, 1871, he was rescued by sovereign grace, and gave himself fully to the Saviour. He began his real religious life as a temperance preacher, and had immense success in New England, where thousands were reclaimed. He enlisted benevolent persons in the work, and built reformatories in many places. In 1877 he extended his mission to California, and in April, 1880, after two years' absence, returned to that State to labor permanently in the gospel, as temperance reformer and pastor. He possesses unusual gifts for persuading men to forsake their evil ways, and in all places stirs the people to active and earnest work to save the fallen and rescue the perishing from temporal and eternal ruin.

McKenzie, William S., D.D., was born in Liverpool, Nova Scotia, Feb. 29, 1832. He was a graduate of Harvard University in the class of 1855. He was ordained in April, 1857, and was pastor of the church in Abington, Mass., one year, and of the church in Andover, Mass., for two years. For six years he was pastor of the Friendship Street church in Providence, R. I., and was pastor in St. John, New Brunswick, also six years. In 1872 he received an appointment as district secretary of the American Baptist Missionary Union, which position he now holds.

McKinlay, Rev. John, was born in Alexandria, Dumbartonshire, Scotland, March 6, 1831. He came to this country in 1855, and was employed as a designer in the Pacific Mills, Lawrence, Mass. While thus occupied he became a subject of converting grace, and feeling it to be his duty to preach the gospel, he pursued his studies at Fairfax, Vt., and at Andover, Mass. He was ordained pastor of the church in Lebanon, N. H., in November, 1862, where he labored with great acceptance until his death, which occurred Sept. 20, 1868.

" He was a close and diligent student of the Scriptures, always bringing well-beaten oil to the sanctuary. Every sermon bore the stamp of his own genius. He could not be a servile copyist.

He was always John McKinlay, and Scotch at that. He had the Scotch acumen to detect the truth, the Scotch tenacity to hold it, the Scotch wit to garnish it in impressive style, and he had withal the Scotch energy and accent of speech to apply it."

McLafferty, Rev. B. S., educated for the law, dedicated himself to the ministry, and was pastor in Illinois. Under appointment of the Home Mission Society he went to the Pacific coast in 1864–65; was pastor at Virginia City, and preached at Carson, the capital of Nevada, until ill health forced him to settle in the better climate of Petaluma, Cal. He had great success here as pastor; sought to establish a Baptist institution at Petaluma; traveled for a time, and did much to enlist the churches in education and in missionary work. He is a busy worker and a vigorous preacher. Continued ill health led him after brief pastorates to take an ocean voyage to China, where he visited missionaries and mission stations. After his return he was pastoral supply of the First Baptist church, San Francisco, for a time pastor at San Diego, and afterwards at Oakland for several years, until near the close of 1878. The Oakland church had large accessions during his ministry. In 1879 he visited the Atlantic States, and on his return made the tour of Oregon, preaching to the churches and assisting in revival meetings. The church at Eugene, the southernmost city in Oregon, and seat of the State University, called him to its pastorate in June, 1879.

McLean, Rev. Thomas George, was born May 18, 1843, of Presbyterian parents, at Montreal, Canada; spent his youth at Chicago and Waukegan, Ill. He was converted at fifteen, and after six years' struggle with doubts as to Presbyterianism, finally yielded to his convictions, was immersed by Dr. Everts, joined the First church of Chicago in 1864, and enlisted in the U. S. army; decided on his return home to enlist in the ministry; graduated in 1869 at the Chicago Theological Seminary, and during his studies had charge of the Erie Street Mission, and preached at Englewood. He settled and was ordained pastor at Cordova, Ill., in 1870. After three years' service at Cordova, with health impaired, he removed to California; was five years pastor at Brooklyn; and in 1878 became missionary and pastor in Santa Barbara County, where he has the oversight of the Carpenteria and Santa Paula churches; preaches at four stations, labors in revivals, and is moderator of Santa Barbara Association.

McLearn, Rev. Richard, was born in Rawdon, Nova Scotia; was converted and baptized when a youth; ordained March 10, 1828, as pastor of the Rawdon Baptist church; subsequently served the church in Windsor, Nova Scotia, as pastor for twelve years, when bronchial disease compelled him to withdraw from the pulpit, but his integrity, piety, and prudence continued to serve the church of Christ until called hence, Aug. 17, 1860.

McLeod, Sir Donald F., Companion of the Bath, and Knight Commander of the Star of India, was born in Fort William, Calcutta, May 6, 1810; his family were Scotch, and to their country he was sent for his education. At eighteen he returned to India, and some time after he was appointed an assistant magistrate.

When about twenty-one, while stationed at Monghir, on the right bank of the Ganges, midway between Calcutta and Allahabad, the Redeemer found and saved him, gave him a new heart and character, and fresh aims and motives. The instrument used in this work was Rev. A. Leslie, a devoted Baptist missionary. Speaking of this change just after it occurred, Sir Donald says, "I have attained a confidence and tranquillity in regard to my worldly duties from which the weakness of my character formerly debarred me, and I have now been freed from despondency and gloominess of spirits, to which for the five previous years I was continually a martyr." And on another occasion, speaking of prayer, he says, "I resort to it in the morning, not only as the most delightful but as the most necessary act of the day, for without it I should have no peace, no power, and during the remainder of the day, whatever of difficulty or annoyance presents itself, my mind flies up to its Creator and is at rest." After obtaining mercy through the blood of the Lamb, he solicited baptism. Mr. Leslie warned him of the contempt which would meet him from the circle in which he moved, but he was ready to follow Christ in the baptismal waters regardless of all consequences, and he was duly immersed in the name of the adorable Trinity, and he continued to the close of his life in communion with the Baptist denomination.

Sir Donald immediately after his conversion began to plan for the secular and religious enlightenment of the people among whom he lived, whose heathenism deeply moved his heart. He gave large sums of money to assist educational efforts and benevolent movements, and his whole soul was enlisted in the work of the missionaries. Rev. Behari Lal Sing, for many years a missionary of the Free Church of Scotland among his countrymen in India, in relating his conversion from heathenism, tells about his education in Dr. Duff's celebrated school, where he read the Bible, and in a medical institution, without any inclination to Christianity, and then says, "It was the pious example of Sir Donald F. McLeod, his integrity, honesty, disinterestedness, and active benevolence, that made me think that Christianity was something living, that there was a loving power in Christ. Here is a man in the receipt of 2000 or 3000 rupees a month; he spends little on himself and gives away the surplus for education and for the temporal and spiritual welfare of my countrymen. This was the turning-point in my religious history, and led to my conversion."

Sir Donald was specially interested in missions to some of the aboriginal races of India, to be found in large numbers in the hilly regions. These being neither Hindoos nor Mohammedans, are held in contempt by both, and as they have neither literature nor a priesthood, they are far more accessible to the gospel. Among them he sustained missionaries at his own expense, and though death hindered the work, yet many of them have been brought to Jesus.

In his official career his fidelity and talents gradually secured his promotion in the civil service, until he became lieutenant-governor of the Punjab; and in the alarming times of the mutiny, when butchery and terror made the bravest British hearts in India tremble, McLeod, like his Baptist brother, Havelock, felt courageous in the Lord his God, and rendered services to his country which will never be forgotten by natives or Britons while the history of English rule in India is read; for these he was made a Companion of the Bath and a Knight Commander of the Star of India.

He died in London, Nov. 28, 1872, full of the peace of God.

McMaster, Hon. Senator William, was born in 1811, in the county of Tyrone, Ireland, and came to Canada at the age of twenty-two. After a short clerkship in a leading Toronto establishment, he became a partner in the business, and ultimately started for himself as a wholesale merchant. The career thus commenced has been eminently successful, and to-day Mr. McMaster's name is almost a household word in the Dominion, as one of its greatest merchants and bankers. For many years past he has given his attention to purely financial, far more than to commercial, transactions. He is officially connected with several great monetary institutions, the most important of which is the Canadian Bank of Commerce. He has held the presidency of this corporation during a period of twenty years, and its splendid success is largely due to his sagacity and prudence. He was also, for many years, chairman of the Canadian board of directors of the Great Western Railway.

In 1862, at the solicitation of friends, Mr. McMaster reluctantly consented to enter political life, and was elected a member of the upper house of the Canadian Legislature by an overwhelming Liberal majority. Immediately after the confederation of the British American provinces, in 1865, he was chosen Senator of the Dominion, and in that capacity he still continues to serve his country. He was ap-

pointed a member in the same year of the council of public instruction, and in 1873 of the senate of Toronto University.

Mr. McMaster was converted in early life, and

HON. SENATOR WILLIAM MᶜMASTER.

united with the Baptist church in Omagh, about forty miles from Belfast, in his native land. To the denomination in Canada he is a tower of much strength. His generous aid secured the erection and re-erection of the Canadian Literary Institute at Woodstock; and he was chiefly instrumental in the formation of the Superannuated Ministers' Society, of which, from its inception, he has been the honored president. Of home and foreign missions he is a steadfast friend; and to many a feeble church, struggling with a building debt, he has rendered timely help. A leading Toronto paper remarks that " the Jarvis Street Baptist church (in which he worships) is one of the costliest and handsomest in the city, and will as long as it stands remain a memorial of his liberality, and of that of the equally liberal-minded lady who has, since 1871, been his wife." But the crowning achievement of his well-spent life is the erection, at his own cost, of the Toronto Baptist College, which occupies a beautiful site in the Queen's Park.

Mr. McMaster has reached the age of threescore years and ten, but "his eye is not dim, nor his natural force abated." He has been twice married, his present wife being Sarah Moulton, widow of the late James Fraser, Esq., of Newburgh, in the State of New York.

McMinnville College is centrally located for

the Baptists of Oregon, at McMinnville. Chartered in 1852, with Rev. G. C. Chandler as president, in spite of many changes it has continued to gain strength, and now is enlisting the hearty support of all the churches. It has already educated some of the most useful men and women in the State. It has a modest building, a college campus of five acres, $15,000 in endowment funds, and nearly $20,000 already secured for the erection of a brick building. It has four professors, and last year there were 100 students. Rev. G. J. Burchett, the president, is one of the best educators on the Pacific coast. He has the confidence of the churches, and under his administration the college is doing good work for the denomination.

McPherson, Hon. William, was born in Boone Co., Ky., Feb. 15, 1813. His father died

HON. WILLIAM M'PHERSON.

when he was a boy, and left him to care for his mother and her little children. While he met this responsibility nobly, at the same time he obtained a good education. In connection with school-teaching he studied law, and mastering all difficulties, he was admitted to the bar at the age of twenty-one. He first practised law in Burlington, Ky., and from it he removed to Helena, Ark., in 1836, and was successful. From Arkansas he removed to St. Louis, Mo., and remained there till his death, in 1872. Mr. McPherson was a man of commanding presence and strong common sense. He took a prominent place among men by general consent. He was a man of vast information. He had one of the finest private libraries in the West. He was

noted for his quick penetration and well-considered plans. He had great magnetic power to sway men, of which he seemed to be unconscious.

He was a decided Baptist. On Jan. 8, 1843, he was baptized by Rev. J. T. Hinton, and united with the Second Baptist church of St. Louis. He was an unconscious leader in Zion. His gifts to his church were large. He inaugurated the building of the house of worship at the corner of Sixth and Locust Streets, and gave to it over $6000. He held official positions in our State and national denominational societies.

The great bridge across the Mississippi at St. Louis was built by capital which he secured in New York, which was necessary to its success, and he was president of the company. The first railroad to St. Louis was established by his aid. He was president of the North Missouri Railroad, and was a prominent mover in the establishment of the Bellefontaine Cemetery. His labors for the growth of the city of St. Louis were not surpassed, if equaled, by any other man. His will to accomplish great things, through difficulties, was imperial.

After a long illness, he came to church for the last time borne in a chair. Strong men wept as he came in. Dr. G. Anderson, his former pastor, preached. Dr. Burlingham, pastor at the time, said, "We fear this is too much for you." He answered, "I was determined to come." Just before he died, he replied to a question in reference to his future hope, "I think I stand on granite." These words are inscribed on his tombstone. There the brave man reposes. "Peaceful be his rest!"

McWhorter, A. B., M.D., a native of Sumterville, S. C., was born Jan. 26, 1791; departed this life Sept. 19, 1859; resided in Montgomery, Ala., from 1830 to his death, and constantly secured in that city the universal regard of the people. It is conceded that the Baptist cause at the capital of our State is more indebted to him for the strong position which it has sustained for forty years than to any other person now living or dead. This is the testimony of Dr. Tichenor, who was his pastor for many years. He was conscientiously particular to meet all his obligations, and a more hospitable home was never kept in that city of rare hospitality. Liberal with his money, generous to the poor, kindly affectionate to all men, wise in counsel, and watchful of the interests of the church and of the pastor, it is but just to say that he was a Christian prince among his brethren.

Meacham, Rev. A. W., an able and eminently successful minister of Little River Association, Ky., was born in Christian Co., Ky., Feb. 13, 1818. He was baptized into the fellowship of Pleasant Hill Baptist church in 1838, where he was licensed to preach in May, 1839, and ordained in December of the same year. A few months after his ordination he accepted a call to the church at Paducah, Ky. From Paducah he removed to Middle Tennessee, where he spent some years in evangelizing. In 1844 he took charge of the church at Shelbyville, Tenn. While laboring with it and with several other churches he was attacked with hemorrhage of the lungs, and was so prostrated that he despaired of life, and returned to his native home, expecting to die. In 1854, having partially recovered, he was called to the care of West Union church, in his native county, to which he still ministers. He has aided in the constitution of 25 churches, and has baptized 4000 persons, 20 of whom are known to have entered the ministry. While he was in Tennessee he was two years moderator of Salem Association and twice moderator of the General Association. Since his return to Kentucky he has been seventeen years moderator of Little River Association.

Meachum, Rev. John Berry, was born May 3, 1789; died Feb. 19, 1864. He was pastor of the First African Baptist church of St. Louis. A marble monument marks his grave in the Baptist burial-ground in Bellefontaine cemetery, erected by the First and Second African churches of St. Louis. He took charge of the First Colored church in 1828; was twenty-five years its pastor. He was born a slave; bought his own freedom, then his father's, a Baptist minister in Virginia. He lived in Kentucky, and married a slave-woman. He worked at the carpenter's trade, and purchased the freedom of his wife and children. He came to Missouri in 1815. He built a steamboat in 1835, and furnished it with a library, and made a temperance boat of it. He was worth $25,000 when he died. He was ordained in 1825, gathered a large church and Sabbath-school, and a deep religious and missionary spirit pervaded his church. He died in his pulpit, with armor on.

Meador, Rev. Christian C., was born in Bedford Co., Va., receiving an elementary education in the common schools of the neighborhood. He was baptized into the fellowship of the New Hope Baptist church, then under the care of the Rev. James Leftwich, in 1844. At this time he was farming, and regarded it as his life-work. Being actively engaged in the prayer-meetings and Sunday-school work of the church, he felt it to be a duty to prepare himself to enter into the Christian ministry. He was licensed to preach by the Mount Hermon church in 1849, and in 1850 went to the school at Botetourt Springs, where he remained for about fifteen months. He then returned to his home, and taught school for nearly a year, frequently preaching in destitute neighborhoods. In 1853 he entered the Columbian College, and graduated in 1857. In 1856, still a student, he started a Sunday-school in South Washington, which was quite successful, and a church was organized in 1857, of which he became the pastor, and which he still serves. Mr. Meador has been greatly blessed in his labors, nearly 500 persons having been added to the church through his instrumentality. His pastoral labors are quite onerous, frequently being called upon by members of other denominations in the neighborhood to visit their sick and bury their dead. Twenty-two years of continuous toil among the same people have given him a strong hold upon their affections. Columbian College conferred upon him in 1860 the degree of A.M. in course.

Medbury, Rev. Arnold Rhodes, missionary secretary of the Wisconsin Baptist State Convention, is a native of Seekonk, R. I., where he was born Dec. 10, 1837. His childhood was spent on a farm in his native town. When seven years old he suffered an irreparable loss in the death of his mother, who was a devoted Christian. He obtained a hope in Christ in 1855, and united with the Third Baptist church in Providence, R. I., of which Rev. Jas. B. Simmons was pastor, and by whom he was baptized. Very early in his Christian experience he had strong impressions that it was his duty to preach the gospel, and began preparation for the work. But in this purpose he met with many hindrances, having to depend upon his own resources to obtain means to secure an education. After a two years' struggle, with but little progress, he determined to join two older brothers in California, hoping the more speedily to obtain the means to educate himself. At the end of six years of varied experiences of success and defeat, he found himself deeply in debt, and apparently farther than ever from realizing his cherished plan for study. At this time the Baptist church of Sonora, Cal., to which he had removed his church membership from Rhode Island, licensed him to preach the gospel, and invited him to do such pastoral work as he could without ordination. This experience only deepened his conviction of his need of more thorough preparation for the Christian ministry, and he gladly availed himself of an offer of pursuing a private course of study, under the direction of Rev. D. B. Cheeney, D.D., pastor of the First Baptist church in San Francisco. This arrangement having been suspended, owing to Dr. Cheeney's extended visit in the East, he entered the University of the Pacific, completing about two-thirds of its prescribed course of study. Leaving the university to engage in mission work in Petaluma, he found himself again, in the autumn of 1865, under the private instruction of Dr. Cheeney, and performing pastoral work for the Third Baptist church of San Francisco. He was ordained by a council convened at the call of the First Baptist church, San Francisco, in March,

1867. In the autumn of the same year he entered the theological seminary at Newton, Mass., and graduated in the class of 1870. Receiving the call (which he accepted) of the First Baptist church in San Francisco, he returned again to California to enter this new field of labor. In 1872, Mr. Medbury became the pastor of the First Baptist church in Portland, Oregon. His pastorate here was in every way successful, the church was greatly strengthened, and reached a highly influential position in the city through his ministrations. From this charge Mr. Medbury was called to the Grand Avenue Baptist church, Milwaukee. After five years of successful pastoral labor with this church he accepted a call to the State Street Baptist church, Rockford, Ill., and entered upon his labors there.

When Mr. Medbury came to Wisconsin, in 1874, he was almost immediately made corresponding secretary of the Wisconsin Baptist State Convention, and secretary of the board and its Executive Committee, for which position he had unusual qualifications. During his entire pastorate at Grand Avenue Baptist church he devoted much time to this important missionary work. It is owing largely to his influence that the State Convention reached its high degree of prosperity and accomplished so much successful missionary work. He gave such value and character to the annual reports of the Convention, especially in its statistical tables, conveying such exact information on all Baptist matters in the State, as to awaken a wide-spread interest not only in the State but in neighboring States. While pastor at Rockford, Ill., the board of the Wisconsin Baptist State Convention extended to him an urgent invitation to take charge of its mission work in the State as missionary superintendent and secretary. He has accepted the position, and entered in September, 1880, upon its duties.

Mr. Medbury is a man of fine native powers, and thorough attainments in literary and theological learning. He is a vigorous thinker and an earnest preacher of the gospel. He has qualifications that fit him pre-eminently for the position he now fills. He brings to it the best of executive and organizing powers, and a supreme love for the work, combined with an unquestioned consecration to Christ and his cause on earth.

Medley, Rev. Samuel, was born at Cheshurst, England, June 23, 1733. In his seventeenth year he entered the British navy as a midshipman. He was full of mirth and frolic, and as a consequence he was a great favorite with his ungodly associates. He was wounded in an action with the French when on service in the Mediterranean, and the opportunities he had for serious reflection during his enforced leisure were of lasting benefit to his soul. Some time afterwards he was led to put his trust in Jesus, and he united by baptism with the church of Dr. Andrew Gifford, in London.

His first settlement in the ministry was at Watford, where he was ordained in July, 1768. In April, 1772, he removed to Liverpool, and in it he labored till his death, in 1799. When Mr. Medley entered upon his pastoral duties at Liverpool the church was small, but under his efficient ministry it prospered greatly, and the house was soon enlarged. Mr. Medley was for some years one of the most influential ministers in Liverpool, or in the north of England. He was greatly beloved by the whole denomination, and by large numbers outside the community whose denominational name he bore and whose principles he ardently loved. He enjoyed great faith, and much of the presence of his Redeemer. His last words were, "Dying is sweet work, sweet work, my Father! my heavenly Father! I am looking up to my dear Jesus, my God, my portion, my all in all, glory! glory! home! home!" He was the author of two works, and of some precious hymns, one of which is familiar wherever the English language is spoken:

> "Awake, my soul, in joyful lays,
> And sing thy great Redeemer's praise;
> He justly claims a song from me;
> His loving kindness, oh, how free!"

Meech, Rev. Levi, son of Capt. Daniel and Zerviah (Witter) Meech, was born in North Stonington, Conn., Feb. 14, 1795; baptized by Rev. Roswell Burrows in 1811, and united with the Baptist church in Preston, Conn.; served in the war of 1812; licensed to preach in 1820; ordained in 1824; an evangelist in spirit from the beginning; served as pastor or supply of churches in Preston, Bozrah, Andover, Salem, Packersville, Voluntown, Colchester, Lebanon, Suffield, Second and Third North Stonington, Mystic, Conn., and Exeter, R. I.; organized the Union Baptist church of Montville, Conn.; greatly blessed in all his work; a wise and successful revivalist; earnest and firm in all reforms; benevolent and devoted to missions; mighty in the Scriptures; strong thinker and sound reasoner; full of sympathy and tenderness; baptized 400 persons; had three sons and two daughters; his oldest son, Levi Witter, a graduate of Brown University, is a distinguished mathematician and actuary; his youngest son, Rev. William W., has been an earnest Baptist minister for thirty years. He died at the homestead in North Stonington, Conn., June 4, 1873, in his seventy-ninth year.

Meek, Rev. John, M.D., a pioneer preacher in South Arkansas, was born in South Carolina in 1791; was first a Methodist preacher, then became a Baptist, and began to preach as such in 1837; removed to Union Co., Ark., in 1840. Here he soon organized a church, the first of the missionary Baptist faith in his region. While supporting his family by the practice of medicine, he was indefatigable in his ministerial labors, and was instrumental in planting many churches and organizing several Associations. He died in 1873.

Mell, Patrick Hughes, D.D., chancellor of the State University, and for many years a leading and

PATRICK HUGHES MELL, D.D.

influential Baptist of Georgia, was born in Walthourville, Liberty Co., Ga., July 19, 1814. In his boyhood he studied in the academies in Liberty County and near Darien, Ga., and then he spent two years at Amherst College, Mass., afterwards teaching in the academy at Springfield, Mass., and in the high school at East Hartford, Conn. In 1838, at twenty-four years of age, he returned to his native State, and, after teaching school in lower and middle Georgia for five or six years, was elected to the professorship of Ancient Languages in Mercer University. He entered upon his duties in February, 1842, and continued a professor in that institution for thirteen years, during which time he became noted for his ability as a professor and for the firmness and excellence of his discipline. His connection with Mercer University was dissolved in November, 1855, but in August, 1856, he was elected Professor of Ancient Languages in the State University at Athens. When Dr. Alonzo Church resigned the presidency of the State University, in 1860, Dr. Mell was elected to the chair of Metaphysics and Ethics, which he still holds, although he was, in August, 1878, elected chancellor of the university, and *ex-officio* president of the State College of Agriculture and Mechanic Arts.

50

His position is one of great dignity, and has been filled by him with distinguished ability and success.

Dr. Mell's religious life began in the summer of 1832, when he was baptized by Rev. Samuel Law, at North Newport church, Liberty Co., Ga. He began to preach at Oxford, Ga., in 1840, and was ordained by order of the Penfield church at the request of the Greensborough church, Nov. 19, 1842, at Penfield. From that time to the present he has preached almost without intermission, having charge of various churches, and some of his pastorates continuing for remarkably long periods. He was pastor of the Greensborough church for ten years; of the Antioch church, in Oglethorpe County, twenty-eight years; and of the Bairdstown church, on the line between Greene and Oglethorpe Counties, thirty-three years. Since his election to the chancellorship of the State University he has resigned all his pastorates and has devoted himself exclusively to the duties of his office.

As a preacher, he is logical and argumentative, delighting in the deep doctrinal subjects of the Bible, and rendering them simple and clear to the comprehension of his hearers. The power and penetration of his intellect enable him to grasp a doctrine forcibly and present it clearly; and his skill in the art of thinking and reasoning is so great that he always speaks logically, his conclusions having the force of demonstrations.

As an author, Dr. Mell has issued several works which have been accepted as standards, among which are his works on " Baptism," on " Corrective Church Discipline," and on " Parliamentary Practice." He has also published small works on " Predestination," " Calvinism," " God's Providential Government," the " Philosophy of Prayer," and part of a work, " Church Polity," which promises to be of great value.

As a presiding officer, Dr. Mell has manifested pre-eminent excellence, which has been recognized by his repeated re-election to the presidency of the Southern Baptist Convention and of the Georgia Baptist Convention.

During the late civil war, in response to a call by the governor of the State for six months' troops, Dr. Mell, although professor in the State University, raised a company, of which he was elected captain, and when the regiment to which he belonged was organized, he was elected colonel. As such he remained in actual service six months at different points within the State.

Few, if any, have exerted a wider and more healthful influence in the denomination in Georgia than Dr. Mell.

Melvin, Rev. R. E., a preacher and writer of note in Mississippi, was born in Pennsylvania in 1811; received a good education, and engaged in teaching; made a profession of Christ in 1852, and was baptized near Brandon, Miss.; engaged in the practice of law in the city of Jackson until the close of the war. He then again commenced teaching near Meridian, where he soon began to preach, although not ordained until 1878. Recently a number of well-written articles in the *Mississippi Baptist Record* have attracted notice, and given him reputation as a writer of ability.

Menno and the Mennonites.—Simon Menno was born in Witmarsum, near Bolswert, in Friesland, in 1505. His education must have been of a high order, and his talents were such as to have given boundless success in any worldly calling, or in the leadership of any community except his Anabaptist disciples. He was persuasive and eloquent. He was familiar with the springs that open the hearts of men, and he wielded an astonishing influence for years over large numbers of persons scattered over several countries of Europe, many of whom would have died for him without murmur, and some of whom were martyred because they entertained him, and they knew the penalty before they gave him a hearty welcome to refresh himself in their homes.

In 1529 he became a priest of the Catholic church at Pinningen, in Friesland. At this time he had never read the Scriptures lest they might draw him away from his fidelity to Rome. In this respect he was even more hostile to God's Word than some other priests of his acquaintance. In celebrating mass the question naturally came into his mind, Can the bread and the wine be the real body and blood of the Son of God? At first he imagined that this suggestion came from the Wicked One, and he resorted to the confessional and other papal methods to chain and silence common sense, but Menno was too gifted for the successful use of such instrumentalities. He had been accustomed to spend his time with two priests in "playing, drinking, and other indulgences," but these sacerdotal exercises failed to satisfy him about transubstantiation. He finally concluded that he would despise the curses of lordly prelates, and search the New Testament to solve his doubts. In its light the falsehood of the mass vanished like the shades of night before the rising sun, and its brazen idolatry excited his indignation.

On the execution of Seicke Snyder, at Leeuwarden, for being "rebaptized," he was filled with astonishment to hear of a second baptism and the reason for it, that infant baptism had no warrant from the Word of God. As he read the Scriptures he saw that it had no divine authority. Then he says, "As I remarked this I spoke of it to my pastor (the rector of the church in which he was an assistant), and, after several conversations, he acknowledged that infant baptism had no ground in the Scriptures. Yet I dared not trust so much to my understanding. I consulted some ancient authors, who taught me that children must by baptism be washed from their original sin. This I compared with the Scriptures, and perceived that it set at naught the blood of Christ. Afterwards I went to Luther, and would gladly have known from him the ground, and he taught me that we must baptize children on their own faith, because they are holy. This also I saw was not according to God's Word. In the third place I went to Bucer, who taught me that we should baptize children in order to be able the more diligently to take care of them, and bring them up in the ways of the Lord. But this too I saw was a groundless representation. In the fourth place I went to Bullinger, who pointed me to the covenant of circumcision, but I found, as before, that, according to Scripture, the practice could not stand. As I now on every side observed that the writers stood on grounds so very different, and each followed his own reason, I saw clearly that we were deceived with infant baptism." Menno had no temptation to give up infant baptism, and his prejudices and interests, and even his bodily safety, were linked to it. But the truth was not in it, and the truth, which he loved, drove him into the ranks of the Anabaptists. No denomination at this hour has so many men, like Dunster, Judson, and Noel, as the Baptist, whose convictions have constrained them to renounce the most cherished ties, and make other weighty sacrifices.

Menno for a time was rector of the village church where he had been an assistant, and preached the Word of Life to his parishioners with acceptance; but finally, in 1536, his conscience would permit him no longer to retain any connection with Rome, and he withdrew from the priesthood and communion of the popes. In 1537 he listened to the appeal of a few godly Anabaptists and became their religious leader, an office which he held till he fell at the feet of the great Teacher in Paradise.

Menno was twenty-two years younger than Luther, whom he greatly respected, and whose writings he carefully studied, but his supreme regard for the Scriptures kept him from adopting any guide except revelation.

When he accepted his new office he knew the fierce cruelties and the violent death which it invited, and which it was likely to bring upon him, but washed in the Saviour's blood himself, he could not withhold the glorious gospel from the millions of doomed papal bondmen, whose present darkness and prospective torments enlisted the deepest sympathies of his soul. He went everywhere preaching Jesus. As a distinguished writer says, "For about five-and-twenty years he traveled with his wife and children amid perpetual sufferings and daily perils of his life over many districts of country,—first in West Friesland, the territory of Groningen, and East Friesland, and then in Gelderland, Holland, Brabant, Westphalia, and the German provinces along the shores of the Baltic as far as Livonia, and in this way he gathered an immense number of followers." Menno was one of the master-spirits and master-builders of the sixteenth century, whose immediate disciples were multitudes, and whose influence has journeyed far beyond the borders of the religious community bearing his name.

He died in 1561 at Oldesloe, in Holstein, where his ashes rest in peace.

Menno had a new heart given him in 1535. God "led him from the way of death, and through mere mercy called him upon the narrow path of life;" "he was graciously forgiven of his impure conduct, and loose, vain life through the merit of the blood of Christ," and he went in a mightier power than even Whitefield to proclaim the efficacy of atonement to perishing men. The churches he instituted were composed of professed believers alone, and these were the only subjects of his baptism. He disclaimed the use of force to support, spread, or defend his religious opinions. His views of the Lord's Supper were Scriptural. He denounced wars, self-defense, and oaths, and insisted on personal piety with great and appropriate zeal. While in many highly important things Menno agreed with us, facts incline us to the conviction that the mode of baptism with him was indifferent. He was almost a Baptist, though a very decided Anabaptist.

The Mennonites, or the communities founded by Menno, survive the fury of persecution, the hatred of state churches, and the evils that dwell in the heart and tempt in the world. The chief strength of the Mennonites in Europe is in Holland, where, in 1846, they had about 130 churches, and a seminary for ministerial education. They had also communities at that time in East Prussia, in Alsace and Lorraine, in Switzerland, and in the south of Russia. In the United States the Mennonites have about 120 churches and 20,000 members. There are three sects of Mennonites in this country,—the Mennonites, the Reformed Mennonite Society, and the Omish Church. The first and last communities hold the same Confession of Faith, which was adopted in Dortrecht, in Holland, in 1632. The Omish Church differs chiefly from the regular Mennonites in their greater simplicity of dress and strictness of discipline. The Reformed Mennonite Society was instituted to pay special attention to the religion of the heart, and in this respect to restore the spirituality of early times. This denomination has condensed the old creed, but with the other two its members profess to believe that the first lesson of the New Testament is repentance. They baptize only penitent believers (no children); they practise feet-washing; they believe that they should not discharge the duties of a magistrate, or "elevate others to a magisterial office; they forbid the use of carnal weapons and oaths," and "they administer baptism (in the United States) by sprinkling or pouring" ("Confession of Faith of the Mennonites," p. 458, Winchester), though the Rynsburgers, or Collegiants, a branch of the Mennonites, originating in Holland, according to Picart, in 1736, practised immersion (see Burrage's "Act of Baptism," p. 180). The Mennonites of to-day are a little nearer us than orthodox members of the Society of Friends, but they are not Baptists.

Mercer, Rev. Asa S., was born in Georgia in 1790; began to preach in Mississippi in 1812; removed to Louisiana in 1823, and settled on the Ouachita. He long exercised a wide influence, and held many prominent positions. He died in Texas in 1850.

Mercer, Jesse, D.D., was the most distinguished and influential Baptist minister ever reared in the

JESSE MERCER, D.D.

State of Georgia; and it is doubtful if any one, under the providence of God, ever exerted a more beneficial influence among the Baptists of Georgia, or as an instrument in the divine hands ever accomplished more beneficial results for the denomination in the State. "How is Mr. Mercer?" asked Dr. Staughton of a gentleman from Georgia. "He is well," was the answer. "He exerts a great influence in your State," continued Dr. Staughton.

" His word is *law*," the other replied. " I am sure," said the doctor, in return, " it is *gospel.*"

Jesse, the son of Silas Mercer, was born in Halifax Co., N. C., Dec. 16, 1769. His father removed to Georgia about 1775, and settled in Wilkes County, but fled to North Carolina at the outbreak of the Revolution, and did not return until after the war, when Jesse was about fourteen years old. From that time until his death, on the 6th of September, 1841, Jesse Mercer resided in Georgia. His youthful character was free from stain ; not even a profane word was ever used by him, nor was he ever guilty of any deviation from strict truthfulness. He was a sober, staid, discreet youth ; even-tempered in his conduct, never dejected nor morose. He had great command of his passions, and was never known through life to have a personal quarrel with any one. He was a pattern of filial obedience, submitting cheerfully to every command of his parents. He was converted at fifteen, was baptized in his eighteenth year, and soon after began to preach. On the 31st of January, 1788, in his nineteenth year, he was married to Miss Sabrina Chivers ; and before he was twenty years of age he was ordained, on the 7th of November, 1789, by Silas Mercer and Sanders Walker. In succession he then took charge of the churches at Hutton's Fork, Indian Creek, in Oglethorpe County, Sardis, Phillips' Mill, Powelton, Whatley's Mill (now Bethesda), Eatonton, and Washington, his pastoral services extending over a period of fifty years. He by no means confined himself to the churches of his charge, however, but, traveling far and near, he preached the gospel everywhere, with a power never surpassed in the State, and with a pathos and unction productive of the best results.

As a Preacher.—Long will he be held in honorable estimation as a truly able, pious, instructive and powerful minister of the gospel. Said Dr. Basil Manly, Sr., of him, " In his happy moments of preaching he would arouse and enchain the attention of reflecting men beyond any minister I have ever heard. At such times his views were vast, profound, original, striking, and absorbing in the highest degree ; while his language, though simple, was so terse and pithy, so pruned, consolidated, and suited to become the vehicle of the dense mass of his thoughts, that it required no ordinary effort of a well-trained mind to take in all he said." His voice was neither very strong nor distinguished for its compass and melody ; his gesticulations were rather clumsy, and the fastidious could find fault with his manner ; but, notwithstanding all, his appearance in the pulpit was far from being uninteresting.

The fair and comely baldness of his head, his venerable mien, his portly frame, his countenance clothed with meekness, benevolence, intelligence, and devotion, rendered him an object of peculiar interest and respect wherever he stood forth

" To negotiate between God and man,
As God's ambassador, the grand concerns
Of judgment and of mercy."

Whilst he seemed untrammeled by the laws of criticism, he violated not the principles of true taste. His sermons were for the most part doctrinal, yet always tending to practical results. His language had a noble bearing, which made it a suitable vehicle for his noble thoughts. The accurate principles of sound logic ran through his addresses, though its forms were not at all times visible. Ungodly men of cultivated minds listened to his sermons as to an intellectual treat. Religious men enjoyed them as affording a spiritual feast. To the graces of oratory Mr. Mercer made no pretensions, but there was an unction from the Holy One, that breathed from his spirit and beamed from his sweet and heavenly eye, which enchained and animated the hearer, and thus more than supplied the absence of oratorical grace. His words did not often flow down upon the people in a rushing torrent, but rather fell like a refreshing shower. No useless verbiage encumbered his topics. Some preachers are occasionally great because, like a small stream, with a shallow and narrow channel, swollen by a sudden shower, they sometimes dash and roar ; but Mr. Mercer's preaching was like a stream whose channel is wide and deep: it embraced a large scope of religious instruction, exhibited a great variety and richness, and flowed onwards with a mighty and increasing volume.

The Cross of Christ was the fixed, luminous centre of his preaching. He delighted in contemplating the gospel as a scheme which honored God and abased the creature. Upon the majesty of the law ; the exceeding sinfulness of sin ; the amazing obligations of the sinner, and his total inability to rescue himself from his ruined and guilty state ; and upon the infinite virtue of the atonement, and the uncontrolled sovereignty of God, and the glorious efficiency of divine grace, he was truly great. Never was a minister more immovably rooted in the respect, confidence, and affection of his people than was Mr. Mercer, while to all classes of the community he was an object of admiration, reverence, and love.

About 1818 he removed from Greene County to Powelton, where he resided until the end of 1826 or beginning of 1827, when he removed to Washington, which remained his home until death. Of the church at the former place he was pastor for twenty-eight years, and of the church at the latter he was pastor about seventeen years ; but after removing to Washington he resigned the charge of most of his other churches.

Connection with the Index.—In the year 1833 the

Christian Index, published by Dr. Wm. T. Brantly, Sr., at Philadelphia, was purchased by Mr. Mercer and removed to Washington, Ga. For several years he was the editor of the *Index*, assisted by Rev. Wm. H. Stokes, and was the means thus of greatly benefiting the denomination in the State by his wise counsel and skillful expositions of discipline and doctrine. But editorial duties were not congenial to him, and the paper became a pecuniary disadvantage. In 1840 he tendered the *Index*, and all its appendages, to the Georgia Baptist Convention. The gift was accepted, and it was published by the Convention, through a committee, until 1862, when it was sold to Rev. S. Boykin, who for several years had been employed as editor. To Mr. Mercer the denomination in the State is indebted for much of its harmony and prosperity, through the influence exerted for many years by that paper.

Efforts in Behalf of Education.—The cause of education has had no more indefatigable, successful, and liberal advocate in the State of Georgia than Jesse Mercer. He took an active part in the establishment of Mount Enon Academy, in Richmond County, in 1807. He was one of the most munificent supporters of Mercer University from its very inception, and the institution was accordingly named after him. His donations, including legacies to the university, did not amount to less than $40,000.

His Efforts in the Missionary Cause.—No object was dearer to Jesse Mercer than the cause of missions. Through his influence the Powelton Baptist Society for Foreign Missions was established, May 5, 1815; and in the year following he procured the appointment of the Mission Board of the Georgia Association to be a component member of the General Missionary Convention of the Baptist denomination, which board existed for many years, and prosecuted its business with much success. He was uniformly appointed a member of the board, was generally its president, and always one of its most liberal and efficient supporters. In 1820 and in 1826 he represented this board in the General Convention. Not until merged into the operations of the State Convention was this board dispensed with.

For some years Mr. Mercer was an active member, and for a while corresponding secretary of the Board of Trustees of the Co-operating Baptist Associations for Instructing and Evangelizing the Creek Indians, organized under the direction of managers appointed by the Ocmulgee, Georgia, and Ebenezer Associations. By his pen, in the pulpit, and with his purse Mr. Mercer strenuously advocated the mission cause throughout his whole career, and was one of those who organized, and for the ten years of its existence was the master-spirit of, the General Committee of the Georgia

Baptists, which resulted in the establishment of the Georgia Baptist Convention, the grand missionary body of the Georgia Baptists. For eighteen years in succession he was elected president of the Georgia Baptist Convention, and for more than twenty years he was successively elected presiding officer of the Georgia Association.

In the discussion of all weighty and difficult subjects in the religious bodies which he attended he usually took a prominent part, and his views generally decided the question under discussion. On one occasion some important subject was discussed for a considerable time, when a worthy brother rose and said, "Well, I now move that Brother Mercer give us his views, and that the question then be put, without any further debate," intimating that it would be improper for the question to be taken until the Gamaliel of the meeting had expressed his opinion, and that after he should speak little more of importance could well be said.

His Liberality.—He gave hundreds and thousands and tens of thousands. To home and foreign missions, to the Bible, tract, Sunday-school, and publication societies, to Columbian College, and to Mercer University he dedicated many thousands of dollars. His bequests to Mercer University amounted to more than $40,000, and to various other benevolent objects not less than $20,000 or $25,000.

His Character.—With all his greatness and reputation he was lowly and humble. His modesty was conspicuous; yet, though eminently meek and gentle in spirit, he was a man of uncommon firmness and of great moral courage. In matters of principle and conscience he was immovable as a rock. His heart was remarkably tender and sympathetic, and he was kind, courteous, and hospitable. He treated his servants with the greatest humanity and with the most judicious consideration. The mental elevation, the distinguished piety, and the ministerial excellence which were combined in Mr. Mercer partially account for the extensive and wonderful influence he exerted over the minds of men, for no other man has wielded the same power over the Baptists of Georgia, nor is any other Baptist who has ever lived in the State to be compared to him in the beneficial results accomplished by his long ministry. In the denomination in Georgia he stands as a bright and shining light, and while it exists in that State his exalted merit and faithful services will cause him to be held in affectionate and sacred remembrance.

Mercer, Rev. Thomas, an able and zealous Baptist minister, who removed from Georgia in 1818 and settled in Southwestern Mississippi; was an early laborer in spreading Baptist sentiments. To facilitate the cultivation of the song-service of the churches he compiled a collection of excellent hymns. He aided in the formation of the Mississippi Association in 1806. In 1817, Thomas Mercer and Benjamin Davis were requested by the Association to visit the Creek Indians and inquire what could be done towards the establishment of schools and the introduction of the gospel among them, and the funds of the Association were applied for their use, and they were required to account to the Mississippi Society for Baptist Missions, Foreign and Domestic. Upon this journey Mercer died, and was buried among strangers.

Mercer University.—One of the objects of the Georgia Baptist Convention, when organized, as set forth in its constitution, was " to afford an opportunity to those who may conscientiously think it their duty to form a fund for the education of pious young men, who may be called by the spirit and their churches to the Christian ministry." From 1826 to 1832 several beneficiaries were adopted by the Convention, and no less than eight received aid from the Convention in the last-named year. In 1828, Josiah Penfield, a devout deacon of the Savannah Baptist church, offered to give $2500 towards a fund for the education of young ministers, provided the Convention would contribute an equal amount. More than $2500 was subscribed by the delegates at the Convention, in Milledgeville, in March, 1829. From this Penfield legacy, and from annual additions, grew the permanent fund for the education of young ministers, which amounted at one time to $33,400, but which now, owing to losses during the civil war, amounts to about $24,000. Having an educational fund, the Convention resolved, in 1831, to establish a classical and theological school, to be connected with manual labor. This resolution, was offered by Dr. Adiel Sherwood. Lands and money were subscribed, a site was chosen, and on the second Monday in January, 1833, Mercer Institute was opened, so named in honor of Jesse Mercer, who has been called " the most influential minister of his day, and, perhaps, the most distinguished minister of the denomination ever reared up in the State." (Campbell's " Georgia Baptists.")

When it grew into a village the site was named Penfield, in memory of Deacon Penfield. Rev. Billington M. Sanders presided over the institute, and brought to the work indefatigable industry. Under his care the institute attracted students from all parts of the State, and contributed greatly to popularize education in the minds of the people. It was not intended to impart a collegiate education, and its elevation to the dignity of a college was an after-thought, started by the failure to establish the Southern Baptist College at Washington, Wilkes County, for which an endowment fund of $100,000 had been subscribed. Of this sum $20,000 had been contributed by the Central Association, a body of intelligent and liberal brethren, to endow the Central Professorship of Languages and Sacred Literature. That body suggested that Mercer Institute be elevated into a college, and this solved a problem which was puzzling the denomination. The Executive Committee of the Convention took the matter in hand, changed the name of Mercer Institute into Mercer University, procured the transfer of most of the subscriptions which had been made to the Southern Baptist College, and, in December, 1837, obtained a charter for the new university. At its next session, in May, 1838, the Georgia Baptist Convention ratified this charter and elected the first board of trustees. The first meeting of this board was held at Penfield, in July, 1838, when they assumed the management of the institution; and this date may be regarded as the official beginning of Mercer University, though the college classes were not organized until January, 1839.

The board of trustees was composed of the following brethren: Jesse Mercer, C. D. Mallary, V. R. Thornton, Jonathan Davis, John E. Dawson, Malcom Johnson, W. D. Cowdry, J. H. T. Kilpatrick, J. H. Campbell, S. G. Hillyer, Absalom Janes, R. Q. Dickinson, William Richards, Thomas Stocks, T. G. Janes, J. M. Porter, Lemuel Greene, James Davant, F. W. Cheney, E. H. Macon, William Lumpkin, J. G. Polhill, Lott Warren, Mark A. Cooper, John B. Walker, I. T. Irwin, W. H. Pope, men who were representatives of the denomination in piety, wealth, intelligence, and in social and political influence. They gave shape to the institution, and to their wise counsels much of its success is due. Thomas Stocks, a layman, who had labored in building up the institute, was the first president of the board of trustees, and was continuously re-elected for about twenty-five years, until failing health unfitted him for the duties of the office. The university entered upon its career with a liberal endowment for the times. Four agents—Posey, Connor, Davis, and Mallary—were employed in getting the subscriptions to the Washington project transferred, and in obtaining new pledges. In this work Rev. C. D. Mallary was engaged during the years 1837, 1838, and 1839. Rev. Jesse Mercer was by far the largest contributor, as he gave during his life and by will about $40,000. Among those who donated from $1000 to $5000 were Cullen Battle, R. Q. Dickinson, W. H. Pope, James Boykin, T. G. Janes, Absalom Janes, W. Peek, Solomon Graves, and John B. Walker. Within the last twenty years several legacies have been left to the university.

In December, 1844, the manual labor system was indefinitely suspended by the trustees, with the concurrence of the contributors to the university.

The first diplomas were conferred in 1841, and since then there has been a regular succession of graduating classes, with the exception of seven years. An efficient faculty was gradually enrolled. One, Prof. S. P. Sanford, entered the institute as a teacher in 1838, and has served continuously down to the Biblical literature, and it was extended over three years. Two professors usually gave most of their time to instruction in this department of the college. The exigencies of the civil war, in 1862, caused a suspension of the theological department, which has never been revived, owing to a general

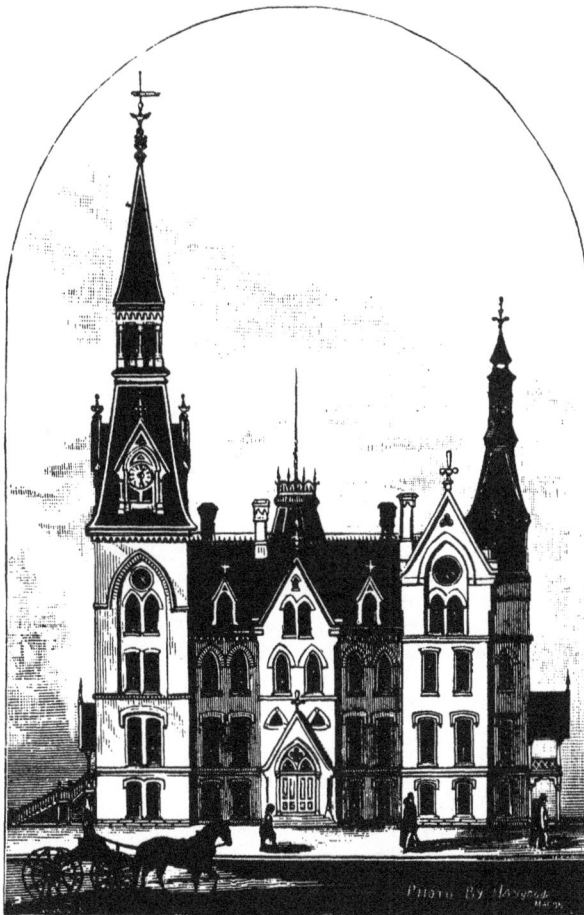

MERCER UNIVERSITY.

present time. Another, Prof. J. E. Willet, an alumnus of 1846, was elected professor in 1847, and has served continuously since that time. In both Mercer Institute and the university a theological education was a primary thought, and was specifically provided for in donations and legacies. Very appropriately, therefore, Rev. Dr. Adiel Sherwood was, in 1840, elected the first theological professor, a position which he occupied three years only, as he then accepted the presidency of Shurtleff College, Ill. In 1845 the theological department was fully organized, embracing Greek, Hebrew, systematic and pastoral theology, ecclesiastical history, and desire to build up the Southern Baptist Theological Seminary.

The curriculum of the classical department in Mercer University embraces the studies usually taught in colleges of respectable grade. The regular course requires four years, and leads to the degree of A.B. A scientific course, including the regular course except ancient languages, is completed in three years, and leads to the degree of B.S.,—Bachelor of Science. Seven have graduated in the scientific course and 440 in the regular course, of whom 77 became ministers of the gospel. Add to these the 12 theological graduates and the

75 who have taken a partial course in the institute and university, and we have a total of 164 Baptist ministers who have received their education in this "classical and theological school" instituted by the Baptist fathers nearly half a century ago.

The law school was organized in 1873. Its course extends through one year, and thus far 24 graduates have received the degree of B.L.

The disasters to the college caused by the civil war led to its dissolution in May, 1865, and the faculty reluctantly closed its doors. The two senior members of the faculty, however, opened a school in the college buildings, and carried on the mixed studies of preparatory and college classes until the close of the year, when the trustees began again the rehabilitation of the university.

There had always been differences of opinion as to the location of the college, and in 1850 a feeble effort was made to remove it to Griffin. About 1853 the Baptists of Northwestern Georgia established the Cherokee Baptist College at Cassville, and soon after those of Western Georgia instituted another at Griffin,—Marshall College. Both failed to secure endowments and passed away. Not long after the war the question of removal was re-opened ; several cities offered valuable pecuniary inducements ; and in April, 1870, the Convention, by a vote of 71 to 16, resolved to remove the university from Penfield ; and at a subsequent conference of a committee of the Convention and the Board of Trustees, it was decided to locate it at Macon, which city gave the university $125,000 of her bonds and seven acres of land on Tatnall Square. A modification of the charter was secured, and the university was removed to Macon in 1871. A large four-story brick building, containing over thirty rooms for recitation purposes and for the library and philosophical apparatus, was erected by the trustees. Another brick building was also reared as a dormitory and dining-hall for the students. A chapel, and a building to contain the museum and to furnish lecture-rooms, were in contemplation also, but the financial panic of 1873 caused a suspension of further building operations.

For more than a quarter of a century the endowment and funds of the university were managed by Thomas J. Burney, treasurer of the Convention, than whom a more faithful and efficient officer never lived. To his discretion the trustees confided the finances of the institution entirely, and that so large a proportion of its funds was saved during the war is due to his wisdom and foresight.

The presidents have been as follows : Rev. B. M. Sanders, 1839 ; Rev. Otis Smith, 1840–43 ; Rev. John L. Dagg, D.D., 1844–54 ; Rev. Nathaniel M. Crawford, D.D., 1855–56 and 1858–65 ; Rev. Henry Holcombe Tucker, D.D., 1866–71 ; and Rev. Archibald J. Battle, D.D., 1872 to date, 1880.

Administration.—Rev. Billington M. Sanders, who had been the central figure in the institute, consented to remain one year as president of the university. It was fitting that he should launch upon its new career of usefulness the bark which he had guided so successfully for six years. Rev. Otis Smith succeeded him, and remained three years. He gave diplomas to the first two graduating classes.

Rev. Dr. Dagg succeeded, in 1844, to a presidency of ten years. With superior mental endowments, solid scholarship, venerable presence, affable manners, aptness in teaching, and steadiness in discipline, he commanded the love and reverence of the whole institution. To the new college he gave dignity and character ; and he made its friends feel that it deserved to take rank among the colleges of the State.

Rev. Dr. Crawford inherited much of the massive intellect of his father, Hon. Wm. H. Crawford. His mind mastered, with equal ease, almost every department of thought. Modest, sincere, sagacious, companionable, independent, and with great clearness and coolness of judgment, he won the respect of his students ; and was a beloved and wise counselor in the assemblies of his brethren. Rev. Dr. Tucker was a president of remarkable originality, acuteness, and readiness. Clear, brilliant, magnetic, he "enthused" his classes as few have the power to do. "You are gentlemen, and the sons of gentlemen," was the key-note of his discipline, which banished from the college all silly tricks and pranks, and encouraged true manliness of character among the students. The fresh vitality of his administration is still felt in the institution.

Rev. Dr. Battle, though a native of Georgia, came from another State, Alabama. His father, Dr. Cullen Battle, had been a prominent Baptist in Georgia until his removal to Alabama, and had been a liberal donor to the university, and his son received a warm welcome on returning to his native State ; and he found friends in all. A Christian gentleman of the highest tone and cultivation, with fine social powers, he has strongly attached to the college the community which contributed so liberally to its endowment.

The university, thus founded in the prayers, sacrifices, and best purposes of the denomination, the centre of its intellectual culture, has ever been the rallying-point of the Georgia Baptists. Sprung from a desire for an educated ministry, it has expanded into a fountain of knowledge for Baptists of every calling. Enlisting their minds and hearts in its great work, the Georgia Baptists have brought to it their offerings of time, money, and wisdom, and when necessary have sacrificed their preferences for locations and measures. Such a fusion of mind and heart has unified and consolidated the denomination, and girded it for the great religious work which it has wrought in the State.

Meredith, Rev. James J., an able minister of Ouachita Baptist Association, La., was born Oct. 27, 1810, and died in Caldwell Parish, La., June 27, 1870.

Meredith, Rev. Thomas, was beyond question the ablest man who has yet appeared among the Baptists of North Carolina, and as the founder, and for nineteen years the editor, of the *Biblical Recorder*, probably did more to develop the denomination than any man who has ever lived in the State. Mr. Meredith was born in Pennsylvania in 1797; came to North Carolina as pastor of the Newbern church in 1820; removed to Georgia in 1822; settled as pastor in Edenton, N. C., in 1825; originated the *Baptist Interpreter* in 1832, which was changed to the *Biblical Recorder* in 1834; removed to Newbern in 1835, and was pastor as well as editor till 1838, when he removed to Raleigh, and taught a female school in connection with editorial labors. Mr. Meredith was the author of the constitution of the North Carolina Baptist State Convention, and of the masterly address of that body when organized in 1830. He was elected a Professor of Mathematics in Wake Forest College in 1835, but did not accept the position. He died in Raleigh in 1851. As an editor, he was the equal of any man in the United States in his day.

Meridian Female College, located at Meridian, Miss., was founded by J. B. Hamberlin since the war. From one to two hundred young ladies are annually taught in this institution. Rev. C. M. Gordon, A.M., is the principal, with whom is associated Rev. M. T. Martin as agent.

Merriam, Rev. Asaph, was born in Gardiner, Mass., in March, 1792; hopefully converted at the age of twenty-five, he united with a Congregational church. Subsequently he became a Baptist, and in 1825 was ordained at Royalston, Mass., and remained here five years. He was afterwards settled over churches in New Ipswich, Canton, Athol, and Bolton. He also supplied one or two churches for a time. His entire ministry extended over a period of about forty years. He died at Bolton, Sept. 19, 1868. He was a useful minister of Christ.

Merrifield, Rev. A. S., was born in Newfane, Vt., April 1, 1837. He belongs to a family of eleven children, all of whom are active members of Baptist churches. Two are in the ministry, three are deacons, and three are ministers' or deacons' wives. He was converted to Christ while a student at Leland Seminary, Townshend, Vt., at the age of seventeen. At this academy he prepared for college, and entered Madison University in 1860. He graduated from college in 1864, and from the theological seminary in 1866. He accepted a call from the Baptist church at Sherman, Chau-

tauqua Co., N. Y., where he was ordained to the ministry Oct. 17, 1866. His pastorate with this church lasted for three years and a half. After this he was pastor at Morris and Sablette, Ill.

Feeling that he might accomplish more good in a new and rising field, he accepted an invitation from a few Baptists in the city of Newton, Kansas, to aid them in starting and building up a Baptist church. With no church organized, no house of worship, and no specified salary, he began labor in this new field in November, 1877. Having no place to hold meetings, these brethren commenced to build a house for that purpose. In January it was completed, and dedicated to the worship of God, free of debt. At that time the church was organized. The preaching of the Word was attended by the power of the Spirit, and many souls were saved. Special meetings were held both in the town and in the country. Thirty persons were baptized, and a goodly number were received by letter and experience. These were the first baptisms that ever took place in the town of Newton. The Baptist church of Newton is a little more than two and a half years old. He has baptized into this church 56 converts, and there have been added in all 164 members.

Mr. Merrifield while in Kansas has, under God, made his own field, and is one of the most judicious, devoted, successful, and able workers in the State.

Merrill, Rev. Daniel, was born March 18, 1765, in Rowley, Mass. He was converted in his thirteenth year; he enlisted in January, 1781, when only fifteen years of age, and fought to the close of the Revolutionary war. He graduated at Dartmouth in 1789 with high honor. He began to preach in 1791, and his first sermon commenced a revival of religion which in a short time brought nearly 100 souls to Jesus. He preached with similar success in several places, staying but a short time in each. In 1793 he formed a church in Sedgwick, Me., of 20 members, on the Congregational platform, and in 1805 it was the largest church of any denomination in the State. Mr. Merrill at this period of great prosperity was filled with doubts about the divine origin of infant baptism, and months after, when he declared himself a Baptist, it produced a great commotion. A Baptist church was then organized of 85 members, and Mr. Merrill was ordained as its pastor. He continued in this field till 1814, when he took charge of a church in Nottingham, N. H., in which he remained seven years. He returned to Sedgwick and again enjoyed extensive revivals, until his death, in June, 1833.

Merrill, Rev. Eliphalet, was born in Stratham, N. H., April 7, 1765. His name is intimately associated with that of Dr. Samuel Shepard, who was the pastor of the church in Brentwood, N. H.

This church has several branches, one of them being in Northwood. Over this branch Mr. Merrill was ordained colleague pastor with Dr. Shepard in 1804, and for thirty years he was the minister of this branch church. He was especially useful in revivals, and made many missionary tours, preaching the gospel and gathering a large number of converts into the churches of New Hampshire. He died in Northwood, Feb. 7, 1853.

Merrill, Rev. Thomas W.—A graduate in the first class that took its full course in Waterville College, and of one of the earliest classes at Newton; commenced missionary work in Michigan in May, 1829. He was the son of Rev. Daniel Merrill, of Maine, who, when a Congregational pastor, was converted to Baptist sentiments, and baptized by Dr. Baldwin, and who was followed by a large part of his church. It was the mission of the son to lead in the commencement and establishment of the educational work of the denomination in Michigan. After teaching in Ann Arbor and Schoolcraft, he enlisted the co-operation of others and gained the charter of what is now Kalamazoo College in 1833. From that time until his death, in 1878, he devoted his life largely to the cause of education, performing gratuitous agency service, and consecrating the accumulations of his life to the endowment of the institution. This is his monument.

Merritt, Rev. W. H., was born in Chatham Co., N. C., in February, 1779; professed faith in Christ in 1801, and began to preach in 1824. He died July 3, 1850, and left $1000 for the erection of a Baptist church at Chapel Hill, and $2000 to Wake Forest College to be appropriated to the education of young ministers.

Merry, Rev. N. G., was born in Christian Co., Ky., July 10, 1824; removed from Kentucky to Tennessee in 1826, where he lived until 1836, when he returned to Kentucky, and remained there until 1840. On the 15th day of May of that year his mistress died, and he was brought again to Tennessee, where he has lived ever since. He removed to Nashville, and resides there at this time. He was converted, and Nov. 1, 1845, he was baptized in the Cumberland River by Dr. R. B. C. Howell. From his conversion he was impressed that he must preach the gospel. He commenced, although with great fear and trembling, to exhort. He tried to shrink from duty, but the more he tried the more forcible became the conviction that of necessity he must preach. In March, 1853, he received a license to fill the pulpit of the colored branch of the First Baptist church. A request was made for his ordination, and a council was called on the 29th of November, 1853, which set him apart to the Christian ministry. Rev. S. Baker, D.D., delivered the ordination sermon. Since then he has preached to the First Colored Baptist

church successfully. He began with 100 members; the church now numbers 2300. During this time he has organized 13 churches. He has had occasion to build four times for his congregation. The present church cost $26,000, and will seat about 1300 persons. The labors of Brother Merry have been wonderfully blessed of the Lord. His influence for good is wide-spread.

Messer, Asa, D.D., LL.D., the third president of Brown University, was born in Methuen, Mass., in 1769. He graduated from Brown University in 1790. He was a tutor in the college for six years. In 1801 he was publicly ordained as a minister of the gospel. Upon the resignation of President Maxcy he was elected to fill his place. He resigned his office in 1826, after having been connected with the university as student and officer nearly forty years. His death occurred at Providence, Oct. 11, 1836.

The estimate in which President Messer was held as a man of scholarly attainments may be inferred from the fact that his own university conferred upon him the honorary degree of Doctor of Divinity in 1806, and Harvard University in 1820. In 1812 the University of Vermont conferred upon him the degree of Doctor of Laws.

His published writings are discourses delivered on different occasions when he was called upon to officiate, on account of his position and his reputation.

Prof. Park and Hon. W. L. Marcy have left on record testimony to the ability and the peculiarities in the character of President Messer, which no one can read without reaching the conclusion that he was a man of mark in the community in which he lived.

Metcalf, Rev. Whitman, was born in Royalston, Mass., Nov. 16, 1797. At an early age he was the subject of serious convictions, and devoted himself to the Lord. It was the desire of his heart that the Lord would honor him by calling him to the work of the ministry. But it was not until June, 1821, that he preached his first sermon by appointment of the Royalston church. The result was a license to preach, which he did as opportunity offered, pursuing his studies at Amherst and Waterville meanwhile. In September, 1825, he was ordained, and sent out by the Baptist Missionary Society of Massachusetts to preach as their missionary in Western New York. He was soon recognized as a leader of the new interests in the western counties of New York, and his services were sought far and near in establishing and fostering churches. He spent six years in Sardinia, Erie Co., building up not only the church there but other flourishing churches in neighboring towns.

The next five years he gave to the church in

Albion, when he returned to Sardinia for three years. He was then appointed by the New York State Convention as their financial secretary, in which service he remained for three years. From 1844 to 1848 he served the church in Brockport, when he was again called from the pastorate by the New York Baptist Education Society to assist for one year in raising funds for her beneficiaries. At the close of this year's service he was employed for one year by the American Baptist Publication Society for New England, when he was called to the church in Springville, which he served from 1850 to 1854, and then removed to Nunda, where he preached with his wonted power and success until 1863, when the infirmities of age compelled him to retire from pastoral work. He resided here, however, until his death, which occurred Nov. 7, 1877. He lived an eventful life, as a missionary, a pastor, and a builder of churches. He came to the close of his earthly career in full age, seeing many communities bearing the precious fruits of his prayers and toils, and loved and lamented by a host of friends.

Michigan, The Baptists of.—The earliest trace of Baptists in the Territory of Michigan is found in Oakland County, in 1818, where the city of Pontiac now stands. Orison Allen and his wife are the first names that appear. In their hands our denominational flag seems to have been brought into the Territory, and over their rude cabin that symbol of our faith and love was first displayed. Others of the same faith accompanied this honored pair, and united with them in efforts to serve the same blessed Master.

After four years, during which these brethren and sisters on this wild shore must have often, like the man of Macedonia, turned wistful looks and pleading calls to the ministers and churches across the lakes for some one to come over and help them, the Paul came over. Rev. Elon Galusha was that Paul. He was the ardent and gifted missionary of the New York Baptist Convention. Brother Galusha reached Pontiac on an itinerant mission in 1822. Here he preached in the wilderness, and led in the organization of the first Baptist church of the Territory.

The population of Michigan, when our first church was planted in it, was about 9000. Detroit was a muddy village of some 1500 inhabitants, among whom, if there was a Baptist, as doubtless there was, his or her memorial has perished.

The first resident Baptist preacher that we learn of in the Territory was Lemuel Taylor, who settled at Stony Creek, in Oakland County. He held the deacon's office, and preached as a licentiate, never desiring ordination. He was a good and useful man, the head of a large family, for whom his hands were diligent, and who perpetuated his use-fulness by their own worth in the churches. As far as in him lay he preached the gospel to his neighbors and in the settlements around, seeking earnestly to plant the virgin soil with true religion and the true church.

The church at this place—Stony Creek—was the second one formed in Michigan. Rev. Nehemiah Lamb and his sons, Revs. C. A. and R. P. Lamb, visiting Pontiac in June, 1824, and breaking bread to the shepherdless flock, organized the brethren at Stony Creek into a church.

The first ordained minister who settled as pastor in our Territory was Elkanah Comstock. As missionary of the New York Convention he volunteered for this remote and solitary service, and took charge of the church in Pontiac in the summer of 1824.

In connection with the labors of Elder Comstock a church was constituted at Troy in 1825, and another at Farmington in 1826, making four churches in the Territory, all in Oakland County.

The Michigan Baptist Association was formed in 1826 of the above four churches, with their two or three ordained ministers.

The second pastor that we learn of was Rev. John Buttolph, who was settled in Troy in 1826. He died with this church the same year. His memory was long perpetuated as that of a loved and successful pastor, a character that was reproduced in his son, also one of the early ministers in the State, who died while yet young, and sleeps by his father's side in Troy.

In Detroit, the year 1826 set the Baptist elements astir, and while they were moving towards securing preaching, Brother Henry Davis, in his studies at Hamilton, was feeling strong impressions impelling him to attempt missionary work in their city. Accordingly, in the summer of this year, he visited Detroit for exploration, and became interested in its few Baptists. The next season (1827) we find him early on the ground with the wife who had given herself to share his life and work. Meetings were established in the academy, and soon baptisms were drawing the interested people to the great river-side to see the new spectacle. The church having formed under covenant, was approved by council of recognition, Oct. 20, 1827. No minister of the Territory was present. The New York Baptist Convention stood nurse to the babe, Elisha Tucker, of Fredonia, presiding and preaching, Jairus Handy, of Buffalo, giving the hand of fellowship, and Asahel Morse, of Ohio, the charge.

Brother Davis, as pastor, addressed himself with enterprise to the building up of the interest. Under his leadership, and with the friendly sympathy and co-operation of Gov. Cass, the grant was secured of the valuable lots, so long occupied, on the corner of Fort and Griswold Streets. But sickness seized and disabled the young pastor, compelling him to abandon his Western work before a year of it was finished.

The next tributary to Baptist influence in Michigan had its rise in the coming of Thomas W. Merrill to this as his adopted field of pioneer work. He entered the Territory in May, 1829, and enjoyed the longest ministerial life in the State which our entire ministry presents. He was from the State of Maine, where his father, a Congregational minister, turned a piece of the world upside down by becoming a Baptist, and by treating his church as "a cake not turned," an "Ephraim who had mixed himself among the people." Thomas had graduated at Waterville College and Newton Theological Seminary. Taking his appointment "not from men nor through man," he started at his graduation from the seminary, and made his way to Michigan at the date aforesaid.

It was his mission, as he had conceived it, and as the event has proved, to start and aid in rearing the Michigan Baptist Institution of Christian and Ministerial Learning, the history of which is detailed in another paper.

Looking across the Territory there is one other quarter in which light was newly breaking at this date, showing that torch-bearers were there setting the fires. It is at the southwest corner, and it reveals Rev. Jacob Price in Cass County. He entered there from Wales in 1831 or 1832, having been furthered on his way by Dr. Cone and others in New York. A Brother Miller, from Virginia, was also working along the Indiana border, adjoining Brother Price's field; and Brother H. J. Hall, from Vermont, was the same year sent as a missionary into that vicinity, and labored with Brother Price happily, and with some cheering ingatherings of souls churches were formed at Liberty, Lagrange, Niles, Edwardsburg, and perhaps over the Indiana line.

Elder Price was the unremitting toiler on that field for forty years. He was benevolence and work personified. God anointed him with the Holy Spirit, and he went about doing good. His kindly countenance was the first preacher's face seen in the cabin doors of the new settlers over a large portion of Southwestern Michigan. Under him numerous churches rose up, and by his wise counsels and Christ-like spirit they guided their affairs with discretion. One generation after another saw his familiar appearance passing along the roads to his scattered preaching-places, and leading the funeral processions of many surrounding towns; and then "he was not, for God took him."

At Comstock, the mother of all the churches in the Kalamazoo River Association was formed by Brother Merrill, Judge Eldred, and others. It is now the Galesburg church.

In 1831 the churches associated in organizing the Michigan Baptist Domestic Mission Society, which kept up its annual meetings, inspired the formation of auxiliaries in all the churches, solicited and appropriated funds, and was in fact what later took the name and form of the State Convention. Foreign missions were alike cared for, and Christian education. Tract circulation was also organized and urged with intelligent liberality and personal labor from the first.

In 1832 there were twenty churches in the Territory and twelve pastors.

Rev. Robert Turnbull became pastor in Detroit in November, 1834, soon after which time the church dedicated their permanent house of worship. During the two and a half years of this pastorate our cause in Detroit advanced well.

At Kalamazoo and vicinity, in 1835, Rev. Jeremiah Hall commenced preaching, and the church was formed the ensuing February. He labored as pastor eight years with discretion and faithfulness, and the church became a steady and central light. The Literary Institute fixed there its permanent location, and began its school-life.

At Schoolcraft, Rev. William Taylor was setting on the candlestick that pure and beneficent light which shone there in such blessing while he lived; ay, and is phosphorescent from his grave there yet, though the storms of more than twenty years have drenched it.

Under these laborers and their co-workers in the churches our growth spread widely. The second Association was called for and formed in 1833 or 1834, bearing then the name of Lagrange, but now the St. Joseph River. And the third, first called the river Raisin, now the Washtenaw Association, was formed on the 14th of January, 1835.

Now came the building and launching of the Baptist Convention of the State of Michigan; for Michigan was becoming a State just in time to allow this name. The story of its organization and growth is reserved for another article.

Of the number of churches and members in the State at the date of the Convention's formation we can only have approximate knowledge. We judge there were about 35 churches and nearly 2000 members.

A large number of ministers came in or were raised up in the churches from 1836 to 1840: Brethren Weaver, Curtiss, Hamlin, J. Harris, N. G. Chase, M. Allen, L. H. Moore, G. B. Day, O. C. Comstock, Fulton, Hendee, Pennell, Rummerey, Wisner, Piper, and others. The American Baptist Home Mission Society came promptly on the field at its origin in 1842, and has been at the front ever since. Almost all the churches, both older and newer, have felt its ready and steady hand of help in their time of need.

In all their efforts, and in general co-operation with missionary, Bible, and other causes, there has been remarkable freedom from partisan divisions and strifes in the churches, Associations, and Conventions. The Baptists of Michigan have been a homogeneous people, respectful towards each other's opinions and modes of action, and determined that no incompatibility should divorce what God had joined together.

The largest number of baptisms in a year was in 1876, when it lacked but little of 3000. The average for fifteen years is a little over 1400. Membership, 27,064. Number of churches, 341, constituting eighteen Associations. For benevolent objects of all kinds, not including what has been done by contributors for their own local churches, they must have given not less than $600,000, all of it in comparatively small sums,— the drops that make the ocean.

Michigan, The Baptist Convention of the State of.

The oldest Baptist church in Michigan —that in Pontiac—was formed in 1822. The first ordained Baptist minister residing in the State entered it in 1824. The first Association was organized in 1827, but no general convention of the Baptists in the State was attempted till 1836. In that year a call was issued to the churches to send delegates to Detroit for a State organization, and in response to the call 26 churches were represented by 55 delegates in Detroit on the 31st of August. Dr. Nathaniel Kendrick, Archibald Maclay, Elon Galusha, Elisha Tucker, and eight others, not residents of the State, were present, and invited to aid the delegates in their work.

The plan of organization then adopted was almost exactly the same as that now in use, after an experience of forty-three years. The design of the Convention was declared to be "to carry out the commission of Christ in giving the gospel to every creature; by multiplying and circulating copies of the Holy Scriptures; aiding home and foreign missions; encouraging Sabbath-school instruction; promoting the circulation of religious tracts; and the cause of education, especially that of the rising ministry." The constitution further provided that the objects contemplated by the Convention "shall be classed in the following order: Bible efforts; home missions; foreign missions; education; general benevolence; and each of the foregoing objects respectively shall be assigned to a specific committee appointed by the Board of Managers."

How little change has been introduced into the general plan of organization after nearly half a century will appear from the following statement of the present plan of work, contained in the by-laws as last printed:

"The board, at its first meeting after its election, shall appoint special boards, consisting of not less than five, nor more than nine members, as follows:

"1. The Board of State Missions.

"2. The Board of Christian and Ministerial Education.

"3. The Board of Foreign Missions.

"4. The Board of Bible Publication and Sunday-school work.

"5. The Board of Home Missions.

"These special boards shall be regarded as co-operative respectively with the general societies of the Baptist denomination for the same objects."

As a result of this organization the American Baptist Missionary Union, and the American Baptist Home Mission Society, and the American Baptist Publication Society, have at their service organized committees to commend their interest to the churches of the State, while other committees are intrusted with the care of new and feeble churches, and with the duty of aiding young men whom God has called to prepare for the gospel ministry. At each annual meeting these subjects come up in turn for consideration, not as intruders, nor simply as welcome visitors, but as the very interests which the Convention was organized to serve.

At the first election of officers, Rev. Robert Powell was chosen president, and Rev. Robert Turnbull secretary, and the Convention entered on its work with hopeful zeal.

Among the objects for which the Convention was formed State missions have naturally occupied a prominent place, both because the demand for missionary work in the State has been great and constant, and because in this work the board was not auxiliary to any broader organization, but responsible for the whole direction and accomplishment of the enterprise. For a few years it co-operated with the American Baptist Home Mission Society in the care of the churches in the State, as was the case in other States, but in 1875 returned to the former plan of separate control. A large proportion of the ablest and largest churches in the State have been fostered by the Convention, and are now glad to recognize their indebtedness.

A second branch of the Convention's work is that of Christian and ministerial education. At the organization of the Convention appreciative recognition was made of the institution at Kalamazoo, and the policy was indicated of having a college with full powers. Funds also were then proposed for theological education. In 1837 a theological school was resolved upon. Funds for beneficiaries were raised and appropriated to students at Hamilton.

In 1846 the establishment of a theological seminary was determined, grounds were purchased in Kalamazoo, and preparations were made for building. The seminary was not, and never became, a separate corporation, but was directly controlled by the Convention, which owned the property, and by its board governed the institution. Prof. James A. B. Stone, pastor at Kalamazoo, and principal of the institute, was placed in charge of the work in the beginning, and retained this place for seventeen years. Instruction began in 1849, and Rev. Samuel Graves was added to the faculty in 1851. After the institute became Kalamazoo College, its professors taught in the seminary as occasion required. In 1866, Dr. Silas Bailey became the principal teacher in the seminary, and remained in this service till the fall of 1869, when the failure of his health compelled him to retire from all severe labor. The funds of the Convention for the support of the seminary had never been adequate, and after the retirement of Dr. Bailey, the seminary at Chicago having been established, it was thought not to provide at present for distinctively theological education. Meanwhile the funds of the Convention which were given for ministerial education are sacredly kept for that purpose, and the income is appropriated in aiding young men in their preparation for the ministry. While the seminary was maintained between 50 and 60 students passed from its studies into the ministry.

In 1869, Rev. Thomas W. Merrill offered to the Convention the sum of $8000 for the support of a professor in Kalamazoo College, who must be a Baptist minister and serve as college pastor. The original endowment was to remain on interest till it should amount to $10,000. In 1874 the same brother proposed to add $14,000 to a previous gift of $1000, for the endowment of scholarships in Kalamazoo College, this addition to become available in 1880 or at his death. These endowments are not at present available, as the notes in which Mr. Merrill made payment are not now paying interest. For one year, however, Rev. Dr. N. S. Burton served in the Merrill Professorship. The funds now in possession of the Convention for educational purposes, besides the Merrill endowments, are about $6000. The Convention also owns the grounds on which the upper buildings of Kalamazoo College are situated, worth about $60,000.

Another enterprise of the Convention was the establishment of a weekly religious paper. Contemplated in the origin of the Convention, and agitated at each of the annual meetings for six years, it was undertaken at the meeting in 1841, and the first number was issued in January, 1842, bearing the name of the *Michigan Christian Herald*. It was put in charge of a committee, of which Rev. Andrew Tenbrook, pastor in Detroit, acted as editor, and R. C. Smith and S. N. Kendrick as publishers. The second year Rev. Miles Sanford performed editorial work. After Prof. Tenbrook was called to the university, Rev. J. Inglis succeeding

him as pastor, also filled the editorial chair. With the year 1848 began Rev. Marvin Allen's proprietorship of the paper, and Rev. Geo. W. Harris assumed editorial care of it. Thence to the death of Mr. Allen, in 1861, these co-laborers supplied the State with the *Herald*. The editor gave eminent satisfaction in his department, and the publisher threw his tireless zeal and rare executive abilities without reserve into the enterprise. On the death of Mr. Allen it was difficult to find a man ready to do his work. The orphaned *Herald* was taken up in Kalamazoo by Brethren Olney, Curtiss, Walden, Clark, and Cadman, and continued to serve the churches well but its publishers ill. In 1867 it was deemed expedient to consolidate the *Herald* with the *Christian Times*, of Chicago, and the *Witness*, of Indianapolis, under the name of the *Standard*, which has since been published in Chicago.

The publication of a weekly Baptist paper for Michigan was, however, commenced again in January, 1873, not by the Convention, but by Rev. L. H. Trowbridge as both publisher and editor. This paper, which bears the name of the *Christian Herald*, is issued from Detroit, and has had a constantly increasing circulation and a continuous growth in power among the churches till now.

Most of the influence which the Convention has exerted has not been of a nature to be easily stated. It has produced unity of action among the churches, has steadily aided in the collection of funds for foreign missions, home missions, and the circulation of religious books, has provided for the support of candidates for the ministry, and has collected and published statistics of the denomination in Michigan. The meetings from the very beginning have been characterized by harmony and an earnest desire to serve the interests of Christ's kingdom.

In Michigan there are 18 Associations, 352 churches, 307 ordained ministers, and 27,285 members.

Middleditch, Robert T., D.D., was born in Bedfordshire, England, May 22, 1825. His father and a brother were Baptist ministers. He became a member of a Baptist church at sixteen years of age, and was educated at an English seminary for missionary students, and in 1844 was sent as a missionary to Jamaica, West Indies, by the English Baptist Missionary Society.

In 1846 he came to the United States, and settled at Lyons Farms, N. J., where he was ordained in 1848. In 1850 he settled at Red Bank, N. J., where he remained as pastor till 1867. He also served the churches of Nyack and Flushing, N. Y., as pastor. In all his settlements he met with success. Since 1872 he has been associate editor of the *Baptist Weekly*. He received the honorary degree of Doctor of Divinity from Madison University.

He is the author of that widely-circulated work, "A Pedobaptist Church no Home for a Baptist;" also a premium mission tract, "The World's Revolution," published for the Southern Baptist Board; "A Baptist Church, the Christian's Home," and "Burmah's Great Missionary." Several sermons preached by him have been published. He is an able and industrious writer and preacher, as his works attest.

Mikels, Wm. S., D.D., was born in Orange Co., N. Y., May 18, 1820. He was graduated from Madison University in 1843, and the theological seminary at Hamilton, N. Y., in 1845. He was ordained pastor of the Baptist church at Rondout, N. Y. After four years of service he then settled in Sing Sing, where he labored six years. In 1856 he accepted the pastorate of the Sixteenth Street Baptist church, New York, which position he filled for seventeen years. This was the great work of his life. It was a continuous revival, and many hundreds were added to the church. Dr. Mikels is a plain, earnest speaker, appealing directly to the hearts of the people. As a friend in need, a counselor in trouble, and as a peace-maker, he has few equals. For some years he has been the pastor of the East Baptist church, located in the Seventh Ward.

Miles, Rev. Edward, was born in the arsenal at Philadelphia, Nov. 15, 1812; baptized in Milesburg, Pa., Nov. 25, 1832; ordained at Milesburg, May 15, 1837, and at different periods served the following churches in Pennsylvania: Alleghany, Meadville, Freeport, Loyalhannock, Uniontown, Zion, Kittanning, New Castle, Brownsville, and Red Stone in Union County. June 4, 1852, he took charge of the Second church in Davenport, Iowa, where he still resides.

Miles, Rev. Frederick W., was born in New Brunswick; was a graduate of King's College, Windsor, Nova Scotia, and was converted while attending that institution. Subsequently adopting Baptist principles, he was baptized. He was for some time pastor of the Baptist church in St. John, New Brunswick, and afterwards pastor of the church at Fredericton, New Brunswick. At the opening of the Baptist seminary, in January, 1836, in Fredericton, Mr. Miles became its principal, and so continued till, to the regret of all, sickness compelled him to resign. Enthusiastic and energetic in his work in the seminary and in the gospel, he had the entire confidence of the Baptist denomination, and their highest commendation. He died February, 1842.

Miles, Rev. George Frederick, was born in Mangerville, New Brunswick; converted and baptized in that province; ordained pastor in 1846, and has been pastor at St. George, Moncton, and Sackville, New Brunswick, and also at Amherst, Nova Scotia, and now performs a vast amount of pastoral and missionary work in Cumberland and Colchester Counties, Nova Scotia.

Miles, Rev. John, in 1662, was ejected from the living of Ilston, in Wales, by the Act of Uniformity. Like a considerable number of Baptists in the time of Cromwell's protectorate he was probably pastor of a Baptist church, and officiated as a preacher in one of the state churches. The law, in 1662, compelled him to surrender his relations to the Establishment, and subjected him otherwise to great sufferings if he would carry out his conscientious convictions. He had been a very active and successful Baptist minister. Backus represents him as the "father of the Baptist churches in Wales, which began in 1649." This statement requires some modification, but it is certain that he was exceedingly useful in spreading the truth in the principality. And had he not been a man of strict conscientiousness he would have retained his living in the national church and sacrificed his religious principles. Many followed this course.

In 1663 he and his Baptist friends of Swansea, in Wales, came to Massachusetts, and located at a place to which they gave the name of their old home. They brought their church records with them, and they joined together "in a solemn covenant" (in a church organization) in the house of John Butterworth. Mr. Miles was the pastor of the American Swanzey church. He was a minister of great industry and zeal, and of fearless courage. When the Boston brethren suffered heavily from the persecuting laws of their Puritan brethren, Mr. Miles went to succor them, and give such counsel and encouragement as his wide experience would readily furnish. He stood his ground in Swanzey against all discouragements and threatenings, and proved himself a tower of strength to the abused and persecuted Baptists. He remained the pastor of Swanzey till his death, in 1683.

Mr. Miles was distinguished for his learning, and remarkable for his piety, and such was the blessed influence which he exerted, and the deep impression which he left, that Backus writes of him in 1777, nearly a hundred years after his death, "his memory is still precious among us." And Mather is compelled to place him and Hanserd Knollys among "some godly Anabaptists" who came from England. "Both of these," he says, "have a respectful character in the churches of this wilderness."

Miles, Gen. Samuel, was born at White Marsh, Montgomery Co., Pa., 1739. His grandfather, one of the first settlers of this State, was a native of Wales. In his sixteenth year Samuel Miles joined a company of militia which was ordered to Northampton County to defend its inhabitants from hostile Indians. In his military duties he showed such skill and courage that the governor of the colony, in 1757, sent him an ensign's commission in the troops of Pennsylvania. He was three

GEN. SAMUEL MILES.

years in active service, during which he was advanced to the command of a company; and he was only once slightly wounded.

At the close of the war he married Catharine, daughter of John Wistar, Esq., and entered upon housekeeping and commercial pursuits in Philadelphia. His talents and industry secured for him such a measure of prosperity that in 1774 he retired from business.

When the Revolutionary agitation began Capt. Miles was among the first to show his patriotic ardor. In 1776 he became colonel of a regiment of riflemen, formed by himself, and composed of his neighbors and friends. This body of brave men, one thousand strong, was attached to the regular army under Washington. On the 28th of August, 1776, he fought with great gallantry at the battle of Long Island, and his riflemen showed a heroism worthy of the glorious cause which they represented. But the army of freedom was not equal to the forces of oppression, and for the time being they were compelled to give way. With Col. Miles, Gens. Sullivan and Stirling, and eighty-one other officers were captured. During his imprisonment he was made a brigadier-general for distinguished services in the field. After his release he was for a time deputy quartermaster of the American army for the State of Pennsylvania. His military services were of the

highest importance in the Revolutionary struggle; and his patriotic example exerted an immense influence in stirring up the lukewarm, and in putting the disloyal to shame.

After the conclusion of peace he was elected mayor of Philadelphia, a position which, for generations, has been regarded by its citizens as an honor of unusual magnitude, the duties of which have generally been discharged by distinguished men. The picture of Gen. Miles adorns the office of the chief magistrate of Philadelphia at this time, surrounded by the portraits of his predecessors and successors; and his biography may be consulted in the archives of the mayor's office. Gen. Miles was an alderman of Philadelphia, a member of the Colonial and State Legislatures, and a judge of the Court of Errors and Appeals. He was a man whom his fellow-citizens delighted to honor.

In 1792 he retired again, to a country-seat in Montgomery County. Of this place President Manning, of Rhode Island College (now Brown University), says, "Col. Miles has a most elegant seat, gardens, meadows, etc., and a most remarkable spring, which turns three wheels in one-fourth of a mile from its source. I spent three days very agreeably" (there). In that beautiful home, in gratifying refined tastes, and in extending a generous hospitality to his numerous friends, he spent the remainder of his days. He died Sept. 29, 1805, in the sixty-seventh year of his age.

Gen. Miles was a zealous Baptist, and a warm friend to every Baptist interest. A lady, a relative of the general, who wrote a sketch of his life for *The Assembly's Magazine* of 1806, a Presbyterian periodical, says, "A Scotch nobleman was once complimented upon the number of offices he had filled under the British government, each of which was mentioned to him; 'You have forgotten,' said he, 'to mention one of my honors, which I prize more than all the rest, and that is the office of an elder in my parish church, which I have filled for many years.' The same pre-eminence in ecclesiastical over civil honors was possessed by Gen. Miles for many years in the Baptist church of Philadelphia."

The writer means that the general was a Baptist deacon, and that he esteemed that office his chief honor. Grace had so completely moulded the heart and character of Gen. Miles, that an intimate friend of nearly twenty years' standing "had never once seen him angry." "He loved and cherished his country as if he expected to live in it forever, and yet he served his God as if he constantly felt that he was a stranger in this world, and that his citizenship and home were in heaven."

Miller, Rev. Andrew Jackson, was born in Hardin Co., Ky., Jan. 7, 1839. He was educated at Madison College, Tenn.; was baptized into the fellowship of Mount Zion Baptist church, in Ohio Co., Ky.; licensed to preach in 1859, and was ordained at Cool Spring church, in the same county, in 1861. He was pastor for a time at Henderson, Ky. Afterwards he preached several years at Carrollton, Mo. In 1877 he returned to Kentucky, and took charge of the church at Cloverport. At present he is pastor of Zion church in Henderson County. He has baptized over 1000 persons, and has served the Henderson County Association as moderator during the last three years. He is a brother of Rev. Dr. A. B. Miller, of Evansville, Ind., an able preacher and an efficient pastor.

Miller, D. Henry, D.D., was born in the Isle of Jersey, Oct. 31, 1827. His mother was the daughter of one of the heroes of Bunker Hill. His father was a native of England. On the death of his father Mrs. Miller returned to Boston, where her son received his first training. He was graduated from the Wesleyan Institution in 1845. In 1849 he received the degree of A.M. from Madison University. Soon after the time of his graduation he embraced the views of the Baptists, and was licensed to preach by the Stanton Street Baptist church in New York. In 1847 he was ordained as pastor of the Baptist church in North Stonington, Conn. In 1849 he organized a church of seven members under an old elm-tree in Yonkers, N. Y., where he remained until 1857. In that year he settled in Meriden, Conn., and in 1861 was commissioned as chaplain of the 15th Regiment Conn. Vols. After two years of service in the field, he settled as pastor of the First Baptist church of Trenton, N. J. In 1866 he received the degree of D.D. from Lewisburg University, Pa. In 1867 he accepted the pastorate of the Broad Street church of Elizabeth, N. J. In 1872 he settled with the Worthen Street church in Lowell, Mass., and in 1873 accepted a call from the Plymouth church in New York. In 1875 he took charge of the Noble Street church, Brooklyn, where he has been eminently successful.

Dr. Miller succeeded Rev. Dr. Dowling, some years since, in the editorship of the *Baptist Memorial*, in which he continued for several years, until its sale and removal from New York.

Miller, Rev. Harvey, son of Rev. Samuel Miller (pastor of old Wallingford church, and first pastor of Meriden church in 1817), was born in Wallingford, Conn., April 3, 1814; baptized on the day he was seventeen years of age by Rev. Simon Shailer; soon began to preach; in 1832 entered Hamilton Theological and Literary Institution, and remained four years; ordained at Ann Arbor, Mich., Nov. 23, 1836; returned to Connecticut in 1838, and became pastor of Baptist church in Meriden, where he successfully labored eighteen years

till his death; died Aug. 27, 1856; had an active and quick mind; an extensive reader; often quaint in his mode of expression; laborious worker; realized excellent results in his ministry; beloved and honored.

Miller, Hon. James, was born in West Philadelphia, Pa., Oct. 22, 1822; was baptized into the fellowship of the Blockley church, Philadelphia, by Rev. Joseph Hammett, Oct. 22, 1843. He soon after became one of the constituent members of the First church, West Philadelphia; but subsequently returned to the Blockley church, where for many years he was a faithful member, an honored office-bearer, and an efficient Sunday-school superintendent. In 1872 he connected himself with the Mantua mission interest in West Philadelphia, and by his labors and benefactions largely aided the organization and growth of the present Mantua church. He was prominently identified with the establishment of the Baptist Home of Philadelphia, and is still a member of its board of trustees. He is also a member of the board of curators of the university at Lewisburg, and is treasurer of the Pennsylvania Baptist General Association and the Philadelphia City Mission. In other religious and secular enterprises he is officially connected with the management of important trusts. For several years he was editor and proprietor of the *Philadelphia Progress*. In 1864-65, and again in 1869-70, he was chosen to represent his fellow-citizens in the Pennsylvania State Legislature. In all these varied and responsible positions he has shown himself to be an able officer, a wise counselor, an upright man, and a consistent Christian. He was especially devoted to Sunday-school work, and much of his time has been spent in earnest and successful efforts to so address himself to the young as to make early religious impressions upon their hearts. Of those whom he has thus influenced many will doubtless shine as stars in the crown of his rejoicing.

Miller, Rev. John, was born at Voluntown, Conn., Feb. 3, 1775; experienced a saving change in his eighteenth year; removed to Abington, Luzerne Co., Pa., Feb. 18, 1802. Here he lived and labored until his decease, Feb. 19, 1857, in his eighty-third year. His wife was the fifth lady in the settlement. On the 18th of October, 1802, the Abington Baptist church was recognized, and the same day he was ordained as its pastor, and he served them with singular ability and success until 1853,—a period of over fifty years. But service in this single church was not enough to satisfy the longing desires of his heart. " He cultivated as his field the northern part of Luzerne County, with portions of Wyoming and Susquehanna Counties, embracing the large area commencing on the summit of the Moosic Mountain on the

51

northeast, and extending down its southwestern slope over the Abington hills, and beyond the waters of the Susquehanna." The immense labor required for the work could not easily be conceived, much less performed, by ministers used to the ordinary comforts of the present day. Benton, Blakely, Clifford, Carbondale, Eaton, Exeter, Newton, Northmoreland, Pittston, Providence, Greenfield, and Tunkhannock are churches located now in what was then the geographical field of this hardy missionary and pastor. Such were the herculean labors of this man, performed without remuneration, amid winter's cold and summer's heat, on foot or on horseback, in dangers seen and unseen, but with unfaltering faith and glowing desire to fulfill the ministry given him in the dispensation of grace. And the fruits were more abundant than the labor. He baptized not far from 2000 converts, attended nearly as many funerals. Six whole churches, and parts of six others, the results of his ministry, have become independent bodies; seven preachers of the gospel have been raised up in the one church, and an influence all-pervading had leavened the entire field.

After a ministry of fifty-three years he lingered for a few weeks in great pain, but was calmly released, in the full possession of his mental powers, on Thursday, Feb. 19, 1857.

Miller, Col. John Blount, was born in Charleston, S. C., on the 16th of September, 1782. He studied law at an early age, and was the first notary public ever appointed for Sumter County. His diligence and accuracy in business soon gave him a large and lucrative practice, and the highest respect of the bench and bar.

He joined the Baptist church, High Hills of Santee, in early life, and his devotion as a Christian was even greater than he had exhibited in his legal profession.

In 1817 he was appointed commissioner and register in equity, which office he held until his death, on the 21st of October, 1851. He was elected to the Legislature in the next winter, and re-elected for each term while he lived.

He was a captain, major, and lieutenant-colonel successively in the war of 1812. Hence the title of colonel, by which he was ever afterward known.

Miller, Rev. Manoah D., of Madison, Wis., was born Feb. 15, 1811, in Elizabethtown, N. J. His parents were Manoah and Elizabeth Miller. They were Baptists, and their Christian lives and example made a deep impression on him, and contributed largely in shaping the future of their son. His father was a judge of the Supreme Court of New York. In early life he obtained a hope in Christ and united with the Baptist Church. He completed the full literary and theological course of Hamilton Literary and Theological Institution. He was ordained at Monkton, Vt., and became the pastor of the Baptist church in that place. He subsequently served as pastor the churches at Springfield, Danville, Windham, Wilmington, and Addison, in Vermont. He received the honorary degree of A.M. from Middlebury College. In January, 1853, he came to Madison, Wis., which has been his place of residence since that time. When he came to Madison the Baptist church there had no church edifice. He at once led the church in the work of building, and succeeded in enlisting the city generally in the movement to such an extent as to secure the best edifice for the church, and the most centrally located of any in the place. He was in that early day an active and very useful pastor. He did much outside of his church to organize the missionary and educational work of the State.

In June, 1857, owing to impaired health requiring his retirement from the active work of the ministry, he organized the Wisconsin Bank of Madison, which institution he managed with honor and success until 1861, when he closed it. He continued banking in other forms and connected with other business until 1876, when he withdrew from active business. He is now living in retirement near the city of Madison. He has always taken the liveliest interest in the Baptist church of which he was the pastor, and of which he has continued an active and useful member.

Miller, Rev. R. M., was born in Sevier Co., Tenn., Nov. 3, 1815. He died April 22, 1871. Professed religion when fifteen years of age, and began to preach in early life. He was ordained July 8, 1843. Revs. John Woody, Thos. Jackson, and John Avery composed the Presbytery. Mr. Miller labored in Johnson, Cass, and Pulaski Counties. He was unwearied in work, and he was successful. He was stricken with paralysis, and died soon after.

Miller, Rev. T. Doughty, was born in New York, Sept. 19, 1835. He was brought up in the Episcopal Church. He was converted in 1850; shortly afterwards he pursued classical and theological studies at St. Augustine's Institute, N. Y., with a view to the ministry of the Episcopal Church. He was principal of a public school in Trenton for three years, and he held the same position subsequently in Newburgh, N. Y. In 1856, having learned the truth more perfectly, he was baptized in the Hudson River with his wife at Newburgh. In August, 1858, he was ordained pastor of the Mount Zion Colored Baptist church, of New Haven, Conn. In this church and in Albany his labors were greatly blessed in winning souls to Jesus.

In 1864 he accepted a call from the First African Baptist church of Philadelphia. In this old community he soon became a great favorite, and the seal of the Spirit was given to his ministrations. The membership is three times more numerous than when he assumed the pastorate. Under his guidance the church purchased a larger edifice in a better locality, which is now entirely paid for through the liberality of the members and the generous gifts of friends in the white churches, who appreciate the talents and piety of Mr. Miller. His enlarged edifice is filled, and his usefulness is visible to all that know the community over which he so worthily presides.

Since his settlement in Philadelphia the First African church has sent out a missionary to the land of their fathers, and four young men who have become successful pastors in Wilmington, Baltimore, New Bedford, and in the Indian Territory.

Mr. Miller was appointed to preach the introductory sermon before the Philadelphia Association in 1879; he was the first colored man that ever occupied the position, and he was not placed in it through political bias, but as a simple recognition of his Christian worth; his sermon showed the propriety of the choice. Mr. Miller is a man of scholarly tastes ; he is the best colored preacher ever located in Philadelphia, and his piety is of a high order.

Millett, Rev. Joshua, was born in Leeds, Me., Jan. 26, 1803. He took part of the collegiate course of study at Waterville, and then went to the Newton Theological Institution, where he graduated in the class of 1835. His ordination took place at Charleston, Me., Jan. 6, 1836, where he remained two years, and then went to Cherryfield, where he was pastor five years. Afterwards he removed to Wayne, where he continued until his death, March 10, 1848.

Mr. Millett was the author of "A History of the Baptists in Maine," in which he has gathered up many facts about men and things in that State which were fast passing into oblivion. Future historians of denominational matters in Maine will be grateful for the careful and useful work which he has done.

Milliken, Rev. L. H., was born Aug. 21, 1813, in Logan Co., Ky. He was educated in Nashville, Tenn., graduating Oct. 3, 1838. He professed religion Dec. 27, 1832, in Logan Co., Ky., and was baptized into the fellowship of the Whippoorwill Baptist church, Law County, by Rev. R. T. Anderson, and ordained at the instance of Pleasant Grove church, by Revs. Wm. Warder, O. H. Morrow, and R. T. Anderson. Mr. Milliken spent a year in evangelistic labors in North Alabama; came to Memphis, Tenn., in the winter of 1839, and took charge of the First Baptist church one year. In the winter of 1841 went to Somerville, Fayette Co.,

Tenn., where he remained teaching, and preaching to Somerville Baptist church until the winter of 1851, when, upon invitation of the church of that city, he removed to Aberdeen, Miss., where he labored six years. In the spring of 1856 he accepted a call to Jackson, Miss., where nearly four years were spent. In 1860 he removed to his plantation in Hardeman Co., Tenn., near Grand Junction, to recruit his health from excessive and long-continued labor. In 1862 he became chaplain of the 13th Tenn. Regiment, C. S. A., and he continued in that office until the winter before the close of the war.

Since the war he has been engaged in teaching and preaching the gospel. Through his efforts a substantial house of worship has been built in La Grange, Tenn., costing $5000, and the foundation of another has been laid in Somerville, Tenn., the county seat of Fayette County, the estimated cost of which is $8000, with a fair prospect of completion. Mr. Milliken is possessed of more than ordinary ability and of great piety.

Mills, J. H., was born in Halifax Co., Va., July 9, 1831; was baptized by his father; graduated with first distinction at Wake Forest in the class with Judge W. T. Faircloth of the Supreme Court of North Carolina and Dr. T. H. Pritchard; became president of Oxford Female College in 1855; bought the *Biblical Recorder* in 1867, which he conducted with success for six years; organized the Oxford Orphan Asylum in 1873, of which he has been the superintendent ever since. This noble charity, which has fed, clothed, and educated hundreds of poor orphan children, has been sustained almost altogether by the unaided efforts of this most benevolent and energetic man, and a rich heritage of blessing will rest upon him and his forever for his "works of faith and labors of love."

Mills, Prof. L. R., was born in Halifax Co., Va., Aug. 17, 1840; baptized by Dr. Wingate, Oct. 19, 1859. He graduated at Wake Forest College in 1861, and served four years in the late war. He has been Professor of Mathematics in Wake Forest College since 1871. Prof. Mills was for several years secretary of the board of education, and is a very effective speaker. He is now bursar of Wake Forest College, and one of the rising men of the State.

Milton, John, was born in London, Dec. 9, 1608. His father was a man of taste and of ample resources, and John had everything to contribute to his proper training. When he was only twelve years of age he had an irresistible desire to acquire information, and would sit up till midnight reading, though seriously afflicted with weak eyes and with severe pains in the head. At fifteen he turned some of the Psalms into beautiful stanzas. Before he went to the University of Cambridge, which he entered when he was sixteen years and two months old, he was an advanced classical scholar, and he was well acquainted with ancient and modern theories of philosophy. He studied seven years in Cambridge.

JOHN MILTON.

When he left the university he came to reside with his father at Horton, in Buckinghamshire, with whom he stayed for several years. This period he spent in reading, in learned investigations, and in giving to the world several pieces of exquisite poetry. He could translate with the greatest ease Hebrew, Greek, Latin, French, Italian, and Spanish, and his works carried marks of the wealth of universal learning. They speedily became known all over Europe, and especially in Italy, so that when he visited that country, in 1639, he was received with extraordinary enthusiasm and honor, the leading men in literary and scientific pursuits treating him as if he were Virgil or Dante returning to visit the glorious land in which they spent their earthly lives. Milton was rudely recalled from his Italian ovations by the fierce conflicts of his countrymen, and for twenty years he wielded his pen for liberty with a power almost surpassing that of the sword of Cromwell, the greatest warrior of the whole Anglo-Saxon race. Milton was a republican arsenal stored with intellectual weapons, which he could use with so much ease, and with such fatal effect, that no man could stand before him. Among his countrymen there was not another with his intellect, his culture, and his skill in using his mighty arms. The royalists, with good reason, dreaded and hated him. Cromwell and his followers cherished him with a tender affection.

He was the Latin secretary of Cromwell during his entire protectorate. Latin was the language of diplomacy and of courts in their business relations with each other. It was Milton that wrote the dispatches which made the Duke of Savoy tremble on his petty throne and drop the bloody sword with which he was inflicting martyrdom upon the godly Waldenses. If Cromwell forged his own thunderbolts, his Latin secretary hurled them forth with such a force that their execution was fatal to every plot conceived against Protestantism or England.

Milton was married three times. His last wife survived him for many years, and was buried in Nantwich, Cheshire, in the Baptist chapel. She had been for a long period a member of the Baptist church of Nantwich.

The work with which Milton's fame is now chiefly connected is " Paradise Lost." It was published in 1667. The author was paid £5 for it, and he was to receive £5 more for every 1300 copies sold. He received £10 from the immortal poem, and his widow sold the copyright for £8. " Paradise Lost" altogether brought the author and his wife less than ninety dollars ! Such compensation for the most sublime production ever created by human genius !

How Milton escaped the axe or the halter of Charles II. history does not tell. It is a circumstance so singular that it seems almost miraculous.

Milton had very decided religious convictions. His principal error was a peculiar view about the person of Christ, tending somewhat towards Arianism. His general opinions, however, were those of the Baptist denomination. He believed, for example, that it was not lawful for any power on earth to exercise compulsion over the conscience in religious matters ; that the Word of God was the only authority in Christ's earthly kingdom ; that the government of a church was purely congregational, as contrasted with the usurpations of popes, prelates, and presbyteries ; and that the members of a church should be regenerated persons. His opinion about imputation is sounder than the doctrine of the great theologian of Kittering. He says, " As therefore our sins are imputed to Christ, so the merit or righteousness of Christ is imputed to us through faith. It is evident therefore that this justification, in so far as we are concerned, is gratuitous ; in so far as Christ is concerned, not gratuitous, inasmuch as Christ paid the ransom for our sins, which he took upon him by imputation." The great poet and the great apostle see alike on this blessed subject.

In his " Treatise on Christian Doctrine" Milton

gives a clear account of his views of the mode and subjects of baptism. He says, "Under* the gospel the first of the sacraments, commonly so called, is baptism, wherein the bodies of believers who engage themselves to pureness of life are immersed in running water to signify their regeneration by the Holy Spirit, and their union with Christ in his death, burial, and resurrection. Hence it follows that infants are not to be baptized, inasmuch as they are incompetent to receive instruction or believe, or to enter into a covenant, or to promise or answer for themselves, or even to hear the Word. For how can infants that understand not the Word be purified thereby, any more than adults can receive edification by hearing an unknown language? For it is not the outward baptism which purifies only the filth of the flesh, but the answer of a good conscience, as Peter testifies, of which infants are incapable." The poet then proceeds to refute the arguments, now threadbare, by which Pedobaptists in that day urged the baptism of children. And when Milton concludes he has left infant baptism without any authority or even pretext for its existence.

In regard to the mode and subjects of baptism, Milton, in "Paradise Lost," expresses the same opinion as he gives in his "Treatise on Christian Doctrine,"—

> .... "them who shall believe
> Baptizing in the profluent stream, the sign
> Of washing them from guilt of sin to life
> Pure, and in mind prepared, if so befall
> For death, like that which the Redeemer died."
> xii. 441.

His "Treatise on Christian Doctrine" was written in Latin, and translated in 1825 by Sumner, who afterwards became bishop of Winchester.

Milton in his old age was blind. The Conventicle Act suspended heavy penalties over all who attended religious services other than Episcopalian, for which Milton had no relish, and he stayed at home and read his Bible, determined to give the government no opportunity to inflict vengeance on the most talented enemy of the house of Stuart. He died Nov. 8, 1674. Macaulay says, "Though there were many clever (talented) men in England during the latter half of the seventeenth century, there were only two minds which possessed the imaginative faculty in a very eminent degree ; one of these produced 'Paradise Lost,' the other 'The Pilgrim's Progress.' " John Bunyan and John Milton† were both Baptists.

Mims, Prof. James S., was born in Columbus Co., N. C., Feb. 10, 1817. He wished to be baptized before he was twelve years of age, but his father, fearing he might be acting prematurely, kept him back until he was about thirteen.

He desired immediately to commence preaching, but his father again restrained him for a short time. Having heard his son speak in a prayer-meeting, he gave his consent, and the church at Fayetteville licensed him to preach.

He went first to Chapel Hill, but close application injuring his health, he was compelled to return home. He next studied privately with Prof. J. C. Furman for eighteen months, and then entered Furman Theological Institution. Having spent a year there, he went to Newton, where he graduated in 1842.

In the autumn of the same year he was elected Professor of Theology in Furman University, and entered on the duties of his office in January, 1843, and continued there until his death, which happened in June, 1855.

He was ordained at Society Hill, S. C., in July, 1843, by Brethren J. C. and Richard Furman, J. O. B. Dargan, and John Culpepper. Although eminently fitted for the pastorate, his brethren claimed his services in preparing others for that office.

His face correctly and plainly indicated the leading features of his mind,—gentleness and firmness, native talent and high culture, in short, every characteristic of the highest order of a Christian gentleman. But his "sun went down while it was yet day."

Miner, Rev. Ashur, was born in North Stonington, Conn., Jan. 30, 1772; ordained in 1805; for ten years associate pastor with Rev. Simeon Brown of the Second Baptist church in North Stonington; on the death of the aged minister, Nov. 24, 1815, he became sole pastor, and continued in that office until his death; was the cotemporary of Revs. Jonathan Miner, John G. Wightman, Roswell Burrows, Elihu Chesebrough, John Sterry, Wm. Palmer, the Darrows, and the Babcocks; enjoyed a number of powerful revivals; received nearly 500 into the church ; died Sept. 1, 1836, in his sixty-fifth year.

Miner, Rev. Bradley, was born in North Stonington, Conn., July 18, 1808. He joined the Baptist church in his native place when he was but thirteen years of age. He began to preach at seventeen. He taught for four or five years, combining study with teaching. He was for some time at Newton, and then went to Hamilton, N. Y. His ordination occurred in 1830, when he accepted a call to the First Baptist church in Fall River. After three years of service with this church, he spent the next three years partly in Pawtucket and partly in Woonsocket, R. I., from which place he removed to Neponset, Mass., and was pastor of the church in that village for nine years. In 1846 he went to Pittsfield, Mass., and, as in other places,

---

* Treatise on Christian Doctrine, pp. 431-2. London, 1825.

† Ivimey's Life of Milton, p. 104. London, 1833.

a rich blessing attended his labors. He removed to the South Baptist church in Providence, with which the Fifth Baptist church united, and the church thus composed, under the guidance of their energetic pastor, erected the Friendship Street church. After a ministry of nearly twenty-eight years, Mr. Miner died in October, 1854. With a warm, ardent temperament, and thoroughly consecrated to his work, he was the means of accomplishing no small amount of good in the different fields in which he was called to labor.

Miner, Rev. George Herman, son of Deacon Leland and Bridget W. (Main) Miner, was born in North Stonington, Conn., Sept. 15, 1835, of a historic Baptist family; well trained; taught two years in Bacon Academy, Conn., and two years in Marion Collegiate Institute in New York; prepared for college in the Connecticut Literary Institution, at Suffield; graduated with honor from Brown University in 1863; studied theology; ordained as pastor of the Central Falls Baptist church in Lincoln, R. I., in August, 1864, and remained four years; in September, 1868, became pastor of the Second Baptist church in Cambridge, Mass., and continued until 1872; in October of that year settled as pastor of the Baptist church in Newburyport, Mass., and labored four years; in October, 1876, accepted the pastorate of the Baptist church in New Britain, Conn., where he is now laboring with his characteristic ability and wonted success; devoutly wields a ready eloquence and good pen.

Miner, Rev. Jonathan, was ordained by the First Baptist church in Groton, Conn., in February, 1814; the same year settled as fourth pastor of the First Baptist church in North Stonington, Conn., and remained twenty years; his labors were followed by very powerful revivals in 1814, 1822, 1828, and in 1831; a man of strong native talents, fervent piety, and clear doctrinal views; a superior preacher; died in 1844. The second pastor of this church was Rev. Eleazar Brown; ordained Jan. 24, 1770; died June 20, 1795. The third pastor was Rev. Peleg Randall; ordained Oct. 25, 1792; settled, 1795; resigned, 1813.

Miner, Rev. Simon G., was born in Brookfield, Madison Co., N. Y., March 8, 1808, being the son of Absalom and Mary Miner. He believes that his conversion took place when he was at the age of five years. When twelve years old he was strongly convinced of his duty to be baptized and unite with the church; but the scruples then so common with reference to early conversion caused a postponement until his twenty-first year. He was then baptized into the fellowship of the church of his native town by Rev. Mr. Kelsey. The family having removed to Friendship, Alleghany Co., his impressions, for some time enter-

tained, as to his duty to preach the gospel, then took more decided form. They were shared also by the deacons of the church, in which he was at length, in the absence of the pastor, quite unexpectedly called upon to fill the pulpit. He complied, and was then regularly licensed by the church, the date of this official act being January, 1830. Up to this time he had been engaged in farming. He now abandoned this business, and began a course of study at Hamilton. His health failing, by advice of the faculty and of his physician he left the institution and began the active duties of the ministry, being ordained at Rushford in August, 1834. His pastorates in the State of New York were with the Rushford, Farmerville, and Penfield churches, some months, meanwhile, being spent in the service of the Genesee Sunday-School Union. In 1837, in association with Rev. Alfred Bennett, he was appointed by the New York State Convention a delegate to the General Convention of Western Baptists, held that year in Cincinnati. This resulted in his removal to the West. His first field of labor was at Lafayette and Crawfordsville, Ind. In July, 1841, he became pastor of the church in Franklin, after one year being recalled to Lafayette, where his labors were resumed, and a house of worship built. In 1847 he accepted an appointment as agent of the Missionary Union, serving one year. He then became pastor of the church in Canton, Ill., the pastorate continuing some ten years, characterized by rich blessings, so that the church grew to be one of the strongest in the State, 490 being added by baptism. After a year of service as secretary of the General Association, Mr. Miner was recalled to Canton, and continued in this second pastorate until 1861. He then entered the service of the Union as a chaplain in the army, remaining in it three years. His health becoming impaired, he engaged in business at Bloomington at the close of the war, and has since served churches as a supply, or acting pastor. His whole period of service has been one of signal usefulness, alike in the gathering of converts and the successful administration of church affairs.

Ministers.—The office of the Christian minister was created by God himself, and its existence is to be defended by all the power of the churches. It is the province of the minister to feed the flock of Christ committed to his charge, to preach the glorious gospel of the blessed God to the perishing, to see that the church is kept free from heresy and sin, and to administer baptism and the Lord's Supper. The minister should be "blameless, the husband of one wife, vigilant, sober, of good behavior, given to hospitality, apt to teach." He should be free from all vices, and "have a good report of them who are without."

The official authority of all ministers is exactly

equal; they are all bishops, and each bishop is but an elder. Prelacy and diocesan episcopacy are unknown in the New Testament. The church of Ephesus, a single congregation, recent in organization, had elders or presbyters, and these elders were called overseers (πρεσβυτέρους επισκόπους) by the apostle Paul, that is, *bishops*, as the Greek text informs us, Acts xx. 17, 28. A bishop, like a Romish, Greek, Anglican, or Methodist prelate, had no existence among the officers of apostolic churches, as there were several bishops in one congregation. St. Jerome, in the fourth century, repeatedly confirms this statement, one quotation from whom we will give. Commenting on Titus i. 5, 7, he says, "A presbyter is the same as a bishop, and until, by the instigation of the devil, there arose divisions in religion, and it was said among the people, 'I am of Paul, and I of Apollos, and I of Cephas,' churches were governed by a common council of the presbyters. Afterwards truly, every one reckoned those to be his, not Christ's, whom he baptized. Then it was decreed over the world that one of the presbyters should be placed over the rest, to whom the whole care of the church should belong,"* etc. Jerome was undoubtedly right about the original equality of gospel ministers, and about the agency which reared Christian hierarchies.

Ministers should be supported by the people for whom they labor. "Even so," says Paul, "hath the Lord ordained that they who preach the gospel should live of the gospel."

Ministers are chosen by the churches, and ordained by brethren summoned for that purpose by the authority and invitation of the churches. God calls every true minister to his work, the churches recognize his voice and obey it, by placing those whom he has selected as watchmen upon the walls of Zion.

Minnesota Baptists, Historical Sketch of.— The First Baptist church of St. Paul was the first church of our denomination organized in the State of Minnesota. The Rev. John P. Parsons, under the appointment of the Baptist Home Mission Society, came to St. Paul in May, 1849. After a search of six months for Baptists he found twelve persons in St. Paul and vicinity who were ready for the formation of a church. The organization took place Dec. 30, 1849. The first baptism was administered in April, 1851. The first meeting-house was built the same year, and the funeral service of its pastor was the first held within its walls.

The church grew in numbers, both by conversion and by letter, until they were compelled to

* Idem est ergo presbyter, qui et episcopus et antequam diaboli instinctu, studia in religione fierent, et diceretur in populis . . . communi presbyterorum concilio, ecclesiæ gubernabantur. Hierom., tom. vi. 198. Coloniæ, 1616. For a full discussion of this subject, see Cathcart's " Papal System," p. 57. Philadelphia.

build a larger house of worship, which they entered on New Year's morning, 1863. The little Indian trading-post had now become a commercial city. The church continued to enjoy the divine presence until it was again found necessary to erect a more spacious house, which was built, and for the first time occupied May 30, 1875. The edifice cost $130,000, and it is now free from debt, with money in the treasury of the church. This church is a child of the American Baptist Home Mission Society, as indeed most of the churches in Minnesota are. It has had eight good pastors. The longest pastorate was that of Rev. J. D. Pope, covering a period of nine years. Some of the membership have fallen asleep. Prominent among these we mention the name of the Hon. Horace Thompson, a brother of great wealth, and a generous giver to the cause of Christ. Others who have gone to the better land have left a worthy record. Among the living we mention Deacon A. H. Cavender, a constituent member, and D. D. Merill, who for a period of about sixteen years has held the position of treasurer of the Minnesota Baptist State Convention. Many others are worthy, and would receive honorable mention if space permitted. Five of the Sunday-school scholars and one Sunday-school superintendent are now preaching the gospel.

The First Baptist church, Minneapolis, was organized March 5, 1853, with ten members. It was publicly recognized June 23, 1853. For one year it was supplied with occasional preaching by Rev. Edwin W. Cressey and Rev. T. B. Rogers, both of whom were missionaries of the Baptist Home Mission Society. They have since enjoyed the labors of seven worthy pastors, viz.: Rev. A. A. Russell, Rev. Amory Gale, Rev. J. R. Manton, L. B. Allen, D.D., Rev. W. T. Lowry, Rev. T. W. Powell, Rev. H. C. Woods. This church and the First church of St. Paul are and have been towers of strength to the cause of Christ in Minnesota.

In June, 1852, Rev. T. R. Cressey became pastor of the Baptist church of St. Paul, and incipient measures were taken by him for the organization of the Minnesota Baptist Association. A call having been extended, delegates from four churches convened in St. Paul, Sept. 24, 1852. The churches represented were St. Paul, St. Anthony, Stillwater, and Willow River, now Hudson, Wis. The combined membership of these four churches was 82 ; 60 of this number were residents of Minnesota. This was the entire number of Baptists then in Minnesota so far as known. At the second annual meeting the aggregate membership of the churches was 180. The third annual meeting showed a constituency in the churches of 202. The fourth a membership of 331. The fifth anniversary was held in Minneapolis, at which sixteen churches were represented, having in all 349 members.

STATE CONVENTION.

The following statement pertaining to the organization of the Minnesota Baptist State Convention we copy from the minutes of the Convention of 1861:

" As early as the summer of 1858, many brethren thought that a State organization was demanded by the interests of the denomination. At the anniversary of the Minnesota Baptist Association of that year a committee was appointed to take the matter into consideration. This committee recommended the formation of a State Convention, and immediately after the adjournment of the Association a meeting was called for that purpose, when a preliminary organization was effected, of which Hon. J. H. Keith was President, Rev. J. D. Pope, Secretary, and William Wakefield, Esq., Treasurer."

But little was done that year, except to procure a charter and prepare the way for future operations.

The first annual meeting was held at Winona, Aug. 29, 1859, when the Convention assumed a permanent form by the adoption of the charter and constitution. The principal officers were re-elected. The board agreed to raise $200 towards the salary of Rev. A. Gale, exploring missionary of the American Baptist Home Mission Society for Minnesota.

The second anniversary of the Convention was held at Minneapolis, Sept. 7, 1860. The meeting was largely attended, and manifested a commendable interest in the work of the Convention. J. D. Ford, M.D., was elected President, Rev. J. D. Pope, Secretary, and Wm. Wakefield, Esq., Treasurer. The members of the Convention pledged $200 for colporteur work, with the understanding that two colporteurs would be employed through the year. The services of Rev. B. Wharton and Brother G. L. Case were secured in connection with the American Baptist Publication Society.

The third anniversary of the State Convention was held in Owatonna in 1861, and reveals a gratifying advance. The number of ministers then in the State was 68 ; number of churches, 96 ; number of Associations, 6 ; with a total membership of 2384. At the close of the first decade of conventional work (1868) the statistics show seven Associations, with a membership of 3940. In 1869 the board report that ten of the churches in the State are self-supporting. The whole number of Associations reported at the last anniversary (1879), counting the Scandinavian Baptist Conference as one, is eight, and the total membership in the State is 6854. The three churches reporting the largest membership are First Minneapolis, 421 ; First St. Paul, 346 ; First Rochester, 245.

EDUCATIONAL HISTORY.

Early in the history of the State an effort was made to found a university. A charter was ob-

tained and a primary building erected in the city of Hastings, but the financial embarrassments which occurred in 1857 and 1858 were so severe as to fatally cripple the enterprise. For a number of years no further effort was made to found a literary institution, but at the annual meeting of the State Convention, in the autumn of 1874, a " centennial committee" was appointed, who reported favorably, and at the annual meeting of the Convention, in 1875, three committees were appointed : 1. On location for an academy. 2. On finance. 3. On charter. The committee on location recommended the city of Owatonna as an eligible place for Minnesota Academy. The report was adopted. The committee on finance were authorized at the same meeting to erect an academic building, and if their judgment approved, to commence a school. At the next Conventional meeting (1877) a building had been erected at an expense of $4400, five teachers were employed, and a school in successful operation having 101 students. During the following winter the committee on charter obtained from the Legislature a revision of the old university charter, under which the Minnesota Academy was organized. The finance committee is to be perpetual, having entire charge of the pecuniary affairs of the institution. The endowment fund now amounts to $5500. The academy is already doing a noble service for sound learning. It receives much encouragement from Congressman M. H. Dunnell, a member of the Baptist church in Owatonna, who is deeply interested in the educational affairs of the State, and from other enlightened and liberal Baptists.

In 1880 there were in Minnesota 9 Associations, 154 churches, 112 ordained ministers, and 7056 church members.

Mirick, Rev. Stephen H., was born in Salem, Mass., Jan. 9, 1819. After having been prepared for college in the Latin grammar-school in his native town, he entered Waterville College, Me., and graduated in August, 1838, receiving in course the degree of A.M. in 1841. Removing South, he taught school in St. Helena Parish, La., during 1839 ; and during 1840 was engaged in the preparatory department of the University of Louisiana. In the fall of 1840 he entered Newton Theological Seminary, and finished the course there in 1843. After leaving the seminary, he preached for the Central Baptist church, Philadelphia, for six months, and was ordained in November, 1843, the sermon being delivered by the Rev. R. E. Pattison, D.D., and the charge by the Rev. Stephen Chapin, D.D. Removing to Charlottesville, Va., he supplied the Baptist church in that place for some months, after which he opened a seminary for young ladies, in 1845, which he conducted with much success during eight years. He then removed to Washington, D. C., where he succeeded the Rev. R. W. Cushman, D.D., as principal of a young ladies' school. After four years' labor in this field, he felt it to be his duty to relinquish teaching and give himself wholly to the work of the ministry. Accordingly he became pastor of the First Baptist church in Camden, N. J., remaining a year, and removed, in 1859, to Lewisburg, Pa., where he took charge of the Baptist church, continuing pastor until 1866. During his pastorate in Lewisburg, he acted as Professor of Greek in the university at that place, while the president was absent completing the endowment fund. Owing to a bronchial disease contracted mainly by exposure during the war, he removed to Washington, D. C., where he entered into government employ in February, 1867. Mr. Mirick has frequently contributed to our religious newspapers and periodicals ; was the Washington editor of the *True Union*, Baltimore ; and has contributed to the *Religious Herald* Expositions of the International Sunday-School Lessons for the past seven years. The same Expositions have also been furnished for the *Index and Baptist*, of Atlanta, Ga. During his residence in Washington, Mr. Mirick has been quite active in promoting Sunday-school interests and in supplying churches destitute of pastors. He is now pastor of the Metropolitan Baptist church, a body gathered and organized under his lead, and in a part of the city where a Baptist church is greatly needed.

Missionary Union, American Baptist.—The General Missionary Convention of the Baptist denomination in the United States of America for Foreign Missions, sometimes called the Triennial Convention, was established in Philadelphia, May 18, 1814, and it continued under that name until 1845.

The agitation produced by the slavery question led to an amicable separation of the Southern and Northern Baptists in their foreign mission efforts, after which, at a Convention held in the Baptist Tabernacle, New York, on the third Wednesday of November, 1845, the present Foreign Missionary Society of the Northern Baptists was organized, and it went into operation in May, 1846, under the name of the "American Baptist Missionary Union." The new body assumed all the indebtedness of its predecessor, and became heir to all its effects. Our Southern brethren, immediately after retiring from the General Convention, formed the Southern Baptist Convention, an honored society, a record of whose toils and triumphs is to be found in another part of this work. The Missionary Union has had its representatives preaching Jesus in several quarters of the world, and rich blessings have descended upon its self-sacrificing men and saintly women as they have carried the tidings of salvation to the perishing. The missions to the

Karens and Teloogoos are the most prosperous fields of labor at this moment in the heathen world ; the seal of heaven rests upon them in a more signal manner than upon any other organized efforts upon earth to bring pagans to Jesus. Marvelous success has attended the labors of our missionaries in Germany and Sweden.

The Missionary Union in 1880 had in Burmah 88 missionaries, 448 native preachers, 433 churches, and 21,594 members.

In Assam there were 17 missionaries, 49 native preachers, 13 churches, and 1331 members.

Among the Teloogoos there were 21 missionaries, 77 native preachers, 11 churches, and 15,660 members.

Among the Chinese there were 24 missionaries, 37 native preachers, 16 churches, and 1426 members.

In Japan we had 12 missionaries, 5 native preachers, 2 churches, and 76 members.

In all our Asiatic missions there were 162 missionaries, 616 native preachers, 475 churches, and 40,087 members.

In Sweden we had 150 native ministers, 298 churches, and 18,851 members.

In Germany there were 270 native ministers, 121 churches, and 25,497 members.

In France there were 12 native ministers, 9 churches, and 726 members.

In Spain there were 3 native ministers, 4 churches, and 140 members.

In Greece there was 1 native minister and 1 church, with 7 members.

In our various foreign missions we had 162 American missionaries, 1052 native preachers and pastors, 908 churches, and 85,308 members. In 1880 there were 8419 converts baptized in our different mission stations. The income of the Missionary Union in that year was $290,851.63.

See separate articles on the missions just named, and on AFRICA, ASSAM ; and for foreign missions conducted by our brethren of the South, see article on SOUTHERN BAPTIST CONVENTION, and the TRIENNIAL CONVENTION.

Mississippi, The Baptists of.—In 1780 a company of Baptists from South Carolina and Georgia settled on Cole's Creek, about twenty miles southeast of Natchez, and in the latter part of the same year organized a church, which they called Salem. These consisted of Richard Curtis, Sr., and his wife, Phebe Curtis, his stepson, John Jones, and his wife, and his three sons, William, Benjamin, and Richard Curtis, Jr., with their wives, together with John Courtney, who married Hannah Curtis, and John Stampley, who married Phebe Curtis, Daniel Ogden and wife, and a man named Perkins and his wife ; Jacob Stampley, the brother of John, and James Cole, who married Jemima Curtis, probably accompanied them. Most of these were church members. Richard Curtis, Jr., was a licensed preacher, and John and Jacob Stampley both became ministers afterwards. Upon the organization of the church Richard Curtis, Jr., was chosen pastor. His labors were greatly blessed, and in a short time sinners were converted and desired baptism. As Mr. Curtis was only a licentiate some perplexity arose about the propriety of his administering the ordinance. But it was very properly decided that Curtis, under the authority of the church, might lawfully baptize them. Among the converts baptized was a Spanish Catholic named Stephen de Alvo, who publicly renounced Catholicism. This greatly incensed the Catholics, but as yet they had no power to punish the offense. At this time the country was nominally under the government of Great Britain, but at the peace of 1783 the territory passed for a time into the hands of the Spanish.

People continued to come into the country, and among them some Baptists. William Chaney, a Baptist deacon, and his son, Bailey E. Chaney, a licensed preacher, came from South Carolina. There came also one Harigail from Georgia, and also Barton Hannon and William Owen, all of whom were, or became, Baptist preachers. Harigail proved to be a man of more zeal than discretion, and proceeded to denounce the Catholics in unmeasured terms. This, together with the conversion and active labors of De Alvo, who had become a deacon, incensed them, and they determined to make an example of some of the leaders. William Hamberlin, Richard Curtis, Jr., and Stephen de Alvo were selected as the chief offenders. This was about 1793 or 1794. A letter was written by Gayoso, the Spanish commandant, to Curtis, expostulating with him upon his course. To this Curtis replied bluntly, and an order for his arrest was issued, and he was brought before Gayoso, April 6, 1795. After threatening to send Curtis, Hamberlin, and De Alvo to work in the mines of Mexico, they were discharged, with an injunction not to offend again. An edict was also issued that " if nine persons were found worshiping together, except according to the forms of the Catholic Church, they should suffer imprisonment." But the church continued to meet privately for worship, and Mr. Curtis officiated publicly in a marriage ceremony in 1795. This was considered a violation of the law, and an attempt was made to arrest him, but he made good his escape, in company with Hamberlin and De Alvo, and they made their way on horseback across the country to South Carolina, where they arrived in the fall of 1795. A number of others were also persecuted. At the end of two years and a half Curtis returned, having been ordained during his stay in South Carolina. The country having passed into the hands of the United States, the Baptists henceforward had rest, and prospered greatly. In 1798 an arm of Salem church was extended into Williamson County, and " the Baptist church on Buffaloe" was constituted. Another church was formed in the same county in 1800, called Good Hope, and two in Amite County, Providence, in 1805, and Ebenezer in 1806. These churches, in 1806, united, and formed the Mississippi Baptist Association. Thomas Mercer came into this region in 1800, and David Cooper, a learned and pious man, in 1802. They were soon joined by a number of young ministers, who afterwards distinguished themselves in this part of the State, and through whose instrumentality Baptist sentiments were propagated in Mississippi and Louisiana. The Association became an active body, and its missionaries penetrated to the remotest settlements.

In 1820 the churches contiguous to Pearl River were dismissed to form the Pearl River Association. In the decade from 1830 to 1840 the churches were torn by internal dissensions, on account of Masonry, missions, and Campbellism. In the conflict old Salem suffered her light to be extinguished. From that time forward population rapidly increased, and many able and zealous ministers entered the field, and Baptist sentiments took a deep hold upon the people.

In 1880 there were in Mississippi 59 Baptist Associations, 1537 churches, 831 ordained ministers, and 122,369 members.

Mississippi Baptist, a religious paper, established by the Mississippi Baptist Convention about 1857. Previous to this it had been struggling for existence as a private enterprise. Under the patronage of the Convention a new life was infused into the paper. Rev. J. T. Freeman, an able writer and an editor of experience, was secured to take charge of it. It was removed to Jackson, the capital of the State, and under the management of Mr. Freeman it was winning a fine success, when it was suspended by the events of the war.

Mississippi Baptist Convention.—This body was organized in 1839. Its object has been to foster a missionary and educational spirit. As the fruit, a number of missionaries are laboring in foreign fields, and one of the best colleges in the South has been built up.

The officers elected in 1880 were Col. W. H. Hardy, of Meridian, President; A. J. Miller, Port Gibson, Recording Secretary ; J. T. Buck, Jackson, Corresponding Secretary ; W. T. Ratcliff, Treasurer. The Convention, through its Board of Ministerial Education, contributed $800 to aid thirty ministerial students, and contributed $6000 to support twenty missionaries, three district evangelists, and one State evangelist. Eastern Louisiana and New Orleans are embraced in their field.

Mississippi Baptist Record is published under the patronage of the Mississippi Baptist Convention. It was started in 1876 to promote the work of the State Convention, and J. B. Gambrell, formerly pastor at Oxford, was selected as editor. It was at first issued at Clinton, but subsequently removed to Jackson. Its circulation is full of encouragement.

Mississippi College, located at Clinton, Hinds Co., Miss., was chartered as Hempstead Academy in 1826. In 1827 the name was changed to Mississippi Academy, by an act of the Legislature authorizing the board of trustees to raise by lottery $25,000. The rents of thirty-six sections of the school land, donated by the United States to the State, were given to the academy for four years. In 1830 the name was changed to Mississippi College, and in 1842 it was transferred to the Presbyterians, and remained under their control until 1850, when it was again surrendered to the people. The Baptist State Convention met that year in the city of Jackson, when the college was offered to the Baptists, and accepted by them. An agent was placed in the field, and by 1860 a cash endowment of $100,000 was raised, with $30,000 more pledged, and buildings costing $20,000 erected. Unfortunately the whole endowment was lost by the war, and the college suspended. In 1867, Dr. Walter Hillman found it disorganized, with a mortgage of $10,000 resting upon it, and only eleven students in attendance. At the end of his administration, in 1873, the debts had all been paid, the building thoroughly repaired, $40,000 towards an endowment raised, a faculty of eight professors engaged, and 190 students in attendance. He was succeeded by W. S. Webb, D.D., under whom the institution has continued to prosper until the present time. From 20 to 30 young ministers have been educated annually for some time, many of whom are now filling the most prominent pulpits in Mississippi, Louisiana, and Arkansas; 191 students were in attendance during the term ending in June, 1880.

Mississippi General Association.—This body operates in the eastern part of the State of Mississippi, and was organized some years ago in opposition to the State Convention. But it is believed that a better state of feeling is beginning to prevail, and the two bodies now seem to be co-operating. The jealousies out of which the division grew are passing away, and the day of entire unification is not far distant. The work of the Association is missionary. A long neglected tribe of Indians in their bounds is receiving special attention, and a converted Indian is employed to preach to them. We have not received the data to be able to state particulars of their work.

Missouri Baptist General Association.—In the year 1833 an informal and small meeting of Baptists was held in the town of Columbia, Mo., to devise ways and means for further promoting Christianity in that State. The anti-mission spirit then ruled the Baptist churches of that region, and the few who possessed the progressive spirit of the gospel labored under great disadvantages in all efforts and plans for the spread of divine truth. They were met at every step by the violent and almost virulent opposition of anti-mission brethren.

The meeting at Columbia was composed of Ebenezer Rogers, Thos. Fristoe, Roland Hughes, Joseph Hughes, Tilman Bell, and Wm. Mansfield. These men of God resolved to secure the services of some good minister of the gospel to do missionary work in the central counties of the State. They contributed of their own limited resources the sum of $600 for the remuneration of the men who might be secured for the work. Rev. Wm. Mansfield was selected to correspond with suitable persons until a missionary should be obtained. He wrote to Anderson Woods and Wm. Duncan, both of whom responded favorably to the call. The duty of making arrangements for the proposed mission work was intrusted to Mr. Mansfield. He attended a meeting of the Mount Pleasant Association for the purpose and in the hope of securing some co-operation. At that meeting he was informed by anti-mission Baptists that if he went on the " stand" he should be forcibly ejected from it. At a convenient time in the progress of the meeting he took a position near the stand and read aloud a list of appointments for Woods and Duncan, and then quietly gave a statement of the reasons why he was not on the stand. Mr. Mansfield was a good man, a plain, earnest, and effective preacher, who supported a large family by successful farming. Woods and Duncan were preachers of no mean ability, and while the work they did under Mansfield's arrangements was much opposed, it was greatly blessed in the conversion of souls and in awakening the spirit of missions.

As a result of this effort a meeting was held at Providence church, in Calloway County, in 1834, to effect a permanent organization for doing mission work. The anti-mission spirit was still rife. In this year the churches and Associations were much troubled with contentions and divisions. At the Providence meeting, Thos. Fristoe, Ebenezer Rogers, Wm. Suggett, Noah Flood, and others were present. The meeting adopted preliminary measures for the permanent organization of the Baptist Central Society. This organization was completed the subsequent year. Out of the Central Society grew the present Missouri Baptist General Association, which held its forty-third annual session in October, 1879.

The objects of the General Association are to promote the preaching of the gospel and the spread of divine truth in the State. For the attainment of these objects the constitution provides mission work, Christian education, and the circulation of religious literature.

A mission board of seventeen members and a corresponding secretary have the management of the missionary department. The board endeavors to develop and enlarge the spirit of progress and beneficence, procure the preaching of the gospel to the destitute, and help weak churches to become self-sustaining. This work has contributed largely to making the Baptist denomination the largest and most influential in the State. From $3000 to $5000 are annually expended by the board in State mission work. The local Associations expend about the same sum in their missionary efforts.

William Jewell College—a history of which is given in another part of this work—is an outgrowth of the progressive spirit of the General Association, and is provided for by its constitution. Stephens College, for the education of young ladies, is likewise organically recognized. At each session of the Association a report is heard from a standing committee on schools and colleges, in which the condition of Baptist institutions of education within the State is made known. Of such institutions there are nine in number, each doing a good work.

The Association at each session hears a report on denominational publications, and seeks to encourage religious literature as a means of spreading divine truth. The American Baptist Publication Society receives encouragement, and Baptist journals in the State in harmony with the purposes and plans of the Association, receive a hearty moral support. At this writing (1880) *The Central Baptist*, an able weekly journal, conducted by Rev. Wm. Ferguson, and *Ford's Christian Repository*, edited by Rev. Dr. and Mrs. S. H. Ford, an excellent magazine of long standing, both published in the city of St. Louis, are indorsed and commended.

All along the history of this organization down to the present time its records are adorned by the names of the best men of the denomination in and out of the ministry. Of ministers who have gone to their reward are such names as Wm. Suggett, Wm. Thompson, D.D., Thos. Fristoe, I. T. Hinton, James E. Welch, S. W. Lynd, D.D., Noah Flood, J. B. Jeter, D.D., X. X. Buckner, Wm. Crowell, D.D., Y. R. Pittz, Jerry Vardeman, and A. P. Williams, D.D. Of deceased laymen there are such men as Judge R. E. McDaniel, Hons. Wade Jackson, David Hickman, Wm. Carson, Marshal Brotherton, Jos. Flood, and Wm. Jewell, M.D., D. L. Shouse, Wm. McPherson, and others, the presence of any of whom would have adorned the most honorable assembly on earth.

The chief living Baptists of the State, ministers and laymen, and honorable women not a few, are now the active friends and hearty supporters of the General Association, which is, no doubt, the organization through which the power and usefulness of an influential denomination in a great State are to reach their highest and broadest development.

Missouri, Baptist Sunday-Schools in.—

The Missouri Baptist Sunday-School Convention was organized in August, 1868. Rev. S. W. Marston, D.D., served as the secretary during the first five years.

The following table will show how he found Sunday-school work in Missouri, and how it has increased for eleven years:

Year.	Number of Associations.	Number of Churches.	Number of Preachers.	Number of Church Members.	Net Gain.	Number of Bible-Schools Reported.	Number of Officers and Teachers.	Number of Scholars.
1868...	45	.. ....	.....	52,996	....	74	....	....
1869...	...	....	.....	....	....	.....	....	....
1870..	50	1003	506	57,089	4,091	430	3494	25,781
1871...	57	1166	846	67,501	10,414	754	5873	44,871
1872...	...	1210	.....	71,717	4,216	.....	....	....
1873...	60	1212	920	74,274	2,557	806	6247	48,261
1874...	...	1264	706	76,072	1,798	816	6250	49,260
1875...	...	1274	750	78,144	....	.....	....	....
1876...	..	....	.....	....	....	.....	....	....
1877...	66	1328	802	79,546	....	.....	....	....
1878...	...	....	.....	....	....	.....	....	....
1879...	66	1381	823	88,491	....	450	3076	41,173
1880...	...	....	.....	....	....	820	6300	50,000

There were about 5937 church members working in the schools during 1879, and 4605 conversions among the scholars. The libraries comprise 26,000 volumes. The churches expended on their own schools, in 1879, $9997; for organs and other objects, $7687; for State Bible-school work, $1023.96.

In 1873 about two-thirds of all the district Associations had within them organized Sunday-school Conventions.

The Rev. M. L. Laws is the able corresponding secretary of the society at this time, upon whose noble work so rich a blessing has descended.

Missouri Baptists, Sketch of.—

The first Christians of any denomination, save Catholic, that ever set foot upon the soil of Upper Louisiana, now the State of Missouri, were Baptists. So far as we have been able to learn, Thomas Bull, his wife, and her mother, Mrs. Lee, were the first to come. They settled in Cape Girardeau County in 1796. The following year they were joined by Enos Randall and wife, and Mrs. Abernathy. At that time Missouri was under the dominion of Spain, and the Roman Catholic was the established church. In 1799, Rev. Thomas Johnson, of Georgia, visited these pioneers, preached the gospel to them and their neighbors, and baptized one woman. This was the first administration of baptism west of the great river, and Elder Johnson was the first Baptist minister of the *regular* order who ever visited the Territory.

Rev. David Green removed from Kentucky and settled in Cape Girardeau County in 1805, and commenced at once to gather together the Baptists. He organized, in 1805, the Tywappity Baptist church, in Scott County, of eight or ten members. For want of succor it soon became defunct, but was reorganized in 1809. The Bethel church was the first permanent church organization in the State. It was formed with fifteen members, July 19, 1806, near the town of Jackson, Cape Girardeau Co. Elder Green was the first pastor of these churches. For some years the Bethel church was an aggressive missionary body, and greatly prospered. It afterwards opposed missions, and as a consequence withered, and finally died. From it sprang, directly or indirectly, all the churches that formed the first Association. Five other churches originated prior to the date next to be mentioned, and together with the two first named, met at the Bethel meeting-house, near Jackson, on the last Saturday in September, 1816, and organized the Bethel Association, the first in the Territory. The constituent churches were Bethel, Tywappity, Providence, Barren, St. François, Bellview, and Dry Creek. The ministers present were Henry Cockerham, John Farrar, Wm. Street, and James P. Edwards. Bethel Association adopted the appellation of "United Baptists."

In 1796 and 1797 a number of Baptist families removed from North Carolina, South Carolina, and Kentucky, most of whom settled in the present limits of St. Louis County. Among them we notice the names of Abraham and Sarah Musick, Jane Sullens, Sarah Williams, and R. Richardson and wife. They came in the face of Catholic restriction. The law said, "Liberty of conscience is not to be allowed beyond the first generation; the children of emigrants must be Catholics." And further, "No preacher of any religion but the Catholic must come into the province." John Clark, a Baptist in sentiment, though not a member, and Thomas R. Musick visited and preached in Missouri in these times of proscription. Clark's first trip was made in 1798; Musick's not long after. Clark was, we presume, the first Protestant minister that ever preached the gospel west of the Mississippi River. Musick settled in the St. Louis district in 1803 or 1804,—the first minister other than Catholic to locate in the Territory. He organized the Fee Fee church, the first in St. Louis County, in 1807, of eighteen members, and became its pastor. This is now the oldest church in the State. Cold Water, the next church in the county, was organized by Musick in 1809.

In November, 1817, at the house of Thomas R. Musick, the Missouri (now St. Louis) Association was formed with the following as constituent churches, viz.: Fee Fee, Cold Water, Bœuf, and Negro Fork, in St. Louis County; and Femme Osage, St. Charles County, and Upper Cuiver in Lincoln County; the aggregate membership of which was 142.

In the autumn of 1817, Revs. John M. Peck and James E. Welch, missionaries of the Baptist General Convention, arrived in St. Louis, then a little French village on the west bank of the Mississippi River. St. Louis is now the fourth city in the Union, extending some fifteen miles up and down the river, with a breadth of four to three miles. Messrs. Peck and Welch organized the First Baptist church of St. Louis, Feb. 8, 1818, with a membership of eleven persons.

Mingled with the tide of emigration westward we find Baptists. Nineteen persons formed a Baptist church near Loutre Island, in Montgomery County, in 1810. Joseph Baker was their pastor. The war of 1812–15 soon afterwards broke out, and most of the membership took refuge in the forts of Howard County. Mount Pleasant church was the first in the upper county. It was organized by Revs. Wm. Thorp and David McLain, near old Franklin, Howard Co. Few meetings for business were held during the war. Thorp and McLain preached to the people in the forts. When the war was over the people began again to hold meetings. The Mount Pleasant Association was formed July 25, 1818, at the old Mount Pleasant meeting-house. The constituent churches were Mount Pleasant, Concord, Cooper Co., organized May, 1817; Bethel, Boone Co., formed June, 1817; and Mount Zion and Salem; their aggregate membership was 161. Ministers present, David McLain, Wm. Thorp, Luke Williams, Edward Turner, and Colden Williams. In less than five years this associational community had extended its limits as far west as Clay and Lafayette Counties, and an average of twenty-five miles on either side of the Missouri River. At its meeting in 1823 it divided its territory, and formed the Fishing River Association, in Clay County, and Concord Association, in Cooper County, in the autumn of that year. Seven churches and six ministers were set off to organize the former, and seven churches to the latter. This left Mount Pleasant with seventeen churches. In 1827 the Mount Pleasant Association again divided for convenience, and the formation of the Salem Association the same year was the result. The new Association took thirteen churches, with 513 members, leaving the old Association with sixteen churches and 734 members.

The Cuivre Association was formed in 1822, of churches in St. Charles, Lincoln, and Warren Counties, eight in number, most or all of which had been dismissed from the Missouri Association for the purpose.

The gospel was early preached in Pike County

by Leroy Jackson, J. M. Peck, and Davis Biggs. Churches were organized as follows: Ramsey's Creek, prior to 1818; Peno, Dec. 25, 1819; Stout's Settlement (now New Hope) Lincoln Co., in 1821. On the 23d of August, 1823, the three churches last named, together with Bethlehem, New London, and Beer Creek, met on Big Peno and organized the Salt River Baptist Association. In 1834 this body sent out a colony of fourteen churches, and formed the Bethel Association, at Bethel meeting-house, Marion Co., the aggregate membership of which was 589. By churches gathered mainly by Elders Lewis and James Williams, situated mostly in Franklin, Washington, and Jefferson Counties, the Franklin Association was organized in 1832, at the house of J. C. Duckworth.

The Cape Girardeau Association, a daughter of the Bethel, was organized in 1824, at Hebron church.

We now pass to Western Missouri. In 1834 the Fishing River Association embraced all the churches west of a line indicated by Grand River. This year it was divided, the Missouri River being made the line, and the ten churches south of the river met in the following October at Little Snibar and organized the Blue River Association. Their total membership was 384.

The twelve Associations now named embraced, in 1834, nearly 200 churches, with a membership of some 7000, scattered over a vast extent of country from St. Genevieve County on the south to Lewis County on the north, from two to three counties deep west of the Mississippi River; and on either side of the Missouri River one to three counties deep, from the eastern to the western boundary of the State.

The General Association for missionary purposes was organized in 1835. This was made the occasion of a fierce and strong war upon boards and benevolent institutions by the anti-missionary party.

In the contest on missions in Missouri the anti-missionaries refused absolutely to fellowship under any circumstances those who favored the missionary enterprise. At the time of the division the regulars numbered over 5000, and the anti-missionaries upwards of 3000. The present strength of the former in the State is 90,000, and of the latter about 6000. (See article on MISSOURI BAPTIST GENERAL ASSOCIATION.)

The Missouri Baptists are warm friends of education.

INSTITUTIONS OF LEARNING.

William Jewell College, with its school of theology, is located at Liberty. Founded by the General Association; chartered February, 1849, and opened about one year after. This is the State denominational school for young men.

Stephens College, for females, is at Columbia. It

was established in 1856 as a "Baptist Female College;" chartered in 1857; adopted by the General Association in 1870. R. P. Rider, President.

Mount Pleasant College, a mixed school, is located at Huntsville. A. S. Worrall, D.D., President.

La Grange College, at La Grange, is for male and female students. J. F. Cook, LL.D., President.

Lexington Baptist Female College is located at Lexington. President, Jno. F. Lanneau.

St. Joseph Female College, at St. Joseph. E. S. Dulin, President.

Hardin College, located at Mexico; female. Mrs. P. A. Baird, President.

Grand River College, at Edinburg. The president is T. H. Storts.

South-West Baptist College, located at Bolivar. J. R. Maupin, President.

These are the Baptist institutions of learning of this State, the most or all of which are doing a noble work.

NEWSPAPERS.

The first Baptist newspaper published in Missouri was issued in 1842 under the auspices of the General Association, called the *Missouri Baptist*. I. T. Hinton and R. S. Thomas were editors. It was abandoned in 1844, and in 1848 it was succeeded by the *Western Watchman*. Another *Missouri Baptist* was established by the Missouri Baptist Publication Society in 1860, edited by S. H. Ford. Both the last-named papers were suspended early in the war. In 1865, John Hill Luther commenced the publication, at Palmyra, of the *Missouri Baptist Journal*, which was recognized as the "State paper" by the General Association in 1866. This is now the *Central Baptist*, published at St. Louis, by Wm. Ferguson. In 1875, Dr. D. B. Ray established the *Baptist Battle-Flag*, now the *Baptist Flag*, devoted to church history and polemic theology. It was first issued from La Grange, but was subsequently removed to St. Louis. And last, *Ford's Christian Repository*, a monthly, is published at St. Louis, and edited by S. H. Ford, LL.D., and Mrs. S. R. Ford.

The Baptists of Missouri have an important position in this great central State, and are wielding a potent influence for good in the evangelical and educational enterprises of the West.

Baptist Progress in Missouri by Decades.

Date.	Number of Associations.	Number of Churches.	Number of Ministers.	Number of Communicants.
1796	...	...	...	12
1806	...	2	3	50
1816	1	14	11	426
1826	8	91	52	2,984
1836	18	230	126	8,723
1846	...	410	201	19,667
1856	31	539	349	31,358
1866	37	749	432	44,877
1876	65	1284	842	89,786
1880	70	1449	839	95,967

Missouri, Central Baptist of.—The first number of the *Missouri Baptist Journal* was issued Jan. 1, 1866, in Palmyra, Mo., as the acknowledged organ of the General Association. About a year later the *Baptist Record* made its appearance in St. Louis, under the editorial conduct of Rev. A. A. Kendrick, D.D. In 1868 these two papers were consolidated, and the name of the *Central Baptist* was given to the journal, whose chief aim was to unite the Baptists of Missouri on a common platform of doctrinal truth, missionary effort, and educational interest.

The result of the consolidation was most gratifying. The circulation of the *Central Baptist* soon reached 8000. Its conciliatory spirit, sturdy defense of our distinctive principles, and the literary ability of its contributors, representing every section of our country, won for it the confidence of Missourians and the respect of Baptists throughout the land. Its principal editors have been successively Dr. J. H. Luther, Dr. W. Pope Yeaman, and Rev. W. Ferguson, aided at different periods by Rev. Norman Fox, President A. A. Kendrick, and Rev. J. C. Armstrong.

The aim of the managers of the *Central Baptist* has always been to establish for the valley of the Missouri a journal of conservative character, maintaining in its editorial conduct pronounced views on every question relating to evangelical religion, and encouraging a spirit of free inquiry in the ministry and among the masses. The enlightened and working element of the denomination has recognized it as a necessity in the region of which St. Louis is the centre, and has generously supported it as one of the permanent agencies in the furtherance of the grand mission intrusted to us as a people. It has an honorable record, with the promise of a brilliant future.

Rev. Wm. Ferguson, the present proprietor and managing editor of the *Central Baptist*, was born in Saline Co., Mo., July 15, 1845. In early life he found the Saviour, and, being impressed with the duty of preaching the gospel, in 1868 he gave up the study of law and entered William Jewell College, at Liberty, Mo., to prepare for the ministry. Here, from the very start, he took the first place in his classes, and secured the abiding love and respect of his instructors and fellow-students. On his graduation, in 1873, he was united in marriage to Miss Florence M. Chandler, of Liberty, and assumed the pastorate of the Baptist church at Fulton, Mo. After one year of successful labor he was elected to the responsible position of financial agent of the Missouri Baptist Ministerial Education Society, and of William Jewell College, which position he held with great acceptance and success until January, 1877, when he purchased a partnership interest with Rev. W. P. Yeaman, D.D., in

the *Central Baptist*, of which, in 1878, he became sole proprietor. Under his management of rare tact and ability the paper has been lifted out of financial embarrassments and placed within the

REV. WILLIAM FERGUSON.

first rank of denominational exponents. He possesses many qualifications which mark the born journalist. To a well-balanced mind, holding decided convictions, and exercising a positiveness in their maintenance, he joins a heart of keen sensibilities and broad sympathies, which enable him to weigh and deal fairly with all the questions which interest the church and humanity. These qualities, combined with unassuming modesty and geniality, secure the respect, esteem, and love of all who know him.

Missouri, Colored Baptists of, are a significant force. They have a State Convention and six district Associations, and claim 30,000 members, with 300 ministers. Among the leaders now living are W. W. Brooks, W. T. Jones, Thos. Jefferson, John Marshall, Henry Burton, L. T. Vealman, Samson Lewis, Hardin Smith, and Daniel Sawyer, men of piety and influence. Some of their churches have a thousand members. Four of their ministers have sketches in this work.

Missouri, Southwest, Baptist College of, is located at Bolivar, Southwest Missouri, and was founded by the Southwest Baptist Convention. It opened at Lebanon, Sept. 17, 1878. Rev. J. R. Maupin, A.M., a graduate of Lagrange College, Mo., is its first president. He was chosen for five years. The curriculum of the institution compares favorably with other colleges. It has a three years' preparatory course and a four years' collegiate. The faculty is composed of ten able instructors. The charter of the college was granted March 19, 1879. It is one of the most liberal in the State. The school is open to male and female students. One hundred and thirty-nine students attended the first year. A large number of students have been converted the past year. The college has a new and beautiful building and six acres of ground. Rev. N. T. Allison is principal of the preparatory department.

Mitchel, Rev. George, was born in England, Sept. 5, 1820. He was converted and baptized in 1838. He studied at Horton College, in Bradford, England, and in Edinburgh University, Scotland. He was ordained in England in July, 1847, and became pastor of the Baptist church at Horsforth, England, where he labored four years, and three at Irwell, Terrace chapel, Bacup. He came to America in 1855; had charge of the church at Beverly, N. J., for three years: was pastor of the Fourth Baptist church of St. Louis, Mo., for two years, in which he built the present house of worship; the church prospered under his ministry. In 1860 he became pastor at Lebanon. During the war he practised medicine and preached Christ. After the war he organized churches in Southwest Missouri. He was pastor at Bolivar, Mo. In 1874 he went to California, and returned soon after to Kansas, and preached at Hiawatha for two years with success,—a stroke of palsy closed his labors there. He returned to Bolivar, Mo., and bore his affliction with patience. He died May 27, 1879.

In both his pastorates in England he was popular and useful, and in this country his labors were successful.

Mitchell, Rev. Edward, was born in the island of Martinique in 1794. He followed the sea in his early life, but having been hopefully converted and baptized by Rev. Dr. Staughton, his attention was at once turned to the Christian ministry. He entered Dartmouth College, and graduated with honor in 1828. Soon after leaving college he was called to become pastor of the Baptist church in Burke, Vt. In 1834 he became pastor of the church in Eaton, Canada East, where he remained until 1838, when he was called to the church in West Hatley, Canada East, where he continued until his death, which occurred March 31, 1872. "He was regarded as the most profound theologian ever settled in the section in which he passed so many years of his useful life."

Mitchell, Edward C., D.D., was born at East Bridgewater, Mass., Sept. 20, 1829. His early religious training was of the Unitarian type. While a student in Waterville College, Me., he was converted, and became a member of a Baptist church.

He was graduated in 1849. He entered Newton Theological Seminary, and was graduated in 1853. He was first settled as pastor in Calais, Me., where he was ordained in 1854. After three years he removed to Rockford, Ill., where he founded the State Street Baptist church, and remained the pastor for five years. In 1862 he was appointed Professor of Biblical Interpretation in the theological department of Shurtleff College, in Illinois, which position he filled during seven years. In 1870 he was elected to the professorship of Hebrew and Old Testament Literature in the Baptist Union Theological Seminary, Chicago. He filled this chair eight years. Then he accepted an appointment to the professorship of Biblical Interpretation in Regent's Park Baptist College, in London, England. He then became the president of the Baptist Theological School of Paris, France. He is the author of "The Critical Hand-Book, a Guide to the Study of the Authenticity, the Canon, and the Text of the Greek New Testament," also "Gesenius's Hebrew Grammar, Translated by Davis, thoroughly Revised and Enlarged." He is a fine scholar, and eminently successful in the line of labor to which he has devoted his life.

Mitchell, John, D.D.—This gentleman, known as "the beloved disciple," was born in Bertie Co., N. C., in 1829; professed faith in Christ at Wake Forest College in 1851; graduated in 1852; studied theology at Greenville, S. C.; was agent for the endowment of Wake Forest College in 1856–57; was pastor at Hillsborough and Greensborough; settled as pastor in Chowan Association after the war; took charge of the Asheville church in 1875; returned to Murfreesborough in 1879, where he now resides. Dr. Mitchell is a trustee of Wake Forest, and also of Chowan Female Institute, and was made a D.D. by his *alma mater* in 1876.

Mitchell, Rev. J. F., a leading minister in Spring River Association, Ark., was born in North Carolina in 1823. He subsequently removed to Georgia, where he began to preach in 1853. He spent five years preaching in that State, and just at the commencement of the civil war he was called to the pastorate at Jacksonville, Florida, but owing to the disturbed state of the country he removed to Texas, where he remained until after the war. His labors were greatly blessed in that State. After laboring in Texas five years, he removed to Benton Co., Ark., where he has been an active co-worker with Jasper Dunegan. He has baptized during his ministry 615 persons.

Mitchell, Rev. S. H., was born in Washington Co., Ind., Feb. 20, 1830. He removed to Iowa in 1855. He was baptized at Oskaloosa in 1859. At the time of his baptism he looked upon teaching as his probable life-work. In 1862 he was licensed to preach, and not long after he was ordained. In

1863 he was appointed general missionary and financial agent of the Iowa Baptist State Convention, and continued in this position till October, 1869. During this period he traveled 30,000 miles over the State, 25,000 of which were by horseback and buggy. It was a time of great activity and growth in the Convention work, as is shown by the increased number of missionaries employed, and the amount of funds collected. In 1862 there were only six missionaries employed, and less than $1000 collected. In 1868 there were thirty, and nearly $6500 were collected.

Jan. 1, 1870, Mr. Mitchell settled as pastor at Ames, Iowa, and remained five years, doing a good work. Lots were purchased, and a substantial meeting-house built. During 1875 he labored as financial agent for the University of Des Moines. In February, 1876, he became pastor at Shell Rock, Iowa, and in July, 1877, began his ministry at Grundy Centre, Iowa, where he still labors, having now entered upon his fourth year of service. There are few men in Iowa so well and favorably known among the Baptists, or whose labors have had as wide a range or as marked effects in State missions.

Mize, Rev. T. S., was born Jan. 29, 1840, at Carrollton, Carroll Co., Ill. He made a profession of religion at the age of twelve years; was graduated at Shurtleff College at twenty years of age; pursued his theological studies at Rochester, N. Y.; ordained at Faribault, Minn.; settled at Clinton Junction, Wis., January, 1867, and died April 29, 1872. Great humility and modesty, and great fidelity to Christ and the church were his crowning characteristics.

Moffat, Judge John S., a well-known Baptist layman of Hudson, Wis., was born on the 25th of November, 1814, in Lansing, Tompkins Co., N. Y. His grandfather, Rev. John Moffat, emigrated from Ireland with a colony, with which also came the Clintons, who settled in New York. He was a Presbyterian clergyman of fine classical and theological attainments. Judge Moffat's parents were Samuel and Ann (Shaw) Moffat. They were Christians, and early in life began to instruct him in the principles of morality and religion; he received his education in the schools of the neighborhood. At eighteen he entered the counting-room of a merchant in Dryden, N. Y., as assistant. Here he remained two years. At twenty he entered the academy at Homer. He also studied at the academy at Groton.

In 1840, Mr. Moffat entered the law-office of Coryden Tyler, of Dryden, and, although admitted to the bar, he engaged for several years in mercantile pursuits. In 1854, Mr. Moffat came to Hudson, Wis., which has since been his home. Upon his arrival here he obtained a position in the land-office, which, together with the position of police justice, he held for many years. Since January, 1870, he has held the office of county judge. He also practises extensively in the courts, and presides over one of the largest insurance and collecting agencies in the Northwest.

Judge Moffat is a thorough-going Christian gentleman. For many years he has been a member of the Baptist church. In the church at Hudson he is a deacon and Sunday-school superintendent. He is a man of commanding influence, which he devotes to the best interests of the community where he resides. Temperance and public virtue and morality have in him an ardent friend. He exemplifies these, as well as the graces of pure religion, in his own daily life.

Mrs. Moffat's maiden name was Nancy Ann Bennet. She is a daughter of Phineas Bennet, a well-known inventor of New York. They were married Jan. 24, 1844. She is in perfect accord with Mr. Moffat in all his Christian and philanthropic labors, and an active and influential member of the Baptist church in Hudson.

Monroe Female College.—This institution, situated in the village of Forsyth, Monroe Co., Ga., was founded in the year 1849, under the title of Forsyth Female Collegiate Institute, Rev. E. J. C. Thomas being the first president. A few years afterwards Rev. Wm. C. Wilkes, a graduate of Mercer University, was elected president, and he managed the college with great energy and success until the close of the year 1866, except when it was temporarily suspended during the war. Rev. S. G. Hillyer, a graduate of Franklin College, and for many years a professor in Mercer University, was its next president. Dr. Hillyer, who is both an excellent scholar and an eminent divine, administered its affairs with great success until 1872, when R. T. Asbury succeeded, only to give way in turn to Dr. Hillyer, in the spring of 1880.

The management of this excellent college has always been in Baptist hands, and year after year has sent out large classes of well-educated young ladies. In 1879 its beautiful building was consumed by fire, but it is now being rebuilt in a more handsome style. The exercises, in the meanwhile, are still continued.

Monroe, Rev. John.—No minister in North Carolina of any denomination is more respected for his piety and usefulness than this venerable man. He was born in Richmond Co., N. C., in October, 1804. His parents emigrated from the Highlands of Scotland in 1 03. He was baptized into the fellowship of the Spring Hill Baptist church in 1819; began to preach in 1825; has labored extensively in the counties of Anson, Richmond, and Robeson, N. C., and Marlborough, S. C., and during the fifty-five years of his ministry he has been pastor of the Spring Hill church. For twenty years

52

he was moderator of the Pedee Baptist Association, and would still fill that place did the infirmities of age permit.

Monroe, Rev. William Y., was born in Oldham Co., Ky., April 3, 1824; removed with his father to Scott Co., Ind., in 1834, and joined the Methodist church in 1842. About this time his mind was exercised in respect to his entering upon the work of the ministry. He began a thorough search of the Bible; the result was that he became a minister and a Baptist. He was ordained in 1850, and has been the pastor of the North Madison Baptist church for twenty-three years. He was elected treasurer of his county two consecutive terms, and has been sent to the State Legislature two sessions. He was elected president of the Indiana State Convention in 1878. He is a man of deep piety, modesty, and profound convictions.

Montague, Rev. Howard W., the eldest son of the Rev. Philip Montague, was born in Middlesex Co., Va., Oct. 10, 1810. He was baptized by his father in November, 1831. In 1838 he married Miss Mildred C. Broaddus, daughter of the Rev. Andrew Broaddus. He was ordained to the ministry in 1840. During his ministerial career of thirty-six years he was at different times pastor of the following churches,—Mount Zion, Ephesus, Howerton's, and Upper Essex, in the county of Essex; Bethel, in the county of Caroline; and Shiloh and Round Hill, in King George. In addition to these he had stated appointments at several other churches, besides being a frequent and zealous worker in protracted meetings in his own and neighboring churches. The one great object of his life was to preach the gospel plainly and faithfully to men, and he did it with great earnestness, power, and success. He was a laborious worker in the ministry, forgetting himself and laying all his energies on the altar of the Master. He possessed a vigorous intellect, was a strong thinker, and in his style of preaching was impressive and stimulating. His own life exemplified the doctrines of godliness, and all who were acquainted with him knew that Christ was the moving spring of his entire actions. He died June 9, 1876, leaving to the churches of his love and labors the memories of a character fragrant with the graces of the Spirit.

Montague, Rev. J. E., was born in Granville Co., N. C., in 1818; baptized in 1839; educated at Wake Forest College; was ordained in 1850, Revs. R. I. Devin and S. Creath forming the Presbytery; and has been the successful pastor of Mill Creek and Bethel churches, Person County, for twenty-six years.

Montague, Judge Robert L., was born in Middlesex Co., Va., May 23, 1819. His parents were zealous members of a Baptist church. His education was begun at a small country school. He was afterwards sent to Fleetwood Academy, in the county of King and Queen, conducted by that accomplished teacher, Oliver White, to be prepared for college. From this school he went to William

JUDGE ROBERT L. MONTAGUE.

and Mary College, where, in July of 1842, he received the degree of Bachelor of Laws, graduating also in the school of political economy. He returned to the college the next session, and continued his studies in legal and political science, and then entered upon the practice of law. He was baptized in August, 1842, by the Rev. Mr. Street, and united with the Glebelanding church, of which he has continued a member till the present, being actively identified with all the movements of the denomination, and serving most efficiently for several years the General Baptist Association of Virginia as its president. Having begun the practice of law in 1844, Judge Montague was appointed, in 1845, the Commonwealth's attorney for Middlesex County, which position he held with efficiency and honor for nineteen years and then resigned. In 1850 he was elected a member of the Virginia Legislature, and was re-elected in 1851, but he resigned without serving. In 1852 he was a Presidential elector, and was the messenger of the electoral college to convey the vote of Virginia to Washington; and in 1856 he was again a Presidential elector. In 1859 he was elected lieutenant-governor of the State. This office he held for the constitutional period of four years. In February, 1861, he was elected by the people of Middlesex and Mathews Counties to represent them in the secession convention; and in April of the same year he was chosen by the convention a member of the executive council to aid the governor in his arduous and responsible duties. He was elected president of the convention at its last session, and it is a singular fact that Judge Montague while presiding over this body was also the president of the Virginia senate for nearly a month, both bodies sitting in the same building, so that, in order to accommodate the presiding officer, the hours of meeting for both bodies had to be changed. In 1863 he was elected a member of the Confederate Congress, and served in that body till its last session; after which time, until 1873, he remained in private life, giving himself entirely to the practice of his profession. In 1873 he was elected a member of the Virginia Legislature by the people of Middlesex County, and in March, 1875, he was elected by the Legislature judge of the eighth judicial circuit. Although Judge Montague's numerous official duties prevented him from adding much to the literature of the denomination, he made a great many public addresses on various subjects, many of which have been published and widely read throughout the State. Although much in public and political life, no man sustained a more honorable reputation. He died during the summer of 1880.

Montanye, Rev. Thomas B., was born Jan. 29, 1769, in New York. When seventeen years of age he was baptized by the Rev. John Gano into the fellowship of the First Baptist church of that city. He was ordained pastor of the Baptist church of Warwick, N. Y., when only nineteen years of age. In 1801 he became pastor of the Southampton church, Bucks Co., Pa. He held this position till death summoned him to the church in glory, Sept. 27, 1829. Mr. Montanye was one of the most popular Baptist ministers in the eastern part of Pennsylvania, where his name was familiar to most professors of religion. No man in the Baptist ranks stood higher than he. His church trusted and loved him, and he and his Southampton brethren walked in harmony with the Baptist brotherhood everywhere. In preaching, his theme was the cross, and he possessed great power in setting forth the matchless glories of the suffering Saviour. His memory is tenderly cherished all over Bucks County at this day.

Montgomery, Rev. W. A., was born in Jefferson Co., Tenn., Nov. 16, 1829. He was converted and baptized in his fourteenth year. He entered the University of Tennessee, at Knoxville, in 1845, and graduated with the first honor of his class in 1850; read law with the Hon. E. Alexander, judge of the Knoxville Circuit Court. He was admitted to the bar in the fall of 1851. He removed to Texas in 1855. He served as a member from Wash-

ington County in the secession convention in 1861. He was licensed to preach while in the Confederate army in 1862. He continued in it until the close of the war; removed to Leadvale, Tenn., in 1867. He was ordained to the work of the ministry in 1868. He received his D.D. from Carson College in 1870, and from the University of Tennessee in 1876. He was pastor first of Leadvale and Dandridge churches from 1868 to 1872; then of First church, Lynchburg, Va., until 1877. He was corresponding secretary of the Southwestern Board for eighteen months. He is now the pastor of the First Baptist church of Memphis, Tenn.

Dr. Montgomery possesses rare ability as an evangelist. The numerous protracted meetings held by him, in which his labors were singularly blessed, abundantly show this. In the pulpit his manner is solemn; his words and arguments are logical, instructive, and convincing. He is among the most prominent preachers in the State.

Montreal College.—This institution owes its origin to the conviction among the Baptists of Canada that, in order to prosecute their denominational work in the provinces, a native, educated ministry must be raised up to do this work. The funds necessary to commence the undertaking having been secured, Dr. Benjamin Davies, then living in England, came to Montreal in 1839, and took charge of what was called the Baptist Theological College, the original design being to have but two instructors, a principal and a tutor, to train the young men who proposed to enter the Christian ministry. Buildings were secured, the necessary preparations made, and a few students connected themselves with the new institution. In 1843, Dr. Davies was called to England to take the presidency of Stepney College, now Regent's Park College, London, and Rev. Dr. Fyfe occupied the place thus made vacant for one year. In 1844, Dr. J. M. Cramp entered upon his duties as president of the college. A fine, cut-stone building was erected on a commanding site in the city of Montreal, and the prospects of the institution wore an encouraging aspect. But it was not long before financial embarrassment crippled the energies of those who had been foremost in promoting the interests of the college. The "hard times" of 1848–50 destroyed all hope of raising funds, which it had been thought could be obtained in England. There was no alternative but to sell the college property, to pay off, as far as possible, the debts of the institution. Apparently the experiment to establish a Baptist theological college in Montreal had proved a failure, and the friends of ministerial education must look for success in some other quarter. (See article on CANADIAN LITERARY INSTITUTE.)

Moody, Lady.—This titled lady lived at Lynn, Mass., in 1640. She purchased the estate of Mr.

Humphrey, one of the magistrates, and intended to become a permanent resident. Soon after making her abode at Lynn she embraced the principles of the Baptists ; and then neither her character nor her position in society could avail her anything. She was compelled to withdraw from the Congregational citizens of Lynn and seek a home on Long Island among the Dutch, who, like their liberal country-men in Holland, gave her a generous welcome. And when the Indians came to Long Island to kill its Dutch settlers, forty of them defended the house of Lady Moody at the peril of their lives. In that day to embrace Baptist principles was to invite expatriation, if not something worse, even from American Christians.

Moore, David, D.D., was born in Northumberland, England, March 28, 1822. He came to the United States in 1834. He received a superior education, and being called of God to the ministry, he was ordained, in June, 1852, as pastor of the Gaines and Murray churches, N. Y. In 1855 he accepted a call to the Le Roy church in the same State ; in 1860 he became pastor of the Washington Street church, Buffalo ; and in 1864 he took the oversight of the Washington Avenue church, Brooklyn, from which he retired, through impaired health, in 1876. He is now pastor of the church of Geneva, N. Y.

He has published several occasional sermons, essays, and addresses, and was, till the failure of his health, an active manager of the American Baptist Home Mission Society, the Long Island Mission Board, and of other denominational institutions.

Few men in the Baptist denomination have wielded a wider or more beneficial influence. As a preacher, he is lucid, sound, earnest, and eloquent. As a pastor, sympathizing, magnetic, and faithful, and, in all the councils of his brethren, capable, practical, and prudent.

Moore, Rev. Ferris, was born in Putney, Vt., Dec. 31, 1796, united by baptism with the church June 24, 1816, and was ordained Dec. 30, 1819, at Keene, N. H., where he was the pastor of the church for two years. Subsequently he was settled at New Ipswich, N. H., Canton, Mass., and at Saratoga, N. Y. From April, 1846, to the fall of 1857 he preached every alternate Sabbath at South Lee, Mass., where he died April 7, 1858.

Moore, John L., D.D., one of the pioneer Baptists of Ohio, was born in Lewis Co., N. Y., Feb. 17, 1803, and was converted at the age of twenty-two. In 1831 he graduated from Hamilton, and one week after his graduation was ordained at Watertown, N. Y., with special reference to the Western field. In October of the same year, in company with three of his classmates, William Choffee, Alvin Bailey, and G. Bartlett, he visited Cleveland, then a village of 1000 inhabitants. From it he went to Columbus, where there was a small Baptist church, and thence to Cincinnati, where there were then three Baptist churches. After a short stay in Cincinnati he visited the towns of the Miami valley. At Hamilton he met with a very severe accident, by which his face was terribly burned and the sight of his eyes greatly injured. Nothing daunted at this, however, he accepted in the spring of 1832 an appointment by the Home Mission Society, then just organized. After general missionary work he became pastor of the church of Piqua, and in 1834 gave half his time to the new church at Troy. His next pastorate was with the church at Dayton, where he remained two years.

For eight years subsequent to this Dr. Moore was the general agent for the Ohio State Convention. Part of his time was, however, devoted to the interests of the college at Granville, of which he was a trustee for more than thirty years. On resigning his agency he took pastoral charge of the church in Springfield, O., which position he held for nearly two years, when he gave himself to the work of establishing a theological institution at Fairmount, near Cincinnati. In 1855 he was appointed an exploring missionary for Ohio by the State Convention, and did much effective work. His health becoming greatly impaired he relinquished this position, and gave himself thenceforward to a more quiet life, preaching, however, as he found opportunity, and making himself useful in the general denominational work. In the same year Denison University conferred upon him the degree of D.D. In 1870 he removed to Topeka, Kan., where he remained until his death, Jan. 23, 1878.

Dr. Moore was one of the most influential and wealthy of the early Baptist ministers of Ohio. His memory is treasured by thousands in that State. He was a very acceptable preacher, and a man of most excellent spirit. He leaves a son in the ministry, Rev. A. S. Moore, of Salem, O.

Moore, Rev. Wm., was born near Pisgah, Butler Co., O., Dec. 8, 1821 ; was baptized by Elder Daniel Bryant at the age of twenty ; studied at Farmer's College, and also at Granville ; took his theological course at the Covington Institute, under Dr. Patterson ; was ordained to the ministry in the autumn of 1847, at the Ninth Street church, Cincinnati, and shortly afterwards was married to Miss E. W. Forbes. In company with Dr. Jewett, of the Teloogoo Mission, he was set apart as a foreign missionary, first to Assam, and afterwards, at the death of Mr. Bullard, to the Pwo Karens, Burmah.

He sailed with his wife from Boston, in the ship "Cato," Nov. 2, 1847, in company with Brethren Danforth, Stoddard, and their wives, and also Brethren Simons and Brayton. On reaching the heathen land he entered with energy upon the arduous labor of acquiring a foreign language. This he soon accomplished, and was permitted to visit the Karens in their distant homes, and tell them of a Saviour's dying love. After about five years of labor his health began to fail, and before the sixth year was completed it was manifest to all that his missionary toils were ended, at least for a time. His voice entirely failed, so that he could speak only in a low whisper. With great reluctance he bade adieu to the chosen labors of his life, and returned to this country. He located first at Cincinnati, but, not being able to preach, he went to Middletown, and entered into business, in which he continued twenty-six years, until his death. Being prompt, reliable, and enterprising, he secured a flattering position in the commercial world. His word was the synonym of honor and fair-dealing.

His influence was always on the side of right and morality, and in this direction it was mighty and constant, and it was felt for the improvement of the community. He was a member of the school board for twelve years, and president of the board of education when he died. In the church he was looked upon as one of the main pillars, holding the office of deacon from 1867 until the close of his life. He was also church clerk for fifteen years, until the time of his death, and during his membership he was a constant attendant at the Sabbath-school, having in charge the adult Bible-class. In his teaching he was clear and methodical, and eminently useful. He was not only a faithful teacher, but a true friend, and a wise counselor to all his class. Even after they left the school he never lost sight of them, but watched his opportunity to do them good. It brightens our appreciation of his goodness to remember that he himself was never conscious of its possession, but labored diligently each day as though the results of eternity depended upon the passing hour. Few men have been more honored for Christian integrity. His unfaltering devotion to the church, his familiarity with men, his sound judgment, and his kindness won many hearts to trust the Saviour whom he loved and honored. With an unblemished reputation, he filled up the measure of his days. He died Sept. 29, 1880, in the full enjoyment of the Saviour's love.

Moran, Rev. M. Y., an able minister in Lincoln Co., Ark., was born in North Carolina in 1818; at the age of twenty-two professed Christ, and soon after began to preach. Having settled in Somerville, Tenn., in 1844, he studied for three years, and obtained a fair knowledge of Greek, Latin, and mathematics. He was ordained in 1855; after preaching in Tennessee three years he removed to Bolivar Co., Miss., where he organized the first church in the county. Here he continued to labor until the war. In 1862 he came to Arkansas and settled at his present place of residence, where he has preached successfully until the present time. He has presided several times as moderator of Bartholomew Association, of Arkansas Baptist Convention, and the General Association of Southeast Arkansas.

More, Godwin C., M.D., was born in Hertford Co., N. C., Nov. 7, 1806; graduated at Chapel Hill; read medicine with his brother-in-law, Dr. Fletcher, and graduated in medicine at Transylvania University. In 1831 he represented his native county in the State Legislature; ran for Congress in 1837, and in 1838 became moderator of the Chowan Association, the largest body of the kind in the State, and he held this honorable position for thirty years. He was elected a member of the Legislature again in 1842, and also in 1867. He was a trustee of Wake Forest College, and for many years president of the board of trustees of the Chowan Female Institute. He died in 1880, loved and lamented by all who knew him.

Morehead, Gov. James T., an able lawyer, and one of the most brilliant orators that Kentucky has produced, was born in Bullitt Co., Ky., May 24, 1797. He attended school at Russellville, and completed his education at Transylvania University. He was raised in the faith of the Baptists, but delayed uniting with the church until late in life, for which he expressed much regret. He studied law at Russellville, and commenced practice at Bowling Green in 1818. He was elected to the Legislature in 1828, and served several terms in that body. He was elected lieutenant-governor of Kentucky in 1832, and became governor of the State upon the death of Gov. Breathitt, in February, 1834. He was several years president of the board of internal improvements. In 1841 he was elected to the U. S. Senate, and at the close of his term, in 1847, he located in Covington, Ky. He died Dec. 28, 1854.

Morehead, Rev. Robert W., A.M., was born in Logan Co., Ky., April 13, 1834. He entered Bethel College in 1854, and remained two years. In 1856 he entered Union University, Tenn., where he graduated in 1859. His theological studies were pursued under the supervision of Dr. J. M. Pendleton. He united with Union Baptist church, in his native county, in 1849; was licensed to preach in 1856, and ordained in 1859. In 1860 he took charge of Bethel church, in Christian County. For several years he has been the beloved and honored pastor of the Baptist church at Princeton, Ky. He is a man of culture and great moral worth.

Morehouse, Henry L., D.D., was born in Stanford, Dutchess Co., N. Y., Oct. 2, 1834. Mr. Morehouse was graduated at the University of Rochester in 1858. He entered Rochester Theological Seminary in 1861, and was graduated in 1864. His first settlement was at East Saginaw, Mich., where he remained from 1864 to 1873, when he was called to the pastorate of the East Avenue Baptist church, in Rochester. Mr. Morehouse was prominently identified with educational and State missionary work in Michigan. He was for some time corresponding and financial agent of the New York Baptist Union for Ministerial Education, which has charge of the theological seminary at Rochester. He was elected to that position in 1877. His report in "Vindication of the Beneficiary System" won for him high encomiums from the first educators of the country. He has also published several able sermons. He was poet of the alumni of Rochester University in 1874. His racy and very readable contributions to the *Examiner and Chronicle*, over the signature "Helmo," have earned him a good reputation. His church has greatly prospered under his ministry, and his earnest labors for the seminary have secured for him the respect of all the friends of ministerial education in the State and in the many States where Rochester is represented. He is now the able corresponding secretary of the American Baptist Home Mission Society.

Moreland, Rev. W. C., for nine years pastor at Arcadia, La., was born in Georgia in 1824; for nineteen years a preacher in the Methodist connection; in 1864 he was ordained as a Baptist minister. He came to Louisiana in 1848. He has served the following Baptist churches acceptably: Homer, Rock Spring, and Antioch, in Claiborne Parish, and Liberty, Mount Gilead, and Arcadia churches, in Bienville Parish.

Morell, Rev. Z. N., was born in Tennessee; is now about eighty years old; commenced preaching at an early age after his conversion, and was successful as a minister in Tennessee and Mississippi; removed to Texas in 1835; was intimately associated with the early warriors, civilians, and ministers who founded the republic of Texas and organized the State. He was one of the originators of the State Convention and Education Society of Texas. His book, "Flowers and Fruits; or, Thirty-six Years in Texas," published in 1872, by Gould & Lincoln, Boston, is full of remarkable incidents touching religious, civil, and martial life, written in a style of masculine vigor.

Morey, Rev. Reuben, a native of Fabius, Onondaga Co., N. Y., where he was born Feb. 21, 1805, obtained a hope in Christ in early life, and united with the Baptist Church. Having strong convictions that it was his duty to preach the gospel, he soon after his conversion began the work of preparation. He was educated at Hamilton Literary and Theological Institution and at Brown University. Dr. Wayland was president at Brown while he was there, and he left upon his student the impress of his own strong intellect and powerful grasp of truth. Dr. J. R. Loomis, president of Lewisburg University, Dr. Ives, of Suffield, Conn., and Dr. William Dean, of Bangkok, Siam, were among his intimate friends at college. After his graduation from Brown University he was ordained and settled as pastor of the Baptist church in Madison, Ind. His subsequent pastorates were at Louisville, Ky., North Attleborough, Mass., Homer, Wyoming, and Arcade, N. Y., Delavan and Tonica, Ill., and Merton, Wis. His longest pastorate was at North Attleborough, Mass., where he remained eight years. His preaching was analytical and doctrinal. He had a profound reverence for the ministerial office, and this imparted depth and solemnity to his public services. As a pastor he was peculiarly gifted for efficient labor in the family and with the individual. He was a tower of strength in all his pastoral labors with his flock. His home during the closing years of his life was in Waukesha, Wis. Here he fell asleep in Jesus, Feb. 17, 1880. "Mark the perfect man and behold the upright, for the end of that man is peace."

Morgan, Rev. Abel, was of Welsh descent, and was born at Welsh Tract, Del., April 18, 1713. He was baptized when about twenty years of age, and was soon afterwards ordained. He had laid the foundation of the learning which he subsequently evinced at the academy in Pencador. In 1739 he took charge of the church in Middletown, N. J., and continued there until his death, in 1785. The period of his life was an important one, and he was equal to the work demanded from him. His influence and the history of the denomination in New Jersey and America are inseparably connected. He had a good judgment, unusual literary attainments, a logical mind, and a very valuable library. He was powerful in debate; he was also unsparing in labor by night and by day. In his old springless cart he rode long distances to preach Jesus. Dr. Jones, in his century sermon, called him "the *incomparable Morgan*." Edwards says of him, "He was not a *custom* divine, nor a *leading-string* divine, but a BIBLE DIVINE." He was on different occasions challenged to debate on doctrine, and always maintained his position. In 1742 there was a great revival at Cape May, in which Baptist and Presbyterian ministers preached. Too many of the converts "took to the water" to suit the Presbyterians. Mr. Morgan accepted a challenge from Rev. Samuel Finley, afterwards president of Princeton College, to discuss the baptismal question. He gained a signal triumph. Mr. Finley tried his pen, and wrote "A Charitable Plea for the Speechless." Mr. Morgan had a reply printed, under the title "Anti-Pædo Rantism, or Mr. Samuel Finley's Charitable Plea for the Speechless examined and refuted, the Baptism of Believers maintained, and the Mode of it by Immersion vindicated, by Abel Morgan, of Middletown, in East Jersey. Philadelphia, printed by B. Franklin, in Market Street. MDCCXLVII.'' This little work is so valuable and scarce that it sells for $12 or more.

REV. ABEL MORGAN.

As a patriot, his trumpet gave no uncertain sound. Even while the royal troops were moving through his neighborhood, after the battle of Monmouth, he was outspoken. The next Sunday he had for his text, " Who gave Jacob for a spoil and Israel to the robbers?'' He says in his diary, that the Sunday after that, " Preached in mine own barn, because the enemy had taken out all the seats in the meeting-house.'' He baptized many persons, and was the means of converting and edifying many more. He wrote some of the most important documents issued by the Philadelphia Association, and was frequently called by it to preach and preside. His many manuscripts, neatly written, show careful preparation, sound doctrine, and practical application. The inscription upon his plain tombstone at Middletown is, " In memory of Abel Morgan, pastor of the Baptist church at Middletown, who departed this life Nov. 24, 1785, in the 73d year of his age. His life was blameless, his ministry was powerful; he was a burning and shining light, and his memory is dear to the saints.''

Morgan, T. J., D.D., Professor of Church History in the Baptist Union Theological Seminary at Chicago, is of Welsh descent. His father was

Rev. Lewis Morgan, a pioneer Baptist preacher in Indiana, and he was born at Franklin, in that State, Aug. 17, 1839. His collegiate course he pursued at Franklin College, graduating in 1861. The war being then in progress, he entered the Union service as a private, and, after three years and four months, at the close of the war, resigned as colonel of the 14th U. S. Colored Infantry. He commanded a division at the battle of Nashville, and was made, subsequently, brevet brigadier-general for " gallant and meritorious service during the war.'' The struggle having closed, Gen. Morgan decided to enter upon study for the ministry, and graduated at Rochester in 1868. His first service was as secretary of the New York Baptist Union for Ministerial Education. At the end of three years he resigned this position, and, removing to Nebraska, served in that State as pastor for one year, and two years as president of the Nebraska State Normal School, being complimented, in 1874, with an appointment by President Grant as a member of the Board of Visitors at West Point. In September of the year last named he entered upon his duties as professor in the theological seminary at Chicago, holding, first, the chair of Homiletics, and at present that of Church History. In the year 1879 Dr. Morgan spent four months in study at the University of Leipsic, Germany, and in the year 1880 five months in European travel and in

T. J. MORGAN, D.D.

the prosecution of historical studies. To his fine scholarly attainments and ability as a teacher Dr. Morgan adds the talent of a " ready writer,'' and has contributed largely and most acceptably to the denominational press.

Morgan, Rev. William D., was born in Wales; educated at Pontypool College; came to America, and was ordained as a Baptist minister in Plymouth, Pa.; settled in Chester, Conn., in 1875, and with the Third Baptist church in North Stonington, Conn., in the spring of 1877; here he was thrown from a carriage and instantly killed, May 7, 1878, aged thirty-four years.

Morrill, Rev. Abner, A.M., son of Deacon John Adams and Mary McDonald Morrill, was born in Limerick, Me., Aug. 18, 1827; was converted while a student in college, and, though educated a Pedobaptist, united with the Main Street Baptist church in Brunswick, Me. To this step he was led by a careful study of God's Word, overcoming much opposition. He graduated from Bowdoin College in 1850. He was called to the chair of Mathematics and Natural Sciences in Midbury Academy the same year. In 1852 he became tutor in the West Tennessee College, Jackson, Tenn. After spending several years in teaching in connection with various institutions in the South, he returned to Maine in 1859, and became pastor of the Baptist church in Farmington. He was afterwards pastor at Turner and Mechanic Falls. In 1865 he came to New York, and has been pastor of the churches in Warsaw and Arcade. He is now settled in Painted Post. He is a faithful minister, a good preacher, and a noble-minded citizen.

Morrill, Rev. D. T., the present (1880) pastor of the Upper Alton Baptist church, Ill., was born Oct. 24, 1825, in Danville, Caledonia Co., N. Y. When he was about three years of age the family removed to Potsdam, St. Lawrence Co., in the same State. His preparation for college he received at the St. Lawrence Academy, in Potsdam. In September, 1847, he entered Union College, intending at first to take an eclectic course, but changed his plans subsequently, entering the Junior class, and graduating in 1849. His conversion took place while in college, without apparent special human agency, and partly in connection with a struggle against doubts even of the truth of the Christian religion. Earnest study of the evidences, accompanied by manifest strivings of the Spirit, ended not only in entire acceptance of the Christian system, but also of Christ as a personal Saviour. Deciding to enter the ministry, he took his theological course at Rochester, entering the seminary in 1851 and graduating in 1853. The interval of time since leaving college and before entering the seminary had been spent in teaching in Rahway, N. J., where he was baptized by Rev. W. H. Wines. Mr. Morrill's desire had been towards foreign missionary work, but a field of missionary labor opening to him at Newark, N. J., he decided to enter it. The mission so undertaken in that city resulted in the organization of the Fifth Baptist church, in March, 1855. This church he served as pastor fourteen years. The church grew into a strong one, built a meeting-house and parsonage, and took its place among the vigorous and efficient churches of the city and State. In 1869 he accepted a call to the Fourth Baptist church, St. Louis, continuing there six years, until 1874. Two hundred accessions by baptism were fruits of this ministry. A year and a half as pastor of Park Avenue church and superintendent of missions in St. Louis Association, and nearly a year in the service of the Publication Society as district secretary, brings the record to 1876, when Mr. Morrill accepted the call of the Upper Alton Baptist church, a field made especially interesting by the close relations into which the pastor of that church is necessarily brought with the students and faculty of Shurtleff College.

Morrill, Rev. J. C., was born in Amesbury, Mass., Aug. 16, 1791. Until he was about forty years of age he was in secular business. Impressed that it was his duty to preach the gospel, he received from the First Baptist church in Lowell a license, and was ordained as an evangelist at Waterville, Me., Oct. 25, 1832. He devoted himself with great zeal and energy to the work for which he had thus been set apart, and his preaching was accompanied by the conversion of souls. His successive pastorates were with churches in Augusta, Sidney, Freeport, Wiscasset, and Corinth, in Maine, Manchester, N. H., and Somerset, Mass. For four years he was in the service of the American and Foreign Bible Society. He died at Taunton, Aug. 22, 1858.

Morris, C. D., D.D., of Toledo, O., was born in North Wales, June 6, 1839. His parents, who were Calvinistic Methodists, removed to America in 1840, and settled in Ohio in 1841. In his eleventh year he united with a Presbyterian church, but in 1860, through independent investigation of God's Word, he became a Baptist, and united with the Baptist church at Urbana, O. In 1859 he became a public school teacher, and followed that calling for three years, when he gave himself entirely to preaching, and became pastor of the Baptist church at Fairfield, O. After remaining here a little while, he took a selected course of study in the university and a full course in the theological seminary at Rochester, N. Y., graduating in 1867. Shortly after graduation he became pastor of the First church, Toledo, O., where he still remains, the oldest pastor in the continuous service of one church in Ohio.

Dr. Morris is a scholarly and strong preacher, and makes himself felt not only in the growing city of Toledo, but throughout the State. He received the degree of D.D. from Chicago, Ill., in 1879.

Morris, Rev. Joshua, a celebrated pioneer Baptist preacher of Kentucky, was born in James City Co., Va., about 1750. He was baptized by Elijah Baker about 1773. He preached for a time in the country, and subsequently in Richmond, where he formed the first Baptist church in that city, in June, 1780. Of this church he became pastor, and ministered to it about seven years. In 1788 he removed to Kentucky, and became the pastor of Brashear's Creek church, in Shelby County. Besides ministering to this body about ten years. he constituted several churches in the regions around him. In 1798 he located in what is now Carroll County, and established Ghent church, and two years afterwards he removed to Nelson County, where he ministered to Cedar Creek and Mill Creek churches, and formed one or two new churches. He was a man of high respectability, and was eminently useful. He died about 1837.

Morris, Rev. William La Rue, was of Irish extraction, and was born in Hardin Co., Ky., Jan. 10, 1821. He was educated as a lawyer, and entered upon the practice of his profession at Hodgensville, Ky. He was a fine speaker, and a young man of strict honesty and integrity, and readily gained a good patronage. At this period his conscience was deeply impressed with a call from God to preach the gospel. To this conviction he finally yielded, and having joined a Baptist church while he was a law student, he was ordained pastor of the Baptist church at Hodgensville in January, 1851. He was remarkably active and zealous in his holy calling, and his improvement was such that he soon became one of the most eloquent preachers in the Kentucky pulpit. In 1866 he was appointed by the board of the General Association, general evangelist for the State. He died June 13, 1867.

Morrison, Judge A. W., was born in Jessamine Co., Ky., Nov. 25, 1802 ; removed to Missouri and settled with his mother and family in Howard County, his father having died in Kentucky. He was liberally educated. His known ability and integrity commended him to the people of his county for almost every office at their disposal. He was for four years receiver of the United States land-office for Missouri, under appointment of President James K. Polk. In 1851 he was appointed State treasurer by Gov. King to fill the vacancy occasioned by the death of Peter G. Glover. So thorough was his efficiency in this department, and so great his personal popularity, that he was elected by the people for three succeeding terms to the same office. He was the incumbent at the breaking out of the civil war, and Gov. Gamble insisted on his holding the position, but this he declined, refusing to take the " test oath."

Judge Morrison's ancestry were of the highest respectability in Wales, and afterwards in Virginia and Kentucky. He still lives on a beautiful and valuable estate in Howard Co., Mo.

In 1873 the judge made a profession of faith in Christ, and united with the Baptist church at Glasgow, in Howard County. His integrity as a man and citizen has marked his course as a Christian. He is intelligently active in every good work, a strong friend of his pastors, a liberal helper in missions and Christian education, and he is a member of several denominational boards. He is remarkably active in mind and body, and still wields a mighty influence in public matters.

Morrow, Rev. Orson Holland, a popular, useful, and much esteemed minister of Bethel Association, was born in Rutherford Co., N. C., Nov. 10, 1800. He was taken by his parents to what is now Simpson Co., Ky., in 1807, where he still lives. He was baptized in 1827, licensed to preach a few months later, and ordained in 1833. He became a close Bible student, and was very thorough in his researches. He has been pastor of four churches most of the time since his ordination, until the feebleness of old age rendered him incapable of the work. He has performed a great amount of missionary labor, and has organized a number of new churches.

His pastorates have been Pleasant Grove, Union, Warren Co., and Sulphur Spring, Simpson Co. During his long and faithful service he has been the means of the conversion of large numbers of souls, eighteen of whom are known to have become active ministers of the gospel. Mr. Morrow has been a frequent contributor to the periodical press.

Morse, Rev. Asahel, son of Rev. Joshua and Susannah (Babcock) Morse, was born in Montville, Conn., Nov. 10, 1771 ; removed with his parents to Landisfield, Mass., in 1779 ; was a lover of good books and an apt scholar ; taught schools with success ; was converted in 1798 ; was baptized Nov. 9 of that year, by Rev. Rufus Babcock, of Colebrook, Conn. ; licensed to preach in the spring of 1799 ; removed to Winsted, Conn., in 1800, where he was ordained in May, 1801 ; traveled and preached in almost every town in Connecticut ; settled with the Baptist church in Stratfield, Conn., in 1803, and remained more than nine years, preaching most of the time six sermons a week ; meanwhile he made a missionary tour, by appointment of the Shaftesbury Association, into Upper Canada, and attended fifty-four meetings ; in 1812 settled in Suffield, Conn., as successor to Rev. John Hastings ; in 1818 was a member of the State convention to frame a new State constitution, and penned for it the article on religious liberty,—a marked event in the State's history ; was a man of great power, and a typical Baptist ; in 1820 went to Philadelphia as delegate from the Connecticut Baptist Missionary Board to the Baptist General Convention; for a time supplied a church in Colebrook, and in 1832 became pastor of the Second Baptist church in that town; returned to Suffield in 1836, where he died June 10, 1838, in his sixty-seventh year. He married, Aug. 24, 1795, Rachel Chapel, of New Marlborough, Mass., and had eight children,—all sons. His was a noble life.

Morse, Rev. John Chipman, was born in Annapolis Co., Nova Scotia; converted and baptized when a youth; ordained pastor over the Digby Neck church March 31, 1842, and continues still in that happy relation. Mr. Morse is a deep and enthusiastic student of the Bible and of nature, and a very useful preacher of the gospel.

Morse, Rev. Joshua, was born in South Kingston, R. I., April 10, 1726; was converted under the preaching of Whitefield at the age of sixteen, and commenced preaching the next year as an itinerant; gathered a church in Montville, Conn., where he was ordained May 17, 1751; for aiding the New Lights and preaching Baptist doctrines in North Stonington, he was opposed, arrested, and abused; the distresses of the Revolution on the coast occasioned his removal to Landisfield, Mass., in 1779, where he gathered a church that he lived to see enrol a hundred members. He was an able, zealous, and faithful minister. He died in 1795, in his seventieth year.

Morse, Rev. Levi, was born in Jefferson, Schoharie Co., N. Y., Aug. 23, 1817; was born again, as he trusts, in December, 1835; baptized into the Jefferson Baptist church in 1838; commenced his studies preparatory to the ministry at Jefferson Academy in 1839, and graduated from Madison University in 1844; settled as pastor of the Baptist church of Athens, Pa., Sept. 8, 1844, the church having been raised up under his labors previously, during one of his vacations; remained as pastor five years, leaving a united church, with 112 members and a convenient house of worship. He has since been pastor at Franklin and Deposit, N. Y., of the North Baptist church of Newark, and at Newton and Pittsgrove, N. J., at Unionville, the Orange Baptist church, and the Franklindale Baptist church, New York, and he is now pastor of the Baptist church of Burlingame, Kansas. His settlements have all been pleasant and prosperous.

During the thirty-seven years of his ministry he has baptized into the churches he has served about 800 converts. In his sixty-fourth year, he is still able to undertake as much public speaking as at any previous period of his history.

Morse, Rev. Samuel B., is one of the most successful and beloved pastors in California. He was born Oct. 26, 1834, in Fayette, Me.; was baptized when scarcely twelve years old, by Rev. John

Butler. He graduated at Colby University and at Newton. Having special gifts for teaching, he engaged in that work for a time in Kentucky and at Vacaville, Cal., the seat of the Baptist College in that State, while it was in the hands of the Methodists. He returned East for some years, and was ordained at Newton in August, 1869. Coming back to California, he became pastor at Stockton nine years, and was remarkably blessed in his work. While pastor there he made the tour of Europe, Egypt, and Palestine, and gathered materials for several instructive lectures on the Holy Land, and has given them over one hundred times with ever-increasing favor. Feb. 1, 1878, he accepted the pastorate of the Brooklyn church, which up to that time was greatly discouraged. His unusual pastoral gifts and spiritual power as a preacher have made the church one of the best in California. He occupies a conspicuous position on missionary and college boards, and as moderator of the San Francisco Association and presiding officer at other public meetings he shows fine executive ability.

Morton, Rev. Salmon, was born in Athol, Mass., May 11, 1767. He was convicted of sin in his sixteenth year, and invested with justifying faith several years later. He was baptized at Madison, N. Y., in 1799, and he was ordained in June, 1802, as pastor of the Madison church, for which he labored for eleven years. In 1816 he took charge of the church in Marcellus, Onondaga Co., but he resigned in 1818 to preach as a home missionary. He died at Marcellus, Jan. 22, 1822. By the people among whom his ministry was exercised he was regarded as a great preacher. His usefulness was very extensive, and his Christian worth was of a high order.

Moss, Lemuel, D.D., was born in Owen Co., Ky., Dec. 27, 1829. His father, Demas Moss, was well known among the pioneer Baptists of Southern Indiana as a man of unusually strong native powers. His mother was a woman of fervent piety as well as mental energy. He came with his parents to Dearborn Co., Ind., in 1833. He was converted at the age of thirteen, and joined the Baptist church at Milan. When he was fourteen he entered the office of the *Lawrenceburg Register*. He spent nine years in printing, part of the time as foreman of a stereotyping establishment. While yet a youth his membership was removed to the First Baptist church, Cincinnati, where his prayer-meeting talks and other earnest religious services led his brethren to think that he ought to enter upon the work of the ministry. As this persuasion accorded with his own convictions he decided to give himself to the Master as a minister. He entered Rochester University, N. Y., in 1853. The select course marked out for him by President Anderson was abandoned after a year's preparatory work, and he entered upon the full course. He graduated in 1858, and two years later graduated in Rochester Theological Seminary, under President Robinson. As a student he was always remarkably diligent, and won and held the confidence of his teachers and fellow-students. He was awarded all the honors of the class. His high moral tone and strict integrity were characteristic during his whole course of study, as they have been ever since. He began preaching during his Sophomore year, and soon exhibited rare power as a public speaker.

Immediately upon his graduation from the seminary he was called to the pastorate of the First Baptist church of Worcester, Mass. In 1868 his *alma mater* conferred upon him the degree of Doctor of Divinity. Upon the organization of the United States Christian Commission by Mr. George H. Stuart and others, in 1864, he was chosen its home secretary, and charged with the responsible duty of interesting the people of the North in the work of the Commission. By request of the Commission he wrote and published "Annals of the United States Christian Commission,"—a book full of interesting facts and inferences, and the only authentic record of the doings of the Commission. The work has received the highest praise. In 1865 he accepted the chair of Systematic Theology in the University of Lewisburg, Pa., and, after three years' service, resigned to accept the position of editor of the *National Baptist*, the organ of the American Baptist Publication Society. His editorship was a marked success. After four years he resigned this work to accept the chair of New Testament Interpretation in Crozer Theological Seminary, Pa. While occupying this position he came to Indiana, and was the principal lecturer for a State ministers' institute. During the course it was very manifest that he was able to answer difficult questions in both systematic theology and exegesis.

In the National Baptist Educational Convention, held in Brooklyn, N. Y., in 1870, he presented a paper on "The Organization of our Educational Work." He has also written for the *Baptist Quarterly* two articles,—one on "Our Schools and Foreign Missions," the other on "The Final Condition of the Unregenerate." In 1876 he edited a book entitled "Baptists and the National Centenary," a book of vast value to those who would know the origin and progress of the various enterprises taken up and carried forward by the denomination.

In 1875 he was elected president of Chicago University, Ill. In 1876 he was elected president of the Indiana State University, and he is still carrying forward its work with a vigor and wisdom that give great promise for the future of the university. He was in 1879 made president of the Indiana State College Association.

He is a clear thinker, a genial friend, an inspiring teacher, and a public speaker of rare power.

Mother-Churches among American Baptists, Some.—The First church of Providence, R. I., is regarded by the majority of Baptists as the oldest church of our denomination in America. That venerable community has been the mother of many churches. The First church of Newport, R. I., with John Clarke, the sturdy old Calvinist, and the enlightened statesman, as its founder, has been the mother of a goodly family of churches. Apart from New England successes, from it Thomas Dungan came to Pennsylvania, who formed the first Baptist church in that State; and by him Elias Keach was encouraged to trust Christ when convicted of sin and baptized, and by his church he was ordained. Mr. Keach founded the Pennepek church, the oldest church now existing in Pennsylvania, of which the First church of Philadelphia was a branch, and also some of the oldest churches in New Jersey, the communities that organized the Philadelphia Association. What these churches have done for the States in which they are located, and through communities springing from them, as well as directly in several other States, only the students of Baptist history know. The church at Swanzey, Mass., was constituted by John Miles in 1663. When he and his Welsh brethren came to New England they brought their church records with them. Their American community was a church like the First Newport, with no dependence upon the First church of Providence. The Welsh Tract church, in Delaware, was formed in Wales in the spring of 1701. Thomas Griffith was the first pastor, and he emigrated with the church to Pennepek, Pa., and subsequently removed with it to Welsh Tract, Del., where the church prospered, and exerted an extensive influence in favor of truth and righteousness. These were the most noted of the mother-churches that came into existence in America *independently of each other*.

It should be remarked that the First church of Providence was not the mother of any of the churches named; that the First church of Newport had some connection with the Pennepek church through Thomas Dungan, but no similar relationship with any of the others, and that the Swanzey and Welsh Tract churches had a European existence before they came to America. A sketch of all the great mother-churches of America would be of unspeakable interest, but in this article we can only notice those already mentioned.

Mott, Judge Frederick, was born near Montrose, Susquehanna Co., Pa., Jan. 14, 1828. Longing for an education beyond that afforded by common schools or the neighboring academy, he entered Brown University, from which he graduated in 1851. He was principal of Derby Academy, Vt., for three years, reading law at the same time, and was admitted to the bar in Vermont. In 1854 he took charge of a union school in Upper Sandusky, O., where he remained two years, and then came to Iowa, located at Winterset, Madison Co., and immediately commenced the practice of law. In September, 1862, entered the army, and was made adjutant of the 39th Iowa Infantry in 1863, and was commissioned by President Lincoln as assistant adjutant-general in 1864, serving as such until the close of the war. Returning home in August, 1865, he resumed the practice of law. In 1868 he was elected judge of the fifth judicial district of Iowa, serving the full term of four years. In October, 1870, was elected president of the Iowa Baptist State Convention, and re-elected to that position at each of the three succeeding annual meetings. In 1873 he was appointed to the professorship of Pleading and Practice in the law department of the State University, which position he held for two years, and resigned to accept the presidency of the University of Des Moines. At the close of the centennial year, his health failing him, he resigned his position, and returned to his former home at Winterset, where he now resides, engaged in his profession. He was a Baptist from his youth up, and has always been a persistent worker in the church and Sabbath-school. While devoted to his own church and the general work of his own denomination, he is deeply interested in every good cause, and is regarded by the community in which he has so long lived as an earnest Christian worker and a public-spirited and invaluable citizen.

Mount Carroll Seminary, now exclusively for young ladies, is located at Mount Carroll, in Carroll Co., Ill. It was founded in 1853, by Miss F. A. Wood and Miss C. M. Gregory, graduates of the Normal School at Albany, N. Y. Beginning with 11 pupils, the school has grown to an average yearly attendance of nearly 200. In 1878 Miss Gregory's connection with the institution ceased, and it has since remained under the principalship of her associate, now Mrs. F. A. W. Sheiner, with whom Miss C. A. Jay is at present associated. The school, which opened in a small and inconvenient room, is now accommodated with extensive buildings, three separate additions having been made to that which the principals erected, in the early history of the seminary, upon the delightful and healthful site still occupied. The grounds are very extensive, consisting of twenty-five acres, and are laid out in orchards, gardens, vineyards, botanical garden, conservatory, with a great variety of shade and ornamental trees. The department of instruction consists of a preparatory, a regular four years', and a normal course. The seminary is incorporated by charter, with full college power to confer degrees.

It is proper to say that this institution has been founded and built up entirely by private enterprise. Superior executive ability has characterized its administration from the beginning. It has grown simply through the public appreciation of its merits, no agents having been at any time employed, either to solicit pupils or to raise funds. Apart from the five acres of ground on which the buildings stand, with the sum of $1000 given at the foundation of the school, no aid from either private or public funds has been received. It is gratifying to have this example of a school built up simply through the good management of those in charge, with the appreciative patronage of a discerning public.

Mount Lebanon Female College, Mount Lebanon, La.—Simultaneously with the movement to establish Mount Lebanon University the Mount Lebanon Female College was organized, and the accomplished wife of Rev. Hanson Lee became principal. At the beginning of the war there were over 100 young ladies in attendance. Mrs. Lee was succeeded by Rev. John Q. Prescott, and upon the suspension of the university Dr. Crane became principal. Finally the buildings were sold to the State for a laboratory, where medicines were manufactured, under the direction of Dr. Egan. About the close of the war an effort was made by Mr. Prescott to revive the school. The buildings were destroyed by fire in 1866, and no attempt has since been made to rebuild.

Mount Lebanon University, Mount Lebanon, La.—About 1847, Dr. B. Egan began to agitate the question of a school of high grade at Mount Lebanon. His efforts resulted in the organization of Mount Lebanon University, which was chartered in 1854. A donation of $10,000 was obtained from the State, and about $50,000 raised in subscriptions; a commodious college building and president's house were erected, a large boarding-hall provided, and an able faculty secured. Rev. Jesse Hartwell, D.D., accepted the presidency, and in a short time nearly 200 students were in attendance. Dr. Hartwell died in 1859, and Rev. W. C. Crane, D.D., LL.D., now president of Baylor University, Texas, was called to the presidency. But in the midst of its prosperity the war began, and the students and faculty were dispersed. Early in the war the endowment notes matured, and were paid in Confederate money, invested in Confederate bonds, and consequently lost. After the war an effort was made to revive the institution, but after a few years' struggle the enterprise was virtually abandoned. The academical department is still maintained, but with some irregularity. The revival of prosperity in the State has awakened a new interest in education, and the question of reviving the university is receiving serious attention.

Mount Pleasant College was founded in

Huntsville, Mo., in 1854. A. S. Worrell, D.D., is the president. He is an admirable teacher, and the institution is rapidly advancing. It is for both sexes; 138 were matriculated last year. The instruction includes all, between the lowest primary and a full college course.

The degrees of A.B. and A.M. are conferred, according to the scholarship of the candidates. The students are pledged to temperance and good conduct. This college is in Randolph County, in a fine portion of the State, and it is doing a needed and noble work.

church, Cleveland, O., where he still remains. In June, 1879, was graduated with the degree of A.B. from the University of Rochester. Has published sermons and reviews, and he is regarded as a young man of great energy and promise.

Muir, Rev. William, was born in Scotland in February, 1829. His parents were Presbyterians, and he received a careful religious training from them. For several years he devoted himself to agricultural pursuits. When he was seventeen years of age he was apprenticed to learn a trade, and continued at the same until 1860. When he

MOUNT PLEASANT COLLEGE.

Moxom, Rev. P. S., was born in Palermo, Canada, Aug. 10, 1848. Removed when a child to Ogle Co., Ill. In January, 1862, went out with the 78th Ill. Regiment, as page to Capt. Bewley. A few days after the battle of Fort Donelson, at the age of fifteen, he enlisted in the 17th Ill. Cavalry, and served until Nov. 28, 1865. Jan. 1, 1866, he entered Kalamazoo College, Mich., where he was converted and baptized into the fellowship of the Battle Creek church by his father, Rev. J. H. Moxom. In the autumn of 1868 he entered Shurtleff College, where he remained until 1870, when he returned to Michigan to teach. In 1871 engaged in the study of law, but in a little while abandoned that for the ministry. His first settlement was at Bellevue, Mich., where he received ordination. In October, 1872, became pastor of the church at Albion, Mich., and in 1875 removed to Rochester, N. Y., to pursue theological studies. During the period of his studies in Rochester was pastor of the church at Mount Morris. Was called, in November, 1879, to the pastorate of the First

grew up to manhood he connected himself with the Presbyterian Church, although, as he subsequently had reason to believe, he knew nothing of experimental religion. In 1852 he left his native country and came to Canada, taking up his residence near Toronto. Early in the year 1855 he met with a severe accident, which laid him aside from labor for two months. Having recovered measurably from its effects, he returned to his usual employment. Two days after recommencing work he was caught in the machinery, and came to all appearance within a hair's breadth of losing his life. These providences of God aroused his attention, in connection with the warm appeals of a personal friend, and he became a hopeful Christian. In a little more than a year he and his wife were baptized and joined the church at Cheltenham. Here he remained four years, when he was licensed to preach the gospel. At once he went to the Canadian Literary Institute to acquire an education, in which he spent three years, and then was ordained to the work of the gospel ministry. Having devoted seven years to the pastoral work, he became, in April, 1871, office editor and business manager of the *Canadian Baptist*, the recognized organ of the Baptist denomination in the provinces of Ontario, Quebec, and Manitoba. In 1874 he became managing editor, and virtually, proprietor, which position he still retains.

Mulcahy, Rev. Michael, was born in Fermoy, County of Cork, Ireland, in 1842. He received a good education in England, where he spent his youth ; in 1867 he emigrated to Canada, was converted in 1869, and joined the Baptist church at Boston, where his natural eloquence and pleadings for Jesus led many to believe. He prepared for the ministry at Woodstock, preaching to destitute churches while pursuing his studies. He was successively pastor at Grand Blanc, Canada ; Ovid, Mich. ; South Bend, Ind. ; and Little Rock, Ark., where he was also chaplain of the State senate. An attack of hemorrhage compelled him to seek health in California. Reaching San Francisco, Sept. 4, 1873, he was called to the vacant pulpit of the First church. His fervid eloquence drew large audiences to the church, and he was on the eve of an evident revival when a return of his old disease brought him to an early grave. He died Jan. 4, 1874.

Mulford, Rev. Clarence W., was born at Salem, N. J., June 8, 1805 ; was converted and baptized at nineteen ; studied at Princeton for a time ; was ordained pastor of the Baptist church at Pemberton, N. J., in November, 1830. He was five years there, and nearly ten at Hightstown. His pastorates at Flemington and Holmdel yielded much fruit. He was particularly blessed in leading souls to Christ. He frequently assisted neighboring pastors. His voice had unusual power to attract and impress. He was one of the early friends of the New Jersey State Convention, was for several years its secretary, and its president from 1843 to 1849. In the early days of the temperance reformation he stood almost alone, but he was a brave advocate in the face of opposition. Through failure of health he was obliged to give up preaching for the most part in the latter years of his life, but having studied medicine, he was very useful in that profession, at the same time ministering to the spiritual comfort of his patients. He died June 28, 1864, at Flemington, N. J.

Mulford, Hon. Horatio J., was born at Canton, N. J., Jan. 16, 1818. He was trained to business, and has been engaged for many years in the management of his own, and in taking part in public affairs. He was baptized at Bridgeton, and united with the First Baptist church in 1853. He was elected deacon in 1856, and still holds the office. He was for a long time superintendent of the Sunday-school. He is a member of the university board

at Lewisburg, a trustee of the Crozer Theological Seminary, and a manager of the Baptist Publication Society. He is greatly interested in the education of the ministry ; has been president of the

HON. HORATIO J. MULFORD.

New Jersey Baptist Education Society since 1857, and still holds that office. His earnestness, executive ability, and liberality have been particularly prominent in bringing the South Jersey Institute to its present prosperity. Mr. Mulford's sympathies go far beyond the societies with which he is officially connected. His help is relied upon by those who take the largest views of spreading the gospel.

Mundy, Rev. J. A., was born in Virginia about 1835 ; graduated at Richmond College in 1858, and was pastor of several important churches in Virginia before he removed to North Carolina, in 1875. He has been for more than four years pastor of the Warrenton church. Mr. Mundy is regarded as one of the finest preachers in the State.

Munro, Rev. Andrew Heber, was born in Surrey, England, in 1827, of Scotch parents. He was chiefly educated at home, but went for a time to a private institution in the south of London, and from thence to the Normal College of the British and Foreign School Society. After a short attendance at the college, he was sent out by the society as one of the teachers of a Model and Normal School established by the government of New Brunswick. He afterwards taught for a time in the Methodist College at Sackville, and subsequently became Latin and mathematical tutor in the Baptist Seminary at Fredericton, New Brunswick, where he also read theology with Dr. Spurden. While at the seminary he began preaching, the scene of his labors being the Welsh settlement of Cardigan, nineteen miles distant, and was instrumental in the conversion of a large number of persons. He was ordained at Digby, Nova Scotia, in 1857. In 1860 he took charge of the North Baptist church, Halifax, Nova Scotia, where he remained nearly seven years. From thence he went to the First church, Yarmouth, Nova Scotia, and after a short pastorate removed to Liverpool, in the same province. In 1869 he accepted a cordial invitation to Alexander Street church, Toronto, Ontario, where, during seven years, his ministry was highly appreciated by the church and community. He then entered upon his present charge, the pastorate of the First church, Montreal, and shortly after his settlement the church received into its fellowship nearly the entire membership of the St. Catharine Street church. During his ministry of twenty-four years he has been permitted to see several extensive revivals of religion.

As a public speaker, Mr. Munro is one of the most attractive and popular men in the Dominion of Canada. Both in the pulpit and on the platform he is at once powerful, graceful, and eloquent. He is one of the trustees of the Toronto Baptist College, and secretary of the Eastern Missionary Convention and of the Baptist Union of Canada.

Munro, Rev. James, was born in Scotland in 1784; converted in 1806 in Chester, Nova Scotia; baptized in New York in 1807; returned to Nova Scotia, and commenced preaching in Halifax; evangelized with Rev. Joseph Crandall, in 1815, to the east of Halifax; ordained in 1816, and evangelized on eastern shores of New Brunswick, and in 1818 up the St. John River; became pastor at Onslow in 1819, and continued in this relation until his death, July 3, 1838. Possessing a keen, logical mind, sterling integrity, fervent piety, and sound theology, Mr. Munro's ministry was highly useful.

Munster, The Uproar at.—See article on ANABAPTISTS.

Münzer, Thomas.—See article on ANABAPTISTS.

Murch, William Harris, D.D., was born at Honiton, England, May 17, 1784. He was entered as a student for the ministry at an Independent college when he was quite a lad. Here that most charming little book, Fuller's "Life of Samuel Pearce," fell into his hands, and led him to abandon the Arian belief, in which he had been brought up, and to embrace evangelical truth. In May, 1802, he was baptized by Dr. Rippon, at Carter Lane meeting-house, London, being then seventeen. He continued his studies for two years longer, and subsequently preached in several places without any stated charge. On John Foster's retirement

from the pastorate of Sheppard's Barton church, Frome, Mr. Murch succeeded him, having previously supplied the pulpit for six months during Mr. Foster's affliction. He remained pastor, with many evidences of usefulness, for twenty-one years, when he was invited to the presidency of Stepney College, the Baptist theological seminary in the metropolis. He entered upon his work there in 1827. During his presidency the interests of the college were diligently advanced, and a large number of students prepared for the ministry. When he retired from this position, in 1844, after seventeen years' service, the tutors and students of the colleges at Bristol, Bradford, and Stepney combined to do honor to him for his worth and usefulness. The degree of D.D. was conferred upon him by Brown University during his presidential course. He presided over the church at Rickmansworth for a short time, and rendered occasional services to churches in and around London until compelled by illness to retire from public employments. He died at Bath, July 12, 1859, and was buried at Frome, the scene of his early labors. During his residence in London he identified himself with all the literary and religious institutions of the denomination. He was one of the secretaries of the Baptist Union from 1834 to 1846, secretary of the Baptist Board from 1837 to 1843, and gave his care and interest to the "New Selection Hymn-Book" for several years. His end was peculiarly peaceful and edifying. His mind was unclouded and serene to the last. He had made daily allusion to his approaching departure for several months, and expressed himself as ready and waiting. His last words, an hour before his death, were, "Precious Saviour! all is right; precious Saviour!"

Murdock, John Nelson, D.D., was born in Oswego, N. Y., Dec. 8, 1820, and received his early religious education among the Methodists. His devoted Christian mother named him after one of the co-laborers of John Wesley, and her earnest prayer was that he might become a minister of the gospel. He was fitted for college by teachers well qualified for their work, one of them, Master Hogan, having been educated at Oxford University. In consequence of his father's death he was obliged to give up the idea of taking a collegiate course. Having chosen the legal profession for his future vocation, he commenced his law studies, and while engaged in them carried on special courses of mathematics and languages, including French and German. Having completed his law studies, he was admitted to the bar. At the age of seventeen he became a hopeful Christian, and united with the Methodist Church in his native city. Not long after commencing the practice of his profession his religious life was greatly quickened, and the duty and privilege of serving his Master in the ministry of the Word was so impressed upon him that he was licensed to preach. While supplying the pulpit of a Methodist church in Jordan, N. Y., in 1841, his attention was drawn to the subject of baptism,

JOHN NELSON MURDOCK, D.D.

and as the result of his investigations he was baptized in 1842, at Durhamville, N. Y., by Rev. Seymour W. Adams, late of Cleveland, O. His ordination as a Baptist minister took place at Waterville, N. Y., in May, 1842, when he was but a few months beyond his majority. Here he remained until January, 1846, when he became pastor of the church in Albion, N. Y. In April, 1848, he entered upon his duties as pastor of the South church, in Hartford, from which place he was called to the pastorate of the Bowdoin Square church, Boston, his service there commencing Jan. 1, 1857, and continuing until Jan. 1, 1863, a period of just six years. In July of this year he was elected secretary of the Missionary Union, which position he now holds.

During a part of the time of Dr. Murdock's ministry in Hartford—i.e., 1853-56—he was joint editor with Rev. Dr. R. Turnbull of the *Christian Review*. The number of his published sermons is twenty-one. All of these were called for by the bodies before which they were delivered. The amount of literary work which he has done in his extensive and varied correspondence, and in the preparation of his valuable reports and special papers in his official relations to the Missionary Union, it is impossible to compute. Honored and beloved by the denomination which he has so long and so faithfully served, Dr. Murdock takes a high place in the front

ranks of her most worthy and distinguished members. He received the honorary degree of Doctor of Divinity from Rochester University in 1854.

Murfee, James T., LL.D.—His paternal grandfather was the Rev. Simon Murfee, a prominent Baptist minister of the Portsmouth Association, Southampton Co., Va. His ancestors were a pious people, and they were Baptists. The subject of this sketch was born in Southampton Co., Va., Sept. 13, 1833. His early home surroundings were of the best character. He graduated from the Virginia Military Institute at Lexington in 1853, without a single demerit and with the highest honors of his class. Soon after graduating he was elected Professor of Mathematics and Natural Sciences in Madison College. Thence called to Lynchburg College, where he united with the Baptist Church in 1857; was called to the University of Alabama in 1860 as Professor of Mathematics, and became commandant of cadets in that institution. At the close of the war he was employed as architect to design and erect new buildings for the institution. He then recommended " a new scheme of university organization," which was adopted by the trustees, but was defeated by State reconstruction. He was called to the presidency of Howard College to put in operation a plan which promised results so long felt as most desirable. The work accomplished at Howard College since the introduction of the system of college administration originated by James T. Murfee bears testimony to the superiority of the method employed. This position he still holds to the universal satisfaction of the denomination.

Murphy, John R., D.D., was born Dec. 8, 1820, in Cape May Co., N. J. As he approached manhood he concluded to study law, but after his conversion felt constrained to devote his life to the ministry. He was baptized, in 1841, by Rev. J. H. Kennard, D.D., and united with the Tenth Baptist church, Philadelphia. He pursued his studies for a time at Branchtown, Pa., and at the old Germantown Academy. He graduated from Madison University in August, 1849, and was ordained in Philadelphia in 1849. From 1850 to 1852 he was pastor of the Greenwich Baptist church, Cumberland Co., N. J. From 1853 to 1859 he was pastor of the Marlton church, Burlington Co., N. J. From 1859 to 1872 he was pastor of the First Baptist church, Salem, N. J. During these years of labor in New Jersey he was closely identified with the Baptist enterprises in the State. During 1864 he spent some time at White House and City Point, Va., with the Union army, as a member of the Christian Commission. In 1872 he accepted a call to the pastorate of the First Baptist church, Des Moines, in which position he remained till September, 1879, sharing with his brethren in Iowa the responsibilities of the general work. **At**

present he is residing near Winterset, Iowa, waiting for improved health to resume pastoral work. During his twenty-seven and a half years of ministerial labor he has received into the four churches he has served nearly 1000 members, over 600 of whom came by baptism.

Murphy, Rev. Joseph, like his brother William, was made a happy subject of redeeming grace in early life, and a preacher of the blessed gospel. He and his brother were sneeringly called "the Murphy boys," because of their youth. Joseph gave great diligence to his education after his conversion, that he might be fully qualified to preach the gospel. He had mental power, ready wit, and fearless courage, and he had a heart in which Christ reigned supreme. After preaching with much success in his native Virginia, he took charge of the church in Deep Creek, Surrey Co., N. C. In his new home he was eminently useful, and soon became the leading minister in the Yadkin Association. His influence also had weight in South Carolina. He was living in 1803, and had passed his eightieth year, an honored and happy Christian.

Murphy, Rev. William, was led to the Saviour and baptized by the celebrated Shubal Stearns. His talents were respectable, his faith vigorous, and his zeal burning. He was the chief instrument in leading Col. Samuel Harris to Jesus, and he was also favored in bringing a whole harvest of souls to the same blessed Redeemer. Mr. Murphy had not only a sound Christian experience, but his doctrines were those of Calvin, Augustine, and Paul. In the year 1775, when the churches were agitated by the Arminian controversy, Mr. Murphy, with great ability and success, defended sovereign and efficacious grace. He went to Kentucky for a permanent home, where he labored with the divine approval for a few years, and then was transferred to the church in glory.

Murphy, Hon. William D., was born in New York, June 4, 1796; died Aug. 26, 1877. A full record of the life of Mr. Murphy would present an illustration of the success and intellectual development that so often attend upon young men whose hearts are influenced by correct religious principles, and who are diligent in business. He had received an English education, but with a wonderful memory, great power of observation, and remarkable conversational abilities, he was enabled to make up for any deficiencies in his earlier opportunities. His life was one of continuous study as well as activity. He was greatly respected in his native city, and was often called to fill important trusts. As member of common council in 1841 and 1842, and of the board of education for several years, he manifested great interest in the schools, and conscientiously discharged his duties. In public discussions he displayed much ability,

and was full of quiet wit and humor, and master of an audience.

He was hopefully converted in June, 1813, and joined the Mulberry Street church, New York. In 1828 he removed his membership to the Oliver Street church, of which he was made a trustee, and for many years took a deep interest in its welfare. As a lay preacher, he often delighted in bringing the consolations of the gospel before the destitute in the asylums of New York, and few men were more widely known or more warmly welcomed. He enjoyed a happy old age in the bosom of his family, where he was greatly beloved by an affectionate household. He published, as the result of the leisure of his later years, a volume entitled "The Advent, and other Poems and Hymns." He represented a New York district in the United States Congress for two years.

Murrow, Rev. Joseph Samuel, a missionary to the Choctaw Indians, in the Indian Territory, sent out and supported by the Rehoboth Baptist Association of Georgia, was born in Jefferson Co., Ga., June 7, 1835. He became a Christian at a very early age, and received academical instruction in youth. He joined Green Fork Baptist church, in Burke Co., Ga., at nineteen; was licensed at twenty. In 1855, at the age of twenty, he entered Mercer University, where he pursued his studies diligently until ordained and sent out as a missionary to the Indian Territory in the fall of 1857. In November of that year he began what has proved to be a long, laborious, and useful missionary life, in which much of hardship and suffering has been mingled with great success and joy.

He settled at North Fork town, and began his missionary work among the Creeks, among whom he labored most assiduously for two years. He then removed to Little River, Creek Nation, and began a work among the Seminoles. In 1861 he constituted the first Baptist church ever formed among that tribe. During the war the Seminoles selected him as their agent, in transactions with the government, to receive their food and supplies; and, as he was cut off from the Association which sustained him, he was thus supported; but he never forgot his character as a missionary, nor ceased to maintain it, while performing his official duties to the satisfaction of both the government and tribe. One of the first structures built always was a bush arbor for preaching services. For several years he and his wife lived thus with the Seminoles, during which period he baptized 200 of that nation, and may thus be considered the father of the mission work among the Seminoles. Three-fifths of the adults of that nation are now Baptists.

The war closed in 1865, and his duties as Indian agent came to an end. Being still cut off from his Association, he took refuge for a year in Texas, but returned in 1866, settling at Atoka, Choctaw Nation, the first missionary to return to the Indian field after the war. He found the Choctaw mission in a very demoralized condition, and proceeded at once to reorganize the churches, in which he was very successful, constituting a large Association, and putting the Sunday-school work on a healthy basis. The Baptist Theological School, for training teachers and preachers, now being established at Tallequah, Cherokee Nation, by the Home Mission Society of the North, is the conception of his brain. He has now been a missionary among the Indians for twenty-four years, has preached thousands of sermons, traveled hundreds of thousands of miles, and baptized over a thousand Indians, yet there is no abatement in his desire to live and labor for the triumph of the gospel among the red men of the West.

Mursell, Rev. James, the eldest son of the Rev. J. P. Mursell, was born at Leicester, England, July 22, 1829. He received a liberal education, and after two or three years of secular employment, in connection with the great railway works of Sir Morton Peto, he determined to give himself to ministerial work, having previously been baptized and received into his father's church at Leicester. After a brief period of study and tutorial work at Aberdeen, he entered Bristol College, and at the conclusion of the college course he was invited to the pastorate of the church at Kettering, as successor to the Rev. William Robinson, who had recently removed to Cambridge. For seventeen years Mr. Mursell labored at Kettering, with a zeal, devotion, and power which attracted general interest and encouraged the highest expectations. Few men were more genial in manners, or had more attached friends. A new edifice was erected more worthy of the denominational celebrity of the town, and better adapted to the wants of the congregation. He removed from Kettering to Bradford in 1870, and after a brief pastorate there, settled at Newcastle-on-Tyne in 1872. In the fullness of successful labors and growing influence he died, May 28, 1875, in his forty-sixth year.

Mursell, Rev. James Philippo, was born at Lymington, England, in 1800. His father, Rev. William Mursell, labored for many years in that town and neighborhood as a Baptist pastor. Mr. James P. Mursell was educated at the famous Baptist school conducted by the Rev. James Hinton, of Oxford, and having given abundant evidence of ministerial gifts in village preaching, he was entered at Bristol College in 1822. His remarkable ability as a preacher procured him several overtures from pastorless churches before his course of study was completed, and in 1825 he commenced his stated ministry as pastor of the church at Wells, Somersetshire. In 1826, on the removal of Robert

Hall from Leicester to Bristol, the attention of the church at Leicester was directed to Mr. Mursell, and in the following year he entered upon his ministry as Mr. Hall's successor in the pastorate. For nearly fifty years Mr. Mursell continued to minister to the same church, and he was the recognized leader of the denomination in the midland district. In conjunction with Mr. Edward Miall he took a conspicuous part in organizing the anti-state-church movement, in 1843. He occupied the chair of the Baptist Union in 1864, and presided over the first of the autumnal assemblies of that body. Throughout his long and honorable career Mr. Mursell rendered valuable service to the denominational interests, particularly in connection with the foreign missions, of which for many years he was one of the Committee of Management.

Muscatine, Iowa.—The Baptist church at this place is among the oldest churches of the State. It was constituted in 1841, and has always held a good position among the churches of Iowa. It has a substantial meeting-house, valued at $14,000, and 202 members.

Muse, Rev. Thomas, of Cuthbert, Ga., was born in Middlesex Co., Va., Jan. 6, 1810. His grandparents were natives of England. At seventeen years of age Mr. Muse began to engage in mercantile pursuits, which he continued for fourteen years. In 1832 he was baptized, and four years after removed to Georgia, settling in Blakely, Early Co. While still merchandising he gradually entered into the duties of a minister, led on by his zeal and the necessity for ministerial labor in his neighborhood. In consequence he was licensed May 7, 1837, and ordained in December, 1840, to take charge of a church organized in Blakely out of material resulting from his own personal labors, and which before he left its service numbered 200 members. Mr. Muse moved to Cuthbert to take charge of a church there, and also of one in Randolph County; and has continued to the present time a faithful, laborious, and successful minister and pastor. He has succeeded in winning souls to Christ far beyond what is granted to most pastors, for more than 4000 have been baptized by his own hands. He has been greatly beloved by his churches, and his pastorates have lasted from four to twenty years. He aided in establishing the Baptist Female College in Cuthbert, and became president of its board of trustees. For twenty years he has been moderator of the Bethel Association, and for forty years has been actively engaged in all its interests.

Musgrove, Rev. Thomas Jefferson, was born in Mason Co., Ky., Jan. 30, 1837. His parents removed to Clark Co., Mo., in 1840. The subject of this sketch finished his college course when twenty-four years of age. In May, 1861, he was ordained to the ministry. In 1867 he took charge of the public schools in Alexandria, Mo. Afterwards he established the Pleasant Hill Academy, where he taught for four years. Then he accepted the charge of the schools in Alexandria a second time. After laboring for two years in this capacity he established Alexandria College, of which he is the president. He is a Baptist, and a man of energy, character, and usefulness.

Music, Rev. Thomas R., was born Oct. 17, 1756; was converted at the age of seventeen. He spent his early life in North Carolina. He came to Missouri with his family in 1803. He lived in St. Louis County. In 1807 he organized the Fee Fee church, among the constituent members of which were Adam Martin and his wife Mary, Richard and Jane Sullens, Thos. R. Music and his wife Sarah. Elder Brown, from Kentucky, and John Clark, labored with Mr. Music, who died in 1842. Mr. Music preached in Missouri, where he was persecuted by Catholics, and needed a gun to guard him from Indians. He is buried in the church grounds at Fee Fee. The old people still cherish his memory.

Mynatt, Rev. Wm. C., was born in Knox Co., Tenn., Nov. 16, 1808, and was baptized by Rev. Samuel Love, in 1832; removed to Asheville, Ala., in 1833, and that year he began to preach, and was ordained in 1836, in Cherokee County, where, in connection with other counties, he spent his best days as a minister, living ten years of that time in De Kalb County; spent several years as missionary of the Domestic Mission Board, and was unquestionably the leading minister in that part of the State. In 1857 he removed to Calhoun County, where he still resides and labors for Christ; though seventy-two years old he is constantly active. He has baptized large numbers of converts, and has been a most trustworthy and gifted minister of the gospel. His son, Rev. J. B. Mynatt, and his brother, Rev. Gordon Mynatt, are also worthy Baptist ministers.

N.

Nash, Rev. C. H., was born at North Granville, Washington Co., N. Y., Dec. 6, 1835; and nine years from that time was born again; but for want of proper instruction and encouragement, was not baptized until 1850. He became impressed that it was his duty to preach the gospel, and in 1857 commenced a preparatory course at Troy Conference Academy, Poultney, Vt.; and two years later entered on the regular course at Madison University, Hamilton, N. Y. Completing his studies at Hamilton, he was called, in 1864, to the pastorate of the Baptist church at Westport, N. Y. Here he was ordained. He remained at Westport four years and a half, during which the church was considerably increased and strengthened. In 1869 he visited Glen's Falls, N. Y., and after supplying the pulpit of the Baptist church there for a few months, accepted the call of the church to the pastorate, and labored with much success for ten years and a half. In 1879 he resolved to enter some mission field in the great West. Finding a little discouraged, scattered church at Concordia, Kansas, he commenced labor there under the appointment of the Home Mission Society. During two years this church has doubled in membership, and has now a neat brick edifice nearly completed. With the advantage of this new church, centrally located, and with the Lord's blessing, there is a good work in prospect at Concordia.

Nash, John Anson, D.D., was born in Shelburn, Chenango Co., N. Y., July 11, 1815. In his sixteenth year he united with the Methodist Church, and soon after he embraced Baptist views. Feeling called to preach the gospel, he entered Madison University in 1836, and graduated from college in 1842, and from the seminary in 1844. Having accepted a call from the Baptist church at Watertown, N. Y., he immediately entered upon the duties of his pastorate, and was ordained in September, 1844. He remained at Watertown about six years. In 1850 he came to Iowa. He has preached to the Baptist churches in Des Moines about seventeen and a half years; has extended his labors far into the surrounding country, gathering and organizing nearly thirty Baptist churches. In 1865, on the starting of the University of Des Moines, by the advice of the movers in this enterprise, he resigned his pastorate and entered upon its work; first as financial agent, then as professor, and for several years has been its president, which office he now holds. Much of this time, however, he has spent in supplying destitute churches in the surrounding region. In 1877 he received the degree of D.D. from the University of Chicago.

Nashville, First Colored Church of.—Rev. N. G. Merry became pastor of this community in 1853, when it was a branch of the First church of white Baptists. Since that time the organization has be-

FIRST COLORED BAPTIST CHURCH, NASHVILLE, TENN.

come independent, and it has been unusually prosperous. The church has grown from 100 to 2300 members, and it has built four times since 1853. Their present edifice cost $26,000, and it will seat 1300 persons. It is an honor to the colored Baptists of the State.

Nashville Institute is situated one mile from Nashville, Tenn., upon a property containing thirty acres, adjoining the Vanderbilt University grounds. The site is high, and commands an unsurpassed prospect of the city and surrounding country. The estate was bought in the spring of 1874 for the American Baptist Home Mission Society, at a cost

The institute has a " Normal," an " Academic," a " Scientific," a " Classical," and a " Theological" course. It prepares young men and women for teaching, and it educates students for the Christian ministry. For 1880–81 the institute had 8 instructors and 249 students of both sexes. Nashville Institute has been and is now a rich blessing to the colored Baptists of this country.

Natchez Seminary.—This institution is devoted to the instruction of freedmen. It is located at Natchez, Miss., and is doing a noble work. The spring term of 1880 closed with 117 matriculates, of whom 31 were preparing for the ministry, and

NASHVILLE INSTITUTE.

of $30,000. At the time it had a mansion upon it, 48 by 80 feet, and two stories high. The Society spent about $45,000 in additional buildings, exclusive of the cost of furnishing. The Institute took possession of its home in October, 1876.

The mansion-house now has four stories, and furnishes apartments for the teachers and dormitories for the young women. Centennial Hall, 49 by 185 feet, and four stories in height, in its ample basement provides accommodations for the boarding department. The first story is devoted to public rooms, and the three stories above it furnish dormitories for about 140 young men. For this building the Institute is chiefly indebted to Mr. and Mrs. Nathan Bishop, of New York.

46 design to become teachers. The institution has the hearty sympathy of the Baptists of Mississippi, and is destined to become an important factor in the elevation of the colored race.

National Monitor, The, Brooklyn, N. Y., was established in 1870 by Rev. Rufus L. Perry as the official organ of the colored Baptists of the United States. The condition of the colored people made it necessary for this paper to be of a politico-religious character, which it still maintains. It circulates among the prominent colored people North and South, and is read in Canada, Hayti, and Africa. It is now one of the leading and most influential papers among the colored people. Rev. Rufus L. Perry is still editor.

Neale, Rollin Heber, D.D., was born in South-ington, Conn. He prepared for college in his native town, and graduated at Columbian College, Washington, D. C., in the class of 1830. While a student

ROLLIN HEBER NEALE, D.D.

in college he was ordained as pastor of the Second Baptist church in Washington, and preached there the last two years of his course. While pursuing his studies at the Newton Theological Institution he was the pastor of the South Boston Baptist church. He graduated at Newton in 1833. From the spring of 1834 to September, 1837, he was the pastor of the First Baptist church in Needham, Mass., from which place he was called to the pastorate of the First Baptist church in Boston, Sept. 17, 1837, and continued in that relation until June, 1877, a period of nearly forty years. Few pastorates in Baptist churches have been so long, and few have been more harmonious. The labors of Dr. Neale, extending on through all these years, have been greatly blessed, his church, under the ministrations of their pastor, having been favored with many precious revivals of religion.

The degree of Doctor of Divinity was conferred upon Dr. Neale by Brown University in 1850, and by Harvard College in 1857. He has published a few sermons, a Harvard College Dudleian lecture, a little volume called the "Burning Bush," and he has written much for the public press. Many of the addresses which he made (and in the making of which he had a most happy gift) on funeral occasions of dear friends have found their way into print. They were the outgushings of a warm,

sympathizing heart, and were exceedingly appropriate to the occasions upon which they were uttered.

Dr. Neale visited Europe four times, one of which was in company with Rev. Dr. Kirk, the late eloquent pastor of the Mount Vernon Congregational church, who was his companion while traveling in the Holy Land.

For many years he was a "visitor" and an overseer of Harvard University. He always took an interest in public affairs, and from the pulpit expressed his views upon the great moral questions of the day. He was known to be a minister of a kind and catholic spirit, and while he held a very warm place in the hearts of his own brethren in the ministry, he had the respect and affection of the clerical profession of all denominations in Boston and its vicinity. He entered upon his eternal reward in 1879, from the city where he lived for so many years.

Nebraska.—Nebraska occupies a position near the centre of the republic. Bounded north by Dakota, east by the Missouri River, south by Kansas, and west by Wyoming. It was originally a part of the Louisiana purchase. It was organized as a Territory May 30, 1854, by the Kansas and Nebraska Act. It was admitted into the Union as a sovereign State in March, 1867. The extreme length of the State from east to west is within a fraction of 413 miles, and its extreme width from north to south is 208 miles. In area the State contains nearly 75,995 square miles, or about 48,636,800 acres. The area of Nebraska is 12,359 square miles larger than all the New England States combined.

Emigration into the Territory began in 1849. The first settlements were confined to the neighborhood of the Missouri River and a narrow strip on one side of the Platte. Here were, therefore, laid the foundations of the future churches in Nebraska. For religious enterprises the circumstances were unfavorable. The population was unstable. Some came to speculate in land, whose stay was transient. But others came to remain. These were poor and scattered, but unity in religious beliefs brought these settlers together, at convenient centres, for the service of God and for mutual edification.

THE BAPTIST ASSOCIATION.

The few Baptists who had come to the Territory to remain formed themselves into churches at various points. On the 28th and 29th of May, 1858, at Nebraska City, the Nebraska Baptist Association was organized by seven churches, which had been previously formed. These were, in the order in which they were constituted, Nebraska City, Peru, Plattsmouth, Fontenelle, Cumming City, Rock Bluff, and Florence.

The First Nebraska City church was recognized Aug. 18, 1855.

At the organization of the Nebraska Association the names of only two ordained ministers appear on the minutes,—Rev. J. M. Taggart and Rev. J. G. Bowen, missionaries of the American Baptist Home Mission Society. If the members were few in number, the records of the first meeting show that they were men of large ideas, strong faith, and a clear insight into the future greatness of the Territory. At this meeting vital questions were discussed,—education, Baptist literature, benevolence, temperance. Among the resolutions passed we find the following, so full of wisdom :

" Resolved, That we recommend to the churches of this Association, when practicable, to erect their meeting-houses within the limits of incorporate towns, and that measures be taken at an early day to secure eligible sites for building purposes."

The first effort at church-building by the Baptists in Nebraska was at Omaha in 1860. For years the growth of the churches was slow ; the faith of the early laborers was severely tested.

At the fifth annual meeting of the Association there was an increase of one church and of 84 members. In 1867 four churches were dismissed with prayers, and the Omaha Association was formed. Since then God has greatly blessed our struggling brethren in Nebraska.

STATE CONVENTION.

The Nebraska Baptist State Convention was organized in 1868 to take the place of the Domestic Mission Board, which had been organized under a resolution adopted by the original Association Sept. 10, 1864.

The resolution reads as follows : " Resolved, That a missionary board of five members be appointed at each annual meeting of this Association, whose duty it shall be to ascertain the destitution of Baptist preaching as far as possible, and by corresponding with the American Baptist Home Mission Society, and appealing to the churches composing this Association, to make arrangements for its supply ; and that we recommend to the churches the penny-a-week system for the purpose of carrying out this resolution."

Article 2d of its constitution states the object of the State Convention : " The object of this body shall be to unite the Baptist churches of the State in the dissemination of the principles of the gospel as understood by them into all parts of the State, and especially, in the prosecution of domestic mission work, to co-operate with the Baptist Home Mission Society." In the revised constitution of 1879 the object is substantially the same.

At the annual meeting in 1872 the following resolution was carried :

" Resolved, That for the purpose of carrying out more fully the objects of the Nebraska Baptist State Convention we hereby incorporate ourselves in accordance with the laws of the State, so that we may acquire and hold property with which to educate and sustain ministers, build or aid in building church edifices, make provision for superannuated pastors or preachers, and sustain all other institutions by which the churches may be united in the dissemination of the principles of the gospel as understood by them in all parts of the world."

The aim of the Convention has been hitherto to assist and co-operate with the Baptist Home Mission Society. At each of its annual sessions questions of vital importance to the home field have been discussed. At no meeting has the work abroad been forgotten.

At a meeting of the board held in October, 1877, it was resolved to hold a historical meeting in June, 1878, at Nebraska City. The object of the meeting was to bring the Baptists together and to review the past. An interesting programme was prepared. Eminent men from abroad lent their aid. Rev. J. M. Taggart, the only remaining pioneer missionary, read a historical paper of much interest, in which he reviewed the growth and development of the denomination for twenty years. The meeting resulted in imparting new zeal to the brethren and new life to the State Convention. At the annual meeting in 1879, Rev. H. L. Morehouse, corresponding secretary of the American Baptist Home Mission Society, submitted to the board of the State Convention a plan for practical co-operation with that society, which was adopted. The third and fourth specifications are as follows :

" The Home Mission Society shall appropriate to the mission work in Nebraska a definite sum pro rata to receipts from the State for the fiscal year of the Convention ending Nov. 1, 1880, four dollars additional to each dollar received from the State ; the apportions to be made, so far as possible, at the beginning of the year, upon a reasonable estimate of probable receipts, and to be corrected by actual experience.

" The Convention shall superintend the work in the State, determine fields, nominate missionaries, name their salaries, and determine the time of labor ; the Home Mission Society to appoint and pay those nominated so far as they approve such nominations and terms."

The existence and growth of the Baptist churches in Nebraska are due largely to the American Baptist Home Mission Society. There is scarcely a church in the State which it has not aided. The number of self-supporting churches as yet is small. The majority of the pastors in active service are sustained in part by this society. The need for enlarged liberality in this field is very great.

EDUCATION.

Recognizing the need and value of an educated ministry, the question of higher education received attention in the early history of this Territory. We find the following in the minutes of the State Convention for 1870:

" Your Executive Board, to which was referred, by a resolution passed at the last annual session, the subject of a denominational educational institution for the State, respectfully report that the duty charged upon them has been fulfilled, as will be seen by referring to the proceedings of the board meeting published in last year's minutes. So far as the members of the Executive Board have knowledge, no definite propositions for the location of a Baptist college have as yet been received which were of such a character as to warrant your committee in recommending a location, as was contemplated in that resolution.

" Your committee would further add that the subject of the founding of a Baptist college in Nebraska, while it is one of the greatest importance to our interests, is one which should demand and receive the most careful deliberation at our hands. We are warned on every hand by the experience of our brethren in other States, as well as by that of other denominations in our own State, that the attempt to build up at too early a day in the history of a State such an institution as is contemplated in your resolution of last year is not only full of difficulty, but of real danger to the interests it is designed to support. It imposes a pecuniary burden not easily borne even in wealthy communities and with favorable surroundings,—a burden which, in our estimation, it would be unwise for us at present to assume.

" Your committee are of opinion that the following are essential to success in a denominational college enterprise in Nebraska:

" 1st. That it be located in the midst of earnest and able friends.

" 2d. That it have sufficient local subscriptions to erect suitable buildings in which to open the school, and a fair sum towards an endowment.

" 3d. Denominational unity in the State in reference to its support as a part of the list of agencies for carrying on the work of this Convention.

" We therefore recommend that further action in this matter be dispensed with until God by his providence shall show us that we are in possession of the conditions which will insure success; and that in the mean time the brethren residing in localities where circumstances are favorable aim at the establishment of local seminaries and academies mainly self-supporting, which may in the future, when our wants and our ability warrant it, become the nuclei of such an institution as shall reflect credit upon our denomination and our State."

This question was considered each subsequent year until the meeting of the Executive Board of the State Convention held in Hastings in May, 1880, when Mr. Eddy, a Baptist of Gibbon, was present to invite the attention of the Educational Committee to an opportunity offered at that place. After correspondence on the subject, the chairman of the committee visited Gibbon, and learned that there was a prospect of obtaining a good donation if we would locate our Baptist school there. A report was made at the meeting of the Executive Board in Blair, Aug. 4, 1880, and the following resolution was passed:

"*Resolved*, That we locate our Baptist school at Gibbon, provided the citizens of Gibbon and vicinity will donate a certain brick building, three stories high, 40 by 60 feet, together with five acres of land, and $1000 for repairs and alterations; also $1000 per year for three years as tuition for pupils of the district above the primary department."

A request was made by the Executive Board that the Educational Committee proceed at once to secure the property and open a school as soon as possible.

A special meeting of the Executive Board was called to meet at Lincoln, Aug. 16, at which resolutions were passed appointing the Rev. G. W. Read as principal of the school, and giving it the name of Nebraska Baptist Seminary. The appointment was accepted, and a meeting arranged between the Educational Committee and the citizens of Gibbon for Aug. 23. At this meeting the citizens agreed to comply with the conditions expressed in the resolution.

Papers were drawn and the building transferred to the Nebraska Baptist State Convention. The money promised for repairs was paid, and the building is now undergoing repairs. School will be commenced about Nov. 1, 1880. The property is valued at $15,000.

Statistical Report of Associations.

Associations.	Number of Churches.	Number of Members.
First Nebraska	13	690
Omaha	15	693
Nemaha Valley	16	575
Blue River	11	458
York	21	607
Republican Valley	15	306
Grand Island	17	672
Loup and Elkhorn Valley	11	201
Scandinavian	9	428
German	3	145
Unassociated	7	80
Associations, 10.	138	4855

The following ministers have done noble work in other States, and are at present in active service in Nebraska: Rev. O. A. Buzzell, Juniata; Rev. W. S. Gee, Lincoln; Rev. J. Gunderman, Central City; Rev. N. P. Hotchkiss, Pawnee City; Rev.

J. Lewelling, Weston ; Rev. S. B. Mayo, Beaver City ; Rev. J. W. Osborn, Fremont; Rev. Amos Pratt, Exeter; Prof. C. C. Bush, St. Edward's ; Rev. I. R. Shanafelt, Macon ; Rev. G. W. Taylor, Blair; Rev. E. D. Thomas, Liberty ; Rev. T. K. Tyson, Wahoo ; Rev. A. Weaver, Loup City ; Rev. F. M. Williams, Ashland.

Nelson, Rev. Ebenezer, was born in Middleborough, Mass., Nov. 9, 1787, and received his early education in Taunton and South Reading, and entered upon mercantile pursuits in Providence, R. I. At the age of twenty-nine years he made a public profession of his faith, and was baptized by Rev. Dr. Gano. Soon after he commenced to study for the ministry, being for a part of the time a pupil of Rev. Dr. Chaplin, afterwards president of Waterville College. He was ordained as pastor of the Baptist church in Lynn, Mass., July 26, 1820, where he remained seven years. His health failing, he resigned his pastorate, and was employed for a year in raising funds for the endowment of the Newton Theological Institution. His term of service being completed, he accepted a call to become the pastor of the West Cambridge church, and was installed Sept. 9, 1828. He remained here six years, and was then appointed the secretary of the Northern Baptist Education Society, holding this position for two years and a half, during which time he rendered most efficient service in the cause of ministerial education. A vacancy having occurred in the Central Baptist church in Middleborough, Mass., he accepted a call to that church, and for fourteen years was their pastor, his labors being greatly blessed in the conversion of sinners and the building up of the church. He took also a deep interest in promoting the prosperity of Pierce Academy, an institution which accomplished so much good in the mental and moral training of scores of both sexes. His health failing again, he resigned his ministry. He continued to perform such service as he could for the cause he so much loved, but gradually he wasted away under the disease which finally proved fatal. He died at Lynn, whither he had removed from Middleborough, April 6, 1852.

Few ministers in Massachusetts labored more faithfully or accomplished more good than Ebenezer Nelson. His name and memory are greatly revered to this day in the places where he labored as an ambassador of the Lord Jesus Christ.

Nelson, Rev. James, was born in Mississippi in 1841; was educated at Center College, Danville, Ky. His great work was in connection with the board of ministerial education of Mississippi College. His field was Mississippi, Arkansas, and Louisiana, where his name will long be affectionately remembered. Through his instrumentality a large number of young ministers were stimulated to strive for higher education, and provided with the means to meet their expenses. Some of these have proved to be the most efficient ministers in the Southwest. He died at Clinton. Miss., Jan. 21, 1876. In connection with his educational work he performed a vast amount of evangelical labor.

Nelson, Rev. James, was born in Louisa Co., Va., Aug. 23, 1841 ; was converted at the age of fourteen, and joined the Elk Creek church. He was educated at Richmond and the Columbian College, graduating at the latter in 1866, with the degree of A.M. ; was licensed in 1859, and ordained in 1863. While a chaplain in the Confederate army the great revival which occurred among the troops of Northern Virginia had its origin in his labors in connection with those of the Rev. Mr. Marshall, of Georgia. Immediately after his graduation Mr. Nelson became pastor of the Baptist church in Georgetown, D. C. In 1871 he resigned his charge there, and became the evangelist and Sunday-school missionary for Maryland and the District of Columbia, and during the four years of his services in this capacity hundreds were converted and baptized, and a number of new churches formed. He is at present the useful pastor of the Farmville Baptist church, Va. He is a forcible writer, and occasionally contributes to the religious papers of the denomination.

Nelson, Rev. Stephen S., was born in Middleborough, Mass., Oct. 5, 1772, and became a member of the celebrated Rev. Isaac Backus's church when he was sixteen years of age. He graduated at Brown University in 1794 with the first honors of his class. He pursued his theological studies with Rev. Dr. Stillman, and was licensed to preach in the twenty-fourth year of his age. He was ordained by a council selected from the Warren Association. His first pastorate was in Hartford, Conn., where his labors were greatly blessed. In a memorable revival which occurred in Hartford in 1798 more than 100 were baptized into the fellowship of the Baptist church. While in Connecticut, Mr. Nelson proved himself the warm friend of religious liberty, and took an active part in urging the Baptist petition or remonstrance, addressed to the Legislature of Connecticut, against the unjust law which compelled Baptists and others to contribute to the support of the "standing order." The restrictions were finally removed by the new constitution, which went into force in 1818.

Mr. Nelson received and accepted, in 1801, a call to become pastor of the church in Mount Pleasant, N. Y., and to take charge of a literary institution in that place. In this new relation he met with deserved success. His subsequent pastorates were in Attleborough and Plymouth, Mass., and in Canton, Conn. Having resigned the pastorate of the church in this latter place, he removed to Amherst, Mass., for the purpose of giving his sons an opportunity to take a course of study in Amherst College. Declining again to become a pastor, he preached whenever opportunity presented in the neighboring villages. His closing days were days of peace and religious enjoyment. He died Dec. 8, 1853, at the ripe age of eighty-one years.

Nelson, Rev. W. A., D.D., was born in Jefferson Co., Tenn., July 1, 1837 ; baptized by M. Cate ; graduated at Carson College, Tenn., in 1859 ; ordained in 1860 ; was missionary during the war ; did good work as a pastor at Shelbyville, Tenn., and was very successful at Edgefield, Nashville, where, under his pastorate, the church increased from 31 to 350, and built a fine house and parsonage ; came to North Carolina in search of health in 1879 ; became president of Judson College, and has gone into the pastorate again at Shelby ; a very successful man. He received D.D. from his *alma mater.*

Nevada, one of the States of the American Union, lying east of California, noted for its immense silver and gold mines, yielding many millions every year. Several Baptist churches have been organized. Only two remain, and give promise of permanence and growth,—one at Virginia City, formed in 1873, with eighteen members, and one at Reno, organized about 1875. Both are making good progress. There are only two Baptist ministers in the State engaged in the ministry,—Rev. H. W. Read, of Virginia City, and Rev. Dr. D. B. McKenzie, at Reno. Both churches have good meeting-houses. There are many Baptists in the towns and mining-camps of Nevada, but they are members of churches elsewhere. This great State is ripe for cultivation by faithful Baptist missionaries.

New Birth, The.—Nicodemus, a cultured Israelite, a sincere inquirer after truth, a loved, honored, and blameless citizen, at the time when he came to Jesus first, knew nothing of the second birth, and was destitute of all title to heaven. And the same thing is true of many of the enlightened and worthy of our age. Without this birth there can be no love for Jesus, and no taste for the gratifications of heaven.

God is the author of the second birth : " As many as received him, to them gave he power to become the sons of God, even to them that believe on his name, who were born, not of blood, nor of the will of the flesh, nor of the will of man, but of God."— John i. 12, 13. In these words it is emphatically denied that regeneration springs from any fleshly or human agency, and it is ascribed wholly to God. Again, it is said, " The wind bloweth where it listeth, and thou hearest the sound thereof, but canst not tell whence it cometh, and whither it goeth : so is every one that is born of the Spirit."—John

iii. 8. The Spirit is the regenerator of every believer. The Lord says, in Ezekiel xxxvi. 26, " A new heart also will I give you, and a new spirit will I put within you : and I will take away the stony heart out of your flesh, and I will give you a heart of flesh." The new heart, the new birth, is the work of God's Spirit altogether.

The new birth requires no lengthened preparation ; the Spirit, with his instrument, the truth, can complete it in a second in the worst specimen of humanity. When the Spirit enters the heart the second birth is the work of a moment, no matter how long penitential sorrow, unrelieved by justifying faith, may continue.

The new birth is not Christian baptism, in which it has been said that a person is " made a member of Christ, the child of God, and an inheritor of the kingdom of heaven ;" not a single one of these blessings was ever conferred by that solemn rite. It is a change of affections ; the regards of the soul are lifted by the Spirit of God from ourselves, the world, and sinful objects, and they are made to hunger for the Saviour. This produces an extensive alteration in the internal and external condition of the man. He does not delight in what he once loved. His chief pleasure is the favor of Christ, for which, or for the fuller enjoyment of which, his soul is constantly craving. " He is a new creature : old things are passed away ; behold, all things are become new." His mind is enlightened, his will is corrected, his sins are loathed and forsaken, and his affections are turned Christward.

The regenerated man when he is first born again feels repentance for sin in his heart ; this accompanies the new birth invariably. He always feels a desire to trust in Jesus when he is born again, and he never rests till he has committed his soul to Christ.

The regenerate man loses his old hopes and their foundation as soon as he is born again. His expectations of divine favor were once built upon his good qualities, blameless acts, or commendable intentions. The regenerating grace of the heavenly Spirit sweeps away all his imaginary merits and false hopes, and for a foundation he sees only the crucified Saviour full of gospel hopes.

The new birth removes old treasures and bestows new riches. The wealth of unbelieving days no longer has power to fascinate the soul, and Calvary becomes the pearl of great price for which the regenerated person counts all things but loss.

And the new birth dethrones old despots in the soul,—the world, sinful habits, covetousness, and superstition,—and it never rests until Christ is Master of mind, heart, and life.

A new heart is demanded by the sinner's reproaching conscience, and by the God of infinite goodness. "Heaven is a prepared place for a prepared people," without a taste for the enjoyments of paradise a man cannot be happy in it. An unregenerate man could not gather satisfaction from the religious pleasures of the celestial home; and if he were to enter it he would be rendered still more miserable by its holy conversation and occupations. For him there is no rest in any world without a new heart. Besides, a holy law must hurl its anathemas forever at the man who cherishes sin in his heart. And as his "carnal mind is enmity against God," he would feel himself at war with God in any quarter of his wide dominions, and in any section of everlasting duration. The Saviour utters the doctrine of the glorified in heaven, of all holy angels, of the entire earthly believing family, of the Holy Word, and of the adorable Trinity, when he says, "Marvel not that I said unto thee, Ye must be born again."—John iii. 7.

New Brunswick Baptists.—See article on Nova Scotia Baptists.

Newell, Rev. I. D., was born in Rushville, Schuyler Co., Ill., July 2, 1837; baptized in Upper Alton in 1849; ordained in Moline, Oct. 13, 1871. He is the son of Rev. I. D. Newell. Mr. Newell spent nearly four years in the Union army during the war, being the first to enlist in Bunker Hill, under the President's first call. He served two years in the ranks, during which time he participated in the battles of Fort Henry, Fort Donelson, Pittsburg Landing, and the siege of Corinth, bearing the colors of the regiment in the last-named conflict. At the end of two years' service he was transferred to Ellet's fleet, on the Mississippi River, and promoted to a first lieutenancy, and one month later to a captaincy, both commissions coming from President Lincoln. At the close of the war he entered Shurtleff College. He completed his theological course at Crozer Seminary, graduating in 1871. He was pastor of the Baptist church of Moline, Ill., for one year. Failing in health, he removed to Nebraska, and preached three years in Clay and Adams Counties. At present he gives but a part of his time to the ministry, being county superintendent of public schools in Clay County.

Newfoundland Baptists.—See article on Nova Scotia Baptists.

New Hampshire Baptists.—Hanserd Knollys founded the First church in Dover, N. H., in 1638. A little later he preached Baptist doctrines; and in 1641 he was recognized by the people of Dover as a decided exponent of our principles; the result was two religious communities. After his return to England, the Baptists, it is said, fled to Long Island to avoid persecution, and for the same reason, in 1644, they removed to the neighborhood of the

present New Brunswick, N. J., and called their new home Piscataway, after the original name of Dover. It is not certain that these Baptists were regularly organized into a Baptist church in Dover.

The first church of our faith in New Hampshire, of whose regular formation there are no doubts, was founded at Newton in 1755. In 1770 it is supposed that there were but three Baptist churches in New Hampshire,—Newton, Madbury, and Weare.

In 1770, Rev. Dr. Hezekiah Smith, an able and devoted minister, settled in Massachusetts, preached extensively in New Hampshire, and great blessings attended his ministrations. He baptized the Rev. Eliphalet Smith, a Congregational clergyman, and thirteen others, who the same day were formed into a Baptist church at Deerfield. Two days after Mr. Smith baptized seven persons, among whom was Dr. Samuel Shepard, who became one of the most active and useful ministers that ever labored in New Hampshire. He was afterwards, till death, the pastor of a church gathered in Brentwood, in 1771, with branches at one time in more than twelve different towns, and a membership of nearly 1000. During this year churches were formed in Richmond, Hinsdale, and Chesterfield. In 1780, Dr. Shepard baptized 44 persons at Meredith, and constituted them into a church. Drs. Hezekiah Smith and Samuel Shepard were apostles in New Hampshire, whose labors enjoyed a remarkable measure of the divine favor. There were other early preachers and churches in New Hampshire worthy of our denominational name; and upon them and their brethren the Spirit of God fell, and converts were gathered and churches formed in all directions, until to-day we have 7 Associations, 86 churches, ministers, settled and without charge, 103. The number of members is 9210. In the department of Sunday-schools we find that there are 72 schools, with 814 teachers and 9319 scholars.

In education the Baptists of New Hampshire have taken an active interest. In 1826 they founded the "New Hampton Literary and Theological Institution," at New Hampton. Dr. B. F. Farnsworth was its first principal and Professor of Theology. Dr. E. B. Smith succeeded him in 1833, and retained his position until 1861. In 1838, Dr. J. Newton Brown was made Associate Professor of Theology, and discharged the duties of the office until 1845, when Dr. James Upham was appointed to the professorship. At the death of Dr. Smith, Dr. Upham became president of the institution, and retained the position until 1866. Owing to inadequate financial support the seminary was removed to Fairfax, Vt., in 1853. This institution gave instruction in the higher branches of a general education, and prepared young men for the ministry; and it had in connection with it an academy of a high order for young women. In its two locations it had about 200 theological students, most of whom became very useful in the pastorate and in other departments of Christian work. Few seminaries with its means have rendered such important service.

After the removal of the New Hampton Institution to Vermont in 1853, the Baptists of New Hampshire took immediate steps to establish an academy at New London, which was opened in 1853 ; it now bears the name of Colby Academy. (See article on COLBY ACADEMY.) The report of the benevolent operations for the year covered by the statistics here given is, for the Missionary Union $1848.11 ; for the Woman's Foreign Mission Society, $1074.06 ; home missions, $863.26 ; for the Convention, $2581.19 ; for home objects, $82,114.04. The total for all purposes, $92,254.03.

The State Convention was founded in 1826. It has accomplished great results in New Hampshire, and its affairs have been managed with much ability. In 1880 it aided seventeen churches and two missions, which have become churches. Its officers were Rev. W. V. Garner, President; Rev. W. Hurlin, Secretary ; A. J. Prescott, Treasurer. While in New Hampshire very many of the churches suffer constant diminution by emigration, a review of the last half-century presents many facts, showing how the denomination has grown in that State. Fifty years ago there were in New Hampshire seventy churches and forty-one ministers. The greater part of these churches were poor, and pastors that were settled received but a scanty support. Moreover, there was more or less direct oppression which Baptists were compelled to endure from the "standing order." They were the "sect everywhere spoken against." But a most happy change has taken place in all these respects. The statistics given above will show the present situation of the denomination. Baptists have places of worship which will compare favorably with those of any other denomination. They are firmly planted in all the prominent cities and villages of the State. In the valley of the Merrimack they were but little known fifty years ago; "Now the churches which occupy that valley," says Dr. E. E. Cummings, in his "Ministry of Fifty Years," "are the pride and strength of the denomination throughout the State." There is every reason to expect that continued prosperity will attend the churches in the future as it has in the past, and that the sentiments and practices of the Baptists will continue to have strong hold on the intelligent convictions of no small part of the community.

New Jersey, The Baptists of.—A goodly number of those who came to the early settlements in the New England colonies held our views of Bible doctrine. They found on their arrival that freedom of conscience was only for Puritans.

Persecutions led them to desire a better country, and they warned their friends in Europe to steer for another destination. When Lord Berkeley and Sir George Carteret obtained possession of "Nova Cesarea," or New Jersey, about 1664, they formed a "Bill of Rights," by which "liberty of conscience to all religious sects who shall behave well" was guaranteed. Speedy immigration followed. The Baptists of New Jersey, except a church or two in the northern hill-country, which sprang out of the religious reconstruction following the revivals under Edwards and the men of his time, came from the old country seed. While there may have been isolated Baptist settlers elsewhere, the first companies of baptized believers located at Middletown, near the entrance of New York harbor, at the territory on the lower Delaware, and at "Piscataqua," on the Raritan River.

The churches at Middletown, "Piscataqua," "Cohansick," and Cape May are called original because they are the mothers of the other organizations.

MIDDLETOWN,

in order of time, stands first. The date assigned it is 1688, but there are good reasons for believing that it originated earlier. In 1648 one Richard Stout and five others appear to have settled in Middletown. The Indian title was purchased previous to the patent from "Nicolles," about 1667. This title is said to have been made to thirty-six men, of whom eighteen were Baptists. They seem to have come from the west end of Long Island, and there is a strong probability that some of them were connected with the people who were dealt with in Massachusetts for Baptist sentiments about 1642, and took refuge at Gravesend, Long Island. Tradition states that they consorted for mutual edification, but there is no church record previous to 1688, when they "settled themselves into a church state," after consultation with the brethren at "Pennepek," Pa., who had just taken that course. There were several gifted brethren among them, of whom John Brown, James Ashton, and George Eaglesfield are mentioned.

Thomas Killingsworth was at the constitution of the church, but there is no evidence that he became its pastor. Obadiah Holmes, who was whipped at Boston, Mass., for his Baptist sentiments, was one of the patentees of Monmouth County, but it is not known that he ever resided here, though his son Jonathan did, and in 1668 was a member of Assembly.

Very little is known of the church during the first generation of its existence, except that an unhappy division occurred, which resulted (in 1711) in each party excommunicating the other, and the silencing of two of their gifted preachers,—John Bray and John Okison. They agreed to call a council of neighboring churches, which met May 25, 1711. The ministers who convened were Messrs. Timothy Brooks, of Cohansey; Abel Morgan and Joseph Wood, of Pennepek; Elisha Thomas, of Welsh Tract, and six elders. The office of elder, in distinction from pastor, is referred to frequently as existing among the old churches in the State. It may be interesting to read the finding of this first council probably in New Jersey, convened in a case of church difficulty. Advice was given (1) " to bury their proceedings in oblivion and erase the record of them." This was done, and four leaves are torn out of the church book. (2) " To continue the silence imposed on the two brethren the preceding year." (3) " To sign a covenant relative to their future conduct." Forty-two signed this, and twenty-six did not, though many of them came in afterwards. The first forty-two were declared to be the church to be owned by sister churches. Another direction of the council was, " That the members should keep their places and not wander to other societies." Peace and prosperity followed, and the gospel soon spread over a wide territory.

PISCATAWAY.

A large tract on the east side of the " Rarinton" was bought of the Indians in 1663. Among the first settlers were people from Piscataqua (now Dover, N. H., then in the province of Maine). It is claimed that of these early settlers at least six were Baptists. (Hanserd Knollys preached Baptist sentiments in Piscataqua, N. H., as early as 1638.) These six were constituted into a gospel church by Rev. Thomas Killingsworth in 1689. Three of the constituents—John Drake, Hugh Dunn, and Edmund Dunham—were lay preachers. Mr. Drake was ordained pastor at the constitution of the church, and continued until his death, fifty years afterwards. His descendants are numerous and influential.

The first meeting-house, by order of the town-meeting, was " built forthwith as followeth: dimensions, twenty foot wide, thirty foot long, and ten foot between joints."

COHANSEY.

In 1683 a company of immigrants, members of Cloughketin church, in the County of Tipperary, Ireland, landed at Perth Amboy, and traveled across the country to the " Cohansick" Creek. In 1685, Obadiah Holmes (son of Obadiah who was persecuted) arrived from Rhode Island. His influence was soon felt. He became judge of the Court of Common Pleas for Salem County, and preached acceptably, though he was never ordained. In 1688, Rev. Elias Keach, of Pennepek, administered baptism to three persons. Thomas

Killingsworth having moved into the vicinity, united with the nine males in constituting the church, and he became the first pastor, continuing nearly nineteen years, until his death. He was appointed judge of the court, and served honorably, while he preached faithfully and successfully. He was succeeded by Rev. Timothy Brooks, who died after serving the church six years, and his successor, a young man of much promise, passed away after a two years' pastorate.

The church records for the first hundred years were burned, but Mr. Kelsay, a subsequent pastor, preserved some minutes, among them the following:

" In 1710, Timothy Brooks, with his company, united with the church. They had come from Swanzey, in Plymouth government, about 1687, and had kept a separate society for twenty-three years, on account of difference in opinion relative to predestination, singing of Psalms, laying on of hands, etc.; the terms of union were *bearance* and *forbearance*."

Mr. Kelsay says that Mr. " Brooks was a useful preacher, of a sweet and loving temper, and always open to conviction."

CAPE MAY.

Among some who came over in 1675 were two Baptists,—George Taylor and Philip Hill. Taylor held Bible readings and expositions at his own house. After his death, in 1702, Mr. Hill continued the meeting. Mr. Keach visited the place, and preached as early as 1688, and others labored with success. Most of the converts went to Philadelphia for baptism. In 1712, by advice of the pastor and two deacons of Cohansey, thirty-seven persons constituted themselves into a church, under the pastorate of Nathaniel Jenkins, one of their own number.

Before 1707 there was no Association in America. We find, however, an institution called a yearly meeting, which fostered communication. From one end of Jersey to the other pastors and devoted brethren went by Indian trails and rough roads to these immense gatherings. There are traditions concerning these fraternal " great meetings" that are full of tender, touching memories.

When, at the suggestion of the Pennepek church, the Philadelphia Association was formed, in 1707, three of its first churches were in New Jersey, viz., Middletown, Piscataway, and Cohansey. There are no extended early records of the Association, but the usual heading of the earliest is " The Elders and Messengers of the Baptized Congregations in Pennsylvania and the Jerseys."

The Associational fellowship led to greater interest among the ministers and churches, an increase of doctrinal strength, and a spreading of

Bible sentiments, which took deep root, and in the succeeding half-century brought forth abundantly.

The New Jersey Baptists have had in their ranks some of the strongest men among the early Baptists of this country, and among them have arisen brethren to whom the whole denomination is indebted. Oliver Hart performed a work of the highest importance in South Carolina; James Manning, the first president of Rhode Island College, laid all Baptists under lasting obligations to himself for his services to general and ministerial education; Abel Morgan was a man of learning, and of immense influence for good over the Middle States; Hezekiah Smith, of Hopewell, N. J., was settled in Haverhill, Mass., and was blessed with great success in winning souls to Christ; John Gano, the most eloquent preacher among the Baptists of his day, and a man greatly honored of God in extending his kingdom, was a native of New Jersey; our first institution of learning was located in New Jersey, and worthily conducted by Isaac Eaton, at Hopewell. Quite a number of distinguished men have been identified with the Baptists of New Jersey.

For a long period the New Jersey churches belonged to the Philadelphia Association. Their representatives in that body exerted such an influence that they had no desire to sunder the ties that united them to it until their great growth compelled them.

Their first Association was formed in 1811; it consisted of fourteen churches, and was called the New Jersey Association. The Central New Jersey Association was formed in October, 1828, by the representatives of seven churches. The Sussex Association was formed in 1833, by four churches. The Delaware River Association was constituted in 1835, by Old-School, or Anti-Missionary Baptists; its members were less than five hundred when the Association was organized, and they have not increased since that time. The East New Jersey Association was established in November, 1842, by fourteen churches. There are at present in New Jersey the following five Associations: the Central, East, North, Trenton, and West, representing 178 churches, with 31,936 members.

From their early history the Baptists of New Jersey have been the intelligent and generous friends of education, and at present they have two seminaries of a high order, with spacious and beautiful buildings, known as Peddie Institute and South Jersey Institute, the former with 10 instructors, 125 students of both sexes, property worth $125,000, and an endowment of $1000; the latter with 10 instructors, 150 students, and a property moderately estimated at $75,000. These institutions are owned by the denomination in New Jersey. In addition to the money invested in Peddie and South Jersey Institutes, the New Jersey Baptists gave liberally to Hamilton and Lewisburg.

New Jersey Baptist Education Society is forty-two years old. It has aided many students who are doing successful work in the ministry. Its officers for 1880 are: President, H. J. Mulford; Vice-Presidents, R. F. Young, W. H. Parmly; Secretary, O. P. Eaches; Treasurer, W. V. Wilson. Income, $1922.65.

New Jersey Baptist State Convention was organized in 1830. There were then 55 churches in the State, with a membership of 4164.

OFFICERS OF THE CONVENTION FROM ITS ORGANIZATION TO THE PRESENT TIME.

Presidents.—Daniel Dodge,* 1830 to 1839; G. S. Webb, 1839 to 1843; C. W. Mulford,* 1843 to 1849; S. J. Drake,* 1849 to 1853; D. B. Stout,* 1853 to 1854; C. E. Wilson,* 1854 to 1855; D. M. Wilson,* 1855 to 1873; James Buchanan, 1873 to ——.

Vice-Presidents.—Joseph Maylin,* 1830 to 1834; Henry Smalley,* 1830 to 1834; G. S. Webb, 1834 to 1839, 1849 to ——; J. M. Challiss,* 1847 to 1848, 1849 to 1868; John Rogers,* 1839 to 1848; J. C. Harrison,* 1839 to 1844; J. E. Welch,* 1844 to 1847; D. B. Stout,* 1868 to 1875; J. M. Carpenter, 1875 to ——.

Secretaries.—M. J. Rhees,* 1830 to 1840; C. W. Mulford,* 1840 to 1843; S. J. Drake,* 1843 to 1848; J. M. Carpenter, 1848 to 1865; H. F. Smith, 1865 to 1879; T. E. Vassar, 1879 to ——.

Treasurers.—P. P. Runyon,* 1830 to 1871; S. Van Wickle, 1871 to 1879; A. Suydam, 1879 to ——.

Income in 1880 was $4429.55.

Within the last fifty years about 54,000 hopeful converts have been added to our churches by baptism. Our present membership is 31,936. Fifty years ago we had but 2 churches, with a membership of only 200 each. Now we have 1 with over 1100, 1 with 1000, 1 with 800, 1 with 600, 5 with 500, 8 with 400, 14 with 300, 24 with 200, and 53 with over 100 each.

New Jersey Baptist Sunday-School Union is only nine years old, but in gathering statistics of the work, awakening interest, organizing mission schools, as well as in helping the weak, it has entered upon a field of great usefulness.

Newman, Prof. Albert Henry, was born in Edgefield, S. C., Aug. 25, 1852; entered the Thomson, Ga., high school, then in charge of Rev. E. A. Steed, now a professor in Mercer University, by whom he was baptized into the fellowship of the Thomson Baptist church in 1868. ·

Called to the Christian ministry, and encouraged by brethren of wisdom and piety, he took a place in the Junior class in Mercer University in 1869.

* Deceased.

Here he was specially indebted to Prof. H. H. Tucker, D.D., LL.D., for his inspiring instruction in metaphysics and logic, and to Prof. J. J. Brantly, D.D., who, at great personal cost, gave him private

PROF. ALBERT HENRY NEWMAN.

instruction for a year and a half in the German language. He entered the Rochester Theological Seminary in 1872; in it his favorite studies were Biblical interpretation, under the direction of the learned Dr. Hackett, and systematic theology, under President A. H. Strong, D.D. He spent a year at Greenville, S. C., at the Southern Baptist Theological Seminary, 1875–76, studying Hebrew, Chaldee, Syriac, and Arabic, under Dr. Toy. He also was greatly aided in Greenville by the lectures of Dr. Broadus on the New Testament, the Septuagint, Josephus, and the early Greek fathers. In 1880, Prof. Newman was elected "Pettengill Professor of Church History" in the Rochester Theological Seminary, after he had served as temporary instructor in, and acting professor of, Church History in the same institution.

Prof. Newman, while a careful student of general church history, is devoting himself specially to the records of the Baptists and related bodies. Prof. Newman not long since was offered the professorship of Hebrew in one of our institutions. His attainments are remarkable; his pen is in demand in various parts of the country as contributor to works on theology and church history. The highest estimate is placed upon his acquisitions and talents by competent judges who are familiar with his worth. Before him, if his life is spared, there is undoubtedly a bright future. He has recently accepted a professorship in the Toronto Theological Seminary.

Newman, Judge Thomas W., was born in Somerset Co., Md., Jan. 23, 1829. He pursued his studies in Washington Academy, Princess Anne, Somerset Co., Md., until he removed to Baltimore, and there studied law under Levin Gale, Esq., and was admitted to the bar in 1850, after which he at once removed to the West, and established himself in his profession the same year at Burlington, Iowa, where he still resides. In 1855 he was elected county judge of Des Moines County for two years. When the civil war broke out he warmly embraced the Union cause, and was appointed by President Lincoln captain in the 11th Regiment of the regular army, and commissioned Aug. 1, 1861. He served until the spring of 1863, when, on account of impaired health, he resigned his commission and returned home, and, after six months spent in recuperation and rest, he again entered upon the practice of his profession. From 1855 to 1857 he was a director of the Burlington and Missouri River Railroad, and aided by an active canvass over the entire line, by speeches and otherwise, in raising means for its construction. He was appointed district judge of the first judicial district of Iowa, in 1874, to fill a vacancy. At the October

JUDGE THOMAS W. NEWMAN.

election of the same year he was chosen for the unexpired term of Jan. 1, 1875, and for a full term of four years, to Jan. 1, 1879, which office he filled with credit, and at the end of the term, though strongly urged to continue, declined on account of the inadequate salary. As a judge he was noted for kindness of heart, urbanity of manner, legal acumen, and loyalty to justice. He has been an active director in the Merchants' National Bank of Burlington since its organization, and for some years past its attorney. He became a Baptist the first year of his manhood, in 1850, and has ever since been closely and warmly identified with the interest of the church and denomination. He was president of the State Convention for some years. He has been a trustee in the Burlington Collegiate Institute since its organization, in 1852, and has filled the office of secretary or treasurer of said institution all the time except when in the army.

New Orleans Baptist Chronicle was published at New Orleans, La., by L. Alex. Duncan from 1852 to 1855. Dr. Duncan, having recovered his health, was the principal editor. It was in quarto form and published weekly. Although it had a considerable circulation in the Southwest, it yielded so little profit to the publishers that its publication was discontinued.

Newport, R. I., The First Church of, had its rise in the very beginnings of New England colonial history. The exact date of its origin, however, is *not definitely known*. Those who have studied the subject the most carefully have reached the conclusion that the *probable* date is early in 1638. As this differs from the traditional one (1644), it may be pertinent to give some of the reasons on which this conclusion rests. (1) From the outset the people statedly assembled for public worship, but it is uncertain whether for this purpose they gathered in several congregations, or, as is more probable, they all met in one. (2) There was certainly a church on the island in 1638. Its members were drawn from various sources. Some had been connected with a Congregational church in Boston. It is, however, well known that the church formed here disclaimed any ecclesiastical fellowship with that church. It was of a different order. And if it was the only church on the island, it is certain that there were Baptists among the members, and that they had a Baptist for their minister. (3) Of the church thus formed Mr. Clarke was the pastor or teaching elder. Gov. Winthrop, writing in 1638, speaks of him as "preacher to those of the island." In 1640, Mr. Lechford writes, "On the island there is a church where one Master Clarke is pastor." Describing the controversy which arose shortly after the foregoing sentence was penned, Mr. Hubbard says "their minister, Mr. Clarke, . . . dissented and publicly opposed." (4) The pastor, Mr. Clarke, was undoubtedly a Baptist before leaving England, and as a Baptist refugee came to this country. (a) He is known to have held, and on his arrival, one distinctively Baptist

tenet, viz., that of religious liberty ; a tenet as distinctively Baptist at the time as is a converted church membership to-day. (b) In the discussion which arose in 1640–41, he contended for another Baptist tenet, viz., the sufficiency of Scripture as a rule of religious faith and practice. (c) We have no record of any change in his religious views after his arrival in this country, as we should in all probability have had if any such change had taken place. (d) Just as soon as he touched shore at Boston he was ready for the sake of his principles to remove into the wilderness. (e) He was not caught in a current which was already setting towards a new settlement ; the proposition came from himself. (5) Those who during this early period became Baptists in the neighboring colony of Massachusetts gravitated naturally to Newport, and there sought a church home. (6) Mr. Comer, who has given us the traditional date of 1644,—a mere conjecture of his,—and whom almost all subsequent authors have followed, although painstaking and accurate as a writer, had not access to all the sources of knowledge since put within our reach. (7) Finally, Mr. Backus, who made later researches and with better facilities, inclined to the opinion that an earlier date was the probable one.

The history of the church may be considered as falling into five periods. (I. 1638–1682.) The first pastor, John Clarke, born in Suffolk, England, Oct. 8, 1609, and educated at one of the ancient universities, arrived at Boston, November, 1637, near the close of the famous Antinomian controversy. Because his opinions were obnoxious to the magistrates he proposed to a number of kindred spirits to withdraw and plant a new colony, which they did the following March, on the island of Rhode Island. He at once assumed the functions of a minister, conducting the public religious worship of the inhabitants. The sense of freedom which the settlers enjoyed led some of them into theological vagaries. They broke not only from the authority of the church, but from the authority also of the Scriptures. They claimed to be led by an "inner light." They were ably controverted by "their minister, Mr. Clarke," who was strongly seconded by Mr. Lenthall, Mr. Harding, and others. The Baptists maintained the binding authority of the Bible and the existence upon earth of a visible church with visible ordinances. This controversy gave rise to the "Seekers," many of whom afterwards became "Quakers."

A visit paid to William Witter, a member of the church, during the summer of 1651, by delegates appointed by the church, may be noticed, since it has been rendered memorable both on account of the treatment received from the Massachusetts authorities and of the results that followed. The truths presented by these confessors—John Clarke,

Obadiah Holmes, and John Crandall—led to a serious examination; "divers," as Obadiah Holmes said, "were put upon a way of inquiry." It is interesting to know that among the number of these was the scholarly Henry Dunster, then president of Harvard College, who became convinced of the unscripturalness of infant baptism. These events were preparing the way for the formation of the First Baptist church in Boston, with which this church for several years held correspondence.

In the year 1652, the year after Mr. Clarke went to England as agent for the colony, the question of "laying hands on" all baptized believers began to be discussed in the church, and four years later, in 1656, several members withdrew and formed a church of the "Six Principle" order. The year after Mr. Clarke's return from England, namely, in 1665, the Sabbath question was agitated in the church, and a few members supposing they were thus following still more closely the teachings of the Spirit in his Word, began to observe the seventh day, and in 1671 a small number drew off and formed a Sabbatarian church. On the 20th of April, 1676, Mr. Clarke died, after a laborious life devoted to an extension of the Redeemer's kingdom, and having from its very beginning served the colony with almost unexampled fidelity and distinguished success.

He was succeeded by Obadiah Holmes, who, born in Preston, England, in 1606, and educated at Oxford University, came to this country in 1629 and united with a Congregational church in Salem, Mass., and ten years later, in Rehoboth, was baptized by Mr. Clarke, and with several others formed a Baptist church. Removing to Newport, he united, late in 1650 or early in 1651, with this church. He was one of the delegates to Lynn in 1651, where he severely suffered for the sake of his faith. He assisted in ministering to the church during Mr. Clarke's prolonged absence in England, and finally succeeded to the pastoral office, in which he continued till his death, which occurred October 15, 1682.

Singing in public worship was from the beginning approved and practised. Four members were disfellowshiped in 1673 for denying the deity of Christ. The doctrinal position of the church was strongly Calvinistic. Both pastors, Clarke and Holmes, left on record confessions of their faith. The distinction which appeared in England dividing the Baptists into two bodies, described as "Particular" and "General," obtained likewise in this country. This was from its organization a "Particular" or "Calvinistic" church, and has continued so ever since. It was in early correspondence with the Particular Baptists of London, and with the churches of Swanzey and Boston. It made efforts to disseminate Baptist principles both at home and throughout the neighboring colonies. The church

was furnished with a board of elders; among the earliest were Joseph Torrey, Obadiah Holmes, Mark Lucar, and John Crandall, the first of whom held many offices of trust in the colony. The first deacon was William Weeden, who died in 1676; the second was Philip Smith. It should be mentioned, further, that Robert Lenthall attempted in 1638 to form a Baptist church in Weymouth, Mass.; that Thomas Painter had been publicly whipped in Hingham, Mass., for refusing to carry his child to the baptismal font; that John Cooke, once a Congregational minister in Massachusetts, and the subject of a letter from John Cotton to his nephew, Cotton Mather, "was living in 1694, probably the oldest survivor of the male passengers in the Mayflower;" that Philip Edes was a friend and helper of Oliver Cromwell; that Samuel Hubbard did much by his letters and other manuscripts to preserve the early history of the church and denomination.

(II. 1683–1732.) The third pastor was Richard Dingley, who, coming from England, was received into the Baptist church in Boston in 1684, and four years later was ordained pastor of this church; in 1694 he resigned and went to South Carolina. In November, 1711, William Peckham, one of the members of the church, was ordained to the pastorship, and continued in office until his death, in 1732. His ministry was disturbed by a headstrong elder, Daniel White, who had been procured as an assistant, but who drew off a few members and set up a separate meeting, which, however, continued but a little while. John Comer, the fifth pastor, born in Boston, Aug. 1, 1704, and educated at Yale College, was baptized into the Baptist church in Boston, Jan. 31, 1725, and May 19, 1726, ordained pastor of this church, colleague with Elder Peckham. His change of views respecting the rite of the imposition of hands, and his preaching it as obligatory on the church, led to a severance of the pastoral relation, Jan. 8, 1729.

During this period there were two interregna in the pastoral office, the second extending to more than a decade of years. During the first, however, the church improved its material condition, and during the second for most of the time sat under the ministry of Mr. Bliss, a Seventh-day Baptist preacher. The church not only had a name, but had, and for a long time possessed, a local habitation. The meeting-house in which the church had long worshiped was sold in 1707, and during the following year a new one was built. Though a salary was voted him at his settlement, Mr. Comer early made an effort to induce the church to adopt the method of weekly offerings for the support of the ministry. The church voted, Sept. 8, 1726, "that a weekly contribution for the support of the ministry should be observed." Singing having

54

fallen into disuse, Mr. Comer re-introduced it. He commenced also regular church records, and gathered much material towards a history of the church. Of members during this period we may mention James Barker, an elder in the church; Peter Taylor and Samuel Maxwell, made deacons in 1724, and William Peckham, in 1732; Peter Foulger, the maternal grandfather of Benjamin Franklin, and a successful missionary to the Indians; Thomas Dungan, the first Baptist minister in Pennsylvania; also three sons of the second pastor, namely, Obadiah, John, and Jonathan Holmes, one or two of them pioneers in New Jersey. The church was thus through its members extending its influence; as during the former period throughout New England, so during this to provinces more remote.

(III. 1732–1788.) John Callender, the successor of Mr. Comer, born in Boston in 1706, and graduated at Harvard College in 1723, and the same year baptized into the Baptist church of his native town, was, Oct. 13, 1731, ordained as pastor of this church. The one hundredth anniversary of the settlement of the island was celebrated by the building of a new house of worship, and by a historical discourse of great fullness and accuracy, preached March 24, 1738, by the pastor, in which he reviewed the events of the century. The entire colony was brought under obligation to him for this first history of its beginnings and early progress. His pastoral labors continued till death, Jan. 26, 1748. Before the close of the same year the church called to the pastorship Edward Upham, born in Malden, Mass., in 1709, and graduated at Harvard College in 1734. It was during his term of service that the Baptists of America made an effort to establish a college within the colony, for which Newport made a strong but unsuccessful bid. There were cogent reasons why it should be located elsewhere. Mr. Upham resigned his charge in 1771, to be succeeded by Erasmus Kelley, who was ordained on the 9th of October. He was born in Bucks Co., Pa., July 24, 1748, and received his education at the University of Pennsylvania. His ministry was interrupted by the Revolutionary war and the British occupancy of the town. He died Nov. 7, 1784, and the pastoral office thus made vacant was filled by the choice of Benjamin Foster, who began his labors on the first Lord's day in January, 1785. He was born in Danvers, Mass., June 12, 1750, graduated at Yale College in 1774, and September 4 of the same year was baptized into the Baptist church in Boston. Mr. Foster severed his pastoral relations Sept. 15, 1788, and removed to New York.

The doctrinal position of the church remained unchanged. The last pastor was very pronounced in his Calvinism. Under his leadership the church united with the Warren Association. So early in this period as 1733–34 the church had agreed upon the desirableness of coming into an association with the churches with which it was in ecclesiastical fellowship. We do not know why the idea was not then realized. During Mr. Foster's administration, Tate and Brady's collection of hymns was in the service of song superseded by Dr. Watts's psalms and hymns. A few names may here be mentioned, as follows: Samuel Fowler, member of the last colonial Assembly which passed the bold act that severed the colony from Great Britain; William Claggett, an ingenious maker of astronomical and musical clocks, and who anticipated Franklin in some of his experiments with electricity; Hezekiah Carpenter and Josias Lyndon, both generous benefactors of the church, though the latter, Gov. Lyndon, was never a member; Benjamin Hall and Joseph Pike, made deacons in 1785.

Reviewing the history of the church thus far traversed, we find a noble record made. Strong were many of the men connected with the church, worthy to be leaders in Zion; and the ministry was able and cultivated. With scarcely an exception the pastors were men of university training. Benedict, having in his history (1848) brought his account of this church down to the close of this period, 1788, adds this remark: "We have now followed the succession of pastors of this ancient community for about a century and a half, . . . and of these nine pastors all but Mr. Holmes (he means Mr. Peckham) were men of liberal education."

(IV. 1789–1834.) The next pastor's term of service extended through nearly a half-century. Michael Eddy, born in Swanzey, Mass., in 1760, and ordained in the same town in 1785, was called to the pastorship of this church Aug. 10, 1789. In 1792 the church, without assigning any reason for the action, voted to withdraw from the Warren Association, and it remained unassociated during the remainder of Mr. Eddy's long pastorate. For a number of years a union Sunday-school was maintained by the several churches in town. Subsequently the different churches organized schools of their own. That in connection with this church was formed in 1834, and the same year the First Baptist Society was incorporated. During this period we seem to pass from the ancient into the modern world. Rapid changes were taking place in modes of life. And changes even in matters of faith were beginning to appear. Suspicions of unsoundness in the faith clouded the closing years of the pastor's life. A loosening in the spiritual temple was manifest. Some members became Arminians, a few were tinctured even with Socinianism. Dr. Channing was welcomed to preach in the pulpit. One sermon of his made a strong impresion. Nevertheless, the majority of the church, it is believed, remained true, though it is known that a few in their love for pure orthodoxy left the church. James A. McKenzie was chosen assistant minister in 1833, and the following deacons were elected: Jethro Briggs, in 1803; George Tilley, in 1813; Abner Peckham and Arnold Barker, in 1822; Benjamin W. Smith and Peleg Sanford, in 1833. Mr. Eddy died June 3, 1835.

(V. 1834–1880.) Already the church had called to the pastoral office Arthur Amasa Ross, born in Thomson, Conn., in 1791, and ordained in his native town in 1819, who entered upon his duties as pastor of this church Nov. 9, 1834. His preaching produced consternation among those who had received "another gospel." In 1836 the church reunited with the Warren Association. In commemoration of the two hundredth anniversary of the settlement of the island the pastor preached, April 4 (March 24, O.S.), 1838, a historical sermon, in which he reviewed the second century of progress. He resigned his charge Nov. 1, 1840, and Joseph Smith was invited, Jan. 2, 1841, to succeed him. He was born in Hampstead, N. H., June 31, 1808, studied a year (1831–32) at the Newton Theological Institution, and was graduated at Brown University in 1837, and the same year ordained as pastor of the Baptist church in Woonsocket, R. I. During his pastorate a new meeting-house was built, with galleries on three sides, and containing 120 pews on the floor. It was dedicated, May 13, 1846, "to the worship of God, the Father, the Son, and the Holy Ghost." The Psalmist displaced in the service of song Winchell's edition of Watts. On the 19th of August, 1849, Mr. Smith resigned the pastoral office, and was succeeded by Samuel Adlam, who was called to the pastorship the 14th of the following October. He was born in Bristol, England, Feb. 4, 1798, and at the age of twenty-two came to Boston, where he was baptized into the First Baptist church. He was ordained pastor of the Baptist church in West Medway, Mass., and after two other settlements was graduated at the Newton Theological Institution in 1838. It was during his ministry that twenty churches, of which this was one, withdrew from the Warren Association and formed a new body, which was called the Narragansett Association. Mr. Adlam resigned his charge June 27, 1864, and March 12, 1865, was succeeded by Rev. C. E. Barrows, D.D., who was graduated at Brown University in 1858, and the Newton Theological Institution in 1861, and on the 25th of December of that year was ordained pastor of the Baptist church in Peabody, Mass. The following brethren have during this period been elected deacons: Benjamin B. Howland, in 1837; Samuel S. Peckham, in 1847; Stephen S. Albro and Samuel Eyles, in 1857; Gilbert Tomp-

kins, George M. Hazard, Thomas H. Clarke, and George Nasen, in 1867; and in 1874, Ara Hildreth. Mr. Howland was deacon for forty years, and for fifty years was clerk of the town and city of Newport.

C. E. BARROWS, D.D.

During the nearly two centuries and a half which have elapsed since the first members of the church entered into solemn covenant with one another to observe the public worship of God and keep the ordinances as given by the Head of the church, this body has remained true to its early confessions of faith. Slight changes have been made in the statement of some of the doctrines, nevertheless the essential principles on which the church rests are the same now as at the first. Among the principles at the beginning were these: that Christ " may alone lay commands upon the church with respect to worship;" that " dipping in water is one of these commands, and that only a believer may be baptized;" that " baptized believers have the liberty to speak in the assemblies of the saints for the edification of the whole;" and that " no disciple of Christ has a right to constrain or restrain the conscience of another, or to seek by physical force to compel men to worship God." The church still believes that Christ alone is the rightful sovereign in the realm of religious faith; that his will has been recorded in Holy Scripture, which is a sufficient rule of doctrine and duty; that it is the will of Christ that those who have by faith accepted him as their Saviour should identify themselves with his people by church relations; that the ordinances of baptism and the Lord's Supper belong to the church, and are designed to set forth great spiritual facts,—the first the origin, and the second the maintenance of the new life in the soul, and each in intimate and vital connection with the death of Christ; and finally, that Christ's church, deeply imbued with his Spirit, is the divinely appointed agency for the evangelization of the world.

Newton, Prof. Calvin, was born in Southborough, Mass., Nov. 26, 1800. He entered Brown University in 1820, and graduated at Union College in 1824. While in Brown University he became a Christian and was baptized. He was licensed to preach by the church in Southborough; graduated at Newton in 1829, and was ordained pastor of the church in Bellingham, Mass., the same year. He remained here three years, and then accepted an appointment, in 1832, as professor in Waterville College. He occupied the chair to which he had been elected for five years. Resigning his position in Waterville, he was appointed professor in the newly established theological institution in Maine. With this institution he was associated for four years, when he became pastor of the church in Grafton, Mass. Having decided to become a physician, he pursued his medical studies until he received the degree of M.D. from the medical institution in Pittsfield, Mass. During the remainder of his life, he was for the most of the time a lecturer or professor in the Worcester Medical Institution, and finally its president. He died Aug. 9, 1853.

Newton, Matthew Turner, M.D., son of Deacon Israel and Harriet T. Newton, was born in 1830 in Colchester, Conn.; fitted for college at Bacon Academy; in 1848 chose the medical profession, and in 1851 graduated from the medical department of Yale College; commenced practice in Salem, Conn.; represented Salem in the General Assembly in 1853; at the close of the Legislature removed to Suffield; in the civil war was assistant surgeon of 3d Conn. Vols.; afterwards surgeon of 10th Conn. Vols.; resumed practice in Suffield; elected deacon of Second Baptist church in Suffield in 1875; has been a trustee of Connecticut Literary Institution since 1872; occupies a high position in society, and exerts a broad and happy influence.

Newton Theological Institution commenced its first session on the 28th of November, 1825. The plan for the foundation of a theological institution of a high order had long been under contemplation, but did not take definite shape until the 25th of May, 1825, when at a large meeting of Baptist ministers and laymen, representing different sections of New England, it was decided to establish such an institution, and commence operations at Newton Centre, Mass. The new seminary was opened, with Rev. Irah Chase as the first instructor of its students, with whom was associated, at the

beginning of the second year, Rev. Henry J. Ripley. These two professors constituted the faculty of instruction for six years. In 1834 the trustees added Rev. James D. Knowles to the corps of instructors, and in 1836, Rev. Barnas Sears. Upon the death of Prof. Knowles in 1838, Prof. H. B. Hackett, then a professor in Brown University, was called to Newton. The early history of the institution was marked by the usual experiences of such seminaries of learning. Interest was awakened, some funds raised, students increased faster than there was ability to meet their wants; then a troublesome debt oppressed the hearts of friends and well-wishers; then came attempts to secure, first, an endowment of $30,000, then of $50,000, both of which attempts failed: then another effort to secure $100,000 was made, and that was successful. But the amount was not yet deemed sufficient to meet the wants of the institution, and there followed a scheme to add $200,000 to the endowment already existing, and success crowned the effort, thus placing Newton on such a foundation that there was every reason to believe its future prosperity was placed beyond all ordinary contingencies.

More than 700 students have enjoyed the advantages of the institution, having obtained their theological education in part or wholly within its walls. Of this large number more than three-fourths have been pastors of churches in this country, and about 60 have received appointments as missionaries to the foreign field. Not far from 55 students have been called to occupy prominent positions in our colleges or theological seminaries, either as presidents or professors, while a large number have been useful as authors or editors. The institution has done a noble work for the cause of Christ in connection with the denomination, to whose ministry it has been such a rich blessing.

New York Baptist Home for Aged and Infirm Persons is the name of one of the best institutions in New York. It is the outgrowth of the Ladies' Home Society, organized in 1869 to provide the aged, infirm, or destitute members of the Baptist churches of New York with a comfortable residence, with board, clothing, skillful medical attendance, with their accustomed religious services, and, at their death, with respectable burial. In its application for means to accomplish its end the society met with a generous response, and speedily erected a large building in Sixty-eighth Street. It is six stories high, and nicely furnished. It does not belie its name. It has rooms for the accommodation of over a hundred inmates. To obtain the position applicants must be recommended by the pastor and deacons of the church to which they belong, or shall give other satisfactory evidence of their good standing in a regular Baptist church for

NEWTON THEOLOGICAL SEMINARY, NEWTON CENTRE, MASS.

five years, must have no means of support, nor relatives who will provide for them, and must pay to the treasurer $100. "Patrons," who have paid $1000, can enter one person without the entrance fee, and, in exceptional cases, the trustees may admit applicants without the fee. A matron presides over the institution, who is chosen for her gentleness, piety, and fitness for such a responsible position. It is her duty each day to inquire after the comfort and health of the inmates, and provide promptly all that may be necessary for them. Both male and female members of the churches, becoming poor, and with no friends to support them, find in this building a home in which to abide with comfort until called to the eternal rest.

New York Baptists, Historical Sketch of.— In the latter part of the seventeenth century Rev. William Wickenden, of Rhode Island, a Baptist minister, visited the little town of New York to preach Christ. He labored for two years, meeting with discouragements and persecution. Without a license from the representatives of the British government, he was regarded as a law-breaker, and thrown into prison, where he lingered for months. For several years afterwards no Baptist minister made New York the scene of his labors. In 1712, Rev. Valentine Wightman, of Groton, Conn., came to New York for a short period; during his ministry about a dozen persons were baptized. After his removal Mr. Nicholas Eyers preached to the struggling community which he left. The following petition of his is on record:

"To His EXCELLENCY WILLIAM BURNET, ESQ., Captain-General and Governor-in-Chief of the Province of New York and New Jersey.

"The humble petition of Nicholas Eyers, brewer, a Baptist teacher in the city of New York:

"Sheweth unto your Excellency that on the first Tuesday of Feb., 1715, at a general quarter sessions of the peace, held at the city of New York, the hired house of your petitioner, situated in the broad street of this city, between the houses of John Michel Eyers and Mr. John Spratt, was registered for an Anabaptist meeting-house within this city; that the petitioner has it certified under the hands of sixteen inhabitants, of good faith and credit, that he had been a public teacher to a Baptist congregation within this city for four years, and some of them for less; that he has it certified by the Hon. Rip Van Dam, Esq., one of his Majesty's council for the province of New York, to have hired a house in this city from him January, 1720, only to be a public house for the Baptists, which he still keeps; and as he has obtained from the Mayor and Recorder of this city an ample certificate of his good behavior and innocent conversation, he therefore humbly prays:

"May it please your Excellency,

"To grant and permit this petitioner to execute the ministerial function of a minister within this city to a Baptist congregation, and to give him protection therein, according to his Majesty's gracious indulgence extended towards the Protestants dissenting from the Established Church, he being willing to comply with all that is required by the Act of Toleration from dissenters of that persuasion in Great Britain, and being owned for a reverend brother by other Baptist teachers.

"As in duty bound the petitioner shall ever pray.

"NICHOLAS EYERS."

After this petition was granted the community to which Mr. Eyers ministered enjoyed considerable prosperity, and in 1724 a church was formally organized, and subsequently a meeting-house was built on Golden Hill, near John Street, of which they were deprived in a few years by the action of one of their own trustees, who had the house sold. Mr. Eyers was pastor of the church for seven years. After 1732 the community disbanded. The church of Mr. Eyers is described as an "Arminian" community.

In 1745, Jeremiah Dodge, a member of the Fishkill Baptist church, who lived in the city of New York, opened his house for the Baptist worship, instituted by his Master and precious to himself. Benjamin Miller, of New Jersey, was accustomed to preach in the house of Mr. Dodge. Some of the members of the Free-Will Church, whom the Lord had taught to renounce Arminianism, joined Mr. Dodge in sustaining the new movement. Joseph Meeks, who was baptized the first year that Mr. Dodge had preaching in his house, greatly contributed to the continued existence of this Baptist enterprise. John Pine, a licentiate of the Fishkill church, preached for them for some time. In 1747 the Scotch Plains church, New Jersey, was constituted, and in 1753 the thirteen New York Baptists united with the community at Scotch Plains. Benjamin Miller, the pastor of the church, needed more room for his New York hearers than a dwelling-house could afford, and a rigging-loft was secured in Cart-and-Horse Street, now William Street, in which the future First church of New York held its meetings for several years. They erected their first church edifice on Gold Street, which was opened in March, 1760. On the 19th of June, 1762, twenty-seven persons, who had received letters of dismission for the purpose from the Scotch Plains church, formed the First Regular Baptist church of New York City. The same day John Gano, of New Jersey, entered upon his duties as pastor of the church, and in two or three years the membership exceeded two hundred. The house had to be enlarged, and soon it was filled to overflowing. The eloquence and piety of Mr. Gano made him one of the most popular ministers in the colonies.

During the Revolution the church was dispersed; baptism was not administered from April, 1776, to September, 1784. Mr. Gano was a brave patriot, and he entered the army as a chaplain. This position he held throughout the war. When the enemy evacuated New York he returned, to find only thirty-seven members of his church. The church edifice had been used as a stable, but it was soon renovated; and on the resumption of divine worship the Lord visited them again, and in two years the church numbered more than two hundred. Mr. Gano left it in 1788 for Kentucky, and he continued there until his death, in 1804.

In 1788, Rev. Dr. Benjamin Foster, of Rhode Island, became pastor of the church, who died of yellow fever in 1798, after exercising his ministry with much acceptance and success for nearly ten years. The Rev. William Collier, of Boston, accepted the pastorate in 1800, and in 1803 the church opened a new stone meeting-house, 65 by 80 feet, which cost $25,000. Mr. Collier resigned in 1804. In the same year the Rev. William Parkinson succeeded Mr. Collier, and continued pastor till 1840. In 1841, Rev. Dr. Cone took the oversight of the First church, and held that office till 1855. The Rev. A. Kingman Nott was elected his successor, and was drowned July 7, 1859, and the Rev. Dr. Anderson followed Mr. Nott. Dr. John Peddie is the present pastor. This mother of churches has had an illustrious succession of shepherds, men of God and men of remarkable talents; and she has had, and has still, a membership worthy of her pastors.

In New York, and in its suburbs and surrounding cities, there are now more than one hundred churches, where a century ago our single Baptist church edifice was a stable for British cavalry horses, and its male members were in the Revolutionary army or in the graves of patriots.

There were Baptists settled at Oyster Bay, Long Island, probably not many years after William Wickenden preached in New York City. They were found here in 1700, with William Rhodes, a licentiate, as their preacher, under whose ministrations converts were brought to Jesus, and among them Robert Feeks, who was ordained pastor in 1724. Fishkill had a Baptist church in 1745, of which Jeremiah Dodge was a member, who had removed to New York, and in that year opened his house for Baptist worship. Northeast church was founded in 1751, by men who had been brought to Christ in the great revivals in the time of Whitefield; Simon Dakin was their first pastor. The First church of Dover was constituted in 1757, and the next year Rev. Samuel Waldo became their pastor, and held that position for thirty-

five years. In 1759 the church at Stanford was organized. The Warwick church was formed in 1766, by Rev. James Benedict, and from a small membership it soon began to prosper, and early in its history it established several new churches. From these seed-scattering communities, and from Baptists coming from New England, our principles soon after this date, at the close of the Revolutionary war, began to spread with extraordinary rapidity, and this was especially true in the western part of the State.

The first Baptist meeting in Western New York was held at Butternuts, in 1773, within the present limits of Otsego County. In 1776 another meeting for worship was established by six baptized Indians, at Brothertown, now in the county of Oneida. These red brethren came from Connecticut and Long Island, N. Y. The community at Butternuts was scattered by the Revolutionary war, but four of the families composing it returned after the proclamation of peace, and the next year revived their meetings for public worship, and in August, 1793, they were recognized as a regular Baptist church. In 1789, Rev. William Furman settled in Springfield, Otsego Co., and at once began the preaching of the gospel, which was soon made powerful to the conversion of souls, and a church was formed, consisting of 30 members, in 1789; the church in Franklin, Delaware Co., was constituted in 1792; in 1794 the Kortright church, Delaware County, and the First, Second, and Third Burlington churches, Otsego County, were organized. And the word of God had free course, and was glorified in the conversion of throngs and in the formation of great numbers of churches. On Sept. 2, 1795, under the leadership of Rev. William Furman, ministers and messengers of thirteen churches met at Springfield and formed the Otsego Association. The sessions were full of joy, hope, and the love of Christ. In 1800 this body contained 37 churches, with 1718 members, nearly two-fifths of all the Baptist church members in the State of New York. The advantages conferred by the Otsego Association led to the formation, in 1801, of the Cayuga Association, and similar needs and benefits resulted in the organization of others, and such an era of almost unbounded prosperity blessed the denomination in Western New York that in 1846 there were thirty Associations in that field.

Among the instrumentalities greatly favored of God in spreading the gospel in Western New York was the "Lake Missionary Society," founded in Pompey, Onondaga Co., in the house of Rev. Jonathan Baker, Aug. 27, 1807. This body, at its meeting in German in 1808, assumed the name of the "Hamilton Missionary Society." It employed men of great zeal and ability to preach Christ, and its success was very great. It was nobly assisted by the "Hamilton Female Society" and other women's organizations existing for the same purpose; the first contribution from this source came on Feb. 19, 1812. The Massachusetts Baptist Missionary Society sent laborers into this field. The "New York Missionary Society" performed some mission service among the Tuscarora Indians. On Nov. 21, 1821, at Mentz, Cayuga Co., the "Baptist Domestic Missionary Convention of the State of New York" was founded, and for an account of its growth, changes, and great usefulness, see article on NEW YORK STATE MISSIONARY CONVENTION.

An educated ministry for our rapidly-increasing churches was long felt to be an absolute necessity. To meet this pressing demand, on Sept. 24, 1817, the "Baptist Education Society of the State of New York" was formed. The first applicant for its patronage was Dr. Wade, subsequently of Burmah. Dr. Kincaid, a member of the same class, and a laborer in the same heathen field, was among the earliest to receive its advantages. For two years the students were taught by private instructors, and at academies, until the spring of 1820, when the Hamilton "Literary and Theological Institution" was founded, which finally became Madison University, Hamilton Theological Seminary, and Colgate Academy. The institutions at Hamilton have done more for New York, New England, the Middle and Western States, and Burmah than any human pen will ever record. Rochester University, with its brilliant history, came from Hamilton.

For the Baptist newspapers of New York, see articles on THE EXAMINER AND CHRONICLE, THE BAPTIST WEEKLY, and THE WATCH-TOWER.

The "New York Association" is the best-known body of that character in the State. In the minutes of the Philadelphia Baptist Association for 1790 we find the following: "The request of the churches at Stamford, Warwick, First and Second of New York, King Street, and Staten Island, for permission to join other Associations if it should be found more convenient, is granted." The Association was formed Oct. 19, 1791. The Rev. Elkanah Holmes was chosen moderator, and the Rev. Dr. Foster, pastor of the First church, clerk. Dr. Foster preached the first sermon before the Association from the text, "Many shall run to and fro, and knowledge shall be increased." The meeting was held in the First church of New York. On May 2, 1805, the Fayette Street, better known as the Oliver Street church, was received into the Association; the messengers representing it on that occasion were John Williams, pastor, and John Withington, Jacob Smith, John Cauldwell, and Francis Wayland. The New York Association has been remarkably active and useful in extending the Redeemer's kingdom throughout the State, and its members have ever shown a spirit of enlightened liberality in their contributions to spread the gospel all over this and many other lands.

There are now 44 Associations in the State of New York, 877 churches, 801 ordained ministers, 114,094 church members, and 878 Sunday-schools, with 13,161 officers and teachers, and 91,217 scholars. In New York the Baptist denomination is but of yesterday, and yet its numbers, intelligence, resources, piety, and influence exhibit a miracle of prosperity.

New York, The First Baptist Church of.— This splendid edifice was dedicated to the worship of Almighty God in October, 1871. The church and chapel, with their ground and furniture, cost $197,500. The edifice is free from debt. The spire, like the whole structure, is of brownstone. Dr. John Peddie is the devoted and popular pastor of the venerable community worshiping in the superb edifice represented in our picture.

New York State Missionary Convention, The.—Availing ourselves of facts stated at the annual meeting of the Convention for 1880, it may be interesting to say that the first Baptist church organized in New York State west of the Hudson was in 1789, at Springfield, Otsego Co., and in 1795 the Otsego Association was organized with 13 churches and 5 ministers. In 1802 its churches had increased to 42, and its ministers to 9. There were at this time in the whole State of New York only 86 churches, with not more than 5000 members. In 1817 the number of churches was 310, with 28,000 members. Now, in 1880, the number of churches is 877, with nearly 115,000 members. In 1802 the population of the Empire State was about 650,000; in 1880 it is fully 5,000,000. The Baptist denomination in the same years has increased more than three times faster than the population, and in the decade ending with 1880 its growth has been more rapid than that of the population.

To no other cause than to the character of the first and second generations of pioneer Baptist ministers can this large growth be ascribed. Most of the first generation died early in this century, and few of them lived later than 1825. But how can this generation estimate the debt it owes to such ministers of the Lord Jesus as Joseph Cornell, Ashbel Hosmer, William Furman, Salmon Morton, Obed Warren, David Irish, Emory Osgood, John Lawton, Joel Butler, Sylvanus Haynes, Ora Butler, Lemuel Covill, and Jonathan Ferris? And to such laymen as Squire Munro, Jonathan Olmsted, Samuel Payne, Ebenezer Wakely, and John Keep? These were noble men of the first generation of Baptist pioneers, and before they had entered into rest another generation on whom their mantle had fallen took up their work and bore their responsibilities. They included such ministers as

FIRST BAPTIST CHURCH, NEW YORK.

Alfred Bennett, Nathaniel Kendrick, Daniel Hascall, John Peck, Caleb Douglass, John Blodgett, Lewis Leonard, Cornelius P. Wyckoff, Elon Galusha, John Smitzer, Bartholomew T. Welch, Spencer H. Cone, Oliver C. Comstock, and Elisha Tucker, and such laymen as William Colgate, Friend Humphrey, Alexander M. Beebee, Seneca B. Burchard, Asa Bennett, Oren Sage, and William Cobb.

These men knew how to discern the signs of coming events and obligations, and to make ready for them. In 1807 they formed the Hamilton Missionary Society, and its field was wider than the State. In 1812, Mrs. Betsey Payne and Mrs. Freedom Olmsted attended the annual meeting of the society as delegates from what was called the Hamilton Female Missionary Society, and carried with them twenty yards of fulled cloth as their society's contribution to the larger treasury. This was the first woman's Baptist missionary society known west of the Hudson, but it soon became the mother of a large number of like societies over all the State. In 1814, Rev. John M. Peck attended the annual meeting of the Hamilton Society as the representative of Luther Rice, and the society took immediate measures to awaken a spirited co-operation in the work of foreign missions. In the same year the necessity of a religious paper, devoted largely to religious news, was felt, and a quarterly paper, called *The Vehicle*, was set agoing, which was subsequently merged in the *New York Baptist Register*. In 1817 the New York State Baptist Education Society was organized, and in 1820 the Hamilton Literary and Theological Institution was started upon its beneficent career. In 1821, prompted by the Hudson River Association, the State Missionary Convention was organized at Mentz, near Auburn, and in 1825 the long-desired union of the Hamilton Missionary Society and the State Convention was effected.

What this State Convention, dating back by this union to the year 1807, has done appears in its helping to make strong and self-supporting such churches as Binghamton, Owego, Waverly, Corning, First and Emmanuel, Buffalo, First and Second, Rochester, Ogdensburg, and scores of others in every part of the State. But, like most other good movements, the Convention has had a checkered history. It took several years to bring about a union between it and the Hamilton Missionary Society. But some years after the union was effected a new and rather sharp trial came in settling the relations that should exist between the Convention and the American Baptist Home Mission Society. An auxiliary relationship was finally fixed upon, and it was made the duty of the Convention to act as a collecting agency for the Home Mission Society, so as to avoid two sets of appeals to the churches. But it was found, after some years of

trial, that the plan did not work well. Then came the conflict of a re-adjustment, which ended in making the State of New York open to the agents of both organizations. But the Convention continued to do good work for the means at its command under this arrangement to the year 1868, when the co-operative system was adopted, by which all the home and domestic money of the State went into the Home Mission Society's treasury, and the State missionaries were paid out of that general fund. The effect of this was to make. the State Convention less influential and successful as a purely State organization.

In 1874 the Convention was reorganized at Hornellsville, N. Y., under a new constitution, the main purpose of which was to make it a strictly State organization, more distinctively representative in its character and less complicated in its structure. It was provided that its sole object should be to promote the interests of the State missionary, educational, and Sunday-school work, and that its efforts should be directed by an executive committee of seven men living in the city of New York and vicinity. In these six years a larger and better work has been done within the State than in any other corresponding period in the Convention's history. Each year has been an advance over the one preceding it in the number of missionaries commissioned, the work done, and the amount of money received. In the year closing with October, 1880, the total receipts and disbursements were $11,978.31. During the year 73 missionaries were commissioned, as against 61 the previous year; and from 70 of these reports were received quarterly up to October 1. These show a total of 2344 weeks' labor performed, 6230 sermons preached, 3931 prayer-meetings held, 12,476 religious visits, 242 churches and out-stations supplied, and 260 persons baptized by the missionaries themselves. The late annual meetings of the Convention have been distinguished for their unity and ability, and for their benign influence on all the denominational interests of the State.

New York Watch-Tower, The, is a weekly journal devoted to Christian work in the Baptist denomination. It was at first called *The Baptist Outlook*, edited by Justin D. Fulton, D.D., but in 1878 its name was changed, and John W. Olmstead, D.D., became the editor and proprietor. It appeared at first in the quarto form, but increase of patronage led to enlargement and a change to the folio form. Its plan is to furnish a good Baptist newspaper at so low a price that the less able members of our churches will be induced to take it. In November, 1880, the paper was further enlarged and improved under the auspices of *The Watch-Tower* Publishing Co., Dr. Olmstead, editor-in-chief, with able assistants. It is loyal to Christ and the Baptist faith and practice. It is the special champion of the "Bible Union" principles, of pure versions in the English as well as foreign tongues. As a journalist, Dr. Olmstead, so long the editor of the *Watchman and Reflector*, of Boston, stands deservedly high. A large part of his paper is filled with carefully-written editorial matter. His discussions of religious and denominational matters are calm, dignified, and forcible. *The Watch-Tower* is growing in public favor and patronage.

Niles, Rev. Asa, was born in North Middleborough, Mass., Feb. 10, 1777. He was baptized by Rev. Dr. Baldwin in 1800, and united with the Second Baptist church in Boston. He studied for a time with Rev. W. Williams, of Wrentham, Mass., and at a meeting of the Warren Baptist Association at Warren, R. I., in 1805, he was ordained as an evangelist. He commenced at once to preach, and labored in several places, not remaining long in any one of them. He was also a missionary of the Rhode Island Convention for some time, doing the work of an evangelist in different parts of the State. In 1832 he removed to North Middleborough, and preached there for two years. His death occurred April 15, 1849.

Nisbet, Ebenezer, D.D., was born June 20, 1826, in Edinburgh, Scotland. He came with his

EBENEZER NISBET, D.D.

parents to America in 1834. The family settled in Broome Co., N. Y. After some years they removed to the neighborhood of Owego, N. Y., at whose academy Ebenezer prepared for the University of Rochester, in which he graduated in 1853. He

entered Rochester Theological Seminary the same year, and graduated in 1855. He remained as a resident graduate at Rochester for a year, and then settled at East Avon, N. Y., and was ordained Sept. 5, 1856. He was pastor at East Avon and Brockport, N. Y., at Fond du Lac, Wis., at Rochester, N. Y., at Rock Island, Ill., and he is now pastor at Leavenworth, Kansas. During his labors at East Avon the membership nearly doubled, large accessions were made at Brockport, 342 were admitted to the Fond du Lac church, and above 200 at Rochester. At Rock Island he was instrumental in largely relieving the church of a burdensome debt, while at Leavenworth under his administration a debt of above $16,000 has been removed. The University of Chicago bestowed upon him, in June, 1868, the degree of Doctor of Divinity. He delivered the following year in the university building, before the Ministers' Institute of the Northwest, a course of lectures on "Science and Religion." He was appointed, in 1881, by the governor of Kansas, one of the regents of the State University. He is the author of an able work on the Resurrection, and he has also written several review articles. Quite a number of his sermons have been published by request.

Nix, Rev. Allen, an able pioneer preacher of Ouachita Baptist Association, La., died in Catahoula Parish in 1847. At the time of his death he was pastor of the First Baptist church on Little River.

Noble, Rev. Mark, was born in Old Charlton, Kent, England, Nov. 25, 1836; was converted under the preaching of Rev. C. H. Spurgeon, by whom he was baptized Dec. 1, 1859. He was ordained at Necton, Norfolk, England. Mr. Noble was brought up by his maternal grandparents. In early life he studied architecture. He entered Mr. Spurgeon's college in 1862. He had charge of the Baptist church at Carleton Road, Norfolk, which he resigned to come to America, in 1870. He arrived in Fairbury, Neb., March 10, 1870. Under his labors the Baptist church in Fairbury was organized, July 3, 1870; also, July 5, 1870, the Dry Branch Baptist church. Mr. Noble has served these churches since their formation, and has organized other churches. He has labored industriously and successfully amid many privations.

Noel, Hon. and Rev. Baptist W., was for many years an eminent clergyman of the Church of England, but from 1848 he was identified with the English Baptists. He was the brother of the Earl of Gainsborough. He was educated at Trinity College, Cambridge, graduating with distinction in 1826. Having been ordained, he became minister of St. John's, Bedford-row, London, where he preached to a very numerous audience of the upper classes until his secession from the Established Church.

He was universally regarded as one of the most eminent preachers in the metropolis, and a leader of the evangelical party. He was one of the royal chaplains, and according to common report more

HON. AND REV. BAPTIST W. NOEL.

than once declined promotion to the Episcopal bench. His secession was the leading event in English ecclesiastical affairs for some time. The publication of his book on the "Union of Church and State" excited much curiosity concerning his future course. At length he avowed himself convinced of the Scripturalness of Baptist principles, and was publicly baptized in London, Aug. 9, 1849. He published two essays about the same time on the "External Act of Baptism" and "Christian Baptism." Soon after, he entered upon his ministry in John Street Chapel, as successor to the venerable John Harrington Evans, near the scene of his labors as a State Church clergyman. Here he ministered until 1868, when, having attained his seventieth year, he resigned his pastoral charge, and engaged occasionally in evangelistic services in different parts of the country, as he had done for some time after his retirement from the Church of England. As an Episcopal minister he had wielded a moral influence scarcely second to that of any of his contemporaries. This was due to the fine blending of dignity and independence in his character with high spirituality. When he joined the Baptists these qualities were irradiated by the sacrifices he had made for conscience' sake. Wherever he went to preach, immense throngs, belonging to almost every denomination, assembled

to listen to a man whose sincerity of motive was beyond suspicion, and whose whole demeanor and action seemed a vivid embodiment of the noblest Christian manhood. When he was invited by the Baptist Union to accept the highest honor which his brethren have it in their power to bestow, he willingly, but with characteristic modesty, accepted the position. He filled the chair in 1867, the year preceding his retirement from the pastorate, and at the autumnal meeting at Cardiff, his unwritten address on the work of the ministry produced a singularly powerful impression. When he retired from the pulpit at John Street in the following year, his text at both services was Gal. vi. 14: "God forbid that I should glory, save in the cross of our Lord Jesus Christ," and he uttered scarcely a word of personal reference during the whole day. It is a remarkable fact that until the time of his departure drew near, he was never known to have a day's illness in his life. Dr. Tyng, in his "Recollections of England," published in 1847, described Mr. Noel as "certainly a most interesting and delightful preacher; altogether extemporaneous; mild and persuasive in his manner, yet sufficiently impressive and sometimes powerful, having a very clear and consistent flow of thought." In addition to a variety of occasional sermons, and sermons on special occasions, Mr. Noel published numerous works of greater or less celebrity. Besides his well-known book on Church and State, and the volumes on Baptism, he published "Sermons on the First Five Centuries of the Church," 1839; "Sermons to the Unconverted," 1840; "Sermons at St. James's," 1842; "Sermons at the Chapels Royal," 1842 and 1848; "Case of the Free Church of Scotland," 1844; "Notes of a Tour in Switzerland in 1847;" "Letters on the Church of Rome," 1852, etc. Among pamphlets which excited considerable attention, his letter to the bishop of London on the spiritual destitution of the metropolis was particularly effective for good. Also his publications on the Jamaica Massacres; on the "Duty of Englishmen towards the Hindoos," and on "American Freedom and Slavery," during the civil war in this country, were widely read. He died Sunday afternoon, Jan. 19, 1873, in his seventy-fifth year. His amiable spirit, exemplary character, fidelity to conviction, and complete and life-long consecration to the work of the Lord, are a precious possession to the whole church, and particularly to the Baptist body, with which, constrained by conscience, he spent his maturer years.

Noel, Silas Mercer, D.D., son of Rev. Theodoric Noel, was born near Richmond, Va., Aug. 13, 1783. He received a classical education, after which he studied law, and entered on the practice of his profession at Frankfort, Ky. After a prosperous career of a few years, he abandoned the law for the gospel ministry, and was ordained pastor of the Big Spring Baptist church in Woodford County. A few years later he was appointed judge of the Circuit Court about the year 1817, which position he filled several years, when he resigned and resumed the active duties of the ministry. He traveled and preached extensively, and, during a number of years, his success was so great that it was said " he baptized more people than any other preacher in Kentucky." In 1827 he became pastor of Great Crossing church in Scott County, and during the following year baptized into its fellowship 359 persons. He was an author of more than ordinary ability, and he wrote extensively for the periodicals of his time. He was the publisher of a Baptist monthly in 1813, which, however, was suspended for want of patronage. In 1836 he was called to the pastorate of the First Baptist church in Lexington. His death occurred May 5, 1839.

Noffsinger, Rev. M. V., pastor at Macon, Miss., was born in Virginia, and educated at Union University, Murfreesborough, Tenn. He professed faith at the age of sixteen, and was ordained in 1862. He has labored successfully as pastor at Marion, Va., four years; Jonesborough, Tenn., four years; Morristown, Tenn., four years; agent of Union University, one year, adding $25,000 to the endowment. He has been some time in his present pastorate. He has been successful as a church builder, and in removing debts from churches. He is about forty years of age.

Norris, S. M., an active Sunday-school laborer at Kingston, La., was born in South Carolina in 1813. He came to Louisiana in 1853. Has accomplished great good as colporteur and Sunday-school agent.

Norsworthy, Rev. Galbanum, M.D., a leading minister of Liberty Association, Arkansas, was born in North Carolina in 1815; removed to Arkansas in 1848, and engaged successfully in the practice of medicine; began to preach in 1868, and has done much to supply the destitution about him; is an able preacher and forcible writer.

North Carolina, The Baptists of.—

THEIR ORIGIN.

Moore, in his " History of North Carolina," says, " Sir William Berkeley, governor of Virginia, drove out of that colony, in 1653, the Baptists and Quakers, who found a refuge in the Albemarle region of Carolina." Morgan Edwards says there were Baptists in North Carolina as early as 1695, and Dr. Hawks, in enumerating the freeholders in several eastern counties of North Carolina, mentions the names of many Baptists, and among them two preachers,— Paul Palmer and William Burgess. The first church, however, of which we read was not organized till 1727,—some authorities say 1729,—in the

county of Camden, by Paul Palmer, and was called Shiloh. This church still exists. Palmer was a native of Welsh Tract, Del.

In 1729 the Meherrin church, which still exists, and is located near Murfreesborough, N. C., was constituted by Joseph Parker, who was ordained by Paul Palmer, of Camden County. In 1750 the Meherrin church gave letters for the formation of the Sandy Run church, in Bertie County, and from these three original churches Baptist principles were gradually but slowly disseminated through the eastern part of the State.

In 1742, Elder William Sojourner came with a colony from Berkeley Co., Va., and settled on Kehukee Creek, in Halifax County. In 1752 the church they founded had multiplied into sixteen churches.

It would seem from what Benedict says that the Baptists of both these settlements were Arminian, or Free-Will, for some time, and were accustomed to baptize, certainly in some cases, without requiring regeneration. In 1775, Miller and Vanhorn were sent down by the Philadelphia Association to look after these irregular Baptists, and with the blessing of God were enabled to effect a great reformation among them. They adopted the London Confession of Faith, published in 1689, and in 1765 formed the Kehukee Association.

The reformation of doctrine alluded to above must have been but partial, however, as we find a resolution adopted at a large meeting held at the Falls of Tar River in 1775, described at length by Burkett and Read in their " History of the Kehukee Association," in which non-fellowship was declared with those churches whose members were not converted *before* baptism. Gradually the churches came to the old landmarks of Baptist faith and were united, though for a long time Joseph Parker and the Meherrin church did not come into the union.

The third, and by far the most prosperous, colony of Baptists who settled in North Carolina also came from Berkeley Co., Va., led by Elder Shubal Stearns, and settled on Sandy Creek, then in Guilford, now in Randolph.

Daniel Marshall, the brother-in-law of Mr. Stearns, before a Congregationalist, became a Baptist, and was very successful as an evangelist. The Sandy Creek was a most fruitful mother of churches, though originally composed of but 16 members. In seventeen years it had organized 42 churches, had ordained 115 ministers, and gathered a membership of 600 communicants.

The first Association formed in this State was the Sandy Creek, in 1758. In 1792 the Arminian Baptists of the eastern part of the State united with the Calvinistic Baptists of this Association, and thus the denomination became united, to remain so till

1827, when the Kehukee and Country Line Associations left the Old-School Missionary Baptists and became a new sect of Anti-Missionary Baptists.

In Dr. G. W. Purefoy's "History of the Sandy Creek Association," pp. 51–57, it is abundantly shown that in 1821 the Country Line Association was a Missionary body, and in favor of Sabbath-schools, and the "History of the Kehukee Association," by Burkett and Read, shows that that body was composed of Missionary churches for many years after its organization. The Portsmouth and the Chowan were both daughters of the Kehukee Association, and were in their origin, as they still are, Missionary organizations.

FORMATION OF THE STATE CONVENTION.

There seems to have been no general effort to unite the denomination till about the years 1814–16, when the North Carolina Baptist Society for Foreign and Domestic Missions was formed. Who were the leaders in this movement does not appear, but we find that the address to the churches was written by the Rev. Josiah Crudup, and that the famous Robert T. Daniel was its agent. This effort at organization having failed, another society was formed about 1826, called the Baptist Benevolent Society. It drew together a number of prominent men in Greenville in 1829, and after talking the matter over it was pretty well agreed that they would make an effort to form a State Convention at their next meeting. In a journal of Dr. Samuel Wait it is stated that Rev. Thomas Meredith prepared the constitution of the new Convention before he left his home in Edenton, and that when the Convention was formed, in the barn of Dr. J. C. Gorham, a leading Baptist of Greenville, Pitt Co., March 20, 1830, that constitution was substantially adopted, and that is still the constitution of the North Carolina Baptist State Convention. Its second article reads as follows: "The primary objects of this Convention shall be the education of young men called of God to the ministry and approved of by the churches to which they respectively belong, the employment of missionaries within the limits of the State, and a co-operation with the Baptist General Convention of the United States in the promotion of missions in general."

At the time of the adoption of this constitution the Baptists of North Carolina, including Primitive, or Anti-Missionary, and Free-Will Baptists, numbered but 14 Associations, 272 churches, and 15,360 members. They had no denominational paper, and no school, male nor female, under control of the denomination. Many of the Associations scarcely raised more money at their annual meetings than was necessary to defray the expenses of printing their minutes, but the founders of the Convention were men of large brain, unflagging zeal, and earnest piety. They were the strongest men of their denomination, and some of them the peers of any men in the State. They planned largely, and worked zealously up to their plans.

The officers of the Convention were P. W. Dowd, President; W. P. Biddle, Thomas Meredith, and C. McAlister, Vice-Presidents; R. S. Blount, Recording Secretary; and H. Austin, Treasurer.

The first Board of Directors of the Convention consisted of Charles W. Skinner and Henry A. Skinner, of Perquimans; Elder Thomas D. Mason, of Greenville; Daniel Boon, of Johnson County; Elder Samuel Wait, William Sanders, and Elijah Clark, of Newbern; Elder James D. Hall, of Currituck County; Peter B. Lawrence and James Hartmers, of Tarborough; James B. Outlaw, of Bertie County; W. B. Hinton, I. Holliman, and Elder John Purefoy, of Wake; Elder Jacob Rascow, of Edenton; Samuel Simpson, of Craven; Elder James McDaniel, of Cumberland; and G. Hukeby, of Orange.

The following ministers were appointed as agents of the Convention, and served without pay, viz.: P. W. Dowd, Raleigh; Thomas Meredith, Edenton; William P. Biddle, Craven County; James McDaniel, Cumberland County; John Armstrong, Newbern; Reuben Lawrence, Bertie County; Robert T. Daniel and Eli Phillips, Moore County; James D. Hall, Currituck County; John Purefoy, Wake County; John Culpepper, Montgomery County; William Dowd, Stokes County. Samuel Wait was appointed general agent of the Convention, at a salary of $1.00 a day, and John Armstrong, corresponding secretary.

An address, wise and masterly in an extraordinary degree, was prepared by the Rev. Thomas Meredith and sent forth to the churches, showing the advantages of such an institution, answering objections, and inviting them to unite in the organization. The Convention was a bond of union and a source of development, and thus proved a great blessing to the denomination.

The Convention has three boards or Executive Committees to attend to the four special departments of work, the Board of Missions, Home and Foreign, located in Raleigh; the Board of Education, located at Wake Forest College; and the Sunday-School Board, also located in Raleigh. These boards are composed of prominent men, laymen as well as ministers, chosen from different parts of the State, enough, however, residing in the vicinity of the location of the board to constitute a quorum.

NORTH CAROLINA BAPTISTS WHO HAVE BECOME DISTINGUISHED IN OTHER STATES.

As in the field of politics North Carolina has produced three Presidents of the nation, Jackson,

Polk, and Johnson, each of whom attained distinction in other States, so in the realm of religion it is not immodest to say that many of the wisest and ablest men who have adorned the Baptist Zion of the South have gone forth from this State. Silas Mercer, of Georgia, was a preacher in North Carolina for years before he went South, and his nephew, Jesse Mercer, the leader of the Georgia Baptists and the founder and benefactor of Mercer University, was a native of Halifax Co., N. C. The elder W. T. Brantly and the elder Basil Manly were born in Chatham Co., N. C., within five miles of each other, and entered the ministry in this State. John Kerr, who as an orator was pronounced by Dr. Jeter as first, and no man was second, and who became so celebrated in Virginia, was born in Caswell Co., N. C., where he began to preach, and he died in North Carolina. Dr. R. B. C. Howell, so long identified with Virginia and Tennessee, and among the most distinguished Baptist authors of the South, was a native of Wayne Co., N. C., and began his ministry in North Carolina. Dr. A. M. Poindexter, the prince of agents, and the most eloquent man the writer ever heard, was born in Bertie Co., N. C. And J. S. Mims, the learned professor, and Iverson L. Brooks, the successful pastor, both of South Carolina, were born, the first in Cumberland County, the second in Caswell Co., N. C. All these, with Saunders, the first president of Mercer University, Georgia, and Emerson, of William Jewell College, Missouri, and Solomon, of Kentucky, and hundreds of other useful and honored men among the Baptists, have gone forth from this great Baptist State.

PROGRESS OF THE BAPTISTS IN NORTH CAROLINA.

In 1770 there were but 9 churches in the State. In 1784 there were 42 churches, 47 ministers, 3776 members. In 1812 there were 204 churches, 117 ministers, and 12,567 members. In 1832 there were 332 churches, 211 ministers, and 18,918 members. In 1851 there were 599 churches, 374 ministers, and 41,674 members. In 1860 there were 692 churches, 374 ministers, and 59,778 members. In 1876 there were 1442 churches, 793 ministers, and 137,000 members. Their statistics as reported for 1880 foot up 77 Associations, 1905 churches, and 172,951 members.

These figures place North Carolina third among the States as regards Baptist strength. Georgia is first, Virginia second, and North Carolina third.

North Carolina, The Biblical Recorder of.—

No single agency has done so much to unite and develop the Baptists of North Carolina as the *Biblical Recorder*, which for forty-six years has been their State organ. In 1833, Rev. Thomas Meredith, then pastor in Edenton, issued *The Baptist Interpreter*, a monthly publication, in pamphlet form, with a list of less than a hundred subscribers. In about two years there was a call for a weekly paper, and in January, 1834, *The Biblical Recorder* was originated by the same man, beginning with nearly 1000 subscribers. The paper was removed to Newbern in 1834, and to Raleigh in 1838, where it is now issued. About this time the *Recorder* and *Southern Watchman*, of Charleston, S. C., were united, and, until 1842, it was published under the style of *The Recorder and Watchman*. In 1842 the *Recorder* was suspended for six months, being superseded by a monthly periodical entitled *The Southern Christian Repository*. After six months, however, the publication of the *Recorder* was resumed, and it continued under the management of Mr. Meredith till his death, in 1851. For two or three years it was edited by Rev. T. W. Toby, D.D., pastor of the Raleigh church, and was still the property of Mrs. Meredith. In 1854 the paper was purchased by a joint-stock company, and Rev. J. J. James, one of the proprietors, became editor. Two years afterwards Mr. James bought out his partners, and associated Rev. J. S. Walthal with himself as editor, and they continued these relations until 1861, when Rev. J. D. Hufham, D.D., bought the journal, and edited it throughout the war. In April, 1865, by reason of a want of postal facilities, the *Recorder* was again suspended for a time, but its publication was resumed in the fall of the same year.

In 1867, Dr. Hufham sold the paper to Dr. Walters and Mr. J. H. Mills, who were its joint editors for a time. Mr. Mills, however, became sole proprietor in a few months, and continued to conduct the paper till 1873, when the *Recorder* passed into the hands of Prof. A. F. Read, who, after two years' experience as editor, sold it to Rev. C. T. Bailey, who still owns it, in connection with C. B. Edwards and N. B. Broughton. Dr. J. D. Hufham was associate editor with Mr. Bailey for more than a year after he took charge of the *Recorder*. Dr. T. H. Pritchard was also employed on the editorial staff for two years, and the Rev. Harvey Hatcher is now the associate editor.

The *Recorder* has a subscription-list of about 4500, and is regarded not only as a means of eminent usefulness, but a good property, yielding a handsome income to the proprietors.

North Carolina, The Colored Baptists of.—

There are probably 80,000 colored Baptists in North Carolina in regular Baptist churches. A considerable number also are to be found in Methodist churches who have been immersed, and who do not believe in or practise infant baptism. Up to the close of the war the colored people in most cases were members of the same churches with the whites, having a portion of the meeting-houses set apart for their use, though in a few instances they had distinct organizations and their own pastors. As was naturally to be expected, they withdrew from their white brethren after their liberation, though not in all cases, for the colored members of the First Baptist church of Raleigh did not retire till nearly four years after the war closed.

Since the war they have grown rapidly, and have now 30 Associations, with about 750 churches, and a membership of 80,000, and with probably 30,000 teachers and scholars in their Sunday-schools.

CONVENTION.

Their State Convention was organized at Goldsborough, N. C., Oct. 17, 1867, and they were aided on this occasion by a committee appointed by the Convention of their white brethren, consisting of Revs. J. S. Purefoy, W. M. Young, A. D. Cohen, and C. J. Nelson. Rev. William Warwick was chosen President, and L. W. Boone, Secretary. The objects of their Convention are the promotion of missions, ministerial education, and Sunday-schools. This Convention met in Newbern in October, 1879, and its officers are Rev. Cæsar Johnson, President; Rev. H. A. Powell, Vice-President; E. E. Smith, Secretary; Rev. John Curly, Corresponding Secretary; Rev. A. B. Williams, Treasurer; Rev. G. W. Perry, Auditor.

They also have a Sunday-school Convention, which meets annually, the last session having been held in September, 1879, in Goldsborough. They have a church organ, called the *African Expositor*, which is issued monthly.

Their corresponding secretary travels as an agent, collecting money, and doing missionary work also.

As early as 1868 the Convention voted that a chair of theology should be established for the training of their ministers, and the Rev. H. M. Tupper, of the Shaw University, was chosen to fill this chair.

In addition to the Shaw University they have three academies,—one at Plymouth, one at Garysburg, and one at Goldsborough; the first two are paid for and the other nearly so.

North Carolina, Western Convention of.— In 1789 the French Broad Baptist church was organized in that part of North Carolina known as west of the Blue Ridge. Big Ivy church also claims to have been constituted about the same time. The first Association organized in the west was the French Broad, in 1807, and was formed by the union of six churches,—Little Ivy, Locust's Old Fields, New Found, Cancy River, French Broad, and Cane Creek. The first three were dismissed from the Holston Association of Tennessee; the other three from Broad River, in South Carolina. Its ordained ministers were Thomas Snelson,

Thomas Justice, Sim Blythe, Benjamin King, Humphrey Posey, and Stephen Morgan.

Other churches and Associations having originated in this part of the State, the Western Baptist Convention was organized in 1845 as an auxiliary of the State Convention. In 1857 it became an independent body. At first its territory extended as far east as the Yadkin, but since the late war it has confined its labors principally to the fourteen counties west of the Blue Ridge. This territory contains 9 Associations, representing about 20,000 Baptists. The Convention has three boards,—a Sunday-school board, located at Asheville; a Mission board, located at Waynesville; and an Education board, whose headquarters are at Hendersonville. In 1853 the *Carolina Baptist*, a weekly newspaper, was started at Hendersonville, with Rev. James Blythe as editor. It suspended in 1856, but resumed publication in 1857. Soon afterwards it was succeeded by the *Baptist Telescope*, W. A. G. Bunn editor, but this paper lived only a few years. Rev. N. Bowen originated the *Cottage Visitor*, which continued until 1871. The *Baptist Gleaner*, edited by Rev. John Ammons, appeared in Asheville in 1877, but lived only a year. The *Baptist Telescope* has been revived, and is edited by Rev. N. Bowen.

The Baptists sought to establish a college at Mars Hill, in Madison County, before the war, but the prevalence of hostilities caused the enterprise to be abandoned, and it has not since been revived. A school at Holly Springs, in Macon County, has been under the patronage of the denomination for several years.

In 1858 it was determined to build a Baptist female college at Hendersonville. Rev. N. Bowen, as agent, pushed the work, until stopped by the war. A granite building, three stories high, nearly complete, owned at present by a joint-stock company, but controlled by the Baptists, is the result of this effort. This institution, known as the Judson College, has a patronage of a hundred students of both sexes, and is presided over by Rev. W. A. Nelson, D.D., aided by a competent corps of teachers. The present officers of the Convention are: President, Rev. N. Bowen; Vice-Presidents, Rev. S. M. Collis, Rev. John Ammons; Secretary, Columbus M. Williams; Treasurer, John L. Pleasants; Historian, Rev. D. B. Nelson.

Northrup, G. W., D.D., LL.D., the able and distinguished president of the theological seminary at Chicago, was born at Antwerp, Jefferson Co., N. Y., Oct. 15, 1826. From his earliest childhood he was under strong religious influences, his father being a man of singularly devout character and life. Though converted, as he believes, at the age of twelve, it was at the age of sixteen that he received baptism, at the hands of Rev. Wilbur Tillinghast, becoming a member of the Baptist church in his native town. The school advantages in Antwerp were of an inferior character. His scholarly tendencies, however, very early showed themselves,

G. W. NORTHRUP, D.D., LL.D.

and he began the study of Latin, with such imperfect helps as he could secure, while but a boy. At the age of eighteen he left home, with a view to make a career for himself, though as yet with no distinct purpose as to the line of life he should choose. Some years were spent in teaching at Trenton, near Utica, and at Granville and Hartford, Washington Co. When at about the age of twenty-one a visit to relatives living in Watertown, N. Y., was the means of deciding him to enter upon a regular course of study. He had already, in connection with his teaching, but mainly through private study, become so much a proficient in mathematics that he had in that department passed over most of the ground of a college course. In Latin he had done something; in Greek he had not made even a beginning. Setting himself resolutely to private study, partly under the tuition of A. C. Beach, Esq., since lieutenant-governor of the State of New York, he made such progress that in a year and a half he was prepared to enter the last term of the Sophomore year at Williams College in Massachusetts. At his graduation, in 1854, he took the metaphysical oration, perhaps the highest of the college honors at Williams. Entering the theological seminary at Rochester, he graduated there in 1857.

Immediately upon the conclusion of his theo-

logical course he was appointed instructor in church history in the seminary at Rochester, and at the end of the year full professor in that department. The ten years of service, until his call to Chicago in 1867, made their lasting impression in the seminary and upon the numerous young men who came under his tuition. Better work in church history has probably never been done in any theological seminary in this country. During this period, besides, Dr. Northrup won distinction as a preacher. For one year and a half he supplied the pulpit of the First church in Rochester, 165 being in that time added to the church by baptism. In 1867 he was called to the presidency and the chair of Theology in the seminary about to be organized at Chicago. Marked as had been his adaptation to the form of work assigned him at Rochester, for this at Chicago he was perhaps still better suited. While yet a youth he had become an enthusiastic student of metaphysics. Previous to entering college he had read "Rational Psychology" (not an easy book to master) through no less than five times, and knew pages of it by heart. This intellectual learning and capacity qualified him in an especial manner for a mastery of systematic theology; and his classes at Chicago enthusiastically testify to the grasp he has, and in their measure enables them to take, of the whole subject of Christian doctrine in its classification and in its verification. Although he has not as yet become known as an author, his lectures, alike in church history and in theology, have been made so complete and so full that, if they could be given to the world, they would rank with the most valued of the many books in these lines of theological study. As a preacher and lecturer Dr. Northrup renders eminent service, alike to the denomination and to the general cause of truth, in those departments of it which it is the fashion of these times especially to assail,—more particularly what concerns the relations of science and philosophy with the doctrines of the Christian faith.

Norton, Charles C., D.D., was born in Washington, Conn. He was brought up in the Protestant Episcopal Church. After his conversion his convictions of duty led him to unite with a Baptist church, and he was baptized into the fellowship of the church in Carmel, Putnam Co., N. Y. Soon after his connection with the church he was licensed to preach, and entered the University of New York, and afterwards the University of Rochester, from which he was graduated. He then entered the theological seminary there, and was graduated in 1854. In 1855 he accepted a call from the Sixth Street Baptist church in New York, where he was ordained and commenced his ministerial work. His connection with that church continued nine years, during which a pressing church debt was removed, and about 400 converts were added to it by baptism. For the past seventeen years he has been the successful pastor of the Central Park Baptist church of New York. He is a fine scholar and an able preacher. The honorary degree of D.D. was conferred on him by Shurtleff College. During his ministry he has baptized 704.

Norton, Judge E. H., was born in Logan Co., Ky., Nov. 21, 1821. He entered Centre College, at

JUDGE E. H. NORTON.

Danville, at seventeen years of age. In 1842 he graduated from the law department of Transylvania University, and located in Platte City, Mo., and rapidly built up a legal practice. In 1852 he was elected circuit judge over a district of seven counties. He was re-elected in 1857 without opposition, and served until sent to Congress, in 1861. At this time he was elected to the State convention to consider the relations of Missouri to the general government. In that body he opposed the ordinance of secession. In 1875 he was elected a member of the convention which framed the present constitution of Missouri, and was chairman of the committee on representative districts. In 1876 he was appointed to the Supreme bench by Gov. Hardin to fill a vacancy occasioned by the death of Judge H. M. Varis. He united with the Baptist Church, in Kentucky, when fourteen years of age. In 1853 he aided to organize a Baptist church in Platte City. He is a trustee of William Jewell College, and takes an interest in his denomination in the State. He is an upright and talented judge.

Nott, Rev. Abner Kingman, son of Rev. Han-

del G. and Lydia C. Nott, was born at Nashua, N. H., March 22, 1834, being the fourth son in a family of fifteen children. His early preparation for college was carried on partly under the tuition of Mr. J. H. Hanson, principal of the Waterville, Me., Academy, and partly under the instruction of his father. While thus engaged in study his conversion took place, in January, 1849. His later preparation for college was made at the Connecticut Literary Institution at Suffield, where he spent a little over one year. The question of his future vocation was settled when he entered Rochester University, in the fall of 1851. He was graduated in the class of 1855. Two years were devoted to theological study in the seminary at Rochester. His life both in college and in the seminary was one of constant and unceasing activity, for he was largely dependent on his own efforts to secure the funds needed for the payment of his bills. He preached, taught, and lectured, and thus acquired a remarkable facility as a public speaker. He preached the first time for the First Baptist church, New York, in the fall of 1856, and Dec. 29, 1856, was unanimously called to the pastorate of the church as the successor of Rev. Dr. Spencer H. Cone. This call he accepted, and a few weeks after his graduation, in July, 1857, was ordained. With the most brilliant prospects before him, and in the midst of a career of usefulness such as few young ministers are permitted to see, he was suddenly

REV. ABNER KINGMAN NOTT.

called to his reward while bathing near Perth Amboy, N. J., July 8, 1859. His goodness, intellectual powers, and eloquence gave him immense popularity in New York City, and made his death a public calamity.

Nott, Rev. Richard M., died at Wakefield, Mass., Dec. 21, 1880, after several months of suffering from extreme nervous prostration. He was born in Nashua, N. H., in March, 1831, where his father, Rev. Handel G. Nott, was then a prominent Congregational minister, settled over the leading church in that rapidly-growing place, from which situation he retired a few years later upon becoming a Baptist, in which character his first settlement was over the Federal Street, now Clarendon Street, Baptist church, Boston. At the age of eleven years Richard was converted, and soon after baptized by his father. He graduated at Waterville College when about nineteen years old. During the next five years he taught school in Red Creek, N. Y., three years, and Calais, Me., two years. Then he entered the theological seminary at Rochester, where he graduated in 1859, and entered immediately upon the pastorate of the First Baptist church in Rochester, N. Y., to which he had been called several months before his graduation. In this important position he continued six years. During this time he wrote the exceedingly interesting memoir of his younger brother, A. Kingman Nott, who suddenly closed in death a most brilliant earthly career in July, 1859, while pastor of the First Baptist church in New York City. At length his health failed, and his appreciating people sent him abroad for recuperation, but he never regained the physical vigor then lost. After his return from his foreign tour, having resigned at Rochester, he labored three years at Atlanta, Ga., where he was successful in gathering what is now the Second Baptist church in that city. Next he was pastor of the church in Aurora, Ill., three years. In 1872 he was called to the pastoral charge of the church in Wakefield, Mass., which he accepted and held about two years, when he resigned; but he continued to reside there until his death, supplying most of the time since his resignation the church in Brookville, formerly South Randolph, where his labors were highly valued, and a good work was done by him. In the summer of 1880 his health so failed that he was obliged to abandon his supply at Brookville, and also his valuable work in the Sunday-school department of *The Watchman*, the "Lesson Helps," which were very satisfactorily prepared by him. After this he gradually declined, till his earthly end was reached at the age of nearly fifty years. He was a superior scholar and a clear thinker. His early promise was uncommon. Few men were his equals in critical scholarship and logical acumen. He would have graced a position as a professor or president of a college or a theological institution. In the Boston

Ministers' Meeting, which he constantly attended, he was justly esteemed as a most serviceable member. Probably there was no place during the last five or six years of his life in which he appeared to better advantage than there. His utterances were real contributions, the great worth of which was readily conceded by all his brethren, among whom he is greatly missed.

Nova Scotia, New Brunswick, Prince Edward Island, and Newfoundland, Historical Sketch of the Baptists in.—From the cession of Acadia,—Nova Scotia and New Brunswick were originally included under this designation,—by France to Great Britain, in 1713 till 1776, when Henry Alline, the celebrated New Light preacher, entered on his fervid, trumpet-toned, evangelistic ministry, a dead formalism in religion almost universally prevailed in these provinces, with only here and there a faint glimmer of evangelical doctrine and spiritual experience.

But amid this moral desolation three or four Baptist ministers appeared almost simultaneously in Acadia,—Rev. John Sutton, with a company of emigrants from New Jersey, settled at Newport, Nova Scotia, in 1760, and there preached and baptized converts, and Daniel Dimock also. Rev. James Sutton, brother of John, was also at Newport. Rev. Ebenezer Moulton, of South Brimfield, Mass., came with the first settlers to Yarmouth, Nova Scotia, in 1761, and preached among them, and baptized a Mrs. Burgess, and probably other converts ; and his preaching subsequently in Horton, Nova Scotia, was attended with great success. Rev. Nathan Mason, with a number of Baptists in church order, emigrated from South Swanzey, Mass., and settled at Sackville, New Brunswick, in 1763. No church, however, appears to have been formed here by either of them, and in a few years they returned to their own country.

In 1776, Henry Alline came forth from obscurity like John the Baptist to prepare the way of the Lord ; many were converted under his ministry, and churches, composed of Baptists and Pedobaptists, were formed. The time, however, soon came for a distinct Baptist movement.

The pioneer Baptist church of the Maritime Provinces was formed of ten members, at Horton, Nova Scotia, Oct. 29, 1778. Rev. Nicholas Pierson, one of their number, was ordained as their pastor Nov. 5, 1778. The Second Baptist church in the provinces was formed at Halifax, Nova Scotia, in 1795, Rev. John Burton being pastor. The Third church was organized at Newport, Nova Scotia, in August, 1799; and the Fourth Baptist church was organized at Sackville, New Brunswick, in October, 1799, Rev. Joseph Crandall being ordained their pastor. Six others must have been formed previous to 1800.

The *Nova Scotia and New Brunswick Baptist Association*, the first in these provinces, was formed at Lower Granville, Nova Scotia, June 23, 1800, and comprised ten churches,—Upper Granville, Lower Granville, Digby, Digby Neck, Yarmouth, Cornwallis, Horton, Newport, Chester, and Sackville. Mixed communion was allowed for a time in some of these churches, but was soon discontinued.

The ministers who united in forming this Association were Thomas Handley Chipman, James Manning, Enoch Towner, Harris Harding, Edward Manning, Theodore Seth Harding, Joseph Dimock, and Joseph Crandall.

These churches, located thus widely apart in the two provinces, were true Baptist Christian centres, whence spiritual knowledge and influence were diffused through the surrounding communities ; and the ministers were true watchmen and evangelists, who bore abroad the torch of divine truth and the message of the gospel to guide the perishing to Christ.

The Baptist denomination, whose origin in these provinces has now been briefly traced, is a large and influential body ; and the movements and events which will now be mentioned will indicate its progress, and also the means of its further expansion.

Organized home missionary efforts were originated at the meeting of the Nova Scotia and New Brunswick Association in 1815, and were immediately followed by the most encouraging success, and home mission work has ever since been carried on in Nova Scotia and New Brunswick with great spiritual results.

The Nova Scotia and New Brunswick Association, composed of 31 churches, with 1827 members, and 22 ministers, was divided into two in 1821, the churches in Nova Scotia forming one Association, and those in New Brunswick forming the other. As in 1810 the membership of the Association was 924, the above figures show that it was nearly doubled in eleven years.

In 1825, Rev. Dr. Tupper, from Nova Scotia, and Rev. Joseph Crandall, from New Brunswick, evangelized on Prince Edward Island, and were the first associated Baptist ministers to labor in that gem of the St. Lawrence, though Rev. A. Crawford, a Scotch Baptist, had successfully commenced operations there as early as 1811.

In 1825, 1826, and 1838, Rev. Joseph Dimock evangelized for several months in Cape Breton, and with the happiest results. Now our home missionary enterprise is one of the most interesting and important of the denomination, and the field is as large as the three provinces and Newfoundland.

The use of the press for denominational and Christian purposes indicates life and progress.

The Nova Scotia and New Brunswick *Baptist Magazine* was commenced in St. John, New Brunswick, in 1827, and continued to be the organ of the denomination in the provinces till 1836, when the *Christian Messenger*, published weekly at Halifax, Nova Scotia, took its place.

In 1847 the *Christian Visitor* was issued at St. John, New Brunswick, as the organ of the denomination in that province. Both these papers continue as Baptist organs, and have been very influential in promoting denominational interests.

Education.—The Baptist Association at Horton in 1828 adopted measures for establishing an institution of learning for our youth, and especially with a view to the proper training of young men called of God to the gospel ministry ; and as a result Horton Academy was opened in May, 1829, with more than 40 pupils, under charge of Rev. Asahel Chapin as principal.

In 1833 the New Brunswick Baptist Association originated a similar movement ; and as a result the Baptist Seminary at Fredericton was opened in January, 1836, with Rev. F. W. Miles as principal.

In the autumn of 1838 circumstances in Nova Scotia impelled the Baptists to make a further advance in the work of higher education ; and Acadia College sprung from the resolve then taken, and was opened in January, 1839, with Rev. E. A. Crawley and Rev. John Pryor as professors, to which Prof. Isaac Chipman was added a year later, and continued his valuable services until he was drowned in the basin of the Minas, in June, 1852. Notwithstanding opposition, difficulties, and loss, Acadia College has grown and attained a leading position among the colleges of these provinces. It has now an endowment of $84,112.46, with other sources of income, and six professors, with Rev. Dr. Sawyer as president. Though the college building at Wolfville was destroyed by fire in December, 1877, a new edifice soon adorned College Hill, flanked on the east by Acadia Seminary, a high school for young ladies, and by Horton Collegiate Academy on the west. The Baptists of New Brunswick and Prince Edward Island have an equal share with those of Nova Scotia in the ownership and government of these institutions.

Foreign Missions.—The organized movement to send out missionaries to the heathen world commenced, like that for home missions in 1815, at Chester in 1838, and in this action the New Brunswick Baptist Association cordially concurred, and Rev. R. E. Burpe, of the latter province, was accordingly sent out to Burmah in 1845 by the Baptists of these provinces,—their first missionary to the heathen. The denomination has now four missions established among the Teloogoos, with native preachers and assistants, under the direction of the missionaries.

The New Brunswick Baptist Association, comprising 50 churches, with 4806 members, and 29 ministers, was divided in 1847 into two Associations,—the Eastern and Western. The figures indicate an increase of over ninefold in the membership of that body in twenty-five years.

The Nova Scotia Baptist Association, comprising 72 churches, with 8967 members, and 54 ministers, was also divided in 1850 into three Associations,—the Western, Central, and Eastern.

In July, 1868, the Prince Edward Island Baptist Association was organized, with 13 churches, containing a membership of 600, dismissed for the purpose from the Nova Scotia Eastern Association, and the membership of the denomination in that island is 1622, or nearly three times what it was twelve years ago.

Union.—The leaders of the Baptist denomination in these provinces provided for the union of all the churches and Associations in denominational work, and through their wise forethought the Baptist Convention of Nova Scotia, New Brunswick, and Prince Edward Island was organized in the city of St. John, New Brunswick, in September, 1846. This Convention is now the most influential of the Baptist organizations in the Maritime Provinces. To its direction and management are committed the great public benevolent enterprises of the denomination,—home missions, education, and foreign missions,—and the greatest care is exercised to conduct matters wisely and efficiently, and yet not to intrench on great denominational principles.

Revivals of a genuine type have all along been a vast means of growth, and they are still needed to promote healthful enlargement. Our churches and denomination should aspire wisely and well to realize the highest ideal of Christian life, activity, and progress.

Newfoundland.—There are a few Baptists on this great island, but no Baptist church or minister. Revs. J. B. McDonald, M.D., and George Armstrong, spent a few weeks in missionary work there in 1875, and Rev. George Armstrong evangelized for nine weeks in 1879.

The following figures show the numerical progress of the Baptist denomination in the Maritime Provinces for the past eighty years :

Year.	Churches.	Ministers.	Members.
1800	10	8	*600
1810	14	9	924
1820	29	19	1,785
1830	70	40	4,633
1840	115	64	9,041
1850			13,773
1860	260	139	21,579
1870	257	145	27,460
1880	356	195	36,700

* About.

Novatians, The.—Novatian, the distinguished founder of the community that bore his name, is known among Greek ecclesiastical writers as Novatus. He was not Novatus of Carthage, a presbyter of that city, who sorely vexed the imperious soul of Cyprian, and who came to Rome and united with Novatian in efforts to maintain gospel purity in the churches.

Novatian, before he professed conversion, was a philosopher of remarkable ability, culture, eloquence, and powers of persuasion ; he was a natural leader of men. When attacked by a dangerous disease, from which death was apprehended, in accordance with the opinion then commonly held by Christians, it was judged that he should be baptized to make heaven certain, and, as his weakness rendered immersion impossible without risking his immediate death, he was subjected, on his couch, to a profuse application of water. We are not informed that Novatian desired this ceremony himself, without any persuasions from his alarmed friends. The writer was once sent for to see a dying lady, and, after praying with her, was earnestly pressed by a follower of Irish Romanism, the perverted faith of St. Patrick the Baptist, " to *regenerate* her ;" he declined to exercise the powers of the Spirit of God and the functions of a Pedobaptist minister; had he yielded, the lady was in a condition in which she could not be held responsible for the act. And it is not improbable that this was the situation of Novatian. He was spared by the providence of God for a mighty work in the churches, and when restored to health he became very active in advancing the interests of Christianity in Rome.

At that period the church, in the capital of the world, as Eusebius records, had 46 presbyters, 14 deacons and subdeacons, 50 minor ecclesiastical officials, and widows and sick and indigent persons, numbering in all 1500, whose support had to be provided for. And partly to assist in bearing this burden, but chiefly through a lack of faith and of complete consecration to God, the door of the church was kept very wide for the admission of unconverted professors, and when these persons betrayed the Saviour by sacrificing to idols in times of persecution, their conduct was excused by their lax brethren ; and the excommunication, necessarily pronounced upon them immediately after their apostasy, was speedily removed.

Cornelius, a Roman presbyter, with an eager eye to the support to be gathered from restored apostates, strongly advocated their forgiveness by the church. Novatian very strenuously resisted it; and when a successor to Bishop Fabianus was to be elected, Cornelius was properly made a predecessor of a long line of coming popes, who loved gold more than anything in the Christian religion.

Novatian was condemned by Cornelius and by all his episcopal friends; and the bishop of Rome sent letters everywhere, bringing the most grievous charges against him, and giving the names and positions of the bishops who united with him in his efforts to crush the first great reformer.

Novatian had been made a presbyter by Fabianus against the custom of the church, for, as Cornelius says, in Eusebius,* " It was not lawful that one baptized in his sick-bed by aspersion, as he was, should be promoted to any order of the clergy. . . . If, indeed, it be proper to say that one like him did receive baptism." But this only shows his extraordinary talents and influence.

After Cornelius became bishop Novatian was elevated to the same office by three Italian bishops, and at once founded the purer community, for whose advancement he labored with great success until martyrdom removed him from the presence of wicked church members in full ecclesiastical standing.

Among the charges brought by Cornelius against Novatian, a list of which can be found in Eusebius, was an accusation of cowardice for refusing to perform the duties of his ministerial office in a time of persecution. Novatian set up a new community in defiance of Cornelius and of nearly all the Christian bishops on earth; and in this he showed unusual courage. Opposition to the treachery, charged upon himself by Cornelius, was the chief instrument which he used to establish his pure church, and it is not in human nature to believe that any man could found a new community in Rome itself by denunciations of a cowardly crime of which he himself had given a conspicuous example. Besides, he left the world as a martyr.

It was customary in the time of Ambrose, when the minister distributed the Lord's Supper to the faithful, to say, " The body of Christ," and the recipient answered, " Amen."† Cornelius, in the same calumnious letter in Eusebius, states that Novatian, when he gave a portion of the Eucharist to a communicant, instead of permitting him to say " Amen," according to the usage no doubt then in existence, seized his hand in both of his hands, before he partook of the symbolic bread, and made him " swear by the body and blood of our Saviour, Jesus Christ, that he would never desert him, nor turn to Cornelius." This story carries its own refutation; the idea that the founder of the purest Christian community then in existence should resort to such an infamous procedure is simply incredible. Cornelius, in the same connection, makes slanderous statements about the extraordinary ambition of Novatian, which have come down to us through the " Ecclesiastical History" of Euse-

bius; and his vanity is frequently given as the motive that led to his assumption of the bishop's office, and to the reformation inaugurated by Novatian.

The Novatians called themselves Kathari, or Puritans. The corner-stone of the denomination was purity of church membership. Novatian charged Cornelius and his followers with dishonoring the church of God, and destroying its divine character by admitting apostates into its membership. He maintained that those who had sacrificed to the idols to save their lives should never be permitted to come to the Lord's table again. This theory became popular with the saintly heroes and heroines, who suffered terribly at the hands of Christ's persecuting enemies, but whose lives were spared. And all true Christians felt a strong leaning towards the holy religion advocated and exhibited by Novatian and his followers. Socrates,‡ a candid and intelligent Greek historian, says, " Novatus (Novatian), a presbyter of the Romish Church, separated from it because Cornelius, the bishop, received into communion believers who had sacrificed (to idols) during the persecution which the emperor Decius had raised against the church. . . . On being afterwards elevated to the episcopacy by such prelates as entertained similar sentiments, he wrote to all the churches, insisting that they should not admit to the sacred mysteries those who had sacrificed (to idols), but exhorting them to repentance, leave the pardon of their offense to God, who has the power to forgive all sin. . . . The exclusion of those who, after baptism, had committed any deadly sin from the mysteries appeared to some a cruel and merciless course; but others thought it just and necessary for the maintenance of discipline, and the promotion of greater devotedness of life. In the midst of the agitation of this important question letters arrived from Cornelius the bishop promising indulgence to delinquents after baptism. . . . Those who had pleasure in sin, encouraged by the license thus granted them, took occasion from it to revel in every species of criminality." The Novatians permanently excluded from their community all who were guilty of deadly sins and second marriages, as well as those who sacrificed to idols to save their lives; and they regarded the church universal as having lost the character of a church of Christ by receiving such persons into her membership. As a result of this conviction they baptized again all who came from the old church to them. Their baptism was immersion, the " pouring around" of Novatian on his sick-bed is the only transaction of that kind in their history now known; and as their leader suffered so much from the unscriptural performance, his followers had little encouragement to imitate such an unfortunate example.

---

* Eccles. Hist., lib. vi. cap. 43.

† Ambros. De Sacram., lib. iv. cap. 5.

‡ Eccles. Hist., lib. iv. cap. 28.

The general doctrines of the Novatians were in perfect harmony with those received by the church universal; they only differed from it on questions of discipline, and chiefly on the great subject of consecration to God.

It is creditable to the piety of the centuries during which the Novatians existed that great numbers of Christians adopted their sentiments and their fold; though hated, wickedly calumniated, and fiercely persecuted for a long time, they spread, and they found adherents not only in rural regions, but in great cities and in the palaces of the emperor. Speaking of the law of Constantine the Great by which heretics were forbidden to meet "in their own houses of prayer, in private houses, or in public places, but were compelled to enter into communion with the church universal," Sozomen says, "The Novatians alone, who had obtained good leaders, and who entertained the same opinions respecting the divinity as the Catholic Church, formed a large sect from the beginning, and were not decreased in point of numbers by this law. The emperor, I believe, relaxed the rigor of the enactment in their favor. . . . Acesius, who was then the bishop of the Novatians in Constantinople, was much esteemed by the emperor on account of his virtuous life."*

Novatian himself was a man of fervent piety; and his life after his conversion was above reproach, unless when accusations came from a calumniator whose charges were incapable of proof. He was the author of works on "The Passover," "Circumcision," "The Sabbath," "High-Priests," "The Trinity," and on other subjects. He had many distinguished men among his disciples. His community spread very widely, and enjoyed special prosperity in Phrygia; but declined rapidly in the fifth century. The Novatians, as a people, were an honor to Christianity, and their teachings and example exercised a powerful restraint upon the growing corruptions of the old church.

The Novatians commenced their denominational life when the baptism of an unconscious babe was unknown outside of Africa; and there it had a limited, if not a doubtful, existence. Indeed, if a celebrated letter of Cyprian, about a council of bishops, said to have been held in Carthage half a dozen years after Novatian set up his banner of church purity, be a forgery, and the supposition is by no means an improbable one, unconscious infant baptism has no proof of its existence in the literature of the world. The infant rite, according to the letter of Cyprian just referred to, had Cyprian for its patron, and as he had shown the utmost hostility to Novatian, he and his followers would not be

* Eccles. Hist., lib. ii. cap. 32.

very eager to adopt a ceremony of which his letter, if genuine, shows that he was the special friend. These considerations, together with the holiness of life demanded by Novatian churches, have led many persons to regard them as Baptists. Of the truth of this opinion in the early history of this people there can be no doubt; and that the majority of their churches baptized only instructed persons to the end of their history is in the highest degree probable.

Nowlin, Rev. David W., was born in Pittsylvania Co., Va., April 11, 1812, and died in Montgomery Co., Mo., Oct. 17, 1865. He was educated for the bar, and was noted for clear views of the law, and for a sound judgment. He taught the Bible in his schools where he gave instructions in science, because he believed it to be the foundation of sound civil law. Hence when he was converted he was familiar with Scriptural knowledge. He found the Saviour in 1849, under the preaching of Rev. William Vardeman, by whom he was baptized, in November, 1851, into the fellowship of Zion church. In 1856 he was ordained by Revs. Jas. E. Welch, W. Vardeman, and the venerable J. T. Johnson. Mr. Nowlin's culture, talent, and piety made him exceedingly acceptable as a preacher. He was frequently moderator of his Association. He was honored and loved as a faithful and successful minister of Jesus.

Nugent, Deacon E. J., was born on the 13th of March, 1812, near Philadelphia, Pa. He grew to the age of sixteen and a half years without religious training. In the year 1831 a lady invited him to accompany her to hear a sermon in the First Baptist church of Philadelphia. A stranger, Rev. N. Colver, preached, and for the first time in his life he was awakened to an alarming consciousness of his sinfulness, and was so exercised that he could not work for several days. He was enabled through grace to repent of sin and to embrace Jesus Christ by a living faith, and was baptized by the pastor, W. T. Brantly, Sr., D.D., with thirty-one others, in the river Delaware. He was immediately set to work as a teacher in the Sunday-school, where he served the church for some years. At this period he was led to consider seriously the impropriety of using intoxicating liquors as a beverage, and he has been an earnest advocate of the cause of temperance ever since. He regarded the Lord's day as a sacred time for moral and religious improvement, bodily rest and recuperation, and under the influence of this view he was early led to fixed habits of constant attendance upon the social and public worship of God. In connection with others he conducted religious services in the suburbs of the city. In March, 1835, he removed to Springfield, O. Mr. Nugent assisted in organizing a Baptist prayer-meeting and Sunday-school, and in January, 1837, a church was formed consisting of thirteen members, of which he was chosen a deacon. The church continued public worship, meeting in school-houses until permitted to worship in an old court-house, where, in the year 1841, a series of meetings was commenced, resulting in the first great revival ever experienced in the town. Over 100 were converted, about 50 of whom joined the Baptist church. The deacon, with a few others, was engaged in conducting meetings for prayer and exhortation in country school-houses, thereby creating an interest in the farming community for the Baptist church. This custom, under the blessing of God, was the secret of the remarkable growth and influence of this church. The deacon afterward wrote a history of the church.

About this time he asked a young Presbyterian brother whom he had heard declare that infant baptism was taught in the Scriptures to point out to him some of the proof texts, and promised to pay him handsomely for his time if he would produce them. But the young man never demanded the reward. Conversations were continued on the subject for several months, resulting in his union with the Baptist Church. On the day he was baptized he preached a sermon on the subject of baptism, giving reasons for his change of views, and was baptized in Buck's Creek by Rev. J. L. Moore, and was licensed to preach the gospel by the Baptist Church. That young man is now the beloved and honored superintendent of Baptist Missions of the city of Philadelphia, Rev. James French. The deacon was either a teacher or superintendent of the Sunday-school during his residence in the place. When it became possible for the church at Springfield to build a house, he was appointed on a building committee of two, and they succeeded in erecting a very commodious brick church edifice and parsonage. Mr. Nugent continued his membership there until the church numbered over 300.

In 1852 he removed to Marysville, O. There being no Baptist church in the town, and only four Baptists, he commenced prayer-meetings in private houses.

In the month of March, 1865, he and his family removed to Ottawa, Kansas. The next day after reaching Ottawa was the Lord's day, and the deacon went to the Baptist Sunday-school and into the young men's Bible-class. On the following Sabbath he was appointed teacher of the same class. At the time he arrived in Ottawa the Baptist church had no edifice. The question of building one was discussed, and he was appointed on the building committee. A house was completed at a cost of $3700. In 1872 he was elected to a seat in the Kansas Legislature. He was also chosen to several offices of trust and honor in his own city. Mr. Nugent has led a godly and useful life.

Nugent, Deacon George, was born in Philadelphia, Pa., May 3, 1809. He received a liberal education in Clermont Academy, in the vicinity of the city. Many of his fellow-students have risen

DEACON GEORGE NUGENT.

to distinguished positions; among these may be mentioned the Hon. John Welsh, late minister to England. His father was George Nugent, a highly respected and influential merchant of Philadelphia.

At the age of twenty-three he was converted, and from careful study of the Scriptures was led to unite with the Lower Merion Baptist church, under the pastoral care of the Rev. Dr. Horatio Gates Jones, by whom he was baptized in 1832. From that time he has proved himself a faithful and devoted Christian. He has been a deacon for more than forty years. While visiting among the poor, and witnessing the destitute and sad condition of many aged saints, he conceived the idea of a home for them. This thought was the primal inception of the Baptist Home. Originated by him, it has also received largely of his gifts.

He has been a member of the boards of the American Baptist Publication and Historical Societies for many years, and has also been long identified with the American Sunday-School Union as chairman of its Missionary Committee. He has taken great interest in the education and moral training of the young. Many churches have shared in his practical benevolence. He was one of the founders of the Second Baptist church, Germantown, and a large contributor to its funds. Of this community he is now a member.

Mr. Nugent is one of the leading citizens of Philadelphia,—public-spirited, benevolent, and universally respected.

Nunnally, Rev. G. A., was born in Walton Co., Ga., March 24, 1841. In youth he was very precocious. At fourteen he entered the University of Georgia, and was the youngest graduate that ever received a diploma at the State University. Before his nineteenth year he was elected Professor of Mathematics in Hamilton College, and for ten years he was principal of Johnson Female Institute. He entered the ministry in 1865, preaching in the same field for eleven years. In 1876 he was elected pastor of the Rome Baptist church, which position he still holds. He is a trustee of Mercer University, and, though young, one of the most influential ministers of Georgia. He is a fine orator, and a man of genius. As a preacher he is surpassed by few, and as a worker his zeal, energy, and capacity make him pre-eminent. In the Appalachee Association, of which he was formerly a member, his influence was unbounded, and he was frequently its moderator.

Mr. Nunnally is a thorough friend of education, missions, and the Sunday-school, and he is possessed of great administrative ability. His fine command of language and brilliancy of intellect make him an able and ready debater, and, with his zeal and earnestness, give him great influence in our denominational gatherings.

Nutter, Rev. David, a useful minister in Nova Scotia and New Brunswick, was ordained at St. John, New Brunswick, June 24, 1819; organized the Baptist church at Windsor, Nova Scotia; labored as a missionary in Canso, Greysborough, and Antigonish; organized the Baptist church at Liverpool, Nova Scotia, in 1821; was pastor of the Baptist church in Portland, St. John; died Jan. 15, 1873.

Nutting, James Walton, LL.D., was one of the first graduates from Windsor College, Nova Scotia; was bred to the bar, and became prothonatory of the Supreme Court of Nova Scotia. His conversion was thorough; he was baptized at Halifax, 1827, and became a member of Granville Street church in that city; was the originator of the system of education among the Baptists of Nova Scotia, which took form at the Baptist Association at Horton in 1828. He was a warm friend of Horton Academy and Acadia College; was co-editor with Mr. Ferguson of the *Christian Messenger* until his death, in 1870, aged eighty-three years. Dr. Nutting possessed great integrity of character, and was universally beloved.

O.

Oates, Rev. Samuel, charged with Murder for Baptizing a Lady, who died soon after, was a minister of popular talents, and a disputant whom it was better for antagonists to shun. Visiting Essex, England, in 1646, he preached in several places, and baptized large numbers of people. This created great indignation among Pedobaptists, and especially among the ministers. They endeavored to stir up the magistrates to arrest Mr. Oates, but they had no charge against him, and they were afraid to imprison him.

Among those baptized by Mr. Oates was a young woman, named Anne Martin, who died a few weeks after her baptism. This furnished the clergymen the charge which they required, and forthwith Mr. Oates was sent to jail, accused of murdering Anne Martin by administering immersion to her. He was actually tried for his life at Chelmsford assizes for this dreadful crime. In that day in the writings of Pedobaptists immersion was frequently denounced as a very dangerous practice; and some branded the Baptists as " a cruel and murdering sect for using it." If the trial against Mr. Oates had been successful it would not only have sent him to the gallows, but it would have been a heavy blow at the administration of the Saviour's only baptism. Great efforts, Mr. Crosby tells us, were made to secure the conviction of Oates; it was asserted that he held Miss Martin so long in the water that she immediately became sick, and stated on her death-bed that the dipping caused her fatal illness; all the falsehoods told about her case, on the trial, were completely exposed. Several witnesses were produced, and among them her own mother, whose testimony proved that she had better health for several days after her baptism than she had enjoyed for years before.

Crosby mentions an essay of Sir John Floyer to prove the advantages of bathing in cold water, in which he gives a catalogue of diseases for which it is a remedy. Sir John closes his essay by observing " that the Church of England continued the use of immersion longer than any Christian church in the West. For the Eastern Church yet uses it; and our church (the Episcopal) still recommends the dipping of infants in her Rubric, to which, I believe, the English Church will at last return, when physic has given them a clear proof by divers experiments that cold baths are both safe and useful. And," he says, " they did great injury to their own children, and to all posterity, who first introduced the alteration of this truly ancient ceremony of immersion, and were the occasion of a degenerate, sickly, and tender race ever since." (Crosby's History of the English Baptists, i. 236–240. London, 1738.)

Ober, Levi E., M.D., a native of Vermont, was born at Rockingham, Windham Co., July 31, 1819, and is the son of Wm. and Fanny (Fairbanks) Ober. In 1830 his father's family moved to Claridon, Geauga, O. Here Levi remained on his father's farm until eighteen years of age, in the summer assisting his father and during the winter attending school. He continued his literary and scientific studies, interspersed with manual labor, until 1845, when he began the study of medicine with Dr. Storm Rosa, of Painesville, O. He took medical lectures at the Western Reserve College, Cleveland, and at the Eclectic Medical College, Cincinnati, from which last-named college he received a diploma in March, 1850. He subsequently attended a course of lectures in the Jefferson Medical College of Philadelphia. Dr. Ober began practice in Moline, Ill., in 1850. He came to La Crosse, Wis., in 1857, where he has since resided. He stands at the head of his profession in the State. He has a very extensive practice, reaching far beyond the city of his residence. In 1872 he went to Europe, traveling extensively in England, Belgium, Switzerland, and parts of Germany, and spending the winter of 1872–73 in Italy. He availed himself of every facility for visiting hospitals, attending lectures, and for making the personal acquaintance of the most eminent medical men in the old country, that he might extend and perfect his medical knowledge.

He was one of the founders of the Illinois Homœopathic Medical Association, and also a founder of the Wisconsin Homœopathic Society, and has been president of both organizations. Once he was called upon to preside over the National Society.

But in Wisconsin Dr. Ober is no less widely known as an eminent medical practitioner than as an earnest and active Christian. He is a member of the Baptist church in La Crosse, one of its deacons, and one of its large-hearted, liberal supporters. In all the religious and benevolent work of his denomination in the State he takes a deep interest. He is a member of the board of the State Convention, and is nearly always present at its annual meetings.

Offer, George, was born in London in 1796.

In early life he became a member of the Baptist church at Bow, and subsequently attached himself to the congregation at Mare Street, Hackney. Although actively engaged in business during the greater part of his life, and rendering valuable public services as a magistrate of London, and as member of the metropolitan board of works, he devoted himself with such ardor and persistence to the history of two books,—the English Bible and the "Pilgrim's Progress,"—that he became a chief authority with all students and inquirers, with book-buyers and booksellers. His collection of Bibles and Testaments, and of the works of the Puritan divines, especially of John Bunyan, was without a rival. Mr. Offer's library was the resort of scholars and divines of all ranks and denominations. He edited the works of Bunyan in three volumes, and wrote a memoir which is allowed to be the most complete biography of that illustrious man. He also wrote the " Life of William Tyndale," published by Bagster. He left in manuscript the largest production of his pen, entitled " The History of the Great Bible," embracing the history of Coverdale's translation, Tyndale's, Cranmer's, and the Genevan, each profusely illustrated with fac-similes carefully made by himself. His death took place at his home in London, Aug. 4, 1864.

Ogilvie, Rev. John, was born in Stafford Co., Va., in the year 1793. He seemed inclined at different times to prepare himself for the profession of the law, and again for that of medicine. He taught school for a short time in Culpeper County, then at Jeffersonton, and subsequently in Fauquier County, having taken charge of the New Baltimore Academy. In early life he was quite skeptical in his views, but in 1823, having heard a sermon by Rev. C. George, his conscience was quickened, he saw the folly of his views, and was led to give himself to Christ. One month after his baptism he was licensed to preach, and one year after was ordained to the work of the ministry and became pastor of the Goose Creek (Pleasant Vale) church. With this church he labored most faithfully for more than twenty-five years. Teaching school and at the same time preaching regularly for three or four churches, his labors were necessarily very onerous, and his exposure to all kinds of weather terribly exhausting. The great majority of the Baptist ministers of Virginia twenty-five years ago, supplying as they did five or six churches, often spent at least one-third of their time on horseback, riding to and from their various appointments for preaching, and Mr. Ogilvie had his full share of these wearying labors. As a preacher, he was endowed with rare gifts. His mind was strongly logical, and he could divest a subject of all its ambiguities and present it so plainly to his hearers as to make the most abstruse subjects clear to the humblest capacities. One who knew him well has said that he never heard him preach a sermon from which a man who had never heard the gospel before, and should never hear it again, might not learn enough about the plan of salvation by the cross of Christ to save his soul. In all the relations of life his character was irreproachable. As a citizen, a neighbor, and a friend he was esteemed by all who knew him, while as a Christian he was revered for his unaffected piety and devotion. He died June 2, 1849, in the fifty-sixth year of his age, and his memory is fragrant among the people who knew him and loved him so well.

Ohio Baptists.—The first church of any denomination in Ohio, or the Northwestern Territory, as it was originally called, was a Baptist church. This was organized at Columbia, then five miles above Cincinnati, and now a part of that city, in 1790. A year and a half previous to this twenty-five persons from Pennsylvania and New Jersey had come down the Ohio River to this point. Six of these were Baptists. This number had increased to nine, when Rev. Stephen Gano, subsequently pastor of the First church of Providence, R. I., who was then visiting the colony, one Saturday at the house of Benjamin Davis, presided over their organization, and the next day baptized three believers. The first pastor of the church was Rev. John Smith, who afterwards became a member of the Senate of the United States. A meeting-house—the first Protestant place of worship in Ohio—was built in 1793.

From this point Baptists soon began to scatter through lower Ohio. After Wayne's victory over the Indians, in 1794, it was safer to leave the river, and the Miami valley rapidly became settled. A Baptist church was formed at Staunton, near Troy, in 1804. About the same time the King's Creek and Union churches were organized, as were also the churches at Middletown and Lebanon. In 1808 the Columbia church removed to Duck Creek, and has ever since borne the name of the Duck Creek church. The Miami Association, containing originally but four churches, was formed in 1797, and for several years included all the Baptist churches in Ohio.

The origin of Baptist churches in other parts of the State was somewhat later. One of the oldest of the churches is that at Marietta. The First church, Dayton, O., was constituted and recognized in 1824, though as early as 1806 there are traces of Baptists in the place, and for some time there had been preaching by traveling ministers. The First church in Cleveland was organized in 1833, the First church in Columbus three or four years earlier, and the First church, Toledo, not until 1853. The oldest Association after the Miami is the Scioto, and the next oldest the Mad River.

The progress of the denomination in Ohio was greatly retarded by what is known as the Campbellite schism in 1827–30, which divided a number of churches and carried away some prominent ministers, notably Rev. D. S. Burnett, of Dayton. In the reaction following this movement, Old-School or Anti-Mission tendencies were developed, which produced divisions and resulted in loss of numbers and power.

In later years, however, there has been great progress. The largest contributors to this have been the State Convention, established in May, 1826, Granville College, opened for students December, 1831, and the Education Society, organized in 1834. At present the Baptists in Ohio number 49,950. There are 633 churches and 469 ordained ministers. Connected with the churches there are 645 Sunday-schools, with 6800 officers and teachers, and 58,500 scholars. Granville, Licking Co., is the literary centre of the denomination, being the seat of Denison University, of which Rev. A. Owen, D.D., is president, and of a young ladies' institute, under the charge of Rev. D. Shepardson, D.D. There are other schools in the State also in which Baptists have a controlling interest, notably the Mount Auburn Young Ladies' Institute, Cincinnati, O., and Clermont Academy, in Clermont County.

Old-Landmarkism.—The following sketch was written at the editor's request by one of the ablest Baptist ministers in this country. His account of the opinions of all landmarkers is entirely reliable:

The origin of the term old-landmarkism was as follows: about the year 1850, Rev. J. R. Graves, editor of the *Tennessee Baptist*, published at Nashville, Tenn., began to advocate the position that Baptists cannot consistently recognize Pedobaptist preachers as gospel ministers. For several years he found but few to sympathize with this view. Among the few was Rev. J. M. Pendleton, then of Bowling Green, Ky., who in 1854 was requested by Mr. Graves to write an essay on this question, "Ought Baptists to recognize Pedobaptist preachers as gospel ministers?" The essay was published in four consecutive numbers of the aforesaid paper, and afterwards in the form of a tract. The title given to it by Mr. Graves was "An Old Landmark Reset." The title was considered appropriate, because there had been a time when ministerial recognition and exchange of pulpits between Baptists and Pedobaptists were unknown. This was an old landmark, but in the course of years it had fallen. When it was raised again it was called "an old landmark reset." Hence the term "old-landmarkism," and of late years, by way of abridgment, "landmarkism."

That the doctrine of landmarkism is not a novelty, as some suppose, is evident, because William Kiffin, of London, one of the noblest of English Baptists, advocated it in 1640, and with those who agreed with him formed a church, of which he was pastor till his death, in 1701,—a very long pastorate. These facts are taken from Cramp's "Baptist History," and he refers to Ivimey's "Life of Kiffin."

Benedict, in his "Fifty Years among the Baptists," in referring to the early part of this century, says, "At that time the exchange of pulpits between the advocates and the opponents of infant baptism was a thing of very rare occurrence, except in a few of the more distinguished churches in the Northern States. Indeed, the doctrine of non-intercourse, so far as ministerial services were concerned, almost universally prevailed between Baptists and Pedobaptists." pp. 94, 95.

Truly the old landmark once stood, and having fallen, it was deemed proper to reset it.

The doctrine of landmarkism is that baptism and church membership precede the preaching of the gospel, even as they precede communion at the Lord's table. The argument is that Scriptural authority to preach emanates, under God, from a gospel church; that as "a visible church is a congregation of baptized believers," etc., it follows that no Pedobaptist organization is a church in the Scriptural sense of the term, and that therefore Scriptural authority to preach cannot proceed from such an organization. Hence the non-recognition of Pedobaptist ministers, who are not interfered with, but simply let alone.

At the time the "Old Landmark Reset" was written the topic of non-ministerial intercourse was the chief subject of discussion. Inseparable, however, from the landmark view of this matter, is a denial that Pedobaptist societies are Scriptural churches, that Pedobaptist ordinations are valid, and that immersions administered by Pedobaptist ministers can be consistently accepted by any Baptist church. All these things are denied, and the intelligent reader will see why.

Olmstead, John W., D.D., was born in Saratoga Co., N. Y., Nov. 13, 1816. His parents were members of the Methodist Episcopal Church. When converted his convictions led him to the Baptists, and he was baptized in Schuylerville, N. Y., in 1836, by Rev. C. B. Keyes. He pursued academic studies in Johnstown, N. Y. The honorary degree of A.M. was conferred on him by Yale College, and afterwards that of D.D. by the University of Rochester. He was first, in 1837, settled over the Baptist church of Little Falls, N. Y., where he remained five years. He then became pastor in Chelsea, Mass., where he continued five years. In 1846 he became editor of the *Christian Reflector*, of Boston. In 1848 the *Watchman* was united with it, and he filled the editorial chair of the consolidated papers until 1877. His ability as a religious

journalist was fully demonstrated in his long and successful management of that paper. In 1878 he commenced the New York *Watch-Tower*, a popular Baptist paper, and he is confident of success. He held prominent positions in Roxbury, Mass., in educational work, and was on the executive committee of the Missionary Union. His life has been one of great usefulness and honor.

Olney, Edward, LL.D., Professor of Mathematics in the University of Michigan, and author

EDWARD OLNEY, LL.D.

of a complete set of mathematical text-books, is descended from the Rhode Island Olneys, and was born in Moreau, Saratoga Co., N. Y., July 24, 1827. During most of his childhood and youth he resided in Ohio. His early opportunities for an education were very slight, but he made the most of them. Beginning to teach at the age of nineteen, he prosecuted his own studies with great energy and success, and early became eminent as a teacher. From 1853 to 1863 he was Professor of Mathematics in Kalamazoo College, and acquired a reputation as teacher in this department almost unequaled. In 1863 he became professor in the State University, and still holds that position; but his interest in Kalamazoo College remains unabated. He is a member of its board of trustees, and among its most liberal supporters. He has the warmest interest in Sunday-school work, and is always ready to serve the temperance enterprise. From 1875 to 1879 he was president of the Baptist State Convention, and has since been its treasurer. Although not an ordained minister, he sometimes conducts religious services. No one would deny that his influence is very great, and always on the side of justice and religion. He was made A.M. by Madison University in 1853, and LL.D. by Kalamazoo College in 1874.

Oncken, Rev. John Gerhard.—No one will refuse to this eminent man the designation of

REV. JOHN GERHARD ONCKEN.

apostle of the German Baptists. His life being so intimately connected with the rise and progress of the Baptist denomination in Germany, the reader is referred to the account of them in this work, and this article will confine itself to some brief biographical data.

Mr. Oncken was born in Varel, in the grand duchy of Oldenburg, Jan. 26, 1800. In his youth he came to England, where, by the grace of God, he became a true Christian. Manifesting a peculiar fitness for evangelistic labors, he was sent to Germany in 1823 as a missionary of the British Continental Society,—a society formed in England for the purpose of spreading the gospel on the continent. Filled with zeal and fervent love, he went back to his native land a joyous herald of the truth which he had learned in a foreign clime. He first preached the gospel on the coasts of the German Ocean, in the cities of Hamburg and Bremen, and in the province of East Frisia. His strong religious convictions, his clear insight into the Word, united with a deep spirituality, a pleasing appearance, and considerable oratorical talent, gave him a welcome reception among the people everywhere. Many were converted, and a powerful religious move-

ment manifested itself in all that region. Mr. Oncken labored as a missionary of the British Continental Society till 1828, and then became the agent of the Edinburgh Bible Society.

As a result of faithful Bible study, Mr. Oncken gradually reached the conviction that baptism belongs only to believers, and that immersion is the only Scriptural mode of baptism. After having long waited for an opportunity to receive baptism, Mr. Oncken was at length baptized, together with six others, by Rev. Barnas Sears, then of Hamilton Institution, on the 22d of April, 1834, in the river Elbe, near Hamburg; these seven believers were the first fruit of thousands yet to follow. On the succeeding day these seven were constituted a church, the First German Baptist church in *modern* times; Mr. Oncken was chosen pastor.

Mr. Oncken's baptism created a great sensation in all circles where he was known, and the persecutions which he formerly endured now became still more violent. The clergy, in harmony with the police, were determined to destroy the work in its inception, but all their efforts proved unavailing. Mr. Oncken, full of love and zeal, proved himself a man of firm determination and undaunted courage; he could not be intimidated nor silenced; he paid no heed to the prohibitions of the authorities; he dreaded not the dungeon, and yielded not, even when incarcerated. Under God, the continuance and the prosperity of the work in Germany is due largely, first of all, to the endurance, fearlessness, and determination, and, secondly, to the untiring labors, of this remarkable man. From that day until now Mr. Oncken's life has been one of apostolic toil and blessed success in spreading the gospel through Germany.

Mr. Oncken has always remained pastor of the church in Hamburg, and has made Hamburg the centre of his evangelistic labors, being enabled to do this through the faithful aid of helpers like Koebner and Schauffler and others, who supplied the church in his absence. In addition to his evangelistic labors in Germany and adjoining countries, Mr. Oncken has frequently visited England in the interest of the German Baptist cause, and in 1853, by invitation of the executive committee of the American Baptist Missionary Union, he visited the United States, traveling extensively in the Northwestern as well as in the older States. On that memorable journey Mr. Oncken's life was wonderfully preserved in a fearful railroad accident at Norwalk, Conn. As a result of Mr. Oncken's visit the committee voted to aid the mission in erecting chapels to the extent of $8000 a year for five years.

Looking over his eventful and useful life, it may be said that Mr. Oncken's piety, courage, untiring energy, and his strong organizing faculty have been the foundation-stones of his great success. His influence over the churches and pastors in Germany has been powerful. They have looked upon him as a father, have greatly revered him, and highly respected his judgment. The weakness of advanced age hinders Mr. Oncken engaging any longer in his loved employ; but while he still lingers amid the scenes of his former conflict, throngs of blessings cheer his declining days, and when he shall be no longer walking among his brethren, the memory of his faithful and successful service will be embalmed among the Baptists of Germany in all succeeding generations.

O'Neall, Chief-Justice John Belton, was born on the 10th of April, 1793, near Bobo's Mills, in

CHIEF-JUSTICE JOHN BELTON O'NEALL.

Newberry District, S. C. He was the son of Hugh O'Neall and Ann Kelly, his wife,—his ancestors on both sides being of ancient Irish families. In his youth he had facilities for education that were unusual for that period. In February, 1811, he entered the Junior class of South Carolina College, and in December, 1812, graduated with the second honor of that institution. He devoted himself to the profession of the law, and from the commencement obtained a large and lucrative practice. In 1816 he was elected to the House of Representatives in the Legislature of South Carolina. He was again elected in 1822, 1824, and 1826, and during the last two terms was the Speaker of the House. In December, 1828, he was elected an associate judge, and in 1830 a judge of the Court of Appeals. On the abolition of that court he was

transferred to the Court of Law. In 1850 he became president of the Court of Law Appeals and of the Court of Errors. Upon the reorganization of a separate Court of Appeals, he was with great unanimity appointed chief justice of South Carolina. It would be superfluous to attempt to describe the manner in which these several offices of public trust have been filled. His thorough business habits, his untiring industry, his incorruptible integrity, his conscientious discharge of the duties of every office, together with his great learning, enabled him to establish for himself a position unequaled by any chief justice in the history of this State.

It might seem that surrounded by such cares he would have no time for the performance of other public duties. But, on the contrary, we find him devoting himself in various other ways to what he deemed the vital interests of the country. His attention to agriculture contributed in great part to its advancement in South Carolina, but especially in his native district of Newberry. To his labors and personal influence, too, is the State indebted for the successful completion of the Greenville and Columbia Railroad. His activity in these respects was but an index of his more private labors in every way in which the material prosperity of the State could be advanced.

Outside of his official labors, perhaps Judge O'Neall was known in no respect so well as in the character of an ardent advocate of total abstinence from all intoxicating liquors. To this work he devoted himself during the most vigorous years of his manhood, and continued his efforts until the time of his death. He became known as the apostle of temperance in South Carolina, and occupied the highest position among its most distinguished advocates in North America. No one man has performed more voluntary labor in this cause than he.

It was the privilege, however, of those who knew Judge O'Neall in his private life to appreciate most highly the true worth of his character. His public life displayed the sterner, his private life the gentler, traits of true and noble manhood, each in equal perfection. God blessed him in the selection of a companion whom he spared until the end of his life. On the 25th of June, 1818, he was married to Helen, eldest daughter of Capt. Sampson and Sarah Strother Pope. All the children of this marriage preceded their honored father to the grave. He himself died on Sunday, the 27th of December, 1863, being seventy years, eight months, and seventeen days old.

The Convention of the Baptist denomination in South Carolina suffered a great loss in the death of Chief-Justice O'Neall, because he was an ardent co-worker with his brethren in the advancement of Christ's kingdom. His parents were Friends, or Quakers, but from the time that Brother O'Neall made a profession of Christianity he was an earnest advocate of the religious views held by the Calvinistic Baptists. A great revival in the town of Newberry, in 1831, gave origin to the Baptist church of that place, on the records of which, under date of Saturday, Jan. 26, 1833, is the following : "Received by experience, John B. O'Neall." In the minutes of Saturday, March 22, 1834, is another item of importance : "Resolved, that it is expedient to appoint three additional deacons of this church, who are requested to conduct all prayer-meetings from time to time, and to take part in any other religious exercises to which they may be prompted by the Spirit in aid of the pastor of this church." Under the above resolution were appointed John B. O'Neall, M. T. Mendenhall, and Drayton Nance. In compliance with the above resolution religious meetings were conducted by the brethren named with great regularity for a considerable time. Judge O'Neall's addresses, lectures, and exhortations are still remembered by those who used to hear them. They were characterized by all the vehemence and earnestness which at a later period marked similar efforts in the cause of temperance. He was at that time very active in the church. Afterwards the judge was often absent discharging his official duties, but whenever at home he was a constant attendant upon the public ministry of the gospel, and felt much interest in all that concerned the welfare of the church.

He carried into it the same characteristics which distinguished him in other important relations, —great zeal, energy, ardor, and devotion. These qualities, connected with unusual ability, made him the effective Christian he was. Judge O'Neall was remarkable for his humility as a Christian, and though occupying prominent positions in the State, and receiving at times an homage which was well calculated to foster worldly pride, he always retained that humility which condescends to small things and to men of low estate. His piety, as exhibited at home, around the fireside, and in private life, displayed this quality most strikingly. It was his custom to erect a domestic altar night and morning, when, gathering his family, white and black, around him, he invoked the blessings and pardon of heaven upon them in a most simple and touching manner, and if a friend or stranger happened under his roof, he invariably prayed for him personally. His fervid manner of addressing a throne of grace showed his strong faith in a special providence. He was remarkable for a tender regard for all around him. If his humblest servant was seriously sick, he exhibited a strong sympathy for him and made him a subject of prayer at the family altar, and followed the remains of a servant to the burying-ground, and stood by the grave during the funeral service with a reverence, humility, and awe which showed how deeply his heart was imbued with the spirit of Christ, and how surely he felt that God was no respecter of persons. He was loved and revered in his own district as the friend of the widow and orphan. Indeed, this was his character throughout the State. Enjoying a reputation for liberality, and occupying a position which exposed him to calls of this kind, it is not too much to say that he expended a small fortune in responding to such appeals. He was quite as well known for that charity which marked the good Samaritan,—that gentle and kind sympathy which will observe and even hunt out and relieve the wants and distresses of others by counsel, advice, and sympathy as well as donations of money.

But Judge O'Neall's most distinguishing trait as a Christian was that he was not ashamed of the religion of Christ. It was this that made him so eminently useful. No man, certainly no layman in the Baptist denomination, nor in any other, has exerted so wide-spread an influence for good. Before assembled multitudes, in charging juries, in sentencing criminals, or in making temperance speeches, he always made it a point to enforce directly or indirectly the truths of Christianity.

At home, in his own church, he was in the habit for many years of conducting prayer-meetings and delivering addresses when there was no preaching in the church. He continued this until he was seriously injured by an accident on the railroad, after which he discontinued public speaking of all kinds. His prayers and lectures on such occasions were warm, fervent, and effective. He would usually take a chapter or a portion of one, and make a running comment. Often he would select a psalm, the fervid eloquence, poetic sentiment, and language of which seemed congenial to him, and gave him an opportunity, which seemed to delight him, of expatiating on the goodness, power, and glory of God.

With all his honors he cherished most his privileges as a servant of Christ, who, amid the many duties of a life of extraordinary activity, has always remembered his dependence upon God, and sought his aid, and strove to guide others, too, in the way of life.

It is not surprising that where such piety is united with such greatness his brethren should have loved and honored him. At the session of the Southern Baptist Convention, held in July, 1858, he was elected president, an office in which he continued until July, 1863, when his failing health forbade his further attendance upon its meetings.

Ontario and Quebec, Baptists of.—It is difficult to trace the history of the introduction of Baptists into these provinces, as until a comparatively recent date no attempt was made to preserve the denominational records. But as Baptists are always found wherever the Word of God is freely circulated and devoutly studied, it is to be presumed that there were many converts to our principles, in the upper province at least, before the arrival of Baptist preachers. So far as can be ascertained, the first churches were planted by itinerant missionaries from Nova Scotia, New Brunswick, and the United States. None of these churches has a history extending over a much longer period than eighty-five years. According to a brief sketch published by the late Rev. Dr. Fyfe, in 1859, the first church in the eastern section of the country of which there is any authentic account was formed in Caldwell's Manor, by Rev. E. Andrews, of Vermont, in 1794. This section is indebted to missionaries sent out by a society of which the late venerable Dr. Sharp, of Boston, was secretary. In the same year (1794) the first church in the western section was formed under Elders Hamilton and Turner, at Thurlow, in the county of Northumberland ; and about the same year Elder Winn commenced to labor in the district of Prince Edward. Through this region there once flourished many churches,—in the townships of Rawdon, Sidney, Cramahe, Murray, etc,—but chiefly through emigration westward some of them have become extinct, and others have languished for years.

In 1800 a brother named Finch, from New Brunswick, began to preach at Charlotteville, and in 1804 a church was formed there, of which several neighboring churches are the thriving daughters. Soon after this the church in Beamsville was formed, under the missionary labors of Elders Covell and Warren, from the Shaftsbury Association, Vt. This church has also been a fruitful mother. Beyond these outlines it would be scarcely possible to trace the influences (they have been so varied) which have raised up Baptist churches in different parts of the country. The Baptists were the first anti-Roman Catholic missionaries to Canada, as they were the first missionaries to the heathen, and it is to be regretted that the history of their early trials and labors is so little known.

The numerical increase of the denomination will be indicated by the following statistics : in 1828 there were in Ontario (then called Upper Canada) 45 ministers, 1435 communicants, and 5740 regular hearers. The Baptists in Quebec, or Lower Canada, at that time were very few, and would not have materially altered the above figures. In 1842 the census gave 19,623 Baptists in the two provinces ; six years later they numbered 28,503 ; in four years more (1852) they numbered 49,846 ; and in 1860 the number of ministers was about 190, of communicants 13,715, and of adherents 60,000. Now (1881) there are not fewer than 250 ministers,

356 churches, a membership of more than 27,000, and at least 125,000 adherents. Of these, by far the greater number belong to Ontario. The "Canadian Baptist Year-Book" for 1881 gives the Baptists of Quebec only 26 English-speaking churches, with a total membership of about 2000. If the members of the Grande Ligne Mission churches (French) are added, the number of communicants will not even then exceed 2400. These figures need occasion no surprise, when it is remembered that the entire Protestant population of that province is exceedingly small. The largest churches in the two provinces are Jarvis Street, Toronto, with 751 ; First Brantford, with 525 ; and First Montreal, with 479 members. Several others have from 200 to 350 members. There are 14 Associations.

For Christian enterprise and liberality the Baptists of Ontario and Quebec will compare favorably with their brethren in any part of the world. Their Literary Institute, at Woodstock, for which an adequate endowment is nearly raised, and the new Theological Seminary at Toronto, the land and buildings of which are the donation of one man, stand as monuments of princely giving on the part of the rich, and of the munificence of the body generally. Home mission work is done under the direction of two boards, representing the East and the West respectively. The new province of Manitoba receives missionary aid through a separate organization. A Foreign Missionary Society is also maintained, with which are connected two Women's Auxiliary Societies. Besides these the aid of the denomination is claimed by a Church Edifice Society, a Society for the Relief of Superannuated Ministers, and the Grande Ligne Evangelical Society.

Two weekly newspapers, the *Canadian Baptist* and *Christian Helper*, are published at Toronto ; and also a monthly, the *Canadian Missionary Link*, devoted to the interests of the Women's Foreign Mission Societies. (See also the article BAPTIST UNION OF CANADA.)

O'Quin, Rev. Ezekiel, a pioneer preacher in Rapides Parish, La., was born in North Carolina in 1781, and died in 1823.

O'Quin, Rev. John, son of Ezekiel O'Quin, was born in South Carolina in 1808, and settled in Rapides Parish, La., in 1815 ; began to preach in 1834, and became a pioneer in the St. Landry region. While preaching constantly he engaged successfully in planting, and amassed a large fortune. Since the war he has engaged actively in politics, and has served with ability several terms in the Louisiana Legislature.

Ordination.—When a brother is set apart to the work of the gospel ministry, if he is ordained by the authority of the church to which his services are to be given, his membership is first transferred to that community. They pass resolutions declaring their conviction that he should be ordained, and they summon a council to meet for that purpose on a designated day. They appoint brethren to represent them in the council. The clerk of the church presents the council with its resolutions, a list of the churches invited, and the names of the representatives of the church. When the council is organized, and opened with devotional exercises, the candidate gives an account of his conversion, call to the ministry, and views of doctrine and church order. After a searching examination from the ministers and laymen of the council, he is requested to retire, when his conversion, divine call, character, orthodoxy, and talents are carefully scrutinized. If he is approved by the council a resolution to that effect is passed, and another that the council proceed to his ordination. The candidate is then brought before the council, and the moderator announces to him its decision. A committee is then appointed to arrange for the ordination services; this committee always includes the candidate. The moderator of the council presides at the ordination. Its services include a sermon, the imposition of hands on the head of the kneeling candidate by all the ministers in the pulpit, the hand of fellowship as a herald of the gospel, a charge to the candidate and to the church. If the minister is not yet a member of the church of which he is to become pastor, the church to which he belongs calls the council, and he is ordained by its request and under its authority.

Oregon, a rich agricultural and mining State, with many prosperous cities. It has four universities and colleges, and a splendid common school system. On May 25, 1844, "The West Union Baptist church" was formed on the Tualatin Plains, with eight members. It was the first Baptist church at that date in the United States west of the Rocky Mountains. They met regularly for years to study the Bible and hear a sermon read by one of their number. In February, 1845, Rev. V. Snelling preached the first sermon to the little flock, joined them, with his wife, and David T. Lénox was ordained a deacon. In May, 1845, they celebrated the Lord's Supper for the first time. Other ministers began to arrive, new churches were organized, until now Oregon has nearly eighty churches, five Associations, a monthly paper, *The Beacon,* one college, at McMinnville, its State Convention, Mission, Education, and Sunday-school Conventions and Boards, a Woman's Missionary Society, and about 3000 Baptist members. There is also a flourishing mission for the Chinese in Oregon, located at Portland; the soul of this mission is a converted and ordained Chinaman, Rev. Dong Gong, who became a Christian and a Baptist almost at the peril of his life.

56

Origin of Infant Baptism, The. — Infant baptism came into life in Africa, the country of slavery, cruelty, and ignorance. In the Roman colony stretching along the coast of the Mediterranean Sea, where the warlike and ferocious Carthaginians built up their commerce and sovereignty, this superstitious rite was born. Never in human history is it heard of until African writers mention it. Tertullian, at the very close of the second century, discountenances the baptism of *children,*— not unconscious infants. Speaking of them he says, "They know how to ask for salvation (baptism) that you may seem to have given it to one seeking it." (Norint petere salutem, ut petenti dedisse videaris. De Baptismo, cap. 18. Lipsiæ, 1839.) These candidates for baptism could ask for it, and consequently were not unconscious babes, and he opposes its administration to them on account of their early years. There is no hint given that it was customary to baptize intelligent children of several years of age. Tertullian's little book was written against the Quintillianists, who suffered women to preach and baptize, and who were regarded as heretics. His work affords no hint of the existence of the baptism of unconscious babes. The first case of that sort, if real, in the literature of Christianity, is to be found in a letter of Cyprian, bishop of Carthage, written about A.D. 256, giving an account of the proceedings of a council of sixty-six bishops held at that time in Carthage. Fidus, a country bishop, wanted to know if an infant might be baptized before it was eight days old. There is not a Sunday-school teacher in a Pedobaptist school in Christendom who could not answer that question in a moment, but Fidus, a bishop, could not decide what to do, and Cyprian, a man of superlative presumption, feels compelled to seek the wisdom of sixty-six bishops to guide Fidus. If the letter of Cyprian is genuine, this is the first distinct evidence of the existence of infant baptism among the Saviour's followers; no other intimation of its occurrence in the third century is given, but few instances of it can be found in the fourth, and the baptism of catechized persons was common for ages after; but we doubt the genuineness of this letter.

Beyond all question infant baptism began in Africa, and Augustine of Hippo was the man who lent it the force which gave it victory. Africa had been cursed for ages with human sacrifices to Saturn,—little children were placed in the arms of a metal image intensely heated, with a blazing fire underneath its outstretched arms. Many persons who became nominal Christians practised this ancient and horrid abomination; backsliders from Christianity followed this hideous rite of the Phœnician colonists of North Africa. Robinson has a theory about the origin of the infant ceremony which may contain some truth. His idea is that it was probably used to place God's mark upon the infants, and thereby to protect them from the bloody arms of infamous Saturn, to whose frightful embrace their superstitious parents would consign them. After mentioning various matters connected with his theory, he says, " Collecting into one point of view all the forementioned facts, the eye fixes on Fidus, the honest and humane bishop of a company of Christians in a country place of Africa, where some of his neighbors bought, stole, captured, and burnt children ; where some of his flock returned to paganism ; others intermarried with pagan families and went with them into the old practices of sacrificing children to the gods ; himself filled with Jewish ideas of dedicating children to the true God, and marking them by circumcision ; and sending for advice to Cyprian, exactly such another confused genius as himself, is it a very improbable conjecture that Fidus bethought himself of baptizing new-born infants as an expedient to save the lives of the lambs of his flock? . . . To prevail with such savages to dedicate their infants to God ; to take possession of them by the soft method of dipping them in water ; to procure some persons of more influence than the parents to become sponsors for the babes (adults required sponsors in order to be baptized soon after the apostolic age, to instruct them, and probably to protect persecuted Christians from baptizing spies) ; this resembles the great Alfred's uniting Britons into tens, and forcing every nine to pledge themselves that the tenth should enjoy his liberty and his life." (History of Baptism, 248–9. Nashville.) Whether Cyprian's letter is genuine or a forgery, and whether or not such a man as Fidus ever lived, it is extremely probable that Mr. Robinson's conjecture had some truth in it. The writer, however, is of the opinion that the grand forces which gave success to infant baptism after the application of the rite to them was conceived, were the pernicious falsehoods that Adam's guilt would keep every unbaptized infant out of heaven, and that his iniquity was washed from the soul of the infant by baptism. So soon as these fables were received, men, and surely women, were inclined to favor the dipping of new-born babes.

Original Sin.—Adam and Eve were created in perfect innocence. They could not be invested with infallibility, for that attribute belongs to God alone, and Jehovah could not create a deity : but they were summoned into life without a tendency to sin, and they were as holy as the angels of God.

The human race was created in Adam and Eve, just as millions of oaks were created in the first tree of that kind. Physical defects or material beauties have been transmitted down from the first two parents of our race ; they could come from no other

source. When Adam sinned he forfeited his title to the tree of life in Eden, and as a consequence its leaves and fruit no longer healed his wounds, acted as an antidote against his diseases, and arrested the decay that ever since has wasted declining years. He lost Eden with the tree of life at the fall, and so did his posterity in him. The head of the family recklessly squandered his rich inheritance, and as a matter of course those who were born to him afterwards never enjoyed any part of it. The same thing was true of the divine favor which he forfeited in Eden ; it was lost to him for the time being by the use of the forbidden fruit, and it was never restored unless he repented, and through divinely-appointed sacrifices turned to the Lord his God.

He left Eden with a heart vitiated by sin, and his children subsequently born came into the world with his spiritual defects and temporal disadvantages. He once bore the image of God, but sin destroyed it, and all his descendants have been marked by a guilty likeness to him.

Original sin vitiates the moral tastes of each man ; it leads him to prefer the world, fleshly gratifications, and even the snares of the tempter, to the service of God. And as there is not in human nature a counteracting agency to subdue guilty tastes and restore the transgressor to Jehovah, he must continually sink deeper into sin unless sovereign grace restores him.

Original sin leads directly and surely to total depravity. We prefer *total perversion* as a better description of this sad state. Good and gentle and moral persons who have not been born again are totally perverted from God. If the heart is for Christ, the whole being is on his side ; if the heart is against him, the whole man is his enemy. When Anne Boleyn had the heart of Henry VIII., he slighted Queen Catharine, hurled aside the authority of the pope and the claims of his religion, in the defense of which he had written a book, defied all Europe in his determination to marry her, and befriended the Bible, which he had burned, and the Protestants, whom he had slandered and persecuted, because of his regard for her. But when his heart turned to a rival of Anne, then he was wholly alienated from her. This is the exact situation of each unsaved man : his heart and life are wholly perverted from God. What was true of ancient Israel may be justly applied to all unconverted persons, " Ye will revolt more and more': the whole head is sick, and the whole heart faint. From the sole of the foot even unto the head there is no soundness in it ; but wounds, and bruises, and putrefying sores."—Isa. i. 5, 6.

Original sin has extended over the whole race. Dreadful and undeniable facts prove this statement, and inspiration asserts it. Paul says, " We have before proved both Jews and Gentiles, that they are all under sin; as it is written, 'There is none righteous, no, not one: there is none that understandeth, there is none that seeketh after God. They are all gone out of the way, they are together become unprofitable; there is none that doeth good, no, not one.'"—Rom. iii. 10-12. When he speaks of Jews and Gentiles he intends to describe all men. The race in unbelief is in a state of total perversion from God.

Original sin paralyzes the moral powers of the soul, and forbids any man, unaided by divine grace, to go to Jesus. A young French ecclesiastic, years ago, was supposed to have died, and was in his coffin when the mass for the dead was being read. He heard every word of it, knew his situation exactly, but could not move a finger, nor an eyelid, nor utter a word. Something led to an inspection of the face, when a slight flush was discovered, and the heart was found to be beating. The man was restored to his family, and by proper remedies speedily became well. But without help he would have been buried. So the entire impenitent are dead in sin. "You hath he quickened who were *dead* in trespasses and sins."—Eph. ii. 1. And under the influence of this moral death of themselves they will never go to Jesus. "No man," says Jesus, "can come to me except the Father who hath sent me draw him." Original sin has the first hold of a human heart, and it will never let it go till the all-powerful hand of grace destroys its dominion.

Original sin has doomed the race except where the Spirit of Christ has given a new heart and saving faith. "By the offense of one judgment came upon all men to condemnation."—Rom. v. 18. "He that believeth not is condemned already."—John iii. 18. This is the condition before God of all who have kept away from Jesus over the whole earth: they are in a state of total perversion from God.

Osage, Iowa, the county town of Mitchell County, is widely known and honored for its adherence to temperance principles and the high moral tone of its people. The Baptist church was organized in 1862. It has grown into an efficient body of 170 members. The Cedar Valley Seminary, one of the Baptist schools of Iowa, under the care of the Cedar Valley Baptist Association, is located at Osage.

Osborn, Rev. John W., of Scio, Linn Co., Oregon, was born Oct. 18, 1838. His father was a laborious and successful preacher. He was in his youth wild, worldly, and loved to ridicule religion; but in 1859, during one of his father's meetings, he was converted, and two months later, while studying at Pella University, was baptized by Rev. Elihu Gunn, and joined the Pella church. He was ordained at Concord, Iowa, in March, 1864, preached in many places for two years in Iowa, Nebraska, and Colo-

rado, and in 1866 removed to Oregon, and preached in Polk County until 1873, when he removed to the Forks of Santiam. In 1878, on account of sickness he removed to Eastern Oregon, and spent some time in Washington Territory, doing missionary work at Dayton, Grande Ronde, the Cove, Indian Creek, and other places. Returning in February, 1880, he settled at Scio, and is pastor of the Providence and Union churches, where he has had his greatest successes. Brother Osborn has always preached without a stated salary; he has done a vast amount of mission work in Central Oregon for the Yamhill, McMinnville, Union, Dallas, Lacrole, Providence, Antioch, Oak Creek, Pilgrim's Home, Pleasant Valley, Shiloh, Scio, and other churches; organized many new churches; helped to organize the General Baptist Association of Oregon, in 1868; has been active on missionary boards, and is one of the most earnest, self-denying, and influential Baptist preachers in the Central Association of Oregon.

Osborn, Rev. John Wesley, Sr., was born of Methodist parents, Aug. 19, 1802. His parents afterwards became Baptists, and the father a Baptist minister. The son was converted and baptized in 1821, in St. Clair Co., Ill.; licensed in 1826, ordained in 1830. He traveled extensively in Central and Northern Illinois, Southern Wisconsin, and Iowa, with little or no salary; organized many permanent churches, and baptized over 3000 converts. He preferred to go where there was no preaching, and build up churches from his own labors. He was often bitterly opposed; sometimes his life was threatened; some of his enemies were converted, and became powerful helpers of the truth. In 1866 he removed to Oregon; served the Union, Lacrole, Antioch, Dallas, North Palestine, Providence, and Scio churches. He was doctrinal in preaching, using only brief notes, and swayed his audiences with the eloquence of truth. Died Oct. 16, 1875, and left his youngest son in the work of the ministry; one of Oregon's successful Baptist preachers.

Osborn, Lucien M., LL.D., was born in Ashtabula, O., in 1823; graduated at Madison University in 1847; principal of the grammar-school of Madison University, 1851-56; Professor of Mathematics and Natural Philosophy in the university, 1856-68. Since 1868, Professor of Natural Sciences; degree of LL.D. conferred by Denison University in 1872; associated for some time with the president of Madison University "to take charge of the internal discipline of the university, which delicate and difficult task was performed with high credit." Dr. Osborn has a high standing in the Baptist denomination, and he is among the purest and most useful men in it.

Osgood, S. M., D.D., died at Chicago, July 9,

1875. He was born at Henderson, Jefferson Co., N. Y., March 2, 1807, being the son of Rev. Emory Osgood. At the age of nine years he became a Christian, and was baptized by his father. He entered active life as a printer, in Watertown, N. Y., and in this place, with the exception of brief intervals, lived some ten years, at the end of that time becoming connected with the office of the *Baptist Register*, in Utica, N. Y., uniting with the Broad Street Baptist church in that city. After one year in Utica he removed to Cortland, N. Y., and, in company with Mr. Rufus A. Reed, took charge of the *Cortland Chronicle*. Returning to Watertown in 1831, he had for his pastor there Rev. Jacob Knapp, and was made a deacon in the church. In 1834 he was appointed missionary printer at Maulmain, Burmah, and on July 3 of that year sailed from Boston in the ship "Cashmere." His associates on the voyage were Jonathan Wade, Grover S. Comstock, William Dean, and Miss Ann Gardner. There were, besides, three missionaries of the American board.

Mr. Osgood remained at Maulmain until 1846, rendering most valuable service. One of his reports, covering a period of two years, "showed that in that time the seven iron hand-presses of the mission had turned out nearly seven hundred thousand copies of different publications, including almost nine million pages of the Scriptures in the New Testament and different books of the Old." Returning to this country in 1846, Mr. Osgood was appointed an agent of the Missionary Union for Western New York ; after seven years his field was changed to that of New Jersey, Pennsylvania, Delaware, and the District of Columbia, his residence being at Philadelphia. In 1860 he was appointed district secretary for the West, with his residence at Chicago. This was his work until his death,—a period of fifteen most laborious and useful years. He was a man greatly beloved in all relations, a devout Christian, a judicious adviser, energetic, indefatigable in service, with a singular faculty for engaging the confidence and interest of all whom he approached.

Ottawa University was originated in 1860, under the name of the Roger Williams University. During the meeting of the Kansas Baptist State Convention, held in Atcheson in 1860, the location of the institution was discussed. Several places desired to secure it. Rev. John T. Jones, a delegate from the First Baptist church of Ottawa (Indian), informed the Convention that his people for some time had felt the need of a school of high grade, and, as they were all Baptists, they would unite with their white brethren in their educational efforts. In December, 1860, the trustees of the projected university visited the Ottawa nation, and after a full conference with these Indian Baptists

they agreed to give 20,000 acres of their land, then worth something over $20,000, to aid in the new educational enterprise. This proposed contract became a law in 1862. In 1865 the name of Roger Williams was dropped, and the institution incorporated under the name of the Ottawa University. The change took place in compliance with the express wish of the Ottawas, who desired to perpetuate their name. Owing to the disturbed state of the country the institution was greatly impeded in its progress until 1865. The college edifice was completed in 1869, at a cost of $40,000.

It is located near the thriving city of Ottawa, Kansas, some fifty-five miles southwest of Kansas City. It has an endowment of 640 acres of choice land, on a part of which the university stands. The buildings are large and substantial stone structures. There were ninety-three students in attendance last year, to whom Dr. P. J. Williams, the president, and his able assistants gave thorough instruction. The institution needs an endowment that would enable it to increase the faculty and to meet all current expenses without annual appeals to the churches and its friends. Dr. Williams is unusually well qualified, by talents, acquirements, facility for imparting instruction, and executive ability, for the position he occupies. The vigorous and expanding Baptist denomination of Kansas is in great need of the university. The friends of truth could not make a better investment than to place a generous endowment at the service of Ottawa University.

Ottumwa, Iowa (pop. 9018), county-seat of Wapello County, has two Baptist churches. The First was constituted in 1855, and has a present membership of 139. The Second was constituted in 1869, and is still a small company. There is also a colored Baptist church of twenty-one members.

Overby, Rev. R. R., was born in Dinwiddie Co., Va., Oct. 12, 1827 ; was a licensed preacher in the Methodist Church ; he was baptized in Petersburg, Va., in July, 1850 ; spent two years at Richmond College, and served as pastor of two colored churches in Petersburg while at college ; served as agent of Murfreesborough Female Institute in 1858 ; settled as pastor in Elizabeth City in 1859, and, with the exception of a year spent as agent of Wake Forest College, has lived and labored for twenty-one years in the section where he now resides. A man of power with the people, and possessing many noble qualities.

Owen, Alfred, D.D., was born in Chiva, Me., July 20, 1829, where he spent his boyhood and received his academical education ; graduated from Waterville College after a four years' course of study, in 1853 ; taught an academy two years at Bridgeton, Me., and in 1855 entered Newton Theological Seminary ; supplied the High Street church, of Lynn, Mass., during a large part of his seminary course, and became pastor of this church on his graduation, in 1858. In 1867 he left Lynn and

ALFRED OWEN, D.D.

became pastor of the Lafayette Avenue church, Detroit, Mich., where he remained until July, 1877. The following two years he was pastor of the University Place church, Chicago, Ill. In 1879 he was elected president of Denison University, O., which position he still holds.

Dr. Owen has written much for the papers, and has given courses of lectures in Ministers' Institutes, as well as before the students of Chicago and Newton Theological Seminaries. He has had large experience in educational work, is a scholarly writer and preacher, and gives great satisfaction as a college president. Kalamazoo College conferred the honorary degree of D.D. upon him in 1871.

Owen, Rev. Ezra D., was born near Norristown, Pa., in 1809. His parents came to Scipio, N. Y., in 1810. He was converted and joined the Baptist church of Venice in 1826. He studied in the common schools and under Dr. Smith, and was ordained at Branchport in 1830. He was pastor at Branchport five years. In 1835 he and his wife came by carriage to Springfield, O., where he served as pastor one year. He came next to Cincinnati, and soon had an appointment from the American Baptist Home Mission Society to go to Richmond, Ind. He labored there two years, and was called to the pastorate of the church at Madison. He served this church as pastor ten or twelve years, in the mean time undertaking the issuing of an Indiana Baptist newspaper,—the *American Messenger*. After publishing it at Madison for about three years, he removed it to Indianapolis in the fall of 1846. During the time of his editorship at Indianapolis he was also under appointment by the American Baptist Home Mission Society, and founded the Baptist church at Evansville. The *American Messenger* was sold to the *Cross and Journal*, of Ohio, and thenceforth the name was the *Journal and Messenger*. He then was called by the Lafayette church, which he served three years, after which he was invited back to Madison, which he served till his death, Sept. 26, 1852.

Owens, Deacon Benjamin W., was born in South Carolina in 1818, lived in Alabama and Arkansas, where he was baptized in 1835, and settled at Stockton, Cal., in 1850. He helped to organize the first Baptist church in that city, bought a house for its worship, helped to build another, and paid several thousand dollars for erecting another. In 1868 he settled in San Francisco, and was a deacon of the Tabernacle and Columbia Square churches many years. He is a generous layman, active on mission and educational boards, and never more happy than when engaged with others in revivals.

P.

Page, Rev. J.—Few ministers in Florida have been more useful than Rev. James Page, pastor of the Baptist (colored) church at Tallahassee. For about forty years he has labored in the city and vicinity, and whether as a slave or freedman, has commanded the respect and confidence of all classes. Nor is his influence confined to his immediate section, it is felt for good among the colored Baptists nearly all over the State. He visited Thomasville, Ga., in 1860, and, by invitation, preached acceptably to the white congregation. Mr. Page is a man of good sense and observation; he is an earnest student of the Bible, and he has long been an acceptable preacher of the gospel. He is a man of large frame, robust constitution, and though now quite an old man, is the unaided pastor of a church numbering some 1200 members.

He has been for several years the clerk of the Bethlehem Association, a very large body, and the first organized by the colored Baptists of the State. He is a progressive man, the friend of education, and has earnestly favored the effort to build up a school for the special benefit of the ministry of his race.

Page, Lady Mary, the wife of Sir Gregory Page, was brought to the Saviour in early life. She examined the baptismal question, and the grounds for dissenting from the Episcopal Church, for five years, and, having decided that she could not make any improvement upon the Saviour's example, she was immersed by Mr. Maisters, in the presence of more than two hundred spectators. Further reading, especially during a protracted sickness, but confirmed her in her religious principles and in her attachment to her church home. Says one who knew her, "Her constant regard for the church, her tender concern for pastor and people, her uncommon benefaction upon their removal hither, deserve a particular acknowledgment, as does also her further bounty given in her last will for the relief of the poor members. She distributed vast sums of money in so silent a way that 'her left hand knew not what her right hand did.'" She endured severe afflictions with heaven-given patience. She enjoyed a clear hope through the blood of the Lamb, and without a struggle she fell asleep in Jesus, March 4, 1728. She was buried in Bunhill-fields, in London, in which city she died. She was a great ornament to her holy profession; she lived in the hearts of the members of her church,

and in a multitude of other hearts. Mr. Richardson, her pastor, preached a funeral sermon for her. Mr. Harrison, a neighboring Baptist minister, preached another funeral sermon to commemorate God's grace in her holy life and death. And he delivered a funeral oration when she was interred; he also composed an ode in honor of the deceased, in which he says,—

> "At length the heroine's crowned. Her numerous foes,
> With whom she long conflicted, are subdued;
> Under her feet they're laid, while she, in strains
> Angelic, sings the praises of the Lord."

Page, Stephen B., D.D., was born in Fayette, Me., Oct. 16, 1808; spent his early life in the family of Rev. Justin Edwards, D.D.; was converted at the age of eighteen, and united with the Baptist church at Hartford, Conn., being the first person baptized by Barnas Sears, D.D., then just ordained; pursued his preparatory studies at Hamilton, N. Y., and graduated at Waterville, Me., in 1835. After spending one year in teaching, entered Newton Theological Seminary, which he left in 1839. In September, 1839, became pastor at Masillon, O., and in 1844 at Wooster, O., where he remained six years. In 1850 took charge of the Norwalk, O., Baptist church, and in 1854 of the Third church, in Cleveland, where he continued with much success until 1861, when he assumed the pastoral care of the Second (now Euclid Avenue) church of Cleveland. This church at the time of his settlement was heavily in debt and apparently near extinction, but under his well-directed labors grew largely in numbers and strength. In 1866 he resigned this pastorate, and engaged in a successful effort to complete an endowment of $100,000 for Denison University. Shortly after this he was appointed by the American Baptist Home Mission Society district secretary for Ohio and West Virginia, this latter State being subsequently, however, given to another, and Indiana and Michigan added to his field. In this work he continued nearly twelve years, during which time he collected over $100,000 for home mission work.

Feb. 1, 1880, Dr. Page resigned his secretaryship. He continues to reside in Cleveland, being with one exception the oldest resident minister in the city.

Paine, Rev. John, was born in Pomfret, Conn., in 1793; baptized in 1813, by Rev. Amos Wells; united with the Baptist church in Hampton, Conn.; ordained and settled pastor of the same church in

1819, and remained eight years; in 1827 removed to Auburn, Mass., then to Ward, Mass., where he labored ten years; subsequent pastorates were in Bozrah, Conn., four years; in South Woodstock, eleven years; in Packersville, Conn., five years; always a close student, clear thinker, instructive preacher, judicious pastor; removed to Preston, Conn., in 1863, where he died April 29, 1864, aged seventy-one years. His daughter Mary married Rev. O. W. Gates, now of California.

Painter, Mr., and the Persecuting Laws of Massachusetts.—In 1644 the General Court of Massachusetts decided "That if any person or persons within this jurisdiction shall either *openly condemn or oppose the baptizing of infants, or go about secretly to seduce others from the approbation or use thereof, or shall purposely depart the congregation at the ministration of the ordinance,* or shall deny the ordinance of magistracy, or their lawful right and authority to make war, or to punish the outward breaches of the first table (of the ten commandments), and shall appear to the court wilfully and obstinately to continue therein after due time and means of conviction, every such person or persons shall be sentenced to banishment." Mr. Backus, speaking of this wicked law enacted by our Congregational brethren, says, "I have diligently searched all the books, records, and papers I could come at upon all sides, and have found a *great number* of instances of Baptists suffering for the above points that we own." Baptists "refused to countenance infant baptism and the use of secular force in religious affairs," and Backus found many cases of persons persecuted by law for opposing infant baptism in the methods specified. Painter, in 1644, "a poor man, was suddenly turned Anabaptist, and having a child born, would not suffer his wife to carry it to be baptized. He was complained of for this to the court, and enjoined by them to suffer his child to be baptized. And because he refused to obey them therein, and told them it was an antichristian ordinance, *they tied him up and whipped him,* which he bore without flinching, and declared he had divine help to support him." Gov. Winthrop says that "he belonged to Hingham, and that he was whipped for denying the Lord's ordinance." (History of the Baptists in New England, by Isaac Backus, i. 127–8. Newton.) This stinging argument brought no conviction to the mind of Mr. Painter, and it only showed the dearth of Scriptural reasons for the infant rite, and the lack of justice and common sense in those who tried to secure persuasion with the lash. More than a hundred years earlier the same kind of argument was freely used in Switzerland, and in our own times force has brought the Baptist infant to the font in Germany. But this old argument of the highwayman will gradually

fall into disuse as men see its worthlessness and its thorough wickedness.

Palen, Rev. Vincent, was born Jan. 17, 1810, in Poughkeepsie, N. Y., of Methodist parents. He experienced religion in 1828, although he did not then make a public profession. In 1833 he became a full member of the Methodist Episcopal Church, and a preacher. After filling a circuit appointment he held a protracted meeting at McAllister's church, near Harrisburg, Pa., at which 120 persons professed conversion. From these converts a church was organized, of which he was chosen pastor. Some of the candidates for membership refusing to accept sprinkling as baptism, he was led carefully to investigate the subject of baptism, and became convinced that immersion is the only Scriptural mode. He was baptized in the Susquehanna River at Harrisburg, by Rev. E. Thomas, a Winebrennarian minister, and was ordained to the ministry in that body. After a pastorate here of sixteen months (during which a meeting-house was built), followed by a brief engagement at Baltimore, he united, in 1843, with the High Street Baptist church in that city, May 25, 1845, after which he was ordained, Rev. S. P. Hill, D.D., preaching the sermon. From this time until the outbreak of the war his time was divided among evangelistic, missionary, and pastoral labors. The beginning of the war found him at Portsmouth, Va., from which he was sent to Richmond, and imprisoned as an "alien enemy." He was, however, soon released, and on reaching Washington was appointed a hospital chaplain. He discharged the duties of this office with efficiency and unflagging zeal. In this and other ways he rendered very important service to the government during the great struggle. At the close of the war he was, with one exception, the last hospital chaplain mustered out of the service, and he was then transferred to the regular army as post chaplain. In December, 1869, in consequence of chronic ill health, he was at his own request retired from active service. He has since resided in Camden, N. J. As his health permits he continues to fill up the measure of his usefulness by preaching and other Christian ministries.

Palmer, Albert Gallatin, D.D., son of Luther and Sarah (Kenyon) Palmer, was born in North Stonington, Conn., May 11, 1813; experienced religion at nine years of age; baptized by Rev. Jonathan Miner, in 1829; joined First Baptist church in North Stonington; began early to preach, and supplied for a year the church in Andover, Conn.; pursued academical studies at Kingston and Pawtucket, R. I., and Andover, Mass.; preached for First Baptist church in North Stonington, by which body he was ordained in 1834; was pastor of First Baptist church in Westerly, R. I., from 1837 to 1843, and blessed in his work; pastor of

Stonington Borough church, Conn., from 1843 to 1852, and prospered; enjoyed three revivals of power; pastor of the church in Syracuse, N. Y., for three years; pastor at Bridgeport, Conn.; pastor for three years at Wakefield, R. I., and shared large revivals; in 1861, by urgent solicitation, returned to Stonington Borough; rich and constant blessings followed; he is here now laboring with great honor, having served at this post twenty-seven years; received from Madison University the honorary degree of Doctor of Divinity; in 1844 published a small volume, "The Early Baptists of Connecticut;" in 1872, a "Historical Discourse" (Centennial), given before the Stonington Union Association; above one hundred sermons and sketches in the *Christian Secretary*, of Hartford, various missionary papers of worth, numerous poems and sonnets, and a superior translation of "Dies Iræ;" is a preacher of remarkable gravity, unction, and earnestness; possesses marked talents, guided by strong faith; for years was president of the Connecticut Baptist State Convention; always a strong advo-

Nearly 200 have been baptized since his labors in Bridgeton began, the membership has almost doubled, and the work of the church has been very much enlarged. In connection with the South

ETHAN B. PALMER, D.D.

Jersey Institute, Mr. Palmer has found a large field for his labors, and his counsels on the denominational boards are very serviceable.

Palmer, Henry, M.D., an eminent and widely-known physician and surgeon of Janesville, Wis., was born in New Hartford, Oneida Co., N. Y., July 30, 1827. He is a son of Deacon Ephraim Palmer, a well-known Baptist of Edgerton, Wis. His father was a farmer, and Henry assisted in the management of the farm until he was nineteen years of age. During the winter he attended the district schools of his neighborhood. He subsequently completed a full course of studies at the Academy of Cazenovia, N. Y. From his early boyhood he earnestly desired to prepare himself for the medical profession. Owing, however, to his want of pecuniary resources he was obliged to delay his cherished plan, and several years were devoted to other pursuits, chiefly teaching school. In 1851 he entered the office of Drs. March and Armsby, at Albany, N. Y., both of whom were distinguished physicians and professors in the Albany Medical College, from which he graduated in 1854. In 1857 he established himself in Janesville, Wis., where he has built up a very extensive local practice, and in surgery his field covers the State at large. Since the death of Dr. E. B. Wolcott, of Milwaukee, he ranks as the leading surgeon in Wisconsin.

ALBERT GALLATIN PALMER, D.D.

cate of education, temperance, and missions; a leader among Connecticut Baptists.

Palmer, Ethan B., D.D., was born in Austerlitz, N. Y., March 12, 1836; baptized at East Hillsdale in 1852; graduated from Madison University in 1860, and from the seminary in 1863; was ordained in the city of New York, Jan. 6, 1864; labored in Newbern, N. C., and at other places. In March, 1872, he began his pastorate of the First church, Bridgeton, N. J., where he continues.

On the outbreak of the civil war in 1861, Dr. Palmer offered his services to the State, and was commissioned surgeon of the 7th Wis. Regiment. Subsequently he was appointed director of the hospital service in Baltimore. He was afterwards transferred to the same service in York, Pa. At this post he remained two years. When Gen. Lee's army commenced the invasion of Pennsylvania, York fell into their hands, and he was taken prisoner, but escaped during the progress of the battle of Gettysburg, and immediately took possession of his hospital, filling it with the wounded from the battle-field. In March, 1864, he was assigned to duty as medical inspector of the 8th Corps of the Army of the Potomac. He continued in this position until the end of the war, when he was ordered to Chicago to close up the medical department of the Western district. This service performed, he returned again to the practice of his profession in Janesville, Wis., having won honorable distinction in the army, and the highest place in his profession.

For many years Dr. Palmer has been a Baptist. The numerous demands made upon his time by his professional engagements prevent his sharing largely in the active work of the church of which he is a member. He is a man of exemplary life, thorough conscientiousness, and earnestness in his profession. Twice his fellow-townsmen have elected him mayor of the city. During the late war between Turkey and Russia, Dr. Palmer went to Europe for the purpose of visiting the hospitals of the contending armies, to acquaint himself with the latest results of the science of surgery attained by the profession in those countries. He was freely passed through the lines, and allowed every facility for accomplishing his object.

Dr. Palmer has won an enviable position, but at fifty years of age, in fine physical health, with unimpaired mental powers, he may be said to have but entered upon his professional career. His past splendid success justifies the hope of his friends that his future will be brilliant, and of still larger usefulness to his fellow-men.

Palmer, Rev. Lyman, was born in Dutchess Co., N. Y., Aug. 19, 1818; his parents were both Baptists, and their home was a place of hearty welcome for ministerial brethren at all times. In his early years he listened to many theological discussions in the quiet old farm-house of his parents. After repeated struggles with his conscience, aroused by the truth and the Holy Spirit, he became a subject of redeeming grace at the age of nineteen. He at once united with the Baptist church in East Hillsdale, Columbia Co., N. Y. Soon after making a profession of religion, he had deep convictions of duty in reference to preaching the gospel. The salvation of his soul was so precious an event that he felt he owed his best

services to the Saviour, who had redeemed him. A sense of unfitness and of the magnitude of the work at first appeared an impassable barrier. Through increasing light he was brought to say

REV. LYMAN PALMER.

from the heart, " Yes, Lord, I will do anything thou requirest." After a few months he received a license from the church and a call to supply their pulpit.

He entered Madison University in the autumn of 1843. He had previously attended an academy, where he had made some proficiency in Latin and Greek. After one year of close application to study his health became so precarious that he left the university, and read Greek and Hebrew with a private teacher, and at the same time studied theology with his pastor. On Lord's day he supplied destitute churches. In February, 1845, he was ordained, that he might go to Iowa as a missionary of the American Baptist Home Mission Society. Before he was ready to journey West he was prostrated by fever, and thus prevented from entering his chosen field. With returning health he entered upon missionary work in Columbia Co., N. Y. Here the work of the Lord prospered in his hands, blessed results crowning his labors. He organized a church, nearly all of whom were converted and baptized under his ministry. In 1851 he received an appointment from the American Baptist Home Mission Society to labor in the Territory of Minnesota. In November, 1851, he started for the falls of St. Anthony, but having to cross the State of Illinois with a wagon, he did not reach the Mississippi at Galena until after the last boat of the season had gone up the river. He remained in Galena during the winter and supplied the Baptist pulpit. His first sermon in St. Anthony was preached on Lord's day, April 24, 1852. The church was small, and in debt for their unfinished chapel. After three years' hard labor the church increased to a membership of 67. He then went up the river fifteen miles, to the town of Anoka. Here he preached in private houses, or in school-houses, or on board of steamboats, as opportunity presented. After three years' untiring labor a good meeting-house was dedicated, and; by the generosity of friends, was soon free from debt. He served the Anoka church eight years, leaving them with a good working membership of 50. A part of the time during the war, teachers being very scarce, he engaged in teaching. In August, 1864, he commenced labor as colporteur of the American Baptist Publication Society. With the exception of about one year, he labored either as colporteur or Sunday-school missionary until 1875. While in the employment of the society he traveled 36,700 miles, distributed by sale and donation 12,700 books, 423,000 pages of tracts, besides selling and giving away many Bibles and Testaments. These were years of severe service, traveling in all weathers, by night and by day, summer and winter, lodging in all manner of. places, yet they were happy years, for much good was accomplished in them. Many Christians were strengthened, the weary and heavy-laden were pointed to Christ, and Sunday-schools and churches were organized for the Master.

Palmer, N. J., Esq.—Among the departed worthies of our Zion this earnest man deserves honorable mention. He was a lawyer, an editor, and sometimes preached. For many years he was secretary of the Baptist State Convention, North Carolina, and a trustee of Wake Forest College. He was a devoted Christian, and died where he had lived for many years, in Milton, in 1855.

Palmer, Rev. Wait, the first pastor of the First Baptist church in North Stonington, Conn., was ordained in 1743, at the same time that the church was organized; remained pastor twenty-two years; preached often in destitute regions; baptized Rev. Simeon Brown and Rev. Shubal Stearns; was an actor in the great "New Light," or Separatist movement; also an active patriot in the Revolution, soon after which he died. The Baptist ministry in Connecticut has been honored by the Palmers: Christopher Palmer, ordained in 1782; Abel Palmer, in 1785; Reuben Palmer, in 1785; Gresham Palmer, in 1805; Phineas Palmer, in 1808.

Palmer, Rev. William, son of Rev. Abel and Lois Palmer, was born in Colchester, Conn., Sept. 10, 1785: was a student from boyhood; was converted and baptized at the age of eighteen; re-ceived a license and commenced preaching at the age of twenty; in 1807 was married to Sarah Bennett, sister of Revs. Alfred and Alvin Bennett; in 1809 was ordained at Colchester, sermon preached by Rev. Samuel Bliss, of Stafford; settled in Ashford, Conn., and labored three years; settled in his native town and preached ten years; from 1824 to 1834 was pastor of the First Baptist church in Norwich, Conn., succeeding Rev. John Sterry; blessed with remarkable revivals in 1829 and 1832, in which he baptized more than a hundred; three years with the church in East Lyme, Conn.; four years with the church in North Lyme; revivals attended his labors; again filled the pastoral office in Norwich from 1841 to 1845, when impaired health compelled his retirement from the pulpit except occasionally. He was lovely and loved, meek. quiet, fervent, and faithful. Passionately fond of study, he held a high rank as a preacher. For twenty-five years he was the clerk of the New London Baptist Association. He died in Norwich, Dec. 25, 1853, at the age of sixty-eight, and after a ministry of forty-eight years, and was buried in Yantic cemetery.

Parker, Rev. Carleton, was born in Hopkinton, Mass., Nov. 30, 1806, and was fitted for college at South Reading and Amherst Academies. He graduated at Waterville College, now Colby University, in the class of 1834. He intended to have entered the ministry on graduating, but the state of his health forbade him, and he devoted himself to teaching for nearly twenty years. Four years he was the principal of the Vermont Literary and Scientific Institution at Brandon. From 1841 to 1844 he had charge of Groton Academy, in the State of New York. For three years he had a "Home School for Boys" in Framingham, Mass. Feeling that the state of his health now warranted his entering the ministry, he was ordained pastor of the Baptist church in Wayne, Me., in May, 1852. He held this relation until September, 1856, then went to Hebron, Me., where he was the pastor for seven years. His other pastorates were in Maine, at Canton, Norridgewock, and North Livermore, where he died, Aug. 22, 1874. By his will he bequeathed several thousand dollars to four of the benevolent societies of the denomination which he had served so long and so well.

Parker, Hon. D. McNeil, M.D., deacon of the Baptist church, Granville Street, Halifax, Nova Scotia, was born in 1822, at Windsor, Nova Scotia; graduated M.D. from the University of Edinburgh, Scotland, in 1845; returned immediately to Nova Scotia, and has ever since been practising his profession in Halifax with high reputation for skill; is a member of the Legislative Council, a governor of Acadia College, and a liberal supporter of all denominational objects.

Parker, H. I., D.D., was born of pious parents at Cavendish, Vt., Nov. 12, 1812. At the age of eighteen he was converted, and four years later was baptized by Rev. Joseph Freeman, D.D. After two years' study at the Norwich and the Black River Academies, and one year at Dartmouth College, he spent two years as instructor at "The Old Cambridge Latin School," graduated at Harvard University in 1840, and studied theology at Newton. He was ordained at Factory Point, Vt., in January, 1842, and was pastor at Burlington, Vt., from 1844 to 1854, when he removed to Wisconsin to aid in establishing the Baptist Institution at Beaver Dam, and was pastor there from 1856 to 1861, when, on account of ill health, he removed to Austin, Minn. Here he preached at six different stations, where as many churches were afterwards organized. In 1872 he settled in California, and has ministered to the churches at Visalia, Santa Barbara, and Santa Anna. During the thirty-eight years of his ministry he has enjoyed many revivals, laid the spiritual foundations of many new churches, built four church edifices, helped to endow and manage two institutions of learning, and was for eight years a member of the Minnesota State Normal Board. In May, 1880, California College conferred upon him the degree of D.D.

Parker, Rev. James, was born in 1812, in Aylesford, Nova Scotia; converted and baptized in 1828; he was ordained May 19, 1842, and became in 1843 pastor of the Baptist church of Brookfield, Queen's Co., Nova Scotia; of the Third Cornwallis church in 1855; of the Third Horton church in 1870; of the Kentville church in 1874; died June 26, 1876. His was a useful life and ministry.

Parker, J. W., D.D., was ordained and settled as pastor of the First Baptist church in Cambridge, Mass., in 1836, and continued to serve in that relation with success during twenty years. At the close of that long pastorate he became secretary of the Northern Baptist Education Society, which position he held about ten years, five of which he was pastor of the Shawmut Avenue Baptist church, in Boston. In January, 1865, he resigned the pastorate of this church, and entered upon the work of establishing schools for training colored men as preachers, and young men and women as teachers, among the freedmen of the Southern States. In this labor Dr. Parker continued about five years, visiting all the Atlantic States many times, introducing teachers into destitute fields, and organizing schools in many towns and cities. While thus occupied his health failed, owing to overwork, hardships, and exposures. Settling down for a while on a small farm in Maryland, he engaged in constant out-door work, and soon regained his usual health. He was then invited to accept the pastorate of the Calvary Baptist church in Washington,

D. C., which he did, occupying the pulpit for about six years with marked success. At the close of this period, feeling the need of rest and change of climate, he visited Europe, where he remained upwards of a year. Soon after his return he was urged to become the pastor of the E Street Baptist church, Washington, D. C., which he consented to do, and he still holds that position. While residing in Massachusetts, Dr. Parker acted for a period of sixteen years as a member of the executive committee of the American Baptist Missionary Union, and in 1849 he was delegated by that body to represent them at the first Baptist Association held in Germany, at the old city of Stettin. Accompanied by that pioneer German missionary, the Rev. J. G. Oncken, he visited the Baptist missions in Denmark and Germany. The missionary stations in France he visited with the Rev. Erastus Willard. From these visits he gleaned many interesting facts which were of great use to the committee in the prosecution of their work in those fields. Dr. Parker stands deservedly very high among his Baptist brethren, as well as among his friends in other denominations, who have long known and acknowledged his sterling worth.

Parker, Rev. Uriah H., an aged Baptist minister residing in Bradley Co., Ark., settled in this part of the State about 1846, and shortly after gathered Shady Grove church in the southern part of Bradley County, the oldest missionary Baptist church between the Ouachita and the Mississippi Rivers. An anti-mission church was gathered at Warren a few years before, but it is long since extinct. Mr. Parker also gathered another church in Bradley County, which was afterwards dissolved. He united his labors with Royal in Drew County, and Tommie in Bradley, and by their common labors the foundations of many of the oldest churches in Bartholomew Association were laid. He often preaches yet with great earnestness and power.

Parker, Rev. Willard G., was born in Annapolis Co., Nova Scotia, April 4, 1816; converted and baptized in 1828; ordained pastor at New Albany, Jan. 28, 1843; was pastor at Sackville, New Brunswick, seven years, and in Nova Scotia at the following places: Nictaux, seventeen years, also of Mitton, Queen's County, Lawrencetown, Valley West, and Pine Grove churches; baptized over a thousand converts; died Dec. 6, 1878; an eminent minister of the gospel.

Parkerism in Indiana.—1. *The Doctrine.*—God never made a creature that will suffer eternally. All the elect were created in union with Christ, and so he was bound by covenant to redeem them. These are the "good seed." The non-elect are the children of the devil, begotten in some mysterious manner of Eve. These are the "bad seed."

2. *The Man.*—Reared on the frontiers of Georgia, "he was without education, uncouth in manners, slovenly in dress, diminutive in person, and unprepossessing in appearance." His enthusiasm bordered on insanity. In 1819 he came into Indiana from his home in Illinois, and at once began to attract attention. He opposed missions, education, and Sunday-schools.

3. *The Motive.*—He sought notoriety as a writer, and was anxious to use the columns of the *Columbian Star*, published in Washington City. His articles were rejected. In his revenge he attacked not only the paper, but all it advocated, such as missions, education, etc.

4. *The Effect.*—Scores of churches and hundreds of members were drawn away after him. And they went so far as to pass resolutions denouncing missions, etc. But finally those churches died as a proper result of their heinous heresy. Parker was excluded from his own church.

Parkhurst, Rev. Jabez W., was born in Middletown, Conn., Jan. 10, 1806. At the age of twenty-two he united with the Baptist church in his native town. In the fall of 1831 he removed to Newton, Mass., fitted himself to enter the theological institution there, and graduated in 1836. For seven years after his graduation he was the pastor of the church in Tyngsborough, Mass., and at the end of this period became pastor of the church in West Dedham, Mass. His pastorate of this church continued for six years, and was closed in consequence of his ill health. He was chosen an agent of the American Baptist Home Missionary Society, and performed the duties of his office for fourteen years. Having closed his relations with the society, he supplied different churches for a time, hoping that his health would be so far restored that he would be able to resume his pastoral work. This hope not being realized, he accepted an appointment as an agent of the Hancock Mutual Life Insurance Company, a position which he occupied until his death, March 19, 1871.

Parkinson, Rev. William, was born in Frederick Co., Md., Nov. 8, 1774. He was convicted of sin in his twentieth year, and in June, 1796, he was baptized by the Rev. Absalom Bainbridge, in Israel's Creek, in his native county. He was ordained to the Christian ministry in April, 1798. He delighted in preaching as an itinerating home missionary, a practice very common among our Baptist fathers, and greatly blessed. In December, 1801, and for "three successive seasons," during Jefferson's administrations he was "a chaplain to Congress." He was chosen to this position by a large majority, and without solicitation on his part. On Lord's day morning he preached in the Capitol, and in the afternoon in the Treasury. He says, "The members of Congress attend abundantly better than I expected; I have, moreover, the pleasure of stating that the President has missed but one of my meetings at the Capitol."

On the 20th of December, 1804, Mr. Parkinson came on a visit to the First Baptist church of New York; after preaching to their great satisfaction for about six weeks, he received an earnest call to become their pastor. Early in April he accepted the call, and very soon after a powerful revival of religion came down upon the church from the throne of grace, and it continued for several years, adding large numbers to the membership of the church, and giving a glorious impetus to Baptist influence, and efforts, and prayers in New York. His congregations were very large, and his sermons swept the people along with him with resistless force. He continued pastor of the First church for thirty-five years, and then resigned, after which he went to Frederick, Md. In 1840 the Bethesda church of New York City, composed chiefly of warm friends of Mr. Parkinson, recently connected with the First church, invited him to become their pastor. He accepted the call, and in 1841 commenced his labors. But soon a fall seriously impaired his health and largely unfitted him for future pulpit efforts; he lingered along for several years, and died March 9, 1848. The last words he uttered were a declaration that "he was in the arms of his precious Saviour." Daniel Dodge, of saintly memory, pastor of the Second church of Philadelphia, preached his funeral sermon in the First Baptist church of New York.

Mr. Parkinson was endowed with a powerful mind, a voice said to be like Whitefield's, and with a large measure of the grace of God. He had some enemies that possessed a great faculty for hating, and he did not always try to disarm them, but he had throngs of warm-hearted friends who loved him living and who bitterly lamented his death.

His published writings were "A Treatise on the Ministry of the Word" and "Sermons on XXXIII. Chapter of Deuteronomy," in two volumes.

Parks, Rev. Harrison H., son of Rev. Benj. M. Parks, was born in Ontario Co., N. Y., March 1, 1815; joined Athens church, O., in 1832; removed to Illinois in 1834; helped to organize the Whitney Grove church and the Old Salem Association; entered upon the work of pioneer preaching in "the far West"; and was ordained in 1847 by the Black Creek church, Mo., of which he became pastor. He subsequently preached for the Quincy, Warsaw, Fall Creek, Lamarsh, Union, and Howard Grove churches, Ill.; was missionary of the Burlington Association, Iowa, and of Bethel church, Ill., until 1876, when he removed to California; has done much to encourage and build up feeble churches; is now serving as pastor the church at Willows, Colusa Co., Cal.

Parks, Rev. James H., was born in New York City, July 13, 1829. He was converted in the year 1847, and united with the Reformed Dutch Church. Soon after he commenced a course of preparation for Rutgers College, having the Christian ministry in view. But health failing, and a series of circumstances arising which brought the subject of Christian baptism to his attention, he was compelled to make a thorough examination of Scriptural teachings upon this subject, which resulted in his being immersed on profession of faith on the 2d of July, 1854.

He afterwards pursued a post-graduate course at Columbian College, Washington, D. C., and received the degree of Master of Arts from that institution upon examination. He was also honored with the degree of A.M. from Princeton College, N. J. He was ordained to the ministry May 28, 1856. He has been pastor of the Baptist churches at Stamford, Conn., Bedford, N. Y., Pemberton, N. J., Manayunk and Calvary, Philadelphia, and is now successfully laboring with the Linden Avenue Baptist church at Dayton, Θ. He also performed faithful service as a chaplain in the army at Washington, D. C., during the late war. His pastorates have been successful and efficient. His views of doctrine are clear, strong, and Scriptural, and are always fearlessly enunciated. He is a positive Baptist, perhaps the more so because his own prejudices, instilled from early childhood, were each successively removed by a specific investigation and a conscientious study of the Word of God.

Parmly, Wheelock H., D.D., was born in Braintree, Vt., July 27, 1816 ; graduated at Columbia College, New York City, in 1842, and from the theological department at Hamilton in 1844; a classmate of George C. Baldwin, of Troy, and others ; spent several years preaching in Louisiana and Mississippi, and for three years was pastor at Shelburne Falls, Mass. In 1850 he took charge of the church in Burlington, N. J., and in 1854 he accepted a call to the First church of Jersey City, of which he remains the beloved, honored, and successful pastor. The city has grown rapidly, and the First church has become large and influential, sending out other churches, which are useful and prosperous. He received the degree of Doctor of Divinity from Madison University in 1867. Dr. Parmly has exercised an extensive influence in the moulding and upbuilding of the missionary and educational institutions of the State. He has a place on the board of the American Baptist Home Mission Society. He is loved by his own people and honored by the denomination in the State.

Patch, Rev. George Washington, was born in Boston, April 30, 1817 ; pursued his preparatory studies in Wakefield, Mass., and New London,

N. H. He was a graduate of Brown University in the class of 1839. Having taken the course of theological study at Newton, he was settled first at Wenham, Mass., and then at Sharon, Mass. From this latter place he was called to Marblehead, Mass., where he had a long and most useful ministry of twenty-six years, and ceased to preach only under the pressure of fatal disease. He died, with scarcely a moment's warning, Dec. 25, 1875. Few ministers have left behind them a better record than he.

WHEELOCK H. PARMLY, D.D.

Paterson, James, D.D., of Glasgow, Scotland, was for fifty years pastor of the first regular Baptist church in that city. He was born in 1801 at Dumbarton, and received his early education at the burgh school, then, as now, of considerable reputation. At first he thought of devoting himself to the medical profession, but during his university course he connected himself with the Glasgow City Mission, and eventually entered the ministry. He had joined the Scotch Baptist Church, but never embraced their views of church polity. In 1829 he hired a room and began to preach. A number of university students came to the poor room, a kind of loft, and, after seeing the place and the congregation, they said, " You never mean, Paterson, to make a kirk out of that !" But he did, and the church which originated with three members gradually grew strong and influential, and is now the largest Baptist church in Scotland. He rendered eminent service to the interests of the denomination, and for many years superintended the theological education of students for the Baptist ministry in Scotland. In 1850 he undertook the editorship of the *Scottish Temperance Review*, and subsequently he edited the *Scottish Review*. His ministry was characterized by solidity and strength, and his life was singularly upright, and marked by a severely conscientious regard for duty and integrity. In everything he put his hand to Dr. Paterson proved himself " a workman who needeth not to be ashamed." In the later years of his life he was aided in the pastoral care of the church by the Rev. James Cubross, D.D., as junior pastor, but he continued to minister to his charge until within a short period of his departure, which took place on Jan. 29, 1880.

Patient, Rev. Thomas, was born in England, and educated, we have no doubt, in Oxford or Cambridge. He became a Congregationalist, and emigrated to New England. After laboring in the ministry on this side of the Atlantic, he was convinced that the Saviour and his apostles were Baptists, and he frankly avowed his convictions. He was immediately subjected to violent persecutions, and to escape them he returned to England.

In 1640 he was appointed co-pastor with Mr. Kiffin in London, where he labored for some time. Parliament having voted that six able ministers should be appointed to preach in Dublin, at a salary of £200 per annum, to be paid from the lands formerly owned by bishops, deans, and chapters, Mr. Patient accepted one of these positions, which was offered to him. In the capital of Ireland he became a very popular preacher, and so gifted was he as an eloquent speaker that at times he traveled much through the country, preaching Jesus wherever he went to delighted throngs of British settlers.

In Dublin he acted as chaplain of Col. John Jones, who was married to a sister of the Protector, and who occupied a seat in his "House of Lords." And such a favorite was he with Col. Jones that he selected him to preach before him and the council every Sunday in Christ church cathedral. This church was completed in 1038, and it was repaired and extensively improved by the celebrated English invader of Ireland, Strongbow. In it he was buried in 1176, and his monument is the chief attraction at this day of a superb church. In this grand old temple, before the governor of Dublin and the *élite* of Anglo-Irish society, Mr. Patient proclaimed a living gospel. He was on friendly relations with Oliver Cromwell himself, as the following quotations from a letter written to the Protector by him will show:

"MY LORD,—From that little acquaintance I had with your excellency before you went out of Ireland, and the suitableness I found in that letter of your experiences, of which I was made a partaker, compared with my observation of the goings of God with you for many years, in this great work in which God hath made use of you, it hath, indeed, very thoroughly confirmed my heart in charity and love towards you, as one elect and precious in the sight of God. . . . Truly God hath kept the heart of my lord deputy close to himself. . . . I am at present, and have been at the headquarters ever since a little before my Lady Ireton (Cromwell's daughter) came over. I do by good experience find, so far as I can discover, the power of God's grace in her soul, a woman acquainted with temptations and breathing after Christ. And I am persuaded it hath pleased God to begin a work of grace in the soul of Col. Henry Cromwell, your son. . . . I watch him, and he is crying much to God in secret. . . . Your grandchild hath been very weak, but it is recovered. . . . I think I shall be at Dublin with my lady (Ireton) this summer."

This letter shows that Mr. Patient had received an epistle from Cromwell, and that he was intimately and religiously associated with several members of his family at that time in Ireland.

Mr. Patient baptized a large number of persons in Dublin. He was a wise and experienced Christian, and he rendered substantial service to the Saviour's kingdom in Ireland. He died July 30, 1666, and the Lord was with him as he passed from this world of the dying into the heaven of the living. His only published work was a quarto volume on baptism.

Patrick, Prof. John B., is a native of Barnwell County, the garden spot of South Carolina. He graduated in the State Military Academy in 1855. From 1856 to 1858 he was tutor in Furman University. In 1859 he was second lieutenant and Assistant Professor of Mathematics, and then Professor of Mathematics and first lieutenant, until the war closed the academy. He was with the cadets during their active service.

In 1866 he was principal of the preparatory department of Furman University. In 1870 he opened the Greenville High School, and in 1878 he converted it into the Greenville Military Institute. He is a very modest man. Those who know him think that few men in the State have exercised a better or more extensive influence over the young men who are assuming the places of the old as they pass away.

Patrick, Saint, the Apostle of Ireland, was of Scotch birth. His proper name was Succathus; the name by which we designate him is of Latin origin; *patricius* means noble, illustrious; it was a surname and a title of honor at the same time given to him by his grateful admirers. Patrick was wild and wicked until his sixteenth year, when he remembered the God of his fathers and repented him of his sins, and enlisted in the divine service. There is no ground for doubting but that he preached the gospel of repentance and faith in Ireland, and that his ministrations were attended by overwhelming success. There are accounts extant of a number of his baptisms, but they are all immersions. There is one baptism mentioned by Nennius (History of the Britons, p. 410. Bohn, London) and by Todd (St. Patrick, Apostle of Ireland, p. 449. Dublin), and found in many other histories, of which O'Farrell writes (Popular Life of St. Patrick, p. 110. New York, 1863), "When the saint entered Tirawly the seven sons (of Amalgaidh) assembled with their followers. Profiting by the presence of so vast a multitude, the apostle entered into the midst of them, his soul inflamed with the love of God, and with a celestial courage preached to them the truths of Christianity; and so powerful was the effect of his burning words that the seven princes and over twelve thousand more were converted on that day, and were soon after baptized in a well (a spring or fountain) called Tobar Enadhaire, the well of Enadhaire." A number of other fountain baptisms of St. Patrick may be found in "The Baptism of the Ages," pp. 62–70. Publication Society, Philadelphia. We have strong reasons for regarding St. Patrick as a Baptist missionary, and beyond contradiction his baptism was immersion.

Patterson, Rev. John W., was born in New Kent Co., Va., Dec. 14, 1850. He was baptized in 1868, entered the Richmond Institute, and was graduated from the same in 1874. He served as missionary of the American Baptist Home Mission Society for some time, and was ordained in July, 1872. He was soon called to the pastorate of the First Baptist church (colored), Danville, Va., where, during five years, he has had abundant success, having baptized nearly one thousand persons. He has been greatly honored by his people, and fills a wide sphere of usefulness. He is an excellent preacher, and quite a vigorous writer, several of his sermons having been published and widely circulated. He is deeply interested in all good movements, and is a trusted leader among his people.

Pattison, Robert E., D.D., was born in Benson, Vt., Aug. 19, 1800. His mother was Sarah Everett, daughter of a physician; his father was a Baptist minister, and Robert was his second son. He united with the Baptist Church when a young man, and soon gave up business for an education to enter the ministry. He prepared for college, and entered Amherst in 1826; stood second in a class of forty. He was tutor in Columbian College, Washington, D. C., then Professor of Mathematics in Waterville College, Me. He was pastor in Salem, Mass., then at Providence, R. I. In 1836 he became president of Waterville College until it suspended for want of means, in 1839. He occupied the pulpit of the Second Baptist church for a year, and returned to

his former charge in Providence. In 1842 he became secretary of the home department of the American Baptist Missionary Union. This position was urged upon him, and he reluctantly left his

ROBERT E. PATTISON, D.D.

church in Providence to fill it. After three years of service he was re-elected secretary, but accepted, in 1845, the presidency of the Western Baptist Theological Institute, at Lexington, Ky. This school was suspended by local difficulties, and Dr. Pattison for six years was a professor at Newton Theological Seminary. Then he resumed, by request, the presidency of Waterville College, and held the office until failing health caused him to retire from labor for a time. He removed to Worcester, Mass., to pass his days free from care, but in two years he assumed the proprietorship of Oread Institute.

In the fall of 1864 he was a Professor of Theology in Shurtleff College. In 1870 he removed to Chicago to become a professor in the Union Baptist Theological Seminary, where he remained until his last illness. In the summer of 1874 his energies began to give way, and after a protracted illness he died at the residence of his eldest son, in St. Louis. Dr. Pattison left as his only literary monument a "Commentary on the Epistle to the Ephesians." Few men have impressed their views more deeply upon others. In all circumstances he possessed a resolute hopefulness and a firmness in adhering to his convictions of right and duty. His powers of persuasion were remarkable, and his life was one of great usefulness and of devoted piety.

Pattison, T. Harwood, D.D., was born in England in December, 1838. He was educated by private tuition, and at the London University School: studied architecture for four years in London; spent

T. HARWOOD PATTISON, D.D.

four years at Regent's Park Baptist College, London, from which he graduated in 1862; was pastor at Newcastle-on-Tyne and Rochdale, in England.

In 1874, during a tour in the United States, he received a call to the pastorate of the First Baptist church of New Haven, Conn. After returning to England he accepted the invitation, and came to this country again in March, 1875, and settled in New Haven. His brilliant pastorate in that city attracted the attention of intelligent Baptists everywhere, and when, in 1879, the Pearl Street church of Albany, N. Y., wanted an under-shepherd to succeed Dr. Bridgman, and fill the position which had been occupied by some of the first ministers in the Baptist denomination, they extended a call to Mr. Pattison. His labors in that city have increased his reputation as a fine scholar, an eloquent preacher, a judicious pastor, and a gospel laborer upon whose efforts the favor of heaven specially rests. He received in 1880 the degree of Doctor of Divinity from Madison University, and he has just been chosen to fill one of the most important chairs in Rochester Theological Seminary.

In the history of our denomination in this country no man has ever acquired such distinguished success in a shorter time than Dr. Pattison, and no one more richly deserves it. Those best acquainted with him anticipate an unusually bright future for

him, rich in the fruits of ripe scholarship, great modesty, ardent piety, and intellectual powers of a high order.

Dr. Pattison, in 1872, published "Present Day Lectures." He is the American correspondent of *The Freeman*, one of the organs of the English Baptists.

Patton, Alfred S., D.D., was born in Suffolk. England, Dec. 25, 1825, came to America when a child, and was educated at Columbian College, Washington, D. C., and Madison University, N. Y. He received the degree of Master of Arts from the former, and Doctor of Divinity from the latter. After graduating he spent some months in Europe.

He was settled as pastor in West Chester, Pa., then in Haddonfield, N. J., then for five years in the First Baptist church of Hoboken, N. J.

In 1859 he accepted the pastorate of the church in Watertown, Mass., and for 1862 and 1863 was the chaplain of the Massachusetts senate.

In 1864 he accepted a call from the old Broad Street church of Utica, N. Y. While there the church built the spacious and attractive house of worship known as the Tabernacle Baptist church. It is located in one of the finest sections of the city. His labors in the new field met with marked success. Dr. Patton is an able preacher, and was a good pastor, possessing remarkable tact and superior

ALFRED S. PATTON, D.D.

social qualities. He has been industrious with the pen. He is the author of the following works: "Kincaid, the Hero Missionary," "The Losing and Taking of Man-Soul, or Lectures on the Holy

War," "Light in the Valley," "Live for Jesus," "My Joy and my Crown," and smaller works published by the American Tract Society. He also contributed articles for the *Christian Review* on "The Influence of Physical Debility on Religious Experience," and "Dreams, their Nature and Uses," also for the Boston *Review*, an article on "Liberal Religion," and for the *Congregational Review*, one on "The Temptation."

In 1872 he purchased the *American Baptist*, and soon after changed its form to a quarto and the name to the *Baptist Weekly*, since which time that journal has taken high rank among Baptist periodicals. He is a firm supporter of all the great enterprises of his denomination, and though kind and considerate to all Christian communities, he is a strenuous supporter of Baptist doctrines and polity.

Patton, Rev. Garrett R., pastor of the Baptist church in Juda, Wis., was born in Fayette Co., Pa., in April, 1811. He passed his youth in the place of his birth, and was educated in the common schools of his neighborhood. In 1830 he made a profession of religion, and united with the Baptist church in Smithfield, Fayette Co., Pa. He was licensed to preach the gospel in 1839, and ordained by the church with which he united when converted. He was pastor of the Monongahela Baptist church in 1839. In 1845 he removed to Juda, Greene Co., Wis., and became pastor of the Baptist church in that place, in which relation he has remained until the present time. He gathered and organized churches in the same county at Monticello, Wyota, and Monroe. He has held the same pastorate longer than any minister in Wisconsin. He is a faithful and successful preacher of the gospel. His ministry has been frequently blessed with revivals of great power. In his seventieth year he is preaching with much acceptance to one of the largest churches in the State.

Patton, Rev. John, was born in 1752, in Kent Co., Del. He was baptized by the Rev. Abel Griffith, of Welsh Tract, in 1789. In 1793 he settled in Shamokin, Pa., and became pastor of the church formed the following year in that place. In 1809 he removed to Fayette Co., Pa., and assumed pastoral care of the Mount Moriah Baptist church. This relation continued until his death, in 1839, aged eighty-seven. Half a century was given to the ministry, and judging from the warm expressions of aged members, both in the Eastern and the Western field he occupied for so many years, he must have been a man of more than ordinary ability and of great activity. As the founder of the ancient church of Shamokin his memory will not perish. Thirteen children and a very large circle of grandchildren, as well as the church he so faithfully served, mourned his loss. One son, James, became a preacher, as did also three grand-

sons,—John P. Rockafeller, G. R. Patton, and Wm. R. Patton. The latter is a graduate of the university at Lewisburg, and a graduate of the Crozer Theological Seminary. He is now pastor of two churches, the Flatwoods, Fayette Co., and the Greensborough, Greene Co., Pa., and is highly respected as a Christian, a minister, and a citizen.

Paul, Rev. Thomas, a gifted and eloquent colored preacher, was born in Exeter, N. H., Sept. 3, 1773, and at the age of sixteen became a Christian. At the age of twenty-eight he commenced preaching, and was ordained at Nottingham West, N. H., May 1, 1805, and soon after became the pastor of the African Baptist church in Boston, where he remained for more than twenty years. He had a fine, commanding presence, and a fervent, pleasing address, so that his preaching was exceedingly attractive, and crowds came to hear him when he preached, as he frequently did, in the towns about Boston. Genuine revivals of religion occurred under his ministry, and he was highly respected and beloved wherever he went.

Mr. Paul was much impressed with the need of evangelical labor in the island of Hayti, and in 1823 he offered himself to the Massachusetts Baptist Missionary Society as a missionary to the people of that island. He was accepted, and on reaching the field of his labor, addressed himself with great earnestness to his work. But his ignorance of the French language made it impossible for him to reach the people whom he was especially desirous of influencing, and he returned to this country, once more to preach the gospel here. It has been said of him, "He was not an ordinary man. For without the advantages of a good education in early life he became distinguished as a preacher. His understanding was vigorous, his imagination was vivid, his personal appearance was interesting, and his elocution was graceful. We have heard him preach to an audience of more than one thousand persons, when he seemed to have command of their feelings for an hour together. On baptismal occasions he was truly eloquent. His arguments were unanswerable, and his appeals to the heart were powerful. The slow and gentle manner in which he placed candidates under the water and raised them up again produced an indelible impression on the spectators, that they had indeed seen a 'burial with Christ in baptism.'" Mr. Paul died April 14, 1831.

Paulicians.—See ALBIGENSES.

Paullin, Rev. James Stratton, was born in Eufaula, Ala., June 7, 1837, and united with the Baptist church in that place in 1853; ordained in 1858; then became pastor of the church in Clayton, where he remained until 1873; removed to Midway, and was pastor there for four years; then pastor of Broad Street church, Mobile, one year; then

57

returned to his old charge at Clayton, where he remains. Mr. Paullin is an earnest Christian and a thorough Baptist, a working pastor, and a good preacher of the gospel.

Pavey, Rev. Charles, was born in England, and licensed to preach by the Fifty-third Street church, New York, in 1849. In 1860 he was ordained, and he took charge of the Hilltown church, Bucks Co., Pa., where he died in 1871. His ministry as a licentiate and as a pastor was greatly blessed. He had an unusual measure of consecration to God. His views of the doctrines of sovereign grace were eminently Scriptural, and his presentation of them was very earnest and effective. The Hilltown church, so blessed by the labors of Father Mathias, felt the death of Mr. Pavey to be a heavy affliction. His memory is warmly cherished by the people and church of Hilltown.

Paxton, Rev. James Edwards, a useful pioneer Baptist preacher in North Louisiana, by whose labors many of the churches in Bienville, Natchitoches, Jackson, Claiborne, and Bossier Parishes were founded, was born in Kentucky in 1820; aided in the organization of Red River Association and the Louisiana Baptist State Convention, and as financial agent of Mount Lebanon University raised the principal part of the endowment of that institution. Removing to Texas, he became in succession pastor at Anderson, Washington, Independence, and Brenham; died in 1876.

REV. WILLIAM EDWARDS PAXTON.

Paxton, Rev. William Edwards, was born in Little Rock, Ark., in 1825; graduated at George-

town College, Ky., under the presidency of Howard Malcom, D.D., by whom he was baptized in 1845; removed to Louisiana in 1853, and engaged in the practice of law; during the war served, with the rank of captain, in the Confederate army; entered the ministry in 1864 and became pastor at Minden; in 1873, president of Shreveport University; in 1877, corresponding secretary of the Southern Baptist Publication Society; in 1878, took charge of the Centennial Institute, Warren, Ark., where he now (1880) teaches and preaches. He has contributed largely to the denominational literature of the South. Besides many articles as contributor or editor, he is the author of the following works: "Rights of Laymen," "Apostolic Church," "Faith a Prerequisite to Church Membership," a premium essay published by American Baptist Publication Society, and "Endless Retribution." He is one of the ablest and most cultured ministers in the Baptist denomination.

Pearce, Rev. Samuel, of Birmingham, England, was born in Plymouth, July 20, 1766. In boyhood he occasionally had distressing convictions of sin. When he was fifteen years of age he was in the house of a dying man, who, in despair, exclaimed, "I am damned forever." As the words fell upon the ear of the youth he was filled with horror for the fate of his father's dying friend, and with anguish for his own guilty state; and though his distress on account of sin grew less, it was not until about a year after, when the sermon of a man of God made him grieve over sin more deeply than ever, and pointed out to his hopeless soul the wounded Saviour, that the truth as it is in Jesus gave him peace. His heart was full of Christ, and completely relieved of all fears. He was blessed with full assurance of faith, and as a result, with joy unspeakable and full of glory.

Soon after this he made a covenant with Jehovah, signing it with his own blood, pledging himself completely to the Lord. But though his heart was full of ardor, and his resolution firmly taken, it would seem that he trusted too much to himself, and he partly broke his vows; in consequence of which he was overwhelmed with despair, until the cross with the agonizing Redeemer took the place of his violated covenant as his great source of comfort.

He was educated for the ministry at Bristol College, and during his stay there he was often engaged in preaching Jesus to the poor and neglected in and around that city, and his grand theme on these occasions was "The Sacrifice of Calvary."

In the latter part of 1789 he was ordained pastor of the Cannon Street church, Birmingham, where his ministry was continued till he rested from his labors and his pains.

At one period his mind was a little agitated in

reference to Arminianism and Socinianism : he was then a young man weighing for the first time the shrewdest sophistries of the enemies of truth. But he was completely cured by a dangerous malady which seized him, in the distresses and apprehensions of which he saw that "his diligence, faithfulness, and unspotted life" were no props to sustain a departing soul, that only the omnipotent and guilt-atoning Saviour could protect him, and from that moment the perfect Lamb of his first religious experience was his whole trust till he met him face to face.

He was the friend of Carey and Fuller before Carey went to India, and he was one of the warmest advocates of foreign missions that dwelt on earth since the Son of Mary came from his heavenly home on a foreign mission to this lost world. During his whole life after entering upon the ministry, and while his health was unbroken, he had a continual struggle about going out as a missionary to India. His popularity as a minister was immense, his people loved him tenderly, his usefulness showed that the seal of God was deeply impressed upon his ministry. The board of the Missionary Society, at his request, gave an opinion upon his duty to go to the heathen, and their decision was that as he was more useful to foreign missions in England than he could be in India, he should remain in Birmingham ; nevertheless, his heart was in India with his friend Carey until he was carried by angels to his Saviour's presence in glory. He rendered effective service to the cause of missions by his eloquent appeals in Birmingham and in various parts of England, and also in Ireland. And in 1794 he wrote to Dr. Rogers, of Philadelphia, and made a rousing appeal to him to try and secure the formation of an American Baptist Foreign Missionary Society.

Mr. Pearce died of consumption, Oct. 10, 1799, after a ministry of only ten years. His last illness was full of hope, patience, and the love of Christ. He had great faith in prayer, and he carried everything to the Saviour, with whom he wrestled with persevering importunity till the Lord revealed his will. He continually thirsted for the presence of God; life was nothing without it, nor any amount of earthly success or joy. His peace was unusual, and it was apparent to all that knew him. He was sure that his Saviour loved him, that nothing could hurt him, and that he had a home and a divine welcome awaiting him in the heavens, and he was one of the happiest of men. His love for God was all-engrossing and ever-enduring, and his love for men embraced every one, and in needful situations would give everything. He was like Fenelon, Robert Murray McCheyne, of Dundee, or the apostle John, the friend of God and the friend of man. And in his ten years' ministry he left an impression that lives in Birmingham, and in many parts of England to-day, though he has been in his grave for eighty-one years. Measured by usefulness instead of years this young pastor preached for at least a century.

Peat, Rev. J. B., was born in England, Sept. 24, 1816. His father died in 1818, and his mother in 1824, and he was thus left an orphan at an early age. America had such attractions for the boy that he emigrated to the New World in his young manhood, and when converted gave his whole heart and service to the cause of Christ, and won for himself much esteem as a zealous and conscientious preacher in some of the Western States. About the year 1870 he visited California for his health, and received much benefit. He became pastor at the city of Red Bluff, where he died, Nov. 15, 1876. He was very active in temperance and other reform movements. He was the author of the following published works: "The Baptists Examined," "Sure," and "Parsonage Pencillings."

Peay, Rev. John M., was born in Rutherford Co., Tenn., May 19, 1832. He removed to Kentucky in his youth. After attending the common schools, he finished his education, under the supervision of Rev. Dr. J. S. Coleman, at Beaver Dam, Ohio Co., Ky. He united with the Sandy Creek Baptist church in 1853, was licensed to preach in 1854, and was ordained at Beaver Dam in 1857. In 1858 he took charge of the Baptist church at South Carrollton, where he still labors. He has been pastor of three other churches most of the time since he was ordained. He is a powerful and practical preacher, and has been a very successful pastor. He is a vigorous writer, and has published several works, which have met with popular favor. He is also senior editor of *The Student*, an educational journal, published in South Carrollton.

Peay, Rev. Richard Dawson, A.M., brother of John M. Peay, was born in Coffee Co., Tenn., Nov. 10, 1846. He was baptized into the fellowship of Green River Baptist church, in Ohio Co., Ky., in 1864. Entered Bethel College in 1866, graduated with the honor of his class in 1871, was ordained at South Carrollton in 1872, and immediately took pastoral charge of the Portland Avenue Baptist church in Louisville, Ky. After remaining three years he accepted a call to the church in Henderson, Ky. In 1879 he became the principal of the high school in Henderson, meanwhile preaching on the Lord's day to the church at that place.

Peck, Rev. A. C., was born June 25, 1846, at Munson, Geauga Co., O.; graduated at the University of Wisconsin in 1866; taught high school at Freeport, Ill., one year; united with the Baptist church there, and was licensed to the ministry; took a three years' course in the theological seminary at Rochester, N. Y., graduating in 1870; was called to the pastorate at Mumford, N. Y., but, on account of ill health, did not enter upon it; came to Kansas in 1871; engaged in teaching and farming. In 1872 taught in the university at Ottawa, and was called to the pastorate of the Baptist church there; ordained in January, 1873; resigned on account of failing health in 1874; elected superintendent of schools of Franklin Co., Kansas; called to the First Baptist church, Lawrence, Kansas, in October, 1875, where he still ministers.

Peck, Rev. Elijah, was born May 3, 1767, in Warren, Conn. Early in the spring of 1795 he removed from Cooperstown, N. Y., into the "Beech Woods," and settled in Mount Pleasant, Wayne Co., Pa. This journey, in company with his wife and three children, he performed with an ox-team and sled; modern luxuries were then unknown. In June, 1806, he received ordination. From March 3, 1808, until his decease, March 16, 1835, he was the esteemed pastor of the Mount Pleasant church, but, like all pioneer ministers, he performed a vast amount of work in regions round about. "His general appearance indicated great activity and power of endurance. His voice was musical and pleasant, and his manners affable and modest." "He moved in a sphere of great usefulness," and "served his own generation by the will of God."

Peck, Rev. John, was born in Milan, Dutchess Co., N. Y., Sept. 11, 1780. He found full relief from sin, through faith in Jesus, in his eighteenth year, and was baptized. On the 11th of June, 1806, he was ordained as pastor of the First church in Cazenovia, after preaching to the people for eighteen months. This relation continued until 1835, when he resigned to give himself to more extended usefulness. There was spiritual prosperity among his people when he left them, and his ministry among them had been greatly blessed. Six churches were organized chiefly from members dismissed from Cazenovia, and fifteen of her young men had been ordained as pastors of other churches. It was the greatest trial of his life to break the holy tie that united him to his dear people.

He was a warm friend of the Baptist Education Society of the State of New York, which established the Hamilton Literary and Theological Society, now Madison University. He was an active supporter of the Hamilton Baptist Missionary Society, which accomplished a great work for the Saviour over an extensive section of New York; and when it was merged into the Baptist Missionary Convention of the State of New York, he became the general agent of the new body, and served for fifteen years with abounding success. Mr. Peck was a good man, full of the Holy Spirit, whose name will ever be remembered with gratitude in the wide sphere in which his labors were performed. He died Nov. 15, 1849.

Peck, John Mason, D.D., was born in the parish of Litchfield, South Farms, Conn., Oct. 31, 1789. His conversion took place in 1807, when he was eighteen years of age. He first united with the Congregational church in Litchfield. Removing, in 1811, to Windham, Greene Co., N. Y., he became acquainted with the Baptists through the church, and through the pastor, Rev. H. Harvey, in the adjoining town of New Durham. He had already become doubtful of Pedobaptist views and practices, and now, after further inquiry, having fully abandoned those views, he was baptized, Sept. 14, 1811, uniting with the church in New Durham. On the next day, by invitation of the church, he preached his first sermon, and was immediately licensed, and in 1813 was ordained as pastor of the Baptist church in Catskill. After a brief pastorate here, and another at Amenia, in Dutchess County, he accepted an agency in behalf of foreign missions, laboring under the guidance of Rev. Luther Rice. He then, 1816–17, had a year of study under Dr. Stoughton, of Philadelphia. He was then appointed a missionary of the board of the Triennial Convention, to labor in St. Louis and vicinity. Thus began his Western career. July 25, 1817, he set out, with his wife and three children, in a covered wagon, upon the long journey of 1200 miles to his field of labor, and on the 1st of December reached St. Louis. His associate, Rev. James E. Welch, had reached the field before him. In 1822 he became a resident of Rock Spring, Ill., and this remained his home until his death.

At Rock Spring, Dr. Peck, in connection with his missionary labors, now under the appointment of the Massachusetts Baptist Missionary Society, established a seminary for general and theological education, being aided in this, to some extent, by Eastern friends. The seminary was certainly a successful one. It is said to have had at one time one hundred students. As another sphere of auxiliary labor, he began, April 25, 1828, the publication of a paper,—the *Western Pioneer and Baptist.* His work in preaching, meantime, covered a very wide region; while all the affairs of the Territory, soon to become the State of Illinois, engaged his intelligent and active interest. In due time the Rock Spring Seminary became united with the seminary at Upper Alton, now Shurtleff College. Dr. Peck, aside from other labors, wrote largely. Among his works were "A Biography of Father Clark," "Emigrant's Guide," "Gazetteer of Illinois," "Annals of the West," and other works. He died at Rock Spring, March 24, 1857, in the sixty-eighth year of his age. He was a man of many remarkable qualities, robust in intellect, strong in purpose, positive in his opinions, and bold in their advocacy, a born missionary, and a thorough-going Western man.

Peck, Solomon, D.D., was born in Providence, Jan. 25, 1800. He early developed a taste for study, and was sufficiently advanced to enter the Sophomore class in Brown University when he was but thirteen years of age. He graduated in 1816, taught in the University grammar-school and in the college three years and a half; was a student at Andover four years, and was ordained a minister of the gospel in 1823. He preached for a short time in North Yarmouth, Me., and subsequently for one of the churches in Charleston, S. C. He was appointed Professor of the Latin and Hebrew Languages in Amherst College in 1825. In 1832 he visited France in the service of the American Baptist Board of Foreign Missions. A connection was thus commenced with foreign missions which had its influence on what proved to be the great life-work of Dr. Peck. As the secretary of the executive board for twenty hard-working years he performed an amount of clerical work of the magnitude and importance of which few persons can form any conception. He performed not only this home work, but, as an associate with the Rev. Dr. James N. Granger, he traveled extensively in Europe and Asia, visiting the stations of the Missionary Union, suggesting plans, setting things in order, and in many ways doing what lay in his power to advance the cause he so much loved.

After resigning his position as secretary of the board in Boston he spent some time at Beaufort and Edisto Island, S. C., laboring for the mental and spiritual improvement of the colored race. His last public service was as chaplain to the Home for Disabled Soldiers, in Boston, and as secretary of the Freedmen's Aid Society. Dr. Peck died June 12, 1874.

Peckham, Rev. William Augustus, was born in 1810, in Euclid, O., where he lived until he reached manhood, when he removed with his parents to Ontario, N. Y. In early life he experienced religion, and united with the Methodist Episcopal Church. But about the year 1836 his religious views changed, and he united with the Baptist church in Lyons, N. Y., where he was then residing. In 1840 he was licensed to preach, and in 1845 was ordained by the Baptist church in Cassadaga, N. Y., where he was settled as pastor. In 1847 he came to Wisconsin and settled in Jones County, devoting his ministry to the churches in Franklin and Highland. The following year he removed to Aztalan, Jefferson Co., Wis., where he shortly afterwards died. He is remembered by the older ministers of the State as a very earnest and devout Christian minister, from whom much was hoped in those early pioneer days.

Peckworth, Rev. John P., was born in England about 1770, and came to this country when he was thirteen years of age. He united with the First Baptist church in Wilmington, Del., but afterwards he removed to Philadelphia, and joined the First church in that city. He was ordained in 1808, and the next year he and others formed the Third Baptist church of Philadelphia, of which he became the pastor. The new community prospered greatly under his earnest and godly ministrations, and became a strong body. In 1823 he went to Baltimore, and after some other changes of residence and scenes of labor he died at Wilmington, March 7, 1845, in his seventy-fifth year, in the full enjoyment of a blessed hope through the blood of the Lamb.

Peddie Institute.—Eaton's school at Hopewell was not forgotten when Brown University flourished and academies grew in other States. In 1848 the subject of academic education was agitated in New Jersey, and schools were begun at Salem and Plainfield.

"In 1863 the following decisive action was taken" by the Baptist State Convention held at Bordentown:

"*Resolved,* That a committee be appointed to take into consideration the desirableness and propriety of making arrangements immediately for establishing a *Literary Institution* under the patronage of our denomination in New Jersey."

The next year, 1864, the following was adopted:

"*Resolved,* That the efforts of brethren to establish a first-class school at Hightstown, to be under the control of the Baptists, meet the hearty approval of this body, and that we pledge to it our cordial support."

In the month of March, 1866, a charter was first obtained. In 1867 the subject of a new building began to be earnestly considered, and (two years after) on Oct. 26, 1869, it was formally opened as "The New Jersey Classical and Scientific Institute."

In 1872 the charter was so altered as to change the name to that of Peddie Institute, in honor of its munificent donor, Hon. T. B. Peddie, of Newark. Mr. Peddie's gifts and subscription to this institute now amount to more than $50,000. And besides him the names of such men as Colgate, Trevor, Wyckoff, Van Wickle, Judges Runyon and Cook, Hon. D. M. Wilson, Rev. W. V. Wilson, and many others good and true, are to be remembered for their large donations, as well as the masses of Baptists who gave liberally to secure the valuable property at Hightstown. During its brief existence it has furnished many students who in the professions and in mercantile life have been a credit to the school and the denomination. Under

PEDDIE INSTITUTE, HIGHTSTOWN, N. J.

Prof. E. J. Avery and his corps of teachers it is steadily progressing.

The building consists of a centre and wings in line. It is 255 feet in length, five stories high, including basement and attic. The three middle stories of the wings contain eighty-four rooms for students and teachers, each room designed to accommodate two occupants. In the attics are the rooms for the literary societies, and in the ladies' building, the music-rooms; the rest is occupied for dormitories. The basement in the north wing contains the school-room for the primary department, artists' rooms, suite of rooms for teachers, and four rooms for students.

The kitchen, laundry, steward's private rooms, servants' sleeping-rooms, and steward's office are situated in the basement of the south wing. The basement of the centre contains the dining-room; the first story, the small chapel in the rear, and the parlors in front; the second story, two school-rooms in front, and three recitation-rooms in the rear; the third story, the laboratory and lecture-room in the rear, and three rooms for library cabinets in the front. The attic is designed for a large chapel or temporary gymnasium. Water-tanks are situated at the extreme ends of each wing, under the roof, supplying water to each story, by means of pipes, furnished with faucets, passing down through the end rooms in front. These are also designed for bath-rooms. The whole building is heated by apparatus in the cellar.

Peddie, John, D.D., was born of Scotch parents, in Ancaster, Ontario, May 24, 1838; was converted when seventeen years of age, and pursued a full course of study at Madison University and Hamilton Theological Seminary, graduating from the latter institution in 1865. Settled at Watertown, N. Y., in 1865, and remained nearly three years. Became pastor of the Calvary church, Albany, N. Y., in May, 1868, and remained until March, 1871, when he entered upon the pastorate of the Fourth church, Philadelphia. Here he remained for seven years and a half, when he received and accepted a pressing call to the Second church of Chicago, Ill. In the spring of 1880 he became pastor of the First church of New York City. Received the degree of D.D. from Madison University.

Dr. Peddie possesses remarkable pulpit power. His originality of thought, his clear and manly utterances, and his strong sympathetic nature enable him to present the "glad tidings" with an almost irresistible magnetism. He has already baptized nearly 1000 converts, and has cheered and strengthened the faltering faith of many of God's children. The weak and the unfortunate always find in him a true friend, and few men have so largely won the love and regard of others. His services have been in frequent demand on special occasions, and by his sermons and lectures he has been a generous helper to many enterprises beyond the boundaries of his immediate church work. The close of his pastorate in Philadelphia was made the

JOHN PEDDIE, D.D.

occasion for a special meeting of the Philadelphia Baptist Social Union, at which the farewell greetings were mingled with many tender and eloquent testimonies to the value of his ministry and friendship.

Peddie, Hon. Thomas B., is a native of Edinburgh, Scotland. He received a good education, and in his youth was a great reader. He came to this country in 1833, and settled in Newark, N. J. By strict habits of industry and by remarkable ability his manufacturing establishment is now among the largest of the kind in the country. He has been twice mayor of Newark, the largest city in the State, twice in the State Legislature, and he served in the United States Congress of 1876–78, in which he was placed upon important committees. He has also been president of the board of trade, and in foreign travel has ably represented business interests. When a young man Mr. Peddie made a profession of religion, and was baptized by Rev. Mr. Brown. He united with the First Baptist church in Newark, and as a trustee was particularly active in the building of their fine commodious meeting-house. He takes a deep interest in all the affairs of the church.

When the academy at Hightstown was in great straits Mr. Peddie's sympathies were enlisted, and he gave it at one time a donation of $25,000. His benefactions since have increased this sum to more than $50,000. Mr. Peddie is a generous benefactor

HON. THOMAS B. PEDDIE.

of the Baptist denomination, whose record is an honor to us.

Peirce Academy, Middleborough, Plymouth Co., Mass., was founded by deacon Levi Peirce, of Middleborough. Two purposes were kept in mind in the erection of the academy building in 1808,—one was to furnish a hall suitable to hold public worship in, and the other to secure rooms for the use of the teachers who might have charge of the academy. Like so many institutions of a similar character, the first few years of its existence were years of struggle and varied fortunes. Its history furnishes another illustration of the saying, that "it is hard to get up a Baptist institution, and harder yet to kill it." In 1828, a place for public worship having been built by Deacon Peirce on the lot adjoining the academy, the meeting-house and the academy, with the lots on which they stood, were deeded to the Central Baptist Society; and subsequently the academy passed into the hands of trustees, an act of incorporation having been obtained from the Legislature of Massachusetts for this purpose in 1835. In 1842 it came under the control of Prof. J. W. P. Jenks, and it is due to his energetic efforts and most persistent labors that the institution rose to the high rank which it attained among the academies of New England. A new school building was erected, valuable apparatus and cabinets were secured, and the institution in all its departments was pervaded

with new life. Hundreds of young men and young ladies have been educated within the walls of the academy, and to the entire section of country in which it is located it has proved to be the source of untold good. Too much praise cannot be awarded to Prof. Jenks for the efforts he has put forth and the personal sacrifices he has made in behalf of the institution, to which he has given twenty-nine of the best years of his life. He closed his connection with it in 1871. Its present principal is Mr. George H. Coffin.

Pella, Iowa,—"The City of Refuge,"—was settled by Hollanders. A Baptist church was early organized in it, which has grown in usefulness and numbers. It has a good edifice, recently erected, and its prospects are very encouraging.

The Iowa Central University, one of the educational institutions of the Iowa Baptists, has been located at Pella, and for years has been successfully prosecuting its work.

Pelot, Rev. Francis, a native of Switzerland, was born March 11, 1720. His parents were Presbyterians, and gave their son a fine education. He came to South Carolina in 1734, and joined the Baptists about 1744. He was probably the first pastor of the Euham church, and he continued in the office until his death, in 1774. He held a very high place in the denomination, as was to be expected because of his talents, piety, and wealth. Mr. Edwards once said of him, "He possesses three islands and about 3785 acres on the continent, with slaves and stock in abundance. This (said he) I mention, not to flatter my friend Pelot, but in hope that his conduct may influence other wealthy planters to preach the gospel among the poor Baptists when God inclines their hearts to it." He was very useful in spreading the gospel in South Carolina.

Peltz, George Alexander, D.D., was born in Philadelphia, Pa., May 2, 1833. His ancestry was German on his father's side, and Scotch on his mother's. His father, Alexander M. Peltz, died at an early age, but he had become prominent as a State politician, and especially as an acceptable political speaker. Under the care of a pious mother the subject of this sketch became an attendant at the Spruce Street Baptist church and Sunday-school. This was under the pastorates of the Rev. Dr. Rufus Babcock and the Rev. Thomas O. Lincoln. He subsequently attended the Second Baptist church of Southwark, Philadelphia, afterwards known as the Calvary Baptist church. Here he found the Lord, and was baptized by the Rev. John A. McKean, Jan. 5, 1851. One year later he began preparation for college, and entered the Freshman class at Lewisburg, Pa., in the fall of 1853.

During his college course he labored quite extensively among the churches of the vicinity, especially at Sunbury, Northumberland, Muncy, and Hughesburg. He also took the lectures and other studies of the theological department begun at Lewisburg in 1855. He graduated as valedictorian of his class in 1857, and at once proceeded to New York City, where, on August 1, he took charge of a mission interest founded by two generous Baptists, and located in Continental Hall, corner of Eighth Avenue and Thirty-fourth Street. From this mission the Pilgrim Baptist church was organized, Oct. 7, 1857. Mr. Peltz remained here as pastor for eight years, leaving a united church of 402 members, with a good house of worship and a hopeful outlook.

In October, 1865, he became pastor of the Tabernacle Baptist church of Philadelphia, remaining there until March 31, 1871. During his pastorate the church cleared off its entire indebtedness, thoroughly revised its roll, and was largely increased in membership. Mr. Peltz then devoted himself entirely to Sunday-school work until the end of 1872. In Convention and Institute efforts he traveled over nearly all the States east of the Mississippi. In January, 1873, he settled with the South Baptist church of Newark, N. J. In January, 1876, he returned to Philadelphia to assume the associate editorship of the *The Sunday-School Times*. In November, 1877, he removed into the Chautauqua region, so famous in Sunday-school work, and became pastor of the First Baptist church of Jamestown, N. Y.

In 1869, Mr. Peltz edited the first series of lessons issued by the American Baptist Publication Society. He was the first editor of *The Baptist Teacher*, and held that post for three years. He previously edited a Sunday-school department in *The National Baptist*, and subsequently a similar department in *The Independent*. He contributed largely to the leading Sunday-school papers and lesser publications of the land. He was a member of the Executive Committee of the International Sunday-School Convention for ten years. He presided over this body at its session in Baltimore, in April, 1875. He was chairman of the Baptist National Sunday-School Convention at St. Louis in 1869. For three years he was president of the Pennsylvania State Sunday-School Convention, and for two years its corresponding secretary. He was for nearly two years associate editor of *The Sunday-School Times*. At present he resides in Philadelphia.

Pemberton Baptist Church, at Pemberton (formerly New Mills), a pleasant village in Burlington Co., N. J., surrounded by a rich and beautiful farming country. Its real founder was Francis Briggs, probably a member of the Cohansey church, who settled at New Mills in 1750; invited

Baptist ministers to preach at his house; seven were converted and baptized, and a small meeting-house erected in 1752. A noble example of fidelity and activity worthy of imitation by every isolated Baptist! He died in 1763. In 1764 the church was constituted with nine members, Rev. Peter P. Van Horn pastor. It is counted as the eleventh, as to date of constitution, among existing regular Baptist churches in the State. It immediately united with the Philadelphia Association; in 1812 transferred its membership to the New Jersey Association (now West New Jersey), formed in 1811. Prior to 1816 the following were pastors: Revs. Peter P. Van Horn, David Branson, David Loughborough, Alexander Magowan, Isaac Carlile, Isaiah Stratton. At that date the membership was 164. Rev. John Rogers, who was successful in doctrinating and building up the church, was pastor from 1816 to 1828. A second and larger house of worship was erected in 1823. Then the following pastors: Revs. C. W. Mulford, 1830–35, a time of ingathering; Timothy Jackson, two years; J. G. Collom, seven years, chapel erected in a more central location, for evening meetings and Sunday-school; D. S. Parmalee, about five years; L. C. Stevens, very brief pastorate; S. M. Shute, three years, during which the present parsonage was bought; Thomas Goodwin, three years. Rev. Levi G. Beck's pastorate (1859–64) was signalized by the erection, in 1861, of the present pleasant and commodious house of worship, centrally and conveniently located. Rev. J. H. Parks was pastor from 1864 to 1869; Rev. James W. Willmarth from 1869 to 1878. Various improvements made. Present pastor, Rev. J. C. Buchanan.

From the constitution of the church until now (May, 1880) 911 have been baptized. Present number, 184.

This ancient church is the mother of several churches in the vicinity, has always been self-supporting, has had no debts or mortgages on its property, and has been favored repeatedly with precious revivals. Its membership has been loyal to Baptist principles, kind to pastors, and interested in the general work of the denomination. The field does not, perhaps, give promise of specially rapid growth, but the church is firmly established, has had much faithful instruction, and will doubtless live and prosper. It has sent out several able ministers, has had among its lay members men of steadfast piety and of influence and usefulness, and is dear to all who have been connected with it or have labored with it in the ministry.

Pendleton, James Madison, D.D., was born Nov. 20, 1811, in Spottsylvania Co., Va. His parents, John and Frances J. Pendleton, removed to Christian Co., Ky., when he was one year old, and settled upon a farm near the present village of Pembroke. Upon this farm he lived until he was twenty years old. During the winter seasons he attended the best schools the community afforded, and with the judicious training of his excellent parents he was better educated than the average farmer boy.

At fifteen he became interested in the subject of religion, but his convictions did not result in conversion until he was seventeen, when he united with the Bethel church, near Pembroke. He was baptized by Rev. John S. Wilson, April 14, 1829. In February, 1831, he was licensed to preach, and began the work of the ministry before he was twenty years of age.

He is the only licentiate ever sent forth by the Bethel church to this date (1878). *Unum sed Leonem.* In 1833 he entered the Christian County Seminary at Hopkinsville, and took a three years' course of instruction in the Latin and Greek classics, meantime preaching for the Hopkinsville and Bethel churches alternate Sundays. At the former church he was ordained Nov. 1, 1833. In 1837 he accepted the call of the church in Bowling Green, Ky., and entered upon a pastorate of twenty years. Soon after this settlement he formed the acquaintance of Miss Catharine Stockton Garnett, of Glasgow, Ky., who became his wife in 1838. By her piety and abounding good works she has proved herself to be a model pastor's wife. They have four children living, three of whom are wives of professional gentlemen, and the other, a son, is a lawyer in the city of Philadelphia.

During his twenty years' pastorate at Bowling Green, in 1849, Dr. Pendleton cordially espoused Henry Clay's gradual emancipation measures, and supported them by many newspaper publications. The vote of the State, however, was largely against those measures, and slavery remained unchanged till the "civil war" wrought its overthrow.

In 1857, Dr. Pendleton was elected Professor of Theology in Union University, Murfreesborough, Tenn. He had ever esteemed the pastorate his office and preaching his function in life, and would accept the professorship only with the proviso that he should have a pastorate also. Arrangements were made at once that he should become pastor of the Baptist church in Murfreesborough, and he removed to his new field, where he remained until the civil war laid its paralyzing hand upon church and college. The unquenchable loyalty of the man made it necessary for him to remove to the Northern States. After a short settlement of three years, from 1862 to 1865, at Hamilton, O., he removed, in November, 1865, to Upland, Pa., where he has ever since been the highly esteemed and faithful pastor.

At an early day, Dr. Pendleton became an almost constant writer for the denominational press and for the local papers of his community. Of this kind of literature few men except editors are so prolific. Besides, he has published many books, pamphlets, tracts, and sermons, such as "Three Reasons why I am a Baptist," "Church Manual," "Treatise on the Atonement," "Sermons on Important Subjects," "Christian Doctrines, a Compendium of Theology," the last of which is generally conceded to be a masterly production, concise, logical, orthodox, and comprehensive, and supplying a long felt want in the curriculum of theological education and in the libraries of Christian households.

Dr. Pendleton is a hard student, devoting his morning hours to his study, which he keeps well stocked with only the best and most approved evangelical literature, and history, biography, and philosophy. His impatience with irreverence and looseness guards his library from the intrusion of liberalism and trash.

He preaches as he writes, after a well-defined model or plan, from which he seldom swerves even in the most impassioned efforts. He is methodical in his work, and resolutely follows his prearranged plans, alternating study with pastoral visitation with a regularity few men can maintain. He is devout, serious, conscientious, and yet highly appreciates good wit and humor, and is ready and judicious in the use of them. He is of medium height, well proportioned, firm of step as of convictions, a sincere friend, generous to every good cause according to his ability, unostentatious and affable with his friends, reserved among strangers, and cautious of his associations. His integrity of character and honesty of conviction are absolutely above suspicion, and are due to his abiding, unshaken trust in God.

Pengilly, Rev. Richard, author of the "Scriptural Guide to Baptism," was a native of Penzance, Cornwall, England, where he was born Sept. 14, 1782. In early life he was a member of the Wesleyan Methodist body. Like Samuel, he was devoted to God in his childhood. A baptismal service and a sermon by the Rev. Isaiah Birt attracted his attention to the principles of the Baptists, and in 1802 he was baptized, and became one of the constituent members of the newly-formed Baptist church at Penzance. He had been licensed as a local preacher among the Methodists, and his Baptist brethren encouraging him to exercise his gifts, he was received as a student at Bristol College, and pursued the usual course of study until 1807, when he was sent to Newcastle-on-Tyne as a probationer. Having received a call to the pastorate there, he was ordained Aug. 12, 1807, and continued to minister to the same church until 1845, when he retired from all pastoral work. Although he never accepted another charge, he occupied himself with various evangelical and benevolent engagements which his strength permitted until his death, March 22, 1865, in his eighty-third year. During his long pastorate at Newcastle he did good service. He established the first Sunday-school in the town among the evangelical Non-Conformists, and promoted the formation of the local Bible and tract societies. His denominational work was of great value in the district. He published " Seven Letters to the Society of Friends on the Nature and Perpetuity of Baptism" and several tracts, some of which had a wide circulation. His " Scripture Guide to Baptism" has passed through many editions, and has been translated into the German and other European tongues. Probably no other book on the subject has had such a wide diffusion, or been more generally useful.

Penick, Rev. Wm. Sydnor, was born in Halifax Co., Va., May 12, 1836. His father, William Penick, being a planter in easy circumstances, his early educational advantages were the best that could be secured. After prosecuting his studies for four years under a tutor employed in the family, he entered a school under the care of the Rev. A. M. Poindexter, D.D. At the age of fourteen, his father designing him for mercantile life, he was placed in a store, where he remained for three years. About this time he was converted, and was baptized by the Rev. James Longanacre. At the close of his three years' service in business he resolved to pursue his studies, and entered an academy in his native county. Afterwards, in 1855, he became a student in Richmond College, where he graduated in 1858, with the degree of A.B. In the fall of 1858 he was ordained to the work of the gospel ministry, and early in 1859 took charge of the Baptist church in Chatham, the county-seat of Pittsylvania, Va. In the summer of 1861 he entered the army of the Southern Confederacy as captain of a company. In 1868 he resigned the care of the church in Chatham, and, having removed to the Shenandoah Valley, became pastor of several churches in Jefferson and Berkeley Counties, W. Va. In 1870 he settled in Martinsburg, taking exclusive charge of a church which he had organized there, and directing the building of a handsome house of worship. While a resident of this place he was elected superintendent of the public schools in Martinsburg and Berkeley Counties, and served for two years with great efficiency. About this time Richmond College conferred on him the honorary degree of A.M. In 1874 he entered upon his present field of labor as pastor of the First Baptist church in Alexandria, Va., where his labors have been greatly blessed in enlarging the membership and increasing its influence for good. Mr. Penick is honored for his worth and labors not only by his own congregation but by all who know him.

Penn, Admiral Sir William, was born in England in 1621. His father, the captain of a merchant vessel, taught him his own profession so thoroughly that early in life he was one of the ablest mariners in the British islands. The Mediterranean at that period was full of pirates, whose vessels were the swiftest that plowed its waters ; the crews of these ships were skillful and reckless men, who shed blood without pity, and enslaved freemen without remorse. The son of Captain Giles Penn learned his calling in the ocean specially scourged by the pirates, and as a matter of necessity he was a fighting mariner. At the age of twenty-three William was appointed a captain in the Royal navy, and was ordered to take charge of the " Fellowship," of twenty-eight guns. He rose rapidly to the highest commands in the navy ; before he was thirty years of age he was vice-admiral of the Irish seas ; and, though he died when he was only forty-nine years of age, he was an admiral and general of the British fleet, and had rendered brilliant services to his country.

Some Baptists for years have been under the impression that Penn held their faith. David Benedict and Curtis make this statement; and many others in comparatively recent times. Crosby and Ivimey do not. Neither does a single writer competent to bear testimony on such a question. Southey says that " Sir John Lawson was a rigid Anabaptist," others of an earlier day assert the same thing. But while the religion of the one distinguished admiral is frequently stated, the denomination of the other during the doubtful period of his life is not named. Granville Penn, the great-grandson of Sir William, says, " His church was the Church of England, by whose services he was baptized and buried, and to which he adhered when *it could be found.*" He, no doubt, was baptized in the Episcopal Church, but so were many thousands of Baptists in his day. And his being buried with the Episcopal service affords no evidence that he was an Episcopalian. He died in 1670, under the restored Stuarts, when nothing but the Episcopal service would be tolerated in the parish church of Redclyffe, Bristol, where he was interred. Moreover, a man of Sir William's character under the Stuarts was certain to be a member of the church patronized by the powerful. Granville Penn states that Sir William adhered to the Church of England (Episcopalianism) " when it could be found." Daniel Neal says that in 1641 " the old English hierarchy was suspended, and lay prostrate for about eighteen years." Macaulay says, " The Puritans interdicted (in England), under heavy penalties, the use of the Book of Common Prayer, not only in churches, but even in private houses. It was a crime in a child to read, by the bedside of a sick parent, one of those beautiful collects which had soothed the griefs of forty generations of Christians." Episcopalianism was outlawed in England for years. During this period Sir William Penn never hinted that his preferences were for the Episcopal Church. He would have been, during a large part of the interregnum, instantly removed from his command if he had. It is extremely probable that the politic admiral, especially just before the Protectorate, was a friend of the Baptists. His interests required him to be a Congregationalist or a Baptist, and these were of supreme moment with Sir William Penn. Baptist principles were extensively held in the navy, and they were entertained by his chief friends. So that it is not unlikely that he pretended to favor Baptist doctrines. But we know of no *authority* for the common tradition that Penn was a member of any Baptist church or congregation.

Sir William Penn owed his entire position in the navy to the enemies of the Stuarts. The Parliament first, and Cromwell afterwards, gave him promotion and wealth. When he was about to leave for the West Indies in charge of a fleet of thirty-eight vessels of war, according to Granville Penn, at his own request, he received from Cromwell lands in Ireland worth £300 per annum, "as they were let in 1640," to make up for his losses. On the 4th of December, 1654, the Protector himself wrote to the Lord-deputy and Council in Ireland ordering the speedy selection of the lands given to Penn, and Cromwell directs that they should be chosen "where there is a castle, or convenient house of habitation upon them, and near to some garrison for security." Cromwell gives as a reason for the special interest which he showed in Penn's lands, that the admiral "is now engaged in further service for the Commonwealth in the present expedition by sea, and cannot himself look after the settling of the said estate." The expedition was the disastrous West Indian undertaking led by Penn and Venables.

After all the favors which the Parliament and Cromwell could grant Penn, on the 25th of December, a few days after he left Spithead, he sent word to Prince, subsequently Charles II., that he was ready to place the whole fleet at his disposal, and run it into any port he might designate. Granville Penn admits this, and accounts for it by the desire of his ancestor to see the king supplant Cromwell "as the only means of restoring health and soundness to his disordered country." Clarendon records Penn's treacherous act. Penn's acceptance of the command of the expedition, and his seeking and obtaining a very valuable grant from Cromwell, make the proposed surrender of his fleet to Charles II. an infamous offer. It was the deliberate and wicked expression of a deceitful and selfish heart.

Penn was thrown into prison after his return from the West Indies, and, according to Dixon, he sent a humble petition to the Council, in which he confessed his faults and threw himself upon the mercy of Cromwell, who generously restored him to freedom. After this, pretending to give up politics, he retired to Ireland, and upon the very estate given him by the Protector "he used his whole influence to prepare in secret a way for the return of the exiled princes." And on the deposition of Richard Cromwell, even Monk was not a more unblushing betrayer of the liberties of his country than Admiral Penn. Charles II. knighted him in Holland for his treason to the people of England. Dixon, in his "Historical Biography of William Penn," says of the admiral, "The cavalier who stood by his prince through all the changes of fortune may be admired, even by a Republican; but for the man who seeks a trust merely to betray it, who uses the sword to strike the hand he voluntarily swears to defend, no term of reprehension is too strong. Admiral Penn's case was one of peculiar baseness, for he added ingratitude to treason." The American army, in the Revolution, had one notorious general who tried to serve the king of England in the spirit which governed Admiral Penn.

William Penn, the founder of this State, learned his ideas of liberty from Algernon Sidney, and not from his father, who never was a Baptist. His views of freedom were broad and generous for that day. But the Baptists before and during his time were far in advance of Penn or his teachers in their knowledge and application of religious liberty. Hepworth Dixon says that at Chester, in 1682, Penn's first legislative assembly met in the Friends' meeting-house with the great Quaker, and they passed laws in conformity with Penn's "Frame of Government," issued by him in London some time before. One of these gave liberty to the people to believe "any doctrines not destructive to the peace and honor of civil society," and another declared "that *every Christian man* of twenty-one years of age, unstained by crime, *should be eligible to elect* or *be elected* a member of the Colonial Parliament." According to this law, no Israelite or unbeliever in Christ could vote in Penn's territories. This was William Penn's own doctrine. In Rhode Island, in 1647, under the guidance of Roger Williams, laws were made giving equal liberty to men of all creeds and of none. And this was the doctrine of Baptists for ages before that time.

See Southey's "Lives of the British Admirals," v. 240. London, 1837. "Memorials of Sir William Penn," by Granville Penn, i. 94; ii. 17, 20; ii. 15, 141. London, 1833. Neal's "History of the Puritans," ii. 466. Dublin, 1755. Macaulay's

"History of England," i. 125. Boston, 1854. Clarendon's "History of the Rebellion," iii. 576. Oxford, 1706. William Hepworth Dixon's "Historical Biography of William Penn," 23, 25, 27, 201, 202.

Pennepek, or Lower Dublin Church.

—This is the oldest Baptist church in Pennsylvania. The Cold Spring church existed before it, but dissolved in a few years. Its edifice is in the twenty-third ward of Philadelphia, in a beautiful rural region, a few rods from the Pennepek Creek, where candidates have been immersed from the organization of the church. This church is the *seat* (cathedra) from which the influences and the men went forth who organized the earliest churches in Pennsylvania and in New Jersey.

It was founded by Elias Keach, whose father was a distinguished Baptist minister and author in London, in the month of January, 1688. Its constituent members were Elias Keach, John Eaton, George Eaton and Jane, his wife, Sarah Eaton, Samuel Jones, John Baker, Samuel Vaus, Joseph Ashton and Jane, his wife, William Fisher, and John Watts. Mr. Keach was elected pastor, and Samuel Vaus was chosen and ordained a deacon. Mr. Keach was an apostle in zeal and labors to win souls to Jesus. He preached in Philadelphia, Chester, Salem, Middletown, Cohansey, Burlington, Trenton, and elsewhere. The Lord greatly blessed these missionary efforts, and a branch of the Pennepek church was formed in each preaching station. Morgan Edwards says of these branches, "They were all one church, and Pennepek the centre of union, where as many as could met to celebrate the death of Christ; and for the sake of distant members they administered the ordinance quarterly at Burlington, Cohansey, Salem, and Philadelphia." In about three years Middletown, Piscataqua, and Cohansey became churches. Mr. Keach returned to England in 1692. John Watts, a member of the church, succeeded Mr. Keach as pastor. In 1700, Mr. Watts, at the request of the church, prepared a catechism, which was also intended for a confession of faith, and the work was published that year. In 1707 a house of worship was erected near the site of the present church; the building was 25 feet square. In 1770 a new house was built, 33 by 30. The third church edifice was reared in 1805, and it stands to-day a substantial and capacious structure, around which hallowed memories cluster. Many other churches, including the First Baptist church of Philadelphia, owe their origin to the Pennepek community.

During a period of six years there were no baptisms in the Pennepek church, though it was favored by the pastoral labors of Dr. Samuel Jones, one of the most talented and godly men that preached the gospel in the United States. At the close of this time of barrenness a revival commenced in 1804, which lasted for about six years.

The Pennepek church is a member of the Philadelphia Association at this day, which came into existence under her auspices. The church has had twenty pastors, and has sent forth twenty-two persons to preach the gospel.

Pennsylvania Baptists.

—Thomas Dungan, an old minister, came from Rhode Island to the colony of Penn in 1684. He gathered a church at Cold Spring, near Bristol, Bucks County, "of which," says Morgan Edwards in 1770, "nothing remains but a grave-yard and the names of the families that belonged to it,—the Dungans, Gardners, Woods, Doyles, etc." He died in 1688, and was buried at Cold Spring. Even the grave-yard has disappeared now, and only the foundations of a wall can be traced, which formed a part of the church or a portion of the cemetery wall. The church itself disbanded after a brief but useful existence.

The second church founded in Pennsylvania was the Lower Dublin, or Pennepek. In the year 1686, Elias Keach, of London, a wild young man, arrived in Philadelphia. He dressed in black and wore bands to pass for a minister. He obtained an opportunity to preach in the house of a Baptist in Lower Dublin, and when he had spoken for some time he "stopped short, looked like a man astonished, and the audience concluded that he had been seized with some sudden disorder." But they speedily learned that he was deeply convicted of sin. He went to Father Dungan, of Cold Spring, who pointed him to Jesus; he soon had peace in believing, and he was baptized and ordained by Mr. Dungan. He formed a church of twelve persons at Pennepek in January, 1688, and became their pastor. He labored with burning zeal, and, considering the difficulties, with astonishing success, through Pennsylvania and New Jersey, and established missions at "the Falls (Trenton), Burlington, Cohansey, Salem, Pennsneck, Chester, and Philadelphia," and he maintained preaching at Cold Spring and Middletown. He had the zeal of an enthusiast, and "he was considered the chief apostle of the Baptists in these parts of America." He returned to his birthplace in 1692, but the missions in several cases became churches, and the spirit he planted in these communities created the Philadelphia Association a few years after he left the colony.

The Great Valley church was constituted in 1711. The Brandywine church was formed in 1715. The Montgomery church was organized in 1719. The Tulpehocken church was founded in 1738, and the Southampton in 1746. The Philadelphia church had an existence either as a branch of Lower Dublin or as an independent community from 1698, the former is the more probable. But in 1746, to settle doubts on this question and to protect legacies, the church was formally incorporated. The New Britain church was organized in 1754, and the Vincent in 1770.

Since our national independence was secured, about 200 churches have arisen in the counties east of the Susquehanna River and its North Branch. Some of these became extinct, or changed names and locations, so that a clear and complete sketch of them all, however interesting, would be entirely impracticable in this work.

The first known English Baptist preacher on the Susquehanna was the first person named as slain in the first Wyoming massacre, in 1763. He was William Marsh, a New England Separatist, but came from Wantage, N. J., into Pennsylvania. The first church was formed in Pittston, in December, 1776. The first Baptists in Northern Pennsylvania were from Connecticut, Rhode Island, Massachusetts, Virginia, New York, and New Jersey. They were Revolutionary soldiers and pioneers of the settlements, both ministers and private members.

A portion of Southwestern Pennsylvania was taken up by Virginians. There were Baptists among them, and a church was founded at Aughwick, Huntingdon Co., in 1776; at Konoloway, Bedford, in 1764; at Sideling Hill, Fulton, in 1790; at Turkeyfoot, Somerset, in 1775; at Great Bethel (Uniontown), Fayette, in 1770; at Goshen, Greene, in 1773; at Peter's Creek, Washington, in 1773; at Pigeon Creek, in 1775; Loyalhanna, in 1775; Forks of Yough, in 1777. Enon church arose in 1791; Beulah, Cambria Co., in 1797; Pittsburgh in 1812. These facts show the progress of settlements, without attempting details of the scores of churches which have arisen on and west of the Susquehanna.

ASSOCIATIONS

are yearly meetings of messengers of churches combining for spiritual improvement, to ascertain changes, and to confer as to measures for promoting their sentiments. Their powers are advisory. The following are the regular Baptist Associations in Pennsylvania:

1707.—Philadelphia, the first Association in America, now 174 years old.

1776.—Redstone, in Southwestern Pennsylvania, finally absorbed by others about 1841.

1807.—Abington, in Lackawanna County, and west and north of it.

1809.—Beaver, on west central border of the State.

1821.—Northumberland, in the east-central (Lewisburg) region.

1823.—French Creek, in the northwest corner of the State.

1826.—Bridgewater, out of old Susquehanna, in Susquehanna County and eastern Bradford.

1830.—Centre, a missionary body in the Juniata River region.

1831.—Central Union, in and west of Philadelphia.

1832.—Monongahela, a missionary body, southward of Pittsburgh.

1835.—Bradford, North, mostly from Old-School Chemung.

1837.—Clarion, north-central, west of the Alleghany Mountains.

1839.—Pittsburgh, in and around that city.

1843.—Wyoming, from Bridgewater, in Wyoming and Luzerne Counties.

1843.—Tioga, from Bradford, mostly in Tioga County, northern tier.

1847.—Clearfield, central, both sides of the Alleghanies.

1848.—North Philadelphia, from Philadelphia and Central Union.

1859.—Ten-Mile, southwest corner of the State.

1865.—Oil Creek Association was formed.

1870.—Wayne, from Abington, northeast corner of the State.

1875.—Reading, in east-central, or Schuylkill coal region.

1876.—Indiana, south of Clarion, west of the Alleghanies.

1878.—Wheeling, in Western Pennsylvania and West Virginia.

East Pennsylvania Welsh Association is more than twenty years old.

There are about forty Welsh churches, and half a dozen German, of the regular Baptist faith not connected with English Associations

All our churches in Potter and McKean Counties, and a number of the others on the northern tier, associate with bodies in New York State.

There are 23 Associations in this State, 568 churches, and 64,572 members. There are 503 Sunday-schools reported, with 6120 officers and teachers, and 50,860 scholars. Six Associations make no report of Sunday-schools, when most probably every church has one.

When it is remembered that Pennsylvania was chiefly settled by Scotch-Irish and Germans, that is, by people intensely Presbyterian or tenaciously Lutheran, nearly the most difficult material on earth out of which to make Baptists, and that few members of our denomination, comparatively, came from Europe, the progress of the Baptists is remarkable.

EDUCATION.

Pennsylvanians led in forming the first Baptist academy in this country,—Isaac Eaton's, at Hopewell, N. J., 1756,—and also in establishing their first college,—Brown University, Providence, R. I., in 1766. Dr. Samuel Jones conducted an academy at Lower Dublin from 1766 to 1794. In 1814 an education society for the Middle States was formed in Philadelphia. Its master-spirit, Dr. William Staughton, had for some years taken ministerial students to his home for private instruction, and in 1818 he and Prof. Irah Chase hired rooms for the same object. The institution was removed to Washington City, and in 1821 appeared as Columbian College. The Hamilton (N. Y.) Institution, now called Madison University, received material aid from Pennsylvania. In 1832 the Northumberland Association proposed a Manual Labor Academy, principally to aid ministerial students, but waived it in favor of the proposal of Philadelphia brethren to found an institution at Haddington. And when the Haddington effort failed, the Northumberland friends rallied, and in 1846, Prof. S. W. Taylor opened a high school, which developed into a college, with academic and theological departments, and a female institute, now called the University of Lewisburg. By amicable arrangement, the theological department was, in 1868, transferred to Crozer Theological Seminary, at Upland, Delaware Co.

The academies under the direct control of the Baptists of the State are five in number: the University Academy, at Lewisburg, founded in 1846; the Reid Institute, in Clarion County, established in 1863; Monongahela College Academy, in Greene County, instituted in 1867; Keystone Academy, in Wyoming County, opened in 1868; and Mount Pleasant Institute, in Westmoreland County, founded in 1873. The University Female Institute at Lewisburg is not included in the above list. It is the only ladies' institute within the State, and is connected with the university, thus enjoying peculiar advantages. It embraces a regular college course, and has hitherto been awarded a large share of public patronage.

During the past year the number of instructors attached to these academies was 37, and the number of students 641. At a very low valuation, the amount invested in these schools is $160,000. These institutions are of recent origin, and it is believed that the Baptists of Pennsylvania will soon start new schools in other localities.

LITERATURE.

The first known American work in favor of distinct Baptist principles is attributed to John Watts, of Pennepek, and was printed in the year 1700. It was designed mostly for children and youth. No copy of it is known to the public. Morgan Edwards, of Philadelphia, wrote historical sketches of priceless value of the Baptists in several of the colonies. Doctors S. Jones, Rogers, Staughton, Holcombe, Belcher, Malcom, Curtis, Brantly, Sr.,

Ira M. Allen, Geo. B. Ide, and J. Newton Brown among the dead, and H. G. Jones, Jr., Anderson, Magoon, Cathcart, Pendleton, Dyer, Spencer, J. Wheaton Smith, Dr. W. W. Keen, Francis Jennings, J. Spencer Kennard, Justin R. Loomis, and others among the living. Robert Lowry's hymns are sung around the world. Any attempt to name the books, or other most worthy products from the pen of our people, might seem invidious, and it is hardly possible to make such a record complete.

The following are names of Baptist periodicals that have been or are still issued in Philadelphia: *Latter-Day Luminary, Christian Index, The World as it is and as it should be, Religious Narrator, Christian Gazette, Baptist Record, Christian Chronicle, National Baptist, Baptist Quarterly,* and several for children and Sunday-schools, with millions of pages of tracts and books from the American Baptist Publication Society.

From 1825 to 1827, at Montrose, Davis Dimock issued the *Baptist Mirror, or Christian Magazine.* In 1827, Eugenio Kincaid, at Milton, published a *Literary and Evangelical Register.* And Pittsburgh has furnished one or more periodicals adapted to the wants of Western Pennsylvania.

BENEVOLENCE.

Early minutes of the Philadelphia Association are very meagre, yet they give proofs of efforts to send the gospel to the destitute at home, to use the press for the common good, and to aid young men in preparing to be able ministers of the New Testament. Before and after the Revolution they sent evangelists into the new fields on the Susquehanna, and at an early day they transmitted money to Hindoostan, and to Burmah soon after missions were opened there.

In 1800 a Philadelphia Domestic Mission Society was formed. In 1810 they reported seven men in their service,—Thomas Smiley, on the West Branch; Thomas G. Jones, in Pennsylvania and Ohio; Henry George, at Owl Creek, in Ohio; William West, near Lake Erie; and Brethren Montague, Bateman, and Cooper on both sides of the Delaware. In 1827 the Philadelphia and other similar local societies began their union as the Baptist Missionary Association of Pennsylvania. At its semi-centennial, in 1877, it reported a total expenditure of $282,189 in its fifty years' work, during which it had aided 233 churches and made 1430 appointments of home missionaries, who had reported about 17,000 baptisms.

The Baptist General Tract Society, formed in Washington City in 1824, came to Philadelphia in 1826, and is now known as the American Baptist Publication Society. It has constantly enlarged its power in the production of wholesome reading, its business department aiding its large outlays in benevolence. It was many years located at 530 Arch Street, but now has spacious and eligible accommodations, as denominational and book headquarters, at 1420 Chestnut Street.

The Pennsylvania Baptist Education Society, founded in 1839, has vigorously prosecuted its aims, with great advantages to the rising ministry, and through them to the church and to the world.

Among the promoters of every good enterprise may generally be found a fair proportion of Pennsylvania Baptists. In the first national foreign mission meeting were Staughton, Rogers, Holcombe, Proudfoot, Randall, White, Peckworth, H. G. Jones, Sr., Hough, and Mathias. The Baptists of Pennsylvania are generous contributors to home and foreign objects.

The university at Lewisburg has extensive and beautiful buildings and a handsome endowment. Crozer Theological Seminary, in its home and in its endowment, is a monument of liberality. The white marble house of the American Baptist Publication Society cost $258,000, is entirely out of debt, and was paid for chiefly by Pennsylvanians. The fifty-six Baptist churches of Philadelphia have a greater number of splendid church edifices than any one of the other denominations in the city, and they are nearly all free from debt.

The Baptists of Pennsylvania are thoroughly united, and they are praying, working, and giving to spread the knowledge of Jesus in a way that inspires the hope that in twenty years, with God's blessing, they will double their numbers.

Pennsylvania Baptist Education Society, The, was organized Sept. 18, 1839, in the First Baptist church in Philadelphia. It has extended aid to about 500 students. It is believed that over 300 ministers thus aided are now in active service in home and foreign fields. The experience of the past forty years fully justifies us in stating that such organizations are of vital necessity. In the workings of this society, each year is strictly probationary, and students failing to meet just expectations are dropped from the list. The society is not in formal connection with any institution of learning, but holds itself at liberty to give aid to students studying outside of Pennsylvania, when adequate reasons for the selection are given. The appropriations given to students are designed to cover the cost of cheap boarding and the expense of tuition. They have varied in different periods from $80 annually to $150. The present maximum grant is $110.

The officers for 1881 are Thomas J. Hoskinson, President; Levi Knowles, Treasurer; Rev. G. M. Spratt, D.D., Corresponding Secretary; Rev. Jacob G. Walker, Recording Secretary. Twenty members constitute the board of managers.

Dr. Spratt has made the society, in his many years

of service, the most successful agency for its object in this country. The receipts last year were $12,000, and there were 63 students who received assistance.

Pennsylvania Baptist General Association was founded July 4, 1827, in the Blockley Baptist church, Philadelphia. The organization of the society was perfected in the autumn of the same year. It is purely a State missionary institution. Rev. William E. Ashton was its first president. Hon. James M. Linnard held that office with remarkable usefulness for twenty-seven years. During the first half-century of its existence it has had on an average 29 missionaries a year in its employment, and it issued 1430 commissions. In that period it formed or fostered 233 of the Baptist churches of the State, some of which to-day are the strongest and most flourishing in Pennsylvania. During the fourteen years' secretaryship of the Rev. L. G. Beck the sum of $172,000 was raised for the Association, and the churches increased from 424 to 553, and the members from 40,000 to 63,500. The Association has accomplished a grand work, and it is, at this time, in a state of efficiency that inspires exalted hopes for coming days.

In 1880 it employed 42 missionaries. Its income was $14,914.43. Rev. R. H. Austin was its president, and Rev. W. H. Conard its corresponding secretary.

Pennsylvania, Western, Classical and Scientific Institute is located at Mount Pleasant, Pa., about forty miles southeast of Pittsburgh, with which it is connected by rail. The academy is at the foot of the mountains, in a rich farming region. Its site affords a commanding view of the town and the surrounding country. Its buildings are spacious, and possess every convenience and comfort.

Mount Pleasant has seven evangelical churches, with a substantial membership in each, and other religious bodies, with regular preaching. No intoxicating liquors, according to law, can be sold in Mount Pleasant, or within two miles of it.

The school was organized under the auspices of the Pittsburgh, Monongahela, and Beaver Baptist Associations. It was opened in 1873, and its growth has been constant until it is now self-sustaining. Both sexes are admitted to its advantages, and they are about equally represented in its classes. It has usually six teachers. It imparts a first-class academical education, and it is now a blessing to the section of the State where its advantages have been so extensively enjoyed.

Pentecost, Rev. Hugh O., son of Hugh L. and Emma (Flower) Pentecost, was born Sept. 30, 1848, at New Harmony, Ind.; educated at Madison University, N. Y., where he took a select course; ordained in 1871, at Rockville Centre, Long Island, and settled as pastor; second settlement was with the Calvary Baptist church in Westerly, R. I., Aug. 4, 1875; third settlement with South Baptist church, Hartford, Conn., May 1, 1878; has recently become pastor in Brooklyn, N. Y.; an able, successful, and devoted minister.

Pepper, Prof. George Dana Boardman, D.D., the youngest son of John and Eunice Hutchinson

PROF. GEORGE DANA BOARDMAN PEPPER, D.D.

Pepper, was born in Ware, Mass., Feb. 5, 1833. His parents were members of a Baptist church in which his father was a deacon, so that from infancy the future professor lived in an atmosphere of Christian influence. Though the subject of positive religious experiences when not more than seven or eight years old, it was not until May 4, 1856, that he publicly professed faith in Christ by baptism, and became a member of the Baptist church in his native town. After a thorough academical preparation for college he entered Amherst, in which he graduated in 1857, ranking third in his class. He entered Newton Theological Seminary after leaving Amherst, and took the full course. After leaving Newton he became pastor of the First Baptist church of Waterville, Me., the seat of Colby University. In 1865 he accepted the chair of Ecclesiastical History in Newton Theological Seminary, which he occupied with so much acceptance and success that he was elected to the professorship of Christian Theology in the newly established school at Upland, Pa., the Crozer Theological Seminary. He spent one year in prepara-
58

tion for the duties of the new position, upon the discharge of which he entered in the autumn of 1868; and he continues in that institution still, giving his able co-operation in moulding the principles and characters of men, not a few of whom have already taken an honored place in the Baptist ministry.

Several of his discussions of denominational and other theological questions have been published in reviews, in pamphlets, and otherwise. For eight years he prepared for the *Baptist Teacher* the expositions of the International Sunday-School Lessons. This effort involved and exhibited great learning, given in wisely simple terms. And it is doubtful if the same work was ever performed as well by another. He is the author of a volume of respectable dimensions on "Outlines of Theology," which he has not given to the public, and which he uses in his class with so much success that his students leave him the equals of the best-trained theological graduates in our country, and the superiors of many of their young brethren. Prof. Pepper is a man of extreme gentleness and modesty, of the highest culture, the deepest piety, and the greatest worth. Mrs. Pepper is well and widely known as a very able and efficient worker in every department of the Master's kingdom, especially in the cause of missions.

Periodicals.—See article on BAPTIST LITERATURE.

Perkins, Rev. Isaac, a native of Georgia, removed to Arkansas about 1830, and gathered the first Baptist church in Southwestern Arkansas. He died in Hempstead County in 1852. He was moderator of Saline Association for about twelve years.

Perren, Rev. Charles, the pastor of the Western Avenue Baptist church, Chicago, was born Oct. 22, 1839. His conversion took place when he was fourteen years of age. Deciding to study for the ministry, he entered the Canadian Literary Institute, at Woodstock, Ontario, where he graduated from the department of Arts, and that of Theology. In 1862 he was ordained at Vienna, Ontario. Subsequently he was, upon passing the senior examination of the theological seminary at Chicago, he received the degree of B.D. in that institution. His former pastorates have been at Georgetown and St. Catherine's, Ontario. He has held his present one in Chicago some three years, enjoying to an unusual degree the confidence and affection of the people he serves.

Perry, Hon. Eli, was born in Cambridge, Washington Co., N. Y., Dec. 25, 1799, and died May 17, 1881. In early life he was baptized by Dr. Bartholomew Welsh into the fellowship of the Pearl Street church, Albany. He was possessed of a large mind and a generous heart. Christ was everything to him, and to his cause he consecrated his means and his efforts. He was for many years the personal friend of the strong men who gave a high character to the Pearl Street church, in the Baptist denomination, among whom were Judge Ira Harris, Friend Humphrey, and John N. Wilder. Possessing great force of character, uncommon sagacity, and irreproachable integrity, combined with quiet simplicity and humility, he became an eminent citizen whom every one delighted to honor. For seventeen years he was mayor of Albany, a longer period of service in that office than was rendered by any of his predecessors since the incorporation of the city. As a member of the Legislature, and of Congress for two successive terms, he enjoyed the confidence of the bodies in whose deliberations he shared, and of his constituents. For many years he was president of the board of trustees of his loved church, and for some time an honored deacon. For this community he cherished a warm and an abiding affection. He left $16,000 to Emmanuel church and Sunday-school, and to the Albany Baptist Missionary Union and the Rochester Theological Seminary, at his death; and he made provision in his will that at the decease of his widow, after the payment of several legacies of $1000 each to distant relatives, his entire estate, estimated to be worth $400,000, should be divided into five equal parts, and distributed as follows: one-fifth each to Rochester and Hamilton Theological Seminaries, and one-fifth each to the Hudson River Baptist Association North, the American Baptist Missionary Union, and the American Baptist Home Mission Society. In life, Mr. Perry was a generous contributor to all denominational and charitable objects, and he made arrangements that after death his gifts should send forth streams of beneficence for generations. Few men were more loved in life or more lamented after death.

Perry, Prof. Herman, A.M., was born in Wyoming, N. Y., Feb. 12, 1824. Converted and baptized in early youth, and having remarkable natural grace and great persuasive force in addressing religious meetings, he was believed to be destined to the work of preaching. With the approval of the church he studied for the ministry, graduated at Madison University in 1846, received the degree of A.M. from Rochester University in 1850, and commenced to preach; but was compelled by his delicate health to discontinue. He took charge successively of the academies at Richburgh, N. Y., and Allegan, Mich. For the sake of his health he removed to California in 1863, and established at Sacramento "The Young Ladies' Seminary," which took rank among the best educational institutions of the State. He died Jan. 18, 1876, and his death was felt to be a great loss by the Baptists of the Pacific coast, in whose educational and benevolent enterprises he had been a wise counselor and generous supporter.

Perry, Rev. Joseph, was born in Stanhope, N. J., in November, 1806. While yet a young man he was converted, and united with the First Baptist church of Newark, N. J., Rev. D. Dodge, pastor.

Soon after his marriage he removed to Paterson, N. J., and took a most prominent part in the great Washingtonian temperance movement. Here he was licensed to preach by the First Baptist church. Afterwards removing to Washington, D. C., he was ordained as a minister of the gospel.

Accepting an appointment as a home missionary, he went to Fairfax, Va., his circuit extending to Richmond. From this field he removed, and took charge of the Haverstraw, N. Y., Baptist church. From Haverstraw he was called to New Durham, N. J., where he toiled with wonderful courage to redeem the place from the control of rum. After a struggle such as few men have encountered, with his life almost constantly in danger, he overthrew the liquor power, and transformed the village from a state of riotous Sabbath-breaking to a lovely and quiet abode. After building, by strenuous efforts, a beautiful church, he closed a pastorate of six years, and removed to Manahawkin, N. J., and spent two years of hard and successful labor for Christ.

In 1859 he accepted a call to the Mariners' Baptist Bethel, of Philadelphia, where for twenty years he labored unceasingly among the sailors of the merchant service, and among the seamen of the U. S. navy on the receiving-ship at the Philadelphia navy-yard. At this port, through the generosity of Wm. Bucknell, Esq. (still living), John P. Crozer, Capt. John Levy (both deceased), and others, he built a neat church for seamen. At last, after baptizing hundreds of sailors, and many others, he was compelled by failing strength to retire from the active ministry. Recovering his health soon afterwards, he entered with renewed energy upon general and heaven-blessed work for his divine Master.

Two years of happy unflagging toil followed, when a sudden and fatal attack of pneumonia ended his earthly work, and he went to his reward Feb. 14, 1881, closing a life filled with most thrilling incidents and adorned with Christian graces.

Mr. Perry was one of the best men in the Baptist ministry in Pennsylvania.

Perry, Rev. Lewis.—Lewis Perry, a well-known colored Baptist preacher of North Carolina, was born in 1804, and became the body-servant of Dr. Wiley Perry, an eminent physician of Franklin County, about 1820. He became a lover of Jesus at an early age, and during the great revival which visited the village of Lewisburg in 1830, he was eminently useful in instructing and encouraging struggling penitents. He possessed a voice of great pathos and power, which he used with fine effect in singing and prayer, and his preaching, especially when touching on religious experience, was impressive in a high degree.

His education was quite limited. By his own unaided efforts he learned to read and write, and attained a useful knowledge of the simpler rules of arithmetic. He was a close student of the Bible for many years, and few men were better acquainted with the teachings of the New Testament.

This good man had secretly acquired from his master's books, and a close study of his practice, a very respectable knowledge of medicine ; and such was the esteem in which he was held by the people, and the confidence of his master in his judgment, that when Dr. Perry had become quite old, he would frequently send Lewis to see his patients, especially when called out at night. Indeed, the old Baptist preacher was familiarly known all over the county as "Doctor Perry"; and so much esteemed was he as a physician and a nurse that a young man of his native county left him a legacy of a thousand dollars for his attention to him during his last illness.

He died at the age of fifty-eight, and the respect in which he was held was manifested by the very large number of persons of all classes who attended his funeral services.

Perry, Rev. Rufus L., was born a slave in Smith Co., Tenn., March 11, 1834. He learned to read and write in early life, which inspired him with an irrepressible abhorrence of slavery, and he ran away to Canada in August, 1852. He went to Windsor, opposite Detroit, and by hard study soon became a schoolmaster among the large body of fugitives who had escaped from slavery.

He was hopefully converted in 1854, prepared for the ministry at Kalamazoo Theological Seminary with the class of 1861, and was ordained as pastor of the Second Baptist church of Ann Arbor, Oct. 9, 1861, by a council, of which Rev. Samuel Cornelius was moderator, and Prof. James R. Boise clerk. He afterwards served as pastor at St. Catharines, Ontario, and Buffalo, N. Y. In 1865 he entered upon a general missionary and educational work among the freedmen, and has, until the present, labored for the education, evangelization, and general elevation of his race, serving as superintendent of schools for freedmen, as editor of the *Sunbeam*, co-ordinate editor of the *American Baptist*, editor of the *People's Journal*, and editor and publisher of the *National Monitor*. He was for ten years corresponding secretary of the consolidated American Baptist Missionary Convention, and he is at present corresponding secretary of the American Educational Association and of the American Baptist Free Mission Society, and editor of the *National Monitor*, of Brooklyn, N. Y.

Perryman, Rev. Elisha, one of the most useful pioneer preachers of the Georgia Baptists, was born in Halifax Co., Va., Feb. 6, 1769, of Welsh ancestors, all of whom, on both sides, as far back as known, were stanch Baptists. His father commanded a company, raised by himself, in the Revolutionary war, and, besides other engagements, was present at the battle of Guilford Court-House. Cornwallis's army, and especially Tarleton's troopers, in their ravages, so completely destroyed his property, when encamped within six miles of his house, that he removed to Georgia with his family, and settled on Big Kiokee Creek, twenty-two miles from Augusta. Here Elisha Perryman, after much mental distress, was gloriously converted in May, 1799. On the third Sabbath in August, 1801, he was baptized by Abraham Marshall, and joined Kiokee church. Gradually the conviction that it was his duty to preach grew upon him. He studied by firelight at night; and he made it a point to accompany Jesse Mercer and Abraham Marshall to their appointments, in order to learn the doctrines of Christianity. He gave himself entirely to the work of an evangelist, confining himself to no one section of the country, but going wherever destitution abounded. In January, 1810, he removed to Warner County, and often would make preaching tours afterwards through Montgomery, Emanuel, Tatnall, and Bullock Counties, and, at other times, would make tours through Richmond, Burke, Jefferson, and Severn Counties. Again, he would sally forth among the northern counties, and even sometimes into South Carolina, traveling up and down the Savannah River. It was thus that the Baptist pioneer preachers of Georgia established their principles in the State.

The Lord blessed him with a strong constitution, and, though he died Dec. 1, 1857, in his eighty-ninth year, he continued to preach with vivacity and vigor to the last, calling upon sinners to flee from the wrath to come.

Persecution of Baptists in America.—John Waller, Lewis Craig, and James Childs, three Baptist ministers, were arrested in Spottsylvania Co., Va., "for preaching the gospel contrary to law," and while in prison they proclaimed the good news to listening throngs through the doors and windows of the jail. In Middlesex and Caroline Counties, Va., many Baptist ministers were imprisoned for preaching; they were subjected to the treatment of common felons, and if possible to worse indignities. William Webber and Joseph Anthony were imprisoned in Chesterfield Co., Va., for telling the story of the Cross. James Ireland suffered imprisonment in Virginia, and illegal and wicked efforts were made to kill him in jail because he was a herald of Calvary. To keep the people from hearing the imprisoned preachers, walls were sometimes built around the jails in which they were confined, and half-drunken outcasts were hired to beat drums to drown their voices. When out of prison in the Old Dominion they were mobbed; while immersing converts men on horseback would ride into the water to create a disturbance. They were often interrupted in their discourses and insulted, but they despised the jail, the lash, and the malicious jeers. When hunted like wild beasts, and denounced as wolves in sheep's clothing, they meekly replied, "That if they were wolves and their persecutors the true sheep, it wás unaccountable that they should treat them with such cruelty; that wolves would destroy sheep, but that it was never known till then that sheep would prey upon wolves." (Semple's History of Virginia Baptists, p. 21.)

In New England, outside of Rhode Island, our brethren were frequently arrested for not paying taxes to support the Congregational clergy. Women, too, had their rights recognized, and they were arrested and robbed to support the ministers of their neighbors. The sacred tax-gatherers took from the Baptists "pewter dishes, skillets, kettles, pots and warming-pans, workmen's tools, and spinning-wheels; they drove away geese and swine and cows, and when there was but one it was not spared. A brother recently ordained returned to Sturbridge, Mass., for his family, when he was thrust into prison and kept during the cold winter, till some one paid his fine and secured his release. Mr. D. Fisk was robbed at Sturbridge of five pewter plates and a cow, J. Perry of the baby's cradle and a steer, J. Blunt of andirons, shovel, and tongs, and A. Bloice, H. Fisk, John Streeter, Benjamin Robbins, Phenehas Collier, John Newel, Josiah Perry, Nathaniel Smith, John Corry, and J. Barstow of spinning-wheels, household goods, cows, and of their liberty for a season." (Backus's Church History, ii. 94, 95. Newton.) Sturbridge was but a specimen of what was taking place all over New England, and of the love cherished for our Baptist fathers by men who only differed from them about baptism. Early the persecution of Baptists was commenced in New England; Roger Williams was compelled to fly from Salem to escape illegal violence in 1635; the meeting-house of the First Baptist church of Boston, in 1677, was closed by order of the General Court of Massachusetts, and after a little, when they ventured to use it again, the doors were nailed up and a paper fastened on them, which read, "All persons are to take notice that by order of the court the doors of this house are shut up, and that they are prohibited from holding any meeting therein or to open the doors thereof without license from authority till the Gen-

eral Court take further order, as they will answer the contrary at their peril." (Hildreth's History of the United States, i. 497-499. New York.)

The town of Ashfield, Mass., was settled by Baptists, and when it had a few Congregational families in it they built a church, called a minister, and then laid a tax upon the land to meet the cost of the one and the support of the other. The Baptists refused to pay the church bills of their Puritan neighbors, and immediately the best portion of the cultivated land in the town was seized and sold for trifling sums to pay their iniquitous dues. The house and garden of one man were taken from him, and the young orchards, the meadows, and the cornfields of others. The grave-yard of the Baptists was actually sold to liquidate the debts of a church with which they had nothing to do, and to support a minister with whom they did not intend to worship. These properties were sold in 1770 for £35.10, and they were worth £363.8. The Congregational minister was one of the purchasers. This was but the first payment, and two others were to follow. (Minutes of the Philadelphia Baptist Association for 1770, p. 160.) Such were some of the countless wrongs which our fathers suffered even in this land.

Perseverance, Final.—The Saviour is *the Shepherd* of his believing flock. He says, "The hireling fleeth, because he is a hireling, and careth not for the sheep. I am the good shepherd, and know my sheep, and am known of mine."—John x. 13, 14. Peter, speaking of Jesus, says, "For ye were as sheep going astray; but are now returned unto the Shepherd and Bishop of your souls."—First Epistle ii. 25. Christ will never leave nor forsake his flock. Besides, "He that keepeth Israel shall not slumber nor sleep. The Lord is thy keeper." —Psalm cxxi. 4. Now, as the Saviour is the shepherd of his flock, as he knows every one of them, is always with them, and never slumbers, he can never lose a sheep. David risked his life when a mere stripling in killing a lion and a bear to protect his flock, and is there any likelihood that the omnipotent Master of heaven will be a poorer shepherd than David, and suffer the old lion of the pit to rob his flock?

> " His honor is engaged to save
> The meanest of his sheep;
> All that his heavenly Father gave
> His hands securely keep."

Christ never changes. He knows everything in the most hidden recesses of the pit, in the secret parts of Satan's heart, in the lurking-places of earth, and in the concealed quarters of heaven. He has a perfect knowledge of the past and the present; and the entire future lies bare before him. "All things are naked and opened unto the eyes of him with whom we have to do." He is without any motive to change, and change with him is impossible, unless, indeed, some human weakness should overtake the intellect that has planned and executed the creation. He commands Philip to join the eunuch's chariot and preach to him; the evangelist obeys, and soon the traveler believes and is baptized. Now, why does the Spirit begin this work if it is ever to be abandoned? Could it agree with Christ's wisdom and purposes of love to begin a temple of salvation in the soul which Satan was soon to pull down and destroy? He takes the same interest in every believer which he showed in the eunuch; and as he is the Father of lights, without variableness or the shadow of turning, the work of grace will be carried on in every soul till the man reaches the heavenly rest.

The love of Christ is fixed upon each one whom his Spirit calls to repentance. This is the only reason for the regeneration of a single human being. This love was born in Christ in the distant morning of a past eternity; it led to the election of each believer from everlasting, as Paul says, "According as he hath chosen us in him before the foundation of the world, that we should be holy and without blame before him in love."—Eph. i. 4. What Jehovah declared in ancient times about Israel is true of all the spiritual Israel to-day, "Yea, I have loved thee with an everlasting love, therefore with loving-kindness have I drawn thee." —Jer. xxxi. 3. As Paul says, "But God, who is rich in mercy, for his great love wherewith he hath loved us, even when we were dead in sins, hath quickened (made alive) us together with Christ."—Eph. ii. 4, 5. The love that gave Jesus for us is God's, the love that made us alive as believers when we were dead in sins is Christ's, will that love ever give up one soul which it cherished in its everlasting regards? Will the Saviour permit one chosen and eternally loved friend to drop out of his heart into the abyss? Who shall separate us from the love of Christ? Shall tribulation, or distress, or persecution, or famine, or nakedness, or peril, or sword? Nay, in all these things we are more than conquerors through him that loved us. For I am persuaded that neither death, nor life, nor angels, nor principalities, nor powers, nor things present, nor things to come, nor height, nor depth, nor any other *creature* (creation) shall be able to separate us from the love of God, which is in Christ Jesus our Lord. Nothing created can separate the saint from his Saviour's love, nor shall the Uncreated One.

The believer in his second birth *is made a new creature*, he receives a new heart with new tastes, and while his old love of sin, not wholly subdued, may for a time, through the arts of the tempter, lead him from God, yet he cannot remain in sin, he will one day become dissatisfied with its husks,

and feel the famishing pangs of spiritual starvation; and he will hunger for the soul-bread, which abounds in the house of his Saviour-Father; and will arise and go to his Father. The carrier-pigeon taken five or six hundred miles from its home and set at liberty, immediately and swiftly returns; and so a soul, born from above, will surely awake to its wants and dangers, and nothing out of heaven can keep it from the throne of grace, and no one in the skies shall cast it out.

God's Word speaks of the eternally enduring life given in conversion. In Rom. viii. 29, 30, we read, "Whom he did foreknow, he also did predestinate to be conformed to the image of his Son, that he might be the first-born among many brethren. Moreover, whom he did predestinate, them he also called: and whom he called, them he also justified: and whom he justified, them he also glorified." According to this inspired statement every soul whom God calls to repentance shall be glorified in heaven. The Saviour generally connects faith in himself with everlasting life: "My sheep hear my voice, and I know them, and they follow me: and I give unto them eternal life; and *they shall never perish*, neither shall any pluck them out of my hand. My Father, who gave them to me, is greater than all; and none is able to pluck them out of my Father's hand."—John x. 27, 28. "None," neither the believer himself, nor any one else, shall tear a redeemed soul from the protecting hand of the great Redeemer's Father.

Several Scriptures are supposed to contradict the passage just quoted, and others of kindred meaning, one of which will fully represent the others. It is, "For if we sin willfully after that we have received the knowledge of the truth, there remaineth no more sacrifice for sins, but a certain fearful looking for of judgment and fiery indignation, which shall devour the adversaries."—Heb. x. 26, 27. That these words threaten eternal death to believers who sin *willfully* there is no doubt; but they do not declare that any one ever did sin willfully, or that any one ever shall. They simply warn the children of God of the dreadful results of such a crime, with a view to protect them from it; and this warning and others like it show that the good Shepherd will use every effort to keep his word, in which he declares that he gives them eternal life, and they shall never perish. Paul, in the ocean-storm, received the assurance from God that there would be no loss of any man's life, but of the ship. But when near the shore the sailors were deserting, he said to the soldiers, "Except these abide in the ship ye cannot be saved." Paul in this declaration did not contradict his favorable prediction, he was taking steps to have it fulfilled; and every warning like Paul's in Hebrews x. 26, 27, is but putting forth efforts to make the saints persevere, and to prove the truth of Paul's assurance in Philippians i. 6, "Being confident of this very thing, that he who hath begun a good work in you will perform it, *will complete it* (ἐπιτελέσει), until the day of Jesus Christ." The Saviour never began the needless work of saving a man in part; there is no sinner once truly converted among the myriads of the lost. Every elect soul is regenerated, and every man whom the Spirit calls will be glorified.

Peto, Sir Samuel Morton, Baronet, was born at Woking, England, on Aug. 4, 1809. He served

SIR SAMUEL MORTON PETO, BARONET.

an apprenticeship of seven years with his uncle, a builder engaged in extensive operations, at whose death, in 1830, he succeeded to a moiety of the business. His firm took part in the great work of erecting the new Houses of Parliament at Westminster, and other important undertakings. On the dissolution of his partnership, in 1845, Mr. Peto engaged extensively in railroad-building in England and other countries. In some of these enterprises he was associated with the eminent railroad-builder Thomas Brassey. Towards the close of the Crimean war, he undertook, without prospect of profit, the construction of a railway from the harbor of Balaklava to the British camp before Sebastopol, and most expeditiously accomplished this valuable work, thereby facilitating the military operations and relieving the hardships of the soldiers. In appreciation of this patriotic service he was made a baronet of the United Kingdom, by a royal patent dated Feb. 22, 1855. His conspicuous ability as a man of business had been recognized some years earlier

by the citizens of Norwich, who elected him to Parliament in 1847, and also in 1852. He was one of the members for the metropolitan borough of Finsbury from 1859 to 1865, and in the latter year was elected for Bristol, which seat he held until the bankruptcy of his firm in the financial troubles of 1866–67. Sir S. Morton Peto joined the Baptist church at St. Mary's, Norwich, during the pastorate of the Rev. William Brock, and soon won a distinguished name in the Baptist body. On the death of W. B. Gurney, Esq., he was chosen treasurer of the Missionary Society, and by his zeal and munificence gave a great impetus to the missionary cause. Feeling the need of an enlargement of denominational effort in the metropolis, he built Bloomsbury Chapel at his own cost, and united with the church which Dr. Brock gathered there in 1848. He also purchased the building known as the Diorama, in Regent's Park, and, having converted it into a commodious and elegant place of worship, induced the Rev. Dr. Landels to become the minister of the church afterwards formed there. Both these enterprises soon became prosperous, and the rapid growth of the Baptists in London and the neighborhood during the last twenty-five years is largely due to the liberality and energy of Sir Morton Peto. He was one of the first to discern the remarkable gifts of Mr. Spurgeon, and gave largely towards the erection of the Metropolitan Tabernacle. Regent's Park College and other Baptist institutions of learning shared in his generous regards, and he has latterly taken a deep interest in promoting the efficiency of the schemes of the Baptist Union for a suitable provision for aged and infirm ministers. Whilst in Parliament, Sir Morton Peto was recognized as a leader of the Nonconformists, and was held in high esteem by all parties for his fidelity to his principles and his unfailing courtesy of behavior. He published in 1863 a book on "Taxation, its Levy and Expenditure," and in 1866 "Resources and Prospects of America," the fruit of a sojourn of several weeks in this country.

Petrobrusians, The.—Peter de Bruys was the Catholic priest of an obscure parish in France, which he left, early in the twelfth century, when he became a preacher of the gospel. How he unlearned the gospel of the Seven Hills and was instructed in that of Calvary we cannot tell, but he was educated in both directions. Many Romanists, like Staupitz or Fenelon, have received the saving knowledge of Jesus and retained their connection with the papal church; but Peter abhorred popery.

He taught that baptism was of no advantage to infants, and that only believers should receive it, and he gave a new baptism to all his converts; he condemned the use of churches and altars, no doubt

FIFTH BAPTIST CHURCH, PHILADELPHIA, PA.

for the idolatry practised in them; he denied that the body and blood of Christ are to be found in the bread and wine of the Supper, and he taught that the elements on the Lord's table are but signs of Christ's flesh and blood; he asserted that the offerings, prayers, and good works of the living could not profit the dead, that their state was fixed for eternity the moment they left the earth; like the English Baptists of the seventeenth century, and like the Quakers of our day, he believed that it was wrong to sing the praises of God in worship; and he rejected the adoration of crosses, and destroyed them wherever he found them.

It is said that on a Good-Friday the Petrobrusians once gathered a great multitude of their brethren, who brought with them all the crosses they could find, and that they made a large fire of them, on which they cooked meat, and gave it to the vast assemblage. This is told as an illustration of their blasphemous profanity. Their crucifixes, and along with them probably the images of the saints, were the idols they had been taught to worship, and when their eyes were opened they destroyed them, just as the converted heathen will now destroy their false gods. Hezekiah did a good thing in destroying the serpent of brass, which in the wilderness had miraculous powers of healing, when the Israelites began to worship it as a god.

Peter's preaching was with great power; his words and his influence swept over great masses of men, bending their hearts and intellects before their resistless might. "In Provence," says Du Pin, "there was nothing else to be seen but Christians rebaptized, churches profaned or destroyed, altars pulled down, and crosses burned. The laws of the church were publicly violated, the priests beaten, abused, and forced to marry, and all the most sacred ceremonies of the church abolished."

Peter de Bruys commenced his ministry about 1125, and such was his success that in a few years in the places about the mouth of the Rhone, in the plain country about Thoulouse, and particularly in that city itself, and in many parts of " the province of Gascoigne" he led great throngs of men and women to Jesus, and overthrew the entire authority of popes, bishops, and priests.

Had the life of this illustrious man been spared the Reformation probably would have occurred four hundred years earlier under Peter de Bruys instead of Martin Luther, and the Protestant nations of the earth would not only have had a deliverance from four centuries of priestly profligacy and widespread soul destruction, but they would have entered upon a godly life with a far more Scriptural creed than grand old Luther, still in a considerable measure wedded to Romish sacramentalism, was fitted to give them.

Peter and his followers were decided Baptists,

and like ourselves they gave a fresh baptism to all their converts. They reckoned that they were not believers when first immersed in the Catholic Church, and that as Scripture baptism required faith in its candidates, which they did not possess, they regarded them as wholly unbaptized; and for the same reason they repudiated the idea that they rebaptized them, confidently asserting that because of the lack of faith they had never been baptized.

Peter the Venerable, abbot of Cluny, was born in 1093, and died in 1157. He was distinguished by scholarship, acuteness of mind, and Biblical knowledge. He and St. Bernard were the two leading ecclesiastics of France. Peter would rebuke a pope if he deserved it without hesitation, and no other human being was above his authority. The abbot had assailed the Jews and the Saracens in two distinct works. And such was the extraordinary success of the Petrobrusians, and the great difficulty of refuting their arguments from the Scriptures, that Peter felt compelled to come forth and defend the deserted ecclesiastics and the church threatened with ruin. We shall quote somewhat freely from the abbot to show the doctrines of these grand old Baptists. At the beginning of his pamphlet he states the five heads of the heresy of the Petrobrusians.

In the first he accuses them of "denying that little children under years of responsibility can be saved by the baptism of Christ; and that the faith of another (alienam fidem, the faith demanded from popish sponsors when a child was christened) could benefit those who were unable to exercise their own (faith); because, according to them, not another's faith, but personal faith, saves with baptism, the Lord saying, 'He who shall believe, and be baptized, shall be saved, but he that believeth not shall be condemned.'" This is the abbot's first and heaviest charge against these ancient Baptists. This accusation means that the Petrobrusians refused to baptize children because they were destitute of faith. The charge is repeated frequently by the abbot of Cluny.

"The second *capitulum* says that temples or churches should not be built, and that those existing should be torn down; that sacred places for praying were unnecessary for Christians, since God when addressed in supplication heard equally those who in a warehouse and in a church deserved his attention, in a market-place and in a temple, before an altar or before a stable." By this we understand that the Petrobrusians did not believe in the sanctity of bricks and mortar, and probably thought that as Romish churches were nests of idols and scenes of blasphemous superstition, their destruction would be no crime.

"The third *capitulum* requires holy crosses to be broken and burned, because that frame, or instrument, on which Christ, so fiercely tortured, was so cruelly slain, is not worthy of adoration, or veneration, or of any supplication; but to avenge his torments and death, it should be branded with disgrace, hacked to pieces with the sword, and consumed in the flames." The Petrobrusians detested the worship of the crucifix, and prayers offered to it, and, like the Scotch Covenanters, they urged its destruction as a Christ-dishonoring idol.

"The fourth *capitulum* denied not only the reality of the body and blood of the Lord, as offered daily and constantly in the sacrament (Eucharist) in the church; but judged that it was absolutely nothing, and should not be offered to God." In this opinion all Protestants concur.

"The fifth *capitulum* holds up to ridicule sacrifices, prayers, charitable gifts, and the other good works performed by the faithful living for the faithful departed." Peter then states that he had answered "these five heads," or heresies, "as God had enabled him." He might have added a sixth *capitulum*, that the Petrobrusians wanted Scripture for everything and not the sayings of the fathers. This is admitted in his discussion of their errors. The creed given by Peter to these Baptists is excellent as far as it goes. It is the faith of their brethren to-day. The abbot then proceeds to refute these imaginary heresies separately. And under the heading, " Answer to the Saying of the Heretics that Little Children should not be Baptized (Responsio contra id quod dicunt hæretici parvulos non posse baptizari) he commences his attack on the first *capitulum*. Peter assumes without evidence that the Petrobrusians believed that baptism was essential to salvation; and he takes up their declaration that faith was necessary to baptism, and that not the faith of another but the faith of the subject of baptism, and then he proceeds with great ingenuity to show how the faith of others " saved" persons, as he says, in the Saviour's day. Among the cases which he brings forward is that of the paralytic let down through the roof of the house to the Saviour who was inside, and Peter quotes the gospel narrative. " And when he (Jesus) saw *their faith* he said, Thy sins are forgiven." . . . Peter then says, " What do you say to these things? Behold, I relate this not from Augustine (the godfather of infant baptism, whose arguments have been its defensive weapons for ages, and were very useful to the abbot) but from the Evangel, which you say you trust most of all. At length either concede that some can be saved by the faith of others (aliorum fide alios tandem posse salvari concedite), or deny if you can that the cases I brought forward are from the Evangel." This and several similar instances of healing in the New Testament where the faith of another exercised an influence in securing healing, make the abbot jubi-

lant over the Petrobrusians. But the paralyzed man had faith himself, as well as those who brought him to Jesus.

This theory is probably borrowed entirely from Augustine. In his day the baptism of adults demanded faith continually, and when he put forth enormous efforts to change the subjects of baptism, he still insisted upon faith, the faith of sponsors for unconscious babes. Hence he says, "A little child is benefited by their faith by whom he is brought to be consecrated" (in baptism) (prodesse parvulo eorum fidem a quibus consecrandus offertur*); " a little child believes through another (the sponsor) because it sinned through another" (Adam) ([parvulus] credit in altero quia peccavit in altero†). Again, speaking of a little child, he says, " It has the needful sacrament of the Mediator, so that what could not as yet be done by its faith is performed by the faith of those who love it" (necessarium habet Mediatoris sacramentum, ut quod per ejus fidem nondum potest, per eorum qui diligunt, fiat‡). Speaking of baptism, Augustine says, " Mother-church loans them (little children) the feet of others that they may come (to it), the heart of others that they may believe, and the tongue of others that they may make confession" (accommodat illis mater ecclesia aliorum pedes ut veniant, aliorum cor ut credant, aliorum linguam ut fateantur§). Augustine was in arms to compel all Christendom to adopt infant immersion. He was almost constantly declaring, " Without baptism little children can have no life in themselves" (sine quo [baptismo] nec parvuli possunt habere vitam in semetipsis‖); and as Peter the Venerable is fighting a similar battle with the Petrobrusians, he stores his memory with Augustine's arguments. No doubt it was this that led him to say about the faith of those who carried the palsied man to Jesus, " Behold, I relate this not from Augustine, but from the Evangel."

Another common Pedobaptist argument is presented by Peter, the abbot, in these words, " The unbelieving husband is saved by the believing wife, and the unbelieving wife is saved by the believing husband." This he gives as a quotation from 1 Cor. vii., and commenting upon it, he says, " If the unbelieving wife is saved by the faith of the husband, and the unbelieving husband is saved by the faith of the wife, why should not the child be saved by the faith of husband and wife together?" This is a very natural question. But unfortunately for the abbot, Paul does not speak of either husband or wife as being saved by the faith of the other. He represents the one as being

* Augustini Opera Omnia, i. 1304.   Migne, Parisiis, 1842.
† Idem, v. 1342.   ‡ Idem, iii. 418.
§ Idem, v. 950.   ‖ Idem, x. 615.

SANCTIFIED by the other. And the sanctification he refers to after its work is done leaves its subject an unbeliever. It is the legal righteousness of their wedded relations and the legitimacy of their children of which the apostle is speaking. If indeed a Christian lady could give not only her own heart but the love of Christ and the heavenly inheritance to her unbelieving husband, and allow him still to remain in unbelief and sin, it would make a union with her an unheard-of attraction. And the same would be true of the believing husband. But Peter misquotes the Vulgate, the only copy of the Scriptures which he had. It has not his *salvatur*, but *sanctificatus* and *sanctificata est.*

In ancient times, after the heresy sprang into existence that water baptism was necessary to salvation, it was believed that martyrdom, or a baptism in one's own blood, would supply the place of the saving immersion. Peter turns this to ingenious account. He says, " If the martyrs by a personal faith are saved without baptism (in water), why may not little children, as I have said, be saved by baptism without a personal faith ?" Or WE might add, Why may they not be saved like the martyrs without any baptism ? Treating of the commission of the Saviour, the baptismal creed of the Petrobrusians, he says, "' He who believeth not shall be damned.' You think, forsooth, that little children are held by this chain, and because they are not able to believe, that baptism will profit them nothing. But it is not so ; the sacred words themselves show this ; they do not show it to the blind, but to those who see ; they show it to the humble, not to the haughty. ' Go,' says the Lord, ' into all the world, and preach the gospel to every creature. He that believeth and is baptized shall be saved ; he that believeth not shall be condemned.' These words terrify the rebellious ; they do not condemn the innocent, they strike iniquity ; they do not strike irresponsible infancy, they destroy despisers of grace ; they do not condemn the simplicity of nature (innocent children). . . . Restrain, therefore, the excessive severity which you assume, and do not aim to appear more just than him, all whose ways are mercy and truth, nor shut out little children from the kingdom of heaven (by refusing to baptize them), in reference to whom he has said, ' Of such is the kingdom of heaven.' " Peter's interpretation of the condemnation of the commission is correct ; it does not condemn any who cannot believe. But his inference from it that infants should be baptized is childishness for the imaginary advantage of infants. All infants are saved without baptism, as the Petrobrusians believed. The commission has only to do with believers and their baptism, and the penalty of unbelief when persons have heard the gospel in years when faith is possible.

Peter proceeds to take up the old argument which

Augustine uses, and which has such a modern and familiar sound : " For thus afterwards Christ the Lord placed holy baptism in his church, the sacrament of the New Testament for the circumcision of the flesh." (Sic etiam postquam Dominus Christus in ecclesia sua sacramentum Novi Testamenti pro circumcisione carnis sanctum baptismum dedit. Augustini Opera Omnia, ii. 1087. Migne, Parisiis, 1842.) And he says, " For it is very disgraceful and impious that we should refuse that to the little children of Christians which we grant to the little children of Jews, . . . for neither does the law prevail over the gospel nor Moses over Christ. . . . The little children of the Hebrews were circumcised by divine command on the eighth day, and *purged from original sin.* Where, then, was the faith of the boys ? What was their understanding of the sacrament which they received ? What was their knowledge of divine things ? Where are you who condemn Christian little children ? The little children of Jews *are saved* by the sacrament of circumcision, and shall not the little children of Christians be saved by the sacrament of baptism ? The Jew believes, and his son is cleansed from sin ; the Christian believes, and shall not his child be freed from similar guilt ? There is no faith in the little children of Christians, but neither is there any faith in the little children of Jews, yet they are *saved* by the faith of another when circumcision is received, and these (little children) are saved by the faith of another (the sponsors) when baptism is received."*

We have made these quotations to show how vigorously the Petrobrusians denounced baptism on the "*faith of another*" and insisted on personal faith. Much more might be introduced from the celebrated assault of the abbot of Cluny, but from what has been placed before the reader from Peter the Venerable, it is clear that the Petrobrusians were very decided Bible Baptists,—Baptists ready for anything on earth except a renunciation of their Scriptural principles. The other four charges of Peter are quite as favorable to the general orthodoxy of these ancient brethren.

Their immense strength to resist the church and make converts is seen in the extraordinary pains Peter takes to arm himself with all the weapons of Augustine and with such as he had made himself, and in the extremely skillful use which he makes of them. It is refreshing to read a treatise written seven hundred and thirty-six years ago against a powerful body of Baptists by a very able theologian. Augustine directed the most subtle arguments against the men who held Baptist principles in his day ; but our people, when crushed, have

* Patrl. Lat., clxxxix. pp. 722, 729, 752, 754, 755, 757, 758. Migne, Parisiis, 1854.

MEMORIAL BAPTIST CHURCH, PHILADELPHIA, PA.

only been overcome for a time, and then received fresh life again; and beyond a doubt our doctrines will finally seize the whole race and bless all nations.

Phelps, Mrs. Sophia Emilia, a daughter of Rev. James Harvey Linsley, a Baptist minister, was born Nov. 16, 1823; married, Aug. 26, 1847, Rev. S. D. Phelps, D.D.; a graceful and popular writer; author of a memoir of her father; frequent contributor to journals, especially to the *Christian Secretary;* writer of the expositions of the Sabbath-School Lessons of the International Series in the *Christian Secretary;* successful teacher of Bible-classes; gives to Sunday-school teachers weekly lectures in Hartford, before members of different denominations.

Phelps, Sylvanus Dryden, D.D., editor of *Christian Secretary,* son of Capt. Israel and

SYLVANUS DRYDEN PHELPS, D.D.

Mercy (Stevens) Phelps, grandson of Deacon Judah Phelps, of the Revolutionary war, was born in Suffield, Conn., May 15, 1816; worked on farm and taught winter schools; had great fondness for books; converted in 1834; baptized, in 1838, by Rev. M. G. Clarke; united with Second Baptist church in Suffield while a member of the Connecticut Literary Institution, where he fitted for college; licensed to preach in 1840; taught in Connecticut Literary Institution and Southwick Academy, Mass.; entered Brown University, and graduated in 1844; same year entered Yale Theological Seminary; supplied Baptist church in Bristol, and afterwards First Baptist church in New Haven, where he settled as pastor Jan. 21, 1846, and remained

twenty-eight years, during which time 1217 united with the church, 615 by baptism, and four colonies went out to form new churches. In 1871 the present church had 800 members,—largest evangelical church in the State; called at same time to two churches, but settled, in 1874, with Jefferson Street church in Providence, R. I.; on death of Rev. E. Cushman became proprietor and editor of *Christian Secretary,* Hartford, Conn., for which he had previously largely written; in 1859–60 spent about a year in Europe and the East; a brief trip to Europe in 1872; has written and published; a volume of poems in 1842; another, "Eloquence of Nature, and Other Poems;" yet another, in 1855, "Sunlight and Hearthlight;" in 1865, a volume of selections from previous volumes, with new poems; in 1862, a prose volume, "Holy Land," etc., passing through nine editions; "Sermons in the Four Quarters of the Globe;" delivered poems at college commencements; written numerous articles for reviews and periodicals; often lectured on Egypt and the Nile; easy and graceful writer of prose and poetry; popular and honored preacher; received degree of D.D. from Madison University in 1854; married, Aug. 26, 1847, Sophia Emilia Linsley, of Stratford, Conn.

Philadelphia Baptist Association, The, was formed on the "twenty-seventh day of the seventh month, on the seventh day of the week," in the year 1707. The meeting lasted till the third day of the week following. Before the formation of the Association the churches had a general meeting for preaching and administering the ordinances, which was held in different places. The first was held at Salem, N. J., in 1688; this was about three months after the Lower Dublin church was constituted. The next was held at the latter church, the next at Philadelphia, and the fourth at Burlington. Others were held in various places. The people with whom the brethren met called the gathering a yearly meeting because it met with them but once a year, but those who attended all the sessions of this body spoke of it as a quarterly meeting. The Association was designed to differ from the yearly meeting chiefly in this, that it was to be a body of *delegates representing* churches, and the yearly meeting had no representative character.

The brethren who constituted the Association came from Lower Dublin (Pennepek), Middletown, Piscataqua, Cohansey, and Welsh Tract. The Philadelphia congregation, though giving its name to the Association, is not represented as a constituent member, because it was regarded as a branch of the Lower Dublin church. Morgan Edwards mentions with evident satisfaction, that though the Association was formed of but five churches, "It has so increased since as to contain thirty-four churches (in 1770), exclusive of those which have been detached to form another Association." In 1879 the Association had 81 churches, with a membership of nearly 24,000.

The influence of the Philadelphia Association has been greater in shaping Baptist modes of thinking and working, than any other body in existence. It is older by nearly fifty years than any other Association. Its "Confession of Faith" and "Treatise of Discipline" have wielded an immense power in favor of orthodoxy and piety among our rising churches. It has ever been the warm friend of missions at home and abroad, its ministers making missionary tours all over our country. It has always been the friend of Sunday-schools since

What our denomination would have been in this country without the Philadelphia Association is an interesting question. We cannot suppose that the Associational institution would have had no existence among us. It flourished in England long before 1707. But this mother Association had men of learning even in her early history, with sound Baptist principles, great practical sagacity, and with a love for struggling Baptists in the farthest East and in the most distant South ; and, as a consequence, the Associational plan became popular, and the spirit of the old Philadelphia body was grafted upon every kindred institution all over the land. Nor did this ancient body look coldly upon the

BAPTIST HOME OF PHILADELPHIA.

the system was first presented to its churches. It encouraged the school of Isaac Eaton, of Hopewell, N. J., for the preparation of young men for the ministry, the first Baptist institution of that character in America; and it founded Brown University, formerly Rhode Island College, and through it, indirectly, all our seminaries of learning. As early as 1788 it took its stand in favor of temperance. It was a tower of strength to our persecuted brethren in other colonies in times when they suffered great legal oppression. It gave them financial aid and good counsel, and lent the weight of its great influence in seeking a redress of grievances from men in power, and it has ever demanded liberty for all men to worship God according to the dictates of their consciences.

crushed liberties and the struggling warriors of their country in Revolutionary times. On the 19th of October, 1781, our army made its victorious entry into Yorktown ; on the 23d the Association was in session ; on the night of that day the old watchmen of Philadelphia cried, "Twelve o'clock and all is well, and Cornwallis has surrendered." The next morning the Association met *at sunrise* to bless God for the glorious news, and to record their gratitude in appropriate resolutions. The mother Association of our land has a precious record.

Philadelphia, Baptist Home of, was chartered in 1869. Its object is " to provide a place of residence for members of Baptist churches who may, by reason of age, infirmities, or poverty, become incapable of supporting themselves and their families, and also to afford such persons other relief, and in such other way, as the trustees may deem prudent and advisable." The trustees have authority to admit members of other Christian churches whenever special contributions are made for that purpose.

The management consists of a board of trustees, who must be members of Baptist churches, and of a board of lady managers, consisting of representatives from the Baptist churches of Philadelphia and vicinity. To the former belongs the duty of securing titles, investing trust funds, and other legal matters, and to the lady managers is assigned the entire management of the institution, the admission and care of the inmates, and the procuring of funds to meet the required expenses above the amount furnished by the partial endowment of $30,000.

Mr. George Nugent, President; Hon. H. G. Jones, Secretary; and Mr. Levi Knowles, Treasurer, of the board of trustees, have served from the date of organization with great zeal and fidelity. The officers of the lady managers are Mrs. L. Knowles, President; Mrs. John Mustin, Vice-President; Mrs. P. G. McCollin, Corresponding Secretary; Miss Anna E. Friend, Recording Secretary; Mrs. C. H. Banes, Treasurer. Mrs. Knowles and Mrs. McCollin have filled the offices assigned to them from the founding of the institution, and to the wonderful executive ability of the former and the enthusiasm and persevering zeal of the latter, aided by a noble band of Baptist sisters, the home is largely indebted for its success and popularity.

The building is located at Seventeenth and Norris Streets, upon a plot of ground valued at $30,000, the generous gift of Deacon Joseph F. Page, of the First Baptist church. It has a handsome exterior, and is especially adapted by its plan for the purpose for which it is used. Built with wings forming three sides of a square, and surrounded by ample grounds, laid out with walks and shrubbery, its appearance is one of great beauty. There are rooms for 85 inmates. The charge for admission is $200 when under seventy years, and $150 when over that age.

As its name indicates, it is a home, and it is remarkably free from the cheerlessness that too frequently mars places of public charity, and, on the contrary, it possesses an air of comfort and contentment that reflects the highest credit upon the Christian benevolence of the denomination.

Philadelphia, The Fifth Baptist Church of, was founded in 1824, by members of the Sansom Street church, organized by Dr. Staughton. It cost about $100,000, and was dedicated to the worship of Almighty God, Oct. 13, 1864. It was paid

for before it was used for divine service. Its membership, as reported to the Philadelphia Association in October, 1880, was 584. Rev. B. D. Thomas is its highly esteemed pastor. (See illustration, p. 911.)

Philadelphia, Memorial Baptist Church of, was organized in July, 1868, by Rev. P. S. Henson, D.D.; its chapel was built soon after the formation of the church. The main edifice was completed and dedicated in February, 1876. The latter building will seat 1500 persons. Both structures and lots cost $165,500, and the church has no debt. It had in October, 1880, a membership of 642. (See illustration, p. 915.)

Philadelphia, Second Baptist Church of, was organized in March, 1803. It has had seven pastors since it was formed, six of whom have left the church militant for the heavenly assembly. William Cathcart, D.D., the seventh pastor, has held his office since April, 1857. The church is strongly Calvinistical and warmly missionary. It has paid the present pastor's salary *every month* since April, 1857, a few days before the time, except on two occasions, when it was received on the day it was due. It had a membership in October, 1880, of 707. Its present church edifice is a two-story building, 65 by 100, with a front 76 feet 6 inches wide. It was dedicated in March, 1875. It cost $93,500, and it is entirely paid for. The design of its magnificent front was evidently taken originally from the ancient church of the Abbey of Sainte Geneviève, in Paris, founded by Clovis, and rebuilt from the eleventh to the thirteenth century, an engraving of which is in Lacroix's "Manners, Customs, and Dress of the Middle Ages," p. 40. London.

Philips, Prof. G. Morris, A.M., was born at Penningtonville (now Atglen), Chester Co., Pa., Oct. 28, 1851. He was fitted for college in his native village, and entered the university at Lewisburg in 1867. Having completed the regular classical course, he graduated in 1871, taking the second honors of the largest class which has ever graduated from the university. In the ensuing autumn he assumed the chair of Mathematics in Monongahela College, which position he filled most acceptably for a year and a half. From 1873 to 1878 he held the chair of Higher Mathematics in the State Normal School at West Chester, Pa., where he soon became known most favorably as an enthusiastic and successful instructor. While in that position he declined an appointment to the county superintendency. In 1878 he was appointed Professor of Mathematics and Natural Philosophy in the university at Lewisburg.

Prof. Philips is a most careful and accurate scholar, with great breadth of mind, and a large acquaintance with literature, especially in the line of science. As an instructor he has few equals for clearness of statement, earnestness of manner, and

SECOND BAPTIST CHURCH, PHILADELPHIA, PA.

ability to awaken enthusiasm. His genial manners, thoroughness of work, and large Christian sympathy endear him to all who come under his influence. At the present writing he is engaged with Prof. Sharpless, of Haverford College, in preparing a new text-book on astronomy.

Philips, Judge John W., was born in Wilson Co., Tenn., July 1, 1837. He graduated at Alleghany College, Pa., in 1860. Made a profession of religion in Meadville, Pa., while at college, in the spring of 1859, and joined the Baptist church. He took his letter from the Meadville church to the Round Lick Baptist church in Wilson Co., Tenn., and from it he came to the Second Baptist church of St. Louis, in 1873, of which he is now a member and a deacon. He superintends the Olivet Mission of the Second church.

He was elected judge of the seventh judicial circuit of Tennessee, by the people of that circuit, by a large majority; every vote in the county where he lived was cast for him except six. There were four counties in the circuit. Judge Philips raised a company for the Union army and performed honorable service, and was made colonel of his regiment. He is now a lawyer of successful practice in St. Louis, in the firm of Philips & Stewart.

Philips, Dr. M. W., the veteran agricultural editor of the South, was born in South Carolina in 1806; graduated at South Carolina College in 1826; graduated in the medical department of Pennsylvania University in 1829; settled in Mississippi in 1830; soon became distinguished as a scientific farmer, and contributor to agricultural journals; became a Baptist in 1849, and at once took an active part in church work, especially in the promotion of education, and was chiefly instrumental in the purchase of Mississippi College and the establishment of Central Female College at Clinton, Miss. After the war he removed to Memphis, Tenn., and became editor of the *Southern Farmer*. This he gave up in 1877 to take charge of the Farm and the Agricultural professorship of the University of Mississippi, a position he still holds.

Phillips, Rev. William, was born in Provincetown, Mass., Aug. 24, 1801. In his boyhood his family removed to Pawtucket, R. I. At the age of seventeen he became a Christian, and was baptized by Dr. Benedict, then the pastor of the Baptist church in Pawtucket. At once he began to speak and perform other service in the social meetings, and was so acceptable to his brethren that his pastor sent for him, and asked him if he had ever thought it would be a privilege to preach the gospel. The young man replied that it was a pleasure to him to take part in the religious meetings which he attended, but he felt that an insuperable obstacle lay in the way of his obtaining an educa-

tion, as he was the sole stay and support of a widowed mother. In the providence of God it was found that this obstacle could be removed, and the way was opened for him to fit for college, under the tuition of Dr. Benedict. He entered Brown University in 1822, and graduated in 1826. In the class were several members who were afterwards distinguished in their professions in life. Among these may be mentioned Rev. George Burgess, D.D., the Episcopal bishop of Maine, Hon. John Kingsbury, LL.D., and Prof. Edwards A. Park, D.D. On leaving college Mr. Phillips did not take a course of theological study, but in the March following his graduation he was ordained pastor of the church in North Attleborough, Mass. He remained here until the fall of 1828, when he accepted a call to the Third Baptist church in Providence, R. I., and commenced his ministry there the first Sabbath in November, 1828. He continued with this church eight years, when he was invited to become the pastor of the First Baptist church in Charlestown, Mass. He remained here until the fall of 1841, when, his health having failed, he resigned his office and removed to Providence, R. I., where he has lived ever since. For one year he suspended regular ministerial labor. At the end of that time his health was sufficiently restored to enable him to supply churches, although he has never been a regular pastor since he left Charlestown. For five and a half years he thus supplied the church at Fruit Hill, in the neighborhood of Providence, and for eight years the church at Lonsdale, R. I. While filling this last engagement he went abroad, extending his trip up the Nile as far as Thebes, and visiting also the Holy Land, spending several weeks in Jerusalem.

Mr. Phillips resides at his pleasant home in the suburbs of Providence, respected and beloved by a large circle of friends. He was made a member of the corporation of Brown University in 1836.

Phippen, Rev. George.—At the residence of his daughter, Mrs. J. W. Mills, in Chicago, May 15, 1873, died Rev. George Phippen, in the eighty-fourth year of his age. He was born in Salem, Mass., Feb. 2, 1790, baptized into the fellowship of the Baptist church there by Rev. Lucius Bolles, Aug. 25, 1805, and ordained at Middletown, Conn., June 11, 1812, after graduating at Brown University. His successive pastorates were at Middletown Centre and Suffield, Conn., West Troy and Newburgh, N. Y., Tyringham and Lee, Mass. He had an influential share in the establishment of the Connecticut Literary Institution at Suffield, and was successively secretary and president of the Education Society in that State. He closed, in the peaceful joy of one departing to be with Christ, a long life of marked fidelity and usefulness.

Picket, Rev. John, was born in King and Queen

Co., Va., Jan. 14, 1744. In early life he was fond of sports and frivolous amusements. On a visit to North Carolina the Saviour called him into his peace. He was baptized in 1766. A year after he returned to Virginia. In 1768 a church was formed in Fauquier, Va., chiefly through his instrumentality; the church was called Carter's Run. Mr. Picket was ordained its pastor in 1772. His prosperity in winning souls soon drew persecution upon him. A mob broke into the meeting-house and split the pulpit in pieces. The magistrates sent the pastor to prison, where he preached God's Word to the salvation of great numbers. When he was released from prison he proclaimed Jesus with greater zeal than ever, extending his labors into Culpeper and over the Blue Ridge, where at the first baptism that ever took place in Shenandoah fifty were immersed. Mr. Picket loved the Saviour intensely, was never weary in laboring for him, was honored by great usefulness in the service of Jesus, and he led a saintly life. He died in June, 1803.

Pidge, Rev. John Bartholomew Gough, the son of Edwin and Mary E. Pidge, was born at Providence, R. I., Feb. 4, 1844; was educated in public and private schools at Providence, and subsequently entered Brown University, graduating therefrom in 1866; graduated also at Newton Theological Institution in 1869. While a student at Newton he translated Braune's "Commentary on Philippians," from the German, under the supervision of Dr. Hackett; was ordained Sept. 8, 1869, and became pastor of the church at Lawrence, Mass. In 1871 he declined a call to the professorship of New Testament Exegesis from Crozer Theological Seminary. In April, 1879, he accepted a call to the pastorate of the Fourth church, Philadelphia, in which field of labor he continues a ministry that has greatly endeared him to one of our largest churches.

Mr. Pidge is a man of studious habits, of scholarly attainments, and of marked pulpit power. His sermons are fruitful in the results of close application, and are well calculated to enrich the minds of those who wait upon his ministrations.

Pierson, Rev. Nicholas, an English Baptist, who settled in Horton, Nova Scotia, about 1775; was ordained, Nov. 5, 1778, pastor of the Baptist church at Horton, formed seven days previous; the first Baptist church organized in the Maritime Provinces. Mr. Pierson continued pastor till his removal to New Brunswick in 1791, where he died some years after.

Pike, Rev. James C., an eminent minister of the English General Baptists, and for twenty-two years secretary of their Foreign Missions, was born June 26, 1817. His father, the author of "Persuasives to Early Piety," was gratified to see in his own

son what he so earnestly commended to the young generally. After a course of study at Stepney College, he commenced his ministry at Wisbech, as assistant to the Rev. Joseph Jarrom. He labored here fourteen years, and then removed to Leicester, where, in two pastorates, he spent the remaining years of his life. In 1855 he was chosen secretary of the Foreign Missions, in the place of his father, to whose faith and zeal it owed its origin. His industry and courage, as well as bodily strength, were severely taxed by the burdens laid upon him as a pastor of a large church and the responsible director of the missionary work. But he was a workman who needed not to be ashamed. He died August, 1876, aged fifty-nine years.

Pike, Rev. John G., was born at Edmonton, England, April 6, 1784. His father, the Rev. Dr. Pike, had formerly been a clergyman of the Established Church, from which he seceded for conscience' sake, and became the minister of a Presbyterian congregation in the neighborhood of London. When in his eighteenth year he was entered as a student for the ministry at an Independent college. Whilst pursuing his studies the subject of baptism powerfully attracted his mind, and he was led by his convictions to abandon the Pedobaptist sentiments in which he had been brought up. He was baptized by the only Baptist minister he was acquainted with in August, 1804, but did not join any Baptist church until 1808, when he was received into the church in London under the pastoral care of the eminent General Baptist minister, Dan Taylor, by which he was soon after formally licensed to preach. After preaching for some time without a fixed engagement, he accepted a call to the General Baptist church in Derby. His success was attested by the rapid increase of the congregation and numerous baptisms. The church edifice was inadequate, and, notwithstanding the commercial depression of the period, a new and much larger building was erected. His scanty income obliged him to commence a boarding-school for the support of his family, but his ministerial labors were abundant in Derby and all the neighborhood. He threw himself heartily into the work of foreign missions, and co-operated with Andrew Fuller and the Particular Baptists until the General Baptist Mission was organized. Mr. Pike was immediately chosen secretary of the society. Besides these labors his pen was ever busy. His "Persuasives to Early Piety" and "Guide for Young Disciples" had a wide circulation and were eminently useful. Besides these works, which are everywhere known and deservedly esteemed, he wrote other practical works of great value. During his long pastorate at Derby, which was terminated only by his death, he lived in the affection of his people and enjoyed the esteem of all classes of the community. He died suddenly, seated at his desk with his pen in hand, Sept. 4, 1855, aged seventy.

Pilgrim, Rev. Thomas J., was born in Middlesex Co., Conn., Dec. 19, 1805; was licensed to preach, and spent a time at Hamilton, N. Y., under the tuition of Nathaniel Kendrick and Daniel Hascall. His health failing him, in 1827, he left Hamilton, and by the Western waters came to New Orleans, where, after waiting some time, he succeeded in getting a passage on a schooner to the mouth of the Brazos River, in the then Mexican province of Texas. He accepted service as a teacher of the children of Mexican hidalgos, and assisted Stephen F. Austin in translating from Spanish into English the laws of Mexico, thus acquiring a thorough command of the Spanish language. For the most of his life he was occupied as a teacher with signal success, instructing such men as James H. Bell, M. Austin Bryan, and Guy M. Bryan. He organized and conducted the first Sunday-school ever originated in Texas. In establishing Sunday-schools, teaching Bible - classes, distributing the Bible, and managing Gonzales College he spent most of his life. After coming to Texas he gave up the duties of the ministry, but lived and acted as a consistent, devoted Christian, taking a deep interest in the education of the young men proposing to enter the Christian ministry, and giving liberally to their support. He died at Gonzales, Texas, Oct. 29, 1877.

Pillsbury, Rev. Stephen, was born in Amesbury, Mass., Oct. 30, 1781. Hopefully converted at the age of twenty-one, he was baptized into the fellowship of the church in Sutton, N. H. Having decided to give his life to the work of the ministry he preached as a licentiate in different places. He was ordained in Hebron, N. H., where he remained fifteen years. In 1830 he became pastor of the church in Sutton, where his labors were much blessed during his five years' pastorate. His next pastorates were at Dumbarton and at Londonderry, N. H. In the latter place he died, Jan. 22, 1851.

Pingry, Judge William M., was born at Salisbury, N. H., May 28, 1806, and was admitted to the bar in Vermont in June, 1832. He was baptized in 1831, and at once identified himself with the interests of his denomination in the State of Vermont. In 1841 he removed to Perkinsville, and became a deacon of the Baptist church in that place. He has occupied several of the most prominent positions in Baptist organizations in the State. From 1838 to 1840 he was judge of the Washington County Court. He was a member of the Vermont constitutional convention in 1850, State auditor from 1853 to 1860, a member of the Vermont house of representatives in 1860, 1861, and 1868, and of the senate in 1869, 1870. He has practised his profession since June, 1832, excepting

that from November, 1854, to August, 1857, he was cashier of a bank. Dartmouth College con-

JUDGE WILLIAM M. PINGRY.

ferred on him, in 1860, the honorary degree of Master of Arts.

Pitman, Judge John, the son of Rev. John Pitman, was born in Providence, Feb. 23, 1785. Such was his precocity that he entered Brown University before he had completed his eleventh year. He graduated in the year 1799, and though but a mere lad of fourteen, commenced the study of law, which he pursued for two years and a half, at the end of which time he was prepared to be admitted to the Rhode Island bar. He was too young, however, to practice his profession, and in order to perfect himself in his studies he was placed under the direction of an eminent lawyer of Poughkeepsie, N. Y., Hon. Theodorus Bailey. After various fortunes in different localities he returned to his native city and opened a law-office, and for several years practised in the Rhode Island courts. He then took up his residence in Salem, Mass., and subsequently in Portsmouth, N. H., and thus became familiar with the practice of law in the courts of those States. Once more he returned to Providence, and continued his residence there from 1820 to the close of his life. In 1824 he was appointed U. S. district judge for the district of Rhode Island. During this long period of professional service he proved himself a public-spirited citizen, always throwing the weight of his influence on the side of any plan or organization which had for its object the improvement of his fellow-men. He was a member of the corporation of Brown University for thirty-six years, six years as a trustee and thirty years as a Fellow. His college conferred upon him the degree of Doctor of Laws in 1842.

JUDGE JOHN PITMAN.

Few men have more thoroughly won the respect and affection of the community in which they lived than Judge Pitman. Loyal to the faith of his fathers, he was a firm Baptist, and a devout worshiper in the venerable church in which for so many years he had a seat. Although, like his long cherished friend, Nicholas Brown, he never made a public profession of his faith, he nevertheless "illustrated the strict integrity, the devout humility, and the exemplary life of a Christian man." His death took place in Providence, Nov. 17, 1864, when he was within less than four months of being eighty years of age.

Pitman, Rev. John, was born in Boston, April 26, 1751. Early in life he was apprenticed to learn the business of a rope-maker. He was baptized by Rev. Dr. Stillman, Feb. 24, 1771, and became a member of the First Baptist church in Boston. He removed to Philadelphia in 1774. For some time he was in the Continental army during the Revolutionary war. He began to preach probably in 1777, and in October of this year became pastor of the Baptist church in Upper Freehold, N. J., where he remained until March 10, 1780. For two or three years he was without a settlement. He removed to Providence, R. I., in 1784, and was occupied with secular pursuits and preaching for the next two years, and in October, 1786, was called to the pastorate of the church in Warren, R. I., where he continued until 1790, when he returned to Providence, where he resided for several years, during a few of which he was the pastor of the church in the neighboring town of Pawtucket. In 1797 he became pastor of the church in Rehoboth, Mass., where for nearly all the rest of his life he lived, dying July 22, 1822.

Pitts, Rev. Y. R., was born in Scott Co., Ky., Nov. 8, 1812. His parents were Younger and Elizabeth T. Pitts. His father died when he was but twelve years of age; his mother was left a widow with eight children. She was a remarkable Christian woman, and she was much assisted by her son; between them there existed a tender relation of heart devotion. He removed to Missouri in 1860. He was ordained to the ministry of the Baptist denomination in Georgetown, Ky., Nov. 23, 1841. The ordaining council were J. D. Block, J. M. Frost, Howard Malcom, D.D., president of Georgetown College, R. T. Dillard, B. F. Kinney, and William Craig. He was pastor at Elkhart, Ky., thirteen years. He labored also at Williamstown, Blue Creek, and elsewhere. In Missouri he was pastor at Fayette. At the time of his death he was about to enter upon an agency for William Jewell College. He died at Clinton, Mo., in October, 1870, to which place he had gone to attend the General Association of Missouri. A neat marble monument marks his resting-place in the city cemetery at Huntsville, Mo. He was a man of high character, and a faithful minister of Christ.

Platt, Rev. Edward Francis, was born at Schroon Lake, N. Y., Dec. 16, 1821, and was baptized into the fellowship of the Baptist church of the same place in 1838. At an early period in his Christian life he made choice of the ministry, and pursued a course of studies under the instruction of Rev. W. W. Moore, of Lansingburg, N. Y. He commenced preaching in Cairo, N. Y., in 1845, and in the following year was ordained at that place to the work of the ministry. In 1847 he became pastor of the First church, Catskill, N. Y., where he labored with great success for five and a half years. Being obliged by ill health to resign this pastorate, he went West, and in 1853 became pastor of a young and struggling church at Toledo, O., under the direction of the Home Mission Society. Here he labored with untiring zeal until his death, which occurred Nov. 21, 1866. During this period of thirteen years he won the hearts of all by his purity of life, his devotion to the cause of Christ, and his pulpit abilities. His death was felt to be a great loss not only in Toledo, but in the entire State.

Poindexter, Abram Maer, D.D., was born in Bertie Co., N. C., Sept. 22, 1809. His father was the Rev. Richard Poindexter, of Louisa Co., Va., who, on the occasion of his marriage with Mrs. Jordan, of North Carolina, removed to that State. Young Poindexter's early educational advantages were good, and he applied himself closely to the ordinary studies preliminary to a college course. While still quite young he entered the Columbian College, but owing to feeble health his studies there were interrupted, and after a brief period he was compelled to abandon them and return to his home. In 1831 he made a profession of religion ; in 1832 he was licensed to preach, and in 1834 he was ordained to the work of the gospel ministry. For some time before his ordination he was the companion, student, and co-laborer of the Rev. A. W. Clopton, the popular and useful pastor of Baptist churches in Charlotte Co., Va., from whose gifted mind and heart, as well as varied and ripe experience in pastoral duties, he derived valuable and life-long impressions for good. Quite early in life Dr. Poindexter married Mrs. Eliza Craddock, a lady of great excellence of character, after which he resided in Halifax Co., Va., where most of his mature life was spent. From the very beginning of his ministry he displayed unusual talents, and was esteemed the most promising young minister of his time. As a preacher, Dr. Poindexter was deservedly held in very high regard, especially with large out-door assemblies, such as convene at Associational meetings. On such occasions his preaching was frequently distinguished by great fluency and power of speech, unusual vigor and depth of thought, a beautiful logical consecutiveness in the development of truth, and an earnestness and impetuosity of manner that swayed and moved the masses with resistless power. As a thinker he had but few equals. His intellect was clear, active, strong, and original. His thoughts were pre-eminently his own. He called no man master, excepting always the great Teacher. As an extemporaneous debater he stood almost alone among disputants ; and so accurate was his method, so precise his arguments, so correct his style, that a verbatim report of his remarks would rarely require the least revision for publication. As an agent for the Columbian and Richmond Colleges he was greatly successful, while as secretary of the Southern Baptist Publication Society, and afterwards as co-secretary of the Foreign Mission Board of the Southern Baptist Convention, he won a noble reputation for energy and executive ability. His impressive appeals in behalf of missions and education stimulated the zeal, enlisted the interest, and secured the contributions of large numbers throughout the South, and gave an impetus to those causes which they still feel. He was a man of deep convictions and intense feeling. His words were indeed the outer image of his inmost soul.

He believed, and therefore he spoke ; and when he spoke men had no hesitation in saying, here is a Christian man who will part with his life rather than with his convictions of right and duty. Dr. Poindexter, like many of his brethren in the ministry, was called, in the providence of God, to pass through dark waters of affliction. Two promising sons were taken from him during the war, one by the accidental discharge of his own pistol, and the other at the head of his company, by a bullet of the enemy. The ravages of war swept away his estate ; and to crown his sorrows his estimable wife soon passed away from his desolated home, leaving among the wrecks an only daughter, who has since died, who was married to the Rev. J. B. Taylor, Jr., now of Wilmington, N. C. In 1843 the Columbian College conferred upon him the degree of D.D. He died May 7, 1872.

Pollard, John, Sr., was born in Goochland Co., Va., July 14. 1803. The maiden name of his mother was Catherine Robinson, of the same family with Spenker Robinson, of the house of burgesses of Virginia, who was presiding over that body at the time Patrick Henry made his celebrated speech against the British crown, and who was the first to cry "treason !" when the great orator closed with the startling utterance, "Cæsar had his Brutus," etc." One of his uncles was private secretary to Chief-Justice Marshall, and one of his aunts, wife of the distinguished Judge Pendleton, of the Virginia Court of Appeals. His education was received in a school at Hanover Court-House, and comprised the ordinary English branches and some acquaintance with Latin. He learned much afterwards in the office of his uncle, R. Pollard, clerk of King and Queen Co., Va., with whom he served as deputy from his seventeenth to his twenty-first year. When of age he settled in King and Queen County, farming and practising law. In 1826 he was baptized into the fellowship of the Lower King and Queen church by Rev. Wm. Todd. Subsequently he withdrew, with others, to form the Mattapony church, of which he continued a member until his death, having been thirty-five years one of its deacons, and thirty-four years the superintendent of its Sunday-school. He was an ardent supporter of denominational enterprises, and was noted for his hospitality, especially to Baptist ministers, many of whom, such as Luther Rice, Eli Bell, Valentine Mason, Andrew Broaddus, and William F. Broaddus, were frequently found at his cheerful fireside. He was at different times commissioner of revenue, a justice of the County Court, and high sheriff. Mr. Pollard was very strong in his attachments to the Columbian College, to which he contributed liberally and frequently, and at which institution four of his sons were educated ; while at the same time friendly to other institutions of learning. He was a man of very decided principles, and of remarkable liveliness of temperament. He died Sept. 13, 1877. It is a noteworthy fact, that of his seven children and twenty-eight grandchildren surviving him, all that have attained the age of twelve years are useful members of Baptist churches.

Pollard, John, D.D., son of John Pollard and Juliet Jeffries, sister of Judge J. M. Jeffries, of the second judicial circuit of Virginia, was born Nov. 17, 1839, in King and Queen Co., Va. He began his education at Stevensville Academy, and completed it at the Columbian College, Washington, D. C., where he graduated with the highest honors in 1860. After his graduation he remained as tutor of Greek and Latin in the college during the session of 1860–61, and also took a private course in theology under Rev. G. W. Samson, D.D., at that time president of the college. He was ordained to the ministry July 14, 1861, and became pastor of Hermitage and Clarke's Neck churches, Middlesex Co., Va., with which he remained nine years, until October, 1870, when he accepted a call to the pastorate of Lee Street Baptist church, Baltimore. Mr. Pollard has published a compendious history of the Lee Street church, and was appointed by the Executive Board of the Maryland Union Association to finish the "History of the Churches" connected with that body, begun by the late Dr. G. F. Adams, in which desirable work considerable progress has been made. He has contributed occasional articles also to the religious papers. For three successive sessions of the Maryland Union Association, embracing not only the churches of the whole of Maryland, but also those of the District of Columbia, he has been its efficient moderator. The Columbian College conferred upon him, in 1867, the degree of A.M. in course, and in 1877 the degree of D.D. In 1880, Dr. Pollard became a pastor in Richmond, Va., leaving throngs of friends in Baltimore.

Pomeroy, Caleb M., was born at old Salem, Mass., Aug. 8, 1810. His father died when he was nine years of age. In 1831 he removed to Cincinnati. He became a resident of Quincy, Ill., in 1837, and that city has since been his home. During twenty-four years he was a successful pork-packer; then for fourteen years president of the First National Bank in Quincy. In 1842 he united with the First Baptist church of Quincy, and was elected one of its deacons in the same year. His membership and office he continued to hold until 1857, when he united with others in forming the Vermont Street church, where again he was called to the office of deacon. For thirty-three years he was a teacher in the Sunday-school. Mr. Pomeroy has always been a very liberal man, giving largely to many and various objects of

Christian enterprise, in the time when his business prospered making these gifts in hundreds and thousands of dollars. Reverses in business have reduced his ability, but in no degree affected his interest or his readiness to give. He is, and has always been, a pillar in the church.

Pools of Jerusalem.—Of all cities of antiquity, in proportion to area and population, Jerusalem seems to have been the most abundantly supplied with water. In the worst straits of siege, drought, or famine, during its checkered and eventful history, it seems never to have suffered from such a curtailment of its water-supply as to amount to a serious calamity. While there is no stream in the near vicinity of the city to account for this abundance, the Kedron being but a brook in name, yet such sources of supply as were available seem to have been so utilized that the city could always be guarded against so grave an evil as an inadequate supply of water. The sources of this supply were the natural springs without, and perhaps within the city, and the drainage of the winter rains, gathered into public and private pools, tanks, wells, and cisterns. In most cases the ultimate and most copious source of supply for the larger reservoirs were the springs or fountains mentioned. For ordinary domestic uses the winter rains seem to have been stored in private cisterns and tanks. Public institutions appear to have had larger cisterns and reservoirs for their special wants. Modern exploration beneath the traditional temple area has fully brought to light the elaborate system of water-supply for the wants of the ancient temple service and worshipers. But the public reservoirs or pools, to which we now confine our attention, were the receptacles where the waters were most abundantly collected, and most freely used by the people. Outside the walls of the modern city traces of several large pools can now be discerned which indicate their early existence; but those that remain, in their varying degrees of preservation, fully show the important part they must have performed in the water-supply of the city. For the purposes of convenience we may begin at the large pool located in a valley or basin to the northwest of the modern city. This pool was most probably built by Solomon, and is characterized by the prophet Isaiah as "the old pool" (Isaiah xxii. 11), and also as "the upper pool, which is in the highway of the fuller's field" (2 Kings xviii. 17). It is excavated out of the earth and limestone rock, the walls, like these structures in general, being built up of stones and cement. Here, by the conduit of this upper pool (2 Kings xviii. 17), the envoys of the king of Assyria stood when they delivered the message of their master to Hezekiah. Dr. Robinson carefully measured this pool, and found the length 316 feet; breadth, 218 feet at one end, and 200 feet at the other, with a depth of 18 feet. Steps were found at the corners leading down to the bottom of the reservoir. Originally, the pool received most of its supply, in all probability, from the neighboring springs or fountains that the king sealed when the city was besieged during his reign; but now the drainage of the winter rains from the adjacent hills appears to be the only source of supply. From the dilapidated condition of the pool, this, however, soon disappears. At the northwest angle of the city, within the modern walls, and near the Church of the Holy Sepulchre, is the " Pool of Hezekiah," supposed to be referred to in 2 Kings xx. 20, where the king is represented as making a pool and conduit, and bringing water into the city. The modern name is Birket-el-Hummam,—the Pool of the Bath,—from its supplying a neighboring bath. During the rainy season the water is brought down from the Upper Pool referred to by a small aqueduct that enters the city near the Yâfâ Gate. In October, 1871, when the writer of the present article saw this pool, the quantity of water did not suffice to cover the floor, which sloped considerably from north to south. At the northwest angle there is the usual descent by steps to the bottom of the reservoir. The people of the neighborhood, at the present time, freely use the pool to wash and fill their water-jars. The length of the pool, according to Dr. Robinson, is 240 feet; its breadth, 144 feet. On the opposite side of the city, north of the Mosque of Omar, and near the eastern wall, is an immense excavation, with walls of stone and cement, known as Birket Israel, or Pool of Israel. Almost uniform tradition identifies the modern Birket Israel as the "Pool of Bethesda," in our Lord's time described as having five porches, and where he performed a striking miracle.—John v. 2–7. Dr. Robinson, though standing alone among ancient and modern authorities in his views respecting the identity of the modern pool with " Bethesda," yet admits that it was once used as a reservoir. The limits of this article will not permit any reference in detail to the testimony of such witnesses as Eusebius, Jerome, and others, who describe the pool as, in their time, divided into two sections, filled with water, but evidently the same structure as the single pool that in our Lord's day was surrounded by covered colonnades. In superficial area this pool covers more than an acre of ground. It is 360 feet long, 130 feet broad, and 75 feet deep, now partly choked with rubbish. Emerging from St. Stephen's Gate, and passing a short distance down the bed of the Kedron, the modern traveler comes to a natural cave or grotto, from the bottom of which, reached by a flight of steps cut in the rock, issues a copious supply of water. This fountain at present is known as the "Fountain of the Virgin," and is the same, in all

probability, as the King's Pool mentioned by Nehemiah.—Neh. ii. 14. The general dimensions of the grotto are 15 feet in length, 5 or 6 feet in width, and 6 or 8 feet in height. The water in the basin varies in depth from one to three feet, but can be indefinitely increased in quantity by slightly damming or obstructing the outlet. This fountain is much resorted to by the poorer classes of the modern city. Recent discoveries leave little room to doubt that the "Fountain of the Virgin" derives its supply from the reservoirs beneath the temple area, in turn replenished, it is believed, by subterranean conduits, not yet discovered, from the springs that were sealed by King Hezekiah when the ancient city was besieged. By an underground passage of little more than a quarter of a mile in length, the "Fountain of the Virgin" pours its surplus waters into the Birket-es-Silwân,—the ancient "Pool of Siloam." Accepting the measurement of Dr. Barclay, the pool is 17 feet at the upper end, 14½ feet at the lower, and 18½ feet in depth. It is now never filled, the water easily passing through it by an outlet at the lower end. The walls are very much out of repair, so that it would be impossible for the pool, under existing circumstances, to be charged with the volume of water it must have originally received. A short distance back of the pool, up the hill, is a smaller reservoir, 6 or 8 feet wide by 8 or 10 feet in length. This tank receives first the overflow from the "Fountain of the Virgin," and then pours it into the adjoining "Pool of Siloam." The bottom of this upper basin, or that of the adjacent pool itself, may be reached by a flight of steps, and the water graduated in depth by temporarily damming the outlet of one or the other. "The Lower Pool of Gihon," situated to the west of the city, in the valley of that name, and now known as Birket-es-Sultan, was the largest in or near the city. This pool, or lake, was formed by damming up the bed of the valley, so as to confine the overflow of the Upper Pool, described as situated to the northwest of the city. Dams across the valley form the ends, while its bed, sloping gently on either side, forms the sides of this immense reservoir. By a careful measurement, Dr. Robinson found the length along the centre, 592 feet; the breadth at the north end, 245 feet; at the south, 275 feet. The depth at the north end is 35 feet; at the south, 42 feet. This pool owes its construction most probably to Hezekiah, and may be referred to in 2 Chron. xxxii. 30. It is now dry, and is not unfrequently used as a corral for camels. In the time of the Crusades, from the accounts that have been transmitted, it was abundantly charged with water, and appears to have been a great watering-place for horses. From the Upper Pool, the rains, and the aqueduct passing near by from the pools near Bethlehem, the volume of water in this great reservoir, derived from these several sources, must have been practically inexhaustible. This, of course, could have only been the case when the pools and aqueducts were very different in condition and repair from that seen at the present day.

In any enumeration of the public pools of the ancient city mention at least must be made of three immense pools situated near Bethlehem, constructed by Solomon, and known as "Solomon's Pools." They are fed by natural springs in the vicinity. They were built for the use of the Holy City, and as they now, by an aqueduct, send their wholesome waters within its walls, so in the past they must have played an important part in the water resources of the city.

The pools in or near Jerusalem known to have existed in the time of our Lord, where they can with sufficient positiveness be identified, have now been considered. That they were all in good repair and thoroughly fitted, in the days of the Apostles, to serve the purposes of their construction, there is scarcely reason to doubt; for a generation had not elapsed since Herod carefully repaired and strengthened the pools and reservoirs in and near the capital of his kingdom. The assumption by Pedobaptists that the rite of immersion could not have been administered in connection with the 3000 converts of Pentecost on a single day, because there could have been no facilities for baptism on such a scale, is not only untenable, but preposterous in the light of what has been advanced. These pools at that time, even under unfavorable circumstances, must not only have contained a sufficient *depth* of water for the purpose, but, as a necessary appliance, steps appear to have been built for entering them. In the case of the largest of them, the "Lower Pool of Gihon," the sloping sides of the valley were peculiarly fitted for entering the pool to any required depth. The multitude of sick people lingering and waiting at the "Pool of Bethesda" when the impotent man was healed, indicates that in one of the largest reservoirs, if it does not establish the fact respecting the others, the people were accustomed freely to enter. Even *now* the comparatively small basin at the bottom of the "Fountain of the Virgin" would furnish an excellent baptistery, if there were need of so employing it. The "Pool of Siloam" near by, must have been, as it would be now if in repair, still better fitted for the purpose. Moreover, the sloping floors of "the Upper Pool of Gihon" and the neighboring "Pool of Hezekiah" show conclusively that these pools could be entered to any depth suitable for bathing, and hence for immersion. The first converts appear at the outset to have worshiped in the temple unmolested. "They grew in favor with all the people." Popular sym-

pathy was with them. The spirit of intolerance had hardly begun to manifest itself, as it did so virulently afterwards. It is not likely, therefore, there was any opposition to the use of the public pools in administering the rite of baptism to the Pentecostal converts, or the multitudes subsequently. In the "Lower Pool of Gihon" alone,—the largest, and the one perhaps most extensively used,—with the Apostles and the Seventy as possible administrators, any reasonable objection against the immersion of the 3000 on the day of Pentecost, or any number later, at once vanishes; and when the facilities furnished by the other pools are taken into consideration, the absurdity of the objections against the immersion of a large number, as to time and quantity of water, becomes still more apparent.

Pope, Rev. George.—This useful minister was pastor of Abbott's Creek Church, Davidson Co., N. C. He was repeatedly moderator of the Sandy Creek Association, and during the great revival of 1800 baptized 500 persons. He baptized the elder Dr. W. T. Brantly into the fellowship of May's chapel.

Pope, John Francis, was born in New Bedford, Mass., Jan. 22, 1823; was converted at the age of sixteen, and baptized by Dr. Henry Jackson. He was a graduate of Harvard. Mr. Pope was among the early pioneers to California, arriving there in August, 1849, and, with his wife, joined the First Baptist church, San Francisco, and became one of its most influential members, holding the position of deacon from July, 1854, twenty-five years. He occupied important positions in the school department of the city, and assisted in establishing its high schools. In denominational matters he held high official positions in the Associations, Conventions, and college boards, and did much to impress upon the State his own character as a Christian and an enlightened Baptist. At the quarter centennial of the organization of the San Francisco Baptist Association, in 1874, he was the moderator.

Pope, Rev. O. C., the managing editor of the *Texas Baptist Herald*, was born Feb. 15, 1842, in Washington Co., Ga.; was educated at Mercer University, Penfield, Ga., and graduated regularly from its theological department; connected himself with the Baptist church in August, 1858. Since entering the ministry he has served Louisville church, Ga., Morristown, Tenn., and Central Baptist church, Nashville, Tenn. He has acted as secretary of Mercer Association, Ga., Nolachucky Association, Tenn., and corresponding and recording secretary of the General Association of East Tennessee. He founded and edited for two years the *Baptist Reflector*, at Nashville, Tenn. He is in the vigor of his manhood, and promises to make the *Herald* a power for good in Texas.

Porter, Rev. William, was born in Erie Co., Pa., May 3, 1803, of Congregational parents; was married, converted, and baptized in Delaware Co., O.; joined the Mill Creek church, and was ordained by it in 1838. He was pastor and missionary in and around the region of the church till 1847, when he moved to Oregon, settled on the "West Plain," near Forest Grove; served the West Union church,—the first Baptist church organized west of the Rocky Mountains,—the West Tualatin and other churches, and for twenty years kept alive (with the aid of Deacon D. T. Lenox) the Baptist denomination in the lower part of the Willamette Valley, west of the river. He was both doctrinal and practical, extempore and pathetic, swaying his hearers with a wonderful power. Having done much work for Christ, he died Nov. 29, 1872, mourned by a multitude who revered him as their spiritual father and guide in religious life.

Posey, Rev. Humphrey, an eminent Baptist minister, was distinguished for his benevolent spirit

REV. HUMPHREY POSEY.

and great abilities. He was above the ordinary size, with a large frame and fine face and head. Born in Henry Co., Va., Jan. 12, 1780, he commenced preaching in 1803, and was ordained in 1805, in Buncombe Co., N. C., and, among others, preached to the Cherokee Indians. He was regularly appointed a missionary to the Cherokees at Valley Town, in North Carolina, by the Baptist Mission Board, of Philadelphia, in 1817, and maintained his connection with the mission until 1824, accomplishing great good. In 1824 he settled in

Cherokee, Ga., and became a very successful agent for the Hearn School, relieving it of much pecuniary embarrassment. In 1844 he married a second time, and removed to Newnan, where he died, Dec. 28, 1846. Dr. J. H. Campbell, in his "Georgia Baptists," records it "as his deliberate conviction that Humphrey Posey was naturally one of the greatest men, and, for his limited opportunities, one of the greatest preachers he has ever known. His person, his countenance, his voice, the throes of his gigantic mind, the conceptions of his large Christian soul, —all proclaimed him great." The first time Dr. Campbell ever met him was at the Georgia Baptist Convention, in 1835, near Penfield, and the doctor says, "Such men as Mercer, Sanders, Dawson, Thornton, Mallary, Brooks, and others were there, but Posey was a giant among them all." Dr. C. D. Mallary wrote and published a "Life of Humphrey Posey."

Post, Rev. Albert L., was born in 1809, at Montrose, Pa. Montrose was founded in 1800 by Capt. Bartlett Hinds, who survived the storming of Stony Point, a worthy pioneer magistrate and Baptist. His daughter, Susanna, and his stepson, Maj. Isaac Post, were the parents of the subject of this sketch. He was educated at Union College, Schenectady, N. Y.; was admitted to the bar, and soon after became prosecuting attorney for Susquehanna County. In 1836 he started *The Spectator*, a paper devoted to the freedom

REV. ALBERT L. POST.

of the colored race. In 1841 he was ordained to the ministry at Montrose, which has still continued to be his residence. He has rendered valuable service in protracted meetings and in partial pastorates. He was president for many years of "The American Baptist Free Mission Society," in whose interests he visited England. He is a vigorous opponent of secret societies. Mr. Post is a man of mind and a model of Christian integrity. He would suffer the loss of everything, and the worst form of death, rather than sacrifice a principle. Stern, the embodiment of the martyr spirit, with a keen intellect and a generous heart, all men love him, though not a few differ from his opinions. Pennsylvania never had a purer Baptist.

Post, Rev. John Clark, was born at Montpelier, Vt., April 20, 1814; spent most of his childhood and early youth in Connecticut; went West in 1832; was converted and baptized into the fellowship of the Baptist church of Aurora, Ind. (the pastor being Rev. Jesse L. Holman), on Nov. 4, 1838; was licensed there to preach in 1839; was ordained at Charlestown, Ind., in 1840. He has been pastor at Charlestown, Franklin, Delphi, and other places in Indiana; of Aledo, Edgington, Andalusia, and other churches in Illinois, and was settled at Fort Scott, Wichita, Hutchinson, and other places in Kansas; has been blessed with extensive revivals, and built several meeting-houses. At sixty-six years of age he enjoys good health, and occupies an extensive mission field in Southwest Kansas.

Potter, Albert K., D.D., was born in Coventry, R. I., and was a graduate of Brown University in the class of 1859. He studied at the Newton Theological Institution, and was ordained Sept. 27, 1860, as pastor of South Berwick, Me., where he remained for four years. He removed to Springfield, Mass., in 1864, and became pastor of the State Street church in that city. He has held this position ever since.

Dr. Potter is endowed with a fine intellect, whose vigorous power is unsurpassed in the State which his labors have long blessed. His reading extends over a very wide range; he is one of the most cultured men in the Baptist ministry; his usefulness in Springfield and in the denomination generally is very great. As a writer he is regarded with admiration. The friends of truth wish him a long life for the exercise of his great talents in the Master's cause.

Potter, Rev. C. W., was born in Voluntown, Conn., in 1821; at the age of fourteen united with the Baptist Church; baptized by Dr. A. G. Palmer,—his first candidate; studied in Bacon Academy; licensed in Colchester in 1842; preached two years in East Haddam; ordained at Avon, Sept. 23, 1846; subsequent settlements were at North Haven, Cromwell, Lee, and Sturbridge, Mass.; at Willington, Suffield, and other places in

Connecticut; has had five sons and a daughter; one son, Rev. George B., was pastor of Baptist church in Ashland, but is now dead; one son, Rev. Lester L., is now pastor at Everett, Mass.

Potter, Rev. Daniel C., was born in Stonington, Conn., March 15, 1850. He was baptized in Jersey City in 1865, into the North church. He graduated at Madison University in 1873, and was settled and ordained as pastor in the Sixth Street Baptist church, New York, in 1873.

Special public attention has been called to him by his series of illustrated lectures, by the aid of stereopticon views, on European manners, art, and architecture. By travel abroad and by correspondence he has secured photographs of rivers, pools, and baptisteries in Oriental countries, which, with the temples connected with them, make his lectures on the mode of baptism of the ancients interesting and convincing. By an invention of his own, not yet disclosed, his magic lantern gives a better representation than any other in use. His pastorate in Sixth Street is successful, and promises to be a long one. For several years he has officiated as secretary of the New York Baptist Ministers' Conference. Mr. Potter's ministry is marked by talent and spirituality.

Potter, Deacon Giles, son of Elisha P. and Abigail (Lathrop) Potter, was born in Lisbon, Conn., Feb. 22, 1829; educated in common schools and at Leicester Academy, Mass., and graduated at York College in 1855, and converted in same year; baptized by Rev. S. D. Phelps, D.D., and united with First Baptist church in New Haven; taught in the academy in East Hartford, in Connecticut Literary Institution, Suffield, and in Hill's Academy and Essex Seminary; chosen superintendent of Sunday-school in Essex in 1860, and remains in that position to the present (1880); chosen deacon in 1865, and now holds the office; represented Essex in the Legislature for three years,— from 1870 to 1873; selectman and justice of peace in Essex; school visitor for fourteen years; elected in 1873 agent of State board of education, and still holds the position; of marked abilities, energy, prudence, and fidelity.

Potter, Rev. Lester Lewis, son of Rev. C. W. Potter, was born in Colebrook, Conn., March 30, 1858; educated at Connecticut Literary Institution, and at Rochester, N. Y.; baptized at the age of ten; licensed by the Baptist church in Willington, Conn., at the age of sixteen; during studies at Rochester supplied churches in Avon and West Somerset, N. Y.; in April, 1879, settled with the Baptist church in Everett, Mass.

Potter, Rev. Walter McD., was a native of Rhode Island. He graduated the second in his class in Brown University, and pursued his theological studies in Andover and Rochester. He was the first Baptist minister in Colorado. The Baptist church at Denver was gathered under his labors. He collected the means for, and superintended in the construction of, the basement of the first Baptist house of worship, when his health failed; he returned to Providence, where he died, April 9, 1866, aged twenty-nine years and eleven months. Few men have accomplished so much in so short a time. With a remarkable foresight he secured lands in and around Denver, which he bequeathed to the Home and Foreign Mission Societies, out of which they will realize together probably nearly $100,000. On account of the great interest that he felt in the Denver church, the Home Mission Society has transferred a large portion of its share of their legacy to this church, which has enabled it to pay some $12,000 of debts, leaving a handsome balance of about as much more as a beginning towards the erection of another church edifice as a monument to its founder's memory. He was noted for positive convictions and a conscientious adherence to what he believed to be duty. He had tact to adapt himself to circumstances, so as to be successful in whatever he undertook. His life was brief, but long enough to form an established character as an able, devoted servant of Jesus Christ.

Potter, Hon. William H., was born on Potter Hill, in the town of Westerly, R. I., Aug. 26, 1816. His father, Col. Henry Potter, commanded the 3d R. I. Regiment in the war of 1812. Col. Potter was a warm friend of education, and he took great pains to secure its advantages for his only son, Wil-

REV. WALTER M'D. POTTER.

liam. He sent him to Yale College, after he had been for years at schools and academies, that he might receive the best culture that New England could impart. He was compelled, through impaired sight, to leave Yale before he graduated, but that institution recognized his literary standing, and in 1852 bestowed upon him the honorary degree of A.M.

For many years he made teaching his profession, and he obtained such a measure of success in that calling as cheered himself and gratified his friends, and bound the hearts of throngs of the young to him for life.

By President Lincoln he was appointed assistant United States assessor of internal revenue, an office which he held for several years. He was State senator in the Connecticut Legislature from the seventh district for some time, and during that period his great worth as an instructor was abundantly proved. He was appointed chairman of the committee on education, and took an important part in the revision of the school code of his adopted State. So satisfactory were his labors in connection with legislation for education that he was appointed one of the four elective members of the State board of education. This position he held for two successive terms of four years each. He is now judge of probate for the district in which he resides. He has been for many years a deacon of the Union Baptist church of Mystic River, Conn.; loved and honored by the entire community in which he lives.

He is a vigorous Baptist. While his love for other Christians is large, his admiration for the Baptist denomination, the first community that bore the name of Christ, is unbounded. He knows the history of his religious ancestors, and can write it better than almost any other man in the "Land of Steady Habits;" he knows their principles of liberty and love, and he would like to spread them everywhere; he is a worthy man in all the relations of life.

Potts, Col. D. G., was born in Sussex Co., Va., Aug. 27, 1810, and was educated in the neighboring schools. He served for several years most efficiently as sheriff of the county, being also engaged in farming and merchandising until 1844, when he removed to Petersburg, Va., and engaged in the commission business. In 1856 he was elected treasurer of the Petersburg Railroad Company, which position he held with rare fidelity during nineteen years, up to 1875. In 1877 he was appointed by the President postmaster at Petersburg, which office he still holds. Col. Potts has always taken a deep interest in the well-being of the communities where he has lived, and his integrity and experience have made him a valuable counsellor in public affairs. He served in the city council of Petersburg from 1853 to 1868, and was senior alderman and chairman of the committee on public property during all that long period. He is as active and useful in church affairs as he is in public. In 1836 he united with the Baptist church at Newville, Sussex Co. When he removed to that neighborhood in 1834 there was but one professor of religion there. Through his efforts and the preaching of Rev. J. L. Gwaltney, a church building was erected and a church organized, and when he left there, in 1844, there was a large and flourishing congregation, and one of the most prosperous county Sunday-schools in the State. For more than forty years Col. Potts has been an active worker in the Sunday-school as teacher or superintendent, and, what is something worthy of special mention, he was never once late at school. He has also served as deacon during all his long Christian life, and in all the spheres in which he moves no man is more highly honored and justly esteemed.

Powell, Rev. Joab, was one of the most remarkably successful and eccentric preachers in Oregon. Whenever it was known that he would preach the entire population crowded to hear him. He was born in Claiborne Co., Tenn., July 16, 1799. He was baptized in 1824, and joined the Berean church; removed to Missouri; licensed in 1830, and soon after was ordained by the Salem church, which was anti-mission, while he was a missionary Baptist. Soon after he went to the Blue Springs. The county judge, Richard Stanley, said to him, as he had said to others, supposing that he also was anti-mission, "If your mission is only to preach to the sheep and lambs, you need not come here, for we have no sheep and lambs." Mr. Powell replied, "My mission is to poor sinners." The judge said, "Then you can preach for us." He did so, built a large church, and baptized 150. He continued many years as a frontier preacher; removed to Oregon in 1852; went about everywhere, sometimes acting as pastor, but was almost constantly doing the work of an evangelist. His discourses were earnest and full of sharp points. His audiences were kept in tears and smiles, and when the sermon was over he would sing, exhort, pray, and entreat by times, until the most obdurate would yield. After a long and useful life, beloved by his church, he died Jan. 25, 1873.

Powell, Rev. Robert, was a native of Massachusetts, but removed with his parents to Hamilton, N. Y., in 1805, where he experienced religion while yet a child. He commenced preaching when young, and was permitted to enjoy the service nearly sixty years. In 1817 he was one of the thirteen who in prayer together, and the offering of a dollar each to the object, organized the Hamilton Institution. He was for some years the last survivor of that honored band. Coming to Michi-

gan in 1832, he was, until his death, in 1875, one of the most trusted and loved standard-bearers of the denomination. Highly gifted in voice and song, of an excellent spirit, with clearness of reason and native eloquence, he was a good and able minister of Christ. He died at Clinton, his home in Michigan, in his eightieth year.

Powell, Rev. Thomas.—No name is linked in more interesting ways with early Baptist history in Illinois than that of Rev. Thomas Powell. He was born, Dec. 9, 1801, in the town of Abergavenny, Monmouthshire, South Wales. In his fifteenth year he experienced conversion, and united with the Baptist church in his native town. In the year 1818 he emigrated to New York, and united with the Mulberry Street Baptist church in that city, under the pastoral care of Dr. Archibald Maclay. At that time there were in the city only six Baptist churches, namely, Gold Street, Fayette Street, afterwards called Oliver Street, Mulberry Street, Van Dam Street, Broome Street, and Anthony Street. In Brooklyn there was no Baptist church. In the year 1822, Mr. Powell was licensed by the Mulberry Street church, and although not ordained, was called out and encouraged to preach in Hoboken, Brooklyn, Newark, and other places in the vicinity. He had enjoyed advantages of education, which enabled him then to begin at once an active ministry, which may be said to date from the year named, 1822. Subsequently he was ordained, and appointed a missionary to labor at Newburgh and Cornwall, in Orange County. He was later called to the pastorate of the church in Hudson, but after some months resigned, and became pastor in Milton, Saratoga Co., where he remained in care of the church nearly ten years.

While Mr. Powell resided in Milton members of the church and others were from time to time removing to the West. This circumstance, and the representations then made as to the religious destitution of the Valley of the Mississippi, induced him, contrary to the opinion and advice of many warm friends in the church at Milton, to volunteer as missionary of the Home Mission Society. He accordingly removed to Illinois in 1836. Rev. Jonathan Going, D.D., was at that time the corresponding secretary of the society. He made his home at first in La Salle County, although the first churches organized by him were in Putnam County, at Hennepin and Granville. At this time there was no Association organized between the northern boundary of the State and Springfield save one, the Northern Association, including the one church in Chicago. Nearly all the churches now included in the Ottawa Association were organized by Mr. Powell, and some connected with other Associations. He shared also in organizing the Illinois

River Association. In the various forms of denominational activity within the State he has actively shared, while engaged during many years in fruitful missionary labors over wide districts of country. To no man is the denomination more indebted for its prosperity and growth, especially in the earlier history of the State.

Powell, Rev. T. W., was born Sept. 12, 1836, at Chesterville, O. He graduated at Denison University, Granville, O., in 1863, having paid his way mostly by teaching. He took a select course in theology at Hamilton Theological Seminary, N. Y. He became pastor at Tiffin, O., in 1865. He was called to Davenport, Iowa, in September, 1868. Here the church enjoyed almost a constant revival for a year and a half, during which time he baptized over 130 persons. From overwork in long continuous meetings his health gave way, and he resigned in the autumn of 1870. After a year's rest, during which he did some mission work at Tama City, he settled with the First Baptist church in Minneapolis, Minn., in October, 1871. After two and a half years his health failed again, and he spent a year and a half in recruiting, mostly in the South. In the summer of 1875 he once more returned to Iowa. After supplying the church at Pella for a few months, he was recalled to Davenport. After three years in a second pastorate with this church, he resigned to enter upon work at Marshalltown. Here the church has paid a cumbersome debt of many years' standing, and is enjoying prosperity.

Powell, Vavasor, was born in Radnorshire, Wales, in 1617. Through his parents he was connected with the first families in North Wales. When young he was taught the learned languages, and he became a successful student in pursuit of general knowledge. He received his university education at Jesus College, Oxford. In his youth he was the most mischievous boy in the neighborhood in which he lived. When he first officiated as an Episcopal minister, he says that " he was a reader of common prayers, in the habit of a foolish shepherd, that he slighted the Scriptures, was a stranger to secret and spiritual prayer, and a great profaner of the Sabbath."

By reading Puritan books, hearing sermons which they preached, and by conversations with them, Mr. Powell was led to the Saviour, and his heart and character were completely changed. Soon after this he forsook the Episcopal Church. His preaching now became the most powerful agency in Wales. Wherever he went multitudes waited upon his ministry, and large numbers were renewed by the Holy Spirit and became followers of the Lamb. Opposition was stirred up by his burning eloquence and his unexampled success ; and in 1642 he went to London, where his popularity was nearly

as great, in a little time, as it was in Wales. He received a pressing invitation to settle in Dartford, in Kent, which he accepted, and there he founded a church, and brought many souls to the Redeemer.

In 1646, Mr. Powell was frequently importuned to return to Wales. He knew its language better than he understood any other. The people regarded him as an apostle. That country seemed more free from a persecuting spirit than it had been, and its people were in the most deplorable ignorance about the salvation of the Saviour, with but few ministers to point them to the light of Christ ; and having received a testimonial to his godly life, and to his " able gifts for the work of the ministry," signed by Charles Herte and seventeen members of the Westminster Assembly of Divines, he returned to Wales and resumed his labors among his countrymen. Crosby says that " he frequently preached in two or three places in a day, and he was seldom two days in a week throughout the year out of the pulpit ; nay, he would sometimes ride an hundred miles in a week and preach in every place where he might have admittance, either night or day ; so that there was hardly a church, chapel, or town hall in all Wales where he had not preached." He proclaimed Jesus at fairs, markets, and wherever there was a gathering of people. He preached the glorious gospel upon mountains, in jails, and even in the houses of persecuting magistrates. He was once arrested in Brecknockshire, about 10 P.M., with fifty or sixty of his hearers, and confined during the night in a church. At midnight he preached a sermon to his companions and captors from the words, " Fear not them who kill the body." During the service the most malevolent of his persecutors wept bitterly. Next morning when brought to the house of the justice that functionary was temporarily absent, and while waiting for his return Mr. Powell preached again. The justice was indignant to find his house turned into a conventicle, but two of his daughters were deeply moved by the truth which fell from the lips of the fearless man of God. Before 1660 Mr. Powell had formed more than twenty churches, of which some had two, some three, and some four or five hundred members. Mr. Powell at one time had 20,000 followers in Wales, and has been properly designated the Whitefield of that principality.

Mr. Powell was a Calvinist, holding and preaching election, effectual calling, final perseverance, full justification by faith, and the absolute need of the Divine Spirit to give a man power to will and to do the things that please God. He was also a Baptist.

He had no fear of men, or jails, or death in his heart. He was a strong republican, and he openly denounced the protectorship of Cromwell when his power was dreaded by all Europe; and Cromwell was so apprehensive of his influence that he arrested him. He spent eight years in thirteen prisons. And he died in the Fleet jail, in London, in the eleventh year of his incarceration, Oct. 27, 1671. His death was unusually blessed; the power and love of God filled his soul with enthusiasm in the miseries of a cell and in the agonies of a distressing complaint.

He was the author of nine works, one of which was a Concordance. Mr. Powell was an ardent lover of the Bible.

The footprints of Powell are seen all over Wales to-day, and many of his religious descendants have crossed the Atlantic to build up the mighty denomination whose name is dear to us, and whose liberty of conscience has given freedom to the churches of America.

Powers, Rev. J. Pike, a talented minister, and one who is greatly esteemed for his piety and usefulness, was born in Westmoreland Co., Va., Aug. 4, 1842. He removed to Kentucky in 1855, was engaged some years in mercantile business at Augusta, and was afterwards president of the Exchange Bank of Kentucky at Mount Sterling. He was educated at Augusta and Georgetown Colleges, and afterwards spent two years at the Southern Baptist Theological Seminary. He united with the Baptist church at Georgetown, Ky., in 1857, and was ordained to the ministry at Augusta in 1869, and immediately appointed missionary of Bracken Association. Among the churches he founded while acting in this capacity was the church at Mount Sterling, of which he was chosen pastor, in which capacity he has since labored. Mr. Powers has performed much missionary work, and caused to be erected three good houses of worship and one parsonage.

Pratt, Rev. Dura D., was born in Marlborough, Vt., July 13, 1806. Having removed to Worcester, Mass., he was brought under the influence of the ministry of Rev. Jonathan Going, by whom he was baptized into the fellowship of the First Baptist church in that city. Called of God, as he believed, to the ministry of his Son, he prepared himself for his work, and in 1832 was invited to take the pastorate of the Baptist church in Nashua, N. H., where he had a most successful ministry for twenty-three years, baptizing during that period not far from 600 individuals. He died of paralysis Nov. 13, 1855. "Mr. Pratt was among the best ministers of the Baptist denomination in the State of New Hampshire. He was uncompromising in his opinions and fearless in defending them, yet kind and conciliatory in treating of the views of others. He was remarkable for his clear foresight and judicious management in times of difficulty and trial. He studied to know his people and adapt his labors

to their wants. He was highly evangelical and practical in his preaching, seizing on those points of Scripture with great vigor which were appropriate to the existing state of affairs." These are words of warm commendation, but justly deserved.

Pratt, John, D.D, educator, and founder of Denison University, O., was born in Windham Co., Conn., Oct. 12, 1800. He spent most of his early life on a farm and in a mill. By dint of undaunted energy and much lonely night study he succeeded in fitting himself to teach a public school. At the age of twenty he went to Amherst Academy, Mass., where he prepared for college. After spending nearly four years in Columbian College, Washington, D. C., he entered Brown University, and graduated in 1827, and, after a short professorship in Transylvania University, Ky., became pastor of the First church, New Haven, Conn. In 1831 he was principal of South Reading Academy for six months, and then accepted a call from the trustees of Granville Literary and Theological Institution to take charge of the same. In 1833 this school, then very weak and badly housed, was incorporated, and Prof. Pratt was made president. In 1837 he resigned the presidency, and became Professor of Ancient Languages, which position he retained, with slight interruptions, until 1859, when he retired to private life. In 1878 the degree of D.D. was conferred upon him by Denison University. He has been twice married. His first wife, Miss Mary Glover Corey, to whom he was married in 1830, was a sister of Mrs. Dr. B. Sears. In 1855 he married Susan C. Wheeler, of Licking Co., O.

Dr. Pratt has been one of the most prominent and foremost of Ohio Baptists. His work in Denison University is his monument. As a teacher, he was unrivaled. Dr. Turney, late of Washington, D. C., said of him that he had no superiors and but few equals in the professor's chair. His long life has been characterized by signal devotion to the cause of education and religion, and his sacrifices for these objects have been numerous and great. Taking in view the struggles of his early life, his career has been very remarkable. His closing days are being spent on his farm near Granville, the scene of his life-long toil.

Pratt, William M., D.D., was born in Madison Co., N. Y., Jan. 13, 1817. After a common school and academic preparation, he entered Hamilton University, where he took the full course in letters and theology, graduating in 1839. He married Miss Julia A., daughter of Rev. John Peck, and subsequently removed to Crawfordsville, Ind., where he preached, and taught a school for young ladies. In 1845 he took charge of the First Baptist church in Lexington, Ky., to which he ministered seventeen years. He was several years corresponding secretary of the board of the General Association of Baptists in Kentucky. In 1869 he removed to New Albany, Ind., where he preached two years to Bank Street church, after which he located in Louisville, Ky., and engaged in the book-trade, at the same time preaching on the Lord's day for Broadway and Walnut Street churches. In 1871 he became pastor of the church at Shelbyville, Ky. In a few years he returned to Lexington, where he now lives, and is supplying several churches in the vicinity. He is an able preacher, an excellent business man, and has contributed largely towards establishing Baptist interests in Kentucky.

Predestination is one of the revealed doctrines of God's Word. Moses says, " Secret things belong unto the Lord our God, but those which are revealed belong unto us and to our children forever."—Deut. xxix. 29. Predestination is frequently noticed by the inspired writers, and consequently, as a portion of God's revelation, it belongs to us. We should lovingly receive it, and try to understand it, and never slight the Mighty One by whose authority prophets, apostles, and evangelists penned the sacred writings, by attempting to argue it out of the Scriptures, or to pass it by as a dreaded mystery, of which we should not think, and which the Spirit ought not to have revealed.

προορίζω in the New Testament means to predetermine, to predestinate. Paul says, " In whom also we have obtained an inheritance, being *predestinated*, according to the purpose of him who worketh all things after the counsel of his own will."—Eph. i. 11. According to this statement saints enjoy an inheritance because God predestinated them to it, and the same Almighty Ruler " worketh *all things* after the counsel of his own will," in heaven and on earth. Predestination is the foreordination of believers to heaven, and the instrumentalities by which they are to be converted, preserved, and rendered triumphant, and it is the foreordination of all the occurrences of earth. The celestial worlds are governed by laws ordained ages ago, and constraining such exact obedience that men can tell everything, with unerring certainty, about various changes that are to take place in the sun, moon, and stars from the past movements of these heavenly bodies. Calvin beautifully says, " There is no power among all the creations more wonderful or illustrious than that of the sun ; for, besides his illumination of the whole world by his splendor, how astonishing it is that he cherishes and enlivens all animals by his heat ; with his rays inspires fecundity into the earth ; from the seeds genially warmed in her bosom produces a green herbage, which, being supported by fresh nourishment, he increases and strengthens until it rises into stalks ; feeds them

with perpetual exhalations till they grow into blossoms, and from blossoms to fruit, which he then by his influences brings to maturity ; that trees likewise and vines by his genial warmth first put forth leaves, then blossoms, and from the blossoms produce their fruit." But the sun, and every plant and animal on earth, are governed by predestinated laws, enacted at their creation. This doctrine applies to all human events.

Speaking of the decrees of God in reference to the transactions affecting men for good or evil in this life, the celebrated Jonathan Edwards says, " Whether God hath decreed all things that ever came to pass or not, all that own the being of a God, own that he knows all things beforehand. Now it is self-evident, that if he knows all things beforehand, he either doth approve of them, that is, he either is willing they should be, or he is not willing they should be. But to will that they should be is to decree them. . . . That we should say, that God has decreed every action of men, yea, every action that is sinful, and every circumstance of those actions, that he predetermines that they shall be in every respect as they afterwards are ; that he determines that there shall be such actions, and just so sinful as they are, and yet that God does not decree the actions that are sinful, *as sin*, but decrees them as good, is really consistent. For we do not mean by decreeing an action *as sinful* the same as decreeing an action so that it shall be sinful. . . . So God, though he hates a thing as it is simply, may incline to it with reference to the universality of things. Though he hates sin in itself, yet he may will to permit it for the greater promotion of holiness in this universality, including all things, and at all times. So, though he has no inclination to a creature's misery, considered absolutely, yet he may will it for the greater promotion of happiness in this universality. . . . He wills to permit sin, it is evident, because he *does* permit it."* This account of predestination is clear, almost complete, and in harmony with the Word of God. It may be summed up in these words : God governs the world by decrees of *permission* for evils, and of appointment, for proper things, and in this way he foreordains everything on earth, and is the absolute ruler of all things.

The late Dr. Richard Fuller says, " The Libertarians reject the doctrine of predestination ; they deny that God has foreordained all things. But how can this negation be even mentioned without shocking our reason and our reverence for the oracles of God ? I might easily show that nothing is gained by this denial, that it only removes the difficulty a little farther back. This system rejects predestination, and maintains that God has left all

---

* Works of Jonathan Edwards, ii. 525, 527, 528. London, 1840.

men to act as they choose. But what is meant by a man's acting as he chooses? It is of course that he obeys the impulses of his own feelings and passions. Well, did not God endow him with these passions? Did not God know that if certain temptations assailed the creature to whom he had given these passions he would fall? Did he not foresee that these temptations would assail him? Did he not permit these temptations to assail him? Could he not have prevented these temptations? Why did he form him with these passions? Why did he allow him to be exposed to these temptations? Why, in short,—having a perfect foreknowledge that such a being, so constituted and so tempted, would sin and perish,—why did he create him at all? None will deny the divine foreknowledge; and I at once admit that the mere foreseeing an event, which we cannot hinder, and have no agency in accomplishing, does not involve us in any responsibility. But when the Creator, of his own sovereign pleasure, calls an intelligent agent into being, fashions him with certain powers and appetites, and places him amid scenes where he clearly sees that temptations will overcome him,—in such a case it is self-evident that our feeble faculties cannot separate foreknowledge from foreordination. The denial of preordination does not, therefore, at all relieve any objection, it only conceals the difficulty from the ignorant and unthinking.

"But even if the theory of the Libertarians were not a plain evasion, it would be impossible for us to accept such a solution; for it dethrones Jehovah; it surrenders the entire government of the world to mere chance, to wild caprice and disorder. According to this system, nature, providence, are only departments of atheism; God has no control over the earth and its affairs; or, if that be too monstrous and revolting, he exercises authority over matter, but none over the minds and hearts of men. 'The king's heart is in the hands of the Lord, as rivers of water he turneth it whithersoever he will,'—such is the declaration of the Holy Spirit; but this theory rejects this truth. God exercises no control over men's hearts, consequently prophecy is an absurdity, providence is a chimera, prayer is a mockery, since God does not interfere in mortal events, but abandons all to the wanton humors and passions of myriads of independent agents, none of whose whims and impulses he restrains, by whom his will is constantly defeated and trampled under foot. A creed so odious, so abhorrent to all reason and religion, need only to be carried out to its consequences and no sane mind can adopt it."[*]

The Scriptural authority for this doctrine is unquestionable. Nebuchadnezzar dreams of a great image (Daniel ii.) with a golden head, the breast

---

* Baptist Doctrines, pp. 483-85. St. Louis, 1880.

and the arms of silver, a brazen body and thighs, legs of iron, and feet part of iron and part of clay; a stone cut without hands destroys the image, becomes a great mountain, and fills the world. The golden head was the kingdom of Nebuchadnezzar, the silver arms the Medo-Persian empire, the brazen body the Macedonian dominion, and the iron legs, and feet partly iron and partly clay, the government of Rome. The stone cut without hands was Christ's coming kingdom and conquests that would destroy all existing empires and fill the whole world with the agencies of its universal authority. These events, except the destruction of Nebuchadnezzar's kingdom, were ages in the future, but they were predetermined and absolutely certain. The same thing was true of the second dream of the king,—the dream of the cutting down of the great tree "whose height reached unto heaven, and the sight unto the end of all the earth." It foretold the insecurity of the king and his removal from the throne for seven years; this heaven-preordained calamity fell upon the king soon after. The present condition of the Jews, and their state for ages, was preordained of God: "I will deliver them, saith the Lord, to be removed to all the kingdoms of the earth, to be a curse and an astonishment, and a hissing, and a reproach, among all the nations whither I have driven them."—Jer. xxix. 18. "I will sift the house of Israel among all nations, like as corn is sifted in a sieve, yet shall not the least grain fall upon the earth."—Amos ix. 9. Isaiah (vi. 11, 12) foretelling evils for the Jews, says, "Lord, how long? And he answered, 'Until the cities be wasted without inhabitant, and the houses without man, and the land be utterly desolate.'" "Be not dismayed, O Israel, for, behold, I will save thee from afar off, and thy seed from the land of their captivity; and Jacob shall return, and be in rest and at ease, and none shall make him afraid. I will make a full end of all the nations whither I have driven thee: but I will not make a full end of thee, but correct thee in measure: yet will I not utterly cut thee off, or leave thee wholly unpunished."—Jer. xlvi. 27, 28. The Jews have been scattered into all lands, and they are everywhere unjustly regarded as a "reproach and a hissing"; they have been sifted among the nations, but no grain of Israel has taken root in the lands of their exile; their country and their cities are desolate; he has not wholly cut off Israel, and he is evidently awaiting the right time to restore them to their country and their God. These events were predestinated and foretold thousands of years ago.

In the fifth chapter of Revelation, the Lamb standing in the midst of the throne took the wonderful book with seven seals, the book of providential decrees; for he has all power in heaven and on earth, and he opened seal after seal, ushering in a vast train of events running over many ages; but these great issues were all predestinated, foretold, and recorded in a book before any of them became realities. Peter, addressing the Jews, says of Christ, "Him, being delivered by the *determinate counsel and foreknowledge of God*, ye have taken, and by wicked hands have crucified and slain."—Acts ii. 23. "For of a truth against thy holy child Jesus, whom thou hast anointed, both Herod and Pontius Pilate, with the Gentiles and the people of Israel, were gathered together, for to do whatsoever *thy hand and thy counsel determined before* (literally, *predestinated*) *to be done.*"—Acts iv. 27, 28. Every item in the Saviour's death occurred by the determinate counsel and foreknowledge of God, even to the carrying out of the prophetic record, "A bone of him shall not be broken." The Jews actuated by malice, Satan prompted by murderous hate, Pilate controlled by cruel selfishness, and the people misled by base slanders, demanded the Saviour's blood, and without intending or desiring it, they inflicted upon Jesus "Whatsoever God's hand and counsel determined before should be done;" and what occurred in the Saviour's death governs the whole transactions of earth; as Augustine, quoted approvingly by Calvin, says, "Nothing could be more absurd than for anything to happen independently of the ordination of God, because it would happen at random."* "Our days are determined, the number of our months is with him, he has appointed our bounds that we cannot pass, he doeth according to his will in the army of heaven, and among the inhabitants of the earth."

The Philadelphia Confession of Faith says, "God hath decreed in himself from all eternity, by the most wise and holy counsel of his own will, freely and unchangeably all things whatsoever comes to pass; yet so as thereby is God neither the author of sin, nor hath fellowship with any therein, nor is violence offered to the will of the creature, nor yet is the liberty or contingency of second cause taken away, but rather established, in which appears his wisdom in disposing all things, and power and faithfulness in accomplishing his *decree*.

"Although God knoweth whatsoever may, or can come to pass upon all supposed conditions, yet hath he not decreed anything, because he foresaw it as future, or as that which would come to pass upon such conditions."—Chap. iii. 1, 2.

The Westminster Confession of Faith† has the two clauses of the Philadelphia Confession just quoted; the only change is "ordain" for "decreed," in the first section of the Philadelphia article, and the words "in which appears his wisdom in disposing all things, and power and faithfulness in accomplishing his decree."

The seventeenth article of the Episcopal Church of England says, "Predestination to life is the everlasting purpose of God, whereby, before the foundations of the world were laid, he hath constantly decreed by his counsel, secret to us, to deliver from curse and damnation those whom he hath chosen in Christ out of mankind, and to bring them by Christ to everlasting salvation, as vessels made to honor. Wherefore they which be endued with so excellent a benefit of God be called according to God's purpose by his Spirit working in due season; they through grace obey the calling; they be justified freely; they be made sons of God by adoption; they be made like the image of his only-begotten Son Jesus Christ; they walk religiously in good works, and at length by God's mercy they attain to everlasting felicity."

Predestination, the foreordination of all the elect to heaven, and of all the instrumentalities to secure their conviction and preservation until they reach the skies, and the preappointment of all earthly occurrences, is the doctrine of all British Presbyterians, and their American religious descendants, of all regular Baptists, and of the celebrated Thirty-Nine Articles of the Episcopal Church.

In no sense does this doctrine interfere with our responsibility for our acts. The Jews on the day of Pentecost who heard from Peter that by "the determinate counsel and foreknowledge of God" they had killed the Lord, gathered no comfort from the divine predestination of the Saviour's death; on the contrary, as they heard Peter's sermon "they were pricked in their heart, and said unto Peter, and to the rest of the apostles, 'Men and brethren, what *shall we do?*'" They knew the act was theirs, and nothing in the universe could make them think otherwise.

Dr. Thomas Reid,‡ one of the most eminent mental philosophers of modern times, says, "We have by our constitution a natural conviction or belief that we act freely; a conviction so early, so universal, and so necessary in most of rational operations, that it must be the result of our constitution, and the work of him that made us. If any one of our natural faculties be fallacious there can be no reason to trust to any of them, for he that made one made all." We are conscious that a particular sin is ours; *if we cannot believe our consciousness about that, we can be sure of nothing, we must doubt everything.* Men sin because they desire to do it; they transgress without constraint, and they know it. Judas did not pretend to charge

* Calvin's Institutes, lib. i. cap. 16, sec. 8.

† The Constitution of the Presbyterian Church in the United States of America, p. 256. Philadelphia.

‡ Essays on the Powers of the Human Mind, vol. iii. p. 245. London, 1822.

his crime on predestination, nor did the three thousand on the day of Pentecost, and no man true to his own consciousness ever will in this or any other world.

The Scriptures assume that all sinners perpetrate their iniquities of their own free will, and hence the publican is represented by the Saviour as praying, "Lord, be merciful to me, a sinner," and the prodigal, "I have sinned against heaven and in thy sight, and I am no more worthy to be called thy son." This language would be absurdly false if the publican and prodigal were compelled by a decree of God or man to sin. If he who made a mother's heart, and gave a Saviour to die for us, by his undoubted predestination of all events compelled men to sin, there would be pity for unfortunate and unwilling transgressors in his bosom, but no pains from him for them in any world, and no day of judgment. But our *own consciousness*,— by which we are aware that we see, hear, feel pain, and have the Saviour in our affections,—the instrumentality by which we learn everything outside of ourselves, tells us that we sin of our own choice, and that the guilt is ours. It makes each of us say, "Against thee, thee only, have I sinned and done this evil in thy sight." And its statements must be true. The whole Scriptures charge their iniquities upon men, and it would indicate insanity, or a hypocrisy never developed in the most outrageous deceivers of our race, to charge them upon others than those who perpetrate them.

We do not pretend to reconcile predestination and human freedom to sin. God asserts both, and has not seen fit to show us how they agree; and while we are absolutely certain that both doctrines are true, we leave any *apparent* lack of harmony between them to the light of an eternal morning. As Dr. Richard Fuller, speaking of these two great facts, says, " I have shown that both these doctrines are true, and of course that there is no discrepancy between them. I have shown that it is impossible for us to resist either of these great truths, and it is equally impossible for our minds to reconcile them. But here, as everywhere, faith must come to our aid, teaching us to repose unquestionably upon God's veracity."

God has predestinated the continuance of harvest while the earth remaineth, but he has also predestinated the perpetual return of seed-time, and both are preappointed together. If a farmer were to say, "God has foreordained the annual coming of a harvest forever, therefore I shall sow nothing," his Scripture-reading neighbor would inform him that he had also foreordained the planting of seed just before and in connection with the predestinated harvest. "While the earth remaineth, *seedtime and harvest*, and cold and heat, and summer and winter, and day and night, shall not cease."

So is it with spiritual blessings, and the means of securing them. If a man is predestinated to eternal life, it is foreordained that he shall repent, that he shall strive to enter in at the strait gate, that he shall believe upon Jesus, that he shall lead a holy life, that he shall be a man of prayer, that he shall be anxious to lead sinners to Christ, and that he shall in some measure be faithful unto death, Paul, in his passage to Rome, when the storm was very alarming, said to his companions in peril, " there should be no loss of any man's life among you, but of the ship." God had predetermined this : but when the sailors were about to desert the vessel, he said to the soldiers and prisoners on board, " Except these abide in the ship, ye cannot be saved."—Acts xxvii. 22, 31. It was also foreordained of God that the sailors should stay and work the vessel. So is it with the saint's predestination to life eternal; with this there are the following foreordinations of God : " I am the vine, ye are the branches : He that abideth in me, and I in him, the same bringeth forth much fruit: for without me ye can do nothing. If a man abide not in me, he is cast forth as a branch, and is withered; and men gather them, and cast them into the fire, and they are burned. If ye abide in me, and my words abide in you, ye shall ask what ye will, and it shall be done unto you. Herein is my Father glorified, that ye bear much fruit; so shall ye be my disciples. Ye have not chosen me, but I have chosen you, and ordained you, that you should go and bring forth fruit, and that your fruit should remain."—John xv. 5–8, 16. And when a believer sees these evidences of predestination in himself, the words of the poet are true of him,—

> " More happy, but not more secure,
> The glorified spirits in heaven."

Prescott, Rev. John Q., a distinguished preacher and educator in Louisiana, was born in New Hampshire in 1820; while teaching in Alabama was ordained to the ministry; for six years at the head of a large school at Macon, Miss.; removed to Louisiana in 1852; was successively financial agent of Baptist State Convention, Professor of Mathematics in Mount Lebanon University, and principal of Mount Lebanon Female College; died in 1867.

Pressley, Judge B. C., was born in York County, S. C. He is between fifty and sixty years of age, and has long been regarded as one of the ablest lawyers in the State. Gen. Connor, for some time attorney-general of South Carolina, once said to the writer, " Mr. Pressley prides himself on his skill in planting, at which he has never succeeded, and thinks very little of himself as a lawyer. But I would as soon encounter any other man at the bar." This is not the first instance in which men of high order of talent have mistaken both their strong and their weak points. He has been a circuit judge for several years, and there is not an abler or a purer on the bench. He carries his natural urbanity and kindness into his high position as well as into private life. He is everywhere the same Christian gentleman, and never ashamed of being a Baptist.

Pressley, Judge John Gotea, was born in Williamsburg Co., S. C., May 24, 1833 ; descended on his father's side from the Scotch Covenanters, and on his mother's from the French Huguenots. His father was an eminent citizen and Presbyterian ruling elder. His mother, a woman of great piety. In 1851 he graduated high in his class from the South Carolina Military Academy, at Charleston. Studied law with a relative, Judge Benjamin C. Pressley, a man of great piety, through whose friendly conversation he was led to investigate the faith of Baptists, in order to vindicate the faith of his ancestors, but the result was that he became a Baptist, and joined, by baptism, the Second church of Charleston, in 1854. In June, 1854, he was admitted to the bar before he was of age, by special dispensation of Presiding Judge J. B. O'Neall, a name dear to all Baptists in South Carolina. He settled in Kingstree ; joined the Baptists ; helped to make the Bethlehem church respected and influential ; was ordained a deacon in 1856 ; had a fine legal practice ; became a member of the State Legislature in 1858 ; and at the beginning of the war, in 1861, joined the Confederate army as a captain ; rose to the rank of lieutenant-colonel of 25th S. C. Vol. Regiment ; commanded it in every battle but one, until disabled by wounds, and often prayed with his men around the camp-fire. He was a brave soldier. He was trustee of Furman University, a frequent member of Baptist State Conventions, and in 1868 a member of the Southern Baptist Convention at Baltimore, which inaugurated the good feeling then fast growing between Southern and Northern Baptists. In 1869 he removed to California ; located at Suisun City ; joined the Dixon church ; entered into a lucrative practice ; helped to organize California College ; was a trustee and secretary of the college board until his removal to Santa Rosa, in 1873, when he joined the church there ; was chosen deacon and Sunday-school superintendent, and is a leader in the church. Moderator of Association, and known everywhere as an earnest Baptist. In 1875 he was elected county judge. In 1879 he was nominated by Democrats, and indorsed by Republicans, Workingmen, and the Temperance parties for superior judge, and elected, which position he occupies with distinguished ability. There are few happier Christian homes than the one occupied by Judge Pressley and his wife at Santa Rosa, Cal.

Prevaux, Rev. Francis Edward, was born in Amesbury, Mass., in 1822, and was a graduate of Brown University in the class of 1846, and pursued his theological studies at Newton. On leaving the institution he received an appointment from the American Baptist Home Missionary Society to go to California as a missionary to the new settlements of that State. He not only preached but engaged also in the work of teaching. Although his connection with the Home Missionary Society was not of long continuance, he remained in the vocation to which he deemed himself called by the voice of Providence. Ten years were devoted to his work, when the disease which terminated fatally compelled him to return to his Eastern friends in Salisbury, Mass., where he died May 12, 1860.

Price, Rev. Jonathan D., in early life was a Presbyterian, and had studied at Princeton College. He was born and reared in New Jersey. Expecting to go as a missionary, in order to increase his usefulness he took a course in a medical college at Philadelphia. While reading the news from the Baptist missions he was led to investigate the subject of the ordinances, became a Baptist, was ordained at Philadelphia, shared with Judson the savage barbarities of Oung-pen-la, afterwards had a prospect of great influence with the king and court because of his medical skill, but died in 1828. His wife was the first female missionary laid in the grave in Burmah. This early link between the Baptists of New Jersey and foreign missions is calculated to animate zeal and activity in conquering the world for Christ.

Price, Rev. Thomas, Ph.D., was born in Breconshire, Wales, on the 17th of April, 1820. He was baptized into the fellowship of the Watergate Baptist church, Brecon, by the Rev. John Evans. At the age of twenty-one he left the rural scenes of this ancient Welsh town for the metropolis. Here he united at first with the Welsh church at Moorfields, and subsequently with the Eagle Street church, whence, in 1841, he was sent to Pontypool College to pursue his studies for the Christian ministry.

In 1845, Mr. Price was invited to assume the pastoral charge of the Calvaria Baptist church in Aberdare. It was at the time a feeble interest, and the only church of the Baptist faith (with perhaps one exception) in the whole of that vicinity. The growth of the town, in consequence of the development of large iron and coal interests, was rapid and substantial, but not more so than the growth of the Baptist cause under the vigorous administration of Mr. Price. In 1851 a new building was decided upon, with a seating capacity for 1000 hearers. The work of the succeeding ten years is unprecedented in the history of the denomination in Wales. Large and commodious churches were built at Llwydcoed, Mill Street, Cwmdare, Gadlys Ynislwyd, Aberaman, Cwmaman, Capcouch, and the edifice previously occupied by the Welsh church was fitted up and used by a flourishing English congregation.

In 1862 there were 3096 members in full communion in the Aberdare Valley, over 1000 at Calvaria, the parent church, alone. No such record of aggressive work can be instanced of any other single pastor within the boundaries of the principality.

Nor has the great strength of this indefatigable worker been confined to the interests of his own church. All the great movements of a social and political character find in him an energetic and commanding supporter. He has been, and still is, a prominent leader and moulder of public sentiment on every great question of social, national, and religious interest. The citizens have on frequent occasions testified their appreciation of his services in a befitting manner. His pleasant home is a perfect gallery of costly testimonials, indicating a life of remarkable activity and a versatility of talent rarely found in the same person.

Dr. Price has been for many years on the staff of the *Seren Gomer*, and was for a considerable period co-editor of the *Gweon*, an undenominational newspaper of wide influence. He was likewise joint editor of the *Gweithewo*, a social and political paper, devoted mainly to the interests of the working classes. He was principal promoter and one of the editors of the *Gwyliedydd* and the *Medelwo Iewane*, and was for many years chief editor of the *Seren Cymru*, the leading organ of the Welsh Baptists in the principality.

As lecturer and preacher, Dr. Price is known throughout the length and breadth of Great Britain. His realistic power is remarkable. He speaks of the remote past with a quaint familiarity which sometimes borders on the grotesque, but which is immensely effective on the popular mind. The simple narratives of Scripture seldom glow with a purer lustre than when garnished with his peculiar genius. In every form of descriptive speech he is an accomplished master.

Long life and a glory-tinted old age to the veteran who has been so true and brave in the moral and spiritual conflicts of his country and his times!

Price, Rev. Thomas Jones, was born in the town of Hay, Breconshire, North Wales, March 9, 1805 ; came with his parents to America in 1818, and settled in Clark Co., O. ; was converted at the age of fifteen, and soon after began to preach, being then known as the boy preacher. His work was for the most part within the bounds of the Mad River Association, Ohio, over which he presided for thirty-nine years, and in which he exercised a controlling influence. He was somewhat eccentric

in his methods of work, and had a special liking for the itinerant system, preaching at the same time for a number of churches. Being blessed with a competency, it was his delight to supply feeble churches, to help the poor, and to give to the cause of missions at home and abroad. Under the title of "Elder" Price he was known far and near, and is remembered most affectionately by thousands of people. He died April 15, 1876, and was buried at Urbana, O.

Prichard, John, D.D., was born in the parish of Llaneilian, near Amlwch, Wales, in the month of March, 1796. He was led to the acceptance of the Baptist faith from hearing a sermon preached by a distinguished Calvinistic Methodist (Rev. John Prytherch) on the sufferings of Christ, from the text, " I have a baptism to be baptized with, and how am I straitened until it is accomplished?" He was immersed by the Rev. Thomas Rees Davies. He entered the college at Abergavenny at the age of twenty-five. His first and only settlement was Llangollen. He was a most indefatigable worker in the cause of Christ. His influence was felt more widely than that of any other pastor in the northern counties of the principality for many years. He labored diligently to establish an English church in Llangollen, and not without effect. In 1862 a college for the training of young men for the Christian ministry was established largely through his influence, of which he became the president.

Dr. Prichard wrote much for the press. Early in his ministry he started a monthly magazine for the use of Baptist Sunday-schools, called *Yr Athraw* (The Teacher), which he conducted single-handed for many years. He likewise published a compendium of doctrines, called " The First Catechism," upwards of thirty thousand copies of which were sold, not to mention the reprint of the same in this country. Many pamphlets of great value were likewise the production of his pen.

He was an able and instructive preacher. Many of his contemporaries exceeded him in brilliancy, but in sanctified common sense and exalted piety he was unsurpassed. Few men served their age more faithfully and well. He died on the 7th of September, 1875, in his eightieth year.

Prichard, Rev. John Lamb, was born in Pasquotank Co., N. C. Prof. John Armstrong found him, at the age of twenty-three, a carpenter, and awakened in him a thirst for knowledge. The next year, 1835, he presented himself at Wake Forest Institute, then a manual labor school, with his kit of tools on his shoulder, and asked the privilege of working for an education. In 1840 he graduated with honor, spent a year as master of an academy in Murfreesborough, N. C., and then, at the instance of the Rev. John Kerr, settled as pastor of the Danville Baptist church, in Virginia. Here he remained ten years, preaching a part of the time for the churches of Yanceyville and Milton, in North Carolina. In 1852 he removed to Lynchburg, Va., where for four years he labored with intense ardor and distinguished success.

In 1856 he became pastor of the First Baptist church of Wilmington, N. C., and at once entered upon the enterprise of erecting a new house of worship. He was not permitted to finish this work, but he lived long enough to see that his labors would be rewarded by giving the Baptists of Wilmington the handsomest church structure in the State.

In 1862 the little blockade steamer "Kate" brought the yellow fever to Wilmington, and among its last and noblest victims was this great and good man. He died a hero and a martyr, and his virtues have been fittingly commemorated in an admirable memoir by the Rev. J. D. Hufham, D.D. Mr. Prichard was twice married, first to Miss Mary B. Hinton, of Wake Co., N. C. His second wife was Miss Jane, eldest daughter of Dr. James B. Taylor, of Richmond, Va. His eldest son, Robert, graduated at Wake Forest College, and was an accepted missionary to China, where he died. His eldest daughter, Mary, is the wife of Prof. Charles E. Taylor, of Wake Forest College.

Prime, Rev. George M., was born in Vermont in 1802; received a liberal education, and entered upon the practice of medicine first in Mississippi and Louisiana. In 1830 he settled in Little Rock, Ark., where he continued some years, and then removed to Camden. He became a Baptist about 1858, while practising his profession in Franklin Parish, La. He was soon after ordained to the ministry, and in a few years returned to Arkansas and devoted himself entirely to the ministry. Dr. Prime was a fine writer, and at one time paid much attention to art as an amateur portrait-painter. He died at Eldorado, Ark., March 1, 1869.

Prince Edward Island Baptists.—See article on NOVA SCOTIA BAPTISTS.

Prior, Rev. John Thomas, a native of Georgia, was born in Madison, Morgan Co., Feb. 27, 1847. At the age of fifteen he was immersed, and joined the Bethlehem church, of which his father was an honored deacon. At the age of twenty-one he entered Mercer University, and graduated from the full course in 1870. He began preaching early in life, under a license from the Bethlehem church. In 1871 he was ordained, and engaged in teaching in important schools of the South. In 1872 he accepted a call from the Dixon church, California, acting as associate pastor for fifteen months. In 1874 he was pastor at Grand Island. The next five years he was pastor of the Hopewell and Woodland churches. In California he gained

general confidence as a writer, and was cordially welcomed to the business and editorial control of the *Evangel*, the duties of which he assumed in 1879. As a pastor and preacher he has been very successful.

Pritchard, T. H., D.D., was born in Charlotte, N. C., Feb. 8, 1832; baptized by Dr. W. T. Burke in 1849; graduated at Wake Forest College in 1854; served the college one year as agent; was ordained pastor of Hartford church, N. C., November, 1855, Dr. Wm. Hooper preaching the sermon; read theology for a while with Dr. J. A. Broadus, in Charlottesville, Va.; was pastor of the Franklin Square church of Baltimore from January, 1860, to July, 1863; filled the pulpit of First church, Raleigh, N. C., from November, 1863, to May, 1865, during the absence of pastor, Dr. T. E. Skinner, in

T. H. PRITCHARD, D.D.

Europe; settled as pastor of First church, Petersburg, Va., in July, 1865; resumed care of the Raleigh church in February, 1868, and remained in this position till called to the presidency of Wake Forest College, in July, 1879. For seven years Dr. Pritchard was chairman of the Board of Missions of State Convention; and was for several years associate editor of *Biblical Recorder.* He received the title of D.D. from the University of North Carolina in 1868. His father, Rev. J. P. Pritchard, has lived in Texas for twenty-five years.

Dr. T. H. Pritchard is doing a noble work for Wake Forest College, and his great ability and piety qualify him for eminent success in any department of ministerial labor.

Progress of Baptist Principles in other Denominations.

The Baptists have increased at a rate within a hundred years which is fitted to excite astonishment. In 1784 we had 471 churches and 35,101 members in this country, now we have 26,060 churches and 2,296,327 members. But our principles have spread very widely in other religious communities.

Ever since the Saviour said, "My kingdom is not of this world; if my kingdom were of this world, then would my servants *fight*," Baptists have repudiated the connection between church and state, by which the latter supports the former. About the middle of the seventeenth century the Quakers and Baptists were severely persecuted in Massachusetts, and numbers of both communities were banished. "Toleration was preached against as a sin in rulers, that would bring down the judgment of heaven upon the land. Mr. Dudley (the deputy governor) died with a copy of verses in his pocket, of which the two following lines make a part

' Let men of God, in court and churches, watch
O'er such as do a *toleration* hatch.' "*

John Adams, subsequently President of the United States, while he was at the Continental Congress, in 1774, declared that it was against the consciences of the people of Massachusetts to make any change in their laws about religion; that Israel Pemberton the Quaker, and Isaac Backus the Baptist minister, who were seeking deliverance for their brethren, suffering imprisonment in Massachusetts jails for their religious opinions, might as well think they could change the movements of the heavenly bodies as alter their religious laws.† This was the doctrine of American Congregationalists during the struggle for independence.

In Virginia the Episcopal state church levied taxes to support her ministry, with an oppressive severity from the settlement of the colony down to the time when Revolutionary liberty and Baptist and Presbyterian growth deprived her of her unjust exactions. But after this an insidious effort was made to pass an assessment law, by which each man should be compelled to pay a tax to support his own minister. Patrick Henry‡ favored the assessment, and Washington and John Marshall, the future chief justice of the United States,§ and the Presbyterian ministers of Virginia, and, of course, the Episcopal Church. But the Baptists and Presbyterian laymen finally secured the rejection of the assessment in 1785. Thomas Jefferson, the great friend of liberty in worshiping God for the Baptists

of Virginia, says, in a letter to Dr. Rush, "There was a hope confidently cherished about 1800 that there might be a state church throughout the United States, and this expectation was specially cherished by Episcopalians and Congregationalists." ‖

To-day, in our broad country, in every denomination of Protestants, the Baptist doctrine, that religion should be free from state guardianship and financial support, is universally accepted.

In the time of Jonathan Edwards, one of the greatest of American thinkers, and one of the most devout Christians that ever ministered in a Congregational meeting-house, his church in Northampton, Mass., admitted to the Lord's Supper "those who really rejected Jesus Christ and disliked the gospel way of salvation in their hearts, and knew that this was true of themselves;" and the church had a method of admitting such members "without lying and hypocrisy." This system "spread very much among ministers and people in that county and in other parts of New England."¶ When Mr. Edwards, in 1749, felt compelled to take the ground that none but real Christians have a right to come to the Lord's Supper, his Baptist platform for the communion table created a great ferment throughout the town, and a general cry for his dismissal was heard, and the next year he was driven from a church where the Lord had so signally honored his ministry. Isaac Backus brought the same charge against the First Congregational church of Norwich, Conn., in 1745. As Dr. Hovey relates it, "Men who entertained no hope themselves, and who gave no evidence to others that they had been renewed by the Spirit of God, were often, if not generally, admitted to all the privileges and ordinances of the Christian church."** This system, out of which Unitarianism grew in New England, was a wide-spread and malignant evil one hundred and thirty years ago.

The Presbyterian Church in America was in the same situation. The Larger Catechism of that church says of baptism, "Whereby the parties baptized are solemnly *admitted into the visible church*, and enter into an open and professed engagement to be wholly and only the Lord's."†† In the time of Edwards this article, framed by the Westminster Assembly, was in full force, the child of church members was admitted into the church by baptism, and in youth on merely repeating the catechism, without any reference to a new heart, was permitted to go to the Lord's table. Curtis states that at the time when Princeton Seminary was founded, "so far from conversion being es-

---

* Grimshaw's History of the United States, pp. 57, 58. Philadelphia, 1836.
† Life and Works of John Adams, ii. 399.
‡ Wirt's Life of Patrick Henry, p. 263. Hartford.
§ Rives's Life and Times of James Madison, i. 601-2.

‖ Memoirs, Correspondence, etc., iii. 341. Charlottesville, 1829.
¶ Works of Jonathan Edwards, i. Pref. clvii. London, 1840.
** Life and Times of Isaac Backus, p. 44. Boston, 1859.
†† The Constitution of the Presbyterian Church, pp. 341-42. Presbyterian Board of Publication Philadelphia.

teemed necessary to full communion, it was a matter of formal discussion whether it was proper to require the credible profession of a change of heart in the ministry, and considered that it was not. Yet even now there is nothing in their Confession of Faith to prevent the reception of unconverted persons as communicants. The Established Church of Scotland, with a similar confession [the same], does not require conversion."*

As late as the Revolution the Episcopalians were lamentably indifferent about the conversion of the clergy as a qualification for their sacred office, and about the regeneration of the laity as a needful preparation for the Eucharist.

In our day the Congregational ministry and membership stand on the Saviour's platform of conversion. No one can unite with the Presbyterian Church of this country without satisfying the minister and elders that he has a new heart. And even in evangelical congregations of the Episcopal Church the godly rector in preparing his "confirmation class" for the bishop will exercise much vigilance to see that each of them is born "from above."

Infant baptism is suffering from a rapid decline. In the time of Edwards every infant in the colonies, whose parents were not Baptists or Quakers, was duly christened shortly after birth, just as every similar child in England is baptized in our day. But with us now there are hosts of unsprinkled children whose parents are pious Pedobaptists. Many of the most devoted members of non-Baptist communities leave their children to select their own form of baptism when they are converted. Curtis, whose work was published in 1855, among other evidences of the decline of infant baptism quotes from a "recent number" of the *Journal of Commerce* the statement of its Boston correspondent, who says, "In our Congregational churches we fear that there is considerable indifference and neglect in reference to infant baptism. In one of our oldest churches in this State there had not been a few years since an instance of infant baptism for the seven preceding years. Last year there were seventy Congregational churches in New Hampshire that reported no infant baptisms. This year ninety-six churches report none. If this indifference continues the ordinance will become extinct in the Congregational churches."

In 1827, Curtis states that there was one infant baptized in the Presbyterian Church in the United States to every 13⅙ communicants, and in 1853 the tables of the Old and New School Presbyterians being counted together, infant baptism had decreased from 13½ to 22⁸⁄₁₀. This is a reduction of not quite a half in a few years.† Among the Meth-

odists the ceremony is treated with even less consideration, and the decay is still in rapid progress.

Our principles have invaded the churches of our brethren of the evangelical denominations, and they have expelled state-churchism from every one of them; they have shown them the Saviour's grand doctrine that a church should be composed of converted members, which has been adopted extensively, and they are breathing a withering decline over the practice of infant baptism. In our own denominational fold, by the blessing of God, we have gathered a host of converts and trained them for the highest usefulness. We have reared many noble institutions of learning, sent out missionaries whom God has greatly blessed, and exerted a powerful influence in favor of true liberty on the State and National institutions of our country, and outside of it in America our work has been almost as great. And it is likely that our influence in other denominations will continue, and even spread, until "alien baptisms" will equal Baptist immersions, and children will be relieved from the initiatory rite altogether, and one great fold will embrace the whole regenerated followers of the Lamb.

Proper, Rev. Datus D., was born in Van Buren Co., Iowa, Jan. 31, 1844. In 1862, during his academic course at Mount Pleasant, he entered the army and served three years. In January, 1866, he united with the Baptist Church. He afterwards engaged for a time in teaching school and farming, and while thus occupied he was impressed with the conviction that it was his duty to preach the gospel. In 1872 he was ordained. In 1873 he went to the Theological Seminary, Chicago, where he graduated from the special course in 1875. In 1875 he settled as pastor at Ames, Iowa, where he remained two years. During this time 56 were added to the church. In 1877 he accepted a call to the church at Iowa Falls. He resigned this pastorate to become State Sunday-School missionary of the American Baptist Publication Society and of the Iowa Baptist State Convention. He gave to this work fifteen months of earnest and successful labor, and then returned to the pastorate, settling with the East Des Moines Baptist church, his present field of labor.

Proselyte Baptism of the Jews is still a living institution, and occasionally in the United States it is administered. Dr. Lightfoot says that "As soon as the proselyte grows whole of the wound of circumcision they bring him to baptism, and placed in the water, they again instruct him in some weightier and in some lighter commands of the law; which being heard, he plunges himself, and comes up, and behold he is an Israelite indeed in all things." To explain what the plunging is he quotes from Maimonides, "Every person baptized must dip his whole body, now stripped and made

* Progress of Baptist Principles, p. 66. Boston, 1855.
† Idem, pp. 131-35. Boston, 1855.

naked, at one dipping." (Whole Works, vol. xi. pp. 59, 61. London, 1826.) This complete dipping is still required for a Pagan or a Christian embracing Judaism. (The Baptism of the Ages, p. 192. Publication Society, Philadelphia.)

Proudfoot, Rev. Richard, was born in the city of London in 1770. He came to America prior to the war of 1812, and became a student under the celebrated Dr. Staughton, of Philadelphia. Soon after his course of preparatory study for the work of the ministry, he settled in Cambria County, when that section was almost an unbroken wilderness. His field of labor stretched over the Alleghanies and eastward to Huntingdon, Stone Creek, Mill Creek, Shirleysburg, and parts adjacent. In all these places the fruits of his labor are very apparent in churches still existing. He traveled over this immense region, sometimes on foot or in the saddle, amid all conditions of weather, until called home to his reward, May 2, 1845, aged seventy-five years. His place of burial is at Three Springs, Huntingdon County. Brother Proudfoot stands among the honored band of twenty-six ministers, from eleven different States, who assembled in Philadelphia, May 18, 1814, and organized the Baptist Triennial Convention, and, at the same time, recognized and appointed Judson and Rice as missionaries in Burmah.

Providence.—That God created the world and everything in it we assume, and that he exercises dominion over these works of his hands his Word unmistakably teaches. His government of the world is plainly to be inferred from the vast and diversified interest he has shown in summoning it into existence. The maker of a powerful engine, requiring great skill and patient toil, would not leave it at work without superintendence, and without protection from the efforts of the evil disposed, who might readily destroy its efficiency. Jehovah has complete control of the world and all its movements, and his government is in continual exercise for the best interests of our race.

The supreme *reason* for each earthly act is the order of Jehovah. We do not speak of the *causes* of events, but the *reasons*, without which they cannot exist in this world. God has two classes of orders, *decrees of permission and decrees of appointment.* By the former he allows men and demons to commit acts of wrong which they have planned, and for the conception and execution of which they are solely responsible. By the latter he directly ordains the existence of pure and merciful events. And by these two classes of divine orders Jesus rules the world. Job's experience furnishes an illustration of God's decrees of permission and of appointment. When Satan turned the fury of the tornado upon the house in which his children were feasting, and his sons were killed, he said, "The

Lord gave and the Lord hath taken away, blessed be the name of the Lord." By divine *appointment* Job's sons came to him ; by divine *permission* Satan destroyed his young men, and Job recognizes the dominion of God in both events. The Saviour says, "All power is given unto me in heaven and in earth." The word power ($\xi\xi o v\sigma i a$) used by Matthew means authority, sovereignty, dominion. Christ, then, has entire control of the birds of the air, the fish of the sea, the beasts of the field, and the whole movements of human beings, and of all the elements, and of all the worlds, of everything, and of every one that can influence mortals favorably, unfavorably, or indifferently. He received this authority to use it, and he cannot be unfaithful to his trust. "He doeth according to his will in the army of heaven, and among the inhabitants of the earth."

Instruments of the Saviour's Providential Government.—He uses what we call *accidents as the instruments* of his providential government. When the voice of God arrested the knife with which Abraham was going to kill Isaac, he found a ram caught in a thicket ready for the altar from which his only son was released. No human being enticed the ram to the thicket, or drove, or bound it there ; Jehovah drew it by the attractive shrubs, or the sweet grass, and unconsciously it pressed forward until its horns were firmly held by the tangled brush ; and by this apparent accident the Lord provided for the necessities of Abraham's situation, as he has done myriads of times since for the needs of others.

The *worst crimes of men are instruments* of God's government. The special love which Jacob cherished for Joseph stirred up the fierce malice of his brothers, and at first they proposed to murder him, and then they concluded to sell him into slavery and tell his father that a wild beast had killed him. A band of Ishmaelites going down to Egypt, no doubt knowing that he was as free as themselves, agreed to buy him and to aid his brothers in their great crime. When Potiphar bought Joseph the wickedness of his wife soon covered the young Hebrew with infamy and cast him into prison. Three parties, by as many distinct iniquities, lent their aid to place Joseph in jail. There he interpreted the dream of a high officer in Pharaoh's palace, he in process of time mentioned Joseph to the king, whose mysterious visions he explained, and Joseph became governor of all Egypt, and saved its people and the inhabitants of the adjacent countries, including his father and brothers, from the horrors of a seven years' famine. The basest passions of men's hearts are often turned by Jehovah into channels of benevolence.

Henry VIII., of England, wrote a book against Luther, and was the strongest partisan of the pa-

pacy in Europe. But the Lord determined to bring him and his people from the odious tyranny of Rome. Henry fell in love with a young lady of his court, and for certain réasons he sought a divorce from his wife Catherine; the pope was afraid to offend Charles V., a near relative of the queen, and a neighbor of his holiness, and he refused Henry's application. The king secured a divorce from his Parliament and married Anne Boleyn. Upon the new marriage the wrath of papal Europe was expended, and Queen Anne, who loved the Bible, led her husband and his kingdom into the ranks of the Reformation. Before, and since, the Jews, out of envy and hatred, were employed by Jehovah to shed the blood of atonement and to purchase our redemption by the wounds they inflicted upon Jesus; in innumerable cases God has used the dark passions of men to execute his plans of love.

The *towering ambition of men* is another agency of his providence. The Medes were once lying outside of Babylon, resolved to increase their glory and their empire by the capture of the mightiest and most magnificent city on earth. Within its walls their power and threats were regarded with contempt. One night the king made a great feast for a thousand of his lords, and during the joyful excitement the sacred vessels carried from the temple of God in Jerusalem by the plundering Babylonians were brought to the favored guests, and they drank wine out of them in honor of the gods of Babylon, and they blasphemed Jehovah. Soon the terrible hand and writing were seen, and speedily the ambitious Medes were in that palace, and that night guilty Belshazzar was slain, and Darius sat upon his throne.

The *suggestions of Jehovah* influence men to perform the behests of his providence. Just as evil spirits can make suggestions in our minds without our knowledge of their presence, so can Jehovah. When Achan concealed the precious metals and the rich robe at the capture of Jericho, his brethren knew nothing of his crime. The rout at Ai proclaimed the fact that some one had sinned, but said nothing about the transgressor. The lots were cast, and Achan was unmasked and he confessed. But the suggestions of God himself were required to guide those who cast the lots. So when Haman was going to hang Mordecai, the man of God, the night before the king's consent was to be solicited, Ahasuerus could not sleep, and instead of music or wine he had the chronicles of his kingdom read, and, singularly enough, that section of them narrating that Mordecai had saved the king from assassination, and that he had never been rewarded. Mordecai was honored the next morning by Haman leading him through the principal street of Babylon with the king's crown upon his head and a

royal robe around him, and making proclamation that he was the man whom the king delighted to honor. God disturbed the king that sleepless night; he suggested the chronicles of his kingdom, and the section about Mordecai, and his providence protected his life and honored him. It was Jehovah that suggested modern missions to William Carey, and by suggestion, beyond all doubt, harvests of acts of God's government are summoned into life. These are some of the agencies employed by divine providence.

Character of the Government.—It *applies to everything* affecting human life, even the smallest matters. The Saviour says, " Are not two sparrows sold for a farthing? And one of them shall not fall on the ground without your Father; but the very hairs of your head are all numbered; fear ye not, therefore, ye are of more value than many sparrows."—Matt. x. 29-31. From the falling of a sparrow to the jar which makes a globe tremble the Saviour's providence controls everything.

It *rules everything wisely.* The wheels of providence, according to Ezekiel, are full of eyes, and they give such abundance of knowledge that there is no room for mistakes; and, according to the same writer, the God-man, enthroned, sat on a crystal firmament, watching every movement of the great wheels of providence, and rendering mistakes impossible. The Stamp Tax and the Tea Duty created the American Revolution, extended and secured the liberties of this land, and have made our country a miracle of progress, without a parallel in human history. Our independence gave the Reform Bill and vastly extended liberty to England and to all her colonies. It gave freedom to all the republics on this side of the Atlantic; and it has given the same blessing to France and Italy, and, in some measure, to Spain, Prussia, and Austria. The providence of God makes no mistakes.

It *draws blessings from all sources.* The foul waters that flow from the sewers of a large city reach the river and the ocean, and the sun draws them up in vapors into the clouds, but in their journey they lose everything poisonous and offensive, and they descend in sweet rains to fill the fountains and the rivers. So the events of providence are all turned into favors for the children of God, "*All things* work together for good to them that love God, to them that are the called according to his purpose." " No weapon that is formed against them shall prosper." While the hands that were pierced with the nails of Calvary hold the reins of earthly movements, started by material, satanic, or human agencies, the child of God is safe; his wants shall be supplied, and his Master will continually, as well as finally, give him the victory.

Providence, First Baptist Church of, was

founded in 1639. This ancient church has a grand history, and deserves a conspicuous place in the "Baptist Encyclopædia." In March, 1639, Ezekiel Holliman baptized Roger Williams. Mr. Williams, immediately after, immersed him and ten others. The church was constituted at this time. Mr. Williams, whose ministerial character was recognized by his brethren in receiving baptism from him instead of Mr. Holliman, after he submitted to the rite, became the minister of the infant community. Some time afterwards he withdrew from them, and was succeeded by Chad Brown, a man of steadfastness, wisdom, and great influence, the founder in America of the distinguished Brown family of Providence, one of whom, Nicholas, gave his name to our oldest university. William Wickenden followed Chad Brown as pastor of the First church of Providence. Gregory Dexter, after Wm. Wickenden, held the same position. Thomas Olney took charge of the church after Mr. Dexter. The Rev. Pardon Tillinghast ministered to the old church after Mr. Olney. This generous man gave his ministerial services for nothing, and at his own expense built a house of worship and presented it as a gift to the church. Ebenezer Jencks was the successor of Pardon Tillinghast, his ministry continuing some seven years. The little church, like a good many other small churches, had its controversies. The question which disturbed it was one to which is attached very little importance in these days. It was whether the "laying on of hands" was necessary to constitute a person a valid member of a church formed, as was believed, after the divine apostolic model. James Brown, the grandson of Chad, succeeded Ebenezer Jencks, and Samuel Winsor followed him. In 1726 a better and more commodious house of worship was erected, through the zeal and enterprise of some of the members of the church, and under the ministry of Samuel Winsor, Jr., the discordant elements appeared to be blending more harmoniously together.

"For one hundred and thirty years," says the historical sketch prepared by Dr. Caldwell and Prof. William Gammell, "the church has been going on, receiving neither from within nor without any strong impulse. Its ministers were natives, bred on the spot, generally advanced in years, at work for their daily bread, and with no special training. The church had been content with their unpaid services, and with such growth as came. It had a small meeting-house. It had but 118 members in a population of 4000, with 400 families. The time had come for advance and enlargement."

The establishment of Rhode Island College, as it was then called, in Providence, and the coming to the town of so gifted a scholar and so eloquent a preacher as Rev. James Manning, the first president of the college, were the harbingers of better days to the church. The weight of Mr. Manning's influence was thrown in the scale against those who insisted on "the imposition of hands" being a prerequisite to full church membership. Mr. Winsor and those who sympathized with him withdrew from the church, determined to have no fellowship with those who either denied or questioned the permanent obligation of those who were to enter a Christian church "passing under hands," as it was termed. Dr. Manning had the rare gift of enlisting the sympathy and co-operation of others in aiding him to carry out the plans upon the accomplishment of which he set his heart. He elevated the tone of public sentiment in the matter of sustaining religious worship. A house "for the public worship of Almighty God, and also for holding commencement in," was erected. Modeled after that of "St. Martin-in-the-Fields" in London, it is a gem of architectural beauty, which even to this day wins the admiration of all persons of good taste, and will ever remain as an illustration of the large benevolence and the generous self-sacrifice of those who were chiefly instrumental in rearing a structure of such noble dimensions and eminent fitness for the purposes for which it was built. It cost not far from £7100, a sum which represents, we venture to say, more than twice that amount in these days.

President Manning died July 29, 1791, in the fifty-fourth year of his age. In spite of the heavy weight of care which rested on him as the presiding officer of an institution which was struggling for life, no ministry of the church in all its previous history had been so successful as his. Although he never regarded himself, in the proper sense of the word, as the pastor of the church, he performed for it a service of great value, and left an impress upon it which is felt to this day.

The pastorate of the next minister, Rev. John Stanford, and that of his successor, the eloquent Maxcy, were of comparatively brief duration. Upon the election of Maxcy to the presidency of the college, a nephew of President Manning, the Rev. Stephen Gano, M.D., was called to succeed him. His ministry continued for thirty-five years, and was blessed as that of few servants of Christ has been. Remarkable revivals attended his preaching. The first one of them, that of 1820, brought an addition of 147 persons to the church by baptism. Dr. Gano died Aug. 18, 1828. The church more than quadrupled during the pastorate of Dr. Gano.

Rev. Robert Everett Pattison was called to fill the important place made vacant by the death of his predecessor, and entered upon the duties of his office March 21, 1831. For a little more than five years he preached and performed the work of a pastor with distinguished success, in building up his people in Christian knowledge and the development of the graces of the Christian character. Such a ministry as that of Dr. Pattison's was most fruitful for good, and its results are felt down to the present hour. Called to the presidency of Waterville College, now Colby University, he resigned his office Aug. 11, 1836. Rev. William Hague was elected pastor of the church June 1, 1837, and sus-

Providence, was the Rev. James Nathaniel Granger, who commenced his labors Nov. 13, 1842, and remained pastor of the church until his death, which occurred Jan. 5, 1857. Having been appointed in connection with Dr. Solomon Peck as one of a deputation to visit the Baptist missionary stations in the East, he was absent from his people a little more than a year and a half. The larger part of this time the pastoral care of the church devolved

FIRST BAPTIST CHURCH, PROVIDENCE, R. I.

tained that relation to it a little more than three years. Over one hundred persons were received into the fellowship of the church by baptism and by letter during his ministry. Upon the resignation of Dr. Hague, Dr. Pattison for a short time performed again the duties of pastor, when his election as one of the secretaries of the Baptist Board of Foreign Missions once more dissolved his connection with the people of his charge. His successor, whose memory is still so greatly revered in

on the Rev. John Calvin Stockbridge, until his call to succeed the venerable Dr. Sharp as pastor of the Charles Street church, in Boston, brought the engagement to a close. During the remainder of Dr. Granger's absence the Rev. Francis Smith supplied the pulpit. After the return of Dr. Granger from the East, the Rev. William Carey Richards was his assistant for a brief period, until the formation of the Brown Street church, of which he was chosen the pastor, dissolved the connection. The Rev

Francis Wayland, D.D., on the death of Dr. Granger, acted as pastor of the church for somewhat more than a year with rare fidelity, and the most conscientious application to the discharge of the duties of what he ever regarded as the most solemn and responsible position to which a mortal can be called, that of a minister of the Lord Jesus Christ. The Rev. Samuel Lunt Caldwell, who for twelve years had been the pastor of the First Baptist church in Bangor, Me., was invited to become the pastor of the church. He commenced his ministry in Providence June 13, 1858, and ended it Sept. 7, 1873. His pastorate covered a period of more than fifteen years, and was closed that he might accept the professorship of Church History in the Newton Theological Institution. The successor of Dr. Caldwell was the present pastor, the Rev. Edward Glenn Taylor, D.D., who commenced his labors April 18, 1875.

The above sketch presents but a meagre outline of the history of what in some respects may be regarded as one of the most prominent Baptist churches in the country. As one proof of the influence for good which has gone forth from it, it is stated that since 1775 sixty ministers of the gospel have been connected with it, besides its pastors, in addition to fifty persons who have received license of the church to preach, all of whom have entered the ministry. Nearly all of these persons have been connected with the college as officers or students.

For more than one hundred years the First church of Providence has enjoyed an unusual amount of peace. In 1774 there was a signal illustration of this union. The church wished to erect the noble edifice to which allusion has already been made, a house 80 feet square, with a spire 196 feet high, a magnificent structure for the 4321 persons who then dwelt in Providence. In such a great enterprise every one commonly has advice to give, and opinions to be respected; John Brown, however, the brother of the celebrated Nicholas, was appointed "a committee of one" to build one of the most spacious and beautiful temples for the worship of God in America. Unity of purpose and feeling have characterized this community in an extraordinary measure for many years.

Patriotism has had its warmest friends in the First church. John Brown, the "committee of one," was a fair representative of the people for whom he built a house of worship. He owned twenty vessels at the commencement of the Revolutionary war, every one of which was likely to be captured or destroyed by the British fleet, if he opposed the measures of the mother-country, and he uttered his Declaration of Independence four years before the document of Jefferson was issued. He destroyed the British armed schooner "Gaspee" in June, 1772, which was sent from Boston to enforce obnoxious revenue laws in Narragansett Bay; Lieut. Duddingston was wounded in the encounter which resulted in the blowing up of his vessel; and his blood was really the first shed in the war of independence.

This church never began to prosper thoroughly until it gave a stated income to its pastors. Nicholas Brown, whose gifts to Brown University amounted to nearly $160,000, belonged to the congregation of this church; and his munificent donations to advance higher education have raised up for it liberal friends in all denominations. Many of the first men in Rhode Island have descended from the pastors and members of the First church.

In the words of the historical sketch to which reference has been made, "For three-quarters of a century this church stood alone, or the same as alone, the only church of its own persuasion, or perhaps of any persuasion, within the large territory then included in the town of Providence. It has held its place and held on its way while a populous city has grown around it, and churches of many names have multiplied on every side. It has twelve sisters of the same polity and faith, all of them organized since the beginning of the present century; the thirteen having 3377 members. Eighty-eight churches, of at least thirteen different denominations, the major part of which have arisen since that time, now occupy the ground where once and for two generations it stood alone. It was either the first in this country, or it stood side by side with Newton in the van of a numerous succession of similar churches, amounting in 1880 to 26,060, with 2,296,327 members."

Pruett, Rev. William Harrison, is one of the pioneer Baptist preachers in Eastern Oregon and Washington Territory, where since his ordination, in 1871, he has traveled extensively, preached the gospel in new settlements, organized many new churches and baptized many converts; labored as pastor or missionary at Weston, Mount Pleasant, Pilot Rock, Walla Walla, Dayton, Pendleton, Butte Creek, Meadowville, Mountain Valley, Heppner, and other places; built several church edifices; and has been one of the most influential and successful laborers in all that new and needy field. He is still in the vigor of manhood. He has a good education, having studied at Jefferson Academy and McMinnville College, Oregon. At the age of three years he removed from Ray Co., Mo., where he was born, to Oregon, in 1847. In 1861 he professed Christianity, and was baptized; but in 1862, believing he had been deceived, he was again baptized, on the confession of what he was sure was the work of the Holy Spirit in his salvation.

Pryor, John, D.D., was born in Halifax, Nova Scotia, and pursued his studies at King's College,

Christ Church College, Oxford, and at the Newton Theological Institution. He was ordained in Providence, R. I., in 1830. For some time he was principal of the Horton Academy, Wolfville, Nova Scotia, and subsequently professor and president of Acadia College. He was associate pastor at Horton, then pastor of the old Cambridge church, the church in Halifax, Nova Scotia, and the churches in Randolph and Lexington, Mass., in which latter place he now resides.

Publication Society, The American Baptist. —On the 25th of February, 1824, a company of twenty-five Baptists met at the house of Mr. George Wood, in Washington City, D. C., to consider the propriety of the formation of a Baptist Geheral Tract Society. The call which brought them together was the result of a letter sent by the Rev. Noah Davis, of Maryland, to his classmate, the Rev. James D. Knowles, then living in Washington City. Mr. Davis had been deeply impressed with the desirableness of such a tract society, and of its importance for the promotion of the welfare of the Baptists in this country, and for the prosecution of their special Christian work. Hence his letter to Mr. Knowles, the call for the meeting at Mr. Wood's, and the organization of the society. It began its work at once, though in a modest way. The receipts of the society for the first year of its existence amounted to $373.80, and it issued 696,000 pages of tracts.

In the year 1826 the society was transferred to Philadelphia, because that city offered greater advantages for publishing and distributing its tracts throughout the country. Its growth from this date was slow but steady. It at length began to issue bound volumes; then to care especially for Sunday-schools, and to prepare books and other publications to meet their needs. In 1840 it was led to employ colporteurs for the circulation of its publications, and for the performance of necessary pioneer Christian work. At length, in 1845, the name of the society was changed, and it became The American Baptist Publication Society, whose object, according to its constitution, is "To promote evangelical religion by means of the Bible, the printing-press, colportage, and the Sunday-school."

The total number of publications on the catalogue of the society on April 1, 1881, was 1326. This was after a thorough examination of the list and the dropping of a number that were once issued. These publications include books, tracts, and periodicals. A few figures will exhibit the increase of its issues from its origin, and show the magnitude of this part of its work. The issues are all reduced to 18mo pages.

In 1824, total issues......		696,000
From 1824–1840, average annual issues......		7,840,198
" 1840–1857, " " "		22,110,645
" 1857–1860, " " "		61,856,066

From 1860–1870, average annual issues......		198,382,395
" 1870–1880, " " "		381,820,429
" 1824–1880, " " "		94,845,010
" 1824–1880, total issues......		5,311,320,610

In regard to the character of the publications of the society, George W. Anderson, D.D., in his little work, "The Baptists in the United States," says, "If the excellence of a denominational literature is to be determined by the strong common sense which pervades it, its reverence for the sacred Scriptures, and habitual and thorough deference to its teachings, by its complete and scholar-like examination of the Word of God, and by its calm, candid, and courteous tone, then the works issued from the press of this society will bear comparison with those of any denomination in the world."

The progress of the society will further appear from a glance at the receipts into its treasury at different periods of its history. These receipts include both those in its business department and the funds specially contributed for its missionary work. The former is self-sustaining; hence all the funds contributed to the latter are used exclusively for that object.

In 1824, total receipts......		$373.80
" 1830, " "		3,094.09
" 1840, " "		12,165.77
" 1850, " "		40,579.71
" 1860, " "		84,783.91
" 1870, " "		332,149.59
" 1880, " "		349,564.46

The increasing work of the society demanded from time to time larger accommodations. At length, in 1876, the present building at 1420 Chestnut Street was completed, at a cost of $258,000, the whole of which was provided for by the liberality of its friends and the proceeds of the sale of its former building. The last $100,000 of the cost was given by Wm. Bucknell, Esq., and members of his family, and by the various members of the family of the late J. P. Crozer, Esq. It is thought that the accommodations furnished in this edifice will be sufficient for many long years to come.

During the fifty-six years of its existence, the society has fulfilled the expectation of its founders, and has proved an efficient means of promoting the unity of the Baptists of the United States in feeling, in doctrinal views, in Scriptural practices, and in the promotion of missionary work at home and abroad. Its publications have gone throughout the land into every State and Territory, as also have its colporteurs and Sunday-school missionaries. Its power for good has been steadily developed, and everything indicates that under the blessing of God it will continue to enlarge its work as the demands of the wide field in which it is called to labor become more numerous and pressing.

MISSIONARY WORK

OF THE AMERICAN BAPTIST PUBLICATION SOCIETY.

This department of the society has been developed to meet the wants which from time to time claimed recognition. At first the gratuitous distribution of tracts, and, subsequently, of books, was undertaken ; then the missionary colporteur agency was óriginated. At length the demands for systematic efforts to increase the number of Sunday-schools, and to promote their efficiency, led to the employment of Sunday-school missionaries. The work, as now carried on, consists in three things :

1. In preaching the gospel *from house to house* by a band of missionary *colporteurs*, who unite with personal efforts to convert the inmates, the circulation of the Holy Scriptures, and the dissemination of a gospel literature.

2. In sustaining *Sunday-school* missionaries to form new schools, to strengthen and improve old ones, and to organize the forces of the different States for efficient Sunday-school work.

3. In making grants of small libraries to poor ministers and Sunday-schools, and of tracts to pastors and to missionaries of other societies and Conventions.

Colporteur missionaries were first employed by the society in 1840, about one year before any other society in this country entered on a similar work. During the forty years that have since elapsed it has employed nearly 1500 such laborers, in the various fields in this country, as well as in Canada, Sweden, Norway, and Italy. In 1880 there were 34 employed in as many States and Territories of our country.

The work in Sweden was commenced in 1855, when the Rev. Andreas Wiberg was sent to that country to originate and direct a system of missionary colportage. His efforts were very successful, and when, in 1866, the work was transferred to the American Baptist Missionary Union, there were in Sweden 176 Baptist churches and an aggregate of 6606 members, and the work had extended into Norway and other adjacent countries. This was all the development of the work undertaken by the society in 1855, when there were only forty Baptists in the kingdom. At the present time there are nearly 300 Baptist churches, with about 20,000 members, though they are sending hundreds of their young and enterprising members to this country every year.

The Sunday-school missionary work was first inaugurated in 1867. In 1880 there were under appointment 21 such missionaries, laboring in as many of our States and Territories, all of them, with one exception, in the South or the West.

The society's donations of tracts and books have been steadily increasing in number from the earliest years of its history, and this work might with great benefit be still vastly enlarged were the necessary means at its disposal.

The extent and results of the work may be partially understood on an examination of the following table, which shows the statistics from the beginning until 1880 :

Days of service	262,342
Miles traveled	2,998,492
Books sold	171,987
Books given away	92,139
Pages of tracts distributed	6,937,445
Sermons and addresses delivered	620,417
Prayer-meetings held	53,086
Families visited	664,580
Persons baptized	13,446
Churches constituted	499
Sunday-schools organized	3,955
Conventions and institutes held or addressed	4,674
Sunday-schools aided by donations	7,931
Pastors and ministerial students furnished with grants of books for their libraries	1,710

It is proper to remark that all the contributions to the society are used exclusively for its missionary work, unless specially directed by the donors to some other end.

PERIODICALS.

In common with religious publication societies in this country and abroad, the society at an early period in its history recognized the periodical press as a powerful agency for the promotion of Christian work. Soon after its organization it began the monthly issue of *The Tract Magazine*, which, during its short life, was a means of extending the circulation of tracts. This was followed by *The Monthly Paper*, afterwards the *Baptist Record*, which was first published in 1836, and was suspended in 1855.

Since that date the periodical department has been gradually becoming more comprehensive in its issues, while their circulation has largely increased, as the following figures will show. They indicate the total number of copies of each periodical issued, from the time of its establishment until April 1, 1881 :

Young Reaper, monthly and semi-monthly, 1857-1881	56,446,930
National Baptist, weekly, 1865-1881	5,307,481
Baptist Quarterly, 1867-1878	59,383
Baptist Teacher, monthly, 1869-1881	4,189,400
Baptist Lesson Monthly, 1869-1881	47,263,500
Baptist Primary Lesson Monthly, 1874-1881	17,791,200
Bible Lesson Quarterly, 1879-1881	1,205,500
Intermediate Lesson Quarterly, 1881	235,000
Our Little Ones, monthly, 1873-1881	15,958,000
Our Young People, monthly, 1881	215,000

Total number of copies issued 148,670,394

Purefoy, Geo. W., D.D.—The Rev. John Purefoy, a wise and good man, gave three sons to the Baptist ministry of North Carolina,—Geo. W., James S., and N. A. Purefoy. George was the oldest of them, and was born in 1809 ; was baptized in 1830, and began to preach at once. In early life he preached much, but for many years before his death his health did not allow him to preach often. He was the author of the "History of the Sandy Creek Association," and of several works on the baptismal controversy. He died in 1880. The State University at Chapel Hill gave him the title of D.D. in 1870.

Purefoy, Rev. James S., the third son of Rev. John Purefoy, was born in 1813, baptized in 1830, began to preach in 1835, and was ordained in 1840, Dr. Samuel Wait and Rev. P. W. Dowd constituting the Presbytery. Most of the pastoral labor of Mr. Purefoy has been performed in Wake and Granville Counties. No man, living or dead, has done so much for Wake Forest College as this unpretending brother. When plowing in the field, before he was twenty-one, he gave $25 to this institution, and through all its checkered history he has been its unfaltering friend. For many years he was its treasurer, without salary. He secured for it, since the war, a contribution of $10,000 from the Baptists of the North, and to him, more than to any other, is due the credit of rescuing the college from loss when it was heavily involved in 1848-49, and by his energy and liberality the handsome Wingate Memorial Hall was erected in 1879-80. Early in life Mr. Purefoy married Mary, the daughter of Deacon Foster Fort, and a kindred spirit, ready for every good work, she proved to be. Many poor young men, and especially many young ministers struggling to obtain an education, have found in this man and his wife friends ready and willing to help them, and it gives the writer of this sketch peculiar pleasure to leave on record the fact that by money voluntarily loaned by Mr. Purefoy he was enabled to complete his course in college. Mr. Purefoy is still a vigorous man, and seems to reckon it the highest glory of his life to labor and sacrifice for Wake Forest College.

Purefoy, Rev. N. A., was born in Wake Co., N. C., in 1811 ; attended Wake Forest College, but took his degree of A.B. from Columbian College, Washington, D. C. He served the Fayetteville church and the church in Warrenton each for several years, but most of his pastoral life has been spent in preaching to country churches. Quiet and unobtrusive, this good man has long been regarded by his brethren as a fine illustration of almost every Christian virtue.

Purinton, Jesse M., D.D., was born in Coleraine, Mass., Aug. 12, 1809 ; baptized in Truxton when eleven years of age ; educated at Hamilton, N. Y., and ordained in 1834 ; was pastor in Coleraine, and in Arcade, N. Y., in Forestville and Mount Moriah, Pa., and in Morgantown, W. Va. He was for several years a missionary in Northwest Virginia. He aided in many revivals, and was instrumental in leading large numbers to Jesus. In 1860 the degree of Doctor of Divinity was conferred upon him. He died at Morgantown, June 17, 1869. Dr. Purinton was an able minister and a devoted follower of the Saviour.

Putnam, Daniel, professor in the Normal School at Ypsilanti, Mich., was born in Lyndeborough, N. H., Jan. 8, 1824. Having fitted for college at New Hampton, he entered Dartmouth College, and graduated in the class of 1851. During the next two

years he taught in the New Hampton Academy, as he had done a part of his Senior year. He remained with it a short time after its removal to Fairfax, Vt., but came to Michigan in 1854, as professor in Kalamazoo College. He resided in Kalamazoo till 1868, but did not hold his professorship the whole interval. For seven years he was superintendent of public schools, for eighteen months county superintendent, and for one year served as president of the college *ad interim*. In 1868 he became professor in the State Normal School at Ypsilanti, and still holds that position. He is a preacher, but was never ordained. He has been chaplain of the State Insane Asylum at Kalamazoo the last eighteen years, and has often preached in other pulpits. He has rendered abundant service to the Baptist State Convention on its different boards, and is at present a valuable member of the Board of State Missions. Mrs. Putnam is a daughter of the late Rev. E. B. Smith, D.D., of Fairfax, Vt.

Puryear, Bennet, LL.D., Professor of Chemistry in Richmond College, Richmond, Va., was born in Mecklenburg Co., Va., July 23, 1826. He graduated at Randolph Macon College, in June, 1847, with the highest honors of his class. After leaving college he taught school one year in Monroe Co., Ala. ; then returned to his native State, and during the session of 1849-50 attended lectures at the University of Virginia. In July, 1850, he was appointed tutor in Richmond College, and in the year following was elected Professor of Natural Science in that institution. In 1859 he resigned his professorship in Richmond College to accept the chair of Chemistry and Natural Philosophy in Randolph Macon College, where he remained until 1866, at which time he was recalled to his former position in Richmond. In 1868, when the college was reorganized and the office of president abolished, he was elected chairman of the faculty, which position he has continued to hold until the present time, being annually chosen thereto by his colleagues. In 1873 the school of natural science was divided into physics and chemistry, and the school of chemistry was assigned to him. At college, Prof. Puryear was distinguished for his attainments in the classics as well as in natural science, and when circumstances have required him to take charge of a class in Greek, or Latin, or mathematics, he has done so with distinguished success. His acquaintance with the subjects of his own school is broad and thorough. As a lecturer, his style is clear and pointed, and often enlivened by sallies of genial humor. The matter of his lectures is so admirably arranged that they are felt to be a growth, and not a mere aggregation of facts. In the experiments of the laboratory he is unusually successful. Prof. Puryear has not given much attention to popular lectures or addresses, but whenever he has spoken in public he has been heard with pleasure. Besides occasional contributions to various periodicals, he published, in 1866–

BENNET PURYEAR, LL.D.

67, in the *Farmer*, a series of articles on "The Theory of Vegetable Growth"; in 1875, in *The Planter and Farmer*, papers on "The Public School in its Relation to the Negro," since printed in pamphlet form; in the same year, in the *Religious Herald*, a series of articles on the "Public School"; and in 1878, also in the *Religious Herald*, papers on the "Virginia State Debt," and also on "The Atmosphere." With the exception of the first series, these papers were all published under the signature of "Civis." These articles evinced ability and fullness of information, but those relating to the public school are specially noticeable. No newspaper articles on questions of public State policy ever awakened in Virginia a more general interest, or produced a profounder impression. Questions which seemed to be settled, and whose discussion was unthought of, were brought again into the field of controversy; and the public school system, established by constitutional enactment, fostered by the spirit of the times, and appealing to the interests of the masses of the people, was shaken to its foundation. The articles were everywhere talked of, and called forth able replies. It was the opinion of many that no papers so fundamental in scope, so vigorous in statement, so brilliant in rhetoric, and so instinct with passion had appeared in Virginia for a long time. Although these articles discussed questions which were largely local, they exerted much more than a local interest. In a few weeks the hitherto but slightly known professor became one of the most widely known men of the whole South; and in acknowledgment of the learning and ability shown in the "Civis" articles, Georgetown College, Ky., and Howard College, Ala., conferred on him the honorary degree of LL.D. (June, 1878). Dr. Puryear is president of the Tuckahoe Club, an association of farmers in the vicinity of Richmond College, and his eminent success in cultivating a small farm is a practical illustration of the value of science in agriculture. Notwithstanding Dr. Puryear's opposition to public schools, he is an earnest advocate of education, and has contributed much to the prosperity of Richmond College. He is among the most honored and influential citizens of Richmond, a man of sound judgment, genial disposition, and inflexible integrity. He is an active member of the Grace Street Baptist church in Richmond.

Q

Quarles, Rev. Frank (colored), is a Baptist minister of great worth, now about sixty years old. He was born in Caroline Co., Va., and came to Georgia in 1850. He was a faithful slave until the close of the war, but his character and abilities may be estimated when it is stated that he was licensed and ordained by the First Baptist church in Atlanta in 1863, previous to emancipation, the Presbytery being composed of Rev. H. C. Hornady and Rev. William T. Brantly, D.D. Since 1863 he has lived in Atlanta, and has served the Friendship Baptist church as pastor since 1866. For twelve years in succession he has been moderator of the Ebenezer (colored) Association, and since the organization of the (colored) Missionary Baptist Convention at Augusta, Ga., in 1868, he has been its president. He exerts a wide and healthful influence in the State, and uses it freely for religious and educational purposes. He married in Virginia, and lived with his wife thirty-eight years, raising two children,—a son and a daughter. He is a man of ability and piety, and as a man and preacher is highly esteemed by all who know him.

Quincy, Hon. Josiah, was born in Lenox, Mass., March 7, 1793. His father, Samuel Quincy, was a lawyer in Roxbury, Mass., where he acquired a large property in the practice of his profession. He indorsed heavily the paper of several mercantile firms in Boston, and the commercial disasters of 1777–78 swept away nearly every vestige of his estate. He then retired to a little cottage among the Berkshire hills, where he soon died of a broken heart. His son Samuel, the brother of Josiah, with a dollar and a half in his pocket, but rich in spirit, left on foot for Boston to seek his fortune. He became in due time a flourishing shipmaster and owner of vessels, and filled many offices of trust and responsibility in that city. Josiah, from a lameness caused by sickness in infancy, was unable to perform much manual labor. He accordingly turned his attention to study as a necessity for his future support. Under many discouraging circumstances he prepared himself at the Lenox Academy to enter as a Sophomore in college. Circumstances prevented him from carrying out his plan to take a full collegiate course, and on leaving his academic studies he entered upon the study of law with Samuel Jones, Esq., of Stockbridge, Mass. He taught school during the day, and his law studies were necessarily carried on at night. It was by these fierce battles with indigence that the latent powers of his nature were largely developed, that his invincible determination for ultimate success was strengthened, and that, by heroic effort, he laid broad and deep the foundations of his future eminence.

On being admitted to the bar, Mr. Quincy practised his profession a few months at Stockbridge, and removed from that place to Sheffield, where he remained a short time, and then went to Rumney, N. H., ever afterwards his home. Soon after settling in Rumney he was married to May

HON. JOSIAH QUINCY.

Grace, daughter of Jabez Weed, of Plymouth. Rumney is a small town among the hills of New Hampshire, but the young lawyer, by industry and perseverance, soon gained a high rank in his profession, his practice extending for a long distance in all directions. Not many years elapsed before he was known as one of the most eminent lawyers of the State, and when he retired from practice in 1864, his professional business was said to have been as large as that of any legal gentleman in New Hampshire. For years he was president of the Grafton County bar. He had under his tuition many law students, and among them the eminent Judge Clifford, of the United States Supreme Court. Mr. Quincy was a prominent politician, and filled many public offices. He was several years a member of the New Hampshire house of representatives, and was twice elected to the State senate, the latter year filling the office of president of that body. He was also a member of the first board of trustees of the State Asylum for the Insane. In financial matters he was favorably known, and for years was one of the directors of the Pemigewassett Bank, in Plymouth, N. H. He was one of the most active of that persevering band of men who originated and carried forward the building of the Boston, Concord and Montreal Railroad, and for fourteen years was the president of its board of directors. The herculean labors he performed in the progress of this enterprise, and the intense anxieties he endured in its behalf, had much to do with the completion of the work upon which he and the gentlemen associated with him had embarked, and with its final, successful accomplishment.

Mr. Quincy was very active in educational matters. Remembering his own early struggles, the needy student always found in him a friend and counselor, and many will always remember with gratitude his generous gifts in their extremity. He was much interested in the schools of the county and the town in which he lived. He was a trustee of the Newton Theological Seminary, and for years was president of the trustees of the New Hampton Academy. He took the deepest interest in the latter, as for many years it was the leading Baptist institution in the State, and had connected with it a theological department. At one time, by his own funds, he removed from it a debt amounting to several thousand dollars.

In his religious belief Mr. Quincy was thoroughly a Baptist, although he had, like all Baptists, a wide catholicity of feeling for true believers of any name. He was converted under the faithful ministry of Rev. Noah Nichols, pastor of the Baptist church in Rumney, and by him was baptized in 1831. He remained a prominent member of this church until his death, always ready to aid it with his wise counsel, and contributing largely to its support. As it had been his early religious home, during his long and eventful life he cherished for it a strong and increasing affection. He loved to attend the gathering of the Associations and the State Conventions, and found these meetings a refreshing rest from the laborious cares of his profession. He was a life member of the Missionary Union, and other Baptist organizations formed for the advancement of the Redeemer's kingdom. In his domestic life he was a kind and indulgent parent, and made home attractive by an exhibition of its sweeter charities. He died in Rumney, his residence for sixty years, Jan. 19, 1875, being almost eighty-two years of age. He passed away as he had lived, in the full hope of a blessed immortality. Two sons and three daughters survive him.

One of the most prominent traits in the character of Mr. Quincy was his invincible and unbending integrity. No temptation could swerve him a hair's breadth from a stern and incorruptible honesty. In his profession he was keen and sharp, but with no smirch of trickery. He was an eminent lawyer, a faithful public officer, an upright business man, and a generous and valuable citizen. In private life he was a most courteous gentleman, highly beloved by a very extensive circle of acquaintances. In his religious faith he was firm and unwavering, trusting for salvation alone in the Lord Jesus Christ, and at the close of his long and active life could well say, "I have finished my course; henceforth there is laid up for me a crown of righteousness."

R.

Rabun, Gov. William, one of the noblest and purest of men, was born in Halifax Co., N. C., April 8, 1771. When he was about fourteen his father, Matthew Rabun, removed to Georgia, and, after residing a short time in Wilkes County, settled in Hancock County. In the year 1788 young William professed faith in Christ, and united with the church at Powelton, having been publicly baptized by Silas Mercer.

Growing up to man's estate he took a high position, both as a church member and a citizen. Without solicitation on his part, he was, for many years, sent to the Legislature from Hancock County, then one of the most influential counties in the State. Being president of the State senate, in March, 1817, he became *ex-officio* governor of the State, on account of the resignation of Gov. Mitchell, and in the following November he was elected governor of Georgia. He died Oct. 24, 1819, while occupying that exalted position.

He was a man of singular piety. Though highly honored by his fellow-citizens, he was not made vain by it; and, though heavily burdened with the affairs of state, he never forgot the claims of his Master's cause. Up to the time of his death he was a regular attendant upon the sessions of the Georgia Association, taking an active part in the deliberations and workings of the body. Even while governor of the State, in the years 1817, 1818, 1819, his familiar name still appears in the minutes of the Association, and it was a pleasing and common sight to witness the governor of the State fulfilling the duties of chorister and clerk in the Powelton church. He was a man of prayer, and his house was the house of prayer. To all the benevolent institutions of the day he gave his influence and his purse. Wise in counsel, firm in purpose, upright in dealing, he was possessed of a piety transparent, unaffected, deep, and ardent; all the elements of true greatness were in him beautifully blended.

Upon the death of Gov. Rabun, Rev. Jesse Mercer, by request of the Legislature, preached before them a memorial sermon, in which occurs the following tribute to his piety and worth: "Your late excellent governor was the pleasant and lovely companion of my youth; my constant friend and endeared Christian brother in advancing years; and until death my unremitting fellow-laborer and able supporter in all the efforts of benevolence and philanthropy in which I had the honor and happiness to be engaged, calculated either to amend or ameliorate the condition of men."

During the Seminole war, in 1818, Gov. Rabun called out the militia, and placed them under the command of Gen. Gaines. They were ordered, under command of Maj. Wright, of the U. S. army, to discover the course of the Indians who had been committing depredations. Capt. Obed Wright, of the Chatham militia, had positive orders from Gov. Rabun to destroy Hoponee and Philemi towns, for committing atrocities on the frontier. By mistake Chehaw town was taken, partly burned, and some Indians killed. An angry correspondence ensued between Gov. Rabun and Gen. Jackson in regard to the matter, a part of which is given. Gen. Jackson wrote, May 7, 1818, "Such base cowardice and murderous conduct as this transaction shows have no parallel in history, and shall meet with their merited punishment. You, sir, as governor of a State within my military division, have no right to give a military order while I am in the field; and this being an open and violent infringement of the treaty with the Creek Indians, Capt. Wright must be prosecuted for this outrageous murder, and I have ordered him to be arrested and confined in irons until the pleasure of the President of the United States is known upon the subject." In his reply, after referring to the communication of Gen. Glasscock, upon which Gen. Jackson based his answer, Gov. Rabun says, "Had you, sir, or Gen. Glasscock, been in possession of the facts that produced this affair, it is to be presumed, at least, that you would not have indulged in a strain so indecorous and unbecoming. I had, on the 21st of March last, stated the situation of our bleeding frontier to you, and requested you, in respectful terms, to detail a part of your overwhelming force for our protection, or that you would furnish supplies, and I would order out more troops, to which you have never yet deigned to reply. You state, in a very haughty tone, that I, a governor of a State under your military division, have no right to give a military order whilst you are in the field. Wretched and contemptible, indeed, must be our situation if this be the fact. When the liberties of the people of Georgia shall have been prostrated at the feet of a military despotism, *then, and not till then,* will your imperious doctrine be tamely submitted to. You may rest *assured* that if the savages continue their depredations on our unprotected frontier, I shall think and act for myself in that respect."

Rambaut, Thomas, D.D., LL.D., is of French descent. He was born in the city of Dublin, Ireland, and was regularly educated in the liberal arts, having studied in the celebrated school of Rev. Henry Lyon, of Portington, and at Trinity College. He came to Savannah, Ga., on attaining his majority, with the intention of studying law, and was converted under the preaching of Rev. Richard Fuller, D.D., of Baltimore, and baptized by Rev. W. T. Brantly, D.D., then in Augusta, Ga. On the Wednesday following he preached his first discourse. He has successively filled the positions of pastor of the Blackswamp church, S. C., Savannah Baptist church, Ga., president of Cherokee Baptist College, Professor of History and Roman Literature in Georgia Military Institute, president of William Jewell College, Mo., and pastor of Tabernacle Baptist church, Brooklyn. He was called to be the successor of Rev. Henry C. Fish, D.D., as pastor of the First church, Newark, N. J., in March, and entered upon this charge on the 1st of April, 1878. He received the degree of LL.D. from Madison University in 1860, and of D.D. from William Jewell College in 1873.

Rand, Theodore Harding, A.M., D.C.L., was born in Cornwallis, Nova Scotia, and is a graduate

THEODORE HARDING RAND, A.M., D.C.L.

of Acadia College; was converted and baptized in Wolfville in 1855, while attending college; taught in the Provincial Normal School, Truro, from 1861

to 1864; then he was chief superintendent of education in Nova Scotia until 1870, and rendered important services in that department; traveled in Europe and observed methods and results of teaching in the best schools there; was appointed, in 1871, chief superintendent of education in New Brunswick, and has there performed similar services to those rendered in Nova Scotia. Admirably adapted for educational work, Dr. Rand performs his responsible duties with enthusiasm and efficiency.

Rand, Rev. Thomas, was born in Manchester, N. H., May 21, 1776, his father being a Presbyterian minister. He was hopefully converted when he was twenty-two years of age, and baptized in Alstead. He began to preach at once, but wishing to secure a better preparation for his work, he entered the school of Rev. William Williams, of Wrentham, and subsequently graduated at Brown University in 1803. He was ordained pastor of the church in Holyoke (then Ireland Parish, West Springfield, Mass.), Oct. 6, 1803. At the time of his ordination his church was the only Baptist church in a circle the diameter of which would be thirty miles, including Hampshire and Hampden Counties. Here he performed his work for twenty-five years, during six months in the year having the charge of a school, in which not a few persons whose after-lives were very useful received their education. In October, 1828, he became the pastor of the church in New Salem, N. H., where he remained six years, then went to Hinsdale, continuing here two years. For five years he was a city missionary in New York City. His closing years were passed in Holyoke, among his former parishioners, where he died, May 31, 1857.

Rand, Rev. Thomas, the son of a minister of the same name, was born in West Springfield, Mass., July 10, 1813; licensed to preach in 1836; graduated at Hamilton Theological Seminary in 1838; ordained at Bayou Chicot, La., in 1841; died at Lake Charles, La., July 1, 1869. He devoted his life to teaching and preaching, and did much to build up the Baptist cause in the Opelousas region. He was a ripe scholar and fine preacher.

Randall, David Austin, D.D., was born in Colchester, Conn., Jan. 14, 1813. At the age of fourteen made a public profession of religion; was licensed to preach June 30, 1838; ordained in Richfield, O., Dec. 18, 1839, where he was pastor of the Baptist church for five years, and where he edited a Washingtonian paper, and gave much time to the temperance cause. In 1845 removed to Columbus, O., and became one of the editors of the *Journal and Messenger*. For several years, after severing his connection with this paper, he engaged in the book business. In 1858 was called to the pastorate of the First Baptist church, Columbus, O., and continued in that position eight years. During this pastorate he made an extensive journey through Oriental countries, the results of which he embodied in a royal octavo volume of 720 pages, entitled "The Handwriting of God in Egypt, Sinai, and the Holy Land." This book has had an extensive sale, and is said by competent critics to be one of the best works on the East. Subsequently he made a minute and extensive tour through continental Europe, and England, Scotland, and Ireland.

Dr. Randall was for six years corresponding secretary of the Ohio Baptist State Convention, and subsequently its treasurer. In 1870 Denison University conferred upon him the honorary degree of D.D. He still resides at Columbus, O., where he devotes his attention to literary pursuits, though he gives much time to lecturing, preaching, and the various educational and missionary enterprises of the day.

Randall, Rev. Nelson Birney, was born in Springville, N. Y., June 14, 1838. After graduating from Hamilton College, Clinton, N. Y., in 1858, and from Rochester Theological Seminary in 1869, he was ordained at Ypsilanti, Mich., the following October. Four years of his previous life had been spent in the practice of law in Gloversville, N. Y. He has sustained with eminent success the relation of pastor in Ypsilanti, Mich., Vineland, N. J., Providence, R. I. (Jefferson Street), and Norristown, Pa., where he now ministers, deeply intrenched in the affections of the church and congregation. No small service has been done in the wiping out of debts, aggregating $16,000, and in important improvements inaugurated under his ministry.

Randall, Judge Samuel, was born in Sharon, Mass., Feb. 10, 1778. A pupil of Rev. William Williams, of Wrentham, Mass., he fitted for Brown University, and graduated in the class of 1804. Hon. Virgil Maxcy and Gov. Marcus Morton were members of the same class. Mr. Randall read law with Judge Howell, but before completing his studies he removed to Warren, to take charge of an academy in that village. Quite a number of his pupils were subsequently students in college, and were an honor to their faithful instructor. For many years he acted as a judge in different courts in Rhode Island. For forty-four years he was a member of the Baptist church in Warren, and took a deep interest in its material and spiritual prosperity. He died at the advanced age of eighty-six, March 5, 1864. Judge Randall was the father of Rev. George M. Randall, D.D., the Episcopal bishop of Colorado. Prof. Gammell says of him, "He died as he lived, universally respected as an upright magistrate, a useful citizen, and a consistent Christian."

Randall, Rev. William H., was licensed to preach in his native town,—North Stonington, Conn.; graduated at Hamilton Theological Seminary, N. Y., in 1850; settled in Frensburg, Phillipsville, and Williamsville, N. Y.; in the late war raised a company, and entered the service as a captain, performing also the duties of a chaplain; for gallant conduct at Chancellorsville he was raised to the rank of major; wounded at Gettysburg, and obliged to leave the field; in 1865 resumed his pastorate at Williamsville; while seeking restoration to health, died at Lake Maitland, Fla., May 7, 1874, in the fifty-sixth year of his age; a pure, noble spirit.

Randall, Rev. William Henry, son of William P. and Marie L. Randall, was born in Groton, Conn., Aug. 23, 1840; converted in February, 1855, and baptized March 25 of same year by Rev. Harvey Silliman, uniting with the Second Baptist church in Groton; graduated with special honor from Brown University in 1861; spent another year at the university in post-graduate studies; taught schools in Mystic and Suffield, Conn., and Providence, R. I., from 1865 to 1872, with the exception of one year—1870–71—spent in travel in Europe and the East, visiting specially the Holy Land; studied at Newton Theological Institution in 1873–74; ordained pastor of Windsor Avenue Baptist church, Hartford, Conn., Dec. 15, 1874; settled with Central Baptist church, Thompson, Conn., in June, 1877, where he is now (1880) laboring; married, July 1, 1874, Mary F. Gallup, daughter of Deacon John Gallup, of Groton, Conn.

Randolph, Judge Joseph F., was born in Plainfield, N. J., about 1800. He was the son of Rev. Robert Randolph. He was baptized at Freehold by Rev. J. M. Challiss. He opened a law-office in Freehold, and afterwards resided and practised in New Brunswick, Trenton, and Jersey City, where he died at an advanced age. He was first elected to Congress in 1838, and served two terms. He also was honored with an appointment to the judgeship of the Supreme Court in New Jersey.

Randolph, Warren, D.D., son of Lewis S. and Hannah (Gilman) Randolph, was born at Piscataway, N. J., March 30, 1826. He was a graduate of Brown University in the class of 1851. Among his classmates were Prof. J. L. Diman, D.D., and Rev. J. B. Simmons, D.D. Soon after his graduation he was ordained as pastor of the High Street Baptist church, Pawtucket, R. I., where he remained but a short time, and then accepted a call to become pastor of the Eighth (now Jefferson) Street church, Providence. He removed to Philadelphia in 1857, and became pastor of the First Baptist church in Germantown, which office he held until 1863, when he was called to the Harvard Street Baptist church, Boston. Four years later, in 1867, he returned to Philadelphia, and was pastor of the Fifth Baptist church until 1870, when his health failing he resigned, and spent not far from a year in foreign travel, extending his trip

WARREN RANDOLPH, D.D.

as far as to Egypt and Palestine. On his return, in 1871, he became Sunday-school secretary of the American Baptist Publication Society. In the discharge of his official duties he traveled very extensively over the United States, and proved himself a most useful agent in promoting the interests of the society which he served.

In 1872 a committee was appointed, by a Sunday-School Convention representing the evangelical denominations of the United States and Canada, to select lessons for a seven years' course of study. Dr. Randolph represented the Baptists in this committee. Its labors were so successful that before the seven years had expired it was calculated that about eight millions of persons were reaping the advantages of the lessons. A second international lesson committee was appointed to serve for the ensuing seven years; of this committee Dr. Randolph was a member. He resigned his secretaryship in 1877, to the sincere regret of the Publication Society, to accept the pastorate of the First Baptist church of Indianapolis, where he remained a little more than two years. On his return to the East he became pastor of the Central Baptist church of Newport, R. I.

Dr. Randolph has been in almost constant service since his ordination, in 1851, and he is admirably qualified for the work of the gospel ministry.

Rangoon Karen College.—In the fifty-sixth annual report presented to the Missionary Union in 1870, among other suggestions Dr. Binney made the following: "Whether we ought not to make some provision for general education for Karens, by which this institution" (the Karen Theological Seminary) "might be relieved of that department." The suggestion of Dr. Binney met with a prompt response, and in the annual report of the executive committee for 1871, we are told that "the effort begun the past year, for the founding of a Karen College at Rangoon, is the logical result of the general educational impulse, which has been felt at the missionary stations." The college was opened on the 28th of May, 1872, Rev. Dr. Binney, president, with three native teachers and seventeen pupils. Rev. John Packer, who had been professor in the State University of Missouri, sailed in October, 1872, to be connected with Dr. Binney, both in the theological institution and the college. The second year of the college opened April 1, 1873, two weeks after the arrival of Prof. Packer, and, with the exception of two weeks' vacation in October, was in continuous session until Jan. 28, 1874. The whole number of students in attendance during the session was 39, of whom 36 were boys. Of course, the work done was of a very elementary character, but it was work well done, and designed to be the foundation work preparatory to something higher in the future. Rev. C. H. Carpenter was appointed president in 1873, and left the United States in January, 1874, to take charge of the college. He remained in office but a short time, when Prof. Packer was chosen in his place. Several circumstances conspired for a year or two to hinder the progress of the college. The report at the end of the session of 1876–77 was more favorable, the number of pupils having been 109, and the last year the number had risen to 127. Through the generosity of one individual an ample site and buildings for the college, including a dormitory, have been secured. A good beginning has been made in the life of the Rangoon College, and the prospect of its future usefulness is very bright.

Rangoon Mission Press.—The first printing-press of which the Baptist missionaries made use was a gift from the English Baptist Mission at Serampore, in 1816. It was sent to Rangoon and placed under the charge of Rev. G. H. Hough, who had learned and practised the trade of printing in the United States. At once Mr. Hough put to press Dr. Judson's "Luminary of Christian Doctrines," a catechism, and a translation of the gospel of Matthew. After the war between England and Burmah, Maulmain became the chief seat of printing operations. In 1861 the Mission Printing-Press, with all that pertained to it, was again established at Rangoon, under the charge of Rev. C. Bennett, and the mission printing was constantly and vigorously prosecuted in the line of Scriptures, books, and tracts. All the movable portion of Mr. Ranney's printing establishment at Rangoon was purchased by the Missionary Union in 1862, and proved a valuable addition to the facilities needed for the publication of a religious literature. From Oct. 1, 1861, to Sept. 30, 1862, there had been published 2,113,000 pages of matter, religious and secular, and during the next year the amount was more than doubled. When Mr. Bennett, who had spent some time in this country, returned to Rangoon in 1865, he was the bearer of important additions to the working material of the printing-office and bindery, which had cost over $6000. During the two years, 1863–65, 8,751,900 pages had been printed. The books and tracts were upon a great variety of subjects, and varied in size from a 16mo to an 8vo,—a revival hymn-book representing the first, and a Burmese and English dictionary the second. The report of the Executive Committee for 1867 estimates the value of the investments made to carry on printing at Rangoon at $18,736.56. From Oct. 1, 1867, to Sept. 30, 1868, the number of pages printed was 10,678,000. Besides the printing done to meet the wants of the missions, a large amount of job work, also, was done, thus enabling the Union to reduce the expenses of running the establishment. Mr. Bennett, who again made a visit to this country, returned to the scene of his labors in the fall of 1872. During his absence the work went on under the superintendence of Rev. I. D. Colburn. In the annual report of the Executive Committee for 1877 the announcement was made that Mr. Bennett had resigned his connection with the press the fall previous. It was stated that "he had been more or less intimately connected with the press for forty-seven years, and during the greater part of this time had taken charge of it. He developed excellent business qualities, and managed its affairs with great prudence and skill till it has become one of the most important factors of our mission work in Burmah." Upon the resignation of Mr. Bennett, Rev. W. H. Sloan was appointed superintendent. He remained in charge for some time, and on returning to this country on account of the health of his family, Mr. Bennett consented, temporarily, to occupy the position he had held for so many years. The report for the year ending Oct. 1, 1877, presents the names of a long list of books and pamphlets printed in the following languages and dialects: English, Burmese, S'gan Karen, Pwo Karen, and Bghai Karen. The number of pages in these books and pamphlets was 4693, and the total of pages printed was 5,843,974. Among the more important of these publications we notice, in Burmese, Judson's English-Burmese Dictionary, completed, royal octavo, the Four Gospels, the Acts, and several of the Epistles, each in royal quarto, together with the Pentateuch in quarto. In S'gan Karen, the English-Karen Dictionary, in medium quarto, several books of the New Testament, and the minutes of six Associations.

Rathbone, Maj.-Gen. John T., was born in Albany, N. Y., Oct. 18, 1821 ; was educated in the academy at Albany and the Collegiate Institute of Brockport, N. Y. His father died when he was fifteen years old, when he left school and accepted a clerkship in Rochester. At seventeen years of age he united with the Baptist church of Brockport. At eighteen he returned to Albany. In 1845 he built his foundry in Albany, which, with the additions since made, is one of the largest in the world.

In 1861, Mr. Rathbone was appointed brigadier-general of the Ninth Brigade of the National Guards of New York, and on the breaking out of the civil war he was appointed commandant of the Albany Depot for Volunteers. On being relieved from this command Gen. Rathbone was highly complimented, not only by the adjutant-general, but by the commander-in-chief, for his great success in raising recruits and performing all the duties of his office. He sent to the front thirty-five regiments from his depot. In 1867, Gen. Rathbone resigned his position as commandant of the Ninth Brigade. When John A. Dix was elected to the governorship of New York he appointed Gen. Rathbone adjutant-general of the State, with the rank of major-general. He served under Gov. Dix's administration with credit to himself and great advantage to the State. He has been asked to accept political nominations, which he invariably declined, ambitious only to serve his fellow-men as a private citizen. He is one of the founders of the Albany Orphan Asylum, of which he has been a trustee for thirty years, and for many years the president. For thirty years he has been superintendent of the Emmanuel Baptist Sunday-school, and he has been a working member of the church for forty years. He founded the Rathbone Library of the University of Rochester, of which he is a trustee, to whose funds he has contributed about $40,000.

Gen. Rathbone is one of the noble Baptists who have conferred honor upon our denomination in the State of New York.

Rauschenbusch, Augustus, D.D., was born at Altena, province of Westphalia, Germany, Feb. 13, 1816. He was the son of A. E. Rauschenbusch, Lutheran pastor in that city, a learned and highly esteemed clergyman, from whom also he received his earliest instructions. In his fifteenth year he entered the gymnasium (college) at Elberfeld, and, having graduated, he went, in his nineteenth year, to the University of Berlin for the purpose of studying for the ministry. Through the instructions of his teacher, the venerable Dr. Neander, and through the influence of pious friends, he was awakened to a sense of his guilt before God, and, after a severe

AUGUSTUS RAUSCHENBUSCH, D.D.

inward struggle, at the age of twenty, he became a decided and joyful believer. Having spent some time at home, he went to the University of Bonn, where he devoted his time both to natural science and theology. At the death of his father, in 1841, the son was chosen by the congregation as his successor. As that congregation numbered about 3000 souls, an important field was thus opened to the youthful minister. His earnest pleading aroused great opposition on the part of the worldly-minded, but, at the same time, it proved the means of awakening many hundreds of persons at Altena and at various places in the vicinity.

After four years of successful labor, Mr. Rauschenbusch felt himself more and more hampered by his ecclesiastical relations, and, after much prayer, he resolved to go to a land where he could preach the gospel untrammeled and unmolested. Having heard of the great religious destitution among the Germans in America, he emigrated to this country in 1846, and immediately went to Missouri to preach to the numerous Germans settled there. In 1847 he was invited by the American Tract Society to come to New York to conduct the publication of their German tracts. Here he became acquainted

with Dr. Somers, a Baptist pastor, and a member of the publishing committee of the Tract Society. Through him he was led to consider the question of baptism. After a long and prayerful investigation of it, he was baptized in May, 1850. He continued his connection with the Tract Society until August, 1853, superintending their seventy German colporteurs, editing their German monthly, the *Botschafter*, and preparing books and tracts. At the same time his influence was strongly and effectively exerted in furthering the Baptist cause among the Germans. In 1851, withdrawing for a time from the Tract Society, he labored as a preacher in Canada, and organized the first German Baptist churches there. Having visited his native land, he returned to this country in 1854 with a number of emigrants, and settled with them in Missouri. In 1855 he organized a German Baptist church in Gasconade Co., Mo., and preached to it until 1858, when, in obedience to a call from the New York Baptist Union for Ministerial Education, he took charge of the German department of the Theological Seminary at Rochester, N. Y. Since that time he has fulfilled, with much ability and success, the duties of his professorship. He is doing a great work. His influence on the young men going forth from Rochester as evangelists and pastors of the German Baptist churches is strongly felt, and his valuable services are gratefully acknowledged by all the churches.

Rawdon College, Yorkshire, England, the theological seminary originally called " the Northern Baptist Education Society," was founded in 1804. Until 1859 the college was located at Horton, near Bradford, and was known as Horton College. Its first president was the Rev. William Steadman, D.D., whose eminent services established the reputation of the seminary and won the confidence of the churches. Dr. Steadman was succeeded by Dr. Acworth, during the latter part of whose presidency the present handsome and commodious building was erected and paid for. The Rev. S. G. Green, D.D., was elected president on the retirement of Dr. Acworth. In 1876, Dr. Green accepted the position of literary editor of the Religious Tract Society, and was succeeded by the Rev. T. G. Rooke, B.A., the present head of the seminary. About 350 ministers and missionaries have been trained in this institution, many of whom have distinguished themselves by faithful and successful service in England, the United States, the British colonies, and in heathen lands. Rawdon College is affiliated to the University of London, and during recent years several students have graduated with distinction. Two scholarships, the " Acworth" and the " Steadman and Godwin," have been founded recently. (See illustration on next page.)

RAWDON COLLEGE, YORKSHIRE, ENGLAND.

Ray, Rev. Ambrose, a distinguished co-laborer with Martin Ball, W. H. Holcome, and others in North Mississippi, was born in South Carolina in 1798. He began to preach about 1833, and, after a successful ministry of seventeen years, he removed to Mississippi in 1850, where he took a high rank among his co-laborers, and was often called to positions of honor and trust among his brethren. He died in 1873, and his remains rest at Union church, Tippah Co., Miss.

Ray, D. B., D.D., was born in Hickman, Ky., March 30, 1830. He was converted, and baptized by Elder White, into the Little Albion Baptist church, Oct. 16, 1844. He was ordained in 1856. He labored in Kentucky and Tennessee till 1870, and then became associated with President Worrell in the editorship of the *Baptist Sentinel* at Lexington, Ky. In 1873 he became pastor at La Grange, Mo., and removed to St. Louis in 1880. He studied in Clinton Seminary, Ky., until ill health compelled him in two years to leave school. His ordination took place in 1856. After this he devoted much time to theological studies, history, and the sciences. Thousands have been converted under his ministry. Not only as an evangelist is he known, but more as a debater on religious questions. He has held forty oral discussions. Most of these have been with Campbellite and Methodist leaders. His discussions have been frequently followed by revivals, as well as by the discomfiture of his opponents.

In 1867 he published his "Text-Book on Camp-

bellism." Seven editions have been issued, and this blighting error has been exposed. In 1870 he issued his "Baptist Succession." It is a convenient

D. B. RAY, D.D.

hand-book of Baptist history, to meet objections against Baptists. Eight editions of it have been issued. "The Church Discussion" is another book he has issued, containing a debate with the Campbellites. He now resides in St. Louis, and is editor and proprietor of the *American Baptist Flag.* He is a man of marked ability and of great courage.

Raymond, John Howard, LL.D., was born in the city of New York, March 7, 1814. His father, Eliachim Raymond, a merchant, was distinguished for his active interest in every religious enterprise, and was a leader among the Baptists of his day. In his earliest school-days J. H. Raymond was the pupil of Gould Brown, and the influence of this master may be traced in his early acquisition of a taste for analytical thinking and correct expression. He was prepared for college at the Hamilton Academy and at the High School of New York. In 1828 he entered Columbia College. Four years later he was graduated at Union College, and immediately began the study of law at New Haven. It was during this period of his life that he was led to an abiding faith in the teachings of the Bible and to an acceptance of Jesus as his Saviour. He united with the First Baptist church of Brooklyn, and shortly after his convictions led him to the study of theology, with the intention of preparing for the ministry. In 1834 he entered the Theological Seminary at Hamilton, N. Y. His talent for acquiring languages made it easy for him to gain distinction as a student of Hebrew, his progress being so marked that he was appointed a tutor of the language at the seminary before he had completed its course of study. In 1839 the chair of Rhetoric and English Literature was established in Madison University, and he was called to the new professorship. He had rare qualities for the work, —habits of thoroughness in study, brilliant oratorical powers, fine rhetorical taste, winning social ways, keen sympathies, ready wit, and the art of teaching. He soon came to believe that he had found his calling, and that he saw his work for life in the profession of the teacher. For ten years Prof. Raymond continued at Madison University, winning reputation as an orator and as a teacher.

He accepted the professorship of Belle-Lettres in the University of Rochester at the time of its organization, in 1850. He remained at Rochester until 1856, when he was selected to organize the Collegiate and Polytechnic Institute in Brooklyn. This work brought him prominently before the educational profession, for he had a difficult task assigned to him, and he accomplished it with brilliant success.

When Matthew Vassar sought the advice of prominent American teachers in selecting the man who should be intrusted with the work of organizing the first great college for women, he found it to be the general opinion that the temperament, the accomplishments, and the experience of Dr.

Raymond made him the man for the position. He was promptly appointed to the presidency and professorship of Mental and Moral Philosophy at Vassar College. His work there began in the summer of 1865. To his task he brought unwearying patience, close observation, and the cautiousness of a man who appreciates the sacredness of a great trust. No man connected with educational institutions in this country has shown more talent for organization than was exhibited by President Raymond. The Collegiate and Polytechnic Institute at its inception was looked upon as a dubious experiment. He there demonstrated that by new and improved organization elements of culture seemingly incongruous could be made coalescent, and that institution became the model after which many high schools and academies have been patterned. This royal talent was yet more brilliantly displayed by him in the organization of Vassar College. His work was accomplished, not by spasmodic efforts, but by patient industry. A careful process of reasoning brought him to a conviction, and for that conviction he could toil unceasingly. Popular appreciation was not a powerful incentive to him. Respect for his own well-considered opinions and faithfulness to trusts placed in his keeping were the constant motives of his earnest life. Such a life gave him an ever-growing influence and an unsought eminence. But success did not dim the glow of his spiritual graces. Humility, calmness, trustfulness, catholicity, and the consecration of his industry and his influence shone brighter and brighter in him till the end of his life.

He gave himself so exclusively to his official work that his graceful pen had little opportunity for exercise. Save a few pamphlets and sermons, all marked with dignity and finish of style, he left no published works. Never physically strong, Dr. Raymond broke down under his labors, and though his physician warned him that he must have rest, he could not release himself from the work he loved. After a year of much suffering, in which his quiet patience and geniality shone brighter than ever before, with no definable disease, but worn out, he died on the 14th of August, 1878. His last words fittingly closed his earnest life as he quietly said to his family, "How easy, how easy, to glide from the work here to the work in heaven!" His death summoned attention to his dignity and worth, calling forth a general tribute of respect to his memory. "His fame, like the fame of Arnold, of Rugby, will live and grow through generations of those to whom and to whose fathers and mothers he was strong guardian, wise guide, dear friend."

Raymond, Rev. Lewis, was born Aug. 3, 1807, at Walton, Delaware Co., N. Y. When he was about seven years of age the family removed to

Sydney, in the same county, now called Sydney Centre. His conversion occurred at twenty-three, when he was baptized by Rev. S. P. Griswold, one of the veteran ministers of New York. In July, 1831, he was licensed by the Sydney church, and for a while united preaching with his business as a builder. His first pastorate was at Laurens, in Otsego County. After two years of successful labor he removed to Cooperstown, where he remained eight and a half years. By this time his brethren had found in him uncommon qualifications for usefulness in revival labor, and in 1841 called him to that sphere of service. Three years were spent in such labor in New York and in Northern Pennsylvania. In June, 1844, he removed to the West, being called to the pastorate of the Baptist church in Milwaukee. The church was very small and feeble, but grew under his ministry, and erected its first house of worship. After four years in Milwaukee he was called to Chicago as pastor of the Tabernacle church, succeeding Rev. H. M. Rice, who had died of cholera. After three years he again engaged in revival labors. In 1854 he removed to Sandusky, O., organizing a church there, which, however, after one year, he gave up to Rev. J. D. Fulton, and he entered the service of the Ohio State Convention. In 1857 he accepted a call to a new organization in Aurora, Ill., the Union Baptist church; in 1859 he went to another new church at Peoria; at the end of a year he entered the army as a chaplain, continuing in that service to the end of the war. Since that time he has been engaged as an evangelist, and in labor with feeble churches. His life has been one of energetic service in a spirit of great enthusiasm and personal devotion. And the fruit, in souls added to the Lord, has been abundant.

Raynor, Samuel, was born on Long Island, Aug. 10, 1810. He was baptized by Dr. Spencer H. Cone in 1833, and became a member of the Oliver Street church, New York, of which he has been a deacon over a quarter of a century. He is a well-known business man in New York. He is distinguished for his liberal support of the great institutions of the Baptist denomination. He is a manager of the American and Foreign Bible Society and of the New York Sunday-School Union. He was for years president of a benevolent institution in New York known as the "Eastern Dispensary," and has official connection with several insurance companies and the Metropolitan Savings-Bank of New York.

Read, Daniel, LL.D., was born in Orangeville, N. Y., April 11, 1825. He was educated at Madison University, and settled at first as pastor of the Big Flats Baptist church, in New York, where he was ordained to the work of the gospel ministry. He was next pastor of the Medina Baptist church,

N. Y., and was then induced to accept the pastorate of the Second Baptist church of St. Louis, Mo. In 1856 he was elected president of Shurtleff College, in Illinois. This old institution was patronized by the Baptists of St. Louis, which enabled Dr. Read to render the special service to it that his influence in that city and his learning promised. Under his charge the college was placed on a firm financial basis, and rose to a position it had not hitherto attained.

In 1873, Dr. Read resigned the presidency of the college and accepted a call of the First Baptist church of Williamsburg, N. Y. He is a faithful pastor and an able preacher. His study of the Bible in the languages in which it was written makes him one of the most instructive expounders of its sacred truth.

Read, Rev. George R., of Alameda, Cal., was born at Attleborough, Mass., March 5, 1841; baptized at North Attleborough in October, 1856; served in the army under Gen. Banks at New Orleans until 1863; studied at Pierce Academy, Mass.; graduated at Brown University in 1868, and at Newton Theological Seminary in 1871; settled as pastor for five years at Lisbon Falls, where he was ordained, Oct. 25, 1871. The church grew under his ministry; many were baptized. He removed to California in December, 1876, and supplied the Stockton church six months, during the pastor's absence in the Holy Land. In July, 1877, he settled at Alameda, organized a church, built a house of worship, and has been favored with growing prosperity. He is greatly beloved, is a self-denying pastor, and zealous worker. He has acted in honorable official positions in Associations and Conventions, and is numbered with the brethren of influence on the Pacific coast.

Read, Rev. Geo. W., was born at Frankfort, Ky., Jan. 16, 1843. Mr. Read spent nearly three years and a half in the Union service during the war, receiving a wound from which he still at times severely suffers. He was baptized Dec. 1, 1866. He entered Shurtleff College preparatory to the work of the ministry, and was ordained at Kinmundy, Ill., June 11, 1871. He was pastor of the Baptist church in Clayton, Ill., five years, and the Union Avenue church, Litchfield, Ill., one year. He removed to Peru, Neb., Jan. 1, 1878. Through his labors a commodious church edifice has been built. He preaches to the Brownville Baptist church in connection with that of Peru.

Read, Rev. Hiram Walter, was born in Jewett City, Conn., July 17, 1819; baptized March 11, 1838, at Oswego, N. Y.; educated at Oswego Academy and Madison University; began his ministry in 1844, at Whitewater, Wis. He was pastor, and chaplain to Wisconsin senate, and labored in many revivals. In 1849 he went to New Mexico,

Index to Names
for all 3 Volumes
is in the back of
Volume 3.